A D V A N C E D

Structured COBOL

A D V A N C E D

Structured COBOL

Gerard A. Paquette
University of Lowell

WCB Wm. C. Brown Publishers

Book Team

Developmental Editor *Linda M. Meehan*
Production Editor *Deborah Daniel Reinbold*
Designer *K. Wayne Harms*
Art Editor *Janice M. Roerig*
Permissions Editor *Karen L. Storlie*
Visuals Processor *Andrêa Lopez-Meyer*

WCB **Wm. C. Brown Publishers**

President *G. Franklin Lewis*
Vice President, Publisher *George Wm. Bergquist*
Vice President, Publisher *Thomas E. Doran*
Vice President, Operations and Production *Beverly Kolz*
National Sales Manager *Virginia S. Moffat*
Advertising Manager *Ann M. Knepper*
Marketing Manager *Craig S. Marty*
Editor in Chief *Edward G. Jaffe*
Managing Editor, Production *Colleen A. Yonda*
Production Editorial Manager *Julie A. Kennedy*
Production Editorial Manager *Ann Fuerste*
Publishing Services Manager *Karen J. Slaght*
Manager of Visuals and Design *Faye M. Schilling*

Cover and interior design by Mary K. Sailer

Library of Congress Catalog Card Number: 90–81594

ISBN 0–697–07771–3

Printed in the United States of America by Wm. C. Brown Publishers, 2460 Kerper Boulevard, Dubuque, IA 52001

10 9 8 7 6 5 4 3 2 1

Contents

4 Relative Files 250

5 Subprograms and Nested Programs 338

6 Interactive COBOL Programs 432

Appendices

Preface

Preface

This text continues the presentation of structured COBOL programming concepts begun in volume 1, *Structured COBOL*. One of the main strengths of volume 1 is the repeated application of a standard problem-solving procedure. The first chapter of volume 2 reviews the problem-solving procedure as it is applied in a sample programming assignment.

The procedure consists of two phases: the design phase and the design implementation phase. In the design phase, students learn to use input/output record layout forms to properly position data, system flowcharts to illustrate basic data flow, structure charts to identify the related tasks the program must process, the program pseudocode to list the detailed processing steps required in each task as well as the order in which the tasks must be processed, and the program flowchart to provide a visual representation of the pseudocode.

In the design implementation phase, students learn to use the design tools to actually code the program, and to complete the task by compiling, debugging, and running the program until all program specifications have been satisfied.

All the sample programs in the text are developed by using the problem-solving procedure as a guide. Many COBOL texts mention the need for systematic analysis in the development of programs, but few actually demonstrate a standard procedure consistently throughout the sample programs of the text. In addition, each chapter contains programming exercises for which some of the design tools are already supplied. As students begin the task of planning the program, the supplied tools enable students to realize the benefits the tools provide in the development of the program.

In the second chapter, students learn how to set up and work with indexed tables, both hard-coded and loadable, with one, two, and three levels. The related concepts of serial and binary searches are also applied. Since binary searches require ordered indexed tables, the sort procedures developed in *Structured COBOL* can be used to properly sort the data before it is loaded into a table.

Chapters 3 and 4 develop the concepts of indexed files and relative files, respectively. Students learn how to create such files and how to update them. Techniques are also developed to provide verification reports or audit trails, an important aspect of working on "invisible" files. Sample programs are carefully selected to illustrate sequential access, random access, and dynamic access.

In Chapter 5, students learn how subprograms and contained (or nested) programs can be used to further enhance the development of structured programs while increasing programming efficiency. The differences in the requirements of subprograms and of contained programs are specified and illustrated. Sample COBOL run units are provided. One run unit consists of a main program and one or more subprograms, another run unit consists of a main program and one or more contained programs, and another run unit consists of a main program that calls both subprograms and contained programs. To maintain students' attention on the new concepts, the programs used as examples are adaptations of previous chapter programs.

In Chapter 6, students are introduced to notions of interactive COBOL programs. The emphasis is on extensive uses of the standard ACCEPT and DISPLAY statements. Students will learn how to create a file interactively, how to perform data validation routines on accepted data, and how to update an existing file interactively. Special nonstandard options of the ACCEPT and DISPLAY statements will be examined in relation to the design of screen formats.

Additional Comments

The COBOL language features developed in this text are in full compliance with the 1985 ANSI COBOL standards. The only exception occurs in the last chapter and concerns videoscreen formatting in interactive COBOL programming.

In each chapter, the sample programs are carefully selected to provide meaningful opportunities for the introduction of new language features. The new concepts are explained and illustrated with one or more examples, depending on their complexity. If appropriate, formats are specified and a summary of related rules is given.

Each chapter ends with a list of the important terms introduced in the chapter. This list is followed by a generous set of exercises. Some exercises can be classifed as drills; others are developmental in the sense that a set of related questions dealing with individual attributes of a concept will gradually lead to an understanding of the general concept itself. Other exercises involve the separate tasks students must perform in the development of a program.

Following the set of standard exercises, each chapter also contains debugging activities. They have been carefully designed to draw students' attention to syntax and logic errors that are typical of those encountered when students write their initial programs related to the chapter material. In general, the first exercise in this set presents a compiler listing of a program with a number of diagnostics, and the students' task is to correct all syntax errors. The second exercise shows the output produced by the program when it is free of syntax errors. But it also shows the output as it should be. The students' task is to find and correct the logic errors that account for the output errors. The source code for the program that contains syntax errors is available to instructors as one of the text's ancillary items.

Each chapter also contains a set of graduated programming exercises. In addition to the statement of the problem in some of these exercises, students are also given fully developed design tools, the task being to code the program, debug it, and run it successfully. For other exercises, fewer design tools are provided, and students are expected to complete the design phase first, and then the design implementation phase. Other exercises are full-scale programming assignments in the sense that only the statement of the problem is given. Students are expected to develop these programs "from scratch."

Students who have mastered the concepts presented in this text are well prepared to enter the job market as entry-level COBOL programmers. In particular, students are able to accomplish the following:

1. Systematically apply an effective and efficient problem-solving procedure that facilitates and documents program development.
2. Load data into a one-level, a two-level, or a three-level table and retrieve table values from static as well as volatile tables.
3. Create and maintain tape files.
4. Create and maintain disk files with sequential, indexed, and relative organization.
5. Design COBOL run units that consist of a main program and one or more subprograms and/or contained programs.
6. Design interactive programs to create and update files.

The author wishes to thank the following reviewers for their comments and suggestions: Ronald M. Bryant, Massasoit Community College; Joyce L. Capen, Central Michigan University; Judith L. Solano, University of North Florida; Sandra M. Stalker, North Shore Community College; and Ron Teemley, DeVry Institute Dallas.

ADVANCED
Structured COBOL

1 Planning Structured Programs

In this introductory chapter, the **problem-solving procedure** that was developed in volume 1, *Structured COBOL,* is revisited mainly for the benefit of students who have not used the first volume. The purpose of the procedure is to establish a systematic approach to the development of structured COBOL programs. In addition, the program development tools that are used within the procedure are retained because they provide very useful documentation for the resulting program. It is a common practice in the business world to periodically make changes to existing programs, and if appropriate program documentation is available, such program maintenance tasks are greatly simplified.

This chapter begins with a presentation of the problem-solving procedure. Brief explanations are provided, and the procedure is shown "at work" in the development of a sample program. ■

Objectives You Should Achieve

After studying this chapter, you should:

1. Know the phases of the problem-solving procedure.
2. Be able to identify the analytical tools used in the design phase of the problem-solving procedure.
3. Be able to apply the analytical tools used in the design phase of the problem-solving procedure, including the following:
   a. Design a system flowchart
   b. Prepare input record layout forms
   c. Prepare a printer spacing chart
   d. Design a structure chart
   e. Write the program pseudocode or design the program flowchart
4. Know and be able to apply the steps of the design implementation phase.
5. Given a programming assignment for which some design tools are provided, be able to complete the design and then implement the design to successful completion.
6. Given the statement of a problem, be able to successfully apply the problem-solving procedure in the development of the required program.

The Problem-Solving Procedure

The problem-solving procedure is listed in Figure 1.1. Note that it consists of two phases, the *design phase* and the *design implementation phase*.

Figure 1.1 The problem-solving procedure

A. Program Design Phase

1. Develop a thorough understanding of the problem. Obtain all program specifications:
   a. Input record layout: identify and name data supplied; indicate position of data on record; name the record.
   b. Output record layout(s): identify the types of records needed; plan the layout of each type; name the data fields; name the records.
2. Plan the solution to the problem.
   a. Determine data flow (system flowchart): source of input data (name input file), function of program, nature of output file (name output file).
   b. Develop the structure chart: identify the overall task, specify functional subcomponents.
   c. Convert each functional component into specific set of processing steps (pseudocode). Walk through with sample data.
   d. For detailed program logic, design a program flowchart. Walk through with sample data.

B. Design Implementation Phase

3. Code the program.
   a. In the IDENTIFICATION DIVISION, name the program, and include program documentation: author, date written, program description.
   b. In the ENVIRONMENT DIVISION, specify the computers and the files.
   c. In the DATA DIVISION, define the files and code all record data specifications. (Use layout forms as guides.)
   d. In the PROCEDURE DIVISION, code all instructions corresponding to processing steps identified in the pseudocode or program flowchart.
4. Key (or enter) the program.
   a. Create a new file.
   b. Use a text editor to add the lines of coding to the file.
   c. Get a listing of the file. (The file is the source program.)
   d. Correct obvious errors.
5. Debug the program.
   a. Use the compiler to identify all syntax errors in the source code.
   b. Correct all syntax errors indicated by the compiler.
   c. Repeat steps a and b until the program is free of syntax errors.
   d. Compile the program, save the object program, and get a compiler listing of the source program.
   e. If available, use the linker to produce an executable image of the program.
6. Test run the program.
   a. Run the executable image with a sample input file; create sample input file if necessary.
   b. Check the output carefully to determine if all objectives are met.
   c. Revise as necessary to meet all objectives.
7. Assemble the complete package.
   a. Input and output record layout forms
   b. System flowchart
   c. Structure chart
   d. Pseudocode
   e. Program flowchart
   f. Program listing produced by the compiler
   g. Sample input file
   h. Sample program output

Figure 1.2 Input record layout example

Record Layout Form

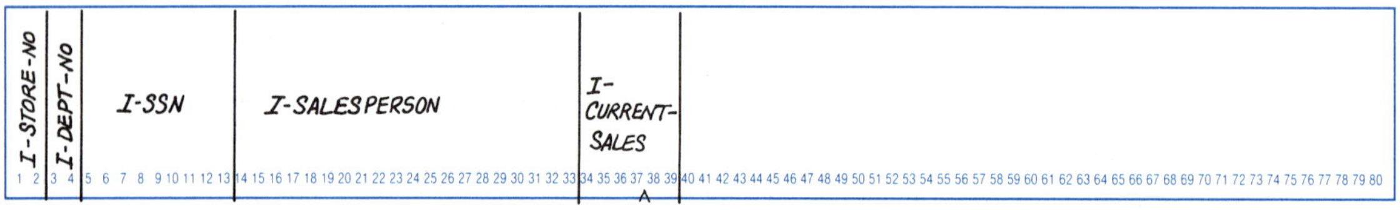

Record Name: SALESPERSON-RECORD

The Program Design Phase

Any serious programmer knows from personal experience that careful planning is essential to achieving an effective and efficient program. The design phase of the problem-solving procedure addresses this issue very directly. Step 1 explicitly calls for the development of a thorough understanding of the problem at hand. This may require several critical readings of the problem as well as discussions to clarify ambiguous, obscure, or insufficiently specific aspects of the problem. Understanding a problem requires a clear identification of the data to be supplied as input to the program, and it requires a clear understanding of the output that must be produced by the program.

To help in this process, input data specifications are recorded on an *input record layout form.* A developed form shows the positioning of data fields on a record, the size of each field, the position of decimal points if they exist, the hierarchical structure of the data items in the record, the names of the fields, and the name of the record itself. Figure 1.2 is an example of a prepared input record layout form. The name of the record is SALESPERSON-RECORD; the names of the data fields in the order in which they occur in the record are I-STORE-NO, I-DEPT-NO, I-SSN, I-SALESPERSON, and I-CURRENT-SALES. The size of the field I-SSN is 9, of the field I-CURRENT-SALES is 6, and there is an assumed decimal point between bytes 4 and 5 of the data item I-CURRENT-SALES.

Output data specifications are also similarly recorded. For instance, if the output of a program is a printed report, a *printer spacing chart* is used to show the report format, that is, the layouts of all the different kinds of lines or records that must be printed on the report. Fields that contain constants actually show the constants, such as column headers; data field positions are indicated as strings of Xs, and needed insertion editing characters are shown in the string; data fields are given names; and each record (line layout) is given a name. Figure 1.3 is an example of a printer spacing chart. In this example, the report contains six different kinds of records (lines), and the names given to these line layouts (records) are, in sequence, DATE-LINE, COMPANY-NAME, REPORT-NAME, HEADINGS, SALES-LINE, and END-LINE. The data field O-REPORT-DATE of DATE-LINE has size 8, and it contains the "slant" or "slash" insertion editing character in bytes 3 and 6. The records COMPANY-NAME, REPORT-NAME, HEADINGS, and END-LINE contain only constants, whereas the record SALES-LINE contains four data fields.

Step 2 of the design phase is the one in which the solution of the problem takes shape and structure. The data flow for the program is established by drawing the *system flowchart,* which identifies the source of the data to be supplied as input to the program and the output to be produced by the program. A sample system flowchart is shown in Figure 1.4. It shows two input files on disks, MASTER-PERSONNEL-FILE and DETAIL-FILE, whose records will be processed by the program, and it shows that the program will produce two output files, the disk file UPDATED-MASTER-FILE and the print file MASTER-PERSONNEL-REPORT.

■ **Figure 1.3** Printer spacing chart example

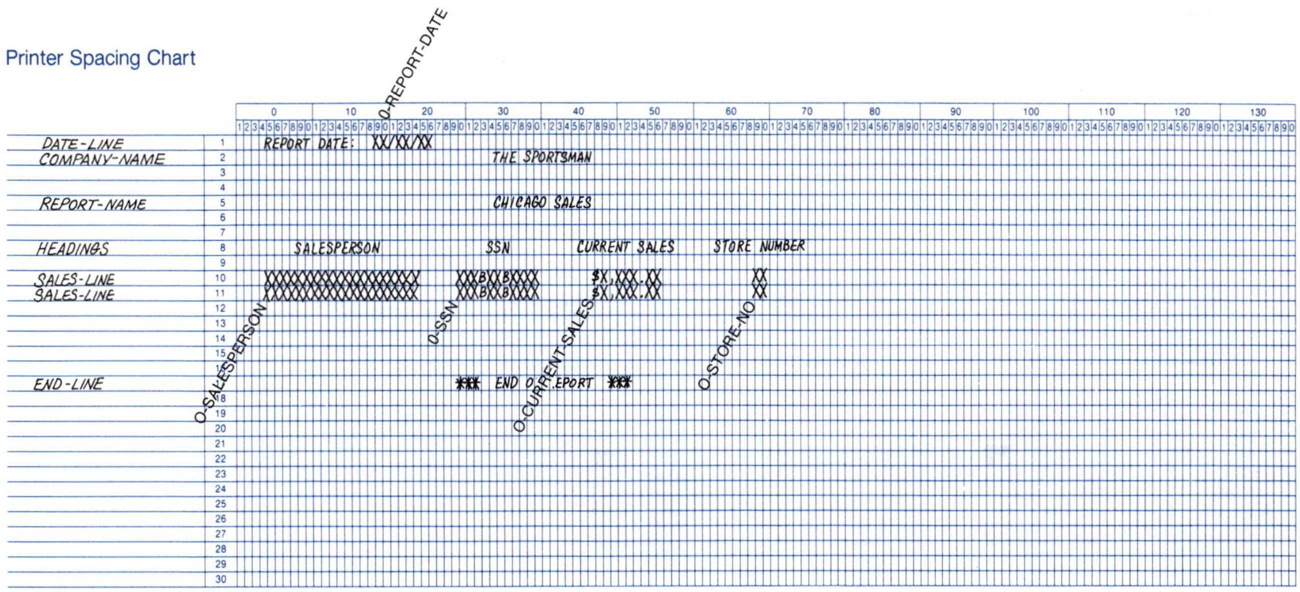

■ **Figure 1.4** System flowchart example

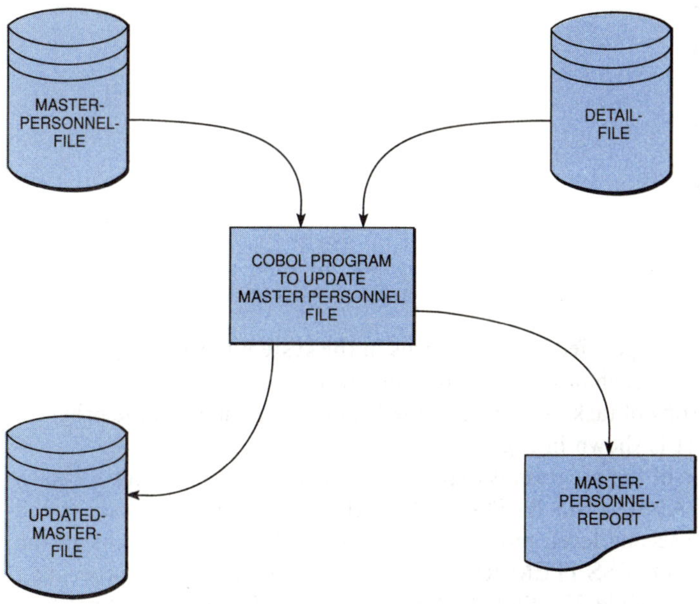

Figure 1.5 Structure chart example

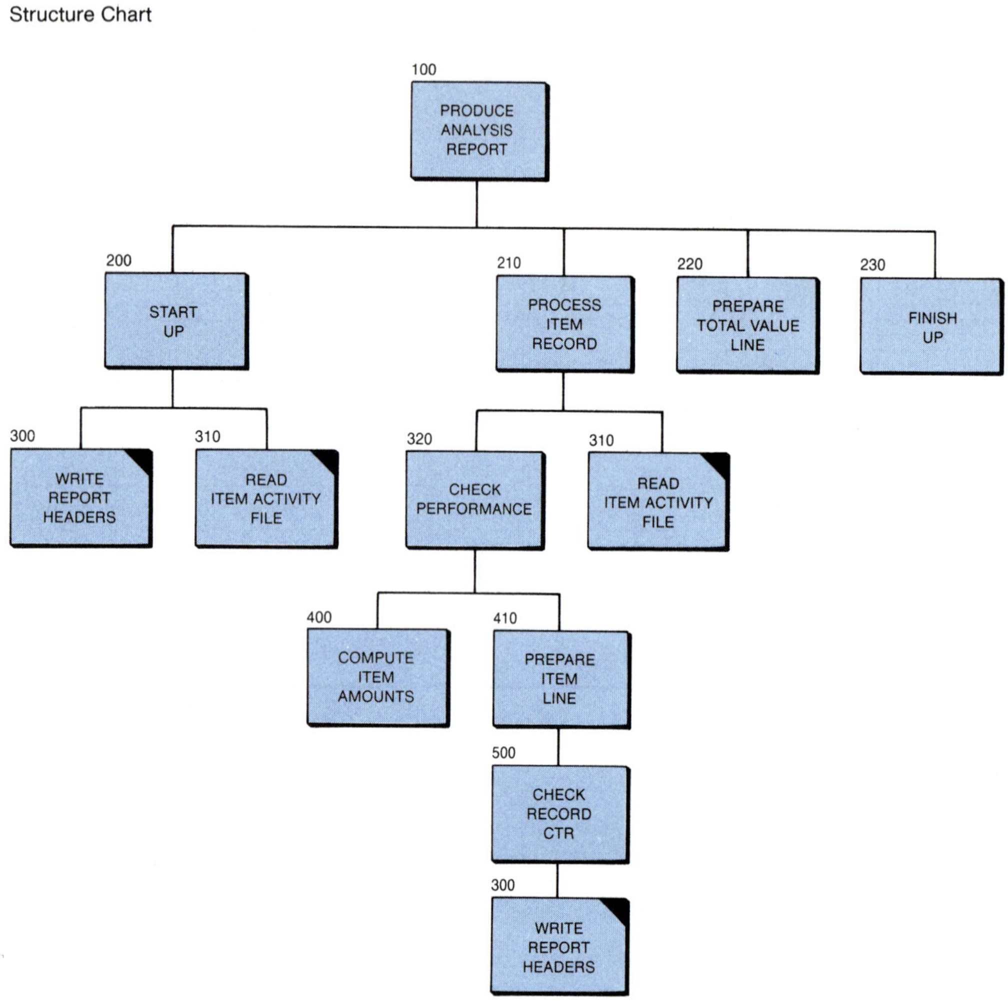

The essential function of the program, specified in broad terms in the system flowchart, must now be broken down into major components, and each of these components in turn is then further separated into subcomponents. The resulting hierarchy of tasks and their related subtasks is shown in the program *structure chart.* A sample structure chart is shown in Figure 1.5.

In this example, the overall function of the program is to produce an analysis report. This is shown as the top-level module 100 PRODUCE ANALYSIS REPORT. Note that this broad task is separated into four components, or modules, at the second level: module 200 START UP, which contains all the needed start-up activities; module 210 PROCESS ITEM RECORD, which contains all the processing activities that pertain to an input record; module 220 PREPARE TOTAL VALUE LINE, whose task is made obvious by the entry in the box; and module 230 FINISH UP, which contains all ending activities, such as closing all opened files. Of the four major tasks, the first two contain certain activities that should be treated as subcomponents at the third level. As subtasks of 200 START UP, module 300 WRITE REPORT HEADERS starts the report, and module 310 READ ITEM ACTIVITY FILE primes the input memory area with the first record of the input file. As subtasks of 210 PROCESS ITEM RECORD, module 320 CHECK PERFORMANCE contains processing steps that are specific to the record currently in input memory, and module 310 READ ITEM ACTIVITY FILE makes the next record of the input file available for processing. Module 320 is further separated into subtasks at the fourth level, namely, 400 COMPUTE ITEM AMOUNTS and 410 PREPARE ITEM LINE. Their functions are made obvious by the names given to them. Also note that module 410 contains submodule

500 CHECK RECORD CTR, and this module in turn contains module 300 as a subtask. (In a structure chart, a particular module that occurs at more than one point in the hierarchy is identified by darkening the upper right-hand corner!) The development of the structure chart requires a very careful analysis of the problem, since this is the structure that will ultimately be transmitted to the program itself.

While the structure chart addresses "what" has to be done by the program, the next step of the problem-solving procedure addresses "how" to get each task done. The two most common design tools for this purpose are the *program pseudocode* and the *program flowchart*. Either tool is sufficient on its own, but in this text, both are presented to allow your instructor to follow his or her preference. Figure 1.6a contains the program pseudocode for a particular program, while Figure 1.6b contains the corresponding flowchart. For instance, the structure chart may contain the task module 320 PREPARE INVENTORY LINE, in which case the corresponding pseudocode paragraph 320-Prepare-Inventory-Line contains the specific processing steps that are required to get the job done, and the flowchart module 320-PREPARE-INVENTORY-LINE shows the same processing steps in visual form. In general, there is one paragraph of specific instructions in the pseudocode and one flowchart module in the program flowchart for each module in the structure chart.

Figure 1.6a Program pseudocode example

100-Produce-Inventory-Report.

1. Perform 200-Start-Up.
2. Perform 210-Process-Item-Record until no more records.
3. Perform 220-Finish-Up.
4. Stop the run.

200-Start-Up.

1. Open the files.
2. Set the end-of-file flag WS-MORE-RECORDS to "YES".
3. Clear the record area Inventory-Line.
4. Perform 300-Write-Report-Headers.
5. Perform 310-Read-Item-Record.

210-Process-Item-Record.

1. Perform 320-Prepare-Inventory-Line.
2. Perform 310-Read-Item-Record.

220-Finish-Up.

1. Close the files.

300-Write-Report-Headers.

1. Move the record Company-Name to the output area Printline.
2. After advancing to the top of a new page, write the output record Printline.
3. Move the record Report-Name to the output area Printline.
4. After advancing 3 lines, write the output record Printline.
5. Move the record Headings-1 to the output area Printline.
6. After advancing 3 lines, write the output record Printline.
7. Move the record Headings-2 to the output area Printline.
8. After advancing 1 line, write the output record Printline.

310-Read-Item-Record.

1. Read an input item-record.
2. Test for the end-of-file record;
   if EOF record reached, move "NO " to the end-of-file flag WS-MORE-RECORDS.

320-Prepare-Inventory-Line.

1. Move input catalog-number to Inventory-Line catalog-number.
2. Move input item-description to Inventory-Line item-description.
3. Move input quantity-on-hand to Inventory-Line quantity-on-hand.
4. Move input unit-purchase-price to Inventory-Line unit-purchase-price.
5. Move input unit-selling-price to Inventory-Line unit-selling-price.
6. Move the record Inventory-Line to the output area Printline.
7. After advancing 2 lines, write the output record Printline.

Figure 1.6b Program flowchart example

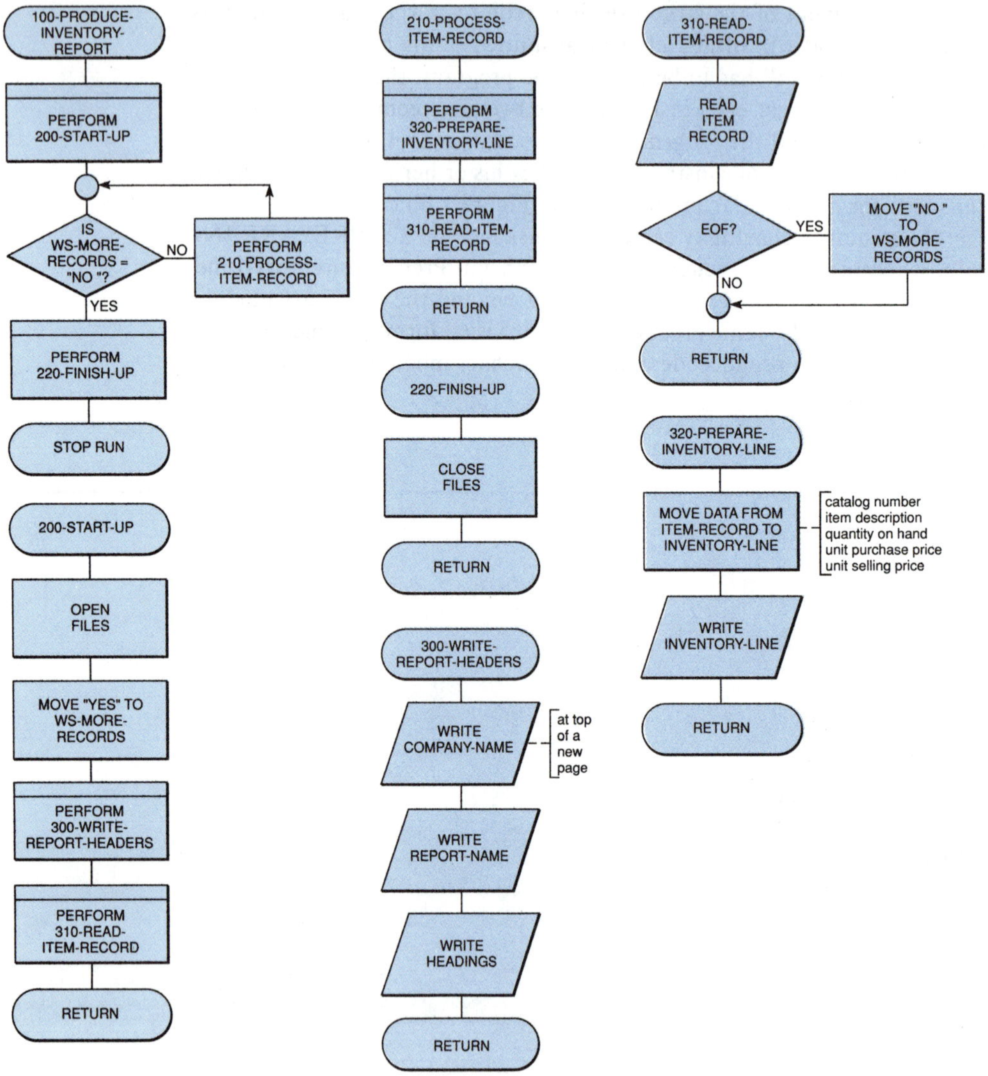

At this point in the development of the program, the design phase is complete, and the programmer should take the time to carefully review the design. Specifically, she or he should play computer with it, that is, take representative records from the input file and walk through the pseudocode or flowchart to verify that the design in fact accomplishes the required results. This is a very important debugging activity which flags logic errors that may have been overlooked. It should be obvious that if the design contains logic errors and no debugging occurs at this point, the errors will simply be passed along to the program and will probably not show up until the program is actually run. In that case, the programmer must still return to the design of the program to make the necessary corrections, and then recode portions of the program, recompile the revised program, and run it again. It is much more economical, in dollars and in time, to debug the logic before proceeding with the implementation of the design.

■ **Figure 1.7** Correspondences between design tools and program entries

a.

```
INPUT-OUTPUT SECTION.

FILE-CONTROL.
    SELECT PHONE-SALES-FILE   ASSIGN TO COB$INPUT.
    SELECT PHONE-SALES-REPORT ASSIGN TO COB$OUTPUT.

DATA DIVISION.

FILE SECTION.

FD  PHONE-SALES-FILE
    RECORD CONTAINS 23 CHARACTERS.

01  PHONE-SALE-RECORD.
    05 I-CUSTOMER-NO    PIC X(4).
    05 FILLER           PIC XX.
    05 I-CATALOG-NO     PIC X(4).
    05 FILLER           PIC XX.
    05 I-UNIT-COST      PIC 999V99.
    05 FILLER           PIC XX.
    05 I-NO-OF-UNITS    PIC 9(4).

FD  PHONE-SALES-REPORT
    RECORD CONTAINS 132 CHARACTERS.

01  PRINTLINE           PIC X(132).

WORKING-STORAGE SECTION.

01  WS-MORE-RECORDS     PIC XXX.

01  HEADINGS.
    05 PIC X(15)    VALUE SPACES.
    05 PIC X(15)    VALUE "CUSTOMER NUMBER".
    05 PIC X(8)     VALUE SPACES.
    05 PIC X(14)    VALUE "CATALOG NUMBER".
    05 PIC X(8)     VALUE SPACES.
    05 PIC X(9)     VALUE "UNIT COST".
    05 PIC X(8)     VALUE SPACES.
    05 PIC X(15)    VALUE "NUMBER OF UNITS".
    05 PIC X(8)     VALUE SPACES.
    05 PIC X(17)    VALUE "PHONE SALE AMOUNT".
    05 PIC X(15)    VALUE SPACES.

01  PHONE-SALE-LINE.
    05 FILLER           PIC X(21).
    05 O-CUSTOMER-NO    PIC X(4).
    05 FILLER           PIC X(18).
    05 O-CATALOG-NO     PIC X(4).
    05 FILLER           PIC X(14).
    05 O-UNIT-COST      PIC $ZZ9.99.
    05 FILLER           PIC X(15).
    05 O-NO-OF-UNITS    PIC ZZZ9.
    05 FILLER           PIC X(17).
    05 O-SALE-AMOUNT    PIC $Z(5)9.99.
    05 FILLER           PIC X(18).
```

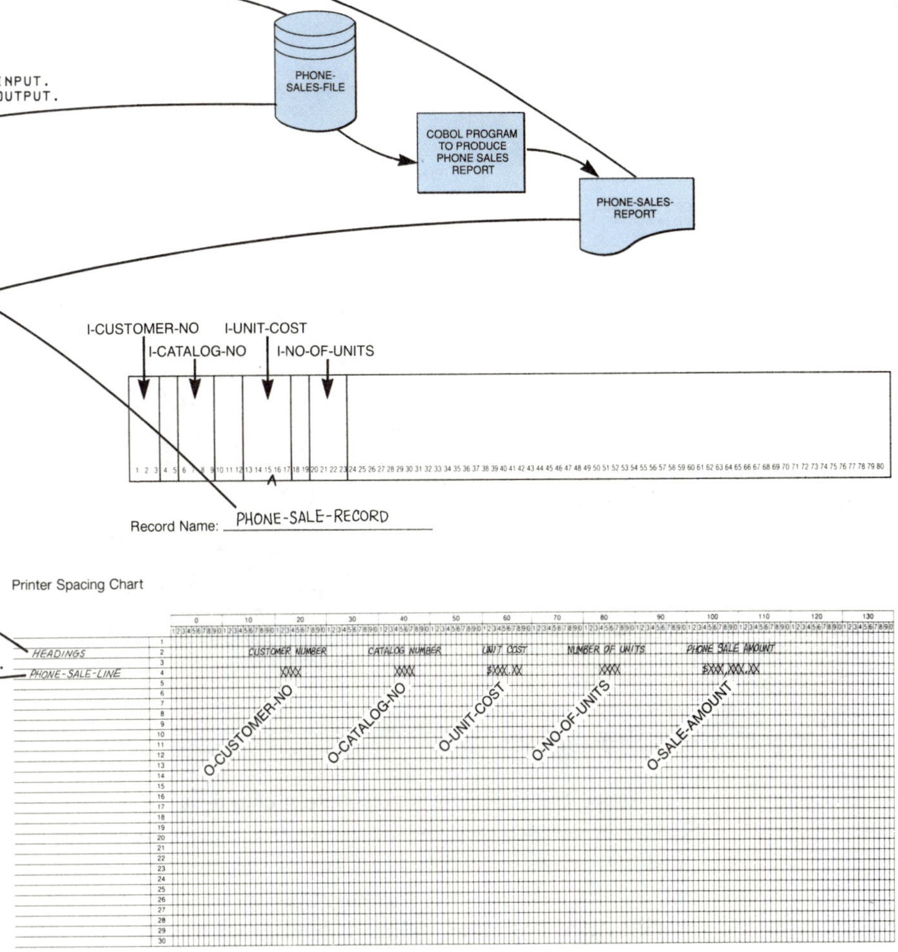

The Design Implementation Phase

The second phase of the problem-solving procedure is much simpler than the first. It simply carries out the design created in the first phase. The first step in this phase, coding the program, is greatly facilitated by the availability of the design tools. Specifically, the system flowchart provides information needed in the FILE-CONTROL paragraph; the input record layout directs the coding of the input records in the FILE SECTION; the printer spacing chart directs the coding of many of the entries in the WORKING-STORAGE SECTION; the pseudocode and/or the program flowchart direct the coding of the PROCEDURE DIVISION. Parts a and b of Figure 1.7 show correspondences between design tools and program entries for a sample program. With all of these aids, coding the program is truly a routine matter.

Figure 1.7 continued

b.

```
PROCEDURE DIVISION.

100-PRODUCE-PHONE-SALES-REPORT.
    PERFORM 200-START-UP.
    PERFORM 210-WRITE-REPORT-HEADERS.
    PERFORM 220-READ-PHONE-SALE-RECORD.
    PERFORM 230-PROCESS-PHONE-SALE-RECORD
        UNTIL WS-MORE-RECORDS = "NO ".
    PERFORM 240-FINISH-UP.
    STOP RUN.

200-START-UP.
    OPEN INPUT PHONE-SALES-FILE.
    OPEN OUTPUT PHONE-SALES-REPORT.
    MOVE "YES" TO WS-MORE-RECORDS.

210-WRITE-REPORT-HEADERS.
    MOVE HEADINGS TO PRINTLINE.
    WRITE PRINTLINE
        AFTER ADVANCING PAGE.
    MOVE SPACES TO PHONE-SALE-LINE.

220-READ-PHONE-SALE-RECORD.
    READ PHONE-SALES-FILE RECORD
        AT END
            MOVE "NO " TO WS-MORE-RECORDS.

230-PROCESS-PHONE-SALE-RECORD.
    PERFORM 300-COMPUTE-PHONE-SALE-AMOUNT.
    PERFORM 310-PREPARE-PHONE-SALE-LINE.
    PERFORM 220-READ-PHONE-SALE-RECORD.

240-FINISH-UP.
    CLOSE PHONE-SALES-FILE.
    CLOSE PHONE-SALES-REPORT.

300-COMPUTE-PHONE-SALE-AMOUNT.
    IF I-NO-OF-UNITS > 100
        THEN
            COMPUTE O-SALE-AMOUNT = I-NO-OF-UNITS *
                                    I-UNIT-COST * .8
        ELSE
            COMPUTE O-SALE-AMOUNT = I-NO-OF-UNITS *
                                    I-UNIT-COST.

310-PREPARE-PHONE-SALE-LINE.
    MOVE I-CUSTOMER-NO TO O-CUSTOMER-NO.
    MOVE I-CATALOG-NO TO O-CATALOG-NO.
    MOVE I-UNIT-COST TO O-UNIT-COST.
    MOVE I-NO-OF-UNITS TO O-NO-OF-UNITS.
    MOVE PHONE-SALE-LINE TO PRINTLINE.
    WRITE PRINTLINE
        AFTER ADVANCING 2 LINES.
```

```
100-Produce-Phone-Sales-Report.
    1. Perform 200-Start-Up.
    2. Perform 210-Write-Report-Headers.
    3. Perform 220-Read-Phone-Sale-Record.
    4. Perform 230-Process-Phone-Sale-Record until no more records.
    5. Perform 240-Finish-Up.
    6. Stop the run.
200-Start-Up.
    1. Open the files.
    2. Set the end-of-file flag WS-MORE-RECORDS to "YES".
210-Write-Report-Headers.
    1. Move Headings to the output area Printline.
    2. After advancing to the top of a new page, write the output record Printline.
    3. Clear the record area Phone-sale-line.
220-Read-Phone-Sale-Record.
    1. Read an input Phone-sale-record.
    2. Test for the end-of-file record; If EOF record reached, move "NO " to the end-of-file flag WS-MORE-RECORDS.
230-Process-Phone-Sale-Record.
    1. Perform 300-Compute-Phone-Sale-Amount.
    2. Perform 310-Prepare-Phone-Sale-Line.
    3. Perform 220-Read-Phone-Sale-Record.
240-Finish-Up.
    1. Close the files.
300-Compute-Phone-Sale-Amount.
    1. If the input number-of-units > 100
         then
              compute the Phone-sale-line amount = input number-of-units times
                                                   input unit-cost times .8
         else
              compute the Phone-sale-line amount = input number-of-units times input unit-cost.
310-Prepare-Phone-Sale-Line.
    1. Move input customer-number to Phone-sale-line customer-number.
    2. Move input catalog-number to Phone-sale-line catalog-number.
    3. Move input unit-cost to Phone-sale-line unit-cost.
    4. Move input number-of-units to Phone-sale-line number-of-units.
    5. Move the Phone-sale-line to the output record area Printline.
    6. After advancing 2 lines, write the output record Printline.
```

Once the program is completely coded, it must be entered into a file, and it must be compiled. Syntax errors detected by the compiler must be corrected, and the program must be compiled again until it is error free. Then a test run of the program must be carried out with a sample input file. The output produced by the program must be checked very carefully to ensure full compliance with the specifications contained in the original problem. Once this has been achieved, the programmer's job is done. He or she assembles the final package, consisting of the original statement of the problem, all the design tools, a listing of the program, a copy of the sample data file, and a copy of the output produced by the program, and submits it to the person who requested the program!

A Sample Program

The preceding pages have examined the steps of the problem-solving procedure in a piecemeal fashion. Now, the procedure will be applied in a systematic manner in the development of the following program.

The Problem

The management of Express Auto Parts Warehouse wants an analysis report for the week that will identify two kinds of items of questionable value to the company: (1) items that have not sold and (2) items that have excessive returns (50 percent or more of sales). For each item, there is a record in the catalog file containing the following data:

cc 1–5	Catalog number
cc 6–25	Item description
cc 26–30	Unit purchase price (format: xxx.xx)
cc 36–39	Quantity on hand at the beginning of the week
cc 40–43	Quantity on order
cc 44–47	Reorder point
cc 48–51	Quantity received during the week
cc 52–55	Quantity sold during the week
cc 56–59	Quantity returned by customers during the week.

The report must be properly documented with a report-date line, company name, report name, and column headings. It must contain the following information for each item of questionable value: the catalog number, the item description, the purchase price, the quantity in stock (on hand + returns + received − sold), the total value of the stock (purchase price × quantity in stock), and the reason for current status (low sales or too many returns or both). At the end of the listing, an entry should specify the total value of the above items.

There should be no more than 30 items listed per page. The pages of the report should be numbered consecutively. An "End of Report" message should terminate the report.

Use the current date as the report date and use Data Set 1X1 as the input file.

The Design Phase for the Sample Program

The programmer must begin by reading and rereading the statement of the problem to become thoroughly familiar with all of its components. Some specific questions are the following: What must the program produce as output? What is provided as input to the program? How should the input data be processed in order to generate the required output?

In the current program, a multipage report must be produced. Each page must contain specific top-of-page documentation and a maximum of 30 detail lines. Additionally, the last page must contain an entry that specifies the total inventory value for the items that have been selected for the report, and it must end with an "End of Report" message. The items that must be selected for this report are those that have had no sales for the week or for which the quantity returned by customers is excessive.

The data supplied as input to the program are the records of the catalog file. Each record contains data related to a particular item in the current inventory. Of special interest are the entries that specify the quantity sold and the quantity returned during the week, since these values must be examined to determine if the item should be selected for the report.

Step 1

Having developed this understanding of the problem, the programmer is ready to work on the various design tools. One of the easiest to prepare is the input record layout, since the data field specifications are supplied in the statement of the problem. On the record layout form, the programmer shows the relative positions of the data fields, gives a name to each field, and also names the record. The form is shown in Figure 1.8. Note that each data name begins with the prefix I- to help document the fact that the field belongs to an input record. Also note the caret (∧) between bytes 3 and 4 of the field I-PURCHASE-PRICE-PER-UNIT to indicate the position of an assumed decimal point.

Since the output is a report, the printer spacing chart is used to prepare the layouts of all the different line formats needed. Sometimes the report format is completely specified in the problem, and, at other times, as in this case, the problem simply states in general terms what the report must contain. It is then the programmer's responsibility to prepare a report format that not only meets the requirements of the problem but that produces a report that is easy to read and aesthetically pleasing to the eye.

Figure 1.8 Input record layout for the sample program

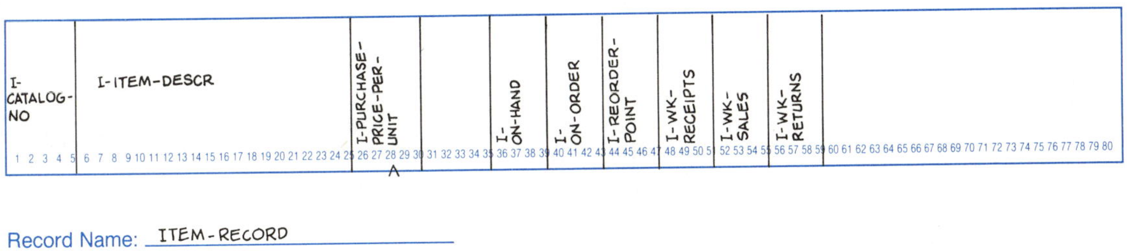

The problem states that the report should be properly documented with a report-date line, company name, report name, and column headers. Since the pages of the report must also be numbered, the top line on each page will contain the report date and the page number. The company name is "Express Auto Parts Warehouse." The report name selected in this example is "Analysis Report." It could have been "Items of Questionable Value" or "Poor Performance Items," or some other descriptive entry. The column headers should adequately describe the data that must be printed for each catalog item selected for this report.

In addition to the formats of top-of-page documentation lines, the format of the detail line must also be prepared. It must contain fields for the catalog number of the selected item, the item description, the purchase price, the quantity in stock, the total value of the stock, and an indication of the reason why the item was selected. Obviously, the positions of these data fields must be coordinated with the column headers.

Two other line formats must also be prepared: the one that will display the total inventory value of the listed items, and the one that contains the "End of Report" message.

All line layouts and data fields should be given descriptive names, and numeric data fields should be properly edited. Data field names begin with the prefix O- to help document the fact that they belong to output records.

The printer spacing chart for the program is shown in Figure 1.9. Note that the company name and report name are centered and the body of the report is balanced across the width of the page.

Figure 1.9 Printer spacing chart for the sample program

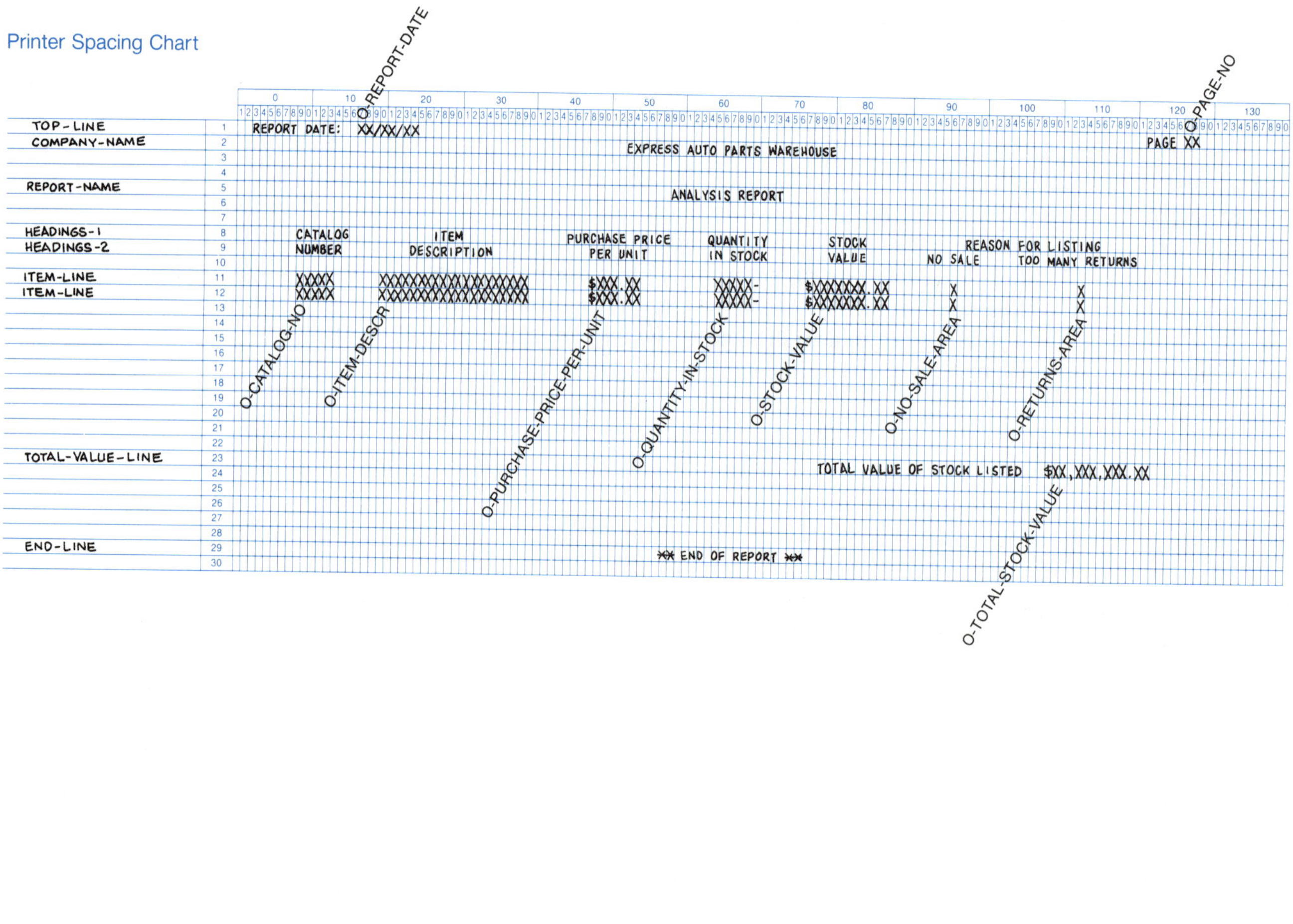

Step 2

Determining the data flow in this program is a simple task. The item records in the catalog file must be accessed and processed by the program. For each selected item, a detail line must be printed on the report. The resulting system flowchart is shown in Figure 1.10. Note that the input file has been named ITEM-ACTIVITY-FILE and the print file that contains the report has been named ANALYSIS-REPORT.

Notice that the system flowchart specifies the global function of the program, namely, to produce the analysis report. This overall task must now be analyzed carefully so that it can be separated into a hierarchy of manageable and clearly defined subtasks. The result of this analysis is the structure chart.

Whenever a program produces a report, the printer spacing chart that shows the report format is a useful guide in identifying task-related aspects of the program. For instance, in Figure 1.9, it's clear that the report must begin with the top-of-page documentation. It consists of five lines. The first of these lines must include the report date, and, consequently, the date must be obtained before the top line can be printed on the report. Once the documentation is printed, up to 30 detail lines are to be printed on the page. Since a detail line prints information related to a record in the input file, the input record must first be read and then processed. Once it has been processed, possibly resulting in a detail line on the report, the next record must be accessed from the input file and processed in turn. In other words, a loop is needed to read and process the records of the catalog file. When 30 detail lines have been printed, a new page must be prepared. And, when all the input records have been processed, a final total must be printed on the last page of the report. This total has to be accumulated during the processing of the records that meet the specified criteria. A computation task should therefore be included in the record-processing loop. And at the very end, an "End of Report" message must be printed.

Figure 1.10 System flowchart for the sample program

System Flowchart

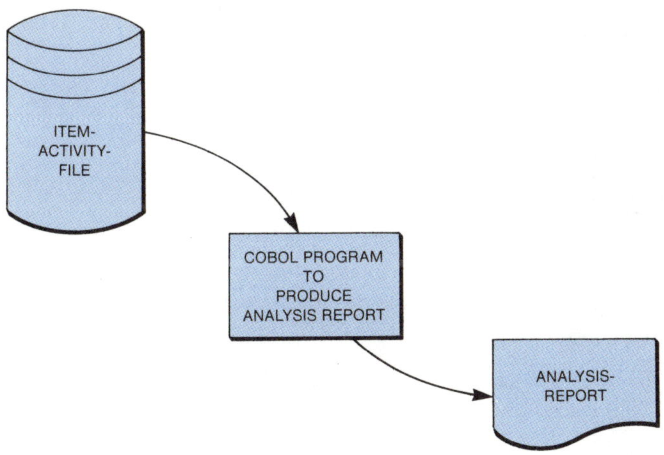

What does it mean to process an item record from the catalog file? Specifically, it means to test the quantity sold and the quantity returned. If the quantity sold is zero, or the quantity returned by customers is at least 50 percent of the quantity sold, the item must be listed on the report. In that case, two tasks must be carried out: (1) the value of the stock in inventory must be computed and it must be subtotaled into the accumulator that will ultimately contain the final total value of all the listed items; (2) a detail line must be prepared and printed on the report. Every time a detail line is printed, a record counter must be incremented and tested in order to satisfy the limit of 30 detail lines per page. When the limit is reached, a new page must be prepared.

The preceding analysis leads to the structure chart shown in Figure 1.11. In this chart, module 200 START UP will contain such items as opening the files, obtaining the report date from the system, initializing the flag that controls the record-processing loop, initializing the total-value accumulator, executing the module that prints the top-of-page documentation on the first page, and executing the read module to prime the input memory area with the first record of the input file. Module 230 FINISH UP will write the "End of Report" message and will close the files.

Figure 1.11 Structure chart for the sample program

Structure Chart

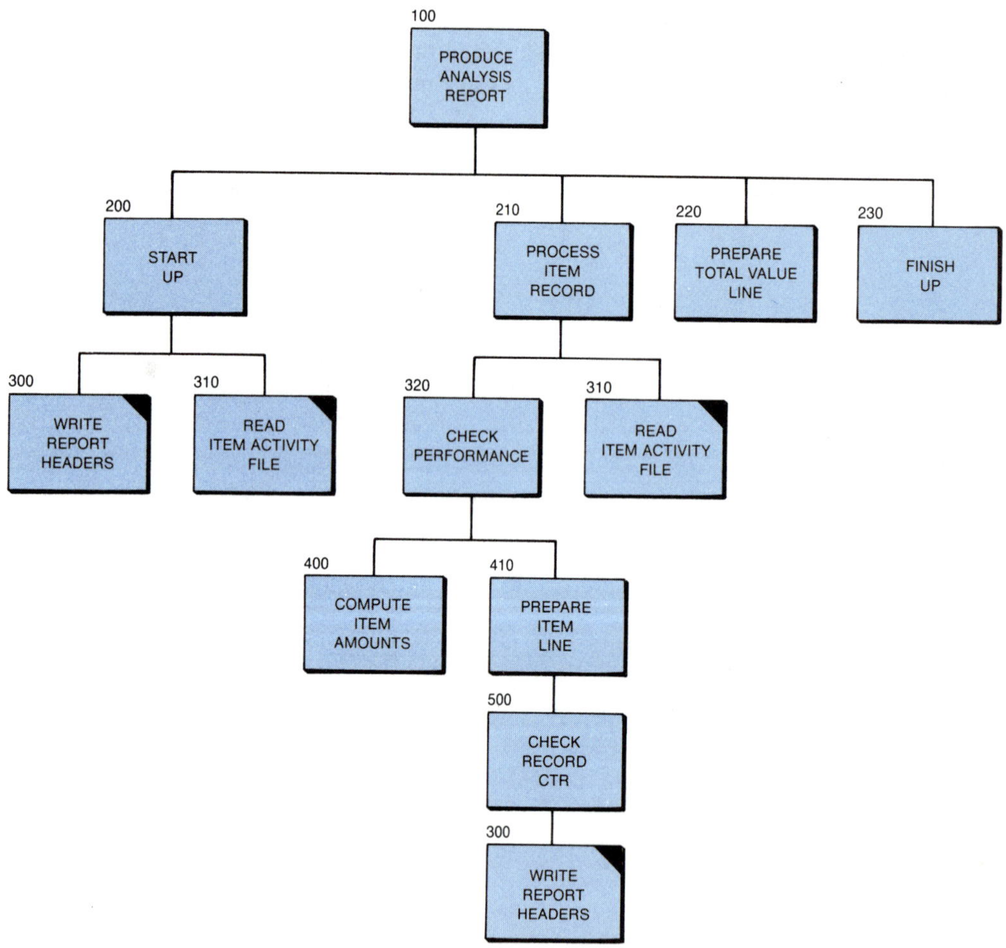

The detailed processing steps required to accomplish the task specified in each module, such as those listed above for modules 200 and 230, are usually itemized in the program pseudocode or the program flowchart. The program pseudocode that corresponds to the structure chart is shown in Figure 1.12.

Figure 1.12 Program pseudocode for the sample program

100-Produce-Analysis-Report.
1. Perform 200-Start-Up.
2. Perform 210-Process-Item-Record until no more records.
3. Perform 220-Prepare-Total-Value-Line.
4. Perform 230-Finish-Up.
5. Stop the run.

200-Start-Up.
1. Open the files.
2. Obtain the date from the system.
3. Move the date to Top-Line date.
4. Set page-number to zero.
5. Set the end-of-file flag WS-MORE-RECORDS to "YES".
6. Set the total-stock-value to zero.
7. Clear the record area Item-Line.
8. Perform 300-Write-Report-Headers.
9. Perform 310-Read-Item-Activity-File.

210-Process-Item-Record.
1. Perform 320-Check-Performance.
2. Perform 310-Read-Item-Activity-File.

220-Prepare-Total-Value-Line.
1. Move total-stock-value to Total-Value-Line total-stock-value.
2. Move Total-Value-Line to the output area Printline.
3. After advancing 5 lines, write the output record Printline.

230-Finish-Up.
1. Move End-Line to the output area Printline.
2. After advancing 10 lines, write the output record Printline.
3. Close the files.

300-Write-Report-Headers.
1. Add 1 to page-number.
2. Move page-number to Top-Line page-number.
3. Move Top-Line to the output area Printline.
4. After advancing to the top of a new page,
   write the output record Printline.
5. Move Company-Name to the output area Printline.
6. After advancing 1 line, write the output record Printline.
7. Move Report-Name to the output area Printline.
8. After advancing 3 lines, write the output record Printline.
9. Move Headings-1 to the output area Printline.
10. After advancing 3 lines, write the output record Printline.
11. Move Headings-2 to the output area Printline.
12. After advancing 1 line, write the output record Printline.
13. Set proper-spacing to 2.
14. Set record-counter to zero.

310-Read-Item-Activity-File.
1. Read an input Item-Record.
2. Test for end-of-file record;
   if EOF record reached, move "NO " to the end-of-file flag WS-MORE-RECORDS.

320-Check-Performance.
1. If input week-sales = zero or
   input week-returns > half of input week-sales,
   perform 400-Compute-Item-Amounts and
   perform 410-Prepare-Item-Line.

400-Compute-Item-Amounts.
1. Add input on-hand, input week-returns, input week-receipts, and then subtract input week-sales to equal quantity-in-stock.
2. Multiply quantity-in-stock by input purchase-price-per-unit to equal stock-value.
3. Add stock-value to total-stock-value.

410-Prepare-Item-Line.
1. Move input catalog-number to Item-Line catalog-number.
2. Move input item-description to Item-Line item-description.
3. Move input purchase-price-per-unit to Item-Line purchase-price-per-unit.
4. Move quantity-in-stock to Item-Line quantity-in-stock.
5. Move stock-value to Item-Line stock-value.
6. If input week-sales = 0, move "X" to Item-Line no-sale-area.
7. If input week-returns > half of input week-sales, move "X" to Item-Line returns-area.
8. Move Item-Line to the output area Printline.
9. After advancing proper-spacing, write the output record Printline.
10. Set proper-spacing to 1.
11. Perform 500-Check-Record-Ctr.

500-Check-Record-Ctr.
1. Add 1 to the record-counter.
2. If record-counter is equal to 30, perform 300-Write-Report-Headers.

Note the following:

1. The pseudocode contains as many paragraphs as there are modules in the structure chart.
2. The pseudocode paragraphs are written in ascending order by their numeric prefixes.
3. Just as the structure chart modules 200, 210, 220, and 230 are directly subordinate to module 100, so is the execution of the pseudocode paragraphs of the same name under the direct control of the primary paragraph 100-Produce-Analysis-Report. That is, the hierarchy built into the structure chart is carried over into the pseudocode.
4. Though modules 300 and 310 are repeated at different points in the structure chart, the paragraphs of the same name are written only once. However, they are referenced (performed) at different points in the pseudocode.
5. The structure chart does not show that module 210 is executed repeatedly; that is not the chart's function. However, the pseudocode does show that paragraph 210-Process-Item-Record is executed repeatedly. See step 2 of the primary paragraph.
6. The structure chart does not show that modules 400 and 410 are executed only if certain criteria are satisfied. Again, that is not the chart's function. However, paragraph 320-Check-Performance does show the conditions under which paragraphs 400-Compute-Item-Amounts and 410-Prepare-Item-Line are executed.

The program flowchart that corresponds to the structure chart is shown in Figure 1.13. Although it has the same objective as the pseudocode, many programmers prefer the visual impact that it provides to the wordiness of the pseudocode. For instance, see how obvious the record-processing loop is in the primary module 100-PRODUCE-ANALYSIS-REPORT and how obvious the selection criteria are in module 320-CHECK-PERFORMANCE.

In a flowchart,

1. Control is assumed to flow from top to bottom and from left to right across the page. Otherwise, arrowheads are used to indicate the direction of flow.
2. Every module begins and ends with a terminal symbol. The one that begins a module contains the name of the module. The one that ends the primary module contains the entry STOP RUN, and all others contain the word RETURN. (EXIT is used in some cases, and this will be explained later.)

Figure 1.13 Program flowchart for the sample program

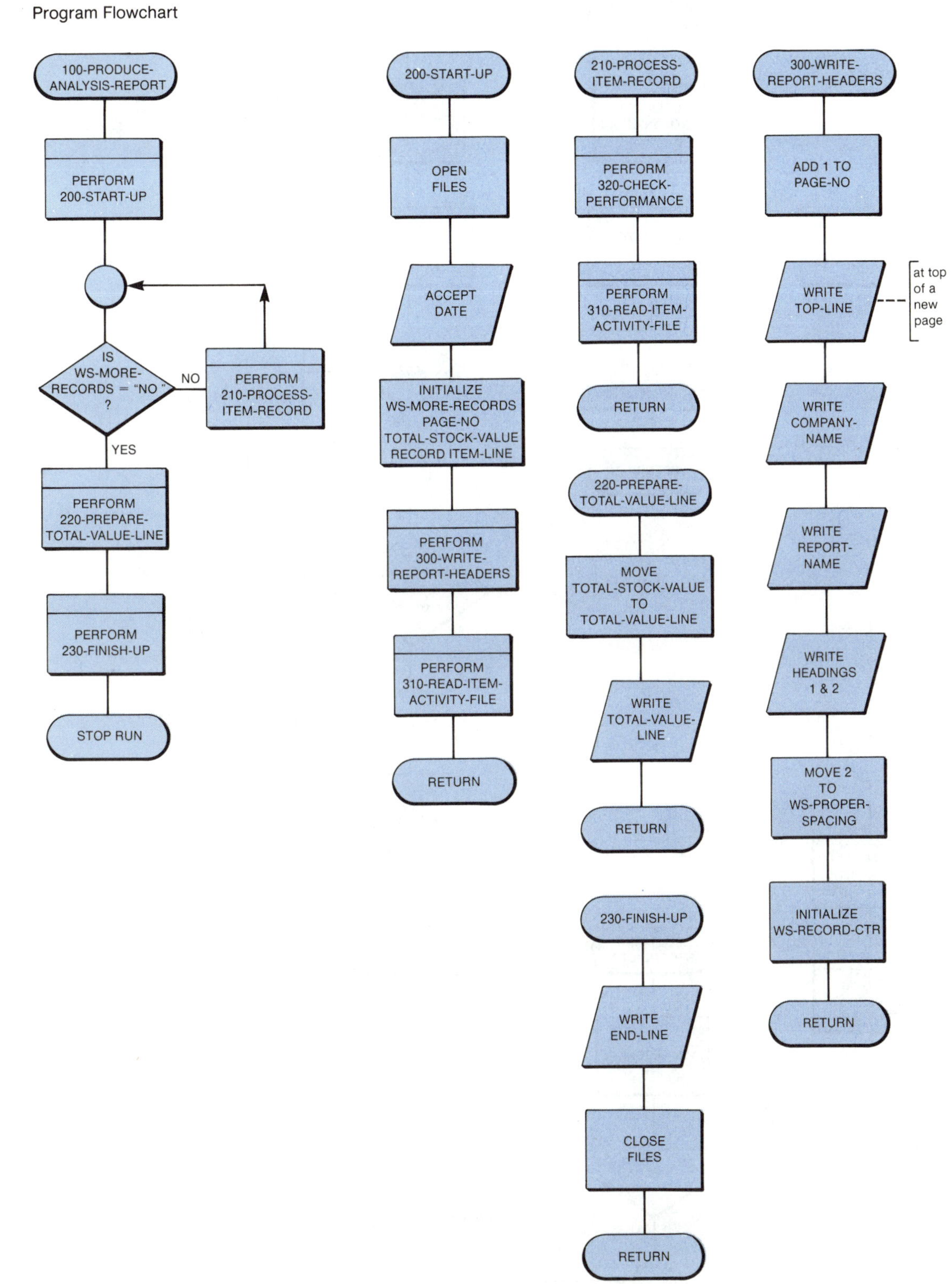

Figure 1.13 continued

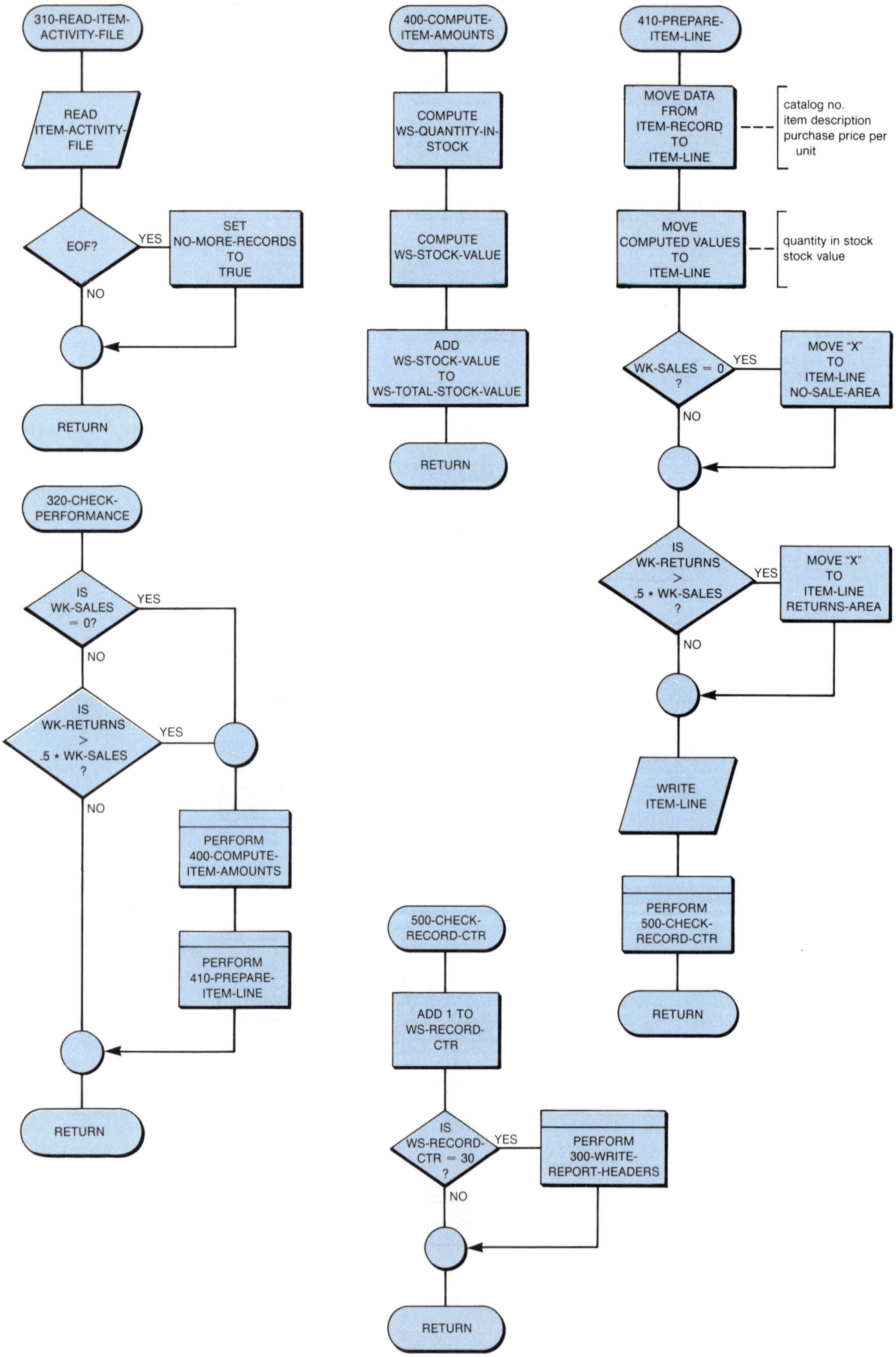

■ **Figure 1.14** Flowchart symbols

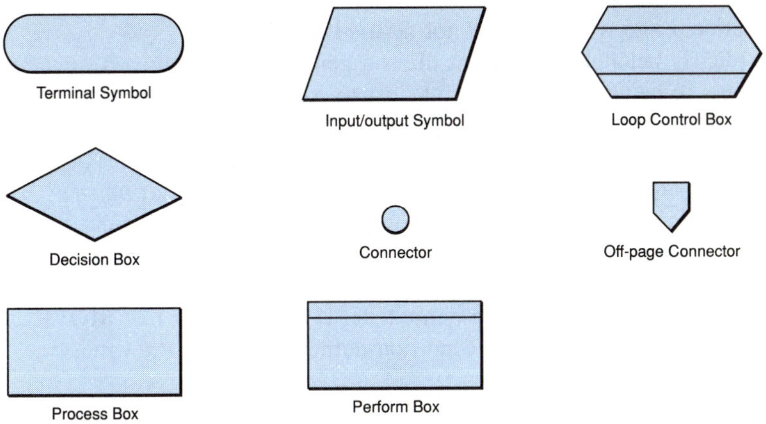

3. There are as many modules in the flowchart as there are modules in the structure chart (or paragraphs in the pseudocode).
4. Control enters a module at exactly one point, namely, the beginning terminal symbol, and control exits a module at exactly one point, namely, the terminal symbol at the end of the module.
5. The symbols, shown in Figure 1.14, indicate specific functions. For instance, a terminal symbol indicates the beginning or the end of a module. A lozenge, or decision box, indicates a test to be executed. A parallelogram indicates an input or an output function. A rectangle or process box indicates a simple process, such as an arithmetic operation or a data transfer. A rectangle with a double bar at the top, called a perform box, indicates a procedure to be performed. A connector or small circle indicates the merging of two branches. A loop control box indicates the intended use of a PERFORM-VARYING-UNTIL statement.

At this point, the programmer should select representative records from the catalog file and execute the processing steps of the pseudocode or flowchart to verify that the program in fact accomplishes the report it has been designed to accomplish. Errors detected here are easier to correct than they will be later. When this debugging phase is complete and the results obtained meet all program specifications, the end of the design phase of the problem-solving procedure has been reached.

The Design Implementation Phase for the Sample Program

In this phase, the program is coded as designed, stored in a file, compiled to detect syntax errors, debugged as needed, and, finally, subjected to a test run. Since you are already familiar with all of these steps, the coded program is simply presented to you in its entirety in Figure 1.15. Note the program entries that are directly related to the design tools prepared earlier.

In this text, all sample programs are coded so as to adhere to the 1985 ANSI (American National Standards Institute) COBOL standards and to programming techniques first presented in this author's volume 1: *Structured COBOL*. Some representative program entries in Figure 1.15 have been numbered in the sequence area, and comments that pertain to them are listed below.

1. The only paragraph in the IDENTIFICATION DIVISION is PROGRAM-ID. All other paragraphs have been labeled as obsolete and will not be used in this text. The documentation that they provided is included in comment lines (denoted by an asterisk in column 7) inserted following the PROGRAM-ID paragraph.
2. All sample programs have been compiled and run on a VAX VMS-8650. You will have to replace system-specific entries with those that apply to your computer system.

3. In the FD paragraph, the RECORD CONTAINS clause is coded for documentation purposes only. The DATA RECORD and LABEL RECORD clauses have been labeled obsolete and are not used in this text.
4. The word FILLER is now optional and will generally not be used in this text.
5. The only record coded as explicitly belonging to a print file is a general-purpose record, such as PRINTLINE. All other records to be written to the print file are coded in the WORKING-STORAGE SECTION.
6. The records that provide top-of-report documentation are coded as group items under a descriptive group name. They are coded in the same sequence in which they appear on the report. This approach increases the self-documentation of the program, decreases the chances of omitting record descriptions, and increases the efficiency of paging functions in virtual memory systems.
7. The SET statement may be used to make a condition-name true. It is equivalent to a MOVE statement that assigns to the data item to which the condition-name is attached the value specified in the definition of the condition-name.
8. The INITIALIZE statement assigns default values of ZERO to numeric and numeric-edited items, and SPACES to nonnumeric items. It may reference elementary or group items. If nondefault initial values are needed, the REPLACING phrase must be used.
9. END-IF is the explicit scope terminator for the IF statement. Many other statements also have scope terminators. (See the COBOL statement formats in Appendix B.)

Figure 1.15 The sample program

```
        IDENTIFICATION DIVISION.

**1     PROGRAM-ID.   EXPRESS-AUTO-ANALYSIS.

       ****************************************************************
       *                                                              *
       *  AUTHOR.          PAQUETTE.                                  *
       *  DATE WRITTEN.    AUGUST 1989.                               *
       *                                                              *
       *  THIS PROGRAM CHECKS THE INVENTORY FILE TO DETERMINE THOSE   *
       *  ITEMS OF QUESTIONABLE VALUE TO THE COMPANY, SPECIFICALLY,   *
       *  ITEMS THAT HAVE NOT SOLD AND ITEMS FOR WHICH TOO MANY       *
       *  RETURNS OCCUR.  THESE ITEMS ARE LISTED ON A REPORT, AND THE *
       *  REASON FOR THE LISTING IS SPECIFIED.                        *
       *                                                              *
       ****************************************************************

**2     ENVIRONMENT DIVISION.

        CONFIGURATION SECTION.

        SOURCE-COMPUTER.   VAX-VMS-8650.
        OBJECT-COMPUTER.   VAX-VMS-8650.

        INPUT-OUTPUT SECTION.

        FILE-CONTROL.
            SELECT ITEM-ACTIVITY-FILE  ASSIGN TO COB$INPUT.
            SELECT ANALYSIS-REPORT     ASSIGN TO COB$OUTPUT.

        DATA DIVISION.

        FILE SECTION.

        FD  ITEM-ACTIVITY-FILE
**3         RECORD CONTAINS 59 CHARACTERS.

        01  ITEM-RECORD.
            05 I-CATALOG-NO                PIC X(5).
            05 I-ITEM-DESCR                PIC X(20).
            05 I-PURCHASE-PRICE-PER-UNIT   PIC 999V99.
**4         05                             PIC X(5).
            05 I-ON-HAND                   PIC 9(4).
            05 I-ON-ORDER                  PIC 9(4).
            05 I-REORDER-POINT             PIC 9(4).
            05 I-WK-RECEIPTS               PIC 9(4).
            05 I-WK-SALES                  PIC 9(4).
               88 NO-SALE                           VALUE ZERO.
            05 I-WK-RETURNS                PIC 9(4).
```

■ **Figure 1.15** continued

```
       FD  ANALYSIS-REPORT
           RECORD CONTAINS 133 CHARACTERS.

**5    01  PRINTLINE        PIC X(133).

       WORKING-STORAGE SECTION.

       01  PROGRAM-CONTROLS.
           05 WS-MORE-RECORDS        PIC X(3).
              88 THERE-IS-A-RECORD             VALUE 'YES'.
              88 NO-MORE-RECORDS               VALUE 'NO '.
           05 WS-RECORD-CTR          PIC S9(2).
              88 PAGE-IS-FULL                  VALUE +30.
           05 WS-PROPER-SPACING      PIC 9.
           05 WS-REPORT-DATE         PIC X(6).
           05 WS-PAGE-NO             PIC S9(2).

       01  WORK-AREAS                COMP.
           05 WS-QUANTITY-IN-STOCK   PIC S9(5).
           05 WS-STOCK-VALUE         PIC S9(5)V99.
           05 WS-TOTAL-STOCK-VALUE   PIC S9(8)V99.

**6    01  REPORT-HEADERS.

           05  TOP-LINE.
               10                PIC X(17)  VALUE '   REPORT DATE:   '.
               10 O-REPORT-DATE  PIC XX/XX/XX.
               10                PIC X(97)  VALUE SPACES.
               10                PIC X(5)   VALUE 'PAGE '.
               10 O-PAGE-NO      PIC Z9.
               10                PIC X(5)   VALUE SPACES.

           05  COMPANY-NAME.
               10 PIC X(52)  VALUE SPACES.
               10 PIC X(28)  VALUE 'EXPRESS AUTO PARTS WAREHOUSE'.
               10 PIC X(53)  VALUE SPACES.

           05  REPORT-NAME.
               10 PIC X(59)  VALUE SPACES.
               10 PIC X(15)  VALUE 'ANALYSIS REPORT'.
               10 PIC X(59)  VALUE SPACES.

           05  HEADINGS-1.
               10 PIC X(8)   VALUE SPACES.
               10 PIC X(7)   VALUE 'CATALOG'.
               10 PIC X(11)  VALUE SPACES.
               10 PIC X(4)   VALUE 'ITEM'.
               10 PIC X(14)  VALUE SPACES.
               10 PIC X(14)  VALUE 'PURCHASE PRICE'.
               10 PIC X(5)   VALUE SPACES.
               10 PIC X(8)   VALUE 'QUANTITY'.
               10 PIC X(8)   VALUE SPACES.
               10 PIC X(5)   VALUE 'STOCK'.
               10 PIC X(13)  VALUE SPACES.
               10 PIC X(18)  VALUE 'REASON FOR LISTING'.
               10 PIC X(18)  VALUE SPACES.

           05  HEADINGS-2.
               10 PIC X(8)   VALUE SPACES.
               10 PIC X(6)   VALUE 'NUMBER'.
               10 PIC X(9)   VALUE SPACES.
               10 PIC X(11)  VALUE 'DESCRIPTION'.
               10 PIC X(13)  VALUE SPACES.
               10 PIC X(8)   VALUE 'PER UNIT'.
               10 PIC X(8)   VALUE SPACES.
               10 PIC X(8)   VALUE 'IN STOCK'.
               10 PIC X(8)   VALUE SPACES.
               10 PIC X(5)   VALUE 'VALUE'.
               10 PIC X(8)   VALUE SPACES.
               10 PIC X(7)   VALUE 'NO SALE'.
               10 PIC X(5)   VALUE SPACES.
               10 PIC X(16)  VALUE 'TOO MANY RETURNS'.
               10 PIC X(13)  VALUE SPACES.
```

```
       01  ITEM-LINE.
           05 CARRIAGE-CONTROL            PIC X.
           05                             PIC X(7).
           05 O-CATALOG-NO                PIC X(5).
           05                             PIC X(6).
           05 O-ITEM-DESCR                PIC X(20).
           05                             PIC X(8).
           05 O-PURCHASE-PRICE-PER-UNIT   PIC $ZZ9.99.
           05                             PIC X(10).
           05 O-QUANTITY-IN-STOCK         PIC ZZZZ9-.
           05                             PIC X(6).
           05 O-STOCK-VALUE               PIC $Z(6)9.99-.
           05                             PIC X(7).
           05 O-NO-SALE-AREA              PIC X.
           05                             PIC X(16).
           05 O-RETURNS-AREA              PIC X.
           05                             PIC X(20).

       01  TOTAL-VALUE-LINE.
           05                       PIC X(78)  VALUE SPACES.
           05                       PIC X(30)  VALUE
                                    'TOTAL VALUE OF STOCK LISTED:   '.
           05 O-TOTAL-STOCK-VALUE PIC $ZZ,ZZZ,ZZ9.99-.
           05                       PIC X(11)  VALUE SPACES.

       01  END-LINE.
           05 PIC X(57)  VALUE SPACES.
           05 PIC X(19)  VALUE '** END OF REPORT **'.
           05 PIC X(57)  VALUE SPACES.

       PROCEDURE DIVISION.

       100-PRODUCE-ANALYSIS-REPORT.
           PERFORM 200-START-UP.
           PERFORM 210-PROCESS-ITEM-RECORD
               UNTIL NO-MORE-RECORDS.
           PERFORM 220-PREPARE-TOTAL-VALUE-LINE.
           PERFORM 230-FINISH-UP.
           STOP RUN.

       200-START-UP.
           OPEN INPUT ITEM-ACTIVITY-FILE
                OUTPUT ANALYSIS-REPORT.
           ACCEPT WS-REPORT-DATE FROM DATE.
           MOVE WS-REPORT-DATE TO O-REPORT-DATE.
           MOVE ZERO TO WS-PAGE-NO.
**7        SET THERE-IS-A-RECORD TO TRUE.
**8        INITIALIZE WS-TOTAL-STOCK-VALUE
                      ITEM-LINE.
           PERFORM 300-WRITE-REPORT-HEADERS.
           PERFORM 310-READ-ITEM-ACTIVITY-FILE.

       210-PROCESS-ITEM-RECORD.
           PERFORM 320-CHECK-PERFORMANCE.
           PERFORM 310-READ-ITEM-ACTIVITY-FILE.

       220-PREPARE-TOTAL-VALUE-LINE.
           MOVE WS-TOTAL-STOCK-VALUE TO O-TOTAL-STOCK-VALUE.
           WRITE PRINTLINE FROM TOTAL-VALUE-LINE
               AFTER ADVANCING 5 LINES.

       230-FINISH-UP.
           WRITE PRINTLINE FROM END-LINE
               AFTER ADVANCING 10 LINES.
           CLOSE ITEM-ACTIVITY-FILE
                 ANALYSIS-REPORT.

       300-WRITE-REPORT-HEADERS.
           ADD 1 TO WS-PAGE-NO.
           MOVE WS-PAGE-NO TO O-PAGE-NO.
           WRITE PRINTLINE FROM TOP-LINE
               AFTER ADVANCING PAGE.
           WRITE PRINTLINE FROM COMPANY-NAME
               AFTER ADVANCING 1 LINE.
           WRITE PRINTLINE FROM REPORT-NAME
               AFTER ADVANCING 3 LINES.
           WRITE PRINTLINE FROM HEADINGS-1
               AFTER ADVANCING 3 LINES.
           WRITE PRINTLINE FROM HEADINGS-2
               AFTER ADVANCING 1 LINE.
           MOVE 2 TO WS-PROPER-SPACING.
           INITIALIZE WS-RECORD-CTR.
```

```
        310-READ-ITEM-ACTIVITY-FILE.
            READ ITEM-ACTIVITY-FILE RECORD
                AT END
                    SET NO-MORE-RECORDS TO TRUE.

        320-CHECK-PERFORMANCE.
            IF NO-SALE OR I-WK-RETURNS > .5 * I-WK-SALES
                PERFORM 400-COMPUTE-ITEM-AMOUNTS
                PERFORM 410-PREPARE-ITEM-LINE
**9         END-IF.

        400-COMPUTE-ITEM-AMOUNTS.
            COMPUTE WS-QUANTITY-IN-STOCK ROUNDED =
                I-ON-HAND + I-WK-RETURNS + I-WK-RECEIPTS -
                I-WK-SALES.
            MULTIPLY WS-QUANTITY-IN-STOCK BY I-PURCHASE-PRICE-PER-UNIT
                GIVING WS-STOCK-VALUE.
            ADD WS-STOCK-VALUE TO WS-TOTAL-STOCK-VALUE.

        410-PREPARE-ITEM-LINE.
            MOVE SPACES TO ITEM-LINE.
            MOVE I-CATALOG-NO TO O-CATALOG-NO.
            MOVE I-ITEM-DESCR TO O-ITEM-DESCR.
            MOVE I-PURCHASE-PRICE-PER-UNIT TO O-PURCHASE-PRICE-PER-UNIT.
            MOVE WS-QUANTITY-IN-STOCK TO O-QUANTITY-IN-STOCK.
            MOVE WS-STOCK-VALUE TO O-STOCK-VALUE.
            IF NO-SALE
                MOVE 'X' TO O-NO-SALE-AREA
            END-IF.
            IF I-WK-RETURNS > .5 * I-WK-SALES
                MOVE 'X' TO O-RETURNS-AREA
            END-IF.
            WRITE PRINTLINE FROM ITEM-LINE
                AFTER ADVANCING WS-PROPER-SPACING.
            MOVE 1 TO WS-PROPER-SPACING.
            PERFORM 500-CHECK-RECORD-CTR.

        500-CHECK-RECORD-CTR.
            ADD 1 TO WS-RECORD-CTR.
            IF PAGE-IS-FULL
                PERFORM 300-WRITE-REPORT-HEADERS
            END-IF.
```

Figure 1.16 shows the data file that was used for a test run of the program, and Figure 1.17 shows the report that it produced.

Obviously, the output should be examined carefully to make sure that it's in full conformity with the specifications of the problem. The results of arithmetic computations should be checked for mathematical accuracy. Are there any omissions? Is the report complete? If a close examination indicates that everything is in order, then the programmer's job is done. The original statement of the problem, the design tools, the program, the sample data file, and the report are assembled and submitted as the complete package to the one who requested the program.

■ Should You Review?

Students who take a second semester of COBOL do so under various circumstances. For some, it may be the continuation of the previous semester's work with only four or five weeks intervening. For others, the time that has elapsed may be three or four months. And for a few, it may be one or two years! Do you feel a need to review? If so, the end-of-chapter material includes review questions and exercises, debugging activities, and programming exercises that should help to refresh your memory and bring COBOL back into focus.

■ Important Terms in Chapter 1

design implementation phase
design phase
flowchart symbols
INITIALIZE
input record layout form
printer spacing chart
problem-solving procedure
program flowchart
program pseudocode
scope terminator
SET
structure chart
system flowchart

Figure 1.16 Data file for the sample program

```
0346RCB ANTENNA              033290399503000400050004000250002 0          03
0348N23 CHANNEL MOBILE CB20829249950190000001000000000050000             05
0359BCB CONVERTER            020790249507500000050000000275000 5          04
0368WFM ANTENNA              006650079805000000030000000030000 00         01
0382NSTEREO SPEAKERS/PR      020790249503500200050000000200005 0          04
0462UFLEXSOCKET WRENCH       001910022902000500080002000175001 0          01
1033WFM RADIO AMPLIFIER      010820129803250000030000000050003 0          07
1048THITCH BALL COVER        000660007906500000050000000350001 0          01
1219XRW DEFOGGER             024980299805250000030000000003001 6          09
1242WRV ALARM SYSTEM         016630199500750100010001000070000 8          08
1263PTORQUE WRENCH           014980179802000300060002000400002 0          03
1264Y8000LB. JACK STAND      010820129801500000080000000000000 1          09
1352VTUNE-UP TESTER          033290399503000200040000000100005 5          04
1503WELECTRONIC FILTER       010820129805000000030000000085000 2          01
1517ASPARE TIRE LOCK         003740044900750100010000000030000 0          02
1584ARV ANTENNA              041630499509500100080001000210000 5          05
1593XHD. TIE DOWN            014980179806000000040000000195002 0          02
1616WAIR DIESEL HORN         014150169800800000005000000001000 0          06
1685TBRAKE CABLE ADJUSTER000660007901000400050003000100000 0             01
1762NBUMPER GUARDS           014150169812500000100000000400005 0          03
1775BBOLT-ON HITCH           056630679505000000040000000200000 0          04
1787A1000-WATT CONVERTER 289963479500120000001000000000000 0              05
1842N16" FULL WHEEL COVER0207902495052000000300000002200000 0             03
1914YC-11 TRAILER HITCH      014150169806000000040000000150000 0          08
2181XEXHAUST HEADERS         056630679505000000010000000050002 8          04
2326RPOWER MUFFLER           014130169502000300050002000190000 0          03
3731W3-2 BBL MANIFOLD        083290999501800000010000000050000 5          08
3734NCAMSHAFT                066630799500900050010000000060000 2          07
5507RBONDED BRAKE SHOE       006650079806000500100004000300006 0          02
5524YDISC BRAKE PADS         012460149505000400100000000280000 8          04
5534AMASTER CYLINDER         012460149505000600100005000350006 0          05
5557PENGINE OIL COOLER       033290399500750100010001000050000 0          06
5577PSOLENOID SWITCH         004580054910000400080002000480005 0          02
5596WHD STAINLESS-ST FAN 014150169800900020010000000001000 4              09
7519YSOLID STATE TACH        033290399503250000020000000150003 0          02
7568Y30-PC TUNE-UP KIT       033290399503000200040000000250000 0          04
7580XRAM AIR SYSTEM          016630199500620000005000000005000 3          01
8419AHOLLEY CARBURETOR       091631099507100100050002000425001 0          03
8572VREAR END LIFT KIT       006650079801800000010000000010000 0          05
8583NWL-BEARING CAPS/PR      003320039803000400080002000150000 0          01
8636ELEAF SPRINGS/PR         074960899503200000002000000000000 2          04
8776NRING & PINION GEARS 083290999503500100030001000125001 5              03
8815PREAR-AXLE SHAFT ASSM014150169800900100020001000030000 0              03
8823UDUAL RHEOSTAT DIMMER010820129804500000030000000080002 5              07
8880WFOG LIGHT KIT           024980299803500200040001000080000 0          04
8896NENGINE COOLER KIT       033290399502500000020000000010000 0          06
8912NREPLACEMENT WHEEL       014150169801000200040002000100000 0          04
8931RSHOCK ABSORBERS/PR      020790249512000600100004000750002 0          03
9977RAIR COMPRESSOR KIT      083290999501100000010000000020000 5          03
9998FFIBERGLASS HARDTOP      283323399800600000005000000001000 2          05
```

Figure 1.17 Report produced by the sample program

```
REPORT DATE:   89/08/30                                                                          PAGE  1
                                            EXPRESS AUTO PARTS WAREHOUSE

                                                  ANALYSIS REPORT

      CATALOG          ITEM               PURCHASE PRICE    QUANTITY       STOCK              REASON FOR LISTING
      NUMBER        DESCRIPTION              PER UNIT       IN STOCK       VALUE          NO SALE     TOO MANY RETURNS

      1033W     FM RADIO AMPLIFIER           $ 10.82          305      $   3300.10                        X
      1219X     RW DEFOGGER                  $ 24.98          511      $  12764.78                        X
      1264Y     8000LB. JACK STAND           $ 10.82          151      $   1633.82        X               X
      1352V     TUNE-UP TESTER               $ 33.29          255      $   8488.95                        X
      1787A     1000-WATT CONVERTER          $289.96           12      $   3479.52        X
      2181X     EXHAUST HEADERS              $ 56.63          478      $  27069.14                        X
      5596W     HD STAINLESS-ST FAN          $ 14.15           93      $   1315.95                        X
      7580X     RAM AIR SYSTEM               $ 16.63           60      $    997.80                        X
      8636E     LEAF SPRINGS/PR              $ 74.96          322      $  24137.12        X               X
      9998F     FIBERGLASS HARDTOP           $283.32           61      $  17282.52                        X


                                                             TOTAL VALUE OF STOCK LISTED:  $    100,469.70




                                                ** END OF REPORT **
```

Exercises

1. Name the two phases of the problem-solving procedure.
2. Name and briefly explain each of the tools developed by the programmer during the first phase of the problem-solving procedure.
3. Briefly explain the functions of the compiler.
4. Briefly explain the functions of the SELECT statement in the FILE-CONTROL paragraph.
5. What are the most basic logic structures?
6. Briefly explain the essential purpose of each division of a COBOL program.
7. Identify the class code and the special characters that may be used in the PIC clause of a numeric data item description. Briefly explain each one.
8. Since the class code X allows any character of the COBOL character set as a valid character, why can it not be used exclusively?
9. Briefly explain the function of the ROUNDED option in an arithmetic statement.
10. Briefly explain the function of the ON SIZE ERROR clause in an arithmetic statement.
11. Explain why it is a good programming practice to insert a trailing minus sign in a numeric-edited PICTURE.
12. Explain the difference between a set of sequential tests and a set of nested tests.
13. List the relational operators that may be coded in a relational test, both in words and symbols.
14. Explain the term "control break."
15. Explain the difference between subtotaling and rolling-forward.
16. Explain the expression "forcing the last footings" in a control break report.
17. Name the three classifications of printed reports and briefly explain each one.
18. **a.** If the values of table elements are specified by the use of VALUE clauses, the resulting table is classified as a ________ table.
    b. If the values of table elements are specified by the execution of statements in the PROCEDURE DIVISION, the resulting table is classified as a ________ table.
19. A table description must always contain at least one ________ clause.
20. The input record layout in Figure 1.18 shows the name and class of each field. Assign a descriptive name to the record, and then write the appropriate record description entries as needed in the FILE SECTION of the DATA DIVISION.

Figure 1.18

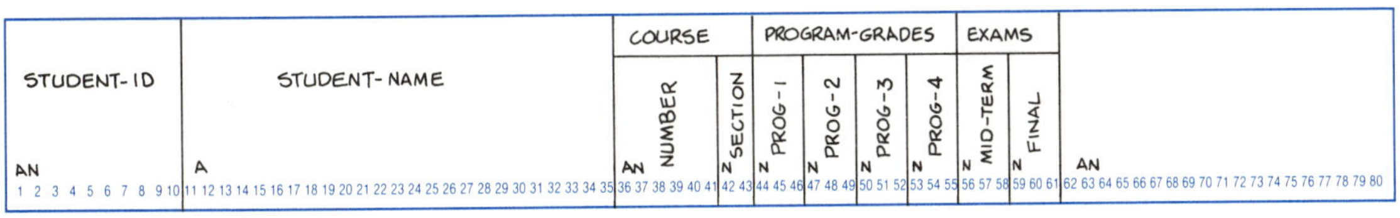

AN: Alphanumeric
A: Alphabetic
N: Numeric

Record Name: ____________________

21. Examine each entry below. If the entry is correct, write OK on the corresponding line. If the entry contains any error, write in the correct coding.

```
A    B                                                        A    B
DATA DIVISION                                                 ____________________
FILE-SECTION.                                                 ____________________
FD   INPUT-FILE.                                              ____________________
     RECORD CONTAINS 50 CHARACTERS.                           ____________________
01   INPUT-RECORD                                             ____________________
     05 I-SSN                          PIC X(9)               ____________________
     05 I-NAME                         PIC X22.               ____________________
     05 I ADRESS                       PIC X(15).             ____________________
     05 I CITY-STATE                   PICX (12.              ____________________
     05 FILLER                         PIC 1X.                ____________________
     05 I-PERSONAL-INFO                PIC X(15).             ____________________
         10 I-SEX                      A1.                    ____________________
         10 I-MARITAL-STATUS           PIC X (1)              ____________________
         10 I-DATE-OF-BIRTH            PIC 6X.                ____________________
             15 I-MONTH BORN           PIC 99.                ____________________
             15 I DAY BORN             PIC 9(2).              ____________________
             15 I YEAR BORN            PIC 2 9s.              ____________________
```

22. Given the flowchart segment in Figure 1.19.

a. Code the statement corresponding to the iteration structure in the module 100-PRODUCE-REPORT:

i. without the use of the TEST option.

ii. with the use of the TEST option.

b. Code the corresponding entries in a PROCEDURE DIVISION. (Show two paragraphs.)

c. Code the procedure 230-PROCESS-RECORD as an in-line PERFORM.

Figure 1.19

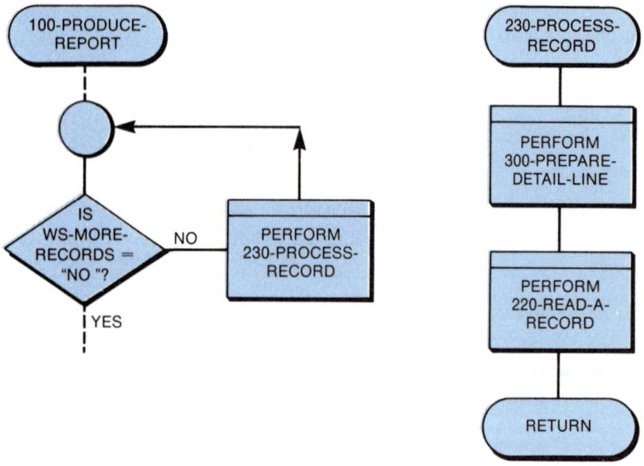

23. Given the following:

```
01  GROUP-ITEM.
    05 ITEM-1               PIC XXX.
    05 ITEM-2               PIC A(4).
    05 SUB-GROUP.
       10 ITEM-3            PIC 999.
       10 ITEM-4            PIC 9V99.
       10 ITEM-5            PIC $ZZ9.99.
    05 ITEM-6               PIC X(10) JUSTIFIED RIGHT.
    05 ITEM-7               PIC XX/XX/XX.
```

a. Describe the contents of each field following the statement INITIALIZE GROUP-ITEM.

b. Identify and describe the contents of the fields affected by each of the following statements:

i.
```
INITIALIZE GROUP-ITEM
    REPLACING ALPHANUMERIC DATA BY "MARY".
```

ii.
```
INITIALIZE SUB-GROUP
    REPLACING NUMERIC DATA BY 18.5.
```

iii.
```
INITIALIZE SUB-GROUP
    REPLACING NUMERIC-EDITED DATA BY 18.5.
```

iv.
```
INITIALIZE GROUP-ITEM
    REPLACING ALPHANUMERIC-EDITED DATA BY "101587".
```

24. Write the complete sequence of statements for the flowchart segments in Figure 1.20.

Figure 1.20

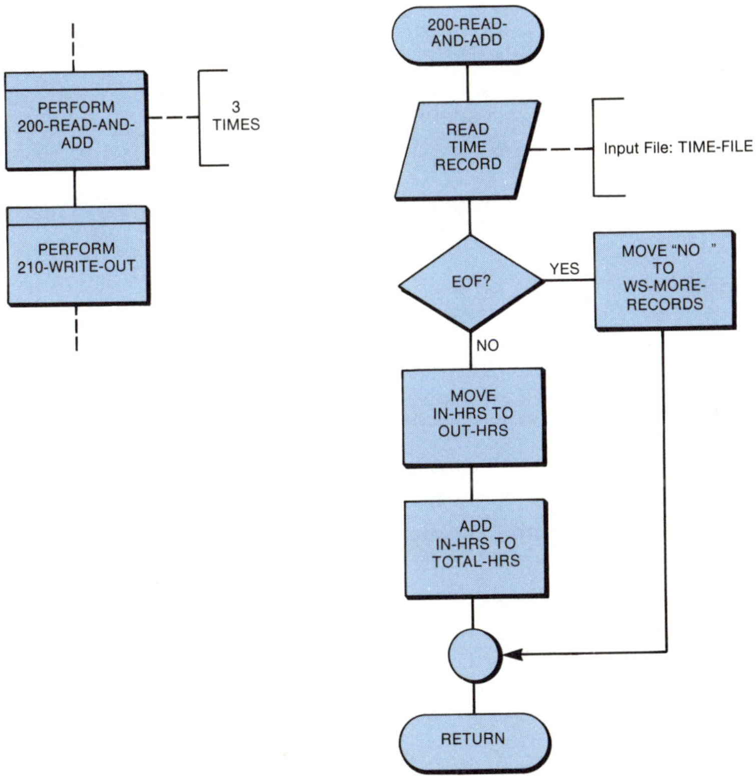

25. In each case, show the value stored in the receiving field after the following MOVE statement is executed:

```
MOVE -123 TO FIELD-X.
```

```
FIELD-X PICTURE:
```

a. 9(4)
b. S9(6)
c. S99
d. S999V99
e. 99V99
f. X(6)

26. Code the PROCEDURE DIVISION entries that correspond to the pseudocode or flowchart of Figure 1.21a and b. Assume the input file is INVENTORY-FILE and the output file is INVENTORY-REPORT.

27. Given the following data items with PICTUREs and initial values as specified.

Data Item	PICTURE	Value Before Execution
FIELD-A	S99999	00300+
FIELD-B	S9999	4533+
FIELD-C	S9999	5800+
FIELD-D	S999V9(4)	125.0554+
FIELD-E	S99	34−
FIELD-F	S99V99	80.25−
FIELD-G	S999V9	750.8+
FIELD-H	$9(4).0099	$0038.0055
FIELD-I	$Z9.99	$ 4.80

In each case below, specify the contents of each data item after the statement is executed.

a. `ADD FIELD-A FIELD-B TO FIELD-C.`

b. `ADD FIELD-A FIELD-B GIVING FIELD-C.`

c.
```
SUBTRACT FIELD-F FROM FIELD-E ROUNDED
      ON SIZE ERROR
          ADD 1 TO FIELD-A
      NOT ON SIZE ERROR
          SUBTRACT 1 FROM FIELD-A.
```

d. `SUBTRACT FIELD-F FROM FIELD-D GIVING FIELD-I ROUNDED.`

e. `MULTIPLY 5 BY FIELD-E GIVING FIELD-A.`

f.
```
MULTIPLY FIELD-F BY FIELD-D
      ON SIZE ERROR
          SUBTRACT FIELD-F FROM FIELD-D GIVING FIELD-E ROUNDED.
```

28. Use the following data items with PICTUREs and initial values as specified to complete the exercises below.

Data Item	PICTURE	Value Before Execution
FIELD-A	S99999	+00300
FIELD-B	S9999	+4533
FIELD-C	S9999	+5800
FIELD-D	S999V9(4)	+125.0554
FIELD-E	S99	−34
FIELD-F	S99V99	−80.25
FIELD-G	S999V9	+750.8
FIELD-H	$9999.0099	$0038.0055
FIELD-I	$Z9.99	$ 4.80

In each case below, specify the contents of each data item after the arithmetic statement is executed.

a. `DIVIDE FIELD-G BY FIELD-E GIVING FIELD-F ROUNDED.`

b.
```
DIVIDE FIELD-C BY FIELD-E GIVING FIELD-I ROUNDED
      ON SIZE ERROR
          MULTIPLY FIELD-C BY FIELD-E GIVING FIELD-A ROUNDED
      NOT ON SIZE ERROR
          SUBTRACT FIELD-E FROM FIELD-B
  END-DIVIDE.
```

c. `COMPUTE FIELD-G ROUNDED = FIELD-C / FIELD-E + FIELD-D * 5.`

Figure 1.21

a.

100-Produce-Inventory-Report.

1. Perform 200-Start-Up.
2. Perform 210-Read-Inventory-File-Record.
3. Perform 220-Process-Inventory-Record until no more records.

.
.

200-Start-Up.

1. Open the files.
2. Set the end-of-file flag WS-MORE-RECORDS to "YES".

210-Read-Inventory-File-Record.

1. Read an input inventory-File record.
2. Test for end-of-file record; if EOF record reached, move "NO " to the flag WS-MORE-RECORDS.

220-Process-Inventory-Record.

.
.
.

9. Move Inventory-Line record to the output area Printline.
10. After advancing 2 lines, write the output record Printline.
11. Perform 210-Read-Inventory-File-Record.

b.

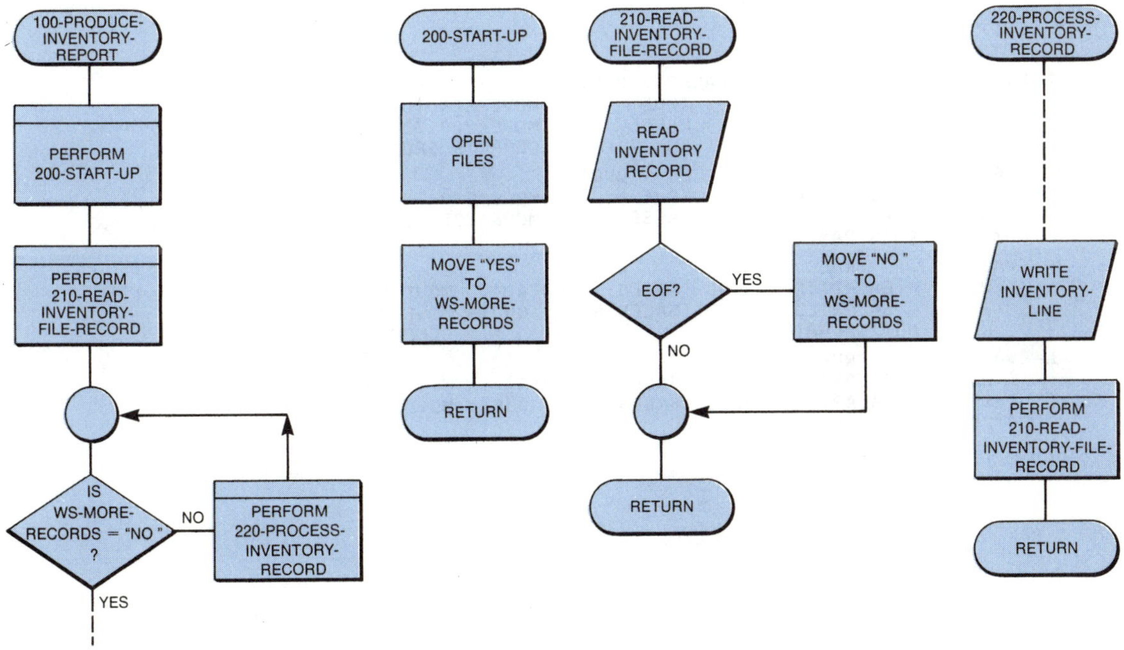

29. Use IF statements to code the logic illustrated in Figure 1.22.

30. Use IF statements to code the logic illustrated in Figure 1.23.

31. Given the flowchart segment in Figure 1.24, which of the following groups contain correct coding?

a.
```
IF SALARIED AND SALES > QUOTA
    MOVE 500 TO BONUS
ELSE
    MOVE 200 TO BONUS
END-IF.
COMPUTE GROSS-PAY = . . .
```

b.
```
IF SALARIED
    IF SALES > QUOTA
        MOVE 500 TO BONUS
    ELSE
        MOVE 200 TO BONUS
ELSE
    COMPUTE GROSS-PAY = . . .
```

c.
```
IF SALARIED
    THEN
        IF SALES > QUOTA
            MOVE 500 TO BONUS
        ELSE
            MOVE 200 TO BONUS
    ELSE
        NEXT SENTENCE.
COMPUTE GROSS-PAY = . . .
```

d.
```
IF SALARIED
    IF SALES > QUOTA
        MOVE 500 TO BONUS
    ELSE
        MOVE 200 TO BONUS
END-IF.
COMPUTE GROSS-PAY = . . .
```

e.
```
IF NOT SALARIED
    NEXT SENTENCE
ELSE
    IF SALES NOT > QUOTA
        MOVE 200 TO BONUS
    ELSE
        MOVE 500 TO BONUS
    END-IF
END-IF.
COMPUTE GROSS-PAY = . . .
```

f.
```
EVALUATE SALARIED ALSO  SALES > QUOTA
    WHEN    TRUE     ALSO    TRUE         MOVE 500 TO BONUS
    WHEN    TRUE     ALSO    FALSE        MOVE 200 TO BONUS
    WHEN    FALSE    ALSO    ANY          COMPUTE GROSS-PAY = . . .
```

g.
```
EVALUATE SALARIED ALSO  SALES > QUOTA
    WHEN    TRUE     ALSO    TRUE         MOVE 500 TO BONUS
    WHEN    TRUE     ALSO    FALSE        MOVE 200 TO BONUS.
COMPUTE GROSS-PAY = . . .
```

h.
```
EVALUATE       TRUE      ALSO        TRUE
    WHEN     SALARIED    ALSO   SALES > QUOTA      MOVE 500 TO BONUS
    WHEN     SALARIED    ALSO   SALES NOT > QUOTA  MOVE 200 TO BONUS
    WHEN   NOT SALARIED  ALSO         ANY          COMPUTE GROSS-PAY = . . .
```

i.
```
EVALUATE       TRUE      ALSO        TRUE
    WHEN     SALARIED    ALSO   SALES > QUOTA      MOVE 500 TO BONUS
    WHEN     SALARIED    ALSO   SALES NOT > QUOTA  MOVE 200 TO BONUS.
COMPUTE GROSS-PAY = . . .
```

■ **Figure 1.22**

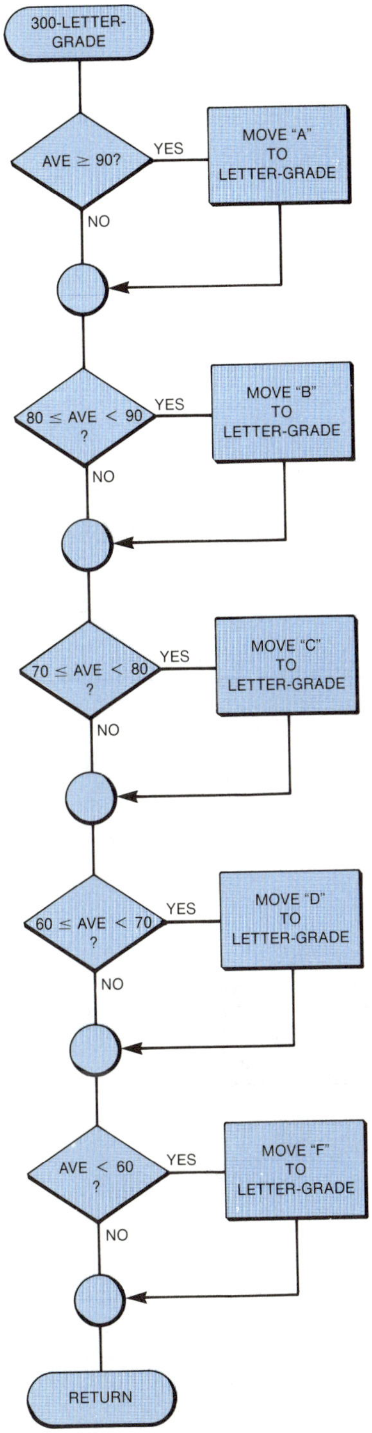

■ **Figure 1.23**

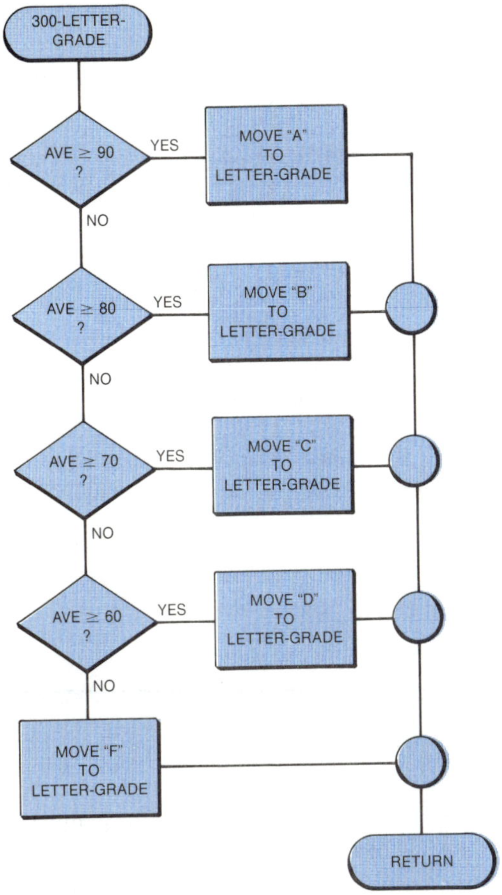

■ **Figure 1.24**

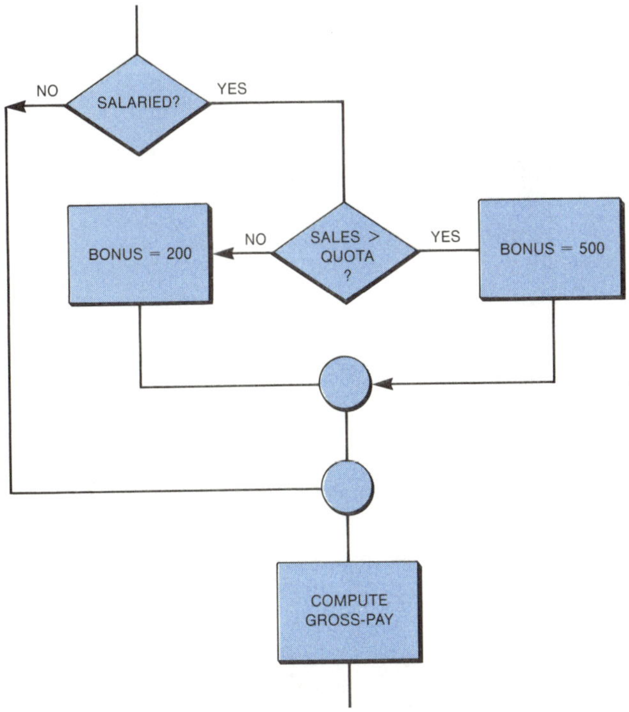

32. Figure 1.25 shows elements needed in a control break.
   - **a.** What is the first value that will be assigned to the store-control field in working storage, WS-STORE-CONTROL?
   - **b.** Code the statement that will be used to test for a control break.
   - **c.** How many records will be read while the first store-control value is in the field WS-STORE-CONTROL? Which ones?
   - **d.** How many records will be processed while the first store-control value is in the field WS-STORE-CONTROL? Which ones?
   - **e.** At which point will the first value in the store-control field WS-STORE-CONTROL be replaced by the second? What will be the second store-control value?
   - **f.** Explain what will signal the printing of the store summary for the first store; the second store; the last store.

33. Refer to Figure 1.26.
   - **a.** Code an INSPECT statement that will replace the region codes 1, 2, 3, and 4 by the letters A, B, C, and D, respectively.
   - **b.** Code an INSPECT statement that will count the spaces in the name field.
   - **c.** Code an INSPECT statement that will count the zeros in a record.
   - **d.** Code an INSPECT statement that will change all uppercase letters to lowercase letters.
   - **e.** Code an INSPECT statement that will replace a period (.) and a comma (,) in the name field by spaces.
   - **f.** Code an INSPECT statement that will count the characters in a person's last name (characters before the first comma!).

Figure 1.25

```
WORKING-STORAGE SECTION.
 .
 .
 .
    05 WS-STORE-CONTROL    PIC XXX.
```

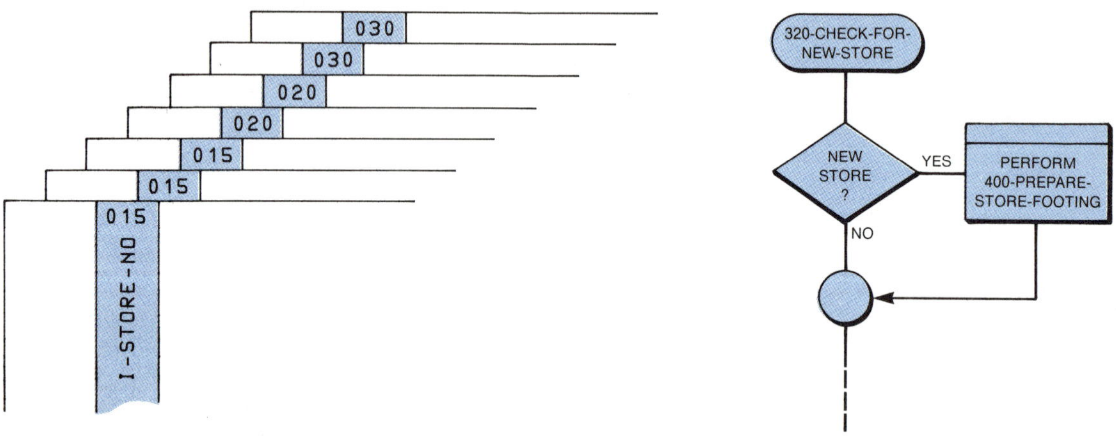

Figure 1.26

Record Layout Form

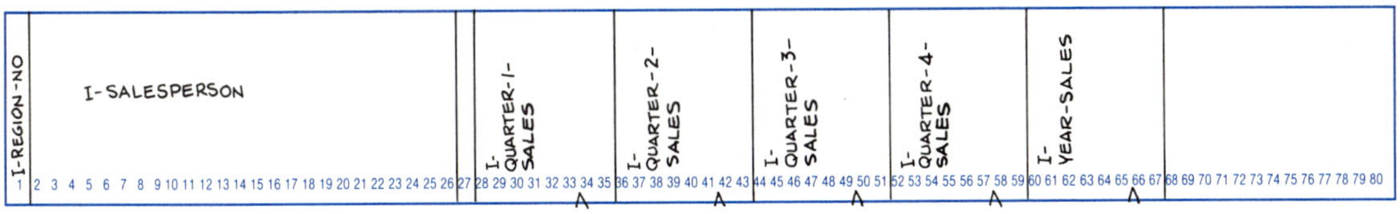

Record Name: SALESPERSON-RECORD

34. Given the following data item descriptions:

```
05 FIELD-A   PIC X(20)   VALUE "ABCDEFGHIJKLMNOPQRST".
05 FIELD-B   PIC 9       VALUE 5.
05 FIELD-C   PIC 99      VALUE 12.
```

Identify the subgroup specified by each of the following reference modifications:

a. FIELD-A (3:2)

b. FIELD-C (1:)

c. FIELD-A (FIELD-C / 2 : FIELD-C - 2 * FIELD-B)

35. The input data file QUARTER-SALES-FILE consists of records formatted as shown in Figure 1.27. One of the records in the file is shown below.

```
MA-32503054300076050067550087000115025 . . .
```

a. What is the salesperson's number?

b. The sales amounts are for which quarter?

c. What are the salesperson's sales for the second week of the quarter? the fifth week?

36. Write record description entries for the table representation shown in Figure 1.28. Assume size 20 for each table element.

37. Write the statement corresponding to the flowchart segment shown in Figure 1.29.

38. Suppose an inventory table is defined as follows:

```
01   INVENTORY-TABLE.
     05 WS-INVENTORY-ITEM   OCCURS 2000 TIMES
                            ASCENDING KEY IS WS-ITEM-NO.
        10 WS-ITEM-NO          PIC 9(4).
        10 WS-ITEM-DESCR       PIC X(15).
        10 WS-ITEM-UNIT-PR     PIC S9(4)V99.
        10 WS-ITEM-SELL-PR     PIC S9(4)V99.
     05 INVENTORY-TABLE-FLAG   PIC XXX.
        88 ITEM-IS-FOUND              VALUE "YES".
     05 ROW-CTR                PIC 9(4).
```

a. A table look-up is needed to retrieve the description and unit price for an input item number I-ITEM-NO. The description and unit price are to be stored in the output record fields O-ITEM-DESCR and O-ITEM-UNIT-PR, respectively. When the values are found, the output record ITEM-LINE is to be written.

i. Design the logic for the table look-up procedure.

ii. Write the COBOL statements needed to implement the table look-up procedure.

Figure 1.27

Record Layout Form

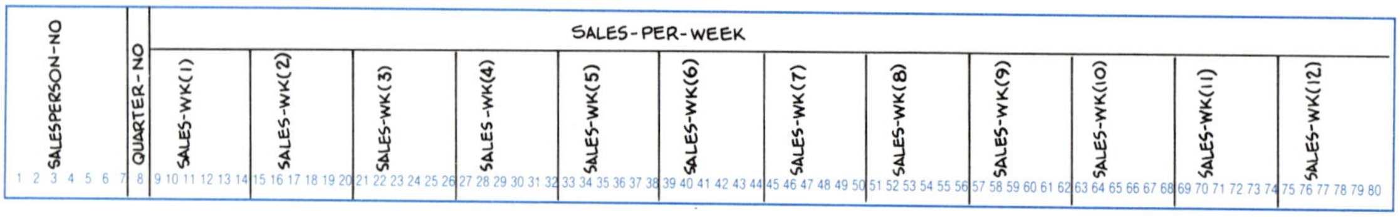

Record Name: QUARTER-SALES-RECORD

Figure 1.28

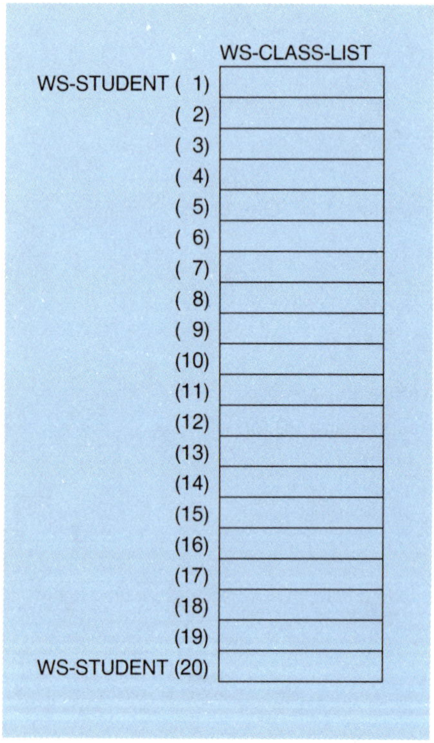

Figure 1.29

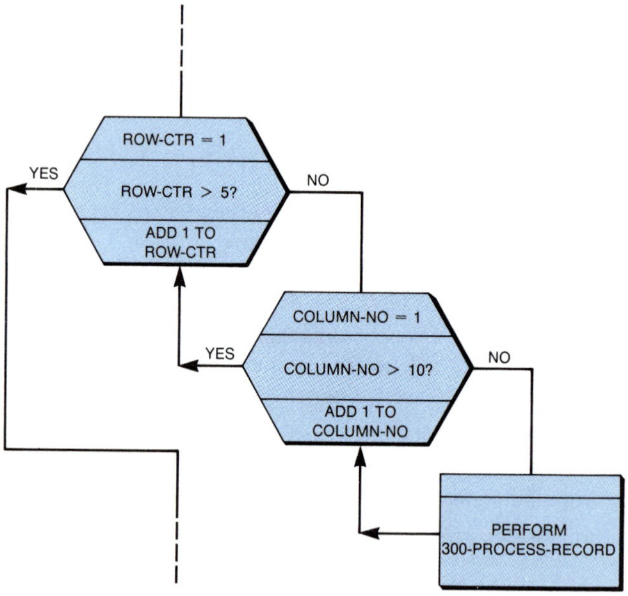

Debugging Activities

1. Given the flowchart segment in Figure 1.30a, a student generated the coding in part b. Identify and correct the errors.
2. A COBOL program was prepared for the purpose described in the IDENTIFICATION DIVISION. The compiler generated the listing shown in Figure 1.31. Correct all the syntax errors.

Figure 1.30

a.

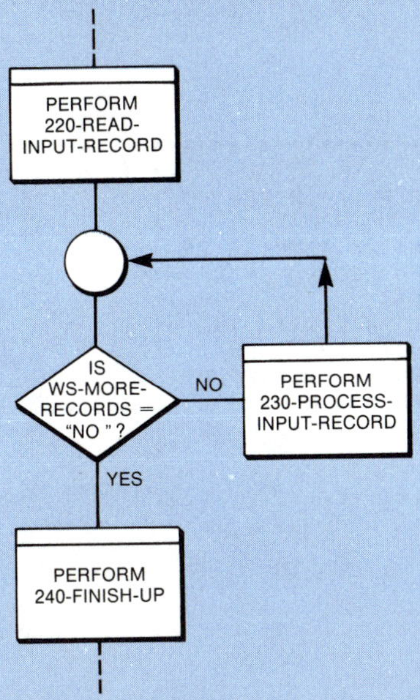

b.

```
PERFORM 220-READ-INPUT-RECORD.
IF WS-MORE-RECORDS NOT = "NO "
    PERFORM 230-PROCESS-INPUT-RECORD.
PERFORM 240-FINISH-UP.
```

3. Assume that all the syntax errors in Figure 1.31 have been corrected. The execution of the program then produced the report shown in Figure 1.32. A cursory examination of the report shows a number of programming errors that were not flagged by the compiler. Find and correct the errors.
4. A COBOL program was prepared for the purposes described in the IDENTIFICATION DIVISION. The compiler generated the listing shown in Figure 1.33. Correct all the syntax errors.
5. The report in Figure 1.34 contains errors as noted. Find the source of each error in the partial program that follows.
6. Refer to Figure 1.35.

   Part a shows relevant portions of the program that produced the report in part b. The catalog file used to load CATALOG-TABLE is in part c. Each record in the detail file in part d contains a catalog part number. The program must retrieve the appropriate table data, compute the markup for the item, and print the information on the report. Unfortunately, the report contains a number of errors, specifically:

   a. The selling price prints as zero.
   b. The markup is negative.
   c. Only three items are printed on the report. There should be five detail lines, followed by an "End of Report" message.
   d. The item numbers and item descriptions (and associated prices) are mismatched.

   Debug the program and run it so as to produce the report shown in Figure 1.36.

■ **Figure 1.31**

```
INT-HAB-PAY-REPORT                    20-Nov-1989 13:44:31    VAX COBOL V3.2-42                   Page    1
Source Listing                        20-Nov-1989 13:43:48    [PAQUETTEG.CHAPTER1]C1FIG31.COB;2 (1)

          IDENTIFICATION DIVISION.

          PROGRAM-ID.    INT-HAB-PAY-REPORT.

          ******************************************************************
          *                                                                *
          *       THE PURPOSE OF THIS PROGRAM IS TO PRODUCE A PAY REPORT   *
          *  FOR THE INTERNATIONAL HABERDASHERY COMPANY.                   *
          *       EACH SALESPERSON RECEIVES A BASE SALARY AND A COMMISSION *
          *  BASED ON THE SALES FOR THE PAY PERIOD.  BOTH PAY COMPONENTS   *
          *  ARE SUPPLIED ON THE SALESPERSON'S INPUT RECORD.               *
          *       THE REPORT MUST BEGIN AT THE TOP OF A NEW PAGE WITH THE  *
          *  COMPANY NAME, FOLLOWED BY THE NAME OF THE REPORT, AND THEN    *
          *  APPROPRIATE COLUMN HEADERS.  FOR EACH SALESPERSON, THE REPORT *
          *  MUST PRINT THE SOCIAL SECURITY NUMBER, THE PERSON'S NAME,     *
          *  THE BASE SALARY, THE COMMISSION, AND FINALLY, THE TOTAL PAY   *
          *  FOR THE CURRENT PAY PERIOD.                                   *
          *                                                                *
          ******************************************************************

          ENVIRONMENT DIVISION.

          CONFIGURATION SECTION.

          SOUCE-COMPUTER.    VAX-VMS-8650.
          1
%COBOL-F-ERROR  117, (1) Invalid syntax
          OBJECT-COMPUTER.  VAX-VMS-8650.
          1
%COBOL-W-ERROR  297, (1) Processing of source program resumes at this point

          INPUT-OUTPUT SECTION.

          FILE-CONTROL.
              SELECT EMPLOYEE-FILE   ASSIGN TO COB$INPUT.
                     1
%COBOL-E-ERROR   17, (1) Longest record is longer than RECORD CONTAINS value - Longest record size
used
              SELECT PAY-REPORT      ASSIGN TO COB$OUTPUT.
                     1
%COBOL-E-ERROR   17, (1) Longest record is longer than RECORD CONTAINS value - Longest record size
used

          DATA DIVISION.

          FILE SECTION.

          FD  EMPLOYEE-FILE
              RECORD CONTAINS 41 CHARACTERS.

          01  SALESPERSON-RECORD.
              05 I-SSN              PIC X(9).
              05 I-SALESPERSON      PIC X(20).
              05 I-SALARY           PIC 9999.99.
              05 I-COMMISSION       PIC 9999.99.

          FD  PAY-REPORT
              RECORD CONTAINS 133 CHARACTERS.

          01  PRINTLINE             PIC X(1332).

          WORKING-STORAGE SECTION.

          01  WS-MORE-RECORDS       PIC XXX.

          01  SALESPERSON-WORK-AREAS.
              05 WS-TOTAL-PAY       PIC XXX.XX-.
                                        1
%COBOL-F-ERROR  156, (1) Invalid PICTURE character-string

          01  COMPANY-NAME
              05 PIC X(54)  VALUE SPACES.
              1
%COBOL-E-ERROR   65, (1) Missing period is assumed
              05 PIC X(26)  VALUE "INTERNATIONAL HABERDASHERY".
              05 PIC X(53)  VALUE SAPCES.
                                  1
%COBOL-F-ERROR  119, (1) Invalid clause in record description
```

```
INT-HAB-PAY-REPORT              20-Nov-1989 13:44:31   VAX COBOL V3.2-42                    Page   2
Source Listing                  20-Nov-1989 13:43:48   [PAQUETTEG.CHAPTER1]C1FIG31.COB;2 (1)

          01  REPORT-NAME.
              05 PIC X(62)  VALUE SPACES.
              05 PIC X(10)  VALUE "PAY REPORT".
              05 PIC X(61)  VALUE SPACES.

          01  HEADINGS.
              05 PIC XXX    VALUE "SSN.
                  1              2
%COBOL-E-ERROR   84, (1) Literal in VALUE clause conflicts with description - clause ignored
%COBOL-F-ERROR  147, (2) Nonnumeric literal improperly continued
              05 PIC X(15)  VALUE SPACES.
              1
%COBOL-E-ERROR   65, (1) Missing period is assumed
              05 PIC X(10)  VALUE "SALESPERSON".
                  1
%COBOL-E-ERROR   84, (1) Literal in VALUE clause conflicts with description - clause ignored
              05 PIC X(15)  VALUE SPACES.
              05 PIC X(6)   VALUE "SALARY".
              05 PIC X(15)  VALUE SPACES.
             05 PIC X(10)  VALUE "COMMISSION".
             05 PIC X(15)  VALUE SAPCES
                                  1
%COBOL-F-ERROR  119, (1) Invalid clause in record description
             05 PIC X(9(   VALUE "TOTAL PAY".
             1  2   3
%COBOL-E-ERROR   65, (1) Missing period is assumed
%COBOL-E-ERROR   84, (2) Literal in VALUE clause conflicts with description - clause ignored
%COBOL-F-ERROR  178, (3) Invalid repetition factor
              05 PIC X(17)  VALUE SPACES.

          01  PAY-LINE.
              05                   PIC X(13).
              05 O-SSN             PIC XXXBXXBXXXX.
              05                   PIC X(7).
              05 O-SALESPERSON     PIC X(20).
              05                   PIC X(9).
              05 O-SALARY          PIC $Z,ZZ9.99.
              05                   PIC X(13).
              05 O-COMMISSION      PIC $Z,ZZ9.99.
              05                   PIC X(16).
              05 O-TOTAL-PAY       PIC $ZZ9.99.
              05                   PIC X(17).

          PROCEDURE DIVISION.

          100-PRODUCE-PAY-REPORT.
              PERFORM 200-START-UP.
              PERFORM 210-WRITE-REPORT-HEADERS.
              PERFORM 220-READ-SALESPERSON-REC.
                      1
%COBOL-F-ERROR  349, (1) Undefined name
              PERFORM 230-PROCESS-SALESPERSON-REC.
              1
%COBOL-W-ERROR  297, (1) Processing of source program resumes at this point
                  UNTIL WS-MORE-RECORDS = "NO ".
                  1
%COBOL-F-ERROR  321, (1) Invalid statement syntax
              PERFORM 240-FINISH-UP.
              1
%COBOL-W-ERROR  297, (1) Processing of source program resumes at this point
              STOP RUN.

          200-START-UP.
              OPEN INPUT EMPLOYEE-FILE
                   OUTPUT PAY-REPORT.
              MOVE "YES" TO WS-MORE-RECORDS.
              MOVE SPACES TO PAY-LINE.

          210-WRITE-REPORT-HEADERS.
              WRITE PRINTLINE FROM COMPANY-NAME
                  AFTER ADVANCING PAGE.
              WRITE PRITLINE FROM REPORT-NAME
                    1
%COBOL-F-ERROR  349, (1) Undefined name
                  AFTER ADVANCING 3 LINES.
              WRITE PRINTLINE FROM HEADINGS
              1
%COBOL-W-ERROR  297, (1) Processing of source program resumes at this point
                  AFTER ADVANCING 3 LINES.

```

Figure 1.31 continued

```
INT-HAB-PAY-REPORT                20-Nov-1989 13:44:31   VAX COBOL V3.2-42                          Page   3
Source Listing                    20-Nov-1989 13:43:48   [PAQUETTEG.CHAPTER1]C1FIG31.COB;2 (1)

             220-READ-SALESPERSON-RECORD.
                 READ EMPLOYEE-FILE RECORD
                     AT END
                         MOVE "NO " TO WS-MORE-RECORDS.

             230-PROCESS-SALESPERSON-REC.
                 PERFORM 300-COMPUTE-TOTAL-PAY.
                 PERFORM 310-PREPARE-PAYLINE.
                         1
%COBOL-F-ERROR  349, (1) Undefined name
                 PERFORM 220-READ-SALESPERSON-REC.
                 1       2
%COBOL-W-ERROR  297, (1) Processing of source program resumes at this point
%COBOL-F-ERROR  349, (2) Undefined name

             240-FINISH-UP.
             1
%COBOL-W-ERROR  297, (1) Processing of source program resumes at this point
                 CLOSE FILES.
                       1
%COBOL-F-ERROR  349, (1) Undefined name

             300-COMPUTE-TOTAL-PAY.
             1
%COBOL-W-ERROR  297, (1) Processing of source program resumes at this point
                 ADD I-SALARY I-COMMISSION GIVING WS-TOTAL-PAY
                     1        2                   3
%COBOL-F-ERROR  276, (1) Operand must be a numeric data-name or a numeric literal
%COBOL-F-ERROR  276, (2) Operand must be a numeric data-name or a numeric literal
%COBOL-F-ERROR  275, (3) Operand must be a numeric or numeric edited data-name
                     ON SIZE ERROR
                         MOVE ZERO TO WS-TOTAL-PAY
                 END-ADD.

             310-PREPARE-PAY-LINE.
                 MOVE I-SSN TO O-SSN.
                 MOVE I-SALESPERSON TO O-SALESPERSON.
                 MOVE I-SALARY TO O-SALARY.
                 MOVE WS-TOTAL-PAY TO O-TOTAL-PAY.
                 WRITE PRINTLINE FROM PAY-LINE
                     AFTER ADVANCING 2 LINES.
```

Figure 1.32

INTERNATIONAL HABERDASHERY

PAY REPORT

SSN	SALESPERSON	SALARY	COMMISSION	TOTAL PAY	
623 45 5100	CAHILL, PAULA R.	$ 985.50	$ 125.00	$ 0.00	
611 72 3510	CUSTER, GEORGE P.	$ 735.40	$ 95.00	$830.40	
315 78 1243	GAMELIN, JOSEPH	$1,230.00	$ 810.00	$ 0.00	
201 86 1752	JONES, EARLE B.	$ 675.00	$ 85.50	$760.50	
795 28 8916	BERARD, NORBERT V.	$1,005.00	$ 225.00	$ 0.00	
186 73 7565	PAQUIN, BRIDGET	$ 960.50	$ 375.50	$ 0.00	
269 31 3905	RENAUD, ANNE	$1,125.00	$ 340.00	$ 0.00	
519 39 2407	LEMAIRE, HERVE	$ 875.50	$ 230.50	$ 0.00	
056 41 9426	IWANSKI, JENNIE	$1,050.25	$ 550.00	$ 0.00	
353 22 8728	MALTAIS, VICTORIA	$ 650.00	$ 100.00	$750.00	

Figure 1.33

```
INT-HAB-PAY-REPORTS                 17-Jul-1989 09:52:48   VAX COBOL V3.2-42                       Page   1
Source Listing                      17-Jul-1989 09:52:25   SCIENCE$DISK:[MA6031.CHAPTER1]C1FIG33.COB;2

           IDENTIFICATION DIVISION.

           PROGRAM-ID.   INT-HAB-PAY-REPORTS.

          ***************************************************************
          *                                                             *
          *      THE PURPOSE OF THIS PROGRAM IS TO PRODUCE A TWO-PART PAY *
          *  REPORT FOR THE INTERNATIONAL HABERDASHERY COMPANY.         *
          *      EACH SALESPERSON RECEIVES A BASE SALARY AND A COMMISSION *
          *  BASED ON THE SALES FOR THE PAY PERIOD.  BOTH PAY COMPONENTS  *
          *  ARE SUPPLIED ON THE SALESPERSON'S INPUT RECORD.            *
          *      THE FIRST PART OF THE REPORT MUST BEGIN AT THE TOP OF A  *
          *  NEW PAGE WITH THE COMPANY NAME, FOLLOWED BY THE NAME OF THE  *
          *  REPORT, AND THEN APPROPRIATE COLUMN HEADERS.  FOR EACH SALES- *
          *  PERSON, THE REPORT MUST PRINT THE SOCIAL SECURITY NUMBER, THE *
          *  PERSON'S NAME, THE BASE SALARY, THE COMMISSION, AND FINALLY, *
          *  THE TOTAL PAY FOR THE CURRENT PAY PERIOD.                  *
          *      THE SECOND PART OF THE REPORT MUST BEGIN ON A SEPARATE   *
          *  PAGE WITH THE COMPANY NAME, FOLLOWED BY THE NAME OF THE RE-  *
          *  PORT, AND THEN SUMMARY INFORMATION FOR THE COMPANY:  TOTAL   *
          *  NUMBER OF EMPLOYEES ON THE CURRENT PAYROLL, THE TOTAL SAL-   *
          *  ARIES, THE TOTAL COMMISSIONS, THE AVERAGE SALARY, AND THE    *
          *  AVERAGE COMMISSION.                                        *
          *                                                             *
          ***************************************************************

           ENVIRONMENT DIVISION.

           CONFIGURATION SECTION.

           SOURCE-COMPUTER.  VAX-VMS-8650.
           OBJECT-COMPUTER.  VAX-VMS-8650.

           INPUT-OUTPUT SECTION.

           FILE-CONTROL.
               SELECT EMPLOYEE-FILE     ASSIGN TO COB$INPUT.
                      1
%COBOL-F-ERROR    52, (1) File has no definition in File Section - definition assumed
               SELECT PAY-REPORT        ASSIGN TO COB$OUTPUT.
                      1
%COBOL-W-ERROR   239, (1) File is CLOSEd but is not OPENed

           DATA DIVISION.

           FILE SECTION.

           FD  EMPLOYE-FILE
               1
%COBOL-E-ERROR    51, (1) File has no definition in FILE-CONTROL paragraph - definition assumed
%COBOL-E-ERROR    17, (1) Longest record is longer than RECORD CONTAINS value - Longest record size
                          used
               RECORD CONTAINS 41 CHARACTERS.

           01  SALESPERSON-RECORD.
               05 I-SSN                PIC X(9).
               05 I-SALESPERSON        PIC X(20).
               05 I-SALARY             PIC $ZZZ9.99.
               05 I-COMMISSION         PIC $ZZZ9.99.

           FD  PAY-REPORT
               RECORD CONTAINS 133 CHARACTERS.

           01  PRINTLINE               PIC X(133).

           WORKING-STORAGE SECTION.

           01  WS-MORE-RECORDS         PIC XXX.
```

■ **Figure 1.33** continued

```
INT-HAB-PAY-REPORTS                    17-Jul-1989 09:52:48   VAX COBOL V3.2-42                       Page   2
Source Listing                         17-Jul-1989 09:52:25   SCIENCE$DISK:[MA6031.CHAPTER1]C1FIG33.COB;2

        01  SALESPERSON-WORK-AREAS.
            05 WS-TOTAL-PAY        PIC $9999.99-   COMP.
               1
%COBOL-E-ERROR   42, (1) COMP and COMP-3 items must have numeric pictures - usage changed to DISPLAY

        01  COMPANY-ACCUMULATORS  COMP.
            05 WS-EMPLOYEE-CTR          PIC S999.
            05 WS-TOTAL-SALARIES        PIC S9(30V99.
                                                1
%COBOL-F-ERROR  178, (1) Invalid repetition factor
            05 WS-TOTAL-COMMISSIONS  PIC S9(3)V99.

        01  COMPANY-WORK-AREAS  COMP.
            05 WS-AVERAGE-SALARY        PIC S99V99.
            05 WS-AVERAGE-COMMISSION PIC S99V99.

        01  COMPANY-NAME.
            05 PIC X(54)  VALUE SPACES.
            05 PIC X(26)  VALUE "INTERNATIONAL HABERDASHERY".
            05 PIC X(53)  VALUE SPACES.

        01  REPORT-NAME.
            05 PIC X(62)  VALUE SPACES.
            05 PIC X(10)  VALUE "PAY REPORT".
            05 PIC X(61)  VALUE SPACES.

        01  HEADINGS.
            05 PIC XXX    VALUE "SSN".
            05 PIC X(15)  VALUE SPACES.
            05 PIC X(11)  VALUE "SALESPERSON".
            05 PIC X(15)  VALUE SPACES.
            05 PIC X(6)   VALUE "SALARY".
            05 PIC X(15)  VALUE SPACES.
            05 PIC X(10)  VALUE "COMMISSION".
            05 PIC X(15)  VALUE SPACES.
            05 PIC X(9)   VALUE "TOTAL PAY".
            05 PIC X(17)  VALUE SPACES.

        01  PAY-LINE.
            05                    PIC X(13).
            05 O-SSN              PIC XXXBXXBXXXX.
            05                    PIC X(7).
            05 O-SALESPERSON      PIC X(20).
            05                    PIC X(9).
            05 O-SALARY           PIC $Z,ZZ9.99.
            05                    PIC X(13).
            05 O-COMMISSION       PIC $Z,ZZ9.99.
            05                    PIC X(16).
            05 O-TOTAL            PIC $Z,ZZ9.99.
            05                    PIC X(17).

        01  SUMMARY-REPORT-LINES.

            05  SUMMARY-REPORT-NAME.
                10 PIC X(10)  VALUE SPACES.
                10 PIC X(14)  VALUE "SUMMARY REPORT".
                10 PIC X(10)  VALUE SPACES.

            05  EMPLOYEE-COUNT-LINE.
                10 PIC X(5)  VALUE "***  ".
                10 PIC X(11) VALUE "EMPLOYEES ON PAYROLL:".
                                   1
%COBOL-E-ERROR   84, (1) Literal in VALUE clause conflicts with description - clause ignored
                10 O-TOTAL-EMPLOYEES PIC ZZZ9.

            05  TOTAL-SALARIES-LINE.
                10 PIC X(5)  VALUE "***  ".
                10 PIC X(15) VALUE "TOTAL SALARIES:".
                10 O-TOTL-SALARIES  PIC $ZZZ,ZZ9.99-.
```

Figure 1.33 continued

```
INT-HAB-PAY-REPORTS                 17-Jul-1989 09:52:48   VAX COBOL V3.2-42                        Page  3
Source Listing                      17-Jul-1989 09:52:25   SCIENCE$DISK:[MA6031.CHAPTER1]C1FIG33.COB;2

            05  TOTAL-COMMISSIONS-LINE.
                10 PIC X(5)  VALUE "***  ".
                10 PIC X(18) VALUE "TOTAL COMMISSIONS:".
                10 O-TOTAL-COMMISSIONS  PIC $ZZZ,ZZ9.99-.

            05  AVERAGE-SALARY-LINE.
                10 PIC X(5)  VALUE "***  ".
                10 PIC X(15) VALUE "AVERAGE SALARY:".
                10 O-AVERAGE-SALARY  PIC $Z,ZZ9.99-.

            05  AVERAGE-COMMISSION-LINE.
                10 PIC X(5)  VALUE "***  ".
                10 PIC X(10) VALUE "AVERAGE COMMISSION:".
                    1
%COBOL-E-ERROR   84, (1) Literal in VALUE clause conflicts with description - clause ignored
                10 O-AVERAGE-COMMISSION PIC $Z,ZZ9.99-.

        PROCEDURE DIVISION.

        100-PRODUCE-PAY-REPORT.
            PERFORM 200-START-UP.
            PERFORM 210-WRITE-REPORT-HEADERS.
            PERFORM 220-READ-SALESPERSON-REC.
            PERFORM 230-PROCESS-SALESPERSON-REC
                UNTIL WS-MORE-RECORDS = "NO ".
            PERFORM 240-PRODUCE-COMPANY-SUMMARY.
            PERFORM 250-FINSH-UP.
                    1
%COBOL-F-ERROR  349, (1) Undefined name
            STOP RUN.
            1
%COBOL-W-ERROR  297, (1) Processing of source program resumes at this point

        200-START-UP.
            OPEN INPUT EMPLOYEE-FILE.
                 OUTPUT PAY-REPORT.
                 1
%COBOL-F-ERROR  321, (1) Invalid statement syntax
            MOVE "YES" TO WS-MORE-RECORDS.
            1
%COBOL-W-ERROR  297, (1) Processing of source program resumes at this point
            MOVE SPACES TO PAY-LINE.
            INITIALIZE COMPANY-ACCUMULATORS.

        210-WRITE-REPORT-HEADERS.
            WRITE PRINTLINE FROM COMPANY-NAME
                AFTER ADVANCING PAGE.
            WRITE PRINTLINE FROM REPORT-NAME
                AFTER ADVANCING 3 LINES.
            WRITE PRINTLINE FROM HEADINGS
                AFTER ADVANCING 3 LINES.

        220-READ-SALESPERSON-REC.
            READ EMPLOYEE-FILE RECORD
                AT END
                    MOVE "NO " TO WS-MORE-RECORDS.

        230-PROCESS-SALESPERSON-REC.
            PERFORM 310-PREPARE-PAY-LINE.
            PERFORM 300-COMPUTE-TOTAL-PAY.
            PERFORM 320-UPDATE-COMPANY-TOTALS.
            PERFORM 220-READ-SALESPERSON-REC.

        240-PRODUCE-COMPANY-SUMMARY.
            PERFORM 330-WRITE-SUMMARY-HEADERS.
            PERFORM 340-COMPUTE-COMPANY-AVERAGES.
            PERFORM 350-PREPARE-SUMMARY-REPORT.

        250-FINISH-UP.
            CLOSE EMPLOYEE-FILE
                  PAY-REPORT.

        300-COMPUTE-TOTAL-PAY.
            ADD I-SALARY I-COMMISSION GIVING WS-TOTAL-PAY
                1        2
```

Figure 1.33 continued

```
INT-HAB-PAY-REPORTS                   17-Jul-1989 09:52:48    VAX COBOL V3.2-42                   Page  4
Source Listing                        17-Jul-1989 09:52:25    SCIENCE$DISK:[MA6031.CHAPTER1]C1FIG33.COB;2

%COBOL-F-ERROR  276, (1) Operand must be a numeric data-name or a numeric literal
%COBOL-F-ERROR  276, (2) Operand must be a numeric data-name or a numeric literal
                     ON SIZE ERROR
                         MOVE ZERO TO WS-TOTAL-PAY
                 END-ADD.

             310-PREPARE-PAY-LINE.
                 MOVE I-SSN TO O-SSN.
                 MOVE I-SALARY TO O-SALARY.
                 MOVE I-COMMISSION TO O-COMMISSION.
                 MOVE WS-TOTAL-PAY TO O-TOTAL-PAY.
                                      1
%COBOL-F-ERROR  349, (1) Undefined name
                 WRITE PRINTLINE FROM PAY-LINE
                     AFTER ADVANCING 2 LINES.

             320-UPDATE-COMPANY-TOTALS.
                 ADD 1 TO WS-EMPLOYEE-CTR.
                 ADD 1-SALARY TO WS-TOTAL-SALARIES
                     1
%COBOL-F-ERROR  349, (1) Undefined name
                     ON SIZE ERROR
                         MOVE ZERO TO WS-TOTAL-SALARIES.
                         1
%COBOL-W-ERROR  297, (1) Processing of source program resumes at this point
                 ADD I-COMMISSION TO WS-TOTAL-COMMISSIONS
                     1
%COBOL-F-ERROR  276, (1) Operand must be a numeric data-name or a numeric literal
                     ON SIZE ERROR
                         MOVE ZERO TO WS-TOTAL-COMMISSIONS.

             330-WRITE-SUMMARY-HEADERS.
                 WRITE PRINTLINE FROM COMPANY-NAME
                     AFTER ADVANCING PAGE.
                 WRITE PRINTLINE FROM SUMMARY-REPORT-NAME
                     AFTER ADVANCING 3 LINES.

             340-COMPUTE-COMPANY-AVERAGES.
                 DIVIDE WS-TOTAL-SALARIES BY WS-EMPLOYEE-CTR
                     GIVING WS-AVERAGE-SALARY ROUNDED
                         ON SIZE ERROR
                             MOVE ZERO TO WS-AVERAGE-SALARY.
                 DIVIDE WS-TOTAL-COMMISSIONS BY WS-EMPLOYEE-CTR
                     GIVING WS-AVERAGE-COMISSION ROUNDED
                            1
%COBOL-F-ERROR  349, (1) Undefined name
                         ON SIZE ERROR
                             MOVE ZERO TO WS-AVERAGE-COMMISSION.
                             1
%COBOL-W-ERROR  297, (1) Processing of source program resumes at this point

             350-PREPARE-SUMMARY-REPORT.
                 MOVE WS-EMPLOYEE-CTR TO O-EMPLOYEE-CTR.
                                         1
%COBOL-F-ERROR  349, (1) Undefined name
                 WRITE PRINTLINE FROM TOTAL-EMPLOYEES-LINE
                                      1
%COBOL-F-ERROR  349, (1) Undefined name
                     AFTER ADVANCING 3 LINES.
                                           1
%COBOL-W-ERROR  297, (1) Processing of source program resumes at this point
                 MOVE WS-TOTAL-SALARIES TO O-TOTAL-SALARIES.
                                           1
%COBOL-F-ERROR  349, (1) Undefined name
                 WRITE PRINTLINE FROM TOTAL-SALARIES-LINE
                     AFTER ADVANCING 2 LINES.
                 MOVE WS-TOTAL-COMMISSIONS TO O-TOTAL-COMMISSIONS.
                 WRITE PRINTLINE FROM TOTAL-COMMISSIONS-LINE
                     AFTER ADVANCING 2 LINES.
                 MOVE WS-AVERAGE-SALARY TO O-AVERAGE-SALARY.
                 WRITE PRINTLINE FROM AVERAGE-SALARY-LINE
                     AFTER ADVANCING 2 LINES.
                 MOVE WS-AVERAGE-COMMISSION TO O-AVERAGE-COMMISSION.
                 WRITE PRINTLINE FROM AVERAGE-COMMISSION-LINE
                     AFTER ADVANCING 2 LINES.
```

Figure 1.34

REPORT DATE: 89/09/15 PAGE 1

THE SPORTSMAN

SALES ANALYSIS REPORT

STORE: 10 - NEW YORK

DEPT NO.	SALESPERSON SSN	SALESPERSON NAME	CURRENT SALES
02	214/36/5025	ALLEN, ROBERT	$1,500.00
02	218/54/6010	BROWN, RAYMOND	$3,022.55
02	641/27/5050	BRANNIGAN, NICOLE	$ 875.25
02	315/46/3030	FOGARTY, JANICE	$1,050.50
02	642/75/4040	MAIN, CHARLES	$1,280.00
04	685/26/4065	CARLSON, HOPE	$ 900.00
04	556/23/4035	CRANE, JOHN	$1,050.50
04	696/99/6055	DANIELS, JULIA	$2,870.50
04	251/34/2020	FARMER, SUSAN	$1,620.00
04	263/45/2070	FEINGOLD, HAROLD	$1,250.50
04	667/45/1060	HARRISON, LILY	$1,425.80
06	521/24/4005	DWYER, TERRENCE	$1,425.80
06	564/45/1045	EDWARDS, PETER	$1,080.50
06	644/35/3075	MANNING, ELIZABETH	$1,350.00
08	377/56/8080	HOWARD, RALPH	$ 560.50
08	482/13/1015	JANKOWSKI, STANLEY	$1,350.00
08	551/16/4090	KELLY, PATRICK	$1,625.00
08	599/23/1085	LANGFORD, SARAH	$1,150.50
08	521/16/6100	PRINGLY, ANNE	$1,098.05
02	408/93/6050	CORDEIRO, ANTONE	$ 100.50
02	509/86/2005	CORTON, ALEXANDRA	$1,000.00
02	509/18/5045	PINEAULT, NORMAN	$ 980.50
02	480/75/5030	TALBOT, JILLIAN	$1,275.80
04	479/21/0065	BARRESI, JOHN	$ 650.00
04	427/56/0010	COCHRANE, RUSSELL	$1,460.50
04	360/90/2035	PENTA, ROBERT	$1,650.25
04	472/84/7080	PROULX, PAULINE	$1,150.00
04	375/70/1060	QUINN, SUZANNE	$1,320.50
06	683/30/9020	COSTELLO, JAMES	$1,670.50
06	418/09/0015	CRAWFORD, SHIRLEY	$1,390.50
06	566/12/7070	FELDMAN, WALTER	$1,470.80
06	433/40/6075	FERNANDEZ, LOUISE	$2,000.00
06	571/90/4025	LEMERISE, DONALD	$1,850.50
06	572/49/5090	WORTHEN, MICHAEL	$1,570.00
08	762/35/5100	GOYETTE, FRANCES	$ 950.00
08	812/13/3085	KOSINSKI, KATHERINE	$1,125.00
08	804/23/3040	VERMETTE, GLORIA	$1,560.50
02	576/40/0892	KING, CHRISTOPHER	$1,890.70
02	416/89/2014	BERNARD, ISIDORE	$2,035.69
02	823/14/4098	MAHFUZ, IRENE	$1,850.25
04	566/73/1251	ROBINSON, GILBERT	$2,105.90
04	788/23/0154	DONOHUE, PHIL	$ 875.00
04	607/04/4132	CORRIGAN, ALENE	$1,875.50
04	745/64/5270	FURTADO, MAUREEN	$2,015.40
06	820/78/8914	ABALLO, NORMA	$2,350.75
06	785/02/3157	DOLLARHIDE, CHRIS	$2,015.70
06	745/63/5164	LINCOURT, LORETTA	$1,495.00
08	466/58/7165	BRAZ, JOAN	$2,315.60
08	557/31/8974	PRATT, ROBIN	$2,155.00
08	487/25/1099	MELANSON, GARY	$1,905.50
02	452/67/7143	BEAUDOIN, ROCKY	$2,215.00
02	787/85/5623	MARKLAND, MARY	$1,987.50
02	674/45/1231	BISBANO, HENRY	$2,190.55
04	720/95/4670	VELOZO, MARIO	$2,423.90
04	624/16/6876	PARISEAU, WILLIAM	$1,785.00
04	712/13/3463	PERRY, MARTA	$1,945.50
06	452/89/2153	CARDIN, FRANCIS	$2,045.90
06	551/50/2546	FORTIN, EMIL	$2,254.50
06	574/93/0461	GALLAGHER, MICHAEL	$1,976.75
06	683/21/5467	NOTTE, LORENZO	$2,005.00
08	721/43/5472	JOBIN, ANTONIO	$2,140.50
08	490/23/4571	MILLER, RENEE	$1,905.70
08	351/56/6178	TRAMONTE, ESTELLE	$2,135.00

Store 10 footing missing

Store 20 footing missing

Store 30 footing missing

TOTAL SALES FOR STORE 40 : $101,558.59 *

Wrong total for store 40

Heading printed after all records have been processed

STORE: 40 - SEATTLE

DEPT NO.	SALESPERSON SSN	SALESPERSON NAME	CURRENT SALES

TOTAL COMPANY SALES : $ 101,558.59 **

*** END OF REPORT ***

■ **Figure 1.34** continued

```
PROCEDURE DIVISION.

100-PRODUCE-SALES-REPORT.
    PERFORM 200-START-UP.
    PERFORM 210-PROCESS-SALES-RECORD
        UNTIL NO-MORE-RECORDS.
    PERFORM 220-PREPARE-COMPANY-FOOTING.
    PERFORM 230-FINISH-UP.
    STOP RUN.

200-START-UP.
    OPEN INPUT SALES-FILE
         OUTPUT SALES-REPORT.
    ACCEPT WS-REPORT-DATE FROM DATE.
    MOVE WS-REPORT-DATE TO O-REPORT-DATE.
    SET THERE-IS-A-RECORD TO TRUE.
    INITIALIZE PROGRAM-ACCUMULATORS
               WS-PAGE-NO.
    MOVE SPACES TO SALES-LINE.
    PERFORM 300-READ-SALES-RECORD.
    PERFORM 310-WRITE-PAGE-HEADING.


210-PROCESS-SALES-RECORD.
    MOVE I-STORE-NO TO WS-STORE-CONTROL.
    PERFORM 320-CHECK-FOR-NEW-STORE.
    PERFORM 330-UPDATE-ACCUMULATORS.
    PERFORM 340-PREPARE-SALES-LINE.
    PERFORM 300-READ-SALES-RECORD.

220-PREPARE-COMPANY-FOOTING.
    PERFORM 410-PREPARE-STORE-FOOTING.
    MOVE WS-COMPANY-ACCUMULATOR TO O-COMPANY-SALES.
    WRITE PRINTLINE FROM COMPANY-FOOTING
        AFTER ADVANCING 6 LINES.

230-FINISH-UP.
    WRITE PRINTLINE FROM END-LINE
        AFTER ADVANCING 10 LINES.
    CLOSE SALES-FILE
          SALES-REPORT.

300-READ-SALES-RECORD.
    READ SALES-FILE RECORD
        AT END
            SET NO-MORE-RECORDS TO TRUE.

310-WRITE-PAGE-HEADING.
    ADD 1 TO WS-PAGE-NO.
    MOVE WS-PAGE-NO TO O-PAGE-NO.
    WRITE PRINTLINE FROM TOP-LINE
        AFTER ADVANCING PAGE.
    WRITE PRINTLINE FROM COMPANY-NAME
        AFTER ADVANCING 1 LINE.
    WRITE PRINTLINE FROM REPORT-NAME
        AFTER ADVANCING 3 LINES.
    INITIALIZE WS-STORES-PER-PAGE-CTR.
    PERFORM 400-WRITE-STORE-HEADING.

320-CHECK-FOR-NEW-STORE.
    IF I-STORE-NO = WS-STORE-CONTROL
        NEXT SENTENCE
    ELSE
        PERFORM 410-PREPARE-STORE-FOOTING.

330-UPDATE-ACCUMULATORS.
    ADD I-CURRENT-SALES TO WS-STORE-ACCUMULATOR
                           WS-COMPANY-ACCUMULATOR.

340-PREPARE-SALES-LINE.
    MOVE I-DEPT-NO TO O-DEPT-NO.
    MOVE I-SSN TO O-SSN.
    MOVE I-SALESPERSON TO O-SALESPERSON.
    MOVE I-CURRENT-SALES TO O-CURRENT-SALES.
    WRITE PRINTLINE FROM SALES-LINE
        AFTER ADVANCING WS-PROPER-SPACING.
    MOVE 1 TO WS-PROPER-SPACING.
```

■ **Figure 1.34** continued

```
400-WRITE-STORE-HEADING.
    EVALUATE I-STORE-NO
        WHEN "10"  MOVE "10 - NEW YORK" TO O-STORE-ID
        WHEN "20"  MOVE "20 - BOSTON" TO O-STORE-ID
        WHEN "30"  MOVE "30 - CHICAGO" TO O-STORE-ID
        WHEN "40"  MOVE "40 - SEATTLE" TO O-STORE-ID
        WHEN OTHER
            DISPLAY " ERROR IN STORE NO. FOR " I-SALESPERSON.
    WRITE PRINTLINE FROM STORE-HEADING-1
        AFTER ADVANCING 3 LINES.
    WRITE PRINTLINE FROM STORE-HEADING-2
        AFTER ADVANCING 3 LINES.
    MOVE 2 TO WS-PROPER-SPACING.

410-PREPARE-STORE-FOOTING.
    MOVE WS-STORE-CONTROL TO O-STORE-NO.
    MOVE WS-STORE-ACCUMULATOR TO O-STORE-SALES.
    WRITE PRINTLINE FROM STORE-FOOTING
        AFTER ADVANCING 3 LINES.
    INITIALIZE WS-STORE-ACCUMULATOR.
    PERFORM 500-CHECK-STORE-CTR.

500-CHECK-STORE-CTR.
    ADD 1 TO WS-STORES-PER-PAGE-CTR.
    IF WS-STORES-PER-PAGE-CTR = 2
        PERFORM 310-WRITE-PAGE-HEADING
    ELSE
        PERFORM 400-WRITE-STORE-HEADING.
```

■ **Figure 1.35**

Part a:

```
FILE SECTION.

FD  CATALOG-FILE
    RECORD CONTAINS 35 CHARACTERS.

01  CATALOG-RECORD.
    05 I-PART-NO          PIC X(5).
    05 I-PART-DESCR       PIC X(20).
    05 I-PURCH-PRICE      PIC 999V99.
    05 I-SELL-PRICE       PIC 999V99.

FD  DETAIL-FILE
    RECORD CONTAINS 5 CHARACTERS.

01  DETAIL-RECORD.
    05 I-DETAIL-PART-NO PIC X(5).

FD  MARKUP-REPORT
    RECORD CONTAINS 80 CHARACTERS.

01  PRINTLINE             PIC X(80).

WORKING-STORAGE SECTION.

01  PROGRAM-CONTROLS.
    05 WS-MORE-DETAIL-RECORDS      PIC XXX.
       88 THERE-IS-A-DETAIL-RECORD         VALUE "YES".
       88 NO-MORE-DETAIL-RECORDS           VALUE "NO ".
    05 WS-MORE-CATALOG-RECORDS     PIC XXX.
       88 NO-MORE-CAT-RECORDS              VALUE "NO ".
    05 WS-PROPER-SPACING           PIC 9.

01  ITEM-WORK-AREAS.
    05 WS-PURCH-PRICE-WORK         PIC S999V99.
    05 WS-SELL-PRICE-WORK          PIC S999V99.
    05 WS-MARKUP-WORK              PIC S999V99.

01  PROGRAM-TABLES.
    05 CATALOG-TABLE.
       10 CAT-ITEM-INFO OCCURS 10 TIMES.
          15 WS-PART-NO            PIC X(5).
          15 WS-PART-DESCR         PIC X(20).
          15 WS-PURCH-PRICE        PIC S999V99.
```

```
    05 CATALOG-TABLE-CONTROLS.
       10 CAT-TABLE-FLAG            PIC XXX.
          88 ITEM-IS-FOUND                  VALUE "YES".
       10 CAT-TABLE-ROW-CTR         PIC S99.


PROCEDURE DIVISION.

100-PRODUCE-MARKUP-REPORT.
    PERFORM 200-START-UP.
    PERFORM 210-PROCESS-DETAIL-RECORD
        UNTIL NO-MORE-DETAIL-RECORDS.
    PERFORM 220-FINISH-UP.
    STOP RUN.

200-START-UP.
    OPEN INPUT CATALOG-FILE
         INPUT DETAIL-FILE
         OUTPUT MARKUP-REPORT.
    MOVE "YES" TO WS-MORE-DETAIL-RECORDS
                  WS-MORE-CATALOG-RECORDS.
    MOVE SPACES TO MARKUP-LINE.
    PERFORM 300-READ-CATALOG-RECORD.
    PERFORM VARYING CAT-TABLE-ROW-CTR FROM 1 BY 1
                UNTIL NO-MORE-CAT-RECORDS
        MOVE CATALOG-RECORD TO CAT-ITEM-INFO (CAT-TABLE-ROW-CTR)
        PERFORM 300-READ-CATALOG-RECORD
    END-PERFORM.
    PERFORM 320-WRITE-REPORT-HEADERS.
    PERFORM 330-READ-DETAIL-RECORD.

210-PROCESS-DETAIL-RECORD.
    PERFORM 340-COMPUTE-MARKUP.
    PERFORM 350-PREPARE-MARKUP-LINE.
    PERFORM 330-READ-DETAIL-RECORD.

220-FINISH-UP.
    WRITE PRINTLINE FROM END-LINE
        AFTER ADVANCING 5 LINES.
    CLOSE CATALOG-FILE
          DETAIL-FILE
          MARKUP-REPORT.

300-READ-CATALOG-RECORD.
    READ CATALOG-FILE RECORD
        AT END
            SET NO-MORE-CAT-RECORDS TO TRUE.

320-WRITE-REPORT-HEADERS.
    WRITE PRINTLINE FROM COMPANY-NAME
        AFTER ADVANCING PAGE.
    WRITE PRINTLINE FROM REPORT-NAME
        AFTER ADVANCING 3 LINES.
    WRITE PRINTLINE FROM HEADINGS
        AFTER ADVANCING 3 LINES.
    MOVE 2 TO WS-PROPER-SPACING.

330-READ-DETAIL-RECORD.
    READ DETAIL-FILE RECORD
        AT END
            SET NO-MORE-DETAIL-RECORDS TO TRUE.

340-COMPUTE-MARKUP.
    MOVE "NO " TO CAT-TABLE-FLAG.
    PERFORM 400-LOOK-UP-CATALOG-TABLE
        VARYING CAT-TABLE-ROW-CTR FROM 1 BY 1
            UNTIL ITEM-IS-FOUND.
    MOVE WS-PURCH-PRICE (CAT-TABLE-ROW-CTR)
        TO WS-PURCH-PRICE-WORK.
    SUBTRACT WS-PURCH-PRICE-WORK FROM WS-SELL-PRICE-WORK
        GIVING WS-MARKUP-WORK.

350-PREPARE-MARKUP-LINE.
    MOVE I-DETAIL-PART-NO TO O-PART-NO.
    MOVE "NO " TO CAT-TABLE-FLAG.
    PERFORM 400-LOOK-UP-CATALOG-TABLE
        VARYING CAT-TABLE-ROW-CTR FROM 1 BY 1
            UNTIL ITEM-IS-FOUND.
```

Figure 1.35 continued

```
    MOVE WS-PART-DESCR (CAT-TABLE-ROW-CTR) TO O-PART-DESCR.
    MOVE WS-PURCH-PRICE-WORK TO O-PURCH-PRICE.
    MOVE WS-SELL-PRICE-WORK TO O-SELL-PRICE.
    MOVE WS-MARKUP-WORK TO O-MARKUP.
    WRITE PRINTLINE FROM MARKUP-LINE
        AFTER ADVANCING WS-PROPER-SPACING.
    MOVE 1 TO WS-PROPER-SPACING.

400-LOOK-UP-CATALOG-TABLE.
    IF I-DETAIL-PART-NO = WS-PART-NO (CAT-TABLE-ROW-CTR)
        SET ITEM-IS-FOUND TO TRUE
    END-IF.
```

Part b:

```
                       EXPRESS AUTO PARTS WAREHOUSE

                               MARK-UPS REPORT

ITEM NO.      ITEM DESCRIPTION       PURCH. PRICE    SELL. PRICE    MARKUP

 5507R       DISC BRAKE PADS           $ 12.46        $   0.00      $ 12.46-
 0359B       FLEXSOCKET WRENCH         $  1.91        $   0.00      $  1.91-
 1242W       TUNE-UP TESTER            $ 33.29        $   0.00      $ 33.29-
```

Part c:

```
0346RCB ANTENNA          0332903995
0359BCB CONVERTER        0207902495
0462UFLEXSOCKET WRENCH   0019100229
1242WRV ALARM SYSTEM     0166301995
1352VTUNE-UP TESTER      0332903995
1616WAIR DIESEL HARN     0141501698
2181XEXHAUST HEADERS     0566306795
5507RBONDED BRAKE SHOE   0066500798
5524YDISC BRAKE PADS     0124601495
7519YSOLID STATE TACH    0332903995
```

Part d:

```
5507R
0359B
1242W
7519Y
1352V
```

Figure 1.36

```
                       EXPRESS AUTO PARTS WAREHOUSE

                               MARK-UPS REPORT

ITEM NO.      ITEM DESCRIPTION       PURCH. PRICE    SELL. PRICE    MARKUP

 5507R       BONDED BRAKE SHOE         $  6.65        $  7.98       $  1.33
 0359B       CB CONVERTER              $ 20.79        $ 24.95       $  4.16
 1242W       RV ALARM SYSTEM           $ 16.63        $ 19.95       $  3.32
 7519Y       SOLID STATE TACH          $ 33.29        $ 39.95       $  6.66
 1352V       TUNE-UP TESTER            $ 33.29        $ 39.95       $  6.66


                         ***  END OF REPORT  ***
```

Programming Exercises

Programming Exercise I

The management of Express Auto Parts Warehouse wants its data processing department to prepare a sales report showing sales figures for the past week for each catalog item. For each item, there is a record in the sales file containing the following data:

cc 1–5	Catalog number
cc 6–25	Item description
cc 26–30	Purchase price per unit
cc 31–35	Selling price per unit
cc 52–55	Quantity sold during the week
cc 56–59	Quantity returned during the week

The sales file is updated weekly.

The sales report must list all the catalog items. For each catalog item, the report must identify the catalog number, the item description, the purchase price per unit, the selling price per unit, the quantity sold during the week, the quantity returned during the week, the gross income from sales during the week, the net income from sales during the week (quantity sold minus quantity returned times selling price), and the net profit or loss.

The report must begin at the top of a new page with appropriate descriptive information: company name, report name, and column headings.

Figure 1.37 contains the layout of the input record, the printer spacing chart, the system flowchart, and the structure chart.

Your assignment is as follows:

a. Complete the design phase by assigning names to the data fields of the output record ITEM-LINE and by developing the program pseudocode or the program flowchart.

b. Code the program, enter it into a file, and debug it.

c. Run the program successfully.

Use Data Set 1X1 as the sales file.

Figure 1.37

Record Layout Form

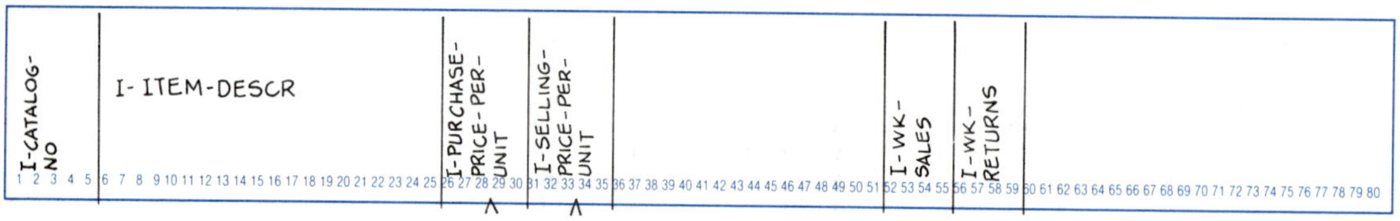

Record Name: SALES-RECORD

Figure 1.37 continued

Printer Spacing Chart

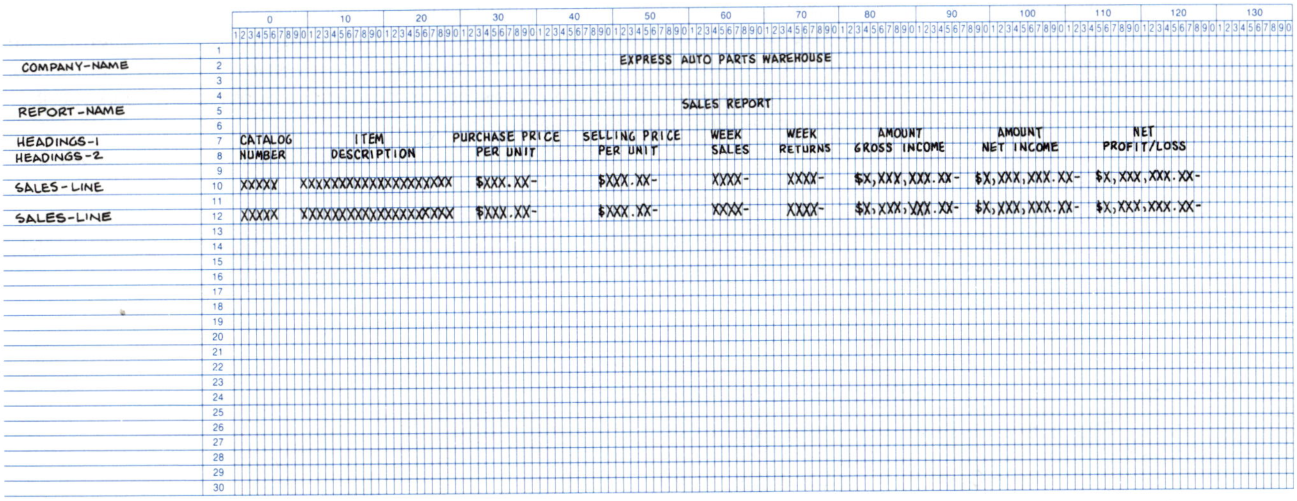

System Flowchart

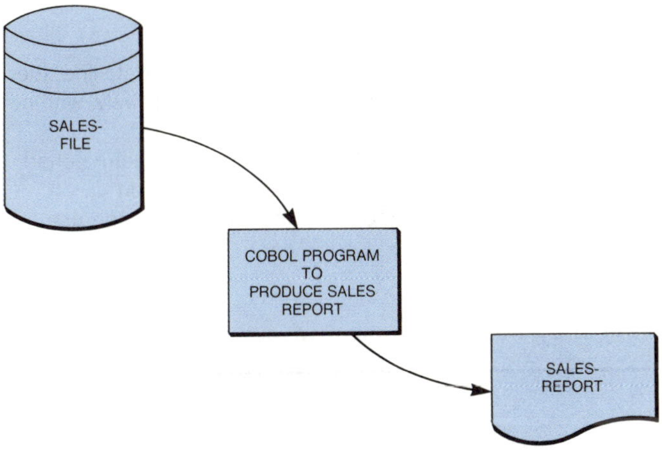

Structure Chart

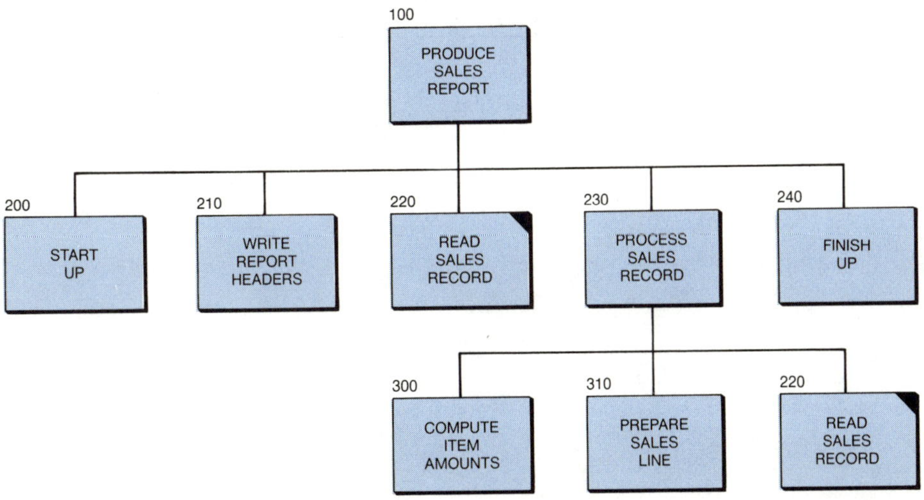

Programming Exercise II

The management of International Haberdashery wants a sales analysis report that will list all of its salespersons. The report is a two-part report. In the first part, it must provide sales information for individual salespersons, and in the second part, it must provide summary information for each store.

For each salesperson, the report must identify the store number, specify the current sales, interpret the current sales as a percent of the salesperson's quota, and provide a rating of the salesperson's performance. The rating will be indicated by a double star if sales are 20 percent or more above quota and by one star if sales are 10 percent or more (but less than 20 percent) above quota.

For each store, the second part of the report must identify the store's location, and it must specify the total number of salespersons at that store, the total sales, the average sales per salesperson, and the top store salesperson.

The input file consists of salespersons' records, arranged alphabetically by store, with store numbers in ascending order. Each record contains the following data:

cc 1–2	Store number
cc 3–22	Salesperson name
cc 48–55	Current sales (format: xxxxxx.xx)
cc 56–63	Sales quota (format: xxxxxx.xx)

The store codes and locations are as follows:

Store Code	Location
10	Providence
20	Hartford
30	Boston
40	Hyannis
50	Worcester

Each part of the report should begin on a new page and be properly documented with a report-date line, the company name, the report name, and headings as needed. Pages are to be numbered consecutively, with no more than 30 detail lines per page.

The layout of the input record, the printer spacing chart, the system flowchart, and the structure chart are provided for you in Figure 1.38. Your task is to complete the design phase and then the design implementation phase of the problem-solving procedure. Use the current date as the report date, and use Data Set 1X2 as the input file.

Figure 1.38

Record Layout Form

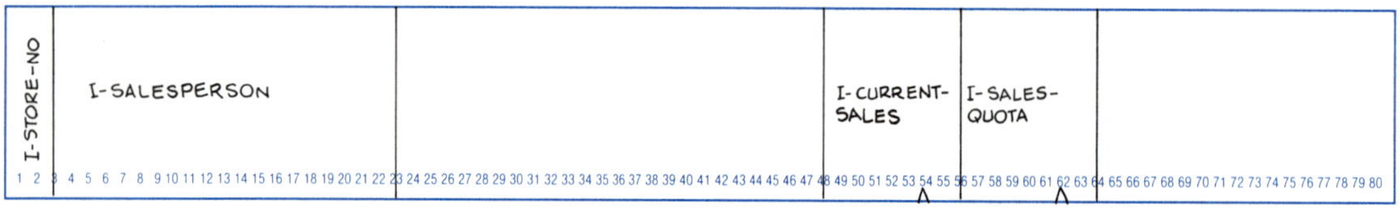

Record Name: SALES-RECORD

Figure 1.38 continued

Printer Spacing Chart

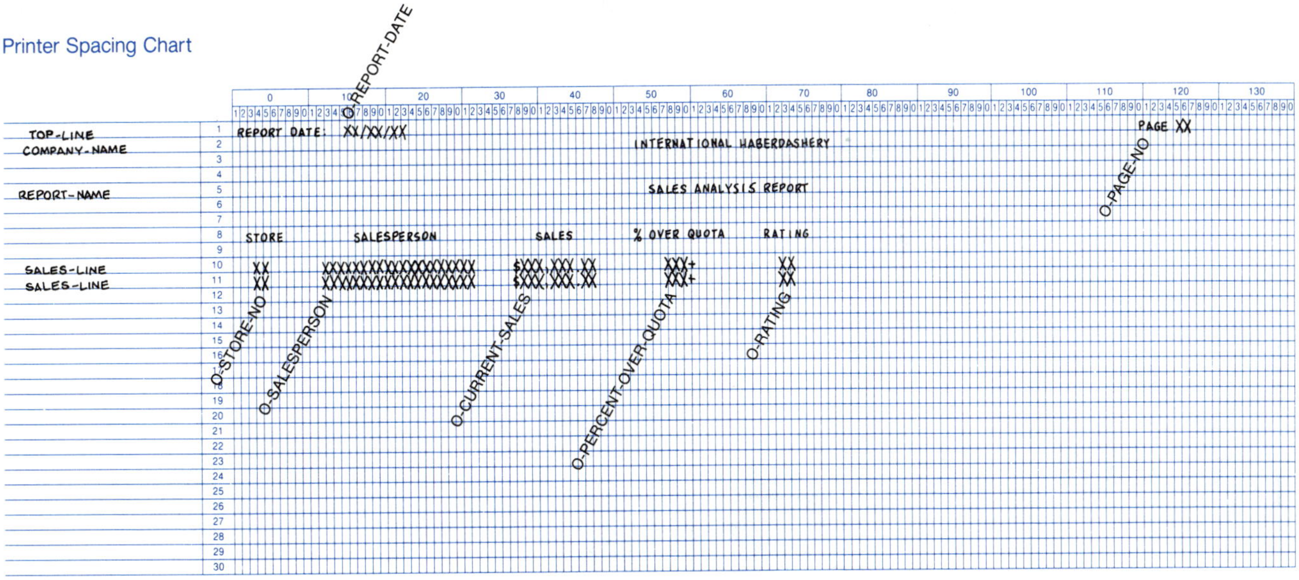

Printer Spacing Chart

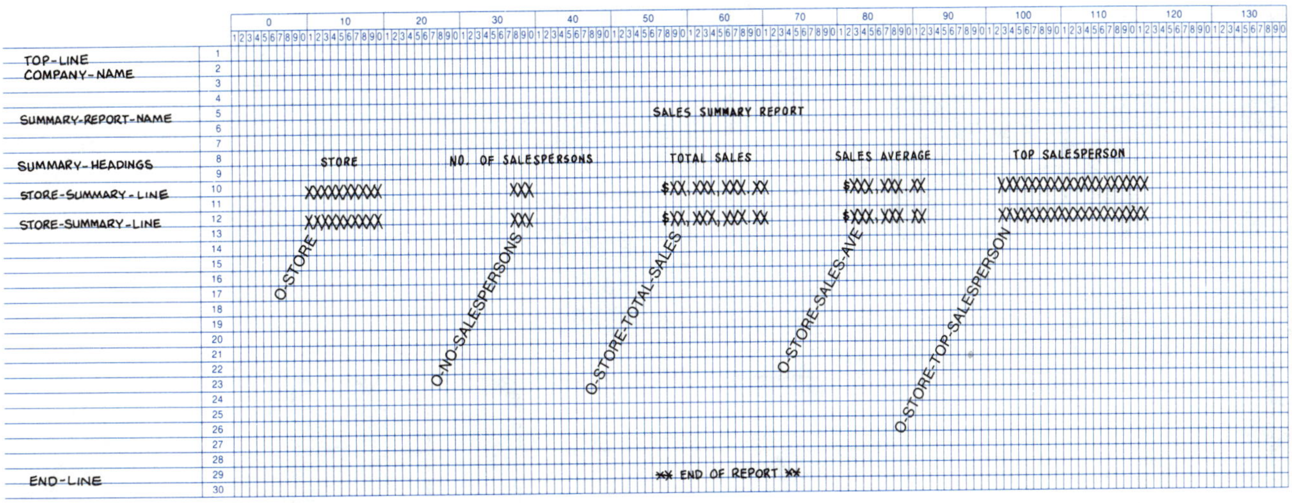

System Flowchart

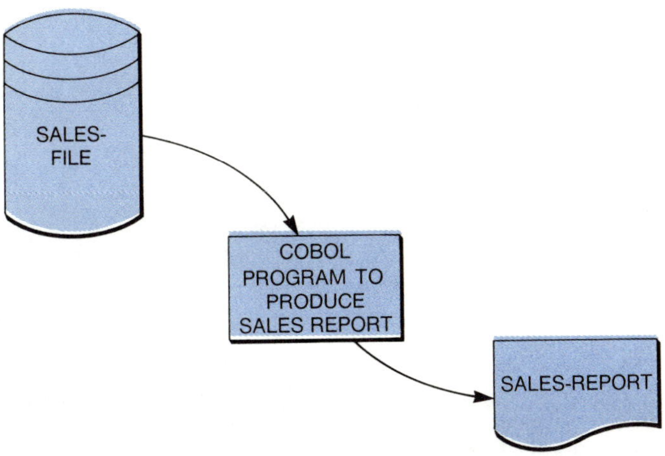

Figure 1.38 continued

Structure Chart

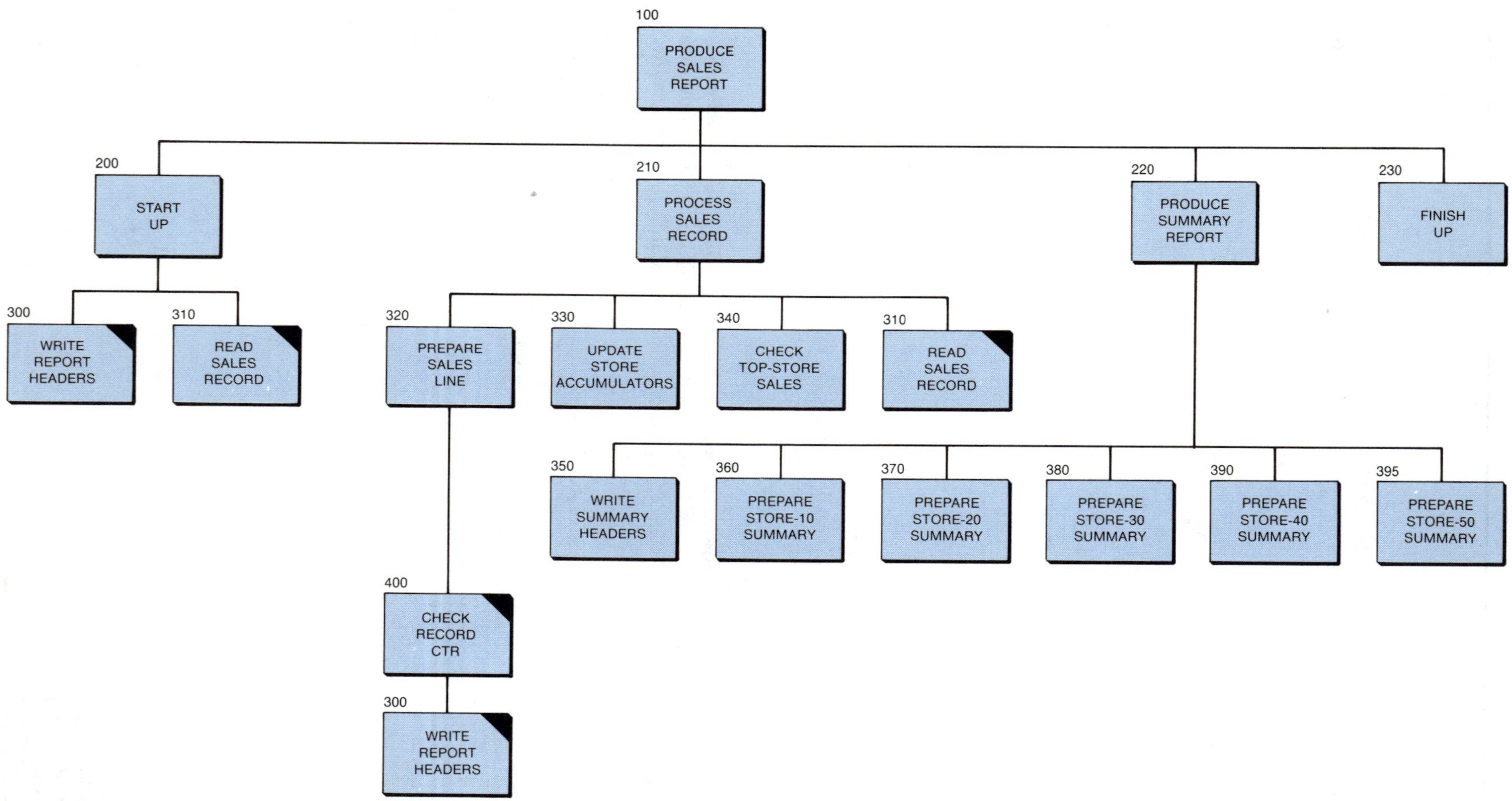

Programming Exercise III

The management of the Ponagansett Electric Company wants a multilevel usage report formatted as shown in Figure 1.39. It must show usage information for each customer of each area, usage information for each area of the company, and usage information for the company as a whole.

Only one area is reported per page. An area report begins with the area heading, then the body of the report contains a detail line for each customer in the area, and the report ends with an area footing that contains summary information for the area. Areas are identified by code and by location. They are as follows:

RI1 - Bristol
RI2 - Essex
RI3 - South

The area heading specifies the area code and location.

A detail line contains the following information for a customer: the classification of the customer as residential or commercial, the rate schedule that applies to the customer, the customer number and name, the previous and current meter readings, the KWH used by the customer for the current period, and the total charge to be assessed to the customer.

The area footing specifies the total KWH sold and the income to be derived from the sale of electricity to each of its customer classifications.

The company footing specifies the total KWH sold and the income to be derived from the sale of electricity to each of its customer classifications as a whole. In addition, the footing identifies the highest user in each classification and the actual number of KWH used.

For each customer, there is a record in the customer file that contains the following data:

cc 1–3	Area code (RI1, RI2, RI3)
cc 4–9	Customer number
cc 10–29	Customer name
cc 30–34	Previous meter reading
cc 35–39	Current meter reading
cc 74–76	Rate schedule

The records in this file are arranged sequentially by customer number within each area code.

The rate schedules are as follows:

1. Residential: A10
   Customer Charge: $1.61 per month
   Energy Charge: 7.974 cents per KWH
2. Residential: A11 (Electric Water Heater)

$2.75	for first	20 KWH or less
10.435 cents per KWH	next	30 KWH
8.381 cents per KWH	next	150 KWH
5.529 cents per KWH	next	350 KWH
6.831 cents per KWH	next	1450 KWH
6.554 cents per KWH	excess of	2000 KWH

3. Residential: A12 (All Electric)
   Same as A11
4. Commercial: C-2 (General Service, Small Business)
   Customer Charge: $4.75 per month
   Energy Charge:

8.913 cents per KWH	first	2000 KWH
8.313 cents per KWH	excess of	2000 KWH

For all rate schedules, the following additional charges apply: .006 cents per KWH for the Uniform Conservation Cost Adjustment, .042 cents per KWH for the Oil Conservation Adjustment, and .01413 cents Fuel Factor per KWH.

Your assignment is to design the program and then to implement it. Use the data in Data Set 1X3, and use the current date as the report date.

Figure 1.39

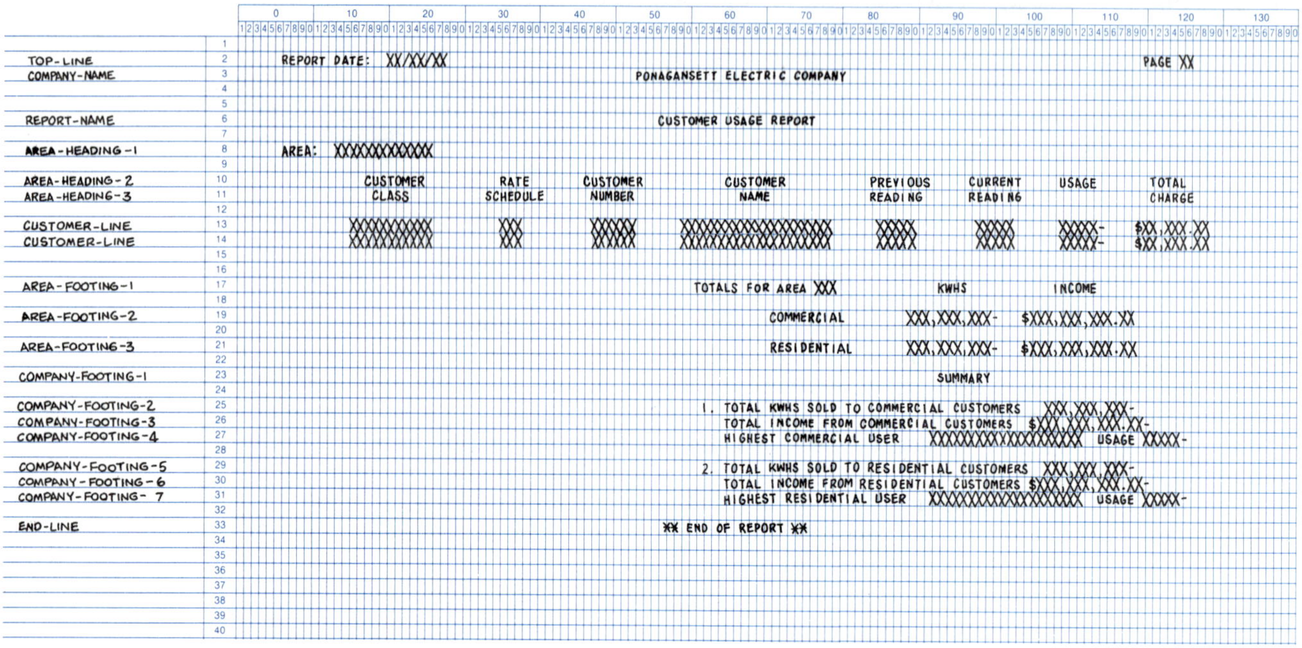

Programming Exercise IV

The management of the Modern Plastics Company wants its data processing department to prepare a weekly payroll tax report. For each employee, the report must list the Social Security number, name, number of allowances claimed, gross income for the week, amount of federal tax to be withheld, and resulting net income for the week. The format of the report is shown in Figure 1.40.

A time records file contains a time record for each employee with the following data:

cc 1–9	Social Security number
cc 10–11	Hours worked at regular pay
cc 12–13	Hours worked at overtime pay (time and a half)

In order to prepare the required report, the program must first load two tables into working storage: an employee information table and a federal withholding tax table. An employee data file is to be used to load the information table. The records in the file contain the following data:

cc 1–9	Social Security number
cc 10–29	Employee name
cc 30–33	Pay rate (format: xx.xx)
cc 34	Number of allowances claimed

The data shown in Figure 1.41 is to be loaded into the tax table. You must enter this data into a tax rate file.

Your assignment, in addition to preparing the above file, is to develop the program. It is recommended that you follow the steps of the problem-solving procedure. Use Data Set 1X4-I as the employee data file and Data Set 1X4-II as the time records file.

Figure 1.40

Printer Spacing Chart

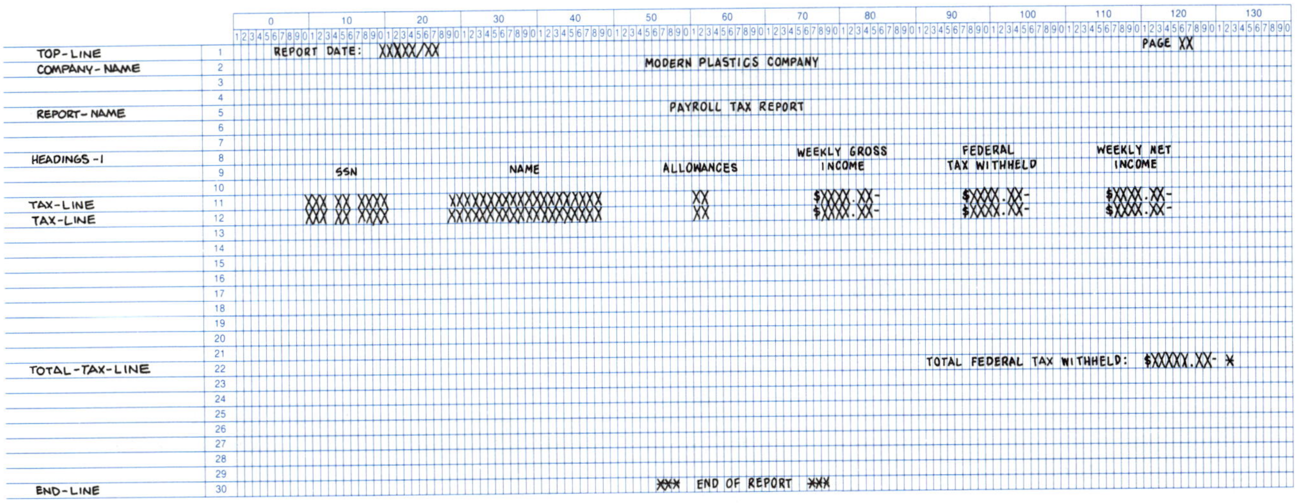

■ **Figure 1.41**

(For Wages Paid After December 1986)
Wage Bracket Percentage Method Table for Computing
Income Tax Withholding from Wages Exceeding Allowance Amount

Weekly Payroll Period				
Married Persons				
If the number of allowances is–	And gross wages are– Over	But not over	Subtract from excess wages	Multiply remainder by–
	$0	$93.00	$36.00	11.0%
	93.00	574.00	51.20	15.0%
0	574.00	901.00	293.93	28.0%
	901.00	1,767.00	415.34	35.0%
	1,767.00	....	538.22	38.5%
	$0	$129.54	$36.00	11.0%
	129.54	610.54	51.20	15.0%
1	610.54	937.54	293.93	28.0%
	937.54	1,803.54	415.34	35.0%
	1,803.54	....	538.22	38.5%
	$0	$166.08	$36.00	11.0%
	166.08	647.08	51.20	15.0%
2	647.08	974.08	293.93	28.0%
	974.08	1,840.08	415.34	35.0%
	1,840.08	....	538.22	38.5%
	$0	$202.62	$36.00	11.0%
	202.62	683.62	51.20	15.0%
3	683.62	1,010.62	293.93	28.0%
	1,010.62	1,876.62	415.34	35.0%
	1,876.62	....	538.22	38.5%
	$0	$239.16	$36.00	11.0%
	239.16	720.16	51.20	15.0%
4	720.16	1,047.16	293.93	28.0%
	1,047.16	1,913.16	415.34	35.0%
	1,913.16	....	538.22	38.5%

Instructions

A. For each employee, use the appropriate payroll period table and marital status section and select the subsection showing the number of allowances claimed.

B. Read across the selected subsection and locate the wage bracket range applicable to the employee's gross wage.

C. From the employee's "excess" wages (gross wages less amount for allowances claimed), subtract the amount shown on the next column of the appropriate row. Amount for each allowance is $38.46. Excess wages = gross wages minus (38.46 times number of allowances claimed).

D. Multiply the remaining amount of wages by the withholding percentage rate shown in the last column. The result of this computation is the amount of tax to be withheld.

2 Table Handling Using Indexes

You are already familiar with the concepts of hard-coded and loaded tables, the various table organizations, table-loading procedures, and procedures to retrieve data from tables. However, these table-handling concepts first presented in volume 1, *Structured COBOL,* used only data items as subscripts. In this chapter, the notions of table handling are extended to include indexes. When tables are defined as indexed tables, more efficient table look-up procedures become available to the programmer. In particular, sequential table searches may be executed through the use of the SEARCH statement, and binary table searches may be executed through the use of the SEARCH ALL statement.

The Monster Burger payroll report program is used as a setting for the introduction of the new table-handling concepts. ■

Objectives You Should Achieve

After studying this chapter, you should:

1. Be able to define an indexed one-level table.
2. Be able to define a two-level table indexed at each level.
3. Be able to define higher-level tables, up to seven levels, indexed at one or more levels.
4. Given the definition of an indexed table of one or more levels, be able to properly reference a table element at any of its levels.
5. Given the definition of an indexed table on one or more levels and appropriate input record descriptions, be able to design the logic needed to input-load the table and then to code the statements corresponding to the specified logic.
6. Given a list of values that must be stored in a two-level table, be able to hard-code an appropriate indexed table.
7. Given the description of a one-level indexed table and a search value, be able to code a SEARCH statement to retrieve an appropriate table element.
8. Given the description of a multilevel indexed table and one or more supplied search values, be able to design the logic and then code the statements needed to retrieve appropriate values from the table.
9. Be able to define an ordered indexed table.
10. Given the description of an ordered indexed table and a data file whose values are to be input-loaded into the table, be able to verify that the records of the file are in the required sequence, and, if they are not, be able to resequence the records as needed.
11. Given a table description, be able to determine if the table can be searched serially or nonserially.
12. Given the assignment of a program whose function is to produce a report containing values that must be retrieved from indexed tables or values that must be computed after retrieving data from an indexed table, be able to design the program and then implement the design to successful completion.

Figure 2.1 Printer spacing chart for the sample program

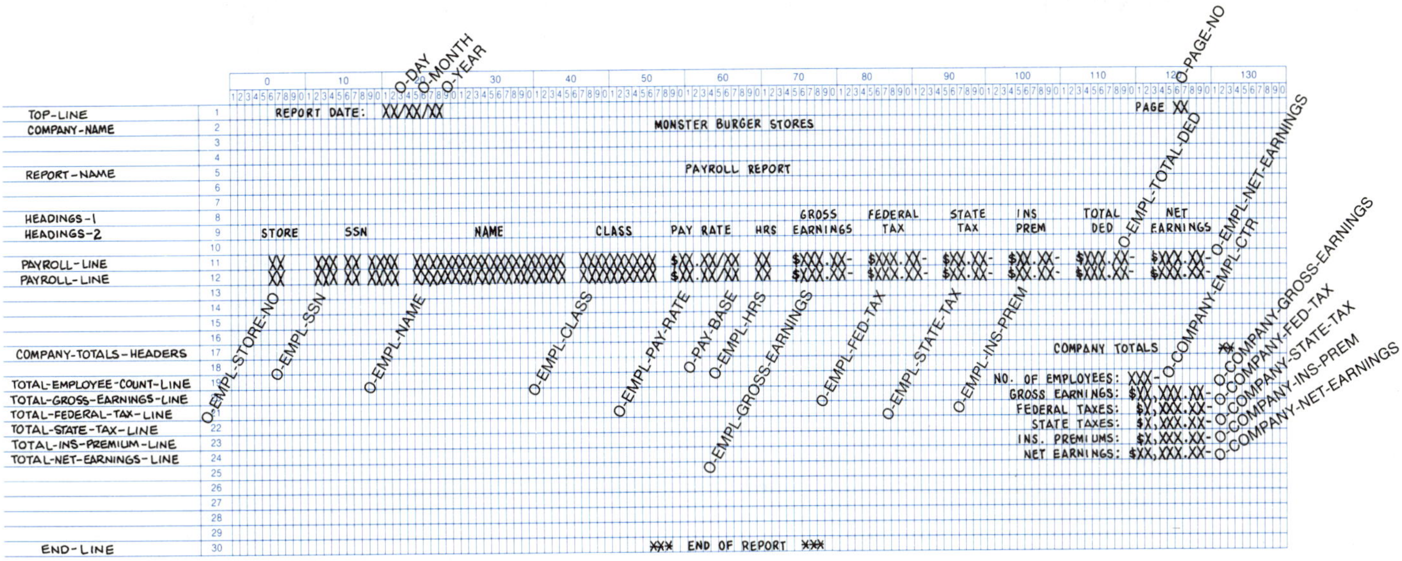

The Problem

The management of the Monster Burger Stores wants a weekly payroll report formatted as shown in Figure 2.1. Each page of the report begins with a page heading and contains a maximum of 30 detail lines. The detail lines must be printed in alphabetic order by employee name within each store, and store codes are to be in ascending order. There are two kinds of detail lines: one is designed for salaried employees, and the other is designed to be used for all other employees. The pay rate for a salaried employee is followed by the suffix "/WK," whereas the pay rate for an employee receiving wages is followed by the suffix "/HR." The hours field for salaried employees is left blank instead of showing the number of hours worked. The last page of the report also contains a company footing area that prints selected totals, and a last line that displays an "End of Report" message.

To prepare this report, the data processing department must use two data files. One file, the employee file, contains a payroll record for each employee on the current payroll. Each payroll record contains the following data:

cc 1–2	Employee classification code
cc 3–11	Employee Social Security number
cc 12–31	Employee name
cc 32–33	Employee store code
cc 34–35	Employee pay code
cc 36–37	Employee hours worked
cc 38–39	Number of store openings or closings (for assistant managers only)
cc 40–41	Employee insurance plan code
cc 42–43	Employee allowances claimed (for tax purposes)

The records in the employee file are sequenced alphabetically by employee name. For purposes of the report, the records must be sorted in ascending order by store number, and, within each store, the records must be sorted alphabetically by employee name.

The other data file, the tables file, contains records that are needed to (1) load federal tax rates into a federal tax rate table, (2) load the company's pay rates into a pay rate table, and (3) load the current insurance rates, for the various insurance plans the company offers, into an insurance rate table.

Each record of the tables file contains an identification code in the first byte. An "I" denotes an insurance rate record, a "P" denotes a pay rate record, and a "T" denotes a tax rate record. The rest of the record is the data that must be stored in one row of the corresponding table.

For purposes of this program, the rates are shown in tables below. The state tax is a "piggyback" tax of 23 percent applied to the federal tax.

Insurance Rates

Individual Coverage	Plan Code	Premium per Week
Basic Plan "A"	IA	$ 6.73
Major Medical Plan "B"	IB	$ 9.14
Family Coverage	**Plan Code**	**Premium per Week**
Basic Plan "A"	FA	$ 8.65
Major Medical Plan "B"	FB	$11.54

Company's Pay Schedule

Code	Pay Rate
01	$3.65/hr
02	$3.90/hr
03	$4.25/hr
04	$4.60/hr
05	$5.10/hr
06	$5.75/hr
07	$6.50/hr
08	$7.30/hr
09	$8.30/hr
10	$9.50/hr
11	$300.00/wk
12	$375.00/wk
13	$450.00/wk
14	$525.00/wk
15	$600.00/wk

Federal Income Tax Withholding Table—Married (Simplified)

Weekly Income	Number of Withholding Allowances				
(Less Than)	0	1	2	3	4
100	.070	.030	.000	.000	.000
200	.100	.075	.045	.020	.000
300	.117	.100	.080	.063	.043
400	.125	.113	.098	.085	.070
500	.130	.120	.108	.098	.086
600	.135	.125	.115	.107	.097
700	.156	.141	.127	.113	.104
800	.171	.159	.146	.134	.121
900	.183	.172	.161	.150	.139
1000	.199	.187	.174	.163	.153

In addition, the employee classifications are as follows:

Code	Classification
01	Apprentice
02	Beginner
03	Yearling
04	Standard
05	Assistant Manager
06	Store Manager

For this company, employee classifications are static; thus, the table is hard-coded into the program.

All employees are paid hourly wages except store managers, who are paid weekly salaries. Only managers and assistant managers are responsible for opening and/or closing stores. Assistant managers receive a weekly bonus of $10 plus an additional $5 for each time they have to open or close a store, in addition to their hourly wages.

Brief Analysis of the Problem

The logical analysis of this problem is as follows.

1. The records in the employee file must be sorted in the required sequence. There are two sort keys: the store number is the major key, and the employee name is the minor key.
2. The federal tax rate table, the pay rate table, and the insurance rate table must be loaded early in the program, since the data they contain must be accessed when employee payroll records in the payroll file are processed. (These tables will be defined as indexed tables in this program.)
3. The report date within the report heading must show the date in the format day/month-name/year. The month name should be retrieved from a table by using the month component of the date as obtained from the operating system. (The month table will also be defined as an indexed table.)
4. The report documentation lines (TOP-LINE, COMPANY-NAME, REPORT-NAME, HEADINGS-1, and HEADINGS-2) are to be printed at the top of each page. And since a maximum of 30 detail lines must be printed on each page, a detail line counter should be set to zero at the top of each page!
5. During the processing of a payroll record,
   a. The employee's gross earnings must be determined. Only store managers are salaried; all other employees are paid hourly wages. Hence, a test must be performed on the employee's classification. If the employee is a manager, the pay rate retrieved from the pay rate table is the gross earnings for the week. For all other employees, the pay rate retrieved from the table must be multiplied by the number of hours worked during the week to determine the gross earnings. In addition, an assistant manager receives a $10 bonus and an extra $5 for each time he or she had to open or close the store. In all cases, the pay code on the employee record is used to select the appropriate pay rate from the table.
   b. The employee's federal tax withholding must be computed. The applicable federal tax rate, which is a function of the gross income level and of the number of allowances claimed by the employee, must be located in the federal tax withholding table. The table shows that the employee's gross earnings corresponds to a specific row of the table. Once the row is located, the number of allowances claimed by the employee is used to select the appropriate tax rate in that row. There are five tax rates in each row: the first is selected for an employee who claims 0 allowances, the second through the fifth are selected for employees who claim 1 to 4 allowances, respectively.
   c. The employee's state tax withholding must be computed. It is 23 percent of the federal tax amount.
   d. The employee's insurance premium must be determined. The amount must be retrieved from the table of insurance premiums by using the insurance plan code on the payroll record.

e. The employee's total deductions must be computed. It is simply the sum of the federal tax, state tax, and insurance premium to be withheld.
f. The employee's net earnings must be computed by subtracting the total deductions from the gross earnings.
g. The employee's computed amounts must be added to the company-level accumulators, and the employee counter must be incremented by 1.
h. The employee's payroll line must be printed on the report. The printer spacing chart shows thirteen fields that must be assigned values. Two of these depend on the employee's classification, namely, O-EMPL-CLASS and O-PAY-BASE. A test is needed to determine the appropriate value of O-PAY-BASE: is the employee a manager or not? And a table look-up, using the employee's classification code, is needed to assign the correct value to the field O-EMPL-CLASS.

   Every time a payroll line is printed on the report, the detail line counter must be incremented by 1, and it must be tested to determine whether the maximum number of lines has been printed on the current page. If so, a new page must be prepared.

6. When all the detail lines have been printed on the report, the company summary must be printed, followed by an "End of Report" message.

The Design Phase

Step 1 of the problem-solving procedure calls for preparing the layouts of the input records. The payroll file contains only one kind of record. Its layout is shown in Figure 2.2a. Even though the records have to be resequenced by the program, the format of each record remains unchanged.

The second input file, the tables file, contains three different kinds of records: one that contains insurance rates, another that contains pay rates, and a third that contains tax rates. Though there are many ways of preparing the data that must be loaded into the program's tables, the most natural way is to prepare one record for each row of data in each of the tables. The first byte of each record is assigned a code used to identify the table that the record is associated with. Other data on a record is planned as follows:

1. A federal tax rate record contains all the entries that must be stored in one row of the federal tax rate table, that is, the upper income limit for that row, and five tax rates. The record's layout is shown in Figure 2.2b. Note that the row entries are grouped under a group name.
2. A pay rate record contains the pay rate to be stored in a row of the pay rate table. The record could be designed to contain the code as well. The code is purposely excluded because we intend to use this table to illustrate a table with positional organization. In this table, a pay rate is to be stored in the row occurrence that corresponds to its code: 3.65 is to be stored in row #1 because its code is 1, 4.60 is to be stored in row #4 because its code is 4, and so on. The layout of this record is shown in Figure 2.2c.
3. An insurance premium record contains a plan code and the corresponding premium amount, since this data is to be stored in one row of the insurance table. Its layout is shown in Figure 2.2d. Note that the plan code and insurance premium are grouped under a group name.

Figure 2.2 Input record layouts for the sample program

Record Layout Forms

a.

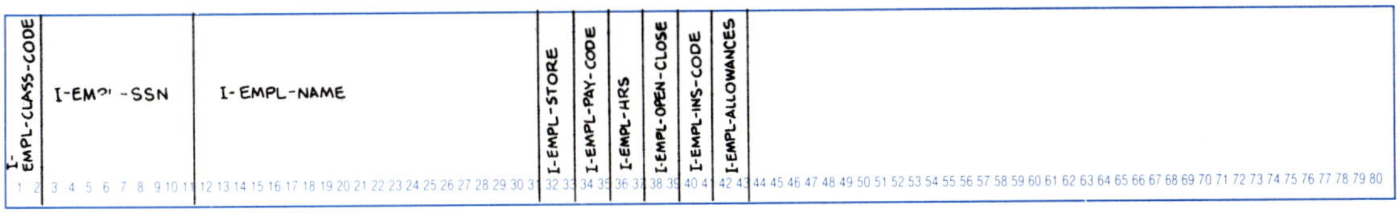

Record Name: PAYROLL-RECORD

b.

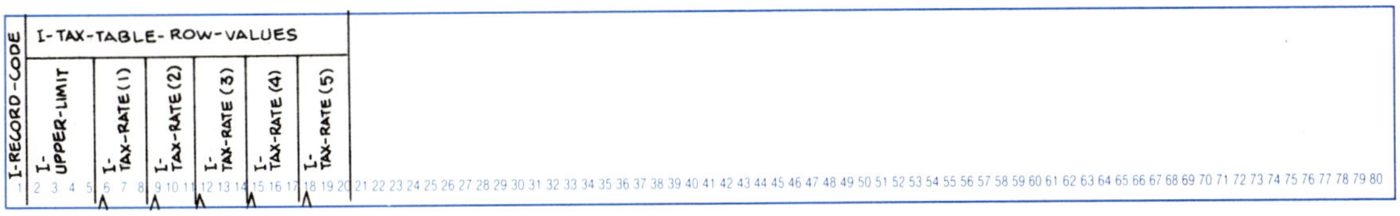

Record Name: FEDERAL-TAX-RATES-RECORD

c.

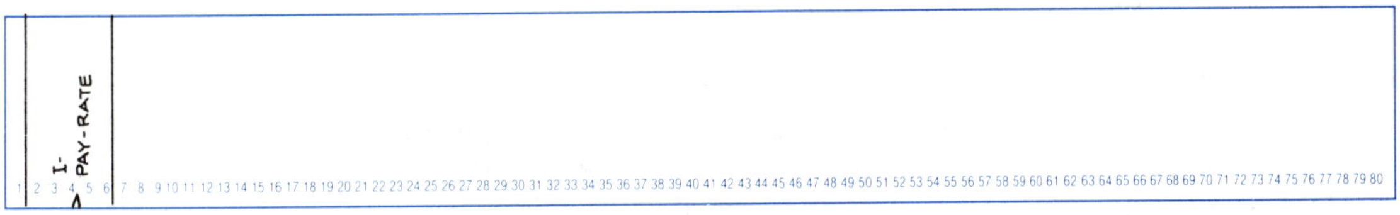

Record Name: PAY-RATE-RECORD

d.

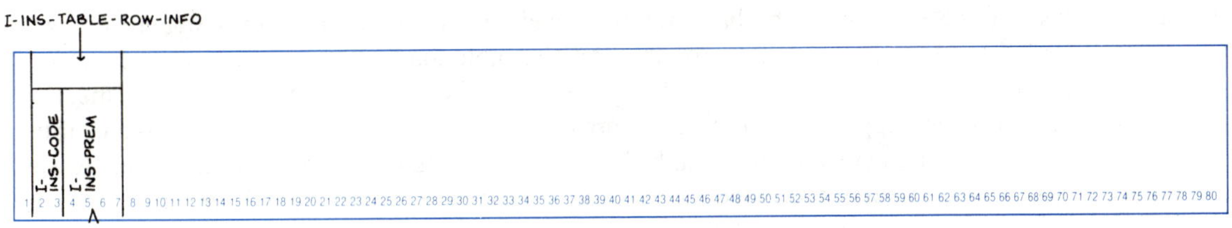

Record Name: INSURANCE-PREMIUM-RECORD

The records in the tables file are sequenced as follows: the ten federal tax rate records in increasing order by upper income limit; the fifteen pay rate records in increasing order by pay rate code; and the four insurance premium records in any order. The sample tables file used in this program is shown below:

```
T0100070030000000000
T0200100075045020000
T0300117100080063043
T0400125113098085070
T0500130120108098086
T0600135125115107097
T0700156141127113104
T0800171159146134121
T0900183172161150139
T1000199187174163153
P00365
P00390
P00425
P00460
P00510
P00575
P00650
P00730
P00830
P00950
P30000
P37500
P45000
P52500
P60000
IIA0673
IIB0914
IFA0865
IFB1154
```

(Recall that the program will also contain two hard-coded tables, one containing month names, the other containing the company's employee classifications. Input records are *not* prepared for these, since the nature of a hard-coded table requires the use of VALUE clauses to assign data to the table elements' occurrences!)

System Flowchart

The system flowchart must show that the program obtains data from **two** input files, TABLES-FILE and PAYROLL-FILE, and it must produce the output file PAYROLL-REPORT. However, since the records in the original employee file must be resequenced for this program, the system flowchart must show the need for a sort file (SORT-FILE) and for the file to be supplied as input to the sort routine, namely, EMPLOYEE-FILE. The output from the sort routine is then the file PAYROLL-FILE. The system flowchart is shown in Figure 2.3.

Structure Chart

The brief analysis of the problem is the basis for the development of the program's structure chart, shown in Figure 2.4. Note that the sorting routine and the table-loading functions have been placed under the control of module 200 START UP. This is because the employee payroll records must be resequenced prior to being supplied as input to the program and because all the program tables must be loaded at the very beginning of the program, before the processing of payroll records begins. Recall that when a payroll record is being processed, numeric data must be retrieved from three tables, namely, the pay rate table (to compute the gross earnings), the federal tax rate table (to compute the federal tax to be withheld), and the insurance premium table. The pay rate retrieval is contained in module 350 COMPUTE EMPLOYEE ITEMS, the federal tax rate retrieval is contained in module 430 COMPUTE TAXES, and the insurance premium retrieval is contained in module 440 SEARCH INSURANCE TABLE.

Figure 2.3 System flowchart for the sample program

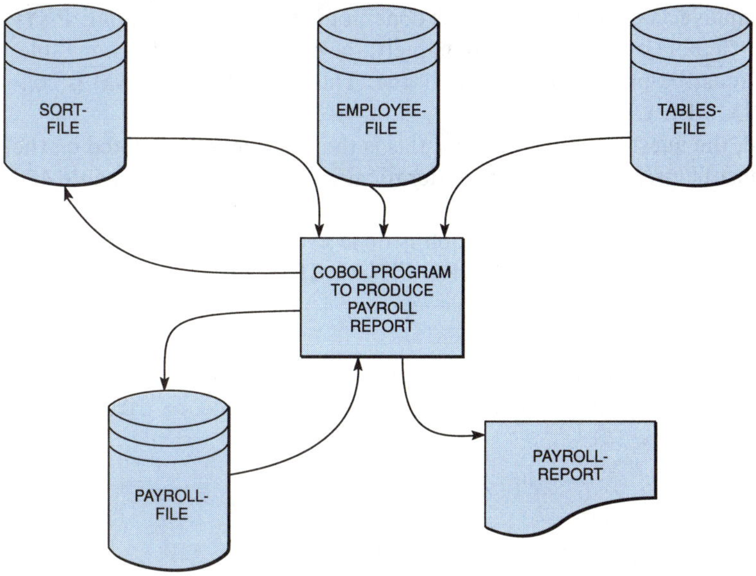

Figure 2.4 Structure chart for the sample program

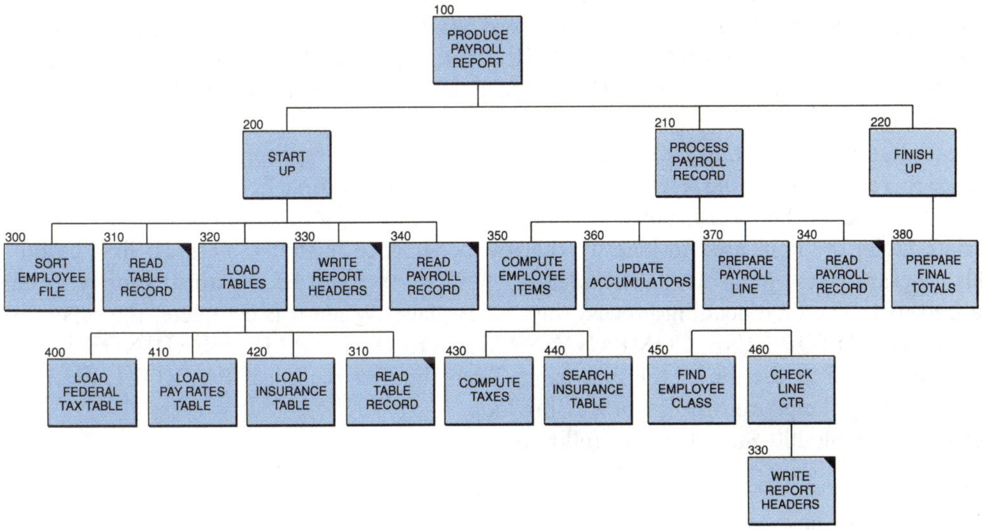

When all the computations have been performed, the company accumulators must be updated. This is done in module 360 UPDATE ACCUMULATORS. Then, the processing of an employee record ends with the preparation of the employee's payroll line. This is done in module 370 PREPARE PAYROLL LINE. In this module, a fourth table must be searched, namely, the employee classification table, since the employee's classification must be printed on the detail line. This table data retrieval is contained in module 450 FIND EMPLOYEE CLASS.

When a payroll line is printed, the question arises whether this is the last line to be printed on the current page. If it is, a new page must be prepared. These considerations are attended to in module 460 CHECK LINE COUNTER.

When all the payroll records have been processed, the job is done except for the printing of the company totals. This is accomplished in module 380 PREPARE FINAL TOTALS.

Program Pseudocode

Since the purpose of the program pseudocode is to show how the tasks specified in the structure chart are to be accomplished, we must now be attentive to details. The primary pseudocode paragraph is simple and straightforward, as follows:

100-Produce-Payroll-Report.

1. Perform 200-Start-Up.
2. Perform 210-Process-Payroll-Record until no more payroll records.
3. Perform 220-Finish-Up.
4. Stop the run.

Within paragraph 200-Start-Up, the employee file must be sorted into the required record sequence; the two input files, TABLES-FILE and PAYROLL-FILE, and the output file PAYROLL-REPORT must be opened. The current date must be obtained from the operating system and its components used to prepare the report date entry of the record TOP-LINE. Two end-of-file flags must be initialized. The flags will be named WS-PAYROLL-RECORDS-FLAG and WS-TABLE-RECORDS-FLAG for the PAYROLL-FILE and TABLES-FILE, respectively, and both must be initialized to "YES." The company accumulators must be initialized to zero.

As noted earlier, a very important task to be accomplished in this paragraph is loading the tables. Recall that for each record in the file TABLES-FILE, the code in the first field identifies the table that must receive the data on the record. Since the contents of records will be stored in successive rows of the appropriate table, the item used to identify the row occurrence in that table must first be initialized. In this program, these items are table *indexes* (table indexes will be explained shortly!) and they are initialized to 1. The table-loading process then takes place. When it is complete, the report is started, that is, the records TOP-LINE, COMPANY-NAME, REPORT-NAME, HEADINGS-1, and HEADINGS-2 are printed at the top of the first page. Then the first record of PAYROLL-FILE is accessed prior to entering the payroll-record-processing loop.

Pseudocode paragraph 200-Start-Up is as follows:

200-Start-Up.

1. Perform 300-Sort-Employee-File.
2. Open Tables-File and Payroll-File as input files, and open Payroll-Report as the output file.
3. Obtain the date from the system and
   a. move the date year-component to Top-Line year;
   b. move the date day-component to Top-Line day;
   c. set month-table-index equal to date month-component;
   d. move month(month-table-index) to Top-Line month.
4. Set the end-of-file flags WS-TABLE-RECORDS-FLAG and WS-PAYROLL-RECORDS-FLAG to "YES".
5. Initialize company-accumulators and page-number to zero.
6. Set the table indexes (Wage-Index, Pay-Rate-Index, Insurance-Index) to 1.
7. Perform 310-Read-Table-Record.
8. Perform 320-Load-Tables until no more table records.
9. Perform 330-Write-Report-Headers.
10. Perform 340-Read-Payroll-Record.

In preparing paragraph 210-Process-Payroll-Record, the structure chart clearly specifies the procedures that must be executed. When they have been executed, the net result is a detail line printed on the report. Then, the next employee record is read and the process continues. The paragraph is as follows:

210-Process-Payroll-Record.

1. Perform 350-Compute-Employee-Items.
2. Perform 360-Update-Accumulators.
3. Perform 370-Prepare-Payroll-Line.
4. Perform 340-Read-Payroll-Record.

Within paragraph 220-Finish-Up, the final totals must be printed on the report, the "End of Report" message must be printed, and the files must be closed. The paragraph is as follows:

220-Finish-Up.

1. Perform 380-Prepare-Final-Totals.
2. Move the record End-Line to the output area Printline.
3. After advancing 5 lines, write the output record Printline.
4. Close the three files.

Sorting the Employee File

Since the records in the employee file are not in the sequence needed for the payroll report, the sort function is used to create a new file, called PAYROLL-FILE, in which the records are in the correct order. The major sort key is the employee's store number, and the minor key is the employee name. Paragraph 300-Sort-Employee-File handles the sorting function, as follows:

300-Sort-Employee-File.

1. Read all input Employee-Record into the Sort-File.
2. Sort the records of Sort-File using the following keys:
   a. major key: input employee-store-number
   b. minor key: input employee-name
3. Write all the sorted records to the file Payroll-File.

Loading the Tables

The data to be loaded into the federal tax rate table, into the pay rate table, and into the insurance rate table is stored on records of the file TABLES-FILE. The code in the first byte of each record identifies the table that must receive the data stored on the record. Module 310 READ TABLE RECORD simply makes a record available in memory, whereas module 320 LOAD TABLES must identify the code so as to move the data to the appropriate table. The code "T" indicates that the record data must be loaded into the federal tax rate table; the code "P" indicates that the record data must be loaded into the pay rate table; and the code "I" indicates that the record data must be loaded into the insurance premium table.

The corresponding pseudocode paragraphs are as follows:

310-Read-Table-Record.

1. Read an input Tables-File record.
2. Test for end-of-file record;
   if EOF record reached, set the flag WS-TABLE-RECORDS-FLAG to "NO ".

320-Load-Tables.

1. Test input record code:
   a. if "T", perform 400-Load-Federal-Tax-Table;
   b. if "P", perform 410-Load-Pay-Rate-Table;
   c. if "I", perform 420-Load-Insurance-Table.
2. Perform 310-Read-Table-Record.

■ **Figure 2.5** Loading the tables

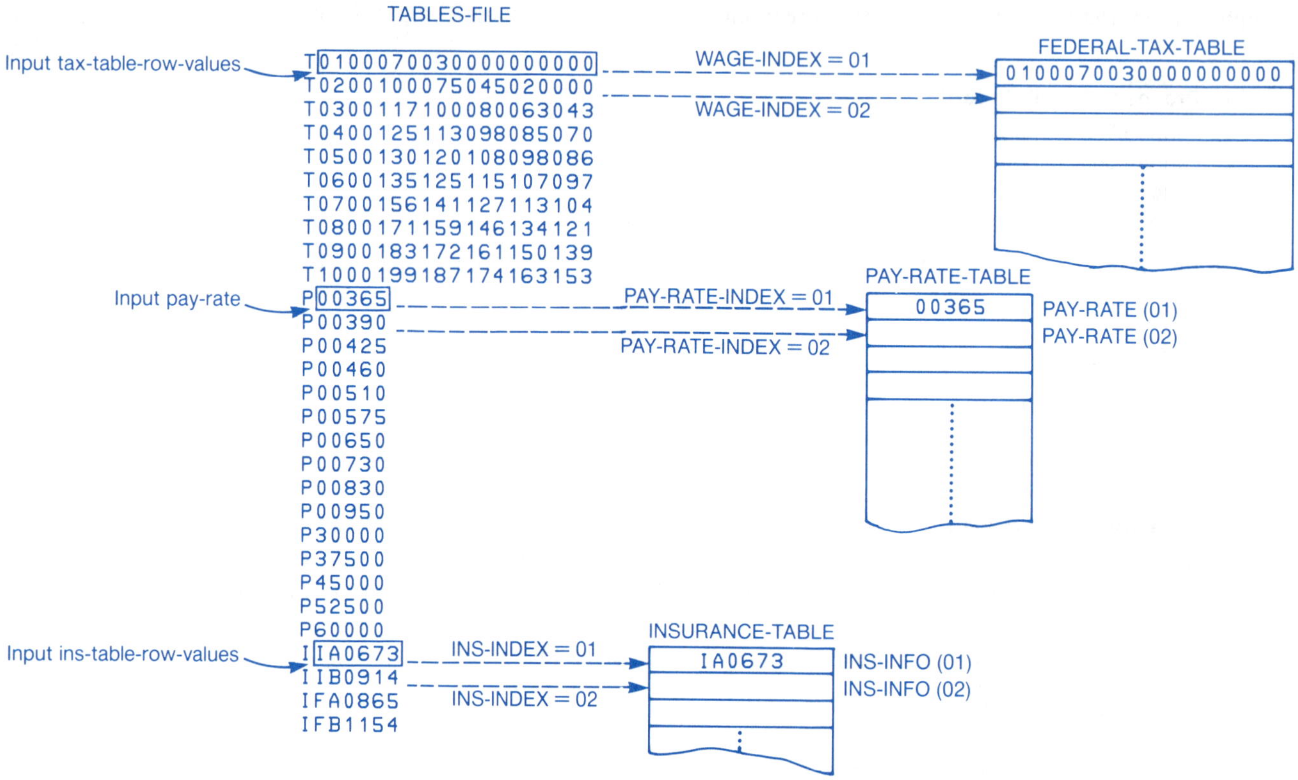

The table-loading process may be illustrated as shown in Figure 2.5. It should be clear that when control is first sent to paragraph 400-Load-Federal-Tax-Table, all the data on the record (except for the code "T") is moved into row #1 of the federal tax rate table, since the value of the index (wage-index) is 1. It was set to 1 in paragraph 200-Start-Up! The index must now be incremented by 1 so that the data on the next record with code "T" can be moved to row #2 of the tax table, and so on. The same reasoning applies to the pay rate table and to the insurance premium table.

The pseudocode paragraphs that load the tables are as follows:

400-Load-Federal-Tax-Table.

1. Move input tax-table-row-values to federal-tax-table wage-level-info(wage-index).
2. Increment wage-index by 1.

410-Load-Pay-Rate-Table.

1. Move input pay-rate to pay-rate-table pay-rate(pay-rate-index).
2. Increment pay-rate-index by 1.

420-Load-Insurance-Table.

1. Move input insurance-table-row-values to insurance-table insurance-info(insurance-index).
2. Increment insurance-index by 1.

Processing a Payroll Record

Paragraph 210-Process-Payroll-Record indicates that the first task is to send control to procedure 350-Compute-Employee-Items to compute the required payroll items. These items are the gross earnings, the federal tax, state tax, and insurance premium withholdings, and finally the net earnings.

In order to compute the gross earnings, the pay rate code specified on the employee's payroll record must be used to retrieve the actual pay rate from the pay rate table. Since this table has positional organization, the pay rate code indicates the pay rate occurrence to retrieve from the table. For instance, if the pay rate code is 05, pay rate (05) is the applicable pay rate for this employee. If the employee is a manager, this pay rate is the gross earnings for the week, but for all other employees, the pay rate must be multiplied by the number of hours worked to determine the gross earnings. (Assistant managers also have increments of $10 and an additional $5 for each time they had to open or close the store!) When the gross earnings have been determined, control is sent to procedure 430-Compute-Taxes.

To compute the federal tax withholding, the gross earnings amount is used to determine the appropriate row of the federal tax rate table, and the number of allowances claimed by the employee is used to select the applicable tax rate in that row. Once found, the tax rate multiplied by the gross earnings amount yields the amount of federal tax to be withheld. Note that upper income limits in the table (the entries in the first column) must be searched to locate the appropriate row. The row is located when the condition

employee-gross-earnings < upper-limit(wage-index)

is satisfied. Recall that wage-index is the item used to reference successive occurrences of income upper limits in the table. Now, since each row contains five tax rates, the first for zero allowances, the second for one allowance, the third for two allowances, the fourth for three allowances, and the fifth for four allowances, a particular tax rate must be specified by two subscripts, the first identifying the row occurrence, and the second specifying the tax rate occurrence within that row. The tax rate occurrence is one more than the number of allowances claimed by the employee. The number of claimed allowances is stored in the field I-EMPL-ALLOWANCES. So, when the condition stated above (employee-gross-earnings < upper-limit(wage-index)) is satisfied, the item

tax-rate(wage-index, input employee-allowances plus 1)

references the correct tax rate.

When the federal tax has been computed, the state tax is simply taken as 23 percent of the federal tax.

Control then passes to the procedure 440-Search-Insurance-Table to determine the insurance premium that must be withheld from the employee's gross earnings. To do this, the insurance plan code specified on the payroll record must be used in a search of the insurance rate table. When a plan code in the table matches the input plan code, the corresponding insurance premium is selected as the amount to be withheld. That is, when the condition

input insurance-code = insurance-table insurance-code(insurance-index)

is satisfied, insurance-table insurance-premium(insurance-index) is the correct premium.

Next, the payroll deductions are totaled, and this total is subtracted from the gross earnings to yield the net earnings.

The pseudocode paragraphs corresponding to these computations are as follows:

350-Compute-Employee-Items.

1. Set pay-rate-index equal to input employee-pay-code.
2. Move pay-rate-table pay-rate(pay-rate-index) to employee-pay-rate.
3. Test input employee-class-code:
   - **a.** if manager, set employee-gross-earnings equal to employee-pay-rate;
   - **b.** if assistant-manager, compute employee-gross-earnings equal to input employee-hours times employee-pay-rate plus (5 times input employee-open-close) plus 10;
   - **c.** if other, compute employee-gross-earnings equal to input employee-hours times employee-pay-rate.
4. Perform 430-Compute-Taxes.
5. Perform 440-Search-Insurance-Table.
6. Add employee-federal-tax, employee-state-tax, employee-insurance-premium to equal employee-total-deductions.
7. Subtract employee-total-deductions from employee-gross-earnings to equal employee-net-earnings.

430-Compute-Taxes.

1. Set wage-index equal to 1.
2. Search federal-tax-table wage-level-info occurrences:
   a. when employee-gross-earnings < upper-limit(wage-index)
      i. move tax-rate(wage-index, input employee-allowances plus 1) to employee-tax-rate;
      ii. multiply employee-gross-earnings by employee-tax-rate to equal employee-federal-tax;
      iii. multiply employee-federal-tax by .23 to equal employee-state-tax.
   b. if the search is unsuccessful, display the message "Gross Earnings out of Range for " input employee-name.

440-Search-Insurance-Table.

1. Set insurance-index to 1.
2. Search insurance-table insurance-info occurrences:
   a. when insurance-code(insurance-index) = input employee-insurance-code move insurance-premium(insurance-index) to employee-insurance-premium.
   b. if the search is unsuccessful, display the message "Ins. Code not Found for " input employee-name.

Now that the employee's payroll computations have been performed, the appropriate amounts must be added to the company accumulators. Procedure 360-Update-Accumulators is as follows:

360-Update-Accumulators.

1. Add 1 to employee-counter.
2. Add employee-gross-earnings to company-gross-earnings.
3. Add employee-federal-tax to company-federal-tax.
4. Add employee-state-tax to company-state-tax.
5. Add employee-insurance-premium to company-insurance-premium.
6. Add employee-net-earnings to company-net-earnings.

Finally, the employee's payroll line must be prepared so that it can be printed on the report. The procedure 370-Prepare-Payroll-Line takes care of the details. The employee's store number, Social Security number, name, and number of hours worked (except for managers) are obtained from the employee's payroll record. The employee's classification is obtained from the employee classification table. The applicable pay base (/WK or /HR) is selected. And the employee's computed amounts are retrieved from the appropriate work areas. The resulting line is printed on the report. The related pseudocode is as follows:

370-Prepare-Payroll-Line.

1. Clear the record area Payroll-Line.
2. Move input store-number to Payroll-Line store-number.
3. Move input Social-Security-number to Payroll-Line Social-Security-number.
4. Move input employee-name to Payroll-Line employee-name.
5. Perform 450-Find-Employee-Class.
6. Move employee-pay-rate to Payroll-Line employee-pay-rate.
7. If input employee-class-code is equal to "06," move "/WK" to Payroll-Line pay-base; otherwise, move "/HR" to Payroll-Line pay-base and move input employee-hours to Payroll-Line employee-hours.
8. Move employee-gross-earnings to Payroll-Line employee-gross-earnings.
9. Move employee-federal-tax to Payroll-Line employee-federal-tax.
10. Move employee-state-tax to Payroll-Line employee-state-tax.
11. Move employee-insurance-premium to Payroll-Line employee-insurance-premium.
12. Move employee-total-deductions to Payroll-Line employee-total-deductions.
13. Move employee-net-earnings to Payroll-Line employee-net-earnings.
14. Move the record Payroll-Line to the output area Printline.
15. After advancing proper-spacing, write the output record Printline.
16. Set proper-spacing to 1.
17. Perform 460-Check-Line-Ctr.

The procedure 460-Check-Line-Ctr is used to determine whether the maximum number of detail lines has been reached for the current page. If it has, another report page is prepared.

The program pseudocode is shown in its entirety in Figure 2.6. (The program flowchart that corresponds to the pseudocode is shown later in Figure 2.18, once the flowchart structures for the SEARCH statement have been examined.)

Figure 2.6 Program pseudocode for the sample program

100-Produce-Payroll-Report.

1. Perform 200-Start-Up.
2. Perform 210-Process-Payroll-Record until no more payroll records.
3. Perform 220-Finish-Up.
4. Stop the run.

200-Start-Up.

1. Perform 300-Sort-Employee-File.
2. Open Tables-File and Payroll-File as input files, and
   open Payroll-Report as the output file.
3. Obtain the date from the system and
   a. move the date year-component to Top-Line year;
   b. move the date day-component to Top-Line day;
   c. set month-table-index equal to date month-component;
   d. move month(month-table-index) to Top-Line month.
4. Set the end-of-file flags WS-TABLE-RECORDS-FLAG and
   WS-PAYROLL-RECORDS-FLAG to "YES".
5. Initialize company-accumulators and page-number to zero.
6. Set the table indexes (Wage-Index, Pay-Rate-Index, Insurance-Index) to 1.
7. Perform 310-Read-Table-Record.
8. Perform 320-Load-Tables until no more table records.
9. Perform 330-Write-Report-Headers.
10. Perform 340-Read-Payroll-Record.

210-Process-Payroll-Record.

1. Perform 350-Compute-Employee-Items.
2. Perform 360-Update-Accumulators.
3. Perform 370-Prepare-Payroll-Line.
4. Perform 340-Read-Payroll-Record.

220-Finish-Up.

1. Perform 380-Prepare-Final-Totals.
2. Move the record End-Line to the output area Printline.
3. After advancing 5 lines, write the output record Printline.
4. Close the three files.

300-Sort-Employee-File.

1. Read all input records Employee-Record into the Sort-File.
2. Sort the records of Sort-File using the following keys:
   a. major key: input employee-store-number
   b. minor key: input employee-name
3. Write all the sorted records to the file Payroll-File.

310-Read-Table-Record.

1. Read an input Tables-File record.
2. Test for end-of-file record;
   if EOF record reached, set the flag WS-TABLE-RECORDS-FLAG
   to "NO ".

320-Load-Tables.

1. Test input record code:
   a. if "T", perform 400-Load-Federal-Tax-Table.
   b. if "P", perform 410-Load-Pay-Rate-Table.
   c. if "I", perform 420-Load-Insurance-Table.
2. Perform 310-Read-Table-Record.

330-Write-Report-Headers.

1. Add 1 to page-number.
2. Move page-number to Top-Line page-number.
3. Move the record Top-Line to the output area Printline.
4. After advancing to a new page, write the output record Printline.

5. Move the record Company-Name to the output area Printline.
6. After advancing 1 line, write the output record Printline.
7. Move the record Report-Name to the output area Printline.
8. After advancing 3 lines, write the output record Printline.
9. Move the record Headings-1 to the output area Printline.
10. After advancing 3 lines, write the output record Printline.
11. Move the record Headings-2 to the output area Printline.
12. After advancing 1 line, write the output record Printline.
13. Initialize line-counter.
14. Set proper-spacing to 2.

340-Read-Payroll-Record.

1. Read an input Payroll-File record.
2. Test for end-of-file record;
   if EOF record reached, set the flag WS-PAYROLL-RECORDS-FLAG
   to "NO ".

350-Compute-Employee-Items.

1. Set pay-rate-index equal to input employee-pay-code.
2. Move pay-rate-table pay-rate(pay-rate-index) to employee-pay-rate.
3. Test input employee-class-code:
   a. if manager, set employee-gross-earnings equal to employee-pay-rate;
   b. if assistant-manager, compute employee-gross-earnings equal to input employee-hours times employee-pay-rate plus (5 times input employee-open-close) plus 10;
   c. if other, compute employee-gross-earnings equal to input employee-hours times employee-pay-rate.
4. Perform 430-Compute-Taxes.
5. Perform 440-Search-Insurance-Table.
6. Add employee-federal-tax, employee-state-tax, employee-insurance-premium to equal employee-total-deductions.
7. Subtract employee-total-deductions from employee-gross-earnings to equal employee-net-earnings.

360-Update-Accumulators.

1. Add 1 to company-employee-counter.
2. Add employee-gross-earnings to company-gross-earnings.
3. Add employee-federal-tax to company-federal-tax.
4. Add employee-state-tax to company-state-tax.
5. Add employee-insurance-premium to company-insurance-premium.
6. Add employee-net-earnings to company-net-earnings.

370-Prepare-Payroll-Line.

1. Clear the record area Payroll-Line.
2. Move input store-number to Payroll-Line store-number.
3. Move input Social-Security-number to Payroll-Line Social-Security-number.
4. Move input employee-name to Payroll-Line employee-name.
5. Perform 450-Find-Employee-Class.
6. Move employee-pay-rate to Payroll-Line employee-pay-rate.
7. If input employee-class-code is equal to "06," move "/WK" to Payroll-Line pay-base;
   otherwise, move "/HR" to Payroll-Line pay-base and
   move input employee-hours to Payroll-Line employee-hours.
8. Move employee-gross-earnings to Payroll-Line employee-gross-earnings.
9. Move employee-federal-tax to Payroll-Line employee-federal-tax.
10. Move employee-state-tax to Payroll-Line employee-state-tax.
11. Move employee-insurance-premium to Payroll-Line employee-insurance-premium.
12. Move employee-total-deductions to Payroll-Line employee-total-deductions.
13. Move employee-net-earnings to Payroll-Line employee-net-earnings.
14. Move the record Payroll-Line to the output area Printline.
15. After advancing proper-spacing, write the output record Printline.
16. Set proper-spacing to 1.
17. Perform 460-Check-Line-Ctr.

380-Prepare-Final-Totals.

1. Move the record Company-Totals-Header to the output area Printline.
2. After advancing 5 lines, write the output record Printline.
3. Move company-employee-counter to Total-Employee-Count-Line company-employee-counter.
4. Move the record Total-Employee-Count-Line to the output area Printline.
5. After advancing 2 lines, write the output record Printline.
6. Move company-gross-earnings to Total-Gross-Earnings-Line company-gross-earnings.
7. Move the record Total-Gross-Earnings-Line to the output area Printline.
8. After advancing 1 line, write the output record Printline.
9. Move company-federal-tax to Total-Federal-Tax-Line company-federal-tax.
10. Move the record Total-Federal-Tax-Line to the output area Printline.
11. After advancing 1 line, write the output record Printline.
12. Move company-state-tax to Total-State-Tax-Line company-state-tax.
13. Move the record Total-State-Tax-Line to the output area Printline.
14. After advancing 1 line, write the output record Printline.
15. Move company-insurance-premium to Total-Ins-Premium-Line company-insurance-premium.
16. Move the record Total-Ins-Premium-Line to the output area Printline.
17. After advancing 1 line, write the output record Printline.
18. Move company-net-earnings to Total-Net-Earnings-Line company-net-earnings.
19. Move the record Total-Net-Earnings-Line to the output area Printline.
20. After advancing 1 line, write the output record Printline.

400-Load-Federal-Tax-Table.

1. Move input tax-table-row-values to federal-tax-table wage-level-info(wage-index).
2. Increment wage-index by 1.

410-Load-Pay-Rate-Table.

1. Move input pay-rate to pay-rate-table pay-rate(pay-rate-index).
2. Increment pay-rate-index by 1.

420-Load-Insurance-Table.

1. Move input insurance-table-row-values to insurance-table insurance-info(insurance-index).
2. Increment insurance-index by 1.

430-Compute-Taxes.

1. Set wage-index equal to 1.
2. Search federal-tax-table wage-level-info occurrences;
   a. when employee-gross-earnings < upper-limit(wage-index)
      i. move tax-rate(wage-index, input employee-allowances plus 1) to employee-tax-rate;
      ii. multiply employee-gross-earnings by employee-tax-rate to equal employee-federal-tax;
      iii. multiply employee-federal-tax by .23 to equal employee-state-tax.
   b. if the search is unsuccessful, display the message "Gross Earnings out of Range for " input employee-name.

440-Search-Insurance-Table.

1. Set insurance-index to 1.
2. Search insurance-table insurance-info occurrences;
   a. when insurance-code(insurance-index) = input employee-insurance-code
      move insurance-premium(insurance-index) to employee-insurance-premium.
   b. if the search is unsuccessful, display the message "Ins. Code not Found for " input employee-name.

450-Find-Employee-Class.

1. Set class-index to 1.
2. Search employee-class-table employee-class-info occurrences;
   when employee-class-code(class-index) = input employee-class-code,
   move employee-class-table employee-class(class-index) to employee-class.

460-Check-Line-Ctr.

1. Add 1 to line-counter.
2. Test line-counter:
   if line counter equal to 30, perform 330-Write-Report-Headers.

The Design Implementation Phase

The first task in this phase is to code the program. The coding is completely directed by the specifications in the original statement of the problem and by the program design that has just been completed. However, we delay the coding in order to learn how to define indexed tables, how to load data into the tables, and how to access table elements using indexes.

Indexed Tables

It is a simple matter to define a table as an *indexed table.* The only new required entry in the table description is the INDEXED BY phrase in the OCCURS clause. It specifies the index (or indexes) that may be used to reference occurrences of table elements, and it must be coded in the entry that contains the OCCURS clause. For instance, the insurance table in the sample program may be defined as follows:

```
01   INSURANCE-TABLE.
     05 WS-INS-INFO  OCCURS 4 TIMES
                     INDEXED BY INS-INDEX.
        10 WS-INS-CODE      PIC XX.
        10 WS-INS-PREM      PIC 99V99.
```

The *index data item* INS-INDEX is completely defined by the INDEXED BY phrase. It is not defined anywhere else in the DATA DIVISION, because it is not a standard data item. That is, it cannot be used in an arithmetic statement, it cannot be redefined, and it cannot be written to a file. However, its value may be specified and/or changed by a SET statement or within a PERFORM-VARYING statement, and its value may be tested in relational statements. For instance, the statement SET INS-INDEX TO 1 assigns the value 1 to INS-INDEX, the statement SET INS-INDEX UP BY 2 adds 2 to the current value of INS-INDEX, and the statement

```
PERFORM 440-SEARCH-INS-TABLE
     VARYING INS-INDEX FROM 1 BY 1
          UNTIL ITEM-IS-FOUND
```

sets INS-INDEX to an initial value of 1 and adds 1 to INS-INDEX every time control returns from the procedure 440-SEARCH-INS-TABLE.

The essential function of an index is to point to an occurrence of a table element. For instance, using the coding above and the data from the insurance table supplied with the statement of the sample problem, the statements

```
SET INS-INDEX TO 3.
DISPLAY WS-INS-INFO (INS-INDEX).
DISPLAY WS-INS-CODE (INS-INDEX).
DISPLAY WS-INS-PREM (INS-INDEX).
```

will display FA0865, FA, and 0865 on three separate lines, that is, they will display the data stored in the fields of the third table element. When used to reference a table element, the index must be a positive integer, and the occurrence that it points to must not exceed the integer specified in the OCCURS clause that defines the table. In the current example, INS-INDEX must not specify a value greater than 4.

The sample program of this chapter needs the following five tables:

1. The table containing the month names, which is a one-level hard-coded table that may be defined as follows:

```
01   MONTH-VALUES.
     05 PIC X(9)  VALUE "JANUARY  ".
     05 PIC X(9)  VALUE "FEBRUARY ".
     05 PIC X(9)  VALUE "MARCH    ".
     05 PIC X(9)  VALUE "APRIL    ".
     05 PIC X(9)  VALUE "MAY      ".
     05 PIC X(9)  VALUE "JUNE     ".
     05 PIC X(9)  VALUE "JULY     ".
     05 PIC X(9)  VALUE "AUGUST   ".
     05 PIC X(9)  VALUE "SEPTEMBER".
     05 PIC X(9)  VALUE "OCTOBER  ".
     05 PIC X(9)  VALUE "NOVEMBER ".
     05 PIC X(9)  VALUE "DECEMBER ".
01   MONTH-TABLE REDEFINES MONTH-VALUES.
     05 WS-MONTH    OCCURS 12 TIMES
                    INDEXED BY MONTH-INDEX PIC X(9).
```

This is the traditional two-step definition of a hard-coded table in which VALUE clauses are coded in one record description and the OCCURS clause is coded in a second record description that REDEFINES the first. The COBOL '85 standards allow the use of the VALUE clause and the OCCURS clause in the same record description. As a result, the month table may be defined as follows:

```
01  MONTH-TABLE      VALUE "JANUARY  FEBRUARY MARCH    APRIL    MA
-   "Y       JUNE     JULY     AUGUST   SEPTEMBEROCTOBER  NOVEMBER
-   " DECEMBER".
    05 WS-MONTH    OCCURS 12 TIMES
                   INDEXED BY MONTH-INDEX PIC X(9).
```

The literal in the VALUE clause is 108 characters long, and the OCCURS clause separates the literal into 12 groupings of 9 characters each. Each group is referenced by WS-MONTH (MONTH-INDEX), where the value of MONTH-INDEX is between 1 and 12. This is the form we will use in the program.

In either case, the index associated with the table is MONTH-INDEX. That is, an occurrence of the data item WS-MONTH may be specified by the index. In general, even though a table contains an INDEXED BY phrase, it does not preclude the use of a standard data item as a subscript. For instance, suppose that I-MONTH-NO is defined by PIC 9(2), and its value is 04. The data item WS-MONTH(I-MONTH-NO) references the fourth occurrence in the table, and WS-MONTH(MONTH-INDEX) also references the fourth occurrence in the table, provided the index has been set to the value of I-MONTH-NO by the statement SET MONTH-INDEX TO I-MONTH-NO.

2. The insurance premium table, as described on page 74. It is a one-level table, since its description contains only one OCCURS clause, and its organization is random, since the row values need not be placed in any specific row.
3. A pay rate table. This one-level table is given positional organization, that is, a pay rate is stored in a row whose occurrence number is the same as its code. For instance, the third pay rate has a value of $4.25, and it is stored in the third row because its numeric code is 03. The fifth pay rate ($5.10) is stored in the fifth row because its numeric code is 05, and so on. The table may be defined as follows:

```
01  PAY-RATE-TABLE.
    05 WS-PAY-RATE   OCCURS 15 TIMES
                     INDEXED BY PAY-RATE-INDEX
                     PIC S999V99.
```

Note that the table has 15 occurrences of the data item WS-PAY-RATE, and the index associated with this table is PAY-RATE-INDEX. (It is not required that an index name contain the word INDEX, but its use increases self-documentation!)

4. A hard-coded employee-class table. This table is also a one-level table, and it is given usage-frequency organization, that is, the most frequently accessed values are placed in occurrences toward the top of the table, and the least frequently toward the bottom of the table. The standard two-step procedure is used to define the table: in step 1, VALUE clauses specify the row contents; in step 2, the REDEFINES clause provides an alternate description so that table elements may be referenced by a subscripted or indexed data name. The table may be defined as follows:

```
01  EMPLOYEE-CLASS-VALUES.
    05 PIC X(12)  VALUE "04STANDARD  ".
    05 PIC X(12)  VALUE "03YEARLING  ".
    05 PIC X(12)  VALUE "02BEGINNER  ".
    05 PIC X(12)  VALUE "01APPRENTICE".
    05 PIC X(12)  VALUE "05ASS'T MGR.".
    05 PIC X(12)  VALUE "06STORE MGR.".
01  EMPLOYEE-CLASS-TABLE REDEFINES EMPLOYEE-CLASS-VALUES.
    05 WS-EMPL-CLASS-INFO   OCCURS 6 TIMES
                            INDEXED BY CLASS-INDEX.
       10 WS-EMPL-CLASS-CODE     PIC 99.
       10 WS-EMPL-CLASS          PIC X(10).
```

The index associated with this table is CLASS-INDEX. Note that since it is specified at the group level, the group item (WS-EMPL-CLASS-INFO) as well as its subordinate items (WS-EMPL-CLASS-CODE and WS-EMPL-CLASS) are indexed. For instance, if the statement SET CLASS-INDEX TO 1 is executed, then WS-EMPL-CLASS-INFO (CLASS-INDEX) = "04STANDARD   ", WS-EMPL-CLASS-CODE (CLASS-INDEX) = 04, and WS-EMPL-CLASS (CLASS-INDEX) = "STANDARD   ".

5. A federal tax rate table. This table is given sequential organization, since row values are sequenced in ascending order by income upper limit. However, it is a two-level table, since each row contains a repeating item, namely, the tax rate. The data description entry for the table must contain two OCCURS clauses, the first specifying the number of row occurrences and the second specifying the number of tax rates in a row. In other words, the second OCCURS clause applies to an item that is subordinate to the subject of the first OCCURS clause. The table may be coded as follows:

```
01  FEDERAL-TAX-TABLE.
    05 WAGE-LEVEL-INFO  OCCURS 10 TIMES
                        ASCENDING KEY IS UPPER-LIMIT
                        INDEXED BY WAGE-INDEX.
       10 UPPER-LIMIT                  PIC S9(4).
       10 WS-TAX-RATE   OCCURS 5 TIMES PIC SV999.
```

The optional clause ASCENDING KEY IS UPPER-LIMIT specifies the field whose values are used to sequence the row entries in the table. The index associated with the first level of the table is WAGE-INDEX, but, by choice, no index is specified at the second level. An index could have been specified for the occurrences of WS-TAX-RATE, such as INDEXED BY ALLOWANCE-INDEX, since the tax rate occurrences are directly related to the number of allowances claimed by the employee. The choice made here illustrates that in a multilevel table, indexing one level of a table does not require the indexing of all levels. Other references will be made to this choice later.

Also note that in this table, WAGE-LEVEL-INFO and UPPER-LIMIT are single-subscripted items, whereas WS-TAX-RATE is a double-subscripted item.

The general format of an indexed table description is contained in Figure 2.7. In this format,

1. *Level-number* must not be 01, 66, 77, or 88.
2. *Data-name-1* is the table element that repeats *integer* times. It is the subject of the OCCURS clause. The OCCURS clause defines the table.
3. *Integer* in the OCCURS clause specifies the exact number of occurrences of the table element specified by *data-name-1*.
4. The KEY clause identifies the data items in the table that serve as the basis for ordering the table elements in ascending or descending order. The use of the KEY clause does not by itself assure the ordering of the table elements.
5. *Data-name-3* is usually a data item subordinate to *data-name-1*, though it may be the same as *data-name-1*. If there is more than one *data-name-3* and the first is the same as *data-name-1*, all others must be subordinate items to *data-name-1*. The order in which multiple *data-name-3* items are listed determines their level of significance, the first being the most significant and the last being the least significant.
6. The INDEXED BY phrase defines the table as an indexed table. It associates one or more indexes with the table, and it allows statements in the PROCEDURE DIVISION to reference occurrences of table elements by indexing. *Index-name-1* is completely defined within the phrase.
7. The PIC clause is coded as part of the entry only if *data-name-1* is not a group name.

Figure 2.7 Table description format

```
level-number data-name-1 OCCURS integer TIMES
    [ {ASCENDING } KEY IS {data-name-3} . . . ] . . .
    [ {DESCENDING}                            ]
    INDEXED BY {index-name-1} . . .
    [ {PICTURE} IS character-string ]
    [ {PIC    }                     ]
```

Loading the Indexed Tables

Refer to Figure 2.2 for the data names supplied on the input records of the file TABLES-FILE, to the table descriptions above, and to the pseudocode paragraphs 200-Start-Up (lines 6,7,8), 310-Read-Table-Record, 320-Load-Tables, 400-Load-Federal-Tax-Table, 410-Load-Pay-Rate-Table, and 420-Load-Insurance-Table. The coding related to the table-loading procedures is the following:

```
200-START-UP.
    .
    .
    .
    SET WAGE-INDEX
        PAY-RATE-INDEX
        INS-INDEX TO 1.
    .
    .
    .
    PERFORM 310-READ-TABLE-RECORD.
    PERFORM 320-LOAD-TABLES
        UNTIL NO-MORE-TABLE-RECORDS.
    .
    .
    .
310-READ-TABLE-RECORD.
    READ TABLES-FILE RECORD
        AT END
            SET NO-MORE-TABLE-RECORDS TO TRUE.
320-LOAD-TABLES.
    EVALUATE I-RECORD-CODE
        WHEN     "T"    PERFORM 400-LOAD-FEDERAL-TAX-TABLE
        WHEN     "P"    PERFORM 410-LOAD-PAY-RATE-TABLE
        WHEN     "I"    PERFORM 420-LOAD-INSURANCE-TABLE.
    PERFORM 310-READ-TABLE-RECORD.
.
.
.
400-LOAD-FEDERAL-TAX-TABLE.
    MOVE I-TAX-TABLE-ROW-VALUES TO WAGE-LEVEL-INFO (WAGE-INDEX).
    SET WAGE-INDEX UP BY 1.
410-LOAD-PAY-RATE-TABLE.
    MOVE I-PAY-RATE TO WS-PAY-RATE (PAY-RATE-INDEX).
    SET PAY-RATE-INDEX UP BY 1.
420-LOAD-INSURANCE-TABLE.
    MOVE I-INS-TABLE-ROW-VALUES TO WS-INS-INFO (INS-INDEX).
    SET INS-INDEX UP BY 1.
```

Note that the SET statement in paragraph 200-START-UP initializes the index of each table to 1, so that when control first enters a table-loading paragraph (400, 410, or 420), the MOVE statement stores the input record value into the first row of the table, and then the statement SET *index* UP BY 1 assures that the next time the MOVE statement is executed, the next occurrence in the table will receive the incoming value! The loop established by the PERFORM-UNTIL statement in paragraph 200-START-UP executes until all the records in the input file TABLES-FILE have been accessed and copied into the appropriate table as selected by the EVALUATE statement in paragraph 320-LOAD-TABLES.

The formats of the SET statements used in this coding are shown in Figure 2.8.

Figure 2.8 SET statement formats

```
1. SET {index-name-1} . . . TO {index-name-2}
       {identifier-1}          {identifier-2}
                               {integer-1   }

2. SET {index-name-3} . . . {UP BY  } {identifier-3}
                            {DOWN BY} {integer-2   }
```

Rules Governing the Use of the SET Statement

1. The SET statement sets values of indexes associated with table elements.
2. In both formats, any index-name must be associated with a table by being named in an INDEXED BY phrase within an OCCURS clause in the table description entry.
3. In format 1,
   a. *Index-name-1* and *identifier-1* are receiving items, and *index-name-2, identifier-2,* and *integer-1* are sending items.
   b. *Identifier-1* and *identifier-2* may be the name of an integer data item or the name of an index data item.* The value of *identifier-2* must be a positive integer.
   c. If *identifier-1* is an integer data item, the sending item must be an index-name.
   d. If *identifier-1* is an index data item, the sending item cannot be an integer.
   e. If there are multiple receiving items, each one is assigned the value of the sending item.
   f. If *index-name-1* is the receiving item and *index-name-2* is the sending item, then the value of *index-name-2* must be an occurrence number for a table entry associated with *index-name-1*.
   g. If *index-name-1* is the receiving item, its value after execution of the SET statement must be the occurrence number of an element in its associated table.

   A summary of the valid combinations of operands for sending and receiving items is contained in Table 2.1. The statement SET receiving-item TO sending-item shows the placement of the operands within SET statement.
4. In format 2,
   a. *Integer-2* may be a signed integer.
   b. *Identifier-3* must be the name of an elementary numeric data item whose value is an integer.
   c. If the UP BY option is used, *index-name-3* is incremented by the number of occurrences specified by the value of *identifier-3* or *integer-2*.
   d. If the DOWN BY option is used, *index-name-3* is decremented by the number of occurrences specified by the value of *identifier-3* or *integer-2*.
   e. If there are multiple indexes being set, each one is incremented or decremented by the number of occurrences specified by the value of *identifier-3* or *integer-2*.
5. In both formats,
   a. Any index-name must be defined in an INDEXED BY phrase within an OCCURS clause in a table description entry.
   b. Following the execution of the SET statement, the value of the result must correspond to the occurrence of a table element as defined by the OCCURS clause.

***Index Data Item:** An index data item is a data item defined in the DATA DIVISION. Its usage is specified by the clause USAGE IS INDEX; its format is the following:

level-number index-data-item-name [USAGE IS] INDEX.

Note that the PIC and VALUE clauses are not allowed. The format of this item is system-specific. Its function is to hold the value of an index outside that item itself. It may also hold the value of another index data item.

An index data item, unlike an index, is not associated with a specific table. Its value may be set initially only by a SET statement, and it may be modified by another SET statement or in the VARYING phrase of the SEARCH statement.

Table 2.1 Valid Combinations of Operands in SET Statements

Receiving Item	Sending Item		
	Index	*Index Data Item*	*Integer Data Item or Integer*
Index	Valid	Valid	Valid
Index Data Item	Valid	Valid	Invalid
Integer Data Item	Valid	Invalid	Invalid

Searching an Indexed Table

One of the most important advantages of attaching an index to a table is the availability of more efficient table look-up procedures under the control of a SEARCH statement as opposed to the control provided by the PERFORM-VARYING statement. Study the following example.

Example:

Suppose a table has been loaded with store-ids and store locations. The task is to find the location of a store for a given store-id.

The table may be defined as an indexed table or a nonindexed table. If the table is not indexed, then a table look-up procedure controlled by a PERFORM-VARYING statement is normally used. The procedure requires a data item that can be used as a subscript to reference row numbers or occurrences in the table, as well as a table search flag that will allow an exit from the procedure as soon as the store location is found. Figure 2.9a shows appropriate flowchart segments to do the table look-up as well as the corresponding coding.

Now, examine Figure 2.9b. It contains the description of the table as an indexed table, the flowchart segment needed to search the table using the SEARCH statement, and the corresponding coding.

The greater simplicity of the logic and the reduced amount of coding make it obvious that a table search under the control of a SEARCH statement is a more efficient procedure. When SEARCH is used, note the following:

1. The table search flag STORE-TABLE-FLAG is not needed. Hence, the data item description is eliminated along with the attached condition-name, the statement that initializes the flag is eliminated, and the statement that changes the value of the flag to provide an exit from the PERFORM-VARYING statement is also eliminated.
2. The data item used as a subscript (ROW-CTR) is not needed. Hence, the data item description is eliminated. The index (STORE-INDEX) is completely defined by the INDEXED BY phrase.
3. The procedure under the control of the PERFORM-VARYING statement, namely 400-SEARCH-STORE-TABLE, is eliminated, since the SEARCH statement itself contains the needed test; hence, there's one paragraph fewer in the PROCEDURE DIVISION.

Figure 2.9a Table search using PERFORM-VARYING

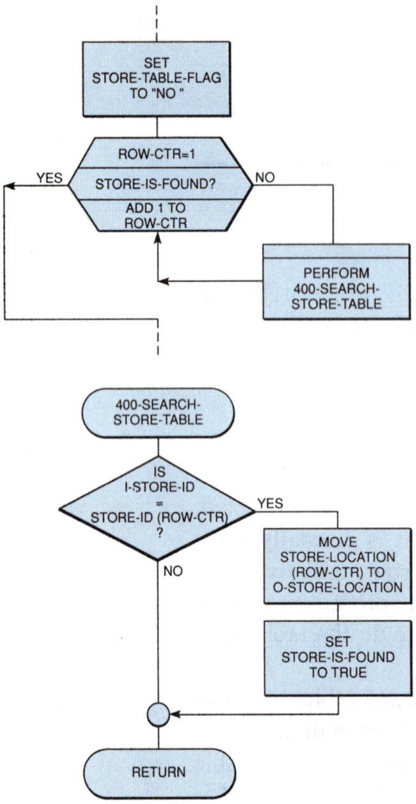


```
WORKING-STORAGE SECTION.
01  STORE-TABLE.
    05 STORE-INFO OCCURS 10 TIMES.
       10 STORE-ID           PIC X(3).
       10 STORE-LOCATION     PIC X(15).
    05 STORE-TABLE-CONTROL.
       10 STORE-TABLE-FLAG   PIC X(3).
          88 STORE-IS-FOUND             VALUE "YES".
       10 ROW-CTR            PIC 9.

PROCEDURE DIVISION.
:
    MOVE "NO " TO STORE-TABLE-FLAG.
    PERFORM 400-SEARCH-STORE-TABLE
       VARYING ROW-CTR FROM 1 BY 1
          UNTIL STORE-IS-FOUND.
    :
400-SEARCH-STORE-TABLE.
    IF I-STORE-ID = STORE-ID (ROW-CTR)
       MOVE STORE-LOCATION (ROW-CTR) TO O-STORE-LOCATION
       SET STORE-IS-FOUND TO TRUE
    END-IF.
```

Figure 2.9b Table search using SEARCH

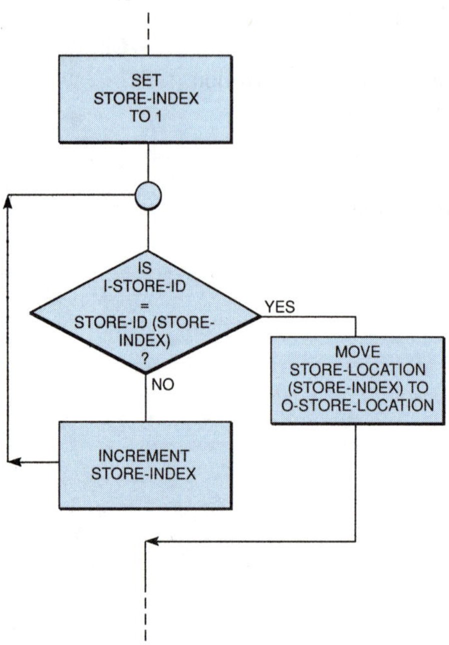


```
WORKING-STORAGE SECTION.

01  STORE-TABLE.
    05 STORE-INFO OCCURS 10 TIMES
                 INDEXED BY STORE-INDEX.
       10 STORE-ID         PIC X(3).
       10 STORE-LOCATION   PIC X(15).

PROCEDURE DIVISION.
:
     SET STORE-INDEX TO 1.
     SEARCH STORE-INFO
         WHEN I-STORE-ID = STORE-ID (STORE-INDEX)
              MOVE STORE-LOCATION (STORE-INDEX)
                      TO O-STORE-LOCATION
     END-SEARCH.
```

Figure 2.10 SEARCH statement format

```
SEARCH identifier-1 [ VARYING { index-name-1 } ]
                              { identifier-2 }

   [AT END imperative-statement-1]

   WHEN condition { imperative-statement-2 }  . . .
                  { NEXT SENTENCE          }

   [END-SEARCH]
```

The SEARCH Statement

The format of the SEARCH statement is contained in Figure 2.10.

Rules Governing the Use of the SEARCH Statement

1. The DATA DIVISION description of *identifier-1* must contain an OCCURS clause and an INDEXED BY phrase. *Identifier-1* must not be a 01-level entry.
2. *Identifier-1* may be subordinate to an item whose definition contains an OCCURS clause. If so, then each dimension of the table must have its own index, but the SEARCH statement modifies only the index associated with *identifier-1*.
3. The VARYING entry is optional. If it is not used, the index used to search the table is the first one named in the INDEXED BY phrase. If the VARYING entry is used, and *index-name-1* is one of the indexes specified in the INDEXED BY phrase associated with the occurrences of *identifier-1*, then *index-name-1* is the index used to search the table and the other indexes remain unchanged. If the VARYING clause is used and *index-name-1* or *identifier-2* is associated with another table, then the value of *index-name-1* or *identifier-2* is incremented so as to reference the same occurrence number as the index of the table being searched. That is, the VARYING entry increments the index of a related table in the same manner as the index of the table being searched. If *identifier-2* is used, it must be an index data item or a numeric integer item.
4. The AT END entry is optional. If it is used, the imperative statement it contains will be executed if the whole table is searched without satisfying the condition in the WHEN clause, and then control will pass to the next statement after the SEARCH. That is, the AT END condition is satisfied when the index is incremented to a value higher than the highest occurrence number in the table. If the AT END clause is not used and this condition occurs, then control passes to the next statement after the SEARCH statement.

5. At least one WHEN clause is required. If more than one is used, the conditions are evaluated in the order in which they occur. The search ends when any one of the tested conditions is satisfied. When a condition is satisfied, the imperative statement that follows will be executed, and control then passes on to the next statement beyond the scope of the SEARCH statement. The index retains the value for which the condition was satisfied. If none of the tested conditions is satisfied for a particular value of the index, the index is incremented to refer to the next occurrence in the table and the conditions are tested again.
6. A condition may take the form of any test: relational, condition-name, class, or sign, simple or compound. It normally references a search value and a search field in the table.
7. The SEARCH statement causes a serial search of the elements in the table. The search begins at the position in the table corresponding to the value of the index. The index is assigned its initial value in a SET statement that precedes the SEARCH statement. The index is automatically incremented by the SEARCH statement if no condition is satisfied for the current value of the index, and then the conditions are tested again.
8. The table being searched may have any organization.
9. END-SEARCH is the explicit scope terminator.

The general logic of the SEARCH statement is illustrated in Figure 2.11. Assume that *table-index* is the index associated with the table being searched, *index-name-1* is an index associated with a related table, and possibly more than one condition is tested. The steps of the table search are as follows:

1. The first step is to set the table index and the index specified in the VARYING phrase, if it is used, to their initial values.
2. The AT END condition is tested. The AT END condition exists if the value specified by *table-index* exceeds the integer in the OCCURS clause that defines the table. If the AT END condition exists, *imperative-statement-1* is executed and control passes beyond the scope of the SEARCH statement, that is, it passes to the first statement that follows the period or the END-SEARCH scope terminator. If the AT END condition does not exist, control passes to the first WHEN clause.
3. The condition in the first WHEN clause (*condition-1*) is tested. If it is satisfied, the imperative statement that follows the condition (*imperative-statement-2*) is executed and control passes to the first statement beyond the scope of the SEARCH statement. If *condition-1* is not satisfied, control passes to the next WHEN clause, if it exists, and its condition is tested as above. Otherwise, the table index is automatically incremented to indicate the next table element occurrence. If the VARYING phrase is used, *index-name-1* is also automatically incremented to indicate the next occurrence in its associated table. Control then returns to test the AT END condition, and the pattern in steps 2 and 3 repeats until an exit from the SEARCH occurs.

Consider the following example.

■ **Figure 2.11** General logic of the SEARCH statement

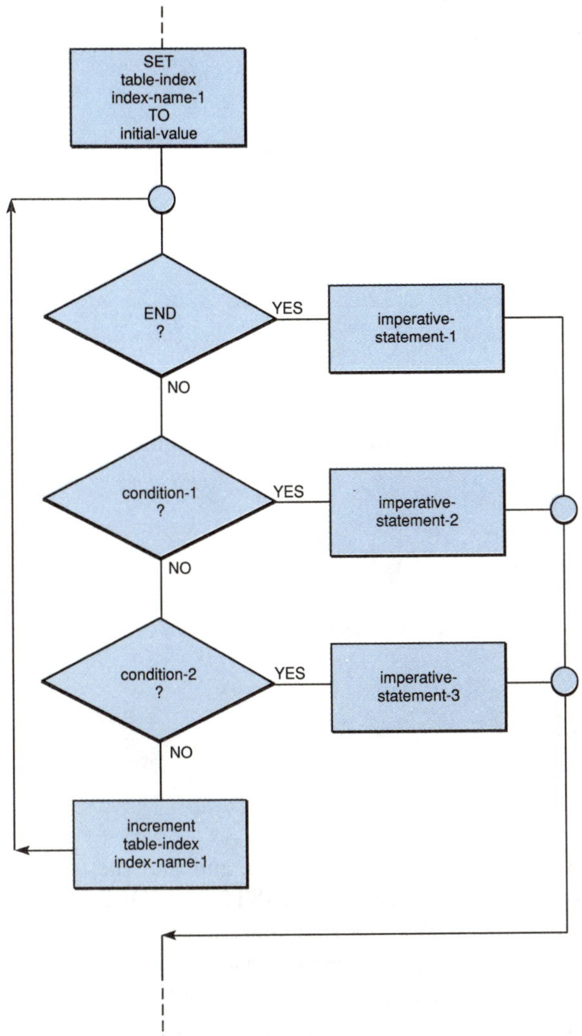

Figure 2.12 Sample table data—example

ROLODEX-TABLE

100	BOSTON	(617) 452-4231
150	HARTFORD	(203) 745-7943
200	NEW YORK	(212) 412-3591
250	ALBANY	(518) 554-7013
300	CHICAGO	(312) 672-8419
350	DETROIT	(313) 532-9905
400	DES MOINES	(515) 857-2620
450	DUBUQUE	(319) 785-4413
500	DALLAS	(214) 375-3692
550	LAS VEGAS	(702) 481-3352

STORE-TABLE

100	HASTINGS, GREGORY W.	75	24500
150	PELADEAU, NANCY M.	50	13650
200	GOMEZ, STELLA	80	26400
250	ROCKFORD, GLEN J.	60	16780
300	KLEIN, KARL M.	70	19800
350	ANDERSON, TIMOTHY L.	70	18450
400	CARLSON, JENNIFER	45	12750
450	MALLON, TERRY	40	09980
500	ROITMAN, WENDY	50	14500
550	PICKERING, ROBERT J.	40	10270

SEARCH-VARYING Example

Suppose that a program contains the following table descriptions and that the tables contain the data shown in Figure 2.12.

```
01  ROLODEX-TABLE.
    05 STORE-DATA   OCCURS 10 TIMES
                    ASCENDING KEY IS STORE-NO
                    INDEXED BY ROLODEX-INDEX.
       10 STORE-NO           PIC X(3).
       10 STORE-LOCATION     PIC X(15).
       10 STORE-PHONE        PIC X(10).
01  STORE-TABLE.
    05 STORE-INFO   OCCURS 10 TIMES
                    ASCENDING KEY IS STORE-NO
                    INDEXED BY STORE-INDEX.
       10 STORE-NO              PIC X(3).
       10 STORE-MGR             PIC X(22).
       10 STORE-EMPL-LIMIT      PIC 99.
       10 STORE-PAYROLL-LIMIT   PIC 9(5).
```

Suppose that a store number is supplied as an input value (I-STORE-NO), and that the task is to prepare an output record with the following data fields: O-STORE-NO, O-STORE-LOCATION, O-STORE-MGR, and O-STORE-PHONE. It is clear that the store location and phone number must be retrieved from ROLODEX-TABLE, whereas the store manager's name must be retrieved from STORE-TABLE. In order to find the correct table values, it is necessary to search one of the two tables, say ROLODEX-TABLE, for the store number that matches the input store number. That is, the search value is taken as I-STORE-NO, and the search field is taken as STORE-NO OF ROLODEX-TABLE. (Note the needed qualification!) When the match is found, the needed output data is available at that occurrence in each of the two tables.

Say that I-STORE-NO = 250. Begin by setting the table indexes (ROLODEX-INDEX and STORE-INDEX) to 1 to indicate that the search should start at the first occurrence of a table element. Then, the test to be performed is whether

```
I-STORE-NO = STORE-NO OF ROLODEX-TABLE (ROLODEX-INDEX).
```

So,

1. When ROLODEX-INDEX = 1, the test fails, since 250 is not equal to 100, and ROLODEX-INDEX and STORE-INDEX are set to 2.
2. When ROLODEX-INDEX = 2, the test fails again since 250 is not equal to 150, and ROLODEX-INDEX and STORE-INDEX are set to 3.
3. When ROLODEX-INDEX = 3, the test fails again since 250 is not equal to 200, and ROLODEX-INDEX and STORE-INDEX are set to 4.
4. When ROLODEX-INDEX = 4, the condition is satisfied and the search ends.

The values that must be retrieved from the tables are STORE-LOCATION (ROLODEX-INDEX), STORE-PHONE (ROLODEX-INDEX), and STORE-MGR (STORE-INDEX), where both indexes point to the fourth table element occurrence.

Figure 2.13 Flowchart segment for table search—example

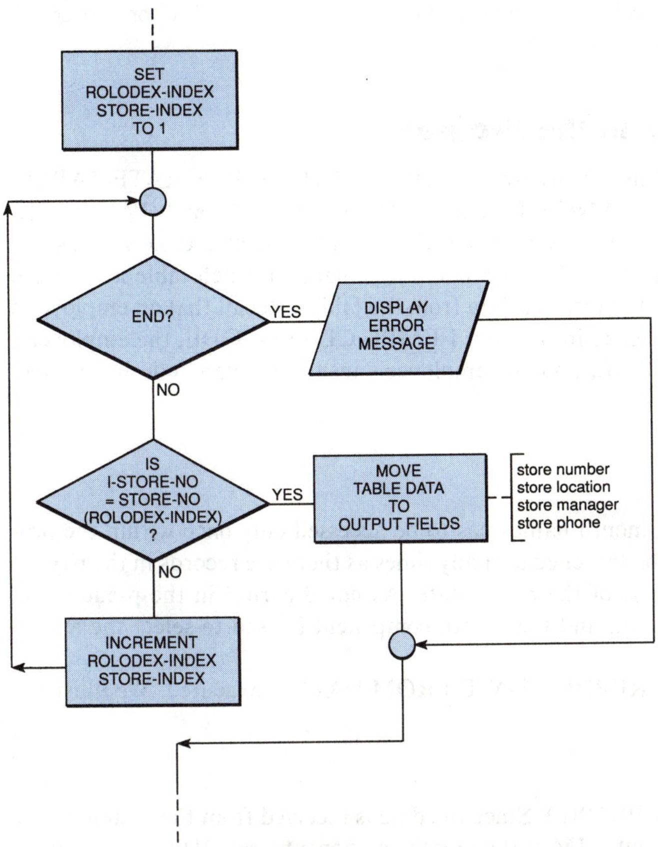

The flowchart segment that represents this search is shown in Figure 2.13, and the formal coding is as follows:

```
SET ROLODEX-INDEX
    STORE-INDEX TO 1.
SEARCH STORE-DATA VARYING STORE-INDEX
    AT END
        DISPLAY "INPUT STORE NUMBER " I-STORE-NO
            " NOT FOUND IN THE TABLE"
    WHEN I-STORE-NO = STORE-NO OF ROLODEX-TABLE (ROLODEX-INDEX)
        MOVE I-STORE-NO TO O-STORE-NO
        MOVE STORE-LOCATION (ROLODEX-INDEX) TO O-STORE-LOCATION
        MOVE STORE-PHONE (ROLODEX-INDEX) TO O-STORE-PHONE
        MOVE STORE-MGR (STORE-INDEX) TO O-STORE-MGR
END-SEARCH.
```

Note the use of the VARYING phrase. It ensures that whenever the ROLODEX-TABLE index ROLODEX-INDEX is incremented, the STORE-TABLE index STORE-INDEX is similarly incremented. The index is incremented every time the condition in the WHEN clause is false for the current value of the index.

Also note the relational operand STORE-NO OF ROLODEX-TABLE (ROLODEX-INDEX). The operand must be qualified with the phrase OF ROLODEX-TABLE, since STORE-NO also names a field of the other table, STORE-TABLE. Whenever qualification is needed, the index (or subscript) is always placed within parentheses *following* the qualification.

The One-level Indexed Tables in the Program

Recall that there are four one-level tables in the program: MONTH-TABLE, PAY-RATE-TABLE, EMPLOYEE-CLASS-TABLE, and INSURANCE-TABLE. MONTH-TABLE and PAY-RATE-TABLE have positional organization. EMPLOYEE-CLASS-TABLE is a hard-coded table with usage-frequency organization, and INSURANCE-TABLE has random organization. Each table is indexed. We now examine procedures that can be used to retrieve data from the tables. Recall that an employee's payroll record contains the employee's class code in the field I-EMPL-CLASS-CODE, the employee's pay rate code in the field I-EMPL-PAY-CODE, and the employee's insurance plan code in the field I-EMPL-INS-CODE.

Accessing the Month Name

It should be clear that the table containing month names has to be accessed only once within the program, but that the other four tables need to be searched as many times as there are records in the payroll file. The month name must be printed as part of the report date. As noted earlier in the pseudocode, the date is obtained from the operating system, and the month component is used to select the appropriate month name in the table.

Suppose the statement ACCEPT WS-REPORT-DATE FROM DATE is executed. We illustrate two different ways of proceeding.

Option 1

Suppose WS-REPORT-DATE is defined by PIC 9(6). Since the date is received from the system in the YYMMDD format, YY is the year component, MM is the month component, and DD is the day component. From the layout of TOP-LINE (Figure 2.1), the day component must be assigned to the data field O-DAY, the year component to the field O-YEAR. These data transfers may be accomplished using reference modification, as in

```
MOVE WS-REPORT-DATE(1:2) TO O-YEAR
MOVE WS-REPORT-DATE(5:2) TO O-DAY
```

Now, the month component must be used to select the month name in the table MONTH-TABLE. One may be tempted to code

```
MOVE WS-REPORT-DATE(3:2) TO MONTH-INDEX
```

and then use direct referencing, as in

```
MOVE WS-MONTH(MONTH-INDEX) TO O-MONTH
```

There are two problems with these statements:

1. An index is assigned a value by a SET statement, not a MOVE statement, as in SET MONTH-INDEX TO WS-REPORT-DATE(3:2).
2. The data transferred by reference modification is treated as an alphanumeric value, whereas the value of MONTH-INDEX must be an unsigned integer. Consequently, the SET statement above is invalid! An intermediate step is needed: define an unsigned integer data item such as 05 WS-MONTH-NO PIC 9(2), and then use the following statements:

```
MOVE WS-REPORT-DATE(3:2) TO WS-MONTH-NO
SET MONTH-INDEX TO WS-MONTH-NO
MOVE WS-MONTH(MONTH-INDEX) TO O-MONTH
```

Option 2

Suppose WS-REPORT-DATE is defined as follows:

```
05  WS-REPORT-DATE.
    10 WS-YEAR      PIC 9(2).
    10 WS-MONTH-NO  PIC 9(2).
    10 WS-DAY       PIC 9(2).
```

The statements

```
MOVE WS-YEAR TO O-YEAR
MOVE WS-DAY TO O-DAY
```

transfer the year and the date components as needed. The month name may be retrieved from the table using direct referencing by the statement

```
MOVE WS-MONTH(WS-MONTH-NO) TO O-MONTH
```

where WS-MONTH-NO is a data item used as a *subscript,* or by the statements

```
SET MONTH-INDEX TO WS-MONTH-NO
MOVE WS-MONTH(MONTH-INDEX) TO O-MONTH
```

where MONTH-INDEX is the table's index.

In the sample program, we will use option 1.

Searching the Insurance Table

For your convenience, the coding that defines the table is repeated below.

```
01   INSURANCE-TABLE.
     05 WS-INS-INFO  OCCURS 4 TIMES
                     INDEXED BY INS-INDEX.
        10 WS-INS-CODE    PIC XX.
        10 WS-INS-PREM    PIC 99V99.
```

The objective of searching this table is to find the insurance premium that must be withheld from the week's earnings. Since the table lists the plan codes and their corresponding premiums, the search procedure must find the plan code in the table that matches the employee's plan code available in the input record field I-EMPL-INS-CODE. The logic of the table search, the corresponding coding, and the representation of the insurance table are shown in Figure 2.14.

The table index INS-INDEX is set to 1 so that the search may begin at the first occurrence of a table element. The AT END condition is tested. If it fails, the condition in the WHEN clause is tested. If this condition fails, the index is incremented, and the AT END condition is tested again. And the pattern is repeated. When a match is found for a particular value of the index, the premium at that occurrence is moved to the work area WS-EMPL-INS-PREM. If no match occurs for any valid value of INS-INDEX, the AT END condition is then satisfied and an appropriate error message is generated.

Note that the SEARCH verb references WS-INS-INFO, the item defined by the OCCURS clause; it does not reference WS-INS-CODE. WS-INS-CODE is the search field, and its values are tested in the WHEN clause.

As an example, suppose that I-EMPL-INS-CODE = "FA". The steps of the table search are as follows:

1. INS-INDEX is set to 1.
2. The pointer (i.e., the occurrence within the table as specified by the value of the index) is at WS-INS-INFO(1).
3. The AT END condition fails, since INS-INDEX is not greater than 4 (the integer in the OCCURS clause).
4. The condition in the WHEN clause fails, since WS-INS-CODE(1)= "IA," not "FA".
5. INS-INDEX is incremented to 2.
6. The pointer is positioned at WS-INS-INFO(2).

Figure 2.14 Procedure to search the insurance table

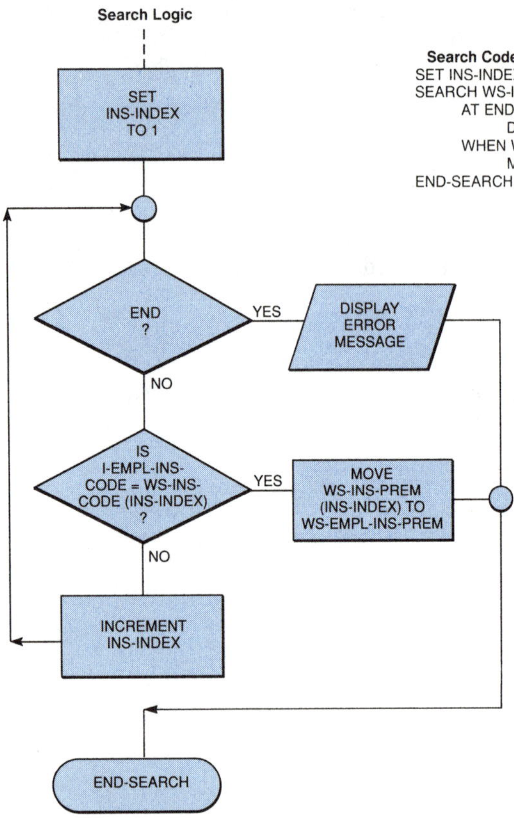

Search Code

```
SET INS-INDEX TO 1.
SEARCH WS-INS-INFO
       AT END
              DISPLAY "INS. CODE NOT FOUND FOR " I-EMPL-NAME
       WHEN WS-INS-CODE (INS-INDEX) = I-EMPL-INS-CODE
              MOVE WS-INS-PREM (INS-INDEX) TO WS-EMPL-INS-PREM
END-SEARCH.
```

Insurance Table

IA	06.73
IB	09.14
FA	08.65
FB	11.54

7. The AT END condition fails.
8. The condition in the WHEN clause fails, since WS-INS-CODE(2)= "IB," not "FA".
9. INS-INDEX is incremented to 3.
10. The pointer is positioned at WS-INS-INFO(3).
11. The AT END condition fails.
12. The condition in the WHEN clause is satisfied, since WS-INS-CODE(3) = "FA", the search value, and the search ends.
13. The MOVE statement in the WHEN clause is executed for INS-INDEX = 3; specifically,

    ```
    MOVE WS-INS-PREM(3) TO WS-EMPL-INS-PREM
    ```

    which copies the numeric value 08.65 into WS-EMPL-INS-PREM.
14. Control exits the SEARCH statement.

Searching the Employee Class Table

The coding for the hard-coded table EMPLOYEE-CLASS-TABLE is shown again below. Its usage-frequency organization makes the search procedure more efficient, since it assures that a minimum number of occurrences will be tested in order to find a match between the employee's class code, contained in the field I-EMPL-CLASS-CODE, and the codes contained in the table.

```
01  EMPLOYEE-CLASS-VALUES.
    05 PIC X(12)   VALUE "04STANDARD  ".
    05 PIC X(12)   VALUE "03YEARLING  ".
    05 PIC X(12)   VALUE "02BEGINNER  ".
    05 PIC X(12)   VALUE "01APPRENTICE".
    05 PIC X(12)   VALUE "05ASS'T MGR.".
    05 PIC X(12)   VALUE "06STORE MGR.".
01  EMPLOYEE-CLASS-TABLE REDEFINES EMPLOYEE-CLASS-VALUES.
    05 WS-EMPL-CLASS-INFO   OCCURS 6 TIMES
                            INDEXED BY CLASS-INDEX.
       10 WS-EMPL-CLASS-CODE    PIC 99.
       10 WS-EMPL-CLASS         PIC X(10).
```

Since the logic is very similar to that shown in Figure 2.14, only the coding of the search procedure is given below:

```
SET CLASS-INDEX TO 1.
SEARCH WS-EMPL-CLASS-INFO
    AT END
        DISPLAY "EMPLOYEE CLASS CODE INVALID FOR " I-EMPL-NAME
    WHEN WS-EMPL-CLASS-CODE (CLASS-INDEX) = I-EMPL-CLASS-CODE
        MOVE WS-EMPL-CLASS (CLASS-INDEX) TO WS-EMPLOYEE-CLASS
END-SEARCH.
```

Note that the table index CLASS-INDEX is set to 1 so as to begin searching the table from the first occurrence on. The SEARCH verb references WS-EMPL-CLASS-INFO, the item defined by the OCCURS clause. At each occurrence of WS-EMPL-CLASS-INFO, the value of the search field WS-EMPL-CLASS-CODE is tested against the search value I-EMPL-CLASS-CODE in the WHEN clause. If the condition in the WHEN clause is satisfied for a particular value of CLASS-INDEX, the search ends because it is successful, and, as a result, the class name stored at that occurrence in the table, namely, WS-EMPL-CLASS (CLASS-INDEX), is moved to the work area WS-EMPLOYEE-CLASS. If the table search is unsuccessful, an appropriate error message is generated.

Searching the Pay Rate Table

The description of the pay rate table and a representation of the table are shown in Figure 2.15. Since this table has positional organization, the pay rates are stored at the occurrences that correspond to their numeric codes. As a result, there are two ways of retrieving a pay rate from the table. One way is to do a table search similar to the searches of the previous tables. In this case, however, it's sufficient to increment the index until its value corresponds to the pay rate code on the employee's payroll record, and then to retrieve the pay rate stored in that occurrence of a table element, as in the following statements:

```
SET PAY-RATE-INDEX TO 1.
SEARCH WS-PAY-RATE
    AT END
        DISPLAY "PAY RATE CODE OUT OF RANGE FOR " I-EMPL-NAME
    WHEN PAY-RATE-INDEX = I-EMPL-PAY-CODE
        MOVE WS-PAY-RATE (PAY-RATE-INDEX) TO WS-EMPL-PAY-RATE
END-SEARCH.
```

However, since the index may be set to any value initially, it is much simpler to set it to the value of the employee's pay rate code, as in SET PAY-RATE-INDEX TO I-EMPL-PAY-CODE, (provided I-EMPL-PAY-CODE is defined as an unsigned integer!) and then to directly retrieve the pay rate stored in that occurrence within the table. This second method consists of the following two simple statements:

```
SET PAY-RATE-INDEX TO I-EMPL-PAY-CODE.
MOVE WS-PAY-RATE (PAY-RATE-INDEX) TO WS-EMPL-PAY-RATE.
```

Figure 2.15 Pay rate table description and representation

Table Description

```
01  PAY-RATE-TABLE.
    05  WS-PAY-RATE OCCURS 15 TIMES
                    INDEXED BY PAY-RATE-INDEX
                    PIC S999V99.
```

Table Representation

WS-PAY-RATE (01)	00365
WS-PAY-RATE (02)	00390
WS-PAY-RATE (03)	00425
WS-PAY-RATE (04)	00460
WS-PAY-RATE (05)	00510
WS-PAY-RATE (06)	00575
WS-PAY-RATE (07)	00650
WS-PAY-RATE (08)	00730
WS-PAY-RATE (09)	00830
WS-PAY-RATE (10)	00950
WS-PAY-RATE (11)	30000
WS-PAY-RATE (12)	37500
WS-PAY-RATE (13)	45000
WS-PAY-RATE (14)	52500
WS-PAY-RATE (15)	60000

PAY-RATE-TABLE

This is referred to as *direct referencing,* and no table search is needed. A table that has positional organization always allows direct referencing of its elements, since the position where the desired element is stored is already known. For instance, if I-EMPL-PAY-CODE = 05, then PAY-RATE-INDEX is set to 05, and the MOVE statement becomes

```
MOVE WS-PAY-RATE (05) TO WS-EMPL-PAY-RATE.
```

As a result, the table element 005.10 is moved to WS-EMPL-PAY-RATE.

The direct referencing procedure may be simplified even more if subscripting rather than indexing is used to refer to the table element. In this case, only one statement is needed, as follows:

```
MOVE WS-PAY-RATE (I-EMPL-PAY-CODE) TO WS-EMPL-PAY-RATE.
```

The only reason this statement will not be used is that the purpose of this chapter is to work with indexes!

Note: Indexing may be used to reference table elements only if the description of the table contains the INDEXED BY phrase. On the other hand, subscripting with data items may always be used, whether the table is indexed or not.

If a table is indexed, it may be searched by means of a SEARCH statement or by using a table look-up procedure under the control of a PERFORM-VARYING statement. If a table is not indexed, it cannot be searched by a SEARCH statement; it must be searched by using a table look-up procedure.

Two-level Indexed Tables

There is one two-level table in the chapter program, namely, the federal tax rate table. Its description is repeated below.

```
01  FEDERAL-TAX-TABLE.
    05 WAGE-LEVEL-INFO   OCCURS 10 TIMES
                         ASCENDING KEY UPPER-LIMIT
                         INDEXED BY WAGE-INDEX.
       10 UPPER-LIMIT                   PIC S9(4).
       10 WS-TAX-RATE   OCCURS 5 TIMES  PIC SV999.
```

Within the program, this table has to be searched to find the employee's tax rate. As noted earlier, the following two items are needed to find the correct tax rate:

1. The income level used to select the correct row in the table. Note that the weekly income must be *less* than the income level specified in the row, and the selected row must be the first row for which this condition is true.
2. The number of allowances claimed by the employee to select the corresponding tax rate in the selected row.

Since the employee's gross earnings amount is stored in the work area WS-EMPL-GROSS-EARNINGS, this item is the search value needed to locate the correct row in the table. The table index WAGE-INDEX is initialized to 1, and the search procedure references the successive occurrences of WAGE-LEVEL-INFO looking for the index value for which the condition

```
WS-EMPL-GROSS-EARNINGS < UPPER-LIMIT (WAGE-INDEX)
```

is first satisfied. When that occurs, the correct row of the tax table is denoted by the value of WAGE-INDEX. Now, the appropriate tax in that row is selected by the reference

```
WS-TAX-RATE (WAGE-INDEX, I-EMPL-ALLOWANCES + 1)
```

where relative subscripting is used to identify the needed tax rate occurrence in the row. So, if I-EMPL-ALLOWANCES = 0, the tax rate occurrence is 1. If I-EMPL-ALLOWANCES = 3, the tax rate occurrence is 4, and so on.

The coding of the needed search procedure is the following:

```
SET WAGE-INDEX TO 1.
SEARCH WAGE-LEVEL-INFO
    AT END
        DISPLAY "GROSS EARNINGS OUT OF RANGE FOR " I-EMPL-NAME
    WHE  WS-EMPL-GROSS-EARNINGS < UPPER-LIMIT (WAGE-INDEX)
        MOVE WS-TAX-RATE (WAGE-INDEX, I-EMPL-ALLOWANCES + 1)
            TO WS-EMPL-TAX-RATE
END-SEARCH.
```

As an example, suppose that an employee's gross earnings are $475 a week, that is, WS-EMPL-GROSS-EARNINGS = 475, and the employee claims 2 allowances, that is, I-EMPL-ALLOWANCES = 2. Use the federal tax rate table in Figure 2.16 to verify the following steps in executing the search procedure.

Step	**Action**
1.	WAGE-INDEX is set to 1.
2.	The pointer is positioned at WAGE-LEVEL-INFO(1).
3.	The AT END condition fails, since WAGE-INDEX is not greater than 10, the integer in the OCCURS clause.
4.	The condition in the WHEN clause fails, since 475 > UPPER-LIMIT(1), where UPPER-LIMIT(1) = 100.
5.	WAGE-INDEX is incremented to 2.
6.	The pointer is positioned at WAGE-LEVEL-INFO(2).
7.	The AT END condition fails.
8.	The condition in the WHEN clause fails, since 475 > UPPER-LIMIT(2), where UPPER-LIMIT(2) = 200.
9.	WAGE-INDEX is incremented to 3.
10.	The pointer is positioned at WAGE-LEVEL-INFO(3).
11.	The AT END condition fails.
12.	The condition in the WHEN clause fails, since 475 > UPPER-LIMIT(3), where UPPER-LIMIT(3) = 300.
13.	WAGE-INDEX is incremented to 4.
14.	The pointer is positioned at WAGE-LEVEL-INFO(4).
15.	The AT END condition fails.
16.	The condition in the WHEN clause fails, since 475 > UPPER-LIMIT(4), where UPPER-LIMIT(4) = 400.
17.	WAGE-INDEX is incremented to 5.
18.	The pointer is positioned at WAGE-LEVEL-INFO(5).
19.	The AT END condition fails.
20.	The condition in the WHEN clause is satisfied, since 475 < UPPER-LIMIT(5), where UPPER-LIMIT(5) = 500.
21.	The MOVE statement in the WHEN clause is executed for WAGE-INDEX = 5 and I-EMPL-ALLOWANCES = 2, specifically, MOVE WS-TAX-RATE(5,3) TO WS-EMPL-TAX-RATE and the value .108 is moved to the receiving field WS-EMPL-TAX-RATE.
22.	Control exits the SEARCH statement.

Figure 2.16 Federal tax rate table

UPPER-LIMIT (01) WS-TAX-RATE (01,1) WS-TAX-RATE (01,2) WS-TAX-RATE (01,3) WS-TAX-RATE (01,4) WS-TAX-RATE (01,5)

WAGE-LEVEL-INFO (01)	0100	070	030	000	000	000
WAGE-LEVEL-INFO (02)	0200	100	075	045	020	000
WAGE-LEVEL-INFO (03)	0300	117	100	080	063	043
WAGE-LEVEL-INFO (04)	0400	125	113	098	085	070
WAGE-LEVEL-INFO (05)	0500	130	120	108	098	086
WAGE-LEVEL-INFO (06)	0600	135	125	115	107	097
WAGE-LEVEL-INFO (07)	0700	156	141	127	113	104
WAGE-LEVEL-INFO (08)	0800	171	159	146	134	121
WAGE-LEVEL-INFO (09)	0900	183	172	161	150	139
WAGE-LEVEL-INFO (10)	1000	199	187	174	163	153

WS-TAX-RATE (05,3)

UPPER-LIMIT (10) WS-TAX-RATE (10,1) WS-TAX-RATE (10,2) WS-TAX-RATE (10,3) WS-TAX-RATE (10,4) WS-TAX-RATE (10,5)

More SEARCH Examples

The format of the SEARCH statement allows any kind of test to be specified in its WHEN clauses. Consider the following examples.

Example 1

Suppose the table STATES-TABLE is defined as follows:

```
01  STATES-TABLE.
    05 STATE-INFO    OCCURS 51 TIMES
                     INDEXED BY ST-INDEX.
       10 ST-ABBREV    PIC X(2).
       10 ST-NAME      PIC X(20).
       10 ST-CAPITAL   PIC X(15).
```

Further suppose that the capital must be retrieved from the table for a given state name, say I-ST-NAME, or for a given state name abbreviation, say I-ST-ABBREV. The table search may be coded as follows:

```
SET ST-INDEX TO 1.
SEARCH STATE-INFO
    WHEN ST-NAME(ST-INDEX) = I-ST-NAME OR
         ST-ABBREV(ST-INDEX) = I-ST-ABBREV
        MOVE ST-CAPITAL(ST-INDEX) TO O-ST-CAPITAL
END-SEARCH.
```

In this statement, the condition in the WHEN clause is a compound relational test. The MOVE statement is executed if either component of the disjunctive test is true.

In general, the condition in a WHEN clause of a SEARCH statement may take the form of any test, such as simple condition-name, relational, sign, or class tests, or compound tests whose components may be any of the above.

Example 2

Suppose the STATES-TABLE must be searched to retrieve the state name and state capital when the input search value is the state name abbreviation, say I-ST-ABBREV, but the data to be retrieved is the state name abbreviation and the state capital when the input search value is the state name, say I-ST-NAME. The following coding may be used:

```
SET ST-INDEX TO 1.
SEARCH STATE-INFO
    WHEN ST-ABBREV(ST-INDEX) = I-ST-ABBREV
        MOVE ST-NAME(ST-INDEX) TO O-ST-NAME
        MOVE ST-CAPITAL(ST-INDEX) TO O-ST-CAPITAL
    WHEN ST-NAME(ST-INDEX) = I-ST-NAME
        MOVE ST-ABBREV(ST-INDEX) TO O-ST-ABBREV
        MOVE ST-CAPITAL(ST-INDEX) TO O-ST-CAPITAL
END-SEARCH.
```

In this statement, when the condition in the first WHEN clause is satisfied, the first two MOVE statements are executed and control passes beyond the scope of the SEARCH statement. If the condition in the first WHEN clause is not satisfied, the condition in the second WHEN clause is tested. If it is satisfied, then the last two MOVE statements are executed, and control passes beyond the scope of the SEARCH statement. If neither condition is satisfied, the index is incremented, and the conditions are tested again. If neither condition is satisfied for any table element occurrence, control simply leaves the SEARCH statement.

Subscripted Data Items

Whenever a table element must be referenced in a statement of the PROCEDURE DIVISION, the reference requires the name of the item, and the name must be accompanied (followed) by one or more subscripts or indexes to indicate the particular occurrence of the item in the table. Attaching subscripts to a data name is called *subscripting. Indexing* is a special subscripting procedure in which indexes are used to denote occurrences of table elements. The general subscripting format is shown in Figure 2.17.

Rules Governing the Use of Subscripts

1. Subscripts may be used only with data names that are defined using the OCCURS clause or with data names that are subordinate to items defined using the OCCURS clause.
2. If a subscripted data name must be qualified, the qualification precedes the parentheses containing the subscripts.
3. If reference modification is applied to a subscripted data name, the reference modification follows the parentheses containing the subscripts.
4. In the format of Figure 2.17,
   a. *Data-name-1* is a data item defined using the OCCURS clause or is subordinate to a data item defined using the OCCURS clause.
   b. Subscripts must be listed within one set of parentheses. There must be as many subscripts as there are OCCURS clauses in the hierarchy that contains *data-name-1*. The subscripts must be listed from left to right in descending order of inclusiveness. They may be separated by a comma, a space, or both. In COBOL '85, the maximum number of subscripts is seven.

      The lowest valid subscript value is 1, and its highest valid value is the integer specified in the OCCURS clause for the table level related to the subscript's position within the parentheses.

      The lowest value of the subscript points to the first occurrence, and the highest value points to the last occurrence within the table level specified by the position of the subscript within the parentheses.
   c. *Data-name-2* must be the identifier of an elementary numeric item whose value is a positive integer. *Data-name-2* may itself be subscripted.
   d. *Integer-1* is an unsigned positive integer.

■ **Figure 2.17** General subscripting format

$$\left\{\begin{array}{l}\text{data-name-1}\\ \text{condition-name}\end{array}\right\}\left(\left\{\begin{array}{l}\text{integer-1}\\ \text{data-name-2 }[\{\pm\}\text{ integer-2}]\\ \text{index-name-1 }[\{\pm\}\text{ integer-3}]\end{array}\right\}\ldots\right)$$

e. A data name followed by its subscripts is called a *subscripted data name.*

f. *Index-name-1* is an index associated with a level of the table by the INDEXED BY phrase of the OCCURS clause that defines that level of the table.

g. In COBOL '85, a data name or an index-name may be incremented or decremented by *integer-2* or *integer-3,* respectively, where *integer-2* and *integer-3* are unsigned integers. The expression is called a *relative subscript;* that is, the occurrence number is specified by the value of *data-name-2* plus or minus *integer-2* or by the value of *index-name-1* plus or minus *integer-3.* For instance, TAX-INDEX + 1 references the next occurrence in the table, and TAX-INDEX − 1 references the prior occurrence relative to the occurrence specified by TAX-INDEX.

h. In COBOL '85, data items and indexes may be mixed as subscripts.

Just a note of caution regarding rules 2 and 3: whenever a subscripted or indexed data item must be qualified, the qualification (OF *identifier* or IN *identifier*) must *precede* the parentheses that contain the subscripts or indexes. But, in reference modification, the parentheses containing the specifications for the reference modification must *follow* the parentheses containing the subscripts or indexes.

Consider the following tables:

```
01  DAY-VALUES.
    05 PIC X(12)  VALUE "MONMONDAY   ".
    05 PIC X(12)  VALUE "TUETUESDAY  ".
    05 PIC X(12)  VALUE "WEDWEDNESDAY".
    05 PIC X(12)  VALUE "THUTHURSDAY ".
    05 PIC X(12)  VALUE "FRIFRIDAY   ".
    05 PIC X(12)  VALUE "SATSATURDAY ".
    05 PIC X(12)  VALUE "SUNSUNDAY   ".
01  DAY-TABLE-1 REDEFINES DAY-VALUES.
    05 WS-DAY-INFO OCCURS 7 TIMES
                   INDEXED BY DAY-INDEX-1.
       10 WS-DAY-ABBREV    PIC X(3).
       10 WS-DAY-NAME      PIC X(9).

01  DAY-TABLE-2 VALUE "MONDAY   TUESDAY  WEDNESDAYTHURSDAY FRIDA
-   "Y   SATURDAY SUNDAY   ".
    05 WS-DAY-NAME OCCURS 7 TIMES
                   INDEXED BY DAY-INDEX-2 PIC X(9).
```

In this example, any reference to WS-DAY-NAME must be qualified, since it names a data item in two distinct tables. Thus, appropriate references may be

```
WS-DAY-NAME OF DAY-TABLE-1(DAY-INDEX-1)
```

and

```
WS-DAY-NAME OF DAY-TABLE-2(DAY-INDEX-2).
```

Now, if reference modification is used to extract a day-name abbreviation from DAY-TABLE-2, the following reference is appropriate:

```
WS-DAY-NAME OF DAY-TABLE-2(DAY-INDEX-2)(1:3).
```

It is clear that this identifier contains qualification as well as reference modification.

Do you see that if DAY-INDEX-1 and DAY-INDEX-2 have the same occurrence value, then

```
WS-DAY-ABBREV(DAY-INDEX-1)
```

and

```
WS-DAY-NAME OF DAY-TABLE-2(DAY-INDEX-2)(1:3)
```

reference the same day-name abbreviation?

As another example, consider the table of month names in the Monster Burger payroll program (see Figure 2.19). The reference

```
WS-MONTH(MONTH-INDEX)(1:3)
```

may be used to retrieve month-name abbreviations.

Back to the Program

Now that we have seen how to define indexed tables, how to load indexed tables, and how to retrieve data from indexed tables, we return to the problem-solving procedure. The last step that we completed was the program pseudocode shown in Figure 2.6. The program flowchart was not presented at that point because the logic of the SEARCH statement remained to be developed. Recall that the flowchart is a visual representation of the detailed processing steps specified in the pseudocode. Please refer to the pseudocode as you examine the flowchart shown in Figure 2.18.

Now, the task of coding the program can be completed by bringing together all the components that have been examined individually, namely, the printer spacing chart (Figure 2.1) that will direct the coding of many entries in the WORKING-STORAGE SECTION of the program, the input record layouts that will direct the coding of FILE SECTION entries, the program pseudocode (Figure 2.6) or the program flowchart (Figure 2.18) that will direct the coding of the PROCEDURE DIVISION, the material on definitions of indexed tables that will direct the coding related to the tables needed in the program, and the new formats introduced in this chapter that will ensure compliance with language syntax.

The program is shown in Figure 2.19. We direct your attention to the following entries:

1. The second SELECT statement specifies SORT-FILE. Recall that the ordering of the employee records in EMPLOYEE-FILE must be changed to accommodate the requirements of the report. The sorting routine (in paragraph 300-SORT-EMPLOYEE-FILE) specifies EMPLOYEE-FILE as the input file (USING EMPLOYEE-FILE), and it specifies PAYROLL-FILE as the output file (GIVING PAYROLL-FILE). The records in PAYROLL-FILE are then in the required sequence, namely, alphabetically by store number, and store numbers are in ascending order.
2. There are three different kinds of records that belong to TABLES-FILE. See the FD paragraph for the file description! Note that the first byte of each record contains a code, but that only the code field of FEDERAL-TAX-RATES-RECORD is given a name. This was done to avoid the need for qualification of the name I-RECORD-CODE. Furthermore, since the three types of records in this file are read into the same input buffer, I-RECORD-CODE always refers to the first byte, regardless of the type of record in the buffer.

   Although three condition-names are defined for the data item I-RECORD-CODE, note that the test in paragraph 320-LOAD-TABLES references the data item I-RECORD-CODE. The condition-names could have been used as follows:

```
310-LOAD-TABLES.
    EVALUATE      TRUE
        WHEN TAX-RATE-RECORD PERFORM 400-LOAD-FEDERAL-TAX-TABLE
        WHEN PAY-RATE-RECORD PERFORM 410-LOAD-PAY-RATE-TABLE
        WHEN INS-PREM-RECORD PERFORM 420-LOAD-INSURANCE-TABLE.
```

Figure 2.18 Flowchart for the chapter program

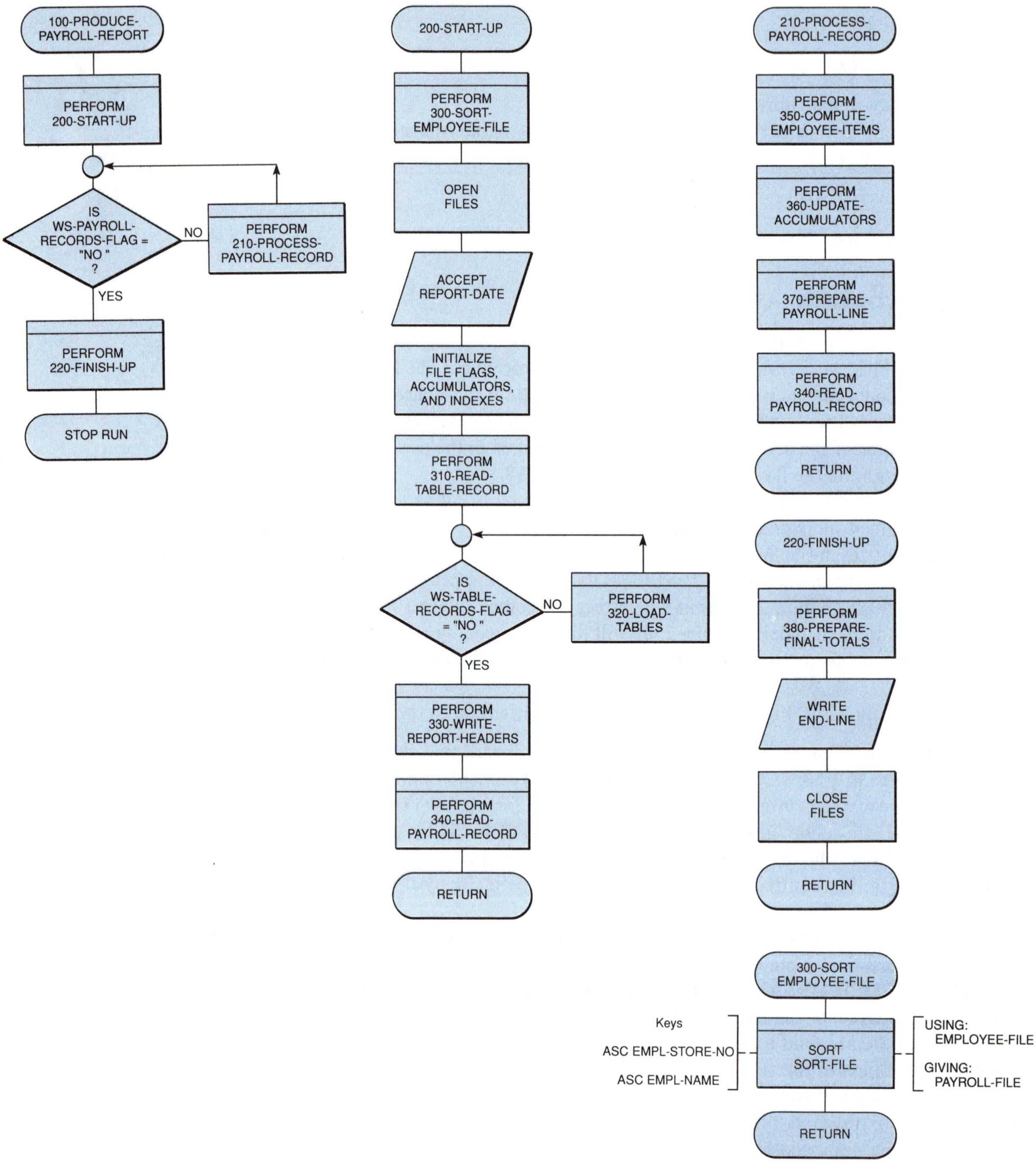

Figure 2.18 continued

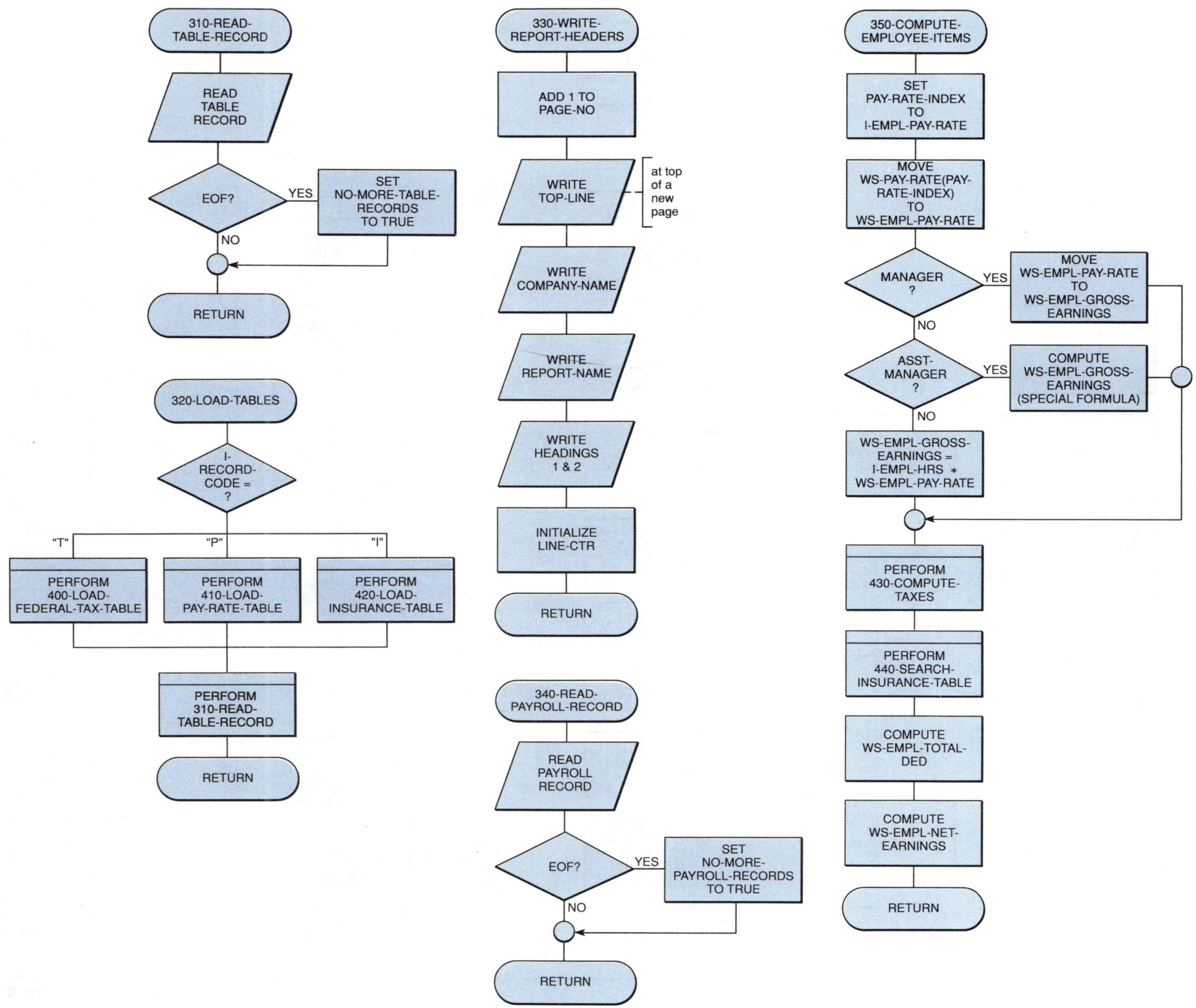

Figure 2.18 continued

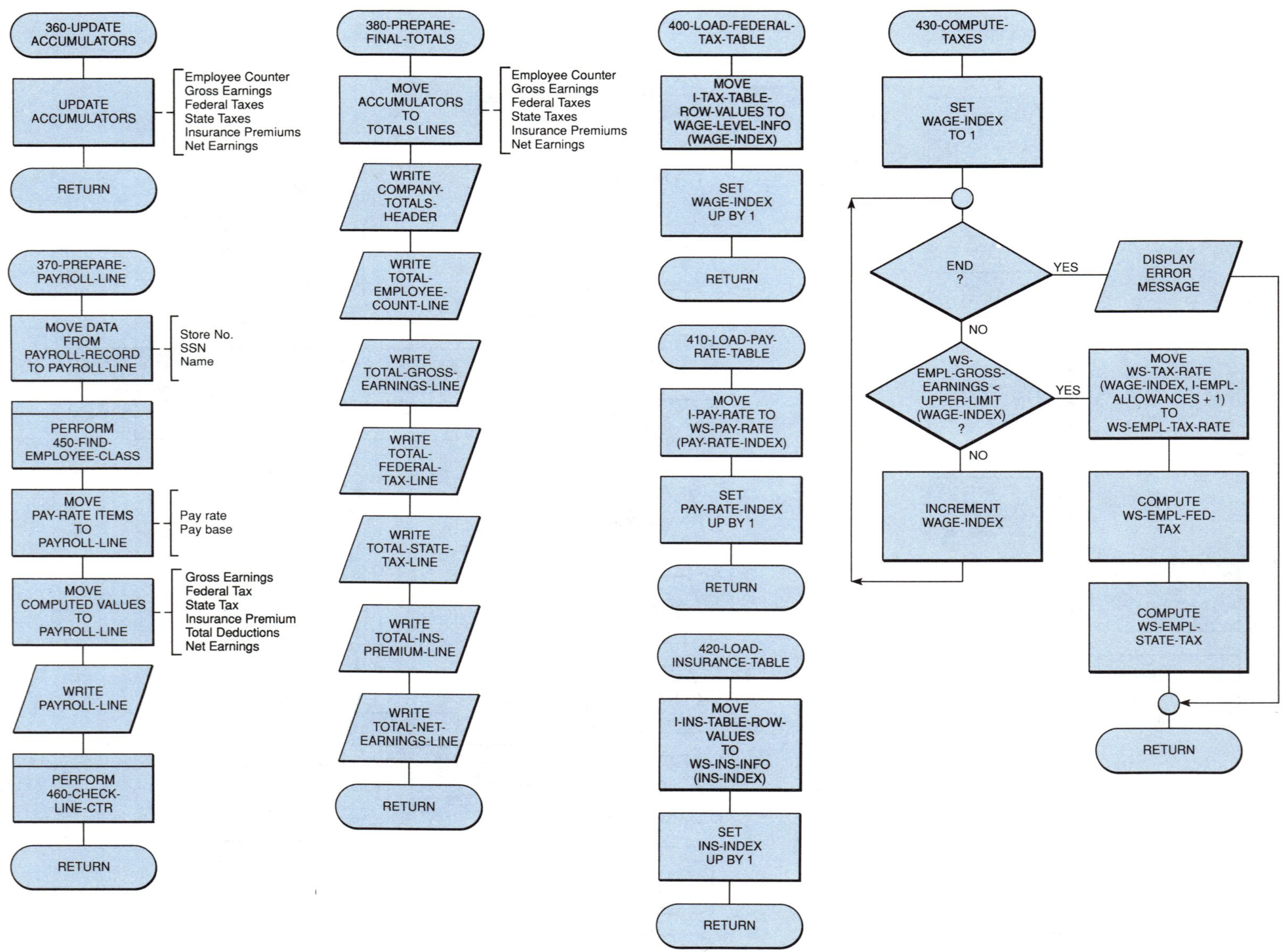

■ **Figure 2.18** continued

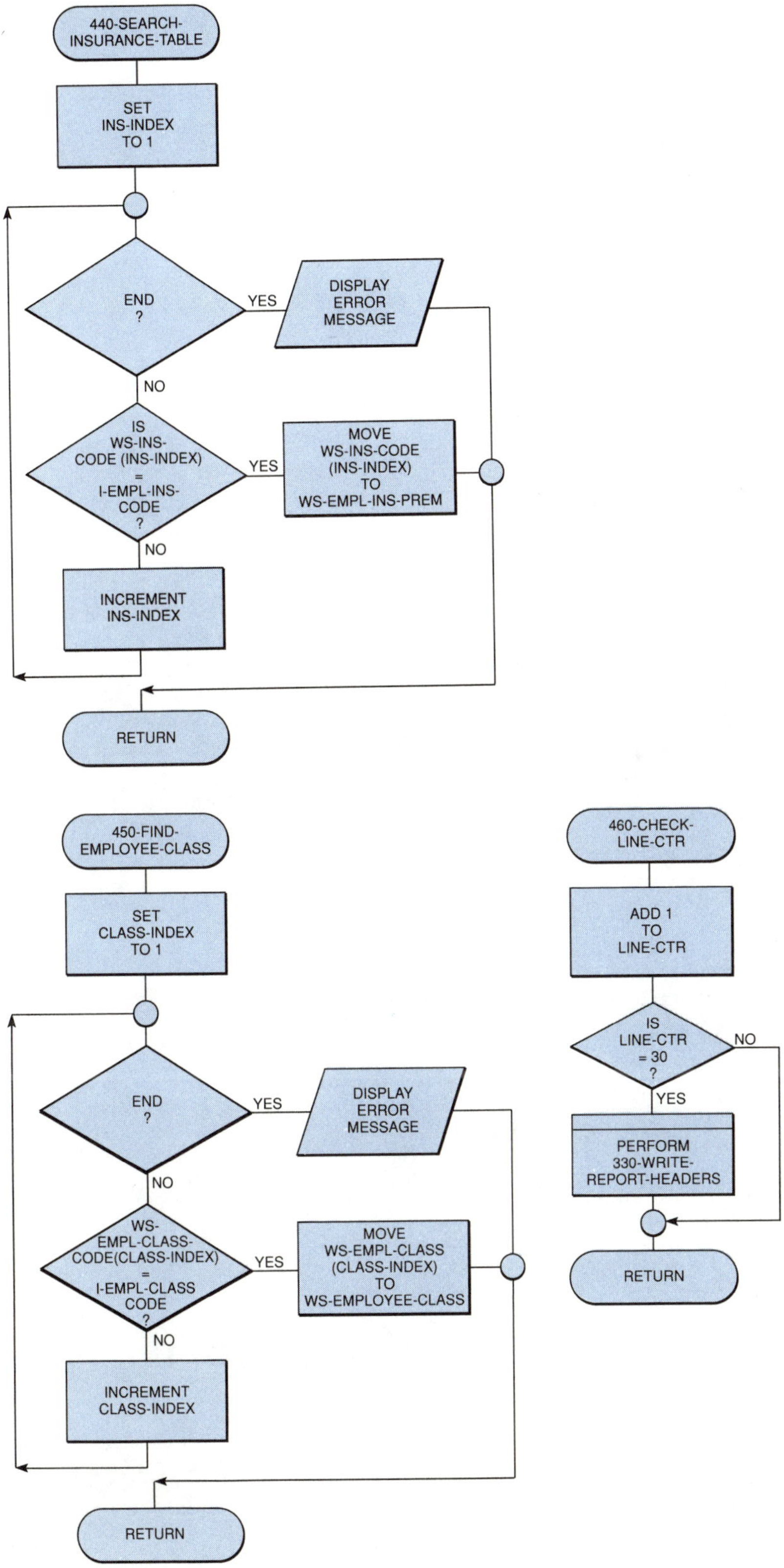

Figure 2.19 COBOL program for the chapter problem

```
 IDENTIFICATION DIVISION.

 PROGRAM-ID.  MONSTER-BURGER-PAYROLL.

*****************************************************************
*                                                               *
*  AUTHOR.          PAQUETTE.                                   *
*  DATE WRITTEN.  FEBRUARY 1989.                                *
*                                                               *
*****************************************************************

 ENVIRONMENT DIVISION.

 CONFIGURATION SECTION.

 SOURCE-COMPUTER.  VAX-VMS-8650.
 OBJECT-COMPUTER.  VAX-VMS-8650.

 INPUT-OUTPUT SECTION.

 FILE-CONTROL.
     SELECT EMPLOYEE-FILE  ASSIGN TO COB$INPUT.
     SELECT SORT-FILE      ASSIGN TO SORTDISK.
     SELECT TABLES-FILE    ASSIGN TO TABLESDATA.
     SELECT PAYROLL-FILE   ASSIGN TO 'PAYROLL.DAT'.
     SELECT PAYROLL-REPORT ASSIGN TO COB$OUTPUT.

 DATA DIVISION.

 FILE SECTION.

 FD  EMPLOYEE-FILE
     RECORD CONTAINS 43 CHARACTERS.

 01  EMPLOYEE-RECORD          PIC X(43).

 SD  SORT-FILE
     RECORD CONTAINS 43 CHARACTERS.

 01  SORT-RECORD.
     05                       PIC X(11).
     05 S-EMPL-NAME           PIC X(20).
     05 S-EMPL-STORE-NO       PIC X(2).
     05                       PIC X(10).

 FD  TABLES-FILE
     RECORD CONTAINS 6 TO 20 CHARACTERS.

 01  FEDERAL-TAX-RATES-RECORD.
     05 I-RECORD-CODE                  PIC X.
        88 TAX-RATE-RECORD                     VALUE 'T'.
        88 PAY-RATE-RECORD                     VALUE 'P'.
        88 INS-PREM-RECORD                     VALUE 'I'.
     05 I-TAX-TABLE-ROW-VALUES.
        10 I-UPPER-LIMIT               PIC 9(4).
        10 I-TAX-RATE   OCCURS 5 TIMES PIC V999.

 01  PAY-RATE-RECORD.
     05                       PIC X.
     05 I-PAY-RATE            PIC 999V99.

 01  INSURANCE-PREMIUM-RECORD.
     05                       PIC X.
     05 I-INS-TABLE-ROW-VALUES.
        10 I-INS-CODE         PIC X(2).
        10 I-INS-PREM         PIC 99V99.
```

Figure 2.19 continued

```
FD  PAYROLL-FILE
    RECORD CONTAINS 43 CHARACTERS.

01  PAYROLL-RECORD.
    05 I-EMPL-CLASS-CODE    PIC 9(2).
       88 MANAGER                    VALUE 06.
       88 ASST-MANAGER               VALUE 05.
       88 REG-EMPLOYEE               VALUES 01 THRU 04.
    05 I-EMPL-SSN           PIC X(9).
    05 I-EMPL-NAME          PIC X(20).
    05 I-EMPL-STORE-NO      PIC X(2).
    05 I-EMPL-PAY-CODE      PIC 9(2).
    05 I-EMPL-HRS           PIC 9(2).
    05 I-EMPL-OPEN-CLOSE    PIC 9(2).
    05 I-EMPL-INS-CODE      PIC X(2).
    05 I-EMPL-ALLOWANCES    PIC 9(2).

FD  PAYROLL-REPORT
    RECORD CONTAINS 133 CHARACTERS.

01  PRINTLINE               PIC X(133).

WORKING-STORAGE SECTION.

01  PROGRAM-CONTROLS.
    05 WS-PAYROLL-RECORDS-FLAG     PIC X(3).
       88 MORE-PAYROLL-RECORDS             VALUE 'YES'.
       88 NO-MORE-PAYROLL-RECORDS          VALUE 'NO '.
    05 WS-TABLE-RECORDS-FLAG       PIC X(3).
       88 MORE-TABLE-RECORDS               VALUE 'YES'.
       88 NO-MORE-TABLE-RECORDS            VALUE 'NO '.
    05 WS-LINE-CTR                 PIC S9(2).
       88 PAGE-IS-FULL                     VALUE +30.
    05 WS-REPORT-DATE              PIC 9(6).
    05 WS-MONTH-NO                 PIC 9(2).
    05 WS-PAGE-NO                  PIC S9(2).
    05 WS-PROPER-SPACING           PIC 9.

01  EMPLOYEE-WORK-AREAS            COMP.
    05 WS-EMPL-PAY-RATE            PIC S9(3)V99.
    05 WS-EMPL-GROSS-EARNINGS      PIC S9(3)V99.
    05 WS-EMPL-TAX-RATE            PIC V999.
    05 WS-EMPL-FED-TAX             PIC S9(3)V99.
    05 WS-EMPL-STATE-TAX           PIC S9(2)V99.
    05 WS-EMPL-INS-PREM            PIC S9(2)V99.
    05 WS-EMPL-TOTAL-DED           PIC S9(3)V99.
    05 WS-EMPL-NET-EARNINGS        PIC S9(3)V99.

01  COMPANY-ACCUMULATORS           COMP.
    05 WS-COMPANY-EMPL-CTR         PIC S9(3).
    05 WS-COMPANY-GROSS-EARNINGS   PIC S9(5)V99.
    05 WS-COMPANY-FED-TAX          PIC S9(5)V99.
    05 WS-COMPANY-STATE-TAX        PIC S9(5)V99.
    05 WS-COMPANY-INS-PREM         PIC S9(5)V99.
    05 WS-COMPANY-NET-EARNINGS     PIC S9(5)V99.

01  PROGRAM-TABLES.

    05 MONTH-TABLE  VALUE 'JANUARY  FEBRUARY MARCH    APRIL    MA
-   'Y        JUNE     JULY     AUGUST   SEPTEMBEROCTOBER  NOVEMBER
-   ' DECEMBER'.
       10 WS-MONTH OCCURS 12 TIMES
                   INDEXED BY MONTH-INDEX  PIC X(9).
```

```
       05 FEDERAL-TAX-TABLE.
          10 WAGE-LEVEL-INFO    OCCURS 10 TIMES
                                ASCENDING KEY UPPER-LIMIT
                                INDEXED BY WAGE-INDEX.
             15 UPPER-LIMIT                        PIC S9(4).
             15 WS-TAX-RATE     OCCURS 5 TIMES PIC SV999.

       05 PAY-RATE-TABLE.
          10 WS-PAY-RATE    OCCURS 15 TIMES
                            INDEXED BY PAY-RATE-INDEX   PIC S999V99.

       05 INSURANCE-TABLE.
          10 WS-INS-INFO    OCCURS 4 TIMES
                            INDEXED BY INS-INDEX.
             15 WS-INS-CODE            PIC X(2).
             15 WS-INS-PREM            PIC 99V99.

       05 EMPLOYEE-CLASS-VALUES.
          10 PIC X(12)   VALUE '04STANDARD  '.
          10 PIC X(12)   VALUE '03YEARLING  '.
          10 PIC X(12)   VALUE '02BEGINNER  '.
          10 PIC X(12)   VALUE '01APPRENTICE'.
          10 PIC X(12)   VALUE '05ASS'T MGR.'.
          10 PIC X(12)   VALUE '06STORE MGR.'.
       05 EMPLOYEE-CLASS-TABLE REDEFINES EMPLOYEE-CLASS-VALUES.
          10 WS-EMPL-CLASS-INFO   OCCURS 6 TIMES
                                  INDEXED BY CLASS-INDEX.
             15 WS-EMPL-CLASS-CODE       PIC 9(2).
             15 WS-EMPL-CLASS            PIC X(10).

   01  REPORT-HEADERS.

       05 TOP-LINE.
          10                  PIC X(6)   VALUE SPACES.
          10                  PIC X(14)  VALUE 'REPORT DATE:  '.
          10 O-DAY            PIC X(3).
          10 O-MONTH          PIC X(9).
          10                  PIC X(3)   VALUE ' 19'.
          10 O-YEAR           PIC X(2).
          10                  PIC X(83)  VALUE SPACES.
          10                  PIC X(5)   VALUE 'PAGE '.
          10 O-PAGE-NO        PIC Z9.
          10                  PIC X(6)   VALUE SPACES.

       05 COMPANY-NAME.
          10 PIC X(56)   VALUE SPACES.
          10 PIC X(21)   VALUE 'MONSTER BURGER STORES'.
          10 PIC X(56)   VALUE SPACES.

       05 REPORT-NAME.
          10 PIC X(60)   VALUE SPACES.
          10 PIC X(14)   VALUE 'PAYROLL REPORT'.
          10 PIC X(59)   VALUE SPACES.

       05 HEADINGS-1.
          10 PIC X(75)   VALUE SPACES.
          10 PIC X(5)    VALUE 'GROSS'.
          10 PIC X(4)    VALUE SPACES.
          10 PIC X(7)    VALUE 'FEDERAL'.
          10 PIC X(4)    VALUE SPACES.
          10 PIC X(5)    VALUE 'STATE'.
          10 PIC X(4)    VALUE SPACES.
          10 PIC X(3)    VALUE 'INS'.
          10 PIC X(6)    VALUE SPACES.
          10 PIC X(5)    VALUE 'TOTAL'.
          10 PIC X(6)    VALUE SPACES.
          10 PIC X(3)    VALUE 'NET'.
          10 PIC X(6)    VALUE SPACES.
```

■ **Figure 2.19** continued

```
05 HEADINGS-2.
   10 PIC X(4)    VALUE SPACES.
   10 PIC X(5)    VALUE 'STORE'.
   10 PIC X(6)    VALUE SPACES.
   10 PIC X(3)    VALUE 'SSN'.
   10 PIC X(14)   VALUE SPACES.
   10 PIC X(4)    VALUE 'NAME'.
   10 PIC X(12)   VALUE SPACES.
   10 PIC X(5)    VALUE 'CLASS'.
   10 PIC X(5)    VALUE SPACES.
   10 PIC X(8)    VALUE 'PAY RATE'.
   10 PIC X(3)    VALUE SPACES.
   10 PIC X(3)    VALUE 'HRS'.
   10 PIC X(2)    VALUE SPACES.
   10 PIC X(8)    VALUE 'EARNINGS'.
   10 PIC X(4)    VALUE SPACES.
   10 PIC X(3)    VALUE 'TAX'.
   10 PIC X(7)    VALUE SPACES.
   10 PIC X(3)    VALUE 'TAX'.
   10 PIC X(5)    VALUE SPACES.
   10 PIC X(4)    VALUE 'PREM'.
   10 PIC X(6)    VALUE SPACES.
   10 PIC X(3)    VALUE 'DED'.
   10 PIC X(5)    VALUE SPACES.
   10 PIC X(8)    VALUE 'EARNINGS'.
   10 PIC X(3)    VALUE SPACES.

01  PAYROLL-LINE.
    05                         PIC X(5).
    05 O-EMPL-STORE-NO         PIC X(2).
    05                         PIC X(4).
    05 O-EMPL-SSN              PIC XXXBXXBXXXX.
    05                         PIC X(2).
    05 O-EMPL-NAME             PIC X(20).
    05                         PIC X(2).
    05 O-EMPL-CLASS            PIC X(10).
    05                         PIC X.
    05 O-EMPL-PAY-RATE         PIC $ZZ9.99.
    05 O-PAY-BASE              PIC X(3).
    05                         PIC X(2).
    05 O-EMPL-HRS              PIC Z9.
    05                         PIC X(3).
    05 O-EMPL-GROSS-EARNINGS PIC $ZZ9.99-.
    05                         PIC X(2).
    05 O-EMPL-FED-TAX          PIC $ZZ9.99-.
    05                         PIC X(2).
    05 O-EMPL-STATE-TAX        PIC $Z9.99-.
    05                         PIC X(2).
    05 O-EMPL-INS-PREM         PIC $Z9.99-.
    05                         PIC X(2).
    05 O-EMPL-TOTAL-DED        PIC $ZZ9.99-.
    05                         PIC X(2).
    05 O-EMPL-NET-EARNINGS     PIC $ZZ9.99-.
    05                         PIC X(3).

01  COMPANY-TOTALS.

    05 COMPANY-TOTALS-HEADER.
       10 PIC X(109)              VALUE SPACES.
       10 PIC X(14)               VALUE 'COMPANY TOTALS'.
       10 PIC X(8)                VALUE SPACES.
       10 PIC X(2)                VALUE '**'.
```

```
       05 TOTAL-EMPLOYEE-COUNT-LINE.
          10 PIC X(101)                VALUE SPACES.
          10 PIC X(18)                 VALUE 'NO. OF EMPLOYEES: '.
          10 O-COMPANY-EMPL-CTR        PIC ZZ9-.
          10 PIC X(10)                 VALUE SPACES.

       05 TOTAL-GROSS-EARNINGS-LINE.
          10 PIC X(103)                VALUE SPACES.
          10 PIC X(16)                 VALUE 'GROSS EARNINGS: '.
          10 O-COMPANY-GROSS-EARNINGS PIC $ZZ,ZZ9.99-.
          10 PIC X(3)                  VALUE SPACES.

       05 TOTAL-FEDERAL-TAX-LINE.
          10 PIC X(104)                VALUE SPACES.
          10 PIC X(16)                 VALUE 'FEDERAL TAXES:  '.
          10 O-COMPANY-FED-TAX         PIC $Z,ZZ9.99-.
          10 PIC X(3)                  VALUE SPACES.

       05 TOTAL-STATE-TAX-LINE.
          10 PIC X(106)                VALUE SPACES.
          10 PIC X(14)                 VALUE 'STATE TAXES:  '.
          10 O-COMPANY-STATE-TAX       PIC $Z,ZZ9.99-.
          10 PIC X(3)                  VALUE SPACES.

       05 TOTAL-INS-PREMIUM-LINE.
          10 PIC X(104)                VALUE SPACES.
          10 PIC X(16)                 VALUE 'INS. PREMIUMS:  '.
          10 O-COMPANY-INS-PREM        PIC $Z,ZZ9.99-.
          10 PIC X(3)                  VALUE SPACES.

       05 TOTAL-NET-EARNINGS-LINE.
          10 PIC X(105)                VALUE SPACES.
          10 PIC X(14)                 VALUE 'NET EARNINGS: '.
          10 O-COMPANY-NET-EARNINGS    PIC $ZZ,ZZ9.99-.
          10 PIC X(3)                  VALUE SPACES.

      05 PIC X(55)  VALUE SPACES.
      05 PIC X(23)  VALUE '***  END OF REPORT  ***'.
      05 PIC X(55)  VALUE SPACES.

 PROCEDURE DIVISION.

 100-PRODUCE-PAYROLL-REPORT.
     PERFORM 200-START-UP.
     PERFORM 210-PROCESS-PAYROLL-RECORD
         UNTIL NO-MORE-PAYROLL-RECORDS.
     PERFORM 220-FINISH-UP.
     STOP RUN.

 200-START-UP.
     PERFORM 300-SORT-EMPLOYEE-FILE.
     OPEN INPUT TABLES-FILE
          INPUT PAYROLL-FILE
          OUTPUT PAYROLL-REPORT.
     ACCEPT WS-REPORT-DATE FROM DATE.
     MOVE WS-REPORT-DATE(1:2) TO O-YEAR.
     MOVE WS-REPORT-DATE(5:2) TO O-DAY.
     MOVE WS-REPORT-DATE(3:2) TO WS-MONTH-NO.
     SET MONTH-INDEX TO WS-MONTH-NO.
     MOVE WS-MONTH(MONTH-INDEX) TO O-MONTH.
     MOVE 'YES' TO WS-TABLE-RECORDS-FLAG
                   WS-PAYROLL-RECORDS-FLAG.
     INITIALIZE COMPANY-ACCUMULATORS
                WS-PAGE-NO.
     SET WAGE-INDEX
         PAY-RATE-INDEX
         INS-INDEX TO 1.
```

```
    PERFORM 310-READ-TABLE-RECORD.
    PERFORM 320-LOAD-TABLES
        UNTIL NO-MORE-TABLE-RECORDS.
    PERFORM 330-WRITE-REPORT-HEADERS.
    PERFORM 340-READ-PAYROLL-RECORD.

210-PROCESS-PAYROLL-RECORD.
    PERFORM 350-COMPUTE-EMPLOYEE-ITEMS.
    PERFORM 360-UPDATE-ACCUMULATORS.
    PERFORM 370-PREPARE-PAYROLL-LINE.
    PERFORM 340-READ-PAYROLL-RECORD.

220-FINISH-UP.
    PERFORM 380-PREPARE-FINAL-TOTALS.
    WRITE PRINTLINE FROM END-LINE
        AFTER ADVANCING 5 LINES.
    CLOSE TABLES-FILE
          PAYROLL-FILE
          PAYROLL-REPORT.

300-SORT-EMPLOYEE-FILE.
    SORT SORT-FILE
        ON ASCENDING KEY S-EMPL-STORE-NO
                         S-EMPL-NAME
        USING EMPLOYEE-FILE
        GIVING PAYROLL-FILE

310-READ-TABLE-RECORD.
    READ TABLES-FILE RECORD
        AT END
            SET NO-MORE-TABLE-RECORDS TO TRUE.

320-LOAD-TABLES.
    EVALUATE I-RECORD-CODE
        WHEN 'T'  PERFORM 400-LOAD-FEDERAL-TAX-TABLE
        WHEN 'P'  PERFORM 410-LOAD-PAY-RATE-TABLE
        WHEN 'I'  PERFORM 420-LOAD-INSURANCE-TABLE.
    PERFORM 310-READ-TABLE-RECORD.

330-WRITE-REPORT-HEADERS.
    ADD 1 TO WS-PAGE-NO.
    MOVE WS-PAGE-NO TO O-PAGE-NO.
    WRITE PRINTLINE FROM TOP-LINE
        AFTER ADVANCING PAGE.
    WRITE PRINTLINE FROM COMPANY-NAME
        AFTER ADVANCING 1 LINE.
    WRITE PRINTLINE FROM REPORT-NAME
        AFTER ADVANCING 3 LINES.
    WRITE PRINTLINE FROM HEADINGS-1
        AFTER ADVANCING 3 LINES.
    WRITE PRINTLINE FROM HEADINGS-2
        AFTER ADVANCING 1 LINE.
    INITIALIZE WS-LINE-CTR.
    MOVE 2 TO WS-PROPER-SPACING.

340-READ-PAYROLL-RECORD.
    READ PAYROLL-FILE RECORD
        AT END
            SET NO-MORE-PAYROLL-RECORDS TO TRUE.

350-COMPUTE-EMPLOYEE-ITEMS.
    SET PAY-RATE-INDEX TO I-EMPL-PAY-CODE.
    MOVE WS-PAY-RATE (PAY-RATE-INDEX) TO WS-EMPL-PAY-RATE.
    IF MANAGER
        MOVE WS-EMPL-PAY-RATE TO WS-EMPL-GROSS-EARNINGS
```

```
    ELSE
        IF ASST-MANAGER
            COMPUTE WS-EMPL-GROSS-EARNINGS ROUNDED =
                I-EMPL-HRS * WS-EMPL-PAY-RATE +
                5 * I-EMPL-OPEN-CLOSE + 10
        ELSE
            MULTIPLY I-EMPL-HRS BY WS-EMPL-PAY-RATE
                GIVING WS-EMPL-GROSS-EARNINGS ROUNDED
        END-IF
    END-IF.
    PERFORM 430-COMPUTE-TAXES.
    PERFORM 440-SEARCH-INSURANCE-TABLE.
    ADD WS-EMPL-FED-TAX WS-EMPL-STATE-TAX WS-EMPL-INS-PREM
        GIVING WS-EMPL-TOTAL-DED.
    SUBTRACT WS-EMPL-TOTAL-DED FROM WS-EMPL-GROSS-EARNINGS
        GIVING WS-EMPL-NET-EARNINGS.

360-UPDATE-ACCUMULATORS.
    ADD 1 TO WS-COMPANY-EMPL-CTR.
    ADD WS-EMPL-GROSS-EARNINGS TO WS-COMPANY-GROSS-EARNINGS.
    ADD WS-EMPL-FED-TAX TO WS-COMPANY-FED-TAX.
    ADD WS-EMPL-STATE-TAX TO WS-COMPANY-STATE-TAX.
    ADD WS-EMPL-INS-PREM TO WS-COMPANY-INS-PREM.
    ADD WS-EMPL-NET-EARNINGS TO WS-COMPANY-NET-EARNINGS.

370-PREPARE-PAYROLL-LINE.
    MOVE SPACES TO PAYROLL-LINE.
    MOVE I-EMPL-STORE-NO TO O-EMPL-STORE-NO.
    MOVE I-EMPL-SSN TO O-EMPL-SSN.
    MOVE I-EMPL-NAME TO O-EMPL-NAME.
    PERFORM 450-FIND-EMPLOYEE-CLASS.
    MOVE WS-EMPL-PAY-RATE TO O-EMPL-PAY-RATE.
    IF MANAGER
        MOVE '/WK' TO O-PAY-BASE
    ELSE
        MOVE '/HR' TO O-PAY-BASE
        MOVE I-EMPL-HRS TO O-EMPL-HRS.
    MOVE WS-EMPL-GROSS-EARNINGS TO O-EMPL-GROSS-EARNINGS.
    MOVE WS-EMPL-FED-TAX TO O-EMPL-FED-TAX.
    MOVE WS-EMPL-STATE-TAX TO O-EMPL-STATE-TAX.
    MOVE WS-EMPL-INS-PREM TO O-EMPL-INS-PREM.
    MOVE WS-EMPL-TOTAL-DED TO O-EMPL-TOTAL-DED.
    MOVE WS-EMPL-NET-EARNINGS TO O-EMPL-NET-EARNINGS.
    WRITE PRINTLINE FROM PAYROLL-LINE
        AFTER ADVANCING WS-PROPER-SPACING.
    MOVE 1 TO WS-PROPER-SPACING.
    PERFORM 460-CHECK-LINE-CTR.

380-PREPARE-FINAL-TOTALS.
    WRITE PRINTLINE FROM COMPANY-TOTALS-HEADER
        AFTER ADVANCING 5 LINES.
    MOVE WS-COMPANY-EMPL-CTR TO O-COMPANY-EMPL-CTR.
    WRITE PRINTLINE FROM TOTAL-EMPLOYEE-COUNT-LINE
        AFTER ADVANCING 2 LINES.
    MOVE WS-COMPANY-GROSS-EARNINGS TO O-COMPANY-GROSS-EARNINGS.
    WRITE PRINTLINE FROM TOTAL-GROSS-EARNINGS-LINE
        AFTER ADVANCING 1 LINE.
    MOVE WS-COMPANY-FED-TAX TO O-COMPANY-FED-TAX.
    WRITE PRINTLINE FROM TOTAL-FEDERAL-TAX-LINE
        AFTER ADVANCING 1 LINE.
    MOVE WS-COMPANY-STATE-TAX TO O-COMPANY-STATE-TAX.
    WRITE PRINTLINE FROM TOTAL-STATE-TAX-LINE
        AFTER ADVANCING 1 LINE.
    MOVE WS-COMPANY-INS-PREM TO O-COMPANY-INS-PREM.
    WRITE PRINTLINE FROM TOTAL-INS-PREMIUM-LINE
         AFTER ADVANCING 1 LINE.
```

Figure 2.19 continued

```
    MOVE WS-COMPANY-NET-EARNINGS TO O-COMPANY-NET-EARNINGS.
    WRITE PRINTLINE FROM TOTAL-NET-EARNINGS-LINE
        AFTER ADVANCING 1 LINE.

400-LOAD-FEDERAL-TAX-TABLE.
    MOVE I-TAX-TABLE-ROW-VALUES TO WAGE-LEVEL-INFO (WAGE-INDEX).
    SET WAGE-INDEX UP BY 1.

410-LOAD-PAY-RATE-TABLE.
    MOVE I-PAY-RATE TO WS-PAY-RATE (PAY-RATE-INDEX).
    SET PAY-RATE-INDEX UP BY 1.

420-LOAD-INSURANCE-TABLE.
    MOVE I-INS-TABLE-ROW-VALUES TO WS-INS-INFO (INS-INDEX).
    SET INS-INDEX UP BY 1.

430-COMPUTE-TAXES.
    SET WAGE-INDEX TO 1.
    SEARCH WAGE-LEVEL-INFO
        AT END
            DISPLAY '*** GROSS EARNINGS OUT OF RANGE FOR '
                I-EMPL-NAME
        WHEN WS-EMPL-GROSS-EARNINGS < UPPER-LIMIT (WAGE-INDEX)
            MOVE WS-TAX-RATE (WAGE-INDEX, I-EMPL-ALLOWANCES + 1)
                TO WS-EMPL-TAX-RATE
    END-SEARCH.
    MULTIPLY WS-EMPL-GROSS-EARNINGS BY WS-EMPL-TAX-RATE
        GIVING WS-EMPL-FED-TAX ROUNDED.
    MULTIPLY WS-EMPL-FED-TAX BY .23
        GIVING WS-EMPL-STATE-TAX ROUNDED.

440-SEARCH-INSURANCE-TABLE.
    SET INS-INDEX TO 1.
    SEARCH WS-INS-INFO
        AT END
            DISPLAY '*** INS. CODE NOT FOUND FOR ' I-EMPL-NAME
        WHEN  WS-INS-CODE (INS-INDEX) = I-EMPL-INS-CODE
            MOVE WS-INS-PREM (INS-INDEX) TO WS-EMPL-INS-PREM
    END-SEARCH.

450-FIND-EMPLOYEE-CLASS.
    SET CLASS-INDEX TO 1.
    SEARCH WS-EMPL-CLASS-INFO
        AT END
            DISPLAY '*** INVALID CLASS CODE FOR ' I-EMPL-NAME
        WHEN WS-EMPL-CLASS-CODE (CLASS-INDEX) = I-EMPL-CLASS-CODE
            MOVE WS-EMPL-CLASS (CLASS-INDEX) TO O-EMPL-CLASS
    END-SEARCH.

460-CHECK-LINE-CTR.
    ADD 1 TO WS-LINE-CTR.
    IF PAGE-IS-FULL
        PERFORM 330-WRITE-REPORT-HEADERS
    END-IF.
```

3. To enhance program structure, the five tables needed in the program have been grouped under the group name PROGRAM-TABLES. Note that all the tables have been indexed, but that the second level of FEDERAL-TAX-TABLE is not indexed. Recall that this was done deliberately to illustrate that the subscripts in an identifier may contain both data names and indexes. The second level of the table could have been indexed, as follows:

```
15 WS-TAX-RATE OCCURS 5 TIMES
               INDEXED BY ALLOWANCE-INDEX  PIC SV999.
```

   Had this been done, the index could then be used in paragraph 430-COMPUTE-TAXES as follows:

   a. Insert a second SET statement to set ALLOWANCE-INDEX to the value specified by the data item I-EMPL-ALLOWANCES, as in

   ```
   SET ALLOWANCE-INDEX TO I-EMPL-ALLOWANCES.
   ```

   b. Change the MOVE statement of the WHEN clause (of the SEARCH statement) to

   ```
   MOVE WS-TAX-RATE (WAGE-INDEX, ALLOWANCE-INDEX + 1)
       TO WS-EMPL-TAX-RATE
   ```

   where ALLOWANCE-INDEX + 1 is a relative index. The results would be the same.

4. The hard-coded table EMPLOYEE-CLASS-TABLE could have been defined without using the REDEFINES clause, as follows:

```
05 EMPLOYEE-CLASS-TABLE
   VALUE "04STANDARD  03YEARLING  02BEGINNER  01APPRENTICE05A
-        "SS'T MGR.06STORE MGR.".
   10 WS-EMPL-CLASS-INFO  OCCURS 6 TIMES
                          INDEXED BY CLASS-INDEX.
      15 WS-EMPL-CLASS-CODE  PIC 99.
      15 WS-EMPL-CLASS       PIC X(10).
```

   Recall that COBOL '85 allows the use of the VALUE clause and of the OCCURS clause in the same item description. The literal continuation (the hyphen to the left of the literal) is used, since the characters in the literal must not be coded beyond column 72. In COBOL '85, the maximum size of a nonnumeric literal is 160 characters. In COBOL '74, the maximum is 120.

5. The headers for the first part of the report have been grouped under the group name REPORT-HEADERS, and the description of the lines needed for the summary part of the report have been grouped under the group name COMPANY-TOTALS.

6. In paragraph 200-START-UP,

   a. Note that an essential start-up activity is to sort the records of EMPLOYEE-FILE. Recall that the file produced by the sorting routine, namely PAYROLL-FILE, must subsequently be open in input mode for the rest of the program.

   b. Note that the date components are manipulated by using reference modification and that the required month name is obtained by direct referencing in the statement

   ```
   MOVE WS-MONTH(MONTH-INDEX) TO O-MONTH.
   ```

   c. The company accumulators are set to zero by means of the INITIALIZE statement.

   d. Note that the table indexes are initialized by the SET statement prior to loading the tables.

7. In paragraph 220-FINISH-UP, the PERFORM statement sends control to paragraph 380-PREPARE-FINAL-TOTALS in order to produce the summary report. Upon returning control, the "End of Report" message is printed, and then the files are closed.

8. In paragraph 350-COMPUTE-EMPLOYEE-ITEMS, the first MOVE statement illustrates direct referencing of a table element. This is a consequence of the positional organization of the table PAY-RATE-TABLE. Also note that an effort was made here to use the index (PAY-RATE-INDEX) associated with the table. This is not necessary! Since the input field I-EMPL-PAY-CODE contains the pay rate occurrence that must be referenced in the table, the SET and MOVE statements could both be replaced by the single statement

```
MOVE WS-PAY-RATE (I-EMPL-PAY-CODE) TO WS-EMPL-PAY-RATE.
```

9. Whenever table elements are to be serially searched by the SEARCH statement, the first occurrence to be looked at must be specified in a SET statement prior to the SEARCH statement. The SET statements in paragraph 450-FIND-EMPLOYEE-CLASS, 430-COMPUTE-TAXES, and 440-SEARCH-INSURANCE-TABLE clearly indicate that the searches begin at the "top" of the table.
10. In paragraph 430-COMPUTE-TAXES, note that in the MOVE statement, the reference to an occurrence of WS-TAX-RATE uses an index (WAGE-INDEX) and a relative subscript (I-EMPL-ALLOWANCES + 1). COBOL '85 allows mixing indexes and data items as subscripts.

The Payroll Report

The employee file that was used as an input file to the COBOL program in Figure 2.19 is shown in Figure 2.20a; the sorted file, now called Payroll File, is shown in Figure 2.20b; and the report produced by the program is shown in Figure 2.21.

Figure 2.20a The sample input employee file

```
02379443987ALMEIDA, PAULA      200335  IB01
04374476512AMBROSE, GUS        100650  FB02
06526934075AUDET, LILLIAN      101500  FB03
04421332564BALL, GEORGE        010645  FB03
05446225388BLAIR, CYNTHIA      20085204FB03
05315641932BLANCHARD, SUZANNE  01075505IB01
04265346992BOOTH, JOAN         300748  FA02
01572162344BOUVIER, DIANNE     100122  IA01
04470156712BRIEN, RAYMOND      200854  FB02
05280015447BUNDY, LISA         30085202FB03
02450152349COVILL, COLINE      010330  IA01
03312317593CROUCH, JOAN        050540  IB01
04299217365CZARNECKI, STANLEY  050650  FB05
02415817943DAILEY, MARSHA      050235  IA01
03493043217DANIELS, JULIA      100445  IB01
04319789442DEAN, MARY          300750  IA01
05468201726DONALDSON, MARC     10095505FA02
06239419615DORR, PAUL          011200  FB04
06532660045FINEMAN, ERNEST     301300  FB04
01510025113GAGNON, GERARD      200122  IA01
02552974388GALLIGAN, FRANCIS   100330  IB01
03494123371GARBER, JULIE       300545  FA02
03311863712GENERI, AMY         010540  FA03
04375443176HAMMOND, GAIL       050848  FA02
05304772224HEALEY, NAOMI       20095503IB01
05519641139HEIMER, CYNTHIA     10085206FB04
06622506073HILL, MICHAEL       051100  FB03
01437116528JARVIS, RICHARD     010122  IA01
05364522332JEFFERDS, CHARLES   30105506FB04
01519378294KALIN, OLIVIA       050120  IA01
01481975521KENNEY, MARTIN      100118  IA01
02319253744KOPECKY, AGNES      100334  IA01
05473649512LACOURSE, IRENE     05105406FB03
03566197327LAPIERRE, GARY      200340  IB01
02614116693LATOUR, JOAN        300333  IA01
04323693173LAVIN, YVONNE       100948  FA02
05519732561MAGUIRE, JAMES      10105803FB05
01537051635MCDONALD, PATRICIA  300120  IA01
06440155771MCELROY, ROSE MARIE 201400  FB03
04624559502MCGARRY, ANNA       010948  IA01
02362799176NELSON, PETER       200234  IA01
04481322217NESTOR, ELEANOR     051045  FB04
04501227532PALUMBO, ROSE       201045  FB04
02367113215PERNAL, RICHARD     050335  IA01
05566315679PETRUSKA, ANGELA    01075206IB01
04444697143RABINOWICZ, MAE     301048  FB03
04549663412RAGOSTA, TERRY      200550  IA01
04540525640RAINVILLE, SHARON   100946  IB01
05326523966RIANNA, MILDRED     05085804FA02
05560771115SCHERER, ANGELA     30085404FB02
03147523318SILVA, GEORGE       010344  FB02
04370229876SOFORENKO, WILLIAM  300552  IB01
03409554662STUDLEY, SANDRA     200540  IB01
05505200792TOUPIN, ADA         20085505FB03
04307231962TOURTELLOT, MARJORIE100850  FB02
04419617752ULMANN, SUSAN       010850  FA02
03338521873WINSLOW, EILEEN     300344  IB01
```

■ Figure 2.20b The sorted payroll file

```
04421332564BALL, GEORGE        010645  FB03
05315641932BLANCHARD, SUZANNE  01075505IB01
02450152349COVILL, COLINE      010330  IA01
06239419615DORR, PAUL          011200  FB04
03311863712GENERI, AMY         010540  FA03
01437116528JARVIS, RICHARD     010122  IA01
04624559502MCGARRY, ANNA       010948  IA01
05566315679PETRUSKA, ANGELA    01075206IB01
03147523318SILVA, GEORGE       010344  FB02
04419617752ULMANN, SUSAN       010850  FA02
03312317593CROUCH, JOAN        050540  IB01
04299217365CZARNECKI, STANLEY  050650  FB05
02415817943DAILEY, MARSHA      050235  IA01
04375443176HAMMOND, GAIL       050848  FA02
06622506073HILL, MICHAEL       051100  FB03
01519378294KALIN, OLIVIA       050120  IA01
05473649512LACOURSE, IRENE     05105406FB03
04481322217NESTOR, ELEANOR     051045  FB04
02367113215PERNAL, RICHARD     050335  IA01
05326523966RIANNA, MILDRED     05085804FA02
04374476512AMBROSE, GUS        100650  FB02
06526934075AUDET, LILLIAN      101500  FB03
01572162344BOUVIER, DIANNE     100122  IA01
03493043217DANIELS, JULIA      100445  IB01
05468201726DONALDSON, MARC     10095505FA02
02552974388GALLIGAN, FRANCIS   100330  IB01
05519641139HEIMER, CYNTHIA     10085206FB04
01481975521KENNEY, MARTIN      100118  IA01
02319253744KOPECKY, AGNES      100334  IA01
04323693173LAVIN, YVONNE       100948  FA02
05519732561MAGUIRE, JAMES      10105803FB05
04540525640RAINVILLE, SHARON   100946  IB01
04307231962TOURTELLOT, MARJORIE100850  FB02
02379443987ALMEIDA, PAULA      200335  IB01
05446225388BLAIR, CYNTHIA      20085204FB03
04470156712BRIEN, RAYMOND      200854  FB02
01510025113GAGNON, GERARD      200122  IA01
05304772224HEALEY, NAOMI       20095503IB01
03566197327LAPIERRE, GARY      200340  IB01
06440155771MCELROY, ROSE MARIE 201400  FB03
02362799176NELSON, PETER       200234  IA01
04501227532PALUMBO, ROSE       201045  FB04
04549663412RAGOSTA, TERRY      200550  IA01
03409554662STUDLEY, SANDRA     200540  IB01
05505200792TOUPIN, ADA         20085505FB03
04265346992BOOTH, JOAN         300748  FA02
05280015447BUNDY, LISA         30085202FB03
04319789442DEAN, MARY          300750  IA01
06532660045FINEMAN, ERNEST     301300  FB04
03494123371GARBER, JULIE       300545  FA02
05364522332JEFFERDS, CHARLES   30105506FB04
02614116693LATOUR, JOAN        300333  IA01
01537051635MCDONALD, PATRICIA  300120  IA01
04444697143RABINOWICZ, MAE     301048  FB03
05560771115SCHERER, ANGELA     30085404FB02
04370229876SOFORENKO, WILLIAM  300552  IB01
03338521873WINSLOW, EILEEN     300344  IB01
```

■ **Figure 2.21** Payroll report produced by the program

REPORT DATE: 10 FEBRUARY 1989 PAGE 1

MONSTER BURGER STORES

PAYROLL REPORT

STORE	SSN	NAME	CLASS	PAY RATE	HRS	GROSS EARNINGS	FEDERAL TAX	STATE TAX	INS PREM	TOTAL DED	NET EARNINGS
01	421 33 2564	BALL, GEORGE	STANDARD	$ 5.75/HR	45	$258.75	$ 16.30	$ 3.75	$11.54	$ 31.59	$227.16
01	315 64 1932	BLANCHARD, SUZANNE	ASS'T MGR.	$ 6.50/HR	55	$392.50	$ 44.35	$10.20	$ 9.14	$ 63.69	$328.81
01	450 15 2349	COVILL, COLINE	BEGINNER	$ 4.25/HR	30	$127.50	$ 9.56	$ 2.20	$ 6.73	$ 18.49	$109.01
01	239 41 9615	DORR, PAUL	STORE MGR.	$375.00/WK		$375.00	$ 26.25	$ 6.04	$11.54	$ 43.83	$331.17
01	311 86 3712	GENERI, AMY	YEARLING	$ 5.10/HR	40	$204.00	$ 12.85	$ 2.96	$ 8.65	$ 24.46	$179.54
01	437 11 6528	JARVIS, RICHARD	APPRENTICE	$ 3.65/HR	22	$ 80.30	$ 2.41	$ 0.55	$ 6.73	$ 9.69	$ 70.61
01	624 55 9502	MCGARRY, ANNA	STANDARD	$ 8.30/HR	48	$398.40	$ 45.02	$10.35	$ 6.73	$ 62.10	$336.30
01	566 31 5679	PETRUSKA, ANGELA	ASS'T MGR.	$ 6.50/HR	52	$378.00	$ 42.71	$ 9.82	$ 9.14	$ 61.67	$316.33
01	147 52 3318	SILVA, GEORGE	YEARLING	$ 4.25/HR	44	$187.00	$ 8.42	$ 1.94	$11.54	$ 21.90	$165.10
01	419 61 7752	ULMANN, SUSAN	STANDARD	$ 7.30/HR	50	$365.00	$ 35.77	$ 8.23	$ 8.65	$ 52.65	$312.35
05	312 31 7593	CROUCH, JOAN	YEARLING	$ 5.10/HR	40	$204.00	$ 20.40	$ 4.69	$ 9.14	$ 34.23	$169.77
05	299 21 7365	CZARNECKI, STANLEY	STANDARD	$ 5.75/HR	50	$287.50	$ 11.50	$ 2.65	$11.54	$ 25.69	$261.81
05	415 81 7943	DAILEY, MARSHA	BEGINNER	$ 3.90/HR	35	$136.50	$ 10.24	$ 2.36	$ 6.73	$ 19.33	$117.17
05	375 44 3176	HAMMOND, GAIL	STANDARD	$ 7.30/HR	48	$350.40	$ 34.34	$ 7.90	$ 8.65	$ 50.89	$299.51
05	622 50 6073	HILL, MICHAEL	STORE MGR.	$300.00/WK		$300.00	$ 25.50	$ 5.87	$11.54	$ 42.91	$257.09
05	519 37 8294	KALIN, OLIVIA	APPRENTICE	$ 3.65/HR	20	$ 73.00	$ 2.19	$ 0.50	$ 6.73	$ 9.42	$ 63.58
05	473 64 9512	LACOURSE, IRENE	ASS'T MGR.	$ 9.50/HR	54	$553.00	$ 59.17	$13.61	$11.54	$ 84.32	$468.68
05	481 32 2217	NESTOR, ELEANOR	STANDARD	$ 9.50/HR	45	$427.50	$ 36.77	$ 8.46	$11.54	$ 56.77	$370.73
05	367 11 3215	PERNAL, RICHARD	BEGINNER	$ 4.25/HR	35	$148.75	$ 11.16	$ 2.57	$ 6.73	$ 20.46	$128.29
05	326 52 3966	RIANNA, MILDRED	ASS'T MGR.	$ 7.30/HR	58	$453.40	$ 48.97	$11.26	$ 8.65	$ 68.88	$384.52
10	374 47 6512	AMBROSE, GUS	STANDARD	$ 5.75/HR	50	$287.50	$ 23.00	$ 5.29	$11.54	$ 39.83	$247.67
10	526 93 4075	AUDET, LILLIAN	STORE MGR.	$600.00/WK		$600.00	$ 67.80	$15.59	$11.54	$ 94.93	$505.07
10	572 16 2344	BOUVIER, DIANNE	APPRENTICE	$ 3.65/HR	22	$ 80.30	$ 2.41	$ 0.55	$ 6.73	$ 9.69	$ 70.61
10	493 04 3217	DANIELS, JULIA	YEARLING	$ 4.60/HR	45	$207.00	$ 20.70	$ 4.76	$ 9.14	$ 34.60	$172.40
10	468 20 1726	DONALDSON, MARC	ASS'T MGR.	$ 8.30/HR	55	$491.50	$ 53.08	$12.21	$ 8.65	$ 73.94	$417.56
10	552 97 4388	GALLIGAN, FRANCIS	BEGINNER	$ 4.25/HR	30	$127.50	$ 9.56	$ 2.20	$ 9.14	$ 20.90	$106.60
10	519 64 1139	HEIMER, CYNTHIA	ASS'T MGR.	$ 7.30/HR	52	$419.60	$ 36.09	$ 8.30	$11.54	$ 55.93	$363.67
10	481 97 5521	KENNEY, MARTIN	APPRENTICE	$ 3.65/HR	18	$ 65.70	$ 1.97	$ 0.45	$ 6.73	$ 9.15	$ 56.55
10	319 25 3744	KOPECKY, AGNES	BEGINNER	$ 4.25/HR	34	$144.50	$ 10.84	$ 2.49	$ 6.73	$ 20.06	$124.44
10	323 69 3173	LAVIN, YVONNE	STANDARD	$ 8.30/HR	48	$398.40	$ 39.04	$ 8.98	$ 8.65	$ 56.67	$341.73

REPORT DATE: 10 FEBRUARY 1989 PAGE 2

MONSTER BURGER STORES

PAYROLL REPORT

STORE	SSN	NAME	CLASS	PAY RATE	HRS	GROSS EARNINGS	FEDERAL TAX	STATE TAX	INS PREM	TOTAL DED	NET EARNINGS
10	519 73 2561	MAGUIRE, JAMES	ASS'T MGR.	$ 9.50/HR	58	$576.00	$ 40.32	$ 9.27	$11.54	$ 61.13	$514.87
10	540 52 5640	RAINVILLE, SHARON	STANDARD	$ 8.30/HR	46	$381.80	$ 43.14	$ 9.92	$ 9.14	$ 62.20	$319.60
10	307 23 1962	TOURTELLOT, MARJORIE	STANDARD	$ 7.30/HR	50	$365.00	$ 35.77	$ 8.23	$11.54	$ 55.54	$309.46
20	379 44 3987	ALMEIDA, PAULA	BEGINNER	$ 4.25/HR	35	$148.75	$ 11.16	$ 2.57	$ 9.14	$ 22.87	$125.88
20	446 22 5388	BLAIR, CYNTHIA	ASS'T MGR.	$ 7.30/HR	52	$409.60	$ 40.14	$ 9.23	$11.54	$ 60.91	$348.69
20	470 15 6712	BRIEN, RAYMOND	STANDARD	$ 7.30/HR	54	$394.20	$ 38.63	$ 8.88	$11.54	$ 59.05	$335.15
20	510 02 5113	GAGNON, GERARD	APPRENTICE	$ 3.65/HR	22	$ 80.30	$ 2.41	$ 0.55	$ 6.73	$ 9.69	$ 70.61
20	304 77 2224	HEALEY, NAOMI	ASS'T MGR.	$ 8.30/HR	55	$481.50	$ 57.78	$13.29	$ 9.14	$ 80.21	$401.29
20	566 19 7327	LAPIERRE, GARY	YEARLING	$ 4.25/HR	40	$170.00	$ 12.75	$ 2.93	$ 9.14	$ 24.82	$145.18
20	440 15 5771	MCELROY, ROSE MARIE	STORE MGR.	$525.00/WK		$525.00	$ 56.18	$12.92	$11.54	$ 80.64	$444.36
20	362 79 9176	NELSON, PETER	BEGINNER	$ 3.90/HR	34	$132.60	$ 9.95	$ 2.29	$ 6.73	$ 18.97	$113.63
20	501 22 7532	PALUMBO, ROSE	STANDARD	$ 9.50/HR	45	$427.50	$ 36.77	$ 8.46	$11.54	$ 56.77	$370.73
20	549 66 3412	RAGOSTA, TERRY	STANDARD	$ 5.10/HR	50	$255.00	$ 25.50	$ 5.87	$ 6.73	$ 38.10	$216.90
20	409 55 4662	STUDLEY, SANDRA	YEARLING	$ 5.10/HR	40	$204.00	$ 20.40	$ 4.69	$ 9.14	$ 34.23	$169.77
20	505 20 0792	TOUPIN, ADA	ASS'T MGR.	$ 7.30/HR	55	$436.50	$ 42.78	$ 9.84	$11.54	$ 64.16	$372.34
30	265 34 6992	BOOTH, JOAN	STANDARD	$ 6.50/HR	48	$312.00	$ 30.58	$ 7.03	$ 8.65	$ 46.26	$265.74
30	280 01 5447	BUNDY, LISA	ASS'T MGR.	$ 7.30/HR	52	$399.60	$ 33.97	$ 7.81	$11.54	$ 53.32	$346.28
30	319 78 9442	DEAN, MARY	STANDARD	$ 6.50/HR	50	$325.00	$ 36.73	$ 8.45	$ 6.73	$ 51.91	$273.09
30	532 66 0045	FINEMAN, ERNEST	STORE MGR.	$450.00/WK		$450.00	$ 38.70	$ 8.90	$11.54	$ 59.14	$390.86
30	494 12 3371	GARBER, JULIE	YEARLING	$ 5.10/HR	45	$229.50	$ 18.36	$ 4.22	$ 8.65	$ 31.23	$198.27
30	364 52 2332	JEFFERDS, CHARLES	ASS'T MGR.	$ 9.50/HR	55	$562.50	$ 54.56	$12.55	$11.54	$ 78.65	$483.85
30	614 11 6693	LATOUR, JOAN	BEGINNER	$ 4.25/HR	33	$140.25	$ 10.52	$ 2.42	$ 6.73	$ 19.67	$120.58
30	537 05 1635	MCDONALD, PATRICIA	APPRENTICE	$ 3.65/HR	20	$ 73.00	$ 2.19	$ 0.50	$ 6.73	$ 9.42	$ 63.58
30	444 69 7143	RABINOWICZ, MAE	STANDARD	$ 9.50/HR	48	$456.00	$ 44.69	$10.28	$11.54	$ 66.51	$389.49
30	560 77 1115	SCHERER, ANGELA	ASS'T MGR.	$ 7.30/HR	54	$424.20	$ 45.81	$10.54	$11.54	$ 67.89	$356.31
30	370 22 9876	SOFORENKO, WILLIAM	STANDARD	$ 5.10/HR	52	$265.20	$ 26.52	$ 6.10	$ 9.14	$ 41.76	$223.44
30	338 52 1873	WINSLOW, EILEEN	YEARLING	$ 4.25/HR	44	$187.00	$ 14.03	$ 3.23	$ 9.14	$ 26.40	$160.60

COMPANY TOTALS *

NO. OF EMPLOYEES: 57
GROSS EARNINGS: $17,334.50
FEDERAL TAXES: $1,598.71
STATE TAXES: $ 367.70
INS. PREMIUMS: $ 533.71
NET EARNINGS: $14,834.38

*** END OF REPORT ***

Higher-level Tables

Suppose that a table is to be defined in a program so that it can be loaded with the year's statistics for each player of each team in each league of professional basketball. The individual player's statistics include the player's name and points scored in each game played during the year. A team's statistics include the team name and the statistics for each player, and a league's statistics include the league name and statistics for each team. In order to delimit the table, suppose there are 50 games in the season, 12 players on each team, 10 teams in a league, and 2 leagues. The tasks to be addressed are the following:

1. Define the table.
2. Determine procedures to load the table.
3. Set up procedures to produce a report that lists for each league all the players who scored at least 40 points in any season game and the number of games in which this occurred.

Defining the Table

It is generally useful to draw a visual representation of the table as an aid in the conceptualization of the table's requirements. Figure 2.22 shows two different ways of representing the table. Do you see that the table is a four-dimensional table? The outermost dimension, or the most inclusive level, is the *league* level; the secondmost inclusive is the *team* level; the thirdmost inclusive is the *player* level; and the fourthmost or least inclusive is the *game* level. All table entries are necessarily subscripted, except for the table name itself. A table entry at the league level requires a single subscript. Its function is to identify the league. A table entry at the team level requires two subscripts, where the first identifies the league and the second identifies the team within that league. A table entry at the player level requires three subscripts, where the first identifies the league, the second identifies the team within that league, and the third identifies the player on that team. A table entry at the game level requires four subscripts, where the first identifies the league, the second identifies the team within that league, the third identifies the player on that team, and the fourth identifies the game number being referenced.

The table may be defined as follows:

```
01  BASKETBALL-STATS.
    05 LEAGUE-INFO  OCCURS 2 TIMES
                    INDEXED BY LEAGUE-INDEX.
       10 LEAGUE-NAME                           PIC X(20).
       10 TEAM-INFO  OCCURS 10 TIMES
                     INDEXED BY TEAM-INDEX.
          15 TEAM-NAME                          PIC X(20).
          15 PLAYER-INFO  OCCURS 12 TIMES
                          INDEXED BY PLAYER-INDEX.
             20 PLAYER-NAME                     PIC X(20).
             20 GAME  OCCURS 50 TIMES
                      INDEXED BY GAME-INDEX     PIC 99.
```

Note that each table level is indexed. Also note that one occurrence of GAME has size 2; one occurrence of PLAYER-INFO has size 120 (50 GAME occurrences and 1 PLAYER-NAME); one occurrence of TEAM-INFO has size 1,460 (12 PLAYER-INFO occurrences and 1 TEAM-NAME); one occurrence of LEAGUE-INFO has size 14,620 (10 TEAM-INFO occurrences and 1 LEAGUE-NAME), and, therefore, the size of the table is 29,240 (2 LEAGUE-INFO occurrences).

Figure 2.22 Table representations

a.

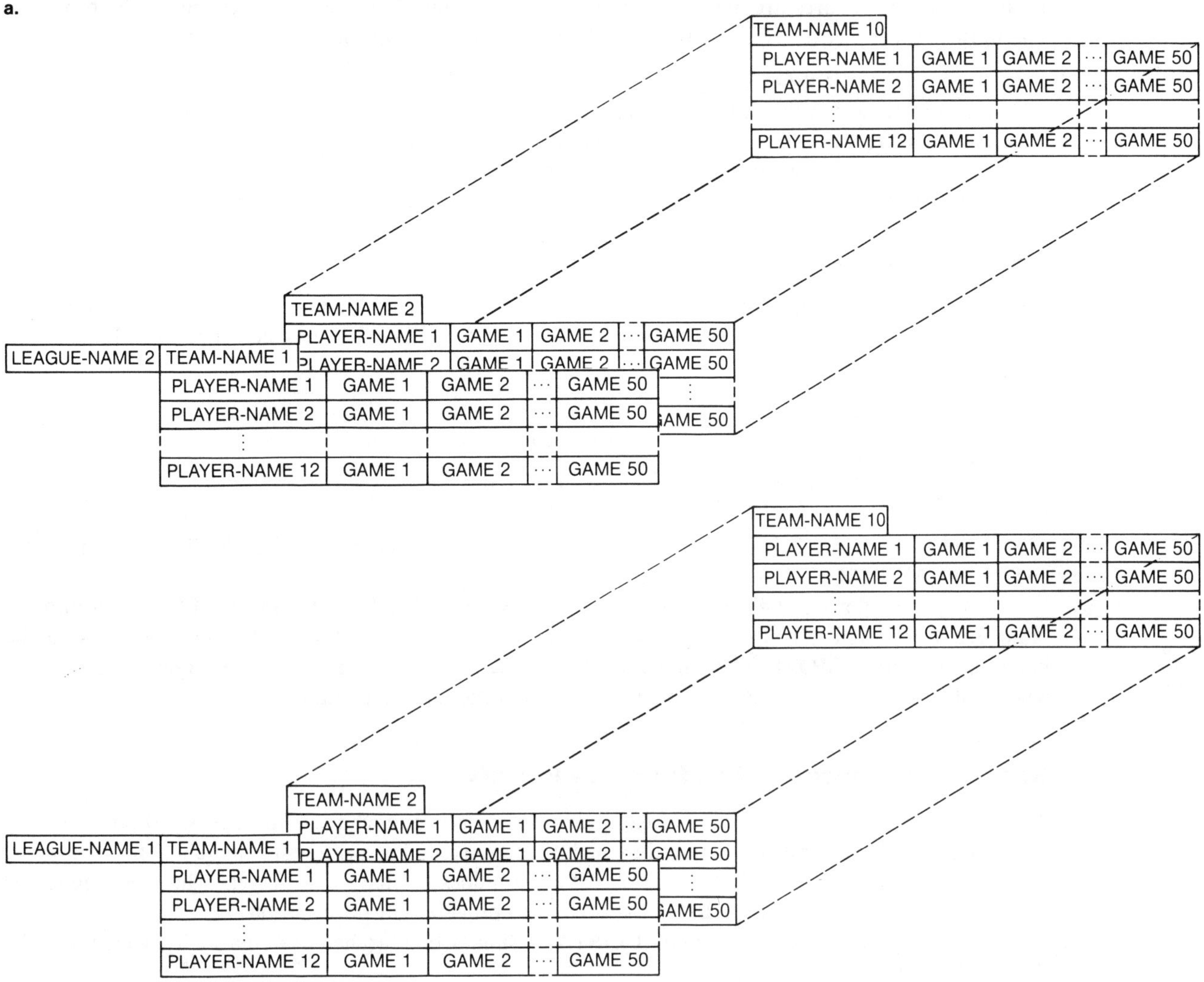

b.

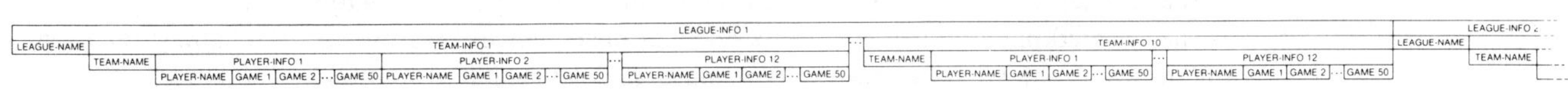

Determine Procedures to Load the Table

Table-loading procedures are always related to the way input data is made available to the program. The most natural way to sequence the records in the data file is in the following order:

1. a record that identifies a league
2. a record that identifies a team of that league
3. twelve player records, one for each member of that team; each record contains the player name and points scored in each of the 50 season games
4. the record sequence specified in items 2 and 3 repeated a total of 10 times, once for each team of the league
5. the record sequence specified in items 1, 2, 3, and 4 to provide the data for the second league.

With this organization, the data file contains three different kinds of records, for a total of 262 records. Let's call the file STATS-FILE. The records of STATS-FILE may be coded as follows:

```
01  LEAGUE-RECORD.
    05 I-LEAGUE-NAME              PIC X(20).
01  TEAM-RECORD.
    05 I-TEAM-NAME                PIC X(20).
01  PLAYER-RECORD.
    05 I-PLAYER-NAME              PIC X(20).
    05 I-GAME   OCCURS 50 TIMES   PIC 99.
```

Note that STATS-FILE contains 2 LEAGUE-RECORD records, 20 TEAM-RECORD records, and 240 PLAYER-RECORD records.

The partial flowchart shown in Figure 2.23 may be used to load the STATS-FILE data into the table BASKETBALL-STATS. As you work your way through the flowchart, keep close tabs on the indexes, and as each MOVE function is executed, check the table representation in Figure 2.22 to "see" where the data is being moved and the order in which the table is being loaded.

Set up Procedures to Produce the Report

The report must list all the players of each team in each league who scored at least 40 points in any season game and the number of games in which this occurred. The printer spacing chart for this report has been prepared in Figure 2.24. Note that if a team does not have any players who meet the stated criteria, a message line (NONE-LINE) is printed to provide that information.

Obviously, the table BASKETBALL-STATS should be searched systematically, which may be done as follows:

1. Select a league, and write LEAGUE-LINE.
2. Within the league, select one team and write TEAM-LINE.
3. For the selected team (they should be selected in sequence), pick a player.
4. For the selected player (they should be selected in sequence), examine all the games; for each game in which the points scored is 40 or more, add 1 to a game counter.
5. After examining all the games and tallying the game counter for a player, if the game counter contains a positive number, print a PLAYER-LINE on the report, and add 1 to a player counter to keep track of the number of players on that team who had one or more 40-point games.
6. Repeat steps 4 and 5 for each player of that team.
7. After examining the table entries for all the players on that team, if the player counter is still 0, print the message line NONE-LINE.
8. Repeat steps 2 through 7 for each team of the selected league.
9. Repeat steps 1 through 8 for the next league.

Figure 2.23 Loading the table BASKETBALL-STATS

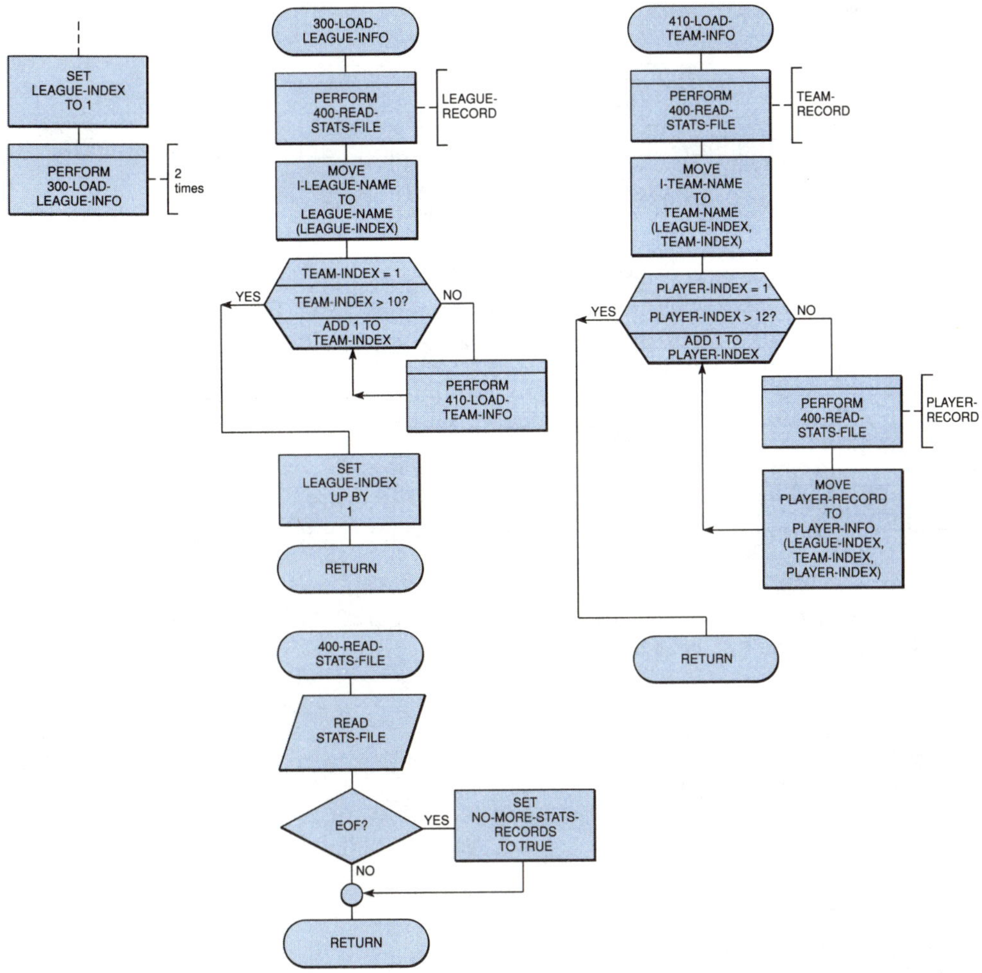

■ **Figure 2.24** Printer spacing chart for the report

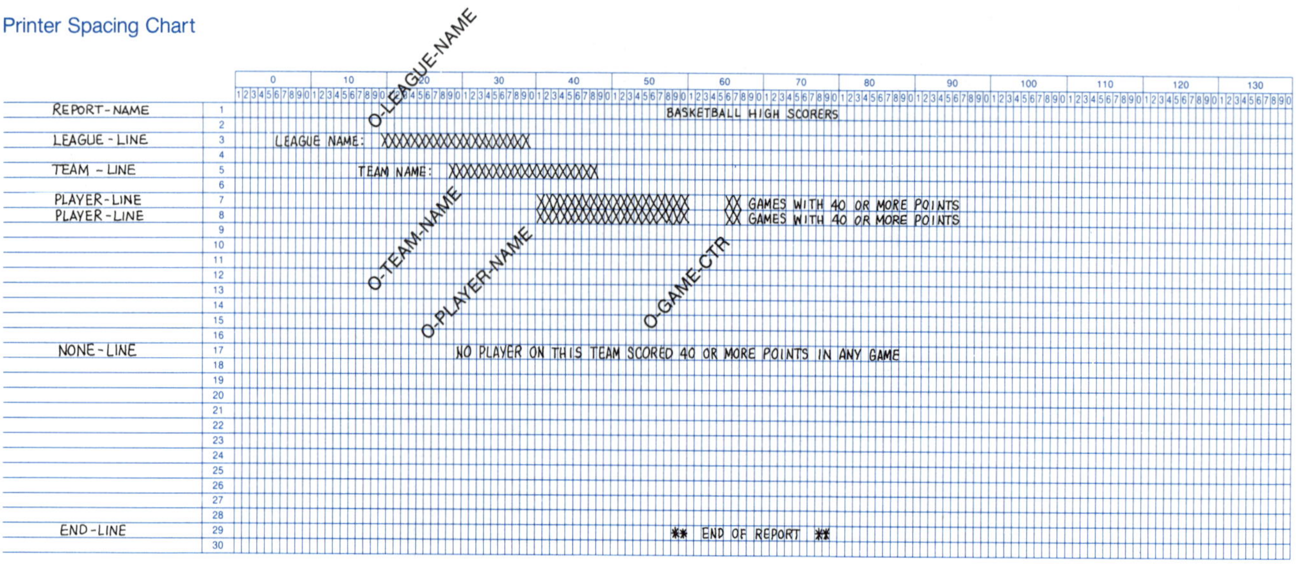

These steps are formalized in the partial flowchart shown in Figure 2.25. The coding corresponding to the partial flowchart of Figure 2.25 is as follows:

```
        .
        .
        .
        SET LEAGUE-INDEX TO 1.
        PERFORM 300-SEARCH-LEAGUE-DATA.
        .
        .
        .
    300-SEARCH-LEAGUE-DATA.
        MOVE LEAGUE-NAME(LEAGUE-INDEX) TO O-LEAGUE-NAME.
        WRITE PRINTLINE FROM LEAGUE-LINE
            AFTER ADVANCING 2 LINES.
        PERFORM 400-SEARCH-TEAM-DATA
            VARYING TEAM-INDEX FROM 1 BY 1
                UNTIL TEAM-INDEX > 10.
        SET LEAGUE-INDEX UP BY 1.
    400-SEARCH-TEAM-DATA.
        MOVE TEAM-NAME(LEAGUE-INDEX, TEAM-INDEX) TO O-TEAM-NAME.
        WRITE PRINTLINE FROM TEAM-LINE
            AFTER ADVANCING 2 LINES.
        MOVE 2 TO PROPER-SPACING.
        INITIALIZE PLAYER-CTR.
        PERFORM 500-SEARCH-PLAYER-DATA
            VARYING PLAYER-INDEX FROM 1 BY 1
                UNTIL PLAYER-INDEX > 12.
        IF PLAYER-CTR = 0
            WRITE PRINTLINE FROM NONE-LINE
                AFTER ADVANCING PROPER-SPACING
        END-IF.
    500-SEARCH-PLAYER-DATA.
        INITIALIZE GAME-CTR.
        PERFORM 600-SEARCH-GAME-DATA
            VARYING GAME-INDEX FROM 1 BY 1
                UNTIL GAME-INDEX > 50.
        IF GAME-CTR IS POSITIVE
            MOVE PLAYER-NAME(LEAGUE-INDEX, TEAM-INDEX, PLAYER-INDEX)
                 TO O-PLAYER-NAME
            MOVE GAME-CTR TO O-GAME-CTR
            WRITE PRINTLINE FROM PLAYER-LINE
                AFTER ADVANCING PROPER-SPACING
            MOVE 1 TO PROPER-SPACING
            ADD 1 TO PLAYER-CTR
        END-IF.
    600-SEARCH-GAME-DATA.
        IF GAME(LEAGUE-INDEX, TEAM-INDEX, PLAYER-INDEX, GAME-INDEX) >= 40
            ADD 1 TO GAME-CTR
        END-IF.
```

Figure 2.25 Procedures to search the table BASKETBALL-STATS

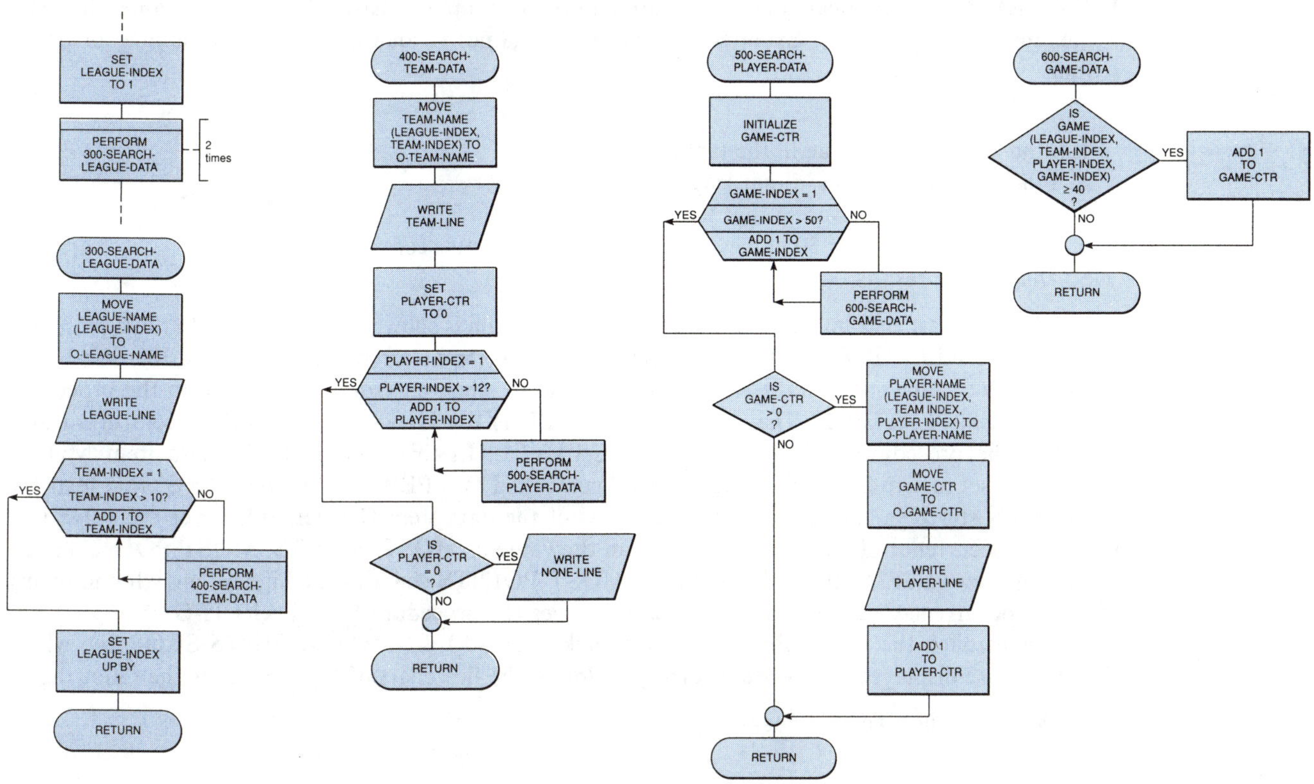

Note the nesting of the PERFORM statements. Successive PERFORMs take you one level deeper into the table. At the outermost level, only one subscript is needed to reference an item at that level, as in

```
MOVE LEAGUE-NAME(LEAGUE-INDEX) TO O-LEAGUE-NAME.
```

At the second level, two subscripts are needed to reference an item at that level, as in

```
MOVE TEAM-NAME(LEAGUE-INDEX, TEAM-INDEX) TO O-TEAM-NAME.
```

At the third level, three subscripts are needed to reference an item at that level, as in

```
MOVE PLAYER-NAME(LEAGUE-INDEX, TEAM-INDEX, PLAYER-INDEX)
    TO O-PLAYER-NAME.
```

And, at the fourth level, four subscripts are needed to reference an item at that level, as in

```
IF GAME(LEAGUE-INDEX,TEAM-INDEX,PLAYER-INDEX,GAME-INDEX) >= 40...
```

In all cases in this problem, the subscripts are the indexes defined in the INDEXED BY phrases of the table description.

Using the SEARCH Statement in Multilevel Tables

Suppose that the BASKETBALL-STATS table must be searched to find the highest number of points scored by a given player in any of the 50 season games. Let's examine some possible situations.

Situation 1

In this case, the player's team and league are known. The input consists of the league name, the team name, and the player name. Examine the player's 50 games to identify the highest number of points scored.

Solution:

1. Find the correct league in the table.
2. Find the correct team in that league.
3. Find the correct player on that team.
4. Examine the player's 50 games to select the most points scored.
5. Display the results.

The flowchart that implements the steps of the solution is shown in Figure 2.26. In the figure, note that the value of LEAGUE-INDEX is known when control is transferred to the procedure 300-SEARCH-TEAM-LEVEL; the value of TEAM-INDEX is known when control is transferred to the procedure 400-SEARCH-PLAYER-LEVEL; and the value of PLAYER-INDEX is known when control is transferred to the procedure 500-SEARCH-GAME-LEVEL. In this procedure, the data item MOST-POINTS is set to zero before entering the loop (controlled by a PERFORM-VARYING) that tests the game points stored in each of the 50 occurrences of the data item GAME. Whenever the value in a particular occurrence of GAME is greater than the value of MOST-POINTS, MOST-POINTS is assigned this new value. At the end of the loop, MOST-POINTS contains the highest entry found in any of the 50 occurrences of GAME. When control leaves the procedure 500-SEARCH-GAME-LEVEL, it returns through the intervening procedures back to 200-FIND-MOST-POINTS-SCORED, where the results are displayed. The coding corresponding to the flowchart of Figure 2.26 is the following:

```
200-FIND-MOST-POINTS-SCORED.
    SET LEAGUE-INDEX TO 1.
    SEARCH LEAGUE-INFO
        WHEN LEAGUE-NAME(LEAGUE-INDEX) = I-LEAGUE-NAME
            PERFORM 300-SEARCH-TEAM-LEVEL
    END-SEARCH.
    DISPLAY "MOST POINTS SCORED BY " I-PLAYER-NAME
            " IS " MOST-POINTS.
300-SEARCH-TEAM-LEVEL.
    SET TEAM-INDEX TO 1.
    SEARCH TEAM-INFO
        WHEN TEAM-NAME(LEAGUE-INDEX, TEAM-INDEX) = I-TEAM-NAME
            PERFORM 400-SEARCH-PLAYER-LEVEL
    END-SEARCH.
400-SEARCH-PLAYER-LEVEL.
    SET PLAYER-INDEX TO 1.
    SEARCH PLAYER-INFO
        WHEN PLAYER-NAME(LEAGUE-INDEX,TEAM-INDEX,PLAYER-INDEX)
                                                    = I-PLAYER-NAME
            PERFORM 500-SEARCH-GAME-LEVEL
    END-SEARCH.
500-SEARCH-GAME-LEVEL.
    INITIALIZE MOST-POINTS.
    PERFORM 600-TEST-GAME-POINTS
        VARYING GAME-INDEX FROM 1 BY 1
            UNTIL GAME-INDEX > 50.
600-TEST-GAME-POINTS.
    IF GAME(LEAGUE-INDEX,TEAM-INDEX,PLAYER-INDEX,GAME-INDEX) > MOST-POINTS
        MOVE GAME(LEAGUE-INDEX,TEAM-INDEX,PLAYER-INDEX,GAME-INDEX)
             TO MOST-POINTS
    END-IF.
```

Again, note that in the SEARCH statement of paragraph 200, the only value that changes is LEAGUE-INDEX, until the condition in the WHEN clause is satisfied; in the SEARCH statement of paragraph 300, the only value that changes is TEAM-INDEX, until the condition in the WHEN clause is satisfied; and in the SEARCH statement of paragraph 400, the only value that changes is PLAYER-INDEX, until the condition is satisfied. These nested SEARCH statements quickly lead to paragraph 500, where the points scored by that player in each of the 50 games are tested for the highest value. In other words, SEARCH LEAGUE-INFO finds the correct league, SEARCH TEAM-INFO finds the correct team, and SEARCH PLAYER-INFO finds the correct player, whereas the PERFORM-VARYING statement controls the testing of the 50 game occurrences for that particular player.

Figure 2.26 Searching the table BASKETBALL-STATS for a player's best game, given team and league

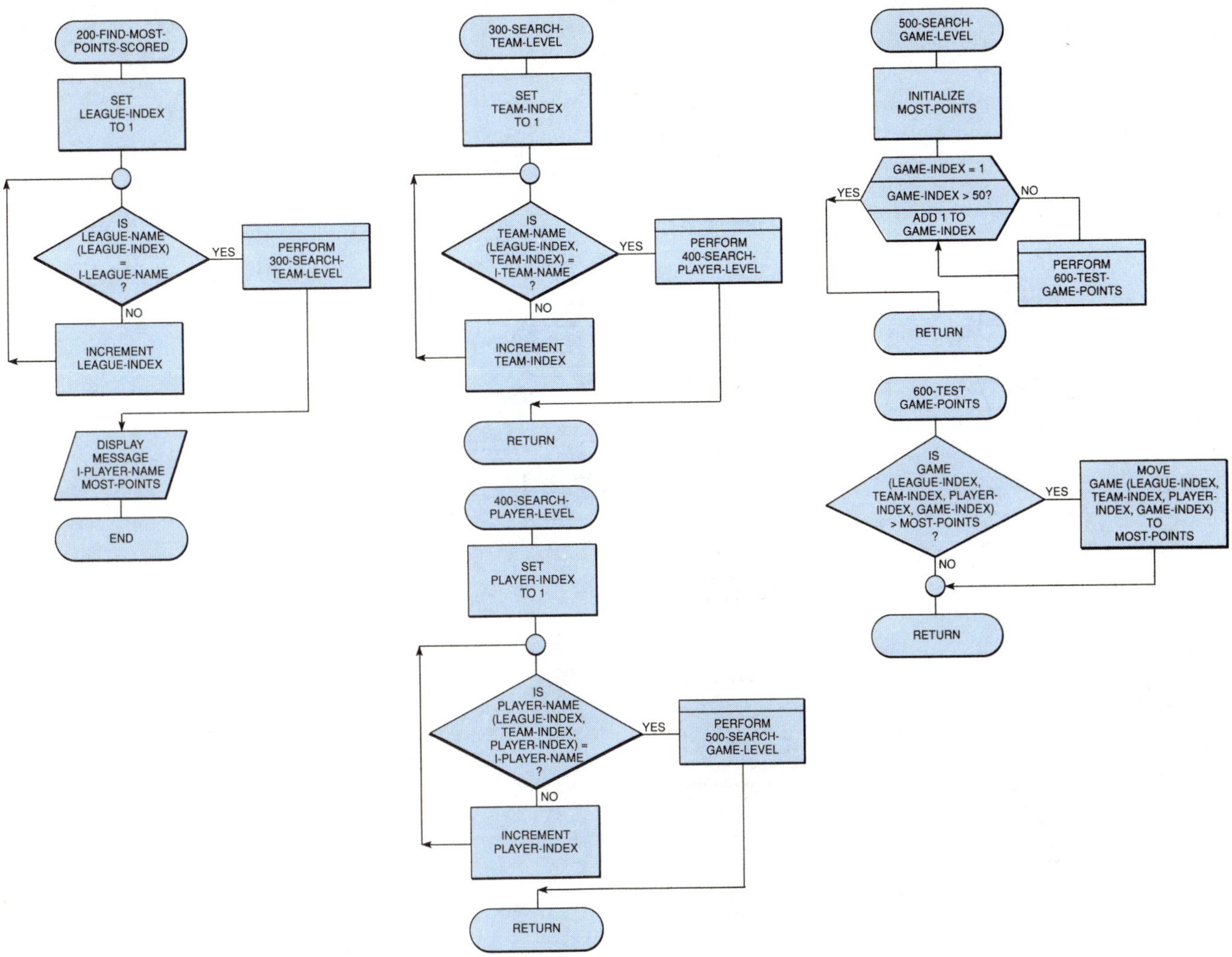

Situation 2

In this case, only the player's name is known. If the player's name is found in the table, also find the player's highest score in any of the 50 games, and provide this information as output along with the player's team and league. If the given player's name is not found in the table, display an error message to that effect.

Solution:

1. Begin with a league.
2. Within that league, select a team.
3. Examine the list of players on that team:
   a. If the given player's name is found, examine the player's 50 games to find the highest score.
   b. If the given player's name is not found, select the next team and repeat step 3.
4. If all the teams in this league have been searched without success, repeat steps 2 and 3 for the next league.
5. a. If the second league has been searched without success, display a message indicating that no such player belongs to either league.
   b. If the player's information has been found, display it.

Figure 2.27 Searching the table BASKETBALL-STATS for a player's best game

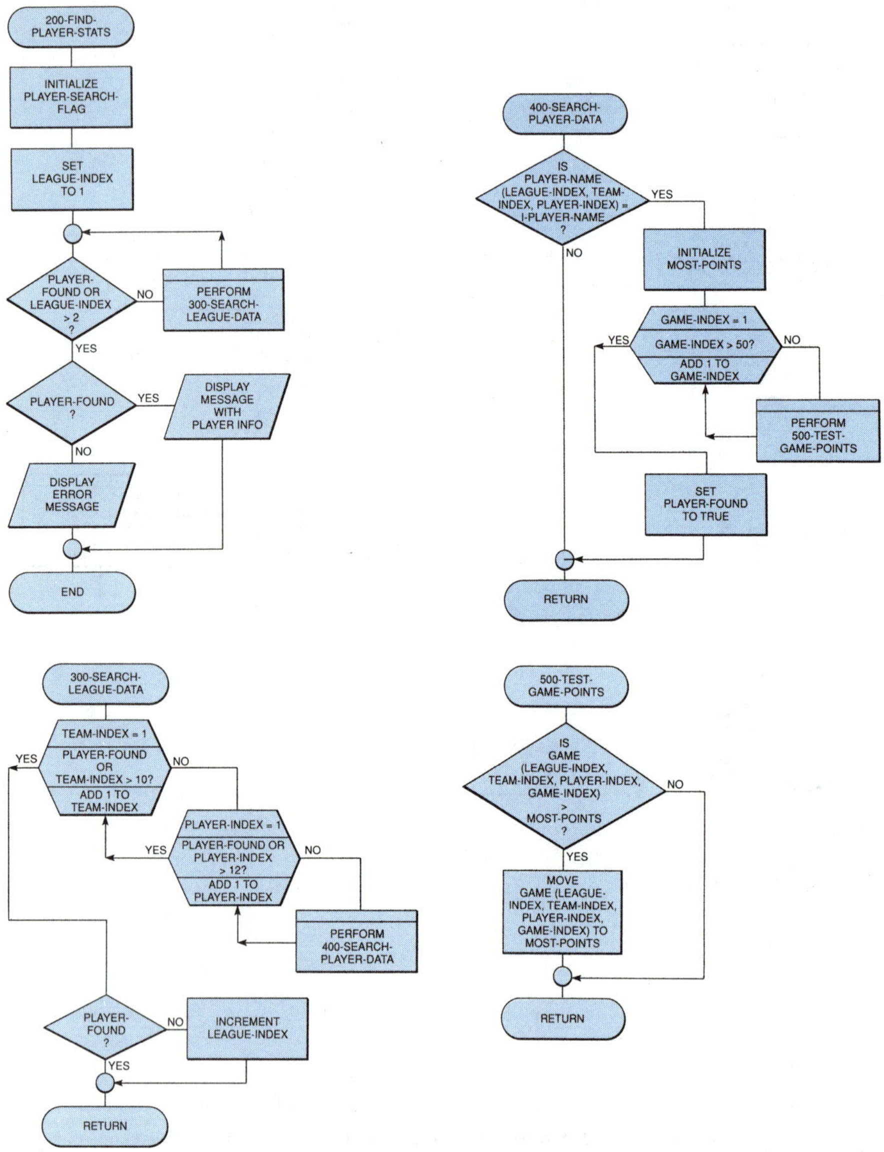

The flowchart that implements the steps of this solution is shown in Figure 2.27. Note the PERFORM-VARYING-AFTER structure in module 300-SEARCH-LEAGUE-DATA. It should be clear that when the player's name is found in module 400-SEARCH-PLAYER-DATA, a PERFORM-VARYING loop is executed to obtain the player's highest score, and then the condition-name PLAYER-FOUND will be set to TRUE. Consequently, upon returning from this module, the test in the PERFORM-VARYING-AFTER structure in module 300 is satisfied, and control will then return to module 200. But also note that both indexes, PLAYER-INDEX and TEAM-INDEX, have been incremented to one occurrence beyond the one for which the condition in module 400 was satisfied. Since the player's team must be identified as part of the output, relative indexing will be required to reference the correct team!

The coding corresponding to the flowchart of Figure 2.27 is shown below. In this coding, assume the following item descriptions:

```
         05  PLAYER-SEARCH-FLAG    PIC X(3).
             88 SEARCH-BEGINS      VALUE "NO ".
             88 PLAYER-FOUND       VALUE "YES".
     .
     .
     .
 200-FIND-PLAYER-STATS.
     SET SEARCH-BEGINS TO TRUE.
     SET LEAGUE-INDEX TO 1.
     PERFORM 300-SEARCH-LEAGUE-DATA
         UNTIL PLAYER-FOUND OR LEAGUE-INDEX > 2.
     IF PLAYER-FOUND
         DISPLAY "MOST POINTS SCORED BY " I-PLAYER-NAME
                 " IS " MOST-POINTS
         DISPLAY "HIS TEAM IS " TEAM-NAME(LEAGUE-INDEX,TEAM-INDEX - 1)
                 "OF THE " LEAGUE-NAME(LEAGUE-INDEX) " LEAGUE"
     ELSE
         DISPLAY I-PLAYER-NAME " DID NOT PLAY ON ANY TEAM OF THE "
                 LEAGUE-NAME(1) " OR " LEAGUE-NAME(2) " LEAGUE!".
 300-SEARCH-LEAGUE-DATA.
     PERFORM 400-SEARCH-PLAYER-DATA
         VARYING TEAM-INDEX FROM 1 BY 1
             UNTIL PLAYER-FOUND OR TEAM-INDEX > 10.
         AFTER PLAYER-INDEX FROM 1 BY 1
             UNTIL PLAYER-FOUND OR PLAYER-INDEX > 12.
     IF PLAYER-FOUND
         NEXT SENTENCE
     ELSE
         SET LEAGUE-INDEX UP BY 1.
 400-SEARCH-PLAYER-DATA.
     IF PLAYER-NAME(LEAGUE-INDEX,TEAM-INDEX,PLAYER-INDEX) = I-PLAYER-NAME
         INITIALIZE MOST-POINTS
         PERFORM 500-TEST-GAME-POINTS
             VARYING GAME-INDEX FROM 1 BY 1
                 UNTIL GAME-INDEX > 50
         END-PERFORM
         SET PLAYER-FOUND TO TRUE
     END-IF.
 500-TEST-GAME-POINTS.
     IF GAME(LEAGUE-INDEX,TEAM-INDEX,PLAYER-INDEX,GAME-INDEX) > MOST-POINTS
         MOVE GAME(LEAGUE-INDEX,TEAM-INDEX,PLAYER-INDEX,GAME-INDEX)
             TO MOST-POINTS
     END-IF.
```

An alternative to the logic of Figure 2.27 is shown in Figure 2.28. Assume that modules 400-SEARCH-PLAYER-DATA and 500-TEST-GAME-POINTS remain unchanged. Note that another variation of the PERFORM structure is being utilized, namely, PERFORM-VARYING-AFTER-AFTER. The coding that corresponds to the flowchart module of Figure 2.28 is the following:

```
 200-FIND-PLAYER-STATS.
     SET SEARCH-BEGINS TO TRUE.
     PERFORM 400-SEARCH-PLAYER-DATA
         VARYING LEAGUE-INDEX FROM 1 BY 1
             UNTIL PLAYER-FOUND OR LEAGUE-INDEX > 2
         AFTER TEAM-INDEX FROM 1 BY 1
             UNTIL PLAYER-FOUND OR TEAM-INDEX > 10
         AFTER PLAYER-INDEX FROM 1 BY 1
             UNTIL PLAYER-FOUND OR PLAYER-INDEX > 12.
     IF PLAYER-FOUND
         DISPLAY "MOST POINTS SCORED BY " I-PLAYER-NAME
                 " IS " MOST-POINTS
         DISPLAY "HIS TEAM IS " TEAM-NAME(LEAGUE-INDEX - 1,TEAM-INDEX - 1)
                 "OF THE " LEAGUE-NAME(LEAGUE-INDEX - 1) "LEAGUE"
     ELSE
         DISPLAY I-PLAYER-NAME " DID NOT PLAY ON ANY TEAM OF THE "
                 LEAGUE-NAME(1) " OR " LEAGUE-NAME(2) " LEAGUE!".
```

In the PERFORM statement above, note that while LEAGUE-INDEX is set to 1, TEAM-INDEX will be allowed to vary from 1 to a maximum of 10 or until the condition PLAYER-FOUND is true, and while TEAM-INDEX is set to a value, PLAYER-INDEX is allowed to vary from 1 to a maximum of 12 or until the condition PLAYER-FOUND is true. Hence, the maximum number of times the procedure 400-SEARCH-PLAYER-DATA will be executed is $2 \times 10 \times 12$, or 240 times, and, naturally, that is the number of players in the two leagues combined!

Figure 2.28 An alternative to the logic of figure 2.27

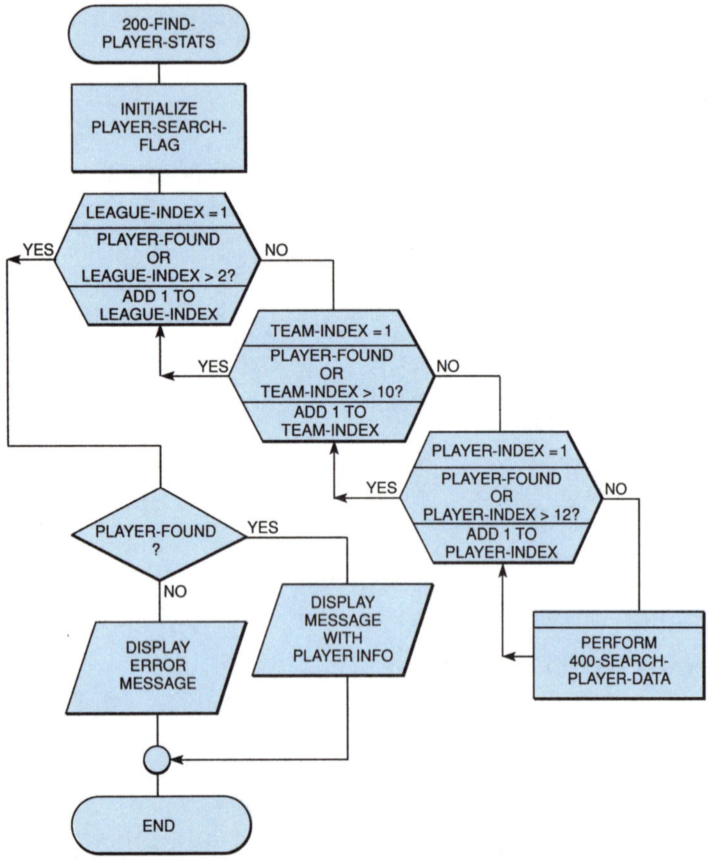

The SEARCH ALL Statement

Recall that the SEARCH statement may be used to execute a *serial search* of elements in an indexed table, regardless of the table's organization. A nonserial search known as a *binary search* is also possible if the table has sequential organization. It is executed under the control of the SEARCH ALL statement.

The SEARCH ALL statement is not as generally applicable as the SEARCH statement because of two important requirements. First, the indexed table must have sequential organization. This fact must be made explicit in the definition of the table by coding one or more KEY clauses in addition to the OCCURS clause and the INDEXED BY phrase. The KEY clauses specify whether the table elements are in ASCENDING or DESCENDING order by the values stored in the fields named in the clauses.

Second, the test in the WHEN clause must compare the search value with the value of a table element by means of a relational test of equality, or its condition-name equivalent. No such restriction exists for the tests used in the WHEN clauses of a serial SEARCH statement. For instance, the federal tax rate table in the sample program of the chapter does in fact have sequential organization. The KEY clause is ASCENDING KEY IS UPPER-LIMIT. But recall that when an employee's gross earnings amount is tested against the values in the various occurrences of UPPER-LIMIT, the needed test is

```
WHEN WS-EMPL-GROSS-EARNINGS < UPPER-LIMIT(WAGE-INDEX).
```

That is, the needed test requires the "less than" relation, and, consequently, the table cannot be searched using the SEARCH ALL statement.

As another example, consider the following INVENTORY-TABLE:

```
01  INVENTORY-TABLE.
    05 PRODUCT-INFO     OCCURS 25 TIMES
                        ASCENDING KEY IS PRODUCT-NO
                        INDEXED BY PRODUCT-INDEX.
       10 PRODUCT-NO              PIC X(8).
       10 PRODUCT-DESCR           PIC X(25).
       10 PRODUCT-PRICE           PIC 9(4)V99.
       10 QUANTITY-ON-HAND        PIC 9(4).
       10 AISLE-NO                PIC X.
       10 BIN-NO                  PIC XX.
```

Suppose the task is to search the table entries to determine the quantity on hand for a given product number, say I-PRODUCT-NO. The condition that has to be tested in the WHEN clause is

```
PRODUCT-NO(PRODUCT-INDEX) = I-PRODUCT-NO
```

for a particular value of the index PRODUCT-INDEX (that is, the needed relation is equality). And since the table is defined as an ordered table (ASCENDING KEY IS PRODUCT-NO), a binary search may be executed on this table. A statement that executes a binary search is the following:

```
SEARCH ALL PRODUCT-INFO
    WHEN PRODUCT-NO(PRODUCT-INDEX) = I-PRODUCT-NO
        MOVE QUANTITY-ON-HAND(PRODUCT-NO) TO O-QUANTITY-ON-HAND.
```

In a binary search, the value of the index is completely determined by the search routine itself. Note that the SET statement is not used to initialize the index PRODUCT-INDEX. The search routine proceeds as follows:

1. It assigns to the index the middle occurrence in the table, say 13 in this example.
2. The test is performed:
   a. If the condition is satisfied for PRODUCT-INDEX = 13, the MOVE statement is executed and control leaves the SEARCH ALL statement.
   b. If the condition is not satisfied, the search routine determines whether the search value I-PRODUCT-NO is in the upper half of the table or the lower half, based on the ordering specified in the KEY clause. If the search value is in the upper half, the lower half is disregarded for the rest of the search procedure, and the index is now assigned the middle occurrence in that portion of the table, namely 7 in this case. If the search value is in the lower half, the upper half of the table is disregarded for the rest of the search procedure, and the index is assigned the middle occurrence in that portion of the table, namely 19 in this case.
3. The condition in the WHEN clause is evaluated again for the index selected in 2b.
   a. If the condition is satisfied, the MOVE is executed and control exits from the search routine.
   b. If the condition is not satisfied, the procedure explained in 2b is repeated for the remaining portion of the table.
4. The procedures explained in steps 2 and 3 are repeated until the item is found or until the search pattern reaches the final table element without satisfying the condition in the WHEN clause. In the latter case, there is no table entry whose value is equal to I-PRODUCT-NO, that is, the search value is not a table element.

Figure 2.29 Sample INVENTORY-TABLE

1852	Parallel PC T-Switch	020500	0150	S	08
1962	Modem Cable	002625	0125	C	01
2537	Rolltop File 5.25	003995	0350	A	24
2591	Floppy Binder 5.25	002495	0112	A	22
3254	DC600A Data Cartridge	003295	0090	A	05
3264	DC2000 Data Cartridge	003495	0105	A	06
4329	Mobile Printer Stand	019900	0015	X	10
4490	Ergon. 5-Star Base Chair	012900	0040	X	15
5521	Plenum Cable 100	015200	0150	C	05
6521	Double-Shielded Cable	007550	0200	C	02
6600	Portable Vacuum	024900	0042	M	30
6644	Surge Protector	008100	0550	E	01
6728	Surge Master Power Strip	008000	0420	E	05
7336	PC Data Module Hard Drive	099500	0032	D	02
7572	Plotter Cable IBM PC	004500	0015	C	10
8006	EC-2400 Modem	074500	0085	E	20
8013	Multiplexer 5000	084500	0074	E	08
8021	Parallel Print Buffer 256	081500	0112	D	08
8043	BNC Transceiver	029500	0065	E	06
8091	25-Pin Connector	001895	0300	C	12
8405	VA Power Line Conditioner	133000	0005	E	02
8426	Back-up Power Supply	069500	0063	E	10
8511	FAX Card 4800 BPS	055900	0040	F	01
8605	IBM Power Center	013000	0175	S	05
8606	Mac Power Center	012000	0220	S	06

Examine the sample inventory table in Figure 2.29. Suppose the value of I-PRODUCT-NO is 8013, and the quantity on hand for that item must be found. When the SEARCH ALL statement is executed, the following sequence of events occurs:

1. PRODUCT-INDEX is set to 13, the middle occurrence in the table.
2. The condition PRODUCT-NO(13) = I-PRODUCT-NO is false, since PRODUCT-NO(13) = 6728, whereas I-PRODUCT-NO = 8013.
3. Since 6728 < 8013, the required table element is in the lower half of the table. The upper half of the table is therefore disregarded, and the index PRODUCT-INDEX is set to 19, the middle occurrence of the lower half.
4. The condition PRODUCT-NO(19) = I-PRODUCT-NO is false, since PRODUCT-NO(19) = 8043.
5. Since 8043 > 8013, the required table element is in the upper half of the remaining portion of the table. The entries from the nineteenth to the twenty-fifth occurrence are now disregarded, and the index PRODUCT-INDEX is set to 16, the middle occurrence between the fourteenth and the eighteenth, the only remaining entries still under consideration.
6. The condition PRODUCT-NO(16) = I-PRODUCT-NO is false, since PRODUCT-NO(16) = 8006.
7. Since 8006 < 8013, the upper half of the remaining portion, namely, occurrences 14 and 15, are disregarded, and PRODUCT-INDEX is set to 17, the lower of the two remaining occurrences 17 and 18.
8. The condition PRODUCT-NO(17) = I-PRODUCT-NO is true, since PRODUCT-NO(17) = 8013, the value of I-PRODUCT-NO.
9. At this point, the search ends and the statement

```
MOVE QUANTITY-ON-HAND(17) TO O-QUANTITY-ON-HAND
```

is executed, and the value 74 is copied into O-QUANTITY-ON-HAND.

The schematic in Figure 2.30 shows the effect of the binary search of the table, that is, the sequence in which portions of the table are eliminated from further consideration.

In the sequence of events enumerated above, note that the condition in the WHEN clause was evaluated four times (steps 2, 4, 6, and 8). Do you see that if a serial search had been conducted, the condition in the WHEN clause would have been tested 17 times?

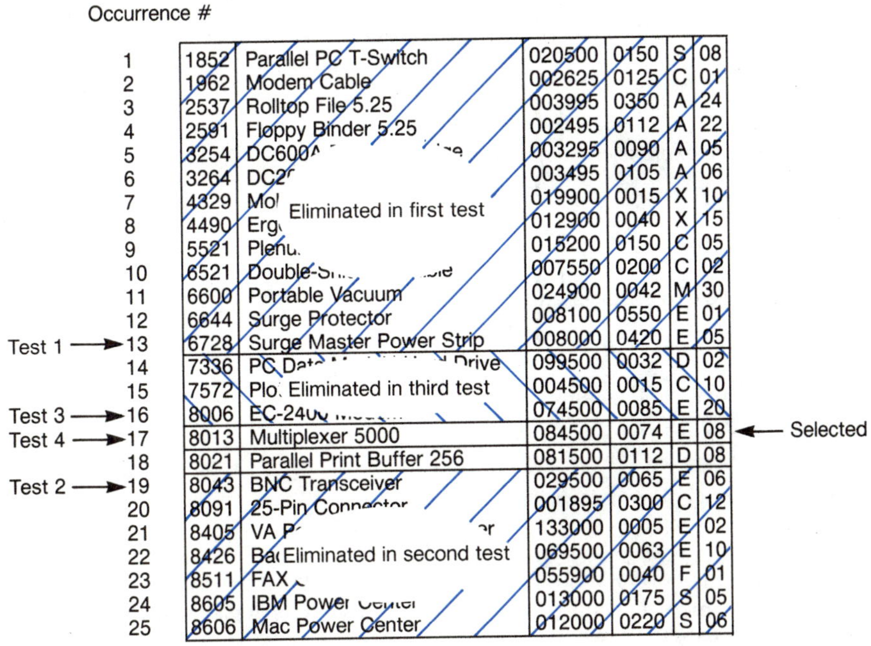

The format of the SEARCH ALL statement is shown in Figure 2.31.

Rules Governing the Use of the SEARCH ALL Statement

1. The SET statement is not used to initialize the index. The index will automatically be controlled by the search routine. It is initially set to the middle occurrence of the table entries.
2. The SEARCH ALL statement causes a nonserial, or binary, search of the table elements.
3. *Identifier-1* is a table identifier. Its description must contain an OCCURS clause with the INDEXED BY phrase, and it must also contain an ASCENDING KEY or DESCENDING KEY clause.
4. The AT END clause is optional. If used, and the condition in the WHEN clause is not satisfied for any index value, *imperative-statement-1* is executed, and control then passes to the first statement beyond the scope of the SEARCH ALL.
5. The test in the WHEN clause must be either a relational test of equality or an equivalent condition-name test.
   a. If the test in the WHEN clause is a relational test, *data-name-1* must be an indexed data item named in the KEY clause. The index must be the first index named in the INDEXED BY phrase. *Data-name-1* may be qualified.

      The value of *identifier-3, literal-1,* or *arithmetic-expression-1* is the search value that is tested against each selected occurrence of *data-name-1*. Neither *identifier-3* nor any data item in *arithmetic-expression-1* may be named in the KEY clause or be indexed by the first index named in the INDEXED BY phrase.
   b. If the test in the WHEN clause is a condition-name test, *condition-name* must be defined as corresponding to only one value, and the associated data item must be named in the KEY clause.
6. If *data-name-1* is not the first data item in the KEY clause, all preceding data items must also be referenced in tests within the WHEN clause.
7. The test in the WHEN clause may be a conjunctive compound test, that is, two or more tests connected by AND.
8. When the test in the WHEN clause is satisfied, *imperative-statement-2* or NEXT SENTENCE is executed. In either case, control is then passed to the first statement beyond the scope of SEARCH ALL, and the index name retains the value for which the test was satisfied.

Figure 2.31 SEARCH ALL statement format

```
SEARCH ALL identifier-1
    [AT END imperative-statement-1]

         { data-name-1 {IS EQUAL TO} {identifier-3            } }
    WHEN {             {IS =       } {literal-1               } }
         {                           {arithmetic-expression-1 } }
         { condition-name-1                                     }

 [       { data-name-2 {IS EQUAL TO} {identifier-4            } } ]
 [ AND   {             {IS =       } {literal-2               } } ] . . .
 [       {                           {arithmetic-expression-2 } } ]
 [       { condition-name-2                                     } ]

    {imperative-statement-2}
    {NEXT SENTENCE         }

    [END-SEARCH]
```

9. If the test in the WHEN clause is never satisfied and the AT END clause is not used, control will simply pass to the first statement beyond the scope of the SEARCH ALL, and the value of the index name is then unpredictable.
10. If *identifier-1* is subordinate to a data item that contains an OCCURS clause, it must be followed by an index name associated with each dimension of the table through the dimension to which it belongs. In that case, the SEARCH ALL statement varies only the index associated with the dimension to which it belongs.
11. If more than one index name is specified in the INDEXED BY phrase, only the first index-name values are manipulated by the search routine. The others remain unchanged.
12. The binary search yields predictable results only if the table elements are in fact ordered as specified by the KEY clauses.

Example

As another example of the use of the SEARCH ALL statement, consider expanding INVENTORY-TABLE to two levels, as follows:

```
01  INVENTORY-TABLE-2.
    05 WAREHOUSE-INFO  OCCURS 4 TIMES
                       ASCENDING KEY IS WAREHOUSE-ID
                       INDEXED BY WH-INDEX.
       10 WAREHOUSE-ID          PIC X(4).
       10 PRODUCT-INFO   OCCURS 1000 TIMES
                         ASCENDING KEY IS PRODUCT-NO
                         INDEXED BY PRODUCT-INDEX.
          15 PRODUCT-NO         PIC X(4).
          15 PRODUCT-DESCR      PIC X(25).
          15 PRODUCT-PRICE      PIC 9(4)V99.
          15 QUANTITY-ON-HAND   PIC 9(4).
          15 AISLE-NO           PIC X.
          15 BIN-NO             PIC XX.
```

Note that the table description accounts for four warehouses, that warehouse data is stored in ascending order by WAREHOUSE-ID value, that each warehouse stocks 1000 different products, and that the products are listed in the table in ascending order by PRODUCT-NO value. The task is to search the table to find the quantity on hand in each warehouse for a particular product number, keep track of the resulting total count, and produce a simple report listing the search results.

Suppose that I-PRODUCT-NO is the product for which the information is needed, and that WS-TOTAL-QUANTITY, O-WAREHOUSE-ID, O-QUANTITY-ON-HAND, O-TOTAL-QUANTITY, WAREHOUSE-LINE, and TOTAL-LINE are properly defined items. Examine the partial flowchart in Figure 2.32, and the corresponding coding below.

■ **Figure 2.32** Searching a two-level table—example

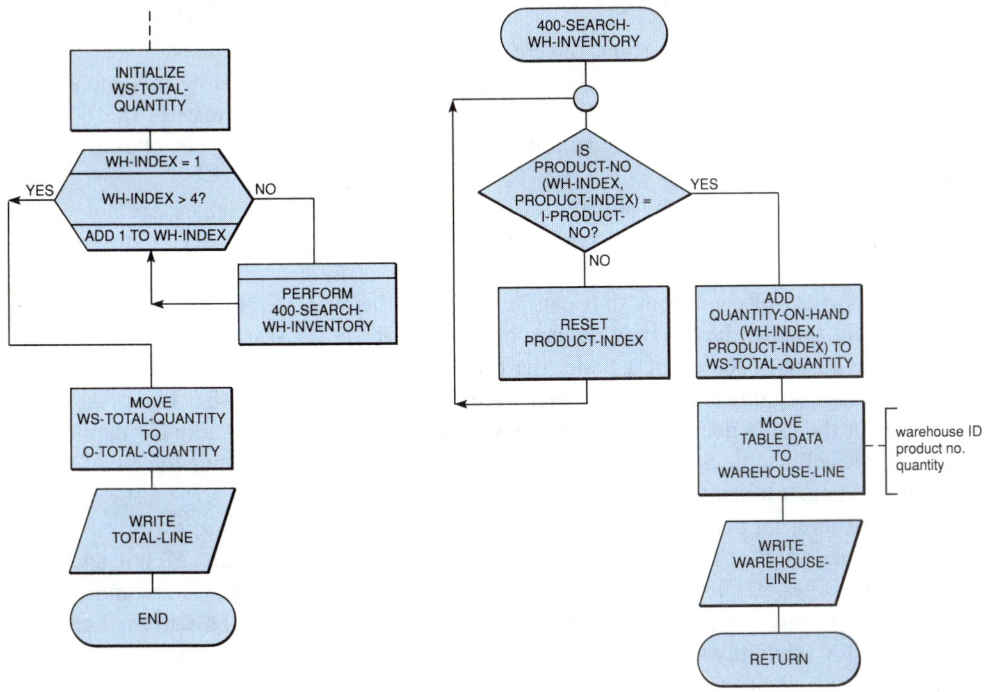


```
    INITIALIZE WS-TOTAL-QUANTITY.
    PERFORM 400-SEARCH-WH-INVENTORY
        VARYING WH-INDEX FROM 1 BY 1
            UNTIL WH-INDEX > 4.
    MOVE WS-TOTAL-QUANTITY TO O-TOTAL-QUANTITY.
    WRITE PRINTLINE FROM TOTAL-LINE
        AFTER ADVANCING 3 LINES.
400-SEARCH-WH-INVENTORY.
    SEARCH ALL PRODUCT-INFO
        WHEN PRODUCT-NO(WH-INDEX, PRODUCT-INDEX) = I-PRODUCT-NO
            ADD QUANTITY-ON-HAND(WH-INDEX, PRODUCT-INDEX)
                TO WS-TOTAL-QUANTITY
            MOVE WAREHOUSE-ID(WH-INDEX) TO O-WAREHOUSE-ID
            MOVE I-PRODUCT-NO TO O-PRODUCT-NO
            MOVE QUANTITY-ON-HAND(WH-INDEX, PRODUCT-INDEX)
                TO O-QUANTITY-ON-HAND
            WRITE PRINTLINE FROM WAREHOUSE-LINE
                AFTER ADVANCING 2 LINES
    END-SEARCH.
```

Note that the PERFORM-VARYING statement selects the first-level occurrence, that is, a particular warehouse, whereas the SEARCH ALL statement examines the table elements at the second level, that is, the product-ids in that warehouse's inventory. Also note that the table element being referenced in the WHEN clause requires as many indexes as there are dimensions associated with the level to which the element belongs. Specifically, PRODUCT-NO belongs to the second level of the table and therefore requires two indexes, WH-INDEX and PRODUCT-INDEX. However, the only index controlled by the SEARCH ALL statement is PRODUCT-INDEX, that is, the index associated with the table level being searched.

SEARCH Versus SEARCH ALL

Following are some guidelines for determining whether to use SEARCH or SEARCH ALL:

1. Unless a table has sequential organization, the SEARCH statement must be used.
2. If a table has sequential organization, that is, its elements are ordered according to some key, either the SEARCH or the SEARCH ALL may be used, provided that the tests in the WHEN clauses of the SEARCH ALL statement are relational tests of equality or corresponding condition-name tests.
3. If a table has sequential organization, but the tests needed in the WHEN clauses are not relational tests of equality (or equivalent condition-name tests), only the SEARCH statement may be used.
4. There is a greater variety of conditions that can be tested in the WHEN clauses of the SEARCH statement than in the WHEN clauses of the SEARCH ALL statement.
5. In order to execute a binary search of a table, the programmer must be certain that the values in the table are in fact organized in the sequence specified by the KEY clauses. The presence of the KEY clauses in the table definition does not ensure internal ordering of table elements.
6. If the characteristics of a table and of search procedures allow the use of either the SEARCH or the SEARCH ALL statements,
   a. Due to required internal preparations for the SEARCH ALL statement, it is a more efficient procedure only for fairly large tables, say tables containing at least 50 entries.
   b. For fairly short tables, say fewer than 50 entries, the SEARCH statement is recommended.
7. If we assume a serial search of a table containing n elements, the table will be searched on average $n/2$ times for randomly selected values. That is, 50 percent of the time the element will be found in the lower half of the table, and 50 percent of the time in the upper half. If the table has 1000 elements, on average it will be searched 500 times before the correct entry is found.
8. If we assume a binary search of a table containing n elements for randomly selected values, the table will be searched at most x times, where 2^x is the smallest power of 2 greater than n. That is, the table size is reduced by a factor of 2 every time the test is not satisfied. If the table has 1000 elements, it will be searched no more than 10 times, since $2^{10} = 1024$.

Both searches are carried out exceedingly fast, so using the binary search is more worthwhile only when used on large tables.

Important Terms in Chapter 2

ASCENDING KEY
binary search
defining an index
DESCENDING KEY
direct referencing
END-SEARCH
index
index data item
INDEXED BY
indexed table
indexing
initializing an index
loading an indexed table
nested OCCURS
SEARCH
SEARCH ALL
search value
searching an indexed table
serial search
SET
SET . . . DOWN BY
SET . . . UP BY
subscripted data name
subscripting
USAGE IS INDEX
varying an index

Exercises

1. a. A hard-coded table must contain the names of the days of the week. Code it as an indexed table in such a way that the correct value can be retrieved by using the digit supplied by the phrase FROM DAY-OF-WEEK when an appropriate ACCEPT statement is executed.
   b. Code an appropriate ACCEPT statement to obtain from the operating system the current day's ordinal number. Also define the data item you specify in the ACCEPT statement so that it can be assigned to the index specified for the table in part a.
   c. Use your work in parts a and b to write the statements needed to assign the correct value to the field O-REPORT-DAY of an output record. Use the table's index.

2. A file called METER-FILE contains records that must be loaded into an indexed table. Each record contains a meter number and a customer number. Assume the meter number is 8 digits long and the customer number is 6 digits long.
   a. Code an appropriate input record description.
   b. Code an appropriate table description so that it can store the contents of 30 records.
   c. Design the logic needed to load the table. Use the table's index.
   d. Code the statements corresponding to your logic of part c.
3. Suppose that the table in exercise 2 has been loaded, and it must now be searched for the customer number that corresponds to an input meter number, say INPUT-METER-NO. When it is found, it must be stored in the field O-CUSTOMER-NO.
   a. Design the logic needed to search the table using a PERFORM-VARYING statement. Use the flag METER-TABLE-FLAG whose definition is

```
05 METER-TABLE-FLAG    PIC X(3).
   88 BEGIN-LOOK-UP              VALUE "NO ".
   88 STOP-LOOK-UP               VALUE "YES".
```

   b. Code the statements corresponding to your logic in part a.
   c. Design the logic needed to search the table using the SEARCH statement.
   d. Code the statements corresponding to the logic in part c.
4. Suppose the two tables described below have been loaded. Code statements as required in parts a and b that will compute the total number of kilowatt-hours used by the customer whose meter number is specified by I-METER-NO, and store the value in WS-KWH-USAGE.

```
01  LAST-MONTH-METER-READINGS.
    05 LM-METER-INFO OCCURS 30 TIMES
                     ASCENDING KEY IS LM-METER-NO
                     INDEXED BY LM-METER-INDEX.
       10 LM-METER-NO        PIC X(8).
       10 LM-METER-READING   PIC 9(5).
01  CURRENT-METER-READINGS.
    05 CURRENT-METER-INFO  OCCURS 30 TIMES
                           ASCENDING KEY IS METER-NO
                           INDEXED BY METER-INDEX.
       10 METER-NO           PIC X(8).
       10 METER-READING      PIC 9(5).
```

   a. Use a SEARCH ALL or a SEARCH statement without the VARYING phrase.
   b. Use a SEARCH statement with the VARYING phrase.
5. Suppose that an electric company charges its customers according to the schedule listed below.

KWH Usage Not More Than (Level Maximums)	Winter Charges November through June Base in dollars	: Rate*	Summer Charges July through October Base in dollars	: Rate*
20	2.68	: 0	2.77	: 0
50	2.68	: 10.040	2.77	: 10.543
200	5.692	: 7.986	5.9329	: 8.4487
550	17.671	: 5.135	18.6634	: 5.636
2000	35.6435	: 6.437	38.3894	: 6.937
99999	128.98	: 6.159	138.9759	: 6.660

*In cents per KWH in excess of previous level maximum.

   a. Provide an appropriate table description. Since the base charge is in dollars and cents, express the rates also in dollars and cents. For instance, 10.040 cents/KWH is .10040 dollars/KWH. Specify an index for each level.
   b. Suppose that the number of kilowatt-hours used is stored in the field WS-KWH-USAGE, and the month number for which the customer's charge must be computed is in the field WS-MONTH-NO. Use your table description in part a and code statements to compute the charge. Store the charge in the field WS-CUSTOMER-CHARGE.
6. Assume that the table below has been loaded with values. Code statements that would add 5 percent to each sales amount in the table. Define any needed data items.

```
01  STORE-TABLE-1.
    05 STORE-NO-1       PIC X(5).
    05 MONTH-SALES-1    OCCURS 12 TIMES
                        INDEXED BY STORE-1-INDEX
                        PIC 9(6)V99.
```

7. Use the table description of exercise 6 and the following table description and record description to complete the exercise which follows:

```
01  STORE-TABLE-2.
    05 STORE-NO-2      PIC X(5).
    05 MONTH-SALES-2   OCCURS 12 TIMES
                       INDEXED BY STORE-2-INDEX
                       PIC 9(6)V99.
01  SALES-LINE.
    05                         PIC X(13).
    05 O-STORE-1-SALES         PIC $Z(5)9.99.
    05                         PIC X(12).
    05 O-STORE-2-SALES         PIC $Z(5).99.
    05                         PIC X(12).
    05 O-TOTAL-MONTH-SALES     PIC $Z(6)9.99.
    05                         PIC X(12).
```

A SALES-LINE must be printed on a report for each of the twelve months. Each line must print the sales for each store and the total sales for the two stores. Code the needed statements.

8. Code a two-level indexed table that could be used to store the sales for each month of the year for each of two stores. (That is, define a two-level table to replace the 2 one-level tables in exercises 6 and 7.)

9. Use your table description in exercise 8 and code statements that would increase the stored sales amounts for each of the 12 months for each store by 5 percent.

10. Use your table description in exercise 8 and the description of SALES-LINE in exercise 7. Code statements to print, for each month, the sales for each store and the total sales for the two stores.

11. Given a store number I-STORE-NO and a month number I-MONTH-NO. Use your table description in exercise 8 and code statements to search the table for the corresponding sales amount. Store the value in the field O-MONTH-SALES.

Debugging Activities

1. Given the following list of transaction codes and descriptions.

Transaction Code	Transaction Type
01	Cash & Carry
02	Charge & Carry
03	Charge & Deliver
04	Deliver COD
05	Layaway
06	Return for Cash
07	Return for Credit
08	Return/Exchange
09	Damaged

The data must be hard-coded into a table. A student provided the following description:

```
                                                    Col. 72
                                                         :
01  TRANSACTION-TABLE  VALUE "01CASH & CARRY02CHARGE& CARRY03CHAR
-   "GE & DELIVER04DELIVER COD05LAYAWAY06RETURN FOR CASH07RETURN
-   "FOR CREDIT08RETURN/EXCHANGE09DAMAGED".
    05 TRANS-INFO  OCCURS 9 TIMES
                   ASCENDING KEY IS WS-CODE
                   INDEXED BY TRANS-INDEX.
       10 WS-TRANS-CODE    PIC X(2).
       10 WS-TRANS-TYPE    PIC X(17).
```

Identify and correct the errors.

2. The purpose of the program in the following listing is to produce a two-level activity report for the previous week for the Express Auto Parts Warehouse Company. Each transaction has been recorded on a transaction record by entering the part number purchased, the quantity purchased, and the transaction code. The transaction file is shown below, and the transaction codes and corresponding transaction types are hard-coded in the table TRANSACTION-TABLE.

The program must load the table CATALOG-TABLE from the records in the CATALOG-FILE. Those records are listed below.

At the first level, the report must contain a detail line corresponding to each transaction. It must identify the part number, the part description, the quantity purchased, and the type of transaction (not its code!).

At the second level, the total number of transactions for each type of transaction must be printed. For this purpose, the program must define a table of counters, one for each type of transaction.

Your task is to correct the syntax errors contained in the program.

Program Listing

```
EXPRESS-ACTIVITY-DBG               1-Mar-1989 13:30:03    VAX COBOL V4.2-40                 Page   1
Source Listing                     1-Mar-1989 13:29:58    [PAQUETTEG.CHAPTER2]V2C3DBG1.COB;3 (1)

       IDENTIFICATION DIVISION.

       PROGRAM-ID.  EXPRESS-ACTIVITY-DBG.

      ****************************************************************
      *                                                              *
      *  AUTHOR.        PAQUETTE.                                    *
      *  DATE WRITTEN.  MARCH 1989                                   *
      *                                                              *
      ****************************************************************

       ENVIRONMENT DIVISION.

       CONFIGURATION SECTION.

       SOURCE-COMPUTER.  VAX-VMS-8650.
       OBJECT-COMPUTER.  VAX-VMS-8650.

       INPUT-OUTPUT SECTION.

       FILE-CONTROL.
           SELECT  CATALOG-FILE       ASSIGN TO CATALOGDATA.
           SELECT  TRANSACTION-FILE   ASSIGN TO COB$INPUT.
           SELECT  ACTIVITY-REPORT    ASSIGN TO COB$OUTPUT.

       DATA DIVISION.

       FILE SECTION.

       FD  CATALOG-FILE
           RECORD CONTAINS 30 CHARACTERS.

       01  CATALOG-RECORD.
           05 I-PART-NO          PIC X(5).
           05 I-PART-DESCR       PIC X(20).
           05 I-UNIT-PRICE       PIC 999V99.

       FD  TRANSACTION-FILE
           RECORD CONTAINS 11 CHARACTERS.

       01  TRANSACTION-RECORD.
           05 I-TRANS-PART-NO  PIC X(5).
           05 I-TRANS-QUANTITY PIC 9(4).
           05 I-TRANS-CODE     PIC XX.

       FD  ACTIVITY-REPORT
           RECORD CONTAINS 133 CHARACTERS.

       01  PRINTLINE           PIC X(133).

       WORKING-STORAGE SECTION.

       01  WS-REPORT-DATE      PIC X(6).

       01  PROGRAM-CONTROLS.
           05 WS-MORE-TRANS-RECORDS       PIC XXX.
              88 THERE-IS-A-TRANS-RECORD           VALUE "YES".
```

```
EXPRESS-ACTIVITY-DBG                1-Mar-1989 13:30:03    VAX COBOL V4.2-40                    Page   2
Source Listing                      1-Mar-1989 13:29:58    [PAQUETTEG.CHAPTER2]V2C3DBG1.COB;3 (1)

                     88 NO-MORE-TRANS-RECORDS           VALUE "NO ".
                  05 WS-MORE-CATALOG-RECORDS    PIC XXX.
                     88 NO-MORE-CAT-RECORDS             VALUE "NO ".
                  05 WS-LINE-CTR                PIC S99.
                     88 PAGE-IS-FULL                    VALUE 40.
                  05 WS-PROPER-SPACING          PIC 9.
                  05 WS-PAGE-NO                 PIC S99.
              01  PROGRAM-TABLES.
                  05 CATALOG-TABLE.
                     10 CAT-ITEM-INFO OCCURS 50 TIMES
                                      ASCENDING KEY WS-CAT-PART-NO.
                                      INDEXED BY CAT-INDEX.
                                      1
%COBOL-F-ERROR  117, (1) Invalid syntax
                        15 WS-CAT-PART-NO       PIC X(5).
                        1
%COBOL-W-ERROR  297, (1) Processing of source program resumes at this point
                        15 WS-CAT-PART-DESCR    PIC X(20).
                        15 WS-CAT-UNIT-PRICE    PIC 999V99.
                  05 TRANSACTION-TYPE-VALUES.
                     10 PIC X(19)  VALUE "01CASH & CARRY     ".
                     10 PIC X(19)  VALUE "02CHARGE & CARRY   ".
                     10 PIC X(19)  VALUE "03CHARGE & DELIVER ".
                     10 PIC X(19)  VALUE "04DELIVER COD      ".
                     10 PIC X(19)  VALUE "05LAYAWAY          ".
                     10 PIC X(19)  VALUE "06RETURN FOR CASH  ".
                     10 PIC X(19)  VALUE "07RETURN FOR CREDIT".
                     10 PIC X(19)  VALUE "08RETURN/EXCHANGE  ".
                     10 PIC X(19)  VALUE "09DAMAGED          ".
                  05 TRANSACTION-TABLE REDEFINES TRANSACTION-TYPE-VALUES.
                     1
%COBOL-E-ERROR   10, (1) REDEFINES item must not be longer than item redefined
                     10 TRANS-INFO OCCURS 9 TIMES
                                   INDEXED BY INFO-INDEX.
                        15 WS-TRANS-CODE              PIC XX.
                        15 WS-TRANS-TYPE              PIC X(17).
                     10 TRANS-TYPE-CTR OCCURS 9 TIMES PIC S999
                                       INDEXED BY CTR-INDEX.
                                       1
%COBOL-E-ERROR   65, (1) Missing period is assumed
%COBOL-F-ERROR  117, (1) Invalid syntax
              01  REPORT-HEADERS.
              1
%COBOL-W-ERROR  297, (1) Processing of source program resumes at this point
                  05 TOP-LINE.
                     10                PIC X(2)       VALUE SPACES.
                     10                PIC X(14)      VALUE "REPORT DATE:  ".
                     10 O-REPORT-DATE  PIC XX/XX/XX.
                     10                PIC X(46)      VALUE SPACES.
                     10                PIC X(5)       VALUE "PAGE ".
                     10 O-PAGE-NO      PIC Z9.
                     10                PIC X(3)       VALUE SPACES.
```

```
EXPRESS-ACTIVITY-DBG                1-Mar-1989 13:30:03    VAX COBOL V4.2-40                    Page   3
Source Listing                      1-Mar-1989 13:29:58    [PAQUETTEG.CHAPTER2]V2C3DBG1.COB;3 (1)

             05 COMPANY-NAME.
                10 PIC X(26)      VALUE SPACES.
                10 PIC X(28)      VALUE "EXPRESS AUTO PARTS WAREHOUSE".
                10 PIC X(26)      VALUE SPACES.

             05 REPORT-NAME.
                10 PIC X(32)      VALUE SPACES.
                10 PIC X(16)      VALUE "ACTIVITY LISTING".
                10 PIC X(32)      VALUE SPACES.

             05 HEADINGS.
                10 PIC X(6)       VALUE SPACES.
                10 PIC X(11)      VALUE "PART NUMBER".
                10 PIC X(6)       VALUE SPACES.
                10 PIC X(16)      VALUE "PART DESCRIPTION".
                10 PIC X(6)       VALUE SPACES.
                10 PIC X(8)       VALUE "QUANTITY".
                10 PIC X(7)       VALUE SPACES.
                10 PIC X(11)      VALUE "TRANSACTION".
                10 PIC X(9)       VALUE SPACES.

         01  ACTIVITY-LINE.
             05                   PIC X(9).
             05 O-PART-NO         PIC X(5).
             05                   PIC X(7).
             05 O-PART-DESCR      PIC X(20).
             05                   PIC X(6).
             05 O-QUANTITY        PIC ZZZ9.
             05                   PIC X(6).
             05 O-TRANS-TYPE      PIC X(17).
             05                   PIC X(6).

         01  SUMMARY-HEADERS.

             05 SUMMARY-NAME.
                10 PIC X(42)  VALUE SPACES.
                10 PIC X(26)  VALUE "TRANSACTION TOTALS BY TYPE".
                10 PIC X(11)  VALUE SPACES.
                10 PIC X      VALUE "*".

             05 SUMMARY-HEADINGS.
                10 PIC X(31)  VALUE SPACES.
                10 PIC X(4)   VALUE "CODE".
                10 PIC X(8)   VALUE SPACES.
                10 PIC X(4)   VALUE "TYPE".
                10 PIC X(9)   VALUE SPACES.
                10 PIC X(22)  VALUE "NUMBER OF TRANSACTIONS".
                10 PIC XX     VALUE SPACES.

         01  SUMMARY-LINE.
             05                  PIC X(32).
             05 O-TRANS-CODE     PIC XX.
             05                  PIC X(3).
             05 O-TRANS-TYPE     PIC X(17).
             05                  PIC X(11).
             05 O-TRANS-TYPE-CTR PIC ZZ9.
```

```
                  05                  PIC X(12).

              01  END-LINE.
                  05 PIC X(33)        VALUE SPACES.
                  05 PIC X(23)        VALUE "***   END OF REPORT   ***".
                  05 PIC X(24)        VALUE SPACES.

              PROCEDURE DIVISION.

              100-PRODUCE-ACTIVITY-LISTING.
                  PERFORM 200-START-UP.
                  PERFORM 210-PROCESS-TRANSACTION-RECORD
                      UNTIL NO-MORE-TRANS-RECORDS.
                  PERFORM 220-PREPARE-SUMMARY-REPORT.
                  PERFORM 230-FINISH-UP.
                  STOP RUN.

              200-START-UP.
                  OPEN INPUT CATALOG-FILE
                       INPUT TRANSACTION-FILE
                       OUTPUT ACTIVITY-REPORT.
                  ACCEPT WS-REPORT-DATE FROM DATE.
                  MOVE WS-REPORT-DATE TO O-REPORT-DATE.
                  MOVE "YES" TO WS-MORE-TRANS-RECORDS
                                WS-MORE-CATALOG-RECORDS.
                  INITIALIZE WS-PAGE-NO.
                  PERFORM VARYING TRANS-TABLE-ROW-CTR FROM 1 BY 1
                                   1
%COBOL-F-ERROR  349, (1) Undefined name
                              UNTIL TRANS-TABLE-ROW-CTR > 9
                                     1
%COBOL-F-ERROR  349, (1) Undefined name
                          MOVE ZERO TO TRANS-TYPE-CTR (TRANS-TABLE-ROW-CTR)
                           1                            2
%COBOL-W-ERROR  297, (1) Processing of source program resumes at this point
%COBOL-F-ERROR  349, (2) Undefined name
                  END-PERFORM.
                              1
%COBOL-W-ERROR  297, (1) Processing of source program resumes at this point
                  MOVE SPACES TO ACTIVITY-LINE.
                  PERFORM 300-READ-CATALOG-RECORD.
                  PERFORM VARYING CAT-INDEX FROM 1 BY 1
                                   1
%COBOL-F-ERROR  349, (1) Undefined name
                              UNTIL NO-MORE-CAT-RECORDS
                      MOVE CATALOG-RECORD TO CAT-ITEM-INFO (CAT-INDEX)
                      1                                      2
%COBOL-W-ERROR  297, (1) Processing of source program resumes at this point
%COBOL-F-ERROR  349, (2) Undefined name
                      PERFORM 300-READ-CATALOG-RECORD
                      1
%COBOL-W-ERROR  297, (1) Processing of source program resumes at this point
                  END-PERFORM.
                  1
%COBOL-F-ERROR  222, (1) "." required at this point
                  PERFORM 320-WRITE-REPORT-HEADERS.
                  1
```

```
%COBOL-W-ERROR  297, (1) Processing of source program resumes at this point
                  PERFORM 330-READ-TRANSACTION-RECORD.

              210-PROCESS-TRANSACTION-RECORD.
                  PERFORM 340-PREPARE-ACTIVITY-LINE.
                  PERFORM 330-READ-TRANSACTION-RECORD.

              220-PREPARE-SUMMARY-REPORT.
                  WRITE PRINTLINE FROM SUMMARY-NAME
                      AFTER ADVANCING 5 LINES.
                  WRITE PRINTLINE FROM SUMMARY-HEADINGS
                      AFTER ADVANCING 3 LINES.
                  MOVE 2 TO WS-PROPER-SPACING.
                  PERFORM VARYING CTR-INDEX FROM 1 BY 1
                                  1
%COBOL-F-ERROR  349, (1) Undefined name
                              UNTIL CTR-INDEX > 9
                                  1
%COBOL-F-ERROR  349, (1) Undefined name
                          MOVE WS-TRANS-CODE (CTR-INDEX)
                          1                   2
%COBOL-W-ERROR  297, (1) Processing of source program resumes at this point
%COBOL-F-ERROR  349, (2) Undefined name
                              TO O-TRANS-CODE
                          MOVE WS-TRANS-TYPE (CTR-INDEX)
                          1                   2
%COBOL-W-ERROR  297, (1) Processing of source program resumes at this point
%COBOL-F-ERROR  349, (2) Undefined name
                              TO O-TRANS-TYPE OF SUMMARY-LINE
                          MOVE TRANS-TYPE-CTR (CTR-INDEX)
                          1                   2
%COBOL-W-ERROR  297, (1) Processing of source program resumes at this point
%COBOL-F-ERROR  349, (2) Undefined name
                              TO O-TRANS-TYPE-CTR
                          WRITE PRINTLINE FROM SUMMARY-LINE
                          1
%COBOL-W-ERROR  297, (1) Processing of source program resumes at this point
                              AFTER ADVANCING WS-PROPER-SPACING
                          MOVE 1 TO WS-PROPER-SPACING
                  END-PERFORM.
                  1
%COBOL-F-ERROR  222, (1) "." required at this point

              230-FINISH-UP.
              1
%COBOL-W-ERROR  297, (1) Processing of source program resumes at this point
                  WRITE PRINTLINE FROM END-LINE
                      AFTER ADVANCING 5 LINES.
                  CLOSE CATALOG-FILE
                        TRANSACTION-FILE
                        ACTIVITY-REPORT.

              300-READ-CATALOG-RECORD.
                  READ CATALOG-FILE RECORD
                      AT END
                          SET NO-MORE-CAT-RECORDS TO TRUE.

```

```
EXPRESS-ACTIVITY-DBG                     1-Mar-1989 13:30:03   VAX COBOL V4.2-40                  Page  6
Source Listing                           1-Mar-1989 13:29:58   [PAQUETTEG.CHAPTER2]V2C3DBG1.COB;3 (1)

           320-WRITE-REPORT-HEADERS.
               ADD 1 TO WS-PAGE-NO.
               MOVE WS-PAGE-NO TO O-PAGE-NO.
               WRITE PRINTLINE FROM TOP-LINE
                   AFTER ADVANCING PAGE.
               WRITE PRINTLINE FROM COMPANY-NAME
                   AFTER ADVANCING 1 LINE.
               WRITE PRINTLINE FROM REPORT-NAME
                   AFTER ADVANCING 3 LINES.
               WRITE PRINTLINE FROM HEADINGS
                   AFTER ADVANCING 3 LINES.
               MOVE 2 TO WS-PROPER-SPACING.
               INITIALIZE WS-LINE-CTR.

           330-READ-TRANSACTION-RECORD.
               READ TRANSACTION-FILE RECORD
                   AT END
                       SET NO-MORE-TRANS-RECORDS TO TRUE.

           340-PREPARE-ACTIVITY-LINE.
               MOVE I-TRANS-PART-NO TO O-PART-NO.
               MOVE I-TRANS-QUANTITY TO O-QUANTITY.
               SEARCH ALL CAT-ITEM-INFO
                           1
%COBOL-F-ERROR  301, (1) Operand must be a table with OCCURS INDEXED BY and KEY IS phrase
                   WHEN I-TRANS-PART-NO = WS-CAT-PART-NO (CAT-TABLE-ROW-CTR)
                                                                 1
%COBOL-F-ERROR  349, (1) Undefined name
                       MOVE WS-CAT-PART-DESCR (CAT-TABLE-ROW-CTR)
                       1                         2
%COBOL-W-ERROR  297, (1) Processing of source program resumes at this point
%COBOL-F-ERROR  349, (2) Undefined name
                           TO O-PART-DESCR
               END-SEARCH.
                          1
%COBOL-W-ERROR  297, (1) Processing of source program resumes at this point
               SEARCH TRANS-INFO
                   WHEN I-TRANS-CODE = WS-TRANS-CODE (INFO-INDEX)
                       MOVE WS-TRANS-TYPE (TRANS-INFO-INDEX)
                                             1
%COBOL-F-ERROR  349, (1) Undefined name
                           TO O-TRANS-TYPE OF ACTIVITY-LINE
               END-SEARCH.
                          1
%COBOL-W-ERROR  297, (1) Processing of source program resumes at this point
               ADD 1 TO TRANS-TYPE-CTR (CTR-INDEX).
                                       1         2
%COBOL-F-ERROR  349, (1) Undefined name
%COBOL-W-ERROR  297, (2) Processing of source program resumes at this point
               WRITE PRINTLINE FROM ACTIVITY-LINE
                   AFTER ADVANCING WS-PROPER-SPACING.
               MOVE 1 TO WS-PROPER-SPACING.
               PERFORM 420-CHECK-LINE-CTR.

           420-CHECK-LINE-CTR.
               ADD 1 TO WS-LINE-CTR.
               IF PAGE-IS-FULL
```

```
EXPRESS-ACTIVITY-DBG                  1-Mar-1989 13:30:03    VAX COBOL V4.2[40                   Page   7
Source Listing                        1-Mar-1989 13:29:58    [PAQUETTEG.CHAPTER2]V2C3DBG1.COB;3 (1)

                   PERFORM 320-WRITE-REPORT-HEADERS
               END-IF.
```

CATALOG-FILE Records

```
8815PREAR-AXLE SHAFT ASSM01415
1352VTUNE-UP TESTER      03329
1264Y8000LB. JACK STAND  01082
8823UDUAL RHEOSTAT DIMMER01082
1762NBUMPER GUARDS       01415
5596WHD STAINLESS-ST FAN 01415
7519YSOLID STATE TACH    03329
1775BBOLT-ON HITCH       05663
0368WFM ANTENNA          00665
7568Y30-PC TUNE-UP KIT   03329
5524YDISC BRAKE PADS     01246
1048THITCH BALL COVER    00066
5507RBONDED BRAKE SHOE   00665
1584ARV ANTENNA          04163
9998FFIBERGLASS HARDTOP  28332
1616WAIR DIESEL HORN     01415
1593XHD. TIE DOWN        01498
9977RAIR COMPRESSOR KIT  08329
1685TBRAKE CABLE ADJUSTER00066
0346RCB ANTENNA          03329
8572VREAR END LIFT KIT   00665
0359BCB CONVERTER        02079
1787A1000-WATT CONVERTER 28996
0382NSTEREO SPEAKERS/PR  02079
8583NWL-BEARING CAPS/PR  00332
1033WFM RADIO AMPLIFIER  01082
2181XEXHAUST HEADERS     05663
5557PENGINE OIL COOLER   03329
3734NCAMSHAFT            06663
2326RPOWER MUFFLER       01413
1517ASPARE TIRE LOCK     00374
3731W3-2 BBL MANIFOLD    08329
1263PTORQUE WRENCH       01498
1503WELECTRONIC FILTER   01082
5534AMASTER CYLINDER     01246
8896NENGINE COOLER KIT   03329
5577PSOLENOID SWITCH     00458
8776NRING & PINION GEARS 08329
0462UFLEXSOCKET WRENCH   00191
7580XRAM AIR SYSTEM      01663
8419AHOLLEY CARBURETOR   09163
0348N23 CHANNEL MOBILE CB20829
8636ELEAF SPRINGS/PR     07496
1842N16" FULL WHEEL COVER02079
1914YC-11 TRAILER HITCH  01415
8880WFOG LIGHT KIT       02498
1242WRV ALARM SYSTEM     01663
8912NREPLACEMENT WHEEL   01415
1219XRW DEFOGGER         02498
8931RSHOCK ABSORBERS/PR  02079
```

TRANSACTION-FILE Records

```
0346R025003
0348N000205
0359B000504
0368W021001
0382N005004
0462U001001
1033W003007
1048T001001
1219X003009
1242W000808
1263P002003
1264Y000109
1352V005504
1503W000201
1517A005002
1584A000505
1593X002002
1616W001006
1685T000301
1762N005003
1775B002504
1787A000805
```

```
1842N015003
1914Y000208
2181X002804
2326R003003
3731W000508
3734N000207
5507R006002
5524Y000804
5534A006005
5557P002006
5577P005002
5596W000409
7519Y003002
7568Y000504
7580X000301
8419A001003
8572V000105
8583N004501
8636E000204
8776N001503
8815P000203
8823U002507
8880W000104
8896N003506
8912N015004
8931R002003
9977R000503
9998F000205
```

3. All the syntax errors in the program of exercise 2 have been corrected. When the program was compiled and a trial run made with the catalog file and transaction file listed above, the following report was produced:

```
REPORT DATE:  89/03/03                                                PAGE  1
                         EXPRESS AUTO PARTS WAREHOUSE

                              ACTIVITY LISTING

   PART NUMBER       PART DESCRIPTION       QUANTITY        TRANSACTION

      0346R                                    250       CHARGE & DELIVER
      0348N                                      2       LAYAWAY
      0359B                                      5       DELIVER COD
      0368W                                    210       CASH & CARRY
      0382N                                     50       DELIVER COD
      0462U                                     10       CASH & CARRY
      1033W                                     30       RETURN FOR CREDIT
      1048T        HITCH BALL COVER             10       CASH & CARRY
      1219X        HITCH BALL COVER             30       DAMAGED
      1242W        HITCH BALL COVER              8       RETURN/EXCHANGE
      1263P        HITCH BALL COVER             20       CHARGE & DELIVER
      1264Y        HITCH BALL COVER              1       DAMAGED
      1352V        HITCH BALL COVER             55       DELIVER COD
      1503W        HITCH BALL COVER              2       CASH & CARRY
      1517A        HITCH BALL COVER             50       CHARGE & CARRY
      1584A        HITCH BALL COVER              5       LAYAWAY
      1593X        HITCH BALL COVER             20       CHARGE & CARRY
      1616W        HITCH BALL COVER             10       RETURN FOR CASH
      1685T        HITCH BALL COVER              3       CASH & CARRY
      1762N        HITCH BALL COVER             50       CHARGE & DELIVER
      1775B        HITCH BALL COVER             25       DELIVER COD
      1787A        HITCH BALL COVER              8       LAYAWAY
      1842N        HITCH BALL COVER            150       CHARGE & DELIVER
      1914Y        HITCH BALL COVER              2       RETURN/EXCHANGE
      2181X        HITCH BALL COVER             28       DELIVER COD
      2326R        HITCH BALL COVER             30       CHARGE & DELIVER
      3731W        HITCH BALL COVER              5       RETURN/EXCHANGE
      3734N        HITCH BALL COVER              2       RETURN FOR CREDIT
      5507R        BONDED BRAKE SHOE            60       CHARGE & CARRY
      5524Y        BONDED BRAKE SHOE             8       DELIVER COD
      5534A        BONDED BRAKE SHOE            60       LAYAWAY
      5557P        BONDED BRAKE SHOE            20       RETURN FOR CASH
      5577P        BONDED BRAKE SHOE            50       CHARGE & CARRY
      5596W        BONDED BRAKE SHOE             4       DAMAGED
      7519Y        BONDED BRAKE SHOE            30       CHARGE & CARRY
      7568Y        BONDED BRAKE SHOE             5       DELIVER COD
      7580X        BONDED BRAKE SHOE             3       CASH & CARRY
      8419A        BONDED BRAKE SHOE            10       CHARGE & DELIVER
      8572V        BONDED BRAKE SHOE             1       LAYAWAY
      8583N        WL-BEARING CAPS/PR           45       CASH & CARRY
```

```
REPORT DATE:  89/03/03                                               PAGE  2
                          EXPRESS AUTO PARTS WAREHOUSE

                               ACTIVITY LISTING

   PART NUMBER       PART DESCRIPTION       QUANTITY        TRANSACTION

      8636E        WL-BEARING CAPS/PR           2       DELIVER COD
      8776N        RING & PINION GEARS         15       CHARGE & DELIVER
      8815P        RING & PINION GEARS          2       CHARGE & DELIVER
      8823U        RING & PINION GEARS         25       RETURN FOR CREDIT
      8880W        RING & PINION GEARS          1       DELIVER COD
      8896N        RING & PINION GEARS         35       RETURN FOR CASH
      8912N        RING & PINION GEARS        150       DELIVER COD
      8931R        SHOCK ABSORBERS/PR          20       CHARGE & DELIVER
      9977R        SHOCK ABSORBERS/PR           5       CHARGE & DELIVER
      9998F        SHOCK ABSORBERS/PR           2       LAYAWAY

                               TRANSACTION TOTALS BY TYPE                 *

                    CODE        TYPE            NUMBER OF TRANSACTIONS

                     01   CASH & CARRY                   7
                     02   CHARGE & CARRY                 5
                     03   CHARGE & DELIVER              10
                     04   DELIVER COD                   10
                     05   LAYAWAY                        6
                     06   RETURN FOR CASH                3
                     07   RETURN FOR CREDIT              3
                     08   RETURN/EXCHANGE                3
                     09   DAMAGED                        3

                      ***  END OF REPORT  ***
```

It is obvious that the above report contains errors. Identify the source of the report errors, and explain what must be done to produce the following correct report:

Report to be Produced

```
REPORT DATE:  89/03/03                                               PAGE  1
                          EXPRESS AUTO PARTS WAREHOUSE

                               ACTIVITY LISTING

   PART NUMBER       PART DESCRIPTION       QUANTITY        TRANSACTION

      0346R        CB ANTENNA                 250       CHARGE & DELIVER
      0348N        23 CHANNEL MOBILE CB         2       LAYAWAY
      0359B        CB CONVERTER                 5       DELIVER COD
      0368W        FM ANTENNA                 210       CASH & CARRY
      0382N        STEREO SPEAKERS/PR          50       DELIVER COD
      0462U        FLEXSOCKET WRENCH           10       CASH & CARRY
      1033W        FM RADIO AMPLIFIER          30       RETURN FOR CREDIT
      1048T        HITCH BALL COVER            10       CASH & CARRY
      1219X        RW DEFOGGER                 30       DAMAGED
      1242W        RV ALARM SYSTEM              8       RETURN/EXCHANGE
      1263P        TORQUE WRENCH               20       CHARGE & DELIVER
      1264Y        8000LB. JACK STAND           1       DAMAGED
      1352V        TUNE-UP TESTER              55       DELIVER COD
      1503W        ELECTRONIC FILTER            2       CASH & CARRY
      1517A        SPARE TIRE LOCK             50       CHARGE & CARRY
      1584A        RV ANTENNA                   5       LAYAWAY
      1593X        HD. TIE DOWN                20       CHARGE & CARRY
      1616W        AIR DIESEL HORN             10       RETURN FOR CASH
      1685T        BRAKE CABLE ADJUSTER         3       CASH & CARRY
      1762N        BUMPER GUARDS               50       CHARGE & DELIVER
      1775B        BOLT-ON HITCH               25       DELIVER COD
      1787A        1000-WATT CONVERTER          8       LAYAWAY
      1842N        16" FULL WHEEL COVER       150       CHARGE & DELIVER
      1914Y        C-11 TRAILER HITCH           2       RETURN/EXCHANGE
      2181X        EXHAUST HEADERS             28       DELIVER COD
      2326R        POWER MUFFLER               30       CHARGE & DELIVER
      3731W        3-2 BBL MANIFOLD             5       RETURN/EXCHANGE
      3734N        CAMSHAFT                     2       RETURN FOR CREDIT
      5507R        BONDED BRAKE SHOE           60       CHARGE & CARRY
      5524Y        DISC BRAKE PADS              8       DELIVER COD
      5534A        MASTER CYLINDER             60       LAYAWAY
      5557P        ENGINE OIL COOLER           20       RETURN FOR CASH
      5577P        SOLENOID SWITCH             50       CHARGE & CARRY
      5596W        HD STAINLESS-ST FAN          4       DAMAGED
      7519Y        SOLID STATE TACH            30       CHARGE & CARRY
      7568Y        30-PC TUNE-UP KIT            5       DELIVER COD
      7580X        RAM AIR SYSTEM               3       CASH & CARRY
      8419A        HOLLEY CARBURETOR           10       CHARGE & DELIVER
      8572V        REAR END LIFT KIT            1       LAYAWAY
      8583N        WL-BEARING CAPS/PR          45       CASH & CARRY
```

```
REPORT DATE:  89/03/03                                                       PAGE  2
                                EXPRESS AUTO PARTS WAREHOUSE

                                      ACTIVITY LISTING

     PART NUMBER        PART DESCRIPTION          QUANTITY         TRANSACTION

        8636E         LEAF SPRINGS/PR                 2        DELIVER COD
        8776N         RING & PINION GEARS            15        CHARGE & DELIVER
        8815P         REAR-AXLE SHAFT ASSM            2        CHARGE & DELIVER
        8823U         DUAL RHEOSTAT DIMMER           25        RETURN FOR CREDIT
        8880W         FOG LIGHT KIT                   1        DELIVER COD
        8896N         ENGINE COOLER KIT              35        RETURN FOR CASH
        8912N         REPLACEMENT WHEEL             150        DELIVER COD
        8931R         SHOCK ABSORBERS/PR             20        CHARGE & DELIVER
        9977R         AIR COMPRESSOR KIT              5        CHARGE & DELIVER
        9998F         FIBERGLASS HARDTOP              2        LAYAWAY

                                     TRANSACTION TOTALS BY TYPE                *

                        CODE          TYPE              NUMBER OF TRANSACTIONS

                         01      CASH & CARRY                    7
                         02      CHARGE & CARRY                  5
                         03      CHARGE & DELIVER               10
                         04      DELIVER COD                    10
                         05      LAYAWAY                         6
                         06      RETURN FOR CASH                 3
                         07      RETURN FOR CREDIT               3
                         08      RETURN/EXCHANGE                 3
                         09      DAMAGED                         3

                        ***   END OF REPORT   ***
```

Programming Exercises

Programming Exercise I

At the end of each business day, the data processing department of the Allied Stock Company must prepare a report listing the phone sales made during the day. For each phone sale, a record containing the customer number, the item number of the catalog item that was sold, and the number of units sold has been prepared and stored in a file. This record layout is shown in Figure 2.33a. For each phone sale, the report must print the customer number, the customer's name, the catalog item number, the quantity ordered, the unit price of the item, and the net amount of the sale. It is company policy to give a 20 percent discount on purchases in which the number of units exceeds 100. The report must be formatted as shown on the printer spacing chart of Figure 2.34.

Before processing the phone sales records, it is necessary to load the catalog price list into a table and the customer file records into another table. The layouts of these records are shown in Figures 2.33b and 2.33c, respectively.

Figure 2.33a PHONE-SALE-RECORD layout

Record Layout Forms

a.

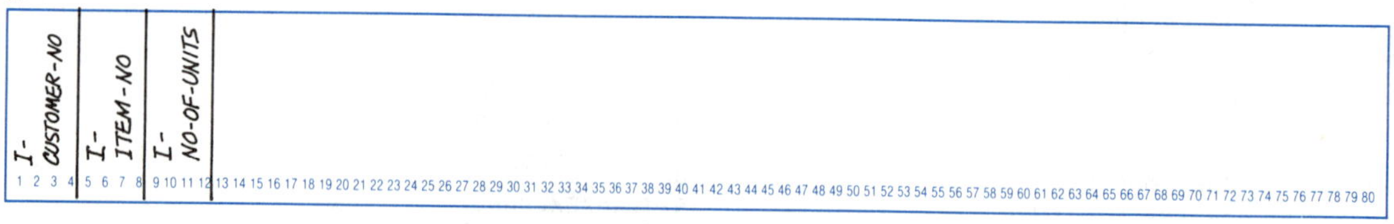

Record Name: PHONE-SALE-RECORD

■ **Figure 2.33b** PRICE-RECORD layout

b.

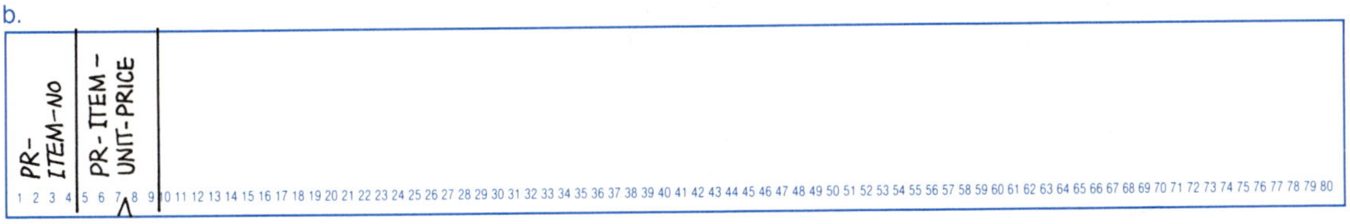

Record Name: *PRICE-RECORD*

■ **Figure 2.33c** CUSTOMER-RECORD layout

c.

Record Name: *CUSTOMER-RECORD*

■ **Figure 2.34** Printer spacing chart for the report

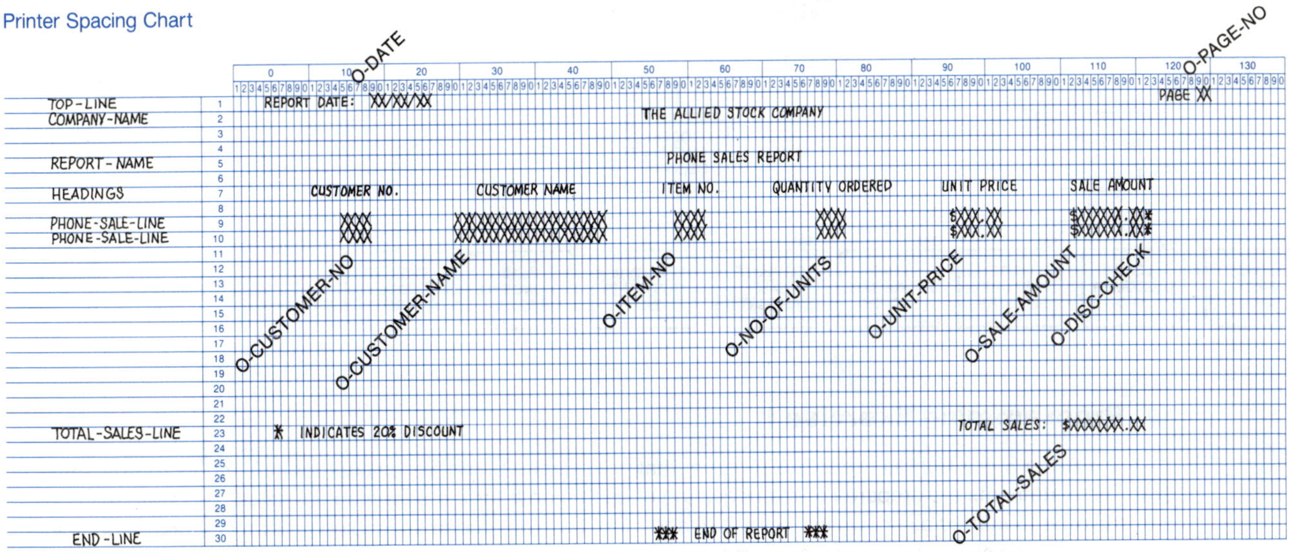

The system flowchart and the structure chart are provided for you in Figures 2.35a and 2.35b.

Your assignment is to complete the design phase, that is, write the program pseudocode or develop the program flowchart, and then to implement the design through a successful execution of the program. Use Data Set 2X1-I for the phone sales file, Data Set 2X1-II for the price list file, and Data Set 2X1-III for the customer file.

Figure 2.35a System flowchart

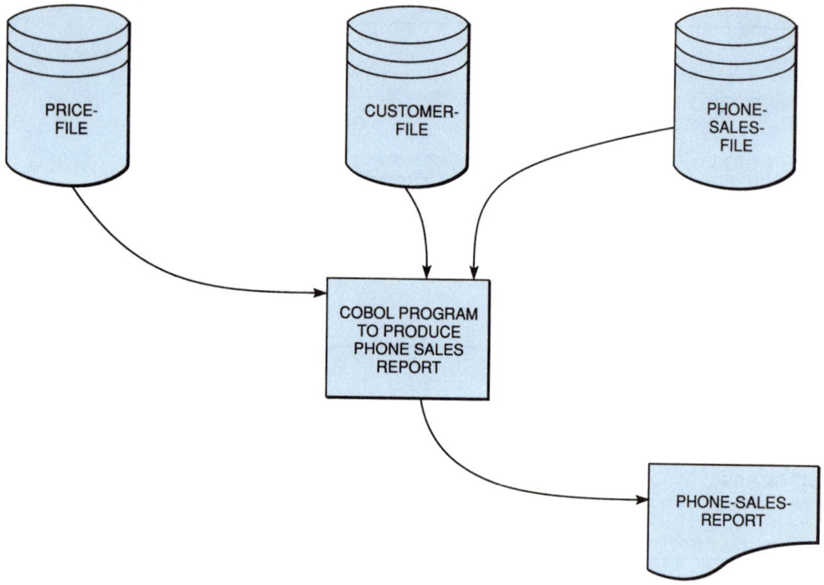

Figure 2.35b Structure chart

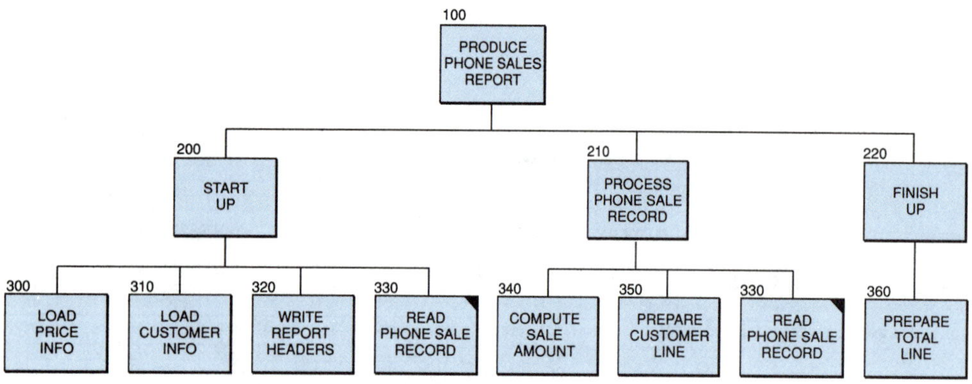

Programming Exercise II

The Allied Stock Company wants a program that will prepare billing statements for its phone sale customers. The statements are prepared at the beginning of each month for the prior month's sales. The statements must be formatted as shown in Figure 2.36 and must be produced in ascending order by customer number.

Phone sale records have been accumulated in a phone transaction file in chronological sequence as they occurred. Each phone sale record contains the date of the transaction, the customer number, the catalog number of the item that was purchased, and the quantity purchased. The phone sale record format is shown in Figure 2.37a.

In order to compute the gross and the net transaction amounts, the price list must be loaded into a table. In order to prepare mailing addresses, the needed customer data must also be loaded into a table. And to identify the month for which the billing statement is prepared, a hard-coded table containing month names must be included in the program. The layout of a customer record and the layout of a price record are shown in Figures 2.37b and 2.37c, respectively.

■ **Figure 2.36** Billing statement format

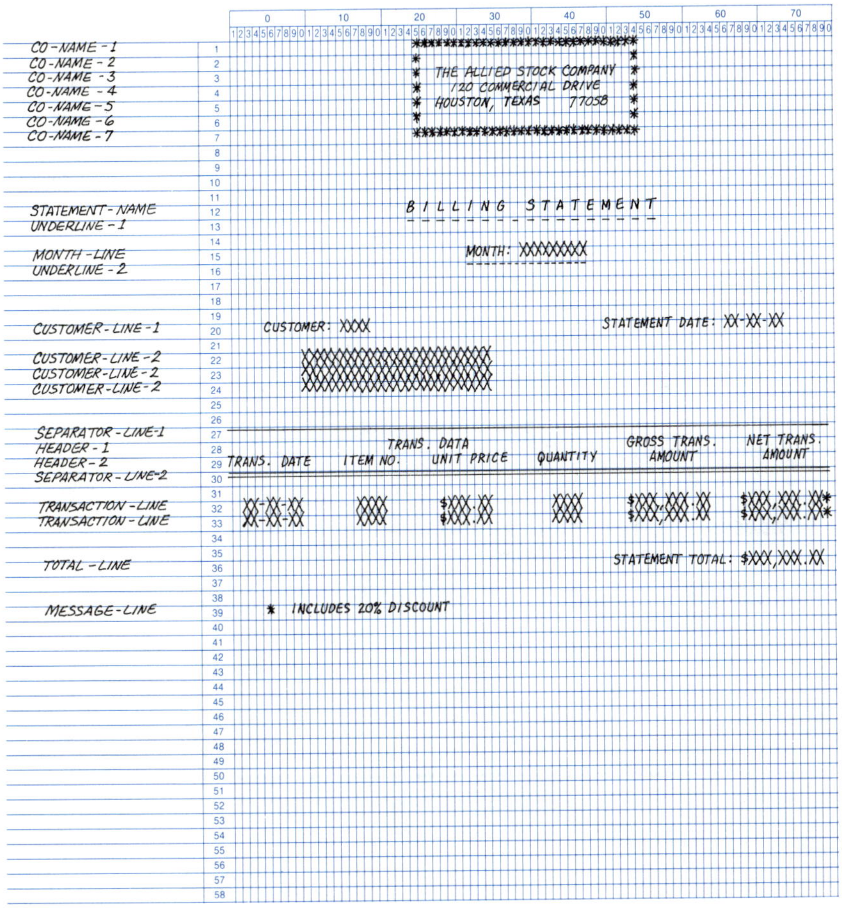

In each billing statement, the transactions must be listed in chronological order. The net transaction amount must include a 20 percent discount if the quantity purchased in that transaction exceeds 100 units. The statement must show the customer's total bill for the billing period.

The system flowchart for this program is shown in Figure 2.38. Note that a sort file is needed to resequence the records in the phone sale transaction file. In addition to a sorting routine, the program must also contain a control break at the customer level, since totals must be produced for a customer before preparing a billing statement for the next customer.

Use Data Set 2X2-I for the phone sale transaction file, Data Set 2X2-II for the customer data file, and Data Set 2X2-III for the price list file.

Your assignment is twofold: first, complete the design phase, that is, develop the structure chart, and the program pseudocode or flowchart; second, implement the design through a successful execution of the program.

Figure 2.37a TRANSACTION-RECORD layout

Record Layout Forms

a.

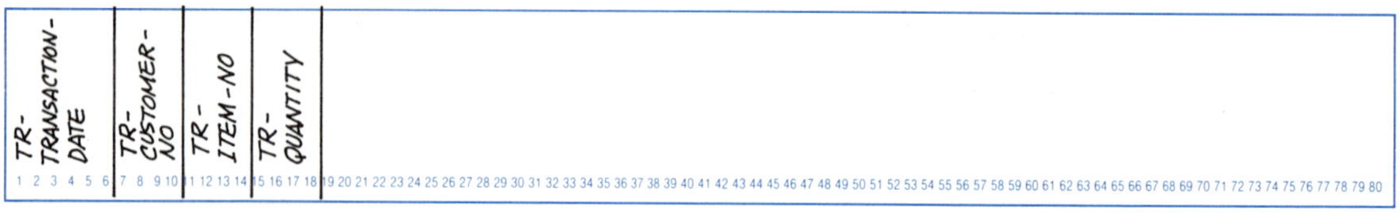

Record Name: TRANSACTION-RECORD

Figure 2.37b CUSTOMER-RECORD layout

b.

Record Name: CUSTOMER-RECORD

Figure 2.37c PRICE-RECORD layout

c.

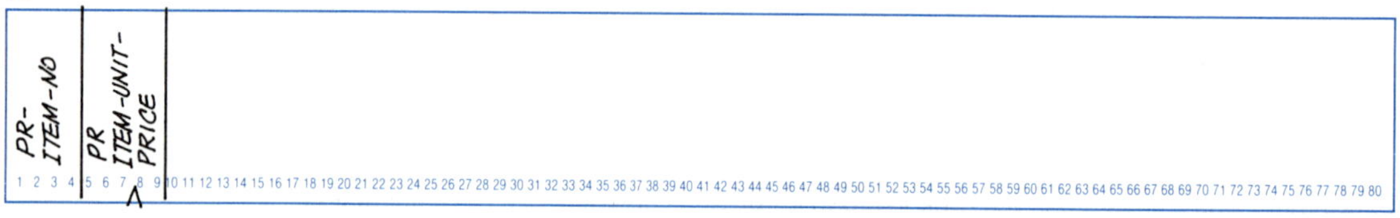

Record Name: PRICE-RECORD

Programming Exercise III

The management of the Allied Stock Company wants the data processing department to prepare a multilevel activity report for the previous month. The report is formatted as shown in Figure 2.39. At the first level, the report lists all the transactions in chronological order for each catalog item. The sale amount must reflect a 20 percent discount if the quantity purchased exceeds 100 units; otherwise there is no discount. At the second level, the report must print the total number of transactions, the total quantity sold, and the total sales amount for each catalog item. The totals for a catalog item are printed before listing the transactions for the next catalog item, that is, the program must contain a control break at the catalog item level. Catalog items are reported in ascending order by catalog item number.

When all catalog items have been reported, the totals for each item are reported in a summary report. An item's summary includes the item number, the total quantity sold, and the total sales amount. A final company summary prints the grand total of all the sales.

The transaction file contains all the transactions of the month in chronological order. Each transaction record contains the customer number, the catalog item number, and the quantity purchased.

Figure 2.38 System flowchart

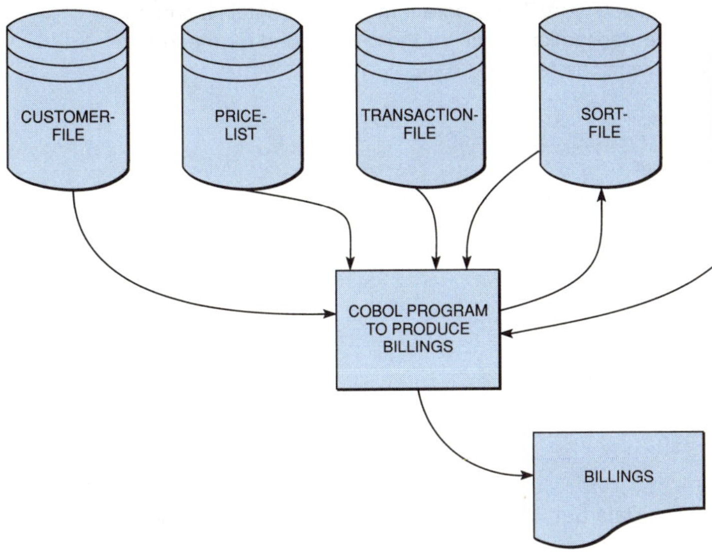

Figure 2.39 Printer spacing chart for the program

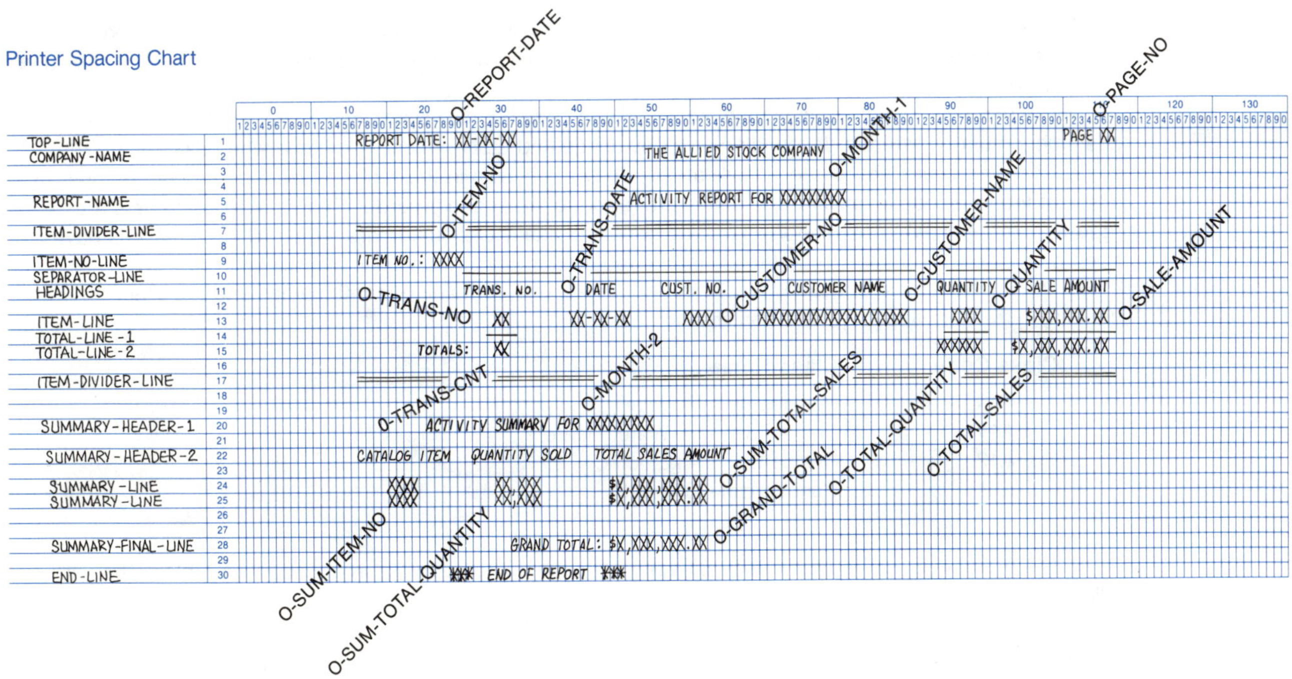

The program must load a customer data file and a price list file into tables in order to have access to data needed to prepare the report. A hard-coded table containing month names is needed, and a fourth table must be set up to contain the totals for each catalog item. The program must also contain a sorting procedure, since the sequence of records in the transaction file is not the one needed for the report.

Each record in the customer data file contains the following data:

cc 1–4	Customer number
cc 5–24	Customer name
cc 25–49	Customer's street address
cc 50–72	Customer's city, state, and zip code

Each record in the price list file contains the following data:

cc 1–4	Item number
cc 5–9	Item unit price (format: xxx.xx)

Each record in the transaction file contains the following data:

cc 1–6	Transaction date (format: yymmdd)
cc 7–10	Customer number
cc 11–14	Item number purchased
cc 15–18	Quantity purchased

Use Data Set 2X3-I as the transaction file, Data Set 2X3-II as the customer file, and Data Set 2X3-III as the price list file.

Your task is to design the program and then implement the design through a successful execution.

Programming Exercise IV

The Ponagansett Electric Company wants its data processing department to design a program to produce a multilevel KWH usage report for the current billing period. The printer spacing chart for the report is shown in Figure 2.40.

The report must list all the customers within each electric rate classification. For each rate class, the customers must be listed in descending order by usage and alphabetically by name when usages are the same. There are four electric rate classifications. They are shown in the table below. A control break must occur at the rate code level, and rate codes are reported in ascending order. That is, A10 customers are reported first, then A11 customers, A12 customers, and finally C-2 customers. When all input records have been processed, a summary report must list the required totals for each rate classification.

The program must contain two hard-coded tables, one containing month names and the other containing the following customer classification data:

Class Code	Class Name
A10	Residential - Regular
A11	Residential - El. Water Heater
A12	Residential - All Electric
C-2	Commercial - General

The program must load the rates that apply for each customer class into respective tables. They are as follows:

Class A10

Minimum Monthly Charge: $1.61

Energy Charge: Nov.–June 7.578 cents/KWH

July–Oct. 8.082 cents/KWH

Figure 2.40 Printer spacing chart for the report

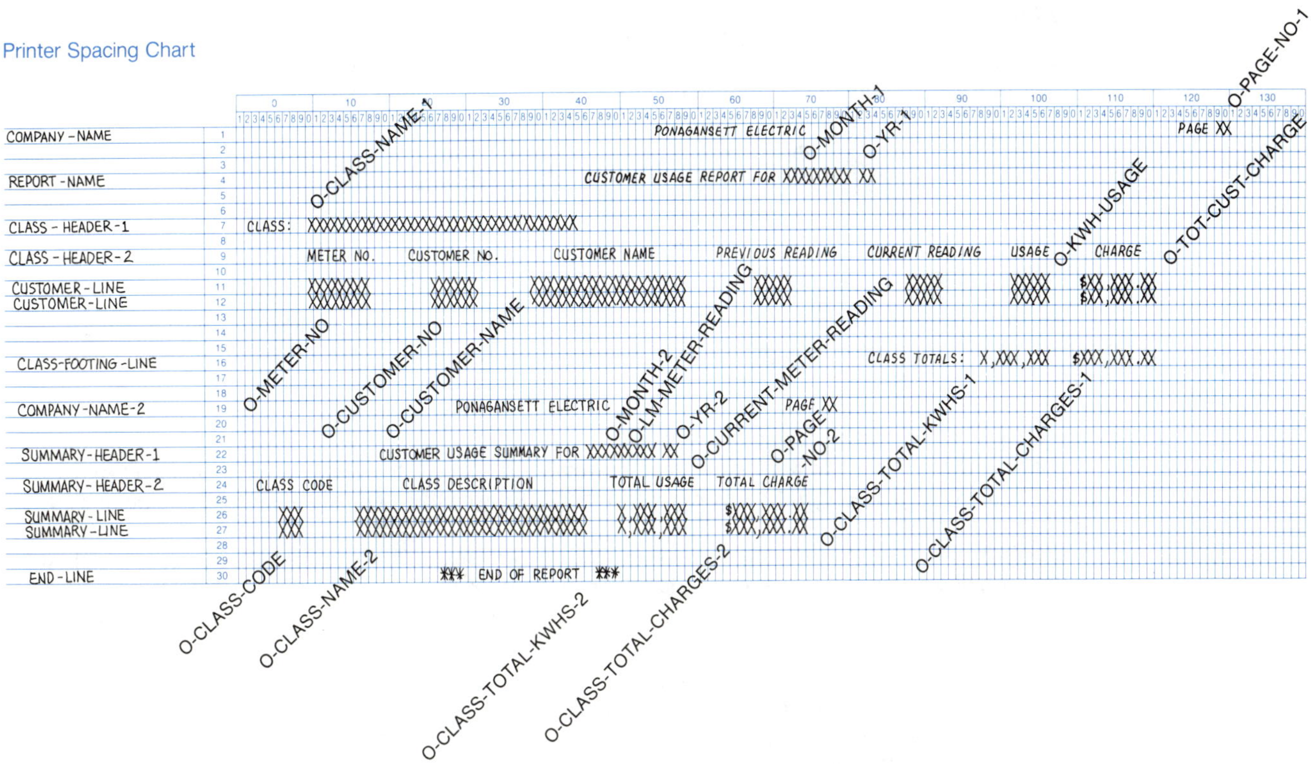

Class A11

Monthly Charge:

KWH Usage	Winter Charges November through June Base in dollars	: Rate*	Summer Charges July through October Base in dollars	: Rate*
0	2.54	0	2.63	0
0–20	2.68	0	2.77	0
21–50	2.68	10.040	2.77	10.543
51–200	5.692	7.986	5.9329	8.4487
201–550	17.671	5.135	18.6634	5.636
551–2000	35.6435	6.437	38.3894	6.937
2001–99999	128.98	6.159	138.9759	6.660

*In cents per KWH in excess of previous level maximum.

Class A12

Same as Class A11.

Class C-2

Customer Charge: $4.75
Energy Charge:

KWH Usage	Winter Charges November through June Base in dollars : Rate	Summer Charges July through October Base in dollars : Rate
0	0 : 0	0 : 0
1–1000	0 : 8.519	0 : 9.019
1001–99999	85.19 : 7.919	90.19 : 8.419

In each row of the tables for class A11 and class C-2, the rate in cents per KWH is applied to the KWH in excess of the usage limit of the previous row. For instance, in class A11, if usage is 140 KWH and the month is February, then the excess over the limit of the previous row is 90KWH (140 − 50), and the applicable rate is 7.986 cents/KWH. Thus, 90 × .07986 = 7.1874, and this amount is added to the base charge of 5.692 for an energy charge of $12.8794.

Two extra charges are also added to each customer bill, namely, the Uniform Conservation Cost Adjustment (UCCA) charge of .011 cents/KWH and the Oil Conservation Adjustment (OCA) charge of .009 cents/KWH.

Records have been prepared for the above rates and are stored in a rates file. Their layouts are shown in Figure 2.41, and a listing of these records is shown in Figure 2.42.

The program must also load customer data records into a table. Each record contains the following data:

cc 1–8	Customer's meter number
cc 9–11	Customer's rate code
cc 12–17	Customer number
cc 18–37	Customer name
cc 38–62	Customer address
cc 63–85	Customer city, state, and zip code

These records are in a customer file in ascending order by meter number.

The program must also load the customers' meter readings for the previous month. This data is available in a file labeled Last Month File. Its records are sequenced in ascending order by meter number, and they contain the following data:

cc 1–8	Customer meter number
cc 9–13	Customer's last month meter reading

When all the tables have been loaded, the program must process the records in the current meter readings file. The records in this file are in ascending order by meter number, and they contain the following data:

cc 1–8	Customer's meter number
cc 9–13	Customer's current meter reading

Since the report specifications require listing customers within each rate classification in descending order by KWH usage, the program must contain a sorting routine that includes an input procedure and an output procedure. Every customer class report should begin on a new page, and the usage summary report should be on a separate last page. The data field of the record CLASS-HEADER-1 must contain the code and the name of the class being reported, whereas in the record SUMMARY-LINE, a class code and its corresponding class name are assigned to distinct fields.

The system flowchart is shown in Figure 2.43. Your task is to design the program and then implement the design to successful completion.

Use Data Set 2X4-I for the rates file, Data Set 2X4-II for the customer file, Data Set 2X4-III for the last month readings file, and Data Set 2X4-IV for the current readings file.

Figure 2.41 Record layouts for the rates records

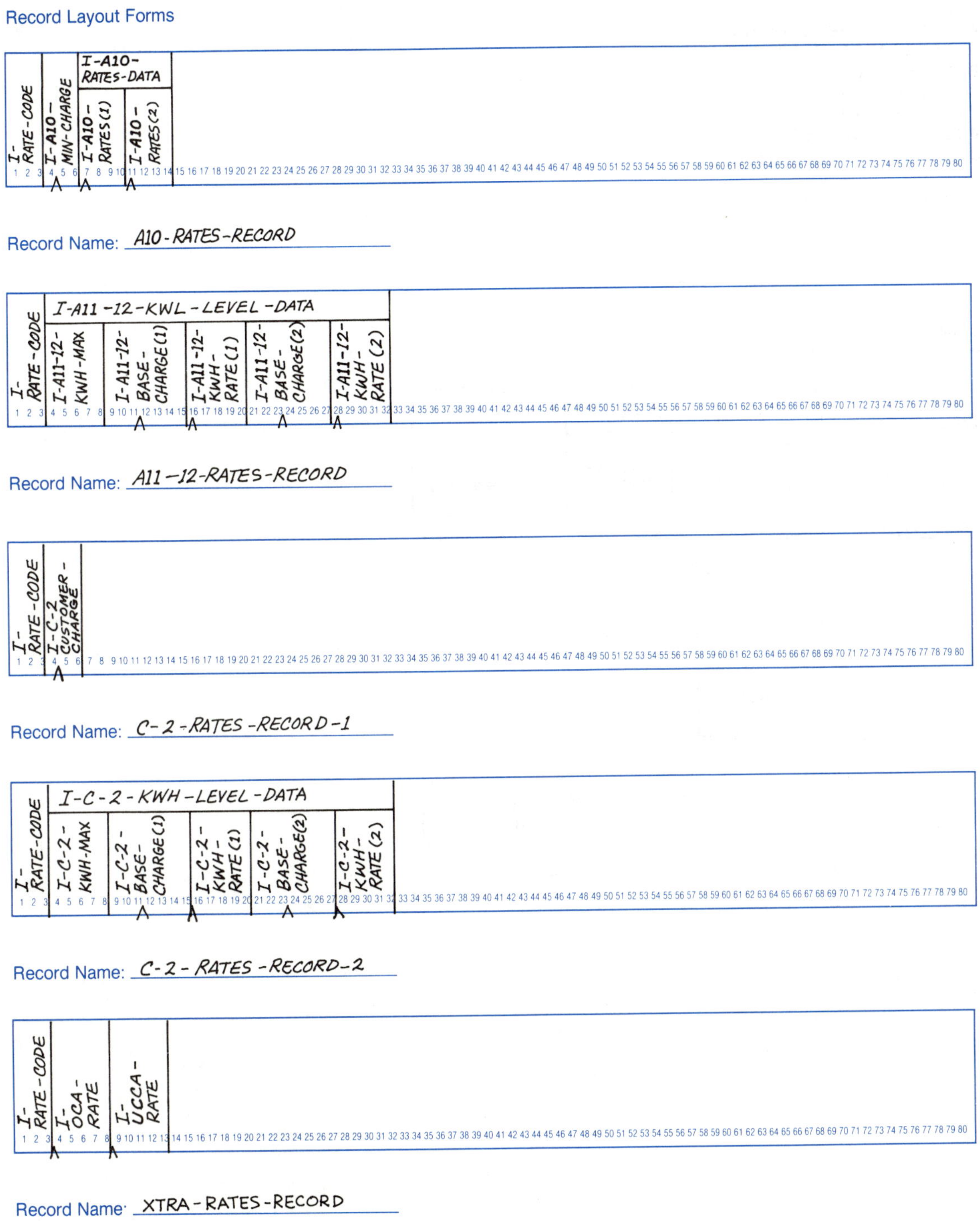

Figure 2.42 Records in RATES-FILE

```
A101610757808082
A110000000254000000000002630000000
A110002000268000000000002770000000
A110005000268001004000027700105430
A110020000569200798600593290848700
A110055001767100513501866340563600
A110200003564350643703838940693700
A119999912898000615913897590666000
C-2475
C-2000000000000000000000000000000
C-2010000000000008519000000009019
C-2999990851900079190901900084190
XXX0001100009
```

Figure 2.43 System flowchart for the program

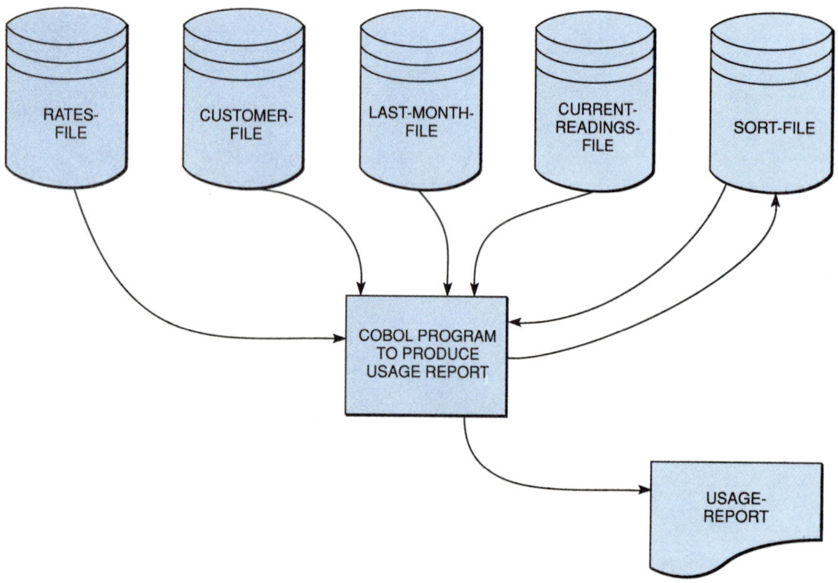

3 Indexed Files

This chapter presents indexed file concepts and procedures to create and to process indexed files. Unlike sequential files, which may be stored on magnetic tape, indexed files (and relative files presented in the next chapter) require the use of a direct-access storage device, such as magnetic disks. This requirement is due to the fact that the essential function of an indexed file is to allow direct access to a record without being concerned with the records that precede it or follow it in the file. Magnetic tapes simply do not provide this facility.

A file is classified as an indexed file if, when it is created, an index entry is generated for each record of the file. The index entry, which must be unique to a record, contains the address of the record in the file.

Indexed files are also referred to as indexed-sequential files (or key-sequenced files in a VSAM IBM environment) because the records are stored sequentially in ascending order by key field values. A procedure developed by IBM to access records of an indexed-sequential file is known as the *Indexed-Sequential Access Method*. As a result, indexed-sequential files are often called ISAM files. ■

Objectives You Should Achieve

After studying this chapter, you should

1. Be able to explain the terms "indexed organization," "random access," and "dynamic access."
2. Given a record description, be able to determine which field, if any, could be specified as a prime record key and which field, if any, could be specified as an alternate record key for an indexed file.
3. Be able to identify the correct form of I/O statements that may be coded in relation to an indexed file when its access and open modes are specified.
4. Given that the function of a program is to create an indexed file for which the prime record key and, possibly, one or more alternate record keys are specified, be able to correctly code the SELECT and OPEN statements for the file.
5. Given that the records of an indexed file must be accessed sequentially by using the prime record key or by using an alternate record key as the key of reference, be able to code the correct SELECT, OPEN, and I/O statements for the file.
6. Given that the records of an indexed file must be accessed randomly by using the prime record key or by using an alternate record key as the key of reference, be able to code the correct SELECT, OPEN, and I/O statements for the file.
7. Given a programming problem in which a master file with indexed organization must be maintained, that is, existing records must be changed or deleted and/or new records must be added, and for which an audit report of the file's activity must be produced, be able to correctly design the program and implement the design to successful completion.

Direct-Access Files Versus Sequential Files

If a file is stored on magnetic tape, then it must be designed as a sequential file. This restriction is due to the physical characteristics of tapes and their drive mechanisms. It is impossible to reach the 100th record on the tape without running the preceding 99 records through the read-write heads. Consequently, in order to organize a file as an indexed file, it is necessary to store it on a direct-access storage device. In this chapter, we limit our attention to the most common DASD, namely, the magnetic disk. Recall that the movable arms of the disk drive can be positioned very quickly to access a record on a specified track of a surface and then be repositioned very quickly to access a record on a track of another surface. A file that will be stored on a disk can then be organized to take advantage of this feature of disk drives.

A file that is set up to allow its records to be accessed directly, that is, not necessarily in the specific physical sequence in which they reside on the file, is classified as a *direct-access file.* The two most common direct-access file organizations are *indexed organization* and *relative organization.*

When a programmer is assigned the task of creating a file that will serve as a master file, serious consideration must be given to the file organization, since the selected organization cannot be changed for the life of the file. It should be obvious that the available physical components of the computer system must be taken into account. If there is no DASD within the computer installation, there is no choice as to file organization; it must be sequential. If there are DASDs, then the programmer must obtain all relevant information relating to the anticipated uses and file maintenance activities for that file. If it is anticipated that every file maintenance activity will require addressing all or most of the records of the file, then a valid argument can be made for a sequential organization. On the other hand, if it is anticipated that most file maintenance activities for that file will involve relatively few records, then this argues in favor of a direct-access file organization.

Creating an Indexed File

Generally, in order to create an indexed file, the records of the input file are sorted on the basis of some key field of each record whose value is unique to that record. The following are examples of such fields: the Social Security number field of records in an employee file, the catalog number field of records in an inventory file, the customer number field of records in an accounts receivable file, and so on. Examples of fields that should not be used as key fields would include the date-of-birth field of records in an employee file and the unit-price field of records in an inventory file. The date-of-birth and unit-price fields are not useful as key fields because the same entry may be found on more than one record of the file. An appropriate key field is one whose value identifies a unique record.

Given that the records of the input file have been sorted in ascending order by the values in the key field, they are accessed from the input file and are then written to the disk file in sequential order. As a record is written to the file, an index associated with the key field value is established for that record in an index table stored in the file itself. The index stores the key field value and specifies the location of the record on the disk. The result is illustrated in Figure 3.1. Note that the file contains two kinds of records, index records and data records. When a data record must be accessed, the index table is searched serially for the index record containing the key value of the data record. When the matching key value is found, the pointer in the index record indicates where the data record is located in the file. The read-write mechanism is positioned accordingly, and the data record is then retrieved directly.

If the records of the disk file are blocked, one index record is prepared for each block. This index record contains the highest key value of the data records in the block, and the pointer indicates the address where the block begins. These index records are stored in the file in ascending order of key values. When a data record must be accessed, a serial search of the index records occurs. The search ends when the key value of the index record is equal to the key value of the target data record or when the key value of the index record is the first one that is greater than the key value of the target record.

Figure 3.1 Index file with index records and data records

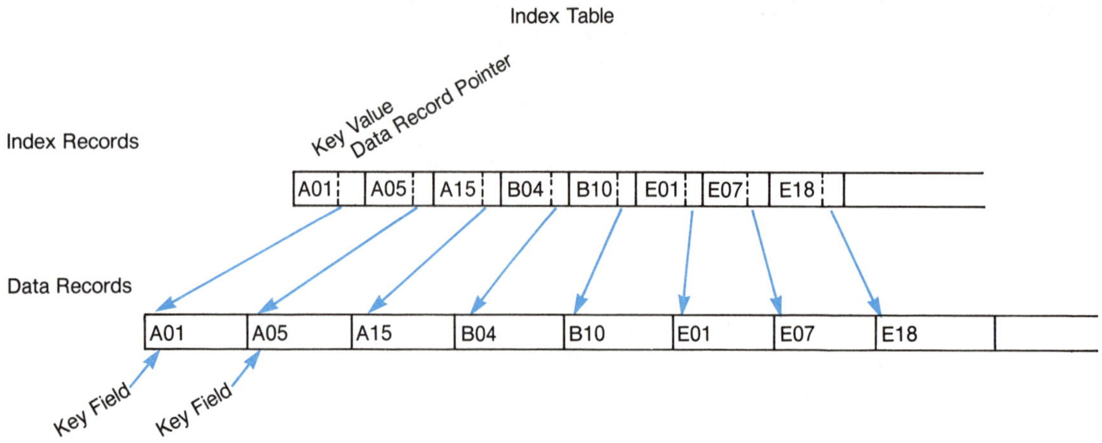

Figure 3.2 Searching for a data record in a block

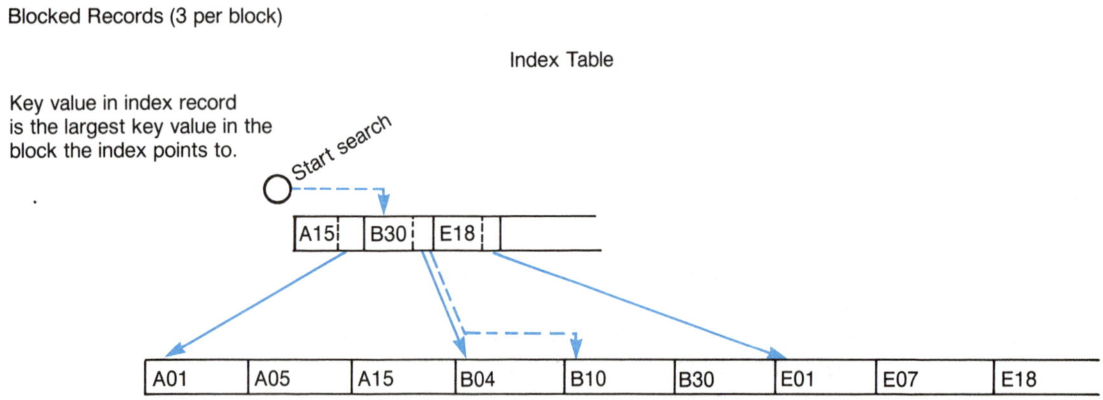

Example: Search for data record with record key value "B10" (follow dotted line):
1. In index table, locate index record with the smallest value ≥ "B10".
2. Follow the pointer to the block.
3. Search data records in the block serially for a key value match.

In either case, the pointer indicates the location of the block that contains the target record. The data records in this block are searched serially until the target record is located. Figure 3.2 illustrates how the data record with key value B10 is located. This illustration shows three records per block.

Though it is possible to create an indexed file by writing records to it in a random fashion, the most common and the most efficient procedure is to write the records to the file in ascending order by the key field values, that is, by specifying that the access mode is sequential. Once the indexed file has been created, its records may be processed sequentially, and, because of the indexes that are associated with the records, they may be retrieved randomly as well. In a way, a file with indexed organization provides the best of both worlds: its records may be accessed sequentially or they may be accessed randomly. The access mode selected is determined on the basis of the particular application that requires the use of the indexed file. If all or most of the records must be processed, the access mode is specified as sequential; but, if relatively few records must be processed, then the access mode is specified as random.

A file is created as an indexed file only once, and thereafter it is maintained periodically for the rest of its life.

Figure 3.3 Printer spacing chart for the audit report

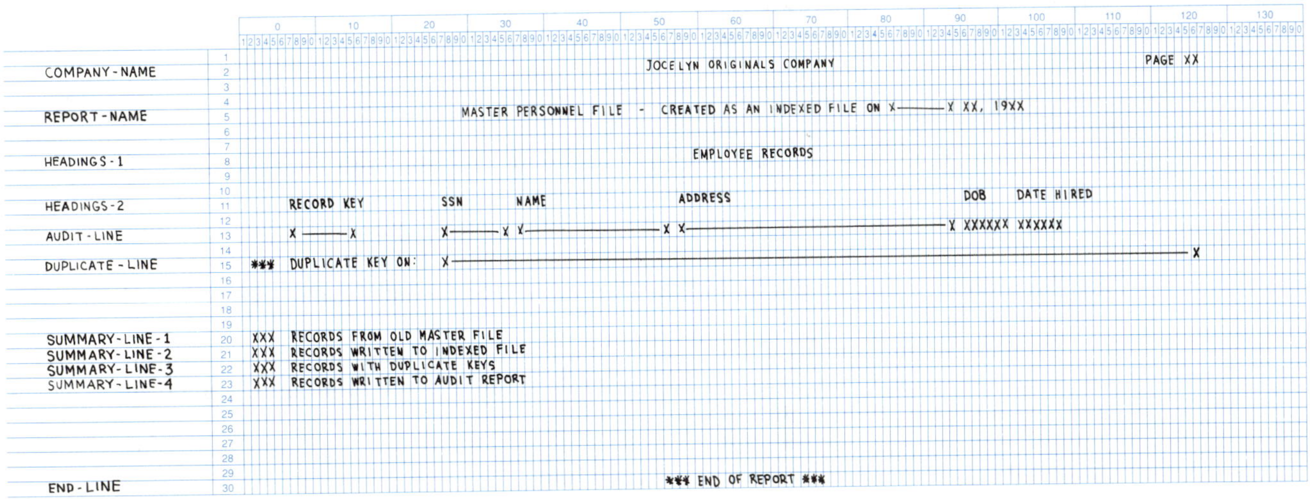

The Problem

The Jocelyn Originals Company is upgrading its computer operations from a tape-based environment to a disk-based environment. The decision is made to set up the master personnel file as an indexed file. The records in the current master file are ordered alphabetically by employee name and are formatted as follows:

cc 1–20	Employee name
cc 21–57	Employee address
cc 58–66	Employee Social Security number
cc 67–72	Employee date of birth (format: MMDDYY)
cc 73–78	Employee date of hire (format: MMDDYY)
cc 79–100	Not used

The indexed file must use the Social Security number field as the prime record key, and the records of the indexed file are to be formatted as follows:

cc 1–9	Employee Social Security number
cc 10–29	Employee name
cc 30–66	Employee address
cc 67–72	Employee date of birth (format: YYMMDD)
cc 73–78	Employee date of hire (format: YYMMDD)
cc 79–100	Not used

An audit trail report, formatted as shown in Figure 3.3, must list the employee records in the same order as they are written to the indexed file, that is, in ascending order by Social Security number.

Brief Analysis of the Problem

Since the records in the current master personnel file are stored in alphabetic order and the key field that will be used in creating the indexed file is the Social Security number field, it is clear that the tape records must be resequenced in ascending order by Social Security number. There are various ways of sorting the tape master personnel file.

Figure 3.4 Sample VAX sort statement

```
SORT/KEY=(POSITION:58,SIZE:9,ASCENDING)MASTER1.DAT MASTER2.DAT
```

Option 1

Use an external sort utility. This is a routine generally packaged with the operating system for the computer. The exact system commands and parameters that must be specified are system dependent, so you must obtain this information from your computer center. Figure 3.4 shows a sort utility available on the VAX. This system command directs the computer to sort all the records of input file MASTER1.DAT in ascending order by the values in bytes 58 through 66 and to store the sorted records in the output file MASTER2.DAT.

If this procedure were used, then the file MASTER2.DAT would have to be supplied as input to the COBOL program whose functions would be to prepare reformatted records, write them to the indexed file, and produce the audit report.

Option 2

Write a COBOL program that uses the COBOL SORT statement to sort the records of the old master file. Following the sort, the program must reformat the master records as specified, write them to the indexed file, and produce the audit report. This is the procedure that we will develop.

Program Design

The system flowchart is shown in Figure 3.5. Note that OLD-MASTER-FILE is the input file. Its records must be accessed (and counted) and released to the sort file. The sort file must resequence the records in ascending order by Social Security number. As a record is returned from the sort file, its data items are copied to a new master record (formatted as specified) and the record is then written to the indexed master file. If the write function is completed successfully, the indexed file record counter is incremented and the corresponding audit line is produced on the report. If the write function is not successful, the cause is an error in the key field value (the Social Security numbers must be in ascending order) and, as a result, the record is written to the audit report along with an appropriate message and the duplicate key record counter is incremented.

When all the records have been returned from the sort file and processed as described, the summary information is written on the report and the job is done!

The summary information on the report shows the total number of records read from the file OLD-MASTER-FILE, the total number of records written to the file INDEXED-MASTER-FILE, the total number of records that were not written to the file INDEXED-MASTER-FILE because of errors in the sequencing of the Social Security numbers, and the total number of detail lines written to the report. Note that since the employee records are sorted in ascending order by Social Security number by the SORT statement, the only kind of sequencing error that can occur is a *duplicate* Social Security number. No two employees can have the same Social Security number, and consequently, if a duplicate is detected, it means a data entry error exists on one of the records with the duplicate values. Since these records are printed in succession on the audit report, it is then a simple matter to call the employees and verify which one contains the error.

Since the records retrieved from the current tape master file must be counted prior to their being released to the sort file, the INPUT PROCEDURE option of the SORT statement is required. And, since the records returned from the sort file must be reformatted before being written to the indexed master file and to the audit report, the OUTPUT PROCEDURE option of the SORT statement is also required. Consequently, the PROCEDURE DIVISION of the program must contain three sections. They will be named 0-MAIN-CONTROL, 1-GET-OLD-RECORDS, and 2-PRODUCE-INDEXED-FILE. Obviously, the report must be produced within section 2-PRODUCE-INDEXED-FILE.

The structure chart is shown in Figure 3.6, and the program pseudocode follows:

Figure 3.5 System flowchart to create the indexed master file

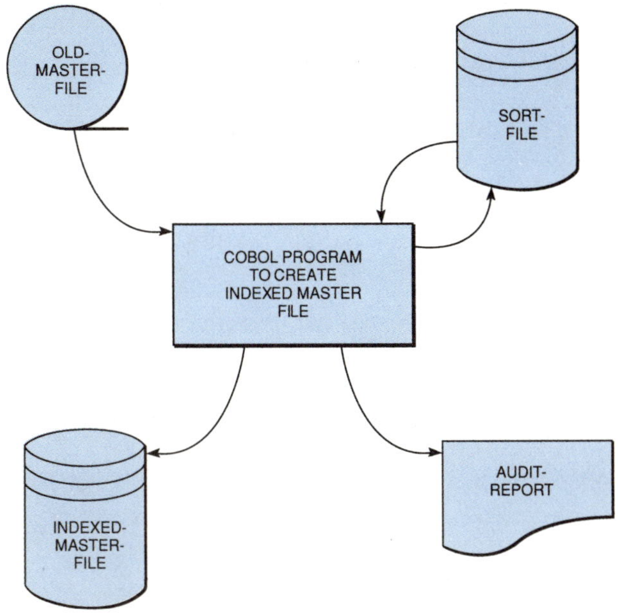

Figure 3.6 Structure chart to create the indexed master file

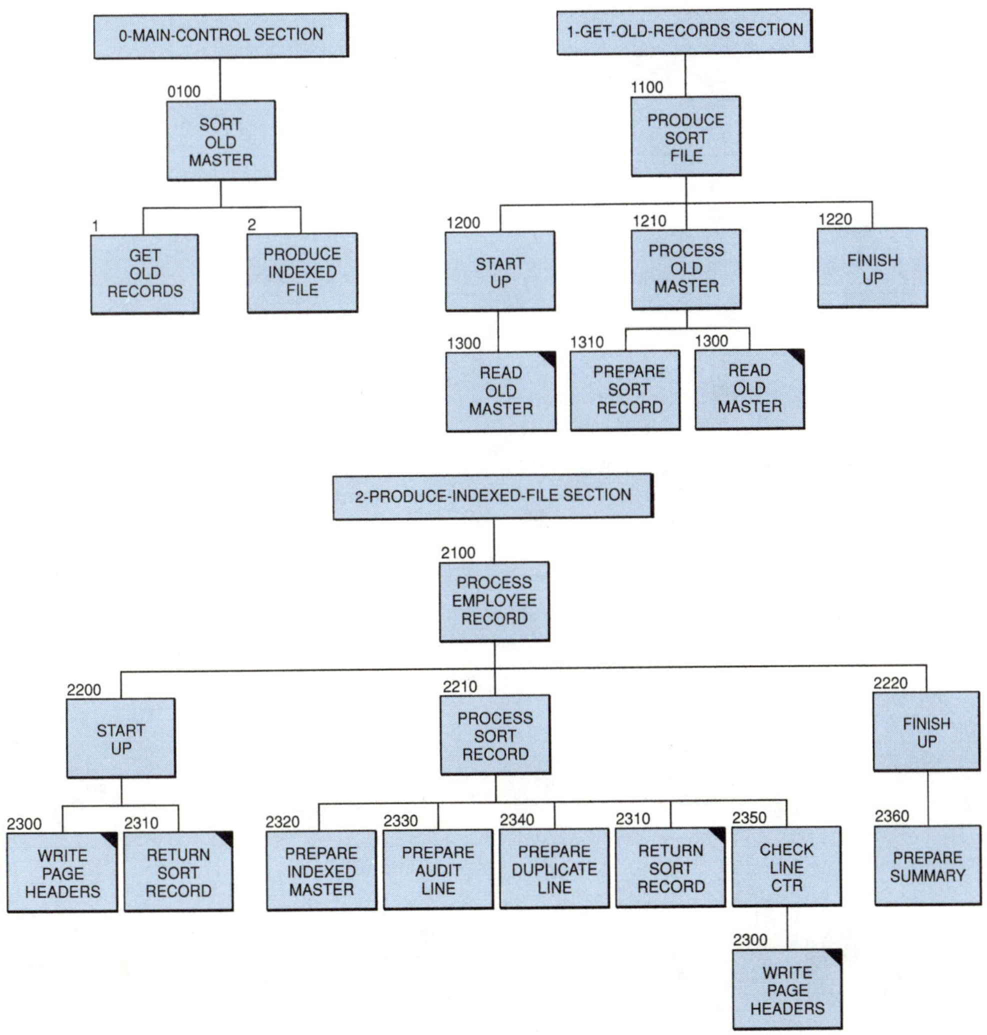

0-Main-Control Section.

0100-Produce-Sort-File.

1. Perform the input procedure 1-Get-Old-Records.
2. Sort the records of Sort-File in ascending order using the major key Social Security number.
3. Perform the output procedure 2-Produce-Indexed-File.
4. Stop the run.

1-Get-Old-Records Section.

1100-Produce-Sort-File.

1. Perform 1200-Start-Up.
2. Perform 1210-Process-Old-Master until no more old master records.
3. Perform 1220-Finish-Up.
4. Exit from the input procedure.

1200-Start-Up.

1. Open Old-Master-File as an input file.
2. Set old-master-record-counter to zero.
3. Set the flag WS-MORE-OLD-RECORDS to "YES".
4. Perform 1300-Read-Old-Master.

1210-Process-Old-Master.

1. Perform 1310-Prepare-Sort-Record.
2. Perform 1300-Read-Old-Master.

1220-Finish-Up.

1. Close Old-Master-File.

1300-Read-Old-Master.

1. Read input Old-Master-File record.
2. Test for end-of-file record:
   a. If EOF record reached, move "NO " to the flag WS-MORE-OLD-RECORDS.
   b. If EOF record is not reached, add 1 to old-master-record-counter.

1310-Prepare-Sort-Record.

1. Move old-master-record to sort-record.
2. Release sort-record to Sort-File.

2-Produce-Indexed-File Section.

2100-Process-Employee-Record.

1. Perform 2200-Start-Up.
2. Perform 2210-Process-Sort-Record until no more sort records.
3. Perform 2220-Finish-Up.
4. Exit from the output procedure.

2200-Start-Up.

1. Open Indexed-Master-File and Audit-Report as output files.
2. Set the counters indexed-file-record-counter, duplicate-record-counter, audit-line-counter, and page-number to zero.
3. Set the flag WS-MORE-SORT-RECORDS to "YES".
4. Obtain the date from the operating system.
5. Set month-table month-index to date month-number.
6. Move month-table month(month-index) to report-name month.
7. Move date day-number to report-name day.
8. Move date year-number to report-name year.
9. Perform 2300-Write-Page-Headers.
10. Perform 2310-Return-Sort-Record.

2210-Process-Sort-Record.

1. Perform 2320-Prepare-Indexed-Master.
2. Test Indexed-Master-File-status-flag value:
   a. If "00", perform 2330-Prepare-Audit-Line.
   b. If not "00", perform 2340-Prepare-Duplicate-Line.
3. Add 1 to audit-line-counter.
4. Perform 2310-Return-Sort-Record.
5. If more-sort-records = "YES", perform 2350-Check-Line-Counter.

2220-Finish-Up.

1. Perform 2360-Prepare-Summary.
2. Move the record End-Line to the output area Printline.
3. After advancing 5 lines, write the output record Printline.
4. Close Indexed-Master-File and Audit-Report.

2300-Write-Page-Headers.

1. Add 1 to page-number.
2. Move page-number to Company-Name page-number.
3. Move the record Company-Name to the output area Printline.
4. After advancing to a new page, write the output record Printline.
5. Move the record Report-Name to the output area Printline.
6. After advancing 3 lines, write the output record Printline.
7. Move the record Headings-1 to the output area Printline.
8. After advancing 3 lines, write the output record Printline.
9. Move the record Headings-2 to the output area Printline.
10. After advancing 3 lines, write the output record Printline.
11. Set proper-spacing to 2.
12. Set line-counter to zero.

2310-Return-Sort-Record.

1. Return a Sort-File record.
2. Test for end-of-file record:
   if EOF record reached, set the flag WS-MORE-SORT-RECORDS to "NO ".

2320-Prepare-Indexed-Master.

1. Move sort-record master-name to indexed-master-record master-name.
2. Move sort-record master-address to indexed-master-record master-address.
3. Move sort-record master-SSN to indexed-master-record master-SSN.
4. Move sort-record master-DOB month to indexed-master-record master-DOB month.
5. Move sort-record master-DOB day to indexed-master-record master-DOB day.
6. Move sort-record master-DOB year to indexed-master-record master-DOB year.
7. Move sort-record master-date-hired month to indexed-master-record master-date-hired month.
8. Move sort-record master-date-hired day to indexed-master-record master-date-hired day.
9. Move sort-record master-date-hired year to indexed-master-record master-date-hired year.
10. Write indexed-master-record to Indexed-Master-File, and test for invalid key:
    a. If invalid record key, set Indexed-Master-File-status-flag to "21".
    b. If not invalid record key, add 1 to Indexed-Master-File-record-counter.

2330-Prepare-Audit-Line.

1. Move sort-record master-SSN to Audit-Line record-key and SSN.
2. Move sort-record master-name to Audit-Line name.
3. Move sort-record master-address to Audit-Line address.
4. Move sort-record master-DOB month to Audit-Line DOB month.
5. Move sort-record master-DOB day to Audit-Line DOB day.
6. Move sort-record master-DOB year to Audit-Line DOB year.
7. Move sort-record master-date-hired month to Audit-Line date-hired month.
8. Move sort-record master-date-hired day to Audit-Line date-hired day.
9. Move sort-record master-date-hired year to Audit-Line date-hired year.
10. Move the record Audit-Line to the output area Printline.
11. After advancing proper-spacing, write the output record Printline.
12. Set proper-spacing to 1.

2340-Prepare-Duplicate-Line.

1. Move sort-record to Duplicate-Line record.
2. Move the record Duplicate-Line to the output area Printline.
3. After advancing proper-spacing, write the output record Printline.
4. Set proper-spacing to 1.
5. Add 1 to duplicate-counter.

2350-Check-Line-Ctr.

1. Add 1 to line-counter.
2. Test line-counter;
   if line-counter = 30, perform 2300-Write-Page-Headers.

2360-Prepare-Summary.

1. Move old-master-counter to Summary-Line-1 old-master-counter.
2. Move the record Summary-Line-1 to the output area Printline.
3. After advancing 5 lines, write the output record Printline.
4. Move indexed-file-counter to Summary-Line-2 indexed-file-counter.
5. Move the record Summary-Line-2 to the output area Printline.
6. After advancing 1 line, write the output record Printline.
7. Move duplicate-counter to Summary-Line-3 duplicate-counter.
8. Move the record Summary-Line-3 to the output area Printline.
9. After advancing 1 line, write the output record Printline.
10. Move audit-line-counter to Summary-Line-4 audit-line-counter.
11. Move the record Summary-Line-4 to the output area Printline.
12. After advancing 1 line, write the output record Printline.

The flowchart that corresponds to the program pseudocode is contained in Figure 3.7.

Figure 3.7 Program flowchart to create the indexed master file

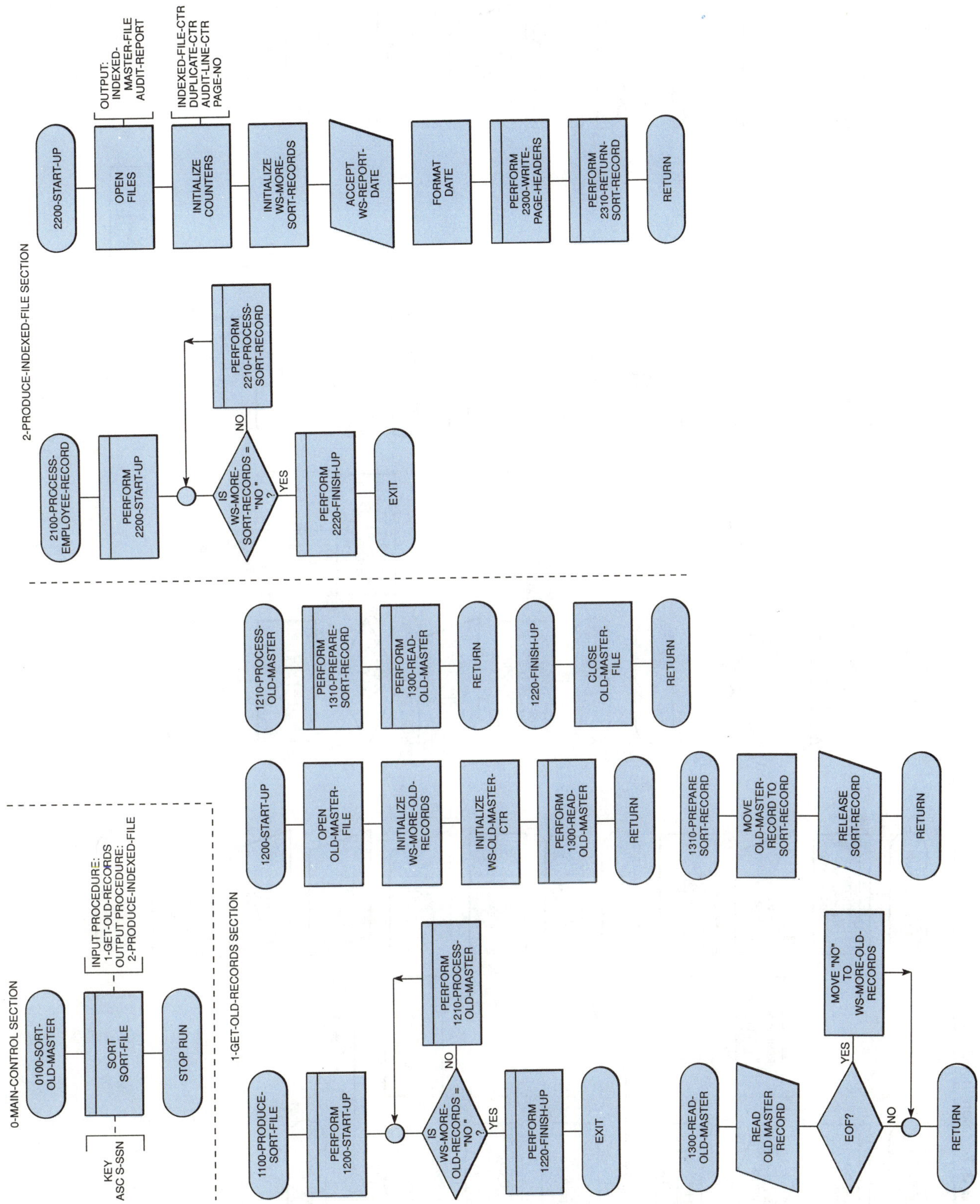

■ **Figure 3.7** continued

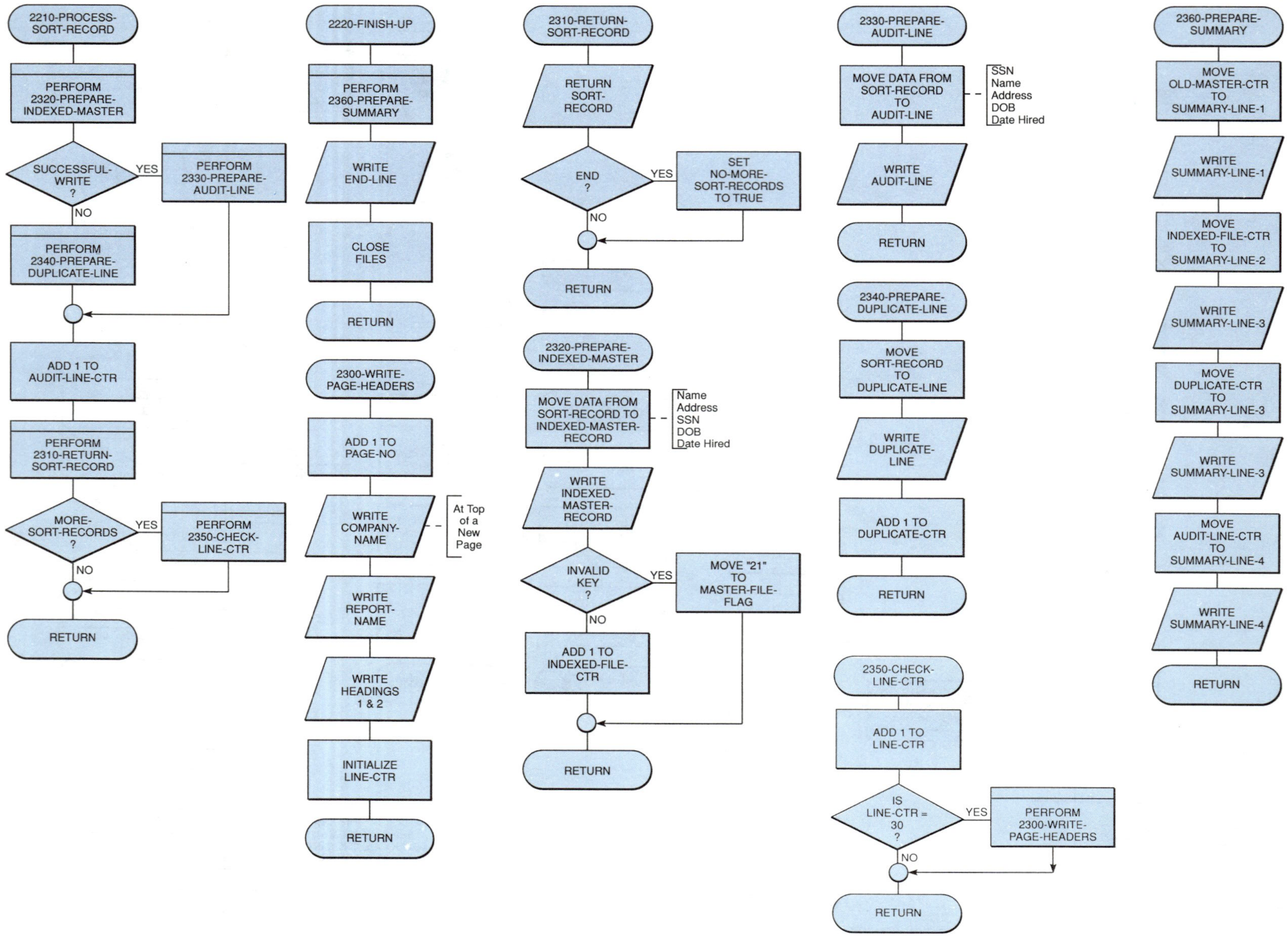

Figure 3.8 FILE-CONTROL paragraph entries for indexed files

```
SELECT [OPTIONAL] file-name-1 ASSIGN TO {implementor-name-1}
                                        {literal-1         }

    [RESERVE integer-1 [AREA ]]
    [                  [AREAS]]
    [ORGANIZATION IS] INDEXED
    [                {SEQUENTIAL}]
    [ ACCESS MODE IS {RANDOM    }]
    [                {DYNAMIC   }]
    RECORD KEY IS data-name-1
    [ALTERNATE RECORD KEY IS data-name-2 [WITH DUPLICATES]] . . .
    [FILE STATUS IS data-name-3]
```

Program Entries Related to Indexed Files

Before coding the program, we must examine program entries related to indexed files. Recall that the FILE-CONTROL paragraph is the first one that contains file-related specifications. The general format of this paragraph for indexed files is shown in Figure 3.8.

The FILE-CONTROL Paragraph

In this format,

1. *File-name-1* is the internal name of the file, and it must be defined in an FD entry of the FILE SECTION.
2. The word OPTIONAL can be specified only for files opened in input mode, and it must be specified for input files that need not be present when the program is run.
3. *Implementor-name-1* is the name of a system-specific device that connects the internal file with an external file. The device must be a direct-access storage device.
4. *Literal-1* is a file specification or a logical name used in connecting the internal file with an external file. The file must reside on a direct-access storage device, and the logical name must be defined to correspond to a direct-access storage device.
5. The RESERVE clause specifies the number of buffers in main memory that must be reserved for the file. If it is not used, the operating system supplies a default value.
6. The clause ORGANIZATION IS INDEXED specifies the file's logical structure as an indexed file. Its use causes the operating system to generate an index for each record written to the file. All indexes are stored in the file itself. A file created as an indexed file remains an indexed file for the rest of its life. A file's organization cannot be changed.
7. The ACCESS MODE clause specifies the order in which the records of the file must be accessed. If the clause is not coded, access mode is sequential by default.
   a. If the access mode is SEQUENTIAL, the records of the file are accessed in ascending order by the record key value.
   b. If the access mode is RANDOM, the value currently stored in a RECORD KEY data item indicates the record to be accessed.
   c. If the access mode is DYNAMIC, the records of the file may be accessed sequentially or randomly.
   d. If the access mode is SEQUENTIAL, the file may be open in INPUT, OUTPUT, I-O, or EXTEND mode.
   e. If the access mode is RANDOM or DYNAMIC, the file may be open in INPUT, OUTPUT, or I-O mode.

8. The RECORD KEY clause names the prime record key for the file. When the indexed file is created, the records are stored in ascending order of the prime record key values.
   a. *Data-name-1* must be described within a record description entry for the file. It may be defined as alphanumeric or alphabetic or as an unsigned numeric item. It may also be a group item, provided the group does not contain a variable-occurrence data item.
   b. The value of the prime record key must be unique to a record. That is, prime record key values must not be duplicated in the records of the file.
   c. The prime record key must have the same location in every record.
   d. The data description entry that defines the prime record key and its location within the record must be identical to the ones used when the indexed file was first created. (Programs that reference the indexed file may use different names for the prime key field, but its location within the record and the PIC clause must remain the same.)
9. The ALTERNATE RECORD KEY clause provides one or more alternate paths by which the records of the indexed file may be accessed.
   a. *Data-name-2* must be described within a record description entry for the file. It may be defined as alphanumeric or alphabetic or as an unsigned numeric item. It may also be a group item, provided the group does not contain a variable-occurrence data item.
   b. Within a record, the field named by *data-name-2* must not begin at the same character position as the field that contains the prime record key.
   c. If more than one alternate record key is specified for the file, these keys must not share the same leftmost character position within the record.
   d. If alternate record keys are specified in the program that creates the file, every program that references the file must contain the same ALTERNATE KEY clauses, in the same sequence, and the record description in those programs must maintain the initial location and description of all the file's keys.
   e. The DUPLICATES phrase allows the file to contain records with duplicate values within corresponding alternate record keys. If the phrase is not used, no two records must have the same alternate record key values.
10. The FILE STATUS clause names a data item that contains the code generated by the operating system that results from an input or output operation on the file.
   a. *Data-name-3* is the name of a two-character alphanumeric data item usually defined in the WORKING-STORAGE SECTION.
   b. *Data-name-3* receives a two-digit code from the operating system subsequent to every input or output operation on the file.
   c. The value in *data-name-3* may be tested to determine the success or failure of an I/O operation on the file, as well as the cause of a failure.

In the current program, the SELECT statement for the indexed file that must be created by the program is as follows:

```
SELECT INDEXED-MASTER-FILE  ASSIGN TO "INDMSTR.DAT"
                            ORGANIZATION IS INDEXED
                            ACCESS MODE IS SEQUENTIAL
                            RECORD KEY IS INDEXED-MR-SSN
                            FILE STATUS IS MASTER-FILE-FLAG.
```

1. INDMSTR.DAT is an external file specification. It names the file in the user's directory that will contain the newly created indexed file, known as INDEXED-MASTER-FILE within the program, when program execution is complete. The file must be stored in a direct-access storage device.
2. The clause ORGANIZATION IS INDEXED specifies that the file INDEXED-MASTER-FILE is an indexed file.
3. The clause ACCESS MODE IS SEQUENTIAL specifies that the master records will be written to this file in ascending order by the prime record key value. This is the most efficient way of creating an indexed file.
4. The clause RECORD KEY IS INDEXED-MR-SSN names the data field INDEXED-MR-SSN of the file's records as the prime record key. The records that will be written to the indexed file must be presorted in ascending order by the values stored in this data field. The brief problem analysis above indicates that the sorting will be done within the program by means of the COBOL SORT statement.

5. The clause FILE STATUS IS MASTER-FILE-FLAG specifies that the I/O operation status codes generated by the operating system relative to the indexed file will be stored in the data item MASTER-FILE-FLAG. This data item must be defined in the WORKING-STORAGE SECTION by the picture clause PIC X(2). In this program, the indexed file will be opened in output mode, and the only I/O operations that will reference it are the OPEN, CLOSE, and WRITE statements. The file status codes that are most applicable in this situation are the following:

   "00" to denote a successful I/O operation;

   "21" to denote an attempt to WRITE a record whose prime record key value is not greater than the prime record key value of the previous record written to the file;

   "30" to denote permanent errors such as a transmission error, a parity error, or a data check.

   The standard file status codes are listed in Appendix C. (*Note:* In addition to the ANSI standard codes, other implementor-specific codes may also be produced by the system; these are in the range from "90" to "99". For instance, the VAX generates the code "94" to denote an attempt to write to an unopened file, or to denote an open mode that is not compatible with a WRITE operation.)

The RANDOM and DYNAMIC options of the ACCESS MODE clause and the ALTERNATE RECORD KEY clause will be examined later.

The next program entry that we examine briefly is the FD paragraph for the indexed file INDEXED-MASTER-FILE. Recall that the record layout has been specified in the statement of the problem. The coding is as follows:

```
FD  INDEXED-MASTER-FILE
    RECORD CONTAINS 100 CHARACTERS
    BLOCK CONTAINS 5 RECORDS.
01  INDEXED-MASTER-RECORD.
    05 INDEXED-MR-SSN          PIC X(9).
    05 INDEXED-MR-NAME         PIC X(20).
    05 INDEXED-MR-ADDRESS      PIC X(37).
    05 INDEXED-MR-DOB          PIC X(6).
    05 INDEXED-MR-DATE-HIRED   PIC X(6).
    05                         PIC X(22).
```

In the FD paragraph, the record size has been maintained at 100 characters to match the size of the records in the old master file. Realize that the record size could have been increased. The blocking factor has been reduced to 5 records. It should be selected after consulting a systems analyst. Note that the prime record key has been positioned at the beginning of the record. Although this is not necessary, it increases record processing efficiency, since fewer record bytes have to be searched to find the prime record key value. Note that INDEXED-MR-SSN is defined as an alphanumeric item. It could have been defined by PIC 9(9). (In a later program, we will specify INDEXED-MR-NAME as a key in the ALTERNATE RECORD KEY clause, to allow access to employee records by using employee names as an alternative to their Social Security numbers.)

In the WORKING-STORAGE SECTION, the only entry that is directly related to the file INDEXED-MASTER-FILE is the file status data item MASTER-FILE-FLAG. It will be coded as follows:

```
05 MASTER-FILE-FLAG        PIC X(2).
   88 SUCCESSFUL-WRITE               VALUE "00".
   88 DUPLICATE-KEY                  VALUE "21".
```

The condition-names are included for additional documentation. (Other status codes will be specified later.)

In the PROCEDURE DIVISION, the indexed file is opened in OUTPUT mode within 2-PRODUCE-INDEXED-FILE SECTION. For each record returned from the sort file, an indexed master record must be prepared. Recall that the record layout for these new master records is not the same as the record layout of the old master records. Specifically, the first data field of the new records must contain the Social Security number, and the data of birth and date hired formats must be YYMMDD. Reference modification will be used in MOVE statements to transfer the date components properly. Once the record has been assigned all of its data item values, it must be written to the indexed file. Recall that it is during this write operation that the index associated with the record is produced and stored in an index record within the index table.

Figure 3.9 WRITE-INVALID KEY statement format

```
WRITE record-name-1 [FROM identifier-1]
        [INVALID KEY imperative-statement-1]
        [NOT INVALID KEY imperative-statement-2]
        [END-WRITE]
```

The WRITE-INVALID KEY Statement

The format of the WRITE statement that must be used when writing records to an indexed file is shown in Figure 3.9.

Rules Governing the Use of the WRITE-INVALID KEY Statement for Indexed Files

1. *Record-name-1* must be the name of a logical record defined in the FD entry for the file being written to.
2. *Identifier-1* is the name of a data item containing data to be transferred to *record-name-1*.
3. *Imperative-statement-1* and *imperative-statement-2* are imperative statements.
4. The file being written to must be opened in OUTPUT, I-O, or EXTEND mode at the time the WRITE statement executes.
5. A WRITE statement is successful only if the prime record key value is unique to the record being written. The value must be assigned to the prime record key data item prior to executing the WRITE statement.
6. If the SELECT statement for the indexed file contains the ALTERNATE RECORD KEY clause, the alternate record key values do not have to be unique to a record if the WITH DUPLICATES option is specified. In this case, later sequential retrieval of records based on alternate record keys will be in the same sequence in which they were written to the file.
7. If access mode is sequential, and the file is opened in
   a. OUTPUT mode, the records must be written in ascending order of prime record key values.
   b. EXTEND mode, the records must be written in ascending order of prime record key values, and the first of these new records must have a prime record key value greater than the highest one that currently exists in the file.
8. If access mode is random or dynamic, records may be written to the file in any order of prime record key values.
9. Following a successful execution of the WRITE statement,
   a. Indexes, based on the record keys, are stored in the index table to enable later retrieval of the record.
   b. The record is no longer available in the record area *record-name-1*.
   c. If the FROM phrase is used, the value of *identifier-1* remains unchanged.
   d. The code "00" is assigned to the data item named in the FILE STATUS clause for the file, or the code "02" is assigned if the record contains a duplicate alternate record key value and the DUPLICATES option is specified in the ALTERNATE RECORD KEY clause.
   e. If the NOT INVALID KEY clause exists, *imperative-statement-2* is executed.
   f. If there is no NOT INVALID KEY clause, control passes to the first statement beyond the scope of the WRITE statement.
10. The INVALID KEY clause specifies the course of action the program must take if the WRITE operation is unsuccessful due to an invalid key condition. When the invalid key condition occurs,
    a. A two-digit code representing that condition is assigned to the data item defined in the FILE STATUS clause for the file. For an indexed file, the various codes are as follows:

       "21" to denote an attempt to write a record whose prime record key value is not greater than the prime record key value of the previous record written to the file, when access mode is sequential;

"22" to denote an attempt to write a record whose prime record key value duplicates an existing prime record key value, when access mode is random or dynamic, or an attempt to write a record for which an alternate record key value duplicates an existing alternate record key value when duplicates are not allowed;

"24" to denote an attempt to write a record beyond the externally defined boundaries for the file;

"30" to denote a permanent system error, such as a transmission error, data check, or parity error.

b. The record is not written to the file, and it remains available in the record area *record-name-1*.

c. Program execution continues as specified by *imperative-statement-1*.

11. END-WRITE is the explicit scope terminator for the WRITE statement.

The WRITE statement needed in the program is the following:

```
WRITE INDEXED-MASTER-RECORD
    INVALID KEY
        SET DUPLICATE-KEY TO TRUE
    NOT INVALID KEY
        ADD 1 TO WS-INDEXED-FILE-CTR
END-WRITE.
```

The SET statement in the INVALID KEY clause duplicates the action the operating system takes if the record being written contains the same Social Security number as the previous record written to the file. The ADD statement in the NOT INVALID KEY clause increments by 1 the counter that keeps track of the number of records written to the indexed file whenever the WRITE operation is successful.

Coding the Program

The complete COBOL program to create the indexed file and to produce the audit report is shown in Figure 3.10. Some lines have been numbered to facilitate references to certain program entries. The numbered comments follow.

1. In this program, INDEXED-MASTER-FILE is created as an indexed file. Any later use of this file requires that its SELECT statement contain the clause ORGANIZATION IS INDEXED and the RECORD KEY clause. The data name in the RECORD KEY clause must always reference the same record position as the one referenced by INDEXED-MR-SSN in the creation run of the file, specifically, the first 9 bytes of the record.

    The access mode is sequential because that is the most efficient way to create an indexed file. The access mode may be changed in later programs that reference the file. *Note well:* The organization of a file cannot be changed, but the mode of access to the records of the file may be changed by the programmer from one program to another and even within a program. Access mode options are a direct consequence of the file's organization!

    The FILE STATUS clause names the data item that receives the status codes produced by the operating system in response to any I/O operation that references the file. It remains an optional entry, but its use allows the program to specify different courses of action related to the conditions specified by the status codes.
2. For each record, the value in the field INDEXED-MR-SSN is its prime record key value. No two records in the indexed file can have the same prime record key value. Later access to records of this file will use the indexes associated with the record key values when the records were initially written to the file.
3. The data item MASTER-FILE-FLAG is named in the FILE STATUS clause of the SELECT statement for the indexed file INDEXED-MASTER-FILE. Every I/O operation that references this file, namely OPEN, CLOSE, and WRITE in this program, causes a two-digit code to be stored in MASTER-FILE-FLAG. Conditional statements in the PROCEDURE DIVISION may test MASTER-FILE-FLAG and provide for the execution of different procedures depending on the code it contains. Two of these codes are specified by the attached condition-names.

■ **Figure 3.10** COBOL program to create the indexed file

```
    IDENTIFICATION DIVISION.

    PROGRAM-ID.  CREATE-INDEXED-MASTER-STANDARD.

   *****************************************************************
   *                                                               *
   *  THE MAIN FUNCTION OF THIS PROGRAM IS TO CREATE AN INDEXED    *
   *  MASTER PERSONNEL FILE FOR THE JOCELYN ORIGINALS COMPANY.     *
   *                                                               *
   *  THE MASTER FILE IS CURRENTLY ON TAPE.  SINCE THE RECORD KEY  *
   *  FOR THE INDEXED FILE IS TO BE THE SOCIAL SECURITY NUMBER, AND *
   *  THE RECORDS ARE CURRENTLY IN ALPHABETIC ORDER BY EMPLOYEE    *
   *  NAME, THE RECORDS MUST BE SORTED IN ASCENDING SSN SEQUENCE   *
   *  AND THEY MUST BE REFORMATTED PRIOR TO BEING WRITTEN TO THE   *
   *  INDEXED MASTER FILE.  THE SSN FIELD MUST BE THE FIRST DATA   *
   *  FIELD OF THE NEW MASTER RECORDS, AND THE DATE-OF-BIRTH AND   *
   *  DATE-HIRED FIELDS MUST BE IN YYMMDD FORMAT.  ON THE OLD      *
   *  RECORDS, THESE DATES ARE IN MMDDYY FORMAT.                   *
   *                                                               *
   *  THE PROGRAM ALSO PRODUCES AN AUDIT REPORT.                   *
   *                                                               *
   *****************************************************************

    ENVIRONMENT DIVISION.

    CONFIGURATION SECTION.

    SOURCE-COMPUTER.  VAX-VMS-8650.
    OBJECT-COMPUTER.  VAX-VMS-8650.

    INPUT-OUTPUT SECTION.

    FILE-CONTROL.
        SELECT OLD-MASTER-FILE      ASSIGN TO COB$INPUT
                                    ORGANIZATION IS SEQUENTIAL
                                    ACCESS MODE IS SEQUENTIAL.
        SELECT SORT-FILE            ASSIGN TO SORTDISK.
1       SELECT INDEXED-MASTER-FILE ASSIGN TO 'INDMSTR.DAT'
                                    ORGANIZATION IS INDEXED
                                    ACCESS MODE IS SEQUENTIAL
                                    RECORD KEY IS INDEXED-MR-SSN
                                    FILE STATUS IS MASTER-FILE-FLAG.
        SELECT AUDIT-REPORT         ASSIGN TO COB$OUTPUT.

    DATA DIVISION.

    FILE SECTION.

    FD  OLD-MASTER-FILE
        RECORD CONTAINS 100 CHARACTERS
        BLOCK CONTAINS 10 RECORDS.

    01  OLD-MASTER-RECORD.
        05 OLD-MR-NAME          PIC X(20).
        05 OLD-MR-ADDRESS       PIC X(37).
        05 OLD-MR-SSN           PIC X(9).
        05 OLD-MR-DOB           PIC X(6).
        05 OLD-MR-DATE-HIRED    PIC X(6).
        05                      PIC X(22).

    SD  SORT-FILE
        RECORD CONTAINS 100 CHARACTERS.

    01  SORT-RECORD.
        05 S-MR-NAME            PIC X(20).
        05 S-MR-ADDRESS         PIC X(37).
        05 S-MR-SSN             PIC X(9).
        05 S-MR-DOB             PIC X(6).
        05 S-MR-DATE-HIRED      PIC X(6).
        05                      PIC X(22).

    FD  INDEXED-MASTER-FILE
        RECORD CONTAINS 100 CHARACTERS
        BLOCK CONTAINS 5 RECORDS.

    01  INDEXED-MASTER-RECORD.
2       05 INDEXED-MR-SSN           PIC X(9).
        05 INDEXED-MR-NAME          PIC X(20).
        05 INDEXED-MR-ADDRESS       PIC X(37).
        05 INDEXED-MR-DOB           PIC X(6).
        05 INDEXED-MR-DATE-HIRED    PIC X(6).
        05                          PIC X(22).
```

Figure 3.10 continued

```
       FD  AUDIT-REPORT
           RECORD CONTAINS 132 CHARACTERS.

       01  PRINTLINE                   PIC X(132).

       WORKING-STORAGE SECTION.

       01  PROGRAM-CONTROLS.
           05 WS-MORE-OLD-RECORDS    PIC X(3).
              88 MORE-OLD-RECORDS              VALUE 'YES'.
              88 NO-MORE-OLD-RECORDS           VALUE 'NO '.
           05 WS-MORE-SORT-RECORDS   PIC X(3).
              88 MORE-SORT-RECORDS             VALUE 'YES'.
              88 NO-MORE-SORT-RECORDS          VALUE 'NO '.
3          05 MASTER-FILE-FLAG       PIC X(2).
              88 SUCCESSFUL-WRITE              VALUE '00'.
              88 DUPLICATE-KEY                 VALUE '21'.
           05 WS-REPORT-DATE.
              10 WS-YR-NO              PIC 9(2).
              10 WS-MONTH-NO           PIC 9(2).
              10 WS-DAY-NO             PIC 9(2).
           05 WS-PROPER-SPACING        PIC 9(1).
           05 WS-PAGE-NO               PIC 9(2).

4      01  PROGRAM-COUNTERS.
           05 WS-OLD-MASTER-CTR        PIC S9(3).
           05 WS-INDEXED-FILE-CTR      PIC S9(3).
           05 WS-DUPLICATE-CTR         PIC S9(3).
           05 WS-AUDIT-LINE-CTR        PIC S9(3).
           05 WS-LINE-CTR              PIC S9(3).

       01  MONTH-VALUES.
           05 PIC X(9) VALUE 'JANUARY  '.
           05 PIC X(9) VALUE 'FEBRUARY '.
           05 PIC X(9) VALUE 'MARCH    '.
           05 PIC X(9) VALUE 'APRIL    '.
           05 PIC X(9) VALUE 'MAY      '.
           05 PIC X(9) VALUE 'JUNE     '.
           05 PIC X(9) VALUE 'JULY     '.
           05 PIC X(9) VALUE 'AUGUST   '.
           05 PIC X(9) VALUE 'SEPTEMBER'.
           05 PIC X(9) VALUE 'OCTOBER  '.
           05 PIC X(9) VALUE 'NOVEMBER '.
           05 PIC X(9) VALUE 'DECEMBER '.

5      01  MONTH-TABLE REDEFINES MONTH-VALUES.
           05 WS-MONTH   OCCURS 12 TIMES
                         INDEXED BY MONTH-INDEX   PIC X(9).

       01 REPORT-HEADERS.
           05 COMPANY-NAME.
              10            PIC X(53)  VALUE SPACES.
              10            PIC X(25)  VALUE
                             'JOCELYN ORIGINALS COMPANY'.
              10            PIC X(41)  VALUE SPACES.
              10            PIC X(4)   VALUE 'PAGE'.
              10 O-PAGE-NO  PIC Z9.
              10            PIC X(6)   VALUE SPACES.

           05 REPORT-NAME.
              10            PIC X(29)  VALUE SPACES.
              10            PIC X(55)  VALUE
             'MASTER PERSONNEL FILE  -  CREATED AS AN INDEXED FILE ON'.
              10            PIC X(1)   VALUE SPACES.
              10 O-MONTH    PIC X(9).
              10 O-DAY      PIC 9(2).
              10            PIC X(4)   VALUE ', 19'.
              10 O-YEAR     PIC 9(2).
              10            PIC X(29)  VALUE SPACES.

           05 HEADINGS-1.
              10 PIC X(59)  VALUE SPACES.
              10 PIC X(16)  VALUE 'EMPLOYEE RECORDS'.
              10 PIC X(57)  VALUE SPACES.
```

```
       05 HEADINGS-2.
          10 PIC X(6)    VALUE SPACES.
          10 PIC X(10)   VALUE 'RECORD KEY'.
          10 PIC X(10)   VALUE SPACES.
          10 PIC X(3)    VALUE 'SSN'.
          10 PIC X(7)    VALUE SPACES.
          10 PIC X(4)    VALUE 'NAME'.
          10 PIC X(17)   VALUE SPACES.
          10 PIC X(7)    VALUE 'ADDRESS'.
          10 PIC X(31)   VALUE SPACES.
          10 PIC X(3)    VALUE 'DOB'.
          10 PIC X(4)    VALUE SPACES.
          10 PIC X(10)   VALUE 'DATE HIRED'.
          10 PIC X(20)   VALUE SPACES.

   01  AUDIT-LINE.
       05                PIC X(6).
       05 O-RECORD-KEY   PIC X(9).
       05                PIC X(11).
       05 O-SSN          PIC X(9).
       05                PIC X(1).
       05 O-NAME         PIC X(20).
       05                PIC X(1).
       05 O-ADDRESS      PIC X(37).
       05                PIC X(1).
       05 O-DOB          PIC X(6).
       05                PIC X(1).
       05 O-DATE-HIRED   PIC X(6).
       05                PIC X(24).

   01  DUPLICATE-LINE.
       05                PIC X(26)   VALUE
                         ' ***  DUPLICATE KEY ON:    '.
       05 O-RECORD       PIC X(100).
       05                PIC X(6)    VALUE SPACES.

   01  REPORT-ENDERS.
       05 SUMMARY-LINE-1.
          10                      PIC X(1)    VALUE SPACES.
          10 O-OLD-MASTER-CTR     PIC ZZ9.
          10                      PIC X(30)   VALUE
                           '  RECORDS FROM OLD MASTER FILE'.

       05 SUMMARY-LINE-2.
          10                      PIC X(1)    VALUE SPACES.
          10 O-INDEXED-FILE-CTR   PIC ZZ9.
          10                      PIC X(33)   VALUE
                           '  RECORDS WRITTEN TO INDEXED FILE'.

       05 SUMMARY-LINE-3.
          10                      PIC X(1)    VALUE SPACES.
          10 O-DUPLICATE-CTR      PIC ZZ9.
          10                      PIC X(29)   VALUE
                           '  RECORDS WITH DUPLICATE KEYS'.

       05 SUMMARY-LINE-4.
          10                      PIC X(1)    VALUE SPACES.
          10 O-AUDIT-LINE-CTR     PIC ZZ9.
          10                      PIC X(33)   VALUE
                           '  RECORDS WRITTEN TO AUDIT REPORT'.

       05 END-LINE.
          10 PIC X(55)   VALUE SPACES.
          10 PIC X(21)   VALUE '*** END OF REPORT ***'.
          10 PIC X(55)   VALUE SPACES.

   PROCEDURE DIVISION.

  *********************************
   0-MAIN-CONTROL SECTION.
  *********************************

   0100-SORT-OLD-MASTER.
       SORT SORT-FILE
6          ON ASCENDING KEY S-MR-SSN
           INPUT PROCEDURE IS 1-GET-OLD-RECORDS
           OUTPUT PROCEDURE IS 2-PRODUCE-INDEXED-FILE.
       STOP RUN.

  *********************************
   1-GET-OLD-RECORDS SECTION.
  *********************************
```

Figure 3.10 continued

```
 1100-PRODUCE-SORT-FILE.
     PERFORM 1200-START-UP.
     PERFORM 1210-PROCESS-OLD-MASTER
         UNTIL NO-MORE-OLD-RECORDS.
     PERFORM 1220-FINISH-UP.
     GO TO 1999-EXIT-SECTION.

 1200-START-UP.
     OPEN INPUT OLD-MASTER-FILE.
     INITIALIZE WS-OLD-MASTER-CTR.
     SET MORE-OLD-RECORDS TO TRUE.
     PERFORM 1300-READ-OLD-MASTER.

 1210-PROCESS-OLD-MASTER.
     PERFORM 1310-PREPARE-SORT-RECORD.
     PERFORM 1300-READ-OLD-MASTER.

 1220-FINISH-UP.
     CLOSE OLD-MASTER-FILE.

 1300-READ-OLD-MASTER.
     READ OLD-MASTER-FILE RECORD
         AT END
             SET NO-MORE-OLD-RECORDS TO TRUE
7        NOT AT END
             ADD 1 TO WS-OLD-MASTER-CTR
     END-READ.

 1310-PREPARE-SORT-RECORD.
     RELEASE SORT-RECORD FROM OLD-MASTER-RECORD.

 1999-EXIT-SECTION.
     EXIT.

*********************************
 2-PRODUCE-INDEXED-FILE SECTION.
*********************************

 2100-PROCESS-EMPLOYEE-RECORD.
     PERFORM 2200-START-UP.
     PERFORM 2210-PROCESS-SORT-RECORD
         UNTIL NO-MORE-SORT-RECORDS.
     PERFORM 2220-FINISH-UP.
     GO TO 2999-EXIT-SECTION.

 2200-START-UP.
     OPEN OUTPUT INDEXED-MASTER-FILE
                 AUDIT-REPORT.
     INITIALIZE WS-INDEXED-FILE-CTR
                WS-DUPLICATE-CTR
                WS-AUDIT-LINE-CTR
                WS-PAGE-NO.
     SET MORE-SORT-RECORDS TO TRUE.
     ACCEPT WS-REPORT-DATE FROM DATE.
8    SET MONTH-INDEX TO WS-MONTH-NO.
     MOVE WS-MONTH(MONTH-INDEX) TO O-MONTH.
     MOVE WS-DAY-NO TO O-DAY.
     MOVE WS-YR-NO TO O-YEAR.
     PERFORM 2300-WRITE-PAGE-HEADERS.
     PERFORM 2310-RETURN-SORT-RECORD.

 2210-PROCESS-SORT-RECORD.
     PERFORM 2320-PREPARE-INDEXED-MASTER.
9    IF SUCCESSFUL-WRITE
         PERFORM 2330-PREPARE-AUDIT-LINE
     ELSE
         PERFORM 2340-PREPARE-DUPLICATE-LINE
     END-IF.
     ADD 1 TO WS-AUDIT-LINE-CTR.
     PERFORM 2310-RETURN-SORT-RECORD.
     IF NO-MORE-SORT-RECORDS
         NEXT SENTENCE
     ELSE
         PERFORM 2350-CHECK-LINE-CTR.

 2220-FINISH-UP.
     PERFORM 2360-PREPARE-SUMMARY.
     WRITE PRINTLINE FROM END-LINE
         AFTER ADVANCING 5 LINES.
     CLOSE INDEXED-MASTER-FILE
           AUDIT-REPORT.
```

Figure 3.10 continued

```
       2300-WRITE-PAGE-HEADERS.
           ADD 1 TO WS-PAGE-NO.
           MOVE WS-PAGE-NO TO O-PAGE-NO.
           WRITE PRINTLINE FROM COMPANY-NAME
               AFTER ADVANCING PAGE.
           WRITE PRINTLINE FROM REPORT-NAME
               AFTER ADVANCING 3 LINES.
           WRITE PRINTLINE FROM HEADINGS-1
               AFTER ADVANCING 3 LINES.
           WRITE PRINTLINE FROM HEADINGS-2
               AFTER ADVANCING 3 LINES.
           MOVE 2 TO WS-PROPER-SPACING.
           INITIALIZE WS-LINE-CTR.

       2310-RETURN-SORT-RECORD.
           RETURN SORT-FILE RECORD
               AT END
                   SET NO-MORE-SORT-RECORDS TO TRUE.

       2320-PREPARE-INDEXED-MASTER.
           MOVE S-MR-NAME TO INDEXED-MR-NAME.
           MOVE S-MR-ADDRESS TO INDEXED-MR-ADDRESS.
           MOVE S-MR-SSN TO INDEXED-MR-SSN.
           MOVE S-MR-DOB(1:2) TO INDEXED-MR-DOB(3:2).
           MOVE S-MR-DOB(3:2) TO INDEXED-MR-DOB(5:2).
           MOVE S-MR-DOB(5:2) TO INDEXED-MR-DOB(1:2).
           MOVE S-MR-DATE-HIRED(1:2) TO INDEXED-MR-DATE-HIRED(3:2).
           MOVE S-MR-DATE-HIRED(3:2) TO INDEXED-MR-DATE-HIRED(5:2).
           MOVE S-MR-DATE-HIRED(5:2) TO INDEXED-MR-DATE-HIRED(1:2).
10         WRITE INDEXED-MASTER-RECORD
               INVALID KEY
                   SET DUPLICATE-KEY TO TRUE
               NOT INVALID KEY
                   ADD 1 TO WS-INDEXED-FILE-CTR
           END-WRITE.

       2330-PREPARE-AUDIT-LINE.
           MOVE S-MR-SSN TO O-RECORD-KEY
                            O-SSN.
           MOVE S-MR-NAME TO O-NAME.
           MOVE S-MR-ADDRESS TO O-ADDRESS.
           MOVE S-MR-DOB(5:2) TO O-DOB(1:2).
           MOVE S-MR-DOB(1:2) TO O-DOB(3:2).
           MOVE S-MR-DOB(3:2) TO O-DOB(5:2).
           MOVE S-MR-DATE-HIRED(5:2) TO O-DATE-HIRED(1:2).
           MOVE S-MR-DATE-HIRED(1:2) TO O-DATE-HIRED(3:2).
           MOVE S-MR-DATE-HIRED(3:2) TO O-DATE-HIRED(5:2).
           WRITE PRINTLINE FROM AUDIT-LINE
               AFTER ADVANCING WS-PROPER-SPACING.
           MOVE 1 TO WS-PROPER-SPACING.

       2340-PREPARE-DUPLICATE-LINE.
           MOVE SORT-RECORD TO O-RECORD.
           WRITE PRINTLINE FROM DUPLICATE-LINE
               AFTER ADVANCING WS-PROPER-SPACING.
           MOVE 1 TO WS-PROPER-SPACING.
           ADD 1 TO WS-DUPLICATE-CTR.

       2350-CHECK-LINE-CTR.
           ADD 1 TO WS-LINE-CTR.
           IF WS-LINE-CTR = 30
               PERFORM 2300-WRITE-PAGE-HEADERS
           END-IF.

       2360-PREPARE-SUMMARY.
           MOVE WS-OLD-MASTER-CTR TO O-OLD-MASTER-CTR.
           WRITE PRINTLINE FROM SUMMARY-LINE-1
               AFTER ADVANCING 5 LINES.
           MOVE WS-INDEXED-FILE-CTR TO O-INDEXED-FILE-CTR.
           WRITE PRINTLINE FROM SUMMARY-LINE-2
               AFTER ADVANCING 1 LINE.
           MOVE WS-DUPLICATE-CTR TO O-DUPLICATE-CTR.
           WRITE PRINTLINE FROM SUMMARY-LINE-3
               AFTER ADVANCING 1 LINE.
           MOVE WS-AUDIT-LINE-CTR TO O-AUDIT-LINE-CTR.
           WRITE PRINTLINE FROM SUMMARY-LINE-4
               AFTER ADVANCING 1 LINE.

       2999-EXIT-SECTION.
           EXIT.
```

4. The counter WS-OLD-MASTER-CTR is incremented in paragraph 1300-READ-OLD-MASTER every time the READ statement executes successfully for the file OLD-MASTER-FILE. Its final value indicates the number of records in the old master file. It is printed as part of the summary report.

   The counter WS-INDEXED-FILE-CTR is incremented in paragraph 2320-PREPARE-INDEXED-MASTER every time the WRITE statement executes successfully for the file INDEXED-MASTER-FILE. Its final value indicates the number of records written to the indexed file. It is printed in the summary report.

   The counter WS-DUPLICATE-CTR is incremented by 1 within the procedure 2340-PREPARE-DUPLICATE-LINE. This procedure is executed from within paragraph 2210-PROCESS-SORT-RECORD whenever the status code in MASTER-FILE-FLAG is not "00" due to an invalid key condition in the WRITE statement of paragraph 2320-PREPARE-INDEXED-MASTER. The final value in the counter WS-DUPLICATE-CTR indicates the total number of master records not written to the indexed file because their prime record key values were duplicates of existing ones. It is printed as part of the summary report.

   The counter WS-AUDIT-LINE-CTR is incremented by 1 within the procedure 2210-PROCESS-SORT-RECORD every time a sort record is processed. Its final value indicates the total number of detail lines written on the audit report. It is printed on the last line of the summary report.
5. The record MONTH-TABLE is included because the printer spacing chart for the report calls for the *name* of the month in the report date area. The current date is obtained from the system and the month component is assigned to the table index MONTH-INDEX in paragraph 2200-START-UP. The statement MOVE WS-MONTH(MONTH-INDEX) TO O-MONTH then retrieves the month name from the table.
6. The SORT statement is used to resequence the master records from an alphabetic ordering to ascending order by Social Security number. The records will be returned from the sort file and will be written to the indexed file in this new sequence.
7. When the READ statement executes successfully, the NOT AT END condition is satisfied and the ADD statement is executed. This procedure counts the number of records accessed from the old master file.
8. The data item WS-MONTH-NO is the month component of the date stored in WS-REPORT-DATE, and its value is assigned to the MONTH-TABLE index MONTH-INDEX. The table element is referenced by WS-MONTH(MONTH-INDEX) and the next MOVE statement retrieves the appropriate month name from the table.
9. When control returns from the procedure 2320-PREPARE-INDEXED-MASTER, the status code in the file status data item MASTER-FILE-FLAG is tested to determine if it is "00". If it is, then the master record was successfully written to INDEX-MASTER-FILE and, as a result, the procedure 2330-PREPARE-AUDIT-LINE is executed. If the status code is not "00", an invalid key condition occurred during the WRITE operation due to a duplicate key and the procedure 2340-PREPARE-DUPLICATE-LINE is executed.
10. When this WRITE operation executes successfully, an index is generated for the record being written to the file. The index is stored in an index table, and it will allow later access to the record by specifying its location in the file.

    If an invalid key condition occurs, the record is not written to the file and no index is generated.

    The ADD statement in the NOT INVALID KEY clause is executed every time the WRITE operation is successful. The final value of the counter WS-INDEXED-FILE-CTR is the number of records written to the indexed file.

The audit report produced by the program is shown in Figure 3.11, and the records of the new indexed file are shown in Figure 3.12.

Figure 3.11 Audit report for the indexed file creation program

```
                                          JOCELYN ORIGINALS COMPANY                                  PAGE  1

                        MASTER PERSONNEL FILE  -  CREATED AS AN INDEXED FILE ON NOVEMBER  14, 1989

                                                   EMPLOYEE RECORDS

   RECORD KEY           SSN        NAME                  ADDRESS                                     DOB    DATE HIRED

   005589243            005589243 BUXBAUM, JOAN M.      172 EARLE DR    GRAND ISLAND, NE 68802 480214 700608
   013407206            013407206 MCGEE, BERNARD W.     2420 CARR LA    CENTRAL CITY, NE 68826 301215 490615
   014766691            014766691 ARMSTRONG, GEORGE     105 STATE ST    PLATTE, NE          68653 480320 830816
   016493017            016493017 COUGHLIN, AILEEN M.   133 DAVIS RD    LEXINGTON, NE       68850 500310 680706
   026307625            026307625 VELTRI, JOHN A.       312 PERCH DR.   HASTINGS, NE        68901 470115 820820
   032561579            032561579 MAYO, EVANGELINA      895 POTTERS AVEGENEVA, NE           68361 620805 830807
   032567781            032567781 AITKEN, THOMAS R.     260 FOUNTAIN STAURORA, NE           68818 260805 460820
   033281512            033281512 PEARSON, ARTHUR       1020 GOLDEN RD HASTINGS, NE         68901 501125 830802
   039764715            039764715 GAFFNEY, MARYLYN      76 MAIN ST      PLATTE, NE          68653 521205 770608
   042750015            042750015 COLETTI, SARAH T.     51 BROAD ST     HASTINGS, NE        68901 380902 640615
   124670325            124670325 MOONEY, RONALD        220 N MAIN ST   HASTINGS, NE        68901 410920 640810
   130043962            130043962 MARKARIAN, MARIAN     984 N MAIN ST   HASTINGS, NE        68901 320507 520820
   144217773            144217773 ALTERMAN, MAUREEN E. 10 MARTIN AVE    YORK, NE            68467 350524 600610
   149201475            149201475 PACCASASSIE, DEBBIE  341 BRANCH AVE NORMAN, NE            68963 282612 570912
   150246389            150246389 PRIMEAU, ISABEL       78 NORTH ST     KEARNEY, NE         68847 470930 720820
   179623741            179623741 BLAZUCK, JOSEPH A.    81 DORIS AVE    GENEVA, NE          68361 450521 750610
   211384406            211384406 KACHADOURIAN, NATALI 922 LOCUST ST    HEBRON, NE          68370 350221 560820
   215137814            215137814 CUMMINGS, DOROTHEA    97 POWER AVE    NORMAN, NE          68963 530407 830822
   226153911            226153911 OVERDEEP, CYNTHIA     130 CANAL ST    YORK, NE            68467 350524 700715
   234891533            234891533 SHERIDAN, RICHARD J. 850SUN CIRCLE    AURORA, NE          68818 421205 650610
   253749144            253749144 LAKE, SUE             252 EAST RD     CRETE, NE           68333 410707 830815
   314764532            314764532 DESROSIERS, RICHARD   92 REGAN RD     LOUP CITY, NE       68853 581221 830815
   322150642            322150642 STURDAHL, DEBRA       2541 RICE ST    CRETE, NE           68333 340614 550715
   364923752            364923752 DURANT, MARIE L.      1250 HIGH RD    GENEVA, NE          68361 430924 540910
   381662514            381662514 BAHR, LENA M.         304 CORY LANE   GENEVA, NE          68361 411110 600820
   432157258            432157258 ROMA, GILDA           25 MAPLE DR     SUPERIOR, NE        68978 500708 720610
   623514793            623514793 CARTER, AMEKIA L.     59 BARK ST      LOUP CITY, NE       68853 320513 620820
   743142265            743142265 ABRUZZI, KENNETH L.   51 RAYMOND ST   HASTINGS, NE        68901 521205 720820
   771894263            771894263 CYR, ROSARIO          205 SUNSET DR   FAIRFIELD, NE       68938 350524 550820


29  RECORDS RETRIEVED FROM OLD MASTER FILE
29  RECORDS WRITTEN TO INDEXED FILE
 0  RECORDS WITH DUPLICATE KEYS
29  RECORDS WRITTEN TO AUDIT REPORT

                                     ***  END OF REPORT  ***
```

Figure 3.12 Records of INDEXED-MASTER-FILE

```
005589243BUXBAUM, JOAN M.    172 EARLE DR    GRAND ISLAND, NE 68802480214700608
013407206MCGEE, BERNARD W.   2420 CARR LA    CENTRAL CITY, NE 68826301215490615
014766691ARMSTRONG, GEORGE   105 STATE ST    PLATTE, NE       68653480320830816
016493017COUGHLIN, AILEEN M. 133 DAVIS RD    LEXINGTON, NE    68850500310680706
026307625VELTRI, JOHN A.     312 PERCH DR.   HASTINGS, NE     68901470115820820
032561579MAYO, EVANGELINA    895 POTTERS AVEGENEVA, NE        68361620805830807
032567781AITKEN, THOMAS R.   260 FOUNTAIN STAURORA, NE        68818260805460820
033281512PEARSON, ARTHUR     1020 GOLDEN RD HASTINGS, NE      68901501125830802
039764715GAFFNEY, MARYLYN    76 MAIN ST      PLATTE, NE       68653521205770608
042750015COLETTI, SARAH T.   51 BROAD ST     HASTINGS, NE     68901380902640615
124670325MOONEY, RONALD      220 N MAIN ST   HASTINGS, NE     68901410920640810
130043962MARKARIAN, MARIAN   984 N MAIN ST   HASTINGS, NE     68901320507520820
144217773ALTERMAN, MAUREEN E.10 MARTIN AVE   YORK, NE         68467350524600610
149201475PACCASASSIE, DEBBIE 341 BRANCH AVE NORMAN, NE        68963282612570912
150246389PRIMEAU, ISABEL     78 NORTH ST     KEARNEY, NE      68847470930720820
179623741BLAZUCK, JOSEPH A.  81 DORIS AVE    GENEVA, NE       68361450521750610
211384406KACHADOURIAN, NATALI922 LOCUST ST   HEBRON, NE       68370350221560820
215137814CUMMINGS, DOROTHEA  97 POWER AVE    NORMAN, NE       68963530407830822
226153911OVERDEEP, CYNTHIA   130 CANAL ST    YORK, NE         68467350524700715
234891533SHERIDAN, RICHARD J.850SUN CIRCLE   AURORA, NE       68818421205650610
253749144LAKE, SUE           252 EAST RD     CRETE, NE        68333410707830815
314764532DESROSIERS, RICHARD 92 REGAN RD     LOUP CITY, NE    68853581221830815
322150642STURDAHL, DEBRA     2541 RICE ST    CRETE, NE        68333340614550715
364923752DURANT, MARIE L.    1250 HIGH RD    GENEVA, NE       68361430924540910
381662514BAHR, LENA M.       304 CORY LANE   GENEVA, NE       68361411110600820
432157258ROMA, GILDA         25 MAPLE DR     SUPERIOR, NE     68978500708720610
623514793CARTER, AMEKIA L.   59 BARK ST      LOUP CITY, NE    68853320513620820
743142265ABRUZZI, KENNETH L. 51 RAYMOND ST   HASTINGS, NE     68901521205720820
771894263CYR, ROSARIO        205 SUNSET DR   FAIRFIELD, NE    68938350524550820
```

Processing an Indexed File Sequentially

Once an indexed file has been created, its records may be accessed either sequentially or randomly. As a simple example of sequential access, suppose that the management of the Jocelyn Originals Company has decided to offer a fringe benefit to employees hired before it went public on July 1, 1980, and it needs a count and an alphabetical list of those employees.

It should be clear that each employee record in the master personnel file INDEXED-MASTER-FILE has to be accessed so that the date hired entry can be tested. If the date hired entry is prior to July 1, 1980, the employee record must be sent to the sort file. When the master personnel file has been completely processed, the selected records in the sort file are sorted alphabetically by employee name.

This very brief analysis indicates a need for an input procedure and an output procedure under control of the SORT statement. The essential functions of the input procedure are as follows:

1. Read a record of INDEXED-MASTER-FILE.
2. Test the date hired field: if its value is less than "800701", copy the employee record to the sort record, release it to the sort file, and increment the employee counter.
3. Repeat steps 1 and 2 until there are no more records in the indexed file.

The essential functions of the output procedure are as follows:

1. Return a record from the sort file.
2. Prepare a report line for the employee record.
3. Repeat steps 1 and 2 until there are no more sort records.

Since this situation does not present any new COBOL procedures, we restrict our attention to the following program entries:

Item 1.

```
SELECT INDEXED-MASTER-FILE ASSIGN TO COB$INPUT
                           ORGANIZATION IS INDEXED
                           ACCESS MODE IS SEQUENTIAL
                           RECORD KEY IS INDEXED-MR-SSN
                           FILE STATUS IS MASTER-FILE-FLAG.
SELECT PRINT-FILE          ASSIGN TO COB$OUTPUT.
```

Item 2.

```
05 MASTER-FILE-FLAG  PIC X(2).
   88 NO-MORE-RECORDS          VALUE "10".
```

Item 3.

```
READ INDEXED-MASTER-FILE RECORD
     AT END
          SET NO-MORE-RECORDS TO TRUE.
```

Item 4.

```
IF INDEXED-MR-DATE-HIRED < "800701"
    RELEASE SORT-RECORD FROM INDEXED-MASTER-RECORD
    ADD 1 TO WS-EMPLOYEE-CTR
END-IF.
```

In item 1, the SELECT clause for the indexed file must contain the clause ORGANIZATION IS INDEXED and the RECORD KEY clause. The data name in the KEY clause must name the same field of the record that was specified as the prime record key when the file was created. In this KEY clause, it is INDEXED-MR-SSN.

Since the program must process the records of the indexed file sequentially, the clause ACCESS MODE IS SEQUENTIAL is the appropriate one to use. It is not required, however, since the default is SEQUENTIAL. In this example, it is coded to increase program self-documentation.

The FILE STATUS clause is always optional. It is included in this example, and the data item MASTER-FILE-FLAG, defined in item 2, will receive the status codes from the operating system every time an I/O operation references the indexed file. The availability of the data item MASTER-FILE-FLAG makes it unnecessary to define the familiar end-of-file flag WS-MORE-RECORDS. This is because the AT END condition causes the system to store the status code "10" in MASTER-FILE-FLAG. Thus the familiar condition-name NO-MORE-RECORDS can be defined to correspond to "10" in the data item MASTER-FILE-FLAG. These alternatives are illustrated in Figure 3.13.

Figure 3.13 Using a FILE STATUS data item as the end-of-file flag

Option 1

```
05 WS-MORE-RECORDS        PIC X(3).
   88 NO-MORE-RECORDS                VALUE "NO ".
```

Sample PROCEDURE DIVISION statements:

```
    MOVE "YES" TO WS-MORE-RECORDS.
    PERFORM 310-READ-MASTER-RECORD.
    .
    .
    .
    PERFORM 210-PROCESS-MASTER-RECORD
        UNTIL NO-MORE-RECORDS.
    .
    .
    .
310-READ-MASTER-RECORD.
    READ INDEXED-MASTER-FILE RECORD
        AT END
            SET NO-MORE-RECORDS TO TRUE.
```

Option 2

```
05 MASTER-FILE-FLAG       PIC X(2).
   88 NO-MORE-RECORDS                VALUE "10".

    PERFORM 310-READ-MASTER-RECORD.
    .
    .
    .
    PERFORM 210-PROCESS-MASTER-RECORD
        UNTIL NO-MORE-RECORDS.
    .
    .
    .
310-READ-MASTER-RECORD.
    READ INDEXED-MASTER-FILE RECORD
        AT END
            SET NO-MORE-RECORDS TO TRUE.
```

In option 1 of Figure 3.13, when the AT END condition occurs in the READ statement, the clause SET NO-MORE-RECORDS TO TRUE moves the literal "NO " to the data item WS-MORE-RECORDS. In the statement

```
PERFORM 210-PROCESS-MASTER-RECORD
    UNTIL NO-MORE-RECORDS
```

the procedure 210-PROCESS-MASTER-RECORD is performed repeatedly until the data item WS-MORE-RECORDS contains the value "NO ".

In option 2, when the AT END condition occurs in the READ statement, the system automatically stores the status code "10" in MASTER-FILE-FLAG and the SET statement, coded in item 3, duplicates this data transfer. In the statement

```
PERFORM 210-PROCESS-MASTER-RECORD
    UNTIL NO-MORE-RECORDS
```

the procedure 210-PROCESS-MASTER-RECORD is performed repeatedly until the data item MASTER-FILE-FLAG contains the status code "10".

In item 3, note that when the records of an indexed file are to be accessed sequentially, the READ statement must contain the AT END clause, since at some point the end-of-file record will be encountered. We will see shortly that when the access mode is specified as RANDOM, the READ statement must contain the INVALID KEY clause, not the AT END clause!

In item 4, the test INDEXED-MR-DATE-HIRED < "800701" is used to select the records for employees hired prior to July 1, 1980. Recall that the date hired format is YYMMDD.

Processing an Indexed File Randomly

The advantage that a file with indexed organization offers over files with sequential organization is the ability to access records in a random manner. As an example, consider the following situation.

The Problem

Some employees of the Jocelyn Originals Company have changed their addresses recently. Management wants the master personnel file to be brought up to date. This file is the one that was created as an indexed file earlier.

Brief Analysis of the Problem

In order to update addresses in the master file, a detail file is prepared containing a record for each employee with a new address. Each detail record contains the Social Security number and the new address of the employee. The Social Security number is required, since it is the prime record key for

Figure 3.14 Detail record and system flowchart for random field update in the indexed file

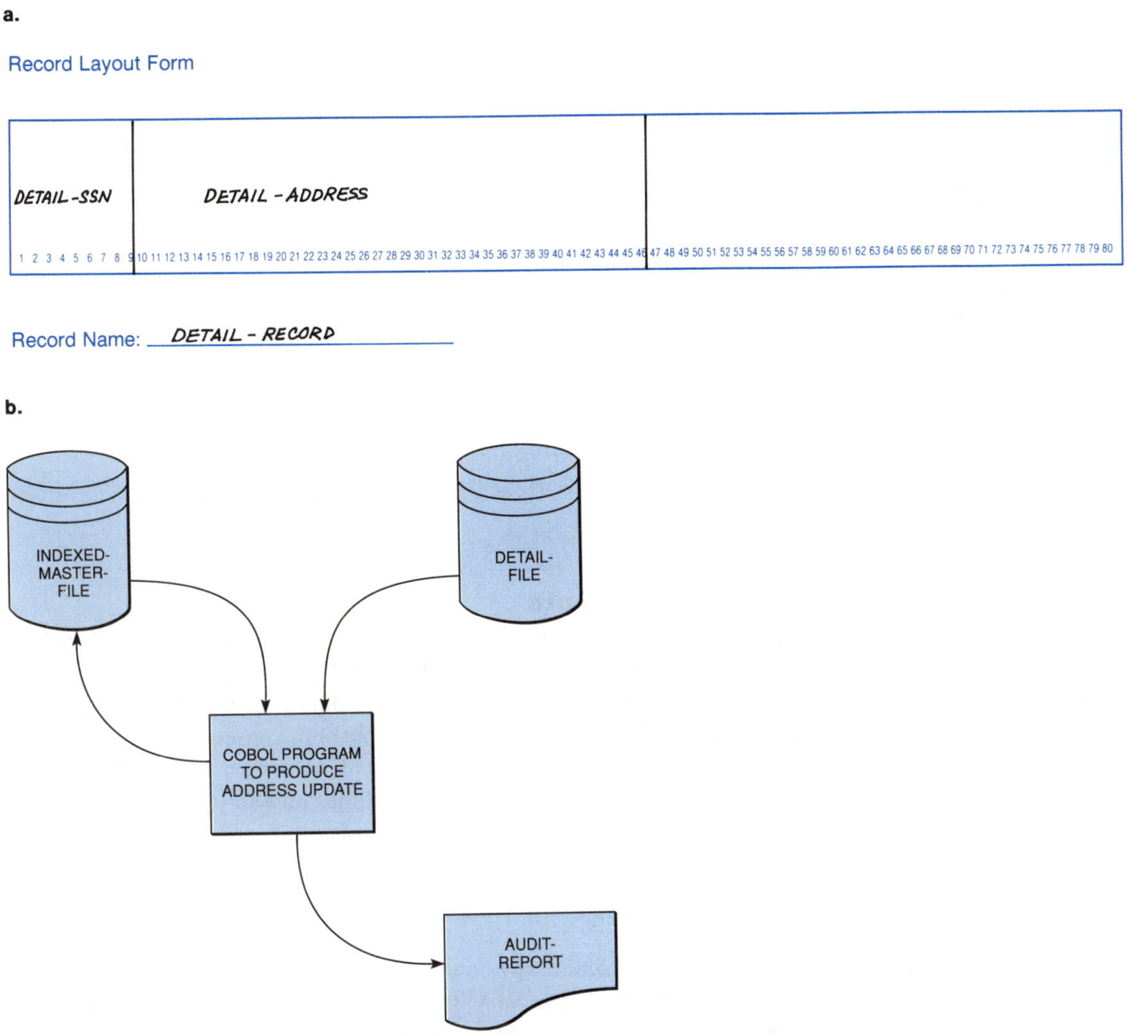

the master personnel file. (Recall that the RECORD KEY data item specified during the creation phase of the indexed file remains, for the life of the file, the value by which the record itself will be located on the file.) The detail record layout and the system flowchart are shown in Figure 3.14.

Note that INDEXED-MASTER-FILE is shown to be an input file since a record to be updated must be accessed from the file, and it is also an output file since an updated record must be rewritten onto the same master file. Consequently, INDEXED-MASTER-FILE has to be open in I-O mode. The overall procedure is fairly straightforward, as follows:

1. Read a detail file record.
2. Retrieve from the master personnel file the record specified by the Social Security number on the detail record.
3. Copy the new address into the master record.
4. Rewrite the corrected record into the master file.
5. Prepare an appropriate entry on the audit report.

However, two potential problems must be taken into account.

Figure 3.15 Printer spacing chart for the audit report

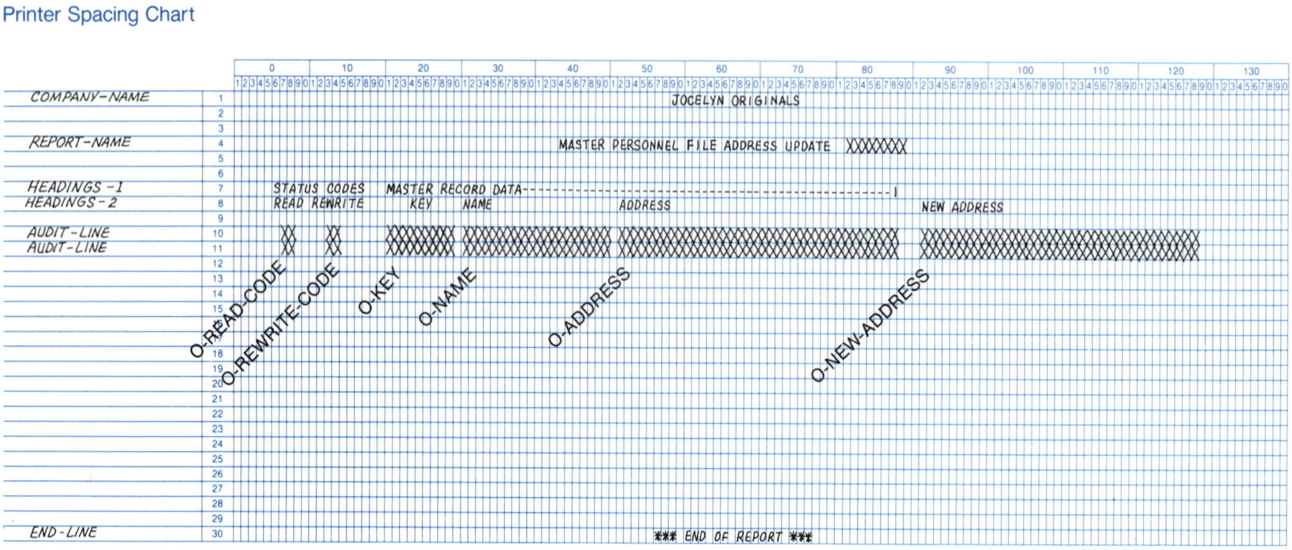

Problem 1: Unable to Find a Master Record

Since the Social Security number is the prime record key for the indexed file, a record is retrieved by specifying its prime record key value, namely, the Social Security number that it contains. If a data entry error occurred when a Social Security number was entered on a detail record, and this value is assigned to the prime record key, it will not be found in the index table and, consequently, the desired record will not be retrieved from the file. This situation is referred to as an invalid key condition. The format of the READ statement that must be used to read an indexed file randomly contains a test for this condition. The READ statement is of the following form:

```
READ indexed-file RECORD
    INVALID KEY
        imperative-statement-1.
```

Obviously, INVALID KEY is the test for an invalid key condition. If it exists, the system stores the status code "23" in the data item named in the FILE STATUS clause and *imperative-statement-1* is executed. It is the programmer's responsibility to plan for a specific course of action if this condition occurs. In this program, we want to print a line on the audit report that shows the status code resulting from the READ operation, the key value for which no record was found, and the error message "No master record with this key value."

Problem 2: Unable to Rewrite the Master Record

Assuming that the READ operation is successful and the new address is copied into the master record, the updated record must then be rewritten to the master file. During this process, the prime record key value for this record must not be changed. If it is, then the REWRITE operation will fail. This situation is also referred to as an invalid key condition. The format of the REWRITE statement that must be used to rewrite a record to an indexed file tests for such a condition. The statement is of the following form:

```
REWRITE record-name
    INVALID KEY
        imperative-statement-1.
```

If an invalid key condition occurs, the system stores the status code "23" in the data item named in the FILE STATUS clause and *imperative-statement-1* is executed. Here also it is the programmer's responsibility to plan for an appropriate course of action. In this program, we want to print a line on the audit report that shows the status code resulting from the REWRITE operation, the record key value that was used to read the record, and the error message "Cannot rewrite record to master file."

■ **Figure 3.16** Structure chart to update addresses

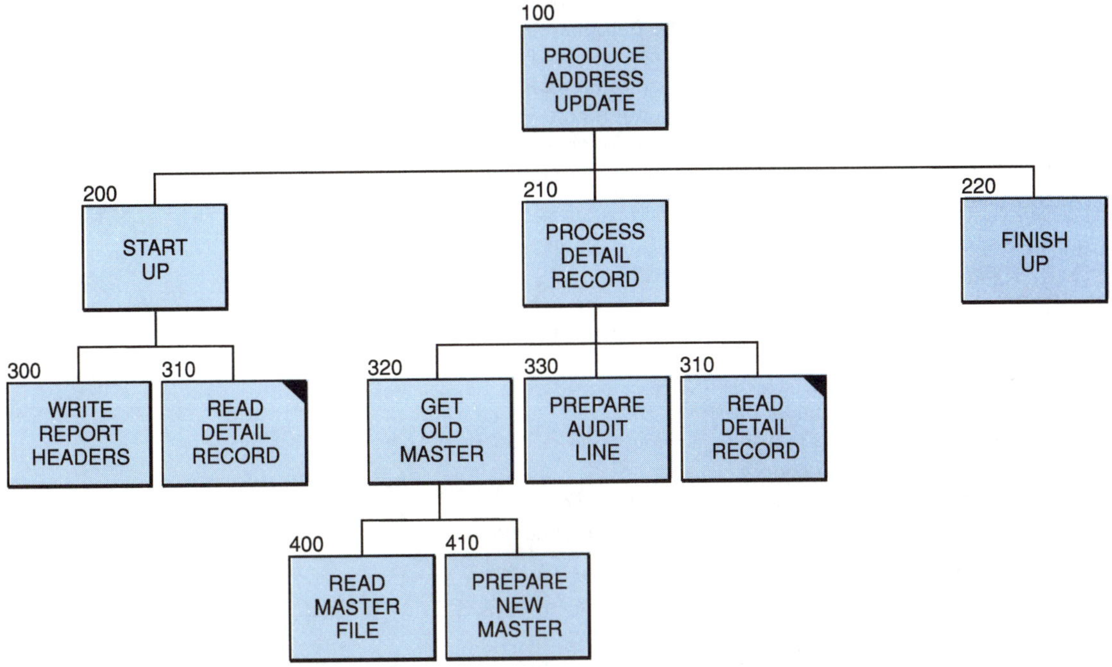

The printer spacing chart for the audit report is shown in Figure 3.15, and the structure chart for the program is shown in Figure 3.16.

The program pseudocode is as follows:

100-Produce-Address-Update.

1. Perform 200-Start-Up.
2. Perform 210-Process-Detail-Record until no more records.
3. Perform 220-Finish-Up.
4. Stop the run.

200-Start-Up.

1. Open Indexed-Master-File as an input-output file, Detail-File as an input file, and Audit-Report as an output file.
2. Obtain the date from the system.
3. Move the date to Report-Name date.
4. Set WS-MORE-RECORDS to "YES".
5. Perform 300-Write-Report-Headers.
6. Perform 310-Read-Detail-Record.

210-Process-Detail-Record.

1. Move spaces to the record area Audit-Line.
2. Move input Social-Security-number to indexed-master-record Social-Security-number.
3. Perform 320-Get-Old-Master.
4. Perform 330-Prepare-Audit-Line.
5. Perform 310-Read-Detail-Record.

220-Finish-Up.

1. Move the record End-Line to the output area Printline.
2. After advancing 5 lines, write the output record Printline.
3. Close the files.

300-Write-Report-Headers.

1. Move the record Company-Name to the output area Printline.
2. After advancing to a new page, write the output record Printline.
3. Move the record Report-Name to the output area Printline.
4. After advancing 3 lines, write the output record Printline.
5. Move the record Headings-1 to the output area Printline.
6. After advancing 3 lines, write the output record Printline.
7. Move the record Headings-2 to the output area Printline.
8. After advancing 1 line, write the output record Printline.
9. Move 2 to proper-spacing.

310-Read-Detail-Record.

1. Read an input Detail-Record.
2. Test for end-of-file:
   if EOF-record reached, set WS-MORE-RECORDS to "NO ".

320-Get-Old-Master.

1. Perform 400-Read-Master-File.
2. Move master-file-flag to Audit-Line read-code.
3. Test Audit-Line read-code:
   if "00", perform 410-Prepare-New-Master, and
   move master-file-flag to Audit-Line rewrite-code.

330-Prepare-Audit-Line.

1. Move input Social-Security-number to Audit-Line key.
2. Test Audit-Line read-code and rewrite-code:
   a. If both = "00", move working-storage master-record name to Audit-Line name,
      move working-storage master-record address to Audit-Line address,
      move input detail-address to Audit-Line new-address.
   b. If read-code = "00" and rewrite-code = "23", move the Rewrite-Error message to Audit-Line message. (Rewrite-Error message: "***** Cannot rewrite record to master file *****")
   c. If read-code = "23", move the Read-Error message to Audit-Line message. (Read-Error message: "***** No master record with this key value *****")
3. Move the record Audit-Line to the output area Printline.
4. After advancing proper-spacing, write the output record Printline.
5. Move 1 to proper-spacing.

400-Read-Master-File.

1. Read Indexed-Master-File record.
2. Test for invalid key:
   a. If so, move "23" to master-file-flag.
   b. If not, move indexed-master-record to working-storage master-record.

410-Prepare-New-Master.

1. Move input address to indexed-master-record address.
2. Rewrite indexed-master-record.
3. Test for invalid key:
   if so, move "23" to master-file-flag.

In pseudocode paragraph 200-Start-Up, note that the indexed file Indexed-Master-File is opened in input-output mode, since the file must be read and it must be written to. In paragraph 210-Process-Detail-Record, step 2 transfers data between two record areas in main memory. Specifically, the value in the field DETAIL-SSN of the record area DETAIL-RECORD is moved to the field INDEXED-MR-SSN of the record area INDEXED-MASTER-RECORD, as shown in Figure 3.17. This is a most crucial step, since the value in the field INDEXED-MR-SSN is the record key value for the record that

Figure 3.17 Initializing the prime record key INDEXED-MR-SSN

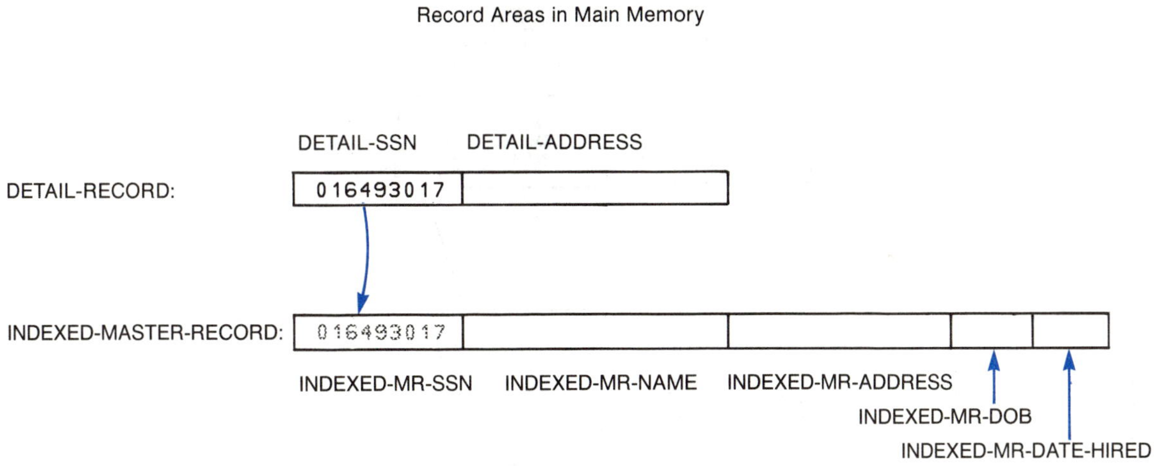

will be retrieved from INDEXED-MASTER-FILE. Step 3 then sends control to paragraph 320-Get-Old-Master, and step 1 in this paragraph sends control to paragraph 400-Read-Master-File. When the read operation in this paragraph is executed, the operating system will look in the index table of Indexed-Master-File for this key value. When the key value is found in the index table, the pointer associated with the key value will specify where the record itself is located within Indexed-Master-File. The read-write mechanism will immediately be directed to that location, the record will be read into the record area Indexed-Master-Record, and a copy will be stored in the working storage item WS-MASTER-RECORD. The reason for making a copy of the record in working storage is to facilitate the printing of the related audit line on the report. The audit line must contain the employee name and old address, and these items must be retrieved from the master record. However, when the updated record is re-written to the master file, its data items can no longer be referenced. Since the audit line is prepared subsequent to rewriting the master record, a copy must be retained in working storage!

On the other hand, if the prime record key value is not found in the index table, the invalid key condition occurs, and status code "23" is moved to the file status item master-file-flag.

In either case, control then returns to step 2 of 320-Get-Old-Master. Here, the value in the file status item master-file-flag, either "00" or "23", is moved to the read-code field of the audit line. In step 3, the code is tested to determine if the read operation was successful or not. If it was not successful, a new master cannot be prepared and, as a result, control returns to paragraph 210-Process-Detail-Record.

If the read operation was successful, control is sent to paragraph 410-Prepare-New-Master to move the new address to the master record and then to rewrite the updated record into the master file. The rewrite operation must be tested for an invalid key. This condition occurs if the prime record key value has been changed since the previous read operation. In that case, the status code "23" is moved to the file status item master-file-flag. Upon returning to paragraph 320-Get-Old-Master, the code in master-file-flag is moved to the audit line rewrite-code. Control returns to paragraph 210-Process-Detail-Record, where it is then sent to paragraph 330-Prepare-Audit-Line to print the appropriate line on the report.

The program flowchart corresponding to the pseudocode is shown in Figure 3.18.

Figure 3.18 Program flowchart for the random field update program

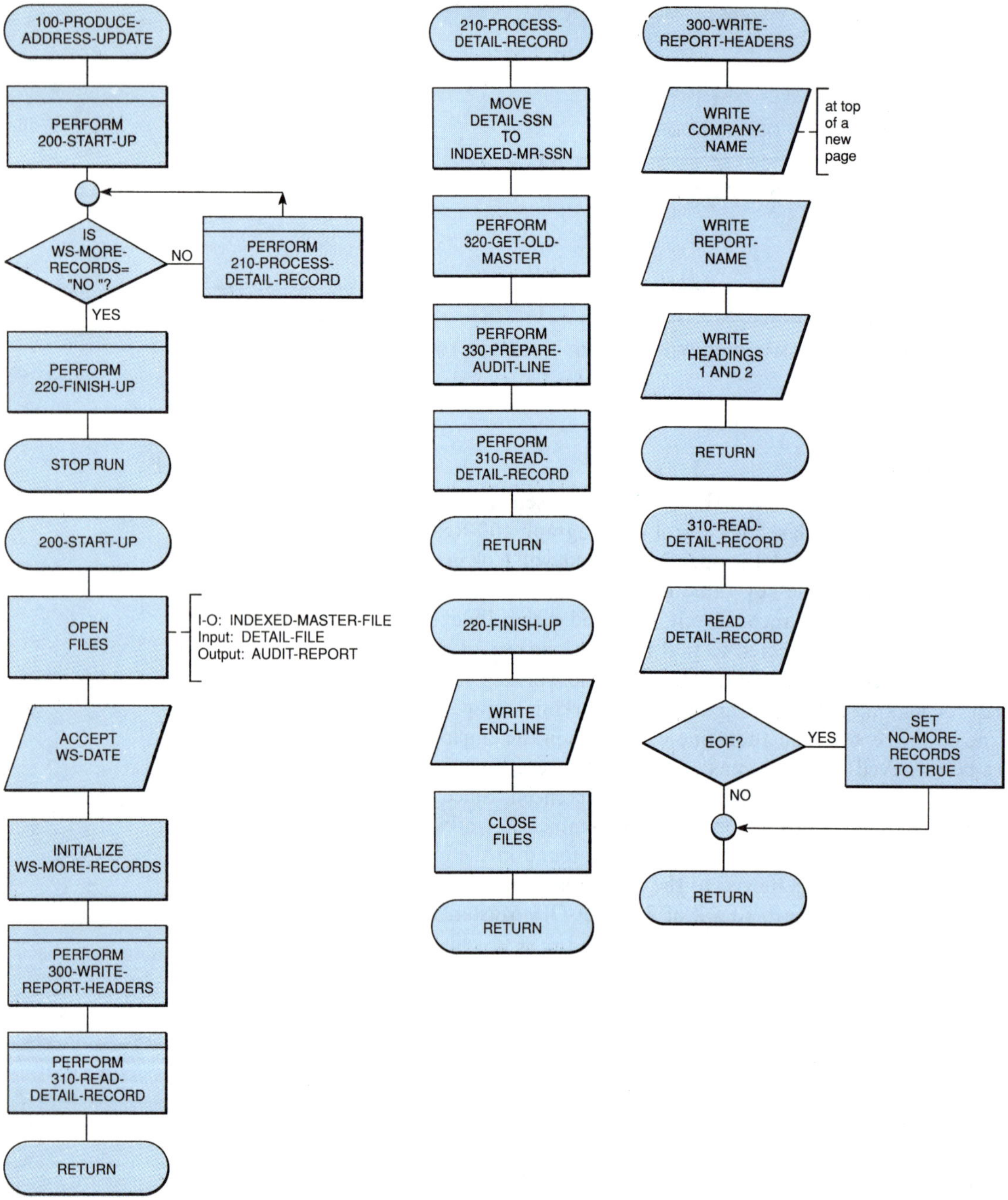

■ **Figure 3.18** continued

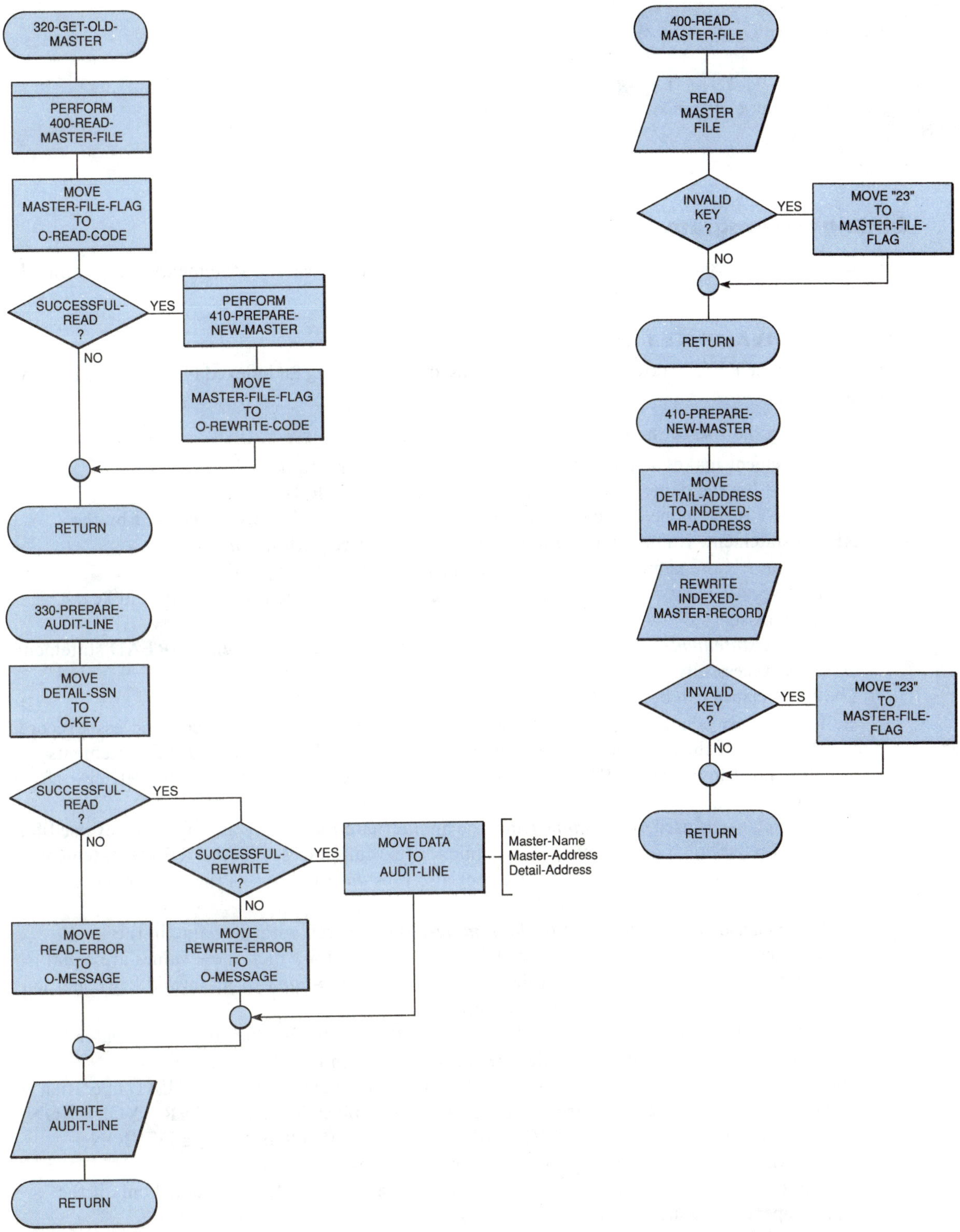

Figure 3.19 READ-INVALID KEY statement format

```
READ file-name-1 RECORD [INTO identifier-1]
     [KEY IS data-name-1]
     [INVALID KEY imperative-statement-1]
     [NOT INVALID KEY imperative-statement-2]
     [END-READ]
```

Coding the Program

We are now ready to code the program. However, since it contains two new statements, we examine the formats and list the rules that govern their use.

The READ-INVALID KEY Statement

The format for the READ statement that must be used when reading an indexed file randomly is shown in Figure 3.19.

Rules Governing the Use of the READ-INVALID KEY Statement

1. This statement makes a specified record available to the program.
2. *File-name-1* is the name of a file defined in the FILE SECTION.
3. *Identifier-1* is the name of a data item that receives a copy of the record accessed by the READ statement. It must not be the record area associated with *file-name-1*.
4. *Date-name-1* is the name of a record key defined for the file being read.
5. *Imperative-statement-1* is an imperative statement that is executed when an invalid key condition exists.
6. *Imperative-statement-2* is an imperative statement that is executed when the READ statement executes successfully.
7. The KEY clause can be used for indexed files only.
   a. If the clause is not used, the prime record key is necessarily the key used to access a record of the file. If the access mode is dynamic, the execution of sequential READ statements subsequent to a random READ statement also uses the prime record key for retrieval of records.
   b. If the clause is used, *data-name-1* may be an alternate record key and it is the key used for record retrieval. If access mode is dynamic, the execution of sequential READ statements subsequent to a random READ statement also uses *data-name-1* as the key for retrieval of records.
   c. If the clause is used, the value of *data-name-1* is compared with the value in the corresponding field of the file's records. The first record for which these values are equal is retrieved. If no record contains a field value equal to *data-name-1,* an invalid key condition exists and the READ operation is unsuccessful.
   d. If a record with a matching key value is retrieved from the file, but its size is greater than the maximum specified for the file, the READ operation is unsuccessful.
8. The INVALID KEY clause contains the statement(s) to be executed if the READ operation is unsuccessful. The clause is required unless there is an applicable USE AFTER EXCEPTION procedure within the DECLARATIVES SECTION of the PROCEDURE DIVISION. (DECLARATIVES sections are not used in the programs of this chapter.)
9. The optional NOT INVALID KEY clause contains statement(s) to be executed only if the READ operation is successful.
10. END-READ is the explicit scope terminator for the READ statement.
11. This statement is used to retrieve records randomly from an indexed file whose access mode is random or dynamic.
12. *File-name-1* must be open in INPUT or I-O mode when the statement executes.

Figure 3.20 REWRITE-INVALID KEY statement format

```
REWRITE record-name-1 [FROM identifier-1]
        [INVALID KEY imperative-statement-1]
        [NOT INVALID KEY imperative-statement-2]
        [END-REWRITE]
```

13. The execution of the READ statement updates the code in the data item named in the FILE STATUS clause. The most applicable standard codes are as follows:

    "00" to denote a successful operation;

    "04" to denote that the size of the record read does not match the size specified in the record description;

    "23" to denote an invalid key, that is, no record in the file contains the record key value;

    "30" to denote a permanent system error;

    "47" to denote that the file is not open, or its open mode is incompatible with the READ statement.

14. A successful READ operation makes a record available in the record area associated with *file-name-1*. If the FD for the file contains more than one record description, the logical records share the same record area. A second record read into the record area replaces only as many characters as it contains. The contents in the excess bytes of the record area are undefined.
15. If a READ operation is not successful, the contents of the record area associated with the file are undefined. In particular, the record key value is undefined.
16. If *file-name-1* is specified as an optional file in its SELECT statement and it is not available to the program, the execution of a READ statement for the file is unsuccessful and the error is classified as an invalid key condition.

The REWRITE-INVALID KEY Statement

The format of the REWRITE statement that must be used to replace a record previously read from an indexed file by an updated version of the record is shown in Figure 3.20.

Rules Governing the Use of the REWRITE Statement for Indexed Files

1. This statement logically replaces an existing record in a file stored on a mass storage device.
2. *Record-name-1* is the name of a logical record defined in the FD for the file from which a record was previously retrieved.
3. *Identifier-1* is the name of a data item that contains the source data.
4. *Identifier-1* and *record-name-1* cannot share the same storage area.
5. *Imperative-statement-1* is an imperative statement that is executed when an invalid key condition exists.
6. *Imperative-statement-2* is an imperative statement that is executed when the REWRITE statement executes successfully.
7. The INVALID KEY clause is required for an indexed file unless there is an applicable USE AFTER EXCEPTION procedure in the DECLARATIVES SECTION of the PROCEDURE DIVISION. It contains statements to be executed if the REWRITE operation is unsuccessful.
8. The optional NOT INVALID KEY clause contains statements to be executed whenever the REWRITE operation is successful.
9. END-REWRITE is the explicit scope terminator.
10. The file that contains *record-name-1* must be open in I-O mode, and it must be on a mass storage device.
11. If a REWRITE statement is successful, the record referenced by *record-name-1* is no longer available in the record area associated with the file.

12. The execution of a REWRITE statement updates the code in the data item named in the FILE STATUS clause for the file. The most applicable standard codes are as follows:

"00" to denote a successful operation;

"02" to denote that a duplicate alternate key was created for a key that allows duplicates;

"21" to denote that the prime record key value changed after a successful READ operation when the access mode is sequential;

"22" to denote that an invalid key condition occurred due to a duplicate alternate key;

"23" to denote that an invalid key condition occurred because no record in the file has the record key value;

"30" to denote a permanent system error.

13. An invalid key condition occurs if
    a. The prime record key value for the record to be rewritten is not the same as the prime record key value for the last record read, when the access mode is sequential.
    b. The prime record key value is not the same as that of any record in the file.
    c. An alternate record key value for the record being rewritten to the file is the same as that of a record already in the file and the DUPLICATES phrase is not specified for the file.
14. When an invalid key condition occurs, the record in the file is not updated and the data in the record area remains unchanged.
15. If the access mode for the indexed file is sequential, the record to be replaced is specified by the value of the prime record key. The value of the prime record key for the record to be rewritten must be the same as the prime record key for the record last read.
16. If the access mode for an indexed file is random or dynamic, the prime record key specifies the record to be replaced.
17. If the record being rewritten has an alternate record key and the REWRITE statement
    a. does not change its value, then the order of record retrieval does not change when the alternate key is used.
    b. changes its value, then the order of record retrieval changes when the alternate key is used.

The COBOL program to randomly update addresses in records of indexed file INDEXED-MASTER-FILE is shown in Figure 3.21. Some entries have been numbered to facilitate references in comments that follow.

Figure 3.21 COBOL program for random field update

```
 IDENTIFICATION DIVISION.

 PROGRAM-ID.        INDEXED-FILE-FIELD-CHANGE.

*****************************************************************
*                                                               *
*   AUTHOR.             PAQUETTE.                               *
*   DATE WRITTEN.       NOVEMBER 1989.                          *
*                                                               *
*   THIS PROGRAM UPDATES A FIELD OF SELECTED RECORDS FROM THE   *
*   MASTER PERSONNEL FILE FOR THE JOCELYN ORIGINALS COMPANY, AN *
*   INDEXED FILE.  RECORDS ARE RETRIEVED RANDOMLY.  THE PROGRAM *
*   ILLUSTRATES THE USE OF THE RECORD KEY IN RELATION TO THE    *
*   READ STATEMENT AND TO THE REWRITE STATEMENT.  THE FILE      *
*   STATUS CLAUSE IS USED TO PROVIDE A FLAG TO TEST FOR SUCCESS-*
*   FUL INPUT-OUTPUT FUNCTIONS.                                 *
*                                                               *
*****************************************************************

 ENVIRONMENT DIVISION.

 CONFIGURATION SECTION.

 SOURCE-COMPUTER.   VAX-VMS-8650.
 OBJECT-COMPUTER.   VAX-VMS-8650.

 INPUT-OUTPUT SECTION.
```

■ **Figure 3.21** continued

```
       FILE-CONTROL.
           SELECT INDEXED-MASTER-FILE  ASSIGN TO DISKMASTER
                                       ORGANIZATION IS INDEXED
1                                      ACCESS MODE IS RANDOM
                                       RECORD KEY IS INDEXED-MR-SSN
                                       FILE STATUS IS MASTER-FILE-FLAG.
           SELECT DETAIL-FILE          ASSIGN TO COB$INPUT.
           SELECT AUDIT-REPORT         ASSIGN TO COB$OUTPUT.

       DATA DIVISION.

       FILE SECTION.

       FD  INDEXED-MASTER-FILE
           RECORD CONTAINS 100 CHARACTERS
           BLOCK CONTAINS 5 RECORDS.

       01  INDEXED-MASTER-RECORD.
2          05 INDEXED-MR-SSN          PIC X(9).
           05 INDEXED-MR-NAME         PIC X(20).
           05 INDEXED-MR-ADDRESS      PIC X(37).
           05 INDEXED-MR-DOB          PIC X(6).
           05 INDEXED-MR-DATE-HIRED   PIC X(6).
           05                         PIC X(22).

       FD  DETAIL-FILE
           RECORD CONTAINS 46 CHARACTERS.

       01  DETAIL-RECORD.
3          05 DETAIL-SSN              PIC X(9).
           05 DETAIL-ADDRESS          PIC X(37).

       FD  AUDIT-REPORT
           RECORD CONTAINS 132 CHARACTERS.

       01  PRINTLINE                  PIC X(132).

       WORKING-STORAGE SECTION.

       01  PROGRAM-FLAGS.
           05 WS-MORE-RECORDS       PIC X(3).
               88 MORE-RECORDS                VALUE 'YES'.
               88 NO-MORE-RECORDS             VALUE 'NO '.
4          05 MASTER-FILE-FLAG      PIC X(2).
               88 SUCCESSFUL                  VALUE '00'.
               88 NO-SUCH-RECORD              VALUE '23'.

       01  PROGRAM-CONTROLS.
           05  WS-DATE              PIC X(6).
           05  WS-PROPER-SPACING    PIC 9.

5      01  WS-MASTER-RECORD.
           05 WS-MR-SSN             PIC X(9).
           05 WS-MR-NAME            PIC X(20).
           05 WS-MR-ADDRESS         PIC X(37).
           05 WS-MR-DOB             PIC X(6).
           05 WS-MR-DATE-HIRED      PIC X(6).
           05                       PIC X(22).

6      01  ERROR-MESSAGES.
           05 READ-ERROR      PIC X(50)  VALUE
              '*****  NO MASTER RECORD WITH THIS KEY VALUE   *****'.
           05 REWRITE-ERROR PIC X(50)  VALUE
              '*****  CANNOT REWRITE RECORD TO MASTER FILE   *****'.

       01  REPORT-HEADERS.
           05 COMPANY-NAME.
              10 PIC X(58) VALUE SPACES.
              10 PIC X(17) VALUE 'JOCELYN ORIGINALS'.
              10 PIC X(57) VALUE SPACES.

           05 REPORT-NAME.
              10 PIC X(43) VALUE SPACES.
              10 PIC X(38) VALUE
                          'MASTER PERSONNEL FILE ADDRESS UPDATE  '.
              10 O-DATE     PIC XX/XX/XX.
              10 PIC X(43) VALUE SPACES.

           05 HEADINGS-1.
              10 PIC X(5)   VALUE SPACES.
              10 PIC X(12)  VALUE 'STATUS CODES'.
              10 PIC X(3)   VALUE SPACES.
              10 PIC X(18)  VALUE 'MASTER RECORD DATA'.
              10 PIC X(49)  VALUE ALL '-'.
              10 PIC X(1)   VALUE '|'.
              10 PIC X(44)  VALUE SPACES.
```

```
           05 HEADINGS-2.
              10 PIC X(5)  VALUE SPACES.
              10 PIC X(12) VALUE 'READ REWRITE'.
              10 PIC X(6)  VALUE SPACES.
              10 PIC X(3)  VALUE 'KEY'.
              10 PIC X(4)  VALUE SPACES.
              10 PIC X(4)  VALUE 'NAME'.
              10 PIC X(17) VALUE SPACES.
              10 PIC X(7)  VALUE 'ADDRESS'.
              10 PIC X(33) VALUE SPACES.
              10 PIC X(11) VALUE 'NEW ADDRESS'.
              10 PIC X(30) VALUE SPACES.

       01  AUDIT-LINE.
           05                                       PIC X(6).
7          05 O-READ-CODE                           PIC X(2).
              88 SUCCESSFUL-READ      VALUE '00'.
           05                                       PIC X(4).
           05 O-REWRITE-CODE                        PIC X(2).
              88 SUCCESSFUL-REWRITE   VALUE '00'.
           05                                       PIC X(6).
           05 O-KEY                                 PIC X(9).
           05                                       PIC X(1).
           05 O-RECORD-DATA.
              10 O-NAME                             PIC X(21).
              10 O-ADDRESS                          PIC X(37).
              10                                    PIC X(3).
              10 O-NEW-ADDRESS                      PIC X(37).
              10                                    PIC X(4).
8          05 O-MESSAGE REDEFINES O-RECORD-DATA PIC X(102).

       01  END-LINE.
           05 PIC X(56)  VALUE SPACES.
           05 PIC X(21)  VALUE '*** END OF REPORT ***'.
           05 PIC X(55)  VALUE SPACES.

       PROCEDURE DIVISION.

       100-PRODUCE-ADDRESS-UPDATE.
           PERFORM 200-START-UP.
           PERFORM 210-PROCESS-DETAIL-RECORD
               UNTIL NO-MORE-RECORDS.
           PERFORM 220-FINISH-UP.
           STOP RUN.

       200-START-UP.
           OPEN I-O INDEXED-MASTER-FILE
                INPUT DETAIL-FILE
                OUTPUT AUDIT-REPORT.
           ACCEPT WS-DATE FROM DATE.
           MOVE WS-DATE TO O-DATE.
           SET MORE-RECORDS TO TRUE.
           PERFORM 300-WRITE-REPORT-HEADERS.
           PERFORM 310-READ-DETAIL-RECORD.

       210-PROCESS-DETAIL-RECORD.
           MOVE SPACES TO AUDIT-LINE.
9          MOVE DETAIL-SSN TO INDEXED-MR-SSN.
           PERFORM 320-GET-OLD-MASTER.
           PERFORM 330-PREPARE-AUDIT-LINE.
           PERFORM 310-READ-DETAIL-RECORD.

       220-FINISH-UP.
           WRITE PRINTLINE FROM END-LINE
               AFTER ADVANCING 5 LINES.
           CLOSE INDEXED-MASTER-FILE
                 DETAIL-FILE
                 AUDIT-REPORT.

       300-WRITE-REPORT-HEADERS.
           WRITE PRINTLINE FROM COMPANY-NAME
               AFTER ADVANCING PAGE.
           WRITE PRINTLINE FROM REPORT-NAME
               AFTER ADVANCING 3 LINES.
           WRITE PRINTLINE FROM HEADINGS-1
               AFTER ADVANCING 3 LINES.
           WRITE PRINTLINE FROM HEADINGS-2
               AFTER ADVANCING 1 LINE.
           MOVE 2 TO WS-PROPER-SPACING.

       310-READ-DETAIL-RECORD.
           READ DETAIL-FILE RECORD
               AT END
                   SET NO-MORE-RECORDS TO TRUE.
```

```
       320-GET-OLD-MASTER.
           PERFORM 400-READ-MASTER-FILE.
           MOVE MASTER-FILE-FLAG TO O-READ-CODE.
           IF SUCCESSFUL-READ
               PERFORM 410-PREPARE-NEW-MASTER
               MOVE MASTER-FILE-FLAG TO O-REWRITE-CODE
           END-IF.

       330-PREPARE-AUDIT-LINE.
           MOVE DETAIL-SSN TO O-KEY.
10         EVALUATE SUCCESSFUL-READ ALSO SUCCESSFUL-REWRITE
               WHEN        TRUE       ALSO        TRUE
                                     MOVE WS-MR-NAME TO O-NAME
                                     MOVE WS-MR-ADDRESS TO O-ADDRESS
                                     MOVE DETAIL-ADDRESS TO O-NEW-ADDRESS
               WHEN        TRUE       ALSO        FALSE
                                     MOVE REWRITE-ERROR TO O-MESSAGE
               WHEN        FALSE      ALSO        ANY
                                     MOVE READ-ERROR TO O-MESSAGE
           END-EVALUATE.
           WRITE PRINTLINE FROM AUDIT-LINE
               AFTER ADVANCING WS-PROPER-SPACING.
           MOVE 1 TO WS-PROPER-SPACING.

       400-READ-MASTER-FILE.
11         READ INDEXED-MASTER-FILE RECORD INTO WS-MASTER-RECORD
               INVALID KEY
                   MOVE '23' TO MASTER-FILE-FLAG.

       410-PREPARE-NEW-MASTER.
12         MOVE DETAIL-ADDRESS TO INDEXED-MR-ADDRESS.
13         REWRITE INDEXED-MASTER-RECORD
               INVALID KEY
                   MOVE '23' TO MASTER-FILE-FLAG.
```

In the program,

1. The access mode is specified as RANDOM. As a result, the record key value of the record to be accessed must be assigned to the record key prior to executing a READ statement (see line 9) and the READ statement must contain the INVALID KEY clause (see line 11), since the program does not contain a USE AFTER EXCEPTION procedure.
2. The prime record key for the file is named INDEXED-MR-SSN, the same one that was specified when the indexed file was first created. Recall that its location within the record and the PIC clause must not change for the life of the file.
3. For each master record that must receive a new address, there is a detail record in DETAIL-FILE. For each detail record, the value in the field DETAIL-SSN must be assigned to the prime record key INDEXED-MR-SSN, and then the READ statement uses that value to locate and retrieve the corresponding master record. See lines 9 and 11.
4. The data item MASTER-FILE-FLAG is named in the FILE STATUS clause for the indexed file. As a result, the operating system automatically stores a two-character status code in MASTER-FILE-FLAG following every input-output operation on the file. In this program, these operations are OPEN, READ, REWRITE, and CLOSE. The program checks status codes for the READ and REWRITE operations only. The READ status codes are tested in the IF statement of paragraph 320-GET-OLD-MASTER, and both the READ and REWRITE status codes are tested in the EVALUATE statement of paragraph 330-PREPARE-AUDIT-LINE. In paragraph 320-GET-OLD-MASTER, the two MOVE statements transfer the codes to the fields O-READ-CODE and O-REWRITE-CODE, respectively.
5. The working storage record WS-MASTER-RECORD receives a copy of the master record retrieved by the READ statement at line 11. Note the INTO phrase. Since the audit line is prepared subsequent to a REWRITE operation and since the master record in the record area INDEXED-MASTER-RECORD is no longer available following a successful REWRITE, a copy of the original master record is retained to supply values needed in the audit line. See the first two MOVE statements in the EVALUATE statement of paragraph 330-PREPARE-AUDIT-LINE.

6. Two error messages are prepared, one related to an invalid key condition in a READ operation, the other related to an invalid key condition in a REWRITE operation. They are printed on the audit report along with the record key value that caused the error. See the last two MOVE statements in the EVALUATE statement of paragraph 330-PREPARE-AUDIT-LINE.
7. The fields O-READ-CODE and O-REWRITE-CODE receive copies of the status codes stored in the file status data item MASTER-FILE-FLAG so as to allow a simultaneous test of the codes in the EVALUATE statement. Recall that any input-output file operation causes a new status code to be stored in the file status flag. These two fields of AUDIT-LINE allow the status codes to be retained!
8. When a READ or a REWRITE error occurs, the REDEFINES clause at line 8 allows the error message to be printed on the audit line in the same area as would otherwise be used to print record data.
9. This MOVE statement assigns to INDEXED-MR-SSN the prime record key value that will be used by the subsequent READ statement to retrieve the desired record from the master file.
10. The EVALUATE statement tests the status codes stored in O-READ-CODE and O-REWRITE-CODE. The test results determine how the audit line is to be prepared for the current detail record.
11. When this READ statement is executed, the current value in INDEXED-MR-SSN is the key that selects the record to be retrieved from the master file. If this key value is not found in the index table, an invalid key condition occurs and the status code "23" is moved to the file status flag MASTER-FILE-FLAG.
12. This MOVE statement replaces the old address in the master record area with the one in the detail record area prior to rewriting the master record to the master file.
13. When the REWRITE statement is executed, the updated record is replaced in the master file at the same location it was previously retrieved from. The prime record key value is used in determining the location, and thus if it has changed since the successful READ, an invalid key condition occurs and the status code "23" is moved to the file status flag MASTER-FILE-FLAG.

The master personnel file shown in Figure 3.12 lists the records before the run of the program. The detail file is shown in Figure 3.22a, and Figure 3.22b shows the master file records after the program run. The report produced by the program is shown in Figure 3.23.

Figure 3.22a Detail file with new addresses

```
01649301785 CROSS ST    LEXINGTON, NE    68850
130043962450 E MAIN ST  HASTINGS, NE     68901
12467032556 MAPLE AVE   LEXINGTON, NE    68850
15024638928 SUNSET ST   KEARNEY, NE      68847
026307625810 PARK DR    AURORA,NE        68818
```

Figure 3.22b Master file with updated addresses

```
005589243BUXBAUM, JOAN M.    172 EARLE DR   GRAND ISLAND, NE 68802480214700608
013407206MCGEE, BERNARD W.   2420 CARR LA   CENTRAL CITY, NE 68826301215490615
014766691ARMSTRONG, GEORGE   105 STATE ST   PLATTE, NE       68653480320830816
016493017COUGHLIN, AILEEN M. 85 CROSS ST    LEXINGTON, NE    68850500310680706
026307625VELTRI, JOHN A.     810 PARK DR    AURORA,NE        68818470115820820
032561579MAYO, EVANGELINA    895 POTTERS AVEGENEVA, NE       68361620805830807
032567781AITKEN, THOMAS R.   260 FOUNTAIN STAURORA, NE       68818260805460820
033281512PEARSON, ARTHUR     1020 GOLDEN RD HASTINGS, NE     68901501125830802
039764715GAFFNEY, MARYLYN    76 MAIN ST     PLATTE, NE       68653521205770608
042750015COLETTI, SARAH T.   51 BROAD ST    HASTINGS, NE     68901380902640615
124670325MOONEY, RONALD      56 MAPLE AVE   LEXINGTON, NE    68850410920640810
130043962MARKARIAN, MARIAN   450 E MAIN ST  HASTINGS, NE     68901320507520820
144217773ALTERMAN, MAUREEN E.10 MARTIN AVE  YORK, NE         68467350524600610
149201475PACCASASSIE, DEBBIE 341 BRANCH AVE NORMAN, NE       68963282612570912
150246389PRIMEAU, ISABEL     28 SUNSET ST   KEARNEY, NE      68847470930720820
179623741BLAZUCK, JOSEPH A.  81 DORIS AVE   GENEVA, NE       68361450521750610
211384406KACHADOURIAN, NATALI922 LOCUST ST  HEBRON, NE       68370350221560820
215137814CUMMINGS, DOROTHEA  97 POWER AVE   NORMAN, NE       68963530407830822
226153911OVERDEEP, CYNTHIA   130 CANAL ST   YORK, NE         68467350524700715
234891533SHERIDAN, RICHARD J.850SUN CIRCLE  AURORA, NE       68818421205650610
253749144LAKE, SUE           252 EAST RD    CRETE, NE        68333410707830815
314764532DESROSIERS, RICHARD 92 REGAN RD    LOUP CITY, NE    68853581221830815
322150642STURDAHL, DEBRA     2541 RICE ST   CRETE, NE        68333340614550715
364923752DURANT, MARIE L.    1250 HIGH RD   GENEVA, NE       68361430924540910
381662514BAHR, LENA M.       304 CORY LANE  GENEVA, NE       68361411110600820
432157258ROMA, GILDA         25 MAPLE DR    SUPERIOR, NE     68978500708720610
623514793CARTER, AMEKIA L.   59 BARK ST     LOUP CITY, NE    68853320513620820
743142265ABRUZZI, KENNETH L. 51 RAYMOND ST  HASTINGS, NE     68901521205720820
771894263CYR, ROSARIO        205 SUNSET DR  FAIRFIELD, NE    68938350524550820
```

Figure 3.23 Audit report produced by the address update program

```
                                     JOCELYN ORIGINALS

                          MASTER PERSONNEL FILE ADDRESS UPDATE  89/11/16

STATUS CODES   MASTER RECORD DATA-------------------------------------------------|
READ REWRITE      KEY     NAME                  ADDRESS                                     NEW ADDRESS

 00     00     016493017 COUGHLIN, AILEEN M.   133 DAVIS RD   LEXINGTON, NE   68850   85 CROSS ST    LEXINGTON, NE   68850
 00     00     130043962 MARKARIAN, MARIAN     984 N MAIN ST  HASTINGS, NE    68901   450 E MAIN ST  HASTINGS, NE    68901
 00     00     124670325 MOONEY, RONALD        220 N MAIN ST  HASTINGS, NE    68901   56 MAPLE AVE   LEXINGTON, NE   68850
 00     00     150246389 PRIMEAU, ISABEL       78 NORTH ST    KEARNEY, NE     68847   28 SUNSET ST   KEARNEY, NE     68847
 00     00     026307625 VELTRI, JOHN A.       312 PERCH DR.  HASTINGS, NE    68901   810 PARK DR    AURORA,NE       68818


                                    *** END OF REPORT ***
```

Indexed File Update

We now consider the development of a complete file updating program for indexed files. Recall from updating a sequential file that a complete file update includes the following functions:

1. Adding new records to the file.
2. Deleting records from the file.
3. Updating existing records, that is, bringing all field values up-to-date.

For instance, in an inventory file, records may have to be added for new items in inventory, records may have to be deleted for those items no longer carried, existing records may require changes in a variety of fields, such as, vendor, purchase price, selling price, quantity in stock, and so on.

In a personnel file, records may have to be added for new employees, records may have to be deleted for employees who quit or were fired, field values for current employees may have to be changed due to a new address, a name change, a new phone number, and so on.

In an accounts receivable file, records may have to be added for new accounts, records may be deleted for accounts that no longer exist, field values may have to be changed in existing accounts to reflect payments received, credits allowed, and so on.

Whenever a master file update is needed, a detail record must be prepared for every record involved in the update. These records are assembled in a detail file. Each record in the detail file contains a code that specifies how the record is to be processed. The codes we will use in the sample program are the same as those used in the sequential file update. They are as follows:

code "1" to mean add this new record to the file;

code "2" to mean delete the corresponding record from the file;

code "3" to mean update field values on the corresponding record in the file.

If the process code is "1", the detail record must be a complete record in the sense that it must contain all the relevant information needed on the master record that it will generate. A very crucial field on this record is the one that contains the prime record key value, since this value will be used by the operating system to place the new record in its appropriate physical and logical position within the indexed file.

If the process code is "2", the detail record need contain only the prime record key value. The operating system will use this value to locate and then to delete the appropriate record from the file.

If the process code is "3", the detail record must contain the prime record key value and the new field values. The operating system will use the record key value to retrieve the corresponding master record in the master file.

While it is not technically necessary that all the records of the detail file have the same description, adhering to a common record description will facilitate the task of generating the program.

The Problem

The Jocelyn Originals Company needs to update its master personnel file. The original master personnel file is the one shown in Figure 3.22b, and the detail file that will be used to update the master file is shown in Figure 3.24.

Figure 3.24 Detail file used to update the master personnel file

```
2743142265ABRUZZI
1106940371CRANDALL, JEAN M.   145 SPRING ST  CENTRAL CITY, NE 68826050945111885
2502422713KRUGER
1310034692MELLO, ALBERT       950 N MAIN ST  HASTINGS, NE     68901050732111885
2262153911OVERDEEP
3124670325MOONEY              10 LOVETT DR   AURORA, NE       68818
1364923752MILTON, ANDREW      741 E MAIN ST  LOUP CITY, NE    68853032553112285
1051642983DONALDSON, LOUISE   42 NORTH ST    KEARNEY, NE      68847093047111885
3026307625VELTRI              24 SUNRISE AVE AURORA, NE       68818
```

Figure 3.25 Detail record layout

Figure 3.26 System flowchart to update the master personnel file

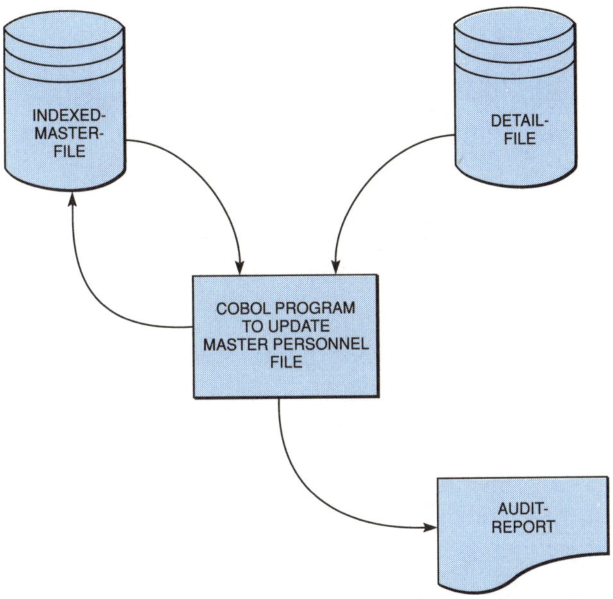

Designing the Program

The detail record layout is shown in Figure 3.25. Note that the first field contains the process code, whereas the second field contains the employee's Social Security number. If the code indicates that a record is to be retrieved from the master file, it is the value of DETAIL-SSN that must be assigned to the prime record key INDEXED-MR-SSN prior to the read operation. If the code indicates that a new record is to be added to the file, the value of DETAIL-SSN is the prime record key value that will be used by the WRITE statement to properly position the new record within the file.

The system flowchart is shown in Figure 3.26, and the printer spacing chart for the audit report is shown in Figure 3.27.

The overall structure of the program is shown in Figure 3.28. Note that within module 210 PROCESS DETAIL RECORD, the process code on the detail record is used to select the appropriate subordinate module 320 ADD NEW RECORD, 330 DELETE OLD MASTER, or 340 CHANGE OLD MASTER. Module 350 PREPARE AUDIT LINE will print a corresponding audit line on the report. Both modules 330 and 340 control subordinate module 400 READ MASTER FILE. In module 330, the record to be deleted is read from the file so that its data may be printed on the audit line. And in module 340, the master record that must receive new field values must be available in main memory so that it can be updated before being rewritten to the master file.

■ **Figure 3.27** Printer spacing chart for the file update audit report

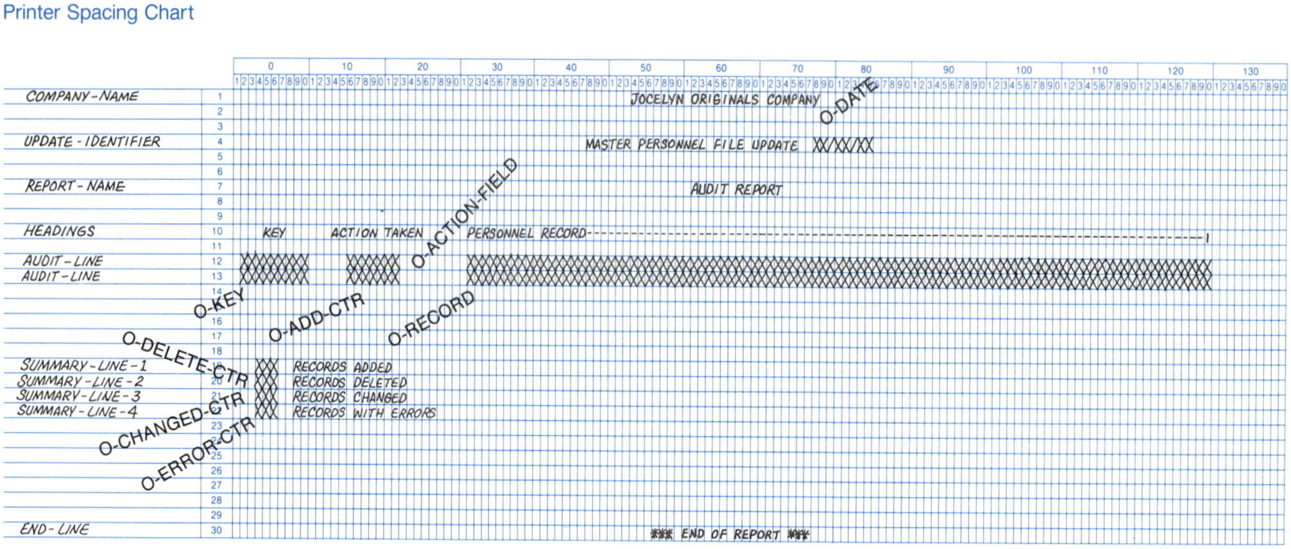

■ **Figure 3.28** Structure chart to update the master personnel file

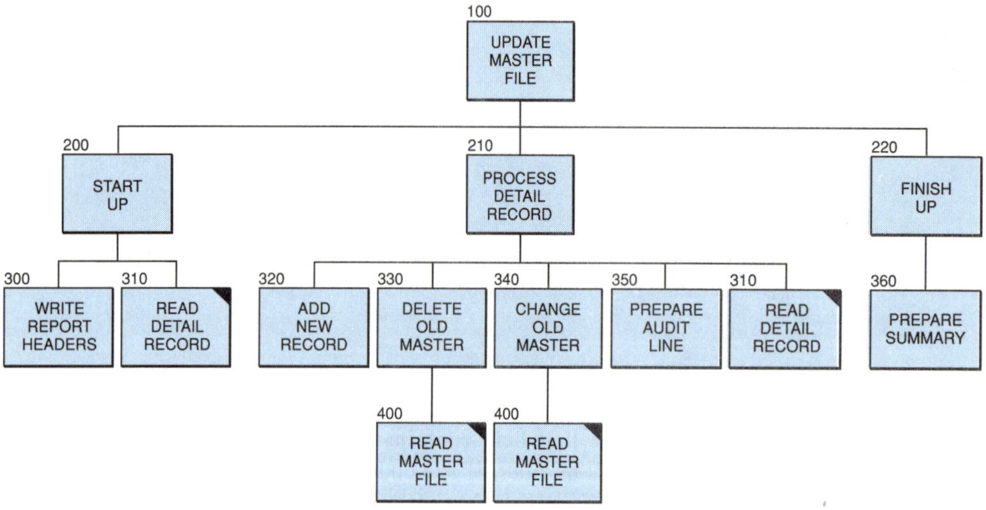

In addition to attending to the major tasks of updating the master file, the programmer must be aware of and make provisions for the possibility of the following input-output errors:

1. When a new record is being added to the master file, the operating system must generate an index based on the record key value for this new record. If a record already exists in the master file with the same prime record key value, a duplicate key condition occurs and the new record will not be copied into the file. In that case, a message should be printed on the audit report to explain the error.
2. If the process code on a detail record indicates that an existing master file record either must be deleted or must have some of its field values changed, the master file record whose key value is specified on the detail record must be read into the record area associated with the master file. If no record is found in the master file with the specified key value, then the read function fails due to an invalid key condition. The programmer should plan an appropriate message to be printed on the audit report to explain the error.

3. If the READ statement required to access an existing master file record is successfully executed, then one of two courses of action will have to be taken: change field values and rewrite the updated record to the master file, or delete the record from the master file. Let us consider each case.
   a. The record must be updated. After copying the new data from the detail record to the appropriate fields of the master record, the updated master record must be rewritten to the master file, and this output function will again use the prime record key value. If any change has occurred in the record key data item between the READ statement that accessed the record and the REWRITE statement that must copy it back to the file, an error condition has developed and the REWRITE function will fail. The programmer should plan to write an appropriate message on the audit report to explain the error.
   b. The record must be deleted. Since the master records are being accessed randomly, a record can be deleted simply by referencing the master file in the DELETE statement. Its format will be examined shortly. When the DELETE function is executed, the record specified by the current value of the prime record key is deleted from the file. If no record is found in the master file with the current prime record key value, an invalid key condition exists. The programmer should prepare an appropriate message to be printed on the audit report to explain the error. You will see that such an error cannot occur in the current program, because a successful read for that record must occur before the DELETE statement is executed. This procedure is used to facilitate the preparation of the required audit line!

In the current program, if any of the input/output errors described above occurs, the file status flag defined for the master personnel file is assigned the specific code that corresponds to the nature of the error. The presence of any of these codes will trigger the printing of appropriate messages. Any message will identify the prime record key value that caused the error.

The Program Pseudocode

The analysis detailed in the previous section leads to the following program pseudocode:

100-Update-Master-File.

1. Perform 200-Start-Up.
2. Perform 210-Process-Detail-Record until no more records.
3. Perform 220-Finish-Up.
4. Stop the run.

200-Start-Up.

1. Open Indexed-Master-File as an input-output file, Detail-File as an input file, and Audit-Report as an output file.
2. Obtain the date from the operating system.
3. Move date to Update-Identifier date.
4. Set the flag WS-MORE-DETAIL-RECORDS to "YES".
5. Set the program counters to zero.
6. Perform 300-Write-Report-Headers.
7. Perform 310-Read-Detail-Record.

210-Process-Detail-Record.

1. Test Detail-Record process-code:
   a. If 1, perform 320-Add-New-record.
   b. If 2, perform 330-Delete-Old-Master.
   c. If 3, perform 340-Change-Old-Master.
   d. If any other, continue.
2. Perform 350-Prepare-Audit-Line.
3. Perform 310-Read-Detail-Record.

220-Finish-Up.

1. Perform 360-Prepare-Summary.
2. Move the record End-Line to the output area Printline.
3. After advancing 5 lines, write the output record Printline.
4. Close the three files.

300-Write-Report-Headers.

1. Move the record Company-Name to the output area Printline.
2. After advancing to a new page, write the output record Printline.
3. Move the record Update-Identifier to the output area Printline.
4. After advancing 3 lines, write the output record Printline.
5. Move the record Report-Name to the output area Printline.
6. After advancing 3 lines, write the output record Printline.
7. Move the record Headings to the output area Printline.
8. After advancing 3 lines, write the output record Printline.
9. Set proper-spacing to 2.

310-Read-Detail-Record.

1. Read an input Detail-Record.
2. Test for end-of-file:
   if EOF record reached, set WS-MORE-DETAIL-RECORDS to "NO ".

320-Add-New-Record.

1. Move input Social-Security-number to Indexed-Master-Record Social-Security-number.
2. Move input name to Indexed-Master-Record name.
3. Move input address to Indexed-Master-Record address.
4. Move input date-of-birth to Indexed-Master-Record date-of-birth.
5. Move input date-hired to Indexed-Master-Record date-hired.
6. Write the record Indexed-Master-Record.
7. Test for invalid key in Write operation:
   if invalid, move the code "22" to master-file-flag.

330-Delete-Old-Master.

1. Move input Social-Security-number to Indexed-Master-Record Social-Security-number.
2. Perform 400-Read-Master-File.
3. If Read operation is successful,
   delete record from Indexed-Master-File.
4. Test for invalid key in Delete operation:
   if invalid, move the code "23" to master-file-flag.

340-Change-Old-Master.

1. Move input Social-Security-number to Indexed-Master-Record Social-Security-number.
2. Perform 400-Read-Master-File.
3. If Read operation is successful,
   a. Move input address to Indexed-Master-Record address and to master-record address.
   b. Rewrite the record Indexed-Master-Record.
   c. Test for invalid key in Rewrite operation:
      if invalid, move the code "23" to master-file-flag.

350-Prepare-Audit-Line.

1. Move input Social-Security-number to Audit-Line key.
2. Test input process-code and related operation on Indexed-Master-File:
   a. If process-code=1 and Write operation is successful,
      move "ADDED" to Audit-Line action-field,
      move input record to Audit-Line record area,
      add 1 to add-counter.

b. If process-code=1 and Write operation is not successful,
move "FAILED" to Audit-Line action-field,
move message-1 to Audit-Line message area
(message-1: "*** Duplicate key—can't add new record with this key"),
add 1 to error-counter.

c. If process-code=2 and Read and Delete operations are successful,
move "DELETED" to Audit-Line action-field,
move master-record to Audit-Line record area,
add 1 to delete-counter.

d. If process-code=2 and Read operation is not successful,
move "FAILED" to Audit-Line action-field,
move message-2 to Audit-Line message area
(message-2: "*** No record found in master file with this key"),
add 1 to error-counter.

e. If process-code=3 and Read and Rewrite operations are successful,
move "CHANGED" to Audit-Line action-field,
move master-record to Audit-Line record area,
add 1 to changed-counter.

f. If process-code=3 and Read operation is not successful,
move "FAILED" to Audit-Line action-field,
move message-2 to Audit-Line message area,
add 1 to error-counter.

g. If other process-code,
move "FAILED" to Audit-Line action-field,
move message-3 to Audit-Line message area
(message-3: "*** Wrong process code on detail record with this key"),
add 1 to error-counter.

3. Move the record Audit-Line to the output area Printline.
4. After advancing proper-spacing, write the output record Printline.
5. Move 1 to proper-spacing.

360-Prepare-Summary.

1. Move add-counter to Summary-Line-1 add-counter.
2. Move the record Summary-line-1 to the output area Printline.
3. After advancing 5 lines, write the output record Printline.
4. Move delete-counter to Summary-Line-2 delete-counter.
5. Move the record Summary-line-2 to the output area Printline.
6. After advancing 1 line, write the output record Printline.
7. Move changed-counter to Summary-Line-3 changed-counter.
8. Move the record Summary-line-3 to the output area Printline.
9. After advancing 1 line, write the output record Printline.
10. Move error-counter to Summary-Line-4 error-counter.
11. Move the record Summary-line-4 to the output area Printline.
12. After advancing 1 line, write the output record Printline.

400-Read-Master-File.

1. Read Indexed-Master-File record with prime record key value.
2. Test for invalid key in Read operation:
   a. If invalid, move the code "23" to master-file-flag.
   b. If not invalid, move indexed-master-record to working-storage master-record.

The program flowchart that corresponds to the pseudocode is shown in Figure 3.29.

Figure 3.29 Program flowchart to update the indexed file

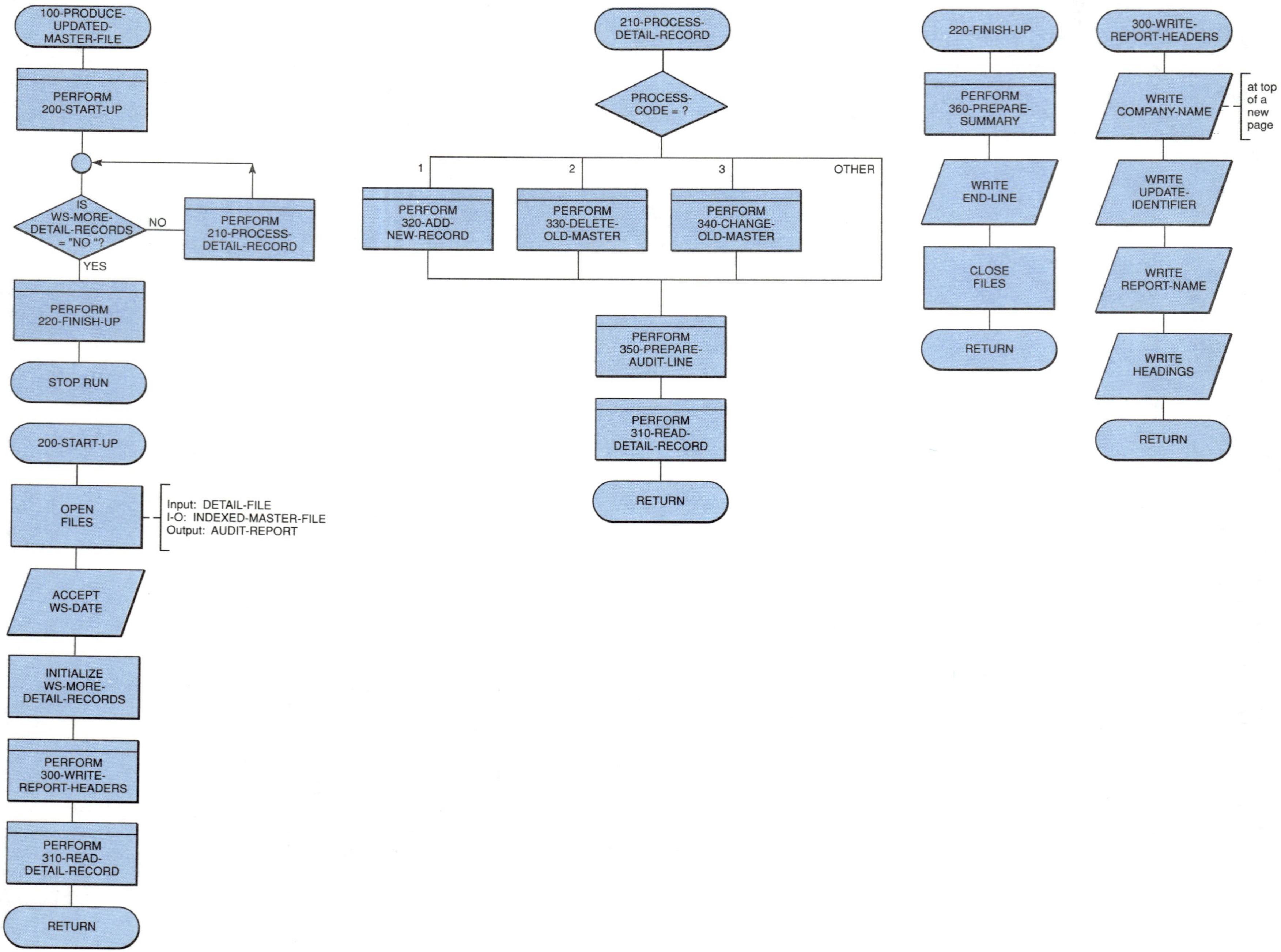

Figure 3.29 continued

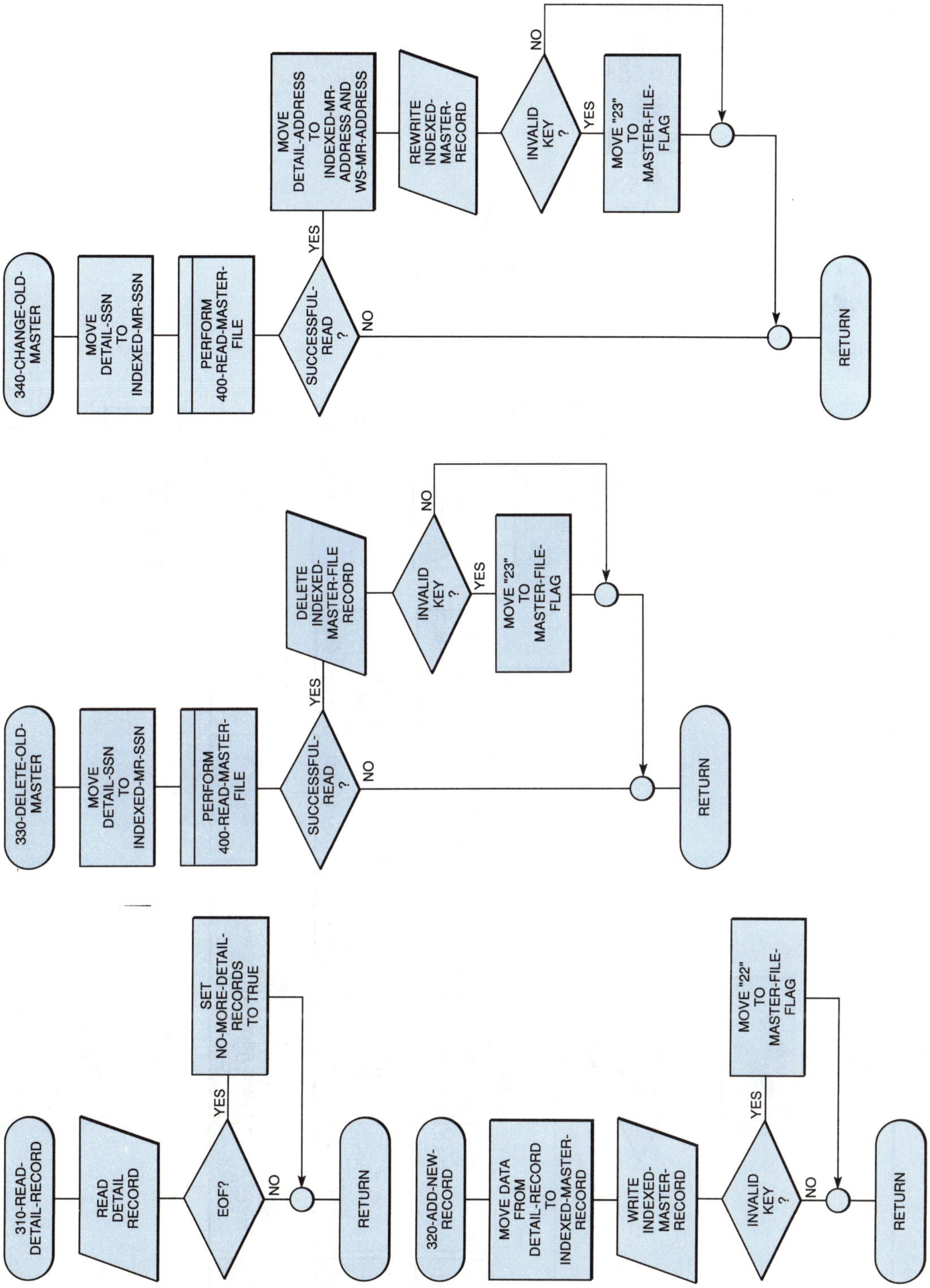

■ **Figure 3.29** continued

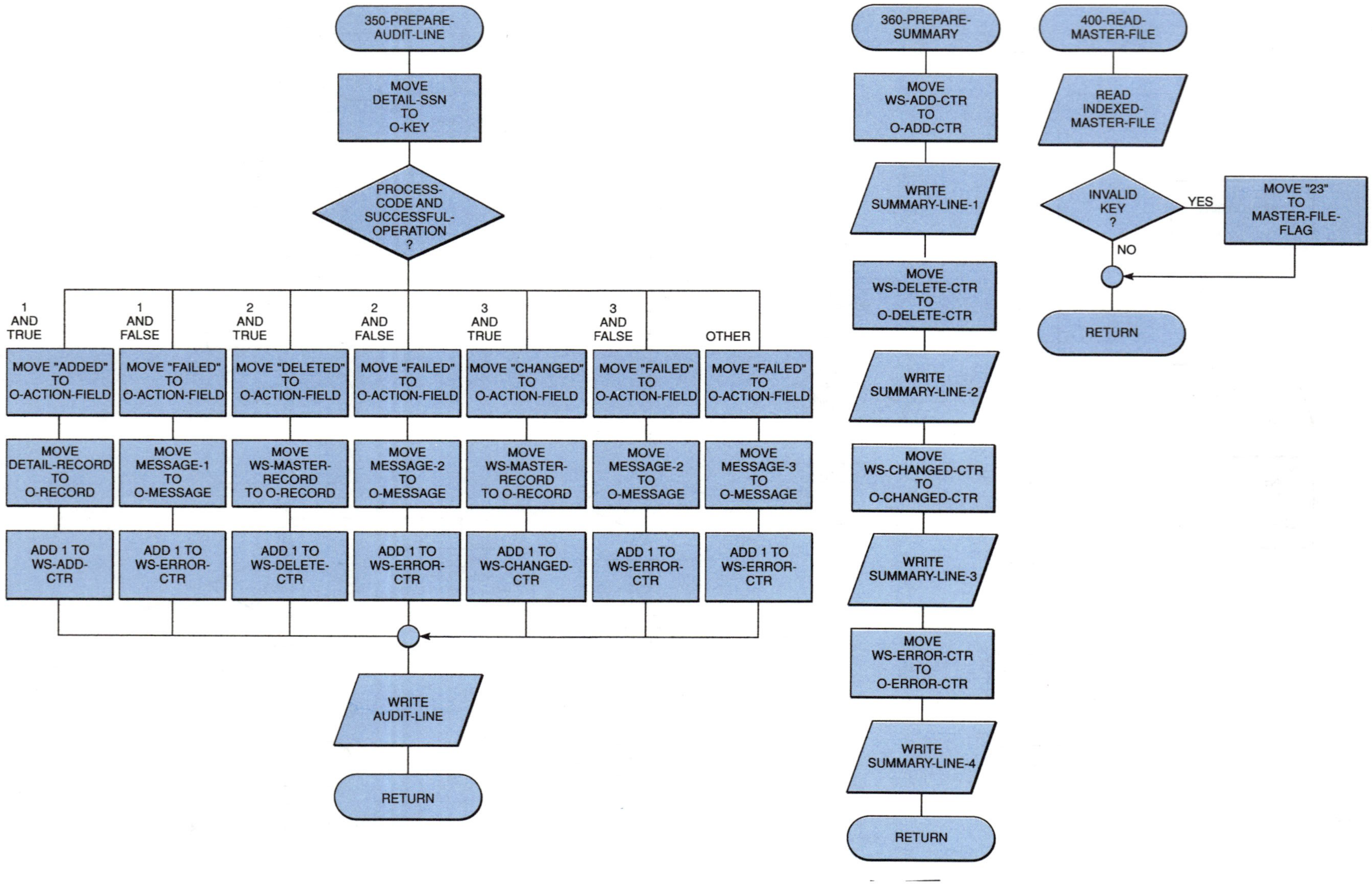

Coding the Program to Update the Indexed File

Before coding the program, we briefly consider two new features in this program, specifically, adding records to an existing indexed file and deleting records from an indexed file.

Recall that when an indexed file is created,

1. The prime record key value of each record is used to generate an index for the record.
2. The indexes are stored in an index table at the beginning of the file.
3. The records are physically written to the file in ascending order of their prime record key values.

When a new record has to be added to the file, where is it positioned within the file? There are generally two different situations that may be encountered. In one situation, if there is space on the cylinder that contains the file, the record is inserted between existing records as determined by the new record's prime key value. Existing records with a greater prime key value are displaced, and corresponding adjustments are made to their indexes in the index table. In the other situation, if not enough space on the cylinder is available, another cylinder will be used as an overflow area for the file. The new record is stored in the overflow area, but the index created for the new record contains additional pointers that allow it to be accessed as if it were physically stored on the original cylinder.

The record management services provided by the operating system make the internal structure of indexed files transparent to the user, and, as a result, the programmer does not have to generate additional code to handle the storage and retrieval of records added to the indexed file. New records are added to the file by using the WRITE-INVALID KEY statement, and they are later accessed, as any other record in the file, by the READ-AT END statement if access mode is sequential and by the READ-INVALID KEY statement if access mode is random.

When a record is to be deleted from an indexed file, there are two available procedures, depending on the access mode in effect at the time. If the access mode is sequential, the target record must be read first to identify it as the correct record to be deleted and then the DELETE statement is executed. If the access mode is random, the prime record key value for the record to be deleted must be moved to the prime record key data item and then the DELETE statement is executed. In either case, the target record is logically removed from the file. The system accomplishes this by performing the following two actions:

1. The system inserts a flag at the beginning of a record to mark it as deleted, so that if the records of the file are being processed sequentially, deleted records will not be accessed.
2. The system removes from the index table the pointers associated with the record to be deleted, so that if it is to be retrieved randomly, the absence of pointers makes it inaccessible.

The DELETE Statement

The format of the DELETE statement is shown in Figure 3.30.

Figure 3.30 DELETE statement format

```
DELETE file-name-1 RECORD
       [INVALID KEY imperative-statement-1]
       [NOT INVALID KEY imperative-statement-2]
       [END-DELETE]
```

Rules Governing the Use of the DELETE Statement

1. The function of the DELETE statement is to logically remove a record from a file on a mass storage device. The file must have indexed organization or relative organization.
2. *File-name-1* must be described in a FD paragraph of the FILE SECTION. It must not be a sequential file, a sort file, or a merge file.
3. *Imperative-statement-1* is an imperative statement that is executed whenever an invalid key condition exists.
4. *Imperative-statement-2* is an imperative statement that is executed whenever the DELETE operation is successful.
5. The INVALID KEY clause is required if the access mode for the file is not sequential, or if the program does not contain a USE AFTER EXCEPTION procedure for the file.
6. The INVALID KEY clause must not be used if the access mode for the file is sequential.
7. The NOT INVALID KEY clause is always optional, and it provides an alternate path to the INVALID KEY clause.
8. END-DELETE is the explicit scope terminator.
9. *File-name-1* must be open in I-O mode at the time the DELETE statement executes.
10. If the access mode for the file is sequential, a successful READ statement must be executed for the record to be deleted prior to executing the DELETE statement. The DELETE statement deletes the last record successfully read from the file.
11. If the access mode for an indexed file is random or dynamic, the prime record key value for the record to be deleted must be moved to the file's prime record key data item prior to executing the DELETE statement. The delete operation is successful if a record in the file has the prime record key value. If a record with the prime record key value cannot be found, an invalid key condition exists and the operation fails.
12. If the delete operation is successful, the record is logically removed from the file and it is no longer accessible, regardless of the access mode. The contents of the record area in main memory are not affected by the operation.
13. The execution of a DELETE statement updates the code in the data item named in the FILE STATUS clause for the file. The standard codes are as follows:

    "00" to denote a successful operation;

    "23" to denote an invalid key because no record in the file has the record key value;

    "30" to denote a permanent system error;

    "43" to denote an attempt to delete a record while the access mode is sequential but without satisfying the condition that the last input-output operation was a successful READ operation;

    "49" to denote an attempt to delete a record from a file whose open mode is not I-O.

The program to update the master personnel file for the Jocelyn Originals Company is contained in Figure 3.31. Some program entries have been numbered to facilitate references to them.

Comments on the Program

The numbered paragraphs that follow correspond to the numbered lines in the program of Figure 3.31.

1. The process code in the first byte of each detail record specifies how the record is to be processed. It is tested in paragraph 210-PROCESS-DETAIL-RECORD. If the code is a valid code, control is sent to the appropriate procedure. However, if there is an error in the code, control immediately leaves the EVALUATE statement and enters paragraph 350-PREPARE-AUDIT-LINE, where an appropriate error message (Message-3) is generated on the report. (Note that if the code is 1, the data in the record must be copied to fields of a new master record, as well as to the audit line, but the code itself is not copied!)

■ **Figure 3.31** COBOL program to update the indexed master file

```
IDENTIFICATION DIVISION.

PROGRAM-ID. UPDATE-INDEXED-FILE.

*****************************************************************
*                                                               *
*   AUTHOR.         PAQUETTE.                                   *
*   DATE WRITTEN.   NOVEMBER 1989.                              *
*                                                               *
*   THIS PROGRAM UPDATES THE MASTER PERSONNEL FILE FOR THE JOCE- *
*   LYN ORIGINALS COMPANY.  THE MASTER FILE IS AN INDEXED FILE.  *
*   THE UPDATE INCLUDES ADDING NEW RECORDS TO THE FILE, DELETING *
*   EXISTING RECORDS, AND CHANGING VALUES ON EXISTING RECORDS.   *
*   THE DETAIL FILE RECORDS CONTAIN A CODE IN COLUMN 1 TO       *
*   SPECIFY HOW THEY ARE TO BE PROCESSED.                       *
*                                                               *
*   AN AUDIT REPORT IS ALSO PRODUCED BY THE PROGRAM.            *
*                                                               *
*****************************************************************

ENVIRONMENT DIVISION.

CONFIGURATION SECTION.

SOURCE-COMPUTER.   VAX-VMS-8650.
OBJECT-COMPUTER.   VAX-VMS-8650.

INPUT-OUTPUT SECTION.

FILE-CONTROL.
    SELECT DETAIL-FILE           ASSIGN TO COB$INPUT.
    SELECT INDEXED-MASTER-FILE   ASSIGN TO DISKMASTER
                                 ORGANIZATION IS INDEXED
                                 ACCESS MODE IS RANDOM
                                 RECORD KEY IS INDEXED-MR-SSN
                                 FILE STATUS IS MASTER-FILE-FLAG.
    SELECT AUDIT-REPORT          ASSIGN TO COB$OUTPUT.

DATA DIVISION.

FILE SECTION.

FD  DETAIL-FILE
    RECORD CONTAINS 101 CHARACTERS.

01  DETAIL-RECORD.
1       05 PROCESS-CODE       PIC 9.
           88 ADDITION           VALUE 1.
           88 DELETION           VALUE 2.
           88 RECORD-UPDATE      VALUE 3.
2       05 DETAIL-SSN         PIC X(9).
        05 DETAIL-NAME        PIC X(20).
        05 DETAIL-ADDRESS     PIC X(37).
        05 DETAIL-DOB         PIC X(6).
        05 DETAIL-DATE-HIRED  PIC X(6).
        05                    PIC X(22).

FD  INDEXED-MASTER-FILE
    RECORD CONTAINS 100 CHARACTERS
    BLOCK CONTAINS 5 RECORDS.

01  INDEXED-MASTER-RECORD.
    05 INDEXED-MR-SSN          PIC X(9).
    05 INDEXED-MR-NAME         PIC X(20).
    05 INDEXED-MR-ADDRESS      PIC X(37).
    05 INDEXED-MR-DOB          PIC X(6).
    05 INDEXED-MR-DATE-HIRED   PIC X(6).
    05                         PIC X(22).

FD  AUDIT-REPORT
    RECORD CONTAINS 132 CHARACTERS.

01  PRINTLINE              PIC X(132).

WORKING-STORAGE SECTION.

01  PROGRAM-CONTROLS.
    05 WS-DATE             PIC X(6).
    05 WS-PROPER-SPACING   PIC 9.
```

```
3       01  PROGRAM-COUNTERS.
            05 WS-ADD-CTR            PIC S9(3).
            05 WS-DELETE-CTR         PIC S9(3).
            05 WS-CHANGED-CTR        PIC S9(3).
            05 WS-ERROR-CTR          PIC S9(3).

        01  PROGRAM-FLAGS.
            05 WS-MORE-DETAIL-RECORDS       PIC X(3).
                88 NO-MORE-DETAIL-RECORDS            VALUE 'NO '.
            05 MASTER-FILE-FLAG             PIC X(2).
                88 SUCCESSFUL-OPERATION              VALUE '00'.
                88 DUPLICATE-KEY                     VALUE '22'.
                88 NO-SUCH-RECORD                    VALUE '23'.

        01  WS-MASTER-RECORD.
            05 WS-MR-SSN           PIC X(9).
            05 WS-MR-NAME          PIC X(20).
            05 WS-MR-ADDRESS       PIC X(37).
            05 WS-MR-DOB           PIC X(6).
            05 WS-MR-DATE-HIRED    PIC X(6).
            05                     PIC X(22).

4       01  ERROR-MESSAGES.
            05 MESSAGE-1           PIC X(53)    VALUE
                '*** DUPLICATE KEY- CAN'T ADD NEW RECORD WITH THIS KEY'.
            05 MESSAGE-2           PIC X(53)    VALUE
                '*** NO RECORD FOUND IN MASTER FILE WITH THIS KEY      '.
            05 MESSAGE-3           PIC X(53)    VALUE
               .'*** WRONG PROCESS CODE ON DETAIL RECORD WITH THIS KEY'.

        01  REPORT-HEADERS.

            05 COMPANY-NAME.
                10 PIC X(53)    VALUE SPACES.
                10 PIC X(25)    VALUE 'JOCELYN ORIGINALS COMPANY'.
                10 PIC X(54)    VALUE SPACES.

            05 UPDATE-IDENTIFIER.
                10 PIC X(47)    VALUE SPACES.
                10 PIC X(30)    VALUE 'MASTER PERSONNEL FILE UPDATE  '.
                10 O-DATE       PIC XX/XX/XX.
                10 PIC X(47)    VALUE SPACES.

            05 REPORT-NAME.
                10 PIC X(60)    VALUE SPACES.
                10 PIC X(12)    VALUE 'AUDIT REPORT'.
                10 PIC X(60)    VALUE SPACES.

            05 HEADINGS.
                10 PIC X(4)     VALUE SPACES.
                10 PIC X(3)     VALUE 'KEY'.
                10 PIC X(6)     VALUE SPACES.
                10 PIC X(12)    VALUE 'ACTION TAKEN'.
                10 PIC X(6)     VALUE SPACES.
                10 PIC X(16)    VALUE 'PERSONNEL RECORD'.
                10 PIC X(82)    VALUE ALL '-'.
                10 PIC X(1)     VALUE '|'.

        01  AUDIT-LINE.
            05                  PIC X(1).
            05 O-KEY            PIC X(9).
            05                  PIC X(5).
            05 O-ACTION-FIELD   PIC X(7).
            05                  PIC X(5).
            05 O-RECORD-AREA.
                10              PIC X(4).
                10 O-RECORD     PIC X(100).
5           05 O-MESSAGE REDEFINES O-RECORD-AREA
                                PIC X(104).

        01  SUMMARY-LINES.

            05 SUMMARY-LINE-1.
                10                  PIC X(3)  VALUE SPACES.
                10 O-ADD-CTR        PIC ZZ9.
                10                  PIC X(15) VALUE '  RECORDS ADDED'.

            05 SUMMARY-LINE-2.
                10                  PIC X(3)  VALUE SPACES.
                10 O-DELETE-CTR     PIC ZZ9.
                10                  PIC X(17) VALUE '  RECORDS DELETED'.
```

```
       05 SUMMARY-LINE-3.
          10                PIC X(3)  VALUE SPACES.
          10 O-CHANGED-CTR  PIC ZZ9.
          10                PIC X(17) VALUE '  RECORDS CHANGED'.

       05 SUMMARY-LINE-4.
          10                PIC X(3)  VALUE SPACES.
          10 O-ERROR-CTR    PIC ZZ9.
          10                PIC X(21) VALUE '  RECORDS WITH ERRORS'.

   01  END-LINE.
       05 PIC X(56)  VALUE SPACES.
       05 PIC X(21)  VALUE '*** END OF REPORT ***'.
       05 PIC X(55)  VALUE SPACES.

   PROCEDURE DIVISION.

   100-PRODUCE-UPDATED-MASTER-FILE.
       PERFORM 200-START-UP.
       PERFORM 210-PROCESS-DETAIL-RECORD
           UNTIL NO-MORE-DETAIL-RECORDS.
       PERFORM 220-FINISH-UP.
       STOP RUN.

   200-START-UP.
       OPEN INPUT DETAIL-FILE
6           I-O INDEXED-MASTER-FILE
            OUTPUT AUDIT-REPORT.
       ACCEPT WS-DATE FROM DATE.
       MOVE WS-DATE TO O-DATE.
       MOVE 'YES' TO WS-MORE-DETAIL-RECORDS.
       INITIALIZE PROGRAM-COUNTERS.
       PERFORM 300-WRITE-REPORT-HEADERS.
       PERFORM 310-READ-DETAIL-RECORD.

   210-PROCESS-DETAIL-RECORD.
7      EVALUATE PROCESS-CODE
           WHEN      1       PERFORM 320-ADD-NEW-RECORD
           WHEN      2       PERFORM 330-DELETE-OLD-MASTER
           WHEN      3       PERFORM 340-CHANGE-OLD-MASTER
           WHEN    OTHER     CONTINUE
       END-EVALUATE.
       PERFORM 350-PREPARE-AUDIT-LINE.
       PERFORM 310-READ-DETAIL-RECORD.

   220-FINISH-UP.
       PERFORM 360-PREPARE-SUMMARY.
       WRITE PRINTLINE FROM END-LINE
           AFTER ADVANCING 5 LINES.
       CLOSE DETAIL-FILE
             INDEXED-MASTER-FILE
             AUDIT-REPORT.

   300-WRITE-REPORT-HEADERS.
       WRITE PRINTLINE FROM COMPANY-NAME
           AFTER ADVANCING PAGE.
       WRITE PRINTLINE FROM UPDATE-IDENTIFIER
           AFTER ADVANCING 3 LINES.
       WRITE PRINTLINE FROM REPORT-NAME
           AFTER ADVANCING 3 LINES.
       WRITE PRINTLINE FROM HEADINGS
           AFTER ADVANCING 3 LINES.
       MOVE 2 TO WS-PROPER-SPACING.

   310-READ-DETAIL-RECORD.
       READ DETAIL-FILE RECORD
           AT END
               SET NO-MORE-DETAIL-RECORDS TO TRUE.

   320-ADD-NEW-RECORD.
       MOVE DETAIL-SSN TO INDEXED-MR-SSN.
       MOVE DETAIL-NAME TO INDEXED-MR-NAME.
       MOVE DETAIL-ADDRESS TO INDEXED-MR-ADDRESS.
       MOVE DETAIL-DOB TO INDEXED-MR-DOB.
       MOVE DETAIL-DATE-HIRED TO INDEXED-MR-DATE-HIRED.
8      WRITE INDEXED-MASTER-RECORD
           INVALID KEY
               MOVE '22' TO MASTER-FILE-FLAG.

9  330-DELETE-OLD-MASTER.
       MOVE DETAIL-SSN TO INDEXED-MR-SSN.
       PERFORM 400-READ-MASTER-FILE.
       IF SUCCESSFUL-OPERATION
           DELETE INDEXED-MASTER-FILE RECORD
               INVALID KEY
                   MOVE '23' TO MASTER-FILE-FLAG
       END-IF.
```

Figure 3.31 continued

```
        340-CHANGE-OLD-MASTER.
            MOVE DETAIL-SSN TO INDEXED-MR-SSN.
            PERFORM 400-READ-MASTER-FILE.
            IF SUCCESSFUL-OPERATION
                MOVE DETAIL-ADDRESS TO INDEXED-MR-ADDRESS
                                       WS-MR-ADDRESS
                REWRITE INDEXED-MASTER-RECORD
                    INVALID KEY
                        MOVE '23' TO MASTER-FILE-FLAG
                END-REWRITE
            END-IF.

10      350-PREPARE-AUDIT-LINE.
            MOVE SPACES TO AUDIT-LINE.
            MOVE DETAIL-SSN TO O-KEY.
            EVALUATE PROCESS-CODE ALSO SUCCESSFUL-OPERATION
                WHEN     1        ALSO        TRUE
                                MOVE 'ADDED' TO O-ACTION-FIELD
                                MOVE DETAIL-RECORD(2:100) TO O-RECORD
                                ADD 1 TO WS-ADD-CTR
                WHEN     1        ALSO        FALSE
                                MOVE 'FAILED' TO O-ACTION-FIELD
                                MOVE MESSAGE-1 TO O-MESSAGE
                                ADD 1 TO WS-ERROR-CTR
                WHEN     2        ALSO        TRUE
                                MOVE 'DELETED' TO O-ACTION-FIELD
                                MOVE WS-MASTER-RECORD TO O-RECORD
                                ADD 1 TO WS-DELETE-CTR
                WHEN     2        ALSO        FALSE
                                MOVE 'FAILED' TO O-ACTION-FIELD
                                MOVE MESSAGE-2 TO O-MESSAGE
                                ADD 1 TO WS-ERROR-CTR
                WHEN     3        ALSO        TRUE
                                MOVE 'CHANGED' TO O-ACTION-FIELD
                                MOVE WS-MASTER-RECORD TO O-RECORD
                                ADD 1 TO WS-CHANGED-CTR
                WHEN     3        ALSO        FALSE
                                MOVE 'FAILED' TO O-ACTION-FIELD
                                MOVE MESSAGE-2 TO O-MESSAGE
                                ADD 1 TO WS-ERROR-CTR
                WHEN   OTHER
                                MOVE 'FAILED' TO O-ACTION-FIELD
                                MOVE MESSAGE-3 TO O-MESSAGE
                                ADD 1 TO WS-ERROR-CTR
            END-EVALUATE.
            WRITE PRINTLINE FROM AUDIT-LINE
                AFTER ADVANCING WS-PROPER-SPACING.
            MOVE 1 TO WS-PROPER-SPACING.

        360-PREPARE-SUMMARY.
            MOVE WS-ADD-CTR TO O-ADD-CTR.
            WRITE PRINTLINE FROM SUMMARY-LINE-1
                AFTER ADVANCING 5 LINES.
            MOVE WS-DELETE-CTR TO O-DELETE-CTR.
            WRITE PRINTLINE FROM SUMMARY-LINE-2
                AFTER ADVANCING 1 LINE.
            MOVE WS-CHANGED-CTR TO O-CHANGED-CTR.
            WRITE PRINTLINE FROM SUMMARY-LINE-3
                AFTER ADVANCING 1 LINE.
            MOVE WS-ERROR-CTR TO O-ERROR-CTR.
            WRITE PRINTLINE FROM SUMMARY-LINE-4
                AFTER ADVANCING 1 LINE.

        400-READ-MASTER-FILE.
            READ INDEXED-MASTER-FILE RECORD INTO WS-MASTER-RECORD
                INVALID KEY
                    MOVE '23' TO MASTER-FILE-FLAG.
```

2. In each detail record, the field DETAIL-SSN contains the value assigned to the prime record key data item (INDEXED-MR-SSN). If the process code is 1, the function of the prime record key is to correctly position the record within the file. If the process code is 2, the function of the prime record key is to specify the master record to be deleted from the master file. And if the process code is 3, the first function of the prime record key is to access the appropriate record from the master file so that its data fields may be updated and the second function is to rewrite the record to its correct location in the file.
3. Program counters are defined because the audit report must print a count of the number of records added to the file, the number of records deleted from the file, the number of master records updated, and the number of detail records not processed properly. The counters are initialized in paragraph 200-START-UP, and each one is incremented within paragraph 350-PREPARE-AUDIT-LINE whenever the required conditions are satisfied.
4. This record contains the error messages that will be printed on the audit report whenever the specified errors occur. MESSAGE-1 is related to status code "22", MESSAGE-2 is related to status code "23", and MESSAGE-3 is related to an erroneous process code. The messages are selected in paragraph 350-PREPARE-AUDIT-LINE.
5. The REDEFINES clause in this entry allows the same print positions of AUDIT-LINE to print either a correctly processed record or the error message that indicates why the record was not processed correctly.
6. The open mode for indexed file INDEXED-MASTER-FILE must be stated as I-O, since the file is referenced in READ, WRITE, REWRITE, and DELETE statements.
7. In this EVALUATE statement, the process code is tested so as to select the appropriate processing paragraph. If the process code is not a 1, 2, or 3, control leaves the EVALUATE statement and then enters paragraph 350-PREPARE-AUDIT-LINE, where the condition in the last WHEN clause is satisfied. This causes MESSAGE-3 to be selected for printout on the audit line.
8. When this WRITE statement is executed, the system uses the record's prime record key (the value of INDEXED-MR-SSN) to determine where the master record should be written. This search occurs in the index table for the file.

   If a record already exists in the file with the current record key value, an invalid key condition occurs, the WRITE function fails, and the code "22" is moved into the status flag MASTER-FILE-FLAG. Control then leaves procedure 320-ADD-NEW-RECORD to return to paragraph 210-PROCESS-DETAIL-RECORD, and it is sent directly to paragraph 350-PREPARE-AUDIT-LINE. In this paragraph, the conditions in the second WHEN clause are satisfied and MESSAGE-1 is selected to be printed on the report.

   If no master record has the current prime record key value, the new record is inserted in the file, either in the primary record area or in the overflow area, and an index is generated in the index table for the new record.
9. In this paragraph, the prime record key value of the record to be deleted, specified by DETAIL-SSN, is assigned to the key data item INDEXED-MR-SSN. The DELETE statement could then be executed immediately. However, because a copy of the record to be deleted is needed on the audit report, the procedure 400-READ-MASTER-FILE is executed first. This read operation, if successful, makes a double copy of the master record, one in the record area INDEXED-MASTER-RECORD and the other in the working-storage item WS-MASTER-RECORD

   Note that the logic of the procedure is such that the DELETE statement is executed only if the preceding read operation was successful. Consequently, the invalid key condition will never occur. Nonetheless, the INVALID KEY clause must still be coded in the DELETE statement.

Also note that the deletion of the record from the master file fails only if the read operation cannot find a master record with the prime record key value specified by DETAIL-SSN.

10. In this paragraph, note that the EVALUATE statement contains two WHEN clauses for each valid process code. One of these clauses formats the audit line if the required operation is successful, whereas the other formats the audit line if the operation is not successful. The last WHEN clause prepares an audit line for a process code error. Each WHEN clause also updates the appropriate counter.

The master file as updated by the program is shown in Figure 3.32. Compare the listing of the updated file with the original file listed in Figure 3.22b. The audit report produced by the program is shown in Figure 3.33.

Figure 3.32 Updated master file

```
005589243BUXBAUM, JOAN M.     172 EARLE DR   GRAND ISLAND, NE 68802480214700608
013407206MCGEE, BERNARD W.    2420 CARR LA   CENTRAL CITY, NE 68826301215490615
014766691ARMSTRONG, GEORGE    105 STATE ST   PLATTE, NE       68653480320830816
016493017COUGHLIN, AILEEN M. 133 DAVIS RD   LEXINGTON, NE    68850500310680706
026307625VELTRI, JOHN A.      24 SUNRISE AVE AURORA, NE       68818470115820820
032561579MAYO, EVANGELINA     895 POTTERS AVEGENEVA, NE       68361620805830807
032567781AITKEN, THOMAS R.    260 FOUNTAIN STAURORA, NE       68818260805460820
033281512PEARSON, ARTHUR      1020 GOLDEN RD HASTINGS, NE     68901501125830802
039764715GAFFNEY, MARYLYN     76 MAIN ST     PLATTE, NE       68653521205770608
042750015COLETTI, SARAH T.    51 BROAD ST    HASTINGS, NE     68901380902640615
051642983DONALDSON, LOUISE    42 NORTH ST    KEARNEY, NE      68847093047111885
106940371CRANDALL, JEAN M.    145 SPRING ST  CENTRAL CITY, NE 68826050945111885
124670325MOONEY, RONALD       10 LOVETT DR   AURORA, NE       68818410920640810
130043962MARKARIAN, MARIAN    984 N MAIN ST  HASTINGS, NE     68901320507520820
144217773ALTERMAN, MAUREEN E.10 MARTIN AVE  YORK, NE         68467350524600610
149201475PACCASASSIE, DEBBIE 341 BRANCH AVE NORMAN, NE       68963282612570912
150246389PRIMEAU, ISABEL      78 NORTH ST    KEARNEY, NE      68847470930720820
179623741BLAZUCK, JOSEPH A.   81 DORIS AVE   GENEVA, NE       68361450521750610
211384406KACHADOURIAN, NATALI922 LOCUST ST  HEBRON, NE       68370350221560820
215137814CUMMINGS, DOROTHEA   97 POWER AVE   NORMAN, NE       68963530407830822
226153911OVERDEEP, CYNTHIA    130 CANAL ST   YORK, NE         68467350524700715
234891533SHERIDAN, RICHARD J.850SUN CIRCLE  AURORA, NE       68818421205650610
253749144LAKE, SUE            252 EAST RD    CRETE, NE        68333410707830815
310034692MELLO, ALBERT        950 N MAIN ST  HASTINGS, NE     68901050732111885
314764532DESROSIERS, RICHARD 92 REGAN RD    LOUP CITY, NE    68853581221830815
322150642STURDAHL, DEBRA      2541 RICE ST   CRETE, NE        68333340614550715
364923752DURANT, MARIE L.     1250 HIGH RD   GENEVA, NE       68361430924540910
381662514BAHR, LENA M.        304 CORY LANE  GENEVA, NE       68361411110600820
432157258ROMA, GILDA          25 MAPLE DR    SUPERIOR, NE     68978500708720610
623514793CARTER, AMEKIA L.    59 BARK ST     LOUP CITY, NE    68853320513620820
771894263CYR, ROSARIO         205 SUNSET DR  FAIRFIELD, NE    68938350524550820
```

Figure 3.33 Audit report for the master file update

```
                                        JOCELYN ORIGINALS COMPANY

                                   MASTER PERSONNEL FILE UPDATE  89/11/28

                                             AUDIT REPORT

   KEY       ACTION TAKEN        PERSONNEL RECORD---------------------------------------------------------------------------|

743142265      DELETED           743142265ABRUZZI, KENNETH L. 51 RAYMOND ST  HASTINGS, NE     68901521205720820
106940371      ADDED             106940371CRANDALL, JEAN M.   145 SPRING ST  CENTRAL CITY, NE 68826050945111885
502422713      FAILED        *** NO RECORD FOUND IN MASTER FILE WITH THIS KEY
310034692      ADDED             310034692MELLO, ALBERT       950 N MAIN ST  HASTINGS, NE     68901050732111885
262153911      FAILED        *** NO RECORD FOUND IN MASTER FILE WITH THIS KEY
124670325      CHANGED           124670325MOONEY, RONALD      10 LOVETT DR   AURORA, NE       68818410920640810
364923752      FAILED        *** DUPLICATE KEY- CAN'T ADD NEW RECORD WITH THIS KEY
051642983      ADDED             051642983DONALDSON, LOUISE   42 NORTH ST    KEARNEY, NE      68847093047111885
026307625      CHANGED           026307625VELTRI, JOHN A.     24 SUNRISE AVE AURORA, NE       68818470115820820


    3  RECORDS ADDED
    1  RECORDS DELETED
    2  RECORDS CHANGED
    3  RECORDS WITH ERRORS


                                          *** END OF REPORT ***
```

Alternate Record Keys

Although the most efficient way of accessing records in an indexed file is by prime record key values, it is also possible to access records by referencing other field values within records of the file. In order to do so, the data fields whose values are to be used to identify records must be specified in the ALTERNATE RECORD KEY clause within the SELECT statement for the file. For instance, in the master personnel file for the Jocelyn Originals Company, if employee records should be accessible by employee name in addition to the employee Social Security number, then the SELECT statement must contain the following clauses:

```
RECORD KEY IS INDEXED-MR-SSN
ALTERNATE RECORD KEY IS INDEXED-MR-NAME
                        WITH DUPLICATES.
```

These clauses must be specified in the program that *creates* the indexed file. When the indexed file is created, the index table will then contain two sets of index records, one associated with the prime record key and one associated with the alternate record key. A prime index record contains the prime record key value of the data record along with a pointer that indicates the location of the data record in the file. The data records in the file are stored in ascending order by prime record key value, and the prime index records are also stored in ascending order by the prime record key values they contain.

A secondary or alternate index record contains the alternate record key value of the data record it corresponds to along with a pointer indicating where the data record is stored in the file. The secondary index records themselves are stored in ascending order by the alternate record key values they contain. The data records remain ordered on the basis of prime record key values.

A simplified illustration of the relationship between the index table and the data records of the master personnel file is shown in Figure 3.34. In this illustration, note that if the data records are to be accessed in ascending order by prime record key value, they are accessed in the order in which they are stored: record #1, record #2, record #3, . . . , record #6. However, if they are to be accessed in ascending order by alternate record key value, they are accessed in the following order: record #4, record #1, record #5, record #2, record #3, and record #6.

An indexed file may have a large number of secondary keys, the number being dictated by the variety of applications the file is likely to be used for. For instance, it may be important to be able to access the records of the master personnel file by employee name, by the date hired, by the date of birth, and so on, in addition to the prime record key, namely, the employee's Social Security number. In that case, the SELECT statement must contain as many ALTERNATE RECORD KEY clauses as there are alternate keys.

It is important to note that program performance degrades as the number of alternate keys increases, but this drawback is generally offset by the greater versatility of the file provided by the extra keys.

The format of the ALTERNATE RECORD KEY clause was shown in Figure 3.8 along with other FILE-CONTROL paragraph entries related to indexed files. The applicable rules are also listed in the general rules that follow the figure.

Figure 3.34 Simplified indexed file structure

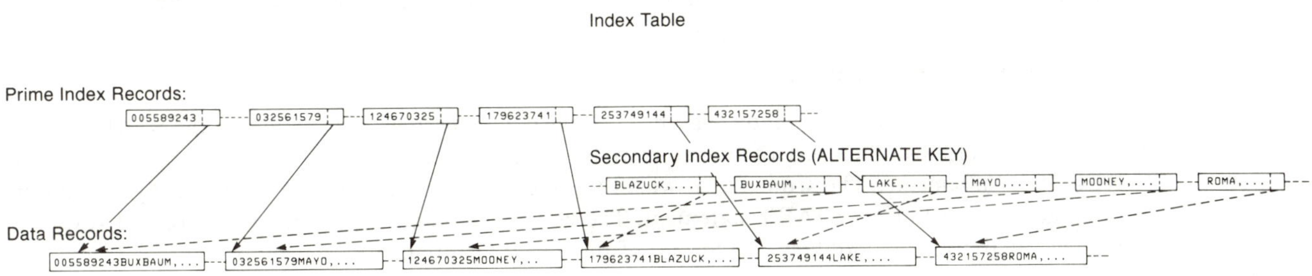

Figure 3.35 Format for DYNAMIC access

```
ACCESS MODE IS DYNAMIC
```

Figure 3.36 Sequential and random READ statement formats for DYNAMIC access

a. Format 1.

```
READ file-name-1 NEXT RECORD [INTO identifier-1]
     [AT END imperative-statement-1]
     [NOT AT END imperative-statement-2]
     [END-READ]
```

b. Format 2.

```
READ file-name-1 RECORD [INTO identifier-1]
     [KEY IS data-name-1]
     [INVALID KEY imperative-statement-3]
     [NOT INVALID KEY imperative-statement-4]
     [END-READ]
```

Note that a prime record key value must be unique to a record. An alternate record key value must also be unique to a record unless the DUPLICATES phrase is included in the ALTERNATE RECORD KEY clause. In the case of the master personnel file of the Jocelyn Originals Company, it should be clear that the DUPLICATES phrase should be specified for the alternate keys, employee name, date hired, and date of birth, since more than one employee may have the same name, or have the same birthday, or have been hired on the same day!

The use of alternate record keys will be illustrated in the next program.

ACCESS MODE IS DYNAMIC

We have seen that records of a file with indexed organization may be accessed either sequentially or randomly. COBOL also allows the access mode to be specified as DYNAMIC. The format is shown in Figure 3.35. By specifying this mode of access, the programmer has the flexibility of freely switching between sequential and random modes of access within the same program. The selection is based strictly on the formats of the input statements coded within the PROCEDURE DIVISION.

To access the records of the file sequentially, the programmer must use the READ format shown in Figure 3.36a. Note the telltale signs: NEXT and AT END! It is possible to read all the records of the file sequentially, beginning with the first logical record. It is also possible to begin sequential access at a specified record other than the first. There are two ways of doing this. In one case, the record key value, prime or alternate, of the target record is assigned to the key of reference, prime or alternate, and a random READ statement is executed. Subsequent execution of READ . . . NEXT RECORD statements will access successive records in increasing order of the key of reference used in the random READ statement. The format of the random READ statement is shown in Figure 3.36b.

The START Statement

In the other case, the record pointer may be positioned anywhere within the file by the START statement, and records can then be accessed sequentially from that point on by executing READ . . . NEXT RECORD statements. The sequence in which the records are accessed is determined by the key of reference specified in the START statement. The key of reference may be the prime record key, or it may be an alternate record key. The format of the START statement is shown in Figure 3.37.

Figure 3.37 START statement format

```
                              ⎧ EQUAL TO                         ⎫
                              ⎪ =                                ⎪
                              ⎪ GREATER THAN                     ⎪
                              ⎪ >                                ⎪
START file-name-1 [KEY IS     ⎨ NOT LESS THAN                    ⎬ data-name-1]
                              ⎪ NOT <                            ⎪
                              ⎪ GREATER THAN OR EQUAL TO         ⎪
                              ⎩ >=                               ⎭
    [INVALID KEY imperative-statement-1]
    [NOT INVALID KEY imperative-statement-2]
    [END-START]
```

Rules Governing the Use of Dynamic READ Statements

1. Format 1 must be used for *sequential access* of records in an indexed file when the access mode is specified as dynamic.
   a. The word NEXT is required. Its use positions the file's record pointer to the next logical record as specified by the key of reference.
   b. The AT END clause is required unless there is a related USE AFTER EXCEPTION procedure in the DECLARATIVES SECTION of the PROCEDURE DIVISION.
   c. When the statement executes, the record indicated by the file's record pointer is copied into the record area associated with the file, the record pointer is then positioned to indicate the next record as specified by the key of reference, and, if the NOT AT END clause is used, *imperative-statement-2* executes. The READ operation is successful.
   d. When the statement executes, if the file's record pointer indicates that there is no next logical record in the file, the AT END condition is satisfied and *imperative-statement-1* is executed. The READ operation is unsuccessful.
2. Format 2 must be used for *random access* of records in an indexed file when the access mode is specified as dynamic.
   a. The INVALID KEY clause is required unless there is a related USE AFTER EXCEPTION procedure in the DECLARATIVES SECTION of the PROCEDURE DIVISION.
   b. If the KEY clause is not present, the prime record key is the default key of reference for the random read operation. If this READ statement is followed by a format-1 READ statement, the prime record key remains the key of reference for subsequent sequential access.
   c. If the KEY clause is used, *data-name-1* is a data item specified as a record key for *file-name-1* either in the RECORD KEY clause or in an ALTERNATE RECORD KEY clause. *Data-name-1* is the key of reference for the random retrieval, and it remains the key of reference for subsequent sequential access by the execution of format-1 READ statements.
   d. When the statement is executed, the value in the key of reference is used to search the corresponding data item in the index records of the file. When a match occurs, the corresponding data record is copied into the record area for the file. If the key of reference is an alternate key that allows duplicates, the first record with a matching value is retrieved. The other records with duplicate key values can be retrieved by sequential access, and if they are retrieved, their order of retrieval is the same as the order in which they were written to the file.
   e. If a random READ statement cannot find a record with a matching key field value, an invalid key condition occurs and the operation is unsuccessful.

3. For both formats, the open mode for the file must be specified as INPUT or as I-O.
4. The execution of either READ statement updates the code in the file status data item. Applicable codes are as follows:

   "00" to denote a successful operation;

   "10" to denote no next logical record during execution of a format-1 READ; this satisfies the AT END condition;

   "23" to denote that no record in the file contains the value of the key of reference; this satisfies the invalid key condition;

   "30" to denote a permanent system error.

   "46" to denote no valid next record during execution of a format-1 READ; this satisfies the AT END condition;

5. Following an unsuccessful read operation, the contents of the file's record area are undefined and the value of the key of reference is also undefined.

(*Note:* See the rules following Figure 3.19 for additional pertinent rules.)

Rules Governing the Use of the START Statement

1. The function of the START statement is to determine the logical position of the file's record pointer prior to sequential access of the file's records.
2. *File-name-1* must be the name of an indexed file, or a relative file, whose access mode is either sequential or dynamic.
3. *Data-name-1* is the name of a record key defined for the file. It may be the prime record key or an alternate record key.
4. *Imperative-statement-1* is an imperative statement. It is executed whenever an invalid key condition occurs.
5. *Imperative-statement-2* is an imperative statement. It is executed whenever the START statement contains the NOT INVALID KEY clause and the start operation is successful.
6. END-START is the explicit scope terminator for the START statement.
7. *File-name-1* must be open either in INPUT mode or in I-O mode.
8. If there is no KEY clause in the statement, the default is KEY IS EQUAL TO *data-name-1*, where *data-name-1* is the prime record key for the file.
9. If there is a KEY clause, *data-name-1* becomes the key of reference for the statement.
   a. A comparison occurs between the value in the key of reference and the corresponding record data item as specified by the relational operator in the KEY clause. All standard rules for the comparison of numeric items and of nonnumeric items apply, except that if the two operands do not have the same size, the longer is truncated to match the size of the shorter.
   b. If the execution of the START statement is successful, the key of reference determines the order in which the records are accessed by subsequent sequential read operations.
   c. If the comparison between the key of reference and the corresponding record data item is not satisfied for any record in the file, the execution of the START statement is unsuccessful and an invalid key condition occurs.
10. The INVALID KEY clause is required unless there is an applicable USE AFTER EXCEPTION procedure in the DECLARATIVES SECTION of the PROCEDURE DIVISION.
11. If execution of the START statement is unsuccessful, the value in the key of reference is undefined.
12. Execution of the START statement
    a. updates the code in the file status data item. Applicable codes are as follows:

       "00" to denote a successful operation;

       "23" to denote that the target record was not found in the file, that is, an invalid key condition occurred;

       "30" to denote other permanent system errors;

       "47" to denote that the file is not open, or its open mode is incompatible.

    b. does not affect the contents of the record area associated with the file.

Program Illustrating Dynamic Access

As an example of the ease of switching from sequential to random retrieval of records of an indexed file provided by the dynamic access mode, consider the following situation.

> The Jocelyn Originals Company wants a program that could be used to list employees hired within a specified period of time, given the beginning date and the number of years in the time span, or to list employees alphabetically, beginning with any employee name.
>
> A master personnel file already exists as an indexed file with the Social Security number as the prime record key and a list of alternate record keys, including the name field and the date hired field.
>
> (For purposes of this program, suppose that alphabetic retrieval of records is limited to five records only.)

Brief Analysis of the Problem

When a date is supplied as input, the date hired data item is selected as the key of reference. Since a starting date may be picked at random, there is no guarantee that a record exists in the file with that date as the employee's date of hire. Consequently, it is not reasonable to issue a READ statement with the given starting date as the record key value. The way to proceed is to use a START statement to position the file's record pointer to indicate the employee record whose date of hire is closest to the specified starting date.

The KEY clause of the START statement supports a number of relational tests. The most appropriate one to use in this case is KEY IS NOT LESS THAN *data-name-1,* where *data-name-1* is the given starting date. Executing a sequential READ statement for which the specified key of reference is the date hired data item then retrieves the first desired record. Records are then accessed sequentially, in order of increasing values of the date hired until the first record is encountered with a date hired that is beyond the specified range.

When an employee name is provided as input, the employee name data item is selected as the key of reference. Since a master record exists in the file for this employee, it can be retrieved by a random READ whose KEY clause specifies the employee name data item as the key of reference. The next four records are accessed in alphabetic order by executing sequential READ statements. These statements use the same key of reference as used in the random READ.

The data that must be provided as input to the program could be supplied by the user at a terminal, and, in this case, the program would access the terminal input by means of an ACCEPT statement. Or, the input data may be stored in a file, and, in this case, the program would access the input records by means of a READ statement. In this sample program, we will use an input file. This file will contain two kinds of records, one that contains an employee name and another that contains data specifying a time frame. The layouts of the input records are shown in Figure 3.38.

Figure 3.38 Input record layouts

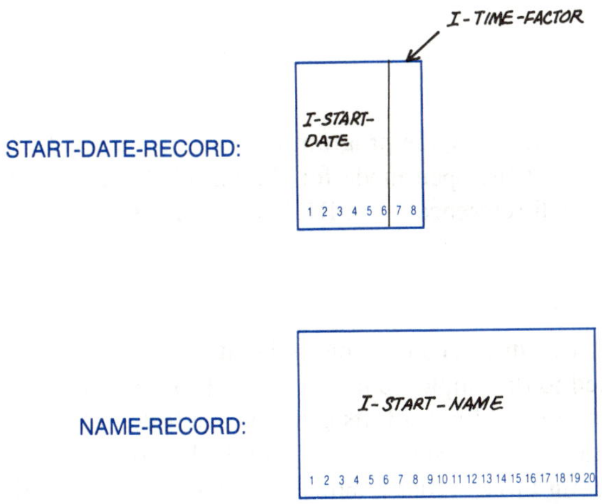

Figure 3.39 Printer spacing chart for the dynamic report

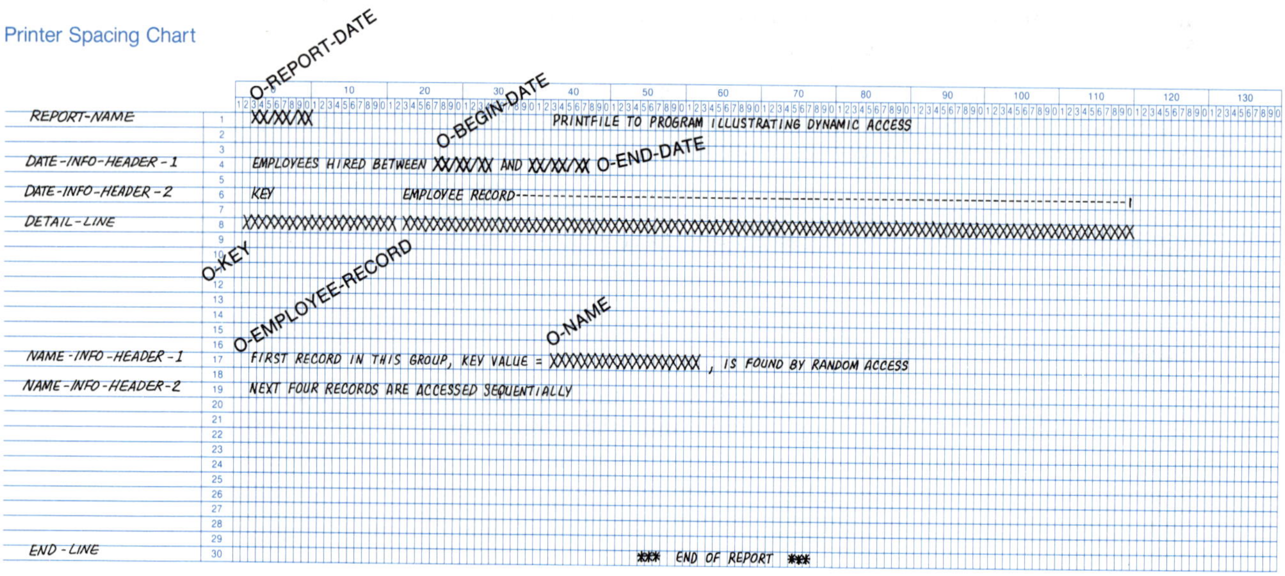

Figure 3.40 System flowchart for the dynamic-access program

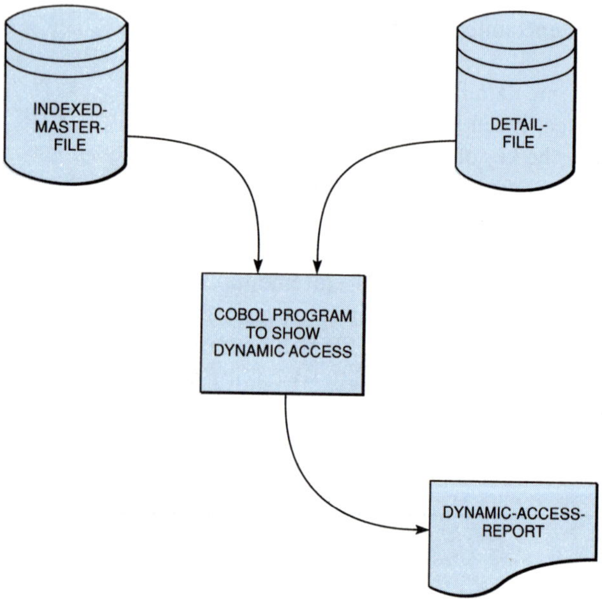

The printer spacing chart for the report to be produced by the program is shown in Figure 3.39. The system flowchart is shown in Figure 3.40. Note that the open mode for the master file is simply INPUT, since the only input/output statements that will reference it are READ statements.

Structure Chart

The design of the program must take into account two distinct tasks, one related to the date hired data item of an employee record and the other related to the employee name. These tasks will be dealt with in distinct sections of the program. When a detail record is read, its contents are tested to determine which section should be executed. The structure chart is shown in Figure 3.41. Note that the PROCEDURE DIVISION of the program will contain three sections, namely, 0-MAIN-CONTROL SECTION, 1-SELECT-BY-DATE SECTION, and 2-SELECT-BY-NAME SECTION.

■ **Figure 3.41** Structure chart for the dynamic-access program

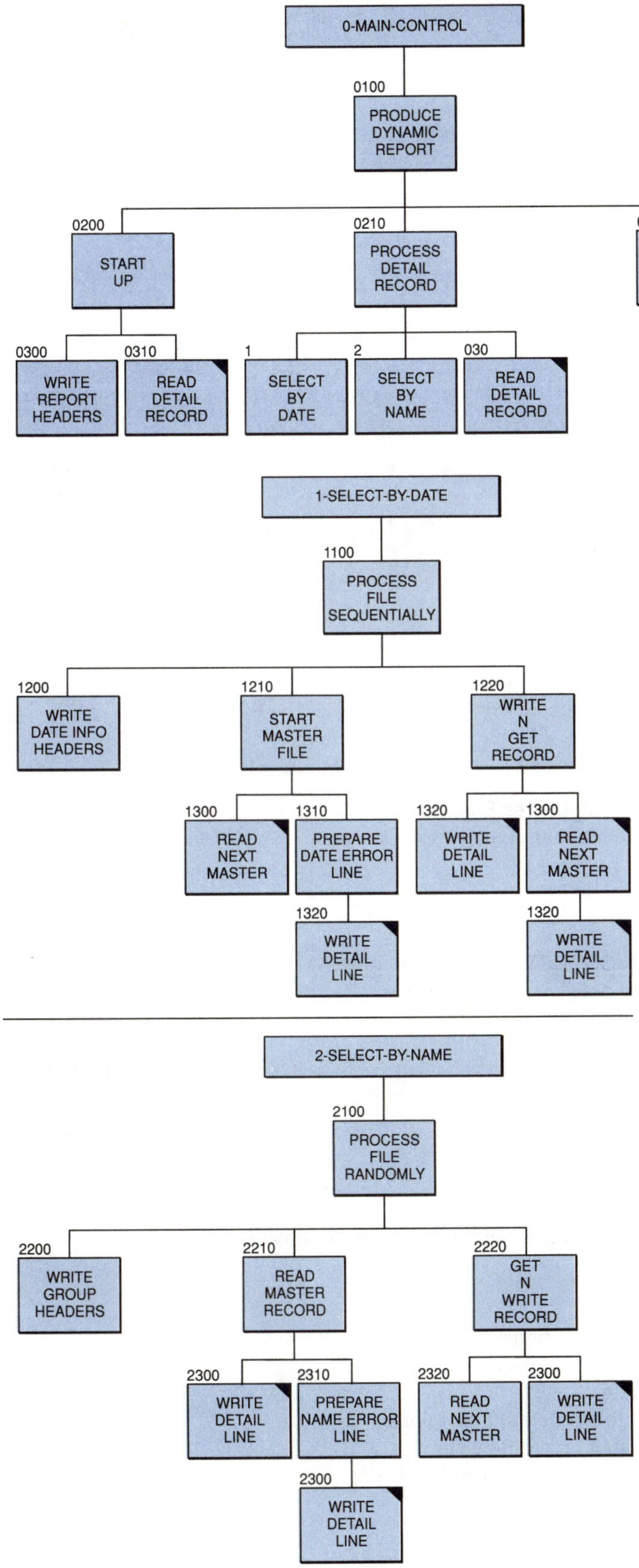

Program Pseudocode

The pseudocode to accomplish the tasks specified in the structure chart follows.

0-Main-Control Section.

0100-Produce-Dynamic-Report.

1. Perform 0200-Start-Up.
2. Perform 0210-Process-Detail-Record until no more records.
3. Perform 0220-Finish-Up.
4. Stop the run.

0200-Start-Up.

1. Open Indexed-Master-File as an input file,
   Detail-File as an input file, and Printfile as an output file.
2. Set the flag WS-MORE-RECORDS to "YES".
3. Obtain the date from the operating system.
4. Move date to Report-Name date.
5. Perform 0300-Write-Report-Headers.
6. Perform 0310-Read-Detail-Record.

0210-Process-Detail-Record.

1. Move spaces to Detail-Line.
2. Test first 6 characters of test-field:
   - **a.** If numeric, perform section 1-Select-By-Date.
   - **b.** If not numeric, perform section 2-Select-By-Name.
3. Perform 0310-Read-Detail-Record.

0220-Finish-Up.

1. Move the record End-Line to the output area Printline.
2. After advancing 4 lines, write the output record Printline.
3. Close the three files.

0300-Write-Report-Headers.

1. Move the record Report-Name to the output area Printline.
2. After advancing to a new page, write the output record Printline.

0310-Read-Detail-Record.

1. Read an input Detail-Record.
2. Test for end-of-file:
   - **a.** If EOF record reached, set WS-MORE-DETAIL-RECORDS to "NO ".
   - **b.** If EOF record not reached, move detail-record to test-field.

1-Select-By-Date Section.

1100-Process-File-Sequentially.

1. Perform 1200-Write-Date-Info-Headers.
2. Perform 1210-Start-Master-File.
3. If start operation is successful,
   - **a.** Move 2 to proper-spacing.
   - **b.** Perform 1220-Write-N-Get-Record
     until Indexed-Master-Record date-hired >= end-date or master-file-flag="10".
4. Exit from section.

1200-Write-Date-Info-Headers.

1. Move input start-date to Date-Info-Header-1 begin-date.
2. Add input time-factor to input start-date to equal end-date
   and Date-Info-Header-1 end-date.
3. Move the record Date-Info-Header-1 to the output area Printline.
4. After advancing 3 lines, write the output record Printline.
5. Move the record Date-Info-Header-2 to the output area Printline.
6. After advancing 2 lines, write the output record Printline.
7. Move 2 to proper-spacing.

1210-Start-Master-File.

1. Move input start-date to Indexed-Master-Record date-hired.
2. Start Indexed-Master-File with key set not less than Indexed-Master-Record date-hired.
3. Test value of key:
   - **a.** If invalid, perform 1310-Prepare-Date-Error-Line.
   - **b.** If valid, perform 1300-Read-Next-Master.

1220-Write-N-Get-Record.

1. Move Indexed-Master-Record date-hired to Detail-Line key.
2. Move Indexed-Master-Record to Detail-line employee-record.
3. Perform 1320-Write-Detail-line.
4. Perform 1300-Read-Next-Master.

1300-Read-Next-Master.

1. Read next record in Indexed-Master-File.
2. Test for end-of-file record;
   if EOF record reached,
   - **a.** Move "10" to master-file-flag.
   - **b.** Move spaces to Detail-Line.
   - **c.** Move symbols to Detail-Line key.
   - **d.** Move message-2 to Detail-Line message
     (message-2: "Reached EOF. No more records in indexed file").
   - **e.** Move 2 to proper-spacing.
   - **f.** Perform 1320-Write-Detail-Line.

1310-Prepare-Date-Error-Line.

1. Move input start-date to Detail-Line key.
2. Move message-1 to Detail-Line message
   (message-1: "Cannot start file for this key").
3. Move 2 to proper-spacing.
4. Perform 1320-Write-Detail-Line.

1320-Write-Detail-Line.

1. Move the record Detail-Line to the output area Printline.
2. After advancing proper-spacing, write the output record Printline.
3. Move 1 to proper-spacing.

2-Select-By-Name Section.

2100-Process-File-Randomly.

1. Move input start-name to Indexed-Master-Record name,
   to Name-Info-Header-2 name, and to Detail-Line key.
2. Perform 2200-Write-Group-Headers.
3. Perform 2210-Read-Master-Record.
4. If read operation is successful,
   - **a.** Move zero to record-counter.
   - **b.** Move 2 to proper-spacing.
   - **c.** Perform 2220-Get-N-Write-Record
     until master-file-flag="10" or record-counter=4.

4. Exit from section.

2200-Write-Group-Headers.

1. Move the record Name-Info-Header-1 to the output area Printline.
2. After advancing 5 lines, write the output record Printline.
3. Move the record Name-Info-Header-2 to the output area Printline.
4. After advancing 1 line, write the output record Printline.
5. Move 2 to proper-spacing.

2210-Read-Master-Record.

1. Read Indexed-Master-File record with key = Indexed-Master-Record name.
2. Test for invalid key:
   a. If so, perform 2310-Prepare-Name-Error-Line.
   b. If not, move Indexed-Master-Record to Detail-Line employee-record
      and perform 2300-Write-Detail-Line.

2220-Get-N-Write-Record.

1. Perform 2320-Read-Next-Master.
2. Test master-file-flag:
   a. If "10", move spaces to Detail-Line,
      move message-2 to Detail-Line message.
   b. If "00", move Indexed-Master-Record name to Detail-Line key,
      move Indexed-Master-Record to Detail-Line employee-record,
      add 1 to record-counter.
3. Perform 2300-Write-Detail-line.

2300-Write-Detail-Line.

1. Move the record Detail-Line to the output area Printline.
2. After advancing proper-spacing, write the output record Printline.
3. Move 1 to proper-spacing.

2310-Prepare-Name-Error-Line.

1. Move 2 to proper-spacing.
2. Move message-3 to Detail-Line message
   (message-3: "No record found in master file with this name").
3. Perform 2300-Write-Detail-Line.

2320-Read-Next-Master.

1. Read next record in Indexed-Master-File.
2. Test for end-of-file record;
   if EOF record reached,
      move "10" to master-file-flag.

In step 2 of paragraph 0210-Process-Detail-Record, note that the characters stored in bytes 1 through 6 of the detail record are tested to determine whether they are numeric or not. If they are numeric, it means that the record contains data specifying a time span, namely, a starting date and the number of years to be included, and, as a result, control is sent to the section 1-Select-by-Date. Otherwise, the record contains an employee name and control is sent to the section 2-Select-by-Name.

In step 2 of paragraph 1200-Write-Date-Info-Headers, the number of years specified on the date record is added to the year component of the starting date to determine the ending date of the time span. For instance, if the starting date is June 1, 1975, and the time span is 2 years, the record contains 750601 as the date and 02 as the time factor. Thus adding 02 to the year component (75), yields 770601 as the ending date. To facilitate the addition, define the 2-character field I-TIME-FACTOR by using PIC 99PPPP.

In step 1 of paragraph 2100-Process-File-Randomly, the employee name on the input record is assigned to the alternate record key INDEXED-MR-NAME, and then in step 1 of paragraph 2210-Read-Master-Record, this input employee name is the value of the key of reference in the random READ statement. If the read operation is successful, the master record for that employee is then available in the record area for the master file. It is copied to the detail line, and the line is written on the report. Then, step 4 of paragraph 2100-Process-File-Randomly will access the next four records in the master file, alphabetically!

The program flowchart corresponding to the pseudocode is shown in Figure 3.42. The COBOL program is shown in Figure 3.43. The records in the indexed file are shown in Figure 3.44a, and the detail file records are shown in Figure 3.44b. Note that the detail file contains two date records, one with a time frame of 10 years, the other with a time frame of 5 years, and it contains three employee name records. The report produced by the program is contained in Figure 3.45.

Figure 3.42 Flowchart for the dynamic-access program

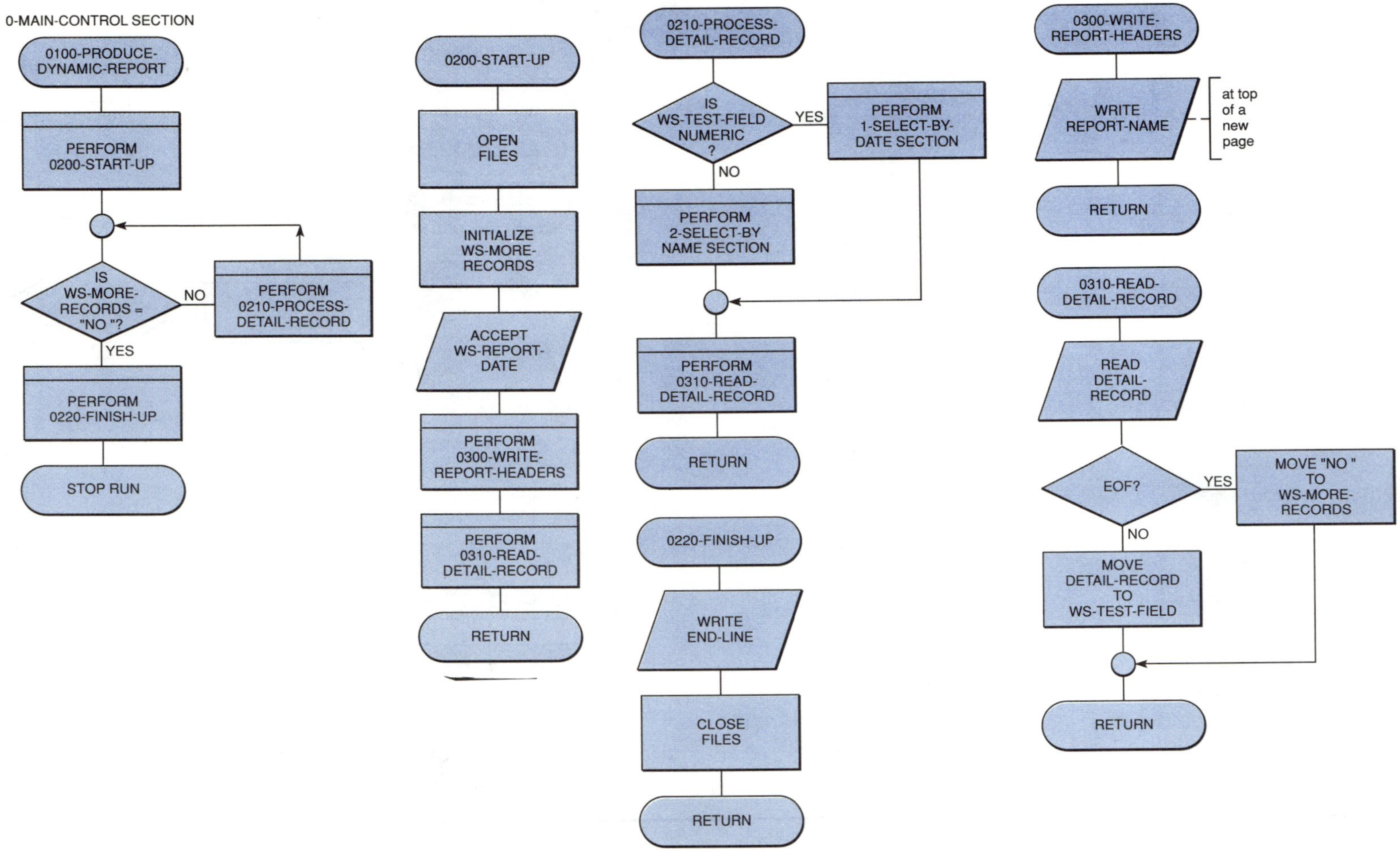

Figure 3.42 continued

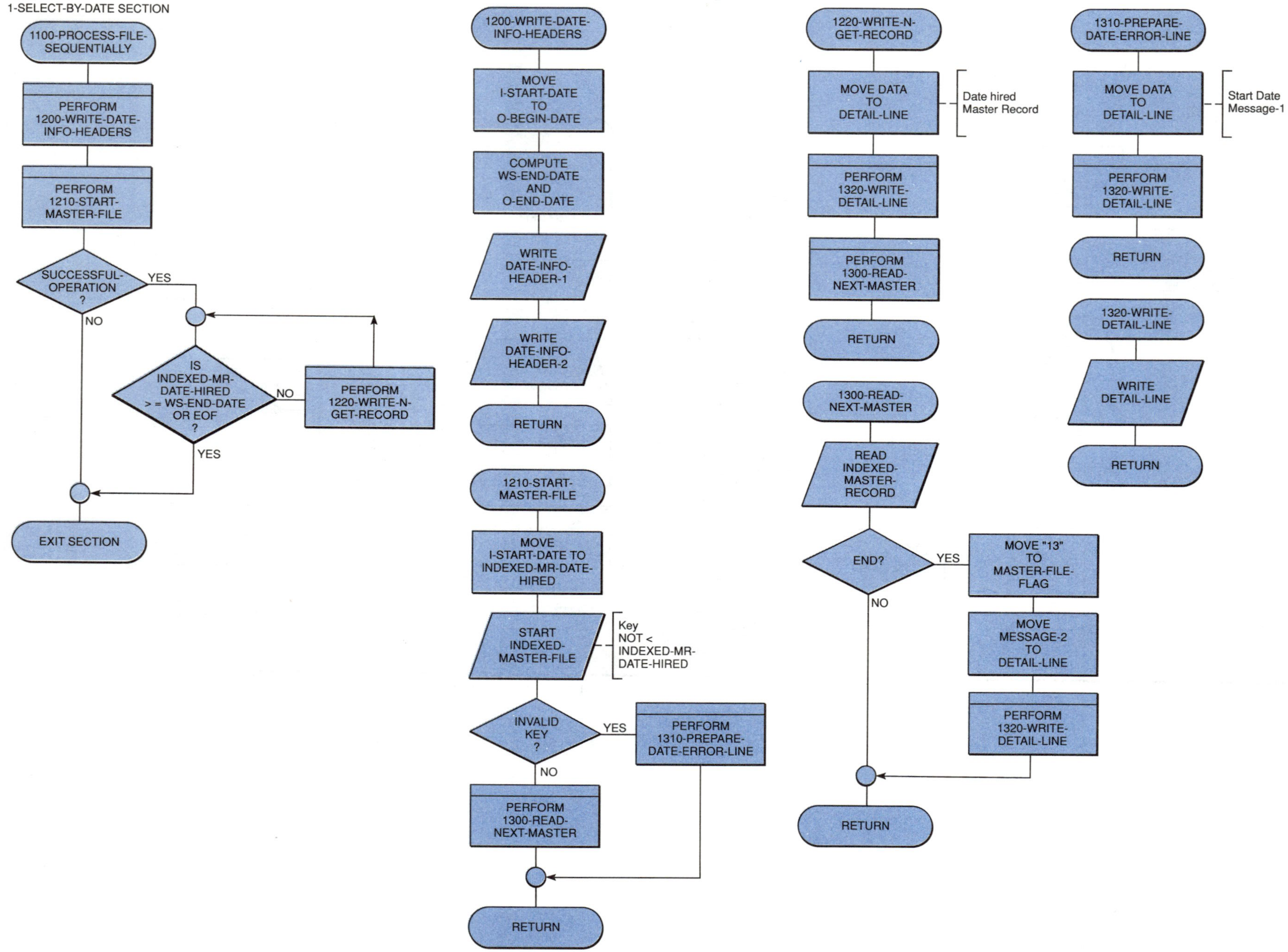

■ **Figure 3.42** continued

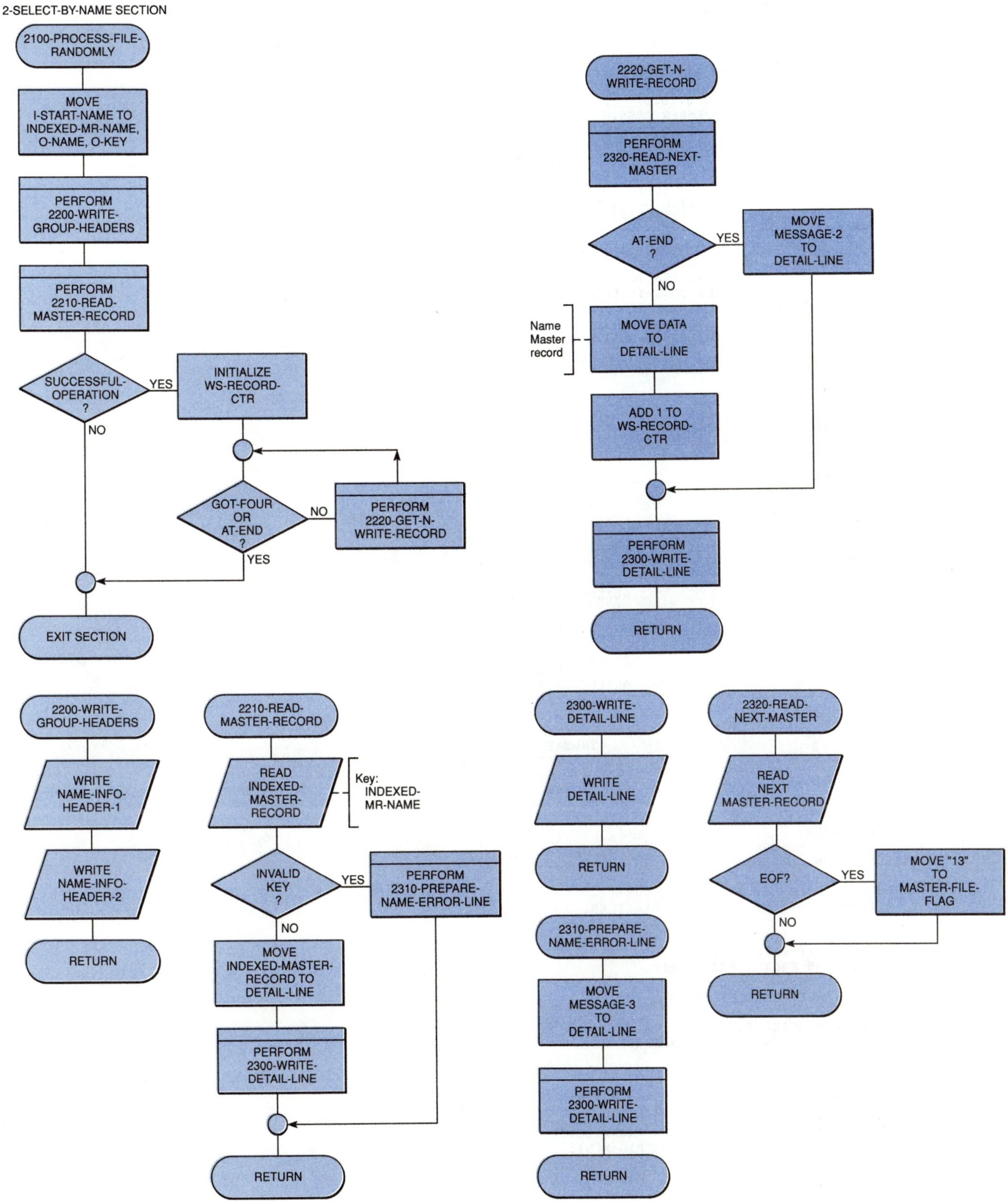

■ **Figure 3.43** COBOL program with dynamic access to the indexed file

```
        IDENTIFICATION DIVISION.

        PROGRAM-ID.        SAMPLE-DYNAMIC.

      *****************************************************************
      *                                                               *
      *   AUTHOR.           PAQUETTE.                                 *
      *   DATE WRITTEN.     NOVEMBER 1989.                            *
      *                                                               *
      *   THIS PROGRAM ILLUSTRATES THE DYNAMIC MODE OF ACCESS.  IT    *
      *   READS A RECORD FROM A DETAIL FILE.  IT TESTS THE INPUT RECORD*
      *   VALUE TO DETERMINE IF IT'S A DATE OR A NAME.  IF IT'S A DATE,*
      *   THE START STATEMENT IS USED TO POSITION THE RECORD POINTER  *
      *   IN THE INDEXED MASTER FILE AND EMPLOYEES HIRED WITHIN THE   *
      *   SPECIFIED NUMBER OF YEARS ARE RETRIEVED FROM THE FILE AND   *
      *   PRINTED ON THE REPORT.                                      *
      *   IF IT'S A NAME, RANDOM ACCESS IS USED TO FIND THE CORRESPOND-*
      *   ING RECORD IN THE INDEXED FILE. IT PRINTS THAT RECORD AND   *
      *   THEN USES SEQUENTIAL ACCESS TO READ AND PRINT THE NEXT 4    *
      *   RECORDS.  THE ABOVE PROCESS IS REPEATED FOR ALL THE RECORDS *
      *   IN THE DETAIL FILE.                                         *
      *                                                               *
      *****************************************************************

        ENVIRONMENT DIVISION.

        CONFIGURATION SECTION.

        SOURCE-COMPUTER.   VAX-VMS-8650.
        OBJECT-COMPUTER.   VAX-VMS-8650.

        INPUT-OUTPUT SECTION.

        FILE-CONTROL.
            SELECT DETAIL-FILE          ASSIGN TO COB$INPUT.
1           SELECT INDEXED-MASTER-FILE  ASSIGN TO MASTERFILE
                                        ORGANIZATION IS INDEXED
                                        ACCESS MODE IS DYNAMIC
                                        RECORD KEY IS INDEXED-MR-SSN
                                        ALTERNATE RECORD KEY IS
                                            INDEXED-MR-NAME
                                                WITH DUPLICATES
                                        ALTERNATE RECORD KEY IS
                                            INDEXED-MR-DOB
                                                WITH DUPLICATES
                                        ALTERNATE RECORD KEY IS
                                            INDEXED-MR-DATE-HIRED
                                                WITH DUPLICATES
                                        ALTERNATE RECORD KEY IS
                                            INDEXED-MR-ZIP
                                                WITH DUPLICATES
                                        FILE STATUS IS
                                            MASTER-FILE-FLAG.
            SELECT PRINTFILE            ASSIGN TO COB$OUTPUT.

        DATA DIVISION.

        FILE SECTION.

        FD  DETAIL-FILE
2           RECORD CONTAINS 8 TO 20 CHARACTERS.

        01  START-DATE-RECORD.
            05 I-START-DATE   PIC 9(6).
            05 I-TIME-FACTOR  PIC 99PPPP.
        01  NAME-RECORD.
            05 I-START-NAME   PIC X(20).

        FD  INDEXED-MASTER-FILE
            RECORD CONTAINS 100 CHARACTERS
            BLOCK CONTAINS 5 RECORDS.

        01  INDEXED-MASTER-RECORD.
            05 INDEXED-MR-SSN               PIC X(9).
            05 INDEXED-MR-NAME              PIC X(20).
            05 INDEXED-MR-ADDRESS           PIC X(32).
            05 INDEXED-MR-ZIP               PIC X(5).
            05 INDEXED-MR-DOB               PIC X(6).
            05 INDEXED-MR-DATE-HIRED        PIC X(6).
            05                              PIC X(22).

        FD  PRINTFILE
            RECORD CONTAINS 132 CHARACTERS.

        01  PRINTLINE            PIC X(132).
```

```
       WORKING-STORAGE SECTION.

       01  PROGRAM-CONTROLS.
3          05 WS-TEST-FIELD             PIC X(20).
           05 WS-REPORT-DATE            PIC X(6).
           05 WS-END-DATE               PIC 9(6).
           05 WS-RECORD-CTR             PIC 9.
              88 GOT-FOUR                          VALUE 4.
           05 WS-MORE-RECORDS           PIC X(3).
              88 NO-MORE-RECORDS                   VALUE 'NO '.
           05 MASTER-FILE-FLAG          PIC XX.
              88 SUCCESSFUL-OPERATION              VALUE '00'.
              88 AT-END                            VALUE '10'.
              88 NO-SUCH-RECORD                    VALUE '20'.
              88 START-ERROR                       VALUE '23'.
           05 WS-PROPER-SPACING         PIC 9.

       01  REPORT-NAME.
           05                 PIC X(2)    VALUE SPACES.
           05 O-REPORT-DATE   PIC XX/XX/XX.
           05                 PIC X(32)  VALUE SPACES.
           05                 PIC X(48)  VALUE
             'PRINTFILE TO PROGRAM ILLUSTRATING DYNAMIC ACCESS'.
           05                 PIC X(42)  VALUE SPACES.

       01  DATE-INFO-HEADER-1.
           05                 PIC X(2)   VALUE SPACES.
           05                 PIC X(24)  VALUE
                              'EMPLOYEES HIRED BETWEEN '.
           05 O-BEGIN-DATE    PIC XX/XX/XX.
           05                 PIC X(5)   VALUE ' AND '.
           05 O-END-DATE      PIC 99/99/99.

       01  DATE-INFO-HEADER-2.
           05 PIC X(2)        VALUE SPACES.
           05 PIC X(3)        VALUE 'KEY'.
           05 PIC X(17)       VALUE SPACES.
           05 PIC X(15)       VALUE 'EMPLOYEE RECORD'.
           05 PIC X(82)       VALUE ALL '-'.
           05 PIC X(1)        VALUE '|'.

       01  NAME-INFO-HEADER-1.
           05                 PIC X(2)     VALUE SPACES.
           05                 PIC X(40)    VALUE
                              'FIRST RECORD IN THIS GROUP, KEY VALUE = '.
           05 O-NAME          PIC X(20).
           05                 PIC X(28)      VALUE
                              ' , IS FOUND BY RANDOM ACCESS'.

       01  NAME-INFO-HEADER-2.
           05 PIC X(2)        VALUE SPACES.
           05 PIC X(44)       VALUE
             'NEXT FOUR RECORDS ARE ACCESSED SEQUENTIALLY'.
           05 PIC X(33)       VALUE SPACES.

       01  MESSAGE-SET.
           05 MESSAGE-1       PIC X(44) VALUE
                 'CANNOT START FILE FOR THIS KEY'.
           05 MESSAGE-2       PIC X(44) VALUE
                 'REACHED EOF. NO MORE RECORDS IN INDEXED FILE'.
           05 MESSAGE-3       PIC X(45) VALUE
                 'NO RECORD FOUND IN MASTER FILE WITH THIS NAME'.

       01  DETAIL-LINE.
           05                                     PIC X(1).
4          05 O-KEY                               PIC X(20).
           05                                     PIC X(1).
           05 O-EMPLOYEE-RECORD                   PIC X(110).
           05 O-MESSAGE REDEFINES O-EMPLOYEE-RECORD PIC X(110).

       01  END-LINE.
           05 PIC X(54)       VALUE SPACES.
           05 PIC X(23)       VALUE '***  END OF REPORT  ***'.

       PROCEDURE DIVISION.

      *********************************

       0-MAIN-CONTROL SECTION.

      *********************************

       0100-PRODUCE-DYNAMIC-REPORT.
           PERFORM 0200-START-UP.
           PERFORM 0210-PROCESS-DETAIL-RECORD
               UNTIL NO-MORE-RECORDS.
           PERFORM 0220-FINISH-UP.
           STOP RUN.
```

```
           0200-START-UP.
               OPEN INPUT DETAIL-FILE
                          INDEXED-MASTER-FILE
                    OUTPUT PRINTFILE.
               MOVE 'YES' TO WS-MORE-RECORDS.
               ACCEPT WS-REPORT-DATE FROM DATE.
               MOVE WS-REPORT-DATE TO O-REPORT-DATE.
               PERFORM 0300-WRITE-REPORT-HEADERS.
               PERFORM 0310-READ-DETAIL-RECORD.

           0210-PROCESS-DETAIL-RECORD.
               MOVE SPACES TO DETAIL-LINE.
5              IF WS-TEST-FIELD(1:6) IS NUMERIC
                   PERFORM 1-SELECT-BY-DATE
               ELSE
                   PERFORM 2-SELECT-BY-NAME.
               PERFORM 0310-READ-DETAIL-RECORD.

           0220-FINISH-UP.
               WRITE PRINTLINE FROM END-LINE
                   AFTER ADVANCING 4 LINES.
               CLOSE DETAIL-FILE
                     INDEXED-MASTER-FILE
                     PRINTFILE.

           0300-WRITE-REPORT-HEADERS.
               WRITE PRINTLINE FROM REPORT-NAME
                   AFTER ADVANCING PAGE.

           0310-READ-DETAIL-RECORD.
6              READ DETAIL-FILE RECORD INTO WS-TEST-FIELD
                   AT END
                       SET NO-MORE-RECORDS TO TRUE.

          *********************************

7          1-SELECT-BY-DATE SECTION.

          *********************************

           1100-PROCESS-FILE-SEQUENTIALLY.
               PERFORM 1200-WRITE-DATE-INFO-HEADERS.
8              PERFORM 1210-START-MASTER-FILE.
               IF SUCCESSFUL-OPERATION
                   MOVE 2 TO WS-PROPER-SPACING
9                  PERFORM 1220-WRITE-N-GET-RECORD
                      UNTIL INDEXED-MR-DATE-HIRED >= WS-END-DATE
                            OR AT-END
               END-IF.
               GO TO 1999-EXIT-SECTION.

           1200-WRITE-DATE-INFO-HEADERS.
               MOVE I-START-DATE TO O-BEGIN-DATE.
10             ADD I-TIME-FACTOR I-START-DATE GIVING WS-END-DATE
                                                     O-END-DATE.
               WRITE PRINTLINE FROM DATE-INFO-HEADER-1
                   AFTER ADVANCING 3 LINES.
               WRITE PRINTLINE FROM DATE-INFO-HEADER-2
                   AFTER ADVANCING 2 LINES.
               MOVE 2 TO WS-PROPER-SPACING.

           1210-START-MASTER-FILE.
               MOVE I-START-DATE TO INDEXED-MR-DATE-HIRED.
               START INDEXED-MASTER-FILE
                   KEY NOT < INDEXED-MR-DATE-HIRED
                   INVALID KEY
                       PERFORM 1310-PREPARE-DATE-ERROR-LINE
                   NOT INVALID KEY
                       PERFORM 1300-READ-NEXT-MASTER
               END-START.

           1220-WRITE-N-GET-RECORD.
               MOVE INDEXED-MR-DATE-HIRED TO O-KEY.
               MOVE INDEXED-MASTER-RECORD TO O-EMPLOYEE-RECORD.
               PERFORM 1320-WRITE-DETAIL-LINE.
               PERFORM 1300-READ-NEXT-MASTER.

           1300-READ-NEXT-MASTER.
11             READ INDEXED-MASTER-FILE NEXT RECORD
                   AT END
                       SET AT-END TO TRUE
                       MOVE SPACES TO DETAIL-LINE
                       MOVE '!!@##&&**@!!' TO O-KEY
                       MOVE MESSAGE-2 TO O-MESSAGE
                       MOVE 2 TO WS-PROPER-SPACING
                       PERFORM 1320-WRITE-DETAIL-LINE
               END-READ.
```

Figure 3.43 continued

```
       1310-PREPARE-DATE-ERROR-LINE.
           MOVE I-START-DATE TO O-KEY.
           MOVE MESSAGE-1 TO O-MESSAGE.
           MOVE 2 TO WS-PROPER-SPACING.
           PERFORM 1320-WRITE-DETAIL-LINE.

       1320-WRITE-DETAIL-LINE.
           WRITE PRINTLINE FROM DETAIL-LINE
               AFTER ADVANCING WS-PROPER-SPACING.
           MOVE 1 TO WS-PROPER-SPACING.

       1999-EXIT-SECTION.
           EXIT.

      *********************************
12     2-SELECT-BY-NAME SECTION.
      *********************************

       2100-PROCESS-FILE-RANDOMLY.
13         MOVE I-START-NAME TO INDEXED-MR-NAME
                                 O-NAME
                                 O-KEY.
           PERFORM 2200-WRITE-GROUP-HEADERS.
           PERFORM 2210-READ-MASTER-RECORD.
           IF SUCCESSFUL-OPERATION
               MOVE ZERO TO WS-RECORD-CTR
               MOVE 2 TO WS-PROPER-SPACING
14             PERFORM 2220-GET-N-WRITE-RECORD
                   UNTIL AT-END OR GOT-FOUR
           END-IF.
           GO TO 2999-EXIT-SECTION.

       2200-WRITE-GROUP-HEADERS.
           WRITE PRINTLINE FROM NAME-INFO-HEADER-1
               AFTER ADVANCING 5 LINES.
           WRITE PRINTLINE FROM NAME-INFO-HEADER-2
               AFTER ADVANCING 1 LINE.
           MOVE 2 TO WS-PROPER-SPACING.

       2210-READ-MASTER-RECORD.
15         READ INDEXED-MASTER-FILE RECORD
               KEY IS INDEXED-MR-NAME
               INVALID KEY
                   PERFORM 2310-PREPARE-NAME-ERROR-LINE
               NOT INVALID KEY
                   MOVE INDEXED-MASTER-RECORD TO O-EMPLOYEE-RECORD
                   PERFORM 2300-WRITE-DETAIL-LINE
           END-READ.

16     2220-GET-N-WRITE-RECORD.
           PERFORM 2320-READ-NEXT-MASTER.
           IF AT-END
               MOVE SPACES TO DETAIL-LINE
               MOVE '!!@##&&**@!!' TO O-KEY
               MOVE MESSAGE-2 TO O-MESSAGE
           ELSE
               MOVE INDEXED-MR-NAME TO O-KEY
               MOVE INDEXED-MASTER-RECORD TO O-EMPLOYEE-RECORD
               ADD 1 TO WS-RECORD-CTR.
           PERFORM 2300-WRITE-DETAIL-LINE.

       2300-WRITE-DETAIL-LINE.
           WRITE PRINTLINE FROM DETAIL-LINE
               AFTER ADVANCING WS-PROPER-SPACING.
           MOVE 1 TO WS-PROPER-SPACING.

       2310-PREPARE-NAME-ERROR-LINE.
           MOVE 2 TO WS-PROPER-SPACING.
           MOVE MESSAGE-3 TO O-MESSAGE.
           PERFORM 2300-WRITE-DETAIL-LINE.

       2320-READ-NEXT-MASTER.
17         READ INDEXED-MASTER-FILE NEXT RECORD
               AT END
                   SET AT-END TO TRUE
           END-READ.

       2999-EXIT-SECTION.
           EXIT.
```

■ **Figure 3.44a** Indexed master file

```
005589243BUXBAUM, JOAN M.    172 EARLE DR   GRAND ISLAND, NE 68802480214700608
013407206MCGEE, BERNARD W.   2420 CARR LA   CENTRAL CITY, NE 68826301215490615
014766691ARMSTRONG, GEORGE   105 STATE ST   PLATTE, NE       68653480320830816
016493017COUGHLIN, AILEEN M. 133 DAVIS RD   LEXINGTON, NE    68850500310680706
026307625VELTRI, JOHN A.     312 PERCH DR.  HASTINGS, NE     68901470115820820
032561579MAYO, EVANGELINA    895 POTTERS AVEGENEVA, NE       68361620805830807
032567781AITKEN, THOMAS R.   260 FOUNTAIN STAURORA, NE       68818260805460820
033281512PEARSON, ARTHUR     1020 GOLDEN RD HASTINGS, NE     68901501125830802
039764715GAFFNEY, MARYLYN    76 MAIN ST     PLATTE, NE       68653521205770608
042750015COLETTI, SARAH T.   51 BROAD ST    HASTINGS, NE     68901380902640615
124670325MOONEY, RONALD      220 N MAIN ST  HASTINGS, NE     68901410920640810
130043962MARKARIAN, MARIAN   984 N MAIN ST  HASTINGS, NE     68901320507520820
144217773ALTERMAN, MAUREEN E.10 MARTIN AVE  YORK, NE         68467350524600610
149201475PACCASASSIE, DEBBIE 341 BRANCH AVE NORMAN, NE       68963282612570912
150246389PRIMEAU, ISABEL     78 NORTH ST    KEARNEY, NE      68847470930720820
179623741BLAZUCK, JOSEPH A.  81 DORIS AVE   GENEVA, NE       68361450521750610
211384406KACHADOURIAN, NATALI922 LOCUST ST  HEBRON, NE       68370350221560820
215137814CUMMINGS, DOROTHEA  97 POWER AVE   NORMAN, NE       68963530407830822
226153911OVERDEEP, CYNTHIA   130 CANAL ST   YORK, NE         68467350524700715
234891533SHERIDAN, RICHARD J.850SUN CIRCLE  AURORA, NE       68818421205650610
253749144LAKE, SUE           252 EAST RD    CRETE, NE        68333410707830815
314764532DESROSIERS, RICHARD 92 REGAN RD    LOUP CITY, NE    68853581221830815
322150642STURDAHL, DEBRA     2541 RICE ST   CRETE, NE        68333340614550715
364923752DURANT, MARIE L.    1250 HIGH RD   GENEVA, NE       68361430924540910
381662514BAHR, LENA M.       304 CORY LANE  GENEVA, NE       68361411110600820
432157258ROMA, GILDA         25 MAPLE DR    SUPERIOR, NE     68978500708720610
623514793CARTER, AMEKIA L.   59 BARK ST     LOUP CITY, NE    68853320513620820
743142265ABRUZZI, KENNETH L. 51 RAYMOND ST  HASTINGS, NE     68901521205720820
771894263CYR, ROSARIO        205 SUNSET DR  FAIRFIELD, NE    68938350524550820
```

■ **Figure 3.44b** Detail file for the sample program run

```
70010110
BAHR, LENA M.
MARKARIAN, MARIAN
60010105
STURDAHL, DEBRA
```

■ **Figure 3.45** Dynamic report produced by the program

```
89/12/05                              PRINTFILE TO PROGRAM ILLUSTRATING DYNAMIC ACCESS

 EMPLOYEES HIRED BETWEEN 70/01/01 AND 80/01/01

 KEY                EMPLOYEE RECORD---------------------------------------------------------------------------|

700608              005589243BUXBAUM, JOAN M.     172 EARLE DR    GRAND ISLAND, NE 68802480214700608
700715              2261539110VERDEEP, CYNTHIA    130 CANAL ST    YORK, NE         68467350524700715
720610              432157258ROMA, GILDA          25 MAPLE DR     SUPERIOR, NE     68978500708720610
720820              150246389PRIMEAU, ISABEL      78 NORTH ST     KEARNEY, NE      68847470930720820
720820              743142265ABRUZZI, KENNETH L.  51 RAYMOND ST   HASTINGS, NE     68901521205720820
750610              179623741BLAZUCK, JOSEPH A.   81 DORIS AVE    GENEVA, NE       68361450521750610
770608              039764715GAFFNEY, MARYLYN     76 MAIN ST      PLATTE, NE       68653521205770608


 FIRST RECORD IN THIS GROUP, KEY VALUE = BAHR, LENA M.         , IS FOUND BY RANDOM ACCESS
 NEXT FOUR RECORDS ARE ACCESSED SEQUENTIALLY

BAHR, LENA M.       381662514BAHR, LENA M.        304 CORY LANE   GENEVA, NE       68361411110600820

BLAZUCK, JOSEPH A.  179623741BLAZUCK, JOSEPH A.   81 DORIS AVE    GENEVA, NE       68361450521750610
BUXBAUM, JOAN M.    005589243BUXBAUM, JOAN M.     172 EARLE DR    GRAND ISLAND, NE 68802480214700608
CARTER, AMEKIA L.   623514793CARTER, AMEKIA L.    59 BARK ST      LOUP CITY, NE    68853320513620820
COLETTI, SARAH T.   042750015COLETTI, SARAH T.    51 BROAD ST     HASTINGS, NE     68901380902640615


 FIRST RECORD IN THIS GROUP, KEY VALUE = MARKARIAN, MARIAN     , IS FOUND BY RANDOM ACCESS
 NEXT FOUR RECORDS ARE ACCESSED SEQUENTIALLY

MARKARIAN, MARIAN   130043962MARKARIAN, MARIAN    984 N MAIN ST   HASTINGS, NE     68901320507520820

MAYO, EVANGELINA    032561579MAYO, EVANGELINA     895 POTTERS AVEGENEVA, NE        68361620805830807
MCGEE, BERNARD W.   013407206MCGEE, BERNARD W.    2420 CARR LA    CENTRAL CITY, NE 68826301215490615
MOONEY, RONALD      124670325MOONEY, RONALD       220 N MAIN ST   HASTINGS, NE     68901410920640810
OVERDEEP, CYNTHIA   2261539110VERDEEP, CYNTHIA    130 CANAL ST    YORK, NE         68467350524700715

 EMPLOYEES HIRED BETWEEN 60/01/01 AND 65/01/01

 KEY                EMPLOYEE RECORD---------------------------------------------------------------------------|

600610              144217773ALTERMAN, MAUREEN E.10 MARTIN AVE    YORK, NE         68467350524600610
600820              381662514BAHR, LENA M.        304 CORY LANE   GENEVA, NE       68361411110600820
620820              623514793CARTER, AMEKIA L.    59 BARK ST      LOUP CITY, NE    68853320513620820
640615              042750015COLETTI, SARAH T.    51 BROAD ST     HASTINGS, NE     68901380902640615
640810              124670325MOONEY, RONALD       220 N MAIN ST   HASTINGS, NE     68901410920640810


 FIRST RECORD IN THIS GROUP, KEY VALUE = STURDAHL, DEBRA       , IS FOUND BY RANDOM ACCESS
 NEXT FOUR RECORDS ARE ACCESSED SEQUENTIALLY

STURDAHL, DEBRA     322150642STURDAHL, DEBRA      2541 RICE ST    CRETE, NE        68333340614550715

VELTRI, JOHN A.     026307625VELTRI, JOHN A.      312 PERCH DR.   HASTINGS, NE     68901470115820820
!!@##&&**@!!        REACHED EOF. NO MORE RECORDS IN INDEXED FILE

                                      *** END OF REPORT ***
```

Comments on the Program

Refer to the numbered lines in Figure 3.43 for the following comments.

1. Indexed file INDEXED-MASTER-FILE has five keys: the prime record key INDEXED-MR-SSN and the four alternate keys INDEXED-MR-NAME, INDEXED-MR-DOB, INDEXED-MR-DATE-HIRED, and INDEXED-MR-ZIP. These keys allow random access and/or sequential access to records of the master file by the employee's Social Security number, name, date of birth, date hired, and zip code. The DUPLICATES phrases specify that more than one record may have the same alternate key values. (Prime record key values *must* be unique.)
2. There are two kinds of records in DETAIL-FILE. One has size 8 and the other has size 20. Note the scalar (P) in the definition of the data item I-TIME-FACTOR. This value must be added to the value of the data item I-START-DATE to yield the ending date for the required time span. For instance, if the record contains 82060105, the starting date of the time span is June 1, 1982, and by adding 050000 to 820601, the ending date is seen to be 870601, or June 1, 1987.
3. The field WS-TEST-FIELD receives a copy of the detail record when it is read by the program. See the INTO phrase in paragraph 0310-READ-DETAIL-RECORD. This field is tested in paragraph 0210-PROCESS-DETAIL-RECORD to determine the section that should be executed.
4. The field O-KEY of the record DETAIL-LINE identifies the key of reference used to access the record printed in the field O-EMPLOYEE-RECORD. In one case, the value is the date hired, and in the other, it is the employee name.
5. This conditional statement uses a class test on the field WS-TEST-FIELD. The field contains a copy of either a START-DATE-RECORD or a NAME-RECORD. If the characters in the first 6 bytes are numeric, the last record read is a START-DATE-RECORD and control is sent to section 1-SELECT-BY-DATE; otherwise, the record in the field is a NAME-RECORD and control is sent to section 2-SELECT-BY-NAME. In either case, when control exits from the section, in paragraph 1999-EXIT-SECTION or in paragraph 2999-EXIT-SECTION, it returns to this paragraph to execute PERFORM 0300-READ-DETAIL-RECORD.
6. This READ statement stores a copy of the detail record into the data item WS-TEST-FIELD. When control enters paragraph 0210-PROCESS-DETAIL-RECORD, WS-TEST-FIELD contains a copy of the last detail record accessed.
7. The key of reference in 1-SELECT-BY-DATE SECTION is the alternate record key INDEXED-MR-DATE-HIRED. It is assigned the input value I-START-DATE in paragraph 1210-START-MASTER-FILE.
8. The procedure 1210-START-MASTER-FILE positions the master file's record pointer based on the condition specified in the KEY clause of the START statement. The clause is KEY NOT < INDEXED-MR-DATE-HIRED, and the key of reference contains the starting date specified in the input field I-START-DATE. Since the relational operator is "NOT <", the record pointer is positioned at a record whose date hired data item value is equal to the value of I-START-DATE, or at the first record whose date hired data item value is greater than the value of I-START-DATE. If a master record is found that meets the KEY clause condition, the PERFORM in the NOT INVALID KEY clause is executed, and, as a result, that master record is copied into the file's record area. (It will be processed in the procedure 1220-WRITE-N-GET-RECORD.)
9. The function of this PERFORM-UNTIL loop is to obtain the records of all the employees hired during the specified time frame. The first of those records was accessed in the procedure 1210-START-MASTER-FILE. The loop terminates under either of two conditions: one, when the date hired on the last accessed master record is beyond (greater than) the ending date for the time span; the other, when the end of file is reached.
10. This ADD statement determines the ending date for the specified time frame.
11. This is the sequential READ statement that accesses the master records in ascending order by the key of reference established in the START statement, namely, INDEXED-MR-DATE-HIRED. If the end of file is reached, an appropriate message is printed on the report.

12. The key of reference in 2-SELECT-BY-NAME SECTION is the alternate record key INDEXED-MR-NAME. It is assigned the input value I-START-NAME in the first paragraph of the section.
13. This MOVE statement assigns the input employee name to the key of reference used in this section.
14. The function of this PERFORM-UNTIL is to obtain the next four master records in alphabetic order by employee name, given that the first record in this group of five records was accessed previously in paragraph 2210-READ-MASTER-RECORD. The loop terminates either when the four records have been accessed or when the end of file has been reached.
15. This READ statement provides random access to records of the file. The record accessed is the one whose alternate record key field (INDEXED-MR-NAME) contains a value equal to that of the key of reference specified in the KEY clause of the statement. If the random READ operation is successful, a corresponding detail line is printed on the report. If it is not successful, an appropriate error message is printed.
16. The functions of this procedure are, first, to access the "next" record in the master file, and, second, to print the corresponding line on the report. The "next" record means "in ascending order of the key of reference," namely, INDEXED-MR-NAME. If the READ operation is not successful, an error message is printed on the report.
17. This is a sequential READ statement. Every time it executes, it uses the key of reference, INDEXED-MR-NAME, established in the random READ statement of paragraph 2210-READ-MASTER-RECORD.

Indexed Files in Brief

1. The records of a file with indexed organization can be accessed sequentially, randomly, and dynamically.
2. In creating an indexed file, one data item of the file's records must be selected as the prime record key. One or more additional data items of the file's records may be selected as alternate record keys. The file's record keys allow different access paths to the file's records.
3. An indexed file's organization must always be specified by the clause ORGANIZATION IS INDEXED in the file's SELECT statement.
4. An indexed file's prime record key must always be specified by the clause RECORD KEY IS *prime-record-key* in the file's SELECT statement.
5. If alternate record keys are defined for an indexed file, any SELECT statement that selects the file must also contain an ALTERNATE RECORD KEY clause for each alternate record key. The clause must include the phrase WITH DUPLICATES if duplicate alternate key values are allowed.
6. The access mode for the file is specified in the file's SELECT statement by the clause ACCESS MODE IS SEQUENTIAL, or ACCESS MODE IS RANDOM, or ACCESS MODE IS DYNAMIC. If the mode is sequential, the clause need not be coded, since that is the default mode.
7. To *create* an indexed file,
   a. The SELECT statement must contain the clause ORGANIZATION IS INDEXED and the RECORD KEY clause. (It may contain one or more ALTERNATE RECORD KEY clauses.)
   b. The access mode should be specified as SEQUENTIAL.
   c. The OPEN mode for the file should be specified as OUTPUT. It may be specified as EXTEND.
   d. For each record to be written to the file, the prime record key value of the record must be assigned to the prime record key data item, and the WRITE-INVALID KEY statement is used to write the record to the file.
8. To READ an indexed file sequentially,
   a. The access mode must be SEQUENTIAL.
   b. The OPEN mode should be specified as INPUT; it may be specified as I-O.
   c. The READ-AT END statement must be used to access the records sequentially from the beginning to the end of the file.

9. To READ an indexed file randomly,
   a. The access mode must be specified as RANDOM.
   b. The OPEN mode may be specified as INPUT or as I-O.
   c. The key of reference, named in the RECORD KEY clause or in an ALTERNATE RECORD KEY clause, must be initialized prior to executing the READ statement.
   d. The READ-INVALID KEY statement must be used to access the record specified by the value in the key of reference. The KEY clause must be coded in the READ statement if the key of reference is an alternate key. It need not be coded if the key of reference is the prime key.
10. To READ an indexed file dynamically,
   a. The access mode must be specified as DYNAMIC.
   b. The OPEN mode may be INPUT or I-O.
   c. To access the records sequentially from the beginning of the file using the prime record key as the key of reference, the READ-NEXT RECORD statement is used.
   d. To access the records sequentially starting at a point other than the beginning of the file, using any key of reference, the START statement is used to position the file's record pointer and then READ-NEXT RECORD statements are used.
   e. To access all the records of the file sequentially using any key of reference, the START statement is used to position the file's record pointer at the record with the lowest value for the specified key of reference and then READ-NEXT RECORD statements are used.
   f. To access the file's records randomly, the key of reference is initialized and then the READ-INVALID KEY statement, with the KEY clause naming the key of reference, is used.
11. An indexed file may be updated sequentially, randomly, or dynamically.
   a. In a sequential update,
      i) Specify access mode as SEQUENTIAL.
      ii) Open the file in I-O mode.
      iii) Access the target record using READ-AT END.
      iv) If field values are to be changed, do so and then rewrite the record using the REWRITE statement.
      v) If the record is to be deleted, verify that it is the correct one and then use the DELETE statement.
   b. In a random update,
      i) Specify the access mode as RANDOM.
      ii) Open the file in I-O mode.
      iii) Initialize the key of reference with the key value of the target record.
         a) If field values are to be changed, access the record with the READ-INVALID KEY statement. Include the KEY clause if the key of reference is not the prime record key. Update the field values, and use the REWRITE-INVALID KEY statement to rewrite the record to the file.
         b) If the record is to be deleted, use the DELETE-INVALID KEY statement to logically delete it from the file.
         c) If a new record is to be added to the file, use the WRITE-INVALID KEY statement to write it to the file.
   c. In a dynamic update,
      i) Specify the access mode as DYNAMIC.
      ii) Open the file in I-O mode.
      iii) For the sequential option,
         a) Initialize the key of reference.
         b) Use the START statement to position the file's pointer.
         c) Use the READ-NEXT RECORD statement to access the record.
         d) If the record is to be deleted, verify it is the correct one and then use the DELETE statement.
         e) If record fields are to be updated, do so and then use the REWRITE statement.
      iv) For the random option, follow step iii of section 11b above.

12. If the OPEN mode for an indexed file is
    a. INPUT and the access mode is SEQUENTIAL, the valid input-output statements are READ-AT END and START.
    b. INPUT and the access mode is RANDOM, the only valid input-output statement is READ-INVALID KEY.
    c. INPUT and the access mode is DYNAMIC, the valid input-output statements are READ-INVALID KEY, START, and READ-NEXT RECORD.
    d. I-O and the access mode is SEQUENTIAL, the valid input-output statements are READ-AT END, REWRITE, DELETE, and START.
    e. I-O and the access mode is RANDOM, the valid input-output statements are READ-INVALID KEY, WRITE, REWRITE, and DELETE.
    f. I-O and the access mode is DYNAMIC, the valid input-output statements are READ-NEXT RECORD, READ-INVALID KEY, WRITE, REWRITE, DELETE, and START.
    g. OUTPUT and the access mode is SEQUENTIAL, RANDOM, or DYNAMIC, the only valid input-output statement is WRITE.
    h. EXTEND and the access mode is SEQUENTIAL, the only valid input-output statement is WRITE.

Important Terms in Chapter 3

ACCESS MODE IS DYNAMIC
ACCESS MODE IS RANDOM
ACCESS MODE IS SEQUENTIAL
alternate record key
ALTERNATE RECORD KEY IS
DASD
DELETE-INVALID KEY
direct-access storage device
direct-access file
dynamic access
dynamic update
END-DELETE
END-REWRITE
END-START
FILE STATUS
file status code
file's record pointer
index
index record
index table
indexed file
indexed organization
indexed-sequential file
ISAM
KEY IS
key of reference
key-sequenced file
ORGANIZATION IS INDEXED
prime record key
random access
random update
READ-INVALID KEY
READ-KEY IS
READ-NEXT RECORD
record key
RECORD KEY IS
relative organization
REWRITE-INVALID KEY
sequential access
sequential update
START-INVALID KEY
VSAM
WITH DUPLICATES
WRITE-INVALID KEY

Exercises

1. What is a file with indexed organization?
2. What main advantage does an indexed file provide over a sequential file?
3. Why is it sometimes important to have a file organization that allows random access to the records of the file?
4. What is the RECORD KEY clause used for?
5. What is the ALTERNATE RECORD KEY clause used for?
6. What is the ACCESS MODE clause used for and what are its options? Explain them.
7. What is the function of the FILE STATUS clause?
8. The Healem Clinic wants to convert its master patient file from sequential to indexed organization. Its records are currently stored alphabetically by patient name in the file SEQ-PATIENT-FILE. The record layout is as follows:

Record Name: OLD-SEQ-RECORD

		Field Names
cc 1–9	Patient number	I-PATIENT-NO
cc 10–29	Patient name	I-PATIENT-NAME
cc 30–79	Patient address	I-PATIENT-ADDRESS
cc 80–99	Patient insurance carrier	I-INS-CARRIER
cc 100–109	Patient insurance code	I-PATIENT-INS-ID
cc 110–115	Patient account balance	I-ACCT-BAL
cc 116–121	Patient last activity date	I-DATE-LAST-ACTIVITY

The new indexed file, named MR-PATIENT-FILE, must use the patient number field as the prime record key and the name field as an alternate record key. The names of the fields of the new records are the same as the ones on the old records, except that the prefix I is replaced by MR. The new record name is MR-PATIENT-RECORD.

a. Code the FILE-CONTROL entries for the old file and for the new file. Use file specifications "OLDFILE.DAT" and "NEWFILE.DAT".

b. Code the FD paragraph for the new file, and assume that each block must contain 650 characters.

c. Code the OPEN statement for each file.

d. Code the I/O statements that will access each file.

e. Explain what could cause an invalid key condition when a record is written to the indexed file.

9. Suppose that the master file MR-PATIENT-FILE created in exercise 8 contains a few records that must be updated with new addresses. The new addresses are contained in DETAIL-FILE.

a. In addition to the new address for a patient, what else must each detail file record contain? Give an appropriate descriptive name to each data field.

b. Code the SELECT statement for MR-PATIENT-FILE.

c. Code the statements needed to properly open each file.

d. Code the statements needed to completely process a detail record (that is, to handle the prime record key and the alternate record key). Assume the record exists in the master file.

10. Suppose the master file MR-PATIENT-FILE created in exercise 8 contains a few records that must be deleted. For each master record to be deleted, a detail record is made available in DETAIL-FILE.

a. What must each detail record contain?

b. Code the SELECT statement for MR-PATIENT-FILE.

c. Code the statements needed to properly open each file.

d. Code the statements needed to delete a master record.

11. Suppose a program is needed to add new records to the master patient file MR-PATIENT-FILE created in exercise 8. A detail record, named DETAIL-RECORD, is prepared in DETAIL-FILE for each new patient, as specified in exercise 8. If a duplicate key is encountered for a new record, the program must display an appropriate error message.

a. Code the SELECT statement needed for MR-PATIENT-FILE.

b. Code the statements needed to properly open each file.

c. Code the statements needed to add a new record to the master file.

12. Suppose the Healem Clinic wants a report, formatted as shown in Figure 3.46, that shows the account balance for each patient record in the master patient file MR-PATIENT-FILE created in exercise 8. The detail lines on the report are to be listed in ascending patient number sequence.

a. Code the SELECT statement needed for MR-PATIENT-FILE.

b. Code the statements needed to properly open the files. Assume the report is contained in the file PATIENT-BALANCE-REPORT.

c. Code the statements that must be executed to obtain the required patient data, prepare the detail line, and write it on the report.

13. Refer to exercise 12 and Figure 3.46. Suppose that the detail lines on the report must be listed in alphabetic order by patient name.

a. Code the statements needed to properly position the file pointer prior to accessing a patient record.

b. Subsequent to properly positioning the file's pointer, code the statements needed to obtain the required patient data, prepare the detail line, and write it on the report.

14. Suppose a random check is to be made of the account balances for the patients of the Healem Clinic. The master patient file is the one created in exercise 8. For each patient number picked at random, that patient's account balance and the balance for the next four in the file are to be reported on a report formatted as shown in Figure 3.46. A program must be prepared for this purpose. A detail record is prepared in DETAIL-FILE for each randomly picked patient number.

a. Code the SELECT statement for MR-PATIENT-FILE.

b. Code the statements needed to properly open the files.

c. Code the procedures needed to access the patient record corresponding to a selected patient number, and to prepare the related set of detail lines on the report. Assume a master record exists for each patient number in the detail file.

Figure 3.46

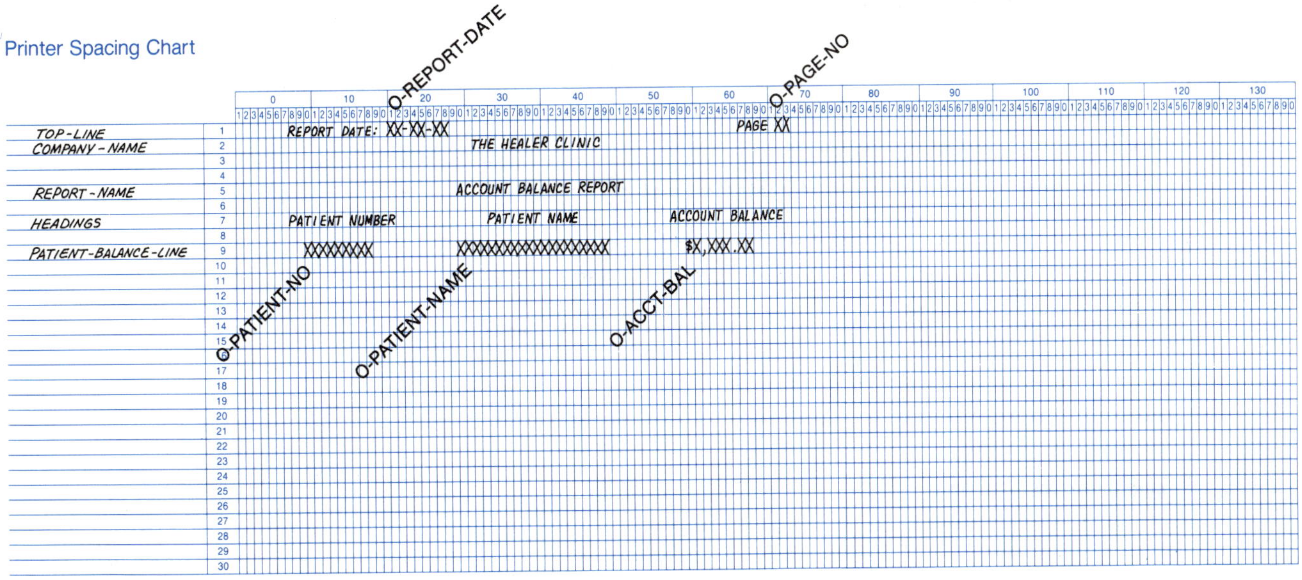

Figure 3.47 Printer spacing chart for the audit report

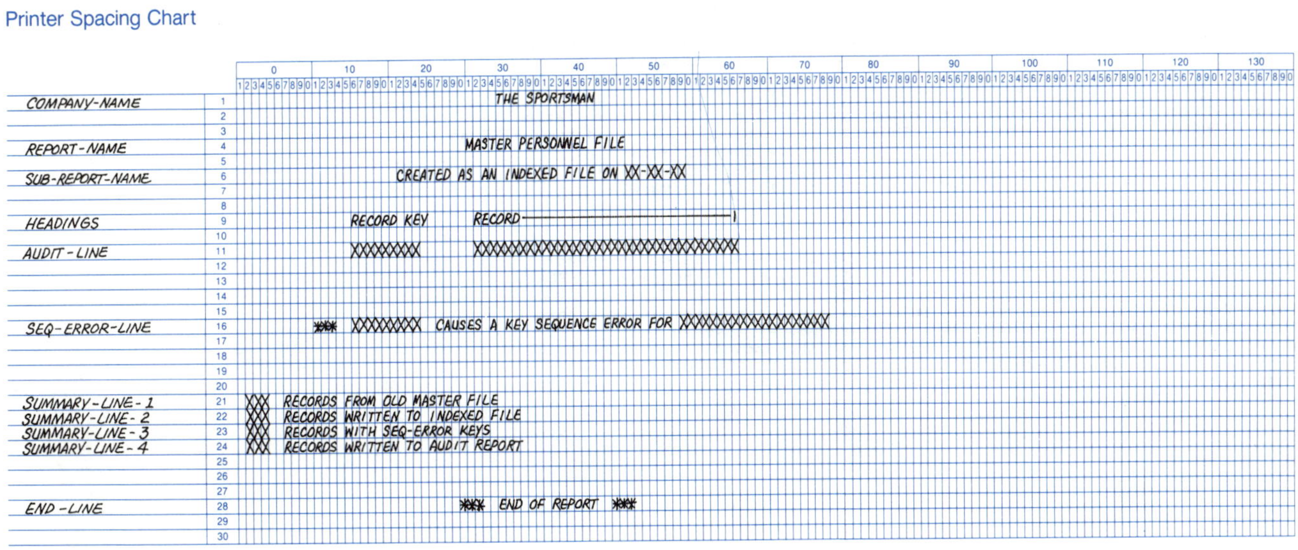

Debugging Activities

1. A student was given the task of designing and coding a program to create a personnel master file for the Sportsman Company. The file must have indexed organization, and its prime record key is the employee Social Security number. Additionally, the file must specify the employee name as an alternate record key. The program must also produce an audit report formatted as shown in Figure 3.47.

   The company's master employee records are currently in a sequential file, and they are sequenced in alphabetic order by employee name.

When the program was compiled, the listing contained a number of diagnostics as shown below. Your task is to correct all the syntax errors in the program.

Program Listing:

```
CREATE-NEW-MASTER-DBG-1                    12-Apr-1989 14:29:24    VAX COBOL V4.2-40                   Page   1
Source Listing                             12-Apr-1989 14:29:02    [PAQUETTEG.CHAPTER6V2]V2C6DBG1.COB;3 (1)

           IDENTIFICATION DIVISION.

           PROGRAM-ID.  CREATE-NEW-MASTER-DBG-1.

          ******************************************************************
          *                                                                *
          *  THE MAIN FUNCTION OF THIS PROGRAM IS TO CREATE AN INDEXED     *
          *  MASTER PERSONNEL FILE FOR THE SPORTSMAN COMPANY.              *
          *                                                                *
          *  THE MASTER FILE IS CURRENTLY A SEQUENTIAL FILE AND THE RECORDS*
          *  ARE IN ALPHABETIC ORDER BY EMPLOYEE NAME.  HOWEVER, THE INDEX-*
          *  ED MASTER FILE MUST USE THE EMPLOYEE SOCIAL SECURITY NUMBER   *
          *  AS THE PRIME RECORD KEY, AND IT MUST SPECIFY THE EMPLOYEE NAME*
          *  AS AN ALTERNATE RECORD KEY.                                   *
          *                                                                *
          *  THE PROGRAM ALSO PRODUCES AN AUDIT REPORT.                    *
          *                                                                *
          ******************************************************************

           ENVIRONMENT DIVISION.

           CONFIGURATION SECTION.

           SOURCE-COMPUTER.  VAX-VMS-8650.
           OBJECT-COMPUTER.  VAX-VMS-8650.

           INPUT-OUTPUT SECTION.

           FILE-CONTROL.
               SELECT OLD-SEQ-FILE        ASSIGN TO COB$INPUT
                      1
%COBOL-W-ERROR  239, (1) File is CLOSEd but is not OPENed
                                          ORGANIZATION IS SEQUENTIAL
                                          ACCESS MODE IS SEQUENTIAL.
               SELECT SORT-FILE           ASSIGN TO SORTDISK.
                      1
%COBOL-W-ERROR   16, (1) RECORD CONTAINS value is greater than length of longest record
               SELECT OLD-SRTD-SEQ-FILE   ASSIGN TO 'OLDSRT.DAT'.
               SELECT NEW-MASTER-FILE     ASSIGN TO 'SPORTSNDX.DAT'
                      1
%COBOL-F-ERROR   89, (1) RECORD KEY clause required for indexed organization
%COBOL-F-ERROR  334, (1) INVALID KEY clause or USE procedure required for WRITE on file
                                          ORGANIZATION IS INDEXED
                                          ACCESS MODE IS SEQUENTIAL
                                          PRIME KEY IS NEW-MR-SSN
                                          1
%COBOL-E-ERROR   65, (1) Missing period is assumed
%COBOL-F-ERROR  117, (1) Invalid syntax
                                          ALTERNATE KEY IS NEW-MR-NAME
                                          FILE STATUS IS MASTER-FILE-FLAG.
                                          1    2
%COBOL-W-ERROR  297, (1) Processing of source program resumes at this point
%COBOL-E-ERROR  452, (1) Missing DATA DIVISION header assumed
%COBOL-F-ERROR  222, (2) 'SECTION' required at this point
               SELECT AUDIT-REPORT        ASSIGN TO COB$OUTPUT.

          DATA DIVISION.
```

```
                 1
%COBOL-W-ERROR  297, (1) Processing of source program resumes at this point
%COBOL-E-ERROR  100, (1) Item already appeared - processing continues

             FILE SECTION.
                 1
%COBOL-E-ERROR  100, (1) Item already appeared - processing continues

             FD  OLD-SEQ-FILE
                 RECORD CONTAINS 33 CHARACTERS.

             01  OLD-MASTER-RECORD.
                 05 OLD-STORE-NO    PIC X(2).
                 05 OLD-DEPT-NO     PIC X(2).
                 05 OLD-SSN         PIC X(9).
                 05 OLD-NAME        PIC X(20).

             FD  SORT-FILE
                 RECORD CONTAINS 80 CHARACTERS.

             01  SORT-RECORD.
                 05 S-STORE-NO    PIC X(2).
                 05 S-DEPT-NO     PIC X(2).
                 05 S-SSN         PIC X(9).
                 05 S-NAME        PIC X(20).

             FD  OLD-SRTD-SEQ-FILE
                 RECORD CONTAINS 33 CHARACTERS.

             01  OLD-SRTD-EMPLOYEE-RECORD.
                 05 OS-STORE-NO    PIC X(2).
                 05 OS-DEPT-NO     PIC X(2).
                 05 OS-SSN         PIC X(9).
                 05 OS-NAME        PIC X(20).

             FD  NEW-MASTER-FILE
                 RECORD CONTAINS 35 CHARACTERS
                 BLOCK CONTAINS 5 RECORDS.

             01  NEW-MASTER-RECORD.
                 05 NEW-MR-RECORD-CODE PIC X(2).
                 05 NEW-MR-STORE-NO    PIC X(2).
                 05 NEW-MR-DEP-NO      PIC X(2).
                 05 NEW-MR-SSN         PIC X(9).
                 05 NEW-MR-NAME        PIC X(20).

             FD  AUDIT-REPORT
                 1
%COBOL-E-ERROR   51, (1) File has no definition in FILE-CONTROL paragraph - definition assumed
%COBOL-E-ERROR   17, (1) Longest record is longer than RECORD CONTAINS value - Longest record size used
                 RECORD CONTAINS 80 CHARACTERS.

             01  PRINTLINE                 PIC X(132).

             WORKING-STORAGE SECTION.

             01  PROGRAM-CONTROLS.
```

```
CREATE-NEW-MASTER-DBG-1                                    12-Apr-1989 14:29:24    VAX COBOL V4.2-40                          Page   3
Source Listing                                             12-Apr-1989 14:29:02    [PAQUETTEG.CHAPTER6V2]V2C6DBG1.COB;3 (1)

                  05 WS-MORE-OLD-RECORDS      PIC X(3).
                     88 MORE-OLD-RECORDS              VALUE 'YES'.
                     88 NO-MORE-OLD-RECORDS           VALUE 'NO '.
                  05 MASTER-FILE-FLAG         PIC 9(2).
                     88 SUCCESSFUL-WRITE              VALUE '00'.
                        1
%COBOL-E-ERROR   83, (1) Condition VALUE conflicts with description of conditional variable
                     88 KEY-SEQ-ERROR                 VALUE '21'.
                        1
%COBOL-E-ERROR   83, (1) Condition VALUE conflicts with description of conditional variable
                  05 WS-REPORT-DATE           PIC X(6).
                  05 WS-PROPER-SPACING        PIC 9(1).

              01  PROGRAM-COUNTERS.
                  05 WS-OLD-MASTER-CTR        PIC S9(3).
                  05 WS-INDEXED-FILE-CTR      PIC S9(3).
                  05 WS-SEQ-ERROR-CTR         PIC S9(3).
                  05 WS-AUDIT-LINE-CTR        PIC S9(3).

              01  WS-NEW-MASTER-RECORD.
                  05 WS-NEW-MR-RECORD-CODE    PIC X(2).
                  05 WS-NEW-MR-STORE-NO       PIC X(2).
                  05 WS-NEW-MR-DEPT-NO        PIC X(2).
                  05 WS-NEW-MR-SSN            PIC X(9).
                  05 WS-NEW-MR-NAME           PIC X(20).

              01 REPORT-HEADERS.
                  05 COMPANY-NAME.
                     10 PIC X(34)  VALUE SPACES.
                     10 PIC X(13)  VALUE 'THE SPORTSMAN'.
                     10 PIC X(33)  VALUE SPACES.

                  05 REPORT-NAME.
                     10 PIC X(30)  VALUE SPACES.
                     10 PIC X(12)  VALUE 'MASTER PERSONNEL FILE'.
                        1
%COBOL-E-ERROR   84, (1) Literal in VALUE clause conflicts with description - clause ignored
                     10 PIC X(1)   VALUE SPACES.

                  05 SUB-REPORT-NAME.
                     10                PIC X(21)  VALUE SPACES.
                     10                PIC X(30)  VALUE
                                       'CREATED AS AN INDEXED FILE ON '.
                     10 O-REPORT-DATE PIC XXBXXBXX.
                     10                PIC X(21)  VALUE SPACES.

                  05 HEADINGS.
                     10 PIC X(15)  VALUE SPACES.
                     10 PIC X(10)  VALUE 'RECORD KEY'.
                     10 PIC X(6)   VALUE SPACES.
                     10 PIC X(6)   VALUE 'RECORD'.
                     10 PIC X(28)  VALUE ALL '-'.
                     10 PIC X(1)   VALUE '|'.
                     10 PIC X(14)  VALUE SPACES.

              01  AUDIT-LINE.
                  05              PIC X(15).
```

```
CREATE-NEW-MASTER-DBG-1                                 12-Apr-1989 14:29:24   VAX COBOL V4.2-40                        Page  4
Source Listing                                          12-Apr-1989 14:29:02   [PAQUETTEG.CHAPTER6V2]V2C6DBG1.COB;3 (1)

                05 O-KEY-1         PIC X(9).
                05                 PIC X(7).
                05 O-RECORD        PIC X(35).
                05                 PIC X(14).

            01  SEQ-ERROR-LINE.
                05                 PIC X(10)  VALUE SPACES.
                05                 PIC X(3)   VALUE '***'.
                05                 PIC X(2)   VALUE SPACES.
                05 O-KEY-2         PIC X(9).
                05                 PIC X(34)  VALUE
                                   ' CAUSES A KEY SEQUENCE ERROR FOR '.
                05 OS-NAME         PIC X(20).
                05                 PIC X(2)   VALUE SPACES.

            01  REPORT-ENDERS.
                05 SUMMARY-LINE-1.
                   10                        PIC X(1)    VALUE SPACES.
                   10 O-OLD-MASTER-CTR       PIC ZZ9.
                   10                        PIC X(30)   VALUE
                                   ' RECORDS FROM OLD MASTER FILE'.

                05 SUMMARY-LINE-2.
                   10                        PIC X(1)    VALUE SPACES.
                   10 O-INDEXED-FILE-CTR     PIC ZZ9.
                   10                        PIC X(33)   VALUE
                                   ' RECORDS WRITTEN TO INDEXED FILE'.

                05 SUMMARY-LINE-3.
                   10                        PIC X(1)    VALUE SPACES.
                   10 O-SEQ-ERROR-CTR        PIC ZZ9.
                   10                        PIC X(29)   VALUE
                                   ' RECORDS WITH SEQ-ERROR KEYS'.

                05 SUMMARY-LINE-4.
                   10                        PIC X(1)    VALUE SPACES.
                   10 O-AUDIT-LINE-CTR       PIC ZZ9.
                   10                        PIC X(33)   VALUE
                                   ' RECORDS WRITTEN TO AUDIT REPORT'.

                05 END-LINE.
                   10 PIC X(29)  VALUE SPACES.
                   10 PIC X(21)  VALUE '*** END OF REPORT ***'.
                   10 PIC X(30)  VALUE SPACES.

             PROCEDURE DIVISION.

             100-CREATE-INDEXED-FILE.
                 PERFORM 200-START-UP.
                 PERFORM 210-PROCESS-OLD-RECORD
                     UNTIL NO-MORE-ODD-RECORDS.
                           1
%COBOL-F-ERROR  349, (1) Undefined name
                 PERFORM 220-FINISH-UP.
                 STOP RUN.

             200-START-UP.
```

```
CREATE-NEW-MASTER-DBG-1                        12-Apr-1989 14:29:24    VAX COBOL V4.2-40                      Page   5
Source Listing                                 12-Apr-1989 14:29:02    [PAQUETTEG.CHAPTER6V2]V2C6DBG1.COB;3 (1)

               OPEN INPUT OLD-SRTD-SEQ-FILE
                    OUTPUT NEW-MASTER-FILE
                           AUDIT-REPORT.
               INITIALIZE PROGRAM-COUNTERS.
               SET MORE-OLD-RECORDS TO TRUE.
               ACCEPT WS-REPORT-DATE FROM DATE.
               MOVE WS-REPORT-DATE TO O-REPORT-DATE.
               INSPECT O-REPORT-DATE
                   REPLACING ALL SPACES BY '-'.
               PERFORM 310-WRITE-REPORT-HEADERS.
               PERFORM 320-READ-OLD-FILE.

           210-PROCESS-OLD-RECORD.
               PERFORM 330-PREPARE-NEW-MASTER.
               IF SEQ-ERROR
                  1
%COBOL-F-ERROR  349, (1) Undefined name
                   PERFORM 350-PREPARE-SEQ-ERROR-LINE
               ELSE
               1
%COBOL-F-ERROR  222, (1) '.' required at this point
                   PERFORM 340-PREPARE-AUDIT-LINE
               END-IF.
               1
%COBOL-F-ERROR  222, (1) '.' required at this point
               ADD 1 TO WS-AUDIT-LINE-CTR.
               1
%COBOL-W-ERROR  297, (1) Processing of source program resumes at this point
               PERFORM 320-READ-OLD-FILE.

           220-FINISH-UP.
               PERFORM 360-PREPARE-SUMMARY.
               WRITE PRINTLINE FROM END-LINE
                   AFTER ADVANCING 5 LINES.
               CLOSE OLD-SEQ-FILE
                     NEW-MASTER-FILE
                     AUDIT-REPORT.

           300-SORT-OLD-FILE.
               SORT SORT-FILE
                    1
%COBOL-F-ERROR  260, (1) Operand must be a file-name defined by SD
                   ON ASCENDING OS-SSN
                   USING OLD-SEQ-FILE
                   GIVING OLD-SRTD-SEQ-FILE.
                                           1
%COBOL-W-ERROR  297, (1) Processing of source program resumes at this point

           310-WRITE-REPORT-HEADERS.
               WRITE PRINTLINE FROM COMPANY-NAME
                   AFTER ADVANCING PAGE.
               WRITE PRINTLINE FROM REPORT-NAME
                   AFTER ADVANCING 3 LINES.
               WRITE PRINTLINE FROM SUB-REPORT-NAME
                   AFTER ADVANCING 2 LINES.
               WRITE PRINTLINE FROM HEADINGS
                   AFTER ADVANCING 3 LINES.
```

```
                  MOVE 2 TO WS-PROPER-SPACING.

              320-READ-OLD-FILE.
                  READ OLD-SRTD-SEQ-FILE RECORD
                      AT END
                          SET NO-MORE-OLD-RECORDS TO TRUE
                  END-READ.

              330-PREPARE-NEW-MASTER.
                  MOVE 'EM' TO NEW-MR-RECORD-CODE.
                  MOVE S-STORE-NO TO NEW-MR-STORE-NO.
                  MOVE S-DEPT-NO TO NEW-MR-DEPT-NO.
                                     1
%COBOL-F-ERROR  349, (1) Undefined name
                  MOVE S-SSN TO NEW-MR-SSN.
                  MOVE S-NAME TO NEW-MR-NAME.
                  MOVE NEW-MASTER-RECORD TO WS-NEW-MASTER-RECORD.
                  WRITE NEW-MASTER-RECORD.
                      INVALID KEY
                       1
%COBOL-F-ERROR  321, (1) Invalid statement syntax
                          SET KEY-SEQ-ERROR TO TRUE
                           1
%COBOL-W-ERROR  297, (1) Processing of source program resumes at this point
                  END-WRITE.
                   1
%COBOL-F-ERROR  222, (1) '.' required at this point

              340-PREPARE-AUDIT-LINE.
              1
%COBOL-W-ERROR  297, (1) Processing of source program resumes at this point
                  MOVE OS-SSN TO O-KEY.
                                  1
%COBOL-F-ERROR  349, (1) Undefined name
                  MOVE NEW-MASTER-RECORD TO O-RECORD.
                  WRITE PRINTLINE FROM AUDIT-LINE
                      AFTER ADVANCING WS-PROPER-SPACING.
                  MOVE 1 TO WS-PROPER-SPACING.

              350-PREPARE-SEQ-ERROR-LINE.
                  MOVE OS-SSN TO O-KEY-2.
                  MOVE OS-NAME TO O-NAME.
                        1          2
%COBOL-F-ERROR  337, (1) Ambiguous reference - check name qualification
%COBOL-F-ERROR  349, (2) Undefined name
                  WRITE PRINTLINE FROM ERROR-LINE
                                         1
%COBOL-F-ERROR  349, (1) Undefined name
                      AFTER ADVANCING WS-PROPER-SPACING.
                                                         1
%COBOL-W-ERROR  297, (1) Processing of source program resumes at this point
                  MOVE 1 TO WS-PROPER-SPACING.

              360-PREPARE-SUMMARY.
                  MOVE WS-OLD-MASTER-CTR TO O-OLD-MASTER-CTR.
                  WRITE PRINTLINE FROM SUMMARY-LINE-1
                      AFTER ADVANCING 5 LINES.
```

```
           MOVE WS-INDEXED-FILE-CTR TO O-INDEXED-FILE-CTR.
           WRITE PRINTLINE FROM SUMMARY-LINE-2
               AFTER ADVANCING 1 LINE.
           MOVE WS-SEQ-ERROR-CTR TO O-SEQ-ERROR-CTR.
           WRITE PRINTLINE FROM SUMMARY-LINE-3
               AFTER ADVANCING 1 LINE.
           MOVE WS-AUDIT-LINE-CTR TO O-AUDIT-LINE-CTR.
           WRITE PRINTLINE FROM SUMMARY-LINE-4
               AFTER ADVANCING 1 LINE.
```

Figure 3.48a Old master file

```
3006820788914ABALLO, NORMA
2004479210065BARRESI, JOHN
4002452677143BEAUDOIN, ROCKY
3002416892014BERNARD, ISIDORE
3008466587165BRAZ, JOAN
4006452892153CARDIN, FRANCIS
2004427560010COCHRANE, RUSSELL
2006683309020COSTELLO, JAMES
1004556234035CRANE, JOHN
1004696996055DANIELS, JULIA
3006785023157DOLLARHIDE, CHRIS
1006521244005DWYER, TERRENCE
1006564451045EDWARDS, PETER
1004251342020FARMER, SUSAN
2006433406075FERNANDEZ, LOUISE
4006574930461GALLAGHER, MICHAEL
2008762355100GOYETTE, FRANCES
1008377568080HOWARD, RALPH
4008721435472JOBIN, ANTONIO
1008599231085LANGFORD, SARAH
2006571904025LEMERISE, DONALD
3006745635164LINCOURT, LORETTA
3002823144098MAHFUZ, IRENE
1006644353075MANNING, ELIZABETH
2004360902035PENTA, ROBERT
4004375701060PERRY, MARTA
3008557318974PRATT, ROBIN
1008521166100PRINGLY, ANNE
2004472847080PROULX, PAULINE
2004375701060QUINN, SUZANNE
4008351566178TRAMONTE, ESTELLE
2008804233040VERMETTE, GLORIA
2006572495090WORTHEN, MICHAEL
```

Figure 3.48b Audit report with serious errors

```
                                   THE SPORTSMAN

                               MASTER PERSONNEL FILE

                       CREATED AS AN INDEXED FILE ON 89-04-12

                 RECORD KEY       RECORD-----------------------------|



0  RECORDS FROM OLD MASTER FILE
0  RECORDS WRITTEN TO INDEXED FILE
0  RECORDS WITH SEQ-ERROR KEYS
0  RECORDS WRITTEN TO AUDIT REPORT


                              *** END OF REPORT ***
```

2. When the program shown in exercise 1 was free of syntax errors, it was compiled and run using the data file shown in Figure 3.48a as the input file. The report it produced is shown in Figure 3.48b. It is clear that the report is incomplete. It should have been the one shown in Figure 3.48c. Your task is to identify and correct the remaining errors in the program so it can produce the correct report and the correct indexed file. The correct indexed file is shown in Figure 3.48d.

Figure 3.48c The correct audit report

```
                              THE SPORTSMAN

                          MASTER PERSONNEL FILE

                  CREATED AS AN INDEXED FILE ON 89-04-12

          RECORD KEY        RECORD----------------------------|

          251342020         EM1004251342020FARMER, SUSAN
          351566178         EM4008351566178TRAMONTE, ESTELLE
          360902035         EM2004360902035PENTA, ROBERT
          375701060         EM2004375701060QUINN, SUZANNE
      *** 375701060  CAUSES A KEY SEQUENCE ERROR FOR PERRY, MARTA
          377568080         EM1008377568080HOWARD, RALPH
          416892014         EM3002416892014BERNARD, ISIDORE
          427560010         EM2004427560010COCHRANE, RUSSELL
          433406075         EM2006433406075FERNANDEZ, LOUISE
          452677143         EM4002452677143BEAUDOIN, ROCKY
          452892153         EM4006452892153CARDIN, FRANCIS
          466587165         EM3008466587165BRAZ, JOAN
          472847080         EM2004472847080PROULX, PAULINE
          479210065         EM2004479210065BARRESI, JOHN
          521166100         EM1008521166100PRINGLY, ANNE
          521244005         EM1006521244005DWYER, TERRENCE
          556234035         EM1004556234035CRANE, JOHN
          557318974         EM3008557318974PRATT, ROBIN
          564451045         EM1006564451045EDWARDS, PETER
          571904025         EM2006571904025LEMERISE, DONALD
          572495090         EM2006572495090WORTHEN, MICHAEL
          574930461         EM4006574930461GALLAGHER, MICHAEL
          599231085         EM1008599231085LANGFORD, SARAH
          644353075         EM1006644353075MANNING, ELIZABETH
          683309020         EM2006683309020COSTELLO, JAMES
          696996055         EM1004696996055DANIELS, JULIA
          721435472         EM4008721435472JOBIN, ANTONIO
          745635164         EM3006745635164LINCOURT, LORETTA
          762355100         EM2008762355100GOYETTE, FRANCES
          785023157         EM3006785023157DOLLARHIDE, CHRIS
          804233040         EM2008804233040VERMETTE, GLORIA
          820788914         EM3006820788914ABALLO, NORMA
          823144098         EM3002823144098MAHFUZ, IRENE


33  RECORDS FROM OLD MASTER FILE
32  RECORDS WRITTEN TO INDEXED FILE
 1  RECORDS WITH SEQ-ERROR KEYS
33  RECORDS WRITTEN TO AUDIT REPORT


                            *** END OF REPORT ***
```

Figure 3.48d The correct indexed file

```
EM1004251342020FARMER, SUSAN
EM4008351566178TRAMONTE, ESTELLE
EM2004360902035PENTA, ROBERT
EM2004375701060QUINN, SUZANNE
EM1008377568080HOWARD, RALPH
EM3002416892014BERNARD, ISIDORE
EM2004427560010COCHRANE, RUSSELL
EM2006433406075FERNANDEZ, LOUISE
EM4002452677143BEAUDOIN, ROCKY
EM4006452892153CARDIN, FRANCIS
EM3008466587165BRAZ, JOAN
EM2004472847080PROULX, PAULINE
EM2004479210065BARRESI, JOHN
EM1008521166100PRINGLY, ANNE
EM1006521244005DWYER, TERRENCE
EM1004556234035CRANE, JOHN
EM3008557318974PRATT, ROBIN
EM1006564451045EDWARDS, PETER
EM2006571904025LEMERISE, DONALD
EM2006572495090WORTHEN, MICHAEL
EM4006574930461GALLAGHER, MICHAEL
EM1008599231085LANGFORD, SARAH
EM1006644353075MANNING, ELIZABETH
EM2006683309020COSTELLO, JAMES
EM1004696996055DANIELS, JULIA
EM4008721435472JOBIN, ANTONIO
EM3006745635164LINCOURT, LORETTA
EM2008762355100GOYETTE, FRANCES
EM3006785023157DOLLARHIDE, CHRIS
EM2008804233040VERMETTE, GLORIA
EM3006820788914ABALLO, NORMA
EM3002823144098MAHFUZ, IRENE
```

Figure 3.49a Printer spacing chart for the audit report

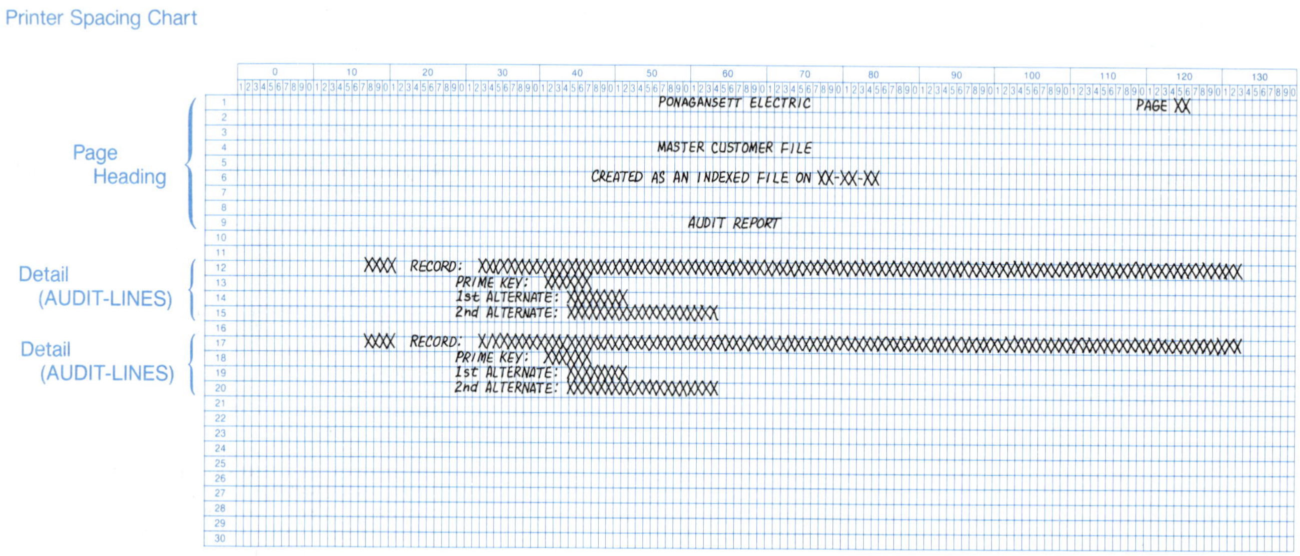

Programming Exercises

Programming Exercise I

The management of the Ponagansett Electric Company has decided to change the organization of its master customer file from sequential to indexed. The decision was based on the fact that customer data must often be updated, and yet every time an update is required, relatively few records of the master file need to be accessed. An indexed organization will provide for faster and more efficient updates, and for billing purposes, the file can still be processed sequentially.

The current master records contain the following data:

cc 1–2	Record code (CM for Customer Master)
cc 3–10	Customer meter number
cc 11–13	Customer rate code
cc 14–19	Customer number
cc 20–39	Customer name
cc 40–64	Customer address
cc 65–87	Customer city, state, and zip code
cc 88–100	Not used

The records in the current master file are blocked with a factor of 10, and they are sequenced in ascending order by meter number.

The new indexed master file to be created by the program must meet the following requirements:

1. The customer number is its prime record key.
2. The meter number and the customer name are its alternate record keys; duplicates are allowed for customer names.
3. The file has a blocking factor of 5.

The sequence and size of data fields in a master record remain as they were in the sequential file.

Since the records in the indexed file must be in ascending order by prime record key value, the old master file must be sorted prior to preparing the new master records.

The system flowchart and the structure chart are shown in Figures 3.49b and 3.49c. Note that an audit report is required, and its format is shown in Figure 3.49a.

Use the current date as the report date, and use Data Set 3X1 as the input file.

Figure 3.49a continued

Printer Spacing Chart

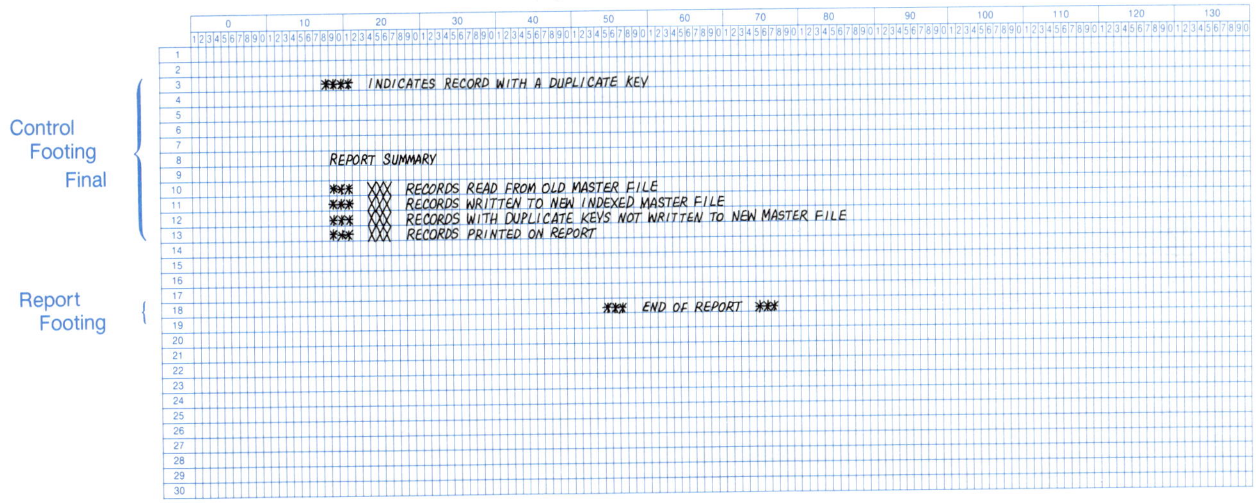

Figure 3.49b System flowchart to create the indexed master file

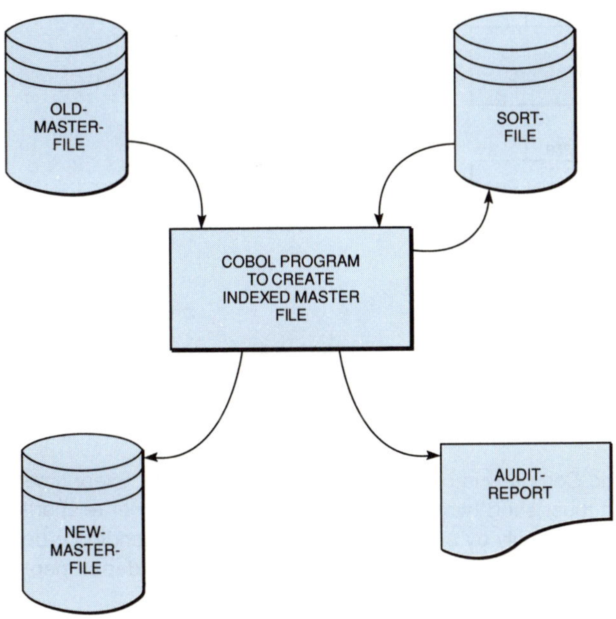

Figure 3.49c Structure chart to create the indexed master file

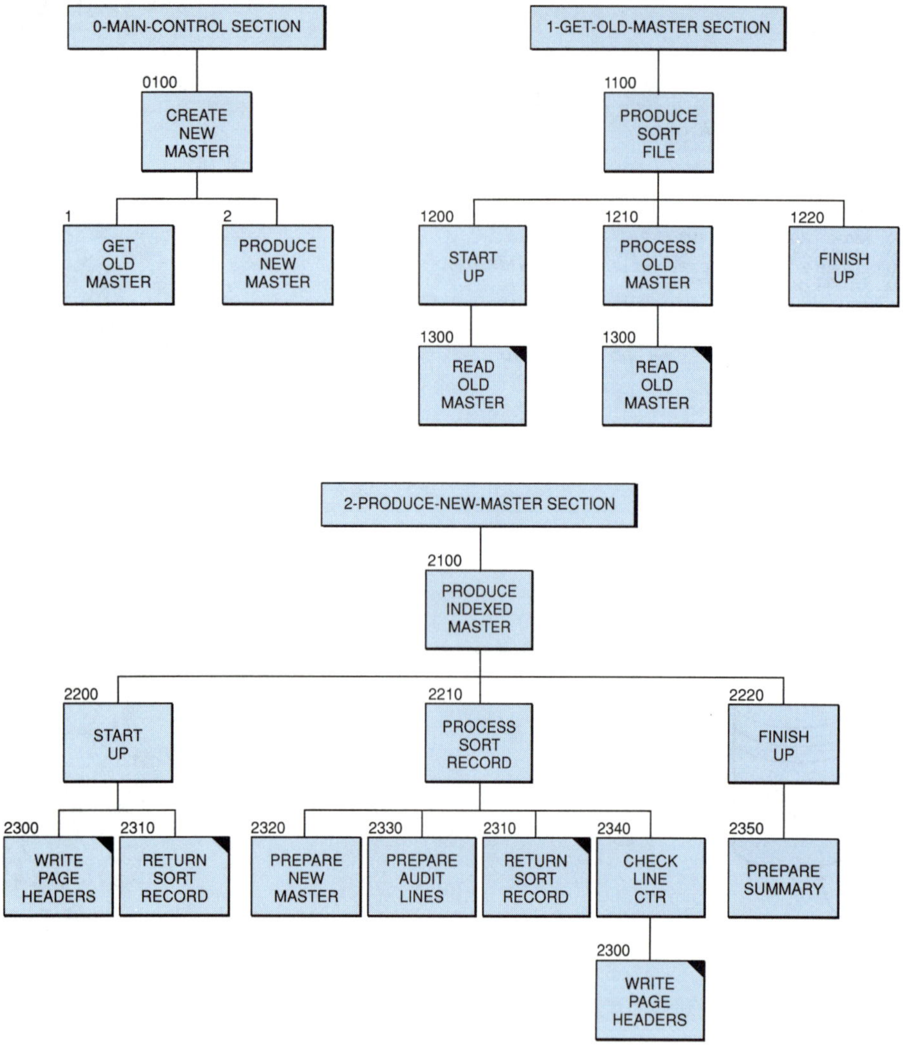

Programming Exercise II

The master customer file of the Ponagansett Electric Company is brought up-to-date periodically. Every time a file update occurs, the data processing department must send two updated copies to the customer relations department: one in which the records are listed alphabetically by customer name and one in ascending order by customer number. In addition, one copy must be sent to the service department. The service department's copy must be in ascending order by meter number.

Your task is to write a program designed to produce these three reports. They are formatted as shown in Figures 3.50a, 3.50b, and 3.50c.

The records in the master customer file contain the following data:

cc 1–2	Record code (CM for Customer Master)
cc 3–10	Customer meter number
cc 11–13	Customer rate code
cc 14–19	Customer number
cc 20–39	Customer name
cc 40–64	Customer street address
cc 65–87	Customer city, state, and zip code
cc 88–100	Not used

The file has indexed organization, and its prime record key is the customer number field. The file also has two alternate keys: the first is the customer meter number, and it does not allow duplicates, the second is the customer name, and it does allow duplicates.

■ **Figure 3.50a** Printer spacing chart for report by name

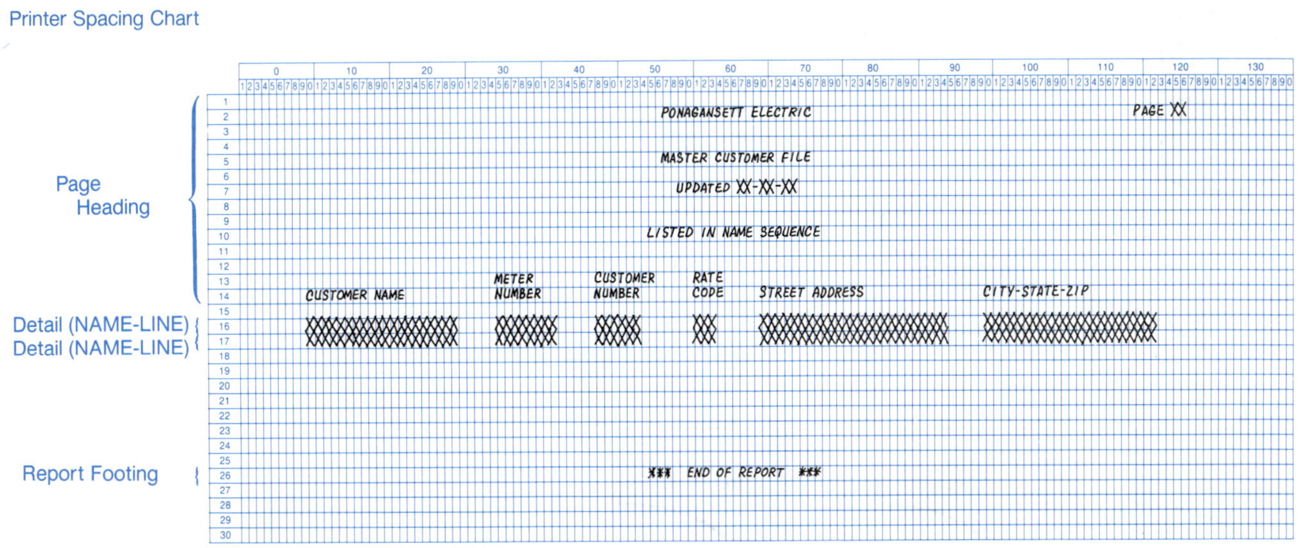

■ **Figure 3.50b** Printer spacing chart for report by customer number

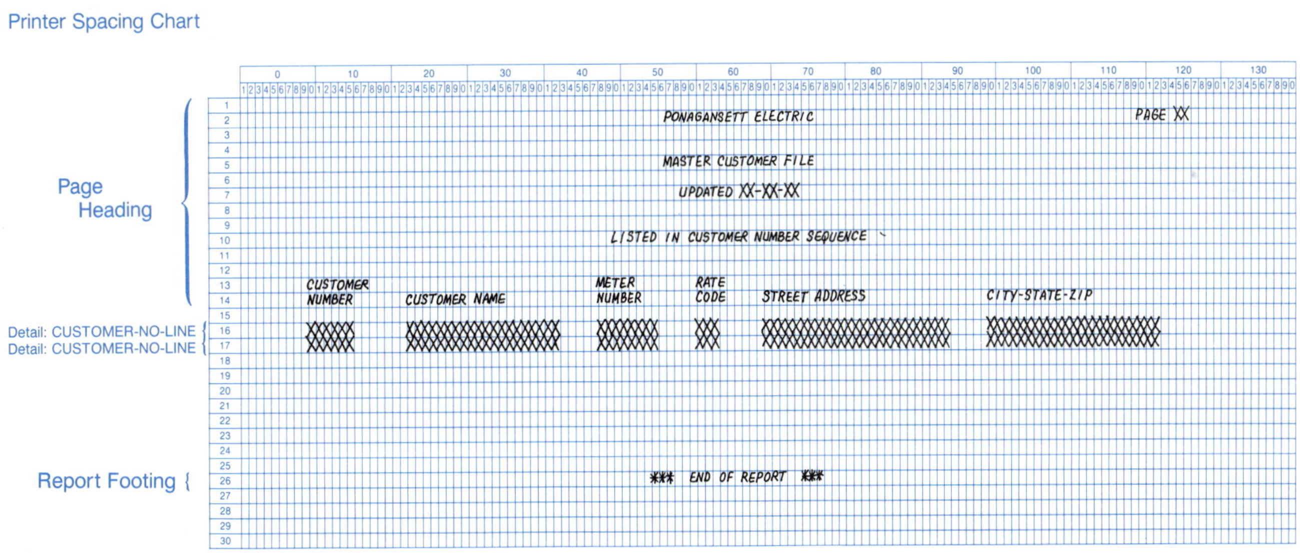

■ **Figure 3.50c** Printer spacing chart for report by meter number

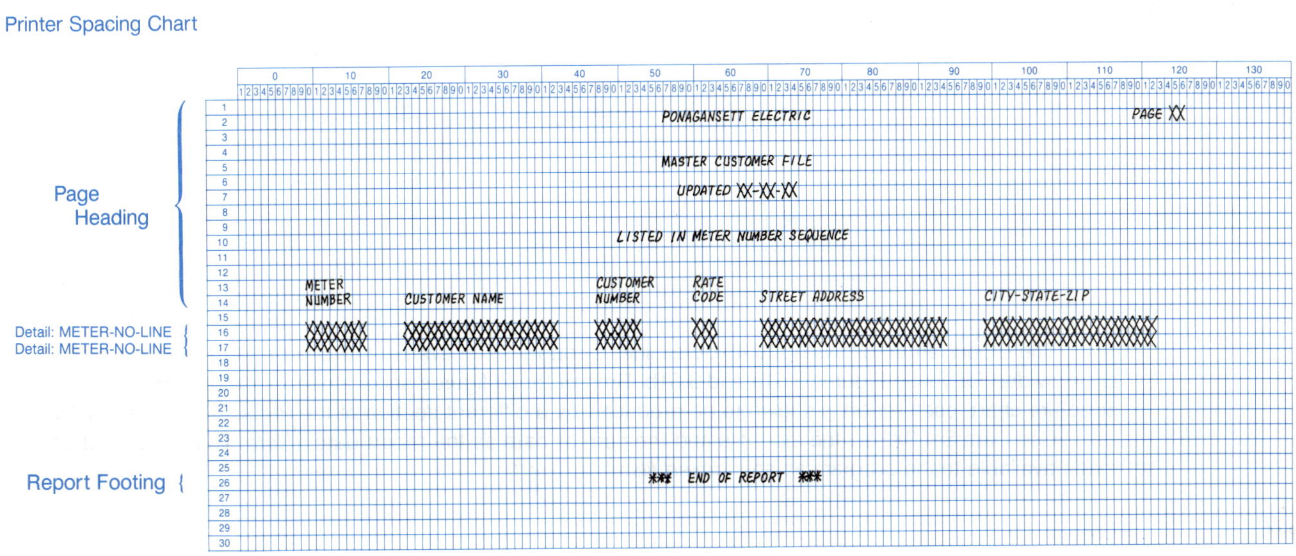

■ **Figure 3.51a** System flowchart to produce the reports

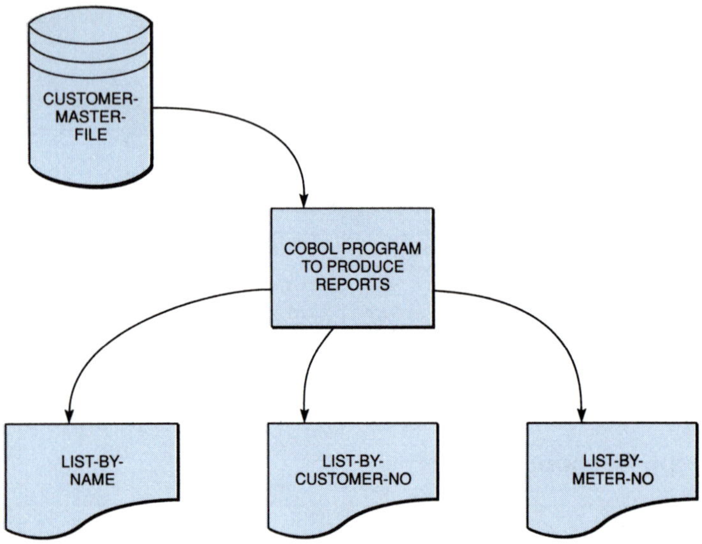

■ **Figure 3.51b** Structure chart to produce the reports

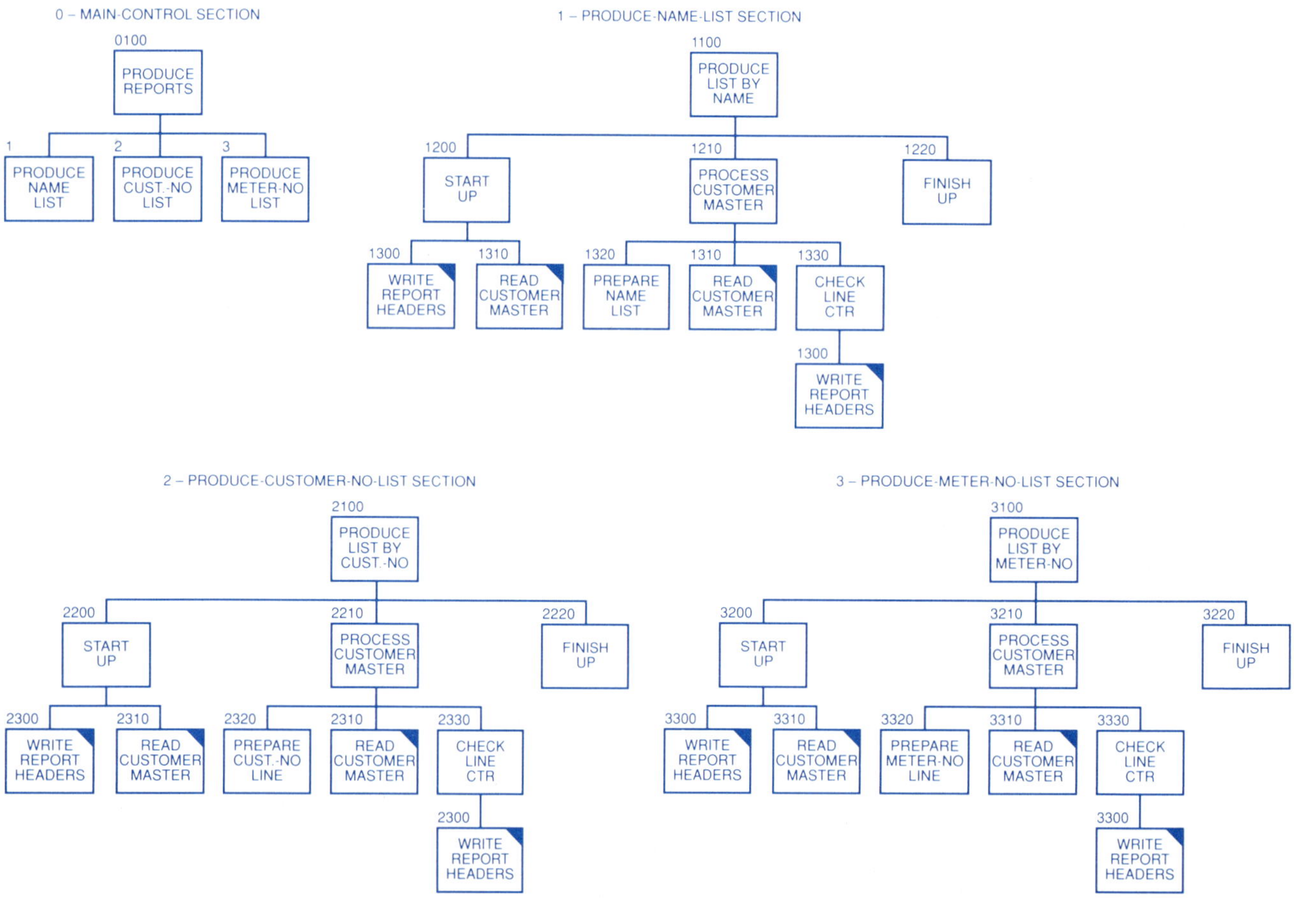

The report format allows up to 45 detail lines per page. The system flowchart and the structure chart are provided for you in Figures 3.51a and 3.51b. Both of these figures show a need for three reports. In the structure chart, each report is shown to be produced by a different section of the PROCEDURE DIVISION.

Use Data Set 3X2 as the input file and the current date as the report date. (*Note:* The input file must be made available to the program as an *indexed file*!)

■ **Figure 3.52** Printer spacing chart for the audit report

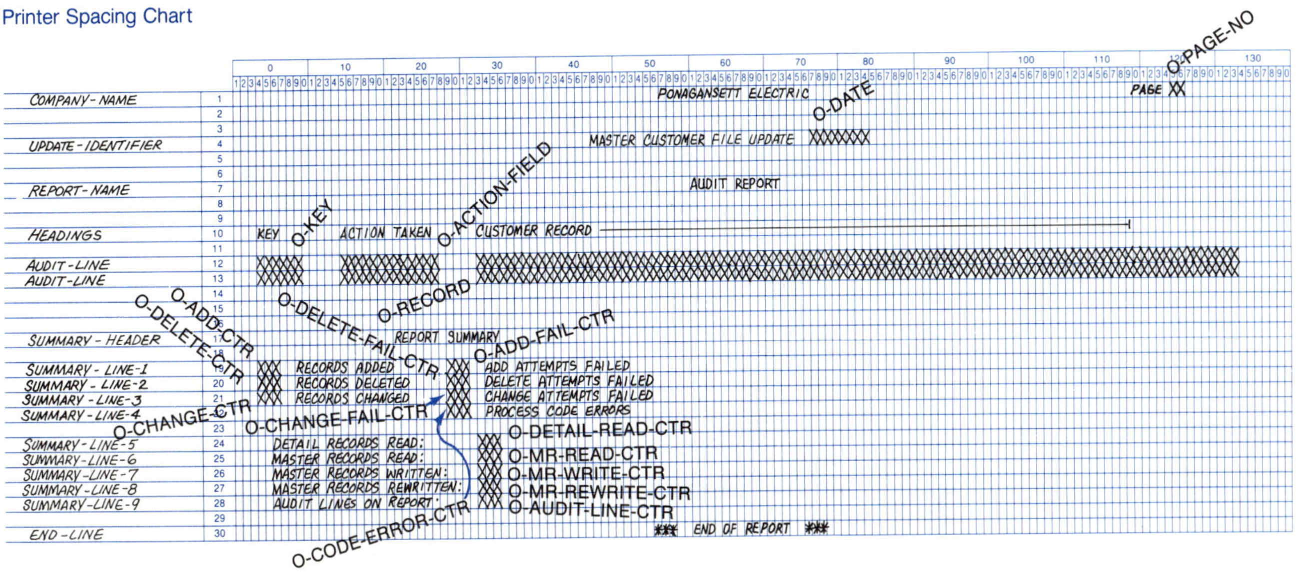

Programming Exercise III

The data processing department of the Ponagansett Electric Company must prepare a program designed to update its master customer file. The master file has indexed organization, and its prime record key is the customer number. Two alternate record keys were also specified when the file was created. The first of these is the customer meter number, without duplicates, and the second is the customer name, with duplicates.

Each master record contains the following data:

cc 1–2	Record code (CM for Customer Master)
cc 3–10	Customer meter number
cc 11–13	Customer rate code
cc 14–19	Customer number
cc 20–39	Customer name
cc 40–64	Customer street address
cc 65–87	Customer city, state, and zip code
cc 88–100	Not used

The program must provide for the addition to the master file of new customer records, for the deletion of records from the file for customers who have left the area, and for the updating of current customer records. Updating of current records is limited to changes in the meter number field, the name field, the address field, and the rate code field.

A detail record is prepared for each customer featured in the master file update. The layout of the detail record is as follows:

cc 1	Process code ("1", "2", or "3")
cc 2–9	Customer meter number
cc 10–12	Electric rate code (A10, A11, A12, or C–2)
cc 13–18	Customer number
cc 19–38	Customer name
cc 39–63	Customer street address
cc 64–86	Customer city, state, and zip code

The process code "1" denotes that a record must be added to the master file, the process code "2" denotes that a master record must be deleted from the master file, and the process code "3" denotes that a current master record must be updated.

The program must update the master customer file, and it must produce an audit report formatted as shown in Figure 3.52.

Use the current date as the report date, Data Set 3X3-I as the detail file, and Data Set 3X3-II as the master customer file. (*Note:* The master customer file must be made available to the program as an *indexed file*!)

Figure 3.53 Printer spacing chart for the audit report

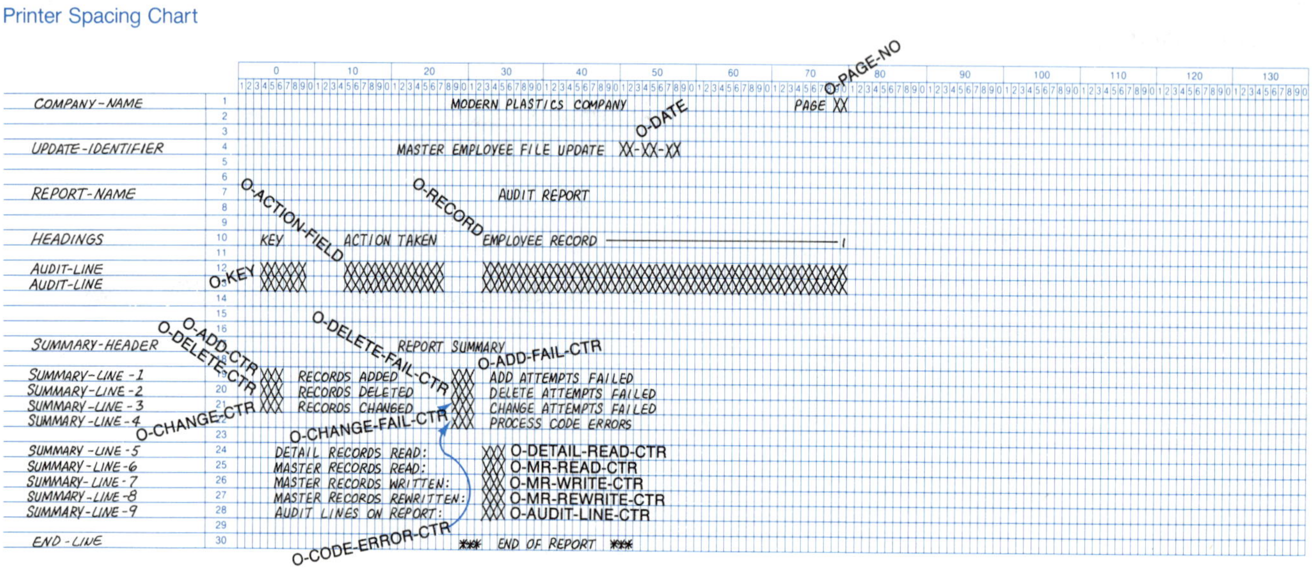

Programming Exercise IV

The master employee file of the Modern Plastics Company must be updated. Over the past few weeks, new employees have been hired, other employees have left their employment, and still other employees require changes to their records. Some have been transferred from one department to another (within the same plant or to another plant), others have had raises in their pay rates, and others have made changes to the number of exemptions they wish to claim for income tax withholdings.

For each employee involved in the master file update, a detail record has been prepared and stored in a detail file. The detail record is formatted as follows:

cc 1	Process code ("1", "2", or "3")
cc 2–3	Plant number (new employees, changes)
cc 4–5	Department number (new employees, changes)
cc 6–14	Employee Social Security number (all records)
cc 15–34	Employee name (new employees only)
cc 35–38	Pay rate (format: xx.xx) (new employees, changes)
cc 39	Number of exemptions claimed (new employees, changes)
cc 40–45	Date hired

Every detail record contains a process code and the employee Social Security number. A process code of "1" denotes a new employee record, a process code of "2" denotes an employee record that must be deleted from the master file, and a process code of "3" denotes an employee record that needs changes in one or more of its data fields. If the process code is "1", the other data fields necessarily contain values, if the process code is "2", the other data fields do not contain values, and if the process code is "3", only the data fields that must be updated contain values.

The master employee file has indexed organization, and its prime record key is the Social Security number field. The file has one alternate record key, namely, the employee name field. Each master record contains the following data:

cc 1–2	Record code (EM for Employee Master)
cc 3–4	Plant number
cc 5–6	Department number
cc 7–15	Employee Social Security number
cc 16–35	Employee name
cc 36–39	Pay rate (format: xx.xx)
cc 40	Number of exemptions claimed
cc 41–46	Date hired

The program that updates the file must also produce an audit report, formatted as shown in Figure 3.53.

Use the current date as the run date, Data Set 3X4-I as the detail file, and Data Set 3X4-II as the master employee file. (*Note:* The master employee file must be made available to the program as an *indexed file*!)

4 Relative Files

Up to this point in your study of COBOL, you have worked with the two most common file organizations, sequential and indexed. Recall that the records of a sequential file must be processed sequentially, whereas the records of an indexed file may be processed either sequentially or randomly. The flexibility that exists in processing the records of an indexed file is achieved by specifying a record key whose value uniquely identifies a record. For each record, this record key value and a pointer indicating the location of the record within the file are stored in an index record. Since all index records are stored in an index block on the disk, the full utilization of the disk for storing data records is compromised to a degree, and since accessing a record requires searching the index records first, actual record access time is increased. ANSI COBOL supports another file organization that does not require reserving a portion of disk space for record indexes and that allows direct access to the data records themselves. It is known as *relative file organization.* Theoretically, the disk space allocated to a relative file is totally formatted to store data records and consequently, disk space is used more efficiently, and a key value associated with a record, known as the record's relative key value (or as the relative record number), is used to directly access the record in the file. ■

Objectives You Should Achieve

After studying this chapter, you should

1. Be able to explain the term "relative organization."
2. Be able to explain the term RELATIVE KEY.
3. Be able to explain how to format a relative file sequentially.
4. Be able to explain how to format a relative file randomly.
5. Be able to explain how to load a relative file sequentially if it has been formatted sequentially.
6. Be able to explain how to load a relative file randomly if it has been formatted sequentially.
7. Be able to explain how to load a relative file sequentially if it has been formatted randomly.
8. Be able to explain how to load a relative file randomly if it has been formatted randomly.
9. Given adequate information about records that must ultimately be loaded into a relative file, be able to determine if it is feasible and reasonable to directly use the value of a particular data field of the records as the record's relative key.
10. Given the access mode and open mode for a relative file, be able to identify the correct form of I/O statements that may be used to reference the file.
11. Given a randomization procedure that must be used to generate the relative key for a record and the record's key field value, be able to compute the record's relative key value.
12. Given a programming problem in which a file must be formatted sequentially, be able to design the program and implement the design to successful completion.
13. Given a programming problem in which a file must be formatted randomly, be able to design the program and implement the design to successful completion.
14. Given a programming problem in which a formatted relative file must be loaded sequentially, and in which an audit report must be produced, be able to design the program and implement the design to successful completion.
15. Given a programming problem in which a formatted relative file must be loaded randomly, in which a relative key value can be obtained without the use of a transformation procedure, and in which an audit report must be produced, be able to design the program and implement the design to successful completion.
16. Given a programming problem in which a formatted relative file must be loaded randomly, in which a randomization procedure is needed to produce a record's relative key value, and in which an audit report must be produced, be able to design the program and implement the design to successful completion.
17. Given a programming problem in which a relative file must be updated, in which a randomization procedure may or may not be required to produce a record's relative key value, and in which an audit report must be produced, be able to design the program and implement the design to successful completion.

Figure 4.1 Sample formatted file

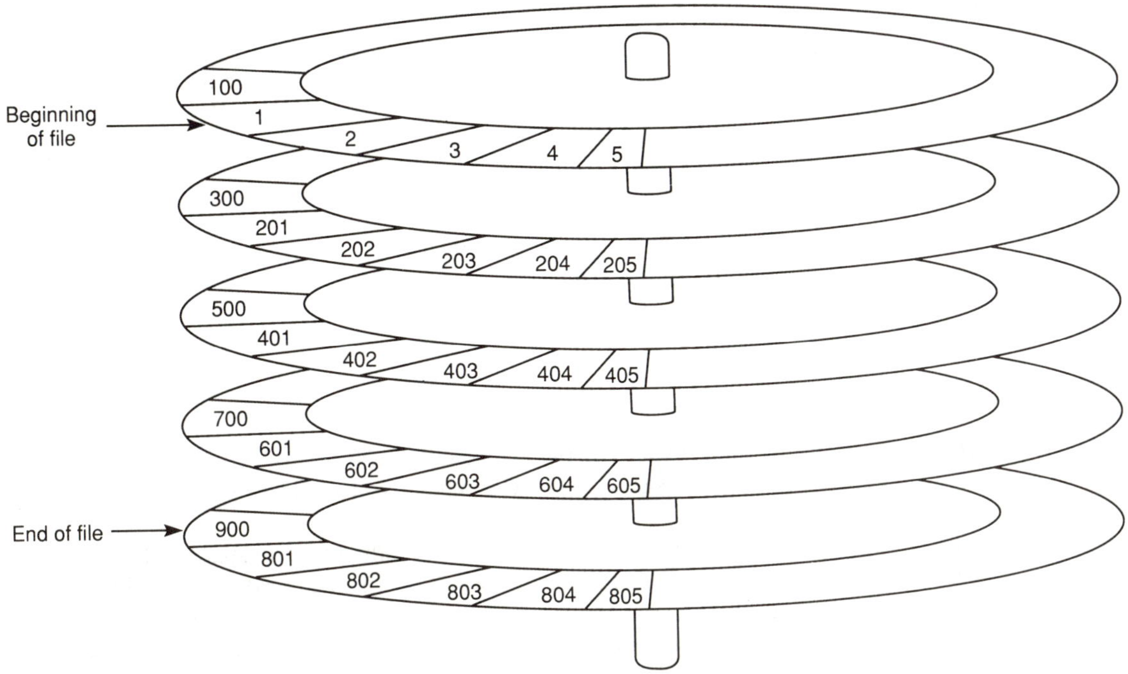

Characteristics of a Relative File

Let's suppose that we need to convert a sequential file to a file with relative organization. Assume that the file will never contain more than 1000 records and that the size of each record is 100 characters. The first task is to format the allocated disk space, that is, separate the disk space into 1000 record areas, each of size 100. These record areas exist in some physical serial sequence on the disk, so that they can be referred to in terms of their "relative" position in the file. That is, there is a first record area, a second record area, a third record area, . . . , and a 1000th record area. As an example, Figure 4.1 shows the file formatted within one cylinder of a disk pack, with 100 record areas per track. Since there are tracks on both surfaces of a disk (or platter), only five disks are needed to completely format the file.

Note that corresponding to each record area there is an ordinal number that specifies its location on the disk relative to the beginning of the file. In an actual file, this ordinal number not only identifies a record area, but it is also the ***relative key*** value for the record, if it exists, that is stored in the area. Specifically, the relative key value for the record stored in record area #1 of a relative file is 1, the relative key value for the record stored in record area #5 is 5, the relative key value for the record stored in record area #50 is 50, the relative key value for the record stored in record area #1000 is 1000. It is not necessary that every record area contain a logical record. There may be many empty record areas, and they may exist anywhere in the file. Preceding every record area, there is a 1-byte field (a flag) that indicates whether or not the record area contains a valid record.

In general, a relative file may be formatted either by using sequential access or by using random access. In sequential-access formatting, a logical record is explicitly written into each record area of the file, whereas in random access, a logical record is explicitly written only into selected record areas. In random-access formatting, the record areas with relative numbers less than the relative number of an explicitly written record are automatically created but do not contain valid logical records. These two procedures are explained briefly on page 252 and are illustrated in Figure 4.2.

Figure 4.2 Formatting a relative file

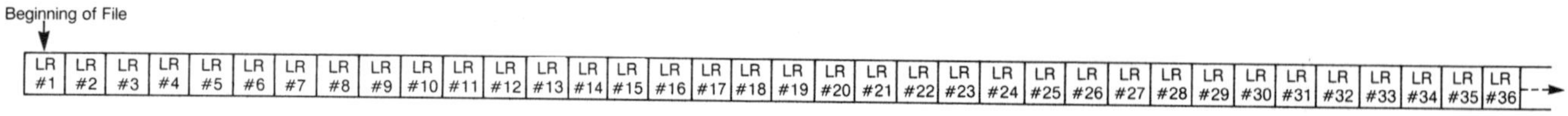

a. Sequential Formatting: Logical record (LR) inserted into each record area

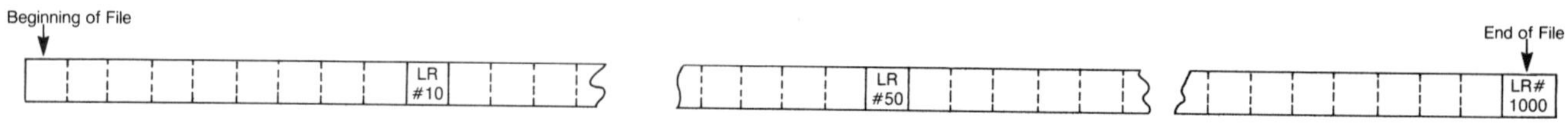

b. Random Formatting: Logical record (LR) inserted into some record areas randomly

Sequential-Access Formatting

In this procedure,

1. The SELECT statement for the file specifies the clause ORGANIZATION IS RELATIVE and the clause ACCESS MODE IS SEQUENTIAL, explicitly or by default.
2. The file is open in OUTPUT mode.
3. The record area may be assigned dummy values or it may be initialized to spaces. (If actual data records were copied to the record areas, the file would be "loaded" rather than simply "formatted." Formatting generally precedes loading for reasons that will become clear later.)
4. The WRITE statement is executed *n* times, where *n* is the number of record areas the file must contain. Records are stored sequentially in the file, and their relative numbers are respectively 1 through *n*. Every record area contains a logical record, namely, the one stored in it by the WRITE statement. See part a of Figure 4.2.

Random-Access Formatting

In this procedure,

1. The SELECT statement for the file specifies the clause ORGANIZATION IS RELATIVE, the clause ACCESS MODE IS RANDOM, and the clause RELATIVE KEY IS relative-key-data-item.
2. The relative key data item specified in the RELATIVE KEY clause is defined as an unsigned integer item, generally in the WORKING-STORAGE SECTION.
3. The file is open in OUTPUT mode.
4. The record area may be assigned dummy values or initialized to spaces.
5. The relative key data item is assigned a value before the WRITE statement is executed. For instance, if it is assigned the value 50, the WRITE statement writes a logical record in record area 50, and record areas 1 through 49 are automatically created but contain no valid record. If the relative key data item is then assigned the value 10, the WRITE statement writes a logical record in record area 10. If it is then assigned the value 1000, the WRITE statement extends the file to 1000 record areas and writes a logical record in record area 1000. At this point, the file contains 1000 record areas, but only three logical records, one in record area 10, one in record area 50, and one in record area 1000.

If the file formatted with sequential access is read sequentially, a logical record is found in each record area. If the file formatted with random access is read sequentially, a logical record is found only in record areas 10, 50, and 1000. The flag that precedes empty record areas causes the read function to skip over them!

In our current example, once the relative file has been formatted, the task of loading the records from the sequential file into the relative file may be completed. However, the loading procedures that must be used are directly related to the access mode that was selected to format the file. We examine the two distinct procedures briefly.

Figure 4.3 Loading a relative file using sequential access

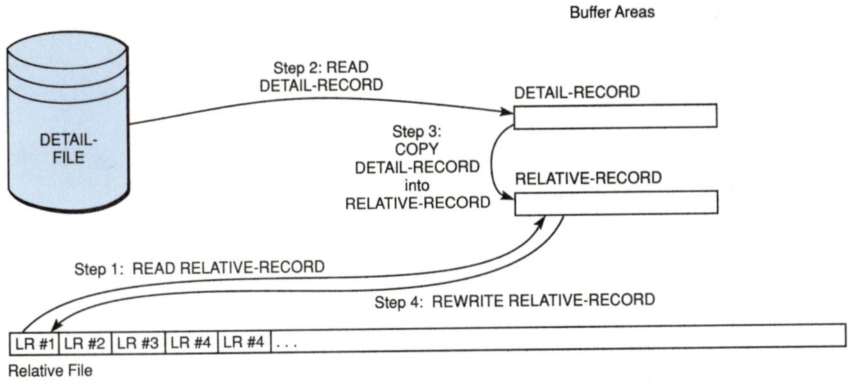

Loading a Relative File Formatted with Sequential Access

A relative file formatted sequentially contains a logical record, albeit a "dummy" record, in each record area. Consequently, any attempt to WRITE a second record in any of these record areas will fail. The record in the target record area must first be read, the data from the input record is then copied into the relative record, and the updated relative record is then rewritten to the file using the REWRITE statement. See Figure 4.3.

Ideally in our example, the records of the sequential file contain a field whose value is unique to a record, is in the range from 1 to 1000, and thus can be used as the relative key for the record. Let's call this "ideal" field I-RECORD-ID. Under these conditions, the most efficient way of loading these records into the relative file is as follows:

1. Sort the sequential file in ascending order by the value in the field I-RECORD-ID. This is the order in which the records are to be stored in the relative file.
2. In the SELECT statement for the relative file, specify ORGANIZATION IS RELATIVE, and specify the access mode as sequential.
3. Open the relative file in I-O mode.
4. Read a relative file record.
5. Read a sequential file record and copy its contents into the record currently in the relative file's buffer.
6. Use the REWRITE statement to rewrite the reconstructed relative record back to the relative file.
7. Repeat steps 4, 5, and 6 until there are no more records in the sequential file, a total of 1000 times in our current example.

Loading a Relative File Formatted with Random Access

A relative file formatted randomly does not necessarily contain a valid record in each record area. If a record area is empty, a data record may be written to it by using the WRITE statement. If a record area is not empty, the record it contains must first be accessed by a READ statement. Its contents are then replaced by the contents of the input data record, and the reconstructed relative record is then rewritten to the relative file using the REWRITE statement.

With this method, the sequential file in our example does not have to be presorted. Its records will be loaded into the relative file randomly. The program must accomplish the following:

1. In the SELECT statement for the relative file, specify the clauses ORGANIZATION IS RELATIVE, ACCESS MODE IS RANDOM, and RELATIVE KEY IS relative-key-data-item. Suppose that the relative key data item is WS-LOCATION-NO.
2. Open the relative file in I-O mode.
3. Read a sequential file record, and move the value of I-RECORD-ID to WS-LOCATION-NO.

Figure 4.4 Loading a relative file using random access

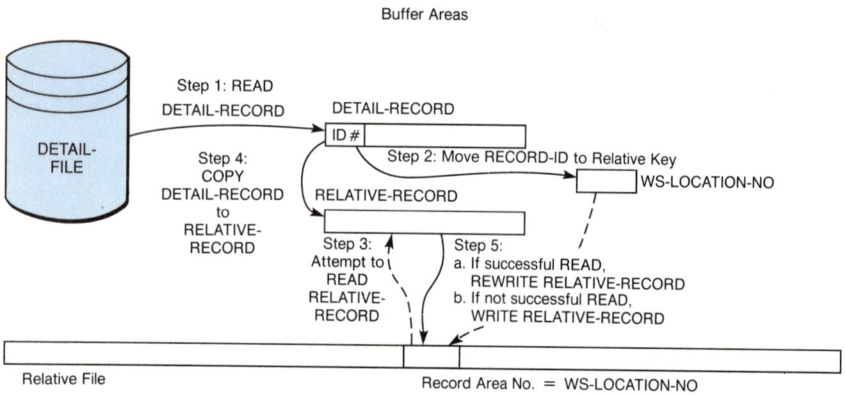

4. Attempt to read the relative file record stored in the record area specified by the relative key WS-LOCATION-NO.
   a. If the read function is successful, it's because that record area contains a logical record. The data on the sequential file record is copied into the relative record, and the reconstructed relative record is then rewritten to the file using the REWRITE statement.
   b. If the read function is not successful, it's because that record area is empty. Consequently, the data on the sequential file record is copied into the relative file buffer, and the WRITE statement is used to write this new record to the relative file.
5. Steps 3 and 4 are repeated until there are no more records in the sequential file. See Figure 4.4.

Once a relative file has been created, that is, formatted and loaded with "real" records, it may be updated by

1. Writing new records into empty record areas, provided of course that the record area number is the relative key for the new record.
2. Deleting records from the file, thereby creating new empty record areas.
3. Replacing data on existing records with new values.

There are two main advantages to relative file organization: first, it makes more efficient use of disk space, provided the number of empty record areas is not excessive; second, records can be accessed more quickly, since there is no need to search an index block to find the location of the record in the file.

In view of the advantages of the relative file organization, it is reasonable to ask why it is not used to a greater extent. One reason is that few files have records with a distinctive field whose values can be used directly as relative keys. In most cases, a field value that uniquely corresponds to a record cannot be used directly to specify a relative position in the file. The value has to be transformed by some procedure, called a *randomization technique,* the result of which can be used as a relative key value. (Some randomization procedures will be examined later in the chapter.) A simple example is a Social Security number field. The value uniquely identifies a record but can hardly be used as an ordinal number, that is, a relative key value, in the range from 1 to *n,* where *n* is the number of record areas in the file. Furthermore, a transformation formula will usually produce the same relative key value for more than one record, thus complicating the process of determining a unique ordinal number for each record.

Even in those cases in which records of a file do contain a field whose value can be used as an ordinal number, the way these numbers are designed often leaves "gaps" in the number sequences. For instance, suppose the product file of a manufacturing company contains a record for each product, and the record contains a product code designed as shown in Figure 4.5.

It's obvious that many of the numbers in the range from 00000001 to 07069999 will never be used as product codes. If the product codes are used to position a record within the relative file, then many of the record areas within the file will never be used to store actual records. As a result, much of the disk space is wasted, thereby making the relative file organization an inefficient one for this kind of situation.

Figure 4.5 Sample record layout with key field PRODUCT-CODE

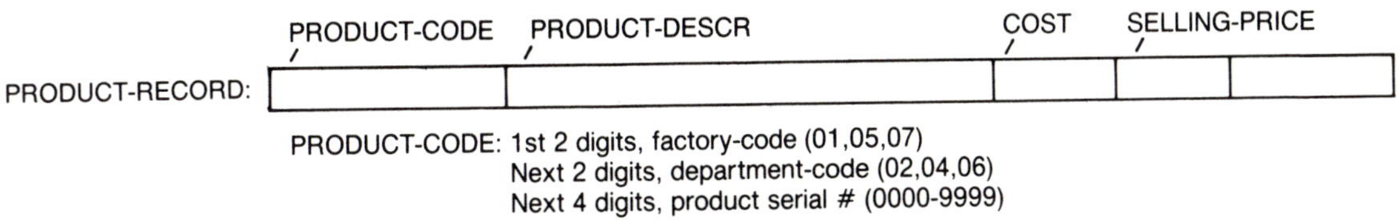

Figure 4.6 Sample record layout with key field CLIENT-NUMBER

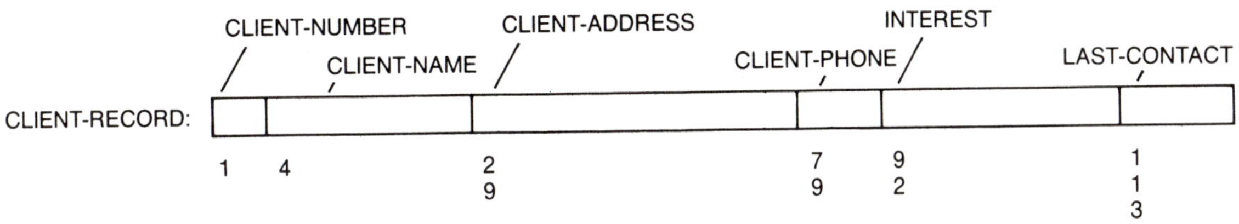

In spite of the difficulties that may be encountered in the use of the relative file organization, we will proceed to illustrate some of its basic concepts, because in those cases where relative organization is appropriate, it provides direct and very efficient access to the relative records.

There are many other file organizations in use in the business world. They are not supported by the COBOL standard but rather are provided as extensions to the standard by the computer manufacturer or vendor to take advantage of a computer's unique architecture. We will not examine any of these.

Creating a File with Relative Organization

As a first example of a relative file, we consider the simplest case possible, namely, that in which each record of the file contains a field whose value is the relative key for the record.

Problem 1

The PR-Consultants Company keeps a file on its clients. Clients have been numbered consecutively as they occur. The company management wants to reorganize the file as a relative file. It intends to process the file sequentially whenever all the clients have to be notified of certain events but wants to access records directly whenever activities involve individual clients.

For the sake of simplicity, assume that there are no more than 10 clients initially, and the file will be set up to accommodate up to 100 client records. The layout of a client record is shown in Figure 4.6. The size of each record is 120 characters.

Brief Analysis of the Problem

From the preceding discussion of relative files, it is clear that the first task is to format the new file, and the second task is to load the client records into it. The file may be formatted sequentially or randomly. The choice is made to format it sequentially. Each record area will receive a dummy record consisting of spaces, except for the field CLIENT-NUMBER, which is assigned zeros.

Since the formatting takes place exclusively on magnetic media, a hard-copy evidence of the process will be provided in the form of an audit report. The report will show the relative key value and the contents of the dummy record stored in every tenth record area, beginning with the first. It will also give a count of the number of record areas in the file.

Figure 4.7 System flowchart to format the client relative file

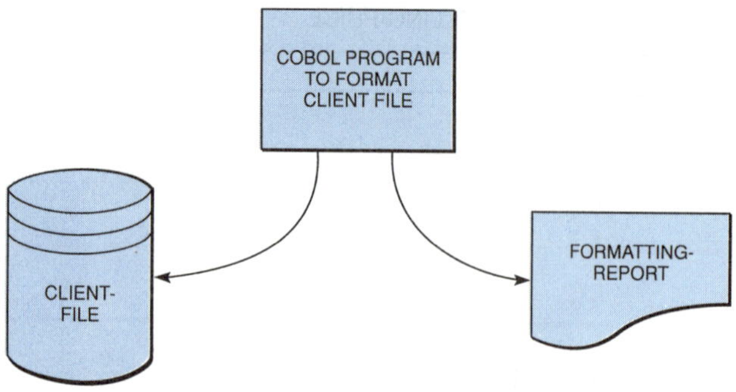

Figure 4.8 Printer spacing chart for the formatting task report

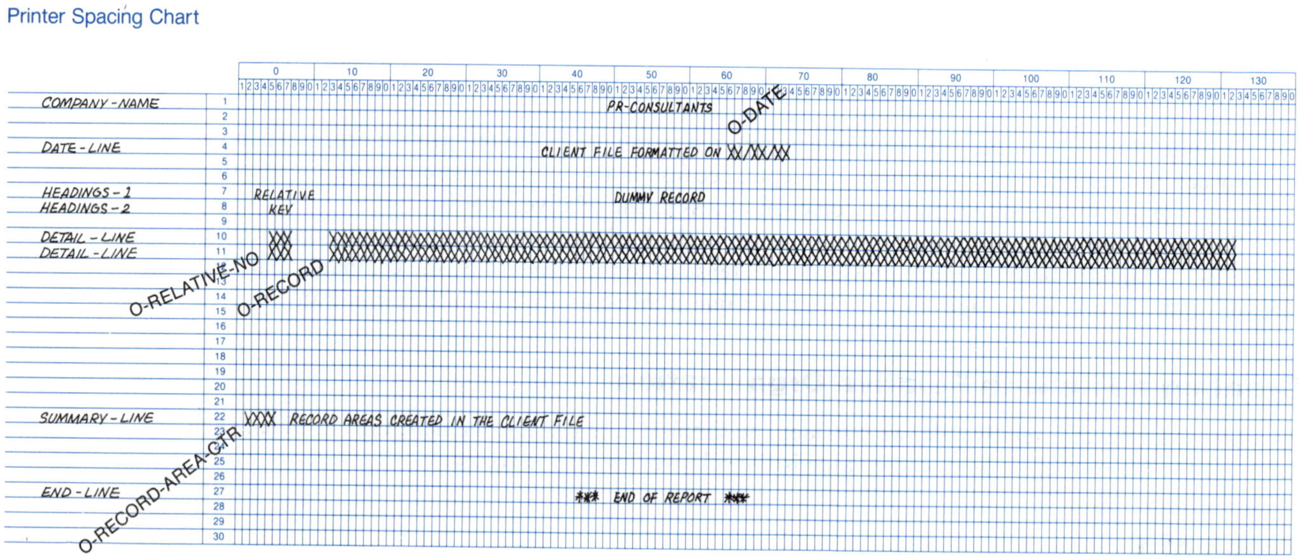

The system flowchart for this task is shown in Figure 4.7, and the printer spacing chart for the report is shown in Figure 4.8. Note that there is no input file for this task, but two output files must be produced, namely, the formatted relative file CLIENT-FILE and the print file FORMATTING-REPORT.

Though the printer spacing chart reserves 120 print positions for a dummy record, only the first three positions will contain printable characters, namely the zeros assigned to the client number field. The remaining characters are all spaces. The dummy record's relative number is obtained from the relative key data item named in the RELATIVE KEY clause of the SELECT statement for the file CLIENT-FILE. This data item will be named WS-LOCATION-NO. **When the access mode is sequential, the operating system automatically stores the record's relative number in the relative key data item when the WRITE statement is executed!**

Since a summary line must indicate the total number of record areas formatted on the file, a counter must be incremented every time a dummy record is written to the file. We will name this counter RECORD-AREA-CTR.

The structure chart for the program is shown in Figure 4.9. Module 200 START UP will open the two files, obtain the date from the system, prepare the standard dummy record, and begin the printed report. Module 210 FORMAT RECORD AREA must be executed a total of 100 times. Within this loop, a test must be performed to determine when a detail line is to be printed on the report. Recall that only every tenth dummy record is to be printed! The test and the steps needed to print a detail line will be contained in module 310 WRITE DETAIL LINE. The printing of the summary line and the end-of-report message will be under the control of module 220 FINISH UP.

The program pseudocode that details the steps needed in the formatting task is the following.

100-Format-Client-File.

1. Perform 200-Start-Up.
2. Perform 210-Format-Record-Area varying record-area-counter from an initial value of 1, and incrementing it by 1 until record-area-counter is greater than 100 or until client-file-flag = "24".
3. Perform 220-Finish-Up.
4. Stop the run.

200-Start-Up.

1. Open the file Client-File and the file Formatting-Report as output files.
2. Obtain the date from the operating system.
3. Move date to Date-Line date.
4. Move spaces to the record areas Client-Record and Detail-Line.
5. Move zeros to Client-Record client-number.
6. Initialize print-number.
7. Move Client-Record to Detail-Line record area.
8. Perform 300-Write-Report-Headers.

210-Format-Record-Area.

1. Write Client-Record to Client-File and test for invalid key:
   a. If invalid key, set client-file-flag to "24", and display "Error Writing to Record Area " location-number.
   b. If not invalid key, perform 310-Write-Detail-Line.

220-Finish-Up.

1. Subtract 1 from record-area-counter.
2. Move record-area-counter to Summary-Line record-area-counter.
3. Move the record Summary-Line to the output area Printline.
4. After advancing 4 lines, write the output record Printline.
5. Move the record End-Line to the output area Printline.
6. After advancing 4 lines, write the output record Printline.
7. Close Client-File and Formatting-Report.

300-Write-Report-Headers.

1. Move the record Company-Name to the output area Printline.
2. After advancing to a new page, write the output record Printline.
3. Move the record Date-Line to the output area Printline.
4. After advancing 3 lines, write the output record Printline.
5. Move the record Headings-1 to the output area Printline.
6. After advancing 3 lines, write the output record Printline.
7. Move the record Headings-2 to the output area Printline.
8. After advancing 1 line, write the output record Printline.
9. Move 2 to proper-spacing.

310-Write-Detail-Line.

1. Test record-area-counter.
   If it is equal to 10 times print-number plus 1, do the following:
   a. Move location-number to Detail-Line relative-number.
   b. Move Detail-Line to the output area Printline.
   c. After advancing proper-spacing, write the output record Printline.
   d. Move 1 to proper-spacing.
   e. Add 1 to print-number.

Figure 4.9 Structure chart to format the client file

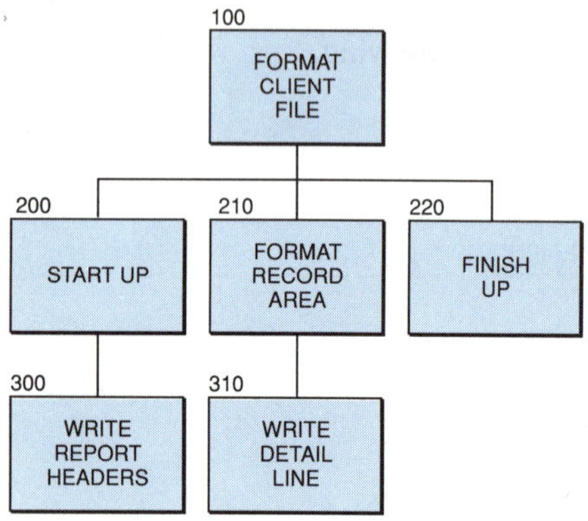

The program flowchart corresponding to the pseudocode is shown in Figure 4.10.

In the primary paragraph, note that the procedure 210-Format-Record-Area is executed until the counter record-area-counter is greater than 100 or until the status flag client-file-flag indicates a write error caused by an invalid key condition. Such a condition should not occur, but if it ever does, an error message will be displayed and the formatting will be terminated. In either case, when control leaves the loop, the number of record areas created in the file is 1 less than the value of record-area-counter.

In paragraph 200-Start-Up, steps 4 and 5 prepare the dummy record that will be written repeatedly to the file Client-File. The data item print-number is used in the procedure 310-Write-Detail-Line to print every tenth record written to the file. (Note the formula in paragraph 310: record-area-counter = 10 * print-number + 1.)

In paragraph 210-Format-Record-Area, it is important to understand that the dummy records are being written sequentially to the file, and as such, the relative key data item location-number is not used *prior* to the WRITE statement to indicate the record area being written to. On the other hand, the execution of the sequential WRITE statement causes the system to store the current record area number into the relative key data item location-number. In paragraph 310-Write-Detail-Line, this is the source of the value assigned to the field Detail-Line relative-number.

Figure 4.10 Program flowchart to format the client file

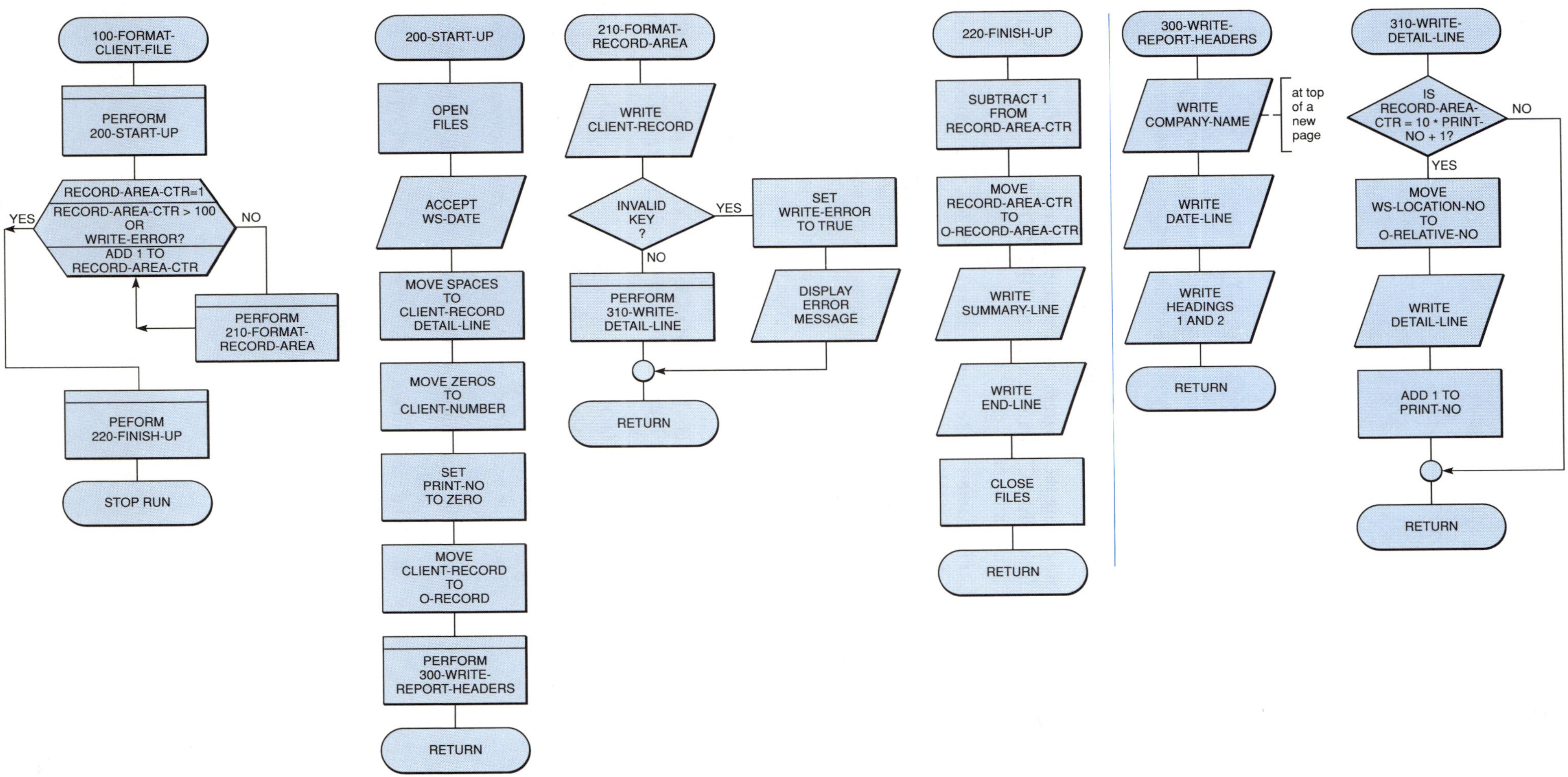

■ **Figure 4.11** FILE-CONTROL paragraph entries for relative files

```
SELECT [OPTIONAL] file-name-1

    ASSIGN TO {implementor-name-1}
              {literal-1         }

  [RESERVE integer-1 [AREA ]]
                     [AREAS]

  [ORGANIZATION IS] RELATIVE

  [                  {SEQUENTIAL [RELATIVE KEY IS data-name-1]}]
  [ACCESS MODE IS    {{RANDOM }                               }]
  [                  {{DYNAMIC} RELATIVE KEY IS data-name-1   }]

  [FILE STATUS IS data-name-2]
```

Coding the Formatting Program

Before coding the program, we examine the program entries that are related to relative files. The first one is the SELECT statement in the FILE-CONTROL paragraph. Its format is shown in Figure 4.11.

In this format,

1. *File-name-1* is the internal name of the file, and it must be defined in an FD entry of the FILE SECTION.
2. The word OPTIONAL may be specified only for files opened in input mode, and it must be specified for input files that need not be present when the program is run.
3. *Implementor-name-1* is the name of a system-specific device that connects the internal file with an external file. The device must be a direct-access storage device.
4. *Literal-1* is a file specification or a logical name used in connecting the internal file with an external file. The file must reside on a direct-access storage device, and the logical name must be defined so as to correspond to a direct-access storage device.
5. The RESERVE clause specifies the number of buffers in main memory that must be reserved for the file. If it is not used, the operating system supplies a default value.
6. The clause ORGANIZATION IS RELATIVE specifies the file's logical structure as a relative file. Once a file is created as a relative file, its organization cannot be changed for the life of the file.
7. The ACCESS MODE clause specifies the order in which the records of the file must be accessed. If the clause is not coded, the access mode is sequential by default.
   a. If the access mode is SEQUENTIAL, the records of the file are accessed in ascending order by the relative key value.
   b. If the access mode is RANDOM, the value currently stored in the relative key data item indicates the record to be accessed.
   c. If the access mode is DYNAMIC, the records of the file may be accessed sequentially or randomly.
   d. If the access mode is SEQUENTIAL, the RELATIVE KEY clause is optional unless a START statement referencing the relative file is to be executed. In that case, the KEY clause is required, and the value of *data-name-1* is used to position the file's pointer.
   e. If the access mode is RANDOM or DYNAMIC, the RELATIVE KEY clause is required, and the value of *data-name-1* indicates the record area referenced by the input/output operation.

f. If the access mode is SEQUENTIAL, the file may be open in INPUT, OUTPUT, I-O, or EXTEND mode.

g. If the access mode is RANDOM or DYNAMIC, the file may be open in INPUT, OUTPUT, or I-O mode.

8. The RELATIVE KEY clause names the file's relative key data item.

   a. *Data-name-1* is the file's relative key data item. It must be an unsigned integer data item, and its PIC clause must not contain the character P. It must not be an elementary item of a record belonging to the file.

   b. The value of *data-name-1* identifies a record's ordinal position within the file. The record in the file's first record area has an ordinal number of 1, that is, its relative key value is 1. Successive records in the file have successively higher relative key values. The record in the *n*th (or last) record area has the highest ordinal number, that is, the highest relative key value, namely, *n*.

   c. The value of *data-name-1* identifies a unique record area within the file. A record area does not necessarily contain a logical record, that is, it may be empty.

9. The FILE STATUS clause names a data item that contains the code generated by the operating system that results from an input or output operation on the file.

   a. *Data-name-3* is the name of a two-character alphanumeric data item usually defined in the WORKING-STORAGE SECTION.

   b. *Data-name-3* receives a two-digit code from the operating system subsequent to every input or output operation on the file.

   c. The value in *data-name-3* may be tested to determine the success or failure of an I/O operation on the file, as well as the cause of a failure.

In our formatting program, the SELECT statement for the relative file is as follows:

```
SELECT CLIENT-FILE  ASSIGN TO "CLIENT.DAT"
                    ORGANIZATION IS RELATIVE
                    ACCESS MODE IS SEQUENTIAL
                    RELATIVE KEY IS WS-LOCATION-NO
                    FILE STATUS IS WS-CLIENT-FILE-FLAG.
```

In this statement,

1. CLIENT.DAT is the name of the file in the user's directory that will contain the newly created relative file. This file must be stored on a direct-access storage device.
2. ORGANIZATION IS RELATIVE specifies that the file CLIENT-FILE has relative organization.
3. ACCESS MODE IS SEQUENTIAL specifies that the file's records will be accessed in ascending order by relative key value. Specifically, since the file will be open in OUTPUT mode, its records will be written in ascending order by record area number, beginning with number 1.
4. RELATIVE KEY IS WS-LOCATION-NO specifies that the data item that will contain a relative key value is WS-LOCATION-NO. In this program, WS-LOCATION-NO will receive, from the operating system, the relative key value of the record being written to the file. This is because the access mode is sequential. If the access mode were random, WS-LOCATION-NO would have to be assigned a relative key value by the program prior to the execution of the WRITE statement. The WRITE statement would then write the current record into the record area specified by WS-LOCATION-NO.

   In this program, WS-LOCATION-NO is the source for the value that will be printed on the report in the field O-RELATIVE-NO of the record DETAIL-LINE.
5. FILE STATUS IS WS-CLIENT-FILE-FLAG specifies that the input/output operation status codes generated by the system relative to the relative file CLIENT-FILE will be stored in the data item WS-CLIENT-FILE-FLAG. As with all other file status data items, WS-CLIENT-FILE-FLAG must be defined as a two-character elementary alphanumeric item. It will be

Figure 4.12 WRITE statement format

```
WRITE record-name-1 [FROM identifier-1]
      [INVALID KEY imperative-statement-1]
      [NOT INVALID KEY imperative-statement-2]
      [END-WRITE]
```

defined in the WORKING-STORAGE SECTION. In this program, since the file CLIENT-FILE is open in OUTPUT mode, the only input/output statements that will reference it are OPEN, WRITE, and CLOSE, and the most applicable status codes are the following:

"00" to denote a successful operation

"22" to denote a duplicate key (a WRITE invalid key)

"24" to denote a boundary violation or a relative key too large for the size specified for the relative key data item (a WRITE invalid key)

"30" to denote all other permanent errors

"35" to denote a file not found (in an OPEN operation)

"37" to denote an inappropriate device type (in an OPEN operation)

"42" to denote a file not open (in a CLOSE operation)

"48" to denote a file not open (in a WRITE operation)

The complete list of status codes is in Appendix C.

In this program, the only status code that is tested is "24" to denote a WRITE error. If such an error is detected, an error message is displayed and the file formatting is terminated.

The only other statement of particular interest is the WRITE statement as applied to relative files. Its format is shown in Figure 4.12.

Rules Governing the Use of the WRITE-INVALID KEY Statement for Relative Files

1. *Record-name-1* must be the name of a logical record defined in the FD entry for the file being written to.
2. *Identifier-1* is the name of a data item containing data to be transferred to *record-name-1*.
3. *Imperative-statement-1* and *imperative-statement-2* are imperative statements.
4. The INVALID KEY clause is required unless the program contains a related USE AFTER EXCEPTION procedure.
5. The file being written to must be open in OUTPUT, I-O, or EXTEND mode prior to the execution of the WRITE statement.
6. If the access mode is sequential, and the file is open in
   a. OUTPUT mode, successive records written to the file have successive relative key values of 1, 2, 3, and so on. The last record has relative key value *n*, where *n* is the number of records written to the file. Furthermore, if the SELECT statement contains the RELATIVE KEY clause, the data item named in the clause receives the relative key number of the record being written to the file.
   b. EXTEND mode, the first record written to the file has a relative key value that is one more than the highest relative key value for any record existing in the file, and records subsequently written to the file have successively higher relative key values.
7. If the access mode is random or dynamic, and the file is open in either OUTPUT mode or in I-O mode, the SELECT statement must contain the RELATIVE KEY clause, and the data item named in the clause must be assigned the relative key value of the record prior to executing the WRITE statement for that record.

8. When the execution of the WRITE statement is successful,
   a. The record is no longer available in *record-name-1*, unless the phrase SAME RECORD AREA is specified for the file.
   b. If the FROM phrase is used, the value of *identifier-1* remains unchanged.
   c. The status code "00" is stored in the data item named in the FILE STATUS clause of the SELECT statement.
   d. If the NOT INVALID KEY option is used, *imperative-statement-2* is executed and then control passes beyond the scope of the WRITE statement.
   e. If the NOT INVALID KEY option is not used, control passes to the first statement beyond the scope of the WRITE statement.
9. Execution of the WRITE statement is not successful if an invalid key condition exists. An invalid key condition occurs if
   a. An attempt is made to write a record beyond the defined file boundaries. The file status code is "24."
   b. The relative key value for the record to be written exceeds the size specified for the relative key data item. The file status code is "24."
   c. The access mode is random or dynamic and the relative key value duplicates that of a record that already exists in the file. The file status code is "22."
10. When an invalid key condition occurs,
   a. *Imperative-statement-1* is executed and control then passes beyond the scope of the WRITE statement.
   b. The FILE STATUS data item receives a code corresponding to the invalid key condition.
   c. The contents of *record-name-1* remain unchanged.

The complete formatting program is shown in Figure 4.13, and the formatting report is shown in Figure 4.14.

Figure 4.13 COBOL program to format the client file

```
 IDENTIFICATION DIVISION.

 PROGRAM-ID.      FORMAT-CLIENT-FILE.

*****************************************************************
*                                                               *
*    AUTHOR.             PAQUETTE.                              *
*    DATE WRITTEN.       JANUARY 1989.                          *
*                                                               *
*    THIS PROGRAM FORMATS A FILE WITH RELATIVE ORGANIZATION FOR *
*    THE PR-CONSULTANTS COMPANY.  IT CREATES 100 RECORD AREAS OF *
*    SIZE 120 AND ASSIGNS ZEROS TO THE CLIENT NUMBER FIELD.     *
*    THE RELATIVE KEY IS WS-LOCATION-NO.                        *
*                                                               *
*    THE AUDIT REPORT PRINTS EVERY TENTH DUMMY RECORD.          *
*                                                               *
*****************************************************************

 ENVIRONMENT DIVISION.

 CONFIGURATION SECTION.

 SOURCE-COMPUTER.  VAX-VMS-8650.
 OBJECT-COMPUTER.  VAX-VMS-8650.

 INPUT-OUTPUT SECTION.

 FILE-CONTROL.
     SELECT CLIENT-FILE          ASSIGN TO 'CLIENT.DAT'
                                 ORGANIZATION IS RELATIVE
                                 ACCESS MODE IS SEQUENTIAL
                                 RELATIVE KEY IS WS-LOCATION-NO
                                 FILE STATUS IS WS-CLIENT-FILE-FLAG.
     SELECT FORMATTING-REPORT ASSIGN TO COB$OUTPUT.

 DATA DIVISION.

 FILE SECTION.

 FD  CLIENT-FILE
     RECORD CONTAINS 120 CHARACTERS.
```

Figure 4.13 continued

```
01  CLIENT-RECORD.
    05 CLIENT-NUMBER     PIC 9(3).
    05 CLIENT-NAME       PIC X(25).
    05 CLIENT-ADDRESS    PIC X(50).
    05 CLIENT-PHONE      PIC X(13).
    05 INTEREST          PIC X(21).
    05 LAST-CONTACT      PIC X(8).

FD  FORMATTING-REPORT
    RECORD CONTAINS 133 CHARACTERS.

01  PRINTLINE            PIC X(133).

WORKING-STORAGE SECTION.

01  RELATIVE-FILE-ITEMS.
    05 WS-LOCATION-NO       PIC 9(3).
    05 WS-CLIENT-FILE-FLAG  PIC XX.
       88 WRITE-ERROR                 VALUE '24'.
    05 RECORD-AREA-CTR      PIC 9(3).

01  PROGRAM-CONTROLS.
    05 PRINT-NO                  PIC 9(3).
    05 WS-DATE                   PIC X(6).
    05 WS-PROPER-SPACING         PIC 9(1).

01  COMPANY-NAME.
    05 PIC X(49)    VALUE SPACES.
    05 PIC X(14)    VALUE 'PR-CONSULTANTS'.
    05 PIC X(70)    VALUE SPACES.

01 DATE-LINE.
    05 PIC X(40)    VALUE SPACES.
    05 PIC X(25)    VALUE 'CLIENT FILE FORMATTED ON '.
    05 O-DATE       PIC XX/XX/XX.
    05 PIC X(60)    VALUE SPACES.

01  HEADINGS-1.
    05 PIC X(2)     VALUE SPACE.
    05 PIC X(8)     VALUE 'RELATIVE'.
    05 PIC X(40)    VALUE SPACES.
    05 PIC X(12)    VALUE 'DUMMY RECORD'.
    05 PIC X(71)    VALUE SPACES.

01  HEADINGS-2.
    05 PIC X(4)     VALUE SPACES.
    05 PIC X(3)     VALUE 'KEY'.
    05 PIC X(126)   VALUE SPACES.

01  DETAIL-LINE.
    05                 PIC X(4).
    05 O-RELATIVE-NO   PIC X(3).
    05                 PIC X(5).
    05 O-RECORD        PIC X(121).

01  SUMMARY-LINE.
    05                     PIC X(1)  VALUE SPACES.
    05 O-RECORD-AREA-CTR   PIC ZZZ9.
    05                     PIC X(41) VALUE
                 ' RECORD AREAS CREATED IN THE CLIENT FILE'.
    05                     PIC X(87) VALUE SPACES.

01  END-LINE.
    05 PIC X(45)    VALUE SPACES.
    05 PIC X(23)    VALUE '*** END OF REPORT ***'.
    05 PIC X(65)    VALUE SPACES.

PROCEDURE DIVISION.

100-FORMAT-CLIENT-FILE.
    PERFORM 200-START-UP.
    PERFORM 210-FORMAT-RECORD-AREA
        VARYING RECORD-AREA-CTR FROM 1 BY 1
            UNTIL RECORD-AREA-CTR > 100 OR WRITE-ERROR.
    PERFORM 220-FINISH-UP.
    STOP RUN.
```

■ **Figure 4.13** continued

```
200-START-UP.
    OPEN OUTPUT CLIENT-FILE
                FORMATTING-REPORT.
    ACCEPT WS-DATE FROM DATE.
    MOVE WS-DATE TO O-DATE.
    MOVE SPACES TO CLIENT-RECORD
                   DETAIL-LINE.
    MOVE ZEROS TO CLIENT-NUMBER.
    INITIALIZE PRINT-NO.
    MOVE [illegible]ENT-RECORD TO O-RECORD.
    PER[illegible] 300-WRITE-REPORT-HEADERS.

210-FORMAT-RECORD-AREA.
    WRITE CLIENT-RECORD
        INVALID KEY
            SET WRITE-ERROR TO TRUE
            DISPLAY ' ERROR WRITING TO RECORD AREA
                WS-LOCATION-NO
        NOT INVALID KEY
            PERFORM 310-WRITE-DETAIL-LINE.

220-FINISH-UP.
    SUBTRACT 1 FROM RECORD-AREA-CTR.
    MOVE RECORD-AREA-CTR TO O-RECORD-AREA-CTR.
    WRITE PRINTLINE FROM SUMMARY-LINE
        AFTER ADVANCING 4 LINES.
    WRITE PRINTLINE FROM END-LINE
        AFTER ADVANCING 4 LINES.
    CLOSE CLIENT-FILE
          FORMATTING-REPORT.

300-WRITE-REPORT-HEADERS.
    WRITE PRINTLINE FROM COMPANY-NAME
        AFTER ADVANCING PAGE.
    WRITE PRINTLINE FROM DATE-LINE
        AFTER ADVANCING 3 LINES.
    WRITE PRINTLINE FROM HEADINGS-1
        AFTER ADVANCING 3 LINES.
    WRITE PRINTLINE FROM HEADINGS-2
        AFTER ADVANCING 1 LINE.
    MOVE 2 TO WS-PROPER-SPACING.

310-WRITE-DETAIL-LINE.
    IF RECORD-AREA-CTR = 10 * PRINT-NO + 1
        MOVE WS-LOCATION-NO TO O-RELATIVE-NO
        WRITE PRINTLINE FROM DETAIL-LINE
            AFTER ADVANCING WS-PROPER-SPACING
        MOVE 1 TO WS-PROPER-SPACING
        ADD 1 TO PRINT-NO
     END-IF.
```

■ **Figure 4.14** Formatting report

```
                                         PR-CONSULTANTS

                                CLIENT FILE FORMATTED ON 89/02/01

RELATIVE                                   DUMMY RECORD
  KEY

  001      000
  011      000
  021      000
  031      000
  041      000
  051      000
  061      000
  071      000
  081      000
  091      000


100  RECORD AREAS CREATED IN THE CLIENT FILE


                                     ***  END OF REPORT  ***
```

Figure 4.15 First ten client records for the PR-Consultants Company

```
001TECHNICAL CERAMICS CORP  525 HOPE ST., LINCOLN, PA 45321               (814)342-7895TV ADV.              11/30/85
002ACE LUMBER               84 SALEM AVE., CENTREDATE, PA 48160           (717)514-6621LOCAL PAPERS         12/05/85
003XTZ FILM PRODUCTIONS     24 DALE ST., PITTSBURG, PA 46010              (412)365-0053TRADE JOURNALS       12/10/85
004BEST FINANCE CORP        1350 WEST RIVER RD., CLIFTON, PA 45436        (814)941-7782TRADE JOURNALS       12/12/85
005CHACE PAINTING CO.       56 VILLA AVE., PITTSBURG, PA 46012            (412)364-5211LOCAL PAPERS         12/20/85
006ATHLETE'S ATTIC          174 WEEDEN DR., SUMMIT, PA 44912              (814)612-3741RADIO ADV.           01/05/86
007TRAVEL-PHONE             150 CAROLINA AVE., PHILADELPHIA, PA 40132     (215)743-9102TV & PAPERS          01/08/86
008CUT-RITE TREE SERVICE    240 HARRIS AVE., MOSHANON, PA 44912           (814)513-6715LOCAL PAPERS         02/15/86
009HAIR LODGE               780 MANTON AVE., PHILADELPHIA, PA 40132       (215)664-3315TV & PAPERS          02/25/86
010SOFTWARE SALES           1284 N. MAIN ST., PITTSBURG, PA 46012         (412)554-3772TRADE JOURNALS       03/20/86
```

Loading the Relative File

Now that the relative file CLIENT-FILE has been formatted, we can proceed to load the client records into the file. Assume that the records shown in Figure 4.15 for the initial 10 clients are currently in the input file DETAIL-FILE. Note that the records are in ascending order by client identification number. As a result, there are two different procedures that may be followed to load the file. One uses sequential access to the relative file CLIENT-FILE; the other uses random access.

Loading Using Sequential Access

In order to load the client records into CLIENT-FILE using sequential access, the following steps must occur:

1. Specify ACCESS MODE IS SEQUENTIAL in the file's SELECT statement.
2. Open CLIENT-FILE in I-O mode.
3. Read a CLIENT-FILE record into the file's record area in main memory and also read a DETAIL-FILE record into its file record area in main memory.
4. Move the contents of the DETAIL-FILE record area to the CLIENT-FILE record area.
5. Rewrite the CLIENT-FILE record to the file.
6. Repeat steps 3, 4, and 5 until there are no more records in DETAIL-FILE.

Note that the first read statement that references CLIENT-FILE accesses the dummy record in record area #1, since the access mode is sequential. Similarly, the first read statement that references DETAIL-FILE accesses the client record with client number equal to 1, since these records are in ascending order by client number. This is the record that must be stored in record area #1 of CLIENT-FILE. Steps 4 and 5 accomplish that.

Every time step 3 is repeated, a corresponding pair of records is accessed, and steps 4 and 5 complete the loading process.

Loading Using Random Access

Loading the records into CLIENT-FILE using random access requires the following steps:

1. Specify ACCESS MODE IS RANDOM in the file's SELECT statement.
2. Open CLIENT-FILE in I-O mode.
3. Read a DETAIL-FILE record into the record area in main memory reserved for the file DETAIL-FILE.
4. Move the value in the CLIENT-NUMBER field to the relative key data item, say WS-LOCATION-NO, and read the CLIENT-FILE record with that relative key value into the record area in main memory reserved for the file CLIENT-FILE.
5. Move the detail record values to the corresponding fields of the CLIENT-FILE record.
6. REWRITE the CLIENT-FILE record to the relative file CLIENT-FILE.

Steps 3 through 6 of the random-access loading procedure are illustrated in Figure 4.16.

Figure 4.16 Steps in loading CLIENT-FILE using random access

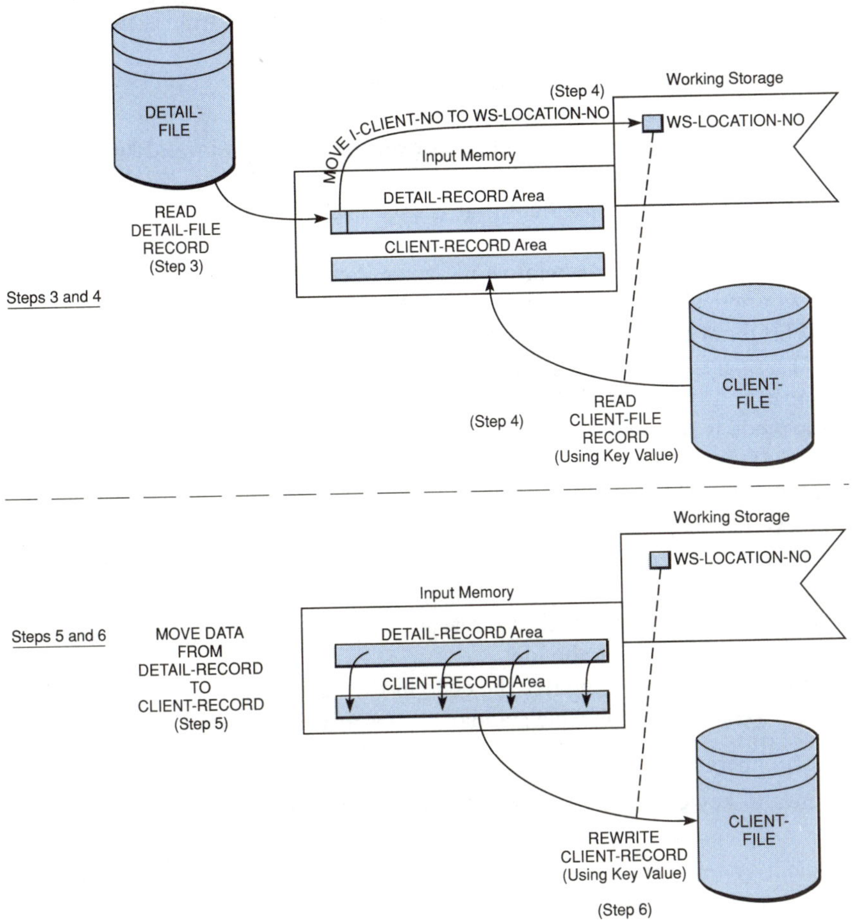

The REWRITE Statement

Note that the two approaches that may be used to load records into a relative file must rewrite the reconstructed record back to the relative file. Within the program, this function will be accomplished by executing the REWRITE statement. The format of the REWRITE-INVALID KEY statement was presented earlier in relation to indexed files. It is repeated here for your convenience, and the applicable rules follow. In particular, note that the INVALID KEY clause is required when the access mode to the file is random or dynamic, but neither KEY clause is allowed when the access mode is sequential.

```
REWRITE record-name-1 [FROM identifier-1]
        [INVALID KEY imperative-statement-1]
        [NOT INVALID KEY imperative-statement-2]
        [END-REWRITE]
```

Rules Governing the Use of the REWRITE Statement for Relative Files

1. This statement logically replaces an existing record in a file stored on a mass storage device.
2. *Record-name-1* is the name of a logical record defined in the FD for the file from which a record was previously retrieved.
3. *Identifier-1* is the name of a data item that contains the source data.
4. *Identifier-1* and *record-name-1* cannot share the same storage area.
5. *Imperative-statement-1* is an imperative statement that is executed when an invalid key condition exists.
6. *Imperative-statement-2* is an imperative statement that is executed when the REWRITE statement executes successfully.
7. The INVALID KEY clause is required for a relative file whose access mode is random or dynamic unless there is an applicable USE AFTER EXCEPTION procedure in the DECLARATIVES SECTION of the PROCEDURE DIVISION. It contains statements to be executed if the REWRITE operation is unsuccessful.
8. The INVALID KEY clause and the NOT INVALID KEY clause must not be used for a relative file whose access mode is sequential.
9. The optional NOT INVALID KEY clause contains statements to be executed whenever the REWRITE operation is successful.
10. END-REWRITE is the explicit scope terminator.
11. The file that contains *record-name-1* must be open in I-O mode, and it must be on a mass storage device.
12. If a REWRITE statement is successful, the record referenced by *record-name-1* is no longer available in the record area associated with the file.
13. The execution of a REWRITE statement updates the code in the data item named in the FILE STATUS clause for the file. The most applicable standard codes are as follows:

    "00" to denote a successful operation

    "23" to denote that an invalid key condition occurred because no record in the file has the specified key value

    "30" to denote a permanent system error

    "43" to denote no successful previous READ statement when the access mode is sequential

    "44" to denote an invalid record size

    "49" to denote an incompatible open mode or an attempt to access an unopen file

14. When an invalid key condition occurs, the record in the file is not updated and the data in the record area remains unchanged.
15. If the access mode for the relative file is sequential, the REWRITE statement replaces the record previously accessed by a successful READ statement. If the previous READ statement was unsuccessful, the execution of the REWRITE statement fails.
16. If the access mode for a relative file is random or dynamic, the record to be replaced is the one specified by the value of the data item in the RELATIVE KEY clause.

Designing the Program to Load CLIENT-FILE

Of the two available procedures to load CLIENT-FILE, we opt to use sequential access. The system flowchart is shown in Figure 4.17. Note that an audit report must be produced by the program to provide evidence that the loading procedure was executed successfully. Its printer spacing chart is shown in Figure 4.18.

The structure chart for the program is shown in Figure 4.19. Note that procedures 310 READ CLIENT RECORD and 320 READ DETAIL RECORD are always executed as a pair. Thus corresponding records from DETAIL-FILE and from CLIENT-FILE are available concurrently in main memory, as specified earlier. In module 330 PREPARE CLIENT RECORD, CLIENT-RECORD receives a copy of the contents of DETAIL-RECORD, and the updated CLIENT-RECORD is then rewritten to the file. In module 340 PREPARE AUDIT LINE, AUDIT-LINE receives a copy of the

Figure 4.17 System flowchart to load CLIENT-FILE

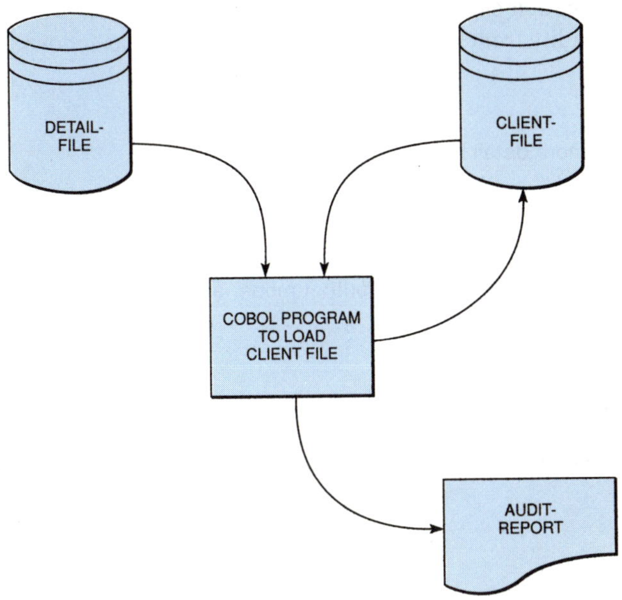

Figure 4.18 Printer spacing chart for the audit report

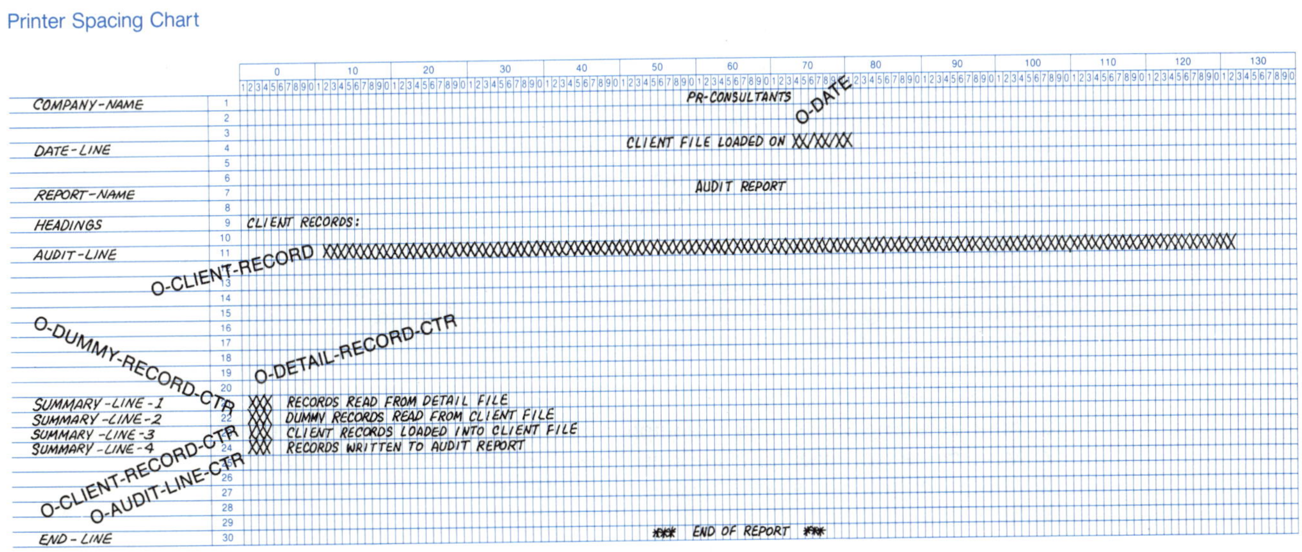

Figure 4.19 Structure chart to load CLIENT-FILE

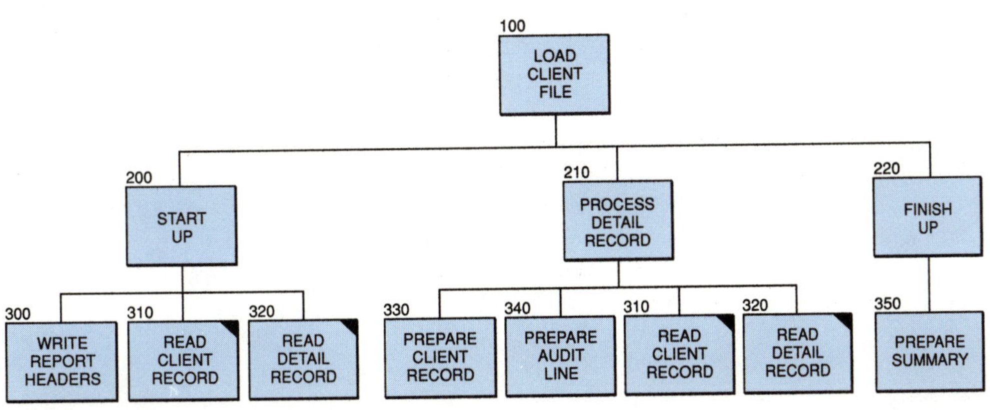

contents of DETAIL-RECORD, and it is then written to the audit report. Module 210 PROCESS DETAIL RECORD is executed repeatedly until there are no more records in DETAIL-FILE. Then, the required summary is printed, and program execution ends.

The program pseudocode can be developed readily from the preceding design tools. It is as follows.

100-Load-Client-File.

1. Perform 200-Start-Up.
2. Perform 210-Process-Detail-Record until no more detail records.
3. Perform 220-Finish-Up.
4. Stop the run.

200-Start-Up.

1. Open the file Detail-File in input mode, the file Client-File in input/output mode, and the file Audit-Report in output mode.
2. Obtain the date from the operating system.
3. Move date to Date-Line date.
4. Set the flag WS-MORE-DETAIL-RECORDS to "YES".
5. Move spaces to the record area Audit-Line.
6. Initialize the program counters: detail-record-counter, dummy-record-counter, client-record-counter, and audit-line-counter.
7. Perform 300-Write-Report-Headers.
8. Perform 310-Read-Client-Record.
9. Perform 320-Read-Detail-Record.

210-Process-Detail-Record.

1. Perform 330-Prepare-Client-Record.
2. Perform 340-Prepare-Audit-Line.
3. Perform 310-Read-Client-Record.
4. Perform 320-Read-Detail-Record.

220-Finish-Up.

1. Perform 350-Prepare-Summary.
2. Move the record End-Line to the output area Printline.
3. After advancing 4 lines, write the output record Printline.
4. Close Detail-File, Client-File, and Audit-Report.

300-Write-Report-Headers.

1. Move the record Company-Name to the output area Printline.
2. After advancing to a new page, write the output record Printline.
3. Move the record Date-Line to the output area Printline.
4. After advancing 3 lines, write the output record Printline.
5. Move the record Report-Name to the output area Printline.
6. After advancing 3 lines, write the output record Printline.
7. Move the record Headings to the output area Printline.
8. After advancing 2 lines, write the output record Printline.
9. Set proper-spacing to 2.

310-Read-Client-Record.

1. Read next record in Client-File.
2. Test for end-of-file record:
   a. If EOF record reached, move "10" to client-file-flag.
   b. If EOF record not reached, add 1 to dummy-record-counter.

320-Read-Detail-Record.

1. Read input Detail-File record.
2. Test for end-of-file record:
   a. If EOF record reached, move "NO " to the flag WS-MORE-DETAIL-RECORDS.
   b. If EOF record not reached, add 1 to detail-record-counter.

330-Prepare-Client-Record.

1. Move the record Detail-Record to the record area Client-Record.
2. Rewrite Client-Record.
3. Add 1 to client-record-counter.

340-Prepare-Audit-Line.

1. Move the record Detail-Record to Audit-Line client-record.
2. Move the record Audit-Line to the output area Printline.
3. After advancing proper-spacing, write the output record Printline.
4. Add 1 to audit-line-counter.
5. Set proper-spacing to 1.

350-Prepare-Summary.

1. Move detail-record-counter to Summary-Line-1 detail-record-counter.
2. Move the record Summary-Line-1 to the output area Printline.
3. After advancing 4 lines, write the output record Printline.
4. Move dummy-record-counter to Summary-Line-2 dummy-record-counter.
5. Move the record Summary-Line-2 to the output area Printline.
6. After advancing 1 line, write the output record Printline.
7. Move client-record-counter to Summary-Line-3 client-record-counter.
8. Move the record Summary-Line-3 to the output area Printline.
9. After advancing 1 line, write the output record Printline.
10. Move audit-line-counter to Summary-Line-4 audit-line-counter.
11. Move the record Summary-Line-4 to the output area Printline.
12. After advancing 1 line, write the output record Printline.

The program flowchart that corresponds to the pseudocode is shown in Figure 4.20.

As you examine the program in Figure 4.21, recall that the decision was made to load the client records into CLIENT-FILE sequentially. As a result, the relative key data item WS-LOCATION-NO is not used to identify the dummy record being read. Records are read sequentially from the beginning of the file. However, it is the programmer's responsibility to make sure that the records in DETAIL-FILE are in ascending order by relative key value, since the first record in DETAIL-FILE will be loaded into record area #1 of CLIENT-FILE, the second record in DETAIL-FILE will be loaded into record area #2 of CLIENT-FILE, and so on! You can verify that the ordering is correct in Figure 4.15. The audit report is shown in Figure 4.22.

■ **Figure 4.20** Program flowchart to load CLIENT-FILE

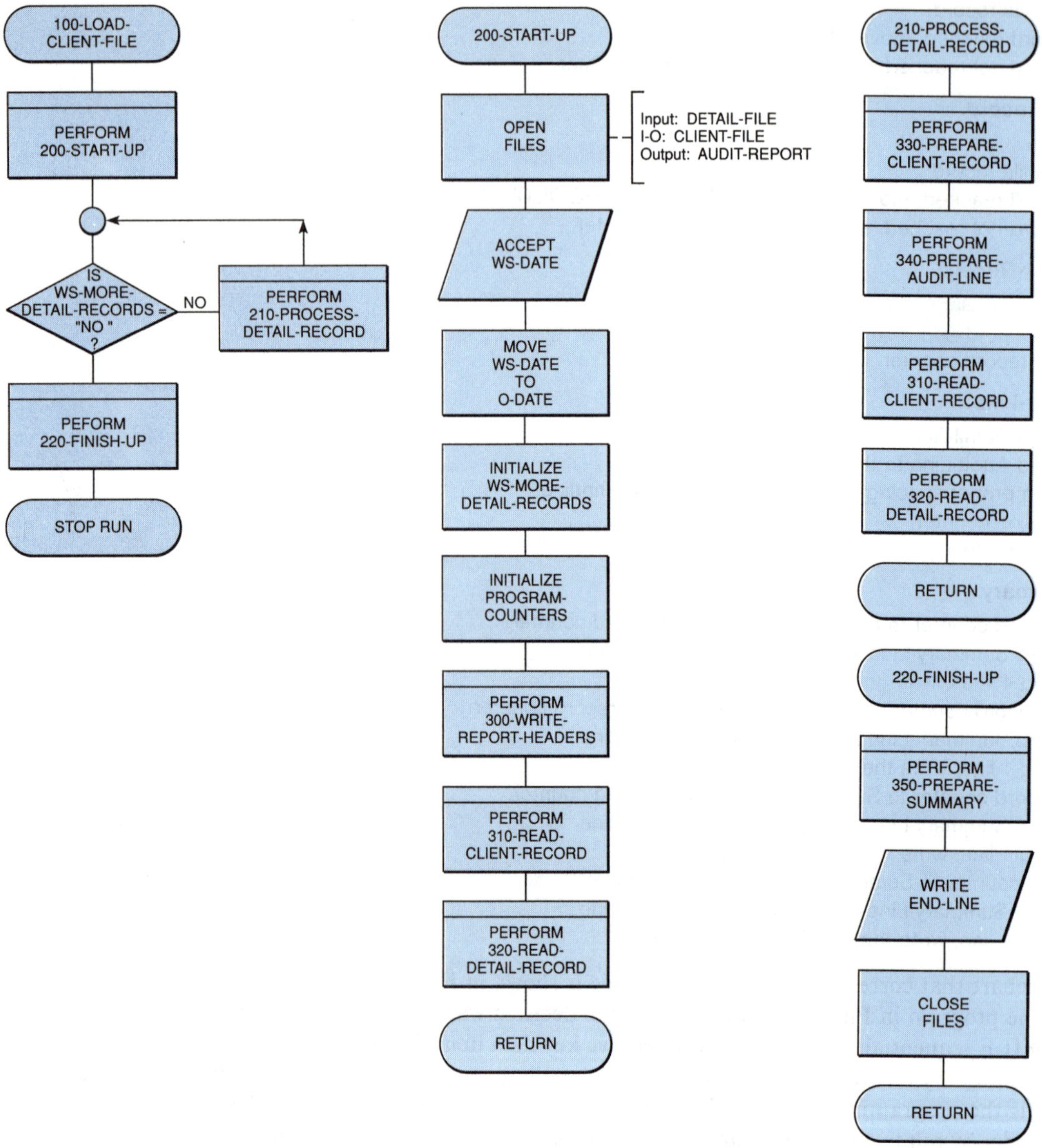

■ **Figure 4.20** continued

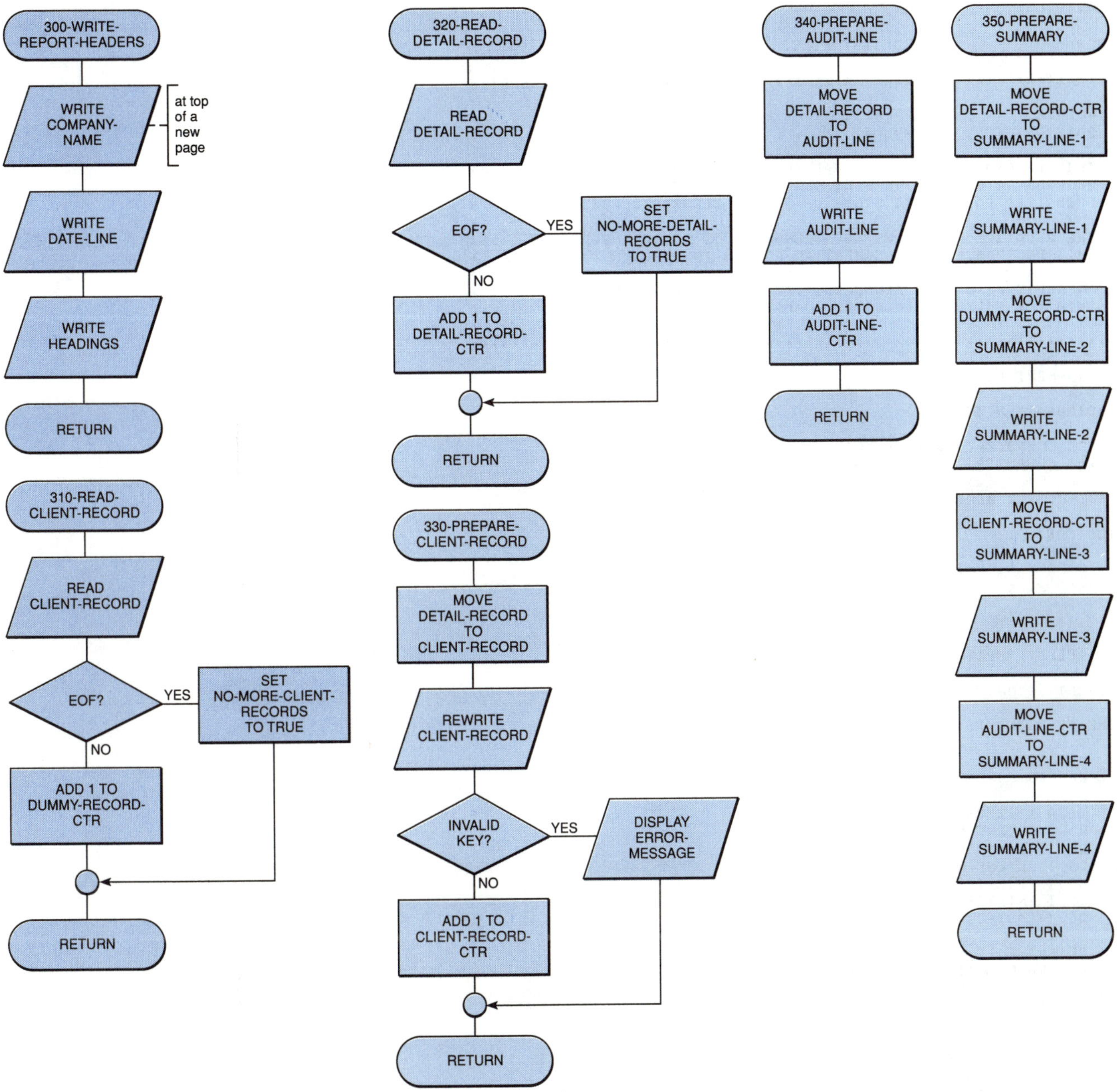

Figure 4.21 COBOL program to load CLIENT-FILE

```
 IDENTIFICATION DIVISION.

 PROGRAM-ID.      LOAD-CLIENT-FILE.

*****************************************************************
*                                                               *
*   AUTHOR.           PAQUETTE.                                 *
*   DATE WRITTEN.     JANUARY 1989.                             *
*                                                               *
*   THIS PROGRAM USES SEQUENTIAL ACCESS TO LOAD 10 CLIENT       *
*   RECORDS INTO RELATIVE FILE CLIENT-FILE.  THIS FILE WAS      *
*   FORMATTED EARLIER TO STORE UP TO 100 RECORDS OF SIZE 120.   *
*                                                               *
*   THE RELATIVE KEY IS WS-LOCATION-NO.  IT IS NOT NEEDED IN    *
*   THIS PROGRAM, SINCE SEQUENTIAL ACCESS IS USED.              *
*                                                               *
*   AN AUDIT REPORT IS PRODUCED.  IT LISTS THE RECORDS LOADED   *
*   INTO THE FILE AND PROVIDES SUMMARY INFORMATION.             *
*                                                               *
*****************************************************************
 ENVIRONMENT DIVISION.

 CONFIGURATION SECTION.

 SOURCE-COMPUTER.  VAX-VMS-8650.
 OBJECT-COMPUTER.  VAX-VMS-8650.

 INPUT-OUTPUT SECTION.

 FILE-CONTROL.
     SELECT DETAIL-FILE     ASSIGN TO COB$INPUT.
     SELECT CLIENT-FILE     ASSIGN TO 'CLIENT2.DAT'
                            ORGANIZATION IS RELATIVE
                            ACCESS MODE IS SEQUENTIAL
                            RELATIVE KEY IS WS-LOCATION-NO
                            FILE STATUS IS WS-CLIENT-FILE-FLAG.
     SELECT AUDIT-REPORT    ASSIGN TO COB$OUTPUT.

 DATA DIVISION.

 FILE SECTION.

 FD  DETAIL-FILE
     RECORD CONTAINS 120 CHARACTERS.

 01  DETAIL-RECORD.
     05 I-CLIENT-NUMBER   PIC 9(3).
     05 I-CLIENT-NAME     PIC X(25).
     05 I-CLIENT-ADDRESS  PIC X(50).
     05 I-CLIENT-PHONE    PIC X(13).
     05 I-INTEREST        PIC X(21).
     05 I-LAST-CONTACT    PIC X(8).

 FD  CLIENT-FILE
     RECORD CONTAINS 120 CHARACTERS.

 01  CLIENT-RECORD.
     05 CLIENT-NUMBER     PIC 9(3).
     05 CLIENT-NAME       PIC X(25).
     05 CLIENT-ADDRESS    PIC X(50).
     05 CLIENT-PHONE      PIC X(13).
     05 INTEREST          PIC X(21).
     05 LAST-CONTACT      PIC X(8).

 FD  AUDIT-REPORT
     RECORD CONTAINS 133 CHARACTERS.

 01  PRINTLINE            PIC X(133).

 WORKING-STORAGE SECTION.

 01  RELATIVE-FILE-ITEMS.
     05 WS-LOCATION-NO           PIC 9(3).
     05 WS-CLIENT-FILE-FLAG      PIC X(2).
        88 SUCCESSFUL                    VALUE '00'.
        88 NO-MORE-CLIENT-RECORDS        VALUE '10'.

 01  PROGRAM-CONTROLS.
     05 WS-MORE-DETAIL-RECORDS PIC X(3).
        88 NO-MORE-DETAIL-RECORDS        VALUE 'NO '.
     05 WS-DATE                  PIC X(6).
     05 WS-PROPER-SPACING        PIC 9.
```

```
01  PROGRAM-COUNTERS.
    05 WS-DETAIL-RECORD-CTR   PIC S9(3).
    05 WS-DUMMY-RECORD-CTR    PIC S9(3).
    05 WS-CLIENT-RECORD-CTR   PIC S9(3).
    05 WS-AUDIT-LINE-CTR      PIC S9(3).

01  COMPANY-NAME.
    05 PIC X(60)  VALUE SPACES.
    05 PIC X(14)  VALUE 'PR-CONSULTANTS'.
    05 PIC X(59)  VALUE SPACES.

01  DATE-LINE.
    05 PIC X(52)  VALUE SPACES.
    05 PIC X(22)  VALUE 'CLIENT FILE LOADED ON '.
    05 O-DATE     PIC XX/XX/XX.
    05 PIC X(51)  VALUE SPACES.

01  REPORT-NAME.
    05 PIC X(61)  VALUE SPACES.
    05 PIC X(12)  VALUE 'AUDIT REPORT'.
    05 PIC X(60)  VALUE SPACES.

01  HEADINGS.
    05 PIC X(2)   VALUE SPACE.
    05 PIC X(15)  VALUE 'CLIENT RECORDS:'.
    05 PIC X(116) VALUE SPACES.

01  AUDIT-LINE.
    05                  PIC X(12).
    05 O-CLIENT-RECORD  PIC X(120).

01  SUMMARY-LINES.
    05 SUMMARY-LINE-1.
       10                       PIC X(2)    VALUE SPACES.
       10 O-DETAIL-RECORD-CTR   PIC ZZ9.
       10                       PIC X(31)   VALUE
            ' RECORDS READ FROM DETAIL FILE'.
    05 SUMMARY-LINE-2.
       10                       PIC X(2)    VALUE SPACES.
       10 O-DUMMY-RECORD-CTR    PIC ZZ9.
       10                       PIC X(37)   VALUE
            ' DUMMY RECORDS READ FROM CLIENT FILE'.
    05 SUMMARY-LINE-3.
       10                       PIC X(2)    VALUE SPACES.
       10 O-CLIENT-RECORD-CTR   PIC ZZ9.
       10                       PIC X(40)   VALUE
            ' CLIENT RECORDS LOADED INTO CLIENT FILE'.
    05 SUMMARY-LINE-4.
       10                       PIC X(2)    VALUE SPACES.
       10 O-AUDIT-LINE-CTR      PIC ZZ9.
       10                       PIC X(33)   VALUE
            ' RECORDS WRITTEN TO AUDIT REPORT'.

01  END-LINE.
    05 PIC X(55)  VALUE SPACES.
    05 PIC X(23)  VALUE '***  END OF REPORT  ***'.
    05 PIC X(55)  VALUE SPACES.

PROCEDURE DIVISION.

100-LOAD-CLIENT-FILE.
    PERFORM 200-START-UP.
    PERFORM 210-PROCESS-DETAIL-RECORD
        UNTIL NO-MORE-DETAIL-RECORDS.
    PERFORM 220-FINISH-UP.
    STOP RUN.

200-START-UP.
    OPEN INPUT DETAIL-FILE
         I-O CLIENT-FILE
         OUTPUT AUDIT-REPORT.
    ACCEPT WS-DATE FROM DATE.
    MOVE WS-DATE TO O-DATE.
    MOVE 'YES' TO WS-MORE-DETAIL-RECORDS.
    MOVE SPACES TO AUDIT-LINE.
    INITIALIZE PROGRAM-COUNTERS.
    PERFORM 300-WRITE-REPORT-HEADERS.
    PERFORM 310-READ-CLIENT-RECORD.
    PERFORM 320-READ-DETAIL-RECORD.

210-PROCESS-DETAIL-RECORD.
    PERFORM 330-PREPARE-CLIENT-RECORD.
    PERFORM 340-PREPARE-AUDIT-LINE.
    PERFORM 310-READ-CLIENT-RECORD.
    PERFORM 320-READ-DETAIL-RECORD.
```

Figure 4.21 continued

```
220-FINISH-UP.
    PERFORM 350-PREPARE-SUMMARY.
    WRITE PRINTLINE FROM END-LINE
        AFTER ADVANCING 5 LINES.
    CLOSE DETAIL-FILE
          CLIENT-FILE
          AUDIT-REPORT.

300-WRITE-REPORT-HEADERS.
    WRITE PRINTLINE FROM COMPANY-NAME
        AFTER ADVANCING PAGE.
    WRITE PRINTLINE FROM DATE-LINE
        AFTER ADVANCING 3 LINES.
    WRITE PRINTLINE FROM REPORT-NAME
        AFTER ADVANCING 3 LINES.
    WRITE PRINTLINE FROM HEADINGS
        AFTER ADVANCING 2 LINES.
    MOVE 2 TO WS-PROPER-SPACING.

310-READ-CLIENT-RECORD.
    READ CLIENT-FILE NEXT RECORD
        AT END
            SET NO-MORE-CLIENT-RECORDS TO TRUE
        NOT AT END
            ADD 1 TO WS-DUMMY-RECORD-CTR.

320-READ-DETAIL-RECORD.
    READ DETAIL-FILE RECORD
        AT END
            SET NO-MORE-DETAIL-RECORDS TO TRUE
        NOT AT END
            ADD 1 TO WS-DETAIL-RECORD-CTR.

330-PREPARE-CLIENT-RECORD.
    REWRITE CLIENT-RECORD FROM DETAIL-RECORD.
    ADD 1 TO WS-CLIENT-RECORD-CTR.

340-PREPARE-AUDIT-LINE.
    MOVE DETAIL-RECORD TO O-CLIENT-RECORD.
    WRITE PRINTLINE FROM AUDIT-LINE
        AFTER ADVANCING WS-PROPER-SPACING.
    ADD 1 TO WS-AUDIT-LINE-CTR.
    MOVE 1 TO WS-PROPER-SPACING.

350-PREPARE-SUMMARY.
    MOVE WS-DETAIL-RECORD-CTR TO O-DETAIL-RECORD-CTR.
    WRITE PRINTLINE FROM SUMMARY-LINE-1
        AFTER ADVANCING 4 LINES.
    MOVE WS-DUMMY-RECORD-CTR TO O-DUMMY-RECORD-CTR.
    WRITE PRINTLINE FROM SUMMARY-LINE-2
        AFTER ADVANCING 1 LINE.
    MOVE WS-CLIENT-RECORD-CTR TO O-CLIENT-RECORD-CTR.
    WRITE PRINTLINE FROM SUMMARY-LINE-3
        AFTER ADVANCING 1 LINE.
    MOVE WS-AUDIT-LINE-CTR TO O-AUDIT-LINE-CTR.
    WRITE PRINTLINE FROM SUMMARY-LINE-4
        AFTER ADVANCING 1 LINE.
```

Figure 4.22 Audit report for the CLIENT-FILE loading program

```
                                        PR-CONSULTANTS

                                CLIENT FILE LOADED ON 89/01/25

                                         AUDIT REPORT
CLIENT RECORDS:

        001TECHNICAL CERAMICS CORP  525 HOPE ST., LINCOLN, PA 45321              (814)342-7895TV ADV.          11/30/85
        002ACE LUMBER               84 SALEM AVE., CENTREDATE, PA 48160          (717)514-6621LOCAL PAPERS     12/05/85
        003XTZ FILM PRODUCTIONS     24 DALE ST., PITTSBURG, PA 46010             (412)365-0053TRADE JOURNALS   12/10/85
        004BEST FINANCE CORP        1350 WEST RIVER RD., CLIFTON, PA 45436       (814)941-7782TRADE JOURNALS   12/12/85
        005CHACE PAINTING CO.       56 VILLA AVE., PITTSBURG, PA 46012           (412)364-5211LOCAL PAPERS     12/20/85
        006ATHLETE'S ATTIC          174 WEEDEN DR., SUMMIT, PA 44912             (814)612-3741RADIO ADV.       01/05/86
        007TRAVEL-PHONE             150 CAROLINA AVE., PHILADELPHIA, PA 40132    (215)743-9102TV & PAPERS      01/08/86
        008CUT-RITE TREE SERVICE    240 HARRIS AVE., MOSHANON, PA 44912          (814)513-6715LOCAL PAPERS     02/15/86
        009HAIR LODGE               780 MANTON AVE., PHILADELPHIA, PA 40132      (215)664-3315TV & PAPERS      02/25/86
        010SOFTWARE SALES           1284 N. MAIN ST., PITTSBURG, PA 46012        (412)554-3772TRADE JOURNALS   03/20/86


 10  RECORDS READ FROM DETAIL FILE
 11  DUMMY RECORDS READ FROM CLIENT FILE
 10  CLIENT RECORDS LOADED INTO CLIENT FILE
 10  RECORDS WRITTEN TO AUDIT REPORT
```

Figure 4.23 START statement format

```
                                 ⎧ EQUAL TO                          ⎫
                                 ⎪ =                                 ⎪
                                 ⎪ GREATER THAN                      ⎪
START file-name-1 [ KEY IS       ⎨ >                                 ⎬ data-name-1 ]
                                 ⎪ NOT LESS THAN                     ⎪
                                 ⎪ NOT <                             ⎪
                                 ⎪ GREATER THAN OR EQUAL TO          ⎪
                                 ⎩ >=                                ⎭
      [INVALID KEY imperative-statement-1]
      [NOT INVALID KEY imperative-statement-2]
      [END-START]
```

Processing a Relative File Sequentially

We have noted earlier that the records of a relative file may be processed sequentially or randomly. The sequential processing of the records may begin at any record location within the file. In the previous program that loaded CLIENT-FILE, processing began with the very first record. However, if processing is to begin with a record other than the first, the starting record area number must be specified within a START statement. (If processing begins with the first record, the START statement is optional.) The format of the START statement has been shown previously in Figure 3.37. For your convenience, it is repeated in Figure 4.23. The rules that follow duplicate some listed earlier but also include others that are specific to the use of the START statement in relation to relative files.

Rules Governing the Use of the START Statement for Relative Files

1. The function of the START statement is to determine the logical position of the file's record pointer prior to sequential access of the file's records.
2. *File-name-1* must be the name of a relative file whose access mode is either sequential or dynamic.
3. *Data-name-1* must be the name of a relative key data item named in the RELATIVE KEY clause for the file identified by *file-name-1*.
4. *Imperative-statement-1* is an imperative statement. It is executed whenever an INVALID KEY condition occurs.
5. *Imperative-statement-2* is an imperative statement. It is executed whenever the START statement contains the NOT INVALID KEY clause and the START operation is successful.
6. END-START is the explicit scope terminator for the START statement.
7. *File-name-1* must be open either in INPUT mode or in I-O mode.
8. If there is no KEY clause in the statement, the default is KEY IS EQUAL TO *data-name-1*, where *data-name-1* is the relative key for the file.
9. If there is a KEY clause, the comparison specified by the relational operator occurs between the relative key value of a record in the file and the value of *data-name-1*.
   a. The file's record pointer is positioned to indicate the first record whose relative key value satisfies the comparison.
   b. If the comparison is not satisfied for any record in the file, an invalid key condition occurs and the execution of the START statement fails.
10. Whenever the START statement is executed, the data item named in the FILE STATUS clause for the file is updated to specify the outcome. The applicable codes are as follows:

    "00" to denote a successful operation

    "23" to denote that the target record was not found, that is, an invalid key condition occurred

    "30" to denote other permanent system errors

    "47" to denote that the file was not previously open, or its open mode is incompatible with the START operation

11. If the START statement is executed for an optional file and the file is not present, an invalid key condition occurs. The status code is "23."
12. The INVALID KEY clause is required unless there is an applicable USE AFTER EXCEPTION procedure in the DECLARATIVES SECTION of the PROCEDURE DIVISION.

If the START operation is successful, the execution of a subsequent READ statement will then access the record specified by the pointer. The format of the READ statement is READ-AT END, since the file is being processed sequentially, and it is possible to encounter the end-of-file record during execution of the READ.

As a simple example, if all the client records of the PR-Consultants Company are to be printed on a report starting with the sixth record, the following statements must be executed in order:

```
    MOVE 006 TO WS-LOCATION-NO.
    START CLIENT-FILE
        KEY = WS-LOCATION-NO
        INVALID KEY
            DISPLAY "ERROR STARTING CLIENT-FILE: " WS-CLIENT-FILE-FLAG
        NOT INVALID KEY
            PERFORM 400-PREPARE-REPORT
    END-START.
    .
    .
    .
400-PREPARE-REPORT.
    PERFORM 500-READ-N-PRINT
        UNTIL NO-MORE-CLIENT-RECORDS OR CLIENT-NUMBER IS ZERO.
.
.
.
500-READ-N-PRINT.
    READ CLIENT-FILE NEXT RECORD INTO O-RECORD
        AT END
            SET NO-MORE-CLIENT-RECORDS TO TRUE
        NOT AT END
            WRITE PRINTLINE FROM RECORD-LINE
                AFTER ADVANCING 1 LINE
    END-READ.
```

Note that WS-LOCATION-NO is the relative key data item. It is assigned the value 006 prior to executing the START statement. The START statement then positions the file at record area number 006, the statement PERFORM 400-PREPARE-REPORT is executed, the statement PERFORM 500-READ-N-PRINT is executed, the READ statement is executed, and, assuming that it is successful, the WRITE statement is executed.

The clause KEY = WS-LOCATION-NO of the START statement is not required since the relation is that of equality. And in paragraph 400, the condition CLIENT-NUMBER IS ZERO is satisfied when the file's pointer has reached the first dummy record. Since no "real" record exists beyond that point, the loop is terminated.

Updating a Relative File

Procedures used to update a relative file are very similar to those used to update an indexed file.

1. Records may be added to a relative file provided their relative key values do not duplicate those of existing records, unless the existing record is a "dummy" record.

   A new record may be written into a record area that does not contain a logical record by using the WRITE statement.

   A new record may be written into a record area that contains a dummy record by first accessing the dummy record by a READ statement, then copying the new record's field values into the dummy record, and finally using a REWRITE statement to rewrite the reconstructed record to the file.
2. Records may be deleted from the file by using either sequential access or random access.

   In sequential access, the target record is first accessed by a READ statement; it is verified to be the correct record; and then the DELETE statement is executed to logically delete the record from the file.

In random access, the record's relative key value is assigned to the file's relative key data item, and the DELETE statement is executed to logically delete it from the file.

In either case, once a record has been deleted from the file by the DELETE verb, it is no longer accessible to the program. Recall that when a relative file is first created, a 1-byte field precedes each record area, and that field serves as a flag to indicate whether or not the record area contains a logical record. The effect of the DELETE verb is to assign the character to the flag field that indicates no logical record in the record area. When a record area is flagged as not containing a logical record, the only input/output statement that can reference it is the WRITE statement.

Another procedure may be used to effectively "delete" an existing record from a relative file. In this procedure, the record to be deleted is read into the file's buffer area, the field values are erased by replacing them with spaces, and the field associated with the record's relative key is assigned the value initially assigned to this field during the creation run, thereby creating a dummy record. The record is then rewritten to the file by means of the REWRITE statement. In other words, a "real" record is replaced by a dummy record!

3. Records that already exist in the file may be changed. Such a record must first be read, new field values are copied into the record as needed, and the record is then rewritten to the file by means of the REWRITE statement. (The procedure is similar to replacing a dummy record with a new record.)

In a program designed to update a relative file, the access mode is normally specified as RANDOM, and the file is opened in I-O mode. Additionally, records in the detail file may be sequenced in descending order by process code, assuming the same codes we have used in the past: a "3" indicating a record to be changed, a "2" indicating a record to be deleted, and a "1" indicating a record to be added. By processing all deletions before additions, more record areas may be made available for new records.

The DELETE statement format is the one shown in Figure 3.30. All the rules specified for indexed files also apply to relative files, with the exception of rule 11. It must be replaced by the following:

Rule 11: If the access mode for a relative file is random or dynamic, the relative key value of the record to be deleted must be moved to the relative key data item prior to executing the DELETE statement. The DELETE operation is successful if the file contains a record with that relative key value. Otherwise, an invalid key condition occurs, and the operation fails.

Loading a Relative File Using a Randomization Procedure

Up to this point, we have used a simple example to examine some important properties of relative files. Specifically, we have seen how to:

1. Format a relative file using sequential access.
2. Format a relative file using random access.
3. Load a relative file using sequential access.
4. Load a relative file using random access.
5. Access records of a relative file in sequential order beginning either with the first record of the file or with a record other than the first.
6. Access records randomly by using the relative key value of the record to be accessed.
7. Update a relative file.

However, as mentioned earlier, it is seldom that a file contains a field whose value can be used directly as a relative key value. Usually, some transformation procedure, called randomization, must be applied to the values of a selected record field to yield numbers that can then be used as relative key values. As an example, we will set up the master personnel file for the Jocelyn Originals Company as a relative file.

Suppose the layout of each record in this file is as follows:

cc 1–9	Social Security number
cc 10–29	Employee name
cc 30–66	Employee address
cc 67–72	Employee date of birth
cc 73–78	Employee date hired
cc 79–100	(not currently used)

The company currently has 200 employees, but in order to allow for the addition of records for new employees, the master file will be formatted for 250 records, that is, the file size will be set to 250. The file is said to have a "packing factor" of 80 percent, that is, only 200 of the 250 record areas will initially contain employee records. If the company growth expectation for the foreseeable future were greater than 25 percent, a lower packing factor would be selected, thus increasing the file size as appropriate.

A number of randomization procedures are available. They are also referred to as *hashing* techniques, since the procedures tend to "make hash" of the contents of the selected field. One such procedure is the *Division Algorithm Method,* and in this program, we illustrate its use as applied to the Social Security number field.

Specifically, in applying the Division Algorithm Method to the Social Security number, the Social Security number is divided by the file size, 250 in this case, or by the largest prime number not greater than 250, namely, 241. If the file size is used, then the remainder will be in the range from 0 to 249. By adding 1 to the remainder, the range of values becomes 1 through 250. This value can then be used as the relative key value for the record.

Example 1

Suppose the SSN (Social Security number) is equal to 743-14-2265. Then, the Division Algorithm yields 743142265 / 250 = 2972569, Remainder 15. By adding 1 to the remainder, the relative key value for the record containing this Social Security number is 16. That is, the number 743142265 has "hashed" to 16. Therefore, the record with SSN = 743-14-2265 will be stored in the 16th record area in the file.

Example 2

Suppose SSN = 032-56-7781. The Division Algorithm yields 032567781 / 250 = 130271, Remainder 31. By adding 1 to the remainder, the relative key value for the record containing this Social Security number is 32. That is, the number 032567781 has been transformed to 32. And so, the record with SSN = 032-56-7781 will be stored in the 32nd record area in the file.

In order to employ this technique, the programmer must code appropriate instructions within the program. Suppose that WS-LOCATION-NO is the relative key data item. Two possible ways of determining the value of WS-LOCATION-NO are as follows:

1.
```
DIVIDE DETAIL-SSN BY 250 GIVING WS-QUOTIENT.
COMPUTE WS-LOCATION-NO =
    (DETAIL-SSN - 250 * WS-QUOTIENT) + 1.
```
2.
```
DIVIDE DETAIL-SSN BY 250 GIVING WS-QUOTIENT
    REMAINDER WS-LOCATION-NO.
ADD 1 TO WS-LOCATION-NO.
```

In both cases, WS-QUOTIENT is defined as an integer, and in number 2 above, note the use of the REMAINDER phrase option of the DIVIDE statement. As a result, the remainder produced by the Division Algorithm is stored directly into WS-LOCATION-NO, and its value is increased by 1 within the ADD statement.

If a record is being written to the relative file, the transformation instructions must precede the WRITE statement, and if a record is to be read from the relative file, the transformation instructions must precede the READ statement.

Randomization and Synonyms

In the randomization procedure illustrated above, it is possible for more than one Social Security number to be transformed into the same relative number. Records for which the same relative number is initially generated by the randomization procedure are called *synonyms.* Obviously, only one record can be stored in a given location on the file, so when a synonym is found, the relative number will be incremented by 1, repeatedly if necessary, until the first unused record location is found. That location number becomes the relative key value for the synonym.

Figure 4.24 Synonyms in a relative file

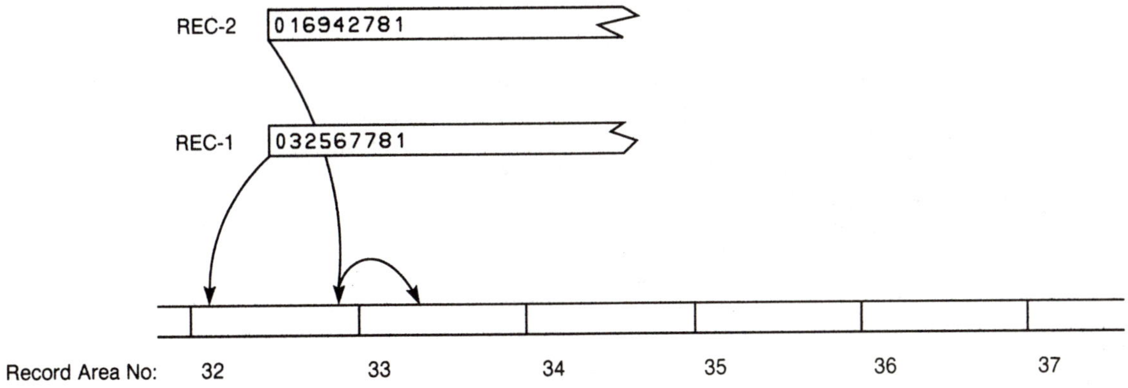

Figure 4.25 Employee records for the Jocelyn Originals Company

```
743142265ABRUZZI, KENNETH L. 51 RAYMOND ST  HASTINGS, NE      68901521205720820
032567781AITKEN, THOMAS R.   260 FOUNTAIN STAURORA, NE        68818260805460820
144217773ALTERMAN, MAUREEN E.10 MARTIN AVE  YORK, NE          68467350524600610
014766691ARMSTRONG, GEORGE   105 STATE ST   PLATTE, NE        68653480320830816
381662514BAHR, LENA M.       304 CORY LANE  GENEVA, NE        68361411110600820
179623741BLAZUCK, JOSEPH A.  81 DORIS AVE   GENEVA, NE        68361450521750610
005589243BUXBAUM, JOAN M.    172 EARLE DR   GRAND ISLAND, NE 68802480214700608
623514793CARTER, AMEKIA L.   59 BARK ST     LOUP CITY, NE     68853320513620820
042750015COLETTI, SARAH T.   51 BROAD ST    HASTINGS, NE      68901380902640615
016493017COUGHLIN, AILEEN M. 133 DAVIS RD   LEXINGTON, NE     68850500310680706
215137814CUMMINGS, DOROTHEA  97 POWER AVE   NORMAN, NE        68963530407830822
771894263CYR, ROSARIO        205 SUNSET DR  FAIRFIELD, NE     68938350524550820
314764532DESROSIERS, RICHARD 92 REGAN RD    LOUP CITY, NE     68853581221830815
364923752DURANT, MARIE L.    1250 HIGH RD   GENEVA, NE        68361430924540910
039764715GAFFNEY, MARYLYN    76 MAIN ST     PLATTE, NE        68653521205770608
211384406KACHADOURIAN, NATALI922 LOCUST ST  HEBRON, NE        68370350221560820
253749144LAKE, SUE           252 EAST RD    CRETE, NE         68333410707830815
130043962MARKARIAN, MARIAN   984 N MAIN ST  HASTINGS, NE      68901320507520820
032561579MAYO, EVANGELINA    895 POTTERS AVEGENEVA, NE        68361620805830807
013407206MCGEE, BERNARD W.   2420 CARR LA   CENTRAL CITY, NE 68826301215490615
124670325MOONEY, RONALD      220 N MAIN ST  HASTINGS, NE      68901410920640810
226153911OVERDEEP, CYNTHIA   130 CANAL ST   YORK, NE          68467350524700715
149201475PACCASASSIE, DEBBIE 341 BRANCH AVE NORMAN, NE        68963282612570912
033281512PEARSON, ARTHUR     1020 GOLDEN RD HASTINGS, NE      68901501125830802
150246389PRIMEAU, ISABEL     78 NORTH ST    KEARNEY, NE       68847470930720820
432157258ROMA, GILDA         25 MAPLE DR    SUPERIOR, NE      68978500708720610
234891533SHERIDAN, RICHARD J.850SUN CIRCLE  AURORA, NE        68818421205650610
322150642STURDAHL, DEBRA     2541 RICE ST   CRETE, NE         68333340614550715
026307625VELTRI, JOHN A.     312 PERCH DR.  HASTINGS, NE      68901470115820820
```

In Figure 4.24, REC-1 has SSN = 032-56-7781. The Division Algorithm Method assigns the relative key value 32 to REC-1. When the algorithm is applied to the Social Security number of REC-2, the Social Security number also "hashes" to 32, a synonym. Obviously, record location 32 is already occupied, so 1 is added to 32 to produce 33. If there is no record already stored in location 33, REC-2 is assigned relative key value 33. Location 33 is unoccupied if it contains no valid record or if it contains only a dummy record.

If record location number 33 is also occupied, successive locations will be checked by adding 1 to the preceding location number. When the first unoccupied location is found, the relative number for that location becomes the relative key value for REC-2.

Loading a Relative File Using the Division Algorithm

Assume that a relative file, called MASTER-FILE, has already been formatted for the Jocelyn Originals Company and has been loaded with dummy records that are blank except for the Social Security number field, which contains zeros. The task now is to load the employee records into the relative file. The employee records are shown in Figure 4.25.

■ **Figure 4.26** Printer spacing chart for the audit report

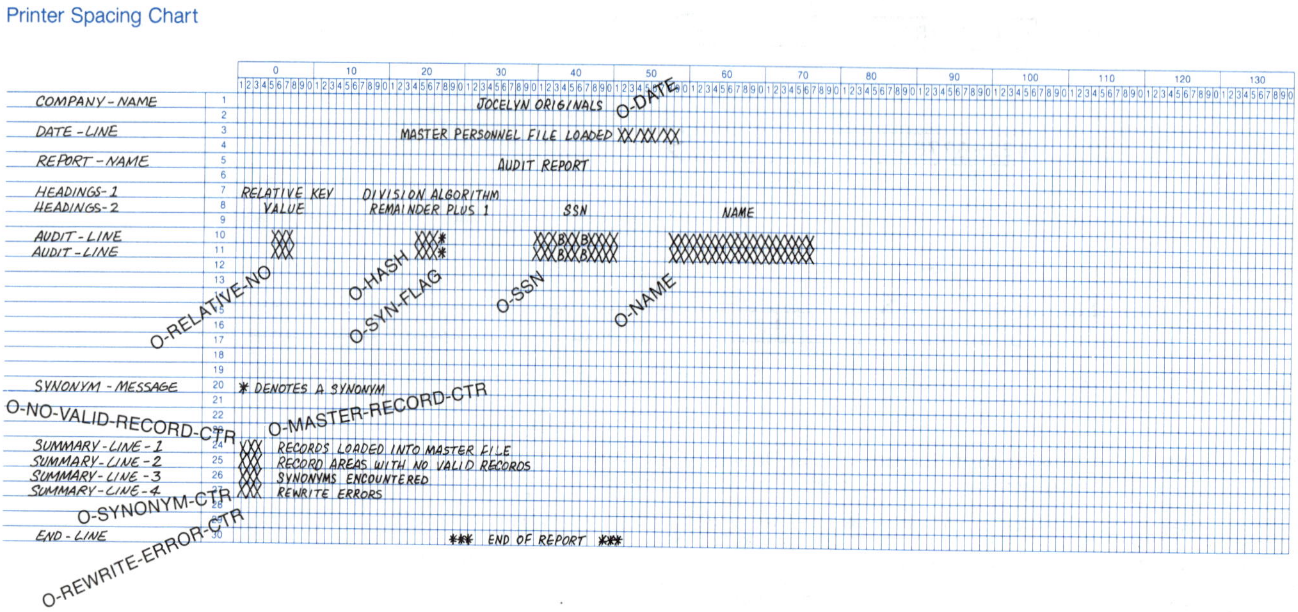

Brief Analysis of the Task

In addition to loading the master records into the relative file, the program should also produce an audit report. The printer spacing chart for the report is shown in Figure 4.26. Note that for each record loaded into the file, the audit line shows its relative key value as well as the initial hash value produced by the Division Algorithm. Asterisks will be used to identify synonyms that occur during the loading process. Only the employee's Social Security number and name will be printed on the report.

The system flowchart is shown in Figure 4.27. The employee records that must be loaded into MASTER-FILE are the ones shown in Figure 4.25. They have been assembled in DETAIL-FILE and are sorted alphabetically by employee name.

The general steps that will be used to load an employee record into the new master file are as follows:

1. Read an employee record from DETAIL-FILE.
2. Apply the Division Algorithm to the employee's Social Security number to determine the initial hashed value for the record. (This number must be greater than zero but not greater than the size of the file!)
3. Move the initial hashed value to the relative key data item, and read the record that is currently stored in that record area of the master file.
   a. If that record area is available, that is, if it contains a dummy record, then prepare the new master record and load it into the master file using the REWRITE statement.
   b. If the record area is not available because it already contains an employee record, then begin a search procedure to find the *next available* record area in the file. This procedure requires a loop that must be executed repeatedly until a record area is found or until it is clear that there are no more available record areas in the file, that is, that the file is full.

      If a record area is found, replace the dummy record with the new master record and load it into the master file using the REWRITE statement.

      If no record area can be found because the file is full, prepare an error message, write it on the report, and then terminate execution of the program.
4. If a master record has been loaded into the master file, prepare the appropriate audit line and write it on the report.

Figure 4.27 System flowchart to load MASTER-FILE

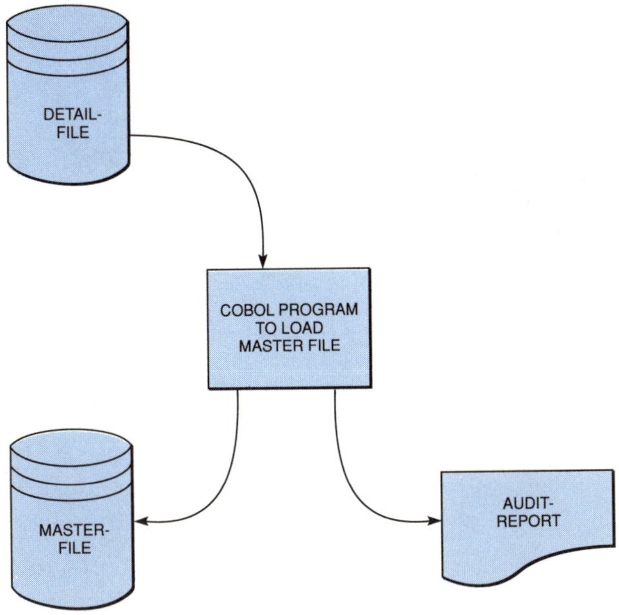

Figure 4.28 Wrapping around to the beginning of the file

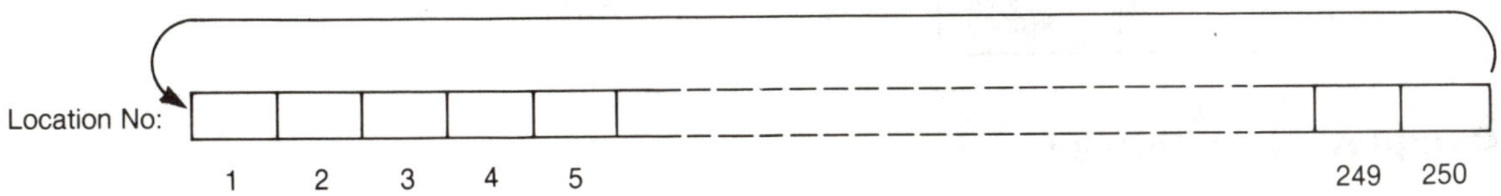

The search referred to in step 3b on page 282 may be conducted as follows:

Since the initial hashed value points to a record area that already contains an employee record, call that value the starting location number. Then, add 1 to the starting location number. Depending upon where this occurs in the file, there may be no problem with this new location number. However, if the hashed value pointed to the last record area in the file, adding 1 will produce a number greater than the size of the file. There are two problems with this situation: first, it's meaningless to consider a record area that does not exist in the file, and second, if an attempt is made to read the file with that relative key value, an INVALID KEY condition will occur because of a boundary violation.

If the last record area of the relative file is reached without finding an available record area, then the search should continue at the beginning of the file. This is easily accomplished by subtracting the file size from the value of the nonexistent record area number.

Example: See Figure 4.28. Assume the file size is 250, and record area 250 is occupied. Adding 1 to the location number yields 251. This number is greater than the file size. Subtracting the file size 250 from 251 yields location number 1, that is, the first record area at the beginning of the file. The search wraps around to the beginning of the file.

Another situation can also be encountered: The file is full. That is, every record location in the file has been searched and every one contains an employee record. To check for this possibility, mark the starting location of the search. If the search reached the end of the file, and it then wrapped around to the beginning of the file, continued searching, and ultimately reached the starting point, then the file is full, since no vacant record area has been found. A message should be produced to explain the event, and the program should be terminated.

These procedures are included in the program that follows.

Figure 4.29 Structure chart to load MASTER-FILE

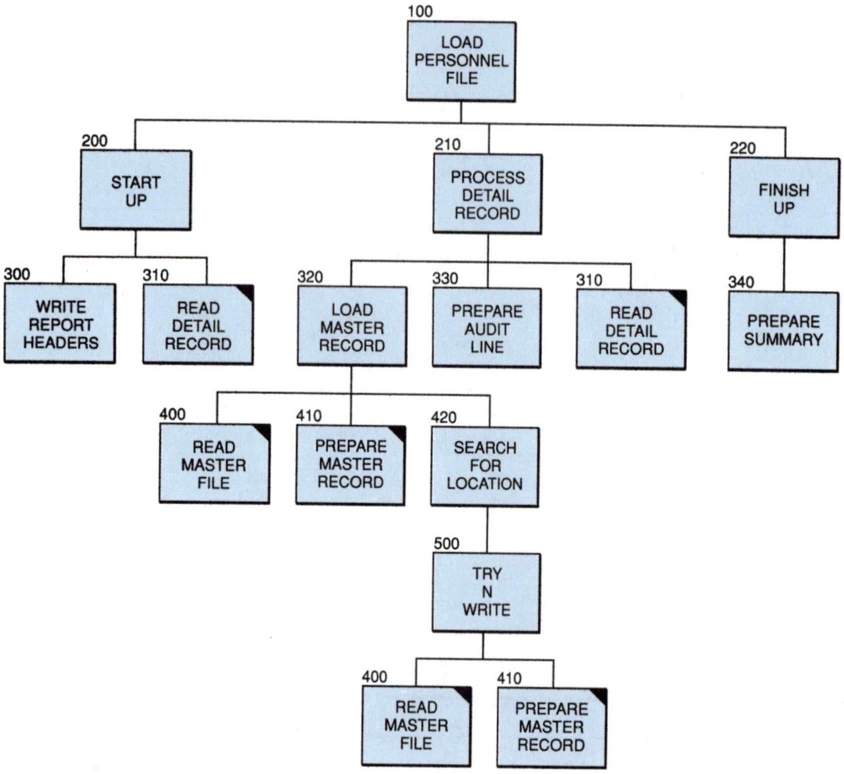

Completing the Design

The requirements of the printer spacing chart and the brief analysis discussed previously lead to the structure chart shown in Figure 4.29.

The detailed steps needed to complete the tasks shown in the structure chart are listed in the pseudocode that follows.

100-Load-Personnel-File.

1. Perform 200-Start-Up.
2. Perform 210-Process-Detail-Record until no more records or until master file is full.
3. Perform 220-Finish-Up.
4. Stop the run.

200-Start-Up.

1. Open the file Detail-File in input mode, the file Master-File in input/output mode, and the file Audit-Report in output mode.
2. Set file-size equal to 250.
3. Obtain the date from the operating system.
4. Move date to Date-Line date.
5. Set the flag WS-MORE-RECORDS to "YES".
6. Set the flag WS-FULL-FILE-FLAG to "NO ".
7. Initialize the program counters: master-record-counter, no-valid-record-counter, synonym-counter, and rewrite-error-counter.
8. Perform 300-Write-Report-Headers.
9. Perform 310-Read-Detail-Record.

210-Process-Detail-Record.

1. Perform 320-Load-Master-Record.
2. Perform 330-Prepare-Audit-Line.
3. Test the flag WS-FULL-FILE-FLAG:

   if it's equal to "NO ", perform 310-Read-Detail-Record.

220-Finish-Up.

1. Move the record Synonym-Message to the output area Printline.
2. After advancing 3 lines, write the record Printline.
3. Perform 340-Prepare-Summary.
4. Move the record End-Line to the output area Printline.
5. After advancing 5 lines, write the output record Printline.
6. Close Detail-File, Master-File, and Audit-Report.

300-Write-Report-Headers.

1. Move the record Company-Name to the output area Printline.
2. After advancing to a new page, write the output record Printline.
3. Move the record Date-Line to the output area Printline.
4. After advancing 2 lines, write the output record Printline.
5. Move the record Report-Name to the output area Printline.
6. After advancing 2 lines, write the output record Printline.
7. Move the record Headings-1 to the output area Printline.
8. After advancing 2 lines, write the output record Printline.
9. Move the record Headings-2 to the output area Printline.
10. After advancing 1 line, write the output record Printline.
11. Set proper-spacing to 2.

310-Read-Detail-Record.

1. Read an input Detail-Record.
2. Test for end-of-file record:
   if EOF record reached, set the flag WS-MORE-RECORDS to "NO ".

320-Load-Master-Record.

1. Divide input Social-Security-number by file-size (250) giving quotient,
   and store remainder as location-number.
2. Add 1 to location-number.
3. Set initial hash equal to location-number.
4. Perform 400-Read-Master-File.
5. Test master-record:
   a. If it's a dummy record, perform 410-Prepare-Master-Record.
   b. If it's not a dummy record, perform 420-Search-For-Location.

330-Prepare-Audit-Line.

1. Move spaces to Audit-Line.
2. Test the flag WS-FULL-FILE-FLAG:
   a. If it's equal to "YES"
      move input Social-Security-number to Full-File-Message Social-Security-number,
      move the record Full-File-Message to the record Audit-Line.
   b. If it's equal to "NO ", test if WS-MASTER-FILE-FLAG = "23".
      If so, move input Social-Security-number to Rewrite-Error-Message Social-Security-number,
      move the record Rewrite-Error-Message to the record Audit-Line.
      If not so, move location-number to Audit-Line relative-number,
      move initial-hash to Audit-Line hash,
      move input Social-Security-number to Audit-Line Social-Security-number,
      move input name to Audit-Line name,
      test the WS-SYNONYM-FLAG: if it's equal to "ON ", move "*" to Audit-Line synonym-flag.
3. Move the record Audit-Line to the output area Printline.
4. After advancing proper-spacing, write the output record Printline.
5. Set proper-spacing to 1.
6. Set the flag WS-SYNONYM-FLAG to "OFF".

340-Prepare-Summary.

1. Move master-record-counter to Summary-Line-1 master-record-counter.
2. Move the record Summary-Line-1 to the output area Printline.
3. After advancing 4 lines, write the output record Printline.
4. Move no-valid-record-counter to Summary-Line-2 no-valid-record-counter.
5. Move the record Summary-Line-2 to the output area Printline.
6. After advancing 1 line, write the output record Printline.
7. Move synonym-counter to Summary-Line-3 synonym-counter.
8. Move the record Summary-Line-3 to the output area Printline.
9. After advancing 1 line, write the output record Printline.
10. Move rewrite-error-counter to Summary-Line-4 rewrite-error-counter.
11. Move the record Summary-Line-4 to the output area Printline.
12. After advancing 1 line, write the output record Printline.

400-Read-Master-File.

1. Read Master-File master-record.
2. Test for invalid key:

   if invalid key condition exists, add 1 to no-valid-record-counter.

410-Prepare-Master-Record.

1. Move input Social-Security-number to master-record Social-Security-number.
2. Move input name to master-record name.
3. Move input address to master-record address.
4. Move input date-of-birth to master-record date-of-birth.
5. Move input date-hired to master-record date-hired.
6. Rewrite master-record.
7. Test for invalid key:
   - **a.** If invalid key condition exists, add 1 to rewrite-error-counter and set WS-MASTER-FILE-FLAG to "23".
   - **b.** If not invalid key condition, add 1 to master-record-counter.

420-Search-For-Location.

1. Set starting-number equal to location-number.
2. Set the flag WS-FILE-SEARCH-FLAG to "ON ".
3. Perform 500-Try-N-Write until the flag WS-FILE-SEARCH-FLAG is equal to "OFF", or until the flag WS-FULL-FILE-FLAG is equal to "YES".

500-Try-N-Write.

1. Add 1 to location-number.
2. Test location-number:

   if location-number is greater than file-size, then subtract file-size from location-number.
3. Test location-number again:
   - **a.** If location-number is equal to starting-number,

     set the flag WS-FULL-FILE-FLAG to "YES".
   - **b.** If location-number is not equal to starting-number,
     - **i.** Perform 400-Read-Master-File.
     - **ii.** Test Master-File master-record:

       If it's a dummy record, then

       set the flag WS-SYNONYM-FLAG to "ON ",
add 1 to synonym-counter,
perform 410-Prepare-Master-Record, and
set the flag WS-FILE-SEARCH-FLAG to "OFF".

The program flowchart corresponding to the pseudocode is shown in Figure 4.30.

Figure 4.30 Program flowchart to load MASTER-FILE

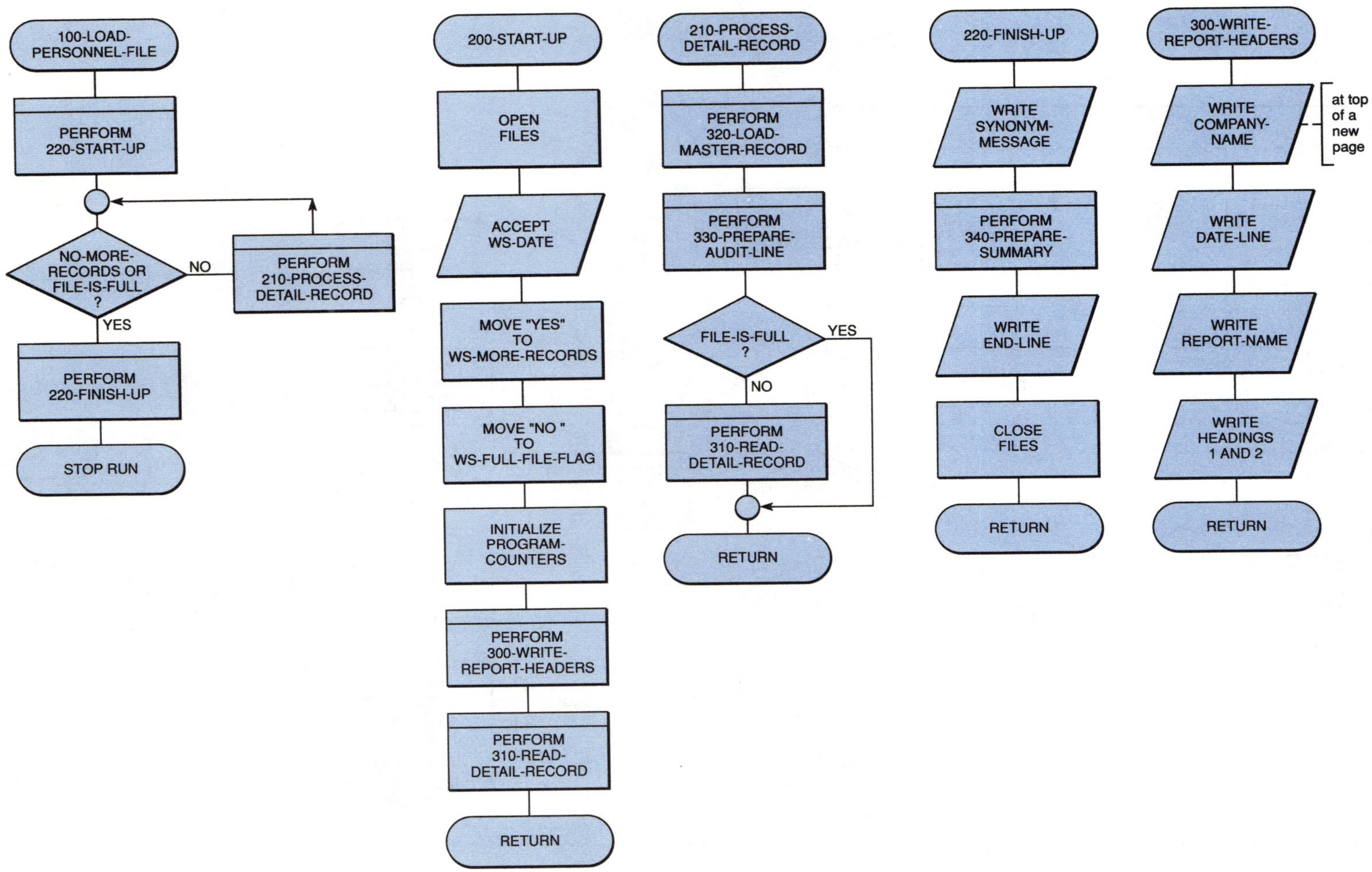

■ **Figure 4.30** continued

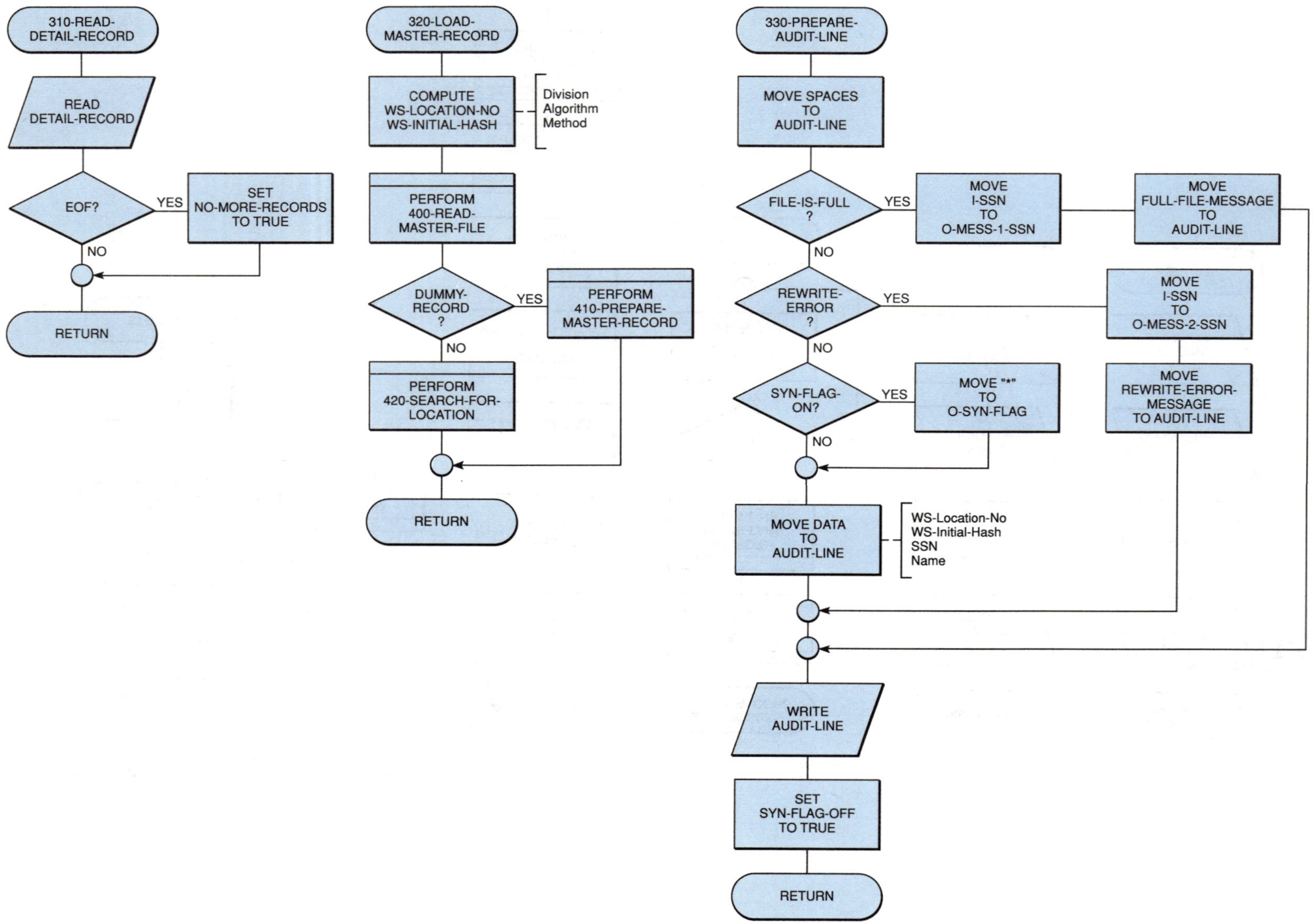

Figure 4.30 continued

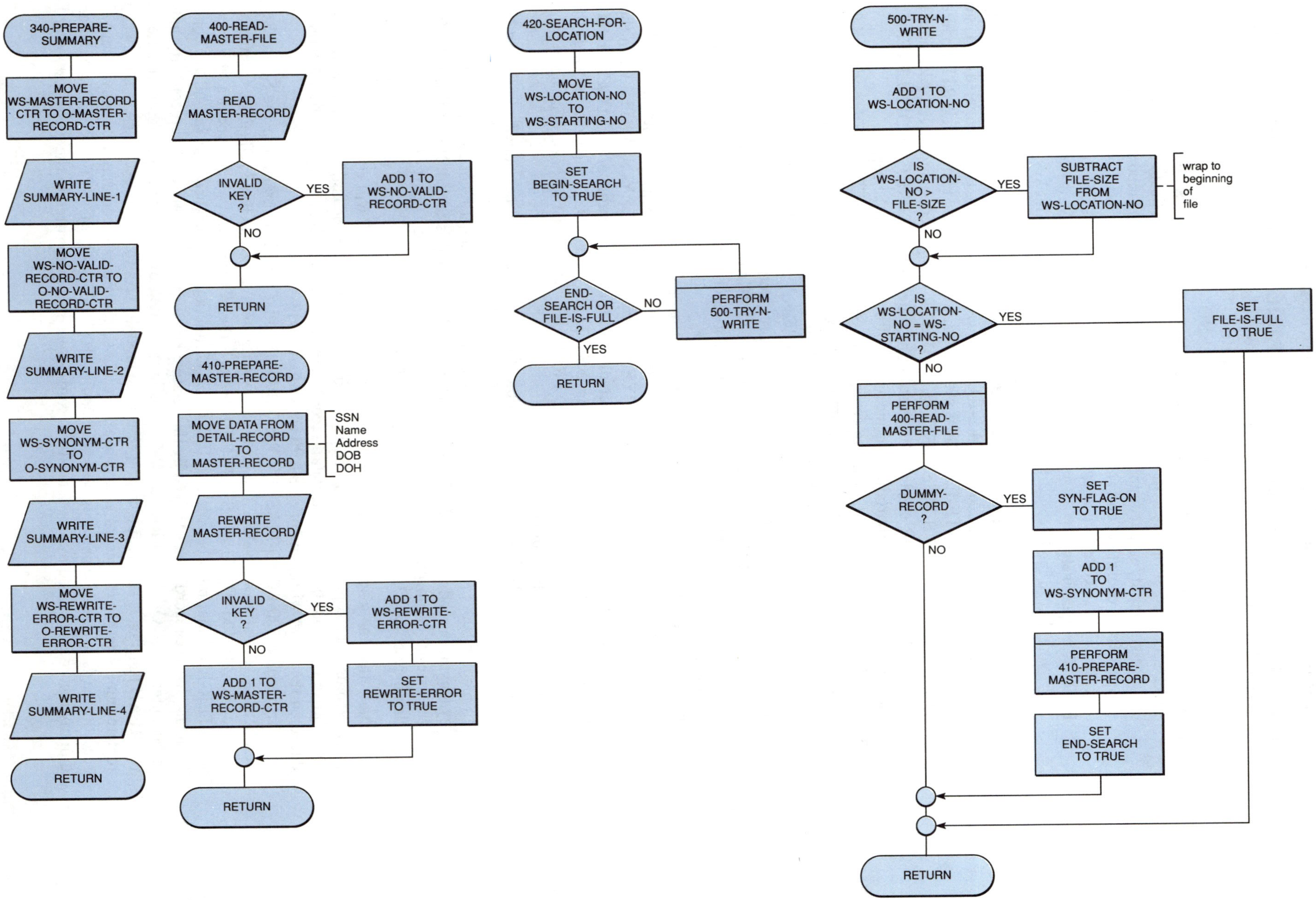

Note that the program will contain a total of five flags, as follows:

1. WS-MORE-RECORDS, used in relation to DETAIL-FILE. It is initialized to "YES" in module 200-START-UP, and its value will be set to "NO " in module 310-READ-DETAIL-RECORD when the AT END condition is satisfied. The condition-name NO-MORE-RECORDS will be used to represent the value "NO ".
2. WS-MASTER-FILE-FLAG, associated with the relative file MASTER-FILE in the FILE STATUS clause of the file's SELECT statement. It is used to indicate successful or unsuccessful input/output functions. The two codes of particular importance are "00" to denote any successful operation, and the code "23" to denote an invalid key condition in a REWRITE operation. These codes are assigned the condition-names SUCCESSFUL and REWRITE-ERROR, respectively.

   Note that in module 400-READ-MASTER-FILE, an invalid key condition during a READ operation causes the counter WS-NO-VALID-RECORD-CTR to be incremented by 1. In module 410-PREPARE-MASTER-RECORD, if an invalid key condition occurs during the REWRITE operation, the counter WS-REWRITE-ERROR-CTR is incremented by 1, and the condition-name REWRITE-ERROR is set to true, whereas a successful REWRITE operation results in the counter WS-MASTER-RECORD-CTR being incremented by 1. Also note that the REWRITE-ERROR condition is tested in module 330-PREPARE-AUDIT-LINE. If the condition exists, an appropriate error message will be printed on the report.
3. WS-FILE-SEARCH-FLAG, used to control the search of MASTER-FILE for an available record area when the Division Algorithm initially yields a synonym. The flag is initialized to "ON " when the search begins, and when a record area is found, the flag is set to "OFF" to provide an exit from the search loop. The values "ON " and "OFF" are assigned the condition-names BEGIN-SEARCH and STOP-SEARCH, respectively.

   The flag is initialized to "ON " in module 420-SEARCH-FOR-LOCATION, and it is set to "OFF" in module 500-TRY-N-WRITE when a record area for the new master record has been found.
4. WS-FULL-FILE-FLAG, associated with the relative file, used to signal that the file is full, and consequently, that no more records can be written to the file. This flag is initialized to "NO " in module 200-START-UP, and it is set to "YES" in module 500-TRY-N-WRITE when the search procedure has been executed repeatedly and the current value of WS-LOCATION-NO has returned to its initial value retained as WS-STARTING-NO. This condition brings the search loop to an end, and, in module 330-PREPARE-AUDIT-LINE, causes an appropriate error message to be printed on the report.
5. WS-SYNONYM-FLAG, used to determine if an asterisk should be printed next to the hashed value produced by the Division Algorithm for a particular employee's Social Security number. In module 500-TRY-N-WRITE, the flag is set to "ON " when a record area is found for a synonym. In module 330-PREPARE-AUDIT-LINE, the flag is tested. If its value is "ON ", the asterisk is moved to the field O-SYN-FLAG and is printed as part of AUDIT-LINE. The flag is reset to "OFF" after AUDIT-LINE is printed.

Note that the loop in module 100-LOAD-PERSONNEL-FILE will continue until there are no more records to be copied from DETAIL-FILE to MASTER-FILE, or until the relative file is full. If the relative file is full before all the detail records have been processed, an appropriate message is produced on the report within module 330-PREPARE-AUDIT-LINE.

In module 320-LOAD-MASTER-RECORD, the first task is to transform the Social Security number into a relative key value. The relative key data item is WS-LOCATION-NO. Control is then sent to module 400-READ-MASTER-FILE, where the relative key value specifies the record of MASTER-FILE that must be accessed. If the READ function fails because of an invalid key condition, it means that the record area specified by the relative key does not contain a valid record. In that case, the counter WS-NO-VALID-RECORD-CTR is incremented by 1 before returning to module 320. If the READ function is successful, control returns to module 320. In either case, a test is now performed to determine whether the record area is available, that is, whether it contains a dummy record. If the record area is available, control is sent to module 410-PREPARE-MASTER-RECORD, where the dummy record is replaced by a new master record before being rewritten to the file. If the record area is not available, control is sent to module 420-SEARCH-FOR-LOCATION, where a search procedure is initiated. The details of the search are contained in module 500-TRY-N-WRITE. Note that module 500 contains the test for a wraparound condition and the test for a full file.

Coding the Program

Now that the design is complete, the program is coded, entered into a file, compiled, and debugged. It is shown in Figure 4.31.

We draw your attention to the following program entries:

1. The SELECT statement for MASTER-FILE.
   a. The ORGANIZATION IS RELATIVE clause is required in any program that needs access to this file.
   b. The ACCESS MODE IS RANDOM clause is required, since access to a record is in terms of its relative key value.
   c. The RELATIVE KEY IS WS-LOCATION-NO clause must be included, since WS-LOCATION-NO is the relative key data item whose value must be specified prior to reading or rewriting a record to the file.
   d. The FILE STATUS IS WS-MASTER-FILE-FLAG clause is needed, since the condition-name REWRITE-ERROR, associated with status code "23," is used in the program to signal the printing of an error message. Recall that the status code "23" is moved to the file status data item when a rewrite error occurs. The program must detect this condition.
2. The WORKING-STORAGE SECTION group item MASTER-FILE-ITEMS.
   a. WS-LOCATION-NO is the master file's relative key data item. It must be an unsigned numeric integer. Its initial value is produced by the Division Algorithm. Its value changes during the search procedure triggered by the presence of a synonym.
   b. WS-INITIAL-HASH contains a copy of the relative key value initially produced by the Division Algorithm. It must be printed on each master record's audit line.
   c. WS-STARTING-NO also contains a copy of the relative key value initially produced by the Division Algorithm. It is used during the search procedure to determine whether the relative file is full.
   d. WS-QUOTIENT is used as a data item in the Division Algorithm. Note that it is defined as an integer, thus assuring that the remainder is also an integer. The remainder is stored in WS-LOCATION-NO.
   e. WS-FILE-SIZE, whose value is 250, is a data item used in the search procedure to allow the search to wrap around to the beginning of the file if necessary.
   f. WS-MASTER-FILE-FLAG is the data item named in the FILE STATUS clause for the master file. It must be defined as a two-character alphanumeric item.
   g. WS-FILE-SEARCH-FLAG is one of two data items used to control the execution of the search loop. The search loop must end when an available record area has been found.
   h. WS-FULL-FILE-FLAG is one of two data items used to control the execution of the search loop. The search loop must end when it is determined that the file is full.
   i. WS-SYNONYM-FLAG is the data item that signals whether an asterisk, denoting a synonym, should be printed as part of a record's audit line.
3. The elementary items of the group PROGRAM-COUNTERS are initialized to zero in paragraph 200-START-UP. Within paragraph 340-PREPARE-SUMMARY, their final values will be printed in the four summary lines required by the report.
4. In paragraph 200-START-UP, the open mode for MASTER-FILE is specified as I-O, since records must be read from the file and newly formed master records must be rewritten to the file.

The audit report produced by the program is contained in Figure 4.32. Note that only one synonym has been flagged on the report. The record with SSN 042-75-0015 should have been stored in record area 16. However, a "collision" occurred, since that location already contained a record. The next record area was checked and found to be available. Hence, relative key value 17 was assigned to the record.

■ **Figure 4.31** COBOL program to load MASTER-FILE using a randomization procedure

```
 IDENTIFICATION DIVISION.

 PROGRAM-ID.    LOAD-MASTER-FILE.

*****************************************************************
*                                                               *
*   AUTHOR.        PAQUETTE.                                    *
*   DATE WRITTEN.  JANUARY 1989.                                *
*                                                               *
*   THIS PROGRAM LOADS A RELATIVE FILE USING A RANDOMIZATION    *
*   PROCEDURE TO GENERATE THE RELATIVE KEY VALUES.  THE         *
*   PROCEDURE USED IS THE DIVISION ALGORITHM METHOD.            *
*   SPECIFICALLY, THE MASTER EMPLOYEE RECORDS OF THE JOCELYN    *
*   ORIGINALS COMPANY ARE LOADED INTO A PREFORMATTED FILE, WITH *
*   FILE SIZE = 250.  WHEN SYNONYMS ARE FOUND, TESTS ARE        *
*   PERFORMED TO ALLOW FOR WRAPAROUND SEARCH AND TO             *
*   DETECT A FULL FILE.                                         *
*                                                               *
*   AN AUDIT REPORT IS ALSO PRODUCED.                           *
*                                                               *
*****************************************************************

 ENVIRONMENT DIVISION.

 CONFIGURATION SECTION.

 SOURCE-COMPUTER.  VAX-VMS-8650.
 OBJECT-COMPUTER.  VAX-VMS-8650.

 INPUT-OUTPUT SECTION.

 FILE-CONTROL.
     SELECT DETAIL-FILE  ASSIGN TO COB$INPUT.
     SELECT MASTER-FILE  ASSIGN TO 'JOCMSTR2.DAT'
                         ORGANIZATION IS RELATIVE
                         ACCESS MODE IS RANDOM
                         RELATIVE KEY IS WS-LOCATION-NO
                         FILE STATUS IS WS-MASTER-FILE-FLAG.
     SELECT AUDIT-REPORT ASSIGN TO COB$OUTPUT.

 DATA DIVISION.

 FILE SECTION.

 FD  DETAIL-FILE
     RECORD CONTAINS 100 CHARACTERS.

 01  DETAIL-RECORD.
     05 I-SSN       PIC 9(9).
     05 I-NAME      PIC X(20).
     05 I-ADDRESS   PIC X(37).
     05 I-DOB       PIC X(6).
     05 I-DOH       PIC X(6).
     05             PIC X(22).

 FD  MASTER-FILE
     RECORD CONTAINS 100 CHARACTERS.

 01  MASTER-RECORD.
     05 MR-SSN      PIC 9(9).
        88 DUMMY-RECORD      VALUE ZEROS.
     05 MR-NAME     PIC X(20).
     05 MR-ADDRESS  PIC X(37).
     05 MR-DOB      PIC X(6).
     05 MR-DOH      PIC X(6).
     05             PIC X(22).

 FD  AUDIT-REPORT
     RECORD CONTAINS 80 CHARACTERS.

 01  PRINTLINE      PIC X(80).
```

Figure 4.31 continued

```
WORKING-STORAGE SECTION.

01  MASTER-FILE-ITEMS.
    05 WS-LOCATION-NO          PIC 9(3).
    05 WS-INITIAL-HASH         PIC 9(3).
    05 WS-STARTING-NO          PIC 9(3).
    05 WS-QUOTIENT             PIC 9(9).
    05 WS-FILE-SIZE            PIC 9(3).
    05 WS-MASTER-FILE-FLAG     PIC X(2).
       88 SUCCESSFUL                       VALUE '00'.
       88 REWRITE-ERROR                    VALUE '23'.
    05 WS-FILE-SEARCH-FLAG     PIC X(3).
       88 BEGIN-SEARCH                     VALUE 'ON '.
       88 STOP-SEARCH                      VALUE 'OFF'.
    05 WS-FULL-FILE-FLAG       PIC X(3).
       88 FILE-IS-FULL                     VALUE 'YES'.
    05 WS-SYNONYM-FLAG         PIC X(3).
       88 SYN-FLAG-ON                      VALUE 'ON '.
       88 SYN-FLAG-OFF                     VALUE 'OFF'.

01  PROGRAM-CONTROLS.
    05 WS-MORE-RECORDS        PIC X(3).
       88 NO-MORE-RECORDS                  VALUE 'NO '.
    05 WS-DATE                PIC X(6).
    05 WS-PROPER-SPACING      PIC 9.

01  PROGRAM-COUNTERS.
    05 WS-MASTER-RECORD-CTR    PIC S9(3).
    05 WS-NO-VALID-RECORD-CTR  PIC S9(3).
    05 WS-SYNONYM-CTR          PIC S9(3).
    05 WS-REWRITE-ERROR-CTR    PIC S9(3).

01  COMPANY-NAME.
    05 PIC X(32) VALUE SPACES.
    05 PIC X(17) VALUE 'JOCELYN ORIGINALS'.
    05 PIC X(31) VALUE SPACES.

01  DATE-LINE.
    05 PIC X(22) VALUE SPACES.
    05 PIC X(29) VALUE 'MASTER PERSONNEL FILE LOADED '.
    05 O-DATE     PIC XX/XX/XX.
    05 PIC X(21) VALUE SPACES.

01  REPORT-NAME.
    05 PIC X(35) VALUE SPACES.
    05 PIC X(12) VALUE 'AUDIT REPORT'.
    05 PIC X(33) VALUE SPACES.

01  HEADINGS-1.
    05 PIC X(1)  VALUE SPACES.
    05 PIC X(12) VALUE 'RELATIVE KEY'.
    05 PIC X(4)  VALUE SPACES.
    05 PIC X(18) VALUE 'DIVISION ALGORITHM'.
    05 PIC X(45) VALUE SPACES.

01  HEADINGS-2.
    05 PIC X(4)  VALUE SPACES.
    05 PIC X(5)  VALUE 'VALUE'.
    05 PIC X(9)  VALUE SPACES.
    05 PIC X(16) VALUE 'REMAINDER PLUS 1'.
    05 PIC X(10) VALUE SPACES.
    05 PIC X(3)  VALUE 'SSN'.
    05 PIC X(18) VALUE SPACES.
    05 PIC X(4)  VALUE 'NAME'.
    05 PIC X(11) VALUE SPACES.

01  AUDIT-LINE.
    05                     PIC X(5).
    05 O-RELATIVE-NO       PIC X(3).
    05                     PIC X(16).
    05 O-HASH              PIC X(3).
    05 O-SYN-FLAG          PIC X.
    05                     PIC X(12).
    05 O-SSN               PIC XXXBXXBXXXX.
    05                     PIC X(4).
    05 O-NAME              PIC X(25).
```

```
01  SYNONYM-MESSAGE      PIC X(20)  VALUE ' * DENOTES A SYNONYM'.

01  ERROR-MESSAGES.
    05 FULL-FILE-MESSAGE.
       10                PIC X(40)  VALUE
             ' FULL FILE OCCURRED AT RECORD WITH SSN= '.
       10 O-MESS-1-SSN   PIC X(9).

    05 REWRITE-ERROR-MESSAGE.
       10                PIC X(24)  VALUE
             ' REWRITE ERROR FOR SSN= '.
       10 O-MESS-2-SSN   PIC X(9).

01  SUMMARY-LINES.
    05 SUMMARY-LINE-1.
       10                       PIC X(1)    VALUE SPACE.
       10 O-MASTER-RECORD-CTR   PIC ZZ9.
       10                       PIC X(33)   VALUE
              '  RECORDS LOADED INTO MASTER FILE'.

    05 SUMMARY-LINE-2.
       10                         PIC X(1)    VALUE SPACE.
       10 O-NO-VALID-RECORD-CTR   PIC ZZ9.
       10                         PIC X(36)   VALUE
              '  RECORD AREAS WITH NO VALID RECORDS'.

    05 SUMMARY-LINE-3.
       10                         PIC X(1)    VALUE SPACE.
       10 O-SYNONYM-CTR           PIC ZZ9.
       10                         PIC X(22)   VALUE
              '  SYNONYMS ENCOUNTERED'.

    05 SUMMARY-LINE-4.
       10                         PIC X(1)    VALUE SPACE.
       10 O-REWRITE-ERROR-CTR     PIC ZZ9.
       10                         PIC X(16)   VALUE
              '  REWRITE ERRORS'.

01  END-LINE.
    05 PIC X(29)   VALUE SPACES.
    05 PIC X(23)   VALUE '***   END OF REPORT   ***'.
    05 PIC X(28)   VALUE SPACES.

PROCEDURE DIVISION.

100-LOAD-PERSONNEL-FILE.
    PERFORM 200-START-UP.
    PERFORM 210-PROCESS-DETAIL-RECORD
        UNTIL NO-MORE-RECORDS OR FILE-IS-FULL.
    PERFORM 220-FINISH-UP.
    STOP RUN.

200-START-UP.
    OPEN INPUT DETAIL-FILE
          I-O MASTER-FILE
         OUTPUT AUDIT-REPORT.
    MOVE 250 TO WS-FILE-SIZE.
    ACCEPT WS-DATE FROM DATE.
    MOVE WS-DATE TO O-DATE.
    MOVE 'YES' TO WS-MORE-RECORDS.
    MOVE 'NO ' TO WS-FULL-FILE-FLAG.
    INITIALIZE PROGRAM-COUNTERS.
    PERFORM 300-WRITE-REPORT-HEADERS.
    PERFORM 310-READ-DETAIL-RECORD.

210-PROCESS-DETAIL-RECORD.
    PERFORM 320-LOAD-MASTER-RECORD.
    PERFORM 330-PREPARE-AUDIT-LINE.
    IF FILE-IS-FULL
        NEXT SENTENCE
    ELSE
        PERFORM 310-READ-DETAIL-RECORD.

220-FINISH-UP.
    WRITE PRINTLINE FROM SYNONYM-MESSAGE
        AFTER ADVANCING 3 LINES.
    PERFORM 340-PREPARE-SUMMARY.
    WRITE PRINTLINE FROM END-LINE
        AFTER ADVANCING 5 LINES.
    CLOSE DETAIL-FILE
          MASTER-FILE
          AUDIT-REPORT.
```

```
300-WRITE-REPORT-HEADERS.
    WRITE PRINTLINE FROM COMPANY-NAME
        AFTER ADVANCING PAGE.
    WRITE PRINTLINE FROM DATE-LINE
        AFTER ADVANCING 2 LINES.
    WRITE PRINTLINE FROM REPORT-NAME
        AFTER ADVANCING 2 LINES.
    WRITE PRINTLINE FROM HEADINGS-1
        AFTER ADVANCING 2 LINES.
    WRITE PRINTLINE FROM HEADINGS-2
        AFTER ADVANCING 1 LINE.
    MOVE 2 TO WS-PROPER-SPACING.

310-READ-DETAIL-RECORD.
    READ DETAIL-FILE RECORD
        AT END
            SET NO-MORE-RECORDS TO TRUE.

320-LOAD-MASTER-RECORD.
    DIVIDE I-SSN BY WS-FILE-SIZE GIVING WS-QUOTIENT
        REMAINDER WS-LOCATION-NO.
    ADD 1 TO WS-LOCATION-NO.
    MOVE WS-LOCATION-NO TO WS-INITIAL-HASH.
    PERFORM 400-READ-MASTER-FILE.
    IF DUMMY-RECORD
        PERFORM 410-PREPARE-MASTER-RECORD
    ELSE
        PERFORM 420-SEARCH-FOR-LOCATION
    END-IF.

330-PREPARE-AUDIT-LINE.
    MOVE SPACES TO AUDIT-LINE.
    IF FILE-IS-FULL
        MOVE I-SSN TO O-MESS-1-SSN
        MOVE FULL-FILE-MESSAGE TO AUDIT-LINE
    ELSE
        IF REWRITE-ERROR
            MOVE I-SSN TO O-MESS-2-SSN
            MOVE REWRITE-ERROR-MESSAGE TO AUDIT-LINE
        ELSE
            MOVE WS-LOCATION-NO TO O-RELATIVE-NO
            MOVE WS-INITIAL-HASH TO O-HASH
            MOVE I-SSN TO O-SSN
            MOVE I-NAME TO O-NAME
            IF SYN-FLAG-ON
                MOVE '*' TO O-SYN-FLAG
            END-IF
        END-IF
    END-IF.
    WRITE PRINTLINE FROM AUDIT-LINE
        AFTER ADVANCING WS-PROPER-SPACING.
    MOVE 1 TO WS-PROPER-SPACING.
    SET SYN-FLAG-OFF TO TRUE.

340-PREPARE-SUMMARY.
    MOVE WS-MASTER-RECORD-CTR TO O-MASTER-RECORD-CTR.
    WRITE PRINTLINE FROM SUMMARY-LINE-1
        AFTER ADVANCING 4 LINES.
    MOVE WS-NO-VALID-RECORD-CTR TO O-NO-VALID-RECORD-CTR.
    WRITE PRINTLINE FROM SUMMARY-LINE-2
        AFTER ADVANCING 1 LINE.
    MOVE WS-SYNONYM-CTR TO O-SYNONYM-CTR.
    WRITE PRINTLINE FROM SUMMARY-LINE-3
        AFTER ADVANCING 1 LINE.
    MOVE WS-REWRITE-ERROR-CTR TO O-REWRITE-ERROR-CTR.
    WRITE PRINTLINE FROM SUMMARY-LINE-4
        AFTER ADVANCING 1 LINE.

400-READ-MASTER-FILE.
    READ MASTER-FILE RECORD
        INVALID KEY
            ADD 1 TO WS-NO-VALID-RECORD-CTR.

410-PREPARE-MASTER-RECORD.
    MOVE I-SSN TO MR-SSN.
    MOVE I-NAME TO MR-NAME.
    MOVE I-ADDRESS TO MR-ADDRESS.
    MOVE I-DOB TO MR-DOB.
    MOVE I-DOH TO MR-DOH.
    REWRITE MASTER-RECORD
        INVALID KEY
            ADD 1 TO WS-REWRITE-ERROR-CTR
            SET REWRITE-ERROR TO TRUE
        NOT INVALID KEY
            ADD 1 TO WS-MASTER-RECORD-CTR.
```

Figure 4.31 continued

```
420-SEARCH-FOR-LOCATION.
    MOVE WS-LOCATION-NO TO WS-STARTING-NO.
    SET BEGIN-SEARCH TO TRUE.
    PERFORM 500-TRY-N-WRITE
        UNTIL STOP-SEARCH OR FILE-IS-FULL.

500-TRY-N-WRITE.
    ADD 1 TO WS-LOCATION-NO.
    IF WS-LOCATION-NO > WS-FILE-SIZE
        SUBTRACT WS-FILE-SIZE FROM WS-LOCATION-NO
    ELSE
        NEXT SENTENCE.
    IF WS-LOCATION-NO = WS-STARTING-NO
        SET FILE-IS-FULL TO TRUE
    ELSE
        PERFORM 400-READ-MASTER-FILE
        IF DUMMY-RECORD
            SET SYN-FLAG-ON TO TRUE
            ADD 1 TO WS-SYNONYM-CTR
            PERFORM 410-PREPARE-MASTER-RECORD
            SET STOP-SEARCH TO TRUE
        END-IF
    END-IF.
```

Figure 4.32 Audit report produced by the relative file loading program

```
                              JOCELYN ORIGINALS

                   MASTER PERSONNEL FILE LOADED 89/06/28

                                 AUDIT REPORT

RELATIVE KEY    DIVISION ALGORITHM
   VALUE         REMAINDER PLUS 1          SSN                  NAME

    016               016             743 14 2265     ABRUZZI, KENNETH L.
    032               032             032 56 7781     AITKEN, THOMAS R.
    024               024             144 21 7773     ALTERMAN, MAUREEN E.
    192               192             014 76 6691     ARMSTRONG, GEORGE
    015               015             381 66 2514     BAHR, LENA M.
    242               242             179 62 3741     BLAZUCK, JOSEPH A.
    244               244             005 58 9243     BUXBAUM, JOAN M.
    044               044             623 51 4793     CARTER, AMEKIA L.
    017               016*            042 75 0015     COLETTI, SARAH T.
    018               018             016 49 3017     COUGHLIN, AILEEN M.
    065               065             215 13 7814     CUMMINGS, DOROTHEA
    014               014             771 89 4263     CYR, ROSARIO
    033               033             314 76 4532     DESROSIERS, RICHARD
    003               003             364 92 3752     DURANT, MARIE L.
    216               216             039 76 4715     GAFFNEY, MARYLYN
    157               157             211 38 4406     KACHADOURIAN, NATALI
    145               145             253 74 9144     LAKE, SUE
    213               213             130 04 3962     MARKARIAN, MARIAN
    080               080             032 56 1579     MAYO, EVANGELINA
    207               207             013 40 7206     MCGEE, BERNARD W.
    076               076             124 67 0325     MOONEY, RONALD
    162               162             226 15 3911     OVERDEEP, CYNTHIA
    226               226             149 20 1475     PACCASASSIE, DEBBIE
    013               013             033 28 1512     PEARSON, ARTHUR
    140               140             150 24 6389     PRIMEAU, ISABEL
    009               009             432 15 7258     ROMA, GILDA
    034               034             234 89 1533     SHERIDAN, RICHARD J.
    143               143             322 15 0642     STURDAHL, DEBRA
    126               126             026 30 7625     VELTRI, JOHN A.

* DENOTES A SYNONYM


 29  RECORDS LOADED INTO MASTER FILE
  0  RECORD AREAS WITH NO VALID RECORDS
  1  SYNONYMS ENCOUNTERED
  0  REWRITE ERRORS


                         ***  END OF REPORT  ***
```

Other Randomization Procedures

If the records that must be loaded into a relative file do not contain a data field whose values can be used directly to specify the record areas in the file where the records are to be stored, it is obvious that some data transformation must occur to provide the needed hashed values. The goal of the data transformation is to generate ordinal numbers that are randomly and evenly distributed within the range specified by the size of the file. Additionally, since data transformation techniques cannot guarantee a one-to-one correspondence between initial field values and the resulting hashed values, a "good" transformation procedure should minimize the number of synonyms that it generates. The most commonly used data transformation or randomization procedure is the Division Algorithm Method applied in the preceding program.

Since the COBOL language does not provide standard randomization procedures, programmers often employ a combination of techniques so as to provide successful results in the particular application at hand. Such an example will be shown shortly.

Another randomization technique that is often used is the Folding Method. It may be applied in a variety of ways. Two examples follow.

Folding Example 1

Suppose a file has 100,000 record areas, and employees' Social Security numbers are to be transformed to generate relative key values. One way of doing this is to fold the last four digits into the first four digits, as illustrated:

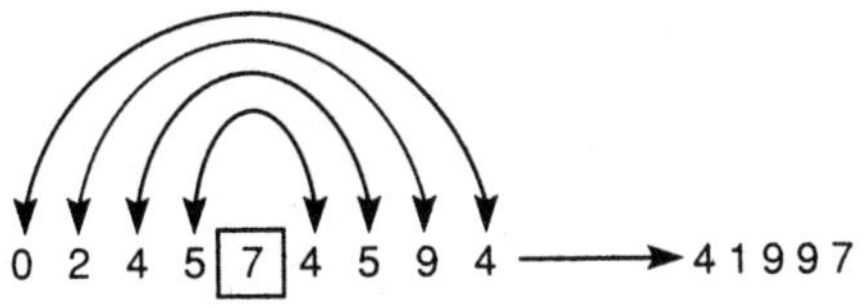

This Social Security number has hashed to 41997. Note that the ninth digit is added to the first (4 + 0 = 4) to produce the first digit of the hashed value; the eighth digit is added to the second digit (9 + 2 = 11), the extra digit in the sum is discarded, and the second digit of the hashed value is 1; the seventh digit is added to the third digit (5 + 4 = 9) to produce the third digit of the hashed value; the sixth digit is added to the fourth digit (4 + 5 = 9) to produce the fourth digit of the hashed value; and the fifth digit remains as is. The resulting hashed values are in the range of 00000 to 99999. By adding 1 to the hashed values, the resulting range is 00001 to 100,000.

Folding Example 2

Suppose a file has 1000 record areas, and employees' Social Security numbers are to be transformed to generate relative key values. In this case, the Social Security number digits can be separated into three parts and the corresponding digits added, as illustrated:

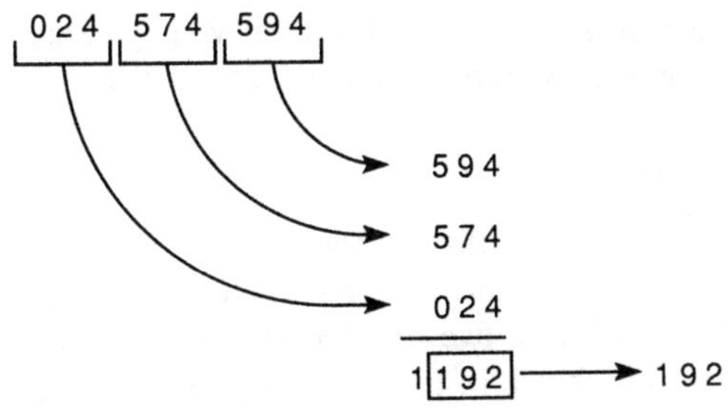

This Social Security number has hashed to 192. The extra digit (1) is dropped. Resulting values are in the range from 000 to 999, and by adding 1 to the results of the transformation, the range is 001 to 1000.

■ **Figure 4.33** Social Security numbers transformed to relative key values

SSN			Relative Key Value	
743	14	2265	151	
032	56	7781	081	
144	21	7773	135	
014	76	6691	172	
381	66	2514	250	
179	62	3741	244	
005	58	9243	138	
623	51	4793	031	
042	75	0015	108	
016	49	3017	227	
215	13	7814	167	
771	89	4263	029	
314	76	4532	011	
364	92	3752	040	
039	76	4715	219	
211	38	4406	002	
253	74	9144	147	
130	04	3962	136	
032	56	1579	173	
013	40	7206	027	
124	67	0325	120	
226	15	3911	241	
149	20	1475	126	
033	28	1512	127	
150	24	6389	186	
432	15	7258	148	
234	89	1533	059	
322	15	0642	115	
026	30	7625	059	060

A close examination of folding example 2 reveals that this procedure would not have been appropriate in the program of Figure 4.31, since the file size is 250. However, by combining a digit transformation to some of the hashed values produced in example 2, relative key values in the range from 1 to 250 may be produced. For instance, apply the following rules in order:

Rule 1. If the folding hashed value is in the range from 1 to 250, accept it as is.

Rule 2.
a. If the leftmost digit is 3, 6, or 9, replace it by 0.
b. If the leftmost digit is 4, 7, or 8, replace it by 1.
c. If the leftmost digit is 5, replace it by 2.

Rule 3.
a. If the leftmost digit is 2 and the middle digit is 6, 7, 8, or 9, decrease the digit's value by 5.
b. If the leftmost digit is 2 and the middle digit is 5, replace the rightmost digit by 0.

Examine the following applications:

1. By folding, 743142265 yields directly 151, and by rule 1, it is retained as the relative key value.
2. By folding, 381662514 yields 558. By rule 2c, 558 becomes 258, and by rule 3b, 258 becomes 250.
3. By folding, 226153911 yields 291. By rule 3a, 291 becomes 241.

If this folding method, combined with the digit transformation specified in these rules, is applied to the Social Security numbers listed in Figure 4.32, nine relative key values fall in the range from 001 to 100, fifteen relative key values fall in the range from 101 to 200, and five relative key values fall in the range from 201 to 250. The complete list of transformations is shown in Figure 4.33. Note that one synonym was produced.

Other randomization techniques are available, but a detailed presentation is beyond the intended scope of this material.

Figure 4.34 System flowchart for master personnel file update

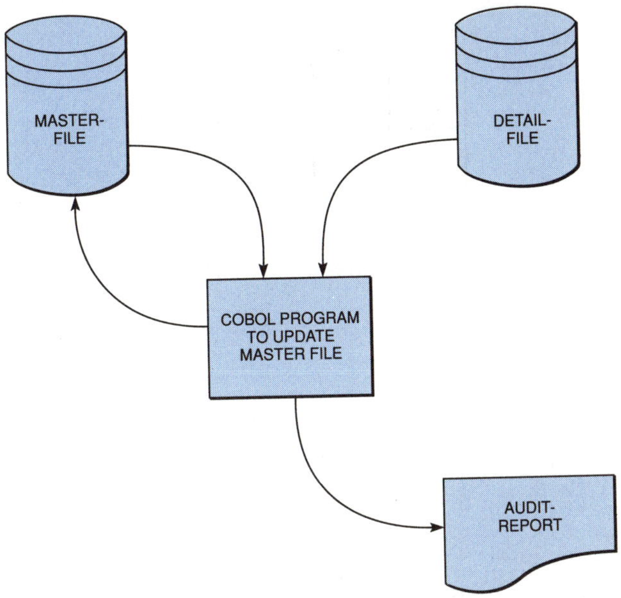

Updating a Relative File Using a Randomization Procedure

We now develop a program to update the master personnel file of the Jocelyn Originals Company. The system flowchart is shown in Figure 4.34.

As expected, the detail file contains a record for each employee record involved in the update. The process codes are the following familiar ones:

> "1" to denote a new employee record that must be added to the file. In addition to the process code, this record must contain the new employee's name, address, Social Security number, date of birth, and date hired.
>
> "2" to denote a record to be deleted from the master file. In addition to the process code, this record contains only the Social Security number, since this is the only employee data needed to identify the master file record that must be deleted.
>
> "3" to denote a master file record for which some field values must be changed. In addition to the process code, this record contains the Social Security number and the new data. In this program, the new data is restricted to a new name and/or a new address.

The records in the detail file will be arranged in descending order by process code. As a result, all records to be updated will be processed first; then, all records to be deleted from the master file will be deleted; and finally, the new employee records will be added to the file.

The layout of the detail record is shown in Figure 4.35. Note that the process code is in the first data field and the employee's Social Security number is in the second data field.

The printer spacing chart for the audit report is shown in Figure 4.36. Note that a detail line is printed for each detail record. It shows the process code on the record, the employee's Social Security number, the relative key value for the corresponding master record, and the action taken with respect to the record. Error messages are also to be printed if related errors occur during the execution of the program.

The critical logic of this program may be analyzed briefly as follows:

1. Read a detail record.
2. Apply the Division Algorithm to obtain the record's initial hashed value.
3. Read the master record in that record area.

Figure 4.35 Detail record layout

Figure 4.36 Layout of audit report for the master personnel file update

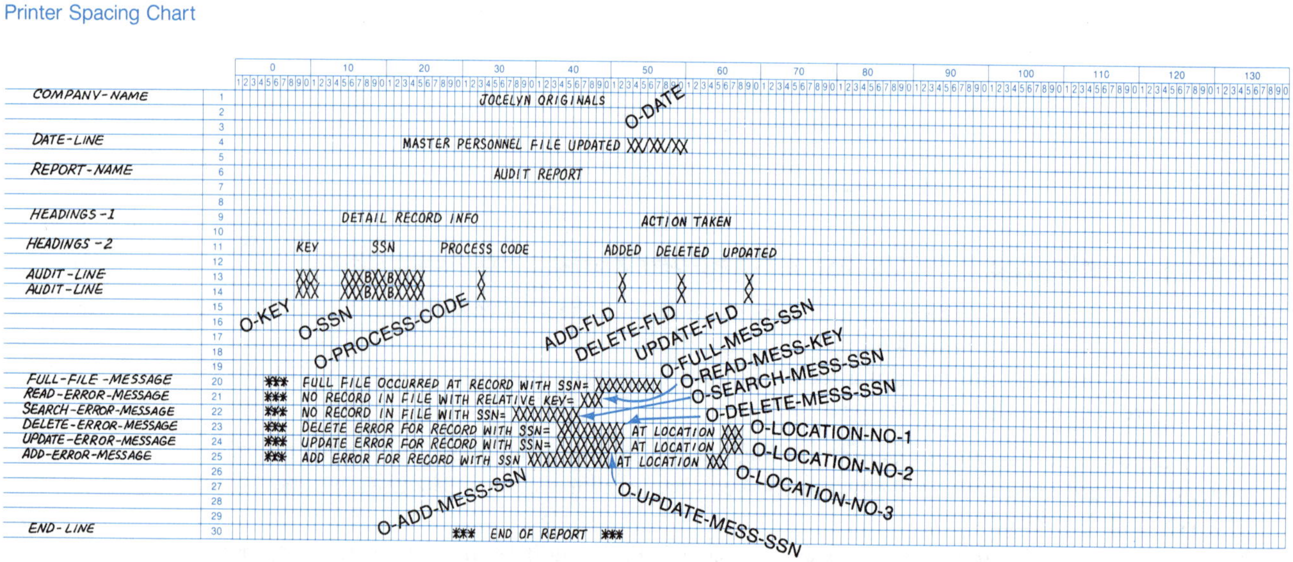

4. Check the process code on the detail record.
   a. If it's a "1," and the read function was not successful, the new record can be inserted here, since there is no logical record in this record area. Move the detail record data to the master record buffer, and write the new master record to the file.
   b. If it's a "1," and the read function was successful, check the master record to see if it is a dummy record. If so, copy the detail record data into the master record, and rewrite the reconstructed record to the master file. If the master record is not a dummy record, then a synonym exists, and a search must begin to locate an available record area. A record area is available if it contains either a dummy record or no logical record. The search continues until a record area is found. If one is not found, the file is full, and an appropriate error message is printed on the report.
   c. If the read function was successful and the process code is a "2," the corresponding master record must be deleted. Before deleting the master record read in step 3, it must be verified as the correct one. It is if its Social Security number matches the one on the detail record. In that case, simply delete the master record. If the master record is not the correct one, due to the presence of a synonym, then a search procedure must be undertaken to find it. It must be found before encountering a dummy record, since the procedure that is used to position records in the file does not allow a dummy or vacant record area between synonyms. If it is found, it must be deleted. If it is not found, an appropriate error message must be printed on the report.

Figure 4.37 Structure chart to update the relative MASTER-FILE

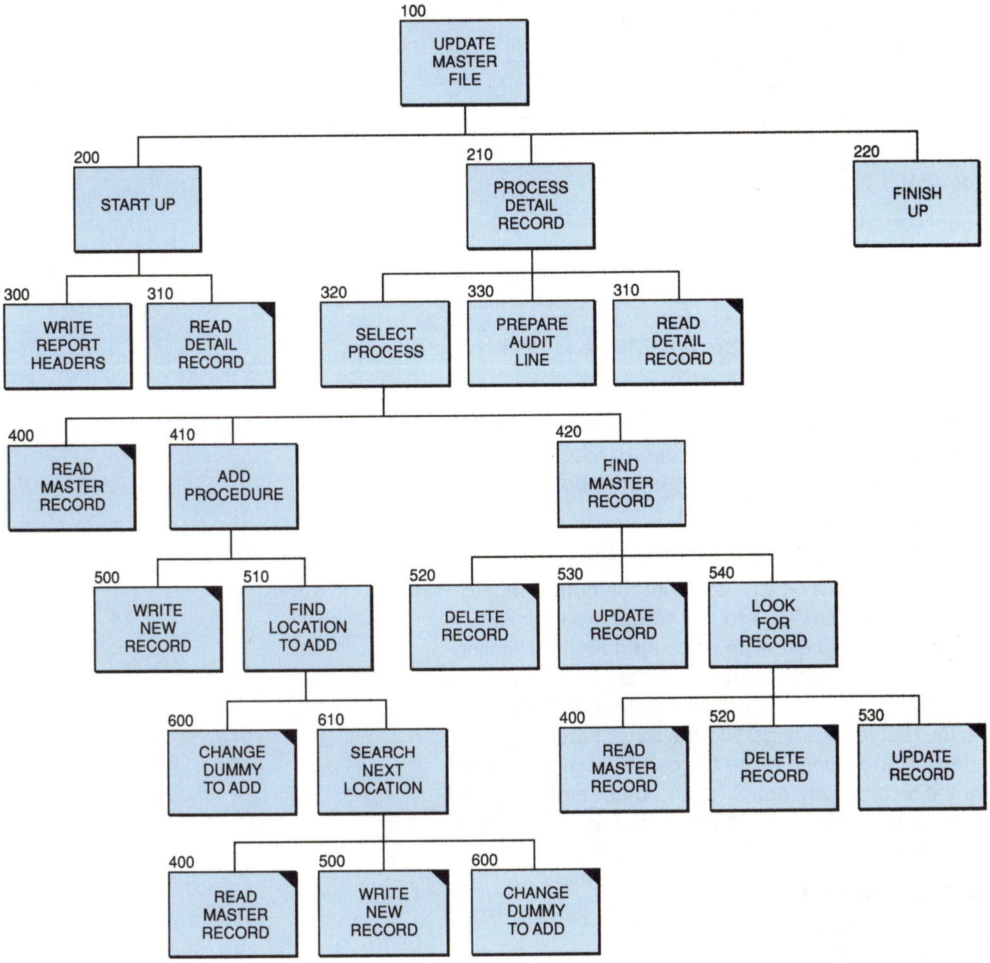

   d. If the process code is a "3," the corresponding master record must be brought up to date. The procedure to find the master record and to update it is similar to the one described in part c on page 300.

   e. If the read function was not successful, and the process code is a "2" or a "3," an appropriate error should be produced on the report.

5. Repeat steps 1 through 4 until there are no more records in the detail file.

The structure chart based on this analysis is shown in Figure 4.37. In particular, note the breakdown of module 320 SELECT PROCESS.

The pseudocode that details the processing steps needed to accomplish the tasks specified in the structure chart and to produce the report as specified in Figure 4.36 is as follows.

100-Update-Master-File.

1. Perform 200-Start-Up.

2. Perform 210-Process-Detail-Record until no more detail records or until master file is full.

3. Perform 220-Finish-Up.

4. Stop the run.

200-Start-Up.

1. Open the file Detail-File in input mode, the file Master-File in input/output mode, and the file Audit-Report in output mode.
2. Set file-size equal to 250.
3. Obtain the date from the operating system.
4. Move date to Date-Line date.
5. Set the flag WS-MORE-DETAIL-RECORDS to "YES".
6. Perform 300-Write-Report-Headers.
7. Perform 310-Read-Detail-Record.

210-Process-Detail-Record.

1. Perform 320-Select-Process.
2. Perform 330-Prepare-Audit-Line.
3. Test the flag WS-FULL-FILE-FLAG:
   if it's equal to "NO ", perform 310-Read-Detail-Record.

220-Finish-Up.

1. Move the record End-Line to the output area Printline.
2. After advancing 5 lines, write the output record Printline.
3. Close Detail-File, Master-File, and Audit-Report.

300-Write-Report-Headers.

1. Move the record Company-Name to the output area Printline.
2. After advancing to a new page, write the output record Printline.
3. Move the record Date-Line to the output area Printline.
4. After advancing 3 lines, write the output record Printline.
5. Move the record Report-Name to the output area Printline.
6. After advancing 2 lines, write the output record Printline.
7. Move the record Headings-1 to the output area Printline.
8. After advancing 3 lines, write the output record Printline.
9. Move the record Headings-2 to the output area Printline.
10. After advancing 2 lines, write the output record Printline.
11. Set proper-spacing to 2.

310-Read-Detail-Record.

1. Read an input Detail-Record.
2. Test for end-of-file record:
   if EOF record reached, set the flag WS-MORE-DETAIL-RECORDS to "NO ".

320-Select-Process.

1. Initialize error-flag to spaces.
2. Divide input Social-Security-number by file-size (250) giving quotient, and store remainder as location-number.
3. Add 1 to location-number.
4. Perform 400-Read-Master-Record.
5. a. If input process-code = "1", perform 410-Add-Procedure.
   b. If input process-code is not = "1" and read is successful, perform 420-Find-Master-Record.
   c. If read is not successful, set error-flag to "R".

330-Prepare-Audit-Line.

1. Move spaces to Audit-Line.
2. If error-flag is not equal to spaces, test error-flag:
   a. If it's equal to "F",
      move input Social-Security-number to Full-File-Message Social-Security-number,
      move the record Full-File-Message to the record area Audit-Line.
   b. If it's equal to "R",
      move input location-number to Read-Error-Message location-number,
      move the record Read-Error-Message to the record area Audit-Line.
   c. If it's equal to "S",
      move input Social-Security-number to Search-Error-Message Social-Security-number,
      move the record Search-Error-Message to the record area Audit-Line.

d. If it's equal to "D",
   move input Social-Security-number to Delete-Error-Message Social-Security-number,
   move location-number to Delete-Error-Message location-number,
   move the record Delete-Error-Message to the record area Audit-Line.
e. If it's equal to "U",
   move input Social-Security-number to Update-Error-Message Social-Security-number,
   move location-number to Update-Error-Message location-number,
   move the record Update-Error-Message to the record area Audit-Line.
f. If it's equal to "A",
   move input Social-Security-number to
   Add-Error-Message Social-Security-number,
   move location-number to Add-Error-Message location-number,
   move the record Add-Error-Message to the record area Audit-Line.

3. If error-flag is equal to spaces,
   a. Move location-number to Audit-Line key.
   b. Move input Social-Security-number to Audit-Line Social-Security-number.
   c. Move input process-code to Audit-Line process-code.
   d. Test input process-code:
      i. If "1", move "X" to Audit-Line add-field.
      ii. If "2", move "X" to Audit-Line delete-field.
      iii. If "3", move "X" to Audit-Line update-field.
4. Move the record Audit-Line to the output area Printline.
5. After advancing proper-spacing, write the output record Printline.
6. Set proper-spacing to 1.

400-Read-Master-Record.

1. Read Master-File master-record.
2. Test for invalid key:
   if invalid key condition exists, move "R" to error-flag.

410-Add-Procedure.

1. Test whether read was successful:
   a. If so, perform 510-Find-Location-to-Add.
   b. If not, perform 500-Write-New-Record.

420-Find-Master-Record.

1. Test if input Social-Security-number is equal to master-record Social-Security-number:
   a. If it is, test input process-code:
      i. If "2", perform 520-Delete-Record.
      ii. If "3", perform 530-Update-Record.
   b. If it is not,
      i. Set search-loop-flag to "ON ".
      ii. Perform 540-Look-For-Record until search-loop-flag is equal to "OFF"
      or until error-flag is equal to "S".

500-Write-New-Record.

1. Move input Social-Security-number to master-record Social-Security-number.
2. Move input name to master-record name.
3. Move input address to master-record address.
4. Move input date-of-birth to master-record date-of-birth.
5. Move input date-hired to master-record date-hired.
6. Write master-record.
7. Test for invalid key:
   if invalid key condition exists, move "22" to master-file-flag,
   move "A" to error-flag.

510-Find-Location-to-Add.

1. If master-record is a dummy-record, perform 600-Change-Dummy-to-Add.
2. If master-record is not a dummy-record,
   a. Set starting-number equal to location-number.
   b. Set search-loop-flag to "ON ".
3. Perform 610-Search-Next-Location until search-loop-flag is equal to "OFF",
   or until file-is-full.

520-Delete-Record.

1. Delete Master-File master-record.
2. Test for invalid key:
   if invalid key condition exists, set error-flag to "D".

530-Update-Record.

1. Test input name:
   if not equal to spaces, move input name to master-record name.
2. Test input address:
   if not equal to spaces, move input address to master-record address.
3. Rewrite master-record.
4. Test for invalid key:
   if invalid key condition exists, set error-flag to "U".

540-Look-For-Record.

1. Add 1 to location-number.
2. Test if location-number is greater than file-size:
   if so, subtract file-size from location-number.
3. Perform 400-Read-Master-Record.
4. Test if master-record is a dummy-record:
   a. If so, set error-flag to "S".
   b. If not a dummy-record, test if input Social-Security-number is equal to master-record Social-Security-number:
      If it is:
      i. Set search-loop-flag to "OFF".
      ii. Test input process-code:
          If "2", perform 520-Delete-Record.
          If "3", perform 530-Update-Record.

600-Change-Dummy-to-Add.

1. Move input Social-Security-number to master-record Social-Security-number.
2. Move input name to master-record name.
3. Move input address to master-record address.
4. Move input date-of-birth to master-record date-of-birth.
5. Move input date-hired to master-record date-hired.
6. Rewrite master-record.
7. Test for invalid key:
   if invalid key condition exists, move "23" to master-file-flag,
   move "A" to error-flag.

610-Search-Next-Location.

1. Add 1 to location-number.
2. Test location-number:
   if location-number is greater than file-size, then subtract file-size from location-number.
3. Test location-number again:
   a. If location-number is equal to starting-number,
      set the condition file-is-full to true.
   b. If location-number is not equal to starting-number,
      perform 400-Read-Master-Record;
      i. If read is not successful, perform 500-Write-New-Record,
         set search-loop-flag to "OFF".
      ii. If read is successful, test Master-File master-record:
          if it's a dummy record, then perform 600-Change-Dummy-to-Add,
          set search-loop-flag to "OFF".

The program flowchart corresponding to the pseudocode is shown in Figure 4.38. Note the wrap-around procedure and the test for a full file in module 610-SEARCH-NEXT-LOCATION.

The program is listed in Figure 4.39, the records of the file DETAIL-FILE are shown in Figure 4.40, and the audit report is shown in Figure 4.41.

Figure 4.38 Program flowchart to update relative MASTER-FILE

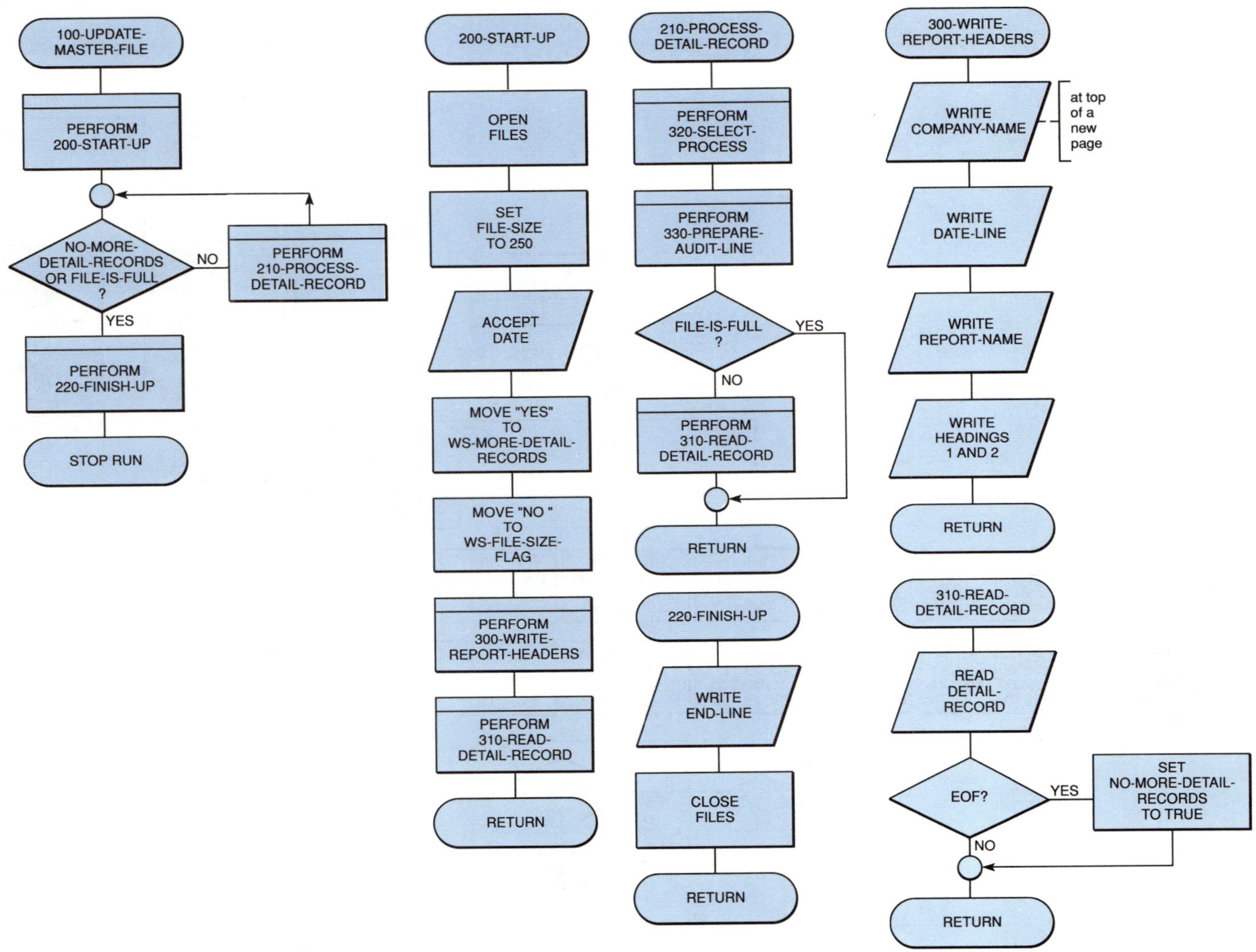

■ **Figure 4.38** continued

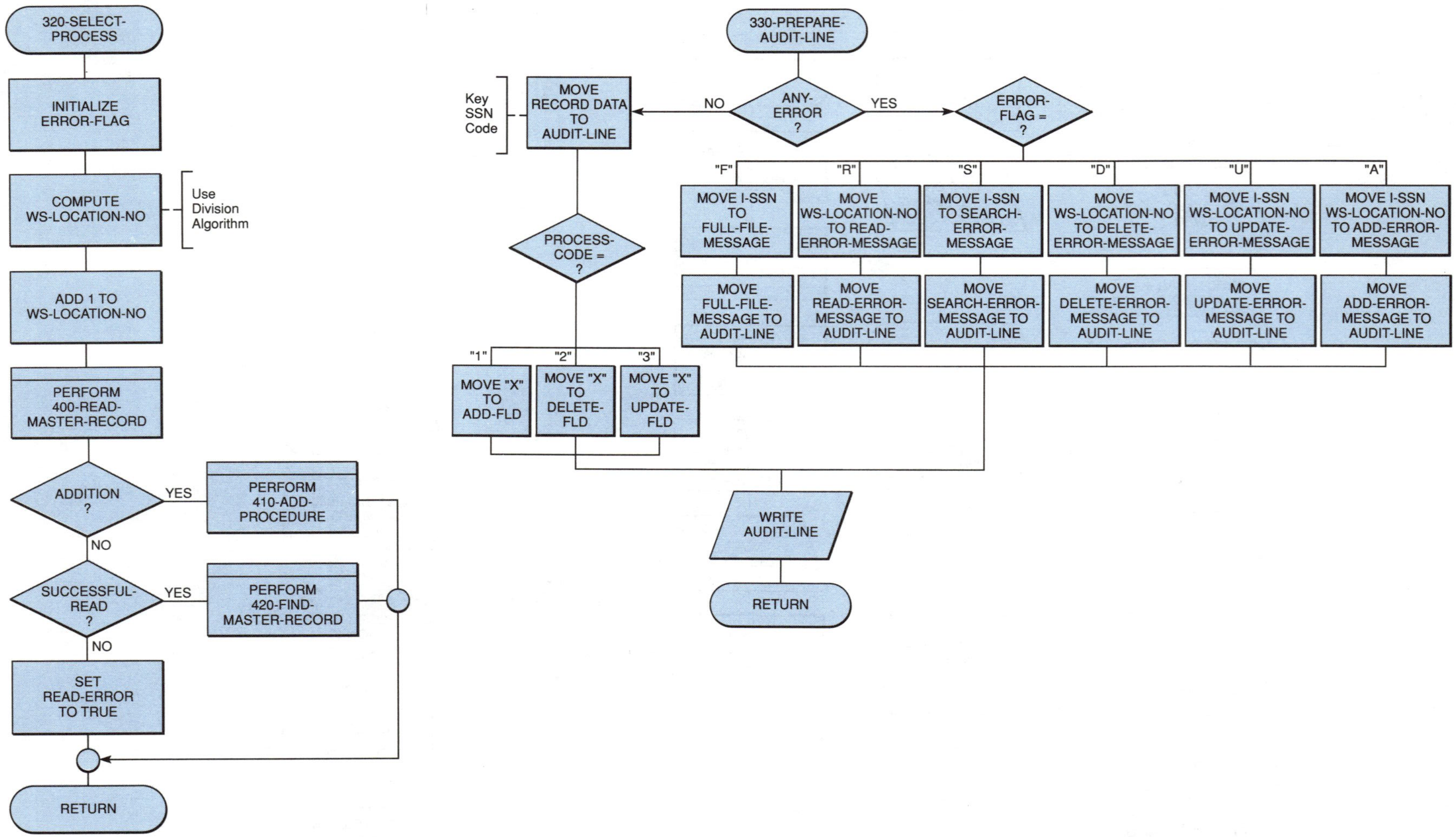

Figure 4.38 continued

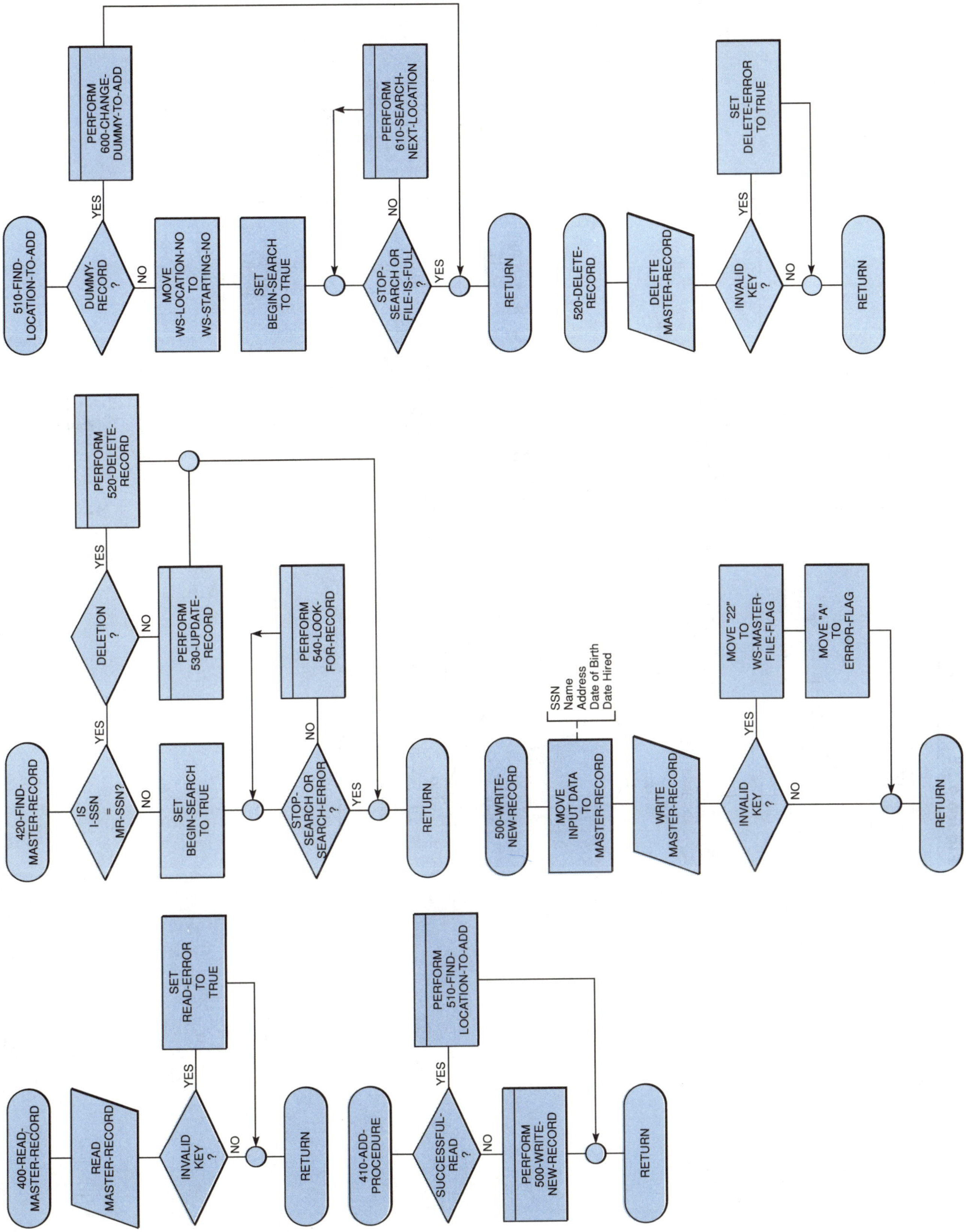

■ **Figure 4.38** continued

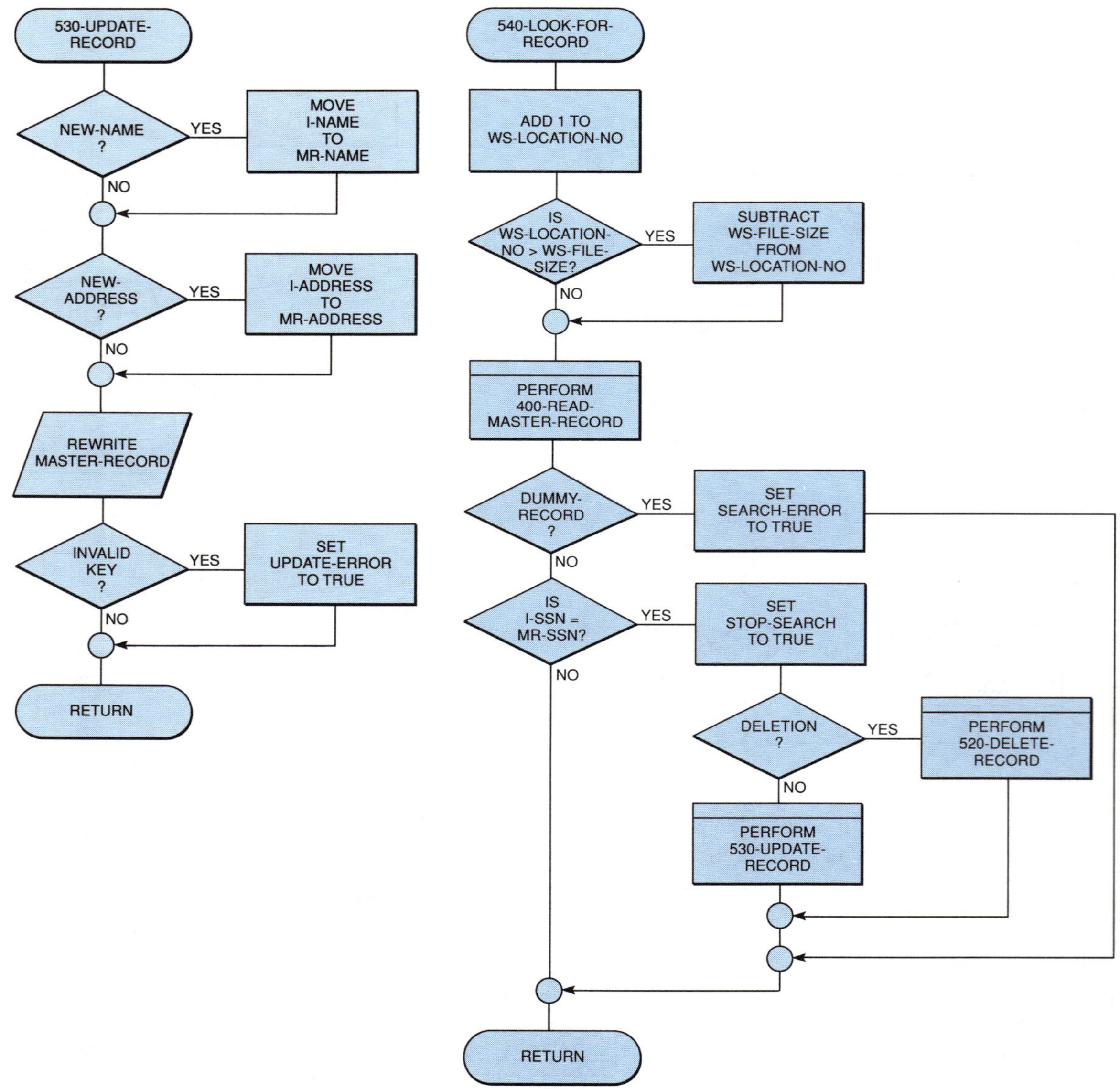

■ **Figure 4.38** continued

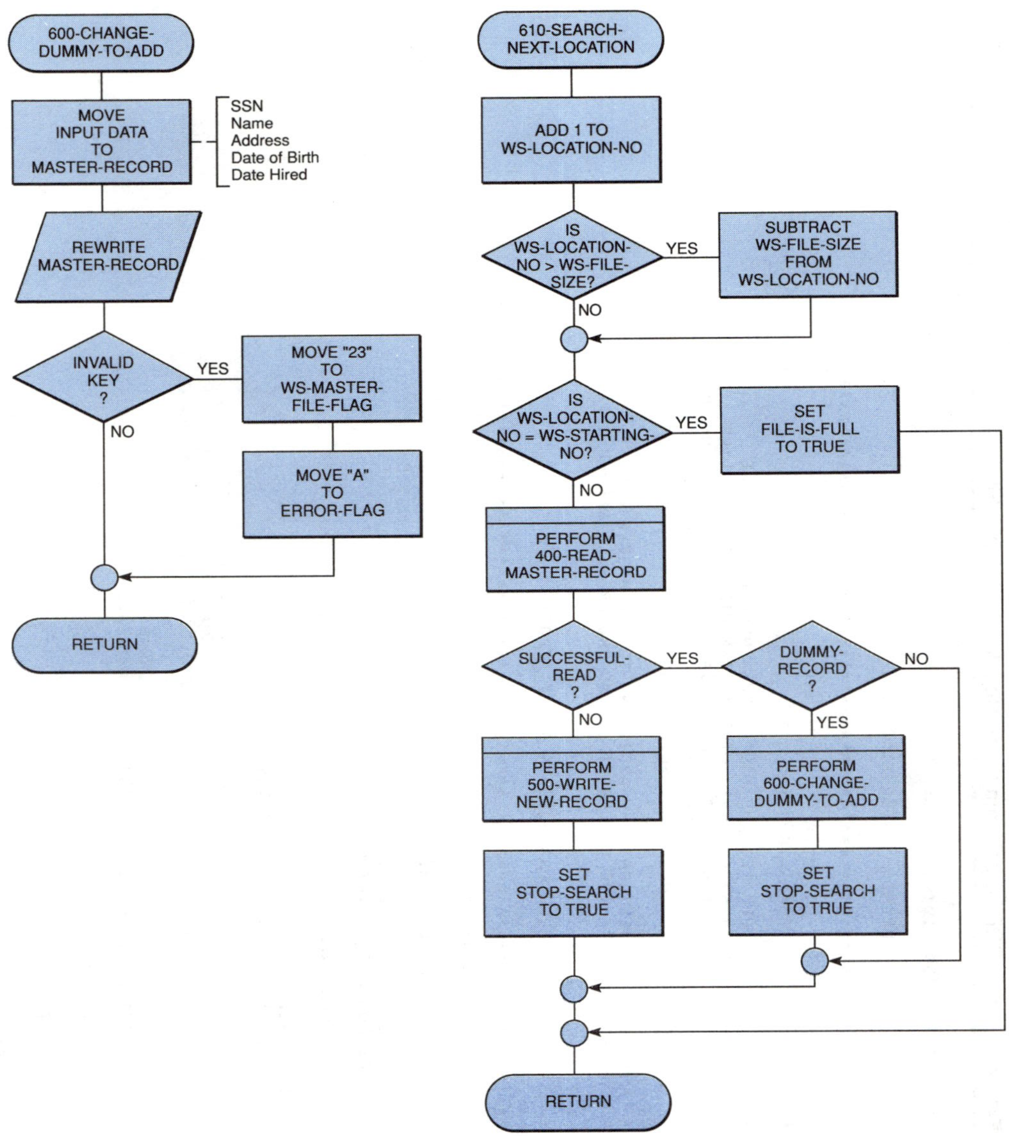

■ **Figure 4.39** COBOL program to update relative MASTER-FILE

```
 IDENTIFICATION DIVISION.

 PROGRAM-ID.    UPDATE-MASTER-FILE-2.

*****************************************************************
*                                                               *
*  AUTHOR.          PAQUETTE.                                   *
*  DATE WRITTEN.  APRIL 1989.                                   *
*                                                               *
*   THIS PROGRAM UPDATES THE MASTER PERSONNEL FILE OF THE       *
*   JOCELYN ORIGINALS COMPANY.  THE MASTER FILE HAS RELATIVE    *
*   ORGANIZATION.  THE RELATIVE KEY DATA ITEM IS WS-LOCATION-NO.*
*   ITS VALUE IS OBTAINED BY USING THE DIVISION ALGORITHM       *
*   METHOD APPLIED TO SOCIAL SECURITY NUMBERS.                  *
*                                                               *
*   THE DETAIL FILE CONTAINS ADDITIONS TO THE MASTER FILE,      *
*   DELETIONS FROM THE MASTER FILE, AND MASTER FILE RECORD      *
*   UPDATES.                                                    *
*                                                               *
*   THE PROGRAM ALSO PRODUCES AN AUDIT REPORT.                  *
*                                                               *
*****************************************************************

 ENVIRONMENT DIVISION.

 CONFIGURATION SECTION.

 SOURCE-COMPUTER.  VAX-VMS-8650.
 OBJECT-COMPUTER.  VAX-VMS-8650.

 INPUT-OUTPUT SECTION.

 FILE-CONTROL.
     SELECT DETAIL-FILE  ASSIGN TO COB$INPUT.
     SELECT MASTER-FILE  ASSIGN TO 'JOCMSTR3.DAT'
                                   ORGANIZATION IS RELATIVE
                                   ACCESS MODE IS RANDOM
                                   RELATIVE KEY IS WS-LOCATION-NO
                                   FILE STATUS IS
                                       WS-MASTER-FILE-FLAG.
     SELECT AUDIT-REPORT ASSIGN TO COB$OUTPUT.

 DATA DIVISION.

 FILE SECTION.

 FD  DETAIL-FILE
     RECORD CONTAINS 101 CHARACTERS.

 01  DETAIL-RECORD.
     05 I-PROCESS-CODE     PIC X(1).
        88 ADDITION                  VALUE '1'.
        88 DELETION                  VALUE '2'.
        88 CHANGE                    VALUE '3'.
     05 I-SSN              PIC 9(9).
     05 I-NAME             PIC X(20).
        88 NOT-NEW-NAME              VALUE SPACES.
     05 I-ADDRESS          PIC X(37).
        88 NOT-NEW-ADDRESS           VALUE SPACES.
     05 I-DOB              PIC X(6).
     05 I-DOH              PIC X(6).
     05                    PIC X(22).

 FD  MASTER-FILE
     RECORD CONTAINS 100 CHARACTERS.

 01  MASTER-RECORD.
     05 MR-SSN         PIC 9(9).
        88 DUMMY-RECORD          VALUE ZEROS.
     05 MR-NAME        PIC X(20).
     05 MR-ADDRESS     PIC X(37).
     05 MR-DOB         PIC X(6).
     05 MR-DOH         PIC X(6).
     05                PIC X(22).

 FD  AUDIT-REPORT
     RECORD CONTAINS 80 CHARACTERS.

 01  PRINTLINE         PIC X(80).
```

Figure 4.39 continued

```
WORKING-STORAGE SECTION.

01  RELATIVE-FILE-ITEMS.
    05 WS-LOCATION-NO         PIC 9(3).
    05 WS-STARTING-NO         PIC 9(3).
    05 WS-QUOTIENT            PIC 9(9).
    05 WS-FILE-SIZE           PIC 9(3).
    05 WS-MASTER-FILE-FLAG    PIC XX.
       88 SUCCESSFUL                     VALUE '00'.
       88 NO-LOGICAL-RECORD              VALUE '23'.
    05 WS-FILE-SEARCH-FLAG    PIC X(3).
       88 RECORD-IS-FOUND                VALUE 'YES'.

01  PROGRAM-CONTROLS.
    05 WS-DATE                PIC X(6).
    05 WS-PROPER-SPACING      PIC 9.

01  PROGRAM-FLAGS.
    05 WS-MORE-DETAIL-RECORDS    PIC X(3).
       88 NO-MORE-DETAIL-RECORDS          VALUE 'NO '.
    05 ERROR-FLAG                PIC X(1).
       88 FILE-IS-FULL                    VALUE 'F'.
       88 READ-ERROR                      VALUE 'R'.
       88 SEARCH-ERROR                    VALUE 'S'.
       88 DELETE-ERROR                    VALUE 'D'.
       88 UPDATE-ERROR                    VALUE 'U'.
       88 ADD-ERROR                       VALUE 'A'.
       88 ANY-ERROR                       VALUES 'F', 'R', 'S',
                                                 'D', 'U', 'A'.
    05 SEARCH-LOOP-FLAG          PIC X(3).
       88 BEGIN-SEARCH                    VALUE 'ON '.
       88 STOP-SEARCH                     VALUE 'OFF'.

01  COMPANY-NAME.
    05 PIC X(32) VALUE SPACES.
    05 PIC X(17) VALUE 'JOCELYN ORIGINALS'.
    05 PIC X(31) VALUE SPACES.

01  DATE-LINE.
    05           PIC X(22) VALUE SPACES.
    05           PIC X(30) VALUE 'MASTER PERSONNEL FILE UPDATED '.
    05 O-DATE    PIC XX/XX/XX.
    05           PIC X(20) VALUE SPACES.

01  REPORT-NAME.
    05 PIC X(34) VALUE SPACES.
    05 PIC X(12) VALUE 'AUDIT REPORT'.
    05 PIC X(34) VALUE SPACES.

01  HEADINGS-1.
    05 PIC X(14) VALUE SPACES.
    05 PIC X(18) VALUE 'DETAIL RECORD INFO'.
    05 PIC X(22) VALUE SPACES.
    05 PIC X(12) VALUE 'ACTION TAKEN'.
    05 PIC X(14) VALUE SPACES.

01  HEADINGS-2.
    05 PIC X(8)  VALUE SPACES.
    05 PIC X(3)  VALUE 'KEY'.
    05 PIC X(7)  VALUE SPACES.
    05 PIC X(3)  VALUE 'SSN'.
    05 PIC X(6)  VALUE SPACES.
    05 PIC X(12) VALUE 'PROCESS CODE'.
    05 PIC X(10) VALUE SPACES.
    05 PIC X(5)  VALUE 'ADDED'.
    05 PIC X(2)  VALUE SPACES.
    05 PIC X(7)  VALUE 'DELETED'.
    05 PIC X(2)  VALUE SPACES.
    05 PIC X(7)  VALUE 'UPDATED'.
    05 PIC X(8)  VALUE SPACES.

01  AUDIT-LINE.
    05                   PIC X(8).
    05 O-KEY             PIC 9(3).
    05                   PIC X(3).
    05 O-SSN             PIC XXXBXXBXXXX.
    05                   PIC X(7).
    05 O-PROCESS-CODE    PIC X.
    05                   PIC X(18).
    05 ADD-FLD           PIC X.
    05                   PIC X(7).
    05 DELETE-FLD        PIC X.
    05                   PIC X(8).
    05 UPDATE-FLD        PIC X.
    05                   PIC X(11).
```

```
01  ERROR-MESSAGES.
    05 FULL-FILE-MESSAGE.
       10                      PIC X(4)    VALUE SPACES.
       10                      PIC X(44)   VALUE
                '***  FULL FILE OCCURRED AT RECORD WITH SSN= '.
       10 O-FULL-MESS-SSN      PIC X(9).
    05 READ-ERROR-MESSAGE.
       10                      PIC X(4)    VALUE SPACES.
       10                      PIC X(42)   VALUE
                '***  NO RECORD IN FILE WITH RELATIVE KEY= '.
       10 O-READ-MESS-KEY      PIC 9(3).
    05 SEARCH-ERROR-MESSAGE.
       10                      PIC X(4)    VALUE SPACES.
       10                      PIC X(33)   VALUE
                '***  NO RECORD IN FILE WITH SSN= '.
       10 O-SEARCH-MESS-SSN PIC X(9).
    05 DELETE-ERROR-MESSAGE.
       10                      PIC X(4)    VALUE SPACES.
       10                      PIC X(39)   VALUE
                '***  DELETE ERROR FOR RECORD WITH SSN= '.
       10 O-DELETE-MESS-SSN PIC X(9).
       10                      PIC X(13)   VALUE ' AT LOCATION '.
       10 O-LOCATION-NO-1      PIC 9(3).
    05 UPDATE-ERROR-MESSAGE.
       10                      PIC X(4)    VALUE SPACES.
       10                      PIC X(39)   VALUE
                '***  CHANGE ERROR FOR RECORD WITH SSN= '.
       10 O-UPDATE-MESS-SSN PIC X(9).
       10                      PIC X(13)   VALUE ' AT LOCATION '.
       10 O-LOCATION-NO-2      PIC 9(3).
    05 ADD-ERROR-MESSAGE.
       10                      PIC X(4)    VALUE SPACES.
       10                      PIC X(36)   VALUE
                '***  ADD ERROR FOR RECORD WITH SSN= '.
       10 O-ADD-MESS-SSN       PIC X(9).
       10                      PIC X(13)   VALUE ' AT LOCATION '.
       10 O-LOCATION-NO-3      PIC 9(3).

01  END-LINE.
    05 PIC X(29)   VALUE SPACES.
    05 PIC X(23)   VALUE '***  END OF REPORT  ***'.
    05 PIC X(28)   VALUE SPACES.

PROCEDURE DIVISION.

100-UPDATE-MASTER-FILE.
    PERFORM 200-START-UP.
    PERFORM 210-PROCESS-DETAIL-RECORD
        UNTIL NO-MORE-DETAIL-RECORDS OR FILE-IS-FULL.
    PERFORM 220-FINISH-UP.
    STOP RUN.

200-START-UP.
    OPEN INPUT DETAIL-FILE
         I-O MASTER-FILE
         OUTPUT AUDIT-REPORT.
    MOVE 250 TO WS-FILE-SIZE.
    ACCEPT WS-DATE FROM DATE.
    MOVE WS-DATE TO O-DATE.
    MOVE 'YES' TO WS-MORE-DETAIL-RECORDS.
    PERFORM 300-WRITE-REPORT-HEADERS.
    PERFORM 310-READ-DETAIL-RECORD.

210-PROCESS-DETAIL-RECORD.
    PERFORM 320-SELECT-PROCESS.
    PERFORM 330-PREPARE-AUDIT-LINE.
    IF FILE-IS-FULL
        NEXT SENTENCE
    ELSE
        PERFORM 310-READ-DETAIL-RECORD.

220-FINISH-UP.
    WRITE PRINTLINE FROM END-LINE
        AFTER ADVANCING 5 LINES.
    CLOSE DETAIL-FILE
          MASTER-FILE
          AUDIT-REPORT.
```

```
300-WRITE-REPORT-HEADERS.
    WRITE PRINTLINE FROM COMPANY-NAME
        AFTER ADVANCING PAGE.
    WRITE PRINTLINE FROM DATE-LINE
        AFTER ADVANCING 3 LINES.
    WRITE PRINTLINE FROM REPORT-NAME
        AFTER ADVANCING 2 LINES.
    WRITE PRINTLINE FROM HEADINGS-1
        AFTER ADVANCING 3 LINES.
    WRITE PRINTLINE FROM HEADINGS-2
        AFTER ADVANCING 2 LINES.
    MOVE 2 TO WS-PROPER-SPACING.

310-READ-DETAIL-RECORD.
    READ DETAIL-FILE RECORD
        AT END
            SET NO-MORE-DETAIL-RECORDS TO TRUE.

320-SELECT-PROCESS.
    INITIALIZE ERROR-FLAG.
    DIVIDE I-SSN BY WS-FILE-SIZE GIVING WS-QUOTIENT
        REMAINDER WS-LOCATION-NO.
    ADD 1 TO WS-LOCATION-NO.
    PERFORM 400-READ-MASTER-RECORD.
    IF ADDITION
        PERFORM 410-ADD-PROCEDURE
    ELSE
        IF SUCCESSFUL
             PERFORM 420-FIND-MASTER-RECORD
        ELSE
             SET READ-ERROR TO TRUE
        END-IF
    END-IF.

330-PREPARE-AUDIT-LINE.
    MOVE SPACES TO AUDIT-LINE.
    IF ANY-ERROR
        EVALUATE   TRUE
            WHEN FILE-IS-FULL
                       MOVE I-SSN TO O-FULL-MESS-SSN
                       MOVE FULL-FILE-MESSAGE TO AUDIT-LINE
            WHEN READ-ERROR
                       MOVE WS-LOCATION-NO TO O-READ-MESS-KEY
                       MOVE READ-ERROR-MESSAGE TO AUDIT-LINE
            WHEN SEARCH-ERROR
                       MOVE I-SSN TO O-SEARCH-MESS-SSN
                       MOVE SEARCH-ERROR-MESSAGE TO AUDIT-LINE
            WHEN DELETE-ERROR
                       MOVE I-SSN TO O-DELETE-MESS-SSN
                       MOVE WS-LOCATION-NO TO O-LOCATION-NO-1
                       MOVE DELETE-ERROR-MESSAGE TO AUDIT-LINE
            WHEN UPDATE-ERROR
                       MOVE I-SSN TO O-UPDATE-MESS-SSN
                       MOVE WS-LOCATION-NO TO O-LOCATION-NO-2
                       MOVE UPDATE-ERROR-MESSAGE TO AUDIT-LINE
            WHEN ADD-ERROR
                       MOVE I-SSN TO O-ADD-MESS-SSN
                       MOVE WS-LOCATION-NO TO O-LOCATION-NO-3
                       MOVE ADD-ERROR-MESSAGE TO AUDIT-LINE
    ELSE
        MOVE WS-LOCATION-NO TO O-KEY
        MOVE I-SSN TO O-SSN
        MOVE I-PROCESS-CODE TO O-PROCESS-CODE
        EVALUATE   TRUE
            WHEN ADDITION  MOVE 'X' TO ADD-FLD
            WHEN DELETION  MOVE 'X' TO DELETE-FLD
            WHEN CHANGE    MOVE 'X' TO UPDATE-FLD
        END-EVALUATE
    END-IF.
    WRITE PRINTLINE FROM AUDIT-LINE
        AFTER ADVANCING WS-PROPER-SPACING.
    MOVE 1 TO WS-PROPER-SPACING.

400-READ-MASTER-RECORD.
    READ MASTER-FILE RECORD
        INVALID KEY
            SET READ-ERROR TO TRUE.

410-ADD-PROCEDURE.
    IF SUCCESSFUL
        PERFORM 510-FIND-LOCATION-TO-ADD
    ELSE
        PERFORM 500-WRITE-NEW-RECORD
    END-IF.
```

```
420-FIND-MASTER-RECORD.
    IF I-SSN = MR-SSN
        THEN
            IF DELETION
                PERFORM 520-DELETE-RECORD
            ELSE
                PERFORM 530-UPDATE-RECORD
    ELSE
        SET BEGIN-SEARCH TO TRUE
        PERFORM 540-LOOK-FOR-RECORD
            UNTIL STOP-SEARCH OR SEARCH-ERROR.

500-WRITE-NEW-RECORD.
    MOVE SPACES TO MASTER-RECORD.
    MOVE I-SSN TO MR-SSN.
    MOVE I-NAME TO MR-NAME.
    MOVE I-ADDRESS TO MR-ADDRESS.
    MOVE I-DOB TO MR-DOB.
    MOVE I-DOH TO MR-DOH.
    WRITE MASTER-RECORD
        INVALID KEY
            MOVE '22' TO WS-MASTER-FILE-FLAG
            SET ADD-ERROR TO TRUE
    END-WRITE.

510-FIND-LOCATION-TO-ADD.
    IF DUMMY-RECORD
        PERFORM 600-CHANGE-DUMMY-TO-ADD
    ELSE
        MOVE WS-LOCATION-NO TO WS-STARTING-NO
        SET BEGIN-SEARCH TO TRUE
        PERFORM 610-SEARCH-NEXT-LOCATION
            UNTIL STOP-SEARCH OR FILE-IS-FULL.

520-DELETE-RECORD.
    DELETE MASTER-FILE RECORD
        INVALID KEY
            SET DELETE-ERROR TO TRUE.

530-UPDATE-RECORD.
    IF NOT-NEW-NAME
        NEXT SENTENCE
    ELSE
        MOVE I-NAME TO MR-NAME.
    IF NOT-NEW-ADDRESS
        NEXT SENTENCE
    ELSE
        MOVE I-ADDRESS TO MR-ADDRESS.
    REWRITE MASTER-RECORD
        INVALID KEY
            SET UPDATE-ERROR TO TRUE.

540-LOOK-FOR-RECORD.
    ADD 1 TO WS-LOCATION-NO.
    IF WS-LOCATION-NO > WS-FILE-SIZE
        SUBTRACT WS-FILE-SIZE FROM WS-LOCATION-NO
    END-IF.
    PERFORM 400-READ-MASTER-RECORD.
    IF DUMMY-RECORD
        SET SEARCH-ERROR TO TRUE
    ELSE
        IF I-SSN = MR-SSN
            SET STOP-SEARCH TO TRUE
            IF DELETION
                PERFORM 520-DELETE-RECORD
            ELSE
                PERFORM 530-UPDATE-RECORD
            END-IF
    END-IF.

600-CHANGE-DUMMY-TO-ADD.
    MOVE SPACES TO MASTER-RECORD.
    MOVE I-SSN TO MR-SSN.
    MOVE I-NAME TO MR-NAME.
    MOVE I-ADDRESS TO MR-ADDRESS.
    MOVE I-DOB TO MR-DOB.
    MOVE I-DOH TO MR-DOH.
    REWRITE MASTER-RECORD
        INVALID KEY
            MOVE '23' TO WS-MASTER-FILE-FLAG
            SET ADD-ERROR TO TRUE
    END-REWRITE.
```

■ **Figure 4.39** continued

```
610-SEARCH-NEXT-LOCATION.
    ADD 1 TO WS-LOCATION-NO.
    IF WS-LOCATION-NO > WS-FILE-SIZE
        SUBTRACT WS-FILE-SIZE FROM WS-LOCATION-NO
    END-IF.
    IF WS-LOCATION-NO = WS-STARTING-NO
        SET FILE-IS-FULL TO TRUE
    ELSE
        PERFORM 400-READ-MASTER-RECORD
        IF NOT SUCCESSFUL
            PERFORM 500-WRITE-NEW-RECORD
            SET STOP-SEARCH TO TRUE
        ELSE
            IF DUMMY-RECORD
                PERFORM 600-CHANGE-DUMMY-TO-ADD
                SET STOP-SEARCH TO TRUE
        END-IF
    END-IF.
```

■ **Figure 4.40** Records of DETAIL-FILE

```
3042750015                        250 S MAIN ST. HASTINGS, NE        68901
3432157258PRINCE, GILDA
3364923752BROWN, MARIE L.         823 GARDENIA RDYORK NE             68467
3039764715ABRAHAM,MARYLYN
3322150642BLAZUCK, DEBRA          85 BELVIEW AVE FAIRFIELD, NE       68938
3432157258                        36 CYPRESS AVE SUPERIOR, NE        68978
2623514793
2234891533
2771984263
2211384406
1011372052NOLAN, ANN MARIE        986 MIDDLE ST  YORK, NE            68467100232021585
1042146254SIMPSON, JAMES R.       9 CHATHAM DR   HASTINGS, NE        68901080547040285
1082682731BEDARD, VINCENT A.      425 ALBANY RD  HEBRON, NE          68370021464082485
1074561032NYMAN, ROGERT P.        784 COUNTY ST  PLATTE, NE          68653072255021786
1037145064DEVINE, VIRGINIA        1240 HARVEY DR GENEVA, NE          68361082457031086
```

■ **Figure 4.41** MASTER-FILE update audit report

```
                              JOCELYN ORIGINALS

                      MASTER PERSONNEL FILE UPDATED 89/04/19

                                AUDIT REPORT


              DETAIL RECORD INFO                       ACTION TAKEN

      KEY        SSN       PROCESS CODE           ADDED   DELETED   UPDATED

      017    042 75 0015        3                                      X
      009    432 15 7258        3                                      X
      003    364 92 3752        3                                      X
      216    039 76 4715        3                                      X
      143    322 15 0642        3                                      X
      009    432 15 7258        3                                      X
      044    623 51 4793        2                           X
      034    234 89 1533        2                           X
***   NO RECORD IN FILE WITH SSN= 771984263
      157    211 38 4406        2                           X
      053    011 37 2052        1                 X
      005    042 14 6254        1                 X
      232    082 68 2731        1                 X
***   NO RECORD IN FILE WITH RELATIVE KEY= 034
      066    037 14 5064        1                 X


                          ***   END OF REPORT   ***
```

Relative Files in Brief

1. The records of a file with relative organization can be accessed sequentially, randomly, and dynamically.
2. A relative file may be formatted using sequential access or random access.
   a. In sequential formatting,
      i. The SELECT statement contains the clause ORGANIZATION IS RELATIVE and the clause ACCESS MODE IS SEQUENTIAL, explicitly or by default.
      ii. The file is open in OUTPUT mode.
      iii. The WRITE statement is executed *n* times, where *n* is the number of record areas the file must contain.
      iv. The record written into each record area may be a structured dummy record or it may be initialized to spaces.
      v. Records are stored sequentially in the file, and their relative key values are successively 1 through *n*.
   b. In random formatting,
      i. The SELECT statement contains the clause ORGANIZATION IS RELATIVE, the clause ACCESS MODE IS RANDOM, and the clause RELATIVE KEY IS relative-key-data-item.
      ii. The file is open in OUTPUT mode.
      iii. The relative key data item is assigned a value, and then the WRITE statement is executed to write a record in the record area specified by the value of the relative key data item. This value is the record's relative key value.
      iv. The record written into each record area may be a structured dummy record, or it may be initialized to spaces.
3. A formatted relative file may be loaded sequentially or randomly.
   a. In sequential loading,
      i. The SELECT statement for the relative file contains the clause ORGANIZATION IS RELATIVE and the clause ACCESS MODE IS SEQUENTIAL, explicitly or by default.
      ii. The relative file is open in I-O mode.
      iii. The records to be loaded into the file are presorted in ascending order by their associated relative key value and are made available to the program in a detail file.
      iv. A record is read from each file. The data is copied from the detail record to the relative record.
      v. The REWRITE statement is used to rewrite the relative record to the relative file.
   b. In random loading,
      i. The SELECT statement contains the clause ORGANIZATION IS RELATIVE, the clause ACCESS MODE IS RANDOM, and the clause RELATIVE KEY IS relative-key-data-item.
      ii. The relative file is open in I-O mode.
      iii. A record is read from the detail file, and its relative key value is determined.
         (a) The relative file record with the specified relative key value is read.
         (b) The data is copied from the detail record to the relative record.
         (c) The REWRITE statement is used to rewrite the relative record to the relative file.
4. A relative file's organization must always be specified by the clause ORGANIZATION IS RELATIVE in the file's SELECT statement.
5. The access mode for the file is specified in the file's SELECT statement by the clause ACCESS MODE IS SEQUENTIAL, or ACCESS MODE IS RANDOM, or ACCESS MODE IS DYNAMIC. If the mode is sequential, the clause need not be coded, since that is the default mode.
6. To READ a relative file sequentially,
   a. The access mode must be SEQUENTIAL.
   b. The file must be open in INPUT mode or in I-O mode.
   c. The file is read with the READ-AT END statement as with any sequential file, or the START statement is used to position the file's pointer at a record other than the first, and then a sequential READ-AT END statement is executed.

7. To READ a relative file randomly,
   a. The access mode must be specified as RANDOM or DYNAMIC.
   b. The file must be open in INPUT mode or in I-O mode.
   c. The relative key value of the record to be read must be moved into the relative key data item.
   d. The record is accessed by executing the READ-INVALID KEY statement.
8. To READ a relative file dynamically,
   a. The access mode must be specified as DYNAMIC.
   b. The OPEN mode may be INPUT or I-O.
   c. To access the records sequentially from the beginning of the file, the READ-NEXT RECORD statement is used.
   d. To access the records sequentially starting at a point other than the beginning of the file, a value is assigned to the relative key data item, the START statement is used to position the file's record pointer, and then READ-NEXT RECORD statements are executed.
   e. To access a record of the file randomly, the relative key value of the record to be read is moved to the relative key data item, and then the READ-INVALID KEY statement is executed.
   f. Access may be switched from sequential to random, and vice versa, simply by executing the appropriate READ statement (or START statement followed by the READ-NEXT RECORD statement for sequential access).
9. A relative file may be updated sequentially or randomly.
   a. In a sequential update,
      i. Access mode is specified as SEQUENTIAL.
      ii. The file is open in I-O mode.
      iii. The target record is accessed by using the READ-AT END statement, or by using the START statement prior to a READ-AT END statement.
      iv. If field values are to be changed, new values are copied to the relative record, and then the record is rewritten to the file using the REWRITE statement.
      v. If the record is to be deleted, it is first verified as the correct one, and then the DELETE statement is used to delete it from the file.
   b. In a random update,
      i. Access mode is specified as RANDOM or DYNAMIC.
      ii. The file is open in I-O mode.
      iii. The relative key data item is assigned the relative key value of the record to be accessed.
         (a) If field values are to be changed, the target record is accessed by using the READ-INVALID KEY statement. The field values are updated, and the REWRITE-INVALID KEY statement is used to rewrite the record to the file.
         (b) If the record is to be deleted, the DELETE-INVALID KEY statement is used to logically delete it from the file.
10. If the OPEN mode for a relative file is
   a. INPUT, and the access mode is SEQUENTIAL, the valid input-output statements are READ-AT END and START.
   b. INPUT, and the access mode is RANDOM, the only valid input-output statement is READ-INVALID KEY.
   c. INPUT, and the access mode is DYNAMIC, the valid input-output statements are READ-INVALID KEY, START, and READ-NEXT RECORD.
   d. I-O, and the access mode is SEQUENTIAL, the valid input-output statements are READ-AT END, REWRITE, DELETE, and START.
   e. I-O, and the access mode is RANDOM, the valid input-output statements are READ-INVALID KEY, WRITE, REWRITE, and DELETE.
   f. I-O, and the access mode is DYNAMIC, the valid input-output statements are READ-NEXT RECORD, READ-INVALID KEY, WRITE, REWRITE, DELETE, and START.
   g. OUTPUT, and the access mode is SEQUENTIAL, RANDOM, or DYNAMIC, the only valid input-output statement is WRITE.
   h. EXTEND, and the access mode is SEQUENTIAL, the only valid input-output statement is WRITE.

Figure 4.42 Important features of various file organizations

File Organization	Common Storage Media	Available Access Modes	File Creation Modes	File Update Modes	Keys	Main Advantages	Main Disadvantages
SEQUENTIAL	Magnetic Disk Magnetic Tape Printer Paper	SEQUENTIAL	SEQUENTIAL	SEQUENTIAL	None required. Records usually key-sequenced.	Uses storage medium efficiently. Ideal if all records are accessed sequentially on each run. Flexible record format. File easily extended. Allows use of variety of storage media.	Limited to sequential access only. Records can be added to end of file only.
INDEXED	Magnetic Disk	SEQUENTIAL RANDOM DYNAMIC	SEQUENTIAL RANDOM DYNAMIC	SEQUENTIAL RANDOM DYNAMIC	RECORD KEY, and optional ALTERNATE RECORD KEYS. Each key must be a record data field.	Allows sequential, random, and dynamic access modes. Allows adding and deleting records randomly and sequentially. Allows updating records randomly and sequentially. Allows for changing record length. Easy to extend file.	Limited to magnetic disks. Requires more disk space because of indexes. Requires more main memory to process records. Random processing may require multiple disk accesses.
RELATIVE	Magnetic Disk	SEQUENTIAL RANDOM DYNAMIC	SEQUENTIAL RANDOM	SEQUENTIAL RANDOM DYNAMIC	RELATIVE KEY A record field value is usually used to produce a key value.	Allows sequential, random, and dynamic access modes. Allows adding, deleting, and updating records randomly or sequentially. Provides fast and direct access to records. Allows for efficient use of disk space.	Limited to magnetic disks. Record areas must all be of the same size. Possibility of synonyms when adding records complicates programming.

File Organization Summary

Files with indexed organization have been discussed in Chapter 3, and files with relative organization have been discussed in this chapter. A summary of some important features of these file organizations is contained in Figure 4.42, and the valid I/O statements that may be used to reference a file, given its organization and its open mode, are listed in Figure 4.43.

Important Terms in Chapter 4

ACCESS MODE IS DYNAMIC
ACCESS MODE IS RANDOM
ACCESS MODE IS SEQUENTIAL
adding a record
DELETE-INVALID KEY
deleting a record
Division Algorithm Method
dummy record
FILE STATUS
Folding Method
format a file
hashing
KEY IS
loading randomly
loading sequentially
logical record
ORGANIZATION IS RELATIVE
packing factor
random-access formatting
randomization procedure
READ-AT END
READ-INVALID KEY
record collision
relative file
relative file organization
relative key data item
RELATIVE KEY IS
relative master file update
REWRITE-INVALID KEY
sequential-access formatting
START-INVALID KEY
synonym
updating a record
wrapping around
WRITE-INVALID KEY

Exercises

1. What is a file with relative organization?
2. What access modes may be used to access records of a relative file?
3. What is the minimum number of record areas that should be formatted for a file if the file must initially be loaded with
   a. 300 records and the file must have a packing factor of 80 percent?
   b. 300 records and the file must have a packing factor of 70 percent?
   c. 900 records and the file must have a packing factor of 75 percent?
   d. 900 records and the file must have a packing factor of 90 percent?

Figure 4.43 Summary of valid input/output statements

File Organization	Access Mode	Open Mode INPUT	OUTPUT	I-O	EXTEND
SEQUENTIAL	SEQUENTIAL	READ	WRITE	READ REWRITE	WRITE
INDEXED	SEQUENTIAL	READ START	WRITE	DELETE READ REWRITE START	WRITE
	RANDOM	READ	WRITE	DELETE READ REWRITE WRITE	
	DYNAMIC	READ READ NEXT START	WRITE	DELETE READ READ NEXT REWRITE START WRITE	
RELATIVE	SEQUENTIAL	READ START	WRITE	DELETE READ REWRITE START	WRITE
	RANDOM	READ	WRITE	DELETE READ REWRITE WRITE	
	DYNAMIC	READ READ NEXT START	WRITE	DELETE READ READ NEXT REWRITE START WRITE	

4. A relative file has been formatted so as to contain 50 record areas. If the file is initially loaded with
   a. 22 records, what is its effective packing factor?
   b. 35 records, what is its effective packing factor?
   c. 40 records, what is its effective packing factor?

5. If a relative file that has been formatted sequentially contains 500 record areas,
   a. Specify the READ statement that may be used to access its records sequentially.
   b. Specify the READ statement that may be used to access its records randomly.

6. Suppose that a relative file has been formatted randomly so as to contain 500 record areas, and that the formatting procedure wrote dummy records to the file by using 20, 100, 250, and 500 as relative key values.
   a. If the access mode is specified as sequential, what form of the READ statement must be used?
   b. If the file is read sequentially, how many records can be accessed?
   c. If the access mode is specified as random, what form of the READ statement must be used?
   d. If records of the file are accessed randomly, under what condition is a READ operation successful?
   e. If records of the file are accessed randomly, under what condition is a READ operation not successful?

7. Suppose that CUSTOMER-FILE is a relative file that has been formatted sequentially and loaded with dummy records, and that DETAIL-FILE contains "real" records that must be loaded randomly into CUSTOMER-FILE. Assume that the data structure of a relative record is the same as that of a detail record.
   a. Code the OPEN statements for each file.
   b. Code the READ statements for each file.
   c. Suppose that the file's relative key data item is WS-LOCATION-NO and that the customer number can be used without transformation as a record's relative key value. Code the sequence of statements needed to load a detail file record into the relative file.

8. Suppose that CUSTOMER-FILE is a relative file that has been formatted randomly and loaded with dummy records for relative key (WS-LOCATION-NO) values 20, 100, 250, and 500. DETAIL-FILE contains "real" records that must be loaded randomly into CUSTOMER-FILE, and the data structure of a relative record is the same as that of a detail record. Suppose that the customer number can be used without transformation as a record's relative key value.

Explain the procedure needed to load a customer record if

   a. `DETAIL-CUSTOMER-NO = 75.`
   b. `DETAIL-CUSTOMER-NO = 100.`

9. A product record contains one of the following product numbers:

```
453789
574123
315245
553144
456239
865899
342195
261799
483189
435049
```

A randomization procedure must be applied to the product number to determine a record's relative key. Assume the relative file into which the product records must be loaded contains 350 record areas. If synonyms occur, the record must be stored in the next available record area.

   a. For each product number, determine its initial hashed value, and determine the relative key for the corresponding product record if the Division Algorithm Method is used and 350 is the divisor.
   b. For each product number, determine its initial hashed value, and determine the relative key for the corresponding product record if the following hashing technique is used:
      i. The first 3 digits are added to the last 3 digits. Any extra digit is dropped.
      ii. If the hundreds digit is 3 and the tens digit is greater than 5, then
      6 converts to 0
      7 converts to 1
      8 converts to 2
      9 converts to 3.
      iii. If the hundreds digit is greater than 3, then
      4, 6, and 8 convert to 1
      5, 7, and 9 convert to 2.
      Example: 150793 → 150
      $\underline{793}$
      943 → 343

   The initial hashed value is 343, and the relative key is 343.

Debugging Activities

1. The owner of Richard's Auto Reconditioning wants his customer records loaded into a relative file. The file has previously been formatted for a total of 50 record areas. Each record area has size 150. The customer records, shown in Figure 4.44a, contain the following data:

cc 1–2	Customer number
cc 3–22	Customer name
cc 23–45	Customer street address
cc 46–70	Customer city, state, zip
cc 71–83	Customer phone
cc 84–108	Customer vehicle
cc 109–114	Customer last date

The customer number is to be used as the relative key for the customer record. Customer numbers are in the range from 1 to 50.

The program that loads the file must also produce an audit report, formatted as shown in Figure 4.44b.

Figure 4.44a Customer records in DETAIL-FILE

```
21ABRAHAM, EDITH E.    53 AZALEA DR.          CLEVELAND, OH     44143(216)678-159782 LINCOLN TOWN CAR        890205
16ANDREWS, ALFRED J.   173 BARKLEY AVE.       YOUNGSTOWN, OH    44515(216)834-087286 TOYOTA P/U              880915
05ASHOOK, MILDRED      840 LAKE FRONT DR.     AKRON, OH         44319(216)741-607868 PONTIAC GRAND PRIX      890420
44BELSHAW, ALICE M.    275 KILLINGTON AVE.    CANTON, OH        44720(216)735-032687 CHEVROLET CELEBRITY     890210
43BILLINGTON, ROLAND G521 CLEARWATER DR.      CANTON, OH        44720(216)735-429588 FORD ESCORT GT          881025
14BRUNEAU, ALICIA      1020 ELMWOOD AVE.      YOUNGSTOWN, OH    44515(216)834-003087 FORD BRONCO             890405
15CARR, CINDY A.       73 TIMBER LANE         YOUNGSTOWN, OH    44511(216)834-291888 MERCURY MARQUIS         890320
06CASSIDY, DAVID M.    212 KLINE AVE.         AKRON, OH         44305(216)741-067486 CHEVROLET S-10          890225
22CAUSEY, KATHY        319 PROFESSOR AVE.     CLEVELAND, OH     44113(216)678-294787 GMC SIERRA              881123
23DACEY, MARK J.       2152 SUPERIOR AVE.     CLEVELAND, OH     44103(216)678-968388 OLDS CUTLASS COUPE      890120
13DEFORGE, JOHN A.     804 PASADENA DR.       YOUNGSTOWN, OH    44507(216)834-361285 JEEP WAGONEER           880520
42DESTON, JOSEPHINE    105 GARDENDALE AVE.    CANTON, OH        44714(216)735-392686 TOYOTA SUPRA            881015
12FAZZINA, GERALD      414 LORETTA AVE.       YOUNGSTOWN, OH    44512(216)834-892189 OLDS CUTLASS CIERA      890317
07GAFFNEY, ALVIN A.    83 JOSEPH AVE.         AKRON, OH         44306(216)741-788488 CADILLAC SEVILLE        881205
24HOOK, FLORENCE       367 PRESTON AVE.       CLEVELAND, OH     44102(216)678-871587 TOYOTA CELICA GT        890212
11KLEK, MICHAEL B.     741 HUDSON AVE.        YOUNGSTOWN, OH    44511(216)834-856385 OLDS CUTLASS SUPREME    881123
08LANCIER, KIM         225 COURTLAND AVE.     AKRON, OH         44320(216)741-804688 JAGUAR XJ6              890217
41MAJEWSKI, CLAIRE M. 10 WOODHAVEN DR.        CANTON, OH        44718(216)735-982487 HONDA ACCORD LX         881020
25POE, STEVEN          642 ARLINGTON BLVD.    CLEVELAND, OH     44139(216)678-881889 CHRYSLER NEW YORKER     890315
26RAULINO, ANNA        35 YORKSHIRE RD.       CLEVELAND, OH     44118(216)678-415688 DODGE DIPLOMAT          890305
40ROUSSIN, PHILLIPE    51 TRUMP AVE.          CANTON, OH        44730(216)735-680462 FORD MUSTANG            880610
10SUMNER, DAVID G.     117 OLD ORCHARD LANE   YOUNGSTOWN, OH    44511(216)834-951989 LINCOLN TOWN CAR        890425
```

Figure 4.44b Printer spacing chart for the audit report

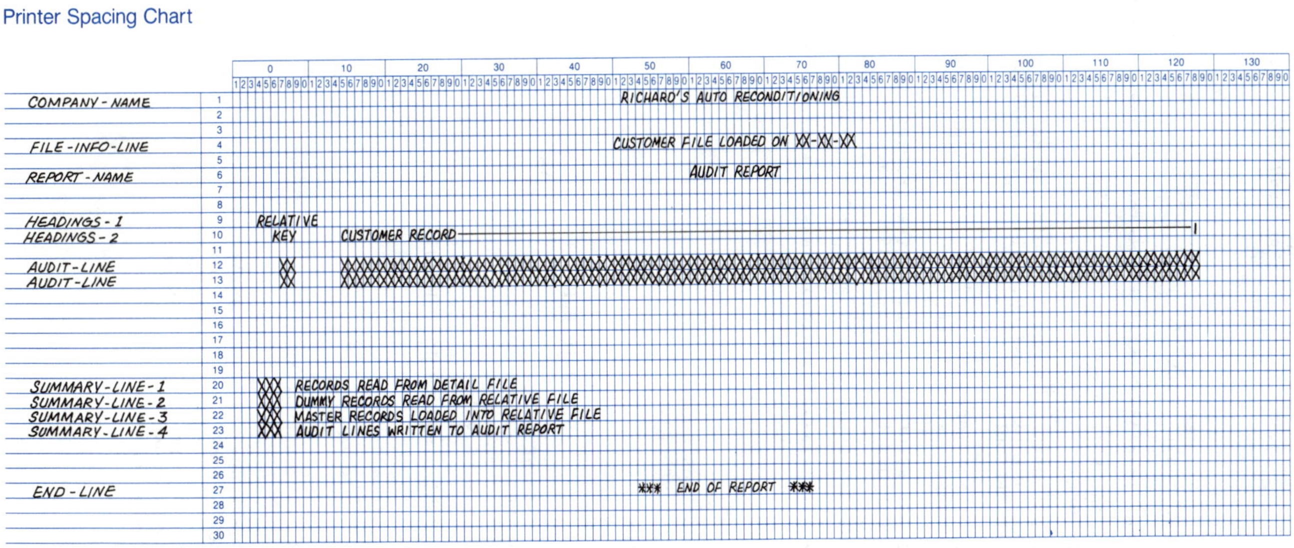

When an attempt was made to compile the program, the compiler generated the diagnostics contained in the following listing. Your task is to correct all the syntax errors.

Program Listing:

```
LOAD-MASTER-FILE-DBG-1                                  26-Apr-1989 15:31:43    VAX COBOL V4.2-40                          Page   1
Source Listing                                          26-Apr-1989 15:31:05    [PAQUETTEG.CHAPTER7V2]V2C7DBG1.COB;2 (1)

               IDENTIFICATION DIVISION.

               PROGRAM-ID.      LOAD-MASTER-FILE-DBG-1.

              ******************************************************************
              *                                                                *
              *   AUTHOR.          PAQUETTE.                                   *
              *   DATE WRITTEN.    APRIL 1989.                                 *
              *                                                                *
              *   THIS PROGRAM LOADS CUSTOMER RECORDS INTO A NEW MASTER ITEM   *
              *   FILE THAT HAS RELATIVE ORGANIZATION.  IT WAS FORMATTED TO    *
              *   STORE UP TO 50 RECORDS OF SIZE 150.                          *
              *                                                                *
              *   THE RELATIVE KEY IS WS-LOCATION-NO.  IT IS ASSIGNED THE      *
              *   VALUE OF THE CUSTOMER NUMBER FIELD.                          *
              *                                                                *
              *   AN AUDIT REPORT IS PRODUCED.  IT LISTS THE RECORDS LOADED    *
              *   INTO THE FILE AND PROVIDES SUMMARY INFORMATION.              *
              *                                                                *
              *   THIS VERSION CONTAINS LOGIC ERRORS AND SYNTAX ERRORS.        *
              *                                                                *
              ******************************************************************

               ENVIRONMENT DIVISION.

               CONFIGURATION SECTION.

               SOURCE-COMPUTER.  VAX-VMS-8650.
               OBJECT-COMPUTER.  VAX-VMS-8650.

               INPUT-OUTPUT SECTION.

               FILE-CONTROL.
                   SELECT DETAIL-FILE     ASSIGN TO COB$INPUT.
                          1
%COBOL-W-ERROR   16, (1) RECORD CONTAINS value is greater than length of longest record
                   SELECT MASTER-FILE     ASSIGN TO "V2C7DBGMR.DAT"
                          1
%COBOL-W-ERROR   16, (1) RECORD CONTAINS value is greater than length of longest record
                                          ORGANIZATION IS RELATIVE.
                   SELECT AUDIT-REPORT    ASSIGN TO COB$OUTPUT.

               DATA DIVISION.

               FILE SECTION.

               FD  DETAIL-FILE
                   RECORD CONTAINS 150 CHARACTERS.

               01  DETAIL-RECORD.
                   05 DETAIL-CUSTOMER-NO          PIC 9(2).
                   05 DETAIL-CUSTOMER-NAME        PIC X(20).
                   05 DETAIL-CUSTOMER-ST-ADDR     PIC X(23).
                   05 DETAIL-CUSTOMER-CITY-ST     PIC X(25).
                   05 DETAIL-CUSTOMER-PHONE       PIC X(13).
                   05 DETAIL-CUSTOMER-VEH         PIC X(25).
```

```
                05 DETAIL-CUSTOMER-LAST-DATE PIC X(6).

            FD  MASTER-FILE
                RECORD CONTAINS 150 CHARACTERS.

            01  MASTER-CUSTOMER-RECORD.
                05 MR-CUSTOMER-NO          PIC 9(2).
                   88 DUMMY-RECORD                VALUE ZEROS.
                05 MR-CUSTOMER-NAME        PIC X(20).
                05 MR-CUSTOMER-ST-ADDR     PIC X(23).
                05 MR-CUSTOMER-CITY-ST     PIC X(25).
                05 MR-CUSTOMER-PHONE       PIC X(13).
                05 MR-CUSTOMER-VEH         PIC X(25).
                05 MR-CUSTOMER-LAST-DATE PIC X(6).

            FD  AUDIT-REPORT
                RECORD CONTAINS 132 CHARACTERS.

            01  PRINTLINE            PIC X(132).

            WORKING-STORAGE SECTION.

            01  RELATIVE-FILE-ITEMS.
                05 WS-LOCATION-NO          PIC X(2).
                05 WS-STARTING-NO          PIC 9(2).
                05 WS-FILE-SIZE            PIC S(2).
                                                1
%COBOL-F-ERROR  156, (1) Invalid PICTURE character-string
                05 WS-ITEM-FILE-FLAG       PIC X(2).
                   88 SUCCESSFUL                    VALUE '00'.
                   88 MASTER-NOT-FOUND              VALUE '23'.

            01  PROGRAM-CONTROLS.
                05 WS-REPORT-DATE                PIC X(6).
                05 WS-PROPER-SPACING             PIC 9.

            01  PROGRAM-FLAGS.
                05 WS-MORE-DETAIL-RECORDS        PIC X(3).
                   88 THERE'S-A-DETAIL-RECORD             VALUE 'YES'.
                           1
%COBOL-F-ERROR  147, (1) Nonnumeric literal improperly continued
%COBOL-F-ERROR  118, (1) Invalid record description
%COBOL-E-ERROR   65, (1) Missing period is assumed
                   88 NO-MORE-DETAIL-RECORDS              VALUE 'NO '.
                05 SEARCH-LOOP-FLAG              PIC X(3).
                1
%COBOL-W-ERROR  297, (1) Processing of source program resumes at this point
                   88 BEGIN-SEARCH                        VALUE 'ON '.
                   88 LOCATON-IS-FOUND                    VALUE 'OFF'.
                05 ERROR-FLAG                    PIC X(1).
                   88 FILE-IS-FULL                        VALUE 'F'.

            01  WS-MASTER-RECORD         PIC X(15).

            01  PROGRAM-COUNTERS.
                05 WS-DETAIL-CTR         PIC S(2).
                                              1
```

```
LOAD-MASTER-FILE-DBG-1                               26-Apr-1989 15:31:43    VAX COBOL V4.2-40                    Page    3
Source Listing                                       26-Apr-1989 15:31:05    [PAQUETTEG.CHAPTER7V2]V2C7DBG1.COB;2 (1)

%COBOL-F-ERROR  156, (1) Invalid PICTURE character-string
  102              05 WS-DUMMY-RECORD-CTR    PIC S(2).
                                                 1
%COBOL-F-ERROR  156, (1) Invalid PICTURE character-string
  103              05 WS-MASTER-CTR          PIC S(2).
                                                 1
%COBOL-F-ERROR  156, (1) Invalid PICTURE character-string
  104              05 WS-AUDIT-LINE-CTR      PIC S(2).
                                                 1
%COBOL-F-ERROR  156, (1) Invalid PICTURE character-string
  105              05 WS-SYN-CTR             PIC S(2).
                                                 1
%COBOL-F-ERROR  156, (1) Invalid PICTURE character-string
  106
  107          01  COMPANY-NAME.
  108              05 PIC X(51)  VALUE SPACES.
  109              05 PIC X(20)  VALUE 'RICHARD'S AUTO RECONDITIONING'.
                      1
%COBOL-E-ERROR   84, (1) Literal in VALUE clause conflicts with description - clause ignored
  110              05 PIC X(52)  VALUE SPACES.
  111
  112          01  FILE-INFO-LINE.
  113              05                 PIC X(50)  VALUE SPACES.
  114              05                 PIC X(24)  VALUE
  115                                 'CUSTOMER FILE LOADED ON '.
  116              05 O-REPORT-DATE PIC XXBXXBXX.
  117              05                 PIC X(49)  VALUE SPACES.
  118
  119          01  REPORT-NAME.
  120              05 PIC X(60)  VALUE SPACES.
  121              05 PIC X(12)  VALUE 'AUDIT REPORT'.
  122              05 PIC X(60)  VALUE SPACES.
  123
  124          01  HEADINGS-1.
  125              05 PIC X(33)  VALUE SPACES.
  126              05 PIC X(8)   VALUE 'RELATIVE'.
  127              05 PIC X(121) VALUE SPACES.
  128
  129          01  HEADINGS-2.
  130              05 PIC X(5)   VALUE SPACES.
  131              05 PIC X(3)   VALUE 'KEY'.
  132              05 PIC X(5)   VALUE SPACES.
  133              05 PIC X(15)  VALUE 'CUSTOMER RECORD'.
  134              05 PIC X(98)  VALUE ALL '-'.
  135              05 PIC X(1)   VALUE '|'.
  136              05 PIC X(4)   VALUE SPACES.
  137
  138          01  AUDIT-LINE.
  139              05            PIC X(6).
  140              05 O-KEY      PIC 9(2).
  141              05            PIC X(6).
  142              05 O-RECORD   PIC X(114).
  143              05            PIC X(4).
  144
  145          01  FULL-FILE-MESSAGE.
  146              05                         PIC X(2)   VALUE SPACES.
  147              05                         PIC X(5)   VALUE ALL '*'.
```

```
LOAD-MASTER-FILE-DBG-1                          26-Apr-1989 15:31:43    VAX COBOL V4.2-40                         Page   4
Source Listing                                  26-Apr-1989 15:31:05    [PAQUETTEG.CHAPTER7V2]V2C7DBG1.COB;2 (1)

           05                      PIC X(50) VALUE
                '  FULL FILE OCCURRED AT RECORD WITH CUSTOMER NO.= '.
           05 O-MESS-CUSTOMER-NO   PIC X(2).

       01  SUMMARY-LINES.

           05 SUMMARY-LINE-1.
              10                   PIC X(4)   VALUE SPACES.
              10 O-DETAIL-CTR      PIC ZZ9.
              10                   PIC X(31)  VALUE
                     '  RECORDS READ FROM DETAIL FILE'.

           05 SUMMARY-LINE-2.
              10                   PIC X(4)   VALUE SPACES.
              10 O-DUMMY-RECORD-CTR PIC ZZ9.
              10                   PIC X(43)  VALUE
                     '  DUMMY RECORDS READ FROM RELATIVE FILE'.

           05 SUMMARY-LINE-3.
              10                   PIC X(4)   VALUE SPACES.
              10 O-MASTER-CTR      PIC ZZ9.
              10                   PIC X(46)  VALUE
                     '  MASTER RECORDS LOADED INTO RELATIVE FILE'.

           05 SUMMARY-LINE-4.
              10                   PIC X(4)   VALUE SPACES.
              10 O-AUDT-LINE-CTR   PIC ZZ9.
              10                   PIC X(37)  VALUE
                     '  AUDIT LINES WRITTEN TO AUDIT REPORT'.

           05 SUMMARY-LINE-5.
              10                   PIC X(4)   VALUE SPACES.
              10 O-SYNONYM-CTR     PIC ZZ9.
              10                   PIC X(22)  VALUE
                     '  SYNONYMS ENCOUNTERED'.

       01  END-LINE.
           05 PIC X(29)  VALUE SPACES.
           05 PIC X(23)  VALUE '***  END OF REPORT  ***'.
           05 PIC X(28)  VALUE SPACES.

       PROCEDURE DIVISION.

       100-LOAD-ITEM-FILE.
           PERFORM 200-START-UP.
           PERFORM 210-PROCESS-DETAIL-RECORD
               UNTIL NO-MORE-RECORDS.
                     1
%COBOL-F-ERROR  349, (1) Undefined name
           PERFORM 220-FINISH-UP.

       200-START-UP.
           OPEN INPUT DETAIL-FILE
                I-O MASTER-FILE
                OUTPUT AUDIT-REPORT.
           ACCEPT WS-REPORT-DATE FROM DATE.
           MOVE WS-REPORT-DATE TO O-REPORT-DATE.
```

```
LOAD-MASTER-FILE-DBG-1                    26-Apr-1989 15:31:43    VAX COBOL V4.2-40                        Page    5
Source Listing                            26-Apr-1989 15:31:05    [PAQUETTEG.CHAPTER7V2]V2C7DBG1.COB;2 (1)

                     SET THERE-IS-A-RECORD TO TRUE.
                         1
%COBOL-F-ERROR  349, (1) Undefined name
                     MOVE SPACES TO AUDIT-LINE.
                     INITIALIZE PROGRAM-COUNTERS.
                     PERFORM 300-WRITE-REPORT-HEADERS.
                     PERFORM 310-READ-DETAIL-RECORD.

                 210-PROCESS-DETAIL-RECORD.
                     PERFORM 320-READ-MR-RECORD.
                             1
%COBOL-F-ERROR  349, (1) Undefined name
                     PERFORM 330-CHECK-LOCATION.
                     1
%COBOL-W-ERROR  297, (1) Processing of source program resumes at this point
                     PERFORM 340-PREPARE-AUDT-LINE.
                             1
%COBOL-F-ERROR  349, (1) Undefined name
                     PERFORM 310-READ-DETAIL-RECORD.
                     1
%COBOL-W-ERROR  297, (1) Processing of source program resumes at this point

                 220-FINISH-UP.
                     PERFORM 360-PREPARE-SUMMARY.
                     WRITE PRINTLINE FROM END-LINE
                         AFTER ADVANCING 5 LINES.
                     CLOSE DETAIL-FILE
                           MASTER-FILE
                           AUDIT-REPORT.

                 300-WRITE-REPORT-HEADERS.
                     WRITE PRINTLINE FROM COMPANY-NAME
                         AFTER ADVANCING PAGE.
                     WRITE PRINTLINE FROM FILE-NFO-LINE
                                          1
%COBOL-F-ERROR  349, (1) Undefined name
                         AFTER ADVANCING 3 LINES.
                                               1
%COBOL-W-ERROR  297, (1) Processing of source program resumes at this point
                     WRITE PRINTLINE FROM REPORT-NAME
                         AFTER ADVANCING 3 LINES.
                     WRITE PRINTLINE FROM HEADINGS-1
                         AFTER ADVANCING 2 LINES.
                     WRITE PRINTLINE FROM HEADINGS-2
                         AFTER ADVANCING 1 LINE.
                     MOVE 2 TO WS-PROPER-SPACING.

                 310-READ-DETAIL-RECORD.
                     READ DETAIL-FILE RECORD
                         AT END
                             SET NO-MORE-DETAIL-RECORDS TO TRUE
                                 1
%COBOL-F-ERROR  349, (1) Undefined name
                     END-READ.

                 320-READ-MASTER-RECORD.
                     READ MASTER-FILE RECORD
```

```
                          INVALID KEY
                          1
%COBOL-F-ERROR  283, (1) File must not have sequential access mode
                               SET MASTER-NOT-FOUND TO TRUE
                     END-READ.

                 330-CHECK-LOCATION.
                     IF DUMMY-RECORD
                          PERFORM 400-WRITE-MR-RECORD
                                     1
%COBOL-F-ERROR  349, (1) Undefined name
                     ELSE
                          ADD 1 TO WS-SYNONYM-CTR
                          1           2
%COBOL-W-ERROR  297, (1) Processing of source program resumes at this point
%COBOL-F-ERROR  349, (2) Undefined name
                          SET BEGIN-SEARCH TO TRUE
                          1
%COBOL-W-ERROR  297, (1) Processing of source program resumes at this point
                          PERFORM 410-SEARCH-NEXT-LOCATION
                               UNTIL LOCATION-IS-FOUND OR FILE-IS-FULL
                                       1
%COBOL-F-ERROR  349, (1) Undefined name
                     END-IF.
                            1
%COBOL-W-ERROR  297, (1) Processing of source program resumes at this point

                 340-PREPARE-AUDIT-LINE.
                     MOVE SPACES TO AUDIT-LINE.
                     IF FILE-IS-FULL
                          MOVE DETAIL-CUSTOMER-NO TO O-MESS-CUSTOMER-NO
                          MOVE FULL-FILE-MESSAGE TO AUDIT-LINE
                     ELSE
                          MOVE WS-LOCATION-NO TO O-RELATIVE-KEY
                                                 1
%COBOL-F-ERROR  349, (1) Undefined name
                          MOVE WS-MASTER-RECORD TO O-RECORD
                     END-IF.
                     WRITE PRINTLINE FROM AUDIT-LINE
                          AFTER ADVANCING WS-PROPER-SPACING.
                     MOVE 1 TO WS-PROPER-SPACING.
                     ADD 1 TO WS-AUDIT-LINE-CTR.

                 360-PREPARE-SUMMARY.
                     MOVE WS-DETAIL-CTR TO O-DETAIL-CTR.
                     WRITE PRINTLINE FROM SUMMARY-LINE-1
                          AFTER ADVANCING 4 LINES.
                     MOVE WS-DUMMY-RECORD-CTR TO O-DUMMY-RECORD-CTR.
                     WRITE PRINTLINE FROM SUMMARY-LINE-2
                          AFTER ADVANCING 1 LINE.
                     MOVE WS-MASTER-CTR TO O-MASTER-CTR.
                     WRITE PRINTLINE FROM SUMMARY-LINE-3
                          AFTER ADVANCING 1 LINE.
                     MOVE WS-AUDIT-LINE-CTR TO O-AUDT-LINE-CTR.
                     WRITE PRINTLINE FROM SUMMARY-LINE-4
                          AFTER ADVANCING 1 LINE.
                     MOVE WS-SYN-CTR TO O-SYN-CTR.
```

```
                                    1
%COBOL-F-ERROR  349, (1) Undefined name
   286              WRITE PRINTLINE FROM SUMMARY-LINE-5
   287                  AFTER ADVANCING 1 LINE.
   288
   289          400-WRITE-MASTER-RECORD.
   290              MOVE DETAIL-CUSTOMER-NO TO MR-CUSTOMER-NO.
   291              MOVE DETAIL-CUSTOMER-NAME TO MR-CUSTOMER-NAME.
   292              MOVE DETAIL-CUSTOMER-ST-ADDR TO MR-CUSTOMER-ST-ADDR.
   293              MOVE DETAIL-CUSTOMER-CITY-ST TO MR-CUSTOMER-CITY-ST.
   294              MOVE DETAIL-CUSTOMER-PHONE TO MR-CUSTOMER-PHONE.
   295              MOVE DETAIL-CUSTOMER-VEH TO MR-CUSTOMER-VEH.
   296              MOVE DETAIL-CUSTOMER-LAST-DATE TO MR-CUSTOMER-LAST-DATE.
   297              REWRITE MASTER-CUSTOMER-RECORD
   298                  INVALID KEY
                        1
%COBOL-F-ERROR  213, (1) File must not have sequential access mode and NEXT phrase must be omitted
   299                      SET MASTER-NOT-FOUND TO TRUE
   300              END-REWRITE.
   301
   302          410-SEARCH-NEXT-LOCATION.
   303              ADD 1 TO WS-LOCATION-NO.
                             1
%COBOL-F-ERROR  277, (1) Operand must be a numeric data-name
   304              IF WS-LOCATION-NO > WS-FULL-SIZE
                                        1
%COBOL-F-ERROR  349, (1) Undefined name
   305                  SUBTRACT WS-FILE-SIZE FROM WS-LOCATION-NO
                                                   1
%COBOL-F-ERROR  277, (1) Operand must be a numeric data-name
   306              END-IF.
                    1
%COBOL-F-ERROR  222, (1) '.' required at this point
   307              IF WS-LOCATION-NO = WS-STARTING-NO
                    1
%COBOL-W-ERROR  297, (1) Processing of source program resumes at this point
   308                  SET FILE-IS-FULL TO TRUE
   309              ELSE
   310                  PERFORM 320-READ-MASTER-RECORD
   311                  IF DUMMY-RECORD
   312                      PERFORM 400-WRITE-MASTER-RECORD
   313                      SET LOCATION-IS-FOUND TO TRUE
                                1
%COBOL-F-ERROR  349, (1) Undefined name
   314                  END-IF
   315              END-IF.
```

2. When the syntax errors flagged in the listing shown in exercise 1 were corrected, the program was compiled and run. The audit report it produced is shown in Figure 4.45a, and the relative file it loaded is shown in Figure 4.45b. However, the report should have been the one in Figure 4.45c, and the relative file should have been loaded as shown in Figure 4.45d. Correct the program as needed.

Figure 4.45a Audit report produced by faulty program

```
                                             RICHARD'S AUTO RECONDITIONING

                                          CUSTOMER FILE LOADED ON 89 04 26

                                                   AUDIT REPORT

 RELATIVE
   KEY      CUSTOMER RECORD----------------------------------------------------------------------------------------------------|

*****  FULL FILE OCCURRED AT RECORD WITH CUSTOMER NO.= 21
*****  FULL FILE OCCURRED AT RECORD WITH CUSTOMER NO.= 16
*****  FULL FILE OCCURRED AT RECORD WITH CUSTOMER NO.= 05
*****  FULL FILE OCCURRED AT RECORD WITH CUSTOMER NO.= 44
*****  FULL FILE OCCURRED AT RECORD WITH CUSTOMER NO.= 43
*****  FULL FILE OCCURRED AT RECORD WITH CUSTOMER NO.= 14
*****  FULL FILE OCCURRED AT RECORD WITH CUSTOMER NO.= 15
*****  FULL FILE OCCURRED AT RECORD WITH CUSTOMER NO.= 06
*****  FULL FILE OCCURRED AT RECORD WITH CUSTOMER NO.= 22
*****  FULL FILE OCCURRED AT RECORD WITH CUSTOMER NO.= 23
*****  FULL FILE OCCURRED AT RECORD WITH CUSTOMER NO.= 13
*****  FULL FILE OCCURRED AT RECORD WITH CUSTOMER NO.= 42
*****  FULL FILE OCCURRED AT RECORD WITH CUSTOMER NO.= 12
*****  FULL FILE OCCURRED AT RECORD WITH CUSTOMER NO.= 07
*****  FULL FILE OCCURRED AT RECORD WITH CUSTOMER NO.= 24
*****  FULL FILE OCCURRED AT RECORD WITH CUSTOMER NO.= 11
*****  FULL FILE OCCURRED AT RECORD WITH CUSTOMER NO.= 08
*****  FULL FILE OCCURRED AT RECORD WITH CUSTOMER NO.= 41
*****  FULL FILE OCCURRED AT RECORD WITH CUSTOMER NO.= 25
*****  FULL FILE OCCURRED AT RECORD WITH CUSTOMER NO.= 26
*****  FULL FILE OCCURRED AT RECORD WITH CUSTOMER NO.= 40
*****  FULL FILE OCCURRED AT RECORD WITH CUSTOMER NO.= 10


      0  RECORDS READ FROM DETAIL FILE
      0  DUMMY RECORDS READ FROM RELATIVE FILE
      0  MASTER RECORDS LOADED INTO RELATIVE FILE
     22  AUDIT LINES WRITTEN TO AUDIT REPORT
     22  SYNONYMS ENCOUNTERED


                            ***  END OF REPORT  ***
```

■ **Figure 4.45b** Relative file improperly loaded

```
00
00
00
00
00
00
00
00
00
00
00
00
00
00
00
00
00
00
00
00
00
00
00
00
00
00
00
00
00
00
00
00
00
00
00
00
00
00
00
00
00
00
00
00
00
00
00
00
00
00
```

■ **Figure 4.45c** Audit report that should have been produced

```
                                                    RICHARD'S AUTO RECONDITIONING

                                                   CUSTOMER FILE LOADED ON 89-04-26

                                                             AUDIT REPORT

RELATIVE
  KEY     CUSTOMER RECORD-------------------------------------------------------------------------------------------------|

   21       21ABRAHAM, EDITH E.   53 AZALEA DR.          CLEVELAND, OH         44143(216)678-159782 LINCOLN TOWN CAR       890205
   16       16ANDREWS, ALFRED J.  173 BARKLEY AVE.       YOUNGSTOWN, OH        44515(216)834-087286 TOYOTA P/U             880915
   05       05ASHOOK, MILDRED     840 LAKE FRONT DR.     AKRON, OH             44319(216)741-607888 PONTIAC GRAND PRIX     890420
   44       44BELSHAW, ALICE M.   275 KILLINGTON AVE.    CANTON, OH            44720(216)735-032687 CHEVROLET CELEBRITY    890210
   43       43BILLINGTON, ROLAND G521 CLEARWATER DR.     CANTON, OH            44720(216)735-429588 FORD ESCORT GT         881025
   14       14BRUNEAU, ALICIA     1020 ELMWOOD AVE.      YOUNGSTOWN, OH        44515(216)834-003087 FORD BRONCO            890405
   15       15CARR, CINDY A.      73 TIMBER LANE         YOUNGSTOWN, OH        44511(216)834-291888 MERCURY MARQUIS        890320
   06       06CASSIDY, DAVID M.   212 KLINE AVE.         AKRON, OH             44305(216)741-067486 CHEVROLET S-10         890225
   22       22CAUSEY, KATHY       319 PROFESSOR AVE.     CLEVELAND, OH         44113(216)678-294787 GMC SIERRA             881123
   23       23DACEY, MARK J.      2152 SUPERIOR AVE.     CLEVELAND, OH         44103(216)678-968388 OLDS CUTLASS COUPE     890120
   13       13DEFORGE, JOHN A.    804 PASADENA DR.       YOUNGSTOWN, OH        44507(216)834-361285 JEEP WAGONEER          880520
   42       42DESTON, JOSEPHINE   105 GARDENDALE AVE.    CANTON, OH            44714(216)735-392686 TOYOTA SUPRA           881015
   12       12FAZZINA, GERALD     414 LORETTA AVE.       YOUNGSTOWN, OH        44512(216)834-892189 OLDS CUTLASS CIERA     890317
   07       07GAFFNEY, ALVIN A.   83 JOSEPH AVE.         AKRON, OH             44306(216)741-788488 CADILLAC SEVILLE       881205
   24       24HOOK, FLORENCE      367 PRESTON AVE.       CLEVELAND, OH         44102(216)678-871587 TOYOTA CELICA GT       890212
   11       11KLEK, MICHAEL B.    741 HUDSON AVE.        YOUNGSTOWN, OH        44511(216)834-856385 OLDS CUTLASS SUPREME   881123
   08       08LANCIER, KIM        225 COURTLAND AVE.     AKRON, OH             44320(216)741-804688 JAGUAR XJ6             890217
   41       41MAJEWSKI, CLAIRE M. 10 WOODHAVEN DR.       CANTON, OH            44718(216)735-982487 HONDA ACCORD LX        881020
   25       25POE, STEVEN         642 ARLINGTON BLVD.    CLEVELAND, OH         44139(216)678-881889 CHRYSLER NEW YORKER    890315
   26       26RAULINO, ANNA       35 YORKSHIRE RD.       CLEVELAND, OH         44118(216)678-415688 DODGE DIPLOMAT         890305
   40       40ROUSSIN, PHILLIPE   51 TRUMP AVE.          CANTON, OH            44730(216)735-680462 FORD MUSTANG           880610
   10       10SUMNER, DAVID G.    117 OLD ORCHARD LANE   YOUNGSTOWN, OH        44511(216)834-951989 LINCOLN TOWN CAR       890425


  22  RECORDS READ FROM DETAIL FILE
  22  DUMMY RECORDS READ FROM RELATIVE FILE
  22  MASTER RECORDS LOADED INTO RELATIVE FILE
  22  AUDIT LINES WRITTEN TO AUDIT REPORT
   0  SYNONYMS ENCOUNTERED


                              ***  END OF REPORT  ***
```

Figure 4.45d Relative file properly loaded

```
00
00
00
00
05ASHOOK, MILDRED     840 LAKE FRONT DR.        AKRON, OH               44319(216)741-607888 PONTIAC GRAND PRIX    890420
06CASSIDY, DAVID M.   212 KLINE AVE.            AKRON, OH               44305(216)741-067486 CHEVROLET S-10        890225
07GAFFNEY, ALVIN A.   83 JOSEPH AVE.            AKRON, OH               44306(216)741-788488 CADILLAC SEVILLE      881205
08LANCIER, KIM        225 COURTLAND AVE.        AKRON, OH               44320(216)741-804688 JAGUAR XJG            890217
00
10SUMNER, DAVID G.    117 OLD ORCHARD LANE      YOUNGSTOWN, OH          44511(216)834-951989 LINCOLN TOWN CAR      890425
11KLEK, MICHAEL B.    741 HUDSON AVE.           YOUNGSTOWN, OH          44511(216)834-856385 OLDS CUTLASS SUPREME  881123
12FAZZINA, GERALD     414 LORETTA AVE.          YOUNGSTOWN, OH          44512(216)834-892189 OLDS CUTLASS CIERA    890317
13DEFORGE, JOHN A.    804 PASADENA DR.          YOUNGSTOWN, OH          44507(216)834-361285 JEEP WAGONEER         880520
14BRUNEAU, ALICIA     1020 ELMWOOD AVE.         YOUNGSTOWN, OH          44515(216)834-003087 FORD BRONCO           890405
15CARR, CINDY A.      73 TIMBER LANE            YOUNGSTOWN, OH          44511(216)834-291888 MERCURY MARQUIS       890320
16ANDREWS, ALFRED J.  173 BARKLEY AVE.          YOUNGSTOWN, OH          44515(216)834-087286 TOYOTA P/U            880915
00
00
00
00
21ABRAHAM, EDITH E.   53 AZALEA DR.             CLEVELAND, OH           44143(216)678-159782 LINCOLN TOWN CAR      890205
22CAUSEY, KATHY       319 PROFESSOR AVE.        CLEVELAND, OH           44113(216)678-294787 GMC SIERRA            881123
23DACEY, MARK J.      2152 SUPERIOR AVE.        CLEVELAND, OH           44103(216)678-968388 OLDS CUTLASS COUPE    890120
24HOOK, FLORENCE      367 PRESTON AVE.          CLEVELAND, OH           44102(216)678-871587 TOYOTA CELICA GT      890212
25POE, STEVEN         642 ARLINGTON BLVD.       CLEVELAND, OH           44139(216)678-881889 CHRYSLER NEW YORKER   890315
26RAULINO, ANNA       35 YORKSHIRE RD.          CLEVELAND, OH           44118(216)678-415688 DODGE DIPLOMAT        890305
00
00
00
00
00
00
00
00
00
00
00
00
00
40ROUSSIN, PHILLIPE   51 TRUMP AVE.             CANTON, OH              44730(216)735-680462 FORD MUSTANG          880610
41MAJEWSKI, CLAIRE M. 10 WOODHAVEN DR.          CANTON, OH              44718(216)735-982487 HONDA ACCORD LX       881020
42DESTON, JOSEPHINE   105 GARDENDALE AVE.       CANTON, OH              44714(216)735-392686 TOYOTA SUPRA          881015
43BILLINGTON, ROLAND G521 CLEARWATER DR.        CANTON, OH              44720(216)735-429588 FORD ESCORT GT        881025
44BELSHAW, ALICE M.   275 KILLINGTON AVE.       CANTON, OH              44720(216)735-032687 CHEVROLET CELEBRITY   890210
00
00
00
00
00
00
```

Programming Exercises

Programming Exercise I

The master customer file of the Allied Stock Company is currently a sequential file. Management wants to have the flexibility of maintaining the master file by randomly accessing records to update field values, to add new customers to the file, and to delete records for customers with whom they are no longer doing business. The decision is made to create a new master file with relative organization, and the current customer number can be assigned, without transformation, to the relative key data item to position the records in the file. The customer records must contain the following data:

cc 1–2	Record code ("CM" for Customer Master)
cc 3–6	Customer number
cc 7–26	Customer name
cc 27–51	Customer street address
cc 52–74	Customer city and state
cc 75–94	Not used
cc 95–100	Customer's last activity date

Your task is to design a program to format the file sequentially, for a total of 9999 record areas, loading each area with a dummy record that contains zeros in the customer number field and spaces elsewhere. In addition, the program must produce an audit report formatted as shown in Figure 4.46a. The system flowchart and structure chart are shown in Figures 4.46b and 4.46c, respectively.

■ **Figure 4.46a** Printer spacing chart for the audit report

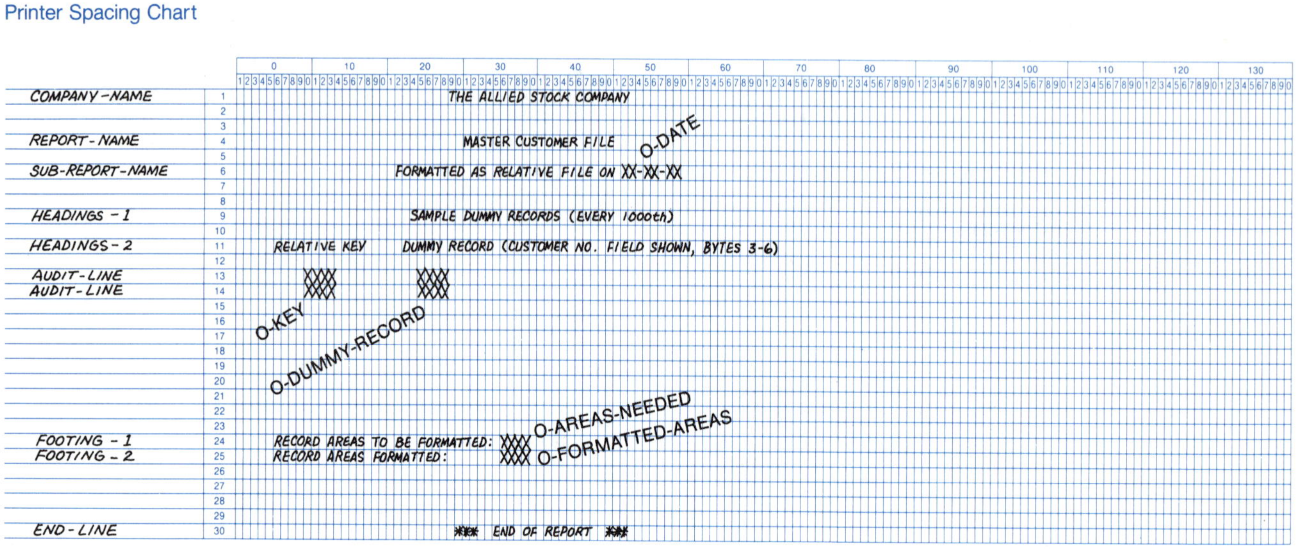

■ **Figure 4.46b** System flowchart for the program

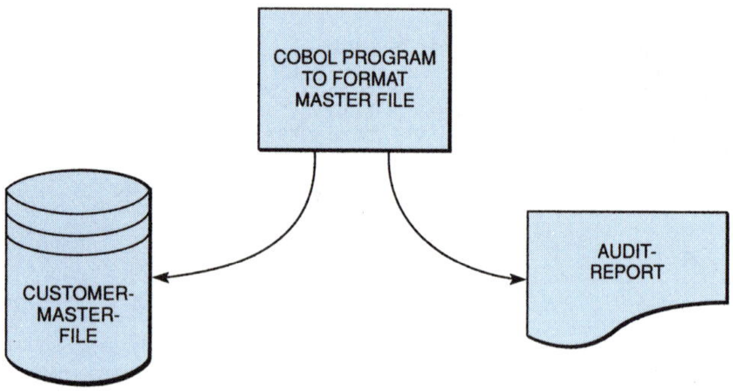

■ **Figure 4.46c** Structure chart for the program

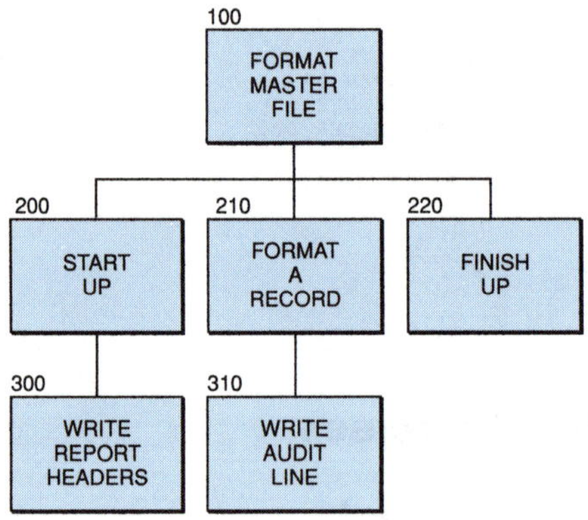

Programming Exercise II

The master customer file of the Allied Stock Company that was created as a relative file in Programming Exercise I must be loaded with the actual master customer records. The relative file contains 9999 record areas, and the customer numbers are in the range from 0001 to 9999. The relative key data item for the file receives the value in the customer number field of the customer's old master record, without transformation.

The current master records are contained in a sequential file, and each record contains the following data:

cc 1–2	Record code ("CM" for Customer Master)
cc 3–6	Customer number
cc 7–26	Customer name
cc 27–51	Customer street address
cc 52–74	Customer city and state
cc 75–94	Not used
cc 95–100	Customer's last activity date (format: YYMMDD)

The data fields of a relative record are identical to the fields listed above. The data on the old record must be copied into the new master record. However, the current date must be specified as the last activity date on each new record.

■ **Figure 4.47a** Printer spacing chart for the audit report

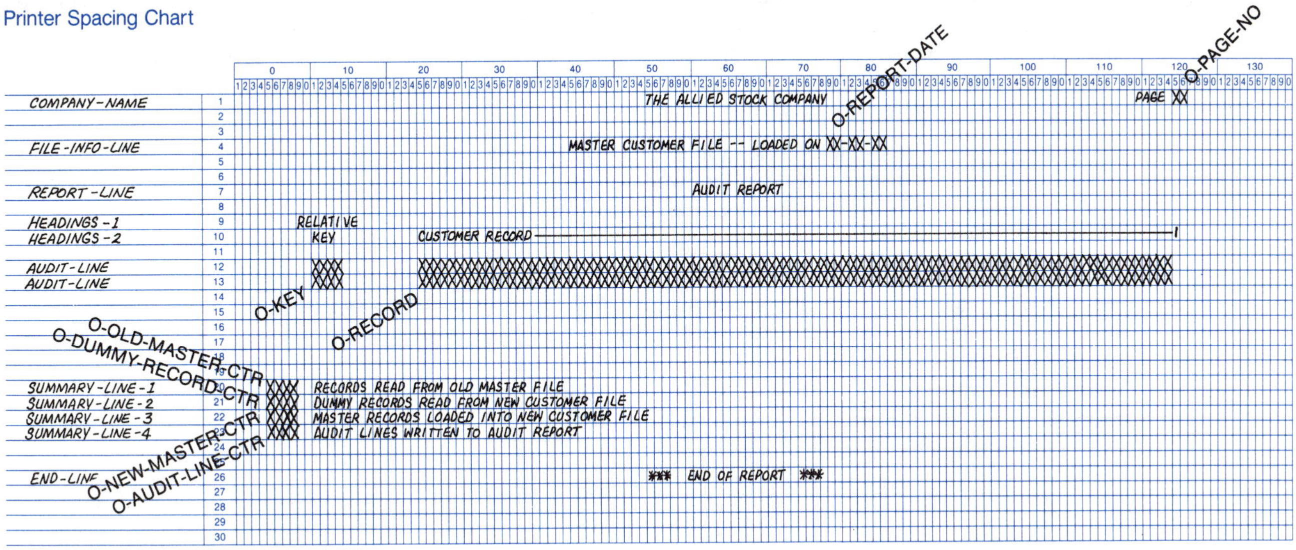

■ **Figure 4.47b** System flowchart for the program

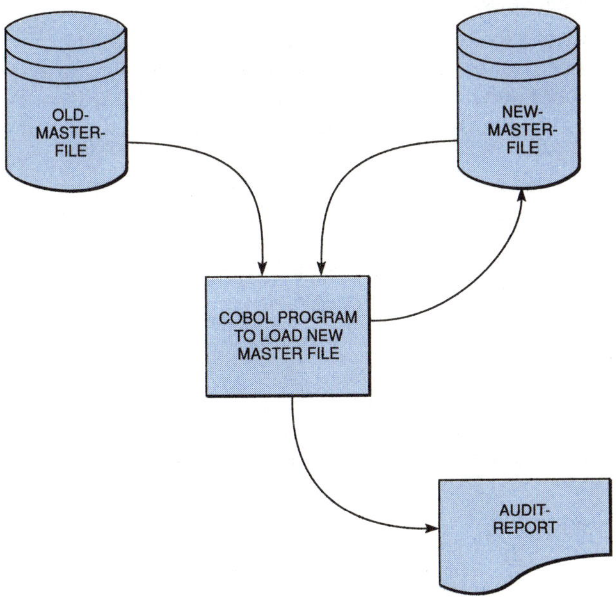

Even though the master records in the sequential file are in ascending order by customer number, the new records must be loaded randomly into the relative file, since the customer numbers are not consecutive numbers.

Your task is to design the program to load the old master records into the new file. The program must also produce an audit report, formatted as shown in Figure 4.47a. Each page of the report must contain no more than 30 audit lines. The system flowchart is shown in Figure 4.47b.

Use Data Set 4X2 as the old master file. You must use the new master customer file produced in Programming Exercise I as the relative file.

Programming Exercise III

The master customer file of the Allied Stock Company, first created as a relative file in Programming Exercise I and loaded in Programming Exercise II, must be updated. The update includes adding new customer records, deleting some customer records from the file, and changing data field values for some records currently in the file. For each customer involved in the update, a detail record is prepared and stored in a detail file. The data fields of the detail record are as follows:

cc 1	Process code (1, 2, or 3) (on every record)
cc 2–5	Customer number (on every record)
cc 6–25	Customer name (for new customers, and name change only)
cc 26–50	Customer street address (for new customers, and address change only)
cc 51–73	Customer city and state (for new customers, and city change only)

A process code of "1" denotes a new customer record to be added to the master file, a "2" denotes a customer record to be deleted from the file, and a "3" denotes a record for which some field values must be changed. Changes in data field values may occur in the name field, the street address field, and the city/state field. A new record and an updated record must indicate the current date as the last activity date. The process codes and customer numbers on the detail file records have been validated.

The data fields of a master record are as follows:

cc 1–2	Record code ("CM" for Customer Master)
cc 3–6	Customer number
cc 7–26	Customer name
cc 27–51	Customer street address
cc 52–74	Customer city and state
cc 75–94	Not used
cc 95–100	Customer's last activity date (format: YYMMDD)

Since the master file contains 9999 record areas, and the relative key for the file used the customer numbers, which range from 0001 to 9999, provisions need not be made in the program to handle synonyms, as they cannot occur. The program should process record updates and deletions prior to adding new records. New records may be added to the file in record areas that either contain no logical record or contain a dummy record.

In addition to updating the file, the program must also produce an audit report, formatted as shown in Figure 4.48. Error messages must be printed if it is not possible to process a detail record as specified by its process code.

Use Data Set 4X3 as the old customer file, and use the relative master file from Programming Exercise II as the file to be updated.

Programming Exercise IV

The Allied Stock Company wants to transfer its catalog item records from a sequential file to one with relative organization. The records are currently in ascending order by catalog item number, and each record contains the following data:

cc 1–2	Record code ("IM" for Item Master)
cc 3–6	Item number
cc 7–26	Item description
cc 27–31	Item purchase price (format: xxx.xx)
cc 32–36	Item selling price (format: xxx.xx)

The records in the new file must contain identical data fields, but they must be extended to a size of 100. The relative file must be formatted for 1000 record areas. Each record area is to be assigned spaces except for the item number field, which is assigned zeros.

The data processing department has decided to transform the item number into the relative key for the corresponding item record.

In this exercise, your task is two-fold. First, design the program to format the file using sequential access and to produce an audit report as shown in Figure 4.49. Second, implement the design to successful completion.

Figure 4.48 Printer spacing chart for the audit report

Printer Spacing Chart

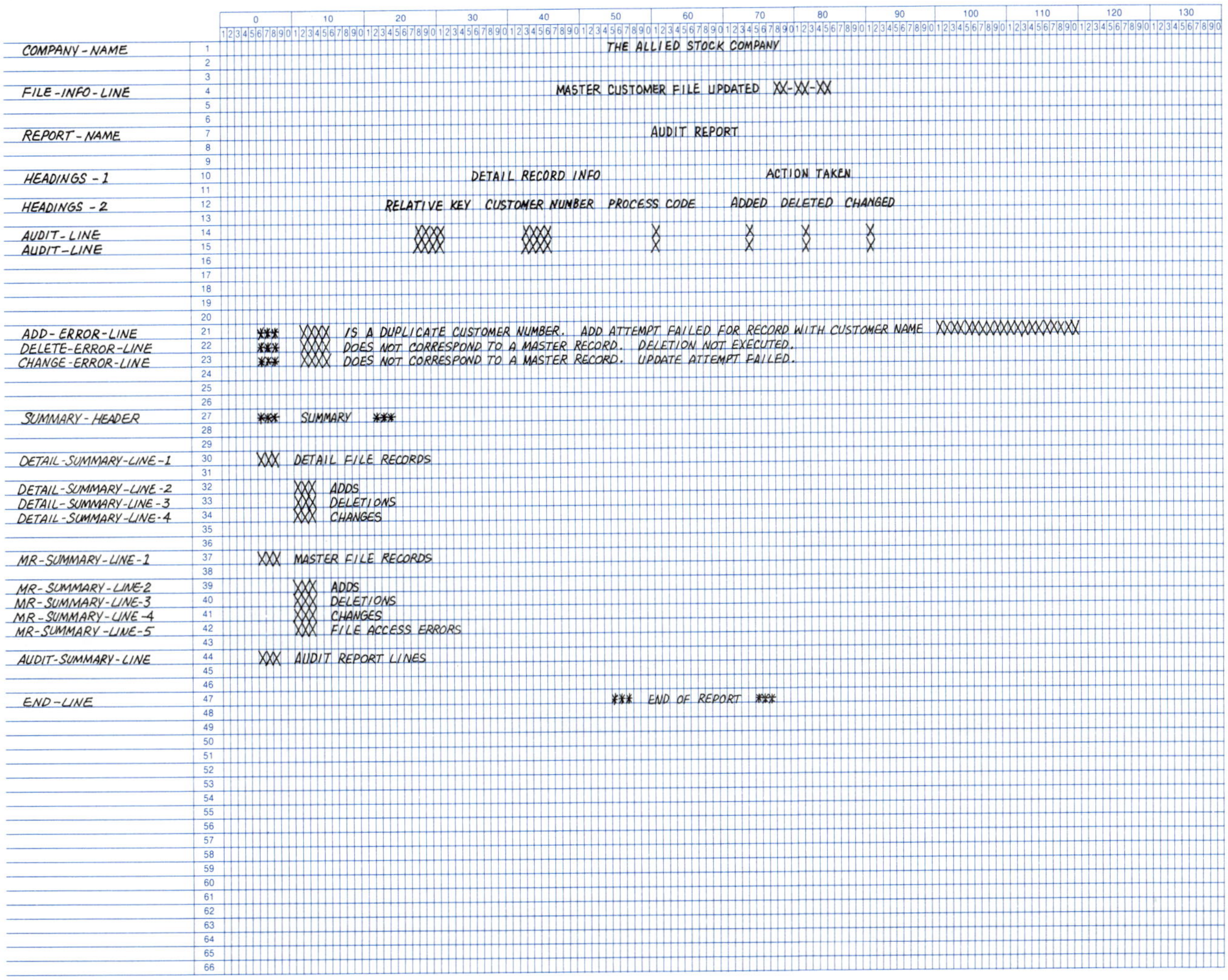

Figure 4.49 Printer spacing chart for the audit report

Printer Spacing Chart

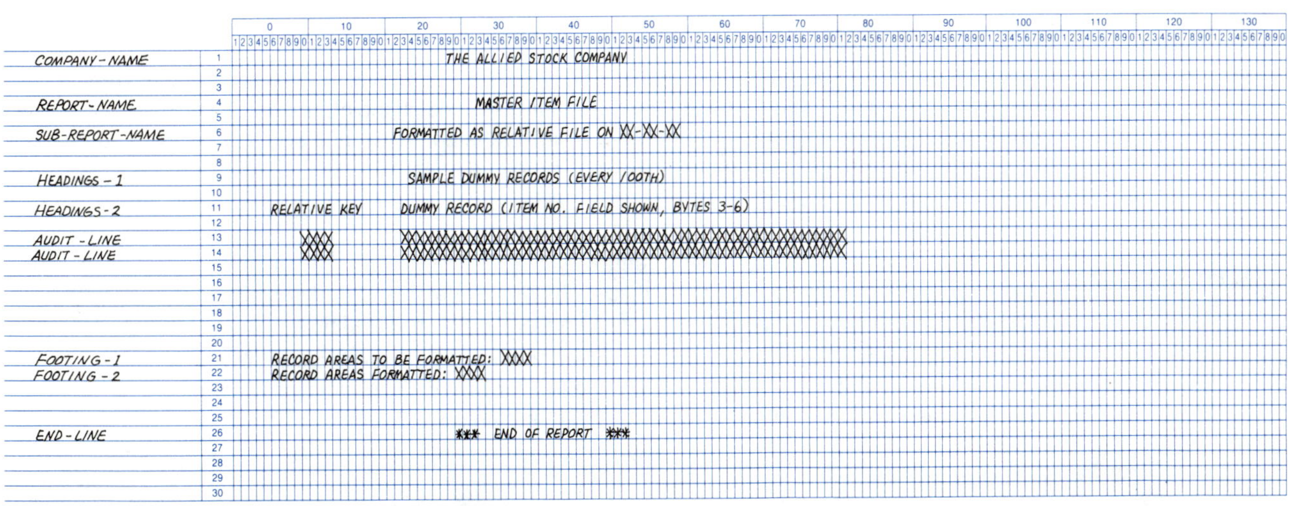

Figure 4.50 Printer spacing chart for the audit report

Printer Spacing Chart

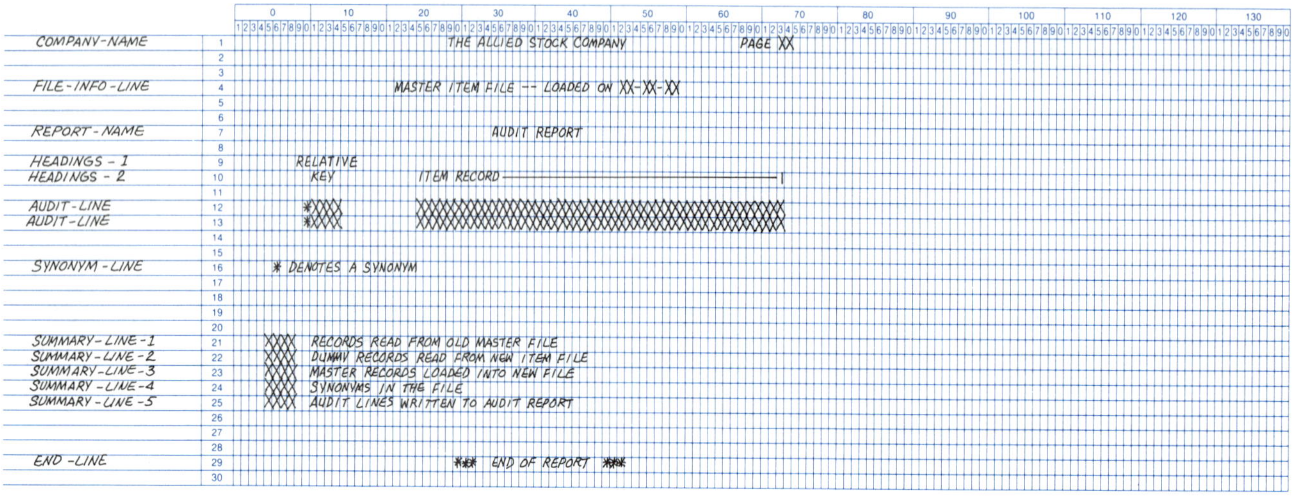

Programming Exercise V

The master item file of the Allied Stock Company, formatted as a relative file in Programming Exercise IV, must now be loaded with the actual item records. The file contains 1000 record areas, and the relative key value for each record is obtained by applying the Division Algorithm to the record's item number value. Since it is possible for the transformation procedure to produce synonyms, the program must make provisions to properly handle the loading of records that collide.

The records that must be loaded into the file are currently in a sequential file, and each record contains the following data:

cc 1–2	Record code ("IM" for Item Master)
cc 3–6	Item number
cc 7–26	Item description
cc 27–31	Item purchase price (format: xxx.xx)
cc 32–36	Item selling price (format: xxx.xx)

The master records in the relative file must contain identical data fields, but their size is set to 100 characters.

The program must also produce an audit report formatted as shown in Figure 4.50.

In this exercise, your task is to design the program and implement the design to successful completion. Use Data Set 4X5 as the current sequential file and the formatted file produced in Programming Exercise IV as the relative master file that must be loaded.

Programming Exercise VI

The master item file of the Allied Stock Company, first created in Programming Exercise IV and loaded in Programming Exercise V, must be updated. The file update includes changing the purchase price and/or the selling price for some items, deleting items no longer sold by the company, and adding new items to the file. For each item involved in the update, a detail record is prepared as follows:

cc 1	Process code (1, 2, or 3) (on every record)
cc 2–5	Item number (on every record)
cc 6–25	Item description (for new items only)
cc 26–30	Item purchase price (format: xxx.xx) (for new items and updates)
cc 31–35	Item selling price (format: xxx.xx) (for new items and updates)

A process code of "1" denotes a new item record that must be added to the file. A code of "2" denotes an item record that must be deleted from the file. A code of "3" denotes an item record for which either the purchase price value or the selling price value or both price values must be changed.

Figure 4.51 Printer spacing chart for the audit report

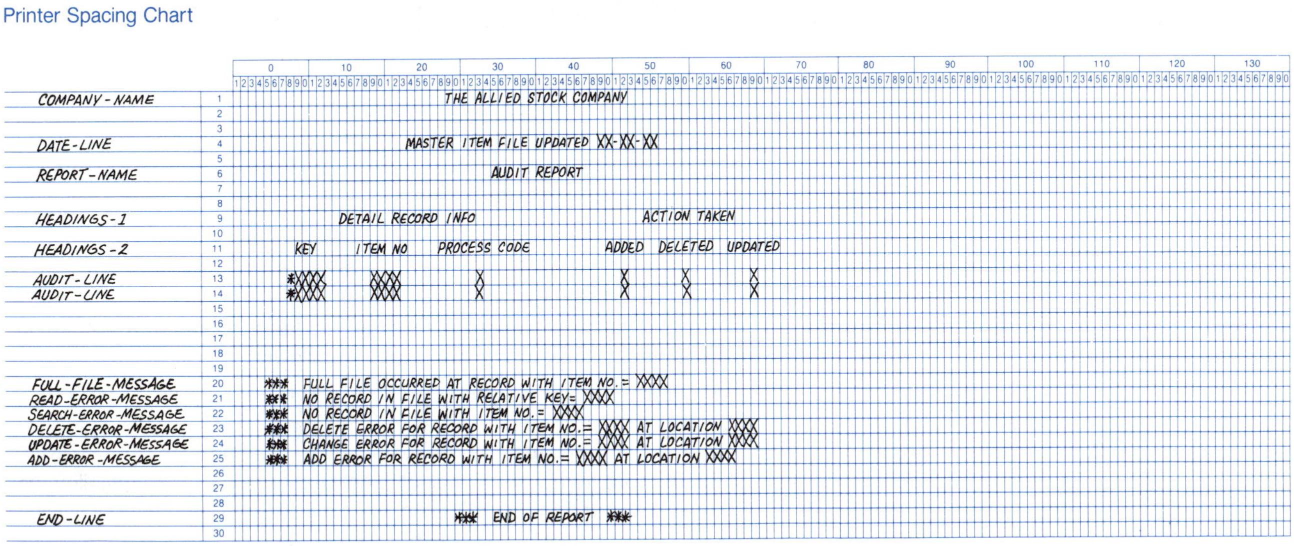

The detail records are stored in a detail file, and the process codes and item numbers in the file have been validated. Furthermore, the records have been sequenced so that price changes will be processed first, then deletions from the master file, and finally additions of new item records to the master file.

The data fields of a master record are as follows:

cc 1–2	Record code ("IM" for Item Master)
cc 3–6	Item number
cc 7–26	Item description
cc 27–31	Item purchase price (format: xxx.xx)
cc 32–36	Item selling price (format: xxx.xx)
cc 37–100	Not used

The program must make provisions to handle synonyms in identifying a record to be deleted or updated, and in inserting new records into the file. (For each record, the relative key value is obtained by transforming the item number by using the Division Algorithm.)

In addition to updating the file, the program must also produce an audit report formatted as shown in Figure 4.51. Error messages must be printed if a detail record cannot be processed as specified by its process code.

Use Data Set 4X6 as the detail file and the master file loaded in Programming Exercise V as the relative file that must be updated.

5 Subprograms and Nested Programs

A major emphasis of structured programming is the development of separate modules for separate tasks. Standard arguments presented to support highly structured programs include the following:

1. Overall logic clarity and program self-documentation are enhanced by subdividing the overall task into an ordered collection of functional subtasks.
2. In the team approach to program development, members of the team can be assigned the responsibility of developing separate modules within the program while the chief programmer retains responsibility for designing the overall structure of the program and for coordinating the activities of team members. The simultaneous development of program modules greatly reduces the time required to complete the programming task.
3. Changes can be made within a module without affecting the overall program logic.
4. A particular function may have to be executed at different points in the program. Instead of recoding the required statements a number of times, it is sufficient to reference the module to be performed.

The implementation of modularity within COBOL programs presented up until now has taken the form of paragraphs and sections, within the PROCEDURE DIVISION, whose execution is controlled by PERFORM statements. In this chapter, the implementation is extended to include *subprograms.* ■

Objectives You Should Achieve

After studying this chapter, you should

1. Be able to identify specific tasks that should be assigned to subprograms.
2. Be able to show in a system flowchart that a main program needs access to subprograms.
3. Be able to indicate in a program's structure chart the need to perform tasks assigned to a subprogram.
4. Be able to indicate a CALL function in a program's flowchart.
5. Be able to design a run unit in which the main program and subprograms are separately compiled.
6. Be able to design a run unit consisting of nested programs.
7. Be able to code the entries in a subprogram related to the USING phrase of the CALL statement that calls the subprogram.
8. Be able to code the entries in programs that have access to data defined as EXTERNAL.
9. Be able to code global entries in a calling program that must make its data available to contained programs.
10. Be able to identify and specify subprograms of a run unit that should be defined as COMMON.
11. Given a programming problem in which the system flowchart and structure chart are provided and in which the charts indicate that the run unit must contain subprograms, be able to complete the task of designing the programs of the run unit, compiling and link-editing them as needed, and obtaining a successful execution of the run unit.
12. Given a programming problem in which the statement of the problem indicates a need for subprograms, be able to completely design the run unit and implement the design to successful completion.

Subprograms

A subprogram is a program designed to accomplish a specific task. It may be coded in any programming language, though the sole interest of this chapter is in COBOL subprograms. Subprograms may be compiled separately into object modules and saved in a library and, when needed, be combined with a main program to form a *run unit*. During execution of the main program, a subprogram is executed by means of a CALL statement. A CALL statement is similar to a PERFORM statement: a PERFORM statement may be paraphrased as "Go execute the procedure and then come back;" a CALL statement may be paraphrased as "Go execute the subprogram and then come back!" Return from a performed paragraph occurs automatically after execution of the last statement in the paragraph. Return from a performed section occurs upon execution of the EXIT statement at the physical end of the section. And, in a similar manner, return from a CALLed subprogram occurs upon execution of the EXIT PROGRAM statement at the end of the subprogram.

Traditionally, the sharing of data between main programs and subprograms was subject to many restrictions. However, the new standards of COBOL '85 have removed a number of restrictions, and in a further effort to facilitate data sharing, the standards now support the *nested program* construct.

In this chapter, we will examine separately compiled subprograms and nested programs.

A First Subprogram Example

As a first example of a program that calls a subprogram, consider the following:

The Problem

The Allied Stock Company wants a program that produces a report listing all the phone sales that occurred during the day. For each phone sale, the report identifies the customer by number, the item purchased by catalog number, the item's unit cost, the number of units purchased, and the net amount of the sale. The report is formatted as shown in Figure 5.1. The report date must specify the month name, day, comma, and year in four digits.

The company usually offers a discount to customers who purchase large quantities of its stock items. However, the discount rate varies periodically. It is raised during special sale events and kept at lower levels otherwise. Currently, the discount rate is 20 percent if the quantity purchased exceeds 100 units.

Figure 5.1 Printer spacing chart for sample program 1

Printer Spacing Chart

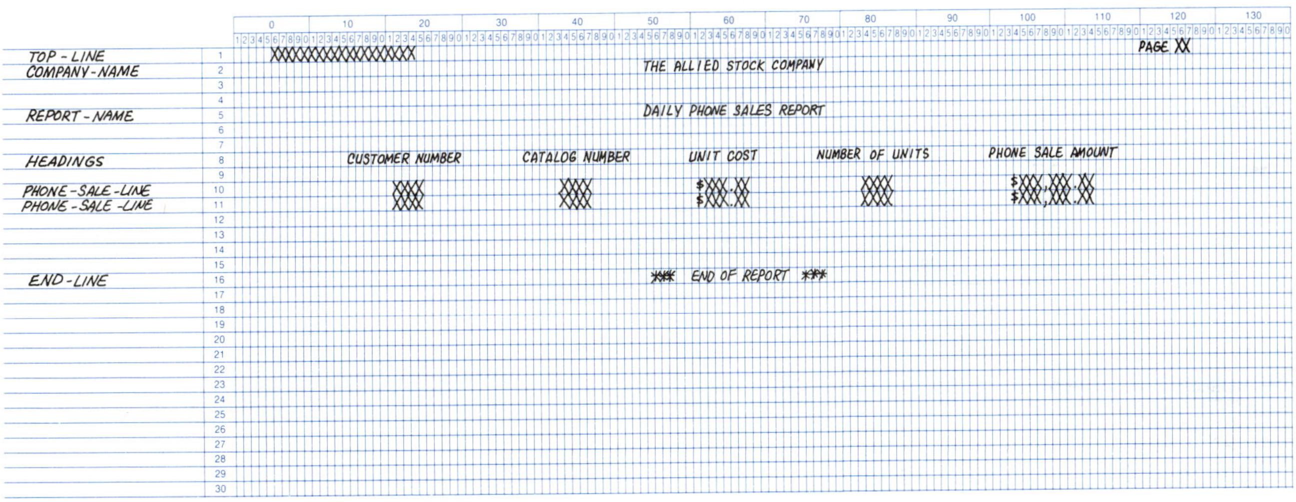

The records of the phone sales for the day are stored in a file. The data structure of a phone sale record is as follows:

cc 1–4	Customer number
cc 7–10	Item catalog number
cc 13–17	Item unit cost (format: xxx.xx)
cc 20–23	Number of units purchased

Brief Analysis

Clearly, producing this report is a simple job. The intent of the problem is to concentrate on those tasks within the program that should be handled by subprograms. There are two such tasks.

Task 1

In order to prepare the report date in the required format, it is necessary to retrieve the month name from a month table. Since this task is common to many programs, the coding has to be repeated in every one of those programs. This is obviously a waste of programmers' time. Preparing a subprogram to perform a task common to many programs is a typical use of subprograms. The details of this subprogram will be examined shortly.

Task 2

Because the company offers discount rates that change from time to time, the program that prepares the report must be edited and recompiled each time the discount rate changes. Such ventures into a working program present opportunities to introduce errors that may result in a program that fails to work properly. Since the program carries out many tasks other than computing discounted sale amounts, it is reasonable to assign the task of computing a customer's net sale amount to a subprogram, thereby maintaining the integrity of the main program. Needed changes can be made to the subprogram without any involvement of the main program.

The System Flowchart

The system flowchart is designed to show that the main program has to have access to subprograms. The system flowchart for this job is shown in Figure 5.2.

It should be clear that the main program has to access subprogram CONVERT-DATE-SUB only once, at the beginning of the job, prior to printing the report headers. On the other hand, subprogram ASC-COMPUTE-SALE-AMT-SUB has to be accessed once for each customer record that is read from the input file PHONE-SALES-FILE.

Figure 5.2 System flowchart for sample program 1

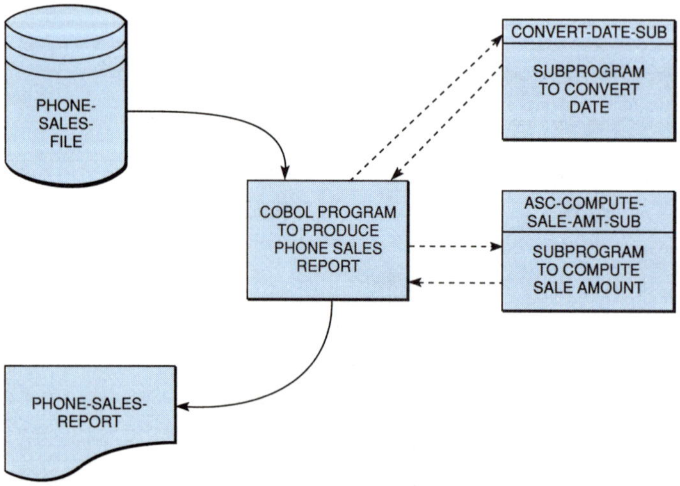

Figure 5.3 Separately compiled programs in the run unit

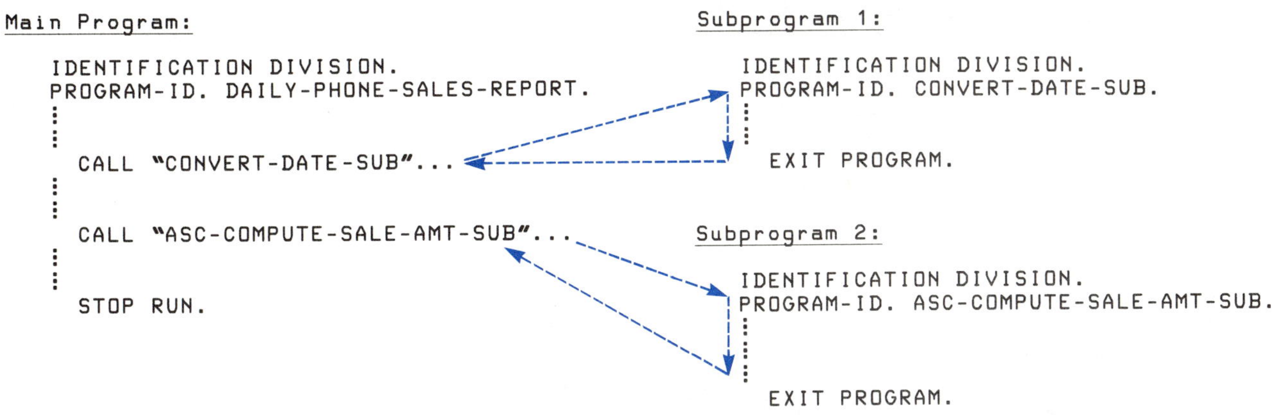

A program that calls a subprogram is referred to as a *calling program,* and a program that is called by another program is referred to as a *called program.* In this example, the main program is the calling program, while CONVERT-DATE-SUB and ASC-COMPUTE-SALE-AMT-SUB are both called programs. A subprogram may itself call another subprogram, in which case it is both a called program and a calling program. A main program is not called by any program, and thus it can only be a calling program.

A *run unit* is the collection of calling and called programs needed for a particular job. In the current example, the run unit consists of the main program, we'll name it DAILY-PHONE-SALES-REPORT, and the two separately compiled subprograms CONVERT-DATE-SUB and ASC-COMPUTE-SALE-AMT-SUB. The run unit may be represented schematically as shown in Figure 5.3.

The Structure Chart

As noted earlier, a subprogram is designed to carry out a specific task that must be accomplished by the calling program. Consequently, the structure chart of the calling program should show the called subprogram as one of its subordinate modules. This is shown in Figure 5.4. Note that the module box contains the telltale CALL entry, and the lined lower half of the box contains the subprogram name. The module box itself is not numbered, since the functional procedures that must be executed are in the called program, not in the calling program.

Note that the structure of each called program is also shown on the same page (since there is enough space to do so!) and it is linked by means of a dotted line to the corresponding module in the structure chart of the calling program. In this example, the structure of each subprogram shows a single functional module.

The function of subprogram CONVERT-DATE-SUB is to prepare the date in the format needed on the report. This requires obtaining the current date from the operating system. Recall that it is received in the YYMMDD form. The subprogram must transform it to the form "month, day, year." For instance, the date "890510" must be converted to "May 10, 1989." The month component of the date must be used to retrieve the month name from the month-name table, the day component must follow the month name, the year component must be used to produce 1989, and a comma must separate the day and the year. When the report date has been properly formatted, it is returned to the calling program.

The function of subprogram ASC-COMPUTE-SALE-AMT-SUB is to compute the net amount of a phone sale. The subprogram must receive the needed data from the calling program, specifically, the unit cost of the item and the number of units (quantity) purchased. It must test the quantity to determine whether a discount applies or not and then select the correct formula to compute the net amount of the sale. The sale amount is then returned to the calling program.

Figure 5.4 Structure chart with CALL modules

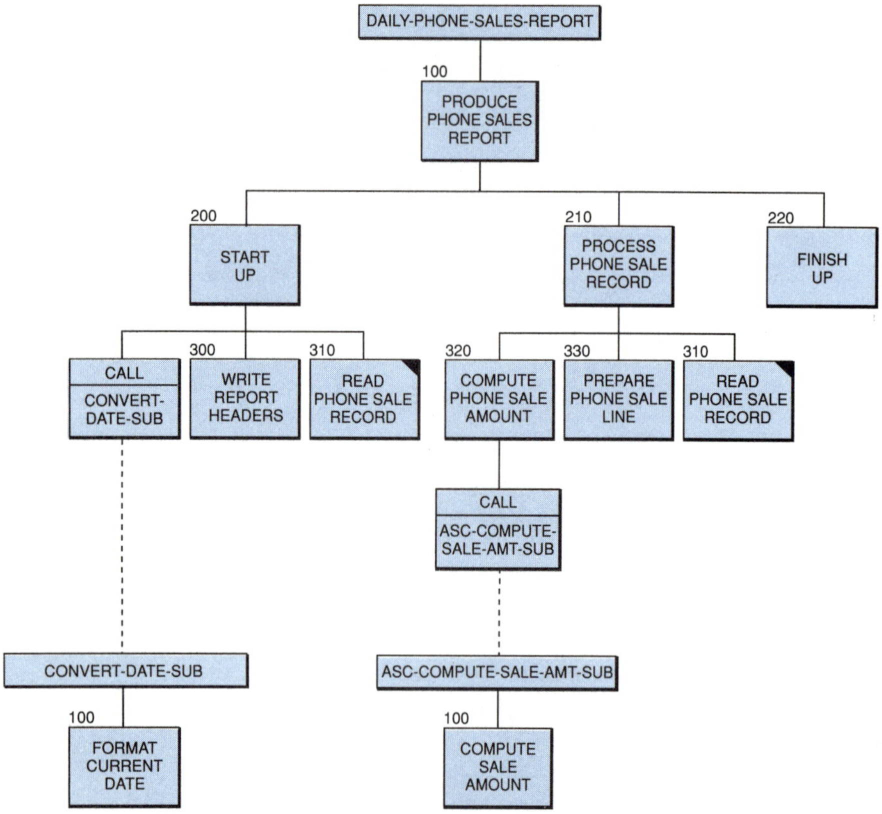

Program Pseudocode and Flowchart

The next step in designing the program is to write the program pseudocode or develop the program flowchart. Both of these tools show specific processing steps needed to do the tasks specified in the modules of the structure chart. Since the run unit consists of a main program and two subprograms, pseudocode is written for each program, or equivalently, a flowchart is developed for each program.

The pseudocode for the main program is as follows:

100-Produce-Phone-Sales-Report.

1. Perform 200-Start-Up.
2. Perform 210-Process-Phone-Sale-Record until the flag WS-MORE-RECORDS is equal to "NO ".
3. Perform 220-Finish-Up.
4. Stop the run.

200-Start-Up.

1. Open the file Phone-Sales-File in input mode, and open the file Phone-Sales-Report in output mode.
2. Initialize the flag WS-MORE-RECORDS to "YES".
3. Move 1 to Top-Line page-number.
4. Call subprogram CONVERT-DATE-SUB, using the data item Top-Line date.
5. Perform 300-Write-Report-Headers.
6. Perform 310-Read-Phone-Sale-Record.

210-Process-Phone-Sale-Record.

1. Perform 320-Compute-Phone-Sale-Amount.
2. Perform 330-Prepare-Phone-Sale-Line.
3. Perform 310-Read-Phone-Sale-Record.

220-Finish-Up.

1. Move the record End-Line to the output area Printline.
2. After advancing 3 lines, write the output record Printline.
3. Close the files.

300-Write-Report-Headers.

1. Move the record Top-Line to the output area Printline.
2. After advancing to a new page, write the output record Printline.
3. Move the record Company-Name to the output area Printline.
4. After advancing 1 line, write the output record Printline.
5. Move the record Report-Name to the output area Printline.
6. After advancing 3 lines, write the output record Printline.
7. Move the record Headings to the output area Printline.
8. After advancing 3 lines, write the output record Printline.
9. Set proper-spacing to 2.

310-Read-Phone-Sale-Record.

1. Read an input Phone-Sale-Record.
2. Test for end-of-file record:
   if EOF record reached, move "NO " to the flag WS-MORE-RECORDS.

320-Compute-Phone-Sale-Amount.

1. Call subprogram ASC-COMPUTE-SALE-AMT-SUB using input number-of-units, input unit-cost, and sale-amount data items.

330-Prepare-Phone-Sale-Line.

1. Move input customer-number to Phone-Sale-Line customer-number.
2. Move input catalog-number to Phone-Sale-Line catalog-number.
3. Move input unit-cost to Phone-Sale-Line unit-cost.
4. Move input number-of-units to Phone-Sale-Line number-of-units.
5. Move sale-amount to Phone-Sale-Line sale-amount.
6. Move the record Phone-Sale-Line to the output area Printline.
7. After advancing proper-spacing, write the output record Printline.
8. Set proper-spacing to 1.

The pseudocode for subprogram CONVERT-DATE-SUB is as follows:

100-Format-Current-Date.

1. Obtain the date from the operating system, storing it in report-date.
2. Add report-date year to data item century.
3. String the following components into formatted-date:
   a. month(report-date month)
   b. 1 space
   c. report-date day
   d. comma (,)
   e. 1 space
   f. year in four digits

999-Exit.

1. Exit from the subprogram.

The pseudocode for subprogram ASC-COMPUTE-SALE-AMT-SUB is as follows:

100-Compute-Sale-Amount.

1. Test number-of-units:
   a. if greater than 100, compute sale-amount equal to number-of-units times unit-cost times .8.
   b. if not greater than 100, multiply number-of-units by unit-cost to equal sale-amount.

999-Exit.

1. Exit from the subprogram.

Figure 5.5 Flowcharts for the programs of the run unit

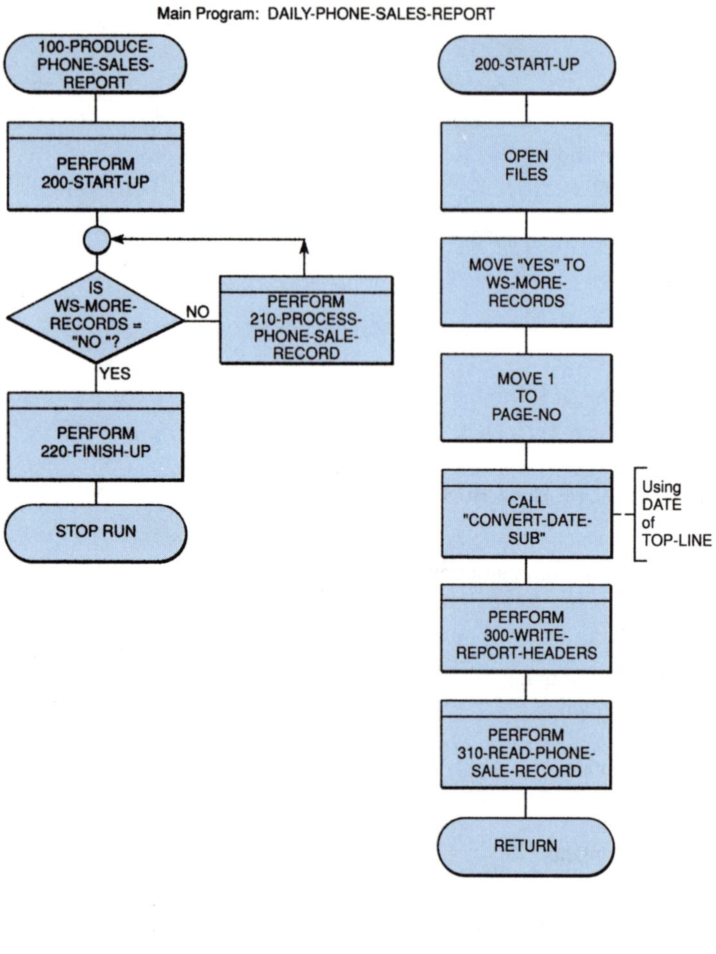

The flowcharts corresponding to the pseudocode are shown in Figure 5.5. Note that in modules 200-START-UP and 320-COMPUTE-PHONE-SALE-AMOUNT, the CALL function is shown within a standard perform symbol. The reason, as explained earlier, is that a CALL statement operates much like a PERFORM statement. That is, it sends control to the subprogram and control returns when the last statement in the subprogram (EXIT PROGRAM) has been executed.

Also note the annotation attached to the CALL box. It specifies the data items that are shared by the calling and called programs.

Figure 5.5 continued

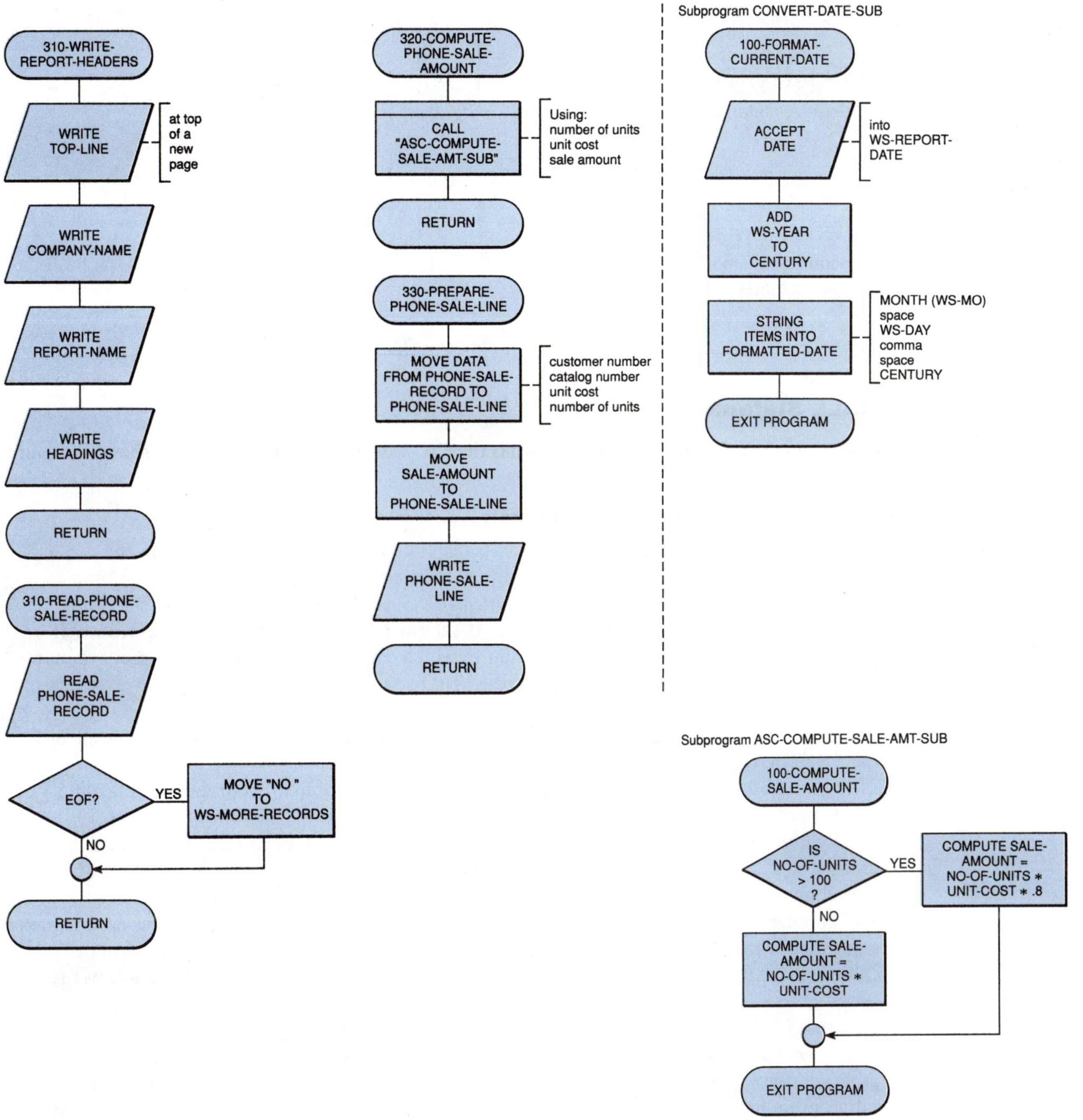

Figure 5.6 CALL statement formats

```
Format 1:
CALL {identifier-1} [USING {[BY REFERENCE] {identifier-2} . . . } . . .]
     {literal-1   }        {BY CONTENT {identifier-2} . . .     }
     [ON OVERFLOW imperative-statement-1]
     [END-CALL]

Format 2:
CALL {identifier-1} [USING {[BY REFERENCE] {identifier-2} . . . } . . .]
     {literal-1   }        {BY CONTENT {identifier-2} . . .     }
     [ON EXCEPTION imperative-statement-1]
     [NOT ON EXCEPTION imperative-statement-2]
     [END-CALL]
```

The CALL Statement

The only new entry needed in the main program is the CALL statement. Its formats are shown in Figure 5.6.

Rules Governing the Use of the CALL Statement

1. The function of the CALL statement is to transfer control to another program in the run unit.
   a. The program containing the CALL statement is the calling program.
   b. The program specified by *literal-1* or *identifier-1* is the called program.
2. *Identifier-1* is an alphanumeric data item. At the time the CALL statement is executed, it contains the name of the COBOL program to which control is transferred. The program name is the one in the called program's PROGRAM-ID paragraph.
3. *Literal-1* is the name of the program to which control is transferred.
4. If the program being called is a COBOL program, *literal-1* is the program name specified in the PROGRAM-ID paragraph of the called program.
5. *Identifier-2* identifies the data that is shared by the calling and called programs. The data item(s) are parameters, and they may be defined in the FILE SECTION or in the WORKING-STORAGE SECTION of the calling program either as elementary items or as group items. The level number in the data item description may be any number from 01 to 49. (Level number 77 is still allowed, but it is scheduled for deletion from the standards.)
6. The qualifier BY REFERENCE means that the called program has access to the storage area associated with *identifier-2*. As a result, when control returns from the called program to the calling program, the value in *identifier-2* may have been changed by statements within the subprogram.
7. The qualifier BY CONTENT means that the called program has access to the value of *identifier-2* but not to its storage area. As a result, when control returns from the called program, the value of *identifier-2* remains as it was before the CALL statement executed. (The subprogram has access to a copy of *identifier-2*. The value in the copy may be changed by the subprogram.)
8. If *identifier-2* has neither qualifier (BY REFERENCE, BY CONTENT), the default is BY REFERENCE.
9. A qualifier applies to every *identifier-2* following the one that explicitly contains the qualifier, until another qualifier is specified.
10. The phrase ON EXCEPTION is equivalent to the phrase ON OVERFLOW.
11. If a CALL statement contains the ON EXCEPTION clause and the program being called is not in the run unit, *imperative-statement-1* executes and control then passes to the end of the CALL statement.

12. If a CALL statement contains the ON EXCEPTION clause and the program being called is in the run unit, control is sent to the called program. Upon returning from the called program, control passes to the end of the CALL statement, or to *imperative-statement-2* if the CALL statement contains the clause NOT ON EXCEPTION, and then to the end of the CALL statement.
13. If a CALL statement does not contain the ON OVERFLOW or ON EXCEPTION clause, and the called program is not in the run unit, program execution simply aborts.
14. END-CALL is the explicit scope terminator for the CALL statement.
15. If a CALL statement contains a USING phrase, then the PROCEDURE DIVISION header of the called program must also contain a USING phrase. The number of parameters in both USING phrases must be the same, and the definitions of the corresponding parameters in both programs must specify the same size. Parameters in the two USING phrases correspond not by name, but strictly on the basis of position within the sets of parameters.
16. The parameters in a CALL statement are made available to the called program when the CALL statement executes.
17. A called program may also contain CALL statements. However, a CALL statement may not call a subprogram's calling program, directly or indirectly.

In paragraph 200-START-UP of the calling program, the CALL statement will be coded as follows:

```
CALL "CONVERT-DATE-SUB" USING O-DATE.
```

In this statement, CONVERT-DATE-SUB is the program name in the PROGRAM-ID paragraph of the subprogram designed to prepare the report date in the appropriate format. The data item being made accessible to the subprogram is O-DATE, which is the data field of the record TOP-LINE that must contain the properly formatted date. Note that its implied qualifier is BY REFERENCE! When the subprogram completes its task, the formatted date will be stored automatically in the field O-DATE.

In paragraph 320-COMPUTE-PHONE-SALE-AMOUNT, the CALL statement will be coded as follows:

```
CALL "ASC-COMPUTE-SALE-AMT-SUB" USING I-NO-OF-UNITS
                                      I-UNIT-COST
                                      WS-SALE-AMOUNT.
```

In this statement, ASC-COMPUTE-SALE-AMT-SUB is the program name in the called program's PROGRAM-ID paragraph. There are three parameters in the USING phrase, and the implied qualifier in each case is BY REFERENCE. The subprogram will use the values of the data items I-NO-OF-UNITS and I-UNIT-COST (these two items are defined in the FILE SECTION of the calling program) in computing the net sale amount for a particular phone sale, and that amount will be stored directly in the field WS-SALE-AMOUNT (a data item defined in the WORKING-STORAGE SECTION of the calling program).

Note that for each phone sale record, the input values of I-NO-OF-UNITS and I-UNIT-COST must be printed in fields of the detail line PHONE-SALE-LINE. That is, those values must not be changed by the subprogram. If the subprogram is correctly designed, there is no reason for it to change those two values. Nonetheless, an extra safeguard can be included by coding the CALL statement as follows:

```
CALL "ASC-COMPUTE-SALE-AMT-SUB"
     USING BY CONTENT I-NO-OF-UNITS
                      I-UNIT-COST
           BY REFERENCE WS-SALE-AMOUNT.
```

The qualifier BY CONTENT assures that the values in I-NO-OF-UNITS and I-UNIT-COST are not changed by the subprogram. On the other hand, the qualifier for WS-SALE-AMOUNT must be BY REFERENCE, implied or explicit, since that field must contain the sale amount as computed by the subprogram subsequent to the execution of the CALL statement.

Coding the Main Program

The coding for the main program is shown in Figure 5.7. As noted earlier, the only new statements that it contains are the CALL statement in paragraph 200-START-UP and the CALL statement in paragraph 320-COMPUTE-SALE-AMOUNT.

Figure 5.7 Main program in the run unit

```
 IDENTIFICATION DIVISION.

 PROGRAM-ID.  DAILY-PHONE-SALES-REPORT.

*****************************************************************
*                                                               *
*  AUTHOR.          PAQUETTE.                                   *
*  DATE WRITTEN:    MAY  1989.                                  *
*                                                               *
*  THIS PROGRAM PRODUCES A REPORT LISTING THE PHONE SALES THAT  *
*  OCCURRED DURING THE DAY.  IT CALLS ONE SUBPROGRAM TO CONVERT *
*  THE DATE INTO THE REQUIRED PRINT FORMAT AND A SECOND SUB-    *
*  PROGRAM TO COMPUTE THE NET AMOUNT OF THE SALE.               *
*                                                               *
*  EACH INPUT RECORD IS A PHONE SALE RECORD THAT CONTAINS THE   *
*  CUSTOMER NUMBER, THE CATALOG NUMBER, THE UNIT COST OF THE    *
*  ITEM, AND THE NUMBER OF UNITS SOLD TO THE CUSTOMER.          *
*                                                               *
*  FOR EACH PHONE SALE, THE PHONE SALE LINE ON THE REPORT MUST  *
*  SHOW THE CUSTOMER NUMBER, THE CATALOG NUMBER, THE UNIT COST, *
*  THE NUMBER OF UNITS SOLD, AND THE NET AMOUNT OF THE SALE.    *
*  THE VALUES ON THE PHONE SALE LINES ARE LISTED UNDER APPRO-   *
*  PRIATE COLUMN HEADINGS.                                      *
*                                                               *
*  THE AMOUNT OF THE SALE IS COMPUTED IN THE SUBPROGRAM.  THE   *
*  DOCUMENTATION WITHIN THE SUBPROGRAM SPECIFIES THE DISCOUNTS  *
*  IN EFFECT AT THE TIME THE PHONE SALE WAS MADE.               *
*                                                               *
*  THE REPORT BEGINS WITH A REPORT DATE LINE, FOLLOWED BY THE   *
*  NAME OF THE COMPANY, THEN THE REPORT NAME, AND FINALLY THE   *
*  APPROPRIATE COLUMN HEADINGS.                                 *
*                                                               *
*****************************************************************

 ENVIRONMENT DIVISION.

 CONFIGURATION SECTION.

 SOURCE-COMPUTER.  VAX-VMS-8650.
 OBJECT-COMPUTER.  VAX-VMS-8650.

 INPUT-OUTPUT SECTION.

 FILE-CONTROL.
     SELECT PHONE-SALES-FILE      ASSIGN TO COB$INPUT.
     SELECT PHONE-SALES-REPORT    ASSIGN TO COB$OUTPUT.

 DATA DIVISION.

 FILE SECTION.

 FD  PHONE-SALES-FILE
     RECORD CONTAINS 23 CHARACTERS.

 01  PHONE-SALE-RECORD.
     05 I-CUSTOMER-NO        PIC X(4).
     05                      PIC X(2).
     05 I-CATALOG-NO         PIC X(4).
     05                      PIC X(2).
     05 I-UNIT-COST          PIC 999V99.
     05                      PIC X(2).
     05 I-NO-OF-UNITS        PIC 9(4).

 FD  PHONE-SALES-REPORT
     RECORD CONTAINS 132 CHARACTERS.

 01  PRINTLINE               PIC X(132).

 WORKING-STORAGE SECTION.

 01  PROGRAM-CONTROLS.
     05 WS-MORE-RECORDS    PIC X(3).
        88 THERE-IS-A-RECORD       VALUE 'YES'.
        88 NO-MORE-RECORDS         VALUE 'NO '.
     05 WS-PROPER-SPACING PIC 9(1).
```

Figure 5.7 continued

```
01  WS-SALE-WORK-AREA.
    05 WS-SALE-AMOUNT      PIC 9(6)V99.

01  TOP-LINE.
    05                 PIC X(5)   VALUE SPACES.
    05 O-DATE          PIC X(19).
    05                 PIC X(96)  VALUE SPACES.
    05                 PIC X(5)   VALUE 'PAGE '.
    05 O-PAGE-NO       PIC 9(2).

01  COMPANY-NAME.
    05 PIC X(54)      VALUE SPACES.
    05 PIC X(24)      VALUE 'THE ALLIED STOCK COMPANY'.
    05 PIC X(54)      VALUE SPACES.

01  REPORT-NAME.
    05 PIC X(54)      VALUE SPACES.
    05 PIC X(24)      VALUE 'DAILY PHONE SALES REPORT'.
    05 PIC X(54)      VALUE SPACES.

01  HEADINGS.
    05 PIC X(15)      VALUE SPACES.
    05 PIC X(15)      VALUE 'CUSTOMER NUMBER'.
    05 PIC X(8)       VALUE SPACES.
    05 PIC X(14)      VALUE 'CATALOG NUMBER'.
    05 PIC X(8)       VALUE SPACES.
    05 PIC X(9)       VALUE 'UNIT COST'.
    05 PIC X(8)       VALUE SPACES.
    05 PIC X(15)      VALUE 'NUMBER OF UNITS'.
    05 PIC X(8)       VALUE SPACES.
    05 PIC X(17)      VALUE 'PHONE SALE AMOUNT'.
    05 PIC X(15)      VALUE SPACES.

01  PHONE-SALE-LINE.
    05                    PIC X(21).
    05 O-CUSTOMER-NO      PIC X(4).
    05                    PIC X(18).
    05 O-CATALOG-NO       PIC X(4).
    05                    PIC X(14).
    05 O-UNIT-COST        PIC $ZZ9.99.
    05                    PIC X(15).
    05 O-NO-OF-UNITS      PIC ZZZ9.
    05                    PIC X(16).
    05 O-SALE-AMOUNT      PIC $ZZZ,ZZ9.99.
    05                    PIC X(18).

01  END-LINE.
    05 PIC X(55)   VALUE SPACES.
    05 PIC X(23)   VALUE '***  END OF REPORT  ***'.
    05 PIC X(55)   VALUE SPACES.

PROCEDURE DIVISION.

100-PRODUCE-PHONE-SALES-REPORT.
    PERFORM 200-START-UP.
    PERFORM 210-PROCESS-PHONE-SALE-RECORD
        UNTIL WS-MORE-RECORDS = 'NO '.
    PERFORM 220-FINISH-UP.
    STOP RUN.

200-START-UP.
    OPEN INPUT PHONE-SALES-FILE
         OUTPUT PHONE-SALES-REPORT.
    SET THERE-IS-A-RECORD TO TRUE.
    MOVE 1 TO O-PAGE-NO.
    CALL 'CONVERT-DATE-SUB' USING O-DATE.
    PERFORM 300-WRITE-REPORT-HEADERS.
    PERFORM 310-READ-PHONE-SALE-RECORD.

210-PROCESS-PHONE-SALE-RECORD.
    PERFORM 320-COMPUTE-PHONE-SALE-AMOUNT.
    PERFORM 330-PREPARE-PHONE-SALE-LINE.
    PERFORM 310-READ-PHONE-SALE-RECORD.

220-FINISH-UP.
    WRITE PRINTLINE FROM END-LINE
        AFTER ADVANCING 3 LINES.
    CLOSE PHONE-SALES-FILE
          PHONE-SALES-REPORT.
```

■ **Figure 5.7** continued

```
300-WRITE-REPORT-HEADERS.
    WRITE PRINTLINE FROM TOP-LINE
        AFTER ADVANCING PAGE.
    WRITE PRINTLINE FROM COMPANY-NAME
        AFTER ADVANCING 1 LINE.
    WRITE PRINTLINE FROM REPORT-NAME
        AFTER ADVANCING 3 LINES.
    WRITE PRINTLINE FROM HEADINGS
        AFTER ADVANCING 3 LINES.
    MOVE 2 TO WS-PROPER-SPACING.

310-READ-PHONE-SALE-RECORD.
    READ PHONE-SALES-FILE RECORD
        AT END
            SET NO-MORE-RECORDS TO TRUE.

320-COMPUTE-PHONE-SALE-AMOUNT.
   CALL 'ASC-COMPUTE-SALE-AMT-SUB' USING I-NO-OF-UNITS
                                         I-UNIT-COST
                                         WS-SALE-AMOUNT.

330-PREPARE-PHONE-SALE-LINE.
    MOVE I-CUSTOMER-NO TO O-CUSTOMER-NO.
    MOVE I-CATALOG-NO TO O-CATALOG-NO.
    MOVE I-UNIT-COST TO O-UNIT-COST.
    MOVE I-NO-OF-UNITS TO O-NO-OF-UNITS.
    MOVE WS-SALE-AMOUNT TO O-SALE-AMOUNT.
    WRITE PRINTLINE FROM PHONE-SALE-LINE
        AFTER ADVANCING WS-PROPER-SPACING.
    MOVE 1 TO WS-PROPER-SPACING.
```

■ **Figure 5.8** Subprogram procedure division header

<u>PROCEDURE</u> <u>DIVISION</u> [<u>USING</u> {data-name-1 . . .]

Coding a Subprogram

Rule 15 that applies to the CALL statement clearly states that a subprogram called by a CALL statement containing the USING phrase must also contain a USING phrase in its PROCEDURE DIVISION header. This USING phrase must contain as many parameters as there are in the USING phrase of the CALL statement that calls the subprogram. For instance, in subprogram CONVERT-DATE-SUB, the PROCEDURE DIVISION header must specify one parameter in its USING phrase, as in

```
PROCEDURE DIVISION USING FORMATTED-DATE.
```

The name given to the parameter need not be the same as its matching parameter in the USING phrase of the CALL statement.

The general format of the PROCEDURE DIVISION header in a called program is shown in Figure 5.8.

Rules Governing the Use of the USING Phrase

1. The USING phrase is required only if the CALL statement in the calling program contains a USING phrase.
2. The USING phrase contains the names used in the subprogram to refer to the parameters it shares with the calling program.
3. The USING phrase in the header must contain as many names as there are in the CALL statement's USING phrase. The data names in the two lists correspond strictly by position.
4. Each *data-name-1* must be defined in the LINKAGE SECTION of the subprogram's DATA DIVISION. The level number of *data-name-1* may be any number from 01 to 49. (Level number 77 may also be used, though it is scheduled for deletion. Pre-1985 compilers allowed only the level numbers 01 and 77.)
5. The description of *data-name-1* must specify a size equal to that of its corresponding item in the USING phrase of the CALL statement. The class need not be the same.

6. References to *data-name-1* in the subprogram's PROCEDURE DIVISION are in terms of its definition in the LINKAGE SECTION.
7. The description of *data-name-1* must not contain a REDEFINES clause. However, *data-name-1* may be the object of a REDEFINES clause.
8. Statements in the PROCEDURE DIVISION of the subprogram may refer to a data item defined in the LINKAGE SECTION only if one of the following conditions is true:
   a. The data item is named in the USING phrase of the PROCEDURE DIVISION header.
   b. The data item is subordinate to a data item named in the USING phrase of the PROCEDURE DIVISION header.
   c. The description of the data item contains a REDEFINES clause, provided the object of the clause is named in the header's USING phrase.
9. A statement in the PROCEDURE DIVISION of the subprogram may refer to a condition-name or to an index defined in the LINKAGE SECTION if the condition-name or index is associated with a data item named in, or subordinate to a data item named in, the USING phrase of the PROCEDURE DIVISION header.

In the current run unit, the PROCEDURE DIVISION header for the called program named CONVERT-DATE-SUB is shown previously, and FORMATTED-DATE must be defined in the subprogram's LINKAGE SECTION. The size of FORMATTED-DATE must be the same as the parameter in the calling program's CALL statement USING phrase, namely O-DATE, and its size is 19.

The PROCEDURE DIVISION header for the called program ASC-COMPUTE-SALE-AMT-SUB will be coded as follows:

```
PROCEDURE DIVISION USING TR-NO-OF-UNITS
                         TR-UNIT-COST
                         TR-SALE-AMOUNT.
```

Positionally, these parameters match up with I-NO-OF-UNITS, I-UNIT-COST and WS-SALE-AMOUNT of the calling program's CALL statement USING phrase. These three items must be defined in the subprogram's LINKAGE SECTION.

The LINKAGE SECTION

The LINKAGE SECTION is a section of a called program's DATA DIVISION. It must be coded after the WORKING-STORAGE SECTION, if there is one, and before the REPORT SECTION, if there is one. It must contain descriptions of the data items it shares with the calling program through the USING phrases of the calling program's CALL statement and of the subprogram's PROCEDURE DIVISION header. If the PROCEDURE DIVISION header of a subprogram is not required to have a USING phrase, the subprogram does not contain a LINKAGE SECTION.

In the subprogram CONVERT-DATE-SUB, the LINKAGE SECTION will be coded as follows:

```
LINKAGE SECTION.
01  FORMATTED-DATE        PIC X(19).
```

In the subprogram ASC-COMPUTE-SALE-AMT-SUB, the LINKAGE SECTION will be coded as follows:

```
LINKAGE SECTION.
01  TR-NO-OF-UNITS        PIC 9(4).
01  TR-UNIT-COST          PIC 999V99.
01  TR-SALE-AMOUNT        PIC 9(6)V99.
```

It could just as well have been coded as follows:

```
LINKAGE SECTION.
01  TRANSACTION-ITEMS.
    05 TR-NO-OF-UNITS     PIC 9(4).
    05 TR-UNIT-COST       PIC 999V99.
    05 TR-SALE-AMOUNT     PIC 9(6)V99.
```

(Note: Pre-1985 COBOL standards required that the level numbers of the data items named in USING phrases be 01 or 77, and furthermore, the level numbers in the called program and in the calling program had to be the same. Those restrictions no longer apply!)

Figure 5.9 Subprogram ASC-COMPUTE-SALE-AMT-SUB

```
IDENTIFICATION DIVISION.

PROGRAM-ID.  ASC-COMPUTE-SALE-AMT-SUB.

*****************************************************************
*                                                               *
*  THE PURPOSE OF THIS SUBPROGRAM IS TO COMPUTE THE AMOUNT TO BE *
*  CHARGED TO CUSTOMERS OF THE ALLIED STOCK COMPANY WHO MADE    *
*  PURCHASES BY PHONE.  THE TOTAL CHARGE IS DISCOUNTED 20% IF   *
*  NUMBER OF UNITS PURCHASED EXCEEDS 100.                       *
*                                                               *
*  THE SUBPROGRAM RECEIVES THE NUMBER OF UNITS PURCHASED AND THE *
*  UNIT COST OF THE ITEM FROM THE CALLING PROGRAM.  IT RETURNS  *
*  TO THE CALLING PROGRAM THE NET SALE AMOUNT FOR THE PURCHASE.  *
*                                                               *
*****************************************************************

ENVIRONMENT DIVISION.

CONFIGURATION SECTION.

SOURCE-COMPUTER.  VAX-VMS-8650.
OBJECT-COMPUTER.  VAX-VMS-8650.

DATA DIVISION.

LINKAGE SECTION.

01  TR-NO-OF-UNITS     PIC 9(4).
01  TR-UNIT-COST       PIC 999V99.
01  TR-SALE-AMOUNT     PIC 9(6)V99.

PROCEDURE DIVISION USING TR-NO-OF-UNITS
                         TR-UNIT-COST
                         TR-SALE-AMOUNT.


100-COMPUTE-SALE-AMOUNT.
    IF TR-NO-OF-UNITS > 100
        COMPUTE TR-SALE-AMOUNT ROUNDED =
            TR-NO-OF-UNITS * TR-UNIT-COST * .8
    ELSE
        COMPUTE TR-SALE-AMOUNT ROUNDED =
            TR-NO-OF-UNITS * TR-UNIT-COST.

999-EXIT.
    EXIT PROGRAM.
```

Coding the Subprogram ASC-COMPUTE-SALE-AMT-SUB

The subprogram ASC-COMPUTE-SALE-AMT-SUB is coded as shown in Figure 5.9. Note the following:

1. The program name in the PROGRAM-ID paragraph is the one specified in the calling program's CALL statement.
2. The DATA DIVISION does not contain a FILE SECTION because this subprogram does not directly access records of files. It does not contain a WORKING-STORAGE SECTION because the subprogram does not need locally defined data items.
3. The LINKAGE SECTION defines the three items that the subprogram shares with the calling program. Note that the PIC clauses have purposely been kept identical to the ones in the calling program.
4. The PROCEDURE DIVISION header contains the USING phrase, and the three items listed are defined in the LINKAGE SECTION.
5. When the calling program statement

```
CALL "ASC-COMPUTE-SALE-AMT-SUB" USING I-NO-OF-UNITS
                                      I-UNIT-COST
                                      WS-SALE-AMOUNT
```

is executed, the values in the data items I-NO-OF-UNITS and I-UNIT-COST are made available to the subprogram but are referenced in the subprogram by the names TR-NO-OF-UNITS and TR-UNIT-COST, respectively. When the appropriate COMPUTE statement is executed, the sale amount, referenced as TR-SALE-AMOUNT in the subprogram, is stored directly into the calling program's data item WS-SALE-AMOUNT.

6. Control is returned to the calling program by executing the EXIT PROGRAM statement. It is shown coded as the sole entry in a separate paragraph of the division. This used to be a requirement, but COBOL '85 has made the use of a separate paragraph optional. The EXIT PROGRAM statement could have been coded as follows:

```
IF TR-NO-OF-UNITS > 100
    COMPUTE TR-SALE-AMOUNT ROUNDED =
        TR-NO-OF-UNITS * TR-UNIT-COST * .8
ELSE
    COMPUTE TR-SALE-AMOUNT ROUNDED =
        TR-NO-OF-UNITS * TR-UNIT-COST.
EXIT PROGRAM.
```

   Furthermore, an implicit EXIT PROGRAM is executed if the subprogram simply runs out of code. However, in line with properly structured programs, that is, to maintain the "one point of entry, one point of exit" construct, the author recommends the use of a separate exit paragraph.

   When the EXIT PROGRAM statement is executed, any PERFORM statement that has not reached the end of its range is reset as if it had. This new feature assures that upon reentering the subprogram, PERFORM statements will execute properly!

Coding the Subprogram CONVERT-DATE-SUB

Recall that the task to be accomplished by subprogram CONVERT-DATE-SUB is to obtain the date from the operating system and generate the report date formatted as specified. The coding for the subprogram is shown in Figure 5.10. Note the following:

1. The ENVIRONMENT DIVISION could have been coded, but it was left out of the source code for the following reasons: (a) Had the CONFIGURATION SECTION been coded, its two paragraphs would have provided documentation only; (b) The INPUT-OUTPUT SECTION is not needed, since the subprogram does not need to access files.
2. The DATA DIVISION does not contain a FILE SECTION, since there are no files to describe.
3. The DATA DIVISION contains a WORKING-STORAGE SECTION. The data item WS-REPORT-DATE receives the current date from the ACCEPT statement. The data item WS-CENTURY is used to construct the year portion of the formatted date. The hard-coded table of month names is needed to convert the month component of the current date into the corresponding month name.
4. The DATA DIVISION contains the LINKAGE SECTION, since the subprogram shares data with the calling program through the use of the USING phrase in the calling program's CALL statement and in the subprogram's PROCEDURE DIVISION header USING phrase. The only item described in the section is FORMATTED-DATE. Recall that it refers to the storage area in the calling program named O-DATE.
5. The PROCEDURE DIVISION header contains the phrase USING FORMATTED-DATE.
6. The ACCEPT statement obtains the current date and stores it in the group item WS-REPORT-DATE. The group's subordinate items allow references to the date's components.
7. The ADD statement produces the current year as a four-digit item.
8. The STRING statement is used to string together the various parts that make up the item FORMATTED-DATE as follows (the STRING statement is explained in Appendix A): WS-MONTH(WS-MO) is retrieved from the table; a space is added to the string; the day number WS-DAY is added to the string; a comma is inserted; the comma is followed by a space; and finally the value of WS-CENTURY completes the string operation.

Figure 5.10 Subprogram CONVERT-DATE-SUB

```
IDENTIFICATION DIVISION.

PROGRAM-ID. CONVERT-DATE-SUB.

********************************************************************
*                                                                  *
*  THE PURPOSE OF THIS SUBPROGRAM IS TO CONVERT THE CURRENT        *
*  DATE FROM YYMMDD FORMAT TO THE REPORT FORMAT THAT NAMES THE     *
*  MONTH, THEN THE DAY NUMBER, AND THE YEAR, AS IN                 *
*                  SEPTEMBER 15, 1990                              *
*                                                                  *
*  THE SUBPROGRAM DEFINES A MONTH TABLE IN WORKING STORAGE.        *
*  IT OBTAINS THE DATE FROM THE SYSTEM, CONVERTS IT TO THE         *
*  APPROPRIATE FORM, AND RETURNS IT TO THE CALLING PROGRAM.        *
*                                                                  *
********************************************************************

DATA DIVISION.

WORKING-STORAGE SECTION.

01  WS-REPORT-DATE.
    05 WS-YR    PIC 9(2).
    05 WS-MO    PIC 9(2).
    05 WS-DAY   PIC 9(2).

01  WS-CENTURY PIC 9(4)  VALUE 1900.

01  MONTH-VALUES.
    05 PIC X(9)  VALUE 'JANUARY'.
    05 PIC X(9)  VALUE 'FEBRUARY'.
    05 PIC X(9)  VALUE 'MARCH'.
    05 PIC X(9)  VALUE 'APRIL'.
    05 PIC X(9)  VALUE 'MAY'.
    05 PIC X(9)  VALUE 'JUNE'.
    05 PIC X(9)  VALUE 'JULY'.
    05 PIC X(9)  VALUE 'AUGUST'.
    05 PIC X(9)  VALUE 'SEPTEMBER'.
    05 PIC X(9)  VALUE 'OCTOBER'.
    05 PIC X(9)  VALUE 'NOVEMBER'.
    05 PIC X(9)  VALUE 'DECEMBER'.
01  MONTH-TABLE REDEFINES MONTH-VALUES.
    05 WS-MONTH OCCURS 12 TIMES  PIC X(9).

LINKAGE SECTION.

01  FORMATTED-DATE    PIC X(19).

PROCEDURE DIVISION USING FORMATTED-DATE.

100-FORMAT-CURRENT-DATE.
    ACCEPT WS-REPORT-DATE FROM DATE.
    ADD WS-YR TO WS-CENTURY.
    STRING WS-MONTH(WS-MO) DELIMITED BY ' '
           ' ' DELIMITED BY SIZE
           WS-DAY DELIMITED BY SIZE
           ',' DELIMITED BY SIZE
           ' ' DELIMITED BY SIZE
           WS-CENTURY DELIMITED BY SIZE
               INTO FORMATTED-DATE.

999-EXIT.
    EXIT PROGRAM.
```

Equivalent results could have been obtained as follows:

1. In the WORKING-STORAGE SECTION, change the description of MONTH-VALUES, as in the following code:

```
01  MONTH-VALUES.
    05 PIC X(9)  VALUE "  JANUARY".
    05 PIC X(9)  VALUE " FEBRUARY".
    05 PIC X(9)  VALUE "    MARCH".
    05 PIC X(9)  VALUE "    APRIL".
    05 PIC X(9)  VALUE "      MAY".
    05 PIC X(9)  VALUE "     JUNE".
    05 PIC X(9)  VALUE "     JULY".
    05 PIC X(9)  VALUE "   AUGUST".
    05 PIC X(9)  VALUE "SEPTEMBER".
    05 PIC X(9)  VALUE "  OCTOBER".
    05 PIC X(9)  VALUE " NOVEMBER".
    05 PIC X(9)  VALUE " DECEMBER".
```

Figure 5.11 Programs of the run unit

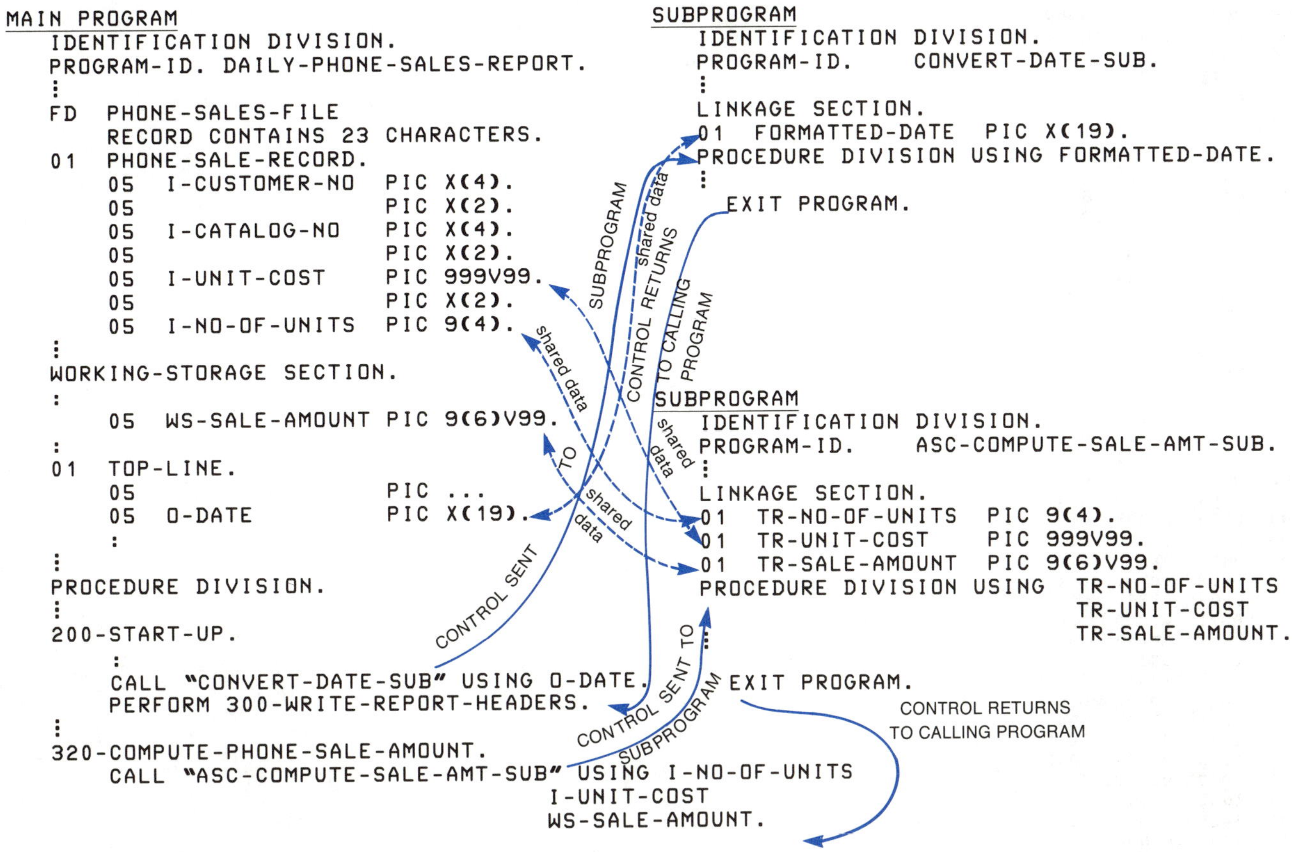

2. In the LINKAGE SECTION, change the description of FORMATTED-DATE to the following:

```
01  FORMATTED-DATE.
    05 MONTH-PART      PIC X(9).
    05 DAY-PART        PIC ZZ9.
    05 COMMA-PART      PIC X(2).
    05 YEAR-PART       PIC 9(4).
```

3. In the PROCEDURE DIVISION, code the following statements:

```
ACCEPT WS-REPORT-DATE FROM DATE.
MOVE WS-MONTH(WS-MO) TO MONTH-PART.
MOVE WS-DAY TO DAY-PART.
MOVE ", " TO COMMA-PART.
ADD WS-YR TO WS-CENTURY GIVING YEAR-PART.
```

The only difference in the results from these two procedures is that the extra spaces due to the length of month names are trailing spaces when the STRING statement is used, but they are leading spaces in the other case!

The Programs in the Run Unit

The schematic in Figure 5.11 shows portions of the programs in the run unit that contain key entries: specifically, the CALL statements in the main program that transfer control to the subprograms, the EXIT PROGRAM statements in the subprograms that return control to the main program, and the data items shared by the calling and called programs.

Figure 5.12 Data file accessed by the main program

```
9999 0001 76750 0600
6001 0003 10500 0016
9009 0007 01000 0013
0046 0012 03800 0082
9551 0013 01250 0040
2150 0036 00999 0003
0008 0064 01510 0001
7752 0369 03999 3500
2200 0400 00100 1200
2201 0401 02199 0003
2203 0403 87500 0002
2205 0405 10000 0001
2207 0407 00300 0610
8611 0408 03650 0009
8612 0409 10130 0004
8614 0501 01299 0016
8617 0503 31000 0001
8618 0506 03100 0063
0105 0561 05915 0045
8619 0583 00250 0027
0061 0600 00900 0010
0700 0601 02800 0002
0701 0602 10001 0001
0702 0603 50000 0005
0703 0604 05112 0010
0704 0605 08999 0003
0705 0606 02500 1001
0706 0607 01289 0004
0707 0608 00500 0013
0708 0609 01389 0102
0709 0611 40000 0007
0711 0613 07189 0003
0713 0615 00125 0017
0715 0617 12589 0003
0717 0619 00360 0100
4121 0801 12009 5000
0037 1010 09999 0005
5213 1012 95000 0002
8515 1022 00399 0120
8633 1022 00399 0005
0530 1025 05500 3010
0003 1030 00099 0041
0210 1034 06760 0031
4203 1091 25099 0002
3200 1200 80050 0002
3201 1201 30000 0001
3203 1203 45000 0004
3205 1205 01199 0011
3207 1207 01500 0004
3209 1209 00500 0017
```

Executing the Run Unit

Now that the programs in the run unit (the main program and the two subprograms) have been coded, they are compiled separately. When they are free of syntax errors, they are link-edited into an executable image. This is a system-specific operation, and you must obtain the appropriate system commands from your instructor. For instance, on the VAX, the programs may be compiled and link-edited as follows:

```
COBOL/ANSI/LIST C5PR1.COB, DATESUB.COB, SUBPR1.COB
LINK C5PR1.OBJ, DATESUB.OBJ, SUBPR1.OBJ
```

where C5PR1.COB is the file that contains the source code for the main program, DATESUB.COB is the file that contains the source code for the subprogram CONVERT-DATE-SUB, and SUBPR1.COB is the file that contains the source code for the subprogram ASC-COMPUTE-SALE-AMT-SUB. The LINK statement produces the executable image C5PR1.EXE, and this is the program version that is executed by the RUN statement.

The input file accessed by the main program is shown in Figure 5.12, and the output produced by the main program is shown in Figure 5.13.

As you examine the report, note that the date printed on the first line was prepared by the subprogram CONVERT-DATE-SUB, and the amounts listed under the header PHONE SALE AMOUNT were prepared by the subprogram ASC-COMPUTE-SALE-AMT-SUB.

Figure 5.13 Report produced by the main program

MAY 08, 1989 | THE ALLIED STOCK COMPANY | PAGE 01

DAILY PHONE SALES REPORT

CUSTOMER NUMBER	CATALOG NUMBER	UNIT COST	NUMBER OF UNITS	PHONE SALE AMOUNT
9999	0001	$767.50	600	$368,400.00
6001	0003	$105.00	16	$ 1,680.00
9009	0007	$ 10.00	13	$ 130.00
0046	0012	$ 38.00	82	$ 3,116.00
9551	0013	$ 12.50	40	$ 500.00
2150	0036	$ 9.99	3	$ 29.97
0008	0064	$ 15.10	1	$ 15.10
7752	0369	$ 39.99	3500	$111,972.00
2200	0400	$ 1.00	1200	$ 960.00
2201	0401	$ 21.99	3	$ 65.97
2203	0403	$875.00	2	$ 1,750.00
2205	0405	$100.00	1	$ 100.00
2207	0407	$ 3.00	610	$ 1,464.00
8611	0408	$ 36.50	9	$ 328.50
8612	0409	$101.30	4	$ 405.20
8614	0501	$ 12.99	16	$ 207.84
8617	0503	$310.00	1	$ 310.00
8618	0506	$ 31.00	63	$ 1,953.00
0105	0561	$ 59.15	45	$ 2,661.75
8619	0583	$ 2.50	27	$ 67.50
0061	0600	$ 9.00	10	$ 90.00
0700	0601	$ 28.00	2	$ 56.00
0701	0602	$100.01	1	$ 100.01
0702	0603	$500.00	5	$ 2,500.00
0703	0604	$ 51.12	10	$ 511.20
0704	0605	$ 89.99	3	$ 269.97
0705	0606	$ 25.00	1001	$ 20,020.00
0706	0607	$ 12.89	4	$ 51.56
0707	0608	$ 5.00	13	$ 65.00
0708	0609	$ 13.89	102	$ 1,133.42
0709	0611	$400.00	7	$ 2,800.00
0711	0613	$ 71.89	3	$ 215.67
0713	0615	$ 1.25	17	$ 21.25
0715	0617	$125.89	3	$ 377.67
0717	0619	$ 3.60	100	$ 360.00
4121	0801	$120.09	5000	$480,360.00
0037	1010	$ 99.99	5	$ 499.95
5213	1012	$950.00	2	$ 1,900.00
8515	1022	$ 3.99	120	$ 383.04
8633	1022	$ 3.99	5	$ 19.95
0530	1025	$ 55.00	3010	$132,440.00
0003	1030	$ 0.99	41	$ 40.59
0210	1034	$ 67.60	31	$ 2,095.60
4203	1091	$250.99	2	$ 501.98
3200	1200	$800.50	2	$ 1,601.00
3201	1201	$300.00	1	$ 300.00
3203	1203	$450.00	4	$ 1,800.00
3205	1205	$ 11.99	11	$ 131.89
3207	1207	$ 15.00	4	$ 60.00
3209	1209	$ 5.00	17	$ 85.00

*** END OF REPORT ***

The Identifier Option of the CALL Statement

In the preceding sample run unit, the CALL statements in the main program are of the form CALL ". . . ," where the subprogram being called is named within literal marks. The other option is to specify an identifier which, at the time the CALL statement is executed, contains the program name of the subprogram being called. To illustrate this option, another familiar problem is presented, albeit with variations that include the use of subprograms.

Sample Problem 2

The Ponagansett Electric Company prepares a sales analysis report on a monthly basis. The report lists all of its customers by area code. For each customer, it prints customer data including KWH usage and charge for the current billing period. For each area, it reports total KWH usage and total income produced from the sale of electricity to its residential customers and its commercial customers. At the company level, it reports the following information: the total KWH usage by its commercial customers,

Figure 5.14 Printer spacing chart for the sales analysis report

Printer Spacing Chart

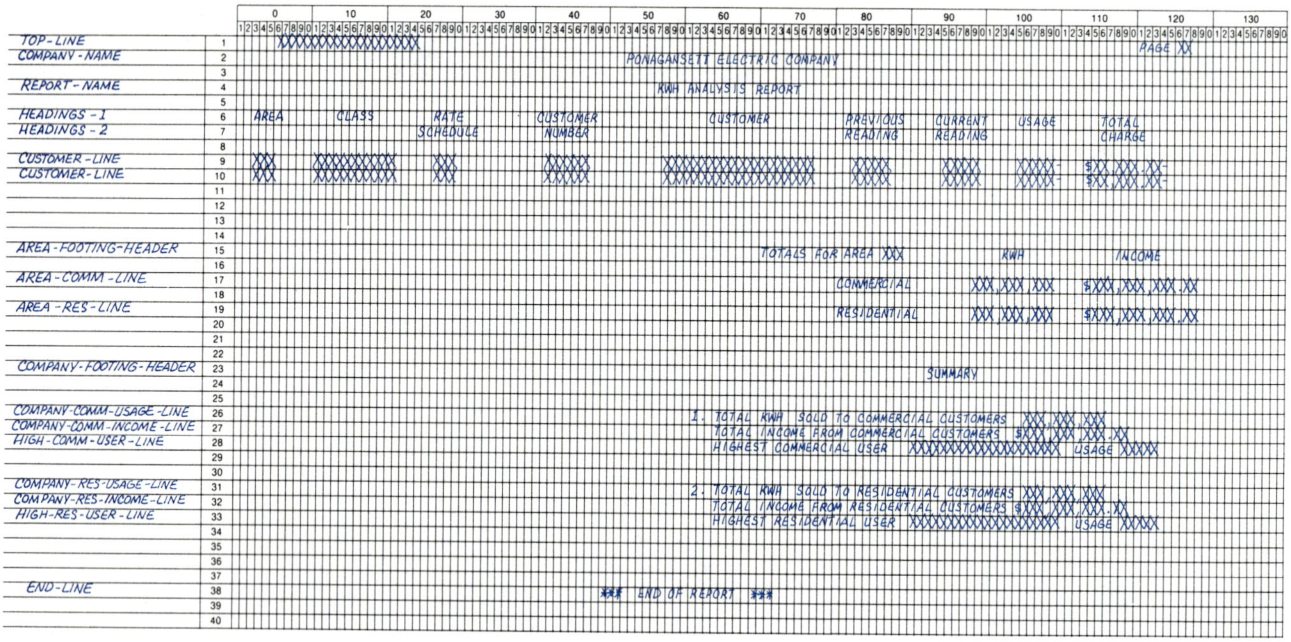

the total income produced by the sale of electricity to its commercial customers, and the name of the commercial customer with the highest KWH usage. It also produces the same kind of information for its residential customers. The report is formatted as shown in Figure 5.14.

For each customer, there is a record in the customer file containing the following data:

cc 1–3	Area code (RI1, RI2, or RI3)
cc 4–9	Customer number
cc 10–29	Customer name
cc 30–34	Previous meter reading
cc 35–39	Current meter reading
cc 40–73	Not used
cc 74–76	Customer rate schedule (A10, A11, A12, or C-2)
cc 77–80	Not used

The file has been presorted in ascending order by customer number within each area code.

There are four rate schedules: A10 for a standard residential customer, A11 for a residential customer who has an electric water heater, A12 for a residential customer who has electric heat, and C-2 for a regular commercial customer. The current details are listed below. In addition to the charge that results from the applicable rate schedule, each customer is also assessed charges related to the Fuel Adjustment Charge program (FAC), the federally mandated Uniform Conservation Cost Adjustment program (UCCA), and the Oil Conservation Adjustment program (OCA). The current charges are as follows:

FAC	.735 cents per KWH
UCCA	.093 cents per KWH
OCA	.009 cents per KWH

A10 Rate Schedule:

Customer charge:	$1.61
Energy charge:	8.082 cents per KWH

A11 Rate Schedule:

First 20 KWH or less	$2.77
Next 30 KWH	10.543 cents per KWH
Next 150 KWH	8.487 cents per KWH
Next 350 KWH	5.636 cents per KWH
Next 1450 KWH	6.937 cents per KWH
All over 2000 KWH	6.660 cents per KWH

A12 Rate Schedule:

Same as A11 Rate Schedule

C-2 Rate Schedule:

Customer charge:	$4.75	
Energy charge:		
First 1000 KWH		9.019 cents per KWH
All over 1000 KWH		8.419 cents per KWH

Analysis of the Problem

This utility company, like all other utility companies, has periodic changes in its rate schedules and in the extra charges it levies for the FAC, UCCA, and OCA programs. It should be apparent that a strong argument can be made to use a subprogram for each rate schedule and for the extra charges that must be levied. When a rate change occurs in a rate schedule, the appropriate subprogram can be updated while the main program and the other subprograms remain intact. Only the affected subprogram has to be recompiled.

To implement this plan, a subprogram named A10-SCHEDULE-SUB will be developed to compute the basic charge for A10 residential customers. A subprogram named A11-SCHEDULE-SUB will be developed to compute the basic charge for A11 and A12 residential customers. A subprogram named C-2-SCHEDULE-SUB will be developed to compute the basic charge for C-2 commercial customers. And a subprogram named XTRA-CHARGE-SUB will be developed to compute the extra charges related to the FAC, UCCA, and OCA programs.

Subprogram XTRA-CHARGE-SUB will be called during the processing of each customer record. However, of the other three subprograms, only one will be called depending on the customer's applicable rate schedule. These subprograms all receive the customer's KWH usage from the main program and return the appropriate charge. The main program must then add the basic charge and the extra charge to determine the customer's total charge.

Additionally, the subprogram CONVERT-DATE-SUB developed in the first sample run unit will be used to produce the report date. Needless to say, this program can be used as is, so no additional coding is required. This serves to illustrate the convenience within a data processing department of having subprograms that are function specific: they have already been compiled and are ready to be accessed by any program that needs the subprogram's function.

Designing the Run Unit

From the preceding discussion, it should be clear that the main program must access records of the input file, and it must produce the required report. It must have access to the subprogram CONVERT-DATE-SUB as it prepares the top-of-report documentation. And while it processes a customer record, it must be able to access subprogram A10-SCHEDULE-SUB, or A11-SCHEDULE-SUB, or C-2-SCHEDULE-SUB, to compute the customer's basic charge, and it must access subprogram XTRA-CHARGE-SUB to compute the customer's extra charge. The resulting system flowchart is shown in Figure 5.15.

Figure 5.15 System flowchart for sample run unit 2

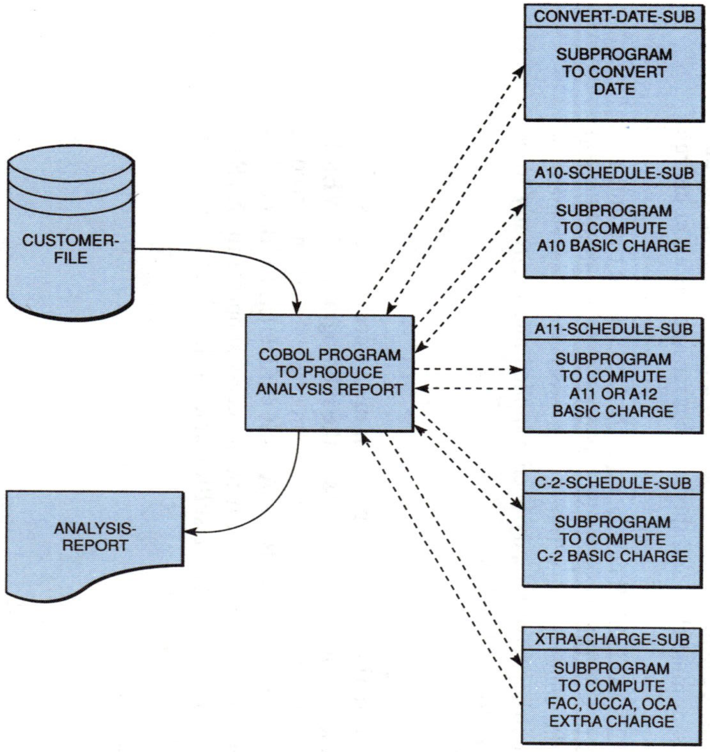

Figure 5.16 Structure chart for sample run unit 2

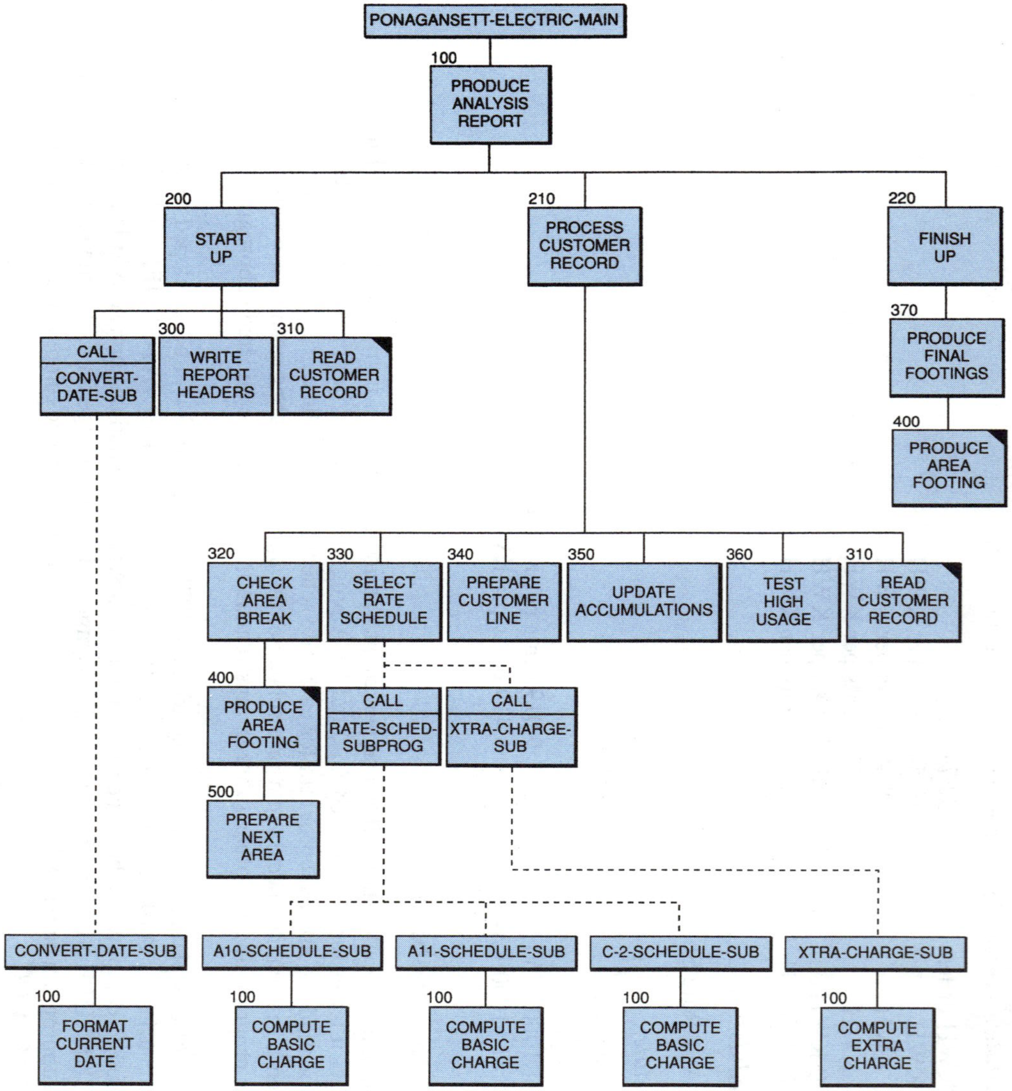

The tasks to be accomplished by the main program and the subprograms are shown in the structure chart of Figure 5.16.

The tasks shown in the structure chart with which you are already familiar will not be analyzed any further. The only module of particular interest at this point is 330 SELECT RATE SCHEDULE.

Examining the Task 330 SELECT RATE SCHEDULE

The structure chart makes it clear that two tasks are to be accomplished in this module: (1) compute the customer's basic charge, and (2) compute the customer's extra charge. Though not shown explicitly in the structure chart, the customer's total charge must also be computed. To compute the customer's basic charge, it is necessary to know two things. One is the customer's KWH usage for the reporting period, and the other is the customer's applicable rate schedule so as to select the correct subprogram.

There are a number of ways of setting up the logic to accomplish these tasks. All must begin by determining the customer's KWH usage. Then, the customer's rate schedule must be tested. It may be tested by using nested selection constructs, or it may be tested by using the case construct. When the customer's rate schedule has been determined, then the appropriate subprogram may be called directly. Figure 5.17a shows the procedure using nested tests, while Figure 5.17b shows the procedure using the case structure.

Figure 5.17a Calling a subprogram from within nested tests

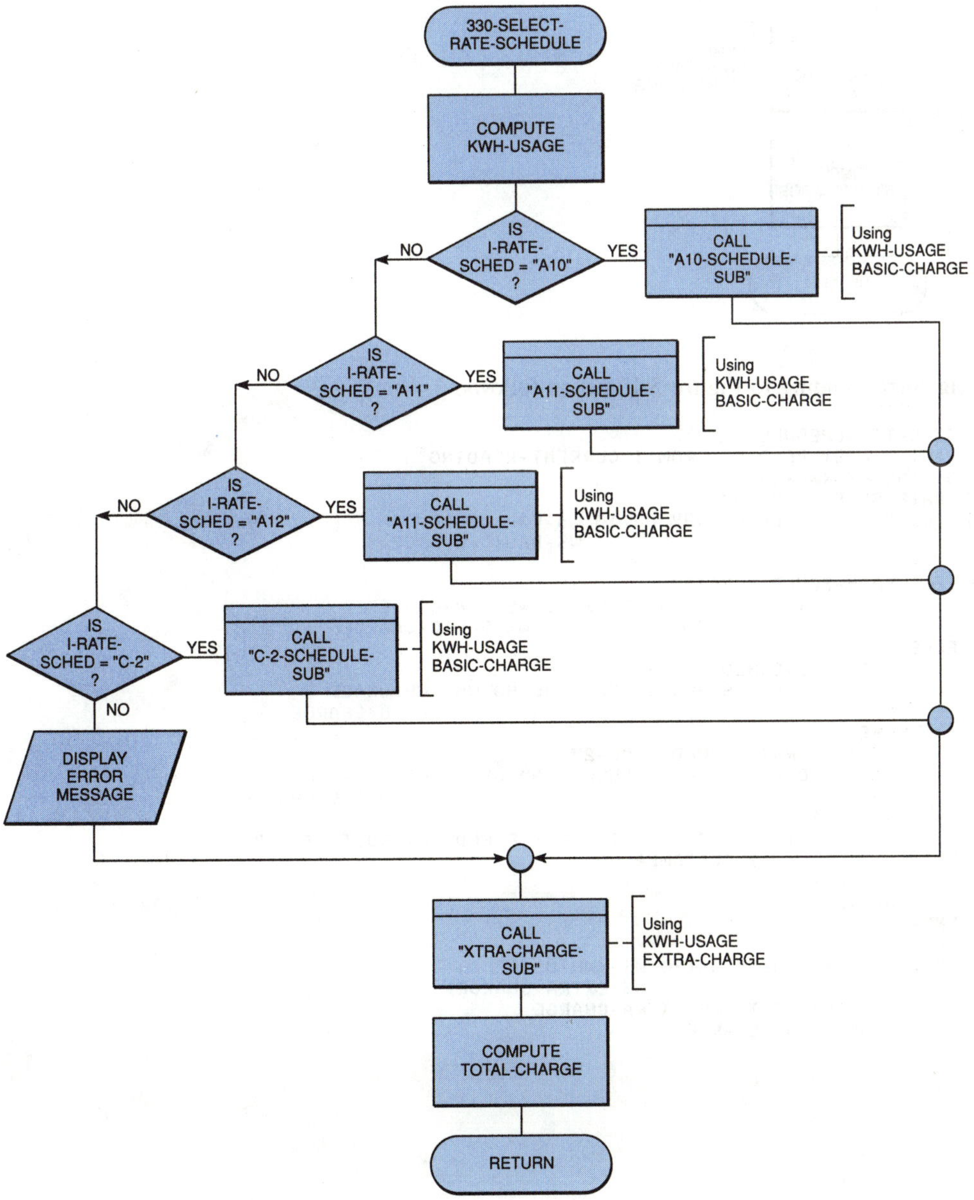

■ **Figure 5.17b** Calling a subprogram from within the case structure

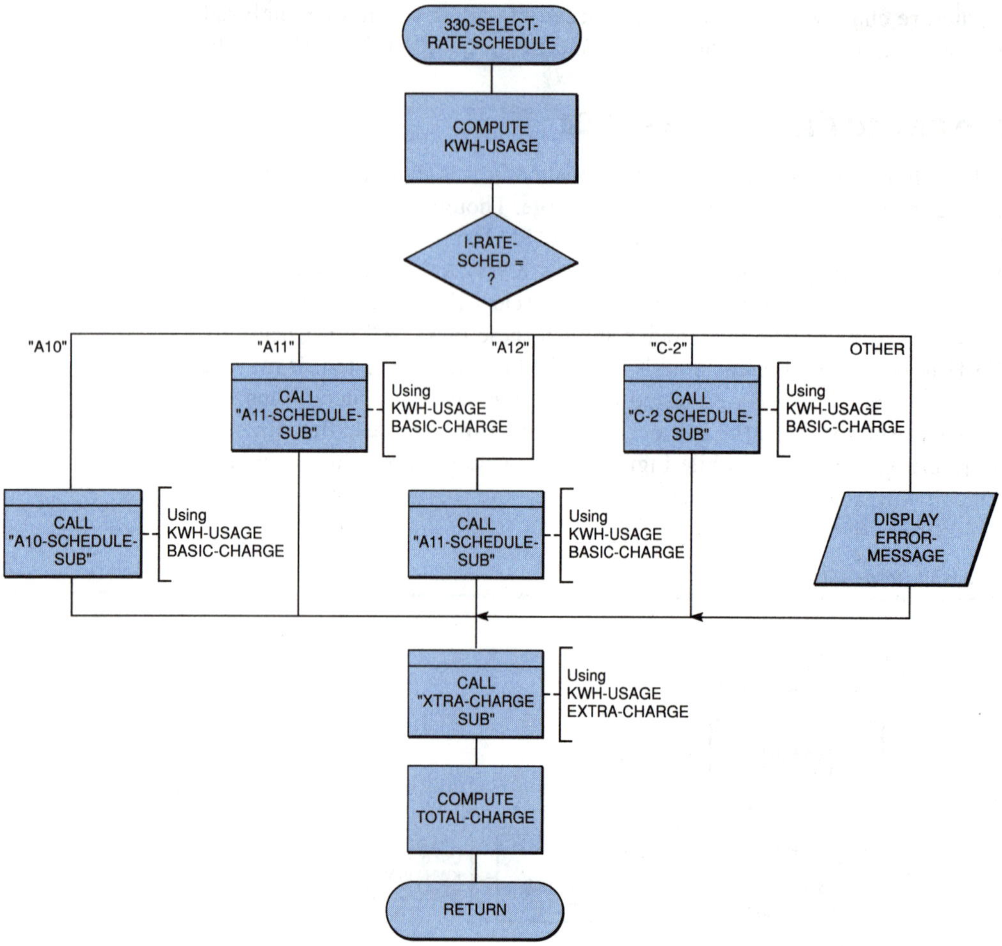

The coding corresponding to Figure 5.17a is as follows:

```
330-SELECT-RATE-SCHEDULE.
    SUBTRACT I-LAST-READING FROM I-CURRENT-READING
        GIVING WS-KWH-USAGE.
    IF I-RATE-SCHED = "A10"
        CALL "A10-SCHEDULE-SUB" USING WS-KWH-USAGE
                                      WS-BASIC-CHARGE
    ELSE
        IF I-RATE-SCHED = "A11"
            CALL "A11-SCHEDULE-SUB" USING WS-KWH-USAGE
                                          WS-BASIC-CHARGE
        ELSE
            IF I-RATE-SCHED = "A12"
                CALL "A11-SCHEDULE-SUB" USING WS-KWH-USAGE
                                              WS-BASIC-CHARGE
            ELSE
                IF I-RATE-SCHED = "C-2"
                    CALL "C-2-SCHEDULE-SUB" USING WS-KWH-USAGE
                                                  WS-BASIC-CHARGE
                ELSE
                    DISPLAY "ERROR IN RATE FIELD FOR CUST. # = "
                        I-CUSTOMER-NO
                END-IF
            END-IF
        END-IF
    END-IF.
    CALL "XTRA-CHARGE-SUB" USING WS-KWH-USAGE
                                 WS-EXTRA-CHARGE.
    ADD WS-BASIC-CHARGE TO WS-EXTRA-CHARGE
        GIVING WS-TOTAL-CHARGE.
```

The coding corresponding to Figure 5.17b is as follows:

```
330-SELECT-RATE-SCHEDULE.
    SUBTRACT I-LAST-READING FROM I-CURRENT-READING
        GIVING WS-KWH-USAGE.
    EVALUATE I-RATE-SCHED
        WHEN    "A10"   CALL "A10-SCHEDULE-SUB" USING WS-KWH-USAGE
                                                      WS-BASIC-CHARGE
        WHEN    "A11"   CALL "A11-SCHEDULE-SUB" USING WS-KWH-USAGE
                                                      WS-BASIC-CHARGE
        WHEN    "A12"   CALL "A11-SCHEDULE-SUB" USING WS-KWH-USAGE
                                                      WS-BASIC-CHARGE
        WHEN    "C-2"   CALL "C-2-SCHEDULE-SUB" USING WS-KWH-USAGE
                                                      WS-BASIC-CHARGE
        WHEN    OTHER   DISPLAY "ERROR IN RATE FIELD FOR CUST. # = "
                            I-CUSTOMER-NO
    END-EVALUATE.
    CALL "XTRA-CHARGE-SUB" USING WS-KWH-USAGE
                                 WS-EXTRA-CHARGE.
    ADD WS-BASIC-CHARGE TO WS-EXTRA-CHARGE
        GIVING WS-TOTAL-CHARGE.
```

Note that the structures in Figures 5.17a and 5.17b require the coding of four CALL statements, all using the literal option. The coding can be simplified by using the identifier option of the CALL statement. The identifier must be an alphanumeric data item of size sufficiently large to store the longest of the subprogram names. Suppose that RATE-SCHED-SUBPROG is the identifier, and that the case construct is selected. The resulting flowchart module is shown in Figure 5.18.

Note that the case structure contains four MOVE operations instead of four CALL operations. The corresponding coding is as follows:

```
330-SELECT-RATE-SCHEDULE.
    SUBTRACT I-LAST-READING FROM I-CURRENT-READING
        GIVING WS-KWH-USAGE.
    EVALUATE I-RATE-SCHED
        WHEN    "A10"   MOVE "A10-SCHEDULE-SUB" TO RATE-SCHED-SUBPROG
        WHEN    "A11"   MOVE "A11-SCHEDULE-SUB" TO RATE-SCHED-SUBPROG
        WHEN    "A12"   MOVE "A11-SCHEDULE-SUB" TO RATE-SCHED-SUBPROG
        WHEN    "C-2"   MOVE "C-2-SCHEDULE-SUB" TO RATE-SCHED-SUBPROG
        WHEN    OTHER   DISPLAY "ERROR IN RATE FIELD FOR CUST. # = "
                            I-CUSTOMER-NO
    END-EVALUATE.
    CALL RATE-SCHED-SUBPROG USING WS-KWH-USAGE
                                  WS-BASIC-CHARGE.
    CALL "XTRA-CHARGE-SUB" USING WS-KWH-USAGE
                                 WS-EXTRA-CHARGE.
    ADD WS-BASIC-CHARGE TO WS-EXTRA-CHARGE
        GIVING WS-TOTAL-CHARGE.
```

Note that the coding is simpler and self-documentation is well served. And because only two CALL statements have to be compiled instead of five, compilation is made more efficient.

■ **Figure 5.18** Using the identifier option of the CALL statement

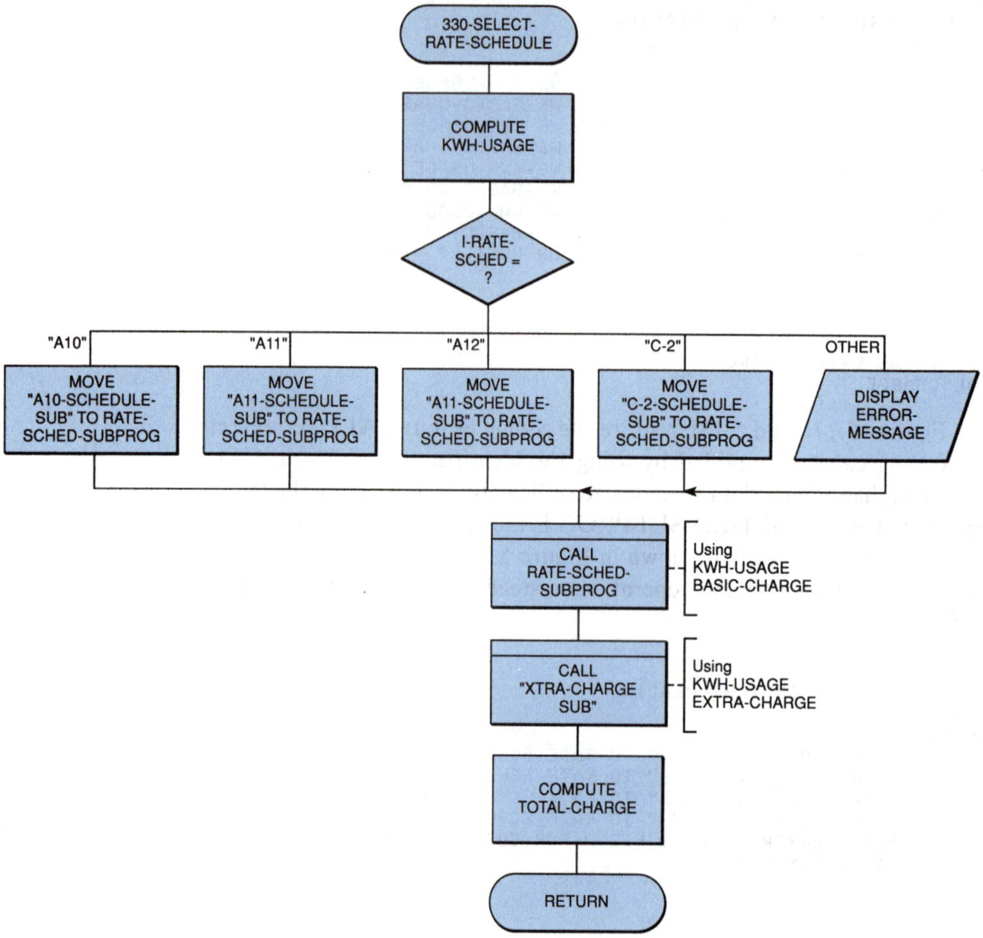

The ON EXCEPTION clause

When a CALL statement is executed, program execution ends abnormally (an ABEND occurs) if the subprogram being called is not in the run unit. The programmer can insert a safeguard against this type of ABEND by coding the ON EXCEPTION or ON OVERFLOW clause in the statement. For instance, the first CALL statement may be coded as follows:

```
CALL RATE-SCHED-SUBPROG USING WS-KWH-USAGE
                              WS-BASIC-CHARGE
    ON EXCEPTION
        DISPLAY "SUBPROGRAM = " RATE-SCHED-SUBPROG " NOT IN RUN UNIT"
END-CALL.
```

Coding the Main Program

As noted earlier, the other aspects of the main program present no new language elements, and therefore the normal development cycle as specified by the problem-solving procedure is bypassed. The main program is simply presented in its entirety in Figure 5.19. The data items that are shared with subprograms and the entries related to the CALL statements have been highlighted for your convenience.

Figure 5.19 Main program of sample run unit 2

```
IDENTIFICATION DIVISION.

PROGRAM-ID.     PONAGANSETT-ELECTRIC-MAIN.

*****************************************************************
*                                                               *
*   AUTHOR.           PAQUETTE.                                 *
*   DATE WRITTEN.     MAY 8, 1989.                              *
*                                                               *
*   THE PURPOSE OF THIS PROGRAM IS TO PRODUCE AN ANALYSIS REPORT *
*   FOR THE CURRENT BILLING PERIOD.  THE PROGRAM CONTAINS A CON- *
*   TROL BREAK AT THE AREA CODE LEVEL.  IT PRODUCES A DETAIL LINE *
*   FOR EACH CUSTOMER IN A SPECIFIED AREA, FOLLOWED BY SUMMARY  *
*   INFORMATION FOR THE AREA.  IT ALSO PRODUCES SUMMARY INFORMA- *
*   TION FOR THE COMPANY AS A WHOLE.                            *
*                                                               *
*   THE PROGRAM CALLS A DATE CONVERSION SUBPROGRAM TO GENERATE A *
*   PROPERLY FORMATTED REPORT DATE.  IT CALLS ANY ONE OF THREE  *
*   SUBPROGRAMS TO COMPUTE THE CUSTOMER'S BASIC ELECTRIC CHARGE, *
*   DEPENDING ON THE CUSTOMER'S APPLICABLE RATE SCHEDULE.  AND IT *
*   CALLS ANOTHER SUBPROGRAM TO COMPUTE AN EXTRA CHARGE BASED ON *
*   THE FUEL ADJUSTMENT CHARGE, THE OIL CONSERVATION ADJUSTMENT *
*   CHARGE, AND THE UNIFORM CONSERVATION COST ADJUSTMENT PROGRAM *
*   CHARGE.                                                     *
*                                                               *
*   THE CALL 'literal' STATEMENT IS USED TO CALL THE DATE CON-  *
*   VERSION PROGRAM AND THE EXTRA-CHARGE PROGRAM, BUT IT USES THE *
*   CALL identifier STATEMENT TO SELECT THE APPROPRIATE BASIC   *
*   CHARGE PROGRAM.                                             *
*                                                               *
*****************************************************************

ENVIRONMENT DIVISION.

CONFIGURATION SECTION.

SOURCE-COMPUTER.  VAX-VMS-8650.
OBJECT-COMPUTER.  VAX-VMS-8650.

INPUT-OUTPUT SECTION.

FILE-CONTROL.
    SELECT CUSTOMER-FILE    ASSIGN TO COB$INPUT.
    SELECT ANALYSIS-REPORT ASSIGN TO COB$OUTPUT.

DATA DIVISION.

FILE SECTION.

FD  CUSTOMER-FILE
    RECORD CONTAINS 80 CHARACTERS.

01  CUSTOMER-RECORD.
    05 I-AREA-CODE             PIC X(3).
    05 I-CUSTOMER-NO           PIC X(6).
    05 I-CUSTOMER-NAME         PIC X(20).
    05 I-LAST-READING          PIC 9(5).
    05 I-CURRENT-READING       PIC 9(5).
    05                         PIC X(34).
    05 I-RATE-SCHED            PIC X(3).
       88 COMMERCIAL                   VALUE 'C-2'.
       88 RESIDENTIAL                  VALUE 'A10', 'A11', 'A12'.
    05                         PIC X(4).

FD  ANALYSIS-REPORT
    RECORD CONTAINS 132 CHARACTERS.

01  PRINTLINE                  PIC X(132).

WORKING-STORAGE SECTION.

01  PROGRAM-CONTROLS.
    05 WS-MORE-RECORDS             PIC X(3).
       88 THERE-IS-A-RECORD                VALUE 'YES'.
       88 NO-MORE-RECORDS                  VALUE 'NO '.
    05 WS-AREA-CONTROL             PIC X(3).
    05 WS-PAGE-NO                  PIC 9(2).
    05 PROPER-SPACING              PIC S9.
    05 RATE-SCHED-SUBPROG          PIC X(16).
```

■ **Figure 5.19** continued

```
01  WS-SHARED-WORK-AREAS.
    05 WS-KWH-USAGE                PIC S9(5).
    05 WS-BASIC-CHARGE             PIC S9(5)V99.
    05 WS-EXTRA-CHARGE             PIC S9(5)V99.

01  WS-WORK-AREAS.
    05 WS-HIGH-KWH-COMM            PIC S9(9).
    05 WS-HIGH-KWH-RES             PIC S9(9).
    05 WS-TOTAL-AMOUNT             PIC S9(5)V99.

01  WS-PROGRAM-ACCUMULATORS        COMP.
    05 WS-AREA-KWH-COMM            PIC S9(9).
    05 WS-AREA-KWH-RES             PIC S9(9).
    05 WS-AREA-COMM-INCOME         PIC S9(9)V99.
    05 WS-AREA-INCOME-RES          PIC S9(9)V99.
    05 WS-COMPANY-KWH-COMM         PIC S9(9).
    05 WS-COMPANY-KWH-RES          PIC S9(9).
    05 WS-COMPANY-COMM-INCOME      PIC S9(9)V99.
    05 WS-COMPANY-INCOME-RES       PIC S9(9)V99.

01  REPORT-HEADERS.

    05 TOP-LINE.
       10              PIC X(5)  VALUE SPACES.
       10 O-DATE       PIC X(19).
       10              PIC X(96) VALUE SPACES.
       10              PIC X(5)  VALUE 'PAGE '.
       10 O-PAGE-NO    PIC Z9.

    05 COMPANY-NAME.
       10 PIC X(52)     VALUE SPACES.
       10 PIC X(28)     VALUE 'PONAGANSETT ELECTRIC COMPANY'.
       10 PIC X(52)     VALUE SPACES.

    05 REPORT-NAME.
       10 PIC X(56)     VALUE SPACES.
       10 PIC X(19)     VALUE 'KWH ANALYSIS REPORT'.
       10 PIC X(57)     VALUE SPACES.

    05 HEADINGS-1.
       10 PIC X(2)      VALUE SPACES.
       10 PIC X(4)      VALUE 'AREA'.
       10 PIC X(7)      VALUE SPACES.
       10 PIC X(5)      VALUE 'CLASS'.
       10 PIC X(8)      VALUE SPACES.
       10 PIC X(4)      VALUE 'RATE'.
       10 PIC X(10)     VALUE SPACES.
       10 PIC X(8)      VALUE 'CUSTOMER'.
       10 PIC X(15)     VALUE SPACES.
       10 PIC X(8)      VALUE 'CUSTOMER'.
       10 PIC X(10)     VALUE SPACES.
       10 PIC X(8)      VALUE 'PREVIOUS'.
       10 PIC X(4)      VALUE SPACES.
       10 PIC X(7)      VALUE 'CURRENT'.
       10 PIC X(4)      VALUE SPACES.
       10 PIC X(5)      VALUE 'USAGE'.
       10 PIC X(6)      VALUE SPACES.
       10 PIC X(5)      VALUE 'TOTAL'.
       10 PIC X(12)     VALUE SPACES.

    05 HEADINGS-2.
       10 PIC X(24)     VALUE SPACES.
       10 PIC X(8)      VALUE 'SCHEDULE'.
       10 PIC X(9)      VALUE SPACES.
       10 PIC X(6)      VALUE 'NUMBER'.
       10 PIC X(34)     VALUE SPACES.
       10 PIC X(7)      VALUE 'READING'.
       10 PIC X(5)      VALUE SPACES.
       10 PIC X(7)      VALUE 'READING'.
       10 PIC X(15)     VALUE SPACES.
       10 PIC X(6)      VALUE 'CHARGE'.
       10 PIC X(11)     VALUE SPACES.
```

```
01  CUSTOMER-LINE.
    05                          PIC X(2).
    05 O-AREA-CODE-1            PIC X(3).
    05                          PIC X(5).
    05 O-CLASS                  PIC X(11).
    05                          PIC X(5).
    05 O-RATE-SCHED             PIC X(3).
    05                          PIC X(12).
    05 O-CUSTOMER-NO            PIC X(6).
    05                          PIC X(10).
    05 O-CUSTOMER-NAME          PIC X(20).
    05                          PIC X(5).
    05 O-LAST-READING           PIC X(5).
    05                          PIC X(7).
    05 O-CURRENT-READING        PIC X(5).
    05                          PIC X(5).
    05 O-KWH-USAGE              PIC ZZZZ9-.
    05                          PIC X(3).
    05 O-TOTAL-AMOUNT           PIC $ZZ,ZZ9.99-.
    05                          PIC X(8).

01  AREA-FOOTING-LINES.

    05 AREA-FOOTING-HEADER.
       10                       PIC X(70) VALUE SPACES.
       10                       PIC X(16) VALUE 'TOTALS FOR AREA '.
       10 O-AREA-CODE-2         PIC X(3).
       10                       PIC X(13) VALUE SPACES.
       10                       PIC XXX   VALUE 'KWH'.
       10                       PIC X(12) VALUE SPACES.
       10                       PIC X(6)  VALUE 'INCOME'.
       10                       PIC X(9)  VALUE SPACES.

    05 AREA-COMM-LINE.
       10                       PIC X(80) VALUE SPACES.
       10                       PIC X(10) VALUE 'COMMERCIAL'.
       10                       PIC X(8)  VALUE SPACES.
       10 O-AREA-KWH-COMM       PIC ZZZ,ZZZ,ZZ9.
       10                       PIC X(4)  VALUE SPACES.
       10 O-AREA-COMM-INCOME    PIC $ZZZ,ZZZ,ZZ9.99.
       10                       PIC X(4)  VALUE SPACES.

    05 AREA-RES-LINE.
       10                       PIC X(80) VALUE SPACES.
       10                       PIC X(11) VALUE 'RESIDENTIAL'.
       10                       PIC X(7)  VALUE SPACES.
       10 O-AREA-KWH-RES        PIC ZZZ,ZZZ,ZZ9.
       10                       PIC X(4)  VALUE SPACES.
       10 O-AREA-INCOME-RES     PIC $ZZZ,ZZZ,ZZ9.99.
       10                       PIC X(4)  VALUE SPACES.

01  COMPANY-FOOTING-LINES.

    05 COMPANY-FOOTING-HEADER.
       10 PIC X(92)     VALUE SPACES.
       10 PIC X(7)      VALUE 'SUMMARY'.
       10 PIC X(33)     VALUE SPACES.

    05 COMPANY-COMM-USAGE-LINE.
       10                       PIC X(61)  VALUE SPACES.
       10                       PIC X(44)  VALUE
               '1. TOTAL KWH  SOLD TO COMMERCIAL CUSTOMERS    '.
       10 O-COMPANY-KWH-COMM PIC ZZZ,ZZZ,ZZ9.
       10                       PIC X(16)  VALUE SPACES.

    05 COMPANY-COMM-INCOME-LINE.
       10                            PIC X(64)  VALUE SPACES.
       10                            PIC X(40)  VALUE
               'TOTAL INCOME FROM COMMERCIAL CUSTOMERS    '.
       10 O-COMPANY-COMM-INCOME PIC $ZZZ,ZZZ,ZZ9.99.
       10                            PIC X(13)  VALUE SPACES.
```

■ **Figure 5.19** continued

```
       05 HIGH-COMM-USER-LINE.
          10                    PIC X(64)   VALUE SPACES.
          10                    PIC X(26)   VALUE
                                'HIGHEST COMMERCIAL USER   '.
          10 O-HIGH-COMM-USER PIC X(20).
          10                    PIC X(8)    VALUE '  USAGE '.
          10 O-HIGH-KWH-COMM   PIC ZZZZ9.
          10                    PIC X(9)    VALUE SPACES.

       05 COMPANY-RES-USAGE-LINE.
          10                     PIC X(61)  VALUE SPACES.
          10                     PIC X(45)  VALUE
               '2. TOTAL KWH  SOLD TO RESIDENTIAL CUSTOMERS   '.
          10 O-COMPANY-KWH-RES PIC ZZZ,ZZZ,ZZ9.
          10                     PIC X(15)  VALUE SPACES.

       05 COMPANY-RES-INCOME-LINE.
          10                        PIC X(64)  VALUE SPACES.
          10                        PIC X(41)  VALUE
               'TOTAL  INCOME FROM RESIDENTIAL CUSTOMERS  '.
          10 O-COMPANY-INCOME-RES PIC $ZZZ,ZZZ,ZZ9.99.
          10                        PIC X(12)  VALUE SPACES.

       05 HIGH-RES-USER-LINE.
          10                   PIC X(64)  VALUE SPACES.
          10                   PIC X(26)  VALUE
                               'HIGHEST RESIDENTIAL USER   '.
          10 O-HIGH-RES-USER PIC X(20).
          10                   PIC X(8)   VALUE '  USAGE '.
          10 O-HIGH-KWH-RES   PIC ZZZZ9.
          10                   PIC X(9)   VALUE SPACES.

   01  END-LINE.
       05 PIC X(49)   VALUE SPACES.
       05 PIC X(23)   VALUE '***  END OF REPORT  ***'.
       05 PIC X(50)   VALUE SPACES.

   PROCEDURE DIVISION.

   100-PRODUCE-ANALYSIS-REPORT.
       PERFORM 200-START-UP.
       PERFORM 210-PROCESS-CUSTOMER-RECORD
           UNTIL NO-MORE-RECORDS.
       PERFORM 220-FINISH-UP.
       STOP RUN.

   200-START-UP.
       OPEN INPUT  CUSTOMER-FILE
            OUTPUT ANALYSIS-REPORT.
       CALL 'CONVERT-DATE-SUB' USING O-DATE.
       INITIALIZE WS-PAGE-NO
                  WS-PROGRAM-ACCUMULATORS
                  WS-HIGH-KWH-COMM
                  WS-HIGH-KWH-RES.
       SET THERE-IS-A-RECORD TO TRUE.
       PERFORM 300-WRITE-REPORT-HEADERS.
       PERFORM 310-READ-CUSTOMER-RECORD.
       MOVE I-AREA-CODE TO WS-AREA-CONTROL.

   210-PROCESS-CUSTOMER-RECORD.
       PERFORM 320-CHECK-AREA-BREAK.
       PERFORM 330-SELECT-RATE-SCHEDULE.
       PERFORM 340-PREPARE-CUSTOMER-LINE.
       PERFORM 350-UPDATE-ACCUMULATORS.
       PERFORM 360-TEST-HIGH-USAGE.
       PERFORM 310-READ-CUSTOMER-RECORD.

   220-FINISH-UP.
       PERFORM 370-PRODUCE-FINAL-FOOTINGS.
       WRITE PRINTLINE FROM END-LINE
           AFTER ADVANCING 5 LINES.
       CLOSE CUSTOMER-FILE
             ANALYSIS-REPORT.
```

■ **Figure 5.19** continued

```
300-WRITE-REPORT-HEADERS.
    ADD 1 TO WS-PAGE-NO.
    MOVE WS-PAGE-NO TO O-PAGE-NO.
    WRITE PRINTLINE FROM TOP-LINE
        AFTER ADVANCING PAGE.
    WRITE PRINTLINE FROM COMPANY-NAME
        AFTER ADVANCING 1 LINE.
    WRITE PRINTLINE FROM REPORT-NAME
        AFTER ADVANCING 2 LINES.
    WRITE PRINTLINE FROM HEADINGS-1
        AFTER ADVANCING 2 LINES.
    WRITE PRINTLINE FROM HEADINGS-2
        AFTER ADVANCING 1 LINE.
    MOVE 2 TO PROPER-SPACING.

310-READ-CUSTOMER-RECORD.
    READ CUSTOMER-FILE RECORD
        AT END
            SET NO-MORE-RECORDS TO TRUE.

320-CHECK-AREA-BREAK.
    IF I-AREA-CODE = WS-AREA-CONTROL
        NEXT SENTENCE
    ELSE
        PERFORM 400-PRODUCE-AREA-FOOTING.

330-SELECT-RATE-SCHEDULE.
    SUBTRACT I-LAST-READING FROM I-CURRENT-READING
        GIVING WS-KWH-USAGE.
    EVALUATE I-RATE-SCHED
        WHEN 'C-2'
            MOVE 'C-2-SCHEDULE-SUB' TO RATE-SCHED-SUBPROG
        WHEN 'A10'
            MOVE 'A10-SCHEDULE-SUB' TO RATE-SCHED-SUBPROG
        WHEN 'A11'
            MOVE 'A11-SCHEDULE-SUB' TO RATE-SCHED-SUBPROG
        WHEN 'A12'
            MOVE 'A11-SCHEDULE-SUB' TO RATE-SCHED-SUBPROG
        WHEN OTHER
            DISPLAY 'ERROR IN RATE FIELD FOR CUST. # = '
                    I-CUSTOMER-NO
    END-EVALUATE.
    CALL RATE-SCHED-SUBPROG USING WS-KWH-USAGE
                                  WS-BASIC-CHARGE
        ON EXCEPTION
            DISPLAY 'RATE-SCHED-SUBPROG = '
                RATE-SCHED-SUBPROG ' IS NOT IN RUN UNIT'
    END-CALL.
    CALL 'XTRA-CHARGE-SUB' USING WS-KWH-USAGE
                                 WS-EXTRA-CHARGE.
    ADD WS-EXTRA-CHARGE TO WS-BASIC-CHARGE
        GIVING WS-TOTAL-AMOUNT.

340-PREPARE-CUSTOMER-LINE.
    MOVE I-AREA-CODE TO O-AREA-CODE-1.
    MOVE I-CUSTOMER-NO TO O-CUSTOMER-NO.
    MOVE I-CUSTOMER-NAME TO O-CUSTOMER-NAME.
    MOVE I-LAST-READING TO O-LAST-READING.
    MOVE I-CURRENT-READING TO O-CURRENT-READING.
    MOVE I-RATE-SCHED TO O-RATE-SCHED.
    IF COMMERCIAL
        MOVE 'COMMERCIAL' TO O-CLASS
    ELSE
        MOVE 'RESIDENTIAL' TO O-CLASS.
    MOVE WS-KWH-USAGE TO O-KWH-USAGE.
    MOVE WS-TOTAL-AMOUNT TO O-TOTAL-AMOUNT.
    WRITE PRINTLINE FROM CUSTOMER-LINE
        AFTER ADVANCING PROPER-SPACING.
    MOVE 1 TO PROPER-SPACING.
```

```
350-UPDATE-ACCUMULATORS.
    IF COMMERCIAL
        ADD WS-KWH-USAGE TO WS-AREA-KWH-COMM
                            WS-COMPANY-KWH-COMM
        ADD WS-TOTAL-AMOUNT TO WS-AREA-COMM-INCOME
                               WS-COMPANY-COMM-INCOME
    ELSE
        ADD WS-KWH-USAGE TO WS-AREA-KWH-RES
                            WS-COMPANY-KWH-RES
        ADD WS-TOTAL-AMOUNT TO WS-AREA-INCOME-RES
                               WS-COMPANY-INCOME-RES.

360-TEST-HIGH-USAGE.
    IF COMMERCIAL
        IF WS-KWH-USAGE > WS-HIGH-KWH-COMM
            MOVE WS-KWH-USAGE TO WS-HIGH-KWH-COMM
            MOVE I-CUSTOMER-NAME TO O-HIGH-COMM-USER
        END-IF
    ELSE
        IF WS-KWH-USAGE > WS-HIGH-KWH-RES
            MOVE WS-KWH-USAGE TO WS-HIGH-KWH-RES
            MOVE I-CUSTOMER-NAME TO O-HIGH-RES-USER
        END-IF
    END-IF.

370-PRODUCE-FINAL-FOOTINGS.
    PERFORM 400-PRODUCE-AREA-FOOTING.
    WRITE PRINTLINE FROM COMPANY-FOOTING-HEADER
        AFTER ADVANCING 5 LINES.
    MOVE WS-COMPANY-KWH-COMM TO O-COMPANY-KWH-COMM.
    MOVE WS-COMPANY-KWH-RES TO O-COMPANY-KWH-RES.
    MOVE WS-COMPANY-COMM-INCOME TO O-COMPANY-COMM-INCOME.
    MOVE WS-COMPANY-INCOME-RES TO O-COMPANY-INCOME-RES.
    MOVE WS-HIGH-KWH-COMM TO O-HIGH-KWH-COMM.
    MOVE WS-HIGH-KWH-RES TO O-HIGH-KWH-RES.
    WRITE PRINTLINE FROM COMPANY-COMM-USAGE-LINE
        AFTER ADVANCING 3 LINES.
    WRITE PRINTLINE FROM COMPANY-COMM-INCOME-LINE
        AFTER ADVANCING 1 LINE.
    WRITE PRINTLINE FROM HIGH-COMM-USER-LINE
        AFTER ADVANCING 1 LINE.
    WRITE PRINTLINE FROM COMPANY-RES-USAGE-LINE
        AFTER ADVANCING 3 LINES.
    WRITE PRINTLINE FROM COMPANY-RES-INCOME-LINE
        AFTER ADVANCING 1 LINE.
    WRITE PRINTLINE FROM HIGH-RES-USER-LINE
        AFTER ADVANCING 1 LINE.

400-PRODUCE-AREA-FOOTING.
    MOVE WS-AREA-CONTROL TO O-AREA-CODE-2.
    MOVE WS-AREA-KWH-COMM TO O-AREA-KWH-COMM.
    MOVE WS-AREA-KWH-RES TO O-AREA-KWH-RES.
    MOVE WS-AREA-COMM-INCOME TO O-AREA-COMM-INCOME.
    MOVE WS-AREA-INCOME-RES TO O-AREA-INCOME-RES.
    WRITE PRINTLINE FROM AREA-FOOTING-HEADER
        AFTER ADVANCING 5 LINES.
    WRITE PRINTLINE FROM AREA-COMM-LINE
        AFTER ADVANCING 2 LINES.
    WRITE PRINTLINE FROM AREA-RES-LINE
        AFTER ADVANCING 2 LINES.
    IF THERE-IS-A-RECORD
        PERFORM 500-PREPARE-NEXT-AREA
    END-IF.

500-PREPARE-NEXT-AREA.
    MOVE ZEROS TO WS-AREA-KWH-COMM
                  WS-AREA-KWH-RES
                  WS-AREA-COMM-INCOME
                  WS-AREA-INCOME-RES.
    MOVE I-AREA-CODE TO WS-AREA-CONTROL.
    PERFORM 300-WRITE-REPORT-HEADERS.
```

Figure 5.20 Subprogram A10-SCHEDULE-SUB

```
IDENTIFICATION DIVISION.

PROGRAM-ID.         A10-SCHEDULE-SUB.

******************************************************************
*                                                                *
*   AUTHOR.            PAQUETTE.                                 *
*   DATE WRITTEN.      MAY 8, 1989.                              *
*                                                                *
*        THIS SUBPROGRAM COMPUTES THE ELECTRIC BILLS FOR         *
*   A10 SERVICE CLASS CUSTOMERS OF PONAGANSETT ELECTRIC          *
*   COMPANY.  IT USES THE LINKAGE SECTION.                       *
*                                                                *
*        THE WORKING-STORAGE SECTION DEFINES THE DATA ITEMS      *
*   CUSTOMER-CHARGE AND ENERGY-RATE AND INITIALIZES THEM.        *
*                                                                *
*        THE FORMULA IS:  KWH * ENERGY-RATE + CUSTOMER-CHARGE.   *
*                                                                *
******************************************************************

ENVIRONMENT DIVISION.

DATA DIVISION.

WORKING-STORAGE SECTION.

01  CUSTOMER-CHARGE      PIC S99V99     VALUE 01.61.

01  ENERGY-RATE          PIC SV9(5)     VALUE .08082.

LINKAGE SECTION.

01  KWHS                 PIC S9(5).

01  BASIC-CHARGE         PIC S99999V99.

PROCEDURE DIVISION USING KWHS
                         BASIC-CHARGE.

100-COMPUTE-BASIC-CHARGE.
    COMPUTE BASIC-CHARGE ROUNDED =
        CUSTOMER-CHARGE + (KWHS * ENERGY-RATE).

999-EXIT.
    EXIT PROGRAM.
```

Coding the Subprograms

1. Subprogram CONVERT-DATE-SUB is the one used in the first example, so it is not repeated here.
2. Subprogram A10-SCHEDULE-SUB must contain the LINKAGE SECTION of the DATA DIVISION, since it is called by a CALL statement that includes the USING phrase. The section must describe the shared items as they are referenced within the subprogram. It also contains the WORKING-STORAGE SECTION to define and initialize the two data items (CUSTOMER-CHARGE and ENERGY-RATE) that may change periodically in this rate schedule. Whenever the company changes these rates, only their VALUE clauses need be changed in the subprogram. The subprogram's PROCEDURE DIVISION header must also contain the USING phrase, and the phrase identifies the items it shares with the calling program. The coding of the subprogram is shown in Figure 5.20.
3. Subprogram A11-SCHEDULE-SUB must contain the WORKING-STORAGE SECTION and the LINKAGE SECTION of the DATA DIVISION. The rate schedule described in the statement of the problem is hard-coded into an indexed table in working storage. This allows periodic changes to be made to entries in the table without requiring any changes in the PROCEDURE DIVISION, so that once the logic of the subprogram has been debugged, it remains intact. The LINKAGE SECTION describes the data items the subprogram shares with the calling program, and the PROCEDURE DIVISION header contains the USING phrase that names the shared items. The subprogram is shown in Figure 5.21.

■ **Figure 5.21** Subprogram A11-SCHEDULE-SUB

```
 IDENTIFICATION DIVISION.

 PROGRAM-ID.        A11-SCHEDULE-SUB.

*****************************************************************
*                                                               *
*    AUTHOR.              PAQUETTE.                             *
*    DATE WRITTEN.        MAY 8, 1989.                          *
*                                                               *
*         THIS SUBPROGRAM COMPUTES THE BASIC CHARGE PORTION OF  *
*    THE ELECTRIC BILL FOR A11 AND A12 SERVICE CLASS CUSTOMERS OF *
*    THE PONAGANSETT ELECTRIC COMPANY.  IT USES THE LINKAGE     *
*    SECTION.                                                   *
*                                                               *
*         THE RATE SCHEDULE IS CONTAINED IN A HARD-CODED        *
*    INDEXED TABLE IN WORKING STORAGE.                          *
*                                                               *
*         THE SEARCH STATEMENT IS USED TO COMPUTE THE           *
*    APPROPRIATE BASIC CHARGE.                                  *
*                                                               *
*****************************************************************

 ENVIRONMENT DIVISION.

 DATA DIVISION.

 WORKING-STORAGE SECTION.

 01   RES-A11-A12-RATE-VALUES.
      05 PIC X(21)    VALUE '000000002000277000000'.
      05 PIC X(21)    VALUE '000200005000277010543'.
      05 PIC X(21)    VALUE '000500020000593308487'.
      05 PIC X(21)    VALUE '002000055001866405636'.
      05 PIC X(21)    VALUE '005500200003839006937'.
      05 PIC X(21)    VALUE '020009999913897706660'.

 01   RES-A11-A12-TABLE REDEFINES RES-A11-A12-RATE-VALUES.
      05 USAGE-LEVEL OCCURS 6 TIMES
                      INDEXED BY RATE-INDEX.
          10 LOW-END        PIC S9(5).
          10 HIGH-END       PIC S9(5).
          10 BASE-AMOUNT    PIC S999V999.
          10 LEVEL-RATE     PIC SV9(5).

 LINKAGE SECTION.

 01   KWH-USAGE               PIC S9(5).

 01   BASIC-CHARGE            PIC S9(5)V99.

 PROCEDURE DIVISION USING KWH-USAGE
                          BASIC-CHARGE.

 100-COMPUTE-BASIC-CHARGE.
     SET RATE-INDEX TO 1.
     SEARCH USAGE-LEVEL
         WHEN KWH-USAGE NOT > HIGH-END (RATE-INDEX)
             COMPUTE BASIC-CHARGE ROUNDED =
             BASE-AMOUNT(RATE-INDEX) + LEVEL-RATE(RATE-INDEX) *
                 (KWH-USAGE - LOW-END(RATE-INDEX)).

 999-EXIT.
     EXIT PROGRAM.
```

4. Subprogram C-2-SCHEDULE-SUB also contains the WORKING-STORAGE SECTION and the LINKAGE SECTION. The rate schedule is hard-coded into a table in working storage, and since commercial customers are also assessed a customer charge, that item is defined and initialized in working storage as well. The LINKAGE SECTION describes the data items the subprogram shares with the calling program, and the PROCEDURE DIVISION header contains the USING phrase that names the shared items. The subprogram is shown in Figure 5.22.
5. Subprogram XTRA-CHARGE-SUB must contain the LINKAGE SECTION to describe the items it shares with the calling program, and the PROCEDURE DIVISION header contains the USING phrase to name the shared items. The subprogram also contains a WORKING-STORAGE SECTION to define and initialize the other data items needed in the PROCEDURE DIVISION to compute the extra charge amount. The subprogram is shown in Figure 5.23.

Figure 5.22 Subprogram C-2-SCHEDULE-SUB

```
 IDENTIFICATION DIVISION.

 PROGRAM-ID.        C-2-SCHEDULE-SUB.

*******************************************************************
*                                                                 *
*   AUTHOR.             PAQUETTE.                                 *
*   DATE WRITTEN.       MAY 8, 1989.                              *
*                                                                 *
*        THIS SUBPROGRAM COMPUTES THE BASIC CHARGE PORTION OF     *
*   THE ELECTRIC BILL FOR C-2 SERVICE CLASS CUSTOMERS OF THE      *
*   PONAGANSETT ELECTRIC COMPANY.  IT USES A LINKAGE SECTION.     *
*                                                                 *
*        THE RATE SCHEDULE IS CONTAINED IN A HARD-CODED           *
*   INDEXED TABLE IN WORKING STORAGE.                             *
*                                                                 *
*        THE SEARCH STATEMENT IS USED TO COMPUTE THE              *
*   APPROPRIATE BASIC CHARGE.                                     *
*                                                                 *
*******************************************************************

 ENVIRONMENT DIVISION.

 DATA DIVISION.

 WORKING-STORAGE SECTION.

 01  CUSTOMER-CHARGE      PIC S99V99   VALUE 04.75.

 01  COM-C2-RATE-VALUES.
     05 PIC X(21)     VALUE '000000100000000009019'.
     05 PIC X(21)     VALUE '010009999909019008419'.

 01  COM-C2-RATE-TABLE REDEFINES COM-C2-RATE-VALUES.
     05 USAGE-LEVEL OCCURS 2 TIMES
                    INDEXED BY RATE-INDEX.
         10 LOW-END       PIC S9(5).
         10 HIGH-END      PIC S9(5).
         10 BASE-AMOUNT   PIC S999V999.
         10 LEVEL-RATE    PIC SV9(5).

 LINKAGE SECTION.

 01  KWH-USAGE                PIC S9(5).
 01  BASIC-CHARGE             PIC S9(5)V99.

 PROCEDURE DIVISION USING KWH-USAGE
                          BASIC-CHARGE.

 100-COMPUTE-BASIC-CHARGE.
     SET RATE-INDEX TO 1.
     SEARCH USAGE-LEVEL
         WHEN KWH-USAGE NOT > HIGH-END (RATE-INDEX)
         COMPUTE BASIC-CHARGE ROUNDED =
             BASE-AMOUNT(RATE-INDEX) +
             LEVEL-RATE(RATE-INDEX) *
             (KWH-USAGE - LOW-END(RATE-INDEX)).
     ADD CUSTOMER-CHARGE TO BASIC-CHARGE.

 999-EXIT.
     EXIT PROGRAM.
```

■ **Figure 5.23** Subprogram XTRA-CHARGE-SUB

```
IDENTIFICATION DIVISION.

PROGRAM-ID.  XTRA-CHARGE-SUB.

******************************************************************
*                                                                *
*  AUTHOR.              PAQUETTE.                                *
*  DATE WRITTEN.        MAY 8, 1989.                             *
*                                                                *
*  THE PURPOSE OF THIS SUBPROGRAM IS TO COMPUTE EXTRA CHARGES    *
*  ASSESSED TO ALL CUSTOMERS OF THE PONAGANSETT ELECTRIC COMPANY.*
*  THESE CHARGES CHANGE PERIODICALLY.  THEY FALL INTO THREE      *
*  CLASSIFICATIONS:  FUEL ADJUSTMENT CHARGE, OIL CONSERVATION    *
*  ADJUSTMENT CHARGE, AND THE UNIFORM CONSERVATION COST ADJUST-  *
*  MENT PROGRAM CHARGE.  THESE EXTRA CHARGES ARE DEFINED AND     *
*  INITIALIZED IN THE WORKING-STORAGE SECTION.                   *
*                                                                *
*  THE SUBPROGRAM RECEIVES THE KWH USAGE FROM THE CALLING PRO-   *
*  GRAM AND RETURNS THE RESULTING EXTRA CHARGE.  IT USES THE     *
*  LINKAGE SECTION.                                              *
*                                                                *
******************************************************************

DATA DIVISION.

WORKING-STORAGE SECTION.

01  EXTRA-CHARGE-RATES.
    05 FAC           PIC SV9(5)   VALUE .00735.
    05 OCA           PIC SV9(5)   VALUE .00093.
    05 UCCA          PIC SV9(5)   VALUE .00009.

LINKAGE SECTION.

01  KWH-USAGE        PIC S9(5).

01  EXTRA-CHARGE     PIC S9(5)V99.

PROCEDURE DIVISION USING KWH-USAGE
                         EXTRA-CHARGE.

100-COMPUTE-EXTRA-CHARGE.
    COMPUTE EXTRA-CHARGE ROUNDED =
        KWH-USAGE * (FAC + OCA + UCCA).

999-EXIT.
    EXIT PROGRAM.
```

Executing the Run Unit

When the new programs of the run unit have been debugged and compiled (recall that subprogram CONVERT-DATE-SUB is already compiled), then all the needed object modules are link-edited into an executable module. Using the data file shown in Figure 5.24 as an input file, the execution of the run unit produced the output shown in Figure 5.25.

Examine the report and note the following:

1. The report date on line 1 was produced by subprogram CONVERT-DATE-SUB.
2. The total charge of the first detail line was produced by the execution of subprogram A11-SCHEDULE-SUB and of subprogram XTRA-CHARGE-SUB.
3. The total charge of the second detail line was produced by the execution of subprogram A10-SCHEDULE-SUB and of subprogram XTRA-CHARGE-SUB.
4. The total charge of the third detail line was produced by the execution of subprogram C-2-SCHEDULE-SUB and of subprogram XTRA-CHARGE-SUB.

Figure 5.24 Input file for sample run unit 2

```
RI1100140NARDONE, MARY E.     1402414997                                A124208
RI1101235FLYNN, ROGER P.      4213142482                                A106508
RI1103041BEST FURNITURE INC. 6656568711                                 C-28608
RI1106176KOLAKOWSKI, CASIMIR 0524005712                                 A106508
RI1110025ASSELIN, JANICE M.   2142122300                                A124208
RI1115722GLORIA'S BEAUTY SHOP3485839208                                 C-28608
RI1120190WAREHAM, JOSEPH F.   1396214387                                A106508
RI1131211KEATING, SUSAN A.    0707008110                                A114208
RI1135400CONNELL, FRED C.     3523536157                                A124208
RI1138625FRYE, LOUISE N.      0110601523                                A106508
RI1150950TINY-TOT NURSERY     1272014355                                C-28608
RI1153276BERGERON, FRANK S.   4103841756                                A114208
RI1155900LOUGHERY, KATRINA    3048131624                                A124208
RI1157133GOUDREAU, ELIZABETH 6565966235                                 A106508
RI1159005COPTER SERVICE       4330945292                                C-28608
RI1160216GATTO, JANICE L.     1051811450                                A114208
RI1161394JOZEFOWICZ, SANDRA   3769238007                                A106508
RI1173731MCFADDEN, MICHAEL R.5808359347                                 A124208
RI1175571LETENDRE, THOMAS F. 4621247210                                 A124208
RI1177505MASSE, EUGENE        0517005703                                A106508
RI1182162EVA'S FRUIT STORE    3257134713                                C-28608
RI1190324MANDEL, ROLANDE J.   1076811240                                A106508
RI1193005SCULLY, CLARA B.     0693407446                                A106508
RI2201055NICOLETTA, JOHN J.   5193552917                                A124208
RI2205182RAY TRUCKING CO.     3482137197                                C-28608
RI2212433DION, GERARD M.      2347423995                                A106508
RI2220020CHOW, SHUI           0978810714                                A124208
RI2223944HODGE, KEVIN J.      7731977824                                A106508
RI2232132PETE'S AUTO SUPPLIES6865270636                                 C-28608
RI2241694LAMOUNTAIN, LOUISE   4024141016                                A114208
RI2245400PATALANO, SAMANTHA   0252703435                                A124208
RI2248375CADY, RAYMOND F.     1517615533                                A106508
RI2252100GASPAR, RAOUL        2357524027                                A106508
RI2262025KLEIN, LAURALYNN     5708257811                                A114208
RI2275364DORIS BAKERY SHOP    7499278134                                C-28608
RI2275690HENNESSY, ROBERT J. 3901539517                                 A106508
RI2278170LUDOVICI, LUIGI      0286003224                                A106508
RI2282985HUMMEL, STELLA       4010741153                                A124208
RI2285374PARKS, EMERY R.      1074611158                                A106508
RI3302010BENNETT, CLARENCE W.2374524228                                 A106508
RI3305327PETRUSKA, MARIE      0124002219                                A124208
RI3320400MARK MARINE SERVICE 4937351447                                 C-28608
RI3331166DIGUILIO, EMILIO M. 5661356997                                 A106508
RI3342314CALLAHAN, JOHN J.    1040611459                                A124208
RI3345943MCCARTHY, EUGENE F. 2753428646                                 A114208
RI3363770GERRY'S SEAFOODS     4519848660                                C-28608
RI3367150BROWN, GEORGE W.     3206532589                                A106508
RI3384000PRECOURT, JEAN M.    0862509562                                A114208
RI3391450DEWEY, FRANCES D.    1121211624                                A106508
RI3394765GARDNER, LEO F.      3543736562                                A124208
```

Figure 5.25 Analysis report produced by sample run unit 2

PAGE 1

MAY 25, 1989

PONAGANSETT ELECTRIC COMPANY

KWH ANALYSIS REPORT

AREA	CLASS	RATE SCHEDULE	CUSTOMER NUMBER	CUSTOMER	PREVIOUS READING	CURRENT READING	USAGE	TOTAL CHARGE
RI1	RESIDENTIAL	A12	100140	NARDONE, MARY E.	14024	14997	973	$ 75.87
RI1	RESIDENTIAL	A10	101235	FLYNN, ROGER P.	42131	42482	351	$ 32.92
RI1	COMMERCIAL	C-2	103041	BEST FURNITURE INC.	66565	68711	2146	$ 209.38
RI1	RESIDENTIAL	A10	106176	KOLAKOWSKI, CASIMIR	05240	05712	472	$ 43.71
RI1	RESIDENTIAL	A12	110025	ASSELIN, JANICE M.	21421	22300	879	$ 68.57
RI1	COMMERCIAL	C-2	115722	GLORIA'S BEAUTY SHOP	34858	39208	4350	$ 413.39
RI1	RESIDENTIAL	A10	120190	WAREHAM, JOSEPH F.	13962	14387	425	$ 39.52
RI1	RESIDENTIAL	A11	131211	KEATING, SUSAN A.	07070	08110	1040	$ 81.08
RI1	RESIDENTIAL	A12	135400	CONNELL, FRED C.	35235	36157	922	$ 71.92
RI1	RESIDENTIAL	A10	138625	FRYE, LOUISE N.	01106	01523	417	$ 38.80
RI1	COMMERCIAL	C-2	150950	TINY-TOT NURSERY	12720	14355	1635	$ 162.08
RI1	RESIDENTIAL	A11	153276	BERGERON, FRANK S.	41038	41756	718	$ 56.05
RI1	RESIDENTIAL	A12	155900	LOUGHERY, KATRINA	30481	31624	1143	$ 89.10
RI1	RESIDENTIAL	A10	157133	GOUDREAU, ELIZABETH	65659	66235	576	$ 52.98
RI1	COMMERCIAL	C-2	159005	COPTER SERVICE	43309	45292	1983	$ 194.30
RI1	RESIDENTIAL	A11	160216	GATTO, JANICE L.	10518	11450	932	$ 72.69
RI1	RESIDENTIAL	A10	161394	JOZEFOWICZ, SANDRA	37692	38007	315	$ 29.71
RI1	RESIDENTIAL	A12	173731	MCFADDEN, MICHAEL R.	58083	59347	1264	$ 98.50
RI1	RESIDENTIAL	A12	175571	LETENDRE, THOMAS F.	46212	47210	998	$ 77.82
RI1	RESIDENTIAL	A10	177505	MASSE, EUGENE	05170	05703	533	$ 49.15
RI1	COMMERCIAL	C-2	182162	EVA'S FRUIT STORE	32571	34713	2142	$ 209.01
RI1	RESIDENTIAL	A10	190324	MANDEL, ROLANDE J.	10768	11240	472	$ 43.71
RI1	RESIDENTIAL	A10	193005	SCULLY, CLARA B.	06934	07446	512	$ 47.28

TOTALS FOR AREA RI1	KWH	INCOME
COMMERCIAL	12,256	$ 1,188.16
RESIDENTIAL	12,942	$ 1,069.38

Figure 5.25 continued

MAY 25, 1989 PAGE 2

PONAGANSETT ELECTRIC COMPANY

KWH ANALYSIS REPORT

AREA	CLASS	RATE SCHEDULE	CUSTOMER NUMBER	CUSTOMER	PREVIOUS READING	CURRENT READING	USAGE	TOTAL CHARGE
RI2	RESIDENTIAL	A12	201055	NICOLETTA, JOHN J.	51935	52917	982	$ 76.58
RI2	COMMERCIAL	C-2	205182	RAY TRUCKING CO.	34821	37197	2376	$ 230.68
RI2	RESIDENTIAL	A10	212433	DION, GERARD M.	23474	23995	521	$ 48.08
RI2	RESIDENTIAL	A12	220020	CHOW, SHUI	09788	10714	926	$ 72.22
RI2	RESIDENTIAL	A10	223944	HODGE, KEVIN J.	77319	77824	505	$ 46.65
RI2	COMMERCIAL	C-2	232132	PETE'S AUTO SUPPLIES	68652	70636	1984	$ 194.39
RI2	RESIDENTIAL	A11	241694	LAMOUNTAIN, LOUISE	40241	41016	775	$ 60.49
RI2	RESIDENTIAL	A12	245400	PATALANO, SAMANTHA	02527	03435	908	$ 70.82
RI2	RESIDENTIAL	A10	248375	CADY, RAYMOND F.	15176	15533	357	$ 33.45
RI2	RESIDENTIAL	A10	252100	GASPAR, RAOUL	23575	24027	452	$ 41.92
RI2	RESIDENTIAL	A11	262025	KLEIN, LAURALYNN	57082	57811	729	$ 56.91
RI2	COMMERCIAL	C-2	275364	DORIS BAKERY SHOP	74992	78134	3142	$ 301.57
RI2	RESIDENTIAL	A10	275690	HENNESSY, ROBERT J.	39015	39517	502	$ 46.38
RI2	RESIDENTIAL	A10	278170	LUDOVICI, LUIGI	02860	03224	364	$ 34.08
RI2	RESIDENTIAL	A12	282985	HUMMEL, STELLA	40107	41153	1046	$ 81.56
RI2	RESIDENTIAL	A10	285374	PARKS, EMERY R.	10746	11158	412	$ 38.36

TOTALS FOR AREA RI2	KWH	INCOME
COMMERCIAL	7,502	$ 726.64
RESIDENTIAL	8,479	$ 707.50

MAY 25, 1989 PAGE 3

PONAGANSETT ELECTRIC COMPANY

KWH ANALYSIS REPORT

AREA	CLASS	RATE SCHEDULE	CUSTOMER NUMBER	CUSTOMER	PREVIOUS READING	CURRENT READING	USAGE	TOTAL CHARGE
RI3	RESIDENTIAL	A10	302010	BENNETT, CLARENCE W.	23745	24228	483	$ 44.69
RI3	RESIDENTIAL	A12	305327	PETRUSKA, MARIE	01240	02219	979	$ 76.34
RI3	COMMERCIAL	C-2	320400	MARK MARINE SERVICE	49373	51447	2074	$ 202.72
RI3	RESIDENTIAL	A10	331166	DIGUILIO, EMILIO M.	56613	56997	384	$ 35.85
RI3	RESIDENTIAL	A12	342314	CALLAHAN, JOHN J.	10406	11459	1053	$ 82.09
RI3	RESIDENTIAL	A11	345943	MCCARTHY, EUGENE F.	27534	28646	1112	$ 86.69
RI3	COMMERCIAL	C-2	363770	GERRY'S SEAFOODS	45198	48660	3462	$ 331.20
RI3	RESIDENTIAL	A10	367150	BROWN, GEORGE W.	32065	32589	524	$ 48.35
RI3	RESIDENTIAL	A11	384000	PRECOURT, JEAN M.	08625	09562	937	$ 73.08
RI3	RESIDENTIAL	A10	391450	DEWEY, FRANCES D.	11212	11624	412	$ 38.36
RI3	RESIDENTIAL	A12	394765	GARDNER, LEO F.	35437	36562	1125	$ 87.70

TOTALS FOR AREA RI3	KWH	INCOME
COMMERCIAL	5,536	$ 533.92
RESIDENTIAL	7,009	$ 573.15

SUMMARY

1. TOTAL KWH SOLD TO COMMERCIAL CUSTOMERS 25,294
   TOTAL INCOME FROM COMMERCIAL CUSTOMERS $ 2,448.72
   HIGHEST COMMERCIAL USER GLORIA'S BEAUTY SHOP USAGE 4350

2. TOTAL KWH SOLD TO RESIDENTIAL CUSTOMERS 28,430
   TOTAL INCOME FROM RESIDENTIAL CUSTOMERS $ 2,350.03
   HIGHEST RESIDENTIAL USER MCFADDEN, MICHAEL R. USAGE 1264

*** END OF REPORT ***

The EXTERNAL Qualifier

COBOL '85 has introduced a number of features designed to facilitate the sharing of data between calling and called programs. One of these new features is the EXTERNAL qualifier. It may be attached to a file description (FD entry) or to a record description (01 level) either in the FILE SECTION or in the WORKING-STORAGE SECTION. Data qualified as EXTERNAL is then accessible by any program in the run unit that contains an identical data description entry. Data items subordinate to records declared as EXTERNAL are also external.

As an example, consider Sample Run Unit 2 developed earlier. The main program shares WS-KWH-USAGE and WS-BASIC-CHARGE with subprograms A10-SCHEDULE-SUB, A11-SCHEDULE-SUB, and C-2-SCHEDULE-SUB, and it shares WS-KWH-USAGE and WS-EXTRA-CHARGE with subprogram XTRA-CHARGE-SUB. By making these three data items external, the subprograms can have direct access to the data, provided the WORKING-STORAGE SECTION of each subprogram contains an exact copy of the description of those items in the calling program.

The calling program already contains the following record description:

```
01  WS-SHARED-WORK-AREAS.
    05 WS-KWH-USAGE        PIC S9(5).
    05 WS-BASIC-CHARGE     PIC S9(5)V99.
    05 WS-EXTRA-CHARGE     PIC S9(5)V99.
```

The record can be declared external as follows:

```
01  WS-SHARED-WORK-AREAS IS EXTERNAL.
    05 WS-KWH-USAGE        PIC S9(5).
    05 WS-BASIC-CHARGE     PIC S9(5)V99.
    05 WS-EXTRA-CHARGE     PIC S9(5)V99.
```

If the four subprograms named above are to have access to this data, the WORKING-STORAGE SECTION of each subprogram must contain an identical record description. For instance, in subprogram A10-SCHEDULE-SUB, the WORKING-STORAGE SECTION would be as follows:

```
WORKING-STORAGE SECTION.
01  CUSTOMER-CHARGE        PIC S99V99     VALUE 01.61.
01  ENERGY-RATE            PIC SV9(5)     VALUE .08082.
01  WS-SHARED-WORK-AREAS IS EXTERNAL.
    05 WS-KWH-USAGE        PIC S9(5).
    05 WS-BASIC-CHARGE     PIC S9(5)V99.
    05 WS-EXTRA-CHARGE     PIC S9(5)V99.
```

With the use of the EXTERNAL qualifier to share data, the USING phrase of the CALL statement in the calling program is no longer needed, and furthermore, in the called program, the USING phrase of the PROCEDURE DIVISION header is not needed, and consequently, the LINKAGE SECTION that defines data items listed in USING phrases is no longer needed! So, in subprogram A10-SCHEDULE-SUB, the DATA DIVISION contains only the WORKING-STORAGE SECTION. The revised subprogram is shown in Figure 5.26. The new entry has been highlighted. Note that the shared data names in the PROCEDURE DIVISION now have the prefix WS-. Also note that there is no LINKAGE SECTION and no USING phrase in the PROCEDURE DIVISION header.

Similar changes have been made to the other subprograms (except CONVERT-DATE-SUB), and they are shown in Figures 5.27a through 5.27c.

In the calling program, the following changes are made:

1. The qualifier IS EXTERNAL is inserted in the description of WS-SHARED-WORK-AREAS.
2. In paragraph 330-SELECT-RATE-SCHEDULE, the USING phrase is removed from the two CALL statements, namely, CALL RATE-SCHED-SUBPROG and CALL "XTRA-CHARGE-SUB".

Figure 5.26 Subprogram A10-SCHEDULE-SUB with EXTERNAL data

```
IDENTIFICATION DIVISION.

PROGRAM-ID.        A10-SCHEDULE-SUB.

*****************************************************************
*                                                               *
*   AUTHOR.             PAQUETTE.                               *
*   DATE WRITTEN.       MAY 1989.                               *
*                                                               *
*        THIS SUBPROGRAM COMPUTES THE ELECTRIC BILLS FOR        *
*   A10 SERVICE CLASS CUSTOMERS OF PONAGANSETT ELECTRIC         *
*   COMPANY.  IT USES THE EXTERNAL QUALIFIER TO SHARE DATA WITH *
*   THE CALLING PROGRAM.                                        *
*                                                               *
*        THE WORKING-STORAGE SECTION DEFINES THE DATA ITEMS     *
*   CUSTOMER-CHARGE AND ENERGY-RATE AND INITIALIZES THEM.  IT   *
*   ALSO DEFINES THE SHARED DATA.                               *
*                                                               *
*        THE FORMULA IS:  KWH * ENERGY-RATE + CUSTOMER-CHARGE.  *
*                                                               *
*****************************************************************

ENVIRONMENT DIVISION.

DATA DIVISION.

WORKING-STORAGE SECTION.

01  CUSTOMER-CHARGE      PIC S99V99      VALUE 01.61.

01  ENERGY-RATE          PIC SV9(5)      VALUE .08082.

01  WS-SHARED-WORK-AREAS    IS EXTERNAL.
    05 WS-KWH-USAGE      PIC S9(5).
    05 WS-BASIC-CHARGE   PIC S9(5)V99.
    05 WS-EXTRA-CHARGE   PIC S9(5)V99.

PROCEDURE DIVISION.

100-COMPUTE-BASIC-CHARGE.
    COMPUTE WS-BASIC-CHARGE ROUNDED =
        CUSTOMER-CHARGE + (WS-KWHS * ENERGY-RATE).

999-EXIT.
    EXIT PROGRAM.
```

Figure 5.27a Subprogram A11-SCHEDULE-SUB with EXTERNAL data

```
IDENTIFICATION DIVISION.

PROGRAM-ID.        A11-SCHEDULE-SUB.

*****************************************************************
*                                                               *
*   AUTHOR.             PAQUETTE.                               *
*   DATE WRITTEN.       MAY 1989.                               *
*                                                               *
*        THIS SUBPROGRAM COMPUTES THE BASIC CHARGE PORTION OF   *
*   THE ELECTRIC BILL FOR A11 AND A12 SERVICE CLASS CUSTOMERS OF *
*   THE PONAGANSETT ELECTRIC COMPANY.  IT USES THE EXTERNAL     *
*   QUALIFIER TO SHARE DATA WITH THE CALLING PROGRAM.  THE DATA *
*   IS DEFINED IN THE WORKING-STORAGE SECTION.                  *
*                                                               *
*        THE RATE SCHEDULE IS CONTAINED IN A HARD-CODED         *
*   INDEXED TABLE IN WORKING STORAGE.                           *
*                                                               *
*        THE SEARCH STATEMENT IS USED TO COMPUTE THE            *
*   APPROPRIATE BASIC CHARGE.                                   *
*                                                               *
*****************************************************************

ENVIRONMENT DIVISION.

DATA DIVISION.

WORKING-STORAGE SECTION.

01  WS-SHARED-WORK-AREAS    IS EXTERNAL.
    05 WS-KWH-USAGE      PIC S9(5).
    05 WS-BASIC-CHARGE   PIC S9(5)V99.
    05 WS-EXTRA-CHARGE   PIC S9(5)V99.
```

Figure 5.27a continued

```
01  RES-A11-A12-RATE-VALUES.
    05 PIC X(21)    VALUE '000000002000277000000'.
    05 PIC X(21)    VALUE '000200005000277010543'.
    05 PIC X(21)    VALUE '000500020000593308487'.
    05 PIC X(21)    VALUE '002000055001866405636'.
    05 PIC X(21)    VALUE '005500200003839006937'.
    05 PIC X(21)    VALUE '020009999913897706660'.

01  RES-A11-A12-TABLE REDEFINES RES-A11-A12-RATE-VALUES.
    05 USAGE-LEVEL OCCURS 6 TIMES
                INDEXED BY RATE-INDEX.
        10 LOW-END       PIC S9(5).
        10 HIGH-END      PIC S9(5).
        10 BASE-AMOUNT   PIC S999V999.
        10 LEVEL-RATE    PIC SV9(5).

PROCEDURE DIVISION.

100-COMPUTE-BASIC-CHARGE.
    SET RATE-INDEX TO 1.
    SEARCH USAGE-LEVEL
        WHEN WS-KWH-USAGE NOT > HIGH-END (RATE-INDEX)
            COMPUTE WS-BASIC-CHARGE ROUNDED =
            BASE-AMOUNT(RATE-INDEX) + LEVEL-RATE(RATE-INDEX) *
                (WS-KWH-USAGE - LOW-END(RATE-INDEX)).

999-EXIT.
    EXIT PROGRAM.
```

Figure 5.27b Subprogram C-2-SCHEDULE-SUB with EXTERNAL data

```
 IDENTIFICATION DIVISION.

 PROGRAM-ID.        C-2-SCHEDULE-SUB.

*****************************************************************
*                                                               *
*  AUTHOR.            PAQUETTE.                                 *
*  DATE WRITTEN.      MAY 1989.                                 *
*                                                               *
*       THIS SUBPROGRAM COMPUTES THE BASIC CHARGE PORTION OF    *
*  THE ELECTRIC BILL FOR C-2 SERVICE CLASS CUSTOMERS OF THE     *
*  PONAGANSETT ELECTRIC COMPANY.  IT USES THE EXTERNAL QUALI-   *
*  FIER TO SHARE DATA WITH THE CALLING PROGRAM.                 *
*                                                               *
*       THE RATE SCHEDULE IS CONTAINED IN A HARD-CODED          *
*  INDEXED TABLE IN WORKING STORAGE.                            *
*                                                               *
*       THE SEARCH STATEMENT IS USED TO COMPUTE THE             *
*  APPROPRIATE BASIC CHARGE.                                    *
*                                                               *
*****************************************************************

 ENVIRONMENT DIVISION.

 DATA DIVISION.

 WORKING-STORAGE SECTION.

 01  CUSTOMER-CHARGE      PIC S99V99   VALUE 04.75.

 01  WS-SHARED-WORK-AREAS    IS EXTERNAL.
     05 WS-KWH-USAGE      PIC S9(5).
     05 WS-BASIC-CHARGE   PIC S9(5)V99.
     05 WS-EXTRA-CHARGE   PIC S9(5)V99.

 01  COM-C2-RATE-VALUES.
     05 PIC X(21)     VALUE '000000100000000009019'.
     05 PIC X(21)     VALUE '010009999909019008419'.

 01  COM-C2-RATE-TABLE REDEFINES COM-C2-RATE-VALUES.
     05 USAGE-LEVEL OCCURS 2 TIMES
                 INDEXED BY RATE-INDEX.
         10 LOW-END       PIC S9(5).
         10 HIGH-END      PIC S9(5).
         10 BASE-AMOUNT   PIC S999V999.
         10 LEVEL-RATE    PIC SV9(5).
```

Figure 5.27b continued

```
PROCEDURE DIVISION.

100-COMPUTE-BASIC-CHARGE.
    SET RATE-INDEX TO 1.
    SEARCH USAGE-LEVEL
        WHEN WS-KWH-USAGE NOT > HIGH-END (RATE-INDEX)
        COMPUTE WS-BASIC-CHARGE ROUNDED =
            BASE-AMOUNT(RATE-INDEX) +
            LEVEL-RATE(RATE-INDEX) *
            (KWH-USAGE - LOW-END(RATE-INDEX)).
    ADD CUSTOMER-CHARGE TO WS-BASIC-CHARGE.

999-EXIT.
    EXIT PROGRAM.
```

Figure 5.27c Subprogram XTRA-CHARGE-SUB with EXTERNAL data

```
IDENTIFICATION DIVISION.

PROGRAM-ID.  XTRA-CHARGE-SUB.

*****************************************************************
*                                                               *
*  AUTHOR.              PAQUETTE.                               *
*  DATE WRITTEN.        MAY 1989.                               *
*                                                               *
*  THE PURPOSE OF THIS SUBPROGRAM IS TO COMPUTE EXTRA CHARGES   *
*  ASSESSED TO ALL CUSTOMERS OF THE PONAGANSETT ELECTRIC COMPANY.*
*  THESE CHARGES CHANGE PERIODICALLY.  THEY FALL INTO THREE     *
*  CLASSIFICATIONS:  FUEL ADJUSTMENT CHARGE, OIL CONSERVATION   *
*  ADJUSTMENT CHARGE, AND THE UNIFORM CONSERVATION COST ADJUST- *
*  MENT PROGRAM CHARGE.  THESE EXTRA CHARGES ARE DEFINED AND    *
*  INITIALIZED IN THE WORKING-STORAGE SECTION.                  *
*                                                               *
*  THE SUBPROGRAM SHARES DATA WITH THE CALLING PROGRAM THROUGH  *
*  THE USE OF THE EXTERNAL QUALIFIER.                           *
*                                                               *
*****************************************************************

DATA DIVISION.

WORKING-STORAGE SECTION.

01  EXTRA-CHARGE-RATES.
    05 FAC            PIC SV9(5)   VALUE .00735.
    05 OCA            PIC SV9(5)   VALUE .00093.
    05 UCCA           PIC SV9(5)   VALUE .00009.

01  WS-SHARED-WORK-AREAS    IS EXTERNAL.
    05 WS-KWH-USAGE       PIC S9(5).
    05 WS-BASIC-CHARGE    PIC S9(5)V99.
    05 WS-EXTRA-CHARGE    PIC S9(5)V99.

PROCEDURE DIVISION.

100-COMPUTE-EXTRA-CHARGE.
    COMPUTE WS-EXTRA-CHARGE ROUNDED =
        WS-KWH-USAGE * (FAC + OCA + UCCA).

999-EXIT.
    EXIT PROGRAM.
```

In addition to facilitating the sharing of data, another benefit of the EXTERNAL qualifier is that it makes more efficient use of main memory allocation. The storage allocation is external to every program that defines it, but it is accessible by every one of them! Most data items defined in a program are internal and local to that program. No other program has access to them (unless access is specifically provided by CALL USING statements or GLOBAL qualifiers). By making data external, the required memory is not allocated to any program, though all programs containing the data description have access to the data. Memory allocation is illustrated in Figure 5.28.

Figure 5.28 EXTERNAL memory allocation and program/memory allocation

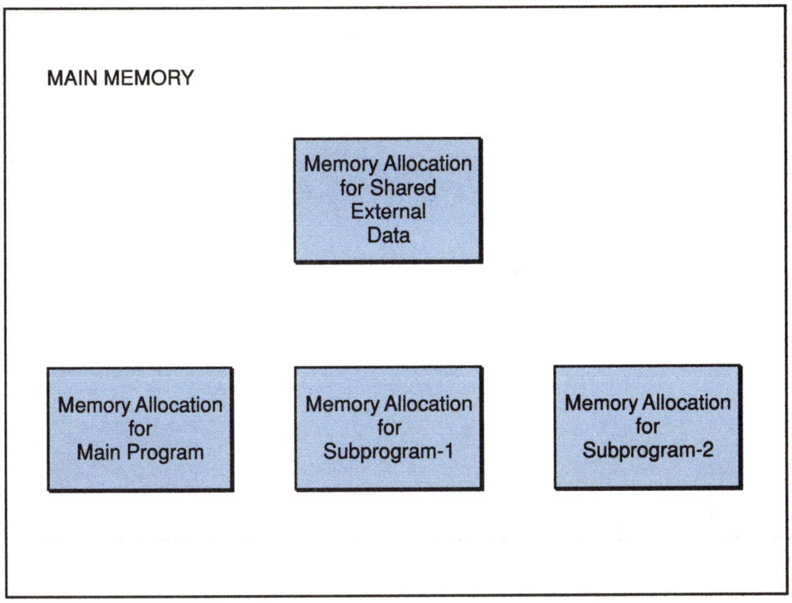

Rules Governing the Use of the EXTERNAL Qualifier

1. The format of the external qualifier is . . . **IS EXTERNAL.**
2. The EXTERNAL qualifier may be specified only in an FD entry or in a level-01 record description in the FILE SECTION or in the WORKING-STORAGE SECTION. (77-level entries may also be defined as EXTERNAL.)
3. The use of the EXTERNAL qualifier in the description of a file or a data item within a program makes that data common to any other program in the run unit that also defines the item as EXTERNAL. All programs sharing the common data must contain identical data description entries.
4. Data items with the EXTERNAL qualifier must be named.
5. Data items that are subordinate to one declared as EXTERNAL are also external.
6. The data names of items declared as EXTERNAL must not be used to name other storage areas in the same program or in contained programs.
7. The data description entry of an item declared as EXTERNAL must not contain a VALUE clause or a REDEFINES clause. Data items subordinate to a declared EXTERNAL item are subject to the same restrictions. (However, a record defined as EXTERNAL may be redefined.)

Nested Programs

Another development in COBOL '85 designed to facilitate the sharing of data among programs while at the same time enhancing modularization in program design is the nested program construct. It allows a program to be completely contained within another program. The nested or inner program is referred to as a *contained* program, and the outer program is referred to as the *containing* program. Both contained and containing programs begin with the IDENTIFICATION DIVISION header followed by the PROGRAM-ID paragraph, and both must end with an END PROGRAM header. (END PROGRAM is technically called a "header" even though its function is to explicitly mark the *end* of the program's source code!)

Just as a called program may also be a calling program, a contained program may also be a containing program. Figure 5.29 illustrates contained programs that are nested at two levels.

The brackets clearly show that program SUB1-LEVEL-2 is completely contained within program SUB1-LEVEL-1, and program SUB1-LEVEL-1 is completely contained within program MAIN-PROGRAM. MAIN-PROGRAM is said to directly contain SUB1-LEVEL-1 and indirectly contain SUB1-LEVEL-2.

Figure 5.29 Schematic of a run unit with a main program and two contained programs

```
IDENTIFICATION DIVISION.
PROGRAM-ID. MAIN-PROGRAM.
:
    CALL "SUB1-LEVEL-1".
:
IDENTIFICATION DIVISION.
PROGRAM-ID. SUB1-LEVEL-1.
:
    CALL "SUB1-LEVEL-2".
:
    EXIT PROGRAM.
IDENTIFICATION DIVISION.
PROGRAM-ID. SUB1-LEVEL-2.
:
    EXIT PROGRAM.
END PROGRAM SUB1-LEVEL-2.
END PROGRAM SUB1-LEVEL-1.
END PROGRAM MAIN-PROGRAM.
```

Figure 5.30 Sample run unit 3

```
IDENTIFICATION DIVISION.                        IDENTIFICATION DIVISION
PROGRAM-ID. DAILY-PHONE-SALES-REPORT.           PROGRAM-ID. CONVERT-DATE-SUB.
:                                               :
    CALL "CONVERT-DATE-SUB" USING...                PROCEDURE DIVISION USING...
:                                                   :
    CALL "ASC-COMPUTE-SALE-AMT-SUB."                EXIT PROGRAM.
:
IDENTIFICATION DIVISION.
PROGRAM-ID. ASC-COMPUTE-SALE-AMT-SUB.
:
    EXIT PROGRAM.
END PROGRAM ASC-COMPUTE-SALE-AMT-SUB.
END PROGRAM DAILY-PHONE-SALES-REPORT.
```

Sample Run Unit 3

One major advantage of nested programs is that files and data items defined in a containing program may be made available to any contained program simply by qualifying the files and/or data as GLOBAL. As a first example, consider the chapter's third sample run unit, illustrated in Figure 5.30. The main program is the one previously used in Sample Run Unit 1, namely, the DAILY-PHONE-SALES-REPORT program for the Allied Stock Company; subprogram CONVERT-DATE-SUB remains separately compiled; and subprogram ASC-COMPUTE-SALE-AMT-SUB is a contained program.

The function of this run unit is still to produce the daily phone sales report as formatted in Figure 5.1. The overall logic to accomplish the task has not changed. The only difference is in the procedure that will be used to share data between the main program and the subprogram that computes the net sale amount.

Differences in the Main Program

There are two changes that will be made to the main program:

1. Since the main program is a containing program, the data it must share with the contained program will be defined as GLOBAL. Global data can be referenced by the program that defines it as well as by any contained program.

The specific data items that must be referenced by the contained program are I-NO-OF-UNITS, I-UNIT-COST, and WS-SALE-AMOUNT. They must be made GLOBAL. However, the GLOBAL qualifier can be specified for 01-level data items only. Since I-NO-OF-UNITS and I-UNIT-COST are elementary items of the record PHONE-SALE-RECORD, the GLOBAL qualifier is simply attached to the record name, as follows:

```
01  PHONE-SALE-RECORD     IS GLOBAL.
    05 I-CUSTOMER-NO      PIC X(4).
    05                    PIC X(2).
    05 I-CATALOG-NO       PIC X(4).
    05                    PIC X(2).
    05 I-UNIT-COST        PIC 999V99.
    05                    PIC X(2).
    05 I-NO-OF-UNITS      PIC 9(4).
```

Similarly, the data item WS-SALE-AMOUNT is an elementary item of the group WS-SALE-WORK-AREA. The group is defined as GLOBAL, as follows:

```
01  WS-SALE-WORK-AREA     IS GLOBAL.
    05 WS-SALE-AMOUNT     PIC 9(6)V99.
```

Whenever a record is defined as GLOBAL, either in the FILE SECTION or in the WORKING-STORAGE SECTION, the record's subordinate items are necessarily also GLOBAL.

2. The CALL statement for subprogram ASC-COMPUTE-SALE-AMT-SUB is coded without the USING phrase. It becomes simply

```
CALL "ASC-COMPUTE-SALE-AMT-SUB".
```

The statement transfers control to the subprogram, and the subprogram has access to the data in the calling program that is defined as GLOBAL.

Differences in Subprogram ASC-COMPUTE-SALE-AMT-SUB

A number of changes must be made to the subprogram.

1. Since the USING phrase has been deleted from the CALL statement in the calling program, the USING phrase in the subprogram's PROCEDURE DIVISION header must also be removed.
2. Because the PROCEDURE DIVISION header does not contain the USING phrase, the LINKAGE SECTION has to be removed. Then, since there are no sections left in the DATA DIVISION, the division header itself may be deleted.
3. A contained program must not specify a CONFIGURATION SECTION. This is required to avoid potential conflicts between the contained and containing program's entries. Consequently, this section is removed from the subprogram, and this leaves the ENVIRONMENT DIVISION without sections, and the division header itself may be removed.
4. The data names in the PROCEDURE DIVISION must now be those of the data items in the main program that were made GLOBAL. Consequently,

   TR-NO-OF-UNITS is changed to I-NO-OF-UNITS,

   TR-UNIT-COST is changed to I-UNIT-COST, and

   TR-SALE-AMOUNT is changed to WS-SALE-AMOUNT.

Now that the needed changes have been made to the main program and the subprogram, the subprogram is appended to the main program, and the resulting file is edited so as to insert the needed END PROGRAM headers. The result is shown in Figure 5.31.

The format of the END PROGRAM header is shown in Figure 5.32.

Figure 5.31 File containing the main program and its contained program

```
 IDENTIFICATION DIVISION.

 PROGRAM-ID.  DAILY-PHONE-SALES-REPORT.

*****************************************************************
*                                                               *
*  AUTHOR.         PAQUETTE.                                    *
*  DATE WRITTEN:   MAY  1989.                                   *
*                                                               *
*  THIS PROGRAM PRODUCES A REPORT LISTING THE PHONE SALES THAT  *
*  OCCURRED DURING THE DAY.  IT CALLS ONE SUBPROGRAM TO CONVERT *
*  THE DATE TO THE REQUIRED PRINT FORMAT AND A SECOND SUB-      *
*  PROGRAM TO COMPUTE THE NET AMOUNT OF THE SALE.               *
*                                                               *
*  THE DATE CONVERSION SUBPROGRAM IS SEPARATELY COMPILED, WHILE *
*  THE OTHER SUBPROGRAM IS NESTED WITHIN THE MAIN PROGRAM.  THE *
*  GLOBAL QUALIFIER IS USED TO SHARE DATA WITH THE NESTED SUB-  *
*  PROGRAM.
*                                                               *
*  EACH INPUT RECORD IS A PHONE SALE RECORD THAT CONTAINS THE   *
*  CUSTOMER NUMBER, THE CATALOG NUMBER, THE UNIT COST OF THE    *
*  ITEM, AND THE NUMBER OF UNITS SOLD TO THE CUSTOMER.          *
*                                                               *
*  FOR EACH PHONE SALE, THE PHONE SALE LINE ON THE REPORT MUST  *
*  SHOW THE CUSTOMER NUMBER, THE CATALOG NUMBER, THE UNIT COST, *
*  THE NUMBER OF UNITS SOLD, AND THE NET AMOUNT OF THE SALE.    *
*  THE VALUES ON THE PHONE SALE LINES ARE LISTED UNDER APPRO-   *
*  PRIATE COLUMN HEADINGS.                                      *
*                                                               *
*  THE AMOUNT OF THE SALE IS COMPUTED IN THE SUBPROGRAM.  THE   *
*  DOCUMENTATION WITHIN THE SUBPROGRAM SPECIFIES THE DISCOUNTS  *
*  IN EFFECT AT THE TIME THE PHONE SALE WAS MADE.               *
*                                                               *
*  THE REPORT BEGINS WITH A REPORT DATE LINE, FOLLOWED BY THE   *
*  NAME OF THE COMPANY, THEN THE REPORT NAME, AND FINALLY THE   *
*  APPROPRIATE COLUMN HEADINGS.                                 *
*                                                               *
*****************************************************************

 ENVIRONMENT DIVISION.

 CONFIGURATION SECTION.

 SOURCE-COMPUTER.  VAX-VMS-8650.
 OBJECT-COMPUTER.  VAX-VMS-8650.

 INPUT-OUTPUT SECTION.

 FILE-CONTROL.
     SELECT PHONE-SALES-FILE     ASSIGN TO COB$INPUT.
     SELECT PHONE-SALES-REPORT   ASSIGN TO COB$OUTPUT.

 DATA DIVISION.

 FILE SECTION.

 FD  PHONE-SALES-FILE
     RECORD CONTAINS 23 CHARACTERS.

 01  PHONE-SALE-RECORD               IS GLOBAL.
     05 I-CUSTOMER-NO       PIC X(4).
     05                     PIC X(2).
     05 I-CATALOG-NO        PIC X(4).
     05                     PIC X(2).
     05 I-UNIT-COST         PIC 999V99.
     05                     PIC X(2).
     05 I-NO-OF-UNITS       PIC 9(4).

 FD  PHONE-SALES-REPORT
     RECORD CONTAINS 132 CHARACTERS.

 01  PRINTLINE              PIC X(132).

 WORKING-STORAGE SECTION.

 01  PROGRAM-CONTROLS.
     05 WS-MORE-RECORDS     PIC X(3).
        88 THERE-IS-A-RECORD        VALUE 'YES'.
        88 NO-MORE-RECORDS          VALUE 'NO '.
     05 WS-PROPER-SPACING PIC 9(1).

 01  WS-SALE-WORK-AREA               IS GLOBAL.
     05 WS-SALE-AMOUNT      PIC 9(6)V99.
```

Figure 5.31 continued

```
01  TOP-LINE.
    05             PIC X(5)  VALUE SPACES.
    05 O-DATE      PIC X(19).
    05             PIC X(96) VALUE SPACES.
    05             PIC X(5)  VALUE 'PAGE '.
    05 O-PAGE-NO   PIC 9(2).

01  COMPANY-NAME.
    05 PIC X(54)    VALUE SPACES.
    05 PIC X(24)    VALUE 'THE ALLIED STOCK COMPANY'.
    05 PIC X(54)    VALUE SPACES.

01  REPORT-NAME.
    05 PIC X(54)    VALUE SPACES.
    05 PIC X(24)    VALUE 'DAILY PHONE SALES REPORT'.
    05 PIC X(54)    VALUE SPACES.

01  HEADINGS.
    05 PIC X(15)    VALUE SPACES.
    05 PIC X(15)    VALUE 'CUSTOMER NUMBER'.
    05 PIC X(8)     VALUE SPACES.
    05 PIC X(14)    VALUE 'CATALOG NUMBER'.
    05 PIC X(8)     VALUE SPACES.
    05 PIC X(9)     VALUE 'UNIT COST'.
    05 PIC X(8)     VALUE SPACES.
    05 PIC X(15)    VALUE 'NUMBER OF UNITS'.
    05 PIC X(8)     VALUE SPACES.
    05 PIC X(17)    VALUE 'PHONE SALE AMOUNT'.
    05 PIC X(15)    VALUE SPACES.

01  PHONE-SALE-LINE.
    05                  PIC X(21).
    05 O-CUSTOMER-NO    PIC X(4).
    05                  PIC X(18).
    05 O-CATALOG-NO     PIC X(4).
    05                  PIC X(14).
    05 O-UNIT-COST      PIC $ZZ9.99.
    05                  PIC X(15).
    05 O-NO-OF-UNITS    PIC ZZZ9.
    05                  PIC X(16).
    05 O-SALE-AMOUNT    PIC $ZZZ,ZZ9.99.
    05                  PIC X(18).

01  END-LINE.
    05 PIC X(55)  VALUE SPACES.
    05 PIC X(23)  VALUE '***  END OF REPORT  ***'.
    05 PIC X(55)  VALUE SPACES.

PROCEDURE DIVISION.

100-PRODUCE-PHONE-SALES-REPORT.
    PERFORM 200-START-UP.
    PERFORM 210-PROCESS-PHONE-SALE-RECORD
        UNTIL WS-MORE-RECORDS = 'NO '.
    PERFORM 220-FINISH-UP.
    STOP RUN.

200-START-UP.
    OPEN INPUT PHONE-SALES-FILE
         OUTPUT PHONE-SALES-REPORT.
    SET THERE-IS-A-RECORD TO TRUE.
    MOVE 1 TO O-PAGE-NO.
    CALL 'CONVERT-DATE-SUB' USING O-DATE.
    PERFORM 300-WRITE-REPORT-HEADERS.
    PERFORM 310-READ-PHONE-SALE-RECORD.

210-PROCESS-PHONE-SALE-RECORD.
    PERFORM 320-COMPUTE-PHONE-SALE-AMOUNT.
    PERFORM 330-PREPARE-PHONE-SALE-LINE.
    PERFORM 310-READ-PHONE-SALE-RECORD.

220-FINISH-UP.
    WRITE PRINTLINE FROM END-LINE
        AFTER ADVANCING 3 LINES.
    CLOSE PHONE-SALES-FILE
          PHONE-SALES-REPORT.

300-WRITE-REPORT-HEADERS.
    WRITE PRINTLINE FROM TOP-LINE
        AFTER ADVANCING PAGE.
    WRITE PRINTLINE FROM COMPANY-NAME
        AFTER ADVANCING 1 LINE.
    WRITE PRINTLINE FROM REPORT-NAME
        AFTER ADVANCING 3 LINES.
    WRITE PRINTLINE FROM HEADINGS
        AFTER ADVANCING 3 LINES.
    MOVE 2 TO WS-PROPER-SPACING.
```

Figure 5.31 continued

```
 310-READ-PHONE-SALE-RECORD.
     READ PHONE-SALES-FILE RECORD
         AT END
             SET NO-MORE-RECORDS TO TRUE.

 320-COMPUTE-PHONE-SALE-AMOUNT.
     CALL 'ASC-COMPUTE-SALE-AMT-SUB'.

 330-PREPARE-PHONE-SALE-LINE.
     MOVE I-CUSTOMER-NO TO O-CUSTOMER-NO.
     MOVE I-CATALOG-NO TO O-CATALOG-NO.
     MOVE I-UNIT-COST TO O-UNIT-COST.
     MOVE I-NO-OF-UNITS TO O-NO-OF-UNITS.
     MOVE WS-SALE-AMOUNT TO O-SALE-AMOUNT.
     WRITE PRINTLINE FROM PHONE-SALE-LINE
         AFTER ADVANCING WS-PROPER-SPACING.
     MOVE 1 TO WS-PROPER-SPACING.

*****************************************************************
*                                                               *
*  THE FOLLOWING SUBPROGRAM IS NESTED WITHIN THE CALLING PROGRAM *
*                                                               *
*****************************************************************

 IDENTIFICATION DIVISION.

 PROGRAM-ID.  ASC-COMPUTE-SALE-AMT-SUB.

*****************************************************************
*                                                               *
*  THE PURPOSE OF THIS SUBPROGRAM IS TO COMPUTE THE AMOUNT TO BE *
*  CHARGED TO CUSTOMERS OF THE ALLIED STOCK COMPANY WHO MADE    *
*  PURCHASES BY PHONE.  THE TOTAL CHARGE IS DISCOUNTED 20% IF   *
*  NUMBER OF UNITS PURCHASED EXCEEDS 100.                       *
*                                                               *
*  THE SUBPROGRAM HAS ACCESS TO THE NUMBER OF UNITS PURCHASED,  *
*  THE UNIT COST OF THE ITEM, AND THE WORKING STORAGE ITEM      *
*  WS-SALE-AMOUNT BECAUSE THEY HAVE BEEN DECLARED 'GLOBAL' IN   *
*  THE CALLING PROGRAM.                                         *
*                                                               *
*****************************************************************

 PROCEDURE DIVISION.

 100-COMPUTE-SALE-AMOUNT.
     IF I-NO-OF-UNITS > 100
         COMPUTE WS-SALE-AMOUNT ROUNDED =
             I-NO-OF-UNITS * I-UNIT-COST * .8
     ELSE
         COMPUTE WS-SALE-AMOUNT ROUNDED =
             I-NO-OF-UNITS * I-UNIT-COST.

 999-EXIT.
     EXIT PROGRAM.

 END PROGRAM ASC-COMPUTE-SALE-AMT-SUB.
 END PROGRAM DAILY-PHONE-SALES-REPORT.
```

Figure 5.32 END PROGRAM header format

END PROGRAM program-name

Rules Governing the Use of the END PROGRAM Header

1. The function of the END PROGRAM header is to indicate the end of a COBOL source program.
2. *Program-name* is the name in the program's PROGRAM-ID paragraph.
3. The END PROGRAM header must be used for every program that contains another program or is contained in another program.
4. A matching pair of PROGRAM-ID and END PROGRAM statements must be completely nested within another pair.
5. An END PROGRAM header may be followed by another END PROGRAM header or by the IDENTIFICATION DIVISION header for another program.
6. The last END PROGRAM header in a set of nested programs must be paired with the outermost PROGRAM-ID paragraph.

Rules Governing the Use of the GLOBAL Qualifier

1. The format of the global qualifier is . . . **IS GLOBAL.**
2. The GLOBAL qualifier may be specified in an FD entry of the FILE SECTION, an RD entry of the REPORT SECTION, or a level-01 record description entry in either the FILE SECTION or the WORKING-STORAGE SECTION. (77-level entries may also be defined as GLOBAL.)
3. The GLOBAL qualifier specifies that the file-name, report-name, or record-name qualified as GLOBAL can be accessed by the program that defines the entry and by any program contained, directly or indirectly, within the program that defines it.
4. All data items subordinate to a global file-name or to a global record-name are also global. Condition-names attached to global data items are also global.
5. If a report-name is global, then the special registers LINE-COUNTER and PAGE-COUNTER are also global.
6. If the GLOBAL qualifier is used in a DATA DIVISION, no two data items may have the same name.
7. If GLOBAL is specified in a REDEFINES clause, only the subject of the REDEFINES is global.

The CANCEL Statement

Recall the function of subprogram CONVERT-DATE-SUB. It was used in each sample run unit in the chapter to convert the current date to a properly formatted date to be printed on a report. It should be clear that it is called only once by the calling program, at the point where the first top-of-page report line is being prepared. Once it has accomplished its function, the subprogram is no longer needed by the program. It may be logically removed from the run unit simply by executing a CANCEL statement that references it, as in

```
CANCEL "CONVERT-DATE-SUB".
```

The appropriate place to cancel the subprogram is subsequent to the CALL statement in the calling program, as in the following example:

```
200-START-UP.
    OPEN INPUT PHONE-SALES-FILE
         OUTPUT PHONE-SALES-REPORT.
    SET THERE-IS-A-RECORD TO TRUE.
    MOVE 1 TO O-PAGE-NO.
    CALL "CONVERT-DATE-SUB" USING O-DATE.
    CANCEL "CONVERT-DATE-SUB".
    PERFORM 300-WRITE-REPORT-HEADERS.
    PERFORM 310-READ-PHONE-SALE-RECORD.
```

The format of the CANCEL statement is shown in Figure 5.33.

Figure 5.33 CANCEL statement format

```
CANCEL {identifier-1} ...
       {literal-1   }
```

Rules Governing the Use of the CANCEL Statement

1. The function of the CANCEL statement is to logically remove a program from a run unit.
2. The CANCEL statement must be in a program from which the program to be canceled is callable.
3. *Identifier-1* is an alphanumeric data item. At the time the CANCEL statement is executed, it contains the name of the program to be canceled. The program name is the one in the program's PROGRAM-ID paragraph.
4. *Literal-1* is the name of the program to be canceled. The program name is the one specified in the program's PROGRAM-ID paragraph.
5. *Identifier-1* or *literal-1* must name a program that has been called and for which an EXIT PROGRAM has been executed.
6. When the CANCEL statement is executed, the program, along with all of its contained programs, is no longer active in the run unit.
7. If a program has been canceled, it may be reactivated in the run unit by the execution of an appropriate CALL statement. The called program is then in its initial state, that is, as it was when it was first called.
8. The CANCEL statement closes files that were left in an open mode in the program being canceled.

The INITIAL Qualifier

When a program or a subprogram in a run unit is executed for the first time, it is said to be in its initial state: internal data items defined with VALUE clauses contain those values, numeric items are automatically set to zero in many operating systems, file pointers are at the beginnings of files, special registers are initialized by the operating system. Subsequent to the execution of a subprogram, some of those values may have been changed. If it is important for the subprogram to be in its initial state *every* time it is called, that can be readily achieved by using the INITIAL qualifier in the subprogram's PROGRAM-ID paragraph, as in

```
PROGRAM-ID.  SUB1 IS INITIAL PROGRAM.
```

or simply

```
PROGRAM-ID.  SUB1 INITIAL.
```

As a result of the INITIAL entry, not only is SUB1 in its initial state every time it is called, but every program contained within it is also in its initial state.

The COMMON Qualifier

When subprograms are compiled separately in a run unit, they are callable not only by the main program but by the other subprograms as well. When subprograms are nested within a main program, they are generally callable only by a containing program that *directly* contains them. For instance, if MAIN-PROGRAM contains subprogram SUB1, and subprogram SUB1 contains subprogram SUB2, then MAIN-PROGRAM can call SUB1 but it cannot call SUB2. SUB2 can be called by subprogram SUB1, however. If subprogram SUB3 is also contained in MAIN-PROGRAM, then it is callable only from its containing program. This situation is illustrated in Figure 5.34, where the arrow points to a callable subprogram.

The restriction that normally applies to calling programs that are nested can be overridden to some extent by qualifying a subprogram as COMMON. For instance, in the illustration of Figure 5.34, if SUB3 is qualified as a COMMON subprogram, then it becomes callable not only by its containing

Figure 5.34 Callable nested programs

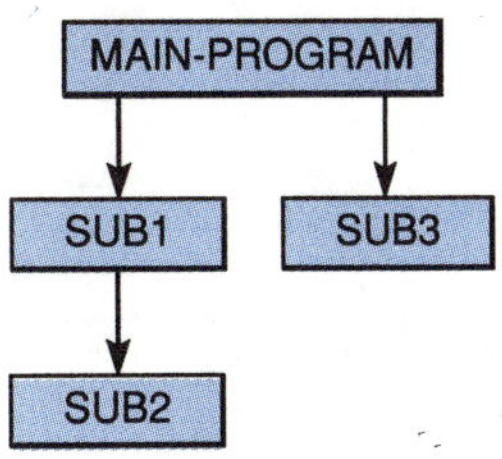

Figure 5.35 A COMMON program in nested programs

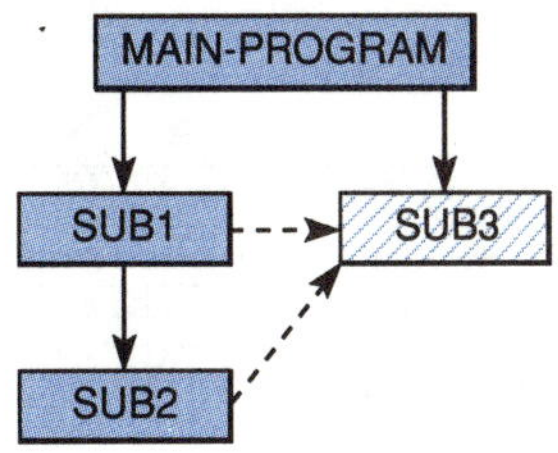

Figure 5.36 COMMON entry format

PROGRAM-ID. program-name-2 [IS { | COMMON / INITIAL | } PROGRAM]

program (MAIN-PROGRAM) but also by subprograms SUB1 and SUB2. This is shown in Figure 5.35, in which SUB3 has been shaded to indicate that it has the COMMON attribute. Note the additional arrows that point to it.

The format of the COMMON entry is shown in Figure 5.36. (The vertical bars indicate that one or more of the choices must be used.)

Rules Governing the Use of the COMMON Entry

In the format of Figure 5.36,

1. *Program-name-2* must be a contained program.
2. The COMMON qualifier may be used only in the PROGRAM-ID paragraph. Its use indicates that *program-name-2* is a common program.
3. A common program may be called by its directly containing program and by any other program directly or indirectly contained in its containing program. However, the common program cannot be called by any of its own contained programs.

Sample Run Unit 4

Sample Run Unit 4 is being developed mainly to illustrate the use of the COMMON qualifier, but it will also use the GLOBAL qualifier, the CALL *literal* and CALL *identifier* statements, and the CANCEL statement.

The Problem

The data processing department of the Ponagansett Electric Company is preparing a run unit consisting of nested programs for the purpose of producing analysis reports for the current billing period for each of its electric rate schedules. (The rate schedules are the familiar ones: A10, A11, A12, and C-2.) For each rate schedule, the program must prepare a report formatted as shown in Figure 5.37. The report must list customers in ascending order by customer number, and it must print totals for the rate schedule being reported. Following the last rate schedule report, company totals must also be printed.

The customer records contain the following data:

cc 1–3	Area code (RI1, RI2, or RI3)
cc 4–9	Customer number
cc 10–29	Customer name
cc 30–34	Previous meter reading
cc 35–39	Current meter reading
cc 40–73	Not used
cc 74–76	Rate schedule
cc 77–80	Not used

The records are stored in ascending order by customer number.

Figure 5.37 Printer spacing chart for the analysis reports

Printer Spacing Chart

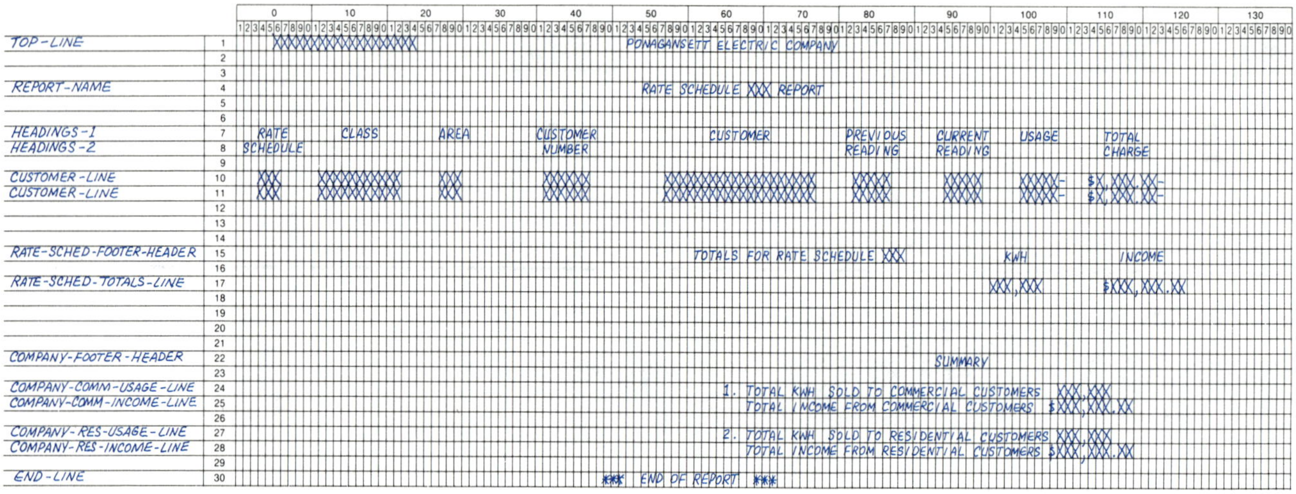

Problem Analysis

In designing this run unit, the following items are determined:

1. Since four reports are to be produced, they will be produced in ascending order by rate schedule code, namely, the "A10" customer report first, followed by the "A11" customer report, the "A12" customer report, and the "C-2" customer report.
2. To accommodate the report sequence, the customer file will be sorted on two keys: the primary key is the rate schedule, and the secondary key is the customer number.
3. As the customers of a particular rate schedule are processed, an appropriate subprogram will be called to compute the applicable basic charge, and another subprogram will be called to compute the extra charge. When all customers of that rate schedule have been processed, the corresponding rate schedule summary will be printed and that rate schedule subprogram will be canceled, since it is no longer needed.
4. Each rate schedule subprogram will be responsible for producing the top-of-report documentation and the rate schedule summary. The detail lines will be produced by the main program, but it will use values computed within the subprograms.
5. A subprogram will be given the task of preparing the top-of-report documentation. It must be called by each rate schedule subprogram. Consequently, it will be specified as a common program.
6. The subprogram that computes a customer's extra charge must also be called by each rate schedule subprogram. Therefore, this subprogram will also be specified as a common program.
7. The subprogram responsible for top-of-report documentation must itself also call a subprogram, namely, the one used to format the date on the report. It should be called only once.
8. Program names are selected as follows:
   a. Main program: PON-ELECTRIC-MAIN.
   b. Top-of-report subprogram: HEADERS-SUB.
   c. Date conversion subprogram: CONVERT-DATE-SUB.
   d. A10 rate schedule subprogram: A10-SCHEDULE-SUB.
   e. A11 rate schedule subprogram: A11-SCHEDULE-SUB.
   f. C-2 rate schedule subprogram: C-2-SCHEDULE-SUB.
   g. Extra charge subprogram: XTRA-CHARGE-SUB.
9. The nesting of the seven programs in the run unit is determined as shown in Figure 5.38. As a result of the nesting scheme, the common subprogram HEADERS-SUB and the common subprogram XTRA-CHARGE-SUB can be called by each rate schedule subprogram, whereas

Figure 5.38 Nesting of programs in the run unit

```
IDENTIFICATION DIVISION.
PROGRAM-ID.    PON-ELECTRIC-MAIN.
:
IDENTIFICATION DIVISION.
PROGRAM-ID.    HEADERS-SUB  COMMON.
:
IDENTIFICATION DIVISION.
PROGRAM-ID.    CONVERT-DATE-SUB.
:
END PROGRAM    CONVERT-DATE-SUB.
END PROGRAM    HEADERS-SUB.
IDENTIFICATION DIVISION.
PROGRAM-ID.    A10-SCHEDULE-SUB.
:
END PROGRAM    A10-SCHEDULE-SUB.
IDENTIFICATION DIVISION.
PROGRAM-ID.    A11-SCHEDULE-SUB.
:
END PROGRAM    A11-SCHEDULE-SUB.
IDENTIFICATION DIVISION.
PROGRAM-ID.    C-2-SCHEDULE-SUB.
:
END PROGRAM    C-2-SCHEDULE-SUB.
IDENTIFICATION DIVISION.
PROGRAM-ID.    XTRA-CHARGE-SUB COMMON.
:
END PROGRAM    XTRA-CHARGE-SUB.
END PROGRAM    PON-ELECTRIC-MAIN.
```

subprogram CONVERT-DATE-SUB is callable only by its containing program HEADERS-SUB. Each subprogram, except CONVERT-DATE-SUB, is callable by the main program PON-ELECTRIC-MAIN.

Additionally, data made GLOBAL in the main program is directly accessible by every subprogram. The items that will be made global are: the customer's input record (subsequent to the sort procedure), the output file (since the different rate schedule subprograms must write to their corresponding reports), work areas (related to computing the KWH usage and charges), company accumulators (since they must be referenced in the rate schedule subprograms), and the rate schedule summary lines (to avoid repeating them in each subprogram).

10. The system flowchart must show the flow of data and transfer of control among the programs of the run unit. It is shown in Figure 5.39. Four files, one main program, and six subprograms are needed.

11. The structure chart must be designed to show the hierarchy of tasks to be performed. The analysis in the preceding steps leads to the structure shown in Figure 5.40. Off-page connectors are used to continue the structure of called subprograms wherever it is determined that insufficient space is available on the current page.

12. Although the overall logic of the main program is fairly straightforward, its flowchart is shown in Figure 5.41 so as to direct your attention to module 320-CHECK-NEW-RATE-SCHEDULE. Note that since a control break occurs at the rate schedule level, procedures are established so as to print summary data for the previous rate schedule. Specifically, the appropriate subprogram is selected, a summary flag is set to "ON " to trigger the printing of summary data within the subprogram, and the subprogram is called. Upon control returning from the subprogram, the subprogram is canceled because it is no longer needed, and the summary flag is reset to "OFF." Finally, the value of I-RATE-SCHED that set off the control break is assigned to RATE-CONTROL.

Also note in this module that the test to select a subprogram is restricted to rate schedules A10, A11, and A12. Since rate schedule C-2 is the last one, a control break will not occur while the literal "C-2" is stored in RATE-CONTROL The summary for the C-2 rate schedule will be forced to occur in module 220-FINISH-UP, prior to the printing of the company summary.

Figure 5.39 System flowchart for run unit 4

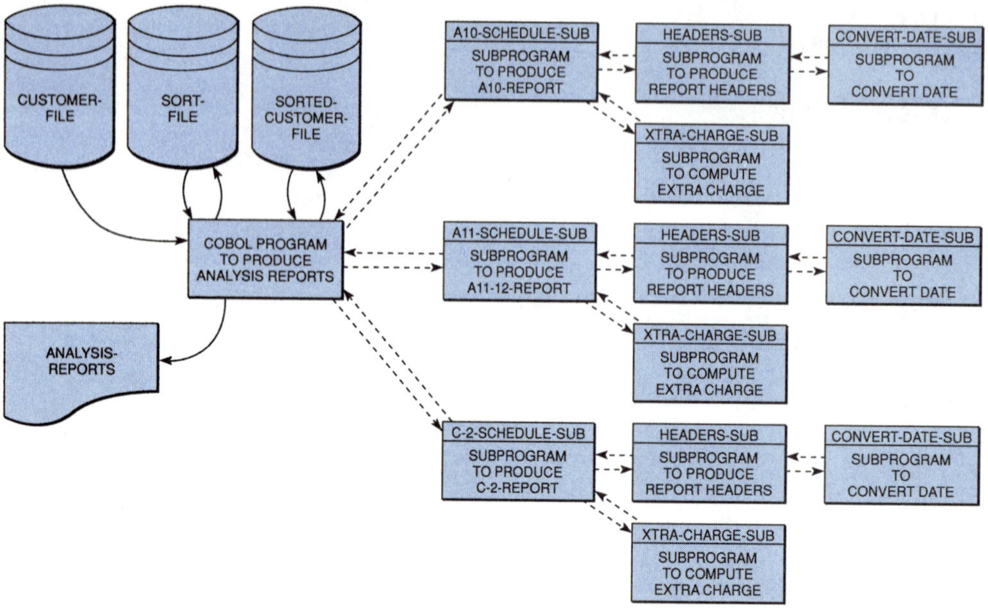

Figure 5.40 Structure chart for run unit 4

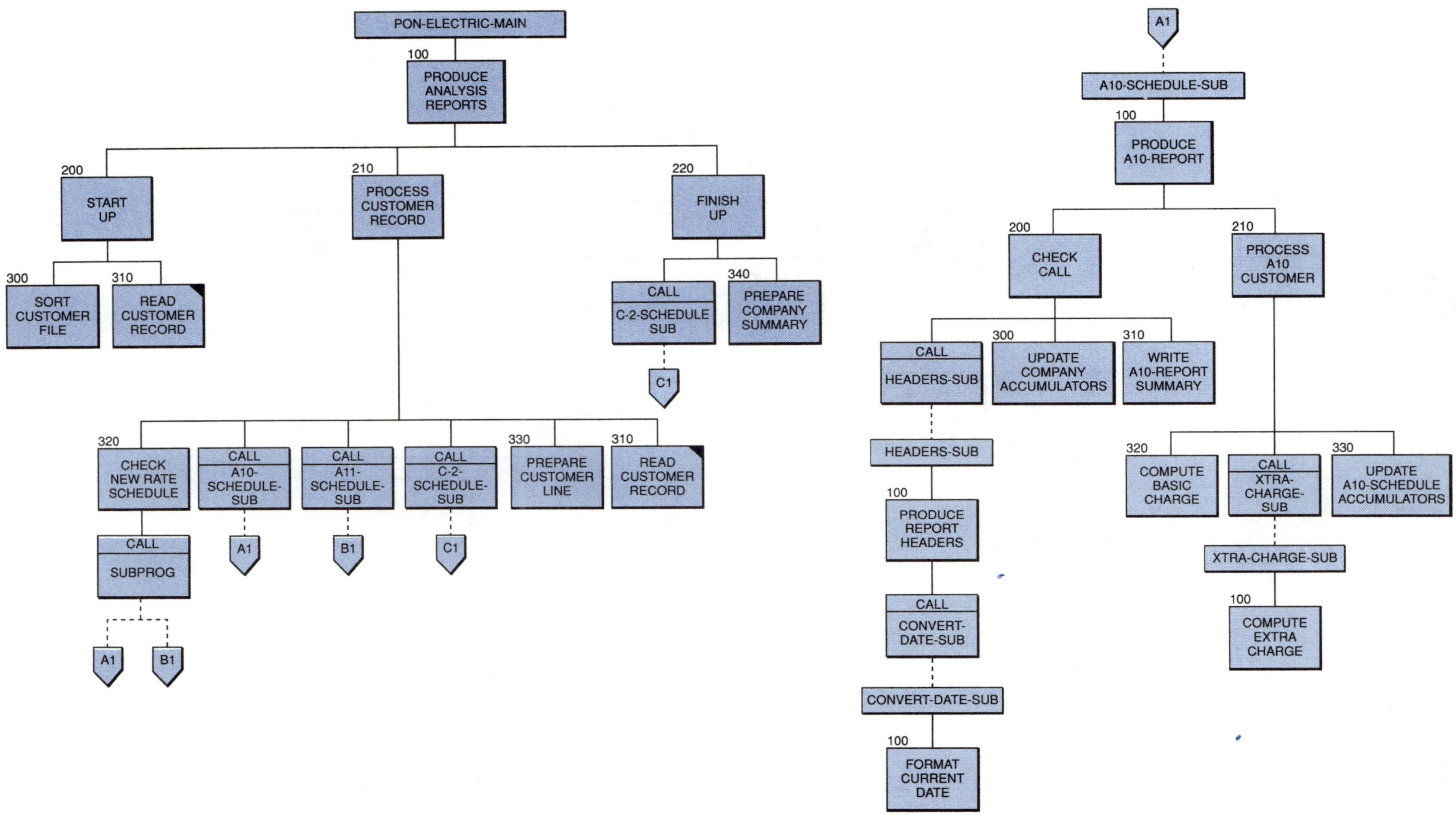

Figure 5.40 continued

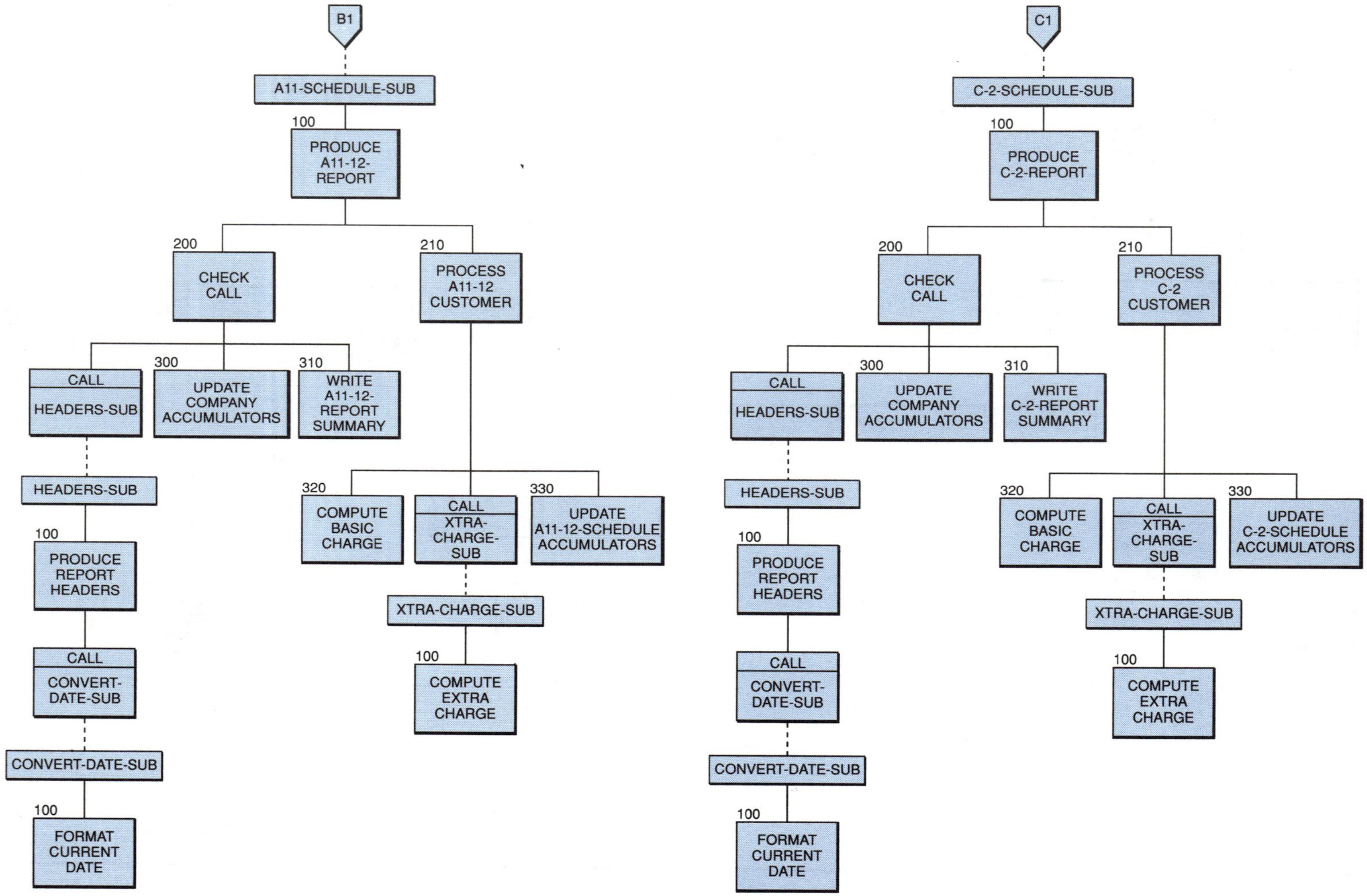

Figure 5.41 Program flowchart for the main program

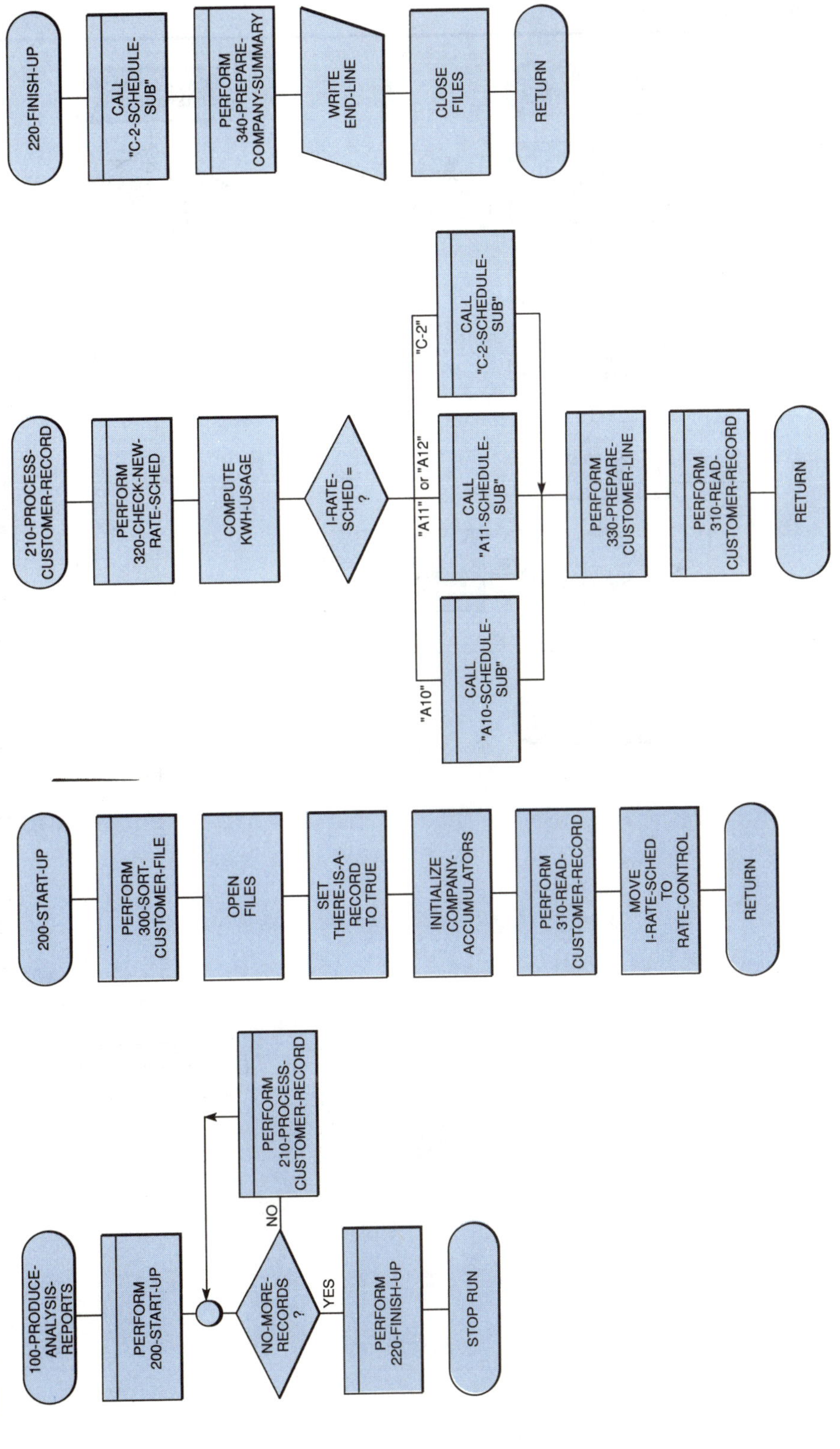

Figure 5.41 continued

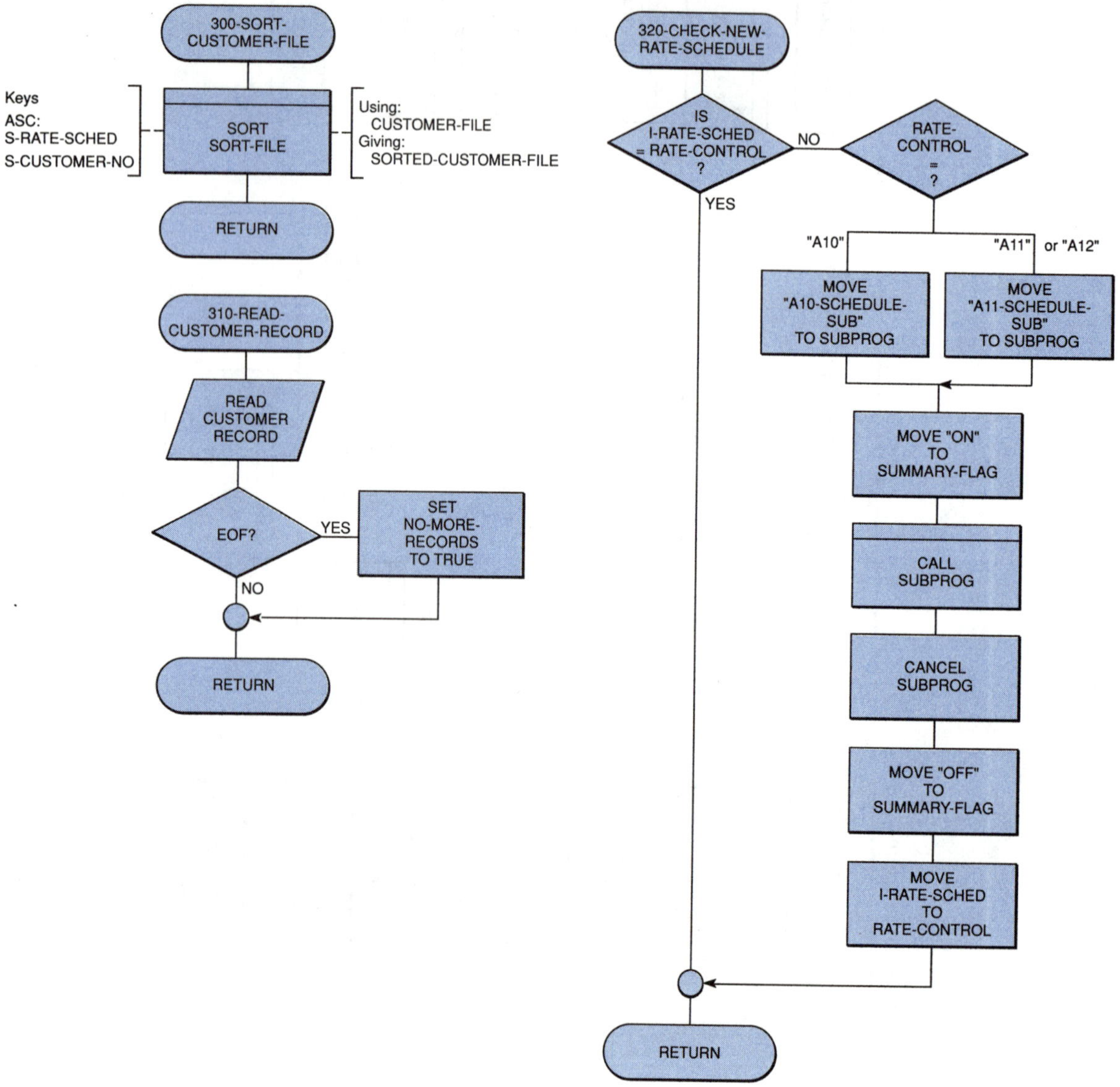

■ **Figure 5.41** continued

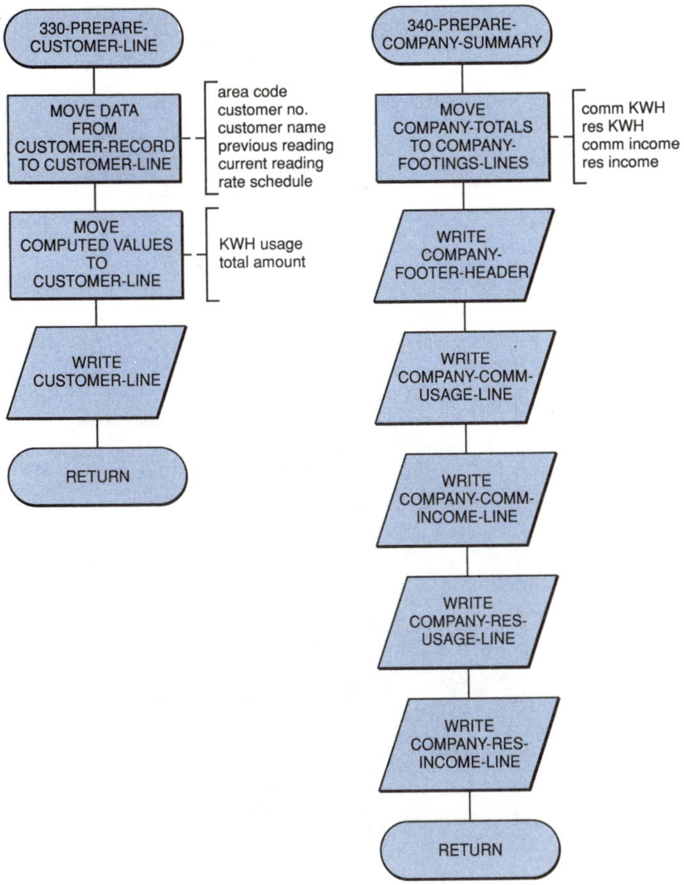

13. The flowchart for subprogram A10-SCHEDULE-SUB is shown as representative of the three rate schedule subprograms. The main difference between these three subprograms is the formula used to determine the customer's basic charge. The representative subprogram flowchart is shown in Figure 5.42.

    Note that in module 200-CHECK-CALL, a call counter within the subprogram is incremented by 1 every time the program is called. When the call counter equals 1, subprogram HEADERS-SUB is called in order to print the top-of-report documentation for this rate schedule's report, and the rate schedule accumulators are initialized. Also note that when the summary flag is "ON ", one procedure updates the company accumulators by using the rolling-forward technique, and a second procedure produces the summary for this rate schedule. If the summary-flag is not "ON ", then module 210-PROCESS-A10-CUSTOMER is executed.
14. The flowchart for subprogram HEADERS-SUB is shown in Figure 5.43. Note that its nested subprogram CONVERT-DATE-SUB is called only once, and that occurs the very first time HEADERS-SUB is called. Also note that a test is used to determine the value to be assigned to the data field of the record REPORT-NAME.
15. The flowcharts for subprogram CONVERT-DATE-SUB and subprogram XTRA-CHARGE-SUB are not shown because these subprograms are very similar to the ones used in Sample Run Unit 2.

Figure 5.42 Flowchart for subprogram A10-SCHEDULE-SUB

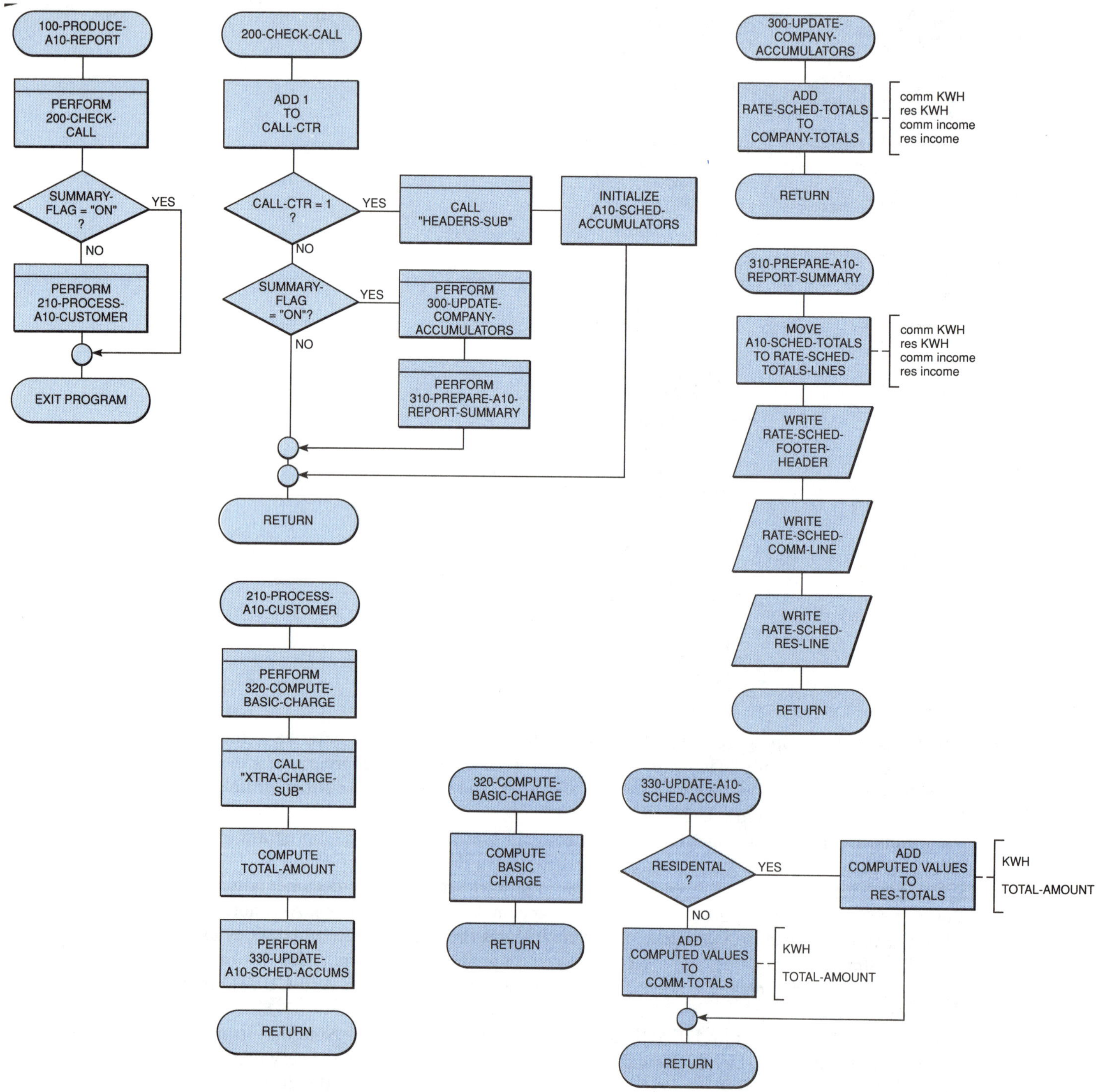

■ **Figure 5.43** Flowchart for subprogram HEADERS-SUB

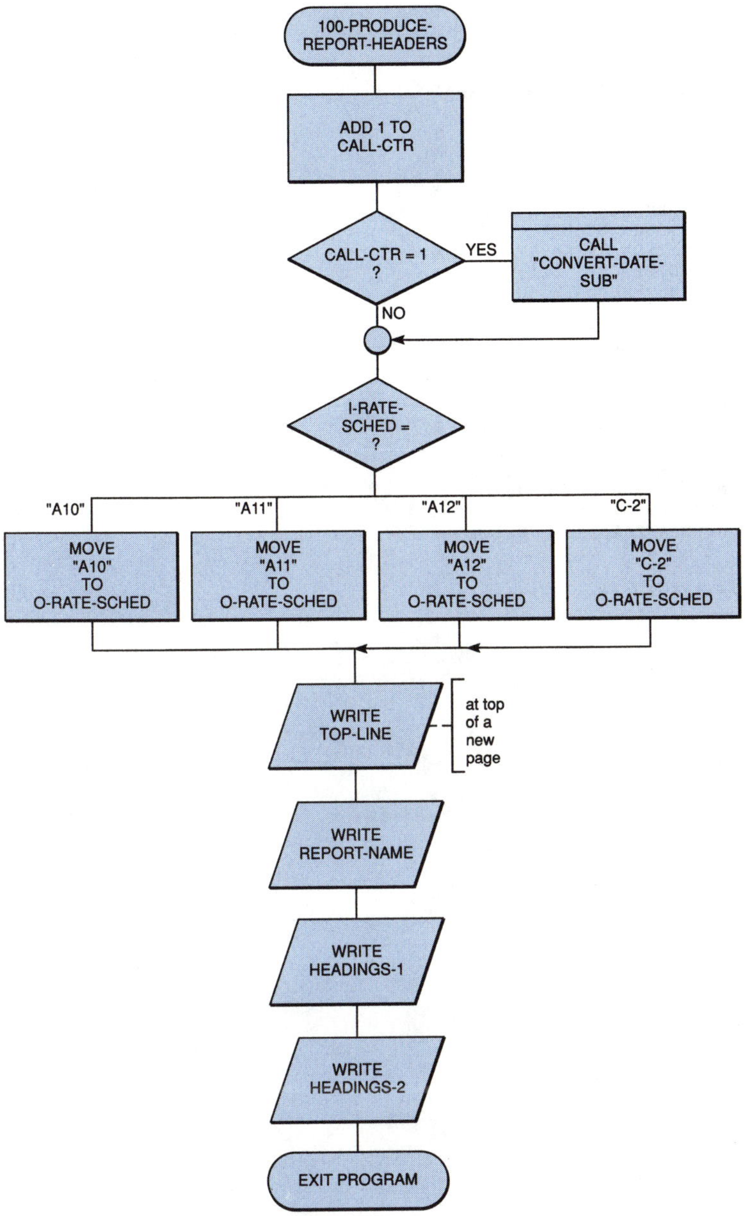

Coding the Nested Programs of the Run Unit

Now that the analysis is complete, the next task is to code the needed programs. And once coded, they must be assembled into the run unit as planned in Figure 5.38. The net result is the run unit shown in Figure 5.44.

The nested programs were compiled, linked, and run using the data file shown in Figure 5.24. The analysis reports that were produced as output are shown in Figure 5.45.

■ Figure 5.44 Nested programs of run unit 4

```
1       IDENTIFICATION DIVISION.

        PROGRAM-ID.      PON-ELECTRIC-MAIN.

       ****************************************************************
       *                                                              *
       *    AUTHOR.          PAQUETTE.                                *
       *    DATE WRITTEN.    MAY 1989.                                *
       *                                                              *
       *    THE PURPOSE OF THIS RUN UNIT IS TO PRODUCE ANALYSIS REPORTS   *
       *    FOR THE CURRENT BILLING PERIOD.  THE MAIN PROGRAM SORTS THE   *
       *    CUSTOMER RECORDS IN ASCENDING ORDER OF CUSTOMER NUMBERS WITHIN*
       *    EACH RATE SCHEDULE.   IT ALSO CONTAINS A CONTROL BREAK AT THE *
       *    RATE CODE LEVEL.   IT SELECTS SUBPROGRAMS TO PROCESS THE      *
       *    CUSTOMER RECORDS.   EACH OF THESE SUBPROGRAMS PRODUCES A DETAIL*
       *    LINE FOR EACH CUSTOMER WITHIN THE RATE SCHEDULE, AS WELL AS   *
       *    SUMMARY INFORMATION FOR THAT RATE SCHEDULE.   THE MAIN PROGRAM *
       *    ALSO PRODUCES SUMMARY INFORMATION FOR THE COMPANY AS A WHOLE. *
       *                                                              *
       *    THE MAIN PROGRAM IS A CONTAINING PROGRAM.   ITS CONTAINED PRO- *
       *    GRAMS ARE: A HEADERS SUBPROGRAM, DEFINED AS COMMON, THREE SUB-*
       *    PROGRAMS USED TO COMPUTE THE CUSTOMER'S BASIC ELECTRIC CHARGE,*
       *    DEPENDING ON THE CUSTOMER'S APPLICABLE RATE SCHEDULE,   AND   *
       *    ANOTHER COMMON SUBPROGRAM TO COMPUTE AN EXTRA CHARGE BASED ON *
       *    THE FUEL ADJUSTMENT CHARGE, THE OIL CONSERVATION ADJUSTMENT   *
       *    CHARGE, AND THE UNIFORM CONSERVATION COST ADJUSTMENT PROGRAM  *
       *    CHARGE.   THE HEADERS SUBPROGRAM ALSO CALLS A DATE CONVERSION  *
       *    SUBPROGRAM.                                               *
       *                                                              *
       ****************************************************************

        ENVIRONMENT DIVISION.

        CONFIGURATION SECTION.

        SOURCE-COMPUTER.   VAX-VMS-8650.
        OBJECT-COMPUTER.   VAX-VMS-8650.

        INPUT-OUTPUT SECTION.

        FILE-CONTROL.
            SELECT CUSTOMER-FILE          ASSIGN TO COB$INPUT.
            SELECT SORT-FILE              ASSIGN TO SORTDISK.
            SELECT SORTED-CUSTOMER-FILE ASSIGN TO 'SRTDCUST.DAT'.
            SELECT ANALYSIS-REPORT        ASSIGN TO COB$OUTPUT.

        DATA DIVISION.

        FILE SECTION.

        FD  CUSTOMER-FILE
            RECORD CONTAINS 80 CHARACTERS.

        01  CUSTOMER-RECORD           PIC X(80).

        SD  SORT-FILE
            RECORD CONTAINS 80 CHARACTERS.

        01  SORT-RECORD.
            05                        PIC X(3).
            05  S-CUSTOMER-NO         PIC X(6).
            05                        PIC X(64).
            05  S-RATE-SCHED          PIC X(3).
            05                        PIC X(4).

        FD  SORTED-CUSTOMER-FILE
            RECORD CONTAINS 80 CHARACTERS.

2       01  SORTED-CUSTOMER-RECORD              GLOBAL.
            05 I-AREA-CODE            PIC X(3).
            05 I-CUSTOMER-NO          PIC X(6).
            05 I-CUSTOMER-NAME        PIC X(20).
            05 I-LAST-READING         PIC 9(5).
            05 I-CURRENT-READING      PIC 9(5).
            05                        PIC X(34).
            05 I-RATE-SCHED           PIC X(3).
               88 COMMERCIAL                    VALUE 'C-2'.
               88 RESIDENTIAL                   VALUE 'A10', 'A11', 'A12'.
            05                        PIC X(4).
```

```
3       FD  ANALYSIS-REPORT                          GLOBAL
            RECORD CONTAINS 132 CHARACTERS.

        01  PRINTLINE               PIC X(132).

        WORKING-STORAGE SECTION.

        01  PROGRAM-CONTROLS.
            05 WS-MORE-RECORDS             PIC X(3).
                88 THERE-IS-A-RECORD             VALUE 'YES'.
                88 NO-MORE-RECORDS               VALUE 'NO '.
            05 SUBPROG                     PIC X(16).

4       01  SHARED-DATA                     GLOBAL.
            05 WS-KWH-USAGE                PIC S9(5).
            05 WS-BASIC-CHARGE             PIC S9(5)V99.
            05 WS-EXTRA-CHARGE             PIC S9(5)V99.
            05 WS-TOTAL-AMOUNT             PIC S9(5)V99.
            05 SUMMARY-FLAG                PIC X(3).
            05 RATE-CONTROL                PIC X(3).
            05 WS-PROPER-SPACING           PIC 9(1).

5       01  COMPANY-ACCUMULATORS            GLOBAL.
            05 WS-COMPANY-KWH-COMM         PIC S9(6).
            05 WS-COMPANY-KWH-RES          PIC S9(6).
            05 WS-COMPANY-INCOME-COMM      PIC S9(6)V99.
            05 WS-COMPANY-INCOME-RES       PIC S9(6)V99.


        01  CUSTOMER-LINE.
            05                       PIC X(3).
            05 O-RATE-SCHED-1        PIC X(3).
            05                       PIC X(5).
            05 O-CLASS               PIC X(11).
            05                       PIC X(5).
            05 O-AREA-CODE           PIC X(3).
            05                       PIC X(11).
            05 O-CUSTOMER-NO         PIC X(6).
            05                       PIC X(10).
            05 O-CUSTOMER-NAME       PIC X(20).
            05                       PIC X(5).
            05 O-LAST-READING        PIC X(5).
            05                       PIC X(7).
            05 O-CURRENT-READING     PIC X(5).
            05                       PIC X(5).
            05 O-KWH-USAGE           PIC ZZZZ9-.
            05                       PIC X(3).
            05 O-TOTAL-AMOUNT        PIC $ZZ,ZZ9.99-.
            05                       PIC X(8).

6       01  RATE-SCHED-FOOTING-LINES          GLOBAL.

            05 RATE-SCHED-FOOTER-HEADER.
                10                       PIC X(61)  VALUE SPACES.
                10                       PIC X(25)  VALUE
                                           'TOTALS FOR RATE SCHEDULE '.
                10 O-RATE-SCHED-2        PIC X(3).
                10                       PIC X(13)  VALUE SPACES.
                10                       PIC X(3)   VALUE 'KWH'.
                10                       PIC X(12)  VALUE SPACES.
                10                       PIC X(6)   VALUE 'INCOME'.
                10                       PIC X(9)   VALUE SPACES.

            05 RATE-SCHED-TOTALS-LINE.
                10                       PIC X(100) VALUE SPACES.
                10 O-RATE-SCHED-KWH      PIC ZZZ,ZZ9.
                10                       PIC X(8)   VALUE SPACES.
                10 O-RATE-SCHED-INCOME   PIC $ZZZ,ZZ9.99.
                10                       PIC X(6)   VALUE SPACES.
```

```
01  COMPANY-FOOTING-LINES.

    05 COMPANY-FOOTER-HEADER.
       10 PIC X(92)     VALUE SPACES.
       10 PIC X(7)      VALUE 'SUMMARY'.
       10 PIC X(33)     VALUE SPACES.

    05 COMPANY-COMM-USAGE-LINE.
       10                      PIC X(65)  VALUE SPACES.
       10                      PIC X(44)  VALUE
               '1. TOTAL KWH  SOLD TO COMMERCIAL CUSTOMERS  '.
       10 O-COMPANY-KWH-COMM PIC ZZZ,ZZ9.
       10                      PIC X(16)  VALUE SPACES.

    05 COMPANY-COMM-INCOME-LINE.
       10                         PIC X(68)  VALUE SPACES.
       10                         PIC X(40)  VALUE
               'TOTAL  INCOME FROM COMMERCIAL CUSTOMERS  '.
       10 O-COMPANY-COMM-INCOME PIC $ZZZ,ZZ9.99.
       10                         PIC X(13)  VALUE SPACES.

    05 COMPANY-RES-USAGE-LINE.
       10                     PIC X(65)  VALUE SPACES.
       10                     PIC X(45)  VALUE
              '2. TOTAL KWH  SOLD TO RESIDENTIAL CUSTOMERS  '.
       10 O-COMPANY-KWH-RES PIC ZZZ,ZZ9.
       10                     PIC X(16)  VALUE SPACES.

    05 COMPANY-RES-INCOME-LINE.
       10                        PIC X(68)  VALUE SPACES.
       10                        PIC X(41)  VALUE
              'TOTAL  INCOME FROM RESIDENTIAL CUSTOMERS '.
       10 O-COMPANY-INCOME-RES PIC $ZZZ,ZZ9.99.
       10                        PIC X(13)  VALUE SPACES.

01  END-LINE.
    05 PIC X(49)    VALUE SPACES.
    05 PIC X(23)    VALUE '***  END OF REPORT  ***'.
    05 PIC X(50)    VALUE SPACES.

PROCEDURE DIVISION.

100-PRODUCE-ANALYSIS-REPORTS.
    PERFORM 200-START-UP.
    PERFORM 210-PROCESS-CUSTOMER-RECORD
        UNTIL NO-MORE-RECORDS.
    PERFORM 220-FINISH-UP.
    STOP RUN.

200-START-UP.
    PERFORM 300-SORT-CUSTOMER-FILE.
    OPEN INPUT  SORTED-CUSTOMER-FILE
         OUTPUT ANALYSIS-REPORT.
    PERFORM 310-READ-CUSTOMER-RECORD.
    MOVE I-RATE-SCHED TO RATE-CONTROL.
    INITIALIZE COMPANY-ACCUMULATORS.
    SET THERE-IS-A-RECORD TO TRUE.

210-PROCESS-CUSTOMER-RECORD.
    PERFORM 320-CHECK-NEW-RATE-SCHEDULE.
    SUBTRACT I-LAST-READING FROM I-CURRENT-READING
        GIVING WS-KWH-USAGE.
7   EVALUATE I-RATE-SCHED
        WHEN    'A10'  CALL 'A10-SCHEDULE-SUB'
        WHEN    'A11'  CALL 'A11-SCHEDULE-SUB'
        WHEN    'A12'  CALL 'A11-SCHEDULE-SUB'
        WHEN    'C-2'  CALL 'C-2-SCHEDULE-SUB'
    END-EVALUATE.
8   PERFORM 330-PREPARE-CUSTOMER-LINE.
    PERFORM 310-READ-CUSTOMER-RECORD.

220-FINISH-UP.
    MOVE 'ON ' TO SUMMARY-FLAG.
9   CALL 'C-2-SCHEDULE-SUB'.
    PERFORM 340-PREPARE-COMPANY-SUMMARY.
    WRITE PRINTLINE FROM END-LINE
        AFTER ADVANCING 5 LINES.
    CLOSE SORTED-CUSTOMER-FILE
          ANALYSIS-REPORT.
```

Figure 5.44 continued

```
       300-SORT-CUSTOMER-FILE.
           SORT SORT-FILE
               ON ASCENDING S-RATE-SCHED
                            S-CUSTOMER-NO
               USING CUSTOMER-FILE
               GIVING SORTED-CUSTOMER-FILE.

       310-READ-CUSTOMER-RECORD.
           READ SORTED-CUSTOMER-FILE RECORD
               AT END
                   SET NO-MORE-RECORDS TO TRUE.

       320-CHECK-NEW-RATE-SCHEDULE.
10         IF I-RATE-SCHED = RATE-CONTROL
               NEXT SENTENCE
           ELSE
               EVALUATE RATE-CONTROL
                   WHEN   'A10'  MOVE 'A10-SCHEDULE-SUB' TO SUBPROG
                   WHEN   'A11'  MOVE 'A11-SCHEDULE-SUB' TO SUBPROG
                   WHEN   'A12'  MOVE 'A11-SCHEDULE-SUB' TO SUBPROG
               END-EVALUATE
               MOVE 'ON ' TO SUMMARY-FLAG
               CALL SUBPROG
               CANCEL SUBPROG
               MOVE 'OFF' TO SUMMARY-FLAG
               MOVE I-RATE-SCHED TO RATE-CONTROL.

       330-PREPARE-CUSTOMER-LINE.
           MOVE I-AREA-CODE TO O-AREA-CODE.
           MOVE I-CUSTOMER-NO TO O-CUSTOMER-NO.
           MOVE I-CUSTOMER-NAME TO O-CUSTOMER-NAME.
           MOVE I-LAST-READING TO O-LAST-READING.
           MOVE I-CURRENT-READING TO O-CURRENT-READING.
           MOVE I-RATE-SCHED TO O-RATE-SCHED-1.
           IF COMMERCIAL
               MOVE 'COMMERCIAL' TO O-CLASS
           ELSE
               MOVE 'RESIDENTIAL' TO O-CLASS.
           MOVE WS-KWH-USAGE TO O-KWH-USAGE.
           MOVE WS-TOTAL-AMOUNT TO O-TOTAL-AMOUNT.
           WRITE PRINTLINE FROM CUSTOMER-LINE
               AFTER ADVANCING WS-PROPER-SPACING.
           MOVE 1 TO WS-PROPER-SPACING.

       340-PREPARE-COMPANY-SUMMARY.
           WRITE PRINTLINE FROM COMPANY-FOOTER-HEADER
               AFTER ADVANCING 5 LINES.
           MOVE WS-COMPANY-KWH-COMM TO O-COMPANY-KWH-COMM.
           MOVE WS-COMPANY-KWH-RES TO O-COMPANY-KWH-RES.
           MOVE WS-COMPANY-INCOME-COMM TO O-COMPANY-COMM-INCOME.
           MOVE WS-COMPANY-INCOME-RES TO O-COMPANY-INCOME-RES.
           WRITE PRINTLINE FROM COMPANY-COMM-USAGE-LINE
               AFTER ADVANCING 2 LINES.
           WRITE PRINTLINE FROM COMPANY-COMM-INCOME-LINE
               AFTER ADVANCING 1 LINE.
           WRITE PRINTLINE FROM COMPANY-RES-USAGE-LINE
               AFTER ADVANCING 2 LINES.
           WRITE PRINTLINE FROM COMPANY-RES-INCOME-LINE
               AFTER ADVANCING 1 LINE.

      *****************************************************************
      *                                                               *
11    *              NESTED SUBPROGRAMS FOLLOW!!                      *
      *              ---------------------------                      *
      *                                                               *
      *****************************************************************

       IDENTIFICATION DIVISION.

12     PROGRAM-ID.  HEADERS-SUB     COMMON.

      *****************************************************************
      *                                                               *
      *   THIS SUBPROGRAM PREPARES THE TOP-OF-REPORT DOCUMENTATION    *
      *   LINES FOR EACH RATE SCHEDULE REPORT.  IT IS DEFINED AS A    *
      *   COMMON PROGRAM SO THAT IT MAY BE ACCESSED BY THE RATE SCHED- *
      *   ULE SUBPROGRAMS.                                            *
      *                                                               *
      *   IT ALSO CALLS A DATE CONVERSION SUBPROGRAM ONCE TO CONVERT  *
      *   THE CURRENT DATE TO THE REQUIRED FORMAT.                    *
      *                                                               *
      *****************************************************************
```

```
DATA DIVISION.

WORKING-STORAGE SECTION.

01  CALL-CTR     PIC 9(2)  VALUE ZERO.

01  REPORT-HEADERS.

    05 TOP-LINE.
       10                      PIC X(5)  VALUE SPACES.
       10 O-DATE               PIC X(19).
       10                      PIC X(28) VALUE SPACES.
       10                      PIC X(28) VALUE
                              'PONAGANSETT ELECTRIC COMPANY'.
       10                      PIC X(52) VALUE SPACES.

    05 REPORT-NAME.
       10                      PIC X(54)  VALUE SPACES.
       10                      PIC X(14)  VALUE 'RATE SCHEDULE '.
       10 O-HEAD-RATE-SCHED    PIC X(3).
       10                      PIC X(7)   VALUE ' REPORT'.
       10                      PIC X(54)  VALUE SPACES.

    05 HEADINGS-1.
       10 PIC X(3)      VALUE SPACES.
       10 PIC X(4)      VALUE 'RATE'.
       10 PIC X(7)      VALUE SPACES.
       10 PIC X(5)      VALUE 'CLASS'.
       10 PIC X(8)      VALUE SPACES.
       10 PIC X(4)      VALUE 'AREA'.
       10 PIC X(9)      VALUE SPACES.
       10 PIC X(8)      VALUE 'CUSTOMER'.
       10 PIC X(15)     VALUE SPACES.
       10 PIC X(8)      VALUE 'CUSTOMER'.
       10 PIC X(10)     VALUE SPACES.
       10 PIC X(8)      VALUE 'PREVIOUS'.
       10 PIC X(4)      VALUE SPACES.
       10 PIC X(7)      VALUE 'CURRENT'.
       10 PIC X(4)      VALUE SPACES.
       10 PIC X(5)      VALUE 'USAGE'.
       10 PIC X(6)      VALUE SPACES.
       10 PIC X(5)      VALUE 'TOTAL'.
       10 PIC X(12)     VALUE SPACES.

    05 HEADINGS-2.
       10 PIC X(1)      VALUE SPACES.
       10 PIC X(8)      VALUE 'SCHEDULE'.
       10 PIC X(32)     VALUE SPACES.
       10 PIC X(6)      VALUE 'NUMBER'.
       10 PIC X(34)     VALUE SPACES.
       10 PIC X(7)      VALUE 'READING'.
       10 PIC X(5)      VALUE SPACES.
       10 PIC X(7)      VALUE 'READING'.
       10 PIC X(15)     VALUE SPACES.
       10 PIC X(6)      VALUE 'CHARGE'.
       10 PIC X(11)     VALUE SPACES.

PROCEDURE DIVISION.

100-PRODUCE-REPORT-HEADERS.
    ADD 1 TO CALL-CTR.
    IF CALL-CTR = 1
13      CALL 'CONVERT-DATE-SUB' USING O-DATE
    END-IF.
    EVALUATE I-RATE-SCHED
        WHEN   'A10'   MOVE 'A10' TO O-HEAD-RATE-SCHED
        WHEN   'A11'   MOVE 'A11' TO O-HEAD-RATE-SCHED
        WHEN   'A12'   MOVE 'A12' TO O-HEAD-RATE-SCHED
        WHEN   'C-2'   MOVE 'C-2' TO O-HEAD-RATE-SCHED
    END-EVALUATE.
    WRITE PRINTLINE FROM TOP-LINE
        AFTER ADVANCING PAGE.
    WRITE PRINTLINE FROM REPORT-NAME
        AFTER ADVANCING 3 LINES.
    WRITE PRINTLINE FROM HEADINGS-1
        AFTER ADVANCING 3 LINES.
    WRITE PRINTLINE FROM HEADINGS-2
        AFTER ADVANCING 1 LINE.
    MOVE 2 TO WS-PROPER-SPACING.

999-EXIT.
    EXIT PROGRAM.
```

■ **Figure 5.44** continued

```
IDENTIFICATION DIVISION.

PROGRAM-ID.  CONVERT-DATE-SUB.

******************************************************************
*                                                                *
*  THE PURPOSE OF THIS SUBPROGRAM IS TO CONVERT THE CURRENT      *
*  DATE FROM YYMMDD FORMAT TO THE REPORT FORMAT THAT NAMES THE   *
*  MONTH, THEN THE DAY NUMBER, AND THE YEAR, AS IN               *
*                    SEPTEMBER 15, 1990                          *
*                                                                *
*  THE SUBPROGRAM DEFINES A MONTH TABLE IN WORKING STORAGE.      *
*  IT OBTAINS THE DATE FROM THE SYSTEM, CONVERTS IT TO THE       *
*  APPROPRIATE FORM, AND RETURNS IT TO THE CALLING PROGRAM.      *
*                                                                *
******************************************************************

DATA DIVISION.

WORKING-STORAGE SECTION.

01  WS-REPORT-DATE.
    05 WS-YR     PIC 9(2).
    05 WS-MO     PIC 9(2).
    05 WS-DAY    PIC 9(2).

01  WS-CENTURY PIC 9(4)  VALUE 1900.

01  MONTH-VALUES.
    05 PIC X(9)   VALUE 'JANUARY'.
    05 PIC X(9)   VALUE 'FEBRUARY'.
    05 PIC X(9)   VALUE 'MARCH'.
    05 PIC X(9)   VALUE 'APRIL'.
    05 PIC X(9)   VALUE 'MAY'.
    05 PIC X(9)   VALUE 'JUNE'.
    05 PIC X(9)   VALUE 'JULY'.
    05 PIC X(9)   VALUE 'AUGUST'.
    05 PIC X(9)   VALUE 'SEPTEMBER'.
    05 PIC X(9)   VALUE 'OCTOBER'.
    05 PIC X(9)   VALUE 'NOVEMBER'.
    05 PIC X(9)   VALUE 'DECEMBER'.
01  MONTH-TABLE REDEFINES MONTH-VALUES.
    05 WS-MONTH OCCURS 12 TIMES  PIC X(9).

LINKAGE SECTION.

01  FORMATTED-DATE    PIC X(19).

PROCEDURE DIVISION USING FORMATTED-DATE.

100-FORMAT-CURRENT-DATE.
    ACCEPT WS-REPORT-DATE FROM DATE.
    ADD WS-YR TO WS-CENTURY.
    STRING WS-MONTH(WS-MO) DELIMITED BY ' '
           ' ' DELIMITED BY SIZE
           WS-DAY DELIMITED BY SIZE
           ',' DELIMITED BY SIZE
           ' ' DELIMITED BY SIZE
           WS-CENTURY DELIMITED BY SIZE
               INTO FORMATTED-DATE.

999-EXIT.
    EXIT PROGRAM.

END PROGRAM CONVERT-DATE-SUB.

END PROGRAM HEADERS-SUB.

******************************************************************
******************************************************************

IDENTIFICATION DIVISION.

PROGRAM-ID.       A10-SCHEDULE-SUB.

******************************************************************
*                                                                *
*  AUTHOR.           PAQUETTE.                                   *
*  DATE WRITTEN.     MAY 1989.                                   *
*                                                                *
*       THIS SUBPROGRAM PREPARES THE ANALYSIS REPORT FOR THE     *
*  A10 RATE SCHEDULE CUSTOMERS OF PONAGANSETT ELECTRIC           *
*  COMPANY.  IT IS A CONTAINED PROGRAM AND IT SHARES DATA WITH   *
*  THE CALLING PROGRAM THROUGH THE GLOBAL QUALIFIER.             *
*                                                                *
******************************************************************
```

Figure 5.44 continued

```
ENVIRONMENT DIVISION.

DATA DIVISION.

WORKING-STORAGE SECTION.

01  A10-SCHED-ACCUMULATORS.
    05 RATE-SCHED-KWH          PIC S9(6).
    05 RATE-SCHED-INCOME       PIC S9(6)V99.

01  CALL-CTR                   PIC S9(2)    VALUE ZERO.

01  CUSTOMER-CHARGE            PIC S99V99   VALUE 01.61.

01  ENERGY-RATE                PIC SV9(5)   VALUE .08082.

PROCEDURE DIVISION.

100-PRODUCE-A10-REPORT.
    PERFORM 200-CHECK-CALL.
    IF SUMMARY-FLAG = 'ON '
        NEXT SENTENCE
    ELSE
        PERFORM 210-PROCESS-A10-CUSTOMER.
    GO TO 999-EXIT.

200-CHECK-CALL.
    ADD 1 TO CALL-CTR.
    IF CALL-CTR = 1
        CALL 'HEADERS-SUB'
        INITIALIZE A10-SCHED-ACCUMULATORS
    ELSE
        IF SUMMARY-FLAG = 'ON '
            PERFORM 300-UPDATE-COMPANY-ACCUMS
            PERFORM 310-PREPARE-A10-REPORT-SUMMARY
        END-IF
    END-IF.

210-PROCESS-A10-CUSTOMER.
    PERFORM 320-COMPUTE-BASIC-CHARGE.
14  CALL 'XTRA-CHARGE-SUB'.
    ADD WS-EXTRA-CHARGE TO WS-BASIC-CHARGE
        GIVING WS-TOTAL-AMOUNT.
    PERFORM 330-UPDATE-A10-SCHED-ACCUMS.

300-UPDATE-COMPANY-ACCUMS.
    ADD RATE-SCHED-KWH TO WS-COMPANY-KWH-RES.
    ADD RATE-SCHED-INCOME TO WS-COMPANY-INCOME-RES.

310-PREPARE-A10-REPORT-SUMMARY.
    MOVE RATE-CONTROL TO O-RATE-SCHED-2.
    MOVE RATE-SCHED-KWH TO O-RATE-SCHED-KWH.
    MOVE RATE-SCHED-INCOME TO O-RATE-SCHED-INCOME.
    WRITE PRINTLINE FROM RATE-SCHED-FOOTER-HEADER
        AFTER ADVANCING 4 LINES.
    WRITE PRINTLINE FROM RATE-SCHED-TOTALS-LINE
        AFTER ADVANCING 2 LINES.

320-COMPUTE-BASIC-CHARGE.
    COMPUTE WS-BASIC-CHARGE ROUNDED =
        CUSTOMER-CHARGE + (WS-KWH-USAGE * ENERGY-RATE).

330-UPDATE-A10-SCHED-ACCUMS.
    ADD WS-KWH-USAGE TO RATE-SCHED-KWH.
    ADD WS-TOTAL-AMOUNT TO RATE-SCHED-INCOME.

999-EXIT.
    EXIT PROGRAM.

END PROGRAM A10-SCHEDULE-SUB.

*********************************************************************
*********************************************************************

IDENTIFICATION DIVISION.

PROGRAM-ID.        A11-SCHEDULE-SUB.

*********************************************************************
*                                                                   *
*  AUTHOR.            PAQUETTE.                                     *
*  DATE WRITTEN.      MAY 1989.                                     *
*                                                                   *
*       THIS SUBPROGRAM PREPARES THE ANALYSIS REPORT FOR THE        *
*  A11 AND A12 RATE SCHEDULE CUSTOMERS OF PONAGANSETT ELECTRIC      *
*  COMPANY.  IT IS A CONTAINED PROGRAM AND IT SHARES DATA WITH      *
*  THE CALLING PROGRAM THROUGH THE GLOBAL QUALIFIER.                *
*                                                                   *
*********************************************************************
```

■ **Figure 5.44** continued

```
DATA DIVISION.

WORKING-STORAGE SECTION.

01  A11-12-SCHED-ACCUMULATORS.
    05 RATE-SCHED-KWH        PIC S9(6).
    05 RATE-SCHED-INCOME     PIC S9(6)V99.

01  CALL-CTR                 PIC S9(2)   VALUE ZERO.

01  RES-A11-A12-RATE-VALUES.
    05 PIC X(21)   VALUE '000000002000277000000'.
    05 PIC X(21)   VALUE '000200005000277010543'.
    05 PIC X(21)   VALUE '000500020000593308487'.
    05 PIC X(21)   VALUE '002000055001866405636'.
    05 PIC X(21)   VALUE '005500200003839006937'.
    05 PIC X(21)   VALUE '020009999913897706660'.

01  RES-A11-A12-TABLE REDEFINES RES-A11-A12-RATE-VALUES.
    05 USAGE-LEVEL OCCURS 6 TIMES
                   INDEXED BY RATE-INDEX.
        10 LOW-END       PIC S9(5).
        10 HIGH-END      PIC S9(5).
        10 BASE-AMOUNT   PIC S999V999.
        10 LEVEL-RATE    PIC SV9(5).

PROCEDURE DIVISION.

100-PRODUCE-A11-REPORT.
    PERFORM 200-CHECK-CALL.
    IF SUMMARY-FLAG = 'ON '
        NEXT SENTENCE
    ELSE
        PERFORM 210-PROCESS-A11-12-CUSTOMER.
    GO TO 999-EXIT.

200-CHECK-CALL.
    ADD 1 TO CALL-CTR.
    IF CALL-CTR = 1
        CALL 'HEADERS-SUB'
        INITIALIZE A11-12-SCHED-ACCUMULATORS
    ELSE
        IF SUMMARY-FLAG = 'ON '
            PERFORM 300-UPDATE-COMPANY-ACCUMS
            PERFORM 310-PREPARE-A11-REPORT-SUMMARY
        END-IF
    END-IF.

210-PROCESS-A11-12-CUSTOMER.
    PERFORM 320-COMPUTE-BASIC-CHARGE.
    CALL 'XTRA-CHARGE-SUB'.
    ADD WS-EXTRA-CHARGE TO WS-BASIC-CHARGE
        GIVING WS-TOTAL-AMOUNT.
    PERFORM 330-UPDATE-A11-12-SCHED-ACCUMS.

300-UPDATE-COMPANY-ACCUMS.
    ADD RATE-SCHED-KWH TO WS-COMPANY-KWH-RES.
    ADD RATE-SCHED-INCOME TO WS-COMPANY-INCOME-RES.

310-PREPARE-A11-REPORT-SUMMARY.
    MOVE RATE-CONTROL TO O-RATE-SCHED-2.
    MOVE RATE-SCHED-KWH TO O-RATE-SCHED-KWH.
    MOVE RATE-SCHED-INCOME TO O-RATE-SCHED-INCOME.
    WRITE PRINTLINE FROM RATE-SCHED-FOOTER-HEADER
        AFTER ADVANCING 4 LINES.
    WRITE PRINTLINE FROM RATE-SCHED-TOTALS-LINE
        AFTER ADVANCING 2 LINES.

320-COMPUTE-BASIC-CHARGE.
    SET RATE-INDEX TO 1.
    SEARCH USAGE-LEVEL
        WHEN WS-KWH-USAGE NOT > HIGH-END (RATE-INDEX)
            COMPUTE WS-BASIC-CHARGE ROUNDED =
            BASE-AMOUNT(RATE-INDEX) + LEVEL-RATE(RATE-INDEX) *
                (WS-KWH-USAGE - LOW-END(RATE-INDEX)).

330-UPDATE-A11-12-SCHED-ACCUMS.
    ADD WS-KWH-USAGE TO RATE-SCHED-KWH.
    ADD WS-TOTAL-AMOUNT TO RATE-SCHED-INCOME.

999-EXIT.
    EXIT PROGRAM.

END PROGRAM A11-SCHEDULE-SUB.
```

```
*****************************************************************
*****************************************************************

 IDENTIFICATION DIVISION.

 PROGRAM-ID.        C-2-SCHEDULE-SUB.

*****************************************************************
*                                                               *
*   AUTHOR.             PAQUETTE.                               *
*   DATE WRITTEN.       MAY 1989.                               *
*                                                               *
*        THIS SUBPROGRAM PREPARES THE ANALYSIS REPORT FOR THE   *
*   C-2 RATE SCHEDULE CUSTOMERS OF PONAGANSETT ELECTRIC         *
*   COMPANY.  IT IS A CONTAINED PROGRAM AND IT SHARES DATA WITH *
*   THE CALLING PROGRAM THROUGH THE GLOBAL QUALIFIER.           *
*                                                               *
*****************************************************************

 DATA DIVISION.

 WORKING-STORAGE SECTION.

 01  C-2-SCHED-ACCUMULATORS.
     05 RATE-SCHED-KWH       PIC S9(6).
     05 RATE-SCHED-INCOME    PIC S9(6)V99.

 01  CALL-CTR                PIC S9(2)    VALUE ZERO.

 01  CUSTOMER-CHARGE         PIC S99V99   VALUE 04.75.

 01  COM-C2-RATE-VALUES.
     05 PIC X(21)     VALUE '000000100000000009019'.
     05 PIC X(21)     VALUE '010009999909019008419'.

 01  COM-C2-RATE-TABLE REDEFINES COM-C2-RATE-VALUES.
     05 USAGE-LEVEL OCCURS 2 TIMES
                    INDEXED BY RATE-INDEX.
         10 LOW-END        PIC S9(5).
         10 HIGH-END       PIC S9(5).
         10 BASE-AMOUNT    PIC S999V999.
         10 LEVEL-RATE     PIC SV9(5).

 PROCEDURE DIVISION.

 100-PRODUCE-C-2-REPORT.
     PERFORM 200-CHECK-CALL.
     IF SUMMARY-FLAG = 'ON '
         NEXT SENTENCE
     ELSE
         PERFORM 210-PROCESS-C-2-CUSTOMER.
     GO TO 999-EXIT.

 200-CHECK-CALL.
     ADD 1 TO CALL-CTR.
     IF CALL-CTR = 1
         CALL 'HEADERS-SUB'
         INITIALIZE C-2-SCHED-ACCUMULATORS
     ELSE
         IF SUMMARY-FLAG = 'ON '
             PERFORM 300-UPDATE-COMPANY-ACCUMS
             PERFORM 310-PREPARE-C-2-REPORT-SUMMARY
         END-IF
     END-IF.

 210-PROCESS-C-2-CUSTOMER.
     PERFORM 320-COMPUTE-BASIC-CHARGE.
     CALL 'XTRA-CHARGE-SUB'.
     ADD WS-EXTRA-CHARGE TO WS-BASIC-CHARGE
         GIVING WS-TOTAL-AMOUNT.
     PERFORM 330-UPDATE-C-2-SCHED-ACCUMS.

 300-UPDATE-COMPANY-ACCUMS.
     ADD RATE-SCHED-KWH TO WS-COMPANY-KWH-COMM.
     ADD RATE-SCHED-INCOME TO WS-COMPANY-INCOME-COMM.

 310-PREPARE-C-2-REPORT-SUMMARY.
     MOVE RATE-CONTROL TO O-RATE-SCHED-2.
     MOVE RATE-SCHED-KWH TO O-RATE-SCHED-KWH.
     MOVE RATE-SCHED-INCOME TO O-RATE-SCHED-INCOME.
     WRITE PRINTLINE FROM RATE-SCHED-FOOTER-HEADER
         AFTER ADVANCING 4 LINES.
     WRITE PRINTLINE FROM RATE-SCHED-TOTALS-LINE
         AFTER ADVANCING 2 LINES.
```

```
320-COMPUTE-BASIC-CHARGE.
    SET RATE-INDEX TO 1.
    SEARCH USAGE-LEVEL
        WHEN WS-KWH-USAGE NOT > HIGH-END (RATE-INDEX)
        COMPUTE WS-BASIC-CHARGE ROUNDED =
            BASE-AMOUNT(RATE-INDEX) +
            LEVEL-RATE(RATE-INDEX) *
            (WS-KWH-USAGE - LOW-END(RATE-INDEX)).
    ADD CUSTOMER-CHARGE TO WS-BASIC-CHARGE.

330-UPDATE-C-2-SCHED-ACCUMS.
    ADD WS-KWH-USAGE TO RATE-SCHED-KWH.
    ADD WS-TOTAL-AMOUNT TO RATE-SCHED-INCOME.

999-EXIT.
    EXIT PROGRAM.

END PROGRAM C-2-SCHEDULE-SUB.

*****************************************************************
*****************************************************************

IDENTIFICATION DIVISION.

15  PROGRAM-ID.  XTRA-CHARGE-SUB        COMMON.

*****************************************************************
*                                                               *
*  AUTHOR.             PAQUETTE.                                *
*  DATE WRITTEN.       MAY 1989.                                *
*                                                               *
*  THE PURPOSE OF THIS SUBPROGRAM IS TO COMPUTE EXTRA CHARGES   *
*  ASSESSED TO ALL CUSTOMERS OF THE PONAGANSETT ELECTRIC COMPANY.*
*  THESE CHARGES CHANGE PERIODICALLY.  THEY FALL INTO THREE     *
*  CLASSIFICATIONS:  FUEL ADJUSTMENT CHARGE, OIL CONSERVATION   *
*  ADJUSTMENT CHARGE, AND THE UNIFORM CONSERVATION COST ADJUST- *
*  MENT PROGRAM CHARGE.  THESE EXTRA CHARGES ARE DEFINED AND    *
*  INITIALIZED IN THE WORKING-STORAGE SECTION.                  *
*                                                               *
*  THE SUBPROGRAM SHARES DATA WITH THE CALLING PROGRAM THROUGH  *
*  THE USE OF THE GLOBAL QUALIFIER.  MOREOVER, IT IS DEFINED AS *
*  A COMMON PROGRAM AND IS ACCESSED BY OTHER SUBPROGRAMS IN THE *
*  RUN UNIT.                                                    *
*                                                               *
*****************************************************************

DATA DIVISION.

WORKING-STORAGE SECTION.

01  EXTRA-CHARGE-RATES.
    05 FAC          PIC SV9(5)   VALUE .00735.
    05 OCA          PIC SV9(5)   VALUE .00093.
    05 UCCA         PIC SV9(5)   VALUE .00009.

PROCEDURE DIVISION.

100-COMPUTE-EXTRA-CHARGE.
    COMPUTE WS-EXTRA-CHARGE ROUNDED =
        WS-KWH-USAGE * (FAC + OCA + UCCA).

999-EXIT.
    EXIT PROGRAM.

END PROGRAM XTRA-CHARGE-SUB.

16  END PROGRAM PON-ELECTRIC-MAIN.

*****************************************************************
*****************************************************************
```

Figure 5.45 Analysis reports of run unit 4

MAY 30, 1989 PONAGANSETT ELECTRIC COMPANY

RATE SCHEDULE A10 REPORT

RATE SCHEDULE	CLASS	AREA	CUSTOMER NUMBER	CUSTOMER	PREVIOUS READING	CURRENT READING	USAGE	TOTAL CHARGE
A10	RESIDENTIAL	RI1	101235	FLYNN, ROGER P.	42131	42482	351	$ 32.92
A10	RESIDENTIAL	RI1	106176	KOLAKOWSKI, CASIMIR	05240	05712	472	$ 43.71
A10	RESIDENTIAL	RI1	120190	WAREHAM, JOSEPH F.	13962	14387	425	$ 39.52
A10	RESIDENTIAL	RI1	138625	FRYE, LOUISE N.	01106	01523	417	$ 38.80
A10	RESIDENTIAL	RI1	157133	GOUDREAU, ELIZABETH	65659	66235	576	$ 52.98
A10	RESIDENTIAL	RI1	161394	JOZEFOWICZ, SANDRA	37692	38007	315	$ 29.71
A10	RESIDENTIAL	RI1	177505	MASSE, EUGENE	05170	05703	533	$ 49.15
A10	RESIDENTIAL	RI1	190324	MANDEL, ROLANDE J.	10768	11240	472	$ 43.71
A10	RESIDENTIAL	RI1	193005	SCULLY, CLARA B.	06934	07446	512	$ 47.28
A10	RESIDENTIAL	RI2	212433	DION, GERARD M.	23474	23995	521	$ 48.08
A10	RESIDENTIAL	RI2	223944	HODGE, KEVIN J.	77319	77824	505	$ 46.65
A10	RESIDENTIAL	RI2	248375	CADY, RAYMOND F.	15176	15533	357	$ 33.45
A10	RESIDENTIAL	RI2	252100	GASPAR, RAOUL	23575	24027	452	$ 41.92
A10	RESIDENTIAL	RI2	275690	HENNESSY, ROBERT J.	39015	39517	502	$ 46.38
A10	RESIDENTIAL	RI2	278170	LUDOVICI, LUIGI	02860	03224	364	$ 34.08
A10	RESIDENTIAL	RI2	285374	PARKS, EMERY R.	10746	11158	412	$ 38.36
A10	RESIDENTIAL	RI3	302010	BENNETT, CLARENCE W.	23745	24228	483	$ 44.69
A10	RESIDENTIAL	RI3	331166	DIGUILIO, EMILIO M.	56613	56997	384	$ 35.85
A10	RESIDENTIAL	RI3	367150	BROWN, GEORGE W.	32065	32589	524	$ 48.35
A10	RESIDENTIAL	RI3	391450	DEWEY, FRANCES D.	11212	11624	412	$ 38.36

TOTALS FOR RATE SCHEDULE A10	KWH	INCOME
	8,989	$ 833.95

MAY 30, 1989 PONAGANSETT ELECTRIC COMPANY

RATE SCHEDULE A11 REPORT

RATE SCHEDULE	CLASS	AREA	CUSTOMER NUMBER	CUSTOMER	PREVIOUS READING	CURRENT READING	USAGE	TOTAL CHARGE
A11	RESIDENTIAL	RI1	131211	KEATING, SUSAN A.	07070	08110	1040	$ 81.08
A11	RESIDENTIAL	RI1	153276	BERGERON, FRANK S.	41038	41756	718	$ 56.05
A11	RESIDENTIAL	RI1	160216	GATTO, JANICE L.	10518	11450	932	$ 72.69
A11	RESIDENTIAL	RI2	241694	LAMOUNTAIN, LOUISE	40241	41016	775	$ 60.49
A11	RESIDENTIAL	RI2	262025	KLEIN, LAURALYNN	57082	57811	729	$ 56.91
A11	RESIDENTIAL	RI3	345943	MCCARTHY, EUGENE F.	27534	28646	1112	$ 86.69
A11	RESIDENTIAL	RI3	384000	PRECOURT, JEAN M.	08625	09562	937	$ 73.08

TOTALS FOR RATE SCHEDULE A11	KWH	INCOME
	6,243	$ 486.99

■ **Figure 5.45** continued

MAY 30, 1989 PONAGANSETT ELECTRIC COMPANY

RATE SCHEDULE A12 REPORT

RATE SCHEDULE	CLASS	AREA	CUSTOMER NUMBER	CUSTOMER	PREVIOUS READING	CURRENT READING	USAGE	TOTAL CHARGE
A12	RESIDENTIAL	RI1	100140	NARDONE, MARY E.	14024	14997	973	$ 75.87
A12	RESIDENTIAL	RI1	110025	ASSELIN, JANICE M.	21421	22300	879	$ 68.57
A12	RESIDENTIAL	RI1	135400	CONNELL, FRED C.	35235	36157	922	$ 71.92
A12	RESIDENTIAL	RI1	155900	LOUGHERY, KATRINA	30481	31624	1143	$ 89.10
A12	RESIDENTIAL	RI1	173731	MCFADDEN, MICHAEL R.	58083	59347	1264	$ 98.50
A12	RESIDENTIAL	RI1	175571	LETENDRE, THOMAS F.	46212	47210	998	$ 77.82
A12	RESIDENTIAL	RI2	201055	NICOLETTA, JOHN J.	51935	52917	982	$ 76.58
A12	RESIDENTIAL	RI2	220020	CHOW, SHUI	09788	10714	926	$ 72.22
A12	RESIDENTIAL	RI2	245400	PATALANO, SAMANTHA	02527	03435	908	$ 70.82
A12	RESIDENTIAL	RI2	282985	HUMMEL, STELLA	40107	41153	1046	$ 81.56
A12	RESIDENTIAL	RI3	305327	PETRUSKA, MARIE	01240	02219	979	$ 76.34
A12	RESIDENTIAL	RI3	342314	CALLAHAN, JOHN J.	10406	11459	1053	$ 82.09
A12	RESIDENTIAL	RI3	394765	GARDNER, LEO F.	35437	36562	1125	$ 87.70

TOTALS FOR RATE SCHEDULE A12	KWH	INCOME
	13,198	$ 1,029.09

MAY 30, 1989 PONAGANSETT ELECTRIC COMPANY

RATE SCHEDULE C-2 REPORT

RATE SCHEDULE	CLASS	AREA	CUSTOMER NUMBER	CUSTOMER	PREVIOUS READING	CURRENT READING	USAGE	TOTAL CHARGE
C-2	COMMERCIAL	RI1	103041	BEST FURNITURE INC.	66565	68711	2146	$ 209.38
C-2	COMMERCIAL	RI1	115722	GLORIA'S BEAUTY SHOP	34858	39208	4350	$ 413.39
C-2	COMMERCIAL	RI1	150950	TINY-TOT NURSERY	12720	14355	1635	$ 162.08
C-2	COMMERCIAL	RI1	159005	COPTER SERVICE	43309	45292	1983	$ 194.30
C-2	COMMERCIAL	RI1	182162	EVA'S FRUIT STORE	32571	34713	2142	$ 209.01
C-2	COMMERCIAL	RI2	205182	RAY TRUCKING CO.	34821	37197	2376	$ 230.68
C-2	COMMERCIAL	RI2	232132	PETE'S AUTO SUPPLIES	68652	70636	1984	$ 194.39
C-2	COMMERCIAL	RI2	275364	DORIS BAKERY SHOP	74992	78134	3142	$ 301.57
C-2	COMMERCIAL	RI3	320400	MARK MARINE SERVICE	49373	51447	2074	$ 202.72
C-2	COMMERCIAL	RI3	363770	GERRY'S SEAFOODS	45198	48660	3462	$ 331.20

TOTALS FOR RATE SCHEDULE C-2	KWH	INCOME
	25,294	$ 2,448.72

SUMMARY

1. TOTAL KWH SOLD TO COMMERCIAL CUSTOMERS 25,294
   TOTAL INCOME FROM COMMERCIAL CUSTOMERS $ 2,448.72

2. TOTAL KWH SOLD TO RESIDENTIAL CUSTOMERS 28,430
   TOTAL INCOME FROM RESIDENTIAL CUSTOMERS $ 2,350.03

*** END OF REPORT ***

Comments on the Nested Programs in Figure 5.45

1. This IDENTIFICATION DIVISION begins the source code for the main and containing program PON-ELECTRIC-MAIN. Note that the last source code line is END PROGRAM PON-ELECTRIC-MAIN.
2. The GLOBAL qualifier makes the record SORTED-CUSTOMER-RECORD and its subordinate items, including condition-names, available to all the subprograms contained directly or indirectly within main program PON-ELECTRIC-MAIN. However, the only data item needed is I-RATE-SCHEDULE, and it is needed in subprogram HEADERS-SUB.
3. The GLOBAL qualifier makes the output file ANALYSIS-REPORT and its record PRINTLINE available to all the subprograms contained within the main program. It is referenced in every subprogram except CONVERT-DATE-SUB and XTRA-CHARGE-SUB.
4. The GLOBAL qualifier makes the subordinate items of SHARED-DATA available to all the subprograms contained within the main program. They are referenced in every subprogram except HEADERS-SUB and its contained subprogram CONVERT-DATE-SUB.
5. The GLOBAL qualifier makes the subordinate items of COMPANY-ACCUMULATORS available to all the subprograms contained within the main program. They are referenced in the three rate schedule subprograms.
6. The GLOBAL qualifier makes the subordinate items of RATE-SCHED-FOOTING-LINES available to all the subprograms contained within the main program. The two subordinate group items RATE-SCHED-FOOTER-HEADER and RATE-SCHED-TOTALS-LINE are referenced in the three rate schedule subprograms.
7. The EVALUATE statement is used to select the appropriate rate schedule subprogram that must be CALLed to properly process a customer record.
8. The detail CUSTOMER-LINE is prepared within the main program to avoid carrying out the same function in each of the three rate schedule subprograms.
9. This CALL statement is needed to force the printing of the summary information for rate schedule C-2.
10. This paragraph contains the rate schedule control break. When it occurs, the EVALUATE statement is used to assign the appropriate rate schedule subprogram name to the identifier SUBPROG and the summary flag is set to "ON ". When the statement CALL SUBPROG is executed, summary information is printed on the report for the appropriate rate schedule. Upon returning control from the subprogram, the statement CANCEL SUBPROG disconnects the subprogram from the run unit and the summary flag is set to "OFF." Note that when summary information has been printed for rate schedule A11, the subprogram A11-SCHEDULE-SUB is disconnected. However, when the first customer record belonging to the A12 rate schedule is processed, subprogram A11-SCHEDULE-SUB is called again. At this point, it is in its *initial* state, and as such, its accumulators, including CALL-CTR, are reset to zero, as they should be to properly process this new group of customer records.
11. Note the nesting of the subprograms that follow. You may wish to draw brackets from a program's IDENTIFICATION DIVISION header to its END PROGRAM header to more clearly see the nesting.
12. Note the use of the COMMON qualifier. This program is callable from every subprogram except its own contained subprogram CONVERT-DATE-SUB. HEADERS-SUB is in fact called by the three rate schedule subprograms.
13. Subprogram CONVERT-DATE-SUB is called when control enters HEADERS-SUB the first time. That is, the report date is formatted only once. Note the USING phrase in the CALL statement.
14. The CALL statement that transfers control to subprogram XTRA-CHARGE-SUB does not specify the USING phrase. Note that the extra charge computed by the subprogram is stored in the data item WS-EXTRA-CHARGE. In the statement that follows the CALL, WS-EXTRA-CHARGE is available, because it is defined as a global item in the main program.
15. Because this subprogram has been defined as common, it is callable by the main program as well as by all the subprograms of the run unit. Specifically, it is called by the three rate schedule subprograms.
16. The last line of source code is the END PROGRAM header for the main program. All other programs of the run unit are completely contained or nested within the main program.

Important Terms in Chapter 5

BY CONTENT
BY REFERENCE
CALL
CALL-USING
callable
called program
calling program
CANCEL
COMMON
contained program
containing program
END PROGRAM
END-CALL
EXIT PROGRAM
EXTERNAL
GLOBAL
INITIAL
link-edit
LINKAGE SECTION
main program
nested programs
ON EXCEPTION
ON OVERFLOW
PROCEDURE DIVISION USING
run unit
separately compiled
sharing data
STRING
subprogram

Exercises

1. Given the following record descriptions in calling program MAIN-PROG,

```
01  EMPLOYEE-RECORD.                 01  WORK-AREAS.
    05 I-SSN        PIC X(9).            05 WS-GROSS-WAGES   PIC S9(4)V99.
    05 I-NAME       PIC X(20).           05 WS-NET-WAGES     PIC S9(4)V99.
    05 I-REG-HRS    PIC 9(2).
    05 I-OT-HRS     PIC 9(2).
    05 I-PAY-RATE   PIC 999V99.
```

   a. code an appropriate CALL statement to make the values stored in the fields I-REG-HRS, I-OT-HRS, and I-PAY-RATE available to subprogram WAGES-SUB such that they cannot be changed by the subprogram.
   b. subject to part a above, name two required entries in subprogram WAGES-SUB.
   c. subject to parts a and b and the record descriptions above, code appropriate required entries in the subprogram.

2. Given the following record descriptions in calling program MAIN-PROG,

```
01  EMPLOYEE-RECORD  EXTERNAL.   01  WORK-AREAS  EXTERNAL.
    05 I-SSN       PIC X(9).         05 WS-GROSS-WAGES   PIC S9(4)V99.
    05 I-NAME      PIC X(20).        05 WS-NET-WAGES     PIC S9(4)V99.
    05 I-REG-HRS   PIC 9(2).
    05 I-OT-HRS    PIC 9(2).
    05 I-PAY-RATE  PIC 999V99.
```

   a. code the statement in MAIN-PROG that transfers control to subprogram WAGES-SUB.
   b. if subprogram WAGES-SUB is to have access to the data items of the records EMPLOYEE-RECORD and WORK-AREAS, code the required entries in the subprogram.
   c. subject to parts a and b above, code the PROCEDURE DIVISION header in subprogram WAGES-SUB.
   d. code the statement in subprogram WAGES-SUB that returns control to the calling program MAIN-PROG.

3. Given the following record descriptions in calling program MAIN-PROG,

```
01  EMPLOYEE-RECORD  GLOBAL.    01  WORK-AREAS  GLOBAL.
    05 I-SSN       PIC X(9).        05 WS-GROSS-WAGES   PIC S9(4)V99.
    05 I-NAME      PIC X(20).       05 WS-NET-WAGES     PIC S9(4)V99.
    05 I-REG-HRS   PIC 9(2).
    05 I-OT-HRS    PIC 9(2).
    05 I-PAY-RATE  PIC 999V99.
```

   a. code the statement in MAIN-PROG that transfers control to contained subprogram WAGES-SUB.
   b. subject to part a and the record descriptions above, identify the entries in contained subprogram WAGES-SUB that are required to make the record data items accessible by the subprogram.
   c. code the statement in contained subprogram WAGES-SUB that returns control to the calling program MAIN-PROG.

4. If a run unit consists of main program MAIN-PROG and the two separately compiled subprograms SUB1 and SUB2,
   a. name the programs that may be calling programs.
   b. name the programs that may be called programs.
   c. name two procedures that may be used to share data between calling and called programs.

5. If data is shared between a calling program and a called program by
   a. the USING phrase of the CALL statement, does the called program have direct access to the storage areas that contain the data?
   b. the EXTERNAL qualifier, does the called program have direct access to the storage areas that contain the data?
   c. the GLOBAL qualifier, does the called program have direct access to the storage areas that contain the data?
6. If a run unit consists of a main program and two nested programs as shown below,
   a. identify the programs that are callable by MAIN-PROG.
   b. identify the programs that are callable by SUB1.
   c. identify the programs that are callable by SUB2.

   Run Unit:

```
IDENTIFICATION DIVISION.
PROGRAM-ID.   MAIN-PROG.
.
.
.
IDENTIFICATION DIVISION.
PROGRAM-ID.   SUB1.
.
.
.
    EXIT PROGRAM.
IDENTIFICATION DIVISION.
PROGRAM-ID.   SUB2.
.
.
.
    EXIT PROGRAM.
END PROGRAM SUB2.
END PROGRAM SUB1.
END PROGRAM MAIN-PROG.
```

7. Given the run unit shown below,

   Run Unit:

```
IDENTIFICATION DIVISION.
PROGRAM-ID.   MAIN-PROG.
.
.
.
IDENTIFICATION DIVISION.
PROGRAM-ID.   SUB1 COMMON.
.
.
.
    EXIT PROGRAM.
IDENTIFICATION DIVISION.
PROGRAM-ID.   SUB2.
.
.
.
    EXIT PROGRAM.
END PROGRAM SUB2.
END PROGRAM SUB1.
IDENTIFICATION DIVISION.
PROGRAM-ID.   SUB3.
.
.
.
    EXIT PROGRAM.
END PROGRAM SUB3.
END PROGRAM MAIN-PROG.
```

   a. name the programs that are callable by MAIN-PROG.
   b. name the programs that are callable by SUB1.
   c. name the programs that are callable by SUB2.
   d. name the programs that are callable by SUB3.
8. In Figure 5.31, recode the divisions of the nested program ASC-COMPUTE-SALE-AMT-SUB (except the IDENTIFICATION DIVISION) such that the discount rate is defined in working storage as the data item DISCOUNT-RATE and is initialized to .80.

Figure 5.46 Printer spacing chart for the social security tax report

Printer Spacing Chart

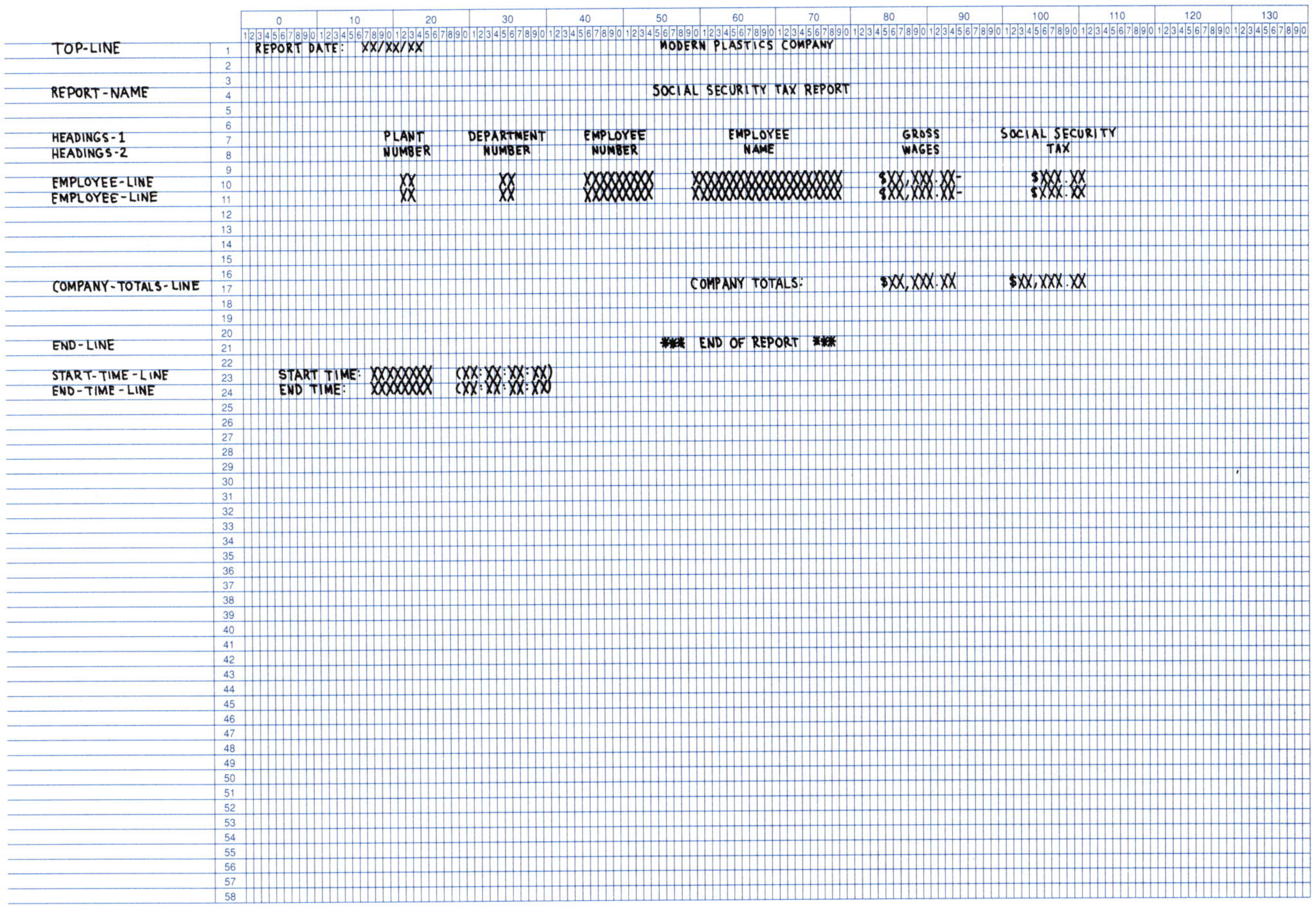

Debugging Activities

1. A student was assigned the task of developing a program whose function is to prepare a report formatted as shown in Figure 5.46.

   The run unit must contain two subprograms, one to compute the Social Security tax that must be levied on an employee's gross wages and the other to obtain the time from the operating system and format it as required for the report. The subprograms have been named SS-TAX-SUB and TIME-SUB, respectively. Subprogram SS-TAX-SUB must be nested within the main program, and subprogram TIME-SUB must be separately compiled. The current Social Security tax rate is 7.51 percent.

   When the time is obtained from the operating system, it is made available to the program as an 8-digit string: a 2-digit hour identifier on a 24-hour clock, a 2-digit minute identifier, a 2-digit second identifier, and a 2-digit hundreths of a second identifier. For instance, 08354275 means 8 hours, 35 minutes, 42 seconds, and 75 hundreths of a second. The subprogram TIME-SUB must convert this time value into two forms, specifically 8:36 A.M. (the time rounded to the nearest minute) and 08:35:42:75, and return them to the main program. (*Note:* The string 15241040 must be converted to 3:24 P.M. and to 15:24:10:40.) The report must print the time when the computer began executing the PROCEDURE DIVISION of the program and the time when it reached the end of program execution.

   Unfortunately, when an attempt was made to compile the programs of the run unit, several syntax errors were flagged. The compiler-generated program listings follow. Your task is to remove all syntax errors from the programs.

```
MODERN-PLASTICS-DBG1\MODERN-PLASTICS-DBG1          10-Aug-1989 13:16:16    VAX COBOL V4.2-40                        Page   1
Source Listing                                     10-Aug-1989 13:15:59    [PAQUETTEG.CHAPTER8V2]V2C8DBG1.COB;4 (1)

        IDENTIFICATION DIVISION.

        PROGRAM-ID.  MODERN-PLASTICS-DBG1.

       ******************************************************************
       *                                                                *
       *  AUTHOR.           PAQUETTE.                                   *
       *  DATE WRITTEN.  AUGUST, 1989                                   *
       *                                                                *
       ******************************************************************

       ENVIRONMENT DIVISION.

       CONFIGURATION SECTION.

       SOURCE-COMPUTER.  VAX-VMS-8650.
       OBJECT-COMPUTER.  VAX-VMS-8650.

       INPUT-OUTPUT SECTION.

       FILE-CONTROL.
           SELECT PAYROLL-FILE     ASSIGN TO COB$INPUT.
           SELECT PAYROLL-REPORT   ASSIGN TO COB$OUTPUT.
                  1
%COBOL-E-ERROR  333, (1) WRITE statement on this file conflicts with its OPEN mode

       DATA DIVISION.

       FILE SECTION.

       FD  PAYROLL-FILE
           RECORD CONTAINS 80 CHARACTERS.

       01  EMPLOYEE-RECORD.
           05                      PIC X(2).
           05 I-PLANT-NO           PIC X(2).
           05 I-DEPT-NO            PIC X(2).
           05 I-SSN                PIC X(9).
           05 I-EMPLOYEE-NAME      PIC X(20).
           05                      PIC X(3).
           05 I-PAYRATE            PIC 99V99.
           05 I-REG-HRS            PIC X(2).
           05 I-OT-HRS             PIC 9(2).
           05                      PIC X(34).

       FD  PAYROLL-REPORT
           RECORD CONTAINS 133 CHARACTERS.

       01  PRINTLINE                PIC X(133).

       WORKING-STORAGE SECTION.

       01  PROGRAM-CONTROLS.
           05 WS-MORE-RECORDS          PIC X(3).
              88 NO-MORE-RECORDS       VALUE "NO ".
           05 WS-PROPER-SPACING        PIC 9.
           05 WS-REPORT-DATE           PIC X(6).
```

```
  1
  1          01  EMPLOYEE-WORK-AREA.
  1              05 WS-GROSS-WAGES        PIC S9(6)V99.
  1              05 WS-SS-TAX             PIC S9(3)V99.
  1
  1          01  COMPANY-ACCUMULATORS.
  1              05 WS-TOTAL-GROSS-WAGES  PIC S9(7)V99.
  1              05 WS-TOTAL-SS-TAX       PIC S9(5)V99.
  1
  1          01  REPORT-HEADERS.
  1
  1              05 TOP-LINE.
  1                  10                 PIC X(16)  VALUE "  REPORT DATE:  ".
  1                  10 O-REPORT-DATE   PIC XX-XX-XX.
                                            1
%COBOL-F-ERROR  156, (1) Invalid PICTURE character-string
  1                  10                 PIC X(31)  VALUE SPACES.
  1                  10                 PIC X(23)  VALUE
  1                                     "MODERN PLASTICS COMPANY".
  1                  10                 PIC X(55)  VALUE SPACES.
  1
  1              05 REPORT-NAME.
  1                  10 PIC X(54)  VALUE SPACES.
  1                  10 PIC X(26)  VALUE "SOCIAL SECURITY TAX REPORT".
  1                  10 PIC X(53)  VALUE SPACES.
  1
  1              05 HEADINGS-1.
  1                  10 PIC X(19)  VALUE SPACES.
  1                  10 PIC X(5)   VALUE "PLANT".
  1                  10 PIC X(6)   VALUE SPACES.
  1                  10 PIC X(10)  VALUE "DEPARTMENT".
  1                  10 PIC X(5)   VALUE SPACES.
  1                  10 PIC X(8)   VALUE "EMPLOYEE".
  1                  10 PIC X(11)  VALUE SPACES.
  1                  10 PIC X(8)   VALUE "EMPLOYEE".
  1                  10 PIC X(15)  VALUE SPACES.
  1                  10 PIC X(5)   VALUE "GROSS".
  1                  10 PIC X(8)   VALUE SPACES.
  1                  10 PIC X(15)  VALUE "SOCIAL SECURITY".
  1                  10 PIC X(18)  VALUE SPACES.
  1
  1              05 HEADINGS-2.
  1                  10 PIC X(19)  VALUE SPACES.
  1                  10 PIC X(6)   VALUE "NUMBER".
  1                  10 PIC X(7)   VALUE SPACES.
  1                  10 PIC X(6)   VALUE "NUMBER".
  1                  10 PIC X(8)   VALUE SPACES.
  1                  10 PIC X(6)   VALUE "NUMBER".
  1                  10 PIC X(14)  VALUE SPACES.
  1                  10 PIC X(4)   VALUE "NAME".
  1                  10 PIC X(17)  VALUE SPACES.
  1                  10 PIC X(5)   VALUE "WAGES".
  1                  10 PIC X(14)  VALUE SPACES.
  1                  10 PIC X(3)   VALUE "TAX".
  1                  10 PIC X(24)  VALUE SPACES.
  1
  1          01  EMPLOYEE-LINE.
```

```
MODERN-PLASTICS-DBG1\MODERN-PLASTICS-DBG1        10-Aug-1989 13:16:16    VAX COBOL V4.2-40             Page   3
Source Listing                                   10-Aug-1989 13:15:59    [PAQUETTEG.CHAPTER8V2]V2C8DBG1.COB;4 (1)

   1              05                     PIC X(21).
   1              05 O-PLANT-NO          PIC X(2).
   1              05                     PIC X(11).
   1              05 O-DEPT-NO           PIC X(2).
   1              05                     PIC X(9).
   1              05 O-SSN               PIC X(9).
   1              05                     PIC X(5).
   1              05 O-EMPLOYEE-NAME     PIC X(20).
   1              05                     PIC X(5).
   1              05 O-GROSS-WAGES       PIC $ZZ,ZZ9.99-.
   1              05                     PIC X(9).
   1              05 O-SSN-TAX           PIC $ZZ9.99.
   1              05                     PIC X(21).
   1
   1          01  COMPANY-TOTALS-LINE.
   1              05                      PIC X(59)  VALUE SPACES.
   1              05                      PIC X(16)  VALUE "COMPANY TOTALS: ".
   1              05                      PIC X(9)   VALUE SPACES.
   1              05 O-TOTAL-GROSS-WAGES PIC $ZZ,ZZ9.99.
   1              05                      PIC X(7)   VALUE.
                                                          1
%COBOL-F-ERROR  119, (1) Invalid clause in record description
   1              05 O-TOTAL-SS-TAX       PIC $ZZ,ZZ9.99.
   1
   1          01  TIME-LINES.
   1              05 START-TIME-LINE.
   1                 10                  PIC X(5)   VALUE SPACES.
   1                 10                  PIC X(12)  VALUE "START TIME: ".
   1                 10 O-START-TIME-1 PIC X(8).
   1                 10                  PIC X(3)   VALUE SPACES.
   1                 10                  PIC X(1)   VALUE "(".
   1                 10 O-START-TIME-2 PIC X(11).
   1                 10                  PIC X(1)   VALUE ")".
   1
   1              05 END-TIME-LINE.
   1                 10                  PIC X(5)   VALUE SPACES.
   1                 10                  PIC X(12)  VALUE "END TIME:   ".
   1                 10 O-END-TIME-1     PIC X(8).
   1                 10                  PIC X(3)   VALUE SPACES.
   1                 10                  PIC X(1)   VALUE "(".
   1                 10 O-END-TIME-2     PIC X(11).
   1                 10                  PIC X(1)   VALUE ")".
   1
   1          01  END-LINE.
   1              05 PIC X(55)  VALUE SPACES.
   1              05 PIC X(23)  VALUE "***  END OF REPORT  ***".
   1              05 PIC X(55)  VALUE SPACES.
   1
   1          PROCEDURE DIVISION.
   1
   1          100-PRODUCE-PAYROLL-REPORT.
   1              PERFORM 200-START-UP.
   1              PERFORM 210-PROCESS-EMPLOYEE-RECORD
   1                  UNTIL NO-MORE-RECORDS.
   1              PERFORM 220-FINISH-UP.
   1
   1          200-START-UP.
```

```
      1           OPEN INPUT PAYROLL-FILE
      1                      PAYROLL-REPORT.
      1           SET THERE-IS-A-RECORD TO TRUE.
                      1
%COBOL-F-ERROR  349, (1) Undefined name
      1           INITIALIZE COMPANY-ACCUMULATORS.
      1           PERFORM 300-WRITE-REPORT-HEADERS.
      1           PERFORM 310-READ-EMPLOYEE-RECORD.
      1
      1       210-PROCESS-EMPLOYEE-RECORD.
      1           PERFORM 320-COMPUTE-EMPLOYEE-ITEMS.
      1           PERFORM 330-PREPARE-EMPLOYEE-LINE.
      1           PERFORM 340-UPDATE-COMPANY-ACCUMULATORS.
      1           PERFORM 310-READ-EMPLOYEE-RECORD.
      1
      1       220-FINISH-UP.
      1           PERFORM 350-PRODUCE-COMPANY-TOTALS.
      1           WRITE PRINTLINE FROM END-LINE
      1               AFTER ADVANCING 5 LINES.
      1           WRITE PRINTLINE FROM START-TIME-LINE
      1               AFTER ADVANCING 2 LINES.
      1           CALL TIME-SUB USING O-END-TIME-1.
                                  1
%COBOL-F-ERROR  349, (1) Undefined name
      1           WRITE PRINTLINE FROM END-TIME-LINE
                  1
%COBOL-W-ERROR  297, (1) Processing of source program resumes at this point
      1               AFTER ADVANCING 1 LINE.
      1           CLOSE PAYROLL-FILE
      1                 PAYROLL-REPORT.
      1
      1       300-WRITE-REPORT-HEADERS.
      1           WRITE PRINTLINE FROM TOP-LINE
      1               AFTER ADVANCING PAGE.
      1           WRITE PRINTLINE FROM REPORT-NAME
      1               AFTER ADVANCING 3 LINES.
      1           WRITE PRINTLINE FROM HEADINGS-1
      1               AFTER ADVANCING 3 LINES.
      1           WRITE PRINTLINE FROM HEADINGS-2
      1               AFTER ADVANCING 1 LINE.
      1           MOVE 2 TO WS-PROPER-SPACING.
      1
      1       310-READ-EMPLOYEE-RECORD.
      1           READ PAYROLL-FILE RECORD
      1               AT END
      1                   SET NO-MORE-RECORDS TO TRUE.
      1
      1       320-COMPUTE-EMPLOYEE-ITEMS.
      1           CALL SS-TAX-SUB.
                        1
%COBOL-F-ERROR  349, (1) Undefined name
      1           COMPUTE WS-GROSS-WAGES ROUNDED =
                  1
%COBOL-W-ERROR  297, (1) Processing of source program resumes at this point
      1               I-PAYRATE * (I-REG-HRS + I-OT-HRS * 1.5).
                                        1
%COBOL-F-ERROR  276, (1) Operand must be a numeric data-name or a numeric literal
```

```
    1
    1          330-PREPARE-EMPLOYEE-LINE.
    1              MOVE I-PLANT-NO TO O-PLANT-NO-1.
                                      1
%COBOL-F-ERROR  349, (1) Undefined name
    1              MOVE I-DEPT-NO TO O-DEPT-NO.
    1              MOVE I-SSN TO O-SSN.
    1              MOVE I-EMPLOYEE-NAME TO O-EMPLOYEE-NAME.
    1              MOVE WS-SSN-TAX TO O-SS-TAX.
                        1               2
%COBOL-F-ERROR  349, (1) Undefined name
%COBOL-F-ERROR  349, (2) Undefined name
    1              WRITE PRINTLINE FROM EMPLOYEE-LINE
                   1
%COBOL-W-ERROR  297, (1) Processing of source program resumes at this point
    1                  AFTER ADVANCING WS-PROPER-SPACING.
    1              MOVE 1 TO WS-PROPER-SPACING.
    1
    1          340-UPDATE-COMPANY-ACCUMULATORS.
    1              ADD WS-GROSS-WAGES TO WS-TOTAL-GROSS-WAGES.
    1              ADD WS-GROSS-WAGES TO WS-TOTAL-GROSS-WAGES.
    1
    1          350-PRODUCE-COMPANY-TOTALS.
    1              MOVE WS-TOTAL-GROSS-WAGES TO O-TOTAL-GROSS-WAGES.
    1              MOVE WS-TOTAL-SS-TAX TO O-TOTAL-SS-TAX.
    1              WRITE PRINTLINE FROM COMPANY-TOTALS-LINE
    1                  AFTER ADVANCING 2 LINES.
```

```
        2
        2    ****************************************************************
        2    *                                                              *
        2    *                     SS-TAX-SUB FOLLOWS                       *
        2    *                                                              *
        2    ****************************************************************
        2
        2     IDENTIFICATION DIVISION.
        2
        2     PROGRAM-ID.  SS-TAX-SUB.
        2
        2     DATA DIVISION.
        2
        2     WORKING-STORAGE SECTION.
        2
        2     01  SS-TAX-RATE     PIC V9999    VALUE ".0751".
                  1
%COBOL-E-ERROR   84, (1) Literal in VALUE clause conflicts with description - clause ignored
        2
        2     PROCEDURE DIVISION.
        2
        2     100-COMPUTE-SS-TAX.
        2         MULTIPLY WS-GROSS-WAGES BY SS-TAX-RATE
                           1
%COBOL-F-ERROR  349, (1) Undefined name
        2             GIVING WS-SS-TAX ROUNDED.
                             1
%COBOL-F-ERROR  349, (1) Undefined name
        2
        2     999-EXIT.
              1
%COBOL-W-ERROR  297, (1) Processing of source program resumes at this point
        2         EXIT-PROGRAM.
                  1
%COBOL-F-ERROR  349, (1) Undefined name
        2
        2     END-PROGRAM SS-TAX-SUB.
              1           2
%COBOL-W-ERROR  297, (1) Processing of source program resumes at this point
%COBOL-E-ERROR   65, (2) Missing period is assumed
%COBOL-F-ERROR  321, (2) Invalid statement syntax
        2
        2    ****************************************************************
        2
        2     END-PROGRAM MODERN-PLASTICS-DBG.
              1           2                  3
%COBOL-W-ERROR  297, (1) Processing of source program resumes at this point
%COBOL-F-ERROR  349, (2) Undefined name
%COBOL-W-ERROR  297, (3) Processing of source program resumes at this point
%COBOL-E-ERROR  465, (3) Program "SS-TAX-SUB" requires an END PROGRAM - error accepted
%COBOL-E-ERROR  465, (3) Program "MODERN-PLASTICS-DBG1" requires an END PROGRAM - error accepted
```

```
TIME-SUB                                                10-Aug-1989 13:22:20    VAX COBOL V4.2-40                   Page   1
Source Listing                                          10-Aug-1989 13:22:04    [PAQUETTEG.CHAPTER8V2]TIMESUB1.COB;2 (1)

             IDENTIFICATION DIVISION.

             PROGRAM-ID.  TIME-SUB.

            *****************************************************************
            *                                                               *
            *  AUTHOR.         PAQUETTE.                                    *
            *  DATE WRITTEN.   AUGUST 1989.                                 *
            *                                                               *
            *****************************************************************

             DATA DIVISION.

             WORKING-STORAGE SECTION.

             01  TIME-DATA.
                 05 HOURS      PIC 9(2).
                 05 MINUTES    PIC 9(2).
                 05 SECONDS    PIC 9(2).
                 05 HUND-SECS  PIC 9(2).

             01  EDITED-TIME-DATA.
                 05 ED-HRS     PIC 9(2).
                 05            PIC X(1)  VALUE ":".
                 05 ED-MIN     PIC 9(2).
                 05            PIC X(1)  VALUE ":".
                 05 ED-SEC     PIC 9(2).
                 05            PIC X(1)  VALUE ":".
                 05 ED-HUN     PIC 9(2).

             01  MERIDIAN      PIC X(2).

             01  EDITED-HOURS  PIC Z9.

             LINKAGE SECTION.

             01  CURRENT-TIME-1   PIC X(8).

             01  CURRENT-TIME-2   PIC X(11).
                 1
%COBOL-E-ERROR  206, (1) Referenced Linkage Section item not in USING phrase - will cause runtime Access Violation if referenced

             PROCEDURE DIVISION.

             100-FORMAT-TIME.
                 ACCEPT TIME-DATA FROM TIME.
                 IF HUND-SECS >= 50
                     ADD 01 TO SECONDS
                 END-IF.
                 IF SECONDS >= 30
                     ADD 01 TO MINUTES
                     IF MINUTES = 60
                         ADD 1 TO HOURS
                         MOVE 0 TO MINUTES
                         IF HOURS = 25
                             MOVE 01 TO HOURS
                         END-IF
```

```
TIME-SUB                                               10-Aug-1989 13:22:20    VAX COBOL V4.2-40                      Page   2
Source Listing                                         10-Aug-1989 13:22:04    [PAQUETTEG.CHAPTER8V2]TIMESUB1.COB;2 (1)

                   END-IF
               END-IF.
               IF HOURS >= 12 AND < 24
                  MOVE "PM" TO MERIDIAN
                  IF HOURS > 12
                       SUBTRACT 12 FROM HOURS
                            GIVING EDITED-HOURS
                  END-IF
               ELSE
                  MOVE "AM" TO MERIDIAN
                  MOVE HOURS TO EDITED-HOURS.
               STRING EDITED-HOURS
                       ":"
                       MINUTES
                       " "
                       MERIDIAN     DELIMITED BY SIZE
                       INTO CURRENT-TIME.
                            1
%COBOL-F-ERROR  349, (1) Undefined name
               MOVE EDITED-TIME-DATA TO CURRENT-TIME-2.
               PERFORM 200-PREPARE-EDITED-TIME-DATA.

           200-PREPARE-EDITED-TIME-DATA.
               MOVE HOURS TO ED-HRS.
               MOVE MINUTES TO ED-MIN.
               MOVE SECONDS TO ED-SEC.
               MOVE HUND-SECS TO ED-HUN.

           999-EXIT.
               EXIT-PROGRAM.
               1          2
%COBOL-F-ERROR  349, (1) Undefined name
%COBOL-W-ERROR  297, (2) Processing of source program resumes at this point
```

Figure 5.47 Data set for the sample run

```
1010456235100PALMER, WALTER R.    11020002005   2                               1960
1010723510611READY, MARIA ELENA   11018003008   1                               1975
1010781207315CAPARCO, DOMENIC A.  11015504000   3                               1982
1020861745201JACKVONY, WEBSTER P.12020003005   2                               1965
1020325123315GRAHAM, JUDITH L.    12012504000   1                               1978
1030017429976PESARE, KAROLYN S.   13018003500   2                               1975
1080724844532CHARNIAK, NELSON T.  18020003005   3                               1970
1080349231175JACKSON, JESSICA     18016504005   1                               1974
1080125263028CANARIO, MARGARETTA  18012504005   2                               1982
2010288916795SILVIA, ROBERTA S.   21018003510   4                               1968
2020231769472LOISELLE, CYNTHIA    22016504005   1                               1970
2040463239232MACDONALD, PHILIP A.24018504000   3                               1964
2040587311472PAINE, JAMES H.      24015954000   4                               1972
2040387428531CALIFANO, CONCETTA   24016004000   1                               1975
2040737565186AFFLECK, SCOTT       24014504000   3                               1978
2070394740218ALMEIDA, RICHARD     27007504005   4                               1972
3010170347173SHERMAN, MILTON L.   31020003005   2                               1970
3020246302715PAPADOPOULOS, JOE E.32018004005   1                               1968
3050227460634GOSSELIN, ANDREW P.  35012004000   3                               1963
3050261197635SANTOS, MANUELA      35010004000   4                               1968
3050177032815JOUBERT, BERTHA M.   35009504000   1                               1970
3050466219366CHAPPELLE, BARBARA   35008004000   1                               1974
3050313905926ANDREWS, EARLE M.    35008004000   2                               1974
3050217415641PERRY, CHARLENE      35006254005   4                               1980
3060235596158KOSTEER, RICHARD G.  36008004010   3                               1975
3060312251653WINFIELD, LEWIS      36006504008   2                               1980
3070346795384LYNCH, WILLIAM S.    37006004000   2                               1976
4010331952867PELLETIER, VINCENT   41020002005   4                               1968
4020433405713POPKIN, ISABELLA M.  42014504005   1                               1974
4050322114268BARBER, MICHELLE K.  45008754005   3                               1972
4050392407915SAULNIER, ROBERT J.  45007504000   2                               1974
4050544287696ROCK, DONALD R.      45007504000   3                               1974
4050419712334ABRUZZI, GENE D.     45007003500   2                               1978
4060585731346HIGGINS, DANIEL J.   46007504000   4                               1977
4070713390477CAMPBELL, ROBIN      47004504000   1                               1980
5010834615944CAPPUCCI, NAOMI      51020002505   1                               1966
5020674337414KLINGER, MICHAEL A.  52016004005   3                               1970
5050419426056SORAFINE, JULIO      55010504006   2                               1970
5050228728353BELANGER, NORMAND    55010504000   2                               1970
5050722199235POTTER, RICHARD      55009004000   4                               1974
5050673372239LOBO, ALBERT P.      55008004000   1                               1978
5050399168704CELANO, LOUISE       55006004005   1                               1980
5060294933154WOLFE, LILETH        56008754005   2                               1976
5060325042172AIKEN, MARTINA       56007004000   4                               1980
5070426435893JUSTINO, KIRA        57006504000   3                               1979
```

2. When the programs shown in exercise 1 were free of syntax errors, they were compiled and the run unit was executed using the data in Figure 5.47. The report produced by the program is shown in Figure 5.48, but it should have been the one shown in Figure 5.49 (except for the actual times at the bottom of the report!). It is clear that a number of logic errors remain in the programs. Your task is to find and correct them, and then obtain a successful run.

■ **Figure 5.48** Erroneous report produced by the run unit

REPORT DATE:

Missing data

MODERN PLASTICS COMPANY

SOCIAL SECURITY TAX REPORT

PLANT NUMBER	DEPARTMENT NUMBER	EMPLOYEE NUMBER	EMPLOYEE NAME	GROSS WAGES	SOCIAL SECURITY TAX
10	10	456235100	PALMER, WALTER R.		$ 0.00
10	10	723510611	READY, MARIA ELENA		$ 41.31
10	10	781207315	CAPARCO, DOMENIC A.		$ 56.78
10	20	861745201	JACKVONY, WEBSTER P.		$ 46.56
10	20	325123315	GRAHAM, JUDITH L.		$ 56.33
10	30	017429976	PESARE, KAROLYN S.		$ 37.55
10	80	724844532	CHARNIAK, NELSON T.		$ 47.31
10	80	349231175	JACKSON, JESSICA		$ 56.33
10	80	125263028	CANARIO, MARGARETTA		$ 58.86
20	10	288916795	SILVIA, ROBERTA S.		$ 44.59
20	20	231769472	LOISELLE, CYNTHIA		$ 67.59
20	40	463239232	MACDONALD, PHILIP A.		$ 58.86
20	40	587311472	PAINE, JAMES H.		$ 55.57
20	40	387428531	CALIFANO, CONCETTA		$ 47.91
20	40	737565186	AFFLECK, SCOTT		$ 48.06
20	70	394740218	ALMEIDA, RICHARD		$ 43.56
30	10	170347173	SHERMAN, MILTON L.		$ 26.75
30	20	246302715	PAPADOPOULOS, JOE E.		$ 56.33
30	50	227460634	GOSSELIN, ANDREW P.		$ 64.21
30	50	261197635	SANTOS, MANUELA		$ 36.05
30	50	177032815	JOUBERT, BERTHA M.		$ 30.04
30	50	466219366	CHAPPELLE, BARBARA		$ 28.54
30	50	313905926	ANDREWS, EARLE M.		$ 24.03
30	50	217415641	PERRY, CHARLENE		$ 24.03
30	60	235596158	KOSTEER, RICHARD G.		$ 22.30
30	60	312251653	WINFIELD, LEWIS		$ 33.04
30	70	346795384	LYNCH, WILLIAM S.		$ 25.38
40	10	331952867	PELLETIER, VINCENT		$ 18.02
40	20	433405713	POPKIN, ISABELLA M.		$ 41.31
40	50	322114268	BARBER, MICHELLE K.		$ 51.73
40	50	392407915	SAULNIER, ROBERT J.		$ 31.21
40	50	544287696	ROCK, DONALD R.		$ 22.53
40	50	419712334	ABRUZZI, GENE D.		$ 22.53
40	60	585731346	HIGGINS, DANIEL J.		$ 18.40
40	70	713390477	CAMPBELL, ROBIN		$ 22.53
50	10	834615944	CAPPUCCI, NAOMI		$ 13.52
50	20	674337414	KLINGER, MICHAEL A.		$ 48.82
50	50	419426056	SORAFINE, JULIO		$ 57.08
50	50	228728353	BELANGER, NORMAND		$ 38.64
50	50	722199235	POTTER, RICHARD		$ 31.54
50	50	673372239	LOBO, ALBERT P.		$ 27.04
50	50	399168704	CELANO, LOUISE		$ 24.03
50	60	294933154	WOLFE, LILETH		$ 21.40
50	60	325042172	AIKEN, MARTINA		$ 31.21
50	70	426435893	JUSTINO, KIRA		$ 21.03
			COMPANY TOTALS:		

Missing data

Wrong values

Wrong values

Missing and incorrect times

*** END OF REPORT

START TIME:
END TIME:

Report must end here!

Figure 5.48 continued

```
REPORT DATE:                                    MODERN PLASTICS COMPANY

                                               SOCIAL SECURITY TAX REPORT

        PLANT     DEPARTMENT     EMPLOYEE          EMPLOYEE              GROSS        SOCIAL SECURITY
        NUMBER      NUMBER        NUMBER             NAME                WAGES              TAX

         10           10        456235100     PALMER, WALTER R.                          $ 19.53

                                              COMPANY TOTALS:         $ 1,100.00     $      0.00


                                           ***  END OF REPORT  ***

  START TIME:           (            )
  END TIME:     :57 PM  (12:57:08:91)
```

This should not be produced!!

Figure 5.49 Correct report to be produced by the run unit

REPORT DATE: 89/08/10

MODERN PLASTICS COMPANY

SOCIAL SECURITY TAX REPORT

PLANT NUMBER	DEPARTMENT NUMBER	EMPLOYEE NUMBER	EMPLOYEE NAME	GROSS WAGES	SOCIAL SECURITY TAX
10	10	456235100	PALMER, WALTER R.	$ 550.00	$ 41.31
10	10	723510611	READY, MARIA ELENA	$ 756.00	$ 56.78
10	10	781207315	CAPARCO, DOMENIC A.	$ 620.00	$ 46.56
10	20	861745201	JACKVONY, WEBSTER P.	$ 750.00	$ 56.33
10	20	325123315	GRAHAM, JUDITH L.	$ 500.00	$ 37.55
10	30	017429976	PESARE, KAROLYN S.	$ 630.00	$ 47.31
10	80	724844532	CHARNIAK, NELSON T.	$ 750.00	$ 56.33
10	80	349231175	JACKSON, JESSICA	$ 783.75	$ 58.86
10	80	125263028	CANARIO, MARGARETTA	$ 593.75	$ 44.59
20	10	288916795	SILVIA, ROBERTA S.	$ 900.00	$ 67.59
20	20	231769472	LOISELLE, CYNTHIA	$ 783.75	$ 58.86
20	40	463239232	MACDONALD, PHILIP A.	$ 740.00	$ 55.57
20	40	587311472	PAINE, JAMES H.	$ 638.00	$ 47.91
20	40	387428531	CALIFANO, CONCETTA	$ 640.00	$ 48.06
20	40	737565186	AFFLECK, SCOTT	$ 580.00	$ 43.56
20	70	394740218	ALMEIDA, RICHARD	$ 356.25	$ 26.75
30	10	170347173	SHERMAN, MILTON L.	$ 750.00	$ 56.33
30	20	246302715	PAPADOPOULOS, JOE E.	$ 855.00	$ 64.21
30	50	227460634	GOSSELIN, ANDREW P.	$ 480.00	$ 36.05
30	50	261197635	SANTOS, MANUELA	$ 400.00	$ 30.04
30	50	177032815	JOUBERT, BERTHA M.	$ 380.00	$ 28.54
30	50	466219366	CHAPPELLE, BARBARA	$ 320.00	$ 24.03
30	50	313905926	ANDREWS, EARLE M.	$ 320.00	$ 24.03
30	50	217415641	PERRY, CHARLENE	$ 296.88	$ 22.30
30	60	235596158	KOSTEER, RICHARD G.	$ 440.00	$ 33.04
30	60	312251653	WINFIELD, LEWIS	$ 338.00	$ 25.38
30	70	346795384	LYNCH, WILLIAM S.	$ 240.00	$ 18.02
40	10	331952867	PELLETIER, VINCENT	$ 550.00	$ 41.31
40	20	433405713	POPKIN, ISABELLA M.	$ 688.75	$ 51.73
40	50	322114268	BARBER, MICHELLE K.	$ 415.63	$ 31.21
40	50	392407915	SAULNIER, ROBERT J.	$ 300.00	$ 22.53
40	50	544287696	ROCK, DONALD R.	$ 300.00	$ 22.53
40	50	419712334	ABRUZZI, GENE D.	$ 245.00	$ 18.40
40	60	585731346	HIGGINS, DANIEL J.	$ 300.00	$ 22.53
40	70	713390477	CAMPBELL, ROBIN	$ 180.00	$ 13.52
50	10	834615944	CAPPUCCI, NAOMI	$ 650.00	$ 48.82
50	20	674337414	KLINGER, MICHAEL A.	$ 760.00	$ 57.08
50	50	419426056	SORAFINE, JULIO	$ 514.50	$ 38.64
50	50	228728353	BELANGER, NORMAND	$ 420.00	$ 31.54
50	50	722199235	POTTER, RICHARD	$ 360.00	$ 27.04
50	50	673372239	LOBO, ALBERT P.	$ 320.00	$ 24.03
50	50	399168704	CELANO, LOUISE	$ 285.00	$ 21.40
50	60	294933154	WOLFE, LILETH	$ 415.63	$ 31.21
50	60	325042172	AIKEN, MARTINA	$ 280.00	$ 21.03
50	70	426435893	JUSTINO, KIRA	$ 260.00	$ 19.53
			COMPANY TOTALS:	$22,635.89	$ 1,699.97

*** END OF REPORT ***

START TIME: 11:42 AM (11:42:13:03)
END TIME: 11:42 AM (11:42:13:63)

■ **Figure 5.50** Printer spacing chart for the daily phone sales report

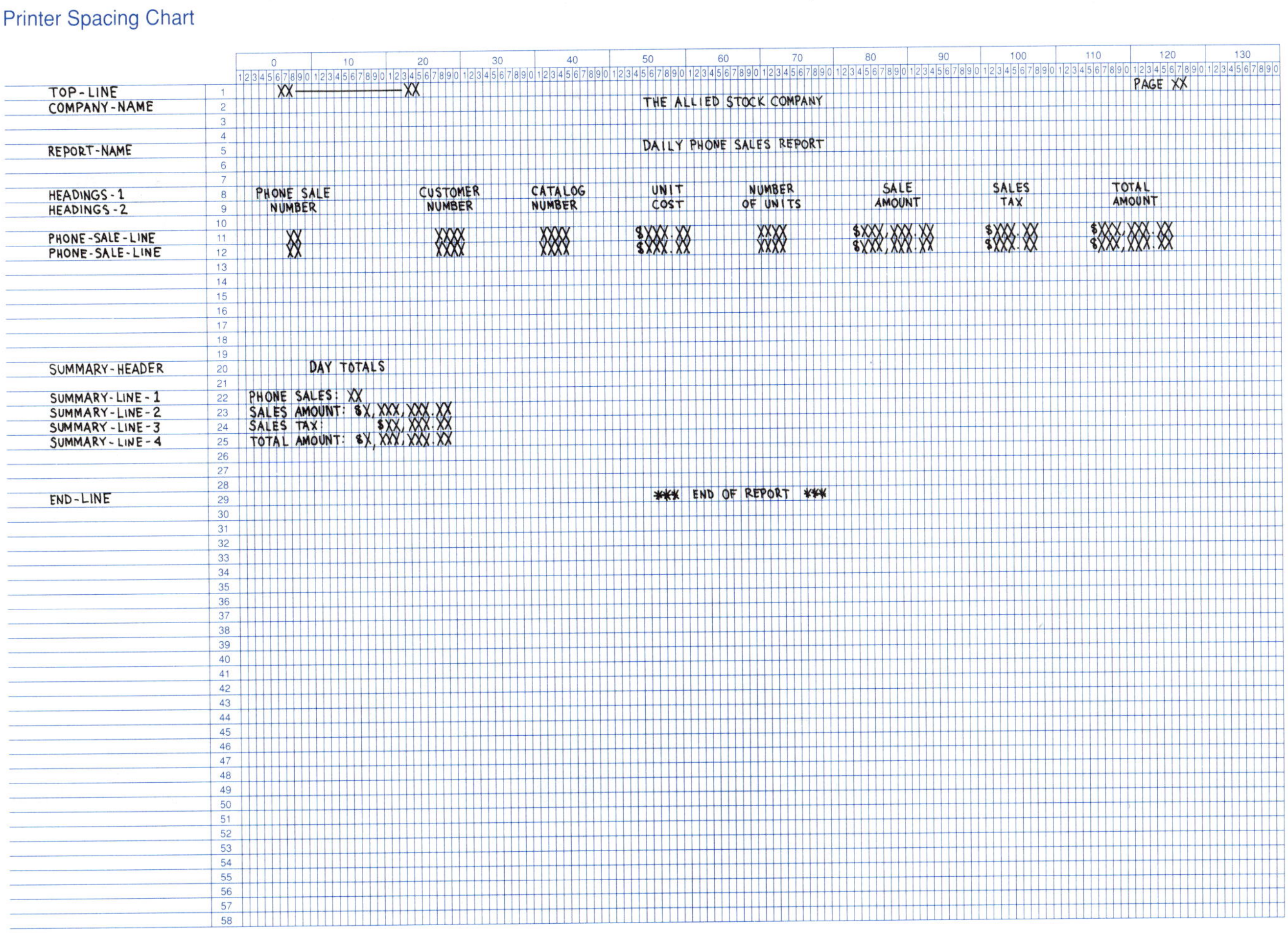

Programming Exercises

Programming Exercise I

Revise the first sample program of this chapter so as to produce a daily phone sales report formatted as shown in Figure 5.50. Two important new features in this program are computing a sales tax on each phone sale and providing summary information on the report.

Since sales tax rates change periodically, it is preferable to use a subprogram to compute the sales tax on a phone sale. In this exercise, assume that the sales tax rate is 5 percent.

Use the original statement of the problem as a starting point. Modify it as noted above and then modify the design tools to take the new features into account. Plan the subprograms as separately compiled subprograms. Then, code the new subprogram and update the main program as needed. Finally, assemble all the programs of the run unit, that is, the main program and the three subprograms, and obtain a successful execution of the run unit. Use Data Set 5X1 as the input file.

Programming Exercise II

In this exercise, a multiple COBOL program run unit, consisting of one separately compiled subprogram and two contained subprograms, must be designed to produce the same report as in Programming Exercise I. The format of the report is the one shown in Figure 5.50. In this run unit, the subprogram that formats the report date is separately compiled, but the subprograms that compute the net amount of a phone sale and the sales tax that must be levied are to be nested within the main program.

Figure 5.51 Printer spacing chart for the payroll report

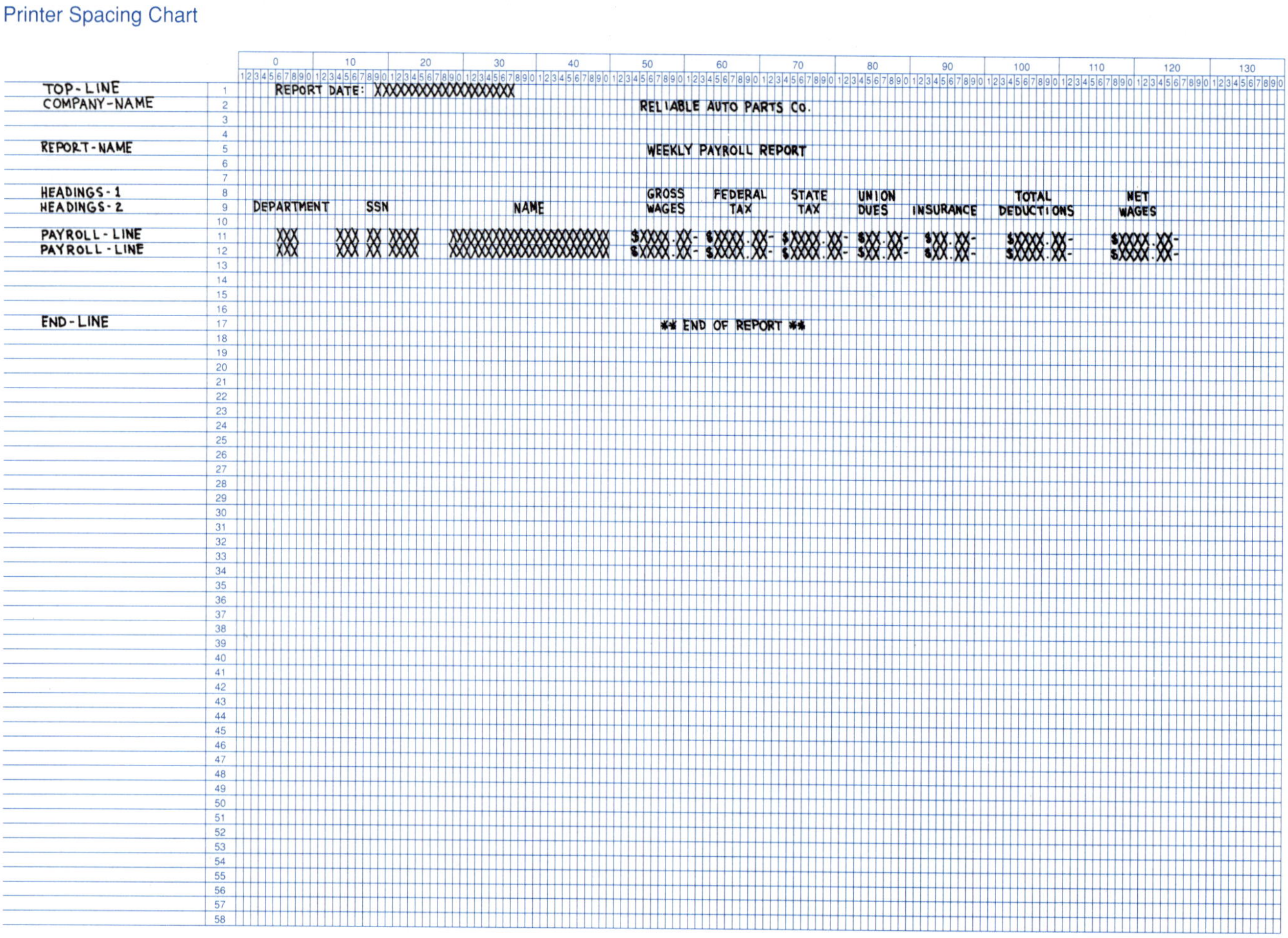

If you have done the previous exercise, revise the main program and the two subprograms that must be nested so as to share data by means of the GLOBAL qualifier. Then append the two subprograms to the main program, and edit the result so that the subprograms are properly nested. Be sure to obtain a successful run of the run unit. Use Data Set 5X1 as the input file.

If you have not done Programming Exercise I, develop it so you can satisfy the requirements of this exercise.

Programming Exercise III

The management of the Reliable Auto Parts Company wants a payroll report formatted as shown in Figure 5.51. The data processing department makes the following determinations:

1. The payroll file contains a payroll record for each employee. Each record contains the following data:

cc 1–3	Department number
cc 4–12	Social Security number
cc 13–34	Name
cc 35–36	Hours worked
cc 37–40	Pay rate (format: xx.xx)
cc 41	Allowances claimed
cc 42	Tax table code (S: single, M: married filing jointly, H: head of household)
cc 43	Insurance plan code (1: individual basic plan, 2: individual major medical plan, 3: family basic plan, 4: family major medical plan).

2. A subprogram will be used to obtain the date from the operating system and format it as needed on the report. The date format is month, day, comma, year.

Figure 5.52 Tax table to be used in the program (Source: Internal Revenue Service)

Tables for Percentage Method of Withholding

(For Wages Paid After December 1988)

Table 1–If the Payroll Period With Respect to an Employee Is Weekly

(a) SINGLE person–including head of household:

If the amount of wages (after subtracting withholding allowances) is:		*The amount of income tax to be withheld shall be:*	
Not over $21		.0	
Over–	*But not over–*		*of excess over–*
$21	–$378	15%	–$21
$378	–$885	$53.55 plus 28%	–$378
$885	–$2,028	$195.51 plus 33%	–$885
$2,028		$572.70 plus 28%	–$2,028

(b) MARRIED person–

If the amount of wages (after subtracting withholding allowances) is:		*The amount of income tax to be withheld shall be:*	
Not over $62		.0	
Over–	*But not over–*		*of excess over–*
$62	–$657	15%	–$62
$657	–$1,501	$89.25 plus 28%	–$657
$1,501	–$3,695	$325.57 plus 33%	–$1,501
$3,695		$1,049.59 plus 28%	–$3,695

3. A subprogram will be used to compute the federal tax to be withheld from the gross wages. The percentage method of withholding will be used. The appropriate table is shown in Figure 5.52. The data from Figure 5.52 must be hard-coded into a two-level table. The first level applies to the "single person" classification, and the second level applies to the "married person" classification.

The withholding allowances must be subtracted from the gross wages to determine the taxable wages. Currently, the allowance amount is $38.46 for each allowance claimed by the employee.

4. A subprogram will be used to compute the applicable state tax. The current state tax rate is 22.4 percent of the federal tax.

5. A subprogram will be used to compute the payroll deductions for union dues and insurance premiums. The dues are currently set at $5.60, and the insurance premiums shown below must be hard-coded into a one-level table with positional organization in working storage.

	Basic	**Major Medical**
Individual	8.06	11.33
Family	12.15	16.00

6. All the subprograms are to be separately compiled.

Your task is to design the multiprogram run unit and implement the design to successful completion. Use Data Set 5X3 as the input file.

Programming Exercise IV

The management of the Jocelyn Originals Company wants its data processing department to prepare an annual report formatted as shown in Figure 5.53.

The company pays bonuses to its sales force based on sales levels. The bonuses are determined on quarterly sales but are paid once a year after year's end. The bonus program consists of three levels: base, level-1, and level-2, with corresponding bonus rates of base-rate, level-1-rate, and level-2-rate. A salesperson whose sales for a quarter do not exceed the base amount receives no bonus. The bonus for any quarter is determined as shown in the following table.

Sales **Greater than**	**But not greater than**	**Bonus computed by**
Base amount	Level-1 amount	(Sales − Base amount) * base-rate
Level-1 amount	Level-2 amount	(Level-1 amount − Base amount) * base-rate + (Sales − Level-1 amount) * level-1-rate
Level-2 amount	(no maximum)	(Level-1 amount − Base amount) * base-rate (Level-2 amount − Level-1 amount) * level-1-rate (Sales − Level-2 amount) * level-2-rate

Figure 5.53 Printer spacing chart for the annual report

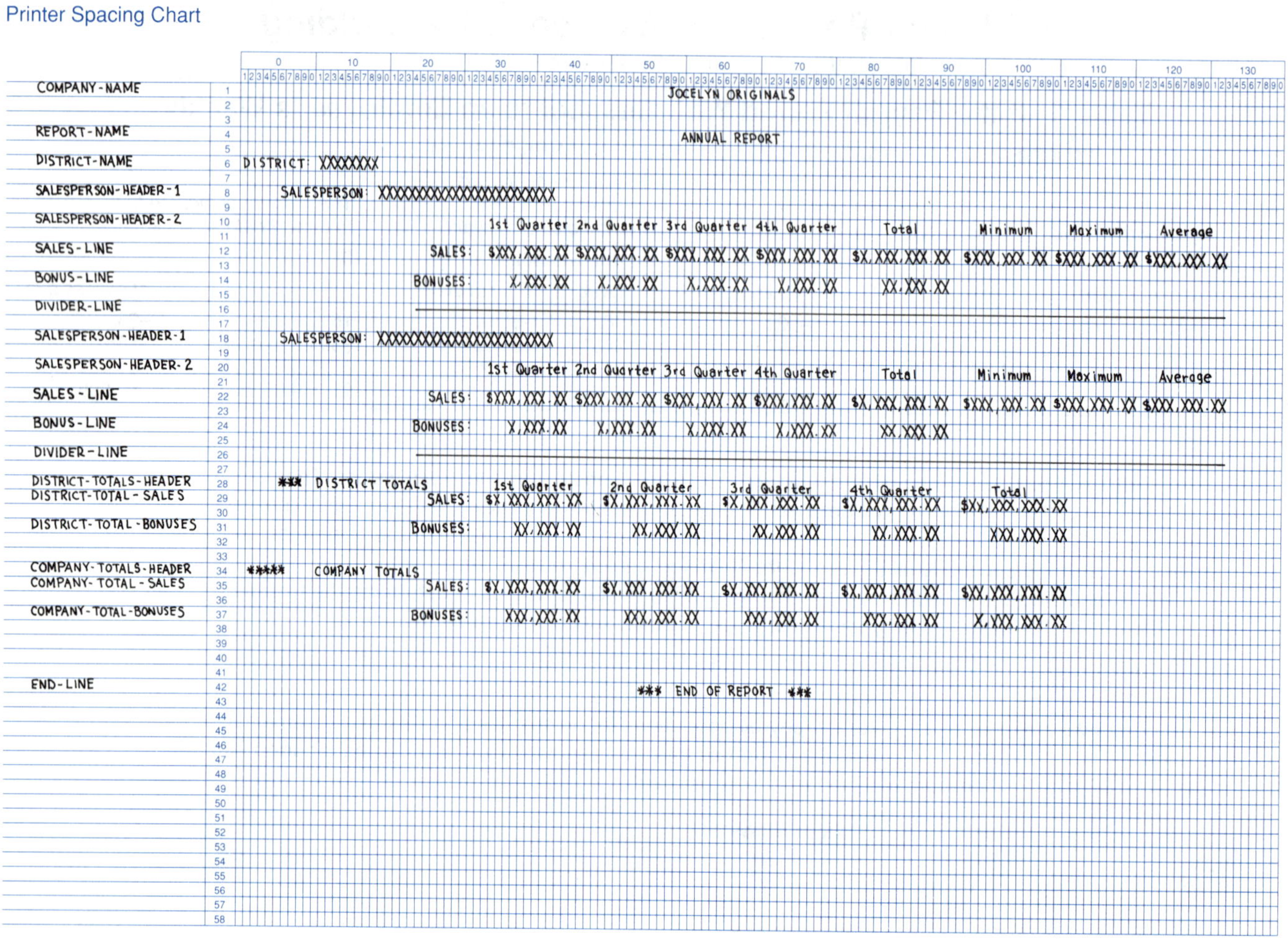

Though the bonus program remains fixed, the company retains flexibility by changing amounts and rates as dictated by the business environment. Currently, the values are as follows:

Base amount = $12,000.00
Level-1 amount = $16,000.00
Level-2 amount = $20,000.00
Base-rate = 5%
Level-1-rate = 10%
Level-2-rate = 15%

A sales file contains a record for each salesperson. The data structure of the record is as follows:

cc 1	District code (1: Eastern, 2: Central, 3: Mountain, 4: Pacific)
cc 2–26	Salesperson's name
cc 27–34	First quarter sales (format: xxxxxx.xx)
cc 35–42	Second quarter sales (format: xxxxxx.xx)
cc 43–50	Third quarter sales (format: xxxxxx.xx)
cc 51–58	Fourth quarter sales (format: xxxxxx.xx)

The records are arranged alphabetically by salesperson name.
The data processing department has made the following determinations:

1. The program must contain a control break at the district level.
2. The salespersons of a district must be reported in alphabetic order by salesperson name.
3. The districts must be reported in ascending order by district code.
4. A subprogram must be used to compute a salesperson's total sales, minimum quarterly sales amount, maximum quarterly sales amount, and average quarterly sales amount.
5. A subprogram must be used to compute a salesperson's quarterly bonuses, as well as the total bonus for the year. The computations must be performed using data names, not specific constants, for sales level amounts and bonus rates. These data items must be defined within the subprogram.
6. The subprograms must be contained within the main program.
7. The report is a continuous report without district page breaks.

Use Data Set 5X4 as the original sales file.

6 Interactive COBOL Programs

When the COBOL language was first developed, its specific end-application was to process data that had been accumulated over time into a "batch file." COBOL programs were traditionally "batch programs," and the execution of COBOL programs that processed batched data was called "batch processing." The advent of video terminals provided the opportunity for the user to supply input data to a program while the program was executing. The rapid advances in video terminal technology and in operating systems that support both concurrent processing and multitasking processes have resulted in a substantial increase in the number of COBOL programs designed as *interactive* programs. The essential difference between batch programs and interactive programs is simply that batch programs obtain input data from files, while interactive programs obtain input data from the user during the execution of the program.

Even though the CODASYL (Conference on Data Systems Languages) Screen Management Committee has released a Screen Management Facility, the features included in this release have not yet been approved by the American National Standards Institute (ANSI) and, consequently, have not been incorporated in the COBOL '85 standards. In the absence of nationally recognized standards, vendors such as IBM, Digital, and Microsoft have developed extensions to the ANSI standards. These extensions are implementor-specific, however, and this fact makes it particularly difficult to develop, in a text such as this one, the concepts of interactive COBOL programs and their related applications. Nonetheless, this chapter is included with the expectation that the similarities between vendor-supplied screen management facilities will allow you to develop a decent grasp of concepts and applications in spite of the differences that exist among them.

Since the programs in this chapter are run on a VAX 8650, it is essential that program entries related to terminal data entry and video data display abide by the Digital extensions to ANSI COBOL '85. Do not attempt to run these programs on your computer without first adapting them to the screen management facility used by your computer. See your instructor for system-specific requirements. **(Note: The first two programs use the standard ACCEPT/DISPLAY statements. They may be run on your computer without any problem.)**

Objectives You Should Achieve

After studying this chapter, you should

1. Be able to code a DISPLAY statement to print a message on the screen.
2. Be able to code a DISPLAY statement to print the value of a data item on the screen.
3. Be able to code an ACCEPT statement to store characters entered at a terminal in a specified data field.
4. Be able to code combinations of DISPLAY and ACCEPT statements to implement specified interactive dialogue using the prompt/response technique.
5. Be able to code combinations of DISPLAY, ACCEPT, and UNSTRING statements to implement specified interactive dialogue using free-form terminal data entry.
6. Be able to use a screen layout form to design a video form for use in an interactive program.
7. Given a video form, be able to code DISPLAY statements to paint the form on the screen.
8. Given a video form, be able to code ACCEPT statements to light up data fields on the screen to facilitate terminal data input.
9. Be able to design an interactive program that implements the simple prompt/response technique.
10. Be able to design an interactive program that implements free-form data entry.
11. Be able to design a menu-driven interactive program.

Creating a Data File Interactively

The problem that follows is presented as a first example of a program that accepts data input from a terminal.

Problem 1

The data processing department of Toucan Enterprises wants a program to create a master personnel file. The file must have indexed organization, and the data for each employee must be supplied interactively. Employee data is currently contained on Rolodex® cards, alphabetized by employee name.

The employee cards must be presorted manually in ascending order by Social Security number, since the prime record key for the master file will be the Social Security number.

The master record layout is as follows:

cc 1–2	Record code (EM for Employee Master)
cc 3–11	Social Security number
cc 12–23	Employee last name
cc 25–35	Employee first name
cc 37	Employee middle initial
cc 38–55	Street address
cc 57–68	City
cc 70–71	State
cc 73–77	Zip code
cc 78–80	Area code
cc 82–88	Phone number

In addition to creating the master file, the program must also prepare a report that lists the records entered into the file. The report is formatted as shown in Figure 6.1.

Figure 6.1 Printer spacing chart for problem 1

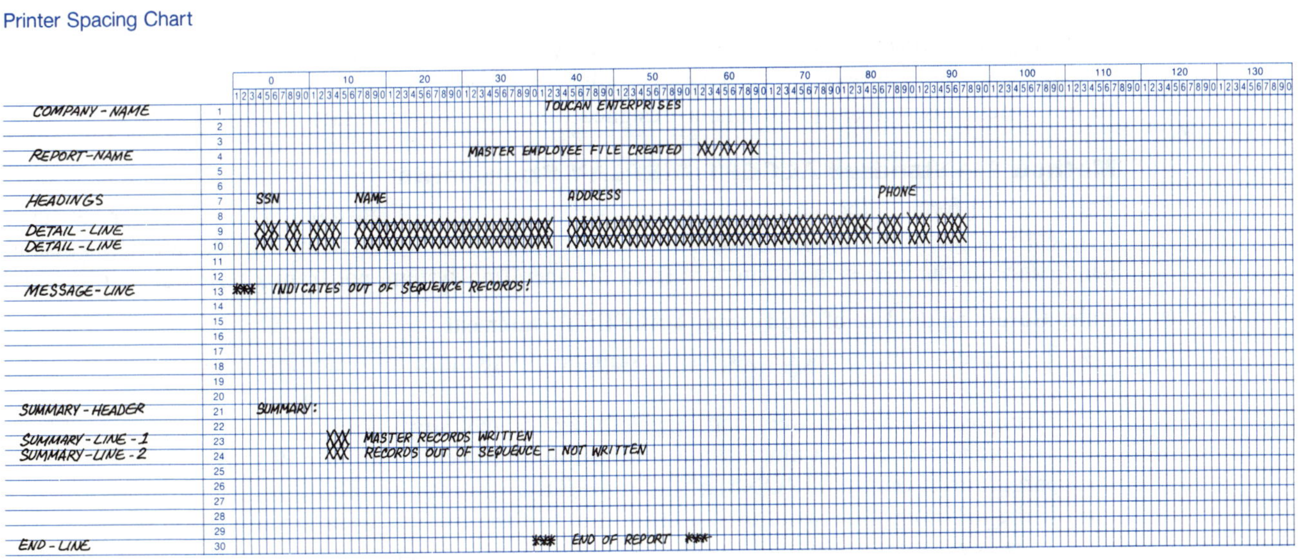

Figure 6.2 System flowchart for problem 1

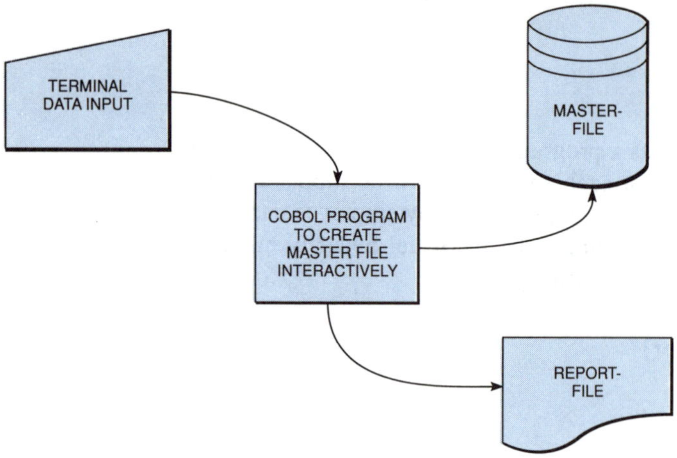

Analysis of Problem 1

Since employee data is to be supplied interactively by the user, there is no input file for this program and, consequently, no read function within the program. However, the program must produce two output files, namely, the master file and the print file containing the report. The system flowchart is shown in Figure 6.2.

The essential task of the program is to create the master file, and a related task is to produce the report. Once the data is available to the program, the processing required to write records to a master file and to prepare detail lines on a report present no new concepts and no challenge. We concentrate our attention on procedures that may be used to input the needed data at a terminal as opposed to making it available in a file. We examine three terminal data input procedures, and they are presented from the simplest to the most complex. The first employs a computer/terminal dialogue based on the ANSI formats of the ACCEPT and DISPLAY statements. The second input procedure uses the standard ACCEPT/DISPLAY statements also, but they are used in conjunction with free-form data entry. And the third procedure, applying Digital Equipment Corporation extensions to the ACCEPT/DISPLAY statements, will use programmer-designed video forms to facilitate data entry.

Method 1—Standard ACCEPT/DISPLAY Statements

The standard formats for the ACCEPT statement are shown in Figure 6.3. The second format, used frequently in previous programs to obtain the current date from the system, is irrelevant to the task at hand, since its function is to obtain data from the operating system, not from a terminal user.

Rules Governing the Use of the Format 1 ACCEPT Statement

1. The general function of the ACCEPT statement is to make low-volume data available to the program.
2. *Identifier-1* is the data item that receives the accepted data.
3. *Mnemonic-name-1* is a mnemonic name that must be defined in the SPECIAL-NAMES paragraph of the ENVIRONMENT DIVISION.
4. If the FROM phrase is not used, the execution of the ACCEPT statement will cause the operating system to obtain data from the system's default input device. (In interactive program applications, the user's terminal must be the system's default input device.)
5. The accepted data is stored left-justified in *identifier-1,* and no editing occurs. That is, it is treated as an alphanumeric data transfer.
6. If the number of characters in the accepted data is less than the size of *identifier-1,* the extra positions are padded with spaces.
7. If the number of characters in the accepted data is greater than the size of *identifier-1,* the extra characters are truncated from the right.

Figure 6.3 ACCEPT statement formats

Format 1: <u>ACCEPT</u> identifier-1 [<u>FROM</u> mnemonic-name-1]

Format 2: <u>ACCEPT</u> identifier-2 <u>FROM</u> { <u>DATE</u> / <u>DAY</u> / <u>DAY-OF-WEEK</u> / <u>TIME</u> }

Figure 6.4 DISPLAY statement format

<u>DISPLAY</u> { identifier-1 / literal-1 } . . . [<u>UPON</u> mnemonic-name-1] [WITH <u>NO</u> <u>ADVANCING</u>]

8. If the FROM phrase is used, data is accepted from the system's device associated with *mnemonic-name-1* in the SPECIAL-NAMES paragraph.
9. If no data is entered, that is if only a carriage return occurs, *identifier-1* is filled with spaces.

When an ACCEPT statement is executed, a prompt, such as a blinking cursor or a question mark, is displayed on the screen and the system waits for an entry. The prompt is specified by the operating system. For instance, on the VAX the prompt is a blinking cursor. When the required characters have been keyed on the keyboard, a carriage return completes the data entry.

Since an interactive program normally executes many ACCEPT statements, it is generally impossible for the user to know what kind of data each prompt is requesting. For that reason, the DISPLAY statement is used to print an appropriate request or a message on the screen prior to requesting data. As a result, a dialogue is established between the system and the user. Specifically, a message or a request is displayed, data is entered as a response, another message or request is displayed, more data is entered, and so on. Such an exchange may be as follows ["(CR)" indicates a carriage return]:

```
ENTER THE EMPLOYEE'S FIRST NAME:
 ROBERT (CR)
ENTER THE EMPLOYEE'S MIDDLE INITIAL:
 E (CR)
ENTER THE EMPLOYEE'S LAST NAME:
 TAITE (CR)
ENTER THE EMPLOYEE'S PHONE NUMBER:
 6784251 (CR)
 .
 .
 .
```

The establishment of a dialogue between the system and the user is called the prompt/response technique. It will be used in the first sample program. Before going on with the sample program, we examine the DISPLAY statement format, shown in Figure 6.4.

Rules Governing the Use of the DISPLAY Statement

1. The general function of the DISPLAY statement is to transmit low-volume data from the program to the system's default output device or the device associated with *mnemonic-name-1*. (In interactive program applications, the user's terminal [screen] must be the default output device.)
2. *Identifier-1* is the name of a source data item. Its value is the transmitted data.
3. *Literal-1* may be any literal, including figurative constants. If *literal-1* is a figurative constant, only one occurrence of the item is displayed.

4. *Mnemonic-name-1* is a mnemonic name that must be defined in the SPECIAL-NAMES paragraph of the ENVIRONMENT DIVISION. (In interactive program applications, *mnemonic-name-1* must be associated with the user's terminal.)
5. If the UPON phrase is not used, the value is displayed on the system's default output device.
6. If the UPON phrase is used, the value is displayed on the device associated with *mnemonic-name-1*.
7. If the NO ADVANCING phrase is not used, an implicit carriage return occurs subsequent to displaying the data. That is, the cursor is positioned at the beginning of the next line.
8. If the NO ADVANCING phrase is used, no carriage return occurs subsequent to displaying the data, and the cursor is placed in the first position to the right of the last character displayed.

To produce the brief dialogue illustrated above, the program would contain the following statements:

```
DISPLAY "ENTER THE EMPLOYEE'S FIRST NAME: ".
ACCEPT FIRST-NAME.
DISPLAY "ENTER THE EMPLOYEE'S MIDDLE INITIAL: ".
ACCEPT MID-INITIAL.
DISPLAY "ENTER THE EMPLOYEE'S LAST NAME: ".
ACCEPT LAST-NAME.
DISPLAY "ENTER THE EMPLOYEE'S PHONE NUMBER: ".
ACCEPT PHONE-NO.
.
.
.
```

The DISPLAY statements display the specified literals, while the ACCEPT statements reference the data fields that store the data entered at the terminal. In this example, the data fields belong to the record MASTER-RECORD. The record might be coded as follows:

```
01  MASTER-RECORD.
    05 NAME.
       10 LAST-NAME     PIC X(12).
       10 FIRST-NAME    PIC X(11).
       10 MID-INITIAL   PIC X(1).
    05 PHONE-NO         PIC 9(7).
    .
    .
    .
```

In the brief dialogue illustrated above, if the NO ADVANCING phrase is included in the DISPLAY statements, a carriage return occurs only after data is entered by the user in response to an ACCEPT statement. On the screen, the dialogue then appears as follows:

```
ENTER THE EMPLOYEE'S FIRST NAME: ROBERT (CR)
ENTER THE EMPLOYEE'S MIDDLE INITIAL: E (CR)
ENTER THE EMPLOYEE'S LAST NAME: TAITE (CR)
```

Note that the number of lines displayed on the screen is cut in half, since the prompt corresponding to the ACCEPT statement is positioned on the same line as the preceding DISPLAY statement! (Note to VAX users: to properly control positioning of the cursor, use the DCL command SET TERMINAL/NOWRAP before running interactive programs.)

Now that we have listed the basic features of the ACCEPT and DISPLAY statements, we return to the development of problem 1.

The Structure Chart

The essential tasks that the program must accomplish are the following:

1. Write the report headers.
2. Get and process employee data entered at the terminal.
3. Prepare and write employee master records to the master file.
4. Prepare corresponding detail lines on the report.
5. Produce summary information on the report.

These tasks may be organized into a structure chart as shown in Figure 6.5.

Figure 6.5 Structure chart for problem 1

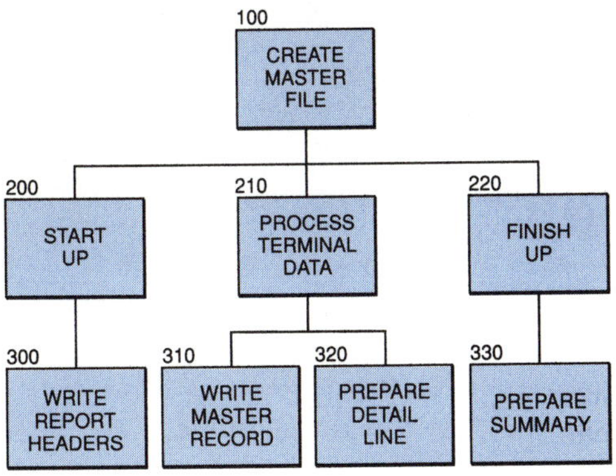

The Program Pseudocode

Since the program is an interactive program, efforts should be made at this point to make the program *user friendly* in addition to making sure that the program carries out all of its essential tasks. User friendly features may include ringing a bell as an attention getter, displaying helpful messages, repeating important reminders, giving the user feedback on actions taken, and the like.

The program pseudocode contains some of these features, and they are highlighted for your convenience.

100-Create-Master-File.

1. Perform 200-Start-Up.
2. Perform 210-Process-Terminal-Data until input-data-flag = "END".
3. Perform 220-Finish-Up.
4. Stop the run.

200-Start-Up.

1. Open Master-File and Report-File in output mode.
2. Obtain report-date from the operating system.
3. Move report-date to Report-Name date.
4. Set program-counters to zero.
5. Perform 300-Write-Report-Headers.
6. Ring bell twice.
7. Display message "Enter employee data by responding to the prompts".
8. Display message "When no more data, enter 'END' at name prompt".
9. Ring bell twice.

210-Process-Terminal-Data.

1. Clear Master-Record and Detail-Line areas.
2. Ring bell once.
3. Display message "Please enter data carefully".
4. Display request "Enter last name".
5. Accept Master-Record last-name.
6. Test Master-Record last-name:
   if "END," set input-data-flag to "END";
   if not "END," then:
   a. Display request "Enter first name".
   b. Accept Master-Record first-name.
   c. Display request "Enter middle initial".
   d. Accept Master-Record middle-initial.
   e. Display request "Enter Social Security number".
   f. Accept Master-Record Social-Security-number.
   g. Display request "Enter street address".
   h. Accept Master-Record street.
   i. Display request "Enter city".
   j. Accept Master-Record city.

k. Display request "Enter state abbreviation".
l. Accept Master-Record state.
m. Display request "Enter 5-digit zip code".
n. Accept Master-Record zip.
o. Display request "Enter phone area code".
p. Accept Master-Record area-code.
q. Display request "Enter 7-digit phone number".
r. Accept Master-Record phone-number.
s. Display message "Thank You!!" and ring bell.
t. Perform 310-Write-Master-Record.
u. Perform 320-Prepare-Detail-Line.

220-Finish-Up.

1. Move the record Message-Line to the output area Printline.
2. After advancing 3 lines, write the output record Printline.
3. Perform 330-Prepare-Summary.
4. Move the record End-Line to the output area Printline.
5. After advancing 5 lines, write the output record Printline.
6. Close the files.

300-Write-Report-Headers.

1. Move the record Company-Name to the output area Printline.
2. After advancing to a new page, write the output record Printline.
3. Move the record Report-Name to the output area Printline.
4. After advancing 3 lines, write the output record Printline.
5. Move the record Headings to the output area Printline.
6. After advancing 3 lines, write the output record Printline.
7. Set proper-spacing to 2.

310-Write-Master-Record.

1. Move "EM" to Master-Record record-code.
2. Write Master-Record.
3. Check for invalid key:
   a. If invalid key condition occurs, ring bell twice,
      display message "SSN for this employee is out of sequence",
      display message "Master record was not created. Note it for later addition",
      display request "Press CR when ready to continue",
      accept user-entry (CR entry),
      add 1 to out-of-sequence-counter.
   b. If not invalid key condition, display message "Master record now in file!",
      display request "Press CR when ready to continue",
      accept user-entry,
      add 1 to master-record-counter.

320-Prepare-Detail-Line.

1. Test master-file-flag:
   if not "00", move "***" to Detail-Line sequence-flag.
2. Move Master-Record Social-Security-number to Detail-Line Social-Security-number.
3. Move Master-Record name to Detail-Line name.
4. Move Master-Record address to Detail-Line address.
5. Move Master-Record phone to Detail-Line phone.
6. Move the record Detail-Line to the output area Printline.
7. After advancing proper-spacing, write the output record Printline.

330-Prepare-Summary.

1. Move master-record-counter to Summary-Line-1 master-record-counter.
2. Move out-of-sequence-counter to Summary-Line-2 out-of-sequence-counter.
3. Move the record Summary-Header to the output area Printline.
4. After advancing 5 lines, write the output record Printline.
5. Move the record Summary-Line-1 to the output area Printline.
6. After advancing 2 lines, write the output record Printline.
7. Move the record Summary-Line-2 to the output area Printline.
8. After advancing 1 line, write the output record Printline.

Note that step 8 of paragraph 200-Start-Up tells the user how to terminate execution of the program. The entry "END" is used within the program as a signal to exit from the terminal-data processing loop. This is similar to the program logic that uses the EOF marker of the input file as a signal to exit from the input-record processing loop. Of course, there is no input file in this program and there are no input records to process. This program processes only terminal input data, so the signal to end the program must come from the terminal!

Also note the series of display and accept functions in paragraph 210-Process-Terminal-Data that implement the prompt/response technique. When all the data has been entered, a user friendly touch displays a "Thank You!" on the screen. Control is then sent to a procedure to write the master record to the master file and then to another procedure to write the detail line on the report. Note in steps 5 and 6 that when the user enters "END" in response to the request for an employee name, the input data flag that controls the processing loop is set to "END", the remaining prompt/response statements are bypassed, and as control returns to step 2 of paragraph 100-Create-Master-File, the loop terminates, the statements in paragraph 220-Finish-Up are executed, and the execution of the program ends.

Paragraph 310-Write-Master-Record contains display/accept functions that inform the user regarding a successful or unsuccessful attempt to write a master record to the master file. Note the technique of requesting the user to press the CR key to continue with the program. This gives the user control over the pace of the interactive dialogue.

Program Flowchart

The flowchart corresponding to the pseudocode is shown in Figure 6.6. Since an interactive dialogue tends to get wordy, a flowchart typically lacks the details that are contained in the numerous prompts within the program. Annotations are used to hint at the nature of the prompts, but the details are left out. If a programmer feels particularly uncomfortable with the results, a separate sheet containing the detailed prompts may be attached to the flowchart.

Figure 6.6 Program flowchart for problem 1

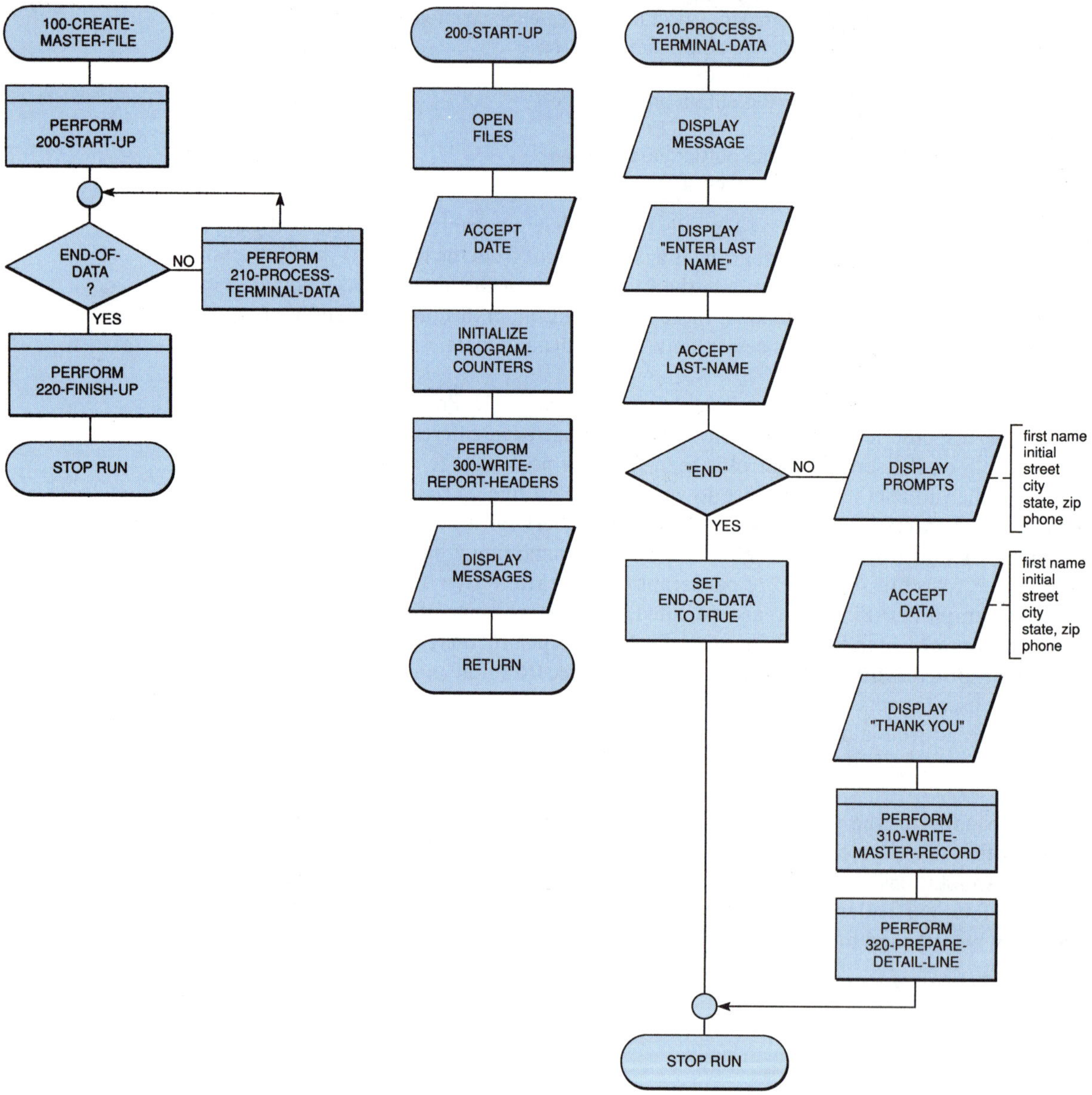

Figure 6.6 continued

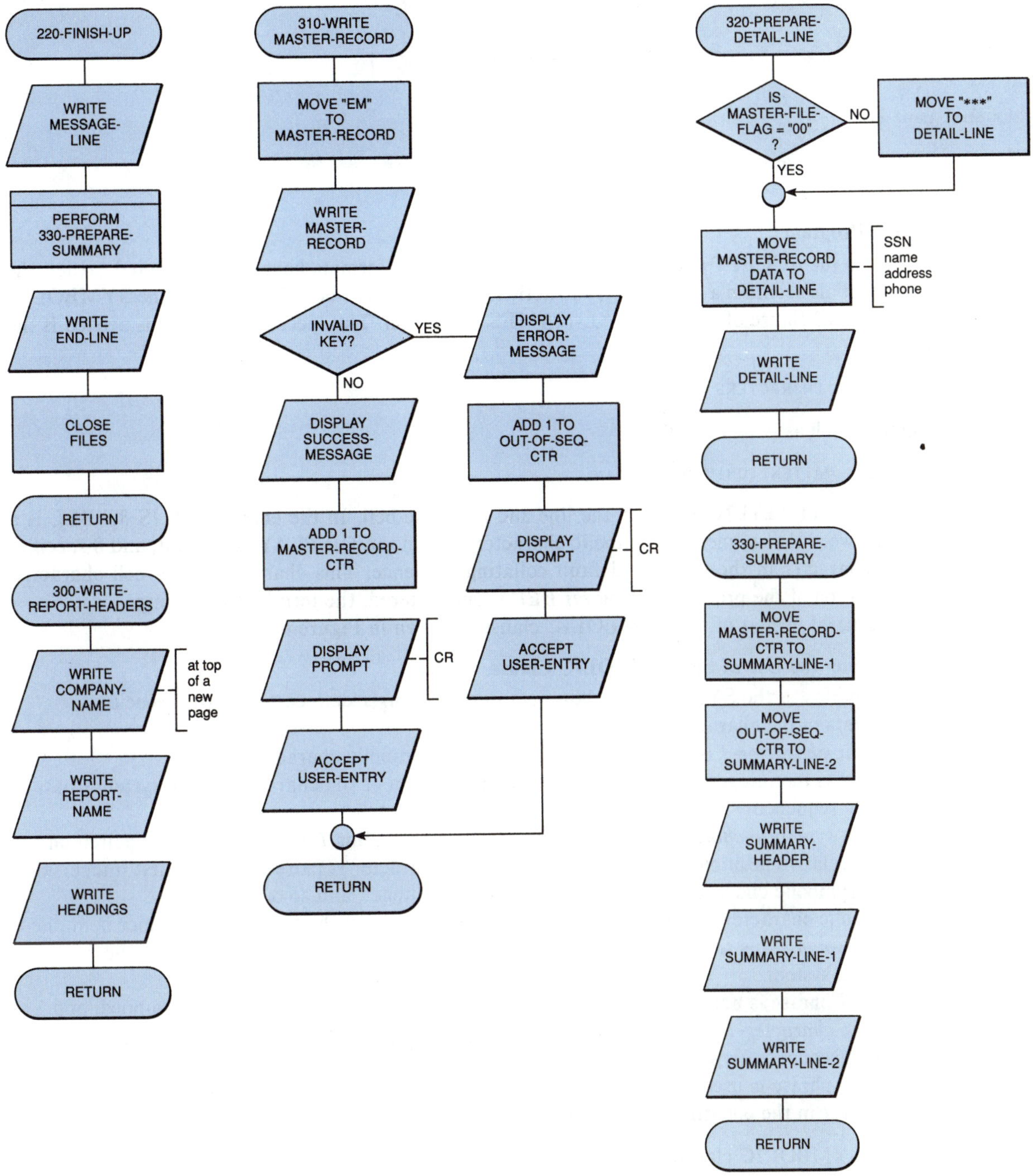

Figure 6.7 SYMBOLIC clause format

$$\left[\underline{\text{SYMBOLIC}}\ \text{CHARACTERS}\ \left\{\left\{\{\text{symbolic-character-1}\}\ldots\begin{Bmatrix}\text{IS}\\\text{ARE}\end{Bmatrix}\{\text{integer-1}\}\ldots\right\}\ldots\ [\underline{\text{IN}}\ \text{alphabet-name-2}]\right\}\right]\ldots$$

Coding the Program

In addition to the ACCEPT and DISPLAY statements whose formats have been presented earlier, the program must also contain a special entry to activate the terminal's bell! This entry is the SYMBOLIC CHARACTERS clause of the SPECIAL-NAMES paragraph. The specific entry that is needed is the following:

```
SYMBOLIC CHARACTERS BEL IS 8.
```

A statement such as

```
DISPLAY "ATTENTION!" BEL
```

displays the literal ATTENTION! on the line and rings the bell. In the entry "BEL IS 8," BEL is a user-defined word that names the symbolic character used in the DISPLAY statement, and 8 specifies the eighth character in the system's default collating sequence. This character is the bell character. During execution of the program, whenever BEL is encountered, the terminal's bell rings.

The general format of the SYMBOLIC clause is shown in Figure 6.7.

Rules Governing the Use of the SYMBOLIC Clause

1. The function of the SYMBOLIC clause is to associate user-defined words with specific characters in the character set used by the program.
2. *Symbolic-character-1* is the user-defined name of a symbolic character.
3. *Integer-1* is the integer that specifies the ordinal position of the character in the system's native collating sequence.
4. For each *symbolic-character-1,* there must be a corresponding *integer-1.* They are paired on the basis of relative position; that is, the first symbolic character is paired with the first integer, the second symbolic character is paired with the second integer, and so on.
5. A symbolic character always has the global attribute, that is, the GLOBAL qualifier is implied.
6. *Alphabet-name-2* is the user-defined name of a collating sequence available within the operating system.
7. If the IN phrase is not used, the system's native (default) collating sequence is implied, and *symbolic-character-1* represents the character whose ordinal number (within the native collating sequence) is specified by *integer-1.*
8. If the IN phrase is used, *symbolic-character-1* represents the character whose ordinal number is *integer-1* in the collating sequence specified by *alphabet-name-2.*

In the SYMBOLIC clause

```
SYMBOLIC CHARACTERS    CR    BEL    ATT
                ARE    14     8      65
```

the symbolic word CR corresponds to the 14th character, the symbolic word BEL corresponds to the 8th character, and the symbolic word ATT corresponds to the 65th character in the system's collating sequence. The statement

```
DISPLAY  CR  " "  ATT  BEL
```

causes a carriage return, followed by the display of a space, followed by the display of the at sign (@) (the 65th character in the ASCII collating sequence), followed by the ring of the terminal's bell. (The complete ASCII collating sequence is shown in Appendix B.)

The coding of the program is shown in Figure 6.8. Some program entries have been numbered to facilitate the following comments.

1. The SYMBOLIC clause defines BEL as the symbolic character that corresponds to the eighth character in the system's collating sequence. The eighth character in the sequence is the terminal bell.
2. MASTER-FILE is defined as an indexed file. Since the access mode is sequential and the master key is MR-SSN, records must be written to the file in ascending order by the values stored in the data field MR-SSN.
3. Some prompts ask the user to press the carriage return to continue execution of the program. When this is done, the characters are accepted into USER-ENTRY. (Actually, depressing any keyboard key allows the program to continue!)
4. This set of DISPLAY statements gets the user's attention and displays informational messages.
5. This set of DISPLAY statements begins the prompts for the required data. The first data item to be entered is the employee's last name.
6. This statement tests the value stored in MR-NAME. If the value is "END", it indicates that the user decided to terminate the execution of the program.
7. If the user did not enter "END", statements prompting for employee data and accepting the data are executed as needed.
8. A "Thank You!" is displayed, and control is then sent to separate paragraphs to write the master record and to prepare a detail line on the report.
9. When the WRITE statement is executed, if an invalid key condition occurs, the bell rings to get the user's attention and informational messages are displayed. If the master record is successfully written, an appropriate message is displayed. And in either case, the user is requested to press the carriage return to continue!

Figure 6.8 Interactive COBOL program implementing the prompt/response technique

```
       IDENTIFICATION DIVISION.

       PROGRAM-ID.  CREATE-FILE-INT1.

      *****************************************************************
      *                                                               *
      *  THIS PROGRAM ILLUSTRATES THE USE OF THE ACCEPT AND DISPLAY   *
      *  STATEMENTS (WITHOUT VENDOR EXTENSIONS TO THE ANSI STANDARDS) *
      *  IN AN INTERACTIVE APPLICATION.  THE PROGRAM ACCEPTS EMPLOYEE *
      *  DATA FROM THE TERMINAL AND WRITES RECORDS TO AN INDEXED FILE.*
      *                                                               *
      *  EACH DATA ITEM IS OBTAINED BY USING THE PROMPT/RESPONSE      *
      *  TECHNIQUE.                                                   *
      *                                                               *
      *  THE PROGRAM ALSO PRODUCES AN AUDIT REPORT.                   *
      *                                                               *
      *****************************************************************

       ENVIRONMENT DIVISION.

       CONFIGURATION SECTION.

       SOURCE-COMPUTER.  VAX-VMS-8650.
       OBJECT-COMPUTER.  VAX-VMS-8650.

       SPECIAL-NAMES.
1.         SYMBOLIC CHARACTERS BEL IS 8.

       INPUT-OUTPUT SECTION.

       FILE-CONTROL.
           SELECT MASTER-FILE      ASSIGN TO 'TOUCAN.DAT"
2.                                 ORGANIZATION IS INDEXED
                                   ACCESS MODE IS SEQUENTIAL
                                   RECORD KEY IS MR-SSN
                                   FILE STATUS IS MASTER-FILE-FLAG.
           SELECT REPORT-FILE      ASSIGN TO COB1$OUTPUT.
```

Figure 6.8 continued

```
DATA DIVISION.

FILE SECTION.

FD  MASTER-FILE
    RECORD CONTAINS 88 CHARACTERS
    BLOCK CONTAINS 5 RECORDS.

01  MASTER-RECORD.
    05 RECORD-CODE          PIC X(2).
    05 MR-SSN               PIC X(9).
    05 MR-NAME.
       10 MR-LAST-NAME      PIC X(12).
       10                   PIC X(1).
       10 MR-FIRST-NAME     PIC X(11).
       10                   PIC X(1).
       10 MR-INITIAL        PIC X(1).
    05 MR-ADDRESS.
       10 MR-STREET         PIC X(18).
       10                   PIC X(1).
       10 MR-CITY           PIC X(12).
       10                   PIC X(1).
       10 MR-STATE          PIC X(2).
       10                   PIC X(1).
       10 MR-ZIP            PIC X(5).
    05 MR-PHONE.
       10 MR-AREA-CODE      PIC X(3).
       10                   PIC X(1).
       10 MR-PHONE-NO       PIC X(7).

FD  REPORT-FILE
    RECORD CONTAINS 100 CHARACTERS.

01  PRINTLINE               PIC X(100).

WORKING-STORAGE SECTION.

01  PROGRAM-CONTROLS.
    05 INPUT-DATA-FLAG      PIC X(4).
       88 END-OF-DATA                VALUE 'END'.
    05 PROPER-SPACING       PIC 9(1).
    05 WS-REPORT-DATE       PIC X(6).
    05 MASTER-FILE-FLAG     PIC X(2).
       88 SUCCESSFUL-WRITE           VALUE '00'.
3.  05 USER-ENTRY           PIC X(10).

01  PROGRAM-COUNTERS.
    05 MASTER-RECORD-CTR       PIC S9(2).
    05 OUT-OF-SEQ-CTR          PIC S9(2).

01  REPORT-LINES.
    05 COMPANY-NAME.
       10 PIC X(41)    VALUE SPACES.
       10 PIC X(18)    VALUE 'TOUCAN ENTERPRISES'.
       10 PIC X(41)    VALUE SPACES.

    05 REPORT-NAME.
       10          PIC X(31)    VALUE SPACES.
       10          PIC X(30)    VALUE
                                'MASTER EMPLOYEE FILE CREATED  '.
       10 O-DATE   PIC XX/XX/XX.
       10          PIC X(31)    VALUE SPACES.

    05 HEADINGS.
       10 PIC X(3)    VALUE SPACES.
       10 PIC X(3)    VALUE 'SSN'.
       10 PIC X(10)   VALUE SPACES.
       10 PIC X(4)    VALUE 'NAME'.
       10 PIC X(24)   VALUE SPACES.
       10 PIC X(7)    VALUE 'ADDRESS'.
       10 PIC X(34)   VALUE SPACES.
       10 PIC X(5)    VALUE 'PHONE'.
       10 PIC X(9)    VALUE SPACES.

    05 DETAIL-LINE.
       10 O-SEQ-FLAG       PIC X(3).
       10 O-SSN            PIC XXXBXXBXXXX.
       10                  PIC X(2).
       10 O-NAME           PIC X(26).
       10                  PIC X(2).
       10 O-ADDRESS        PIC X(40).
       10                  PIC X(1).
       10 O-PHONE          PIC X(11).
       10                  PIC X(3).
```

```
          05 MESSAGE-LINE.
             10 PIC X(3)    VALUE '***'.
             10 PIC X(36)   VALUE
                            '  INDICATES OUT OF SEQUENCE RECORDS!'.

          05 SUMMARY-HEADER.
             10 PIC X(3)    VALUE SPACES.
             10 PIC X(8)    VALUE 'SUMMARY:'.
             10 PIC X(89)   VALUE SPACES.

          05 SUMMARY-LINE-1.
             10                      PIC X(12)   VALUE SPACES.
             10 O-MASTER-RECORD-CTR  PIC ZZ9.
             10                      PIC X(24)   VALUE
                                     '  MASTER RECORDS WRITTEN'.
             10                      PIC X(61)   VALUE SPACES.

          05 SUMMARY-LINE-2.
             10                      PIC X(12)   VALUE SPACES.
             10 O-OUT-OF-SEQ-CTR     PIC ZZ9.
             10                      PIC X(39)   VALUE
                         '  RECORDS OUT OF SEQUENCE - NOT WRITTEN'.
             10                      PIC X(48)   VALUE SPACES.

          05 END-LINE.
             10 PIC X(39)   VALUE SPACES.
             10 PIC X(23)   VALUE '***  END OF REPORT  ***'.
             10 PIC X(38)   VALUE SPACES.

       PROCEDURE DIVISION.

       100-CREATE-MASTER-FILE.
           PERFORM 200-START-UP.
           PERFORM 210-PROCESS-TERMINAL-DATA
               UNTIL END-OF-DATA.
           PERFORM 220-FINISH-UP.
           STOP RUN.

       200-START-UP.
           OPEN OUTPUT MASTER-FILE
                       REPORT-FILE.
           ACCEPT WS-REPORT-DATE FROM DATE.
           MOVE WS-REPORT-DATE TO O-DATE.
           INITIALIZE PROGRAM-COUNTERS.
           PERFORM 300-WRITE-REPORT-HEADERS.
4.         DISPLAY BEL BEL.
           DISPLAY '**************************************************'.
           DISPLAY 'ENTER EMPLOYEE DATA BY RESPONDING TO THE PROMPTS'.
           DISPLAY 'WHEN NO MORE DATA, ENTER 'END' AT NAME PROMPT!'.
           DISPLAY BEL BEL.

       210-PROCESS-TERMINAL-DATA.
           MOVE SPACES TO MASTER-RECORD
                          DETAIL-LINE.
5.         DISPLAY BEL 'PLEASE ENTER DATA CAREFULLY!!'.
           DISPLAY ' '
           DISPLAY 'ENTER LAST NAME: ' WITH NO ADVANCING.
           ACCEPT MR-LAST-NAME.
6.         IF MR-NAME(1:4) = 'END'
               SET END-OF-DATA TO TRUE
           END-IF.
7.         IF NOT END-OF-DATA
               DISPLAY 'ENTER FIRST NAME: ' WITH NO ADVANCING
               ACCEPT MR-FIRST-NAME
               DISPLAY 'ENTER MIDDLE INITIAL: ' WITH NO ADVANCING
               ACCEPT MR-INITIAL
               DISPLAY 'ENTER SOCIAL SECURITY NUMBER: '
                                                WITH NO ADVANCING
               ACCEPT MR-SSN
               DISPLAY 'ENTER STREET ADDRESS: ' WITH NO ADVANCING
               ACCEPT MR-STREET
               DISPLAY 'ENTER CITY: ' WITH NO ADVANCING
               ACCEPT MR-CITY
               DISPLAY 'ENTER STATE ABBREVIATION: ' WITH NO ADVANCING
               ACCEPT MR-STATE
               DISPLAY 'ENTER 5-DIGIT ZIP CODE: ' WITH NO ADVANCING
               ACCEPT MR-ZIP
               DISPLAY 'ENTER PHONE AREA CODE: ' WITH NO ADVANCING
               ACCEPT MR-AREA-CODE
               DISPLAY 'ENTER 7-DIGIT PHONE NUMBER: ' WITH NO ADVANCING
               ACCEPT MR-PHONE-NO
               DISPLAY ' '
8.             DISPLAY 'THANK YOU!!' BEL
               PERFORM 310-WRITE-MASTER-RECORD
               PERFORM 320-PREPARE-DETAIL-LINE
           END-IF.
```

```
       220-FINISH-UP.
           WRITE PRINTLINE FROM MESSAGE-LINE
               AFTER ADVANCING 3 LINES.
           PERFORM 330-PREPARE-SUMMARY.
           WRITE PRINTLINE FROM END-LINE
               AFTER ADVANCING 5 LINES.
           CLOSE MASTER-FILE
                 REPORT-FILE.

       300-WRITE-REPORT-HEADERS.
           WRITE PRINTLINE FROM COMPANY-NAME
               AFTER ADVANCING PAGE.
           WRITE PRINTLINE FROM REPORT-NAME
               AFTER ADVANCING 3 LINES.
           WRITE PRINTLINE FROM HEADINGS
               AFTER ADVANCING 3 LINES.
           MOVE 2 TO PROPER-SPACING.

       310-WRITE-MASTER-RECORD.
           MOVE 'EM' TO RECORD-CODE.
9.         WRITE MASTER-RECORD
               INVALID KEY
                   DISPLAY '*****' BEL BEL
                   DISPLAY
                         'SSN FOR THIS EMPLOYEE IS OUT OF SEQUENCE'
                   DISPLAY
                         'MASTER RECORD WAS NOT CREATED. '
                         'NOTE IT FOR LATER ADDITION'
                   ADD 1 TO OUT-OF-SEQ-CTR
                   DISPLAY 'PRESS CR WHEN READY TO CONTINUE'
                                                WITH NO ADVANCING
                   ACCEPT USER-ENTRY
               NOT INVALID KEY
                   DISPLAY '***  MASTER RECORD NOW IN FILE!'
                   ADD 1 TO MASTER-RECORD-CTR
                   DISPLAY 'PRESS CR WHEN READY TO CONTINUE'
                                                WITH NO ADVANCING
                   ACCEPT USER-ENTRY
           END-WRITE.

       320-PREPARE-DETAIL-LINE.
           IF NOT SUCCESSFUL-WRITE
               MOVE '***' TO O-SEQ-FLAG
           END-IF.
           MOVE MR-SSN TO O-SSN.
           MOVE MR-NAME TO O-NAME.
           MOVE MR-ADDRESS TO O-ADDRESS.
           MOVE MR-PHONE TO O-PHONE.
           WRITE PRINTLINE FROM DETAIL-LINE
               AFTER ADVANCING PROPER-SPACING.

       330-PREPARE-SUMMARY.
           MOVE MASTER-RECORD-CTR TO O-MASTER-RECORD-CTR.
           MOVE OUT-OF-SEQ-CTR TO O-OUT-OF-SEQ-CTR.
           WRITE PRINTLINE FROM SUMMARY-HEADER
               AFTER ADVANCING 5 LINES.
           WRITE PRINTLINE FROM SUMMARY-LINE-1
               AFTER ADVANCING 2 LINES.
           WRITE PRINTLINE FROM SUMMARY-LINE-2
               AFTER ADVANCING 1 LINE.
```

Running the Program

The data in Figure 6.9 was used in a trial run of the program. Figure 6.10 shows the first full screen as entries were made in response to the prompts. A typical screen is a 24 by 80 matrix, that is, 24 lines of 80 characters each. As additional lines are needed, the screen scrolls up one line at a time. In this trial run, a total of 90 lines was needed, which is enough data to fill three screens and display 18 lines on a fourth screen. Lines 25 through 90 are shown in Figure 6.11.

The report produced by the program is shown in Figure 6.12.

Figure 6.9 Sample terminal data

Employee data to be entered at the terminal

1. WALTER R. PALMER
   35 WILLOW DR
   SOMERSET, MA 02750
   PHONE: (508)698-4532
   SSN: 456 23 5100

2. MARIA E. READY
   345 EAST MAIN
   FALL RIVER, MA 02722
   PHONE: (508)678-4534
   SSN: 723 51 0611

3. DOMENIC A. CAPARCO
   415 BARNES ST
   SWANSEA, MA 02764
   PHONE: (508)679-4536
   SSN: 781 20 7315

4. WEBSTER P. JACKVONY
   516 ATLANTIC BLVD
   SEEKONK, MA 02780
   PHONE: (508)679-9432
   SSN: 861 74 5201

5. JUDITH L. GRAHAM
   54 SHADY LANE
   SOMERSET, MA 02750
   PHONE: (508)698-3217

Figure 6.10 First full screen

```
***************************************************
ENTER EMPLOYEE DATA BY RESPONDING TO THE PROMPTS
WHEN NO MORE DATA, ENTER 'END' AT NAME PROMPT!

PLEASE ENTER DATA CAREFULLY!!

ENTER LAST NAME: PALMER
ENTER FIRST NAME: WALTER
ENTER MIDDLE INITIAL: R
ENTER SOCIAL SECURITY NUMBER: 456235100
ENTER STREET ADDRESS: 35 WILLOW DR
ENTER CITY: SOMERSET
ENTER STATE ABBREVIATION: MA
ENTER 5-DIGIT ZIP CODE: 02750
ENTER PHONE AREA CODE: 508
ENTER 7-DIGIT PHONE NUMBER: 6984532

THANK YOU!!
***  MASTER RECORD NOW IN FILE!
PRESS CR WHEN READY TO CONTINUE
PLEASE ENTER DATA CAREFULLY!!

ENTER LAST NAME: READY
```

Figure 6.11 Remaining lines scrolled onto the screen

```
ENTER FIRST NAME: MARIA
ENTER MIDDLE INITIAL: E
ENTER SOCIAL SECURITY NUMBER: 723510611
ENTER STREET ADDRESS: 345 EAST MAIN
ENTER CITY: FALL RIVER
ENTER STATE ABBREVIATION: MA
ENTER 5-DIGIT ZIP CODE: 02722
ENTER PHONE AREA CODE: 508
ENTER 7-DIGIT PHONE NUMBER: 6784534

THANK YOU!!
***  MASTER RECORD NOW IN FILE!
PRESS CR WHEN READY TO CONTINUE
PLEASE ENTER DATA CAREFULLY!!

ENTER LAST NAME: CAPARCO
ENTER FIRST NAME: DOMENIC
ENTER MIDDLE INITIAL: A
ENTER SOCIAL SECURITY NUMBER: 781207315
ENTER STREET ADDRESS: 415 BARNES ST
ENTER CITY: SWANSEA
ENTER STATE ABBREVIATION: MA
ENTER 5-DIGIT ZIP CODE: 02764
ENTER PHONE AREA CODE: 508
ENTER 7-DIGIT PHONE NUMBER: 6794536

THANK YOU!!
***  MASTER RECORD NOW IN FILE!
PRESS CR WHEN READY TO CONTINUE
PLEASE ENTER DATA CAREFULLY!!

ENTER LAST NAME: JACKVONY
ENTER FIRST NAME: WEBSTER
ENTER MIDDLE INITIAL: P
ENTER SOCIAL SECURITY NUMBER: 861745201
ENTER STREET ADDRESS: 516 ATLANTIC BLVD
ENTER CITY: SEEKONK
ENTER STATE ABBREVIATION: MA
ENTER 5-DIGIT ZIP CODE: 02780
ENTER PHONE AREA CODE: 508
ENTER 7-DIGIT PHONE NUMBER: 6799432

THANK YOU!!
***  MASTER RECORD NOW IN FILE!
PRESS CR WHEN READY TO CONTINUE
PLEASE ENTER DATA CAREFULLY!!

ENTER LAST NAME: GRAHAM
ENTER FIRST NAME: JUDITH
ENTER MIDDLE INITIAL: L
ENTER SOCIAL SECURITY NUMBER: 325123315
ENTER STREET ADDRESS: 54 SHADY LANE
ENTER CITY: SOMERSET
ENTER STATE ABBREVIATION: MA
ENTER 5-DIGIT ZIP CODE: 02750
ENTER PHONE AREA CODE: 508
ENTER 7-DIGIT PHONE NUMBER: 6983217

THANK YOU!!
*****
SSN FOR THIS EMPLOYEE IS OUT OF SEQUENCE
MASTER RECORD WAS NOT CREATED. NOTE IT FOR LATER ADDITION
PRESS CR WHEN READY TO CONTINUE
PLEASE ENTER DATA CAREFULLY!!

ENTER LAST NAME: END
```

Figure 6.12 Report produced by the program

```
                                        TOUCAN ENTERPRISES

                                MASTER EMPLOYEE FILE CREATED  89/06/15

   SSN          NAME                          ADDRESS                                    PHONE

   456 23 5100  PALMER      WALTER     R  35 WILLOW DR        SOMERSET     MA 02750 508 6984532

   723 51 0611  READY       MARIA      E  345 EAST MAIN       FALL RIVER   MA 02722 508 6784534

   781 20 7315  CAPARCO     DOMENIC    A  415 BARNES ST       SWANSEA      MA 02764 508 6794536

   861 74 5201  JACKVONY    WEBSTER    P  516 ATLANTIC BLVD   SEEKONK      MA 02780 508 6799432

***325 12 3315  GRAHAM      JUDITH     L  54 SHADY LANE       SOMERSET     MA 02750 508 6983217

***  INDICATES OUT OF SEQUENCE RECORDS!


   SUMMARY:

             4  MASTER RECORDS WRITTEN
             1  RECORDS OUT OF SEQUENCE - NOT WRITTEN


                                      ***  END OF REPORT  ***
```

Method 2—ACCEPT/DISPLAY with Free-form Data Entry

Without changing the primary objective of the program, namely, creating an indexed employee file by obtaining data interactively from the user, we examine another technique that may be used in a prompt/response dialogue between a user and the system. In method 1, each prompt asked for a single data item, such as the employee's first name, the employee's city, and so on. In method 2, a single prompt will request the entry of multiple data items, as in the following:

```
ENTER SSN, LAST NAME, FIRST NAME AND MID INITIAL.
```

The response to this prompt will contain data whose size in number of characters may vary from one employee to another. For instance, not all last names have the same length! Of course, the user could be asked to count spaces to make all last name entries the same size, but that is not practical, since it would likely cause many data entry errors. A better procedure is to employ a free-form data entry in which a delimiter is used to indicate the end of a data item. The following entry is an example of a response to the above prompt in which a semicolon (;) is used as a data item delimiter:

```
456235100;PALMER;WALTER;R
```

As the string of characters is accepted by the program, the components are taken apart on the basis of the presence of delimiters. In our example, all the characters that occur before the first semicolon are assigned to the data field MR-SSN; the next string of characters up to the second semicolon is assigned to the data field MR-LAST-NAME; the third string of characters up to the third semicolon is assigned to the data field MR-FIRST-NAME; and the last string, consisting of a single character, is assigned to the data item MR-INITIAL.

The COBOL statement designed to separate a string of characters into one or more items is the UNSTRING statement. Suppose the program executes the following statements:

```
DISPLAY "PLEASE ENTER DATA CAREFULLY AS SHOWN".
DISPLAY "SSN;LAST NAME;FIRST NAME;INITIAL".
ACCEPT STEP-1-DATA.
```

When the previous string of characters (for PALMER) is entered, it is stored in the data item STEP-1-DATA. Now, the UNSTRING statement is used to separate the components, as follows:

```
UNSTRING STEP-1-DATA
    DELIMITED BY ";"
        INTO MR-SSN        DELIMITER IN WS-DELIM
             MR-LAST-NAME  DELIMITER IN WS-DELIM
             MR-FIRST-NAME DELIMITER IN WS-DELIM
             MR-INITIAL    DELIMITER IN WS-DELIM
END-UNSTRING.
```

Note that the selected delimiter is specified in the clause DELIMITED BY "; " and the data items that receive the "unstrung" components are sequentially MR-SSN, MR-LAST-NAME, MR-FIRST-NAME, and MR-INITIAL. The optional phrase DELIMITER IN WS-DELIM simply moves the encountered delimiter into the data item WS-DELIM.

By applying this technique, the employee data can be obtained by using only two ACCEPT statements. Suppose that the above statements (DISPLAY, DISPLAY, ACCEPT, and UNSTRING) are followed by these statements:

```
DISPLAY "PLEASE ENTER DATA CAREFULLY AS SHOWN!!"
DISPLAY "STREET ADDRESS;CITY;STATE;ZIP;AREA CODE;PHONE NO".
ACCEPT STEP-2-DATA.
UNSTRING STEP-2-DATA
    DELIMITED BY ";"
        INTO MR-STREET      DELIMITER IN WS-DELIM
             MR-CITY        DELIMITER IN WS-DELIM
             MR-STATE       DELIMITER IN WS-DELIM
             MR-ZIP         DELIMITER IN WS-DELIM
             MR-AREA-CODE   DELIMITER IN WS-DELIM
             MR-PHONE-NO    DELIMITER IN WS-DELIM
END-UNSTRING.
```

If the user enters the following data:

```
35 WILLOW DR;SOMERSET;MA;02750;508;6984532
```

then

the string "35 WILLOW DR" is unstrung into MR-STREET,
the string "SOMERSET" is moved into MR-CITY,
the string "MA" is moved into MR-STATE,
the string "02750" is moved into MR-ZIP
the string "508" is moved into MR-AREA-CODE, and
the string "6984532" is moved into MR-PHONE-NO.

The format of the UNSTRING statement is shown in Figure 6.13. The statement is explained in Appendix A.

Figure 6.13 UNSTRING statement format

```
UNSTRING identifier-1
    [DELIMITED BY [ALL] {identifier-2} [OR [ALL] {identifier-3}] . . . ]
                        {literal-1   }           {literal-2   }
    INTO {identifier-4 [DELIMITER IN identifier-5] [COUNT IN identifier-6]} . . .
    [WITH POINTER identifier-7]
    [TALLYING IN identifier-8]
    [ON OVERFLOW imperative-statement-1]
    [NOT ON OVERFLOW imperative-statement-2]
    [END-UNSTRING]
```

Designing the Program

It should be clear that once employee data has been received and stored in the data fields of MASTER-RECORD, program logic remains as it was in the program of Figure 6.8 that implemented method 1. The parts of the program that must be changed are the ones that describe to the user the inputting procedures to be used and the ones related to the DISPLAY and ACCEPT statements that establish the needed dialogue. Additionally, the program must contain the UNSTRING statements that store the accepted data in the appropriate fields of MASTER-RECORD.

Initial DISPLAY statements describing the program's data input procedures are contained in paragraph 200-START-UP, while the actual prompt/response statements are contained in paragraph 210-PROCESS-TERMINAL-DATA.

Consider the logic of flowchart module 210-PROCESS-TERMINAL-DATA shown in Figure 6.14. Note that there are two ACCEPT functions that obtain data from the user, ACCEPT STEP-1-DATA and ACCEPT STEP-2-DATA. The user has been informed to enter "END" at the first prompt for data

Figure 6.14 Flowchart module 210-PROCESS-TERMINAL-DATA

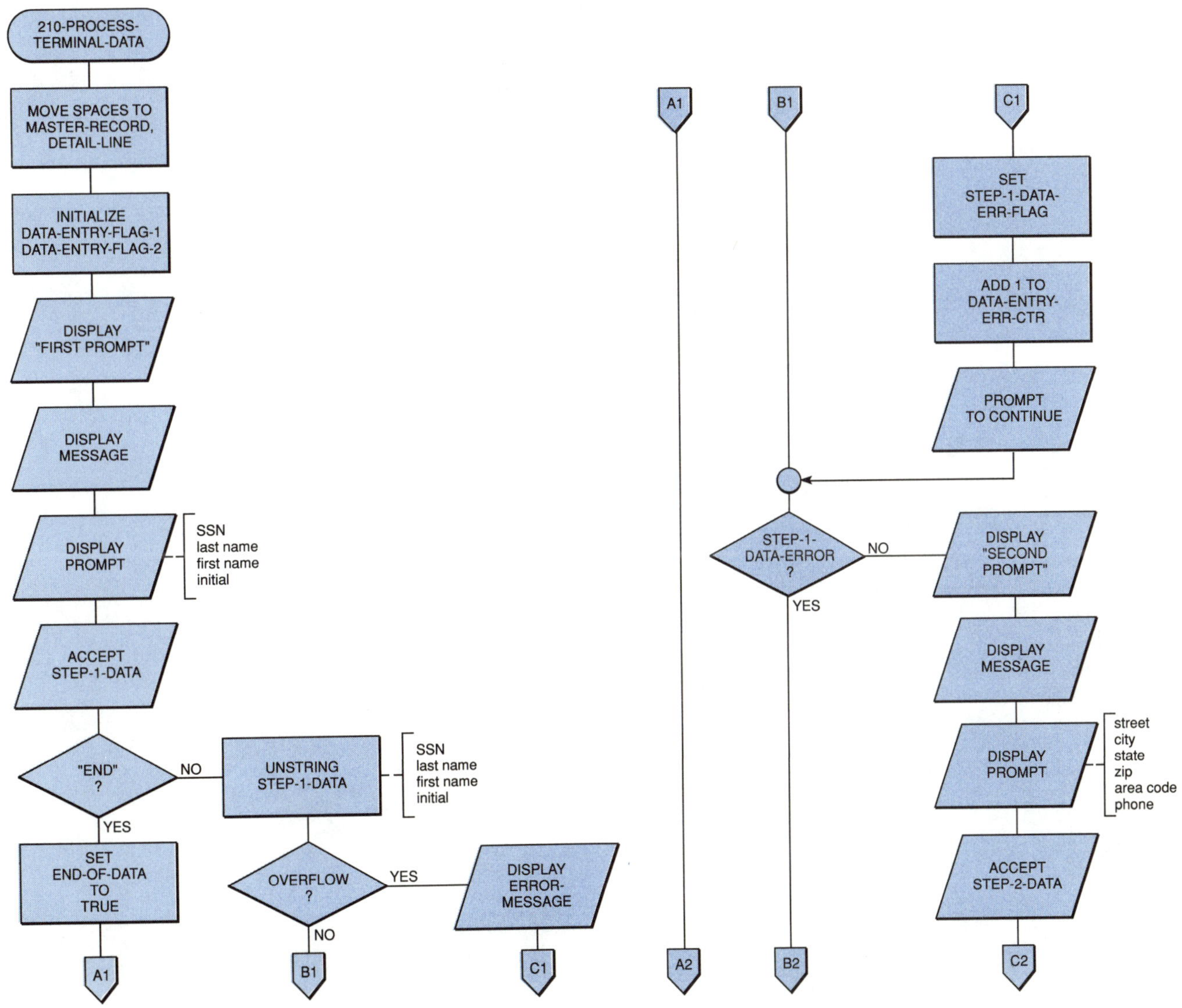

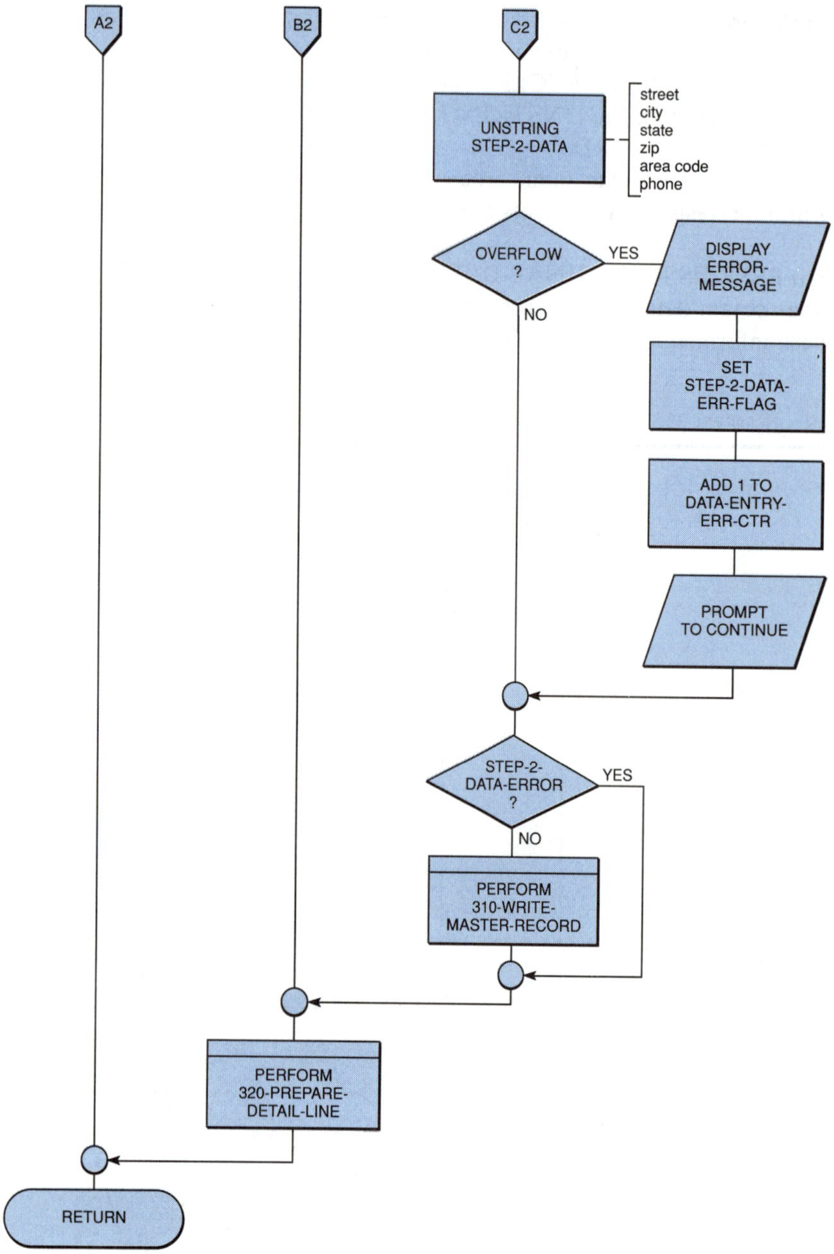
A2
B2
C2
UNSTRING STEP-2-DATA
street
city
state
zip
area code
phone
OVERFLOW ?
YES
NO
DISPLAY ERROR-MESSAGE
SET STEP-2-DATA-ERR-FLAG
ADD 1 TO DATA-ENTRY-ERR-CTR
PROMPT TO CONTINUE
STEP-2-DATA-ERROR ?
YES
NO
PERFORM 310-WRITE-MASTER-RECORD
PERFORM 320-PREPARE-DETAIL-LINE
RETURN

■ **Figure 6.15** Module 320-PREPARE-DETAIL-LINE

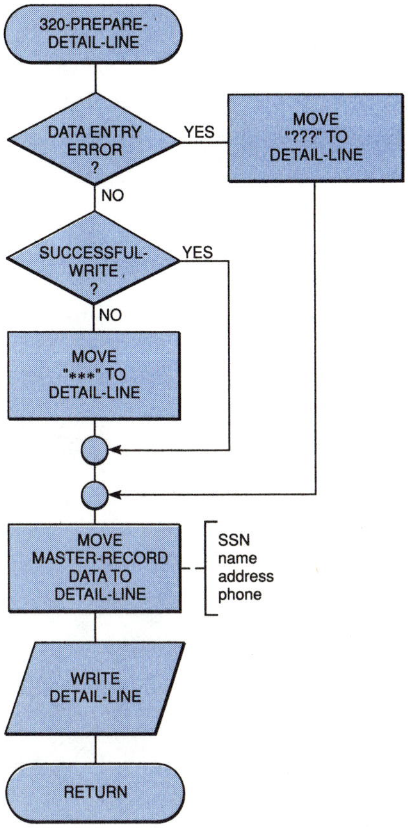

when there is no more data to enter. This will provide an exit from the loop that processes terminal data. If STEP-1-DATA does not contain "END," then its components are taken apart by the UNSTRING function. During the UNSTRING operation, if there are characters left in STEP-1-DATA after the receiving fields have all received their values, this denotes a data entry error. Such an error can be detected by the ON OVERFLOW clause of the UNSTRING statement. If a data entry error occurs, an appropriate message is displayed on the screen to inform the user, a data entry error flag is set, a data entry error counter is incremented, and the user is prompted to enter CR to continue. Note that a step-1 data entry error causes a bypass of the second prompt for data.

On the other hand, if there is no step-1 data entry error, the user is prompted a second time to supply the remaining data for the employee. If there is no step-2 data entry error, control is sent to module 310-WRITE-MASTER-RECORD to write the new master record to the master file. If there is a step-2 data entry error detected by an overflow condition during the UNSTRING operation, the user is informed of the problem and the procedure 310-WRITE-MASTER-RECORD is not executed.

When the detail line is prepared for employee data entered at the terminal, the flag "???" will be printed at the beginning of the line if a data entry error occurred, and the flag "***" will be printed at the beginning of the line if an out-of-sequence write error occurred. This logic is shown in Figure 6.15.

Coding the Program

The program that results from the development above is contained in Figure 6.16. The new entries in this program have been highlighted for your convenience. In particular, note the new informational messages produced by the DISPLAY statements in paragraph 200-START-UP and the implementation of the UNSTRING statements in paragraph 210-PROCESS-TERMINAL-DATA.

Figure 6.16 Interactive COBOL program implementing free-form data entry

```
 IDENTIFICATION DIVISION.

 PROGRAM-ID.  CREATE-FILE-INT2.

************************************************************************
*                                                                      *
*  THIS PROGRAM ILLUSTRATES THE USE OF THE ACCEPT AND DISPLAY          *
*  STATEMENTS (WITHOUT VENDOR EXTENSIONS TO THE ANSI STANDARDS)        *
*  IN AN INTERACTIVE APPLICATION.  THE PROGRAM ACCEPTS EMPLOYEE        *
*  DATA FROM THE TERMINAL AND WRITES RECORDS TO AN INDEXED FILE.       *
*                                                                      *
*  IN THIS PROGRAM, EMPLOYEE DATA IS ENTERED IN TWO STEPS: THE         *
*  FIRST ENTERS THE SSN AND EMPLOYEE NAME; THE SECOND ENTERS           *
*  THE ADDRESS AND PHONE NUMBER.  THE PROGRAM THEN USES THE            *
*  UNSTRING STATEMENT TO ASSIGN DATA TO THE FIELDS OF THE              *
*  MASTER RECORD.                                                      *
*                                                                      *
*  THE PROGRAM ALSO PRODUCES AN AUDIT REPORT.                          *
*                                                                      *
************************************************************************

 ENVIRONMENT DIVISION.

 CONFIGURATION SECTION.

 SOURCE-COMPUTER.  VAX-VMS-8650.
 OBJECT-COMPUTER.  VAX-VMS-8650.

 SPECIAL-NAMES.
     SYMBOLIC CHARACTERS BEL IS 8.

 INPUT-OUTPUT SECTION.

 FILE-CONTROL.
     SELECT MASTER-FILE      ASSIGN TO 'TOUCAN2.DAT'
                             ORGANIZATION IS INDEXED
                             ACCESS MODE IS SEQUENTIAL
                             RECORD KEY IS MR-SSN
                             FILE STATUS IS MASTER-FILE-FLAG.
     SELECT REPORT-FILE      ASSIGN TO COB1$OUTPUT.

 DATA DIVISION.

 FILE SECTION.

 FD  MASTER-FILE
     RECORD CONTAINS 88 CHARACTERS
     BLOCK CONTAINS 5 RECORDS.

 01  MASTER-RECORD.
     05 RECORD-CODE          PIC X(2).
     05 MR-SSN               PIC X(9).
     05 MR-NAME.
        10 MR-LAST-NAME      PIC X(12).
        10                   PIC X(1).
        10 MR-FIRST-NAME     PIC X(11).
        10                   PIC X(1).
        10 MR-INITIAL        PIC X(1).
     05 MR-ADDRESS.
        10 MR-STREET         PIC X(18).
        10                   PIC X(1).
        10 MR-CITY           PIC X(12).
        10                   PIC X(1).
        10 MR-STATE          PIC X(2).
        10                   PIC X(1).
        10 MR-ZIP            PIC X(5).
     05 MR-PHONE.
        10 MR-AREA-CODE      PIC X(3).
        10                   PIC X(1).
        10 MR-PHONE-NO       PIC X(7).

 FD  REPORT-FILE
     RECORD CONTAINS 100 CHARACTERS.

 01  PRINTLINE               PIC X(100).

 WORKING-STORAGE SECTION.

 01  PROGRAM-CONTROLS.
     05 INPUT-DATA-FLAG         PIC X(4).
        88 END-OF-DATA                     VALUE 'END'.
     05 PROPER-SPACING          PIC 9(1).
     05 WS-REPORT-DATE          PIC X(6).
     05 MASTER-FILE-FLAG        PIC X(2).
        88 SUCCESSFUL-WRITE               VALUE '00'.
     05 USER-ENTRY              PIC X(10).
```

```
01  PROGRAM-COUNTERS.
    05 MASTER-RECORD-CTR    PIC S9(2).
    05 OUT-OF-SEQ-CTR       PIC S9(2).
    05 DATA-ENTRY-ERR-CTR   PIC S9(2).

01  TERMINAL-DATA-ITEMS.
    05 STEP-1-DATA          PIC X(37).
    05 STEP-2-DATA          PIC X(53).
    05 DATA-ENTRY-FLAG-1    PIC X(3).
       88 STEP-1-DATA-ERROR           VALUE 'ON '.
    05 DATA-ENTRY-FLAG-2    PIC X(3).
       88 STEP-2-DATA-ERROR           VALUE 'ON '.
    05 WS-DELIM             PIC X(1).

01  REPORT-LINES.
    05 COMPANY-NAME.
       10 PIC X(41)    VALUE SPACES.
       10 PIC X(18)    VALUE 'TOUCAN ENTERPRISES'.
       10 PIC X(41)    VALUE SPACES.

    05 REPORT-NAME.
       10         PIC X(31)    VALUE SPACES.
       10         PIC X(30)    VALUE
                               'MASTER EMPLOYEE FILE CREATED  '.
       10 O-DATE  PIC XX/XX/XX.
       10         PIC X(31)    VALUE SPACES.

    05 HEADINGS.
       10 PIC X(3)    VALUE SPACES.
       10 PIC X(3)    VALUE 'SSN'.
       10 PIC X(10)   VALUE SPACES.
       10 PIC X(4)    VALUE 'NAME'.
       10 PIC X(24)   VALUE SPACES.
       10 PIC X(7)    VALUE 'ADDRESS'.
       10 PIC X(34)   VALUE SPACES.
       10 PIC X(5)    VALUE 'PHONE'.
       10 PIC X(9)    VALUE SPACES.

    05 DETAIL-LINE.
       10 O-ERR-FLAG      PIC X(3).
       10 O-SSN           PIC XXXBXXBXXXX.
       10                 PIC X(2).
       10 O-NAME          PIC X(26).
       10                 PIC X(2).
       10 O-ADDRESS       PIC X(40).
       10                 PIC X(1).
       10 O-PHONE         PIC XXXBXXXBXXXX.
       10                 PIC X(3).

    05 MESSAGE-LINE-1.
       10 PIC X(3)    VALUE '***'.
       10 PIC X(36)   VALUE
          ' INDICATES OUT OF SEQUENCE RECORDS!'.

    05 MESSAGE-LINE-2.
       10 PIC X(3)    VALUE '???'.
       10 PIC X(43)   VALUE
          ' INDICATES RECORDS WITH DATA ENTRY ERRORS!'.

    05 SUMMARY-HEADER.
       10 PIC X(3)    VALUE SPACES.
       10 PIC X(8)    VALUE 'SUMMARY:'.
       10 PIC X(89)   VALUE SPACES.

    05 SUMMARY-LINE-1.
       10                        PIC X(12)   VALUE SPACES.
       10 O-MASTER-RECORD-CTR    PIC ZZ9.
       10                        PIC X(24)   VALUE
                                 ' MASTER RECORDS WRITTEN'.
       10                        PIC X(61)   VALUE SPACES.

    05 SUMMARY-LINE-2.
       10                        PIC X(12)   VALUE SPACES.
       10 O-OUT-OF-SEQ-CTR       PIC ZZ9.
       10                        PIC X(39)   VALUE
                    ' RECORDS OUT OF SEQUENCE - NOT WRITTEN'.
       10                        PIC X(48)   VALUE SPACES.

    05 SUMMARY-LINE-3.
       10                        PIC X(12)   VALUE SPACES.
       10 O-DATA-ENTRY-ERR-CTR   PIC ZZ9.
       10                        PIC X(48)   VALUE
          ' DATA ENTRY ERRORS - MASTER RECORD NOT WRITTEN'.
       10                        PIC X(37)   VALUE SPACES.
```

```
     05 END-LINE.
        10 PIC X(39)  VALUE SPACES.
        10 PIC X(23)  VALUE '***  END OF REPORT  ***'.
        10 PIC X(38)  VALUE SPACES.

 PROCEDURE DIVISION.

 100-CREATE-MASTER-FILE.
     PERFORM 200-START-UP.
     PERFORM 210-PROCESS-TERMINAL-DATA
         UNTIL END-OF-DATA.
     PERFORM 220-FINISH-UP.
     STOP RUN.

 200-START-UP.
     OPEN OUTPUT MASTER-FILE
                 REPORT-FILE.
     ACCEPT WS-REPORT-DATE FROM DATE.
     MOVE WS-REPORT-DATE TO O-DATE.
     INITIALIZE PROGRAM-COUNTERS.
     PERFORM 300-WRITE-REPORT-HEADERS.
     DISPLAY BEL BEL.
     DISPLAY '*-*-*-*-*-*-*-*-*-*-*-*-*-*-*-*-*-*-*-*-*-*-*-*-*-*-*'.
     DISPLAY 'ENTER EMPLOYEE DATA IN 2 STEPS:'.
     DISPLAY 'IN STEP 1,'
     DISPLAY 'ENTER SSN, LAST NAME, FIRST NAME AND MID INITIAL'.
     DISPLAY '** IMPORTANT: SEPARATE DATA BY A SEMICOLON (;)'.
     DISPLAY ' '
     DISPLAY 'IN STEP 2,'
     DISPLAY 'ENTER STREET ADDRESS, CITY, STATE ABBREVIATION,'
             ' ZIP CODE, AREA CODE, AND'.
     DISPLAY '      PHONE NUMBER'.
     DISPLAY '** IMPORTANT: SEPARATE DATA BY A SEMICOLON (;)'.
     DISPLAY ' '
     DISPLAY '*****  YOU WILL BE PROMPTED FOR EACH STEP!'.
     DISPLAY ' '
     DISPLAY '*-*-*-*-*-*-*-*-*-*-*-*-*-*-*-*-*-*-*-*-*-*-*-*-*-*-*'.
     DISPLAY ' '
     DISPLAY 'WHEN NO MORE DATA, ENTER 'END' AT FIRST PROMPT!'.
     DISPLAY ' '
     DISPLAY '*-*-*-*-*-*-*-*-*-*-*-*-*-*-*-*-*-*-*-*-*-*-*-*-*-*-*'.
     DISPLAY ' ' BEL BEL.

 210-PROCESS-TERMINAL-DATA.
     MOVE SPACES TO MASTER-RECORD
                    DETAIL-LINE.
     INITIALIZE DATA-ENTRY-FLAG-1
                DATA-ENTRY-FLAG-2.
     DISPLAY '   ' BEL
     DISPLAY 'FIRST PROMPT!'
     DISPLAY 'PLEASE ENTER DATA CAREFULLY AS SHOWN!!'.
     DISPLAY 'SSN;LAST NAME;FIRST NAME;INITIAL'.
     ACCEPT STEP-1-DATA.
     IF STEP-1-DATA(1:4) = 'END'
         SET END-OF-DATA TO TRUE
     ELSE
         UNSTRING STEP-1-DATA
             DELIMITED BY ';'
                 INTO MR-SSN         DELIMITER IN WS-DELIM
                      MR-LAST-NAME   DELIMITER IN WS-DELIM
                      MR-FIRST-NAME  DELIMITER IN WS-DELIM
                      MR-INITIAL     DELIMITER IN WS-DELIM
             ON OVERFLOW
                 DISPLAY BEL BEL ' '
                     'DATA ENTRY ERROR IN STEP 1 RESPONSE'
                 DISPLAY 'MASTER RECORD WAS NOT CREATED.'
                         ' NOTE IT FOR LATER ADDITION'
                 SET STEP-1-DATA-ERROR TO TRUE
                 ADD 1 TO DATA-ENTRY-ERR-CTR
                 DISPLAY 'PRESS CR WHEN READY TO CONTINUE'
                                        WITH NO ADVANCING
                 ACCEPT USER-ENTRY
         END-UNSTRING
         IF NOT STEP-1-DATA-ERROR
             DISPLAY ' ' BEL
             DISPLAY 'SECOND PROMPT!'
             DISPLAY 'PLEASE ENTER DATA CAREFULLY AS SHOWN!!'
             DISPLAY 'STREET ADDRESS;CITY;STATE;ZIP;AREA CODE;'
                     'PHONE NO'
             ACCEPT STEP-2-DATA
             UNSTRING STEP-2-DATA
                 DELIMITED BY ';'
                     INTO MR-STREET      DELIMITER IN WS-DELIM
                          MR-CITY        DELIMITER IN WS-DELIM
                          MR-STATE       DELIMITER IN WS-DELIM
                          MR-ZIP         DELIMITER IN WS-DELIM
```

```
                        MR-AREA-CODE  DELIMITER IN WS-DELIM
                        MR-PHONE-NO   DELIMITER IN WS-DELIM
                ON OVERFLOW
                    DISPLAY BEL BEL
                         'DATA ENTRY ERROR IN STEP 2 RESPONSE'
                    DISPLAY 'MASTER RECORD WAS NOT CREATED.'
                         ' NOTE IT FOR LATER ADDITION'
                    SET STEP-2-DATA-ERROR TO TRUE
                    ADD 1 TO DATA-ENTRY-ERR-CTR
                    DISPLAY 'PRESS CR WHEN READY TO CONTINUE'
                                           WITH NO ADVANCING
                    ACCEPT USER-ENTRY
            END-UNSTRING
            IF NOT STEP-2-DATA-ERROR
                PERFORM 310-WRITE-MASTER-RECORD
            END-IF
        END-IF
            PERFORM 320-PREPARE-DETAIL-LINE
    END-IF.

220-FINISH-UP.
    WRITE PRINTLINE FROM MESSAGE-LINE-1
        AFTER ADVANCING 3 LINES.
    WRITE PRINTLINE FROM MESSAGE-LINE-2
        AFTER ADVANCING 1 LINE.
    PERFORM 330-PREPARE-SUMMARY.
    WRITE PRINTLINE FROM END-LINE
        AFTER ADVANCING 5 LINES.
    CLOSE MASTER-FILE
          REPORT-FILE.

300-WRITE-REPORT-HEADERS.
    WRITE PRINTLINE FROM COMPANY-NAME
        AFTER ADVANCING PAGE.
    WRITE PRINTLINE FROM REPORT-NAME
        AFTER ADVANCING 3 LINES.
    WRITE PRINTLINE FROM HEADINGS
        AFTER ADVANCING 3 LINES.
    MOVE 2 TO PROPER-SPACING.

310-WRITE-MASTER-RECORD.
    MOVE 'EM' TO RECORD-CODE.
    WRITE MASTER-RECORD
        INVALID KEY
            DISPLAY ' '
            DISPLAY '*****' BEL BEL
            DISPLAY ' '
                    'SSN FOR THIS EMPLOYEE IS OUT OF SEQUENCE'
            DISPLAY 'MASTER RECORD WAS NOT CREATED.'
                    '  NOTE IT FOR LATER ADDITION'
            ADD 1 TO OUT-OF-SEQ-CTR
            DISPLAY 'PRESS CR WHEN READY TO CONTINUE'
                                   WITH NO ADVANCING
            ACCEPT USER-ENTRY
        NOT INVALID KEY
            DISPLAY ' '
            DISPLAY '***  MASTER RECORD NOW IN FILE!'
            ADD 1 TO MASTER-RECORD-CTR
            DISPLAY 'PRESS CR WHEN READY TO CONTINUE'
                                   WITH NO ADVANCING
            ACCEPT USER-ENTRY
    END-WRITE.

320-PREPARE-DETAIL-LINE.
    IF NOT SUCCESSFUL-WRITE
        MOVE '***' TO O-ERR-FLAG
    END-IF.
    IF STEP-1-DATA-ERROR OR STEP-2-DATA-ERROR
        MOVE '???' TO O-ERR-FLAG
    END-IF.
    MOVE MR-SSN TO O-SSN.
    MOVE MR-NAME TO O-NAME.
    MOVE MR-ADDRESS TO O-ADDRESS.
    MOVE MR-PHONE TO O-PHONE.
    WRITE PRINTLINE FROM DETAIL-LINE
        AFTER ADVANCING PROPER-SPACING.

330-PREPARE-SUMMARY.
    MOVE MASTER-RECORD-CTR TO O-MASTER-RECORD-CTR.
    MOVE OUT-OF-SEQ-CTR TO O-OUT-OF-SEQ-CTR.
    MOVE DATA-ENTRY-ERR-CTR TO O-DATA-ENTRY-ERR-CTR.
    WRITE PRINTLINE FROM SUMMARY-HEADER
        AFTER ADVANCING 5 LINES.
    WRITE PRINTLINE FROM SUMMARY-LINE-1
        AFTER ADVANCING 2 LINES.
    WRITE PRINTLINE FROM SUMMARY-LINE-2
        AFTER ADVANCING 1 LINE.
    WRITE PRINTLINE FROM SUMMARY-LINE-3
        AFTER ADVANCING 1 LINE.
```

Figure 6.17 First full screen with method 2

```
*-*-*-*-*-*-*-*-*-*-*-*-*-*-*-*-*-*-*-*-*-*-*-*-*-*
ENTER EMPLOYEE DATA IN 2 STEPS:
IN STEP 1,
ENTER SSN, LAST NAME, FIRST NAME AND MID INITIAL
** IMPORTANT: SEPARATE DATA BY A SEMICOLON (;)

IN STEP 2,
ENTER STREET ADDRESS, CITY, STATE ABBREVIATION, ZIP CODE, AREA CODE, AND
      PHONE NUMBER
** IMPORTANT: SEPARATE DATA BY A SEMICOLON (;)

*****  YOU WILL BE PROMPTED FOR EACH STEP!

*-*-*-*-*-*-*-*-*-*-*-*-*-*-*-*-*-*-*-*-*-*-*-*-*-*

WHEN NO MORE DATA, ENTER 'END' AT FIRST PROMPT!

*-*-*-*-*-*-*-*-*-*-*-*-*-*-*-*-*-*-*-*-*-*-*-*-*-*


FIRST PROMPT!
PLEASE ENTER DATA CAREFULLY AS SHOWN!!
SSN;LAST NAME;FIRST NAME;INITIAL
456235100;PALMER;WALTER;R
```

Executing the Program

The employee data in Figure 6.9 was used in a trial run of the program. This run produced a total of 91 lines on the screen. The first full screen is shown in Figure 6.17, and the remaining 67 lines, which were produced by scrolling up one line at a time, are shown in Figure 6.18.

The report produced by the program is shown in Figure 6.19.

Method 3—Designed Video Forms

Note: You are able to replicate the interactive programs of Methods 1 and 2 on your computer because they rely solely on ANSI formats for the ACCEPT and the DISPLAY statements. However, you may not be able to replicate the programs that follow unless your COBOL compiler supports the same extensions to the ACCEPT and DISPLAY statements as those provided by the Digital Equipment Corporation! Ask your instructor for details.

Extensions to the ANSI COBOL standards allow the programmer of interactive programs to design data entry video forms that are more user friendly than the direct prompt/response technique used earlier. They present at one time a clearer overall picture of the task at hand, which facilitates data entry by the user during the necessary dialogue of interactive applications.

■ **Figure 6.18** Remaining lines from the program run

```
SECOND PROMPT!
PLEASE ENTER DATA CAREFULLY AS SHOWN!!
STREET ADDRESS;CITY;STATE;ZIP;AREA CODE;PHONE NO
85 WILLOW DR;SOMERSET;MA;02720;508;6984532

***  MASTER RECORD NOW IN FILE!
PRESS CR WHEN READY TO CONTINUE

FIRST PROMPT!
PLEASE ENTER DATA CAREFULLY AS SHOWN!!
SSN;LAST NAME;FIRST NAME;INITIAL
723510611;READY;MARIA;E

SECOND PROMPT!
PLEASE ENTER DATA CAREFULLY AS SHOWN!!
STREET ADDRESS;CITY;STATE;ZIP;AREA CODE;PHONE NO
345 EAST MAIN;FALL RIVER;MA;02722;508;6784534

***  MASTER RECORD NOW IN FILE!
PRESS CR WHEN READY TO CONTINUE

FIRST PROMPT!
PLEASE ENTER DATA CAREFULLY AS SHOWN!!
SSN;LAST NAME;FIRST NAME;INITIAL
781207315;CAPARCO;DOMENIC;A

SECOND PROMPT!
PLEASE ENTER DATA CAREFULLY AS SHOWN!!
STREET ADDRESS;CITY;STATE;ZIP;AREA CODE;PHONE NO
415 BARNES ST;SWANSEA;MA;02764;508;6794536

***  MASTER RECORD NOW IN FILE!
PRESS CR WHEN READY TO CONTINUE

FIRST PROMPT!
PLEASE ENTER DATA CAREFULLY AS SHOWN!!
SSN;LAST NAME;FIRST NAME;INITIAL
861745201;JACKVONY;WEBSTER;P

SECOND PROMPT!
PLEASE ENTER DATA CAREFULLY AS SHOWN!!
STREET ADDRESS;CITY;STATE;ZIP;AREA CODE;PHONE NO
616 ATLANTIC BLVD;SEEKONK;MA;02780;508;6799432

***  MASTER RECORD NOW IN FILE!
PRESS CR WHEN READY TO CONTINUE

FIRST PROMPT!
PLEASE ENTER DATA CAREFULLY AS SHOWN!!
SSN;LAST NAME;FIRST NAME;INITIAL
325123315;GRAHAM;JUDITH;L

SECOND PROMPT!
PLEASE ENTER DATA CAREFULLY AS SHOWN!!
STREET ADDRESS;CITY;STATE;ZIP;AREA CODE;PHONE NO
64 SHADY LANE;SOMERSET;MA;02750;508;6983217

*****
SSN FOR THIS EMPLOYEE IS OUT OF SEQUENCE
MASTER RECORD WAS NOT CREATED.  NOTE IT FOR LATER ADDITION
PRESS CR WHEN READY TO CONTINUE

FIRST PROMPT!
PLEASE ENTER DATA CAREFULLY AS SHOWN!!
SSN;LAST NAME;FIRST NAME;INITIAL
END
```

Figure 6.19 Report produced by the program

```
                                        TOUCAN ENTERPRISES

                               MASTER EMPLOYEE FILE CREATED  89/06/15

   SSN           NAME                         ADDRESS                                     PHONE

   456 23 5100   PALMER       WALTER      R  35 WILLOW DR       SOMERSET     MA 02750 508 6984532
   723 51 0611   READY        MARIA       E  345 EAST MAIN      FALL RIVER   MA 02722 508 6784534
   781 20 7315   CAPARCO      DOMENIC     A  415 BARNES ST      SWANSEA      MA 02764 508 6794536
   861 74 5201   JACKVONY     WEBSTER     P  516 ATLANTIC BLVD  SEEKONK      MA 02780 508 6799432
***325 12 3315   GRAHAM       JUDITH      L  54 SHADY LANE      SOMERSET     MA 02750 508 6983217

***  INDICATES OUT OF SEQUENCE RECORDS!
???  INDICATES RECORDS WITH DATA ENTRY ERRORS!


   SUMMARY:

               4  MASTER RECORDS WRITTEN
               1  RECORDS OUT OF SEQUENCE - NOT WRITTEN
               0  DATA ENTRY ERRORS - MASTER RECORD NOT WRITTEN


                                 ***  END OF REPORT  ***
```

Figure 6.20 Video chart

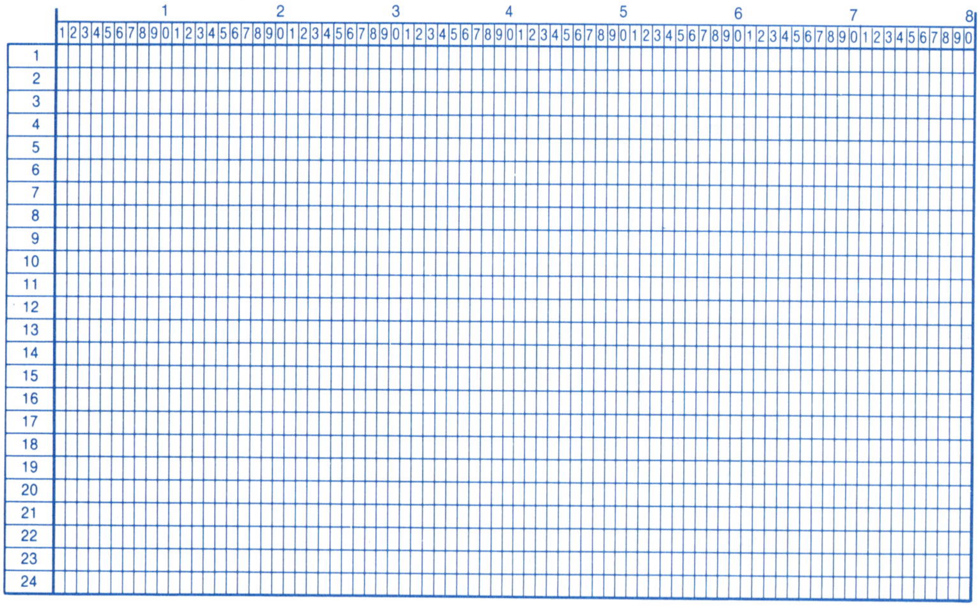

Figure 6.21 Video chart for terminal input of employee data

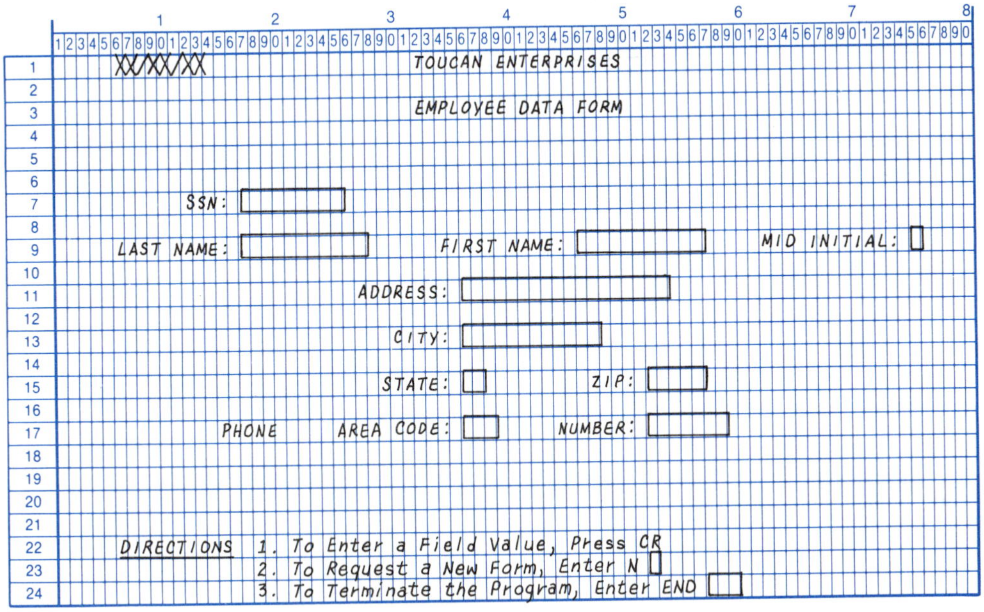

In a manner similar to a printer spacing chart for a printed report, a screen layout form, shown in Figure 6.20, helps the programmer to design a video data entry form. Note that it consists of 24 lines with 80 character positions per line.

Figure 6.21 shows a completed screen layout form with specifications that may be used to prepare a video form to request employee data in the current problem. The printed entries on the form will be produced by DISPLAY statements (including the date in the upper left-hand corner). The rectangular boxes indicate the fields where the user will be prompted to enter the required data. These fields will be associated with ACCEPT statements in the program. The positioning of the printed values and the data entry fields is accomplished by the use of LINE NUMBER and COLUMN NUMBER clauses, in a manner similar to the use of such clauses within the Report Writer.

When the program containing the specifications prepared on the screen layout form is run, the user is presented with the video form shown in Figure 6.22. The cursor is automatically positioned at the SSN data field. In this program, the cursor moves from left to right and from top to bottom across the video form as a result of specifications coded into ACCEPT statements. Therefore, after entering a value in the SSN data field, pressing the carriage return moves the cursor to the LAST NAME field. Following that entry, the cursor moves to the FIRST NAME data field, and so on. After the last data entry (the PHONE NUMBER data field), the cursor is positioned to the right of "Enter N". At this point, if the user enters N, a new video form is displayed. If the user does not want a new form, simply pressing CR advances the cursor to the last line. By entering END, program execution is terminated.

The formats of the ACCEPT and DISPLAY statements provided by the Digital Equipment Corporation as extensions to the ANSI COBOL standards are shown in Figure 6.23. These formats are not explained in detail, since they are not standard across the industry and may be used only with computers whose COBOL compilers support these vendor-specific extensions. However, note the following:

1. Positioning on the screen may be specified in absolute and/or relative numbers in both the ACCEPT and the DISPLAY statements.
2. The ERASE option may be applied to individual lines and to the whole screen, or parts thereof.
3. The BELL option is available as an audio component of the interactive dialogue.

Figure 6.22 Video form displayed by the program

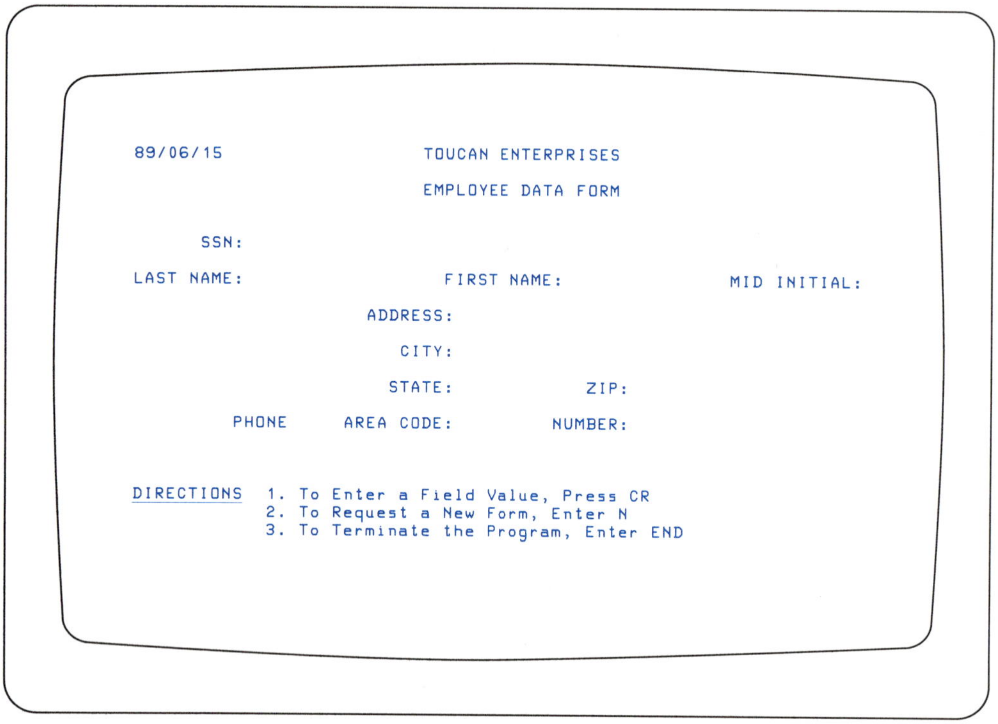

4. Displayed characters and/or data fields may be enhanced by the UNDERLINED, BOLD, BLINKING, and REVERSED (video) options.
5. The CONVERSION option allows for proper internal or external representations of data values.
6. The PROTECTED option limits the number of characters that may be accepted into a data field, thus guarding against truncations.
7. The NO ECHO option accepts characters from the keyboard without displaying them on the screen.
8. The DEFAULT option allows for default values to be specified and accepted.

The program in Figure 6.24 contains entries that create the data entry video form and that accept data in the fields shown in Figure 6.22. The following comments apply to the numbered lines in the program of Figure 6.24.

1. This group of DISPLAY statements presents the user with introductory information. The ACCEPT statement lets the user decide when to continue with the execution of the program.
2. This group of five DISPLAY statements creates the video form. Note the use of LINE and COLUMN phrases to control positioning of displayed characters. Also note the use of the BOLD and UNDERLINED options.
3. This group of ten ACCEPT statements stores the data entered by the user into the data fields of MASTER-RECORD. The use of the LINE and COLUMN options position the cursor at the beginning of the data entry fields on the screen. The use of the REVERSED option provides reversed video display to light up the data entry fields. The use of the PROTECTED option prevents the user from entering more characters than the size of the receiving field (within MASTER-RECORD) allows. If such an attempt is made, the terminal bell rings to advise the user of the problem. The user can then delete characters to the left to repair the entry.
4. This ACCEPT statement positions the cursor to the right of line 2 in the DIRECTIONS at the bottom of the screen. The use of the BLINKING option draws the user's attention to the directions! The user has a choice of entering N to request a new video form or CR (although in reality any other character before the carriage return will do) to advance the cursor to the next choice, namely, the entry field to the right of line 3 in the DIRECTIONS.

■ **Figure 6.23a** DIGITAL extensions to the ACCEPT statement format

```
ACCEPT identifier-1
  ⎧ FROM LINE NUMBER { integer-1
  ⎪                    identifier-2 [PLUS [integer-2]]
  ⎪                    PLUS [integer-2] }
  ⎪ FROM COLUMN NUMBER { integer-3
  ⎪                      identifier-3 [PLUS [integer-4]]
  ⎪                      PLUS [integer-4] }
  ⎪ ERASE [TO END OF] { SCREEN
  ⎪                     LINE }
  ⎪ WITH BELL
  ⎪ UNDERLINED
  ⎪ BOLD
  ⎪ WITH BLINKING
  ⎨ PROTECTED [ { SIZE { integer-5
  ⎪                      identifier-4 }
  ⎪               WITH AUTOTERMINATE
  ⎪               WITH NO BLANK
  ⎪               WITH FILLER literal-1 } ]
  ⎪ WITH CONVERSION
  ⎪ REVERSED
  ⎪ WITH NO ECHO
  ⎪ DEFAULT is { literal-2
  ⎪              identifier-5
  ⎪              CURRENT VALUE }
  ⎩ CONTROL KEY IN identifier-6

  [ { [ON EXCEPTION imperative-statement-1] [NOT ON EXCEPTION imperative-statement-2] } ]
  [ { [AT END imperative-statement-1] [NOT AT END imperative-statement-2]             } ]
[END-ACCEPT]
```

■ **Figure 6.23b** DIGITAL extensions to the DISPLAY statement format

```
DISPLAY { { literal-1
            identifier-1 }
  [ { AT LINE NUMBER { integer-1
                       identifier-2 [PLUS [integer-2]]
                       PLUS [integer-2] }
      AT COLUMN NUMBER { integer-3
                         identifier-3 [PLUS [integer-4]]
                         PLUS [integer-4] }
      ERASE [TO END OF] { SCREEN
                          LINE }
      WITH BELL
      UNDERLINED
      BOLD
      WITH BLINKING
      REVERSED
      WITH CONVERSION                                      } ] } . . .

      [WITH NO ADVANCING]
```

Figure 6.24 Interactive COBOL program with video form features

```
 IDENTIFICATION DIVISION.

 PROGRAM-ID.  CREATE-FILE-INT3.

****************************************************************
*                                                              *
*  THIS PROGRAM ILLUSTRATES THE USE OF THE ACCEPT AND DISPLAY  *
*  STATEMENTS IN AN INTERACTIVE APPLICATION.  IN THIS APPLICA- *
*  TION, A VIDEO FORM IS PREPARED BY USING DIGITAL EXTENSIONS  *
*  TO THE ACCEPT AND DISPLAY STATEMENTS. THE FUNCTION OF THE   *
*  FORM IS TO ACCEPT EMPLOYEE DATA FROM THE TERMINAL. THE PRO- *
*  RAM WRITES RECORDS TO AN INDEXED FILE.                      *
*                                                              *
*  THE PROGRAM ALSO PRODUCES AN AUDIT REPORT.                  *
*                                                              *
****************************************************************

 ENVIRONMENT DIVISION.

 CONFIGURATION SECTION.

 SOURCE-COMPUTER.  VAX-VMS-8650.
 OBJECT-COMPUTER.  VAX-VMS-8650.

 SPECIAL-NAMES.
     SYMBOLIC CHARACTERS BEL IS 8.

 INPUT-OUTPUT SECTION.

 FILE-CONTROL.
     SELECT MASTER-FILE      ASSIGN TO 'TOUCAN3.DAT'
                             ORGANIZATION IS INDEXED
                             ACCESS MODE IS SEQUENTIAL
                             RECORD KEY IS MR-SSN
                             FILE STATUS IS MASTER-FILE-FLAG.
     SELECT REPORT-FILE      ASSIGN TO COB1$OUTPUT.

 DATA DIVISION.

 FILE SECTION.

 FD  MASTER-FILE
     RECORD CONTAINS 88 CHARACTERS
     BLOCK CONTAINS 5 RECORDS.

 01  MASTER-RECORD.
     05 RECORD-CODE        PIC X(2).
     05 MR-SSN             PIC X(9).
     05 MR-NAME.
        10 MR-LAST-NAME    PIC X(12).
        10                 PIC X(1).
        10 MR-FIRST-NAME   PIC X(11).
        10                 PIC X(1).
        10 MR-INITIAL      PIC X(1).
     05 MR-ADDRESS.
        10 MR-STREET       PIC X(18).
        10                 PIC X(1).
        10 MR-CITY         PIC X(12).
        10                 PIC X(1).
        10 MR-STATE        PIC X(2).
        10                 PIC X(1).
        10 MR-ZIP          PIC X(5).
     05 MR-PHONE.
        10 MR-AREA-CODE    PIC 9(3).
        10                 PIC X(1).
        10 MR-PHONE-NO     PIC 9(7).

 FD  REPORT-FILE
     RECORD CONTAINS 100 CHARACTERS.

 01  PRINTLINE             PIC X(100).

 WORKING-STORAGE SECTION.

 01  PROGRAM-CONTROLS.
     05 INPUT-DATA-FLAG    PIC X(4).
        88 END-OF-DATA              VALUE 'END'.
     05 FORM-REQUEST       PIC X(1).
        88 NEW-FORM                 VALUE 'N'.
     05 USER-ENTRY         PIC X(10).
     05 PROPER-SPACING     PIC 9(1).
     05 WS-REPORT-DATE     PIC X(6).
     05 MASTER-FILE-FLAG   PIC X(2).
        88 SUCCESSFUL-WRITE         VALUE '00'.
```

Figure 6.24 continued

```
 01  PROGRAM-COUNTERS.
     05 MASTER-RECORD-CTR    PIC S9(2).
     05 OUT-OF-SEQ-CTR       PIC S9(2).

 01  REPORT-LINES.
     05 COMPANY-NAME.
        10 PIC X(41)    VALUE SPACES.
        10 PIC X(18)    VALUE 'TOUCAN ENTERPRISES'.
        10 PIC X(41)    VALUE SPACES.

     05 REPORT-NAME.
        10          PIC X(31)    VALUE SPACES.
        10          PIC X(30)    VALUE
                                 'MASTER EMPLOYEE FILE CREATED  '.
        10 O-DATE   PIC XX/XX/XX.
        10          PIC X(31)    VALUE SPACES.

     05 HEADINGS.
        10 PIC X(3)    VALUE SPACES.
        10 PIC X(3)    VALUE 'SSN'.
        10 PIC X(10)   VALUE SPACES.
        10 PIC X(4)    VALUE 'NAME'.
        10 PIC X(24)   VALUE SPACES.
        10 PIC X(7)    VALUE 'ADDRESS'.
        10 PIC X(34)   VALUE SPACES.
        10 PIC X(5)    VALUE 'PHONE'.
        10 PIC X(9)    VALUE SPACES.

     05 DETAIL-LINE.
        10 O-SEQ-FLAG      PIC X(3).
        10 O-SSN           PIC XXXBXXBXXXX.
        10                 PIC X(2).
        10 O-NAME          PIC X(26).
        10                 PIC X(2).
        10 O-ADDRESS       PIC X(40).
        10                 PIC X(1).
        10 O-PHONE         PIC XXXBXXXBXXXX.
        10                 PIC X(3).

     05 MESSAGE-LINE.
        10 PIC X(3)    VALUE '***'.
        10 PIC X(36)   VALUE
                       '  INDICATES OUT OF SEQUENCE RECORDS!'.

     05 SUMMARY-HEADER.
        10 PIC X(3)    VALUE SPACES.
        10 PIC X(8)    VALUE 'SUMMARY:'.
        10 PIC X(89)   VALUE SPACES.

     05 SUMMARY-LINE-1.
        10                        PIC X(12)   VALUE SPACES.
        10 O-MASTER-RECORD-CTR    PIC ZZ9.
        10                        PIC X(24)   VALUE
                                  '  MASTER RECORDS WRITTEN'.
        10                        PIC X(61)   VALUE SPACES.

     05 SUMMARY-LINE-2.
        10                        PIC X(12)   VALUE SPACES.
        10 O-OUT-OF-SEQ-CTR       PIC ZZ9.
        10                        PIC X(39)   VALUE
                     '  RECORDS OUT OF SEQUENCE - NOT WRITTEN'.
        10                        PIC X(48)   VALUE SPACES.

     05 END-LINE.
        10 PIC X(39)   VALUE SPACES.
        10 PIC X(23)   VALUE '***  END OF REPORT  ***'.
        10 PIC X(38)   VALUE SPACES.

 PROCEDURE DIVISION.

 100-CREATE-MASTER-FILE.
     PERFORM 200-START-UP.
     PERFORM 210-PROCESS-TERMINAL-DATA
         UNTIL END-OF-DATA.
     PERFORM 220-FINISH-UP.
     STOP RUN.
```

Figure 6.24 continued

```
       200-START-UP.
           OPEN OUTPUT MASTER-FILE
                       REPORT-FILE.
           ACCEPT WS-REPORT-DATE FROM DATE.
           MOVE WS-REPORT-DATE TO O-DATE.
           INITIALIZE PROGRAM-COUNTERS.
           PERFORM 300-WRITE-REPORT-HEADERS.
1.         DISPLAY BEL BEL ' ' ERASE SCREEN.
           DISPLAY '*--*--*--*--*--*--*--*--*--*--*--*--*--*--*'.
           DISPLAY 'YOU WILL BE PRESENTED AN EMPLOYEE DATA FORM'.
           DISPLAY 'FILL IN THE BLANKS AS PROMPTED!'.
           DISPLAY 'PRESS CARRIAGE RETURN WHEN READY TO PROCEED'
                                           WITH NO ADVANCING BEL.
           ACCEPT USER-ENTRY COLUMN PLUS 2.

       210-PROCESS-TERMINAL-DATA.
           MOVE SPACES TO MASTER-RECORD
                          DETAIL-LINE.
           INITIALIZE FORM-REQUEST.
2.         DISPLAY O-DATE                LINE  1  COLUMN 6  ERASE SCREEN
                   'TOUCAN ENTERPRISES' BOLD      COLUMN 32
                   'EMPLOYEE DATA FORM' BOLD
                                         LINE  3  COLUMN 32.
           DISPLAY 'SSN: '               LINE  7  COLUMN 12
                   'LAST NAME: '         LINE  9  COLUMN 6
                   'FIRST NAME: '                 COLUMN 34
                   'MID INITIAL: '                COLUMN 62.
           DISPLAY 'ADDRESS: '           LINE 11  COLUMN 27
                   'CITY: '              LINE 13  COLUMN 30
                   'STATE: '             LINE 15  COLUMN 29
                   'ZIP: '                        COLUMN 47.
           DISPLAY 'PHONE'               LINE 17  COLUMN 15
                   'AREA CODE: '                  COLUMN 25
                   'NUMBER: '                     COLUMN 44.
           DISPLAY 'DIRECTIONS' UNDERLINED BOLD
                                         LINE 22  COLUMN 6
                   "1. To Enter a Field Value, Press CR"
                                                  COLUMN 18
                   "2. To Request a New Form, Enter N"
                                         LINE 23  COLUMN 18
                   "3. To Terminate the Program, Enter END"
                                         LINE 24  COLUMN 18.
3.         ACCEPT MR-SSN          PROTECTED REVERSED
                                         LINE  7  COLUMN 17.
           ACCEPT MR-LAST-NAME    PROTECTED REVERSED
                                         LINE  9  COLUMN 17.
           ACCEPT MR-FIRST-NAME   PROTECTED REVERSED
                                                  COLUMN 46.
           ACCEPT MR-INITIAL      PROTECTED REVERSED
                                                  COLUMN 75.
           ACCEPT MR-STREET       PROTECTED REVERSED
                                         LINE 11  COLUMN 36.
           ACCEPT MR-CITY         PROTECTED REVERSED
                                         LINE 13  COLUMN 36.
           ACCEPT MR-STATE        PROTECTED REVERSED
                                         LINE 15  COLUMN 36.
           ACCEPT MR-ZIP          PROTECTED REVERSED
                                                  COLUMN 52.
           ACCEPT MR-AREA-CODE    PROTECTED REVERSED
                                         LINE 17  COLUMN 36.
           ACCEPT MR-PHONE-NO     PROTECTED REVERSED
                                                  COLUMN 52.
           PERFORM 310-WRITE-MASTER-RECORD.
           PERFORM 320-PREPARE-DETAIL-LINE.
4.         ACCEPT FORM-REQUEST    PROTECTED REVERSED BLINKING
                                         LINE 23  COLUMN 52.
5.         IF NEW-FORM

           END-IF.
6.         ACCEPT INPUT-DATA-FLAG PROTECTED REVERSED BLINKING
                                         LINE 24  COLUMN 57.
7.         IF NOT END-OF-DATA
               DISPLAY BEL BEL 'YOU MUST ENTER ' BOLD
                                         LINE 20  COLUMN  5
               DISPLAY 'END'      BOLD REVERSED BLINKING
                                                  COLUMN 20
               DISPLAY ' TO TERMINATE THE PROGRAM!!' BOLD
                                                  COLUMN 24
               ACCEPT INPUT-DATA-FLAG PROTECTED REVERSED BLINKING
                                         LINE 24  COLUMN 57
           END-IF.
```

```
       220-FINISH-UP.
           WRITE PRINTLINE FROM MESSAGE-LINE
               AFTER ADVANCING 3 LINES.
           PERFORM 330-PREPARE-SUMMARY.
           WRITE PRINTLINE FROM END-LINE
               AFTER ADVANCING 5 LINES.
           CLOSE MASTER-FILE
                 REPORT-FILE.
8.         DISPLAY ' '                  LINE 1 COLUMN 1 ERASE SCREEN.

       300-WRITE-REPORT-HEADERS.
           WRITE PRINTLINE FROM COMPANY-NAME
               AFTER ADVANCING PAGE.
           WRITE PRINTLINE FROM REPORT-NAME
               AFTER ADVANCING 3 LINES.
           WRITE PRINTLINE FROM HEADINGS
               AFTER ADVANCING 3 LINES.
           MOVE 2 TO PROPER-SPACING.

       310-WRITE-MASTER-RECORD.
           MOVE 'EM' TO RECORD-CODE.
           WRITE MASTER-RECORD
               INVALID KEY
9.                 DISPLAY ' ' BEL BEL
                   DISPLAY '*****' BOLD REVERSED BLINKING
                                      LINE 18  COLUMN 2
                   DISPLAY 'SSN FOR THIS EMPLOYEE IS OUT OF SEQUENCE.'
                                      LINE 19  COLUMN 2
                   DISPLAY '  MASTER RECORD WAS NOT CREATED.'
                           '  NOTE IT FOR LATER ADDITION.'
                                      LINE 20  COLUMN 2
                   DISPLAY 'PRESS CR WHEN READY TO CONTINUE'
                                      LINE 21  COLUMN 2
                   ACCEPT USER-ENTRY           COLUMN PLUS 2
                   DISPLAY ' ' LINE 18 ERASE LINE
                   DISPLAY ' ' LINE 19 ERASE LINE
                   DISPLAY ' ' LINE 20 ERASE LINE
                   DISPLAY ' ' LINE 21 ERASE LINE
                   ADD 1 TO OUT-OF-SEQ-CTR
               NOT INVALID KEY
10.                DISPLAY '***  MASTER RECORD NOW IN FILE!'
                                      LINE 19  COLUMN 2
                   DISPLAY 'PRESS CR WHEN READY TO CONTINUE'
                                      LINE 20  COLUMN 2
                   ACCEPT USER-ENTRY           COLUMN PLUS 2
                   DISPLAY ' ' LINE 18 ERASE LINE
                   DISPLAY ' ' LINE 19 ERASE LINE
                   DISPLAY ' ' LINE 20 ERASE LINE
                   ADD 1 TO MASTER-RECORD-CTR
           END-WRITE.

       320-PREPARE-DETAIL-LINE.
           IF NOT SUCCESSFUL-WRITE
               MOVE '***' TO O-SEQ-FLAG
           END-IF.
           MOVE MR-SSN TO O-SSN.
           MOVE MR-NAME TO O-NAME.
           MOVE MR-ADDRESS TO O-ADDRESS.
           MOVE MR-PHONE TO O-PHONE.
           WRITE PRINTLINE FROM DETAIL-LINE
               AFTER ADVANCING PROPER-SPACING.

       330-PREPARE-SUMMARY.
           MOVE MASTER-RECORD-CTR TO O-MASTER-RECORD-CTR.
           MOVE OUT-OF-SEQ-CTR TO O-OUT-OF-SEQ-CTR.
           WRITE PRINTLINE FROM SUMMARY-HEADER
               AFTER ADVANCING 5 LINES.
           WRITE PRINTLINE FROM SUMMARY-LINE-1
               AFTER ADVANCING 2 LINES.
           WRITE PRINTLINE FROM SUMMARY-LINE-2
               AFTER ADVANCING 1 LINE.
```

5. Note the unusual use of the GO TO statement to execute the procedure 210-PROCESS-TERMINAL-DATA. This is the first time in this text (in either volume 1 or volume 2) that a GO TO statement is used to establish a loop in a COBOL program. Interactive dialogue and the use of video forms do not lend themselves too easily to the coding of programs that adhere strictly to the tenets of structured design! Note that the procedure (210-PROCESS-TERMINAL-DATA) is repeated only if the condition NEW-FORM is true. If a new form was not requested, control slips through to the next ACCEPT statement.
6. This ACCEPT statement positions the cursor at the end of line 3 in the set of DIRECTIONS. The expected entry is "END".
7. If the entry in the preceding ACCEPT statement is not "END," the user is reminded, rather forcefully, that it *must* be "END". If the user persists in entering another value, the procedure 210-PROCESS-TERMINAL-DATA is repeated and a new video form is painted on the screen.
8. This statement erases the screen as the program ends.
9. These DISPLAY statements are executed in the event of an invalid key condition when MASTER-RECORD is written to MASTER-FILE. Informational messages are displayed on the screen, just above the set of DIRECTIONS. The user is then asked to enter CR when she or he is ready to continue with the program. The last four DISPLAY statements in the group then delete the message lines from the screen.
10. The first DISPLAY statement informs the user that a master record has been successfully created. The second one prompts the user for a CR to continue. Following the entry, the message lines are erased.

Executing the Program

When the program is executed, the first screen is blank except for general directions. Each screen that follows displays a fresh copy of the video form. The six screens for the sample run of this program are shown in Figures 6.25a through 6.25f.

Figure 6.25 Sample screens produced during a trial run

a.

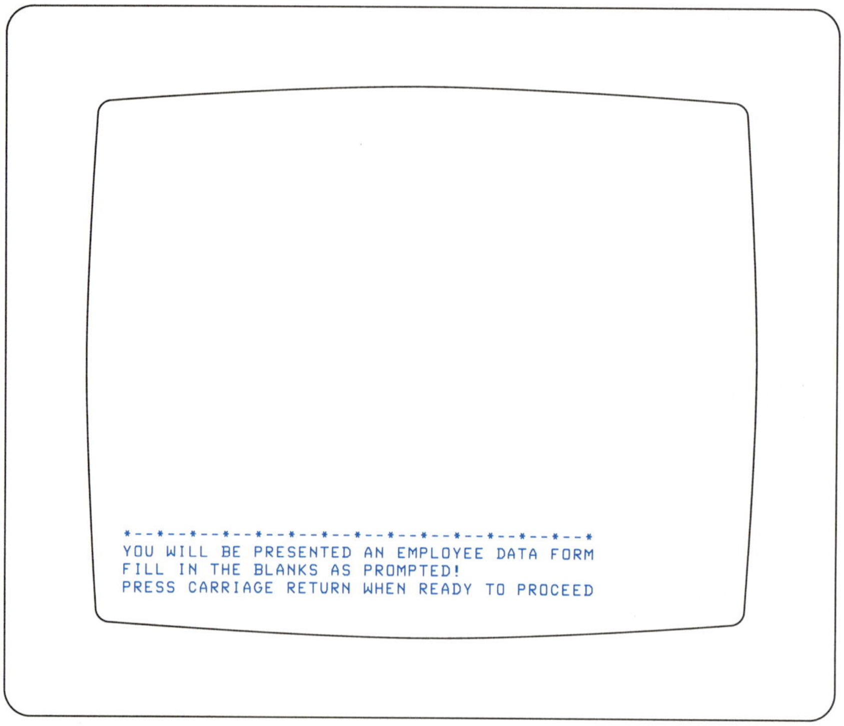

Figure 6.25 continued

b.

```
89/06/15                     TOUCAN ENTERPRISES

                             EMPLOYEE DATA FORM

        SSN: 456235100

LAST NAME: PALMER              FIRST NAME: WALTER        MID INITIAL: R

                          ADDRESS: 35 WILLOW DR

                             CITY: SOMERSET

                            STATE: MA           ZIP: 02750

              PHONE      AREA CODE: 508       NUMBER: 6984532

***  MASTER RECORD NOW IN FILE!
PRESS CR WHEN READY TO CONTINUE

    DIRECTIONS   1. To Enter a Field Value, Press CR
                 2. To Request a New Form, Enter N
                 3. To Terminate the Program, Enter END
```

c.

```
89/06/15                     TOUCAN ENTERPRISES

                             EMPLOYEE DATA FORM

        SSN: 723510611

LAST NAME: READY               FIRST NAME: MARIA         MID INITIAL: E

                          ADDRESS: 345 EAST MAIN

                             CITY: FALL RIVER

                            STATE: MA           ZIP: 02722

              PHONE      AREA CODE: 508       NUMBER: 6784534

***  MASTER RECORD NOW IN FILE!
PRESS CR WHEN READY TO CONTINUE

    DIRECTIONS   1. To Enter a Field Value, Press CR
                 2. To Request a New Form, Enter N
                 3. To Terminate the Program, Enter END
```

Figure 6.25 continued

d.

```
89/06/15                    TOUCAN ENTERPRISES

                            EMPLOYEE DATA FORM

      SSN: 781207315

LAST NAME: CAPARCO            FIRST NAME: DOMENIC     MID INITIAL: A

                       ADDRESS: 415 BARNES ST

                          CITY: SWANSEA

                         STATE: MA          ZIP: 02764

           PHONE      AREA CODE: 508      NUMBER: 6794536

***  MASTER RECORD NOW IN FILE!
PRESS CR WHEN READY TO CONTINUE

    DIRECTIONS   1. To Enter a Field Value, Press CR
                 2. To Request a New Form, Enter N
                 3. To Terminate the Program, Enter END
```

e.

```
89/06/15                    TOUCAN ENTERPRISES

                            EMPLOYEE DATA FORM

      SSN: 861745201

LAST NAME: JACKVONY           FIRST NAME: WEBSTER      MID INITIAL: P

                       ADDRESS: 516 ATLANTIC BLVD

                          CITY: SEEKONK

                         STATE: MA          ZIP: 02780

           PHONE      AREA CODE: 508      NUMBER: 6799432

***  MASTER RECORD NOW IN FILE!
PRESS CR WHEN READY TO CONTINUE

    DIRECTIONS   1. To Enter a Field Value, Press CR
                 2. To Request a New Form, Enter N
                 3. To Terminate the Program, Enter END
```

f.

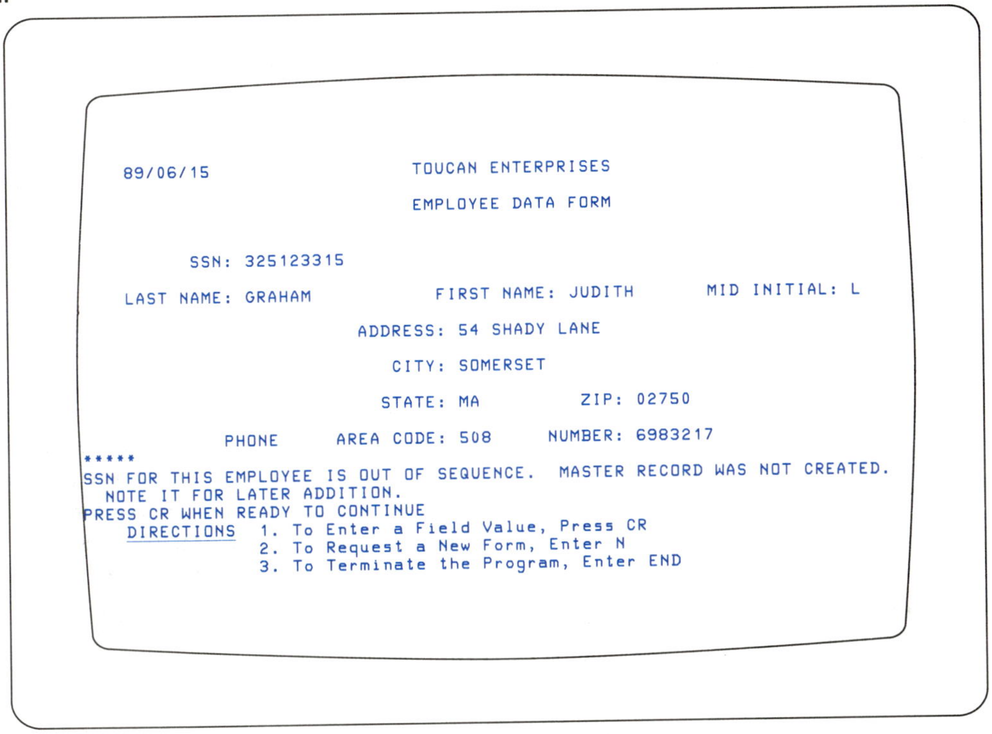

Menu-Driven Master File Update

We now consider an interactive program generally classified as a *menu-driven* program. The master personnel file for Toucan Enterprises that was created earlier as an indexed file needs to be updated periodically. The task is to develop a program to update the file interactively. You are already familiar with the overall logic needed to update an indexed master file. The only new features in this program are the ones related to the interactive aspects of the task. So as not to distract you from these new features, the audit report generally produced to provide a hard-copy record of the update will not be included in this program. The system flowchart is the one shown in Figure 6.26, and the structure chart is shown in Figure 6.27.

To facilitate the interactive dialogue between the program and the user, the first step in module 210 PROCESS TERMINAL DATA presents the user with the MAIN MENU. Its screen layout is shown in Figure 6.28.

The user enters the number (**1**, **2**, or **3**) corresponding to the needed updating action. If **1** is entered, a submenu, namely SUBMENU 1, pops up on the screen. The screen layout for SUBMENU 1 is shown in Figure 6.29.

If the user enters a **2** at the main menu, then SUBMENU 2 appears on the screen. The screen layout for SUBMENU 2 is shown in Figure 6.30.

If the user enters a **3** at the main menu, then SUBMENU 3 comes into view on the screen. The screen layout for SUBMENU 3 is shown in Figure 6.31.

Figure 6.26 System flowchart for menu-driven master file update

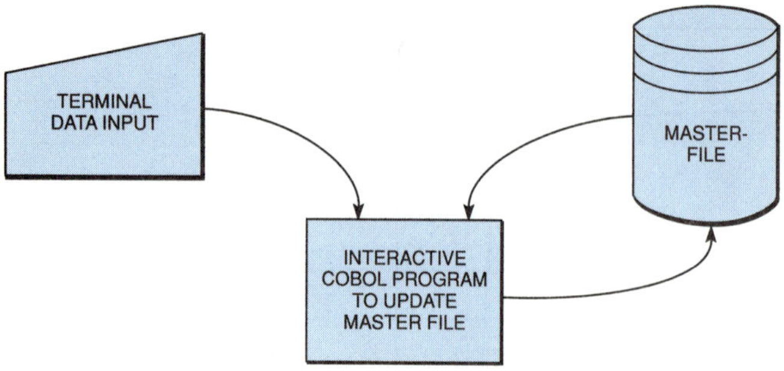

Figure 6.27 Structure chart for menu-driven master file update

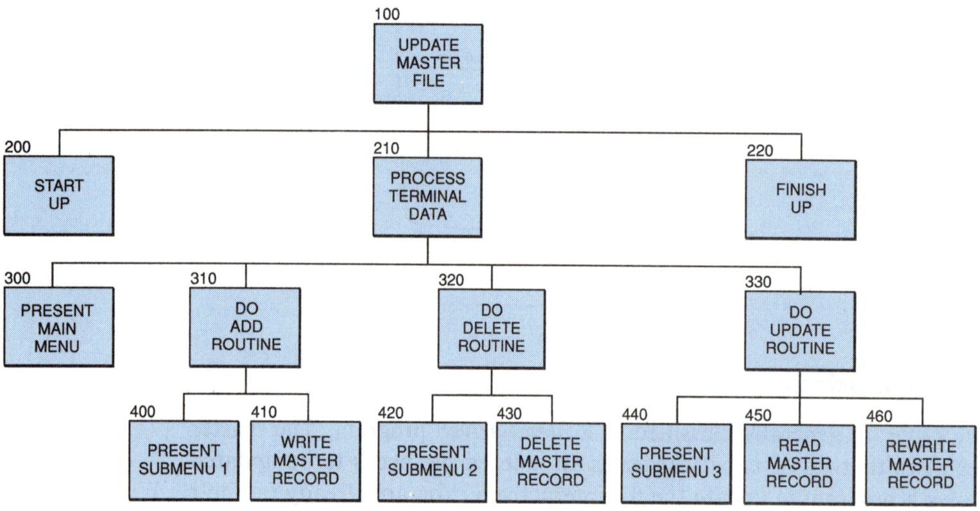

Note that all menus supply directions at the bottom of the screen. Within a submenu, the user has a choice of continuing with a fresh copy of the submenu form or of returning to the main menu. So, for instance, all new employee records could be added to the file before returning to the main menu. It's the user's choice!

Within interactive programs, it is important to provide feedback to the user that keeps him or her apprised of the success or failure of the actions taken at the terminal. On each video form, the blank lines above the DIRECTIONS line are used for this purpose. When the user decides to proceed, the messages are erased! As a result of intense dialogue, interactive programs tend to contain many lines of code. Designing the program to take into account erroneous user responses as well as correct ones and to provide appropriate feedback is a painstaking job, as is the related coding! Nonetheless, the time and effort invested in "covering all the bases" result in a program that is likely to be very effective, even in the hands of a novice, because it has been designed to be user friendly.

Since the program contains nonstandard ACCEPT and DISPLAY statements, it will not be developed systematically as we have done in previous chapters. Rather, it is presented to you in its entirety. Compare the overall structure of the PROCEDURE DIVISION with the structure chart in Figure 6.27. Then, select one updating function at a time, and examine the detailed processing steps while using the corresponding submenu (as shown in Figures 6.29, 6.30, and 6.31) as a guide. They are not difficult to understand.

The program is shown in Figure 6.32. The numbered lines correspond to the comments that follow.

Figure 6.28 MAIN MENU screen layout for master file update

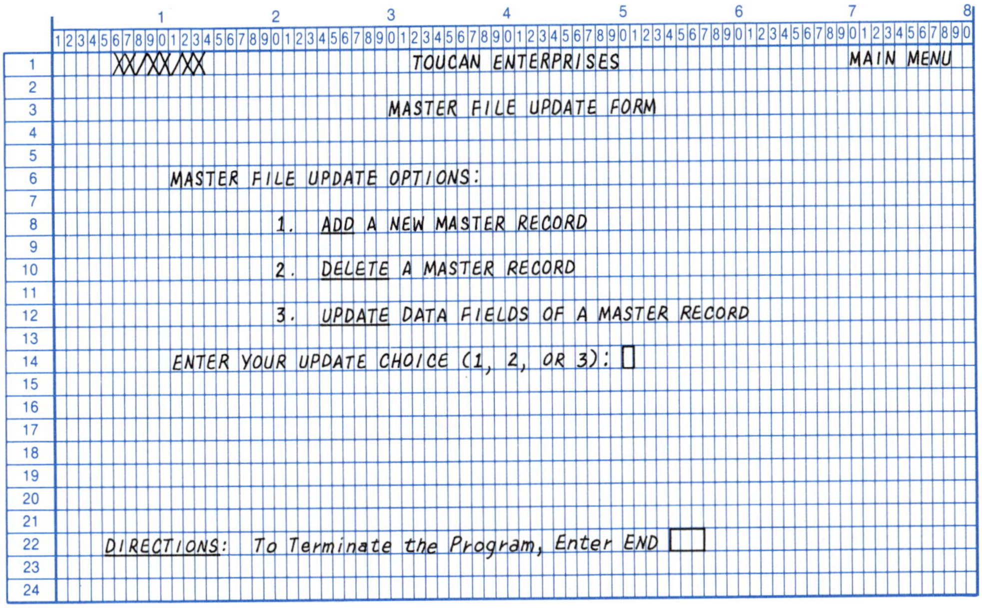

Figure 6.29 SUBMENU 1 screen layout (add a new record)

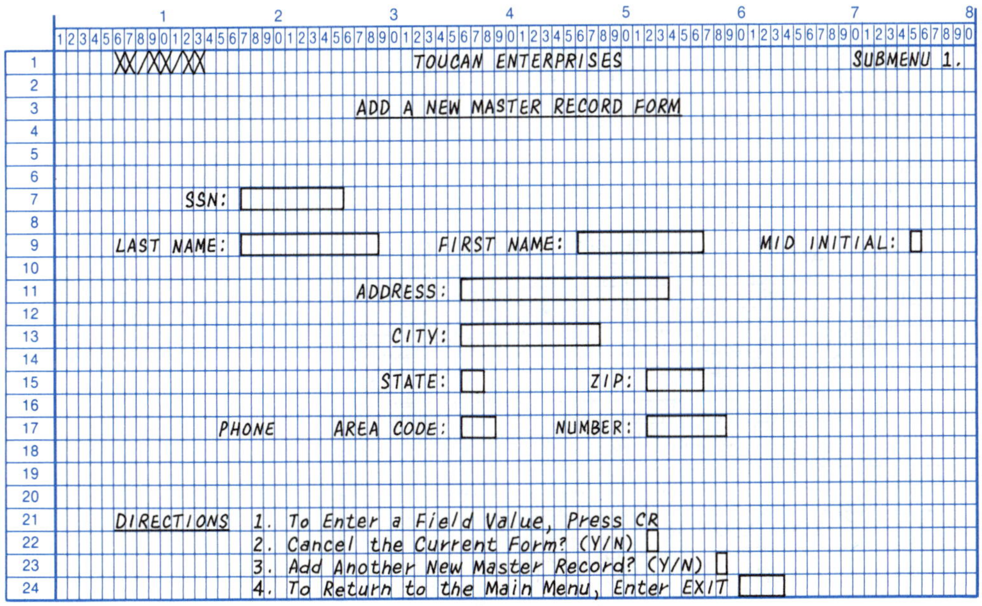

Figure 6.30 SUBMENU 2 screen layout (delete a master record)

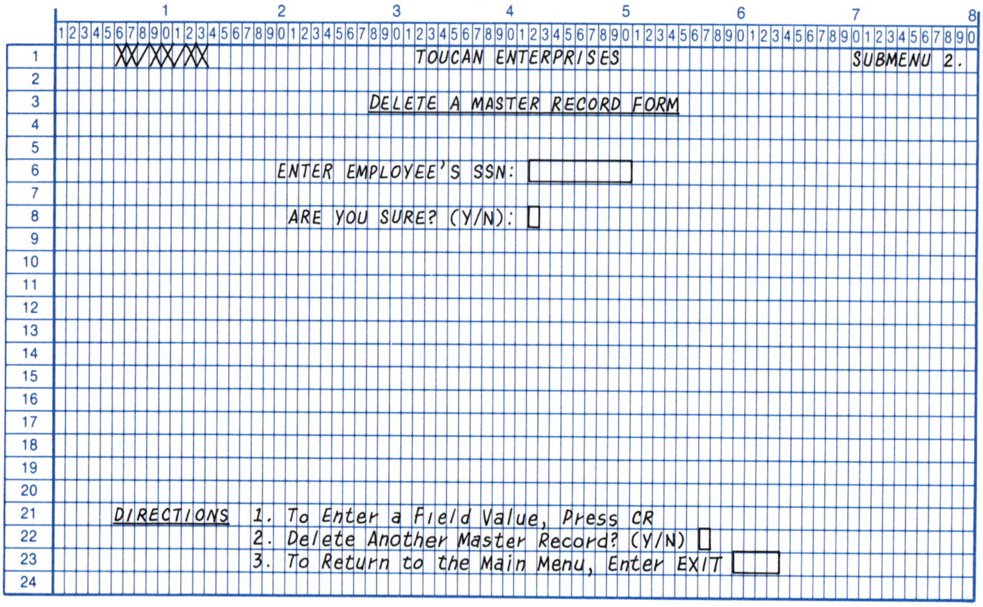

Figure 6.31 SUBMENU 3 screen layout (update a master record)

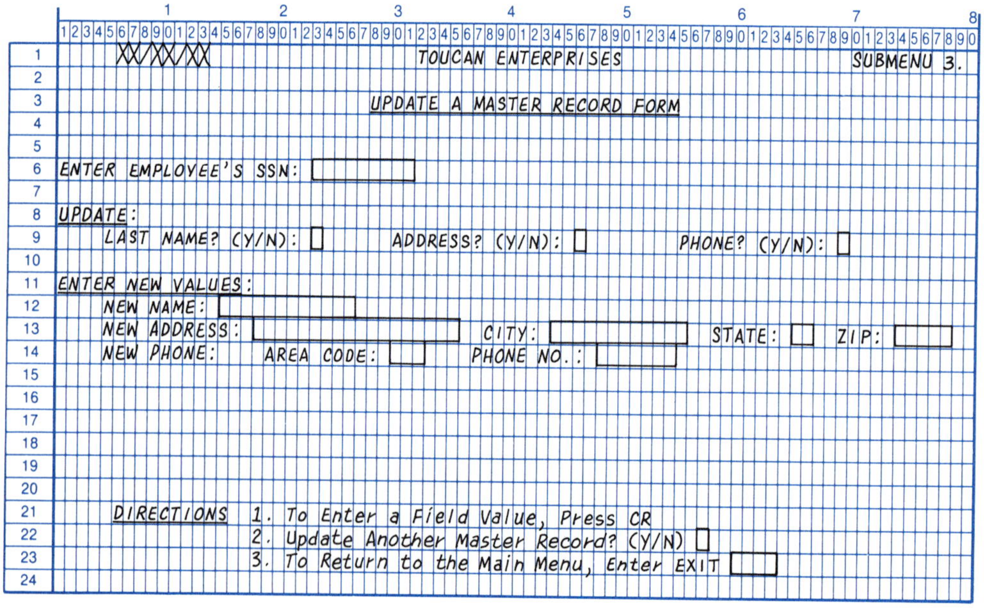

Figure 6.32 Menu-driven interactive program to update a master file

```
 IDENTIFICATION DIVISION.

 PROGRAM-ID.  INTERACTIVE-UPDATE.

************************************************************************
*                                                                      *
*  THIS PROGRAM ILLUSTRATES THE USE OF THE ACCEPT AND DISPLAY          *
*  STATEMENTS IN AN INTERACTIVE UPDATE OF AN INDEXED MASTER            *
*  FILE.  IN THIS APPLICATION, VIDEO FORMS ARE USED TO PRESENT         *
*  A MAIN MENU AND 3 SUBMENUS.  DIGITAL EXTENSIONS TO THE ACCEPT*
*  AND DISPLAY STATEMENTS ARE USED TO CREATE THE MENUS.                *
*                                                                      *
*  SO AS NOT TO CLUTTER THE PROGRAM, AN AUDIT REPORT IS NOT            *
*  PREPARED.                                                           *
*                                                                      *
************************************************************************

 ENVIRONMENT DIVISION.

 CONFIGURATION SECTION.

 SOURCE-COMPUTER.  VAX-VMS-8650.
 OBJECT-COMPUTER.  VAX-VMS-8650.

 INPUT-OUTPUT SECTION.

 FILE-CONTROL.
     SELECT MASTER-FILE        ASSIGN TO 'TOUCAN4.DAT'
                               ORGANIZATION IS INDEXED
                               ACCESS MODE IS RANDOM
                               RECORD KEY IS MR-SSN
                               FILE STATUS IS MASTER-FILE-FLAG.

 DATA DIVISION.

 FILE SECTION.

 FD  MASTER-FILE
     RECORD CONTAINS 88 CHARACTERS
     BLOCK CONTAINS 5 RECORDS.

 01  MASTER-RECORD.
     05 RECORD-CODE         PIC X(2).
     05 MR-SSN              PIC X(9).
     05 MR-NAME.
        10 MR-LAST-NAME     PIC X(12).
        10                  PIC X(1).
        10 MR-FIRST-NAME    PIC X(11).
        10                  PIC X(1).
        10 MR-INITIAL       PIC X(1).
     05 MR-ADDRESS.
        10 MR-STREET        PIC X(18).
        10                  PIC X(1).
        10 MR-CITY          PIC X(12).
        10                  PIC X(1).
        10 MR-STATE         PIC X(2).
        10                  PIC X(1).
        10 MR-ZIP           PIC X(5).
     05 MR-PHONE.
        10 MR-AREA-CODE     PIC 9(3).
        10                  PIC X(1).
        10 MR-PHONE-NO      PIC 9(7).

 WORKING-STORAGE SECTION.

 01  PROGRAM-CONTROLS.
1.   05 INPUT-DATA-FLAG        PIC X(4).
        88 END-OF-DATA               VALUE 'END'.
     05 SELECTION-NO           PIC 9(1).
     05 USER-ENTRY             PIC X(10).
     05 REPORT-DATE            PIC X(6).
     05 EDITED-DATE            PIC XX/XX/XX.
     05 MASTER-FILE-FLAG       PIC X(2).
        88 SUCCESSFUL                VALUE '00'.

2.   01  ADD-ROUTINE-ITEMS.
     05 NEW-ADD-FORM           PIC X(1).
        88 NEW-ADD-REQUEST           VALUE 'Y'.
     05 CANCEL-ADD-FORM        PIC X(1).
        88 CANCEL-FORM               VALUE 'Y'.
     05 ADD-RECORD-FLAG        PIC X(4).
        88 END-ADD-NEW-RECORDS       VALUE 'EXIT'.
```

```
3.      01  DELETE-ROUTINE-ITEMS.
            05 NEW-DELETE-FORM        PIC X(1).
               88 NEW-DELETE-REQUEST       VALUE 'Y'.
            05 VERIFY-DELETE          PIC X(1).
               88 NOT-SURE-DELETE          VALUE 'N'.
            05 DELETE-RECORD-FLAG     PIC X(4).
               88 END-DELETE-RECORDS       VALUE 'EXIT'.

4.      01  UPDATE-ROUTINE-ITEMS.
            05 NEW-UPDATE-FORM        PIC X(1).
               88 NEW-UPDATE-REQUEST       VALUE 'Y'.
            05 UPDATE-RECORD-FLAG     PIC X(4).
               88 END-UPDATE-RECORDS       VALUE 'EXIT'.
            05 NAME-UPDATE-FLAG       PIC X(1).
               88 NAME-UPDATE              VALUE 'Y'.
            05 ADDRESS-UPDATE-FLAG    PIC X(1).
               88 ADDRESS-UPDATE           VALUE 'Y'.
            05 PHONE-UPDATE-FLAG      PIC X(1).
               88 PHONE-UPDATE             VALUE 'Y'.

        PROCEDURE DIVISION.

        100-UPDATE-MASTER-FILE.
            PERFORM 200-START-UP.
            PERFORM 210-PROCESS-FILE-UPDATE
                UNTIL END-OF-DATA.
            PERFORM 220-FINISH-UP.
            STOP RUN.

        200-START-UP.
            OPEN I-O MASTER-FILE.
            ACCEPT REPORT-DATE FROM DATE.
            MOVE REPORT-DATE TO EDITED-DATE.
            INITIALIZE INPUT-DATA-FLAG.
5.          DISPLAY  ' ' BELL ERASE SCREEN.
            DISPLAY  '*---*---*---*---*---*---*---*---*---*---*---*'
                     '---*---*---*---*---*---*---*'.
            DISPLAY 'THE PURPOSE OF THIS PROGRAM IS TO UPDATE THE '
                    'EMPLOYEE MASTER FILE.'
            DISPLAY 'YOU WILL BE PRESENTED WITH A MAIN MENU.  '
                    'IT WILL PROMPT YOU TO SELECT A SUBMENU.'
            DISPLAY '*** IF THIS IS THE WRONG PROGRAM, ENTER 'END' NOW,'
            DISPLAY '    OTHERWISE, ENTER CR AND THE FILE UPDATE '
                    'PROCEDURE WILL BEGIN! '     WITH NO ADVANCING.
            ACCEPT USER-ENTRY.
            IF USER-ENTRY = 'END'
                SET END-OF-DATA TO TRUE
            END-IF.

        210-PROCESS-FILE-UPDATE.
6.          PERFORM 300-PRESENT-MAIN-MENU.
7.          EVALUATE SELECTION-NO
                WHEN     1     PERFORM 310-DO-ADD-ROUTINE
                WHEN     2     PERFORM 320-DO-DELETE-ROUTINE
                WHEN     3     PERFORM 330-DO-UPDATE-ROUTINE
                WHEN   OTHER   CONTINUE

            IF NOT END-OF-DATA
8.              GO TO 210-PROCESS-FILE-UPDATE
            END-IF.

        220-FINISH-UP.
            CLOSE MASTER-FILE.
            DISPLAY ' ' LINE 1 ERASE SCREEN.

9.      300-PRESENT-MAIN-MENU.
            INITIALIZE SELECTION-NO.
            DISPLAY EDITED-DATE           LINE  1  COLUMN  6 ERASE SCREEN
                    'TOUCAN ENTERPRISES'  BOLD     COLUMN 32
                    'MAIN MENU'           BOLD     COLUMN 70
                    'MASTER FILE UPDATE FORM'  BOLD
                                          LINE  3  COLUMN 30.
            DISPLAY 'MASTER FILE UPDATE OPTIONS:'
                                          LINE  6  COLUMN 11
                    '1.'  BOLD            LINE  8  COLUMN 20
                    'ADD' UNDERLINED               COLUMN 24
                    'A NEW MASTER RECORD'          COLUMN 28.
            DISPLAY '2.'  BOLD            LINE 10  COLUMN 20
                    'DELETE' UNDERLINED            COLUMN 24
                    'A MASTER RECORD'              COLUMN 31.
            DISPLAY '3.'  BOLD            LINE 12  COLUMN 20
                    'UPDATE' UNDERLINED            COLUMN 24
                    'DATA FIELDS OF A MASTER RECORD'
                                                   COLUMN 31.
```

```
         DISPLAY 'ENTER YOUR UPDATE CHOICE (1, 2, OR 3):'
                                  LINE 14  COLUMN 11.
         DISPLAY 'DIRECTIONS:' UNDERLINED  BOLD
                                  LINE 22  COLUMN  5
              'To Terminate the Program, Enter END'
                                        COLUMN 18.
         ACCEPT SELECTION-NO  PROTECTED REVERSED DEFAULT IS ZERO
                                  LINE 14  COLUMN 50.
         IF SELECTION-NO IS ZERO
             ACCEPT INPUT-DATA-FLAG  PROTECTED REVERSED BLINKING
                                  LINE 22  COLUMN 54
             IF NOT END-OF-DATA
                 DISPLAY 'YOU MUST ENTER '  BOLD BELL
                                  LINE 18  COLUMN  5
                         'END'  BOLD REVERSED BLINKING
                                        COLUMN 20
                         'TO TERMINATE THE PROGRAM!!'  BOLD
                                        COLUMN 24
                 ACCEPT INPUT-DATA-FLAG  PROTECTED REVERSED BLINKING
                                  LINE 22  COLUMN 54
             END-IF
         END-IF.

10.    310-DO-ADD-ROUTINE.
         PERFORM 400-PRESENT-SUBMENU-1.
         ACCEPT MR-SSN         PROTECTED REVERSED
                                 LINE  7  COLUMN 17.
         ACCEPT MR-LAST-NAME   PROTECTED REVERSED
                                 LINE  9  COLUMN 17.
         ACCEPT MR-FIRST-NAME  PROTECTED REVERSED
                                          COLUMN 46.
         ACCEPT MR-INITIAL     PROTECTED REVERSED
                                          COLUMN 75.
         ACCEPT MR-STREET      PROTECTED REVERSED
                                 LINE 11  COLUMN 36.
         ACCEPT MR-CITY        PROTECTED REVERSED
                                 LINE 13  COLUMN 36.
         ACCEPT MR-STATE       PROTECTED REVERSED
                                 LINE 15  COLUMN 36.
         ACCEPT MR-ZIP         PROTECTED REVERSED
                                          COLUMN 52.
         ACCEPT MR-AREA-CODE   PROTECTED REVERSED
                                 LINE 17  COLUMN 36.
         ACCEPT MR-PHONE-NO    PROTECTED REVERSED
                                          COLUMN 52.
         ACCEPT CANCEL-ADD-FORM  PROTECTED REVERSED BLINKING
                                                    DEFAULT 'N'
                                 LINE 22  COLUMN 52.
         IF NOT CANCEL-FORM
             PERFORM 410-WRITE-MASTER-RECORD
             ACCEPT NEW-ADD-FORM  PROTECTED REVERSED BLINKING
                                                    DEFAULT 'N'
                                 LINE 23  COLUMN 58
             IF NOT NEW-ADD-REQUEST
                 ACCEPT ADD-RECORD-FLAG PROTECTED REVERSED BLINKING
                                 LINE 24  COLUMN 60
                 IF NOT END-ADD-NEW-RECORDS
                     DISPLAY  'YOU MUST ENTER ' BOLD BELL
                                 LINE 18  COLUMN  5
                             'EXIT' BOLD REVERSED BLINKING
                                          COLUMN 20
                             'TO RETURN TO MAIN MENU' BOLD
                                          COLUMN 25
                     ACCEPT ADD-RECORD-FLAG PROTECTED REVERSED
                                                    BLINKING
                                 LINE 24  COLUMN 60
                     IF NOT END-ADD-NEW-RECORDS
                         GO TO 310-DO-ADD-ROUTINE
                     END-IF
                 END-IF
             ELSE
                 GO TO 310-DO-ADD-ROUTINE
         ELSE
```

```
11.           DISPLAY ' '              LINE  7   COLUMN 17 ERASE END LINE
                      " '              LINE  9   COLUMN 17 ERASE END LINE
              DISPLAY 'FIRST NAME:'    LINE  9   COLUMN 34
                      'MID INITIAL:'             COLUMN 62
                      ' '              LINE 11   COLUMN 36 ERASE END LINE
                      ' '              LINE 13   COLUMN 36 ERASE END LINE
                      ' '              LINE 15   COLUMN 36 ERASE END LINE
                      'ZIP:'                     COLUMN 47
                      ' '              LINE 17   COLUMN 36 ERASE END LINE
                      "NUMBER:'                  COLUMN 44
              ACCEPT NEW-ADD-FORM  PROTECTED REVERSED BLINKING
                                                     DEFAULT 'N'
                                       LINE 23   COLUMN 59
              IF NOT NEW-ADD-REQUEST
                  ACCEPT ADD-RECORD-FLAG PROTECTED REVERSED BLINKING
                                       LINE 24   COLUMN 60
                  IF NOT END-ADD-NEW-RECORDS
                      DISPLAY  'YOU MUST ENTER ' BOLD BELL
                                       LINE 18   COLUMN  5
                              'EXIT' BOLD REVERSED BLINKING
                                                 COLUMN 20
                              'TO RETURN TO MAIN MENU' BOLD
                                                 COLUMN 25
                      ACCEPT ADD-RECORD-FLAG PROTECTED REVERSED
                                                      BLINKING
                                       LINE 24   COLUMN 60
                      IF NOT END-ADD-NEW-RECORDS
                          GO TO 310-DO-ADD-ROUTINE
                      END-IF
                  END-IF
              ELSE
                  GO TO 310-DO-ADD-ROUTINE
          END-IF.

12.      320-DO-DELETE-ROUTINE.
          PERFORM 420-PRESENT-SUBMENU-2.
          ACCEPT MR-SSN  PROTECTED REVERSED
                                       LINE  6   COLUMN 42.
          ACCEPT VERIFY-DELETE PROTECTED REVERSED BLINKING
                                       LINE  8   COLUMN 42.
          IF NOT-SURE-DELETE
              DISPLAY 'RE-ENTER CORRECT SSN' BOLD REVERSED BLINKING
                                       LINE 10   COLUMN  6
              DISPLAY 'PRESS CR WHEN READY'
                                       LINE 12   COLUMN  6
              ACCEPT USER-ENTRY  REVERSED
                                       LINE 12   COLUMN 26
              DISPLAY ' '              LINE  6   COLUMN  6 ERASE LINE
              DISPLAY 'ENTER EMPLOYEE'S SSN:'
                                       LINE  6   COLUMN 20
              DISPLAY ' '              LINE 10             ERASE LINE
              DISPLAY ' '              LINE 12             ERASE LINE
              INITIALIZE VERIFY-DELETE
              ACCEPT MR-SSN  PROTECTED REVERSED
                                       LINE  6   COLUMN 42
              ACCEPT VERIFY-DELETE PROTECTED REVERSED BLINKING
                                       LINE  8   COLUMN 42
              IF NOT-SURE-DELETE
                  GO TO 320-DO-DELETE-ROUTINE
              END-IF
          END-IF.
          PERFORM 430-DELETE-MASTER-RECORD.
          ACCEPT NEW-DELETE-FORM  PROTECTED REVERSED BLINKING
                                                     DEFAULT 'N'
                                       LINE 22   COLUMN 57.
          IF NOT NEW-DELETE-REQUEST
              ACCEPT DELETE-RECORD-FLAG PROTECTED REVERSED BLINKING
                                       LINE 23   COLUMN 60
              IF NOT END-DELETE-RECORDS
                  DISPLAY  'YOU MUST ENTER ' BOLD BELL
                                       LINE 18   COLUMN  5
                          'EXIT' BOLD REVERSED BLINKING
                                                 COLUMN 20
                          'TO RETURN TO MAIN MENU' BOLD
                                                 COLUMN 25
                  ACCEPT DELETE-RECORD-FLAG PROTECTED REVERSED
                                                      BLINKING
                                       LINE 23   COLUMN 60
                  IF NOT END-DELETE-RECORDS
                      GO TO 320-DO-DELETE-ROUTINE
                  END-IF
              END-IF
          ELSE
              GO TO 320-DO-DELETE-ROUTINE
          END-IF.
```

Figure 6.32 continued

13.

```
330-DO-UPDATE-ROUTINE.
    PERFORM 440-PRESENT-SUBMENU-3.
    ACCEPT MR-SSN  PROTECTED REVERSED
                            LINE  6  COLUMN 23.
    PERFORM 450-READ-MASTER-RECORD.
    IF SUCCESSFUL
        CONTINUE
    ELSE
        DISPLAY 'ENTER SSN CAREFULLY!' BLINKING
                            LINE 17  COLUMN  6
                'PRESS CR WHEN READY TO CONTINUE'
                            LINE 18  COLUMN  6
        ACCEPT USER-ENTRY            COLUMN 38
        DISPLAY ' '         LINE 17  ERASE LINE
                ' '         LINE 18  ERASE LINE
        GO TO 330-DO-UPDATE-ROUTINE.
    ACCEPT NAME-UPDATE-FLAG  PROTECTED REVERSED
                            LINE  9  COLUMN 23.
    IF NAME-UPDATE
        ACCEPT MR-LAST-NAME  PROTECTED REVERSED
                            LINE 12  COLUMN 15
    END-IF.
    ACCEPT ADDRESS-UPDATE-FLAG  PROTECTED REVERSED
                            LINE  9  COLUMN 46.
    IF ADDRESS-UPDATE
        ACCEPT MR-STREET  PROTECTED REVERSED
                            LINE 13  COLUMN 18
        ACCEPT MR-CITY    PROTECTED REVERSED
                                     COLUMN 44
        ACCEPT MR-STATE   PROTECTED REVERSED
                                     COLUMN 65
        ACCEPT MR-ZIP     PROTECTED REVERSED
                                     COLUMN 74
    END-IF.
    ACCEPT PHONE-UPDATE-FLAG  PROTECTED REVERSED
                            LINE  9  COLUMN 69.
    IF PHONE-UPDATE
        ACCEPT MR-AREA-CODE  PROTECTED REVERSED
                            LINE 14  COLUMN 30
        ACCEPT MR-PHONE-NO   PROTECTED REVERSED
                                     COLUMN 48
    END-IF.
    PERFORM 460-REWRITE-MASTER-RECORD.
    ACCEPT NEW-UPDATE-FORM  PROTECTED REVERSED BLINKING
                                          DEFAULT 'N'
                            LINE 22  COLUMN 57.
    IF NOT NEW-UPDATE-REQUEST
        ACCEPT UPDATE-RECORD-FLAG PROTECTED REVERSED BLINKING
                            LINE 23  COLUMN 60
        IF NOT END-UPDATE-RECORDS
            DISPLAY  'YOU MUST ENTER ' BOLD BELL
                            LINE 18  COLUMN  5
                    'EXIT' BOLD REVERSED BLINKING
                                     COLUMN 20
                    'TO RETURN TO MAIN MENU' BOLD
                                     COLUMN 25
            ACCEPT UPDATE-RECORD-FLAG PROTECTED REVERSED
                                          BLINKING
                            LINE 23  COLUMN 60
            IF NOT END-UPDATE-RECORDS
                GO TO 330-DO-UPDATE-ROUTINE
            END-IF
        END-IF
    ELSE
        GO TO 330-DO-UPDATE-ROUTINE
    END-IF.
```

```
14.     400-PRESENT-SUBMENU-1.
            INITIALIZE ADD-ROUTINE-ITEMS.
            DISPLAY EDITED-DATE         LINE  1  COLUMN  6   ERASE SCREEN
                    'TOUCAN ENTERPRISES' BOLD    COLUMN 32
                    'SUBMENU 1.'        BOLD     COLUMN 70
                    'ADD A NEW MASTER RECORD FORM' BOLD UNDERLINED
                                        LINE  3  COLUMN 27.
            DISPLAY 'SSN: '             LINE  7  COLUMN 12
                    'LAST NAME: '       LINE  9  COLUMN  6
                    'FIRST NAME: '               COLUMN 34
                    'MID INITIAL: '              COLUMN 62.
            DISPLAY 'ADDRESS: '         LINE 11  COLUMN 27
                    'CITY: '            LINE 13  COLUMN 30
                    'STATE: '           LINE 15  COLUMN 29
                    'ZIP: '                      COLUMN 47.
            DISPLAY 'PHONE'             LINE 17  COLUMN 15
                    'AREA CODE: '                COLUMN 25
                    'NUMBER: '                   COLUMN 44.
            DISPLAY 'DIRECTIONS' UNDERLINED BOLD
                                        LINE 21  COLUMN  6
                    '1. To Enter a Field Value, Press CR'
                                                 COLUMN 18
                    '2. Cancel the Current Form? (Y/N)'
                                        LINE 22  COLUMN 18
                    '3. Add Another New Master Record? (Y/N)'
                                        LINE 23  COLUMN 18
                    '4. To Return to the Main Menu, Enter EXIT'
                                        LINE 24  COLUMN 18.

15.     410-WRITE-MASTER-RECORD.
            MOVE 'EM' TO RECORD-CODE.
            WRITE MASTER-RECORD
                INVALID KEY
                    DISPLAY ' ' BELL
                    DISPLAY '*****' BOLD REVERSED BLINKING
                                        LINE 18  COLUMN 2
                    DISPLAY 'DUPLICATE RECORD KEY FOR SSN = ' MR-SSN
                                                 COLUMN 8

                    DISPLAY 'MASTER RECORD WAS NOT CREATED.  '
                            'NOTE IT FOR CORRECTIONS'
                                        LINE 19  COLUMN 2
                    DISPLAY 'PRESS CR WHEN READY TO CONTINUE'
                                        LINE 20  COLUMN 2
                    ACCEPT USER-ENTRY            COLUMN PLUS 2
                    DISPLAY ' '         LINE 18  ERASE LINE
                    DISPLAY ' '         LINE 19  ERASE LINE
                    DISPLAY ' '         LINE 20  ERASE LINE
                NOT INVALID KEY
                    DISPLAY '*** MASTER RECORD NOW IN FILE!'
                                        LINE 19  COLUMN 2
                    DISPLAY 'PRESS CR WHEN READY TO CONTINUE'
                                        LINE 20  COLUMN 2
                    ACCEPT USER-ENTRY            COLUMN PLUS 2
                    DISPLAY ' '         LINE 18  COLUMN 1 ERASE LINE
                    DISPLAY ' '         LINE 19  COLUMN 1 ERASE LINE
                    DISPLAY ' '         LINE 20  COLUMN 1 ERASE LINE
            END-WRITE.

16.     420-PRESENT-SUBMENU-2.
            INITIALIZE DELETE-ROUTINE-ITEMS.
            DISPLAY EDITED-DATE         LINE  1  COLUMN  6   ERASE SCREEN
                    'TOUCAN ENTERPRISES' BOLD    COLUMN 32
                    'SUBMENU 2.'        BOLD     COLUMN 70
                    'DELETE A MASTER RECORD FORM' BOLD UNDERLINED
                                        LINE  3  COLUMN 28.
            DISPLAY 'ENTER EMPLOYEE'S SSN:'
                                        LINE  6  COLUMN 20
                    'ARE YOU SURE? (Y/N):'
                                        LINE  8  COLUMN 21.
            DISPLAY 'DIRECTIONS' UNDERLINED BOLD
                                        LINE 21  COLUMN  6
                    '1. To Enter a Field Value, Press CR'
                                                 COLUMN 18
                    '2. Delete Another Master Record? (Y/N)'
                                        LINE 22  COLUMN 18
                    '3. To Return to the Main Menu, Enter EXIT'
                                        LINE 23  COLUMN 18.
```

■ **Figure 6.32** continued

```
17.     430-DELETE-MASTER-RECORD.
            DELETE MASTER-FILE RECORD
                INVALID KEY
                    DISPLAY '*****' BELL BOLD REVERSED BLINKING
                                        LINE 10  COLUMN  6
                            'NO MASTER RECORD IN FILE WITH SSN= ' MR-SSN
                                        LINE 11  COLUMN  6
                            'NO RECORD DELETED'
                                        LINE 12  COLUMN  6
                            'PRESS CR WHEN READY TO CONTINUE'
                                        LINE 13  COLUMN  6
                    ACCEPT USER-ENTRY REVERSED
                                        LINE 13  COLUMN 38
                    DISPLAY ' '         LINE 10  ERASE LINE
                            ' '         LINE 11  ERASE LINE
                            ' '         LINE 12  ERASE LINE
                            ' '         LINE 13  ERASE LINE
                NOT INVALID KEY
                    DISPLAY '***  MASTER RECORD HAS BEEN DELETED!'
                                        LINE 10  COLUMN  6
                    DISPLAY 'PRESS CR TO CONTINUE'
                                        LINE 11  COLUMN  6
                    ACCEPT USER-ENTRY   LINE 11  COLUMN 27
                    DISPLAY ' '         LINE 10  ERASE LINE
                    DISPLAY ' '         LINE 11  ERASE LINE
            END-DELETE.

18.     440-PRESENT-SUBMENU-3.
            INITIALIZE UPDATE-ROUTINE-ITEMS.
            DISPLAY EDITED-DATE         LINE  1  COLUMN  6  ERASE SCREEN
                    'TOUCAN ENTERPRISES' BOLD    COLUMN 32
                    'SUBMENU 3.'           BOLD  COLUMN 70
                    'UPDATE A MASTER RECORD FORM' BOLD UNDERLINED
                                        LINE  3  COLUMN 28.
            DISPLAY 'ENTER EMPLOYEE'S SSN:'
                                        LINE  6  COLUMN  1.
            DISPLAY 'UPDATE:'  UNDERLINED
                                        LINE  8  COLUMN  1
                    'LAST NAME? (Y/N):'
                                        LINE  9  COLUMN  5
                    'ADDRESS? (Y/N):'            COLUMN 30
                    'PHONE? (Y/N):'              COLUMN 55.
            DISPLAY 'ENTER NEW VALUES:' UNDERLINED
                                        LINE 11  COLUMN  1
                    'NEW NAME:'         LINE 12  COLUMN  5
                    'NEW ADDRESS:'      LINE 13  COLUMN  5
                    'CITY:'                      COLUMN 38
                    'STATE:'                     COLUMN 58
                    'ZIP:'                       COLUMN 69
                    'NEW PHONE:'        LINE 14  COLUMN  5
                    'AREA CODE:'                 COLUMN 19
                    'PHONE NO.:'                 COLUMN 37.
            DISPLAY 'DIRECTIONS' UNDERLINED BOLD
                                        LINE 21  COLUMN  6
                    '1. To Enter a Field Value, Press CR'
                                                 COLUMN 18
                    '2. Update Another Master Record? (Y/N)'
                                        LINE 22  COLUMN 18
                    '3. To Return to the Main Menu, Enter EXIT'
                                        LINE 23  COLUMN 18.

19.     450-READ-MASTER-RECORD.
            READ MASTER-FILE RECORD
                INVALID KEY
                    DISPLAY '*****' BELL BOLD REVERSED BLINKING
                                        LINE 17  COLUMN  6
                            'NO MASTER RECORD IN FILE WITH SSN= ' MR-SSN
                                        LINE 18  COLUMN  6
                            'NO RECORD TO UPDATE'
                                        LINE 19  COLUMN  6
                            'PRESS CR WHEN READY TO CONTINUE'
                                        LINE 20  COLUMN  6
                    ACCEPT USER-ENTRY REVERSED
                                        LINE 20  COLUMN 38
                    DISPLAY ' '         LINE 17  ERASE LINE
                            ' '         LINE 18  ERASE LINE
                            ' '         LINE 19  ERASE LINE
                            ' '         LINE 20  ERASE LINE
                NOT INVALID KEY
                    DISPLAY '***  MASTER RECORD HAS BEEN READ!'
                                        LINE 17  COLUMN  6
                    DISPLAY 'PRESS CR TO CONTINUE'
                                        LINE 18  COLUMN  6
                    ACCEPT USER-ENTRY   LINE 18  COLUMN 27
                    DISPLAY ' '         LINE 17  ERASE LINE
                    DISPLAY ' '         LINE 18  ERASE LINE
            END-READ.
```

Figure 6.32 continued

```
20.   460-REWRITE-MASTER-RECORD.
          REWRITE MASTER-RECORD
              INVALID KEY
                  DISPLAY '*****' BELL BOLD REVERSED
                                    LINE 17   COLUMN  6
                          'NO MASTER RECORD IN FILE WITH SSN= ' MR-SSN
                                    LINE 18   COLUMN  6
                          "NO RECORD UPDATED"
                                    LINE 19   COLUMN  6
                          "PRESS CR WHEN READY TO CONTINUE"
                                    LINE 20   COLUMN  6
                  ACCEPT USER-ENTRY REVERSED
                                    LINE 20   COLUMN 38
                  DISPLAY ' '       LINE 17   ERASE LINE
                          " "       LINE 18   ERASE LINE
                          " "       LINE 19   ERASE LINE
                          " "       LINE 20   ERASE LINE
              NOT INVALID KEY
                  DISPLAY '***  MASTER RECORD HAS BEEN UPDATED!"
                                    LINE 17   COLUMN  6
                  DISPLAY 'PRESS CR TO CONTINUE"
                                    LINE 18   COLUMN  6
                  ACCEPT USER-ENTRY LINE 18   COLUMN 27
                  DISPLAY ' '       LINE 17   ERASE LINE
                  DISPLAY ' '       LINE 18   ERASE LINE
          END-REWRITE.
```

Comments on the Program

1. This item is related to the directions at the bottom of the main menu. The entry END will cause an exit from the loop that processes input data entered at the terminal.
2. These items are related to the directions at the bottom of submenu 1.
3. These items are related to the directions at the bottom of submenu 2.
4. These items are related to the directions at the bottom of submenu 3.
5. This group of DISPLAY statements provides general program information to the user. The user has a choice of continuing with the program or terminating it.
6. Control is sent to the procedure that paints the main menu on the screen.
7. Upon returning from the procedure that presented the main menu to the user, control is sent to the appropriate updating routine, unless the choice made at the bottom of the main menu was to end the program.
8. Note the use of GO TO to loop back to the beginning of the procedure 210-PROCESS-TERMINAL-DATA.
9. This paragraph constructs on the screen the main menu as prepared on the screen layout form in Figure 6.28. Note how the choices are handled at the end of the paragraph. Realize that control returns to paragraph 210, where the user's selection is tested.
10. This paragraph is the add routine. Note that the effect of the first statement is to display submenu 1 on the screen. The ACCEPT statements position the cursor on the submenu form so as to indicate the data to be entered. Note the combinations of ACCEPT and IF statements related to the choices at the bottom of submenu 1.
11. Note how the messages are erased when they are no longer needed.
12. This paragraph is the delete routine. Note that the execution of the first statement paints submenu 2 on the screen. Before going on with the delete operation, the user is prompted for confirmation of the action. Again, note the combination of ACCEPT and IF statements toward the end of the procedure that are related to the user's choices at the bottom of submenu 2.
13. This paragraph is the record update routine. Here the first statement results in bringing up submenu 3 on the screen. The user is then prompted to select the data fields to be updated. Toward the end of the paragraph, the combination of ACCEPT and IF statements checks the user's choice of the selections listed at the bottom of submenu 3.
14. When this paragraph executes, submenu 1 is painted on the screen. This is the form used to add new records to the master file.
15. This paragraph attempts to write a new record to the master file. Whether an invalid key condition occurs or not, feedback is given to the user. Note that message lines are erased once they have served their purpose.

16. When this paragraph executes, submenu 2 pops up on the screen. This is the form used to delete a master record from the master file.
17. The function of this paragraph is to delete a master record. Whether the action is successful or not, the user is apprised of the outcome. When the user is ready to continue, the message lines are erased.
18. When this paragraph executes, submenu 3 is displayed on the screen. This form is used when fields of a master record must be updated.
19. This paragraph attempts to read a master record. It is executed from within the record updating routine. Whether the read operation is successful or not, the user receives appropriate feedback, and he or she decides when to continue.
20. The function of this paragraph is to rewrite a master record that has been updated. Here also, whether the rewrite operation is successful or not, the user is given feedback. When she or he decides to continue, the message lines are erased.

A Sample Run of the Menu-Driven Program

Selected screens from a sample run of the program are shown in the figures that follow. Figure 6.33 shows the main menu in which the user entered **1** as the update action to be taken. As a result, submenu 1 (Add a New Master Record Form) popped up on the screen and the user supplied the data as shown in Figure 6.34. Note in number 2 of the DIRECTIONS that the user indicated the current form should not be canceled. As a result, when "N" was entered, the new master record with SSN = 331952867 was added to the index file and the two message lines

```
***  MASTER RECORD NOW IN FILE!
PRESS CR WHEN READY TO CONTINUE
```

were displayed in the message area of the screen.

The next user entries, not shown in Figure 6.34, were "N" on line 3 of the DIRECTIONS and "EXIT" on line 4. This last entry caused the main menu to be displayed again. This time, the user entered **2** as a file updating action, and as a result, submenu 2 appeared on the screen. The user entered the Social Security number 781207315 and selected Y as a response to the verification prompt. These actions are shown in Figure 6.35. The status shown in Figure 6.35 is just *before* pressing the carriage return after selecting the Y response. If the screen status were shown immediately *after* the carriage return, the messages

```
***  MASTER RECORD HAS BEEN DELETED!
PRESS CR TO CONTINUE
```

would be displayed in the message area of the screen.

The user then entered "N" after line 2 of the DIRECTIONS and "EXIT" at line 3 of the DIRECTIONS. (These actions are not shown.) As a result, the main menu was returned to the screen. This time, the user entered **3** as an updating action and submenu 3 then popped up on the screen. The user entered the employee's Social Security number, 723510611. The program, operating "behind the scene," read the master record from the master file and then displayed the messages

```
***  MASTER RECORD HAS BEEN READ!
PRESS CR TO CONTINUE
```

in the message area of the screen. The messages are not shown in Figure 6.36 because when the user pressed CR to continue, they were erased! At this point, the cursor was positioned at the UPDATE LAST NAME? (Y/N): prompt. The user entered Y, and the cursor moved to the NEW NAME area. Here, the user entered LOBO (replacing the previous last name READY!), and the cursor then moved to the UPDATE ADDRESS? (Y/N): prompt. Here again, the user entered Y, and the cursor then moved to the NEW ADDRESS area. After responding to the four prompts on that line, the cursor went back up to the UPDATE PHONE (Y/N): prompt. In response to the user entering Y here, the cursor

■ **Figure 6.33** Selecting 1 on the main menu

```
89/06/15                    TOUCAN ENTERPRISES                    MAIN MENU
                          MASTER FILE UPDATE FORM

     MASTER FILE UPDATE OPTIONS:

              1.  ADD A NEW MASTER RECORD

              2.  DELETE A MASTER RECORD

              3.  UPDATE DATA FIELDS OF A MASTER RECORD

     ENTER YOUR UPDATE CHOICE (1, 2, OR 3): 1




DIRECTIONS:  To Terminate the Program, Enter END
```

■ **Figure 6.34** Entering a new master record (SUBMENU 1.)

```
   89/06/15                    TOUCAN ENTERPRISES                  SUBMENU 1.
                           ADD A NEW MASTER RECORD FORM


         SSN: 331952867

   LAST NAME: PELLETIER        FIRST NAME: VINCENT         MID INITIAL: J

                          ADDRESS: 1056 EAST MAIN RD

                             CITY: PORTSMOUTH

                            STATE: RI           ZIP: 02950

              PHONE      AREA CODE: 401      NUMBER: 6834598

***  MASTER RECORD NOW IN FILE!
PRESS CR WHEN READY TO CONTINUE
    DIRECTIONS   1. To Enter a Field Value, Press CR
                 2. Cancel the Current Form? (Y/N) N
                 3. Add Another New Master Record? (Y/N)
                 4. To Return to the Main Menu, Enter EXIT
```

Figure 6.35 Deleting a master record (SUBMENU 2.)

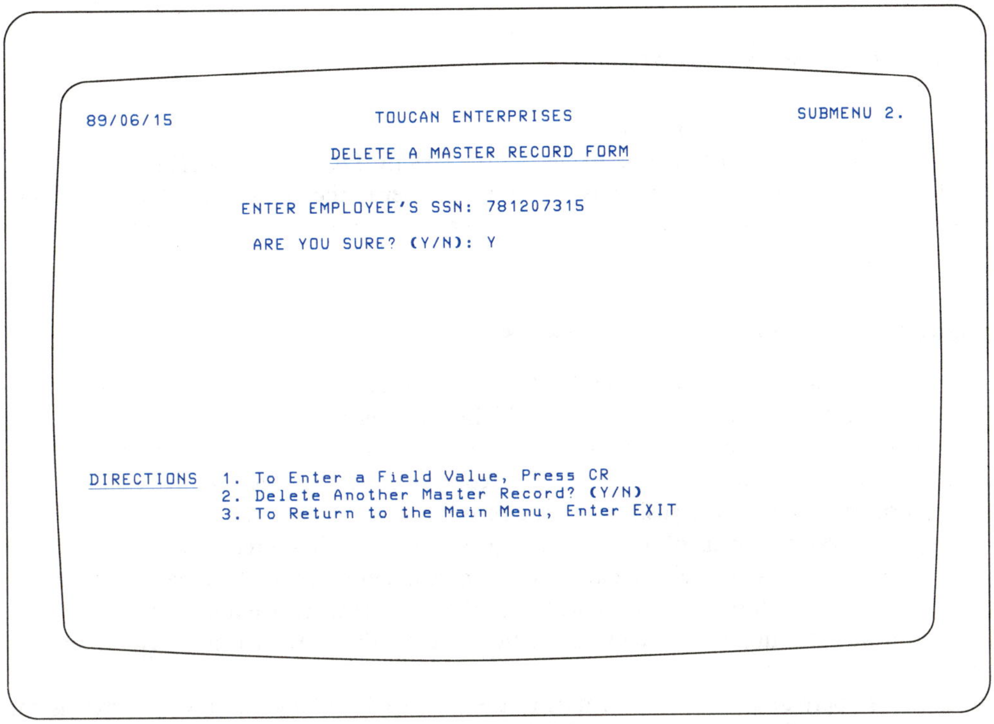

Figure 6.36 Updating a master record (SUBMENU 3.)

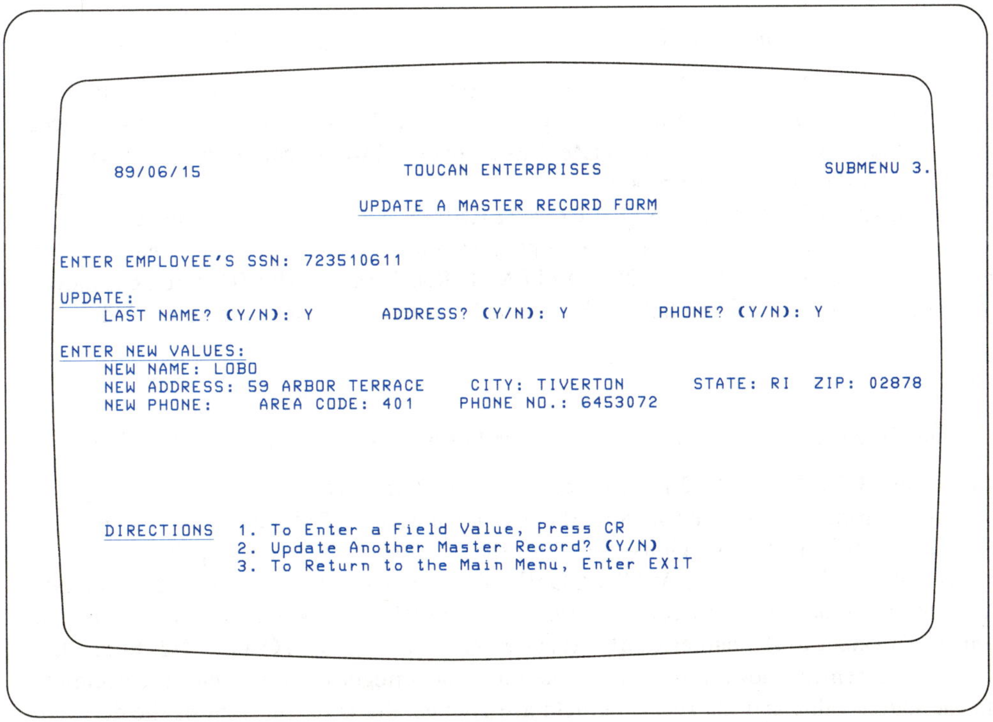

moved to the NEW PHONE area. The user entered the area code and keyed in the new phone number, but the carriage return had not been pressed when this screen dump occurred. If CR had been pressed, then the messages

```
***  MASTER RECORD HAS BEEN UPDATED!
PRESS CR TO CONTINUE
```

would have been displayed in the message area.

To continue, N was entered as a response to line 2 of the DIRECTIONS and "EXIT" was entered as a response to line 3 of the DIRECTIONS, thus returning the user to the main menu. These updating tasks may be continued in any sequence. To end the execution of the program, the user enters "END" at the main menu.

Numeric Data in Interactive Programs

Recall that whenever a record is accessed from a file by a READ statement, the characters are stored left-justified in the record area associated with the file. If there are more characters in the record than can be stored in the record area, the extra characters are truncated from the right. If there are fewer characters in the record than there are positions in the record area, all the characters are stored left-justified and the characters in the extra positions in the record area are undefined.

When data is accessed by means of an ACCEPT statement, the characters being accepted are also transferred left-justified into the receiving data item. If there are more characters than can be stored in the receiving item, the extra characters are truncated on the right. If there are fewer characters than there are positions in the receiving item, the extra positions are padded with spaces. Furthermore, no editing occurs.

These restrictions apply to both ANSI formats of the ACCEPT statement. However, extensions to the ANSI standards generally provide a CONVERSION option that makes the ACCEPT statement much more useful in the handling of data, particularly numeric values. Consider the following examples.

Example 1

The value 25 must be stored in the field ITEM-1, where ITEM-1 is defined by PIC 9(4).

a. If the statement ACCEPT ITEM-1 is executed, the user must enter 0025, since the characters are stored left-justified. By entering only the digits 2 and 5, ITEM-1 would contain two spaces to the right of the 5. An attempt to use ITEM-1 as an operand would cause an INVALID DECIMAL DATA diagnostic to be produced.

b. If the statement ACCEPT ITEM-1 WITH CONVERSION is executed, it is sufficient for the user to enter 25, because the CONVERSION option stores the value in a manner equivalent to the numeric MOVE statement MOVE 25 TO ITEM-1. Recall that a MOVE statement moves an integer into an integer receiving field right-justified and leading spaces are zero-filled.

Example 2

The value 2.35 must be stored in the field ITEM-2, where ITEM-2 is defined by PIC 9(3)V99.

a. If the statement ACCEPT ITEM-2 is executed, the value 2.35 must be entered as a 5-digit item without the decimal point. Specifically, the user must enter 00235. (See ITEM-U in screen 2 of Figure 6.37.) The PIC clause indicates the position of the decimal point.

b. If the statement ACCEPT ITEM-2 WITH CONVERSION is executed, the user may simply enter 2.35 and it will be stored correctly, because the CONVERSION option handles the data in a manner equivalent to the numeric MOVE statement MOVE 2.35 TO ITEM-2. Recall that when a MOVE statement moves a numeric value into a noninteger numeric field, the decimal points in the source value and the receiving field are aligned, digits to the right of the decimal point are stored starting at the decimal, and then the digits to the left of the decimal point are stored starting at the decimal point.

Example 3

The value −2.35 must be stored in the field ITEM-3, where ITEM-3 is defined by PIC S9(3)V99.

a. If the statement ACCEPT ITEM-3 is executed, the value must be entered as a 5-digit negative value in which the sign is stored in the trailing byte along with the digit 5. Specifically, the user must enter 0023N. The PIC clause indicates the position of the decimal point and it also indicates that the item is signed. Since the SIGN clause is not coded in the description of ITEM-3, the default applies, and the sign must be in the trailing byte along with the rightmost digit. (See ITEM-Y in screen 2 of Figure 6.37.)

b. If the statement ACCEPT ITEM-3 WITH CONVERSION is executed, the user may enter −2.35 directly. The CONVERSION option stores the value correctly, since its use is equivalent to the numeric MOVE statement MOVE −2.35 TO ITEM-3. That is, −2.35 is stored as 0023N.

It should be clear from these examples that the use of the CONVERSION option greatly facilitates the entry of numeric values. Zero-filling occurs automatically, and the sign is accepted as if it were in a MOVE statement.

Note the following:

1. In an ACCEPT statement *without* the CONVERSION option,
   - **a.** A digit (0–9) must be supplied for each numeric character position specified by the PIC clause of the receiving item.
   - **b.** The sign must be entered with the rightmost digit, if the default SIGN clause applies to the receiving item. Otherwise, the sign must be entered as specified by the SIGN clause. There are three possibilities: SIGN LEADING, SIGN TRAILING SEPARATE, SIGN LEADING SEPARATE. If SIGN LEADING is indicated, the sign must be entered along with the leftmost digit. If SIGN TRAILING SEPARATE is used, the sign must be the rightmost character. If SIGN LEADING SEPARATE is used, the sign must be the leftmost character. (Obviously, the user must be constantly aware of the applicable SIGN clause!)
2. In an ACCEPT statement *with* the CONVERSION option, the following characters are valid user-entered characters:
   - **a.** leading spaces and trailing spaces. (Spaces between numeric characters, including the decimal point and the sign, are not allowed, and they result in invalid data.)
   - **b.** the digits 0 through 9.
   - **c.** a decimal point.
   - **d.** a sign (+ or −). If a sign is supplied, it must precede all the numeric characters or follow all the numeric characters without intervening spaces. Only one sign is allowed.
   - **e.** the letter E (or e), as used in an exponential form if the receiving item is a COMP-1 or a COMP-2 item. An expression such as −2.53E+5 is valid.
3. When an ACCEPT statement with the CONVERSION option is executed, a conversion error occurs if
   - **a.** a truncation of numeric characters would take place.
   - **b.** invalid characters are entered.

   In either case, the terminal bell rings and the ACCEPT statement is executed again, unless the ON EXCEPTION clause is also coded in the statement. In that case, the input value is stored and the imperative statement in the clause is executed.

   (The preceding three statements apply to accepting *numeric* values. If the receiving field is *alphanumeric,* the CONVERSION option also stores alphanumeric data as if it resulted from MOVE statements. Consequently, editing, right justification, and reference modification are supported! See screen 3 of Figure 6.37.)

■ **Figure 6.37** Illustrations of ACCEPT and DISPLAY operations with and without the CONVERSION option

```
                                   SAMPLE NUMERIC ITEMS                          SCREEN 1.
ITEMS DISPLAYED WITH
                                                  NO CONVERSION       CONVERSION
        ITEM-A:   (VALUE 453)                        00453              453
        ITEM-B:   (VALUE +453)                       0045C              453
        ITEM-C:   (VALUE -453)                       0045L             -453
        ITEM-D:   (VALUE 21.54)                      0215D                21.54
        ITEM-E:   (VALUE -21.54)                     0215M               -21.54
        ITEM-F:   (VALUE 35 COMP)                    #                    35
        ITEM-G:   (VALUE -250.47 COMP)               )                 -250.47
        ITEM-H:   (VALUE +250.47 COMP-1)             zDRx                 2.504700E+02




    ENTER CR TO CONTINUE:
```

```
                                   SAMPLE NUMERIC ITEMS                          SCREEN 2.
ITEMS ACCEPTED WITHOUT CONVERSION
    AND DISPLAYED WITH                            NO CONVERSION       CONVERSION
ITEM-U: (PIC S9(3)V99)        00235                  00235                 2.35
ITEM-X: (PIC S9(3)V99)        0023E                  0023E                 2.35
ITEM-Y: (PIC S9(3)V99)        0023N                  0023N                -2.35
ITEM-Z: (PIC S9(3)V99)        9455R                  9455R              -945.59

ITEMS ACCEPTED WITH CONVERSION
    AND DISPLAYED WITH                            NO CONVERSION       CONVERSION

ITEM-I: (PIC 9(5))             245                   00245              245
ITEM-J: (PIC S9(3))           +125                     12E              125
ITEM-J: (PIC S9(3))           -125                     12N             -125
ITEM-K1: (PIC S9(3)V99)        +54.28                0542H                54.28
ITEM-K2: (PIC S9(3)V99 TRAILING SEPARATE)
                               -54.28                05428-               54.28-
ITEM-L: (PIC S9(3)V99 COMP)    +54.28                4                    54.28
ITEM-L: (PIC S9(3)V99 COMP)    -54.28                Lj                  -54.28
ITEM-M: (PIC $Z,ZZ9.99-)       +25.53                $    25.53         $    25.53
ITEM-M: (PIC $Z,ZZ9.99-)       -25.53                $    25.53-        $    25.53-
ITEM-M: (PIC $Z,ZZ9.99-)     -1470.25                $1,470.25-         $1,470.25-
    ENTER CR TO CONTINUE:
```

Figure 6.37 continued

```
                    SAMPLE ALPHANUMERIC ITEMS                         SCREEN 3

ACCEPTED WITHOUT CONVERSION                          DISPLAYED AS STORED

ITEM-N   (PIC XX/XX/XX)                 062189           062189

ITEM-O   (PIC X(9) JUSTIFIED RIGHT)     JUNE             JUNE

ITEM-P   (PIC XXXBXXBXXX)               234513456        234513456

ACCEPTED WITH CONVERSION                             DISPLAYED AS STORED

ITEM-N   (PIC XX/XX/XX)                 062189           06/21/89

ITEM-O   (PIC X(9) JUSTIFIED RIGHT)     JUNE                  JUNE

ITEM-P   (PIC XXXBXXBXXX)               234513456        234 51 3456


    ENTER CR TO CONTINUE:
```

In screen 2 of Figure 6.37, the items in the first group (ITEM-U through ITEM-Z) receive values through an ACCEPT statement that does not contain the CONVERSION option. Note that in each case, the user must enter five numeric characters. If the value is signed, the sign must be combined with the rightmost digit (since the default applies). Thus, +00235 is entered as 0023E and −00235 is entered as 0023N.

The items in the second group, however, receive converted values, since the ACCEPT statement contains the CONVERSION option. Thus even though the size of ITEM-I is 5, only the digits 245 are entered and the converted value is stored as 00245. The value supplied for ITEM-J consists of four characters, the sign, and three digits, even though the size of ITEM-J is 3. The value +125 is converted and stored as 12E. The value supplied for ITEM-K2 is −54.28. It is stored converted as 05428−, where the minus sign is a trailing separate character, and the implied decimal point is between 4 and 2.

Extensions to the DISPLAY statement usually contain a CONVERSION option as well. The option is useful only when displaying numeric items. The two screens of Figure 6.37 show values displayed without and with the CONVERSION option. If CONVERSION is used,

1. Leading zeros are not displayed (unless they immediately precede a decimal point).
2. The sign is displayed as a leading sign (unless the description of the item specifies TRAILING SEPARATE, in which case it is displayed as a trailing sign).
3. The plus sign (+) is not displayed.
4. An assumed decimal point is displayed as a decimal point.
5. The maximum number of characters displayed is controlled by the size of the source field, increased by 1 for a sign if appropriate, and increased by 1 again for a decimal point if appropriate.
6. COMP-1 and COMP-2 items are displayed in exponential format (see ITEM-H).

Note that COMP items (including COMP-1 and COMP-2) displayed without conversion are absolutely meaningless to the user!

In short, numeric data entry is simplified for the user if the CONVERSION option is used in an ACCEPT statement, and displayed numeric data is most useful to the user if the CONVERSION option is used in DISPLAY statements.

Important Terms in Chapter 6

ACCEPT
ACCEPT FROM
BELL
BLINKING
BOLD
COLUMN NUMBER
CONVERSION
DEFAULT
DELIMITED BY
delimiter
DISPLAY
DISPLAY UPON
END-ACCEPT
END-UNSTRING
ERASE
ERASE LINE
ERASE SCREEN
free-form data entry
interactive dialogue
interactive program
LINE NUMBER
main menu
menu-driven
mnemonic-name
NO ADVANCING
prompt/response technique
PROTECTED
REVERSED
screen layout form
screen management facility
submenu
SYMBOLIC CHARACTERS
terminal bell
terminal input
UNDERLINED
UNSTRING
user friendly
video form

Exercises

1. What is the essential function of an interactive program?
2. Name the two statements used in an interactive program to establish a dialogue between the program and the user.
3. Given the statements in Set 1 and Set 2,

   Set 1.
   ```
   DISPLAY "ENTER EMPLOYEE NUMBER: ".
   ACCEPT EMPLOYEE-NUMBER.
   ```
   Set 2.
   ```
   DISPLAY "ENTER EMPLOYEE NUMBER: " WITH NO ADVANCING.
   ACCEPT EMPLOYEE-NUMBER.
   ```

   explain what happens on the screen when the statements in each set are executed.
4. Records are to be written to a catalog file. The record description is as follows:

   ```
   01  ITEM-RECORD.
       05 ITEM-NO          PIC X(8).
       05 ITEM-DESCR       PIC X(30).
       05 UNIT-PURCH-PRICE PIC 999V99.
       05 UNIT-SELL-PRICE  PIC 999V99.
   ```

   a. Use the simple two-line prompt/response technique to obtain from a terminal user the data needed to prepare a record.
   b. Use the simple one-line prompt/response technique to obtain from a terminal user the data needed to prepare a record.
   c. Use free-form terminal data entry to obtain from a terminal user the data needed to prepare a record.
   d. Use a screen layout form to plan a video form which will facilitate terminal data entry. Suppose the name of the company is Express Auto Parts, and the name given to the video form is Catalog Item Entry Form. Include directions to enter a field value. Underline the word DIRECTIONS but not the message.
   e. Use the video form prepared in item d as a guide, and code the DISPLAY statements needed to paint the form on the screen.
   f. Use the video form prepared in item d as a guide, and code the ACCEPT statements needed to obtain the requested data. Specify reverse video for the screen data fields.
   g. Suppose that the statements needed to paint the video form prepared in item d and to obtain the requested data from the user are contained in paragraph 210-GET-TERMINAL-DATA. A new form must be presented to the user if more catalog items are to be written to the file. Code the statements needed to ask the user if a new form is needed or not, such that if the user replies Y (for YES), a new form is presented on the screen, but if the user replies N (for NO), control exits from the paragraph.

5. Given the following data item descriptions,

```
01  CONSTANT-DATA.
    05 ITEM-1   PIC 9(4)                 VALUE 38.
    05 ITEM-2   PIC S9(3)V99             VALUE -23.52.
    05 ITEM-3   PIC S9(3)V99 LEADING     VALUE +374.83.
```

a. show the characters stored in ITEM-1, ITEM-2, and ITEM-3.

b. show the characters displayed by the statements

```
DISPLAY ITEM-1.
DISPLAY ITEM-2.
DISPLAY ITEM-3.
```

c. show the characters displayed by the statements

```
DISPLAY ITEM-1 WITH CONVERSION.
DISPLAY ITEM-2 WITH CONVERSION.
DISPLAY ITEM-3 WITH CONVERSION.
```

6. Given the following data item descriptions,

```
01  TERMINAL-INPUT-DATA.
    05 ITEM-4   PIC S9(4).
    05 ITEM-5   PIC S(4)V99.
```

a. if ITEM-4 must receive the value −278 and ITEM-5 must receive the value +25.77, what should the user enter when the following statements are executed?

```
ACCEPT ITEM-4.
ACCEPT ITEM-5.
```

b. if ITEM-4 must receive the value −278 and ITEM-5 must receive the value +25.77, what should the user enter when the following statements are executed?

```
ACCEPT ITEM-4 WITH CONVERSION.
ACCEPT ITEM-5 WITH CONVERSION.
```

Debugging Activities

1. A student was assigned the task of planning an interactive program whose function is to obtain data from a data entry operator and prepare a semester's course grade report for the students taking courses at the university. The printer spacing chart for the report is shown in Figure 6.38.

   The data to be supplied interactively for each student consists of the student name, the course number, and the letter grade obtained for each course taken by the student during the semester.

   The program must contain a hard-coded table of letter grades and corresponding numeric grades. The equivalences are the following:

Letter Grade	Numeric Grade
A	4.00
AB	3.50
B	3.00
BC	2.50
C	2.00
CD	1.50
D	1.00
F	0.00

■ **Figure 6.38** Printer spacing chart for the report

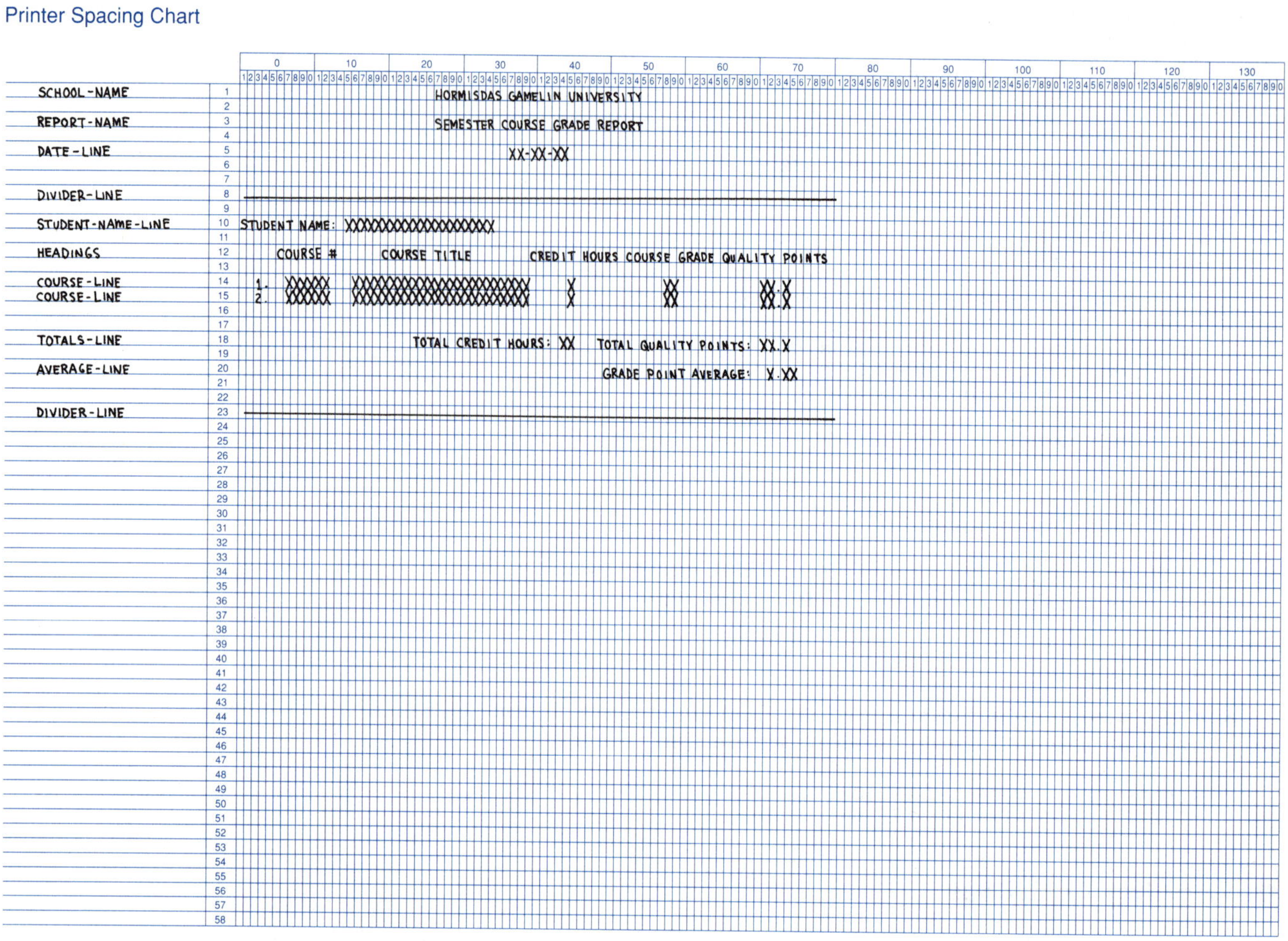

The program must also load a table containing information on each course. This information is contained in a file. The file is shown in Figure 6.39.

The data structure of each record in the file is as follows:

cc 1–6	Course number
cc 7–30	Course title
cc 31	Credit hours

To compute the quality points the students earned in each course, the course's credit hours must be multiplied by the numeric equivalent of the letter grade the student received in the course. The student's grade point average for the semester is obtained by dividing the total quality points by the total credit hours the student earned. Student course data is shown in Figure 6.40.

When the first attempt was made to compile the program, the compiler generated a number of diagnostics, as shown on pages 495–501. Your task is to correct all the syntax errors.

Figure 6.39 Course file records

```
16.202INTRO CIRCUIT THEORY     4
16.208BASIC EE LAB II          2
16.265INTRO LOGIC DESIGN       4
16.312ELECTRONICS LAB II       2
22.211ENGINEERING MECHANICS I 3
22.212MECHANICS OF MATERIALS I3
22.213DYNAMICS                 3
22.214ENGINEERING MECHANICS    4
42.102COLLEGE WRITING II       3
42.224BUSINESS WRITING         3
42.295HIST. AMERICAN LIT II    3
43.106THE MODERN WORLD         3
43.112US HISTORY SINCE 1877    3
43.235CIVIL WAR & RECONSTRUCTI3
45.201INTRO TO PHILOSOPHY      3
45.203INTRO TO ETHICS          3
45.295ETHICAL ISSUES IN TECH   3
46.101INTRO TO AMER POLITICS   3
47.101GENERAL PSYCHOLOGY       3
47.163HUMAN LIFE SPAN          3
47.209SOCIAL PSYCHOLOGY        3
47.272ABNORMAL PSYCHOLOGY      3
48.101INTRO TO SOCIOLOGY       3
59.204TECH & HUMAN VALUES      3
59.206HUMAN VALUES IN W CULT   3
60.201PRINCIPLES OF ACCT I     3
60.202PRINCIPLES OF ACCT II    3
60.301INTERMEDIATE ACCT        3
62.301MARKETING PRINCIPLES     3
62.302MARKETING RESEARCH       3
63.371OPERATIONS MANAGEMENT    3
63.405MGMT INFORMATION SYSTEMS3
64.201ECONOMICS I              3
64.202ECONOMICS II             3
64.211STATISTICS I             3
64.212STATISTICS II            3
66.355PERSONNEL MANAGEMENT     3
66.362BUSINESS LAW I           3
66.498BUSINESS POLICY          3
71.101MUSIC THEORY I           3
71.102MUSIC THEORY II          3
81.112PRINCIPLES OF BIOLOGY    3
81.215MARINE BIOLOGY           2
83.101LIFE SCIENCE I           3
83.102LIFE SCIENCE II          3
83.103LIFE SCIENCE I LAB       1
84.112GEN. CHEMISTRY II        3
84.114GEN. CHEM II LAB         1
84.121CHEMISTRY I              3
84.123CHEMISTRY I LAB          1
91.101INTRO TO COMPUTING       4
91.102INTRO TO COMPUTING II    4
91.204SYSTEMS PROG             3
91.308INTRO TO OPERATING SYS   3
92.115COLLEGE TRIGONOMETRY     3
92.121PRE-CALCULUS MATH        3
92.122DIFFERENTIAL CALCULUS    3
92.131CALCULUS I               4
92.132CALCULUS II              4
92.365COBOL I                  3
92.368COBOL II                 3
95.104GENERAL PHYSICS II       3
95.141PHYSICS I                3
95.144PHYSICS II REC           3
```

Figure 6.40 Student course data

	NAME	COURSE #	GRADE
1.	ROBIN ABRAMS	71.101	A
		47.101	B
		43.106	AB
		45.201	A
		59.204	B
2.	SCOTT ASHLEY	63.371	AB
		92.365	AB
		45.203	B
		43.112	BC
		62.301	A
3.	STELLA BOYKO	92.121	A
		64.201	A
		48.101	A
		42.102	AB
		47.101	B
4.	NORMAN CASEY	16.202	AB
		22.211	C
		42.102	B
		59.204	C
5.	BERTHA CORMIER	64.202	B
		63.405	AB
		62.302	A
		66.362	CD
		42.224	C
		59.204	BC
6.	JULIA DANIELS	95.104	D
		16.202	C
		42.295	B
		47.101	AB
		59.206	B
7.	DONALD FAY	92.131	A
		91.102	AB
		84.121	AB
		84.123	A
		47.163	B
		45.203	AB
8.	ALICIA HARDING	62.301	A
		60.201	A
		47.101	AB
		45.201	B
		42.224	A
9.	ALAN KAPLAN	92.132	F
		83.101	C
		83.103	CD
		59.206	BC
10.	ELEANOR LUCAS	92.368	AB
		63.405	A
		48.101	BC
		47.209	C
		42.295	B
11.	ALMA MORIN	16.202	B
		16.208	AB
		43.112	A
		47.101	A
		45.295	AB
12.	GEORGE PHELAN	91.204	AB
		92.132	AB
		59.206	C
		43.235	BC
13.	LOUISE RAYMOND	63.371	A
		64.202	AB
		92.122	BC
		84.112	B
14.	ROY SALPIETRO	95.104	BC
		92.132	AB
		47.101	B
		45.295	A
		42.295	AB
15.	IDA TISDALE	81.112	BC
		84.112	B
		92.131	C
		45.203	CD
		47.163	BC

```
COURSE-GRADE-DBG-1                                    25-Aug-1989 16:29:13    VAX COBOL V4.2-40                      Page   1
Source Listing                                        25-Aug-1989 16:29:00    [PAQUETTEG.CHAPTER8V2]V2C9DBG1.COB;2 (1)

         IDENTIFICATION DIVISION.

         PROGRAM-ID.  COURSE-GRADE-DBG-1.

        ****************************************************************
        *                                                              *
        *  AUTHOR.          PAQUETTE.                                  *
        *  DATE WRITTEN.  AUGUST 1989.                                 *
        *                                                              *
        ****************************************************************

         ENVIRONMENT DIVISION.

         CONFIGURATION SECTION.

         SOURCE-COMPUTER.  VAX-VMS-8650.
         OBJECT-COMPUTER.  VAX-VMS-8650.
         SPECIAL-NAMES.
             SYMBOLIC CHARACTER BEL IS 8.
                      1
%COBOL-F-ERROR  115, (1) Invalid CONFIGURATION SECTION entry

         INPUT-OUTPUT SECTION.
         1
%COBOL-W-ERROR  297, (1) Processing of source program resumes at this point

         FILE-CONTROL.
             SELECT COURSE-FILE   ASSIGN TO COB1$INPUT.
             SELECT GRADE-REPORT  ASSIGN TO COB1$OUTPUT.

         DATA DIVISION.

         FILE SECTION.

         FD  COURSE-FILE
             RECORD CONTAINS 31 CHARACTERS.

         01  COURSE-RECORD     PIC X(31).

         FD  GRADE-REPORT
             RECORD CONTAINS 80 CHARACTERS.

         01  PRINTLINE         PIC X(80).

         WORKING-STORAGE SECTION.

         01  PROGRAM-CONTROLS.
             05 MORE-COURSE-RECORDS    PIC X(3).
                88 NO-MORE-COURSE-RECORDS    VALUE 'NO '.
             05 STUDENT-INPUT-FLAG     PIC X(3).
                88 NO-MORE-DATA              VALUE 'END'.
             05 COURSE-INPUT-FLAG      PIC X(3).
                88 NO-MORE-COURSES           VALUE 'END'.
             05 REPORT-DATE            PIC X(6).
             05 PROPER-SPACING         PIC 9(1).
             05 USER-ENTRY             PIC X(10).
```

```
COURSE-GRADE-DBG-1                                    25-Aug-1989 16:29:13    VAX COBOL V4.2-40                    Page  2
Source Listing                                        25-Aug-1989 16:29:00    [PAQUETTEG.CHAPTER8V2]V2C9DBG1.COB;2 (1)

          01  STUDENT-ITEMS.
              05 WS-STUDENT-NAME         PIC X(20).
              05 WS-COURSE-NO            PIC X(6).
              05 WS-COURSE-GRADE         PIC X(2).
              05 STUDENT-ACCUMULATORS.
                 10 COURSE-CTR           PIC X(1).
                 10 TOTAL-CREDIT-HRS     PIC 9(2).
                 10 TOTAL-QUALITY-PTS    PIC 9(2)V9.

          01  LETTER-GRADE-VALUES.
              05 PIC X(5)  VALUE 'A 400'.
              05 PIC X(5)  VALUE 'AB350'.
              05 PIC X(5)  VALUE 'B 300'.
              05 PIC X(5)  VALUE 'BC250'.
              05 PIC X(5)  VALUE 'C 200'.
              05 PIC X(5)  VALUE 'CD150'.
              05 PIC X(5)  VALUE 'D 100'.
              05 PIC X(5)  VALUE 'F 000'.

          01  LETTER-GRADE-TABLE REDEFINES LETTER-GRADE-VALUES.
              05 LETTER-GRADE-INFO  OCCURS 5 TIMES
                                    INDEXED BY GRADE-INDEX.
                 10 LETTER-GRADE    PIC X(2).
                 10 NUMERIC-GRADE   PIC 9V99.

          01  COURSE-TABLE.
              05 COURSE-INFO  OCCURS 70 TIMES
                              INDEXED BY COURSE-INDEX.
                 10 COURSE-NO        PIC X(6).
                 10 COURSE-TITLE     PIC X(24).
                 10 CREDIT-HRS       PIC 9(1).

          01  REPORT-HEADERS.
              05 SCHOOL-NAME.
                 10 PIC X(26)  VALUE SPACES.
                 10 PIC X(28)  VALUE 'HORMISDAS GAMELIN UNIVERSITY'.
                 10 PIC X(26)  VALUE SPACES.

              05 REPORT-NAME.
                 10 PIC X(26)  VALUE SPACES.
                 10 PIC X(28)  VALUE 'SEMESTER COURSE GRADE REPORT'.
                 10 PIC X(26)  VALUE SPACES.

              05 DATE-LINE.
                 10                      PIC X(36)  VALUE SPACES.
                 10 O-DATE               PIC XX-XX-XX.
                                                1
%COBOL-F-ERROR  156, (1) Invalid PICTURE character-string
                 10                      PIC X(36)  VALUE SPACES.

          01  STUDENT-LINES.
              05 DIVIDER-LINE            PIC X(30)  VALUE ALL '-'.

              05 STUDENT-NAME-LINE.
                 10                      PIC X(14)  VALUE 'STUDENT NAME: '.
                 10 O-STUDENT-NAME       PIC X(20).
                 10                      PIC X(46)  VALUE SPACES.
```

```

           05 HEADINGS.
              10 PIC X(5)    VALUE SPACES.
              10 PIC X(8)    VALUE 'COURSE #'.
              10 PIC X(6)    VALUE SPACES.
              10 PIC X(12)   VALUE 'COURSE TITLE'.
              10 PIC X(8)    VALUE SPACES.
              10 PIC X(12)   VALUE 'CREDIT HOURS'.
              10 PIC X(1)    VALUE SPACES.
              10 PIC X(12)   VALUE 'COURSE GRADE'.
              10 PIC X(1)    VALUE SPACES.
              10 PIC X(14)   VALUE 'QUALITY POINTS'.
              10 PIC X(1)    VALUE SPACES.

           05 COURSE-LINE.
              10                     PIC X(2).
              10 O-COURSE-CTR        PIC 9..
              10                     PIC X(2).
              10 O-COURSE-NO         PIC X(6).
              10                     PIC X(3).
              10 O-COURSE-TITLE      PIC X(24).
              10                     PIC X(5).
              10 O-CREDIT-HOURS      PIC 9(1).
              10                     PIC X(12).
              10 O-COURSE-GRADE      PIC X(2).
              10                     PIC X(11).
              10 O-QUALITY-PTS       PIC Z9.9.
              10                     PIC X(5).

           05 TOTALS-LINE.
              10                     PIC X(23)  VALUE SPACES.
              10                     PIC X(20)  VALUE
                                     'TOTAL CREDIT HOURS: '.
              10 O-TOTAL-CREDIT-HRS  PIC Z9.
              10                     PIC X(3)   VALUE SPACES.
              10                     PIC X(20)  VALUE
                                     1
%COBOL-E-ERROR   84, (1) Literal in VALUE clause conflicts with description - clause ignored
                                     'TOTAL QUALITY POINTS: '.
              10 O-TOTAL-QUALITY-PTS PIC Z9.9.
              10                     PIC X(5)   VALUE SPACES.

           05 AVERAGE-LINE.
              10                     PIC X(49)  VALUE SPACES.
              10                     PIC X(22)  VALUE
                                     'GRADE-POINT AVERAGE:   '.
              10 O-GRADE-POINT-AVE   PIC Z.99.
              10                     PIC X(5)   VALUE SPACES.

       PROCEDURE DIVISION.

       100-PRODUCE-GRADE-REPORT.
           DISPLAY ' '.
           DISPLAY ' '.
           DISPLAY 'THE PURPOSE OF THIS PROGRAM IS TO PRODUCE THE SEMEST
                   1
%COBOL-F-ERROR  147, (1) Nonnumeric literal improperly continued
```

```
                            'ER'S STUDENT GRADE REPORTS."
                DISPLAY 'IF THIS IS WHAT YOU INTEND TO DO, PRESS CR TO CONTIN
                        1
%COBOL-F-ERROR  147, (1) Nonnumeric literal improperly continued
                        'UE."
                DISPLAY 'OTHERWISE, ENTER 'EXIT' OR 'EX' TO TERMINATE THE PRO
                        1
%COBOL-F-ERROR  147, (1) Nonnumeric literal improperly continued
                        'GRAM!  '  WITH NO ADVANCING.
                ACCEPT USER-ENTRY.
                DISPLAY ' '.
                IF USER-ENTRY(1:2) = 'EX'
                    NEXT SENTENCE
                ELSE
                    PERFORM 200-START-UP
                    PERFORM 210-PROCESS-TERMINAL-DATA
                        UNTIL NO-MORE-DATA
                    PERFORM 220-FINISH-UP.
                STOP RUN.

            200-START-UP.
                OPEN INPUT  COURSE-FILE
                     OUTPUT GRADE-REPORT.
                MOVE 'YES' TO MORE-COURSE-RECORDS.
                PERFORM 300-LOAD-COURSE-TABLE
                    VARYING COURSE-INDEX FROM 1 BY 1
                        UNTIL NO-MORE-COURSE-RECORDS.
                ACCEPT REPORT-DATE FROM DATE.
                MOVE REPORT-DATE TO O-DATE.
                INSPECT O-DATE
                    REPLACING ALL '/' BY '-'.
                PERFORM 310-WRITE-REPORT-HEADERS.
                DISPLAY ' ' BEL.
                            1
%COBOL-F-ERROR  349, (1) Undefined name
                DISPLAY 'FOR EACH STUDENT, YOU WILL BE PROMPTED TO ENTER THE
                        1
%COBOL-F-ERROR  147, (1) Nonnumeric literal improperly continued
                        'STUDENT NAME".
                DISPLAY 'THEN, YOU WILL BE PROMPTED TO ENTER THE COURSE NUMBE
                        1
%COBOL-F-ERROR  147, (1) Nonnumeric literal improperly continued
                        'R AND COURSE GRADE".
                DISPLAY 'FOR EACH COURSE THE STUDENT TOOK DURING THE SEMESTER
                        1
%COBOL-F-ERROR  147, (1) Nonnumeric literal improperly continued
                        "!".
                DISPLAY ' '
                DISPLAY 'THE PROGRAM PRODUCES THE STUDENT'S COURSE GRADE REPO
                        1
%COBOL-F-ERROR  147, (1) Nonnumeric literal improperly continued
                        'RT."
                DISPLAY ' '.
                DISPLAY 'PRESS CR IF YOU ARE READY TO PROCEED!'.
                DISPLAY 'IF YOU DO NOT HAVE THE REQUIRED DATA, ENTER 'EXIT' '
                        WITH NO ADVANCING.
                ACCEPT USER-ENTRY.
```

```
               IF USER-ENTRY(1:2) = 'EX'
                   SET NO-MORE-DATA TO TRUE
               END-IF.

           210-PROCESS-TERMINAL-DATA.
               DISPLAY ' ' BELL.
               DISPLAY 'ENTER THE STUDENT'S NAME: ' WITH NO ADVANCING.
               ACCEPT STUDENT-NAME.
                      1
%COBOL-F-ERROR  349, (1) Undefined name
               PERFORM 320-PREPARE-STUDENT-HEADERS.
               1
%COBOL-W-ERROR  297, (1) Processing of source program resumes at this point
               PERFORM 330-GET-COURSE-INFO
                   UNTIL NO-MORE-COURSES.
               PERFORM 340-PREPARE-STUDENT-SUMMARY.
               DISPLAY ' ' BELL.
               DISPLAY 'ARE THERE ANY MORE STUDENT RECORDS TO PROCESS? (Y/N)
                      1
%COBOL-F-ERROR  147, (1) Nonnumeric literal improperly continued
                   ': ' WITH NO ADVANCING.
               ACCEPT USER-ENTRY.
               IF USER-ENTRY(1:1) = 'N'
                   SET NO-MORE-DATA TO TRUE
               END-IF.

           220-FINISH-UP.
               CLOSE COURSE-FILE
               CLOSE GRADE-REPORT.

           300-LOAD-COURSE-TABLE.
               READ COURSE-FILE RECORD INTO COURSE-INFO(COURSE-INDEX)
                   AT END
                       SET NO-MORE-COURSE-RECORDS TO TRUE.

           310-WRITE-REPORT-HEADERS.
               WRITE PRINTLINE FROM SCHOOL-NAME
                   AFTER ADVANCING PAGE.
               WRITE PRINTLINE FROM REPORT-NAME
                   AFTER ADVANCING 2 LINES.
               WRITE PRINTLINE FROM DATE-LINE
                   AFTER ADVANCING 2 LINES.

           320-PREPARE-STUDENT-HEADERS.
               WRITE PRINTLINE FROM DIVIDE-LINE
                                    1
%COBOL-F-ERROR  349, (1) Undefined name
                   AFTER ADVANCING 3 LINES.
                                      1
%COBOL-W-ERROR  297, (1) Processing of source program resumes at this point
               MOVE STUDENT-NAME TO O-STUDENT-NAME.
                     1
%COBOL-F-ERROR  349, (1) Undefined name
               WRITE PRINTLINE FROM STUDENT-NAME-LINE
               1
%COBOL-W-ERROR  297, (1) Processing of source program resumes at this point
                   AFTER ADVANCING 2 LINES.
```

```
                  WRITE PRINTLINE FROM HEADINGS
                      AFTER ADVANCING 2 LINES.
                  MOVE 2 TO PROPER-SPACING.
                  INITIALIZE STUDENT-ACCUMS.
                           1
%COBOL-F-ERROR  349, (1) Undefined name

               330-GET-COURSE-INFO.
               1
%COBOL-W-ERROR  297, (1) Processing of source program resumes at this point
                  DISPLAY ' '.
                  DISPLAY 'ENTER A COURSE NUMBER: ' WITH NO ADVANCING.
                  ACCEPT WS-COURSE-NO.
                  DISPLAY 'ENTER THE STUDENT'S GRADE IN THAT COURSE: '
                                                    WITHNO ADVANCING.
                                                    1               2
%COBOL-F-ERROR  349, (1) Undefined name
%COBOL-W-ERROR  297, (2) Processing of source program resumes at this point
                  ACCEPT WS-COURSE-GRADE.
                  PERFORM 400-PROCESS-STUDENT-COURSE-DATA.
                  DISPLAY ' '.
                  DISPLAY 'ANY MORE DATA FOR THIS STUDENT? (Y/N): '
                                                     WITH NO ADVANCING.
                  ACCEPT USER-ENTRY.
                  IF USER-ENTRY(1:1) = 'N'
                      SET NO-MORE-COURSES TO TRUE
                  END-IF.

              340-PREPARE-STUDENT-SUMMARY.
                  MOVE TOTAL-CREDIT-HRS TO O-TOTAL-CREDIT-HRS.
                  MOVE TOTAL-QUALITY-PTS TO O-TOTAL-QUALITY-PTS.
                  WRITE PRINTLINE FROM TOTALS-LINE
                      AFTER ADVANCING 2 LINES.
                  DIVIDE TOTAL-CREDIT-HRS BY TOTAL-QUALITY-PTS
                      GIVING O-GRADE-POINT-AVE ROUNDED.
                  WRITE PRINTLINE FROM AVERAGE-LINE
                      AFTER ADVANCING 2 LINES.

              400-PROCESS-STUDENT-COURSE-DATA.
                  ADD 1 TO COURSE-CTR.
                           1
%COBOL-F-ERROR  277, (1) Operand must be a numeric data-name
                  SET COURSE-INDEX TO 1.
                  SEARCH COURSE-INFO
                      WHEN WS-COURSE-NO = COURSE-NO (COURSE-INDEX)
                          NEXT SENTENCE
                  END-SEARCH.
                  SET GRADE-INDEX TO 1.
                  SEARCH LETTER-GRADE-INFO
                      WHEN WS-COURSE-GRADE = LETTER-GRADE (GRADE-INDEX)
                          NEXT SENTENCE
                  END-SEARCH.
                  PERFORM 500-COMPUTE-STUDENT-VALUES.
                  PERFORM 510-PREPARE-COURSE-LINE.

              500-COMPUTE-STUDENT-VALUES.
                  ADD CREDIT-HRS(COURSE-INDEX) TO TOTAL-CREDIT-HRS.
```

```
COURSE-GRADE-DBG-1                                25-Aug-1989 16:29:13    VAX COBOL V4.2-40                      Page   7
Source Listing                                    25-Aug-1989 16:29:00    [PAQUETTEG.CHAPTER8V2]V2C9DBG1.COB;2 (1)

                  MULTIPLY TOTAL-CREDIT-HRS
                      BY NUMERIC-GRADE(GRADE-INDEX)
                          GIVING WS-COURSE-QUALITY-PTS.
                                 1
%COBOL-F-ERROR  349, (1) Undefined name
                  ADD WS-COURSE-QUALITY-PTS TO TOTAL-QUALITY-PTS.
                      1
%COBOL-F-ERROR  349, (1) Undefined name

              510-PREPARE-COURSE-LINE.
              1
%COBOL-W-ERROR  297, (1) Processing of source program resumes at this point
                  MOVE WS-COURSE-CTR TO O-COURSE-CTR.
                       1
%COBOL-F-ERROR  349, (1) Undefined name
                  MOVE WS-COURSE-NO TO O-COURSE-NO.
                  1
%COBOL-W-ERROR  297, (1) Processing of source program resumes at this point
                  MOVE COURSE-TITLE(COURSE-INDEX) TO O-COURSE-TITLE.
                  MOVE CREDIT-HRS(COURSE-INDEX) TO O-CREDIT-HRS.
                                                    1
%COBOL-F-ERROR  349, (1) Undefined name
                  MOVE WS-COURSE-GRADE TO O-COURSE-GRADE.
                  MOVE WS-COURSE-QUALITY-PTS TO O-QUALITY-PTS.
                       1
%COBOL-F-ERROR  349, (1) Undefined name
                  WRITE PRINTLINE FROM COURSE-LINE
                  1
%COBOL-W-ERROR  297, (1) Processing of source program resumes at this point
                      AFTER ADVANCING PROPER-SPACING.
                  MOVE 1 TO PROPER-SPACING.
```

2. When the assignment in exercise 1 was completed, the program was compiled, data was entered at the terminal, and the report that was produced is shown in Figure 6.41. It is obvious that the program still contains a number of errors. The report the program should produce is shown in Figure 6.42. Your task is to find and correct the remaining errors.

Figure 6.41 Course grade report with errors (first four students only)

```
                                 HORMISDAS GAMELIN UNIVERSITY

                                 SEMESTER COURSE GRADE REPORT

                                           89 -08-25

--------------------------------------------------------------------------------

STUDENT NAME: ROBIN ABRAMS

     COURSE #        COURSE TITLE         CREDIT HOURS COURSE GRADE QUALITY POINTS

  1.  71.101   MUSIC THEORY I                  3            A            12.0
  2.  47.101   GENERAL PSYCHOLOGY              3            B            18.0
  3.  43.106   THE MODERN WORLD                3            AB           31.5
  4.  45.201   INTRO TO PHILOSOPHY             3            A            48.0
  5.  59.204   TECH & HUMAN VALUES             3            B            45.0

                            TOTAL CREDIT HOURS: 15    TOTAL QUALITY POINTS: 54.5

                                                       GRADE-POINT AVERAGE:    .28

--------------------------------------------------------------------------------

STUDENT NAME: SCOTT ASHLEY

     COURSE #        COURSE TITLE         CREDIT HOURS COURSE GRADE QUALITY POINTS

                            TOTAL CREDIT HOURS:  0    TOTAL QUALITY POINTS:  0.0

                                                       GRADE-POINT AVERAGE:    .28

--------------------------------------------------------------------------------

STUDENT NAME: STELLA BOYKO

     COURSE #        COURSE TITLE         CREDIT HOURS COURSE GRADE QUALITY POINTS

                            TOTAL CREDIT HOURS:  0    TOTAL QUALITY POINTS:  0.0

                                                       GRADE-POINT AVERAGE:    .28

--------------------------------------------------------------------------------

STUDENT NAME: NORMAN CASEY

     COURSE #        COURSE TITLE         CREDIT HOURS COURSE GRADE QUALITY POINTS

                            TOTAL CREDIT HOURS:  0    TOTAL QUALITY POINTS:  0.0

                                                       GRADE-POINT AVERAGE:    .28
```

Figure 6.42 Course grade report without errors

```
                         HORMISDAS GAMELIN UNIVERSITY

                         SEMESTER COURSE GRADE REPORT

                                   89-08-25

-------------------------------------------------------------------------------

STUDENT NAME: ROBIN ABRAMS

     COURSE #        COURSE TITLE        CREDIT HOURS COURSE GRADE QUALITY POINTS

  1.  71.101    MUSIC THEORY I                 3              A           12.0
  2.  47.101    GENERAL PSYCHOLOGY             3              B            9.0
  3.  43.106    THE MODERN WORLD               3              AB          10.5
  4.  45.201    INTRO TO PHILOSOPHY            3              A           12.0
  5.  59.204    TECH & HUMAN VALUES            3              B            9.0

                      TOTAL CREDIT HOURS: 15   TOTAL QUALITY POINTS: 52.5

                                               GRADE-POINT AVERAGE:  3.50

-------------------------------------------------------------------------------

STUDENT NAME: SCOTT ASHLEY

     COURSE #        COURSE TITLE        CREDIT HOURS COURSE GRADE QUALITY POINTS

  1.  63.371    OPERATIONS MANAGEMENT          3              AB          10.5
  2.  92.365    COBOL I                        3              AB          10.5
  3.  45.203    INTRO TO ETHICS                3              B            9.0
  4.  43.112    US HISTORY SINCE 1877          3              BC           7.5
  5.  62.301    MARKETING PRINCIPLES           3              A           12.0

                      TOTAL CREDIT HOURS: 15   TOTAL QUALITY POINTS: 49.5

                                               GRADE-POINT AVERAGE:  3.30

-------------------------------------------------------------------------------

STUDENT NAME: STELLA BOYKO

     COURSE #        COURSE TITLE        CREDIT HOURS COURSE GRADE QUALITY POINTS

  1.  92.121    PRE-CALCULUS MATH              3              A           12.0
  2.  64.201    ECONOMICS I                    3              A           12.0
  3.  48.101    INTRO TO SOCIOLOGY             3              A           12.0
  4.  42.102    COLLEGE WRITING II             3              AB          10.5
  5.  47.101    GENERAL PSYCHOLOGY             3              B            9.0

                      TOTAL CREDIT HOURS: 15   TOTAL QUALITY POINTS: 55.5

                                               GRADE-POINT AVERAGE:  3.70

-------------------------------------------------------------------------------

STUDENT NAME: NORMAN CASEY

     COURSE #        COURSE TITLE        CREDIT HOURS COURSE GRADE QUALITY POINTS

  1.  16.202    INTRO CIRCUIT THEORY           4              AB          14.0
  2.  22.211    ENGINEERING MECHANICS I        3              C            6.0
  3.  42.102    COLLEGE WRITING II             3              B            9.0
  4.  59.204    TECH & HUMAN VALUES            3              C            6.0

                      TOTAL CREDIT HOURS: 13   TOTAL QUALITY POINTS: 35.0

                                               GRADE-POINT AVERAGE:  2.69
```

Figure 6.42 continued

```
--------------------------------------------------------------------------------

STUDENT NAME: BERTHA CORMIER

     COURSE #        COURSE TITLE        CREDIT HOURS COURSE GRADE QUALITY POINTS

  1.  64.202   ECONOMICS II                  3             B             9.0
  2.  63.405   MGMT INFORMATION SYSTEMS      3             AB           10.5
  3.  62.302   MARKETING RESEARCH            3             A            12.0
  4.  66.362   BUSINESS LAW I                3             CD            4.5
  5.  42.224   BUSINESS WRITING              3             C             6.0
  6.  59.204   TECH & HUMAN VALUES           3             BC            7.5

                       TOTAL CREDIT HOURS: 18    TOTAL QUALITY POINTS: 49.5

                                                  GRADE-POINT AVERAGE:  2.75

--------------------------------------------------------------------------------

STUDENT NAME: JULIA DANIELS

     COURSE #        COURSE TITLE        CREDIT HOURS COURSE GRADE QUALITY POINTS

  1.  95.104   GENERAL PHYSICS II            3             D             3.0
  2.  16.202   INTRO CIRCUIT THEORY          4             C             8.0
  3.  42.295   HIST. AMERICAN LIT II         3             B             9.0
  4.  47.101   GENERAL PSYCHOLOGY            3             AB           10.5
  5.  59.206   HUMAN VALUES IN W CULT        3             B             9.0

                       TOTAL CREDIT HOURS: 16    TOTAL QUALITY POINTS: 39.5

                                                  GRADE-POINT AVERAGE:  2.47

--------------------------------------------------------------------------------

STUDENT NAME: DONALD FAY

     COURSE #        COURSE TITLE        CREDIT HOURS COURSE GRADE QUALITY POINTS

  1.  92.131   CALCULUS I                    4             A            16.0
  2.  91.102   INTRO TO COMPUTING II         4             AB           14.0
  3.  84.121   CHEMISTRY I                   3             AB           10.5
  4.  84.123   CHEMISTRY I LAB               1             A             4.0
  5.  47.163   HUMAN LIFE SPAN               3             B             9.0
  6.  45.203   INTRO TO ETHICS               3             AB           10.5

                       TOTAL CREDIT HOURS: 18    TOTAL QUALITY POINTS: 64.0

                                                  GRADE-POINT AVERAGE:  3.56

--------------------------------------------------------------------------------

STUDENT NAME: ALICIA HARDING

     COURSE #        COURSE TITLE        CREDIT HOURS COURSE GRADE QUALITY POINTS

  1.  62.301   MARKETING PRINCIPLES          3             A            12.0
  2.  60.201   PRINCIPLES OF ACCT I          3             A            12.0
  3.  47.101   GENERAL PSYCHOLOGY            3             AB           10.5
  4.  45.201   INTRO TO PHILOSOPHY           3             B             9.0
  5.  42.224   BUSINESS WRITING              3             A            12.0

                       TOTAL CREDIT HOURS: 15    TOTAL QUALITY POINTS: 55.5

                                                  GRADE-POINT AVERAGE:  3.70
```

■ **Figure 6.42** continued

```
------------------------------------------------------------------------------

STUDENT NAME: ALAN KAPLAN

        COURSE #          COURSE TITLE          CREDIT HOURS COURSE GRADE QUALITY POINTS

  1.   92.132    CALCULUS II                        4            F            0.0
  2.   83.101    LIFE SCIENCE I                     3            C            6.0
  3.   83.103    LIFE SCIENCE I LAB                 1            CD           1.5
  4.   59.206    HUMAN VALUES IN W CULT             3            BC           7.5

                           TOTAL CREDIT HOURS: 11   TOTAL QUALITY POINTS: 15.0

                                                    GRADE-POINT AVERAGE:  1.36

------------------------------------------------------------------------------

STUDENT NAME: ELEANOR LUCAS

        COURSE #          COURSE TITLE          CREDIT HOURS COURSE GRADE QUALITY POINTS

  1.   92.368    COBOL II                           3            AB          10.5
  2.   63.405    MGMT INFORMATION SYSTEMS           3            A           12.0
  3.   48.101    INTRO TO SOCIOLOGY                 3            BC           7.5
  4.   47.209    SOCIAL PSYCHOLOGY                  3            C            6.0
  5.   42.295    HIST. AMERICAN LIT II              3            B            9.0

                           TOTAL CREDIT HOURS: 15   TOTAL QUALITY POINTS: 45.0

                                                    GRADE-POINT AVERAGE:  3.00

------------------------------------------------------------------------------

STUDENT NAME: ALMA MORIN

        COURSE #          COURSE TITLE          CREDIT HOURS COURSE GRADE QUALITY POINTS

  1.   16.202    INTRO CIRCUIT THEORY               4            B           12.0
  2.   16.208    BASIC EE LAB II                    2            AB           7.0
  3.   43.112    US HISTORY SINCE 1877              3            A           12.0
  4.   47.101    GENERAL PSYCHOLOGY                 3            A           12.0
  5.   45.295    ETHICAL ISSUES IN TECH             3            AB          10.5

                           TOTAL CREDIT HOURS: 15   TOTAL QUALITY POINTS: 53.5

                                                    GRADE-POINT AVERAGE:  3.57

------------------------------------------------------------------------------

STUDENT NAME: GEORGE PHELAN

        COURSE #          COURSE TITLE          CREDIT HOURS COURSE GRADE QUALITY POINTS

  1.   91.204    SYSTEMS PROG                       3            AB          10.5
  2.   92.132    CALCULUS II                        4            AB          14.0
  3.   59.206    HUMAN VALUES IN W CULT             3            C            6.0
  4.   43.235    CIVIL WAR & RECONSTRUCTI           3            BC           7.5

                           TOTAL CREDIT HOURS: 13   TOTAL QUALITY POINTS: 38.0

                                                    GRADE-POINT AVERAGE:  2.92
```

```
--------------------------------------------------------------------------------

STUDENT NAME: LOUISE RAYMOND

     COURSE #        COURSE TITLE        CREDIT HOURS COURSE GRADE QUALITY POINTS

  1.  63.371    OPERATIONS MANAGEMENT         3            A             12.0
  2.  64.202    ECONOMICS II                  3            AB            10.5
  3.  92.122    DIFFERENTIAL CALCULUS         3            BC             7.5
  4.  84.112    GEN. CHEMISTRY II             3            B              9.0

                      TOTAL CREDIT HOURS: 12   TOTAL QUALITY POINTS: 39.0

                                                 GRADE-POINT AVERAGE:  3.25

--------------------------------------------------------------------------------

STUDENT NAME: ROY SALPIETRO

     COURSE #        COURSE TITLE        CREDIT HOURS COURSE GRADE QUALITY POINTS

  1.  95.104    GENERAL PHYSICS II            3            BC             7.5
  2.  92.132    CALCULUS II                   4            AB            14.0
  3.  47.101    GENERAL PSYCHOLOGY            3            B              9.0
  4.  45.295    ETHICAL ISSUES IN TECH        3            A             12.0
  5.  42.295    HIST. AMERICAN LIT II         3            AB            10.5

                      TOTAL CREDIT HOURS: 16   TOTAL QUALITY POINTS: 53.0

                                                 GRADE-POINT AVERAGE:  3.31

--------------------------------------------------------------------------------

STUDENT NAME: IDA TISDALE

     COURSE #        COURSE TITLE        CREDIT HOURS COURSE GRADE QUALITY POINTS

  1.  81.112    PRINCIPLES OF BIOLOGY         3            BC             7.5
  2.  84.112    GEN. CHEMISTRY II             3            B              9.0
  3.  92.131    CALCULUS I                    4            C              8.0
  4.  45.203    INTRO TO ETHICS               3            CD             4.5
  5.  47.163    HUMAN LIFE SPAN               3            BC             7.5

                      TOTAL CREDIT HOURS: 16   TOTAL QUALITY POINTS: 36.5

                                                 GRADE-POINT AVERAGE:  2.28
```

Programming Exercises

Programming Exercise I

The data processing department of the Express Auto Parts Warehouse company wants a program to create its master parts file as an indexed file. The master catalog file is currently on Rolodex cards, and each card contains the part number, description, and unit selling price. The cards are arranged in ascending order by part number.

The data structure for the records of the indexed file is as follows:

cc 1–5	Part number
cc 6–25	Part description
cc 26–30	Part unit price (format: xxx.xx)

The record key for the file is the part number.

The program must be designed as an interactive program so that the indexed file can be created by having a data entry operator enter the data on the Rolodex cards at the keyboard during the execution of the program. The program must also produce an audit report of the file creation session. The format of the report is shown in Figure 6.43. (If duplicate key errors or out-of-sequence key errors occur, appropriate error messages must be printed on the report!)

Your task is to design the program to use the prompt/response technique and then implement the design to successful completion. Your program should tell the user to enter "EXIT" or "EX" at the part number prompt to terminate the file creation session.

Use Data Set 6X1 as the Rolodex file.

(*Note:* This task can be accomplished by using the ANSI formats of the ACCEPT and DISPLAY statements.)

■ **Figure 6.43** Printer spacing chart for the report

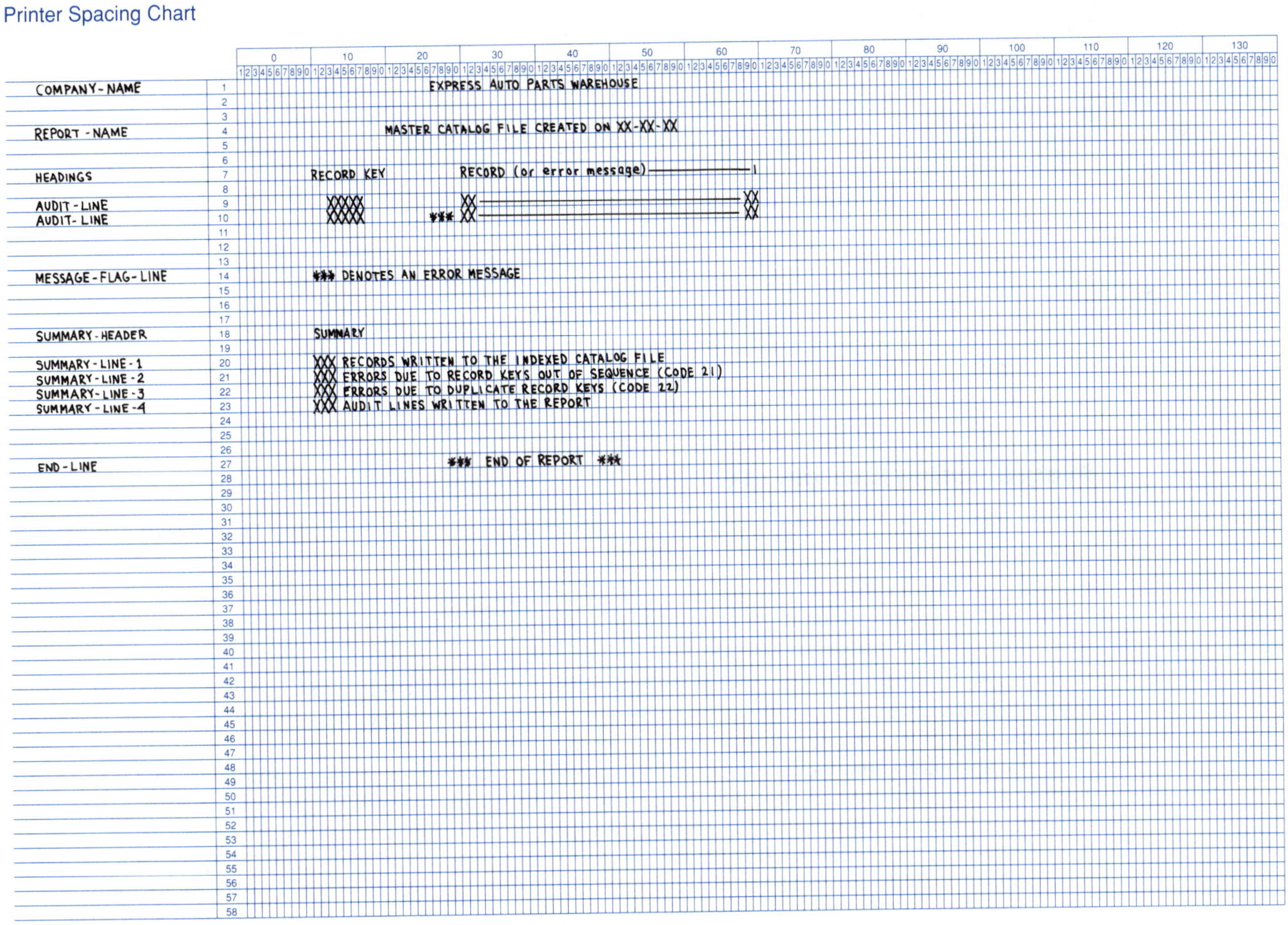

Programming Exercise II

Carry out the task described in Programming Exercise I, but design this program to use the free-form data entry procedure. That is, a single prompt is used to request the data for a part, and the UNSTRING statement is used to move the individual data items into the appropriate fields of a parts record.

(*Note:* This task can be accomplished by using the ANSI formats of the ACCEPT and DISPLAY statements.)

Programming Exercise III

Carry out the task described in Programming Exercise I, but design the interactive program to present the data entry operator with the video form prepared on the screen layout shown in Figure 6.44. Use lines 10 through 18 to display feedback to the operator.

Before presenting the video form, display general information about the use of this program and give the operator the option of exiting from the program.

(*Note:* This program requires the use of a screen management facility. If your compiler does not support extensions to the ANSI standards for the ACCEPT and DISPLAY statement, you will not be able to run the program!)

■ **Figure 6.44** Video chart for terminal data entry

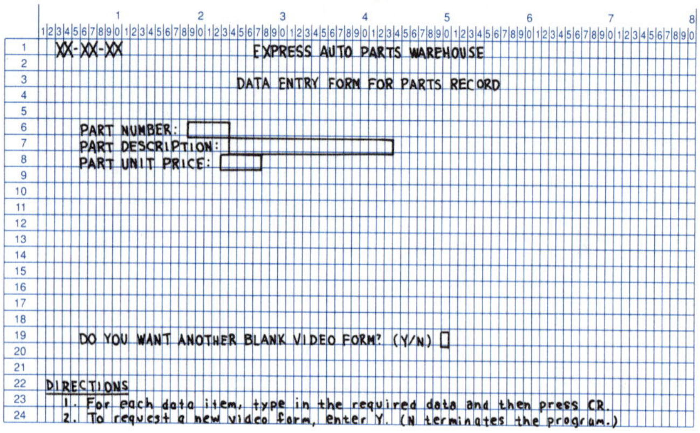

Screen Layout

Programming Exercise IV

The Express Auto Parts Warehouse maintains a catalog file on all items in inventory. Each record in the file contains the following data:

cc 1–5 Part number
cc 6–25 Part description
cc 26–30 Part unit price (format: xxx.xx)

The file has indexed organization and uses the part number as the record key. File maintenance activities include price changes, the addition of new parts to the inventory, and the deletion of catalog items that management has decided to drop from inventory.

Management wants the data processing department to prepare an interactive program that may be used by a data entry operator whenever file updating activities are needed. The program must also produce an audit report of the file maintenance session. The report specifications are shown in Figure 6.45.

If a record is successfully added to the file, an "X" is printed under the header "ADDED" and the part description and unit price are also printed on the line. If the add attempt is not successful, an "X" is printed under the header "NONE" and the message "Addition fails: duplicate part number" is printed on the line.

If a record is successfully deleted from the file, an "X" is printed under the header "DELETED" and the part description is printed on the line to provide additional documentation on the deleted part. If the deletion is not successful, an "X" is printed under the header "NONE" and the message "Deletion fails: no such part number" is printed on the line.

If a price change is successfully completed, an "X" is printed under the header "PRICE CHANGE" and the old and new prices are printed on the line. If the price change attempt fails, the message "Price change fails: no such part number" is printed on the line.

Your task is to design the program as an interactive program. If your compiler supports only the ANSI formats of the ACCEPT and DISPLAY statements, use the prompt/response technique. Otherwise, use designed video forms.

The program should begin by giving general information to the user as to the nature of the task at hand. In the event the user has called the wrong program, an early exit should be provided.

Use Data Set 6X4 as the data to be entered interactively, and use the indexed file created in Programming Exercise I, II, or III as the master file.

■ **Figure 6.45** Printer spacing chart for the file update report

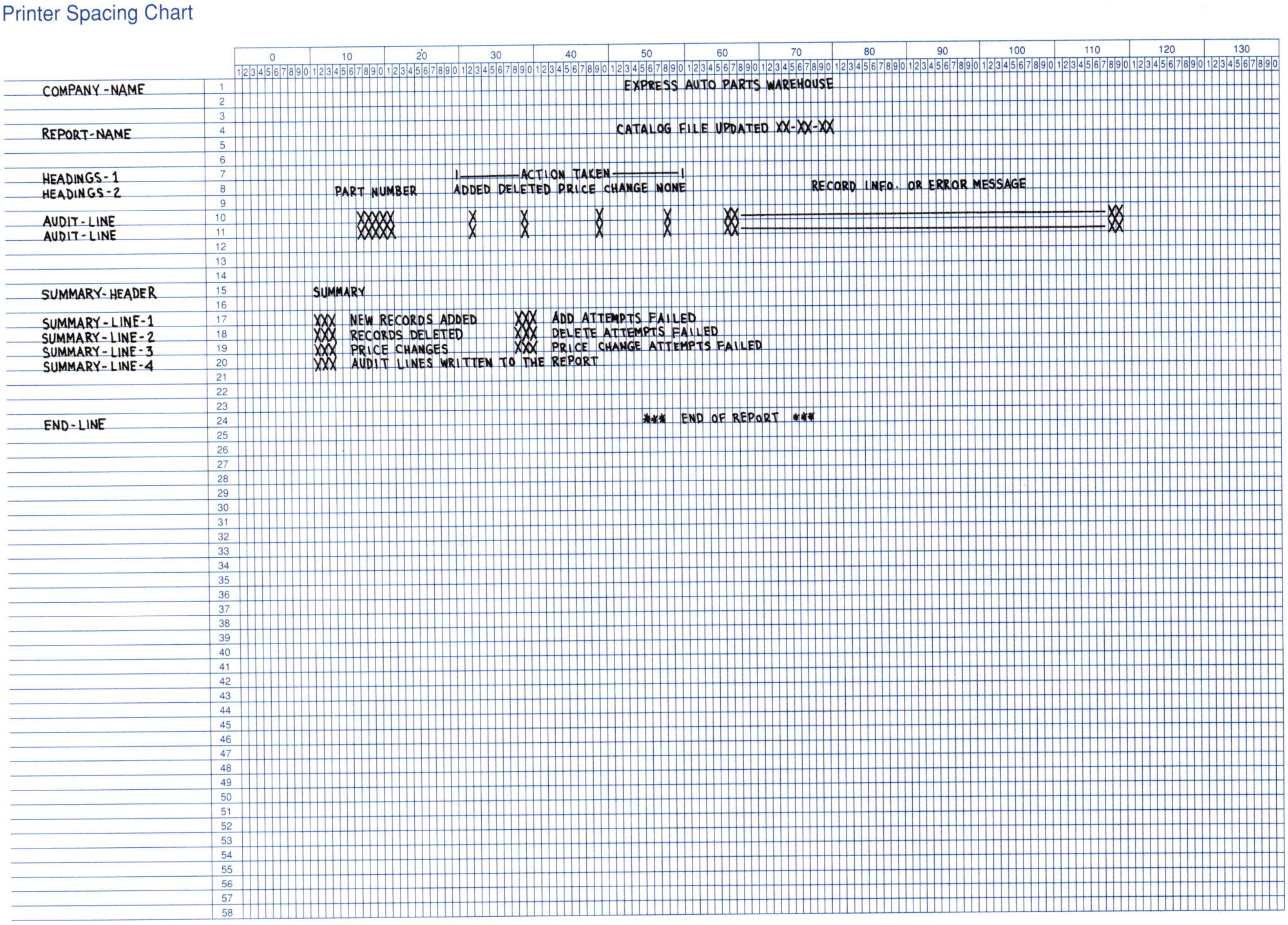

Appendix A

Miscellaneous Statements

Figure A.1 STRING statement format

```
STRING { {identifier-1} . . . DELIMITED BY {identifier-2} } . . .
       { {literal-1   }                    {literal-2   } }
                                           {SIZE        }
    INTO identifier-3
    [WITH POINTER identifier-4]
    [ON OVERFLOW imperative-statement-1]
    [NOT ON OVERFLOW imperative-statement-2]
    [END-STRING]
```

The STRING Statement

The STRING statement is used to join the partial or complete contents of two or more data items into a single field. This is technically referred to as *concatenation.* The format of the STRING statement is shown in Figure A.1

In this format,

1. *Identifier-1* and *literal-1* are the source or sending items. *Literal-1* must be a nonnumeric literal, and *identifier-1* must be in DISPLAY format.
2. *Identifier-2, literal-2,* and SIZE are the delimiters. They delimit the characters to be transferred to the receiving field. The delimiters themselves are not transferred. Literal-2 must be a nonnumeric literal, and identifier-2 must be in DISPLAY format.
3. *Identifier-3* is the receiving field, that is, the concatenated strings are stored in *identifier-3.* This data item must be in DISPLAY format and must not contain editing characters or the JUSTIFIED clause.
4. *Identifier-4,* called the pointer, must be an integer numeric data item. It must be defined such that it can contain a value equal to the size of the receiving field plus 1. (Its PIC clause must not contain the scalar P.) During the STRING operation, the value of the pointer indicates the character position (from the left) in the receiving field where the next transferred character will be stored.
5. *Imperative-statement-1* is an imperative statement. It is executed if an overflow condition occurs, that is, if there are more characters to be transferred but the receiving field is full.
6. *Imperative-statement-2* is an imperative statement. It is executed if no overflow occurs during the STRING operation.
7. *Literal-1* and *literal-2* may be figurative constants other than ALL. The size of any figurative constant is one.
8. Characters are moved from a sending item to the receiving field one by one from the left until the delimiter is encountered. The characters are stored left-justified. If SIZE is specified as the delimiter, all the characters of the source item are transferred. Data transfer also ends if the receiving field is full before encountering the delimiter or if all the characters in the sending item have been transferred.

9. If the POINTER phrase is used, the program must assign to *identifier-4* an integer value greater than zero before the STRING statement executes. The initial value of *identifier-4* indicates the character position in the receiving field where the first transferred character will be stored. If the phrase is not used, the first transferred character is stored in the leftmost character position of the receiving field. As successive characters are transferred, the value of *identifier-4* is increased by 1, so that the current value of *identifier-4* indicates the position where the next transferred character will be stored.
10. If the POINTER phrase is not used, an implicit pointer is defined, but it cannot be referenced by the program.
11. When the STRING operation ends, only the character positions of the receiving field that received transferred characters have changed values. The characters in the remaining positions retain the characters they contained before the STRING operation began.
12. An OVERFLOW condition occurs when the value of *identifier-4* or the implicit pointer is greater than the size of the receiving field.

Example 1

As an example of the STRING statement, examine the subprogram in Figure 5.10 of Chapter 5. The essential parts are repeated here for your convenience.

```
WORKING-STORAGE SECTION.

01  WS-REPORT-DATE.
    05 WS-YR          PIC 9(2).
    05 WS-MO          PIC 9(2).
    05 WS-DAY         PIC 9(2).

01  WS-CENTURY        PIC 9(4)    VALUE 1900.

01  MONTH-VALUES.
    05 PIC X(9)       VALUE "JANUARY  ".
    05 PIC X(9)       VALUE "FEBRUARY ".
    05 PIC X(9)       VALUE "MARCH    ".
    05 PIC X(9)       VALUE "APRIL    ".
    05 PIC X(9)       VALUE "MAY      ".
    05 PIC X(9)       VALUE "JUNE     ".
    05 PIC X(9)       VALUE "JULY     ".
    05 PIC X(9)       VALUE "AUGUST   ".
    05 PIC X(9)       VALUE "SEPTEMBER".
    05 PIC X(9)       VALUE "OCTOBER  ".
    05 PIC X(9)       VALUE "NOVEMBER ".
    05 PIC X(9)       VALUE "DECEMBER ".
01  MONTH-TABLE REDEFINES MONTH-VALUES.
    05 WS-MONTH OCCURS 12 TIMES      PIC X(9).

LINKAGE SECTION.
01  FORMATTED-DATE      PIC X(19).

PROCEDURE DIVISION USING FORMATTED-DATE.

100-FORMAT-CURRENT-DATE.
    ACCEPT WS-REPORT-DATE FROM DATE.
    ADD WS-YR TO WS-CENTURY.
    STRING WS-MONTH(WS-MO) DELIMITED BY " "
           " " DELIMITED BY SIZE
           WS-DAY DELIMITED BY SIZE
           "," DELIMITED BY SIZE
           " " DELIMITED BY SIZE
           WS-CENTURY DELIMITED BY SIZE
           INTO FORMATTED-DATE.
```

In this example, suppose that WS-REPORT-DATE is 890628. The receiving field is FORMATTED-DATE, and its size is 19. The characters transferred into it come from three data items and three literals in the sequence specified by the STRING statement. The first sending item is WS-MONTH(WS-MO). Since WS-MO = 6, the first character transferred is the leftmost character in WS-MONTH(6), namely the letter "J", and this character is stored left-justified in FORMATTED-DATE. The remaining characters of WS-MONTH(6) are transferred one by one until the first space is encountered, as specified by the phrase DELIMITED BY " ".

The second sending item is the space literal denoted by " ", and it is transferred limited only by its size. That is, one space is concatenated into the receiving item.

The third sending item is specified by WS-DAY. Its value is 28, and both characters are transferred into the receiving field, since the delimiter is simply the size of WS-DAY.

The fourth sending item is the literal ",", and the comma is concatenated into the receiving field.

Figure A.2 Date as formatted by the STRING statement

J	U	N	E		2	8	,		1	9	8	9						

The fifth sending item is the literal " ", and a space is stored to the right of the comma.

The sixth and last sending item is WS-CENTURY, and all of its characters are transferred, since the delimiter is the size of WS-CENTURY. Therefore, 1989 is concatenated into the receiving item FORMATTED-DATE.

The six remaining character positions of the FORMATTED-DATE retain their previous characters, namely, spaces in this case. The result is shown in Figure A.2.

Note that if the STRING statement had been coded as

```
STRING WS-MONTH(WS-MO) DELIMITED BY SIZE
         .
         .
         .
```

all the characters in WS-MONTH(6) would have been transferred, specifically, the month name JUNE followed by five spaces, and the resulting date would have been printed as JUNE   28, 1989. The first format is certainly preferable, and that is the main reason for using the STRING statement. It eliminates unnecessary spaces.

Example 2

As another example, suppose that the date of the previous example is to be stored in an unformatted record TOP-LINE instead of the field FORMATTED-DATE. Suppose that TOP-LINE is defined by PIC X(80), and the date must be stored beginning in character position 5. In this case, the POINTER phrase must be used to specify the first character position of the receiving field to receive a transferred character. The identifier used in the phrase must be defined as a positive integer data item. We will name it POSITION-PTR.

The WORKING-STORAGE SECTION of the previous example now contains the additional entry

```
01  POSITION-PTR     PIC 9(2).
```

and the LINKAGE SECTION contains the description

```
01  TOP-LINE         PIC X(80).
```

instead of the description of the item FORMATTED-DATE. The PROCEDURE DIVISION is then coded as follows:

```
PROCEDURE DIVISION USING TOP-LINE.

100-PREPARE-TOP-LINE.
    MOVE SPACES TO TOP-LINE.
    ACCEPT WS-REPORT-DATE FROM DATE.
    ADD WS-YR TO WS-CENTURY.
    MOVE 5 TO POSITION-PTR.
    STRING WS-MONTH(WS-MO) DELIMITED BY " "
           " " DELIMITED BY SIZE
           WS-DAY DELIMITED BY SIZE
           "," DELIMITED BY SIZE
           " " DELIMITED BY SIZE
           WS-CENTURY DELIMITED BY SIZE
           INTO TOP-LINE
           WITH POINTER POSITION-PTR
    END-STRING.
```

Furthermore, since the same delimiter (SIZE) applies to more than one source item in succession, the STRING statement may be coded as follows:

```
STRING WS-MONTH(WS-MO) DELIMITED BY " "
       " " WS-DAY ", " WS-CENTURY DELIMITED BY SIZE
       INTO TOP-LINE
       WITH POINTER POSITION-PTR
END-STRING.
```

Figure A.3 UNSTRING statement format

```
UNSTRING identifier-1
    [ DELIMITED BY [ ALL ] {identifier-2} [ OR [ ALL ] {identifier-3} ] . . . ]
                           {literal-1   }              {literal-2   }
    INTO {identifier-4 [ DELIMITER IN identifier-5] [ COUNT IN identifier-6]} . . .
    [with POINTER identifier-7]
    [ TALLYING IN identifier-8]
    [ON OVERFLOW imperative-statement-1]
    [ NOT ON OVERFLOW imperative-statement-2]
    [ END-UNSTRING ]
```

The UNSTRING Statement

The UNSTRING statement separates data from one source or sending field into one or more receiving fields. Its function is the reverse of that of the STRING statement. The format of the UNSTRING statement is shown in Figure A.3.

In this format,

1. *Identifier-1* is the source or sending field. It must be defined as an alphanumeric item.
2. *Literal-1* and *literal-2* must be nonnumeric literals; *identifier-2* and *identifier-3* must be defined as alphanumeric data items. The selected items are the delimiters for the UNSTRING operation. That is, they are used to separate the characters of the source field into the groups to be transferred into the successive receiving fields. The literals may be figurative constants, other than ALL, and the length of a figurative constant is one character.
3. *Identifier-4* is a receiving field for data transferred from the source field. The data item *identifier-4* may be defined as alphanumeric, alphabetic, or numeric. If it is numeric, it must be in display format and its PIC clause must not contain the scalar P. When the UNSTRING operation begins, the first occurrence of *identifier-4* is the current receiving field.
4. *Identifier-5* is an alphanumeric data item that receives the delimiter(s).
5. *Identifier-6* is a numeric data item defined as an integer. Its function is to count the number of characters transferred from the source field to the receiving field, *identifier-4*. The delimiter is not counted. There may be as many *identifier-6* data items as there are receiving fields.
6. *Identifier-7* is a numeric data item defined as an integer. It is called a *pointer,* and its function is to point to the current character position in the source field. The initial value of the pointer must be set by the program prior to the execution of the UNSTRING operation. The definition of *identifier-7* must allow it to contain an integer value equal to the size of the source field (*identifier-1*) plus 1. Its PIC clause must not contain the scalar P.
7. *Identifier-8* is a numeric data item defined as an integer. Its function is to count the number of receiving fields (*identifier-4*) that received characters during the UNSTRING operation. The initial value of *identifier-8* must be set by the program prior to the execution of the UNSTRING operation. The PIC clause that defines *identifier-8* must not contain the scalar P.
8. *Imperative-statement-1* is an imperative statement that is executed whenever an overflow condition exists.
9. *Imperative-statement-2* is an imperative statement that is executed if no overflow condition exists.
10. An overflow condition exists if either of the following occurs:
    a. All receiving fields (*identifier-4*) have received characters from the source field, but the source field contains characters that have not been examined by the UNSTRING operation.
    b. Before the UNSTRING operation begins, the initial value of the pointer (*identifier-7*) is less than 1 or greater than the number of characters in the source field (*identifier-1*).
11. END-UNSTRING is the explicit scope terminator for the UNSTRING statement.
12. The DELIMITER IN and COUNT IN phrases are permissible options only if the statement contains the DELIMITED BY clause.
13. If the statement contains a POINTER phrase, the UNSTRING operation begins with the character of the source field specified by the pointer (*identifier-7*). Otherwise, the operation begins with the leftmost character of the source field.

14. If the statement contains a DELIMITED BY clause, the UNSTRING operation proceeds to the right (that is, characters are examined and transferred) until a delimiter (*identifier-2, identifier-3, literal-1, literal-2*) is encountered. The UNSTRING operation then resumes with the first character to the right of the delimiter.
15. If the statement does not contain a DELIMITED BY clause, the UNSTRING operation proceeds to the right until every character position of the current receiving field has received a character from the source field. The UNSTRING operation then resumes with the next character in the source field.
16. After data has been transferred to a receiving field, the next receiving field becomes the current receiving field.
17. The UNSTRING operation ends if all receiving fields have been processed or if the rightmost character in the source field is reached before encountering a delimiter or before filling the receiving field.

As an example of the UNSTRING statement, examine the section of Chapter 6 titled "Method 2—ACCEPT/DISPLAY with Free-Form Data Entry." The data entry operator is directed to enter an employee's Social Security number, last name, first name, and middle initial, and to separate these items by semicolons. A sample entry may be "456235100;PALMER;WALTER;R". These characters are stored in (ACCEPTed into!) the data item STEP-1-DATA. The UNSTRING statement then operates "behind the scene" to transfer groups of related characters into appropriate receiving fields. The statement is as follows:

```
UNSTRING STEP-1-DATA
    DELIMITED BY ";"
    INTO MR-SSN          DELIMITER IN WS-DELIM
         MR-LAST-NAME    DELIMITER IN WS-DELIM
         MR-FIRST-NAME   DELIMITER IN WS-DELIM
         MR-INITIAL      DELIMITER IN WS-DELIM
END-UNSTRING.
```

In this statement, STEP-1-DATA is the source field, the semicolon ";" is the delimiter, MR-SSN, MR-LAST-NAME, MR-FIRST-NAME, and MR-INITIAL are the receiving fields, and WS-DELIM stores the delimiter ";". Since there is no POINTER phrase, the UNSTRING operation begins with the leftmost character of STEP-1-DATA. All the characters from the leftmost up to, but excluding, the first semicolon are transferred into the first receiving field, that is, MR-SSN = "456235100". The group of characters beginning with the one to the right of the first delimiter up to, but excluding, the second semicolon is transferred to the second receiving field, that is, MR-LAST-NAME = "PALMER". The group of characters beginning with the character to the right of the second semicolon up to, but excluding, the third semicolon is transferred to the third receiving field, that is, MR-FIRST-NAME = "WALTER". Finally, the remaining character to the right of the third semicolon is transferred to the fourth receiving field, that is, MR-INITIAL = "R".

Note that the DELIMITER IN phrase could have been left out without affecting the outcome of the UNSTRING operation.

Suppose that STEP-1-DATA contains the data specified above, but only the name components are to be accessed and transferred to data fields O-LAST-NAME, O-FIRST-NAME, and O-INITIAL. In this case, the POINTER phrase must be used to position the character pointer at the character to the right of the first semicolon. The character position is 11 (beyond nine character positions for the digits of the Social Security number and one for the first delimiter). Suppose the pointer is defined as POSITION-PTR. It must be initialized prior to the execution of the UNSTRING statement. The statements may be coded as follows:

```
MOVE 11 TO POSITION-CTR.
UNSTRING STEP-1-DATA
    DELIMITED BY ";"
    INTO O-LAST-NAME
         O-FIRST-NAME
         O-INITIAL
    WITH POINTER POSITION-PTR
END-UNSTRING.
```

In this case, the first 10 characters of the source field STEP-1-DATA are not examined, since POSITION-PTR = 11.

Suppose that the data entry operator is instructed to separate the items of STEP-1-DATA by a semicolon (;) or by a hyphen (-) or by a space. The UNSTRING statement may be coded to allow for any of these delimiters and to count the number of receiving fields that actually receive data, as follows:

```
UNSTRING STEP-1-DATA
    DELIMITED BY ";" OR "-" OR SPACE
    INTO MR-SSN          DELIMITER IN WS-DELIM
         MR-LAST-NAME    DELIMITER IN WS-DELIM
         MR-FIRST-NAME   DELIMITER IN WS-DELIM
         MR-INITIAL      DELIMITER IN WS-DELIM
   TALLYING IN FIELD-CTR
END-UNSTRING.
```

(Assume that FIELD-CTR is properly defined.)

■ **Figure A.4** COPY statement format

$$\underline{\text{COPY}}\ \text{text-name-1}\left[\left\{\begin{matrix}\underline{\text{OF}}\\ \underline{\text{IN}}\end{matrix}\right\}\ \text{library-name-1}\right]$$

$$\left[\underline{\text{REPLACING}}\left\{\left\{\begin{matrix}\text{== pseudo-text-1 ==}\\ \text{identifier-1}\\ \text{literal-1}\\ \text{word-1}\end{matrix}\right\}\ \underline{\text{BY}}\left\{\begin{matrix}\text{== pseudo-text-2 ==}\\ \text{identifier-2}\\ \text{literal-2}\\ \text{word-2}\end{matrix}\right\}\right\}\ldots\right]$$

The COPY Statement

Source code that is needed by many programs is often stored in a library and, when needed in a program, is simply copied from the library directly into the program by means of the COPY statement. The format of the COPY statement is shown in Figure A.4.

In this statement,

1. *Text-name-1* is the name of a record in the library.
2. *Library-name-1* is the name of a library file that contains *text-name-1.*
3. *Pseudo-text-1, identifier-1, literal-1,* and *word-1* are entries in *text-name-1*. The selected item must be replaced by a replacement item.
4. *Pseudo-text-2, identifier-2, literal-2,* and *word-2* are replacement items.
5. *Pseudo-text-1* is a string of characters in *text-name-1* that must be replaced by the specified replacement item. The string of characters must not consist of a single comma or of a single semicolon.
6. *Identifier-1* is a data name in *text-name-1* that must be replaced by a replacement item.
7. *Literal-1* is a literal in *text-name-1* that must be replaced by a replacement item. *Literal-1* may be a numeric or a nonnumeric literal. (Nonnumeric literals must be enclosed within quotation marks.)
8. *Word-1* is any COBOL word contained in *text-name-1.*
9. *Pseudo-text-2* is a replacement item that consists of a string of characters. The string may be empty.
10. *Identifier-2* is a data name replacement item.
11. *Literal-2* is a replacement item. It may be numeric or nonnumeric. (Nonnumeric literals must be enclosed within quotation marks.)
12. *Word-2* is a replacement item. It may be any COBOL word.

The function of the COPY statement is to insert text within a COBOL source program. The text is obtained from a library that contains COBOL source text. The text must conform to ANSI formats.

If the COPY statement does not contain a REPLACING phrase, the source text in the library is copied into the program without any change. If the COPY statement does contain the REPLACING phrase, the source text is copied into the program with all replacements made as specified. However, the original source text in the library is not changed.

When a COBOL program contains COPY statements, it is not compiled until all COPY statements have been processed.

Examples:

A library contains the following description:

```
01  EMPLOYEE-RECORD.
    05 SSN         PIC X(9).
    05 NAME        PIC X(35).
    05 ADDRESS     PIC X(40).
    05 DATE-HIRED  PIC X(6).
    05 FILLER      PIC X(30).
```

1. The program EMPLOYEE-ROSTER-1 contains the following entries:

```
IDENTIFICATION DIVISION.
PROGRAM-ID.  EMPLOYEE-ROSTER-1.
 .
 .
 .
```

```
FD  EMPLOYEE-FILE
    RECORD CONTAINS 120 CHARACTERS.
COPY EMPLOYEE-RECORD.
.
.
.
WORKING-STORAGE SECTION.
.
.
.
```

When the compiler processes the COPY statement, the COBOL source program contains the following entries before compilation actually occurs:

```
IDENTIFICATION DIVISION.
PROGRAM-ID.  EMPLOYEE-ROSTER-1.
.
.
.
FD  EMPLOYEE-FILE
    RECORD CONTAINS 120 CHARACTERS.
COPY EMPLOYEE-RECORD.
01  EMPLOYEE-RECORD.
    05 SSN         PIC X(9).
    05 NAME        PIC X(35).
    05 ADDRESS     PIC X(40).
    05 DATE-HIRED  PIC X(6).
    05 FILLER      PIC X(30).
WORKING-STORAGE SECTION.
.
.
.
```

2. The program EMPLOYEE-ROSTER-2 contains the following entries:

```
IDENTIFICATION DIVISION.
PROGRAM-ID.  EMPLOYEE-ROSTER-2.
.
.
.
FD  EMPLOYEE-FILE
    RECORD CONTAINS 120 CHARACTERS.
COPY EMPLOYEE-RECORD
    REPLACING SSN BY I-SSN
              NAME BY I-NAME
              ADDRESS BY I-ADDRESS
              DATE-HIRED BY I-DATE-HIRED
              FILLER BY "        ".
.
.
.
WORKING-STORAGE SECTION.
.
.
.
```

When the compiler processes the COPY statement, the COBOL source program contains the following entries before compilation actually occurs:

```
IDENTIFICATION DIVISION.
PROGRAM-ID.  EMPLOYEE-ROSTER-2.
.
.
.
FD  EMPLOYEE-FILE
    RECORD CONTAINS 120 CHARACTERS.
COPY EMPLOYEE-RECORD
    REPLACING SSN BY I-SSN
              NAME BY I-NAME
              ADDRESS BY I-ADDRESS
              DATE-HIRED BY I-DATE-HIRED
              FILLER BY "        ".
01  EMPLOYEE-RECORD.
    05 I-SSN         PIC X(9).
    05 I-NAME        PIC X(35).
    05 I-ADDRESS     PIC X(40).
    05 I-DATE-HIRED  PIC X(6).
    05               PIC X(30).
WORKING-STORAGE SECTION.
.
.
.
```

3. The program EMPLOYEE-ROSTER-3 contains the following entries:

```
IDENTIFICATION DIVISION.
PROGRAM-ID.  EMPLOYEE-ROSTER-3.
.
.
.
FD  EMPLOYEE-FILE
    RECORD CONTAINS 120 CHARACTERS.
COPY EMPLOYEE-RECORD
    REPLACING ==NAME          PIC X(35)== BY
              ==NAME.
                    10 FIRST-NAME      PIC X(15).
                    10 LAST-NAME       PIC X(20).==
              FILLER BY == ==.
.
.
.
WORKING-STORAGE SECTION.
.
.
.
```

When the compiler processes the COPY statement, the COBOL source program contains the following entries before compilation actually occurs:

```
IDENTIFICATION DIVISION.
PROGRAM-ID.  EMPLOYEE-ROSTER-3.
.
.
.
FD  EMPLOYEE-FILE
    RECORD CONTAINS 120 CHARACTERS.
COPY EMPLOYEE-RECORD
    REPLACING ==NAME          PIC X(35)== BY
              ==NAME.
                    10 FIRST-NAME      PIC X(15).
                    10 LAST-NAME       PIC X(20).==
              FILLER BY == ==.
01  EMPLOYEE-RECORD.
    05 SSN          PIC X(9).
    05 NAME.
       10 FIRST-NAME      PIC X(15).
       10 LAST-NAME       PIC X(20).
    05 ADDRESS      PIC X(40).
    05 DATE-HIRED PIC X(6).
    05          PIC X(30).
WORKING-STORAGE SECTION.
.
.
.
```

Appendix B

Collating Sequences

ASCII (American Standard Code for Information Interchange)

7-bit Code	Decimal Code	Hexadecimal Code	Symbol	Meaning
0000000	000	00	NUL	Null
0000001	001	01	SOH	Start of Heading
0000010	002	02	STX	Start of Text
0000011	003	03	ETX	End of Text
0000100	004	04	EOT	End of Transmission
0000101	005	05	ENQ	Enquiry
0000110	006	06	ACK	Acknowledge
0000111	007	07	BEL	Bell
0001000	008	08	BS	Backspace
0001001	009	09	HT	Horizontal Tabulation
0001010	010	0A	LF	Line Feed
0001011	011	0B	VT	Vertical Tabulation
0001100	012	0C	FF	Form Feed
0001101	013	0D	CR	Carriage Return
0001110	014	0E	SO	Shift Out
0001111	015	0F	SI	Shift In
0010000	016	10	DLE	Data Link Escape
0010001	017	11	DC1	Device Control 1
0010010	018	12	DC2	Device Control 2
0010011	019	13	DC3	Device Control 3
0010100	020	14	DC4	Device Control 4
0010101	021	15	NAK	Negative Acknowledge
0010110	022	16	SYN	Synchronous Idle
0010111	023	17	ETB	End of Transmission Block
0011000	024	18	CAN	Cancel
0011001	025	19	EM	End of Medium
0011010	026	1A	SUB	Substitute
0011011	027	1B	ESC	Escape
0011100	028	1C	FS	File Separator
0011101	029	1D	GS	Group Separator
0011110	030	1E	RS	Record Separator
0011111	031	1F	US	Unit Separator
0100000	032	20	SP	Space (Nonprinting)
0100001	033	21	!	Exclamation Point
0100010	034	22	''	Quotation Mark
0100011	035	23	#	Number Sign
0100100	036	24	$	Dollar Sign
0100101	037	25	%	Percent Sign
0100110	038	26	&	Ampersand
0100111	039	27	'	Apostrophe (Closing single quotation mark)
0101000	040	28	(	Opening Parenthesis
0101001	041	29	)	Closing Parenthesis
0101010	042	2A	*	Asterisk
0101011	043	2B	+	Plus Sign
0101100	044	2C	,	Comma

7-bit Code	Decimal Code	Hexadecimal Code	Symbol	Meaning
0101101	045	2D	-	Hyphen (Minus Sign)
0101110	046	2E	.	Period (Decimal Point)
0101111	047	2F	/	Slant (Forward Slash)
0110000	048	30	0	Digit 0
0110001	049	31	1	Digit 1
0110010	050	32	2	Digit 2
0110011	051	33	3	Digit 3
0110100	052	34	4	Digit 4
0110101	053	35	5	Digit 5
0110110	054	36	6	Digit 6
0110111	055	37	7	Digit 7
0111000	056	38	8	Digit 8
0111001	057	39	9	Digit 9
0111010	058	3A	:	Colon
0111011	059	3B	;	Semicolon
0111100	060	3C	<	Less Than
0111101	061	3D	=	Equals
0111110	062	3E	>	Greater Than
0111111	063	3F	?	Question Mark
1000000	064	40	@	Commercial At
1000001	065	41	A	Uppercase Latin Letter A
1000010	066	42	B	Uppercase Latin Letter B
1000011	067	43	C	Uppercase Latin Letter C
1000100	068	44	D	Uppercase Latin Letter D
1000101	069	45	E	Uppercase Latin Letter E
1000110	070	46	F	Uppercase Latin Letter F
1000111	071	47	G	Uppercase Latin Letter G
1001000	072	48	H	Uppercase Latin Letter H
1001001	073	49	I	Uppercase Latin Letter I
1001010	074	4A	J	Uppercase Latin Letter J
1001011	075	4B	K	Uppercase Latin Letter K
1001100	076	4C	L	Uppercase Latin Letter L
1001101	077	4D	M	Uppercase Latin Letter M
1001110	078	4E	N	Uppercase Latin Letter N
1001111	079	4F	O	Uppercase Latin Letter O
1010000	080	50	P	Uppercase Latin Letter P
1010001	081	51	Q	Uppercase Latin Letter Q
1010010	082	52	R	Uppercase Latin Letter R
1010011	083	53	S	Uppercase Latin Letter S
1010100	084	54	T	Uppercase Latin Letter T
1010101	085	55	U	Uppercase Latin Letter U
1010110	086	56	V	Uppercase Latin Letter V
1010111	087	57	W	Uppercase Latin Letter W
1011000	088	58	X	Uppercase Latin Letter X
1011001	089	59	Y	Uppercase Latin Letter Y
1011010	090	5A	Z	Uppercase Latin Letter Z
1011011	091	5B	[	Opening Bracket
1011100	092	5C	\	Reverse Slant (Back Slash)
1011101	093	5D	]	Closing Bracket
1011110	094	5E	∧	Circumflex
1011111	095	5F	_	Underline
1100000	096	60	`	Opening Single Quotation Mark
1100001	097	61	a	Lowercase Latin Letter a
1100010	098	62	b	Lowercase Latin Letter b
1100011	099	63	c	Lowercase Latin Letter c
1100100	100	64	d	Lowercase Latin Letter d
1100101	101	65	e	Lowercase Latin Letter e
1100110	102	66	f	Lowercase Latin Letter f
1100111	103	67	g	Lowercase Latin Letter g

7-bit Code	Decimal Code	Hexadecimal Code	Symbol	Meaning
1101000	104	68	h	Lowercase Latin Letter h
1101001	105	69	i	Lowercase Latin Letter i
1101010	106	6A	j	Lowercase Latin Letter j
1101011	107	6B	k	Lowercase Latin Letter k
1101100	108	6C	l	Lowercase Latin Letter l
1101101	109	6D	m	Lowercase Latin Letter m
1101110	110	6E	n	Lowercase Latin Letter n
1101111	111	6F	o	Lowercase Latin Letter o
1110000	112	70	p	Lowercase Latin Letter p
1110001	113	71	q	Lowercase Latin Letter q
1110010	114	72	r	Lowercase Latin Letter r
1110011	115	73	s	Lowercase Latin Letter s
1110100	116	74	t	Lowercase Latin Letter t
1110101	117	75	u	Lowercase Latin Letter u
1110110	118	76	v	Lowercase Latin Letter v
1110111	119	77	w	Lowercase Latin Letter w
1111000	120	78	x	Lowercase Latin Letter x
1111001	121	79	y	Lowercase Latin Letter y
1111010	122	7A	z	Lowercase Latin Letter z
1111011	123	7B	{	Opening Brace
1111100	124	7C	|	Vertical Line
1111101	125	7D	}	Closing Brace
1111110	126	7E	~	Tilde
1111111	127	7F	DEL	Delete

EBCDIC (Extended Binary Coded Decimal Interchange Code)*

Left Digit(s)	Right Digit	0	1	2	3	4	5	6	7	8	9
6											
7						¢	.	<	(	+	|
8		&									
9		!	$	*	)	;		-	/		
10								¦	,	%	—
11		>	?								
12			'	:	#	@	'	=	"		a
13		b	c	d	e	f	g	h	i		
14							j	k	l	m	n
15		o	p	q	r						
16			~	s	t	u	v	w	x	y	z
17					[						]
18											
19				{	A	B	C	D	E	F	G
20		H	I							}	J
21		K	L	M	N	O	P	Q	R		
22								S	T	U	V
23		W	X	Y	Z	\					
24		0	1	2	3	4	5	6	7	8	9

Codes 00 to 63 and 250 to 255 represent nonprintable control characters. Code 64 is the blank.

*This table shows decimal codes only, and only printable characters are listed.

CDC Scientific, with 64 Characters*

Left Digit(s)	Right Digit	0	1	2	3	4	5	6	7	8	9
0		:	A	B	C	D	E	F	G	H	I
1		J	K	L	M	N	O	P	Q	R	S
2		T	U	V	W	X	Y	Z	O	1	2
3		3	4	5	6	7	8	9	+	−	*
4		/	(	)	$	=		,	.	≡	[
5		]	%	≠	→	∨	∧	↑	↓	<	>
6		≤	≥		;						

*This table shows decimal codes only.

Appendix C

File Status Codes

File Status	I/O Statements	File Organization	Access Mode	Condition Represented by the Code
00	All	All	All	Successful operation
02	REWRITE WRITE	Indexed	All	Successful operation, but the record just written created a duplicate key value for an alternate record key for which duplicates are allowed.
04	READ	All	All	Successful operation, but the size of the record just read does not agree with the size specified in the program.
05	OPEN	All	All	Successful operation, but the referenced optional file was not present when the statement executed. (If the open mode was I-O or EXTEND, the file was created.)
07	CLOSE OPEN	All	All	Successful operation, but the referenced file is not on a reel-type device. The NOREWIND, REEL/UNIT, or FOR REMOVAL options of the CLOSE statement are overlooked, or the NOREWIND phrase of the OPEN statement is overlooked.
10	READ	All	Sequential	Operation failed because EOF was detected or an optional file was not present.
14	READ	Relative	Sequential	Operation failed because the number of digits in the relative key value is greater than the size specified for the relative key data item.
15	READ	All	Sequential	Operation failed because an optional file was not present, and this was the first attempt to read it.
21	DELETE	Indexed or Relative	Sequential	Operation failed because of a sequence error: prime record (for an indexed file) or relative key (for a relative file) was not the same as the last record read.
	REWRITE	Indexed	Sequential	Operation failed because the prime record key value changed between the previous successful READ and the current REWRITE operation.
	WRITE	Indexed	Sequential	Operation failed because the prime record key value was not greater than that of the last record written. (Prime record key values must be in ascending order.)
22	REWRITE	Indexed	All	Operation failed because it would have created a duplicate alternate record key when duplicates are not allowed.
	WRITE	Indexed	All	Operation failed because a duplicate prime record key, or a duplicate alternate record key when duplicates are not allowed, would have been created.
		Relative	Random or Dynamic	Operation failed because a duplicate relative key would have been created.

File Status	I/O Statements	File Organization	Access Mode	Condition Represented by the Code
23	DELETE READ REWRITE	Indexed or Relative	Random or Dynamic	Operation failed because the record key (prime or alternate for indexed files, relative key for relative files) was not found or an optional file was not present.
	START	Indexed or Relative	Sequential or Dynamic	Operation failed because the record key (prime or alternate for indexed files, relative key for relative files) was not found, or an optional file was not present.
24	WRITE	Indexed or Relative	All	Operation failed because an attempt was made to write beyond the externally defined boundaries for an indexed or relative file; or a sequential write operation was attempted for a relative file but the number of digits in the relative key value exceeded the size specified for the relative key data item.
25	READ START	Indexed or Relative	All	Operation failed because a START statement or a random READ statement was attempted on an optional file that was not present.
30	All	All	All	Operation failed due to an error that cannot be specified by other status codes.
34	WRITE	Sequential	Sequential	Operation failed because an attempt was made to write beyond the externally defined boundaries for the file.
35	OPEN	All	All	Operation failed because an attempt was made to open a nonoptional file in INPUT mode but the file was not present.
37	OPEN	All	All	Operation failed because an attempt was made to open a file in I-O mode when the device does not support a mass storage file.
38	OPEN	All	All	Operation failed because an attempt was made to open a file that was previously closed with a lock.
39	OPEN	All	All	Operation failed because an attempt was made to open a file whose fixed file attributes do not match the ones specified in the program. (Attributes that are checked are organization, index keys (prime and alternate), block size, and maximum record size.)
41	OPEN	All	All	Operation failed because an attempt was made to open a file that was already open.
42	CLOSE	All	All	Operation failed because an attempt was made to close a file that was not open.
43	DELETE REWRITE	All	Sequential	Operation failed because an attempt was made to delete or rewrite a record without a prior successful READ for the record.
44	REWRITE	All	All	Operation failed because an attempt was made to rewrite a record whose size is not the same as the record being replaced.
46	READ	All	Sequential	Operation failed because an attempt was made to read a record from a file open in INPUT or I-O mode when no valid next record has been established within the file.
47	READ START	All	All	Operation failed because an attempt was made to read or start a file that was not open, or was not open in INPUT or I-O mode.
48	WRITE	All	All	Operation failed because an attempt was made to write to an unopen file, or to a file not open in OUTPUT, I-O, or EXTEND mode.
49	DELETE REWRITE	All	All	Operation failed because an attempt was made to delete or rewrite a record of an unopen file, or of a file not open in I-O mode.

Appendix D

Data Sets for Programming Exercises

1X1: Data Set for Chapter 1 sample program problem and Programming Exercise I, Express Auto Parts Warehouse

```
0346RCB ANTENNA          03329039950300040005000400025000020        03
0348N23 CHANNEL MOBILE CB20829249950190000001000000000050000        05
0359BCB CONVERTER        02079024950750000005000000002750005        04
0368WFM ANTENNA          00665007980500000003000000003000000        01
0382NSTEREO SPEAKERS/PR  02079024950350020005000000002000050        04
0462UFLEXSOCKET WRENCH   00191002290200050008000200001750010        01
1033WFM RADIO AMPLIFIER  01082012980325000003000000000500030        07
1048THITCH BALL COVER    00066000790650000005000000003500010        01
1219XRW DEFOGGER         02498029980525000003000000000300016        09
1242WRV ALARM SYSTEM     01663019950075010001000100000700008        08
1263PTORQUE WRENCH       01498017980200030006000200004000020        03
1264Y8000LB. JACK STAND  01082012980150000000800000000000001        09
1352VTUNE-UP TESTER      03329039950300020004000000001000055        04
1503WELECTRONIC FILTER   01082012980500000003000000000850002        01
1517ASPARE TIRE LOCK     00374004490075010001000000000300000        02
1584ARV ANTENNA          04163049950950010008000100002100005        05
1593XHD. TIE DOWN        01498017980600000004000000001950020        02
1616WAIR DIESEL HORN     01415016980080000000500000000010000        06
1685TBRAKE CABLE ADJUSTER00066000790100040005000300001000000        01
1762NBUMPER GUARDS       01415016981250000001000000004000050        03
1775BBOLT-ON HITCH       05663067950500000004000000002000000        04
1787A1000-WATT CONVERTER 28996347950012000000100000000000000        05
1842N16" FULL WHEEL COVER02079024950520000003000000002200000        03
1914YC-11 TRAILER HITCH  01415016980600000004000000001500000        08
2181XEXHAUST HEADERS     05663067950500000001000000000500028        04
2326RPOWER MUFFLER       01413016950200030005000200001900000        03
3731W3-2 BBL MANIFOLD    08329099950180000001000000000500005        08
3734NCAMSHAFT            06663079950090005001000000000600002        07
5507RBONDED BRAKE SHOE   00665007980600050010000400030000060        02
5524YDISC BRAKE PADS     01246014950500040010000000002800008        04
5534AMASTER CYLINDER     01246014950500060010000500003500060        05
5557PENGINE OIL COOLER   03329039950075010001000100000500000        06
5577PSOLENOID SWITCH     00458005491000040008000200004800050        02
5596WHD STAINLESS-ST FAN 01415016980090002001000000000010004        09
7519YSOLID STATE TACH    03329039950325000002000000001500030        02
7568Y30-PC TUNE-UP KIT   03329039950300020004000000002500000        04
7580XRAM AIR SYSTEM      01663019950062000000500000000050003        01
8419AHOLLEY CARBURETOR   09163109950710010005000200004250010        03
8572VREAR END LIFT KIT   00665007980180000001000000000100000        05
8583NWL-BEARING CAPS/PR  00332003980300040008000200001500000        01
8636ELEAF SPRINGS/PR     07496089950320000002000000000000002        04
8776NRING & PINION GEARS 08329099950350010003000100001250015        03
8815PREAR-AXLE SHAFT ASSM01415016980090010002000100000300000        03
8823UDUAL RHEOSTAT DIMMER01082012980450000003000000000800025        07
8880WFOG LIGHT KIT       02498029980350020004000100000800000        04
8896NENGINE COOLER KIT   03329039950250000002000000000100000        06
8912NREPLACEMENT WHEEL   01415016980100020004000200001000000        04
8931RSHOCK ABSORBERS/PR  02079024951200060010000400007500020        03
9977RAIR COMPRESSOR KIT  08329099950110000001000000000200005        03
9998FFIBERGLASS HARDTOP  28332339980060000000500000000010002        05
```

■ 1X2: Data Set for Chapter 1, Programming Exercise II, International Haberdashery

```
10CAHILL, PAULA R.    623455100              0009865000080000
10CUSTER, GEORGE P.   611723510              0007102500080000
10GAMELIN, JOSEPH     315781243              0015250000120000
10JONES, EARLE B.     201861752              0005257500050000
10LAUZON, MARIE L.    315325123              0004652500050000
10MCMAHON, CHERYL     679017429              0009355000080000
10REZENDES, PHILIP    788407265              0011257500080000
10RICHARDS, ROBERT B. 325724844              0006352500050000
10ROSS, ROBERT J.     571349231              0015603000120000
10WHITMAN, ELEANOR    599353423              0010652000120000
10WOOD, RICHARD W.    028125226              0009355000080000
20BERARD, NORBERT V.  795288916              0008705000080000
20DAWICKI, WALTER     472692314              0007705000080000
20HARRINGTON, KATHY   232463239              0010457000120000
20LEONARDO, BARBARA   472587311              0004357500050000
20O'LEARY, KENNY      531387428              0010457000080000
20PAQUIN, BRIDGET     186737565              0016320000120000
20SANDERSON, JED      367215324              0008500000050000
20SHEEHAN, WILLIAM J. 218394740              0008705000080000
30ALBIN, EVELYN C.    173170347              0014355000120000
30FOX, EVA M.         517246302              0026250000200000
30LARSON, ANTHONY     634227460              0011745000120000
30PANKIEWICZ, ALLEN   410425545              0008102000070000
30PURCELL, HARRY C.   356261197              0028150000200000
30RAYMOND, VICTOR     518177032              0007242000070000
30REED, MARGARET      366466219              0014355000120000
30RENAUD, ANNE        269313905              0011745000120000
30RIENDEAU, NORMAN    461217415              0005305000070000
30ROBILLARD, STEPHEN  121315631              0028100000200000
30ROGERS, NANCY A.    581235596              0022405000200000
30SEQUEIRA, PAUL M.   356312251              0018258000120000
30THURSTON, SAMUEL    384346722              0007242000070000
40DAWSON, THOMAS A.   678331952              0010502000080000
40FULLER, ROSE E.     317433405              0007805000050000
40HELGER, ARTHUR      268322166              0010502000080000
40LEMAIRE, HERVE      519392407              0016450000120000
40PECKHAM, PHYLLIS    696544213              0009852500080000
40REAGAN, HELEN P.    334419701              0010050000080000
40SABRA, STEVEN S.    628739394              0006100000050000
40SHEEHAN, CHARLES A. 346585714              0007805000080000
40VACHON, JULIA       477713390              0016400000120000
50CROWLEY, JOHN H.    449834615              0007252500080000
50GAMACHE, NORMAN T.  414674337              0003905000050000
50IWANSKI, JENNIE     056419426              0013275000120000
50MALTAIS, VICTORIA   353228728              0017502000120000
50MELLO, ANTONIO      569461603              0007252500080000
50REGO, FIRMINO       235722152              0006652500050000
50REGO, JOSEPH C.     239673372              0010100000080000
50SANTOS, JOSEPHINE   407399168              0008155000080000
50TREMBLAY, ALPHONSE  451294933              0008695000080000
```

1X3: Data Set for Chapter 1, Programming Exercise III, Ponagansett Electric Company

```
RI1100140NARDONE, MARY E.     1402414997                             A124208
RI1101235FLYNN, ROGER P.      4213142482                             A106508
RI1103041BEST FURNITURE INC. 6656568711                              C-28608
RI1106176KOLAKOWSKI, CASIMIR 0524005712                              A106508
RI1110025ASSELIN, JANICE M.  2142122300                              A124208
RI1115722GLORIA'S BEAUTY SHOP3485839208                              C-28608
RI1120190WAREHAM, JOSEPH F.  1396214387                              A106508
RI1131211KEATING, SUSAN A.   0707008110                              A114208
RI1135400CONNELL, FRED C.    3523536157                              A124208
RI1138625FRYE, LOUISE N.     0110601523                              A106508
RI1150950TINY-TOT NURSERY    1272014355                              C-28608
RI1153276BERGERON, FRANK S.  4103841756                              A114208
RI1155900LOUGHERY, KATRINA   3048131624                              A124208
RI1157133GOUDREAU, ELIZABETH 6565966235                              A106508
RI1159005COPTER SERVICE      4330945292                              C-28608
RI1160216GATTO, JANICE L.    1051811450                              A114208
RI1161394JOZEFOWICZ, SANDRA  3769238007                              A106508
RI1173731MCFADDEN, MICHAEL R.5808359347                              A124208
RI1175571LETENDRE, THOMAS F. 4621247210                              A124208
RI1177505MASSE, EUGENE       0517005703                              A106508
RI1182162EVA'S FRUIT STORE   3257134713                              C-28608
RI1190324MANDEL, ROLANDE J.  1076811240                              A106508
RI1193005SCULLY, CLARA B.    0693407446                              A106508
RI2201055NICOLETTA, JOHN J.  5193552917                              A124208
RI2205182RAY TRUCKING CO.    3482137197                              C-28608
RI2212433DION, GERARD M.     2347423995                              A106508
RI2220020CHOW, SHUI          0978810714                              A124208
RI2223944HODGE, KEVIN J.     7731977824                              A106508
RI2232132PETE'S AUTO SUPPLIES6865270636                              C-28608
RI2241694LAMOUNTAIN, LOUISE  4024141016                              A114208
RI2245400PATALANO, SAMANTHA  0252703435                              A124208
RI2248375CADY, RAYMOND F.    1517615533                              A106508
RI2252100GASPAR, RAOUL       2357524027                              A106508
RI2262025KLEIN, LAURALYNN    5708257811                              A114208
RI2275364DORIS BAKERY SHOP   7499278134                              C-28608
RI2275690HENNESSY, ROBERT J. 3901539517                              A106508
RI2278170LUDOVICI, LUIGI     0286003224                              A106508
RI2282985HUMMEL, STELLA      4010741153                              A124208
RI2285374PARKS, EMERY R.     1074611158                              A106508
RI3302010BENNETT, CLARENCE W.2374524228                              A106508
RI3305327PETRUSKA, MARIE     0124002219                              A124208
RI3320400MARK MARINE SERVICE 4937351447                              C-28608
RI3331166DIGUILIO, EMILIO M. 5661356997                              A106508
RI3342314CALLAHAN, JOHN J.   1040611459                              A124208
RI3345943MCCARTHY, EUGENE F. 2753428646                              A114208
RI3363770GERRY'S SEAFOODS    4519848660                              C-28608
RI3367150BROWN, GEORGE W.    3206532589                              A106508
RI3384000PRECOURT, JEAN M.   0862509562                              A114208
RI3391450DEWEY, FRANCES D.   1121211624                              A106508
RI3394765GARDNER, LEO F.     3543736562                              A124208
```

■ 1X4-I: Data Set for Chapter 1, Programming Exercise IV, Modern Plastics Company

```
456235100PALMER, WALTER R.   20002
723510611READY, MARIA ELENA  18001
781207315CAPARCO, DOMENIC A. 15503
861745201JACKVONY, WEBSTER P.20002
325123315GRAHAM, JUDITH L.   12501
017429976PESARE, KAROLYN S.  18002
407265788KRAUS, DONALD D.    17504
724844532CHARNIAK, NELSON T. 20003
349231175JACKSON, JESSICA    16501
125263028CANARIO, MARGARETTA 12502
288916795SILVIA, ROBERTA S.  18004
231769472LOISELLE, CYNTHIA   16501
463239232MACDONALD, PHILIP A.18503
587311472PAINE, JAMES H.     15954
387428531CALIFANO, CONCETTA  16001
737565186AFFLECK, SCOTT      14503
215311637CANTWELL, CLAUDIA   12501
394740218ALMEIDA, RICHARD    07504
170347173SHERMAN, MILTON L.  20002
246302715PAPADOPOULOS, JOE E.18001
227460634GOSSELIN, ANDREW P. 12003
425545014CHAN, SUKOM         12002
261197635SANTOS, MANUELA     10004
177032815JOUBERT, BERTHA M.  09501
466219366CHAPPELLE, BARBARA  08001
313905926ANDREWS, EARLE M.   08002
217415641PERRY, CHARLENE     06254
315631121SOSNICKI, STANLEY   05503
235596158KOSTEER, RICHARD G. 08003
312251653WINFIELD, LEWIS     06502
346795384LYNCH, WILLIAM S.   06002
331952867PELLETIER, VINCENT  20004
433405713POPKIN, ISABELLA M. 14501
322114268BARBER, MICHELLE K. 08753
392407915SAULNIER, ROBERT J. 07502
544287696ROCK, DONALD R.     07503
419712334ABRUZZI, GENE D.    07002
739394862PROULX, OSCAR R.    06504
585731346HIGGINS, DANIEL J.  07504
713390477CAMPBELL, ROBIN     04501
834615944CAPPUCCI, NAOMI     20001
674337414KLINGER, MICHAEL A. 16003
419426056SORAFINE, JULIO     10502
228728353BELANGER, NORMAND   10502
461602956GREENE, WILMA       09003
722199235POTTER, RICHARD     09004
673372239LOBO, ALBERT P.     08001
399168704CELANO, LOUISE      06001
294933154WOLFE, LILETH       08752
325042172AIKEN, MARTINA      07004
426435893JUSTINO, KIRA       06503
```

■ 1X4-II: Data Set for Chapter 1, Programming Exercise IV, Modern Plastics Company

```
4562351002005
7235106113008
7812073154000
8617452013005
3251233154000
0174299763500
4072657884000
7248445323005
3492311754005
1252630284005
2889167953510
2317694724005
4632392324000
5873114724000
3874285314000
7375651864000
2153116374000
3947402184005
1703471733005
2463027154005
2274606344000
4255450144000
2611976354000
1770328154000
4662193664000
3139059264000
2174156414005
3156311214008
2355961584010
3122516534008
3467953844000
3319528672005
4334057134005
3221142684005
3924079154000
5442876964000
4197123343500
7393948624000
5857313464000
7133904774000
8346159442505
6743374144005
4194260564006
2287283534000
4616029564000
7221992354000
6733722394000
3991687044005
2949331544005
3250421724000
4264358934000
```

■ 2X1-I: Data Set for Chapter 2, Programming Exercise I, Allied Stock Company

```
999900010600
600100030016
900900070013
004600120082
955100130040
215000360003
000800640001
775203693500
220004001200
220104010003
220304030002
220504050001
220704070610
861104080009
861204090004
861405010016
861705030001
861805060063
010505610045
861905830027
006106000010
070006010002
070106020001
070206030005
070306040010
070406050003
070506061001
070606070004
070706080013
070806090102
070906110007
071106130003
071306150017
071506170003
071706190100
412108015000
003710100005
521310120002
851510220120
863310220005
053010253010
000310300041
021010340031
420310910002
320012000002
320112010001
320312030004
320512050011
320712070004
320912090017
```

■ 2X1-II: Data Set for Chapter 2, Programming Exercise I, Allied Stock Company

```
000176750
000310500
000701000
001203800
001301250
003600999
006401510
036903999
040000100
040102199
040387500
040510000
040700300
040803650
040910130
050101299
050331000
050603100
056105915
058300250
060000900
060102800
060210001
060350000
060405112
060508999
060602500
060701289
060800500
060901389
061140000
061307189
061500125
061712589
061900360
080112009
101009999
101295000
102200399
102505500
103000099
103406760
109125099
120080050
120130000
120345000
120501199
120701500
120900500
```

■ 2X1-III: Data Set for Chapter 2, Programming Exercise I, Allied Stock Company

```
0003HALEY, ETHEL        99 SUNSET DR.            PORT LAVACA, TX   77979
0008PANNONNI, NICHOLAS  3 COLT DRIVE             WHARTON, TX       77488
0015HARVEY, SIDNEY      814 REAGAN AVE.          GEORGETOWN, TX    78628
0037CORREIA, HERMAN     293 CRESCENT DR.         AUSTIN, TX        78722
0046WARD, BRUNO         289 ALMY RD.             AUSTIN, TX        78734
0061OLSON, HELENA       2050 EAST KING RD.       WHARTON, TX       77488
0105COUSIN, RAYMOND     698 WALNUT AVE.          MIDLAND, TX       79701
0210TYRELL, ROBERT T.   292 STOCKTON AVE.        FORT WORTH, TX    76106
0432ALVES, HERMANO      350 PILOT DR.            BROWNSVILLE, TX   78521
0530RAPOZA, JUDITH      609 DAVOL ST.            WACO, TX          76704
0700ROY, ALBERT F.      655 N. MAIN ST.          EL PASO, TX       79901
0701O'NEIL, EUGENE      151 RANCHERO DR.         PECOS, TX         79772
0702TAYLOR, MAXINE      64 ANAWAN AVE.           LAREDO, TX        78040
0703FARNHAM, NORMAN     1255 WILSON RD.          BROWNSVILLE, TX   78521
0704FAY, MARGO          815 BEDFORD ST.          CRYSTAL CITY, TX  78839
0705BORDEN REPAIR       1 TINMAN RD.             SWEETWATER, TX    79556
0706GOVERNO, MARY T.    170 WILLIAM ST.          WACO, TX          76705
0707LOU'S PLACE         190 NEWHALL AVE.         LUFKIN, TX        75901
0708POCASSET JEWELERS   201 SOUTH MAIN ST.       LAREDO, TX        78040
0709LOFTY BALLOONS      45 FREEDOM RD.           FORT WORTH, TX    76104
0711PIPEIRA, MARCIA     835 VALENTINE DR.        GEORGETOWN, TX    78626
0713PIELA, ELIZABETH    360 BUFFINGTON AVE.      PECOS, TX         79772
0715TYSON, URSULA       594 MAPLE AVE            ABILENE, TX       79602
0717TRIPLE-A AUTO PARTS 4095 COUNTY RD.          LAREDO, TX        78041
0819DUPRE, DIANE        345 DURFEE AVE.          DALLAS, TX        75223
1723CARPENTER, HAZEL    189 DENHAM DR.           MIDLAND, TX       79705
1765BURNS SERVICE CENTER480 RIDGE RD.            BIG SPRING, TX    79721
2150HAGUE, RUSSELL      126 PRESIDENT AVE.       SAN ANTONIO, TX   78219
2200WALLACE, EDWARD     64 WILLOW LANE           GEORGETOWN, TX    78628
2201BELMORE, ALICE      15 STEVEN AVE.           TEMPLE, TX        76503
2203BARRY, JEAN         177 MARKET DR.           KILLEEN, TX       76544
2205DOSTER, MARY        287 BROADWAY ST.         SAN ANGELO, TX    76902
2207PLUNKETT, GARY A.   750 RODEO BLVD.          ABILENE, TX       79608
2520PLUNKETT, LILLIAN   110 CAMPION AVE.         DALLAS, TX        75223
2875TURCOTTE, THEODORE  530 S. MAIN ST.          CRYSTAL CITY, TX  78839
3200UNDERWOOD, LLOYD    25 ISLAND VIEW RD.       PORT LAVACA, TX   77979
3201HAMILTON, RUTH      13 BAKER ST.             AUSTIN, TX        78721
3203HANCOCK, LENA       229 RIVERSIDE DR.        SWEETWATER, TX    79556
3205LECKY, PAUL M.      111 BORDEN ST.           MIDLAND, TX       79707
3207MCNERNEY, MARIE J.  144 MAPLE AVE            SAN ANTONIO, TX   78212
3209PERRY, MARY T.      75 HIGH HILL RD.         SAN ANGELO, TX    76904
4100PINTO, VICTOR       540 ALDEN ST.            ABILENE, TX       79601
4121AMIDON, PATRICIA    35 BANK ST.              MIDLAND, TX       79701
4203SAHADY, MARY L.     207 STAFFORD RD.         ODESSA, TX        79764
5213HAYES, EDNA         750 MAPLE AVE.           ABILENE, TX       79602
5645CABRAL, CAROL       1530 COUNTY RD.          TEMPLE, TX        76504
6001PRUITT, LARRY       603 ROCK ST.             ATHENS, TX        75751
7752ROY, VICTOR         135 WILCOX ST.           PORT LAVACA, TX   77979
8342LATANO, CATHERINE   2120 MAIN RD.            SEGUIN, TX        78156
8515OLSON, ROBERT M.    108 FRESNO LANE          LAREDO, TX        78040
8611SUTCLIFFE, LOUISE F.1384 PLEASANT ST.        WICHITA FALLS, TX 76304
8612BELANGER, AIME      1685 PLEASANT ST.        WICHITA FALLS, TX 76304
8614GOULART, GALE M.    740 WILLOW RANCH RD.     DALLAS, TX        75244
8617O'NEIL, FRANCIS L.  37 ADAMS RD.             FORT WORTH, TX    76106
8618BARTLETT, MICHELLE  96 BAYSIDE DR.           BIG SPRING, TX    79721
8619HOOKS, TRUDY        491 WARREN AVE.          ODESSA, TX        79763
8633HAYES, TOM          35 COMMONS RD.           BIG SPRING, TX    79721
9009PONTES, EDMUND      195 FROST ST.            HOUSTON, TX       77058
9551DELICIO, RAYMOND    52 KILBURN ST.           ALVIN, TX         77511
9999BENTSON, JAMES R.   254 WEST MAIN RD.        JACKSONVILLE, TX  75766
```

2X2-I: Data Set for Chapter 2, Programming Exercise II, Allied Stock Company

```
890103010504030025
890103600106000010
890103176510100450
890104215006030065
890104861104030040
890105600106000020
890105070804080105
890106320010340005
890106176505610320
890107070804100075
890110010508010002
890110215012010050
890110320006070150
890112215006030080
890112600112090250
890113176510100050
890114070806080200
890117861106130065
890117600112050350
890119320004030010
890120071706020006
890120071705610110
890121010510910008
890121070812050250
890124071705610075
890124215006070230
890124320005030003
890125176504010150
890125172306060001
890125070900640500
890126070808010025
890126320010100015
890127861106090330
890127176505610250
890128861810250001
890128000805610002
890128600112010025
```

2X2-II: Data Set for Chapter 2, Programming Exercise II, Allied Stock Company

```
0003HALEY, ETHEL          99 SUNSET DR.           PORT LAVACA, TX     77979
0008PANNONNI, NICHOLAS    3 COLT DRIVE            WHARTON, TX         77488
0015HARVEY, SIDNEY        814 REAGAN AVE.         GEORGETOWN, TX      78628
0037CORREIA, HERMAN       293 CRESCENT DR.        AUSTIN, TX          78722
0046WARD, BRUNO           289 ALMY RD.            AUSTIN, TX          78734
0061OLSON, HELENA         2050 EAST KING RD.      WHARTON, TX         77488
0105COUSIN, RAYMOND       698 WALNUT AVE.         MIDLAND, TX         79701
0210TYRELL, ROBERT T.     292 STOCKTON AVE.       FORT WORTH, TX      76106
0432ALVES, HERMANO        350 PILOT DR.           BROWNSVILLE, TX     78521
0530RAPOZA, JUDITH        609 DAVOL ST.           WACO, TX            76704
0700ROY, ALBERT F.        655 N. MAIN ST.         EL PASO, TX         79901
0701O'NEIL, EUGENE        151 RANCHERO DR.        PECOS, TX           79772
0702TAYLOR, MAXINE        64 ANAWAN AVE.          LAREDO, TX          78040
0703FARNHAM, NORMAN       1255 WILSON RD.         BROWNSVILLE, TX     78521
0704FAY, MARGO            815 BEDFORD ST.         CRYSTAL CITY, TX    78839
0705BORDEN REPAIR         1 TINMAN RD.            SWEETWATER, TX      79556
0706GOVERNO, MARY T.      170 WILLIAM ST.         WACO, TX            76705
0707LOU'S PLACE           190 NEWHALL AVE.        LUFKIN, TX          75901
0708POCASSET JEWELERS     201 SOUTH MAIN ST.      LAREDO, TX          78040
0709LOFTY BALLOONS        45 FREEDOM RD.          FORT WORTH, TX      76104
0711PIPEIRA, MARCIA       835 VALENTINE DR.       GEORGETOWN, TX      78626
0713PIELA, ELIZABETH      360 BUFFINGTON AVE.     PECOS, TX           79772
0715TYSON, URSULA         594 MAPLE AVE           ABILENE, TX         79602
0717TRIPLE-A AUTO PARTS 4095 COUNTY RD.           LAREDO, TX          78041
0819DUPRE, DIANE          345 DURFEE AVE.         DALLAS, TX          75223
1723CARPENTER, HAZEL      189 DENHAM DR.          MIDLAND, TX         79705
1765BURNS SERVICE CENTER480 RIDGE RD.             BIG SPRING, TX      79721
2150HAGUE, RUSSELL        126 PRESIDENT AVE.      SAN ANTONIO, TX     78219
2200WALLACE, EDWARD       64 WILLOW LANE          GEORGETOWN, TX      78628
2201BELMORE, ALICE        15 STEVEN AVE.          TEMPLE, TX          76503
2203BARRY, JEAN           177 MARKET DR.          KILLEEN, TX         76544
2205DOSTER, MARY          287 BROADWAY ST.        SAN ANGELO, TX      76902
2207PLUNKETT, GARY A.     750 RODEO BLVD.         ABILENE, TX         79608
2520PLUNKETT, LILLIAN     110 CAMPION AVE.        DALLAS, TX          75223
2875TURCOTTE, THEODORE    530 S. MAIN ST.         CRYSTAL CITY, TX    78839
3200UNDERWOOD, LLOYD      25 ISLAND VIEW RD.      PORT LAVACA, TX     77979
3201HAMILTON, RUTH        13 BAKER ST.            AUSTIN, TX          78721
3203HANCOCK, LENA         229 RIVERSIDE DR.       SWEETWATER, TX      79556
3205LECKY, PAUL M.        111 BORDEN ST.          MIDLAND, TX         79707
3207MCNERNEY, MARIE J.    144 MAPLE AVE           SAN ANTONIO, TX     78212
3209PERRY, MARY T.        75 HIGH HILL RD.        SAN ANGELO, TX      76904
4100PINTO, VICTOR         540 ALDEN ST.           ABILENE, TX         79601
4121AMIDON, PATRICIA      35 BANK ST.             MIDLAND, TX         79701
4203SAHADY, MARY L.       207 STAFFORD RD.        ODESSA, TX          79764
5213HAYES, EDNA           750 MAPLE AVE.          ABILENE, TX         79602
5645CABRAL, CAROL         1530 COUNTY RD.         TEMPLE, TX          76504
6001PRUITT, LARRY         603 ROCK ST.            ATHENS, TX          75751
7752ROY, VICTOR           135 WILCOX ST.          PORT LAVACA, TX     77979
8342LATANO, CATHERINE     2120 MAIN RD.           SEGUIN, TX          78156
8515OLSON, ROBERT M.      108 FRESNO LANE         LAREDO, TX          78040
8611SUTCLIFFE, LOUISE F.1384 PLEASANT ST.         WICHITA FALLS, TX   76304
8612BELANGER, AIME        1685 PLEASANT ST.       WICHITA FALLS, TX   76304
8614GOULART, GALE M.      740 WILLOW RANCH RD.    DALLAS, TX          75244
8617O'NEIL, FRANCIS L.    37 ADAMS RD.            FORT WORTH, TX      76106
8618BARTLETT, MICHELLE    96 BAYSIDE DR.          BIG SPRING, TX      79721
8619HOOKS, TRUDY          491 WARREN AVE.         ODESSA, TX          79763
8633HAYES, TOM            35 COMMONS RD.          BIG SPRING, TX      79721
9009PONTES, EDMUND        195 FROST ST.           HOUSTON, TX         77058
9551DELICIO, RAYMOND      52 KILBURN ST.          ALVIN, TX           77511
9999BENTSON, JAMES R.     254 WEST MAIN RD.       JACKSONVILLE, TX    75766
```

■ 2X2-III: Data Set for Chapter 2, Programming Exercise II, Allied Stock Company

```
000176750
000310500
000701000
001203800
001301250
003600999
006401510
036903999
040000100
040102199
040387500
040510000
040700300
040803650
040910130
050101299
050331000
050603100
056105915
058300250
060000900
060102800
060210001
060350000
060405112
060508999
060602500
060701289
060800500
060901389
061140000
061307189
061500125
061712589
061900360
080112009
101009999
101295000
102200399
102505500
103000099
103406760
109125099
120080050
120130000
120345000
120501199
120701500
120900500
```

■ 2X3-I: Data Set for Chapter 2, Programming Exercise III, Allied Stock Company

```
890103010504030025
890103600106000010
890103176510100450
890104215006030065
890104861104030040
890105600106000020
890105070804080105
890106320010340005
890106176505610320
890107070804100075
890110010508010002
890110215012010050
890110320006070150
890112215006030080
890112600112090250
890113176510100050
890114070806080200
890117861106130065
890117600112050350
890119320004030010
890120071706020006
890120071705610110
890121010510910008
890121070812050250
890124071705610075
890124215006070230
890124320005030003
890125176504010150
890125172306060001
890125070900640500
890126070808010025
890126320010100015
890127861106090330
890127176505610250
890128861810250001
890128000805610002
890128600112010025
```

2X3-II: Data Set for Chapter 2, Programming Exercise III, Allied Stock Company

```
0003HALEY, ETHEL        99 SUNSET DR.            PORT LAVACA, TX     77979
0008PANNONNI, NICHOLAS  3 COLT DRIVE             WHARTON, TX         77488
0015HARVEY, SIDNEY      814 REAGAN AVE.          GEORGETOWN, TX      78628
0037CORREIA, HERMAN     293 CRESCENT DR.         AUSTIN, TX          78722
0046WARD, BRUNO         289 ALMY RD.             AUSTIN, TX          78734
0061OLSON, HELENA       2050 EAST KING RD.       WHARTON, TX         77488
0105COUSIN, RAYMOND     698 WALNUT AVE.          MIDLAND, TX         79701
0210TYRELL, ROBERT T.   292 STOCKTON AVE.        FORT WORTH, TX      76106
0432ALVES, HERMANO      350 PILOT DR.            BROWNSVILLE, TX     78521
0530RAPOZA, JUDITH      609 DAVOL ST.            WACO, TX            76704
0700ROY, ALBERT F.      655 N. MAIN ST.          EL PASO, TX         79901
0701O'NEIL, EUGENE      151 RANCHERO DR.         PECOS, TX           79772
0702TAYLOR, MAXINE      64 ANAWAN AVE.           LAREDO, TX          78040
0703FARNHAM, NORMAN     1255 WILSON RD.          BROWNSVILLE, TX     78521
0704FAY, MARGO          815 BEDFORD ST.          CRYSTAL CITY, TX    78839
0705BORDEN REPAIR       1 TINMAN RD.             SWEETWATER, TX      79556
0706GOVERNO, MARY T.    170 WILLIAM ST.          WACO, TX            76705
0707LOU'S PLACE         190 NEWHALL AVE.         LUFKIN, TX          75901
0708POCASSET JEWELERS   201 SOUTH MAIN ST.       LAREDO, TX          78040
0709LOFTY BALLOONS      45 FREEDOM RD.           FORT WORTH, TX      76104
0711PIPEIRA, MARCIA     835 VALENTINE DR.        GEORGETOWN, TX      78626
0713PIELA, ELIZABETH    360 BUFFINGTON AVE.      PECOS, TX           79772
0715TYSON, URSULA       594 MAPLE AVE            ABILENE, TX         79602
0717TRIPLE-A AUTO PARTS 4095 COUNTY RD.          LAREDO, TX          78041
0819DUPRE, DIANE        345 DURFEE AVE.          DALLAS, TX          75223
1723CARPENTER, HAZEL    189 DENHAM DR.           MIDLAND, TX         79705
1765BURNS SERVICE CENTER480 RIDGE RD.            BIG SPRING, TX      79721
2150HAGUE, RUSSELL      126 PRESIDENT AVE.       SAN ANTONIO, TX     78219
2200WALLACE, EDWARD     64 WILLOW LANE           GEORGETOWN, TX      78628
2201BELMORE, ALICE      15 STEVEN AVE.           TEMPLE, TX          76503
2203BARRY, JEAN         177 MARKET DR.           KILLEEN, TX         76544
2205DOSTER, MARY        287 BROADWAY ST.         SAN ANGELO, TX      76902
2207PLUNKETT, GARY A.   750 RODEO BLVD.          ABILENE, TX         79608
2520PLUNKETT, LILLIAN   110 CAMPION AVE.         DALLAS, TX          75223
2875TURCOTTE, THEODORE  530 S. MAIN ST.          CRYSTAL CITY, TX    78839
3200UNDERWOOD, LLOYD    25 ISLAND VIEW RD.       PORT LAVACA, TX     77979
3201HAMILTON, RUTH      13 BAKER ST.             AUSTIN, TX          78721
3203HANCOCK, LENA       229 RIVERSIDE DR.        SWEETWATER, TX      79556
3205LECKY, PAUL M.      111 BORDEN ST.           MIDLAND, TX         79707
3207MCNERNEY, MARIE J.  144 MAPLE AVE            SAN ANTONIO, TX     78212
3209PERRY, MARY T.      75 HIGH HILL RD.         SAN ANGELO, TX      76904
4100PINTO, VICTOR       540 ALDEN ST.            ABILENE, TX         79601
4121AMIDON, PATRICIA    35 BANK ST.              MIDLAND, TX         79701
4203SAHADY, MARY L.     207 STAFFORD RD.         ODESSA, TX          79764
5213HAYES, EDNA         750 MAPLE AVE.           ABILENE, TX         79602
5645CABRAL, CAROL       1530 COUNTY RD.          TEMPLE, TX          76504
6001PRUITT, LARRY       603 ROCK ST.             ATHENS, TX          75751
7752ROY, VICTOR         135 WILCOX ST.           PORT LAVACA, TX     77979
8342LATANO, CATHERINE   2120 MAIN RD.            SEGUIN, TX          78156
8515OLSON, ROBERT M.    108 FRESNO LANE          LAREDO, TX          78040
8611SUTCLIFFE, LOUISE F.1384 PLEASANT ST.        WICHITA FALLS, TX   76304
8612BELANGER, AIME      1685 PLEASANT ST.        WICHITA FALLS, TX   76304
8614GOULART, GALE M.    740 WILLOW RANCH RD.     DALLAS, TX          75244
8617O'NEIL, FRANCIS L.  37 ADAMS RD.             FORT WORTH, TX      76106
8618BARTLETT, MICHELLE  96 BAYSIDE DR.           BIG SPRING, TX      79721
8619HOOKS, TRUDY        491 WARREN AVE.          ODESSA, TX          79763
8633HAYES, TOM          35 COMMONS RD.           BIG SPRING, TX      79721
9009PONTES, EDMUND      195 FROST ST.            HOUSTON, TX         77058
9551DELICIO, RAYMOND    52 KILBURN ST.           ALVIN, TX           77511
9999BENTSON, JAMES R.   254 WEST MAIN RD.        JACKSONVILLE, TX    75766
```

2X3-III: Data Set for Chapter 2, Programming Exercise III, Allied Stock Company

```
000176750
000310500
000701000
001203800
001301250
003600999
006401510
036903999
040000100
040102199
040387500
040510000
040700300
040803650
040910130
050101299
050331000
050603100
056105915
058300250
060000900
060102800
060210001
060350000
060405112
060508999
060602500
060701289
060800500
060901389
061140000
061307189
061500125
061712589
061900360
080112009
101009999
101295000
102200399
102505500
103000099
103406760
109125099
120080050
120130000
120345000
120501199
120701500
120900500
```

2X4-I: Data Set for Chapter 2, Programming Exercise IV, Ponagansett Electric Company

```
A101610757808082
A1100000002540000000002630000000
A1100020002680000000002770000000
A1100050002680010040002770010543
A1100200005692007986005932908487
A1100550017671005135018663405636
A1102000035643506437038389406937
A1199999128980006159138975906660
C-2475
C-2000000000000000000000000000000
C-2010000000000085190000000009019
C-2999990851900079190901900008419
XXX0001100009
```

■ 2X4-II: Data Set for Chapter 2, Programming Exercise IV, Ponagansett Electric Company

```
00154324A12100140NARDONE, MARY E.    152 JEFFERSON ST.        ATLANTA, GA       30315
00154352A10101235FLYNN, ROGER P.     21 NOTRE DAME ST.        N. ATLANTA, GA    30341
00154365C-2103041BEST FURNITURE INC. 550 SAKONNET POINT       EAST POINT, GA    30328
00154381A10106176KOLAKOWSKI, CASIMIR 386 CLARKSON ST.         DECATUR, GA       30035
00154388A12110025ASSELIN, JANICE M.  245 NO. MARION ST.       ATLANTA, GA       30312
00154395C-2115722GLORIA'S BEAUTY SHOP260 WM. SOUZA RD.        HAPEVILLE, GA     30354
00154397A10120190WAREHAM, JOSEPH F.  196 NEWHALL AVE.         MOUNTAIN VIEW, GA 30328
00154405A11131211KEATING, SUSAN A.   106 FAIRHAVEN AVE.       FOREST PARK, GA   30050
00154413A12135400CONNELL, FRED C.    645 CHERRY ST.           EAST POINT, GA    30315
00154417A10138625FRYE, LOUISE N.     43 STEWART ST.           EMORY, GA         30307
00154422C-2150950TINY-TOT NURSERY    142 SPRUCE ST.           ATLANTA, GA       30307
00154427A11153276BERGERON, FRANK S.  73 DOVER ST.             N. ATLANTA, GA    30331
00154438A12155900LOUGHERY, KATRINA   298 SOUTH MAIN ST.       MARIETTA, GA      30060
00154444A10157133GOUDREAU, ELIZABETH 24 DAVIS ST.             DECATUR, GA       30030
00154452C-2159005COPTER SERVICE      29 PERSHING AVE.         COLLEGE PARK, GA  30337
00154469A11160216GATTO, JANICE L.    55 CRESTWOOD AVE.        EAST POINT, GA    30316
00154473A10161394JOZEFOWICZ, SANDRA  45 DUKE AVE.             HAPEVILLE, GA     30354
00154485A12173731MCFADDEN, MICHAEL R.780 ATLANTIC BLVD.       FOREST PARK, GA   30050
00154499A12175571LETENDRE, THOMAS F. 205 MASON ST.            ATLANTA, GA       30349
00154550A10177505MASSE, EUGENE       131 CENTER AVE.          FOREST PARK, GA   30050
00154785C-2182162EVA'S FRUIT STORE   10 SPRING LANE           MARIETTA, GA      30060
00154792A10190324MANDEL, ROLANDE J.  2446 HIGHLAND AVE.       FOREST PARK, GA   30050
00154830A10193005SCULLY, CLARA B.    383 NICHOLS ST.          COLLEGE PARK, GA  30337
00154942A12201055NICOLETTA, JOHN J.  1012 MADISON AVE.        DECATUR, GA       30030
00155010C-2205182RAY TRUCKING CO.    81 STAFFORD RD.          DECATUR, GA       30032
00155100A10212433DION, GERARD M.     315 WASHINGTON ST.       EAST POINT, GA    30344
00155250A12220020CHOW, SHUI          140 ESSEX ST.            ATLANTA, GA       30339
00155520A10223944HODGE, KEVIN J.     560 EASTERN AVE.         EAST POINT, GA    30331
00155723C-2232132PETE'S AUTO SUPPLIES440 JEFFERSON BLVD.      N. ATLANTA, GA    30344
01201413A11241694LAMOUNTAIN, LOUISE  770 BEDFORD ST.          DECATUR, GA       30033
01201450A12245400PATALANO, SAMANTHA  50 AETNA ST.             COLLEGE PARK, GA  30337
01204300A10248375CADY, RAYMOND F.    70 NORTH COURT           N. ATLANTA, GA    30331
01204375A10252100GASPAR, RAOUL       86 COPLEY DR.            MARIETTA, GA      30060
01204423A11262025KLEIN, LAURALYNN    105 ALBION ST.           MABLETON, GA      30059
01204715C-2275364DORIS BAKERY SHOP   74 SIDNEY AVE.           SMYRNA, GA        30080
01523741A10275690HENNESSY, ROBERT J. 46 PALMER ST.            ATLANTA, GA       30305
01523742A10278170LUDOVICI, LUIGI     780 COTTAGE AVE.         FOREST PARK, GA   30050
01524001A12282985HUMMEL, STELLA      228 POWELL ST.           ATLANTA, GA       30316
01524023A10285374PARKS, EMERY R.     131 BARLOW ST.           MABLETON, GA      30059
01530437A10302010BENNETT, CLARENCE W.5021 KNIGHT ST.          SMYRNA, GA        30080
01680142A12305327PETRUSKA, MARIE     379 EAST MAIN RD.        EAST POINT, GA    30312
01702325C-2320400MARK MARINE SERVICE 270 COURTNEY ST.         ATLANTA, GA       30306
01702465A10331166DIGUILIO, EMILIO M. 52 WALNUT AVE.           MARIETTA, GA      30064
01702505A12342314CALLAHAN, JOHN J.   275 DUNCAN DR.           N. ATLANTA, GA    30341
01702580A11345943MCCARTHY, EUGENE F. 68 FARNUM ST.            DECATUR, GA       30032
01702640C-2363770GERRY'S SEAFOODS    86 WARREN AVE.           COLLEGE PARK, GA  30337
01705314A10367150BROWN, GEORGE W.    3964 NORTH MAIN ST.      N. ATLANTA, GA    30318
01705520A11384000PRECOURT, JEAN M.   140 JEPSON LANE          FOREST PARK, GA   30050
01721325A10391450DEWEY, FRANCES D.   532 BEAVER RD.           FOREST PARK, GA   30050
01734250A12394765GARDNER, LEO F.     25 GARDEN AVE.           COLLEGE PARK, GA  30337
```

2X4-III: Data Set for Chapter 2, Programming Exercise IV, Ponagansett Electric Company

```
0015432414024
0015435242131
0015436566565
0015438105240
0015438821421
0015439534858
0015439713962
0015440507070
0015441335235
0015441701106
0015442212720
0015442741038
0015443830481
0015444465659
0015445243309
0015446910518
0015447337692
0015448558083
0015449946212
0015455005170
0015478532571
0015479210768
0015483006934
0015494251935
0015501034821
0015510023474
0015525009788
0015552077319
0015572368652
0120141340241
0120145002527
0120430015176
0120437523575
0120442357082
0120471574992
0152374139015
0152374202860
0152400140107
0152402310746
0153043723745
0168014201240
0170232549373
0170246556613
0170250510406
0170258027534
0170264045198
0170531432065
0170552008625
0172132511212
0173425035437
```

2X4-IV: Data Set for Chapter 2, Programming Exercise IV, Ponagansett Electric Company

```
0015432414997
0015435242482
0015436568711
0015438105712
0015438822300
0015439539208
0015439714387
0015440508110
0015441336157
0015441701523
0015442214355
0015442741756
0015443831624
0015444466235
0015445245292
0015446911450
0015447338007
0015448559347
0015449947210
0015455005703
0015478534713
0015479211240
0015483007446
0015494252917
0015501037197
0015510023995
0015525010714
0015552077824
0015572370636
0120141341016
0120145003435
0120430015533
0120437524027
0120442357811
0120471578134
0152374139517
0152374203224
0152400141153
0152402311158
0153043724228
0168014202219
0170232551447
0170246556997
0170250511459
0170258028646
0170264048660
0170531432589
0170552009562
0172132511624
0173425036562
```

3X1: Data Set for Chapter 3, Programming Exercise I, Ponagansett Electric Company

```
CM00154324A12100140NARDONE, MARY E.    152 JEFFERSON ST.       ATLANTA, GA       30315
CM00154352A10101235FLYNN, ROGER P.     21 NOTRE DAME ST.       N. ATLANTA, GA    30341
CM00154365C-2103041BEST FURNITURE INC. 550 SAKONNET POINT      EAST POINT, GA    30328
CM00154381A10106176KOLAKOWSKI, CASIMIR 386 CLARKSON ST.        DECATUR, GA       30035
CM00154388A12110025ASSELIN, JANICE M.  245 NO. MARION ST.      ATLANTA, GA       30312
CM00154395C-2115722GLORIA'S BEAUTY SHOP260 WM. SOUZA RD.       HAPEVILLE, GA     30354
CM00154395A11120190WAREHAM, JOSEPH F.  196 NEWHALL AVE.        MOUNTAIN VIEW, GA 30328
CM00154405A11131211KEATING, SUSAN A.   106 FAIRHAVEN AVE.      FOREST PARK, GA   30050
CM00154413A12135400CONNELL, FRED C.    645 CHERRY ST.          EAST POINT, GA    30315
CM00154417A10138625FRYE, LOUISE N.     43 STEWART ST.          EMORY, GA         30307
CM00154422C-2150950TINY-TOT NURSERY    142 SPRUCE ST.          ATLANTA, GA       30307
CM00154427A11153276BERGERON, FRANK S.  73 DOVER ST.            N. ATLANTA, GA    30331
CM00154430A12357118DUVAL, ROBERT J.    25 CENTER AVE.          FOREST PARK, GA   30050
CM00154438A12155900LOUGHERY, KATRINA   298 SOUTH MAIN ST.      MARIETTA, GA      30060
CM00154444A10157133GOUDREAU, ELIZABETH 24 DAVIS ST.            DECATUR, GA       30030
CM00154452C-2159005COPTER SERVICE      29 PERSHING AVE.        COLLEGE PARK, GA  30337
CM00154469A11160216GATTO, JANICE L.    55 CRESTWOOD AVE.       EAST POINT, GA    30316
CM00154473A10161394JOZEFOWICZ, SANDRA  45 DUKE AVE.            HAPEVILLE, GA     30354
CM00154485A12173731MCFADDEN, MICHAEL R.780 ATLANTIC BLVD.      FOREST PARK, GA   30050
CM00154499A12175571LETENDRE, THOMAS F. 205 MASON ST.           ATLANTA, GA       30349
CM00154550A10177505MASSE, EUGENE       131 CENTER AVE.         FOREST PARK, GA   30050
CM00154560C-2173502NATIONWIDE TRAVEL   300 SOUTH MAIN ST.      MARIETTA, GA      30060
CM00154785C-2182162EVA'S FRUIT STORE   10 SPRING LANE          MARIETTA, GA      30060
CM00154830A10193005SCULLY, CLARA B.    383 NICHOLS ST.         COLLEGE PARK, GA  30337
CM00154942A12201055NICOLETTA, JOHN J.  1012 MADISON AVE.       DECATUR, GA       30030
CM00155010C-2205182RAY TRUCKING CO.    81 STAFFORD RD.         DECATUR, GA       30032
CM00155100A10212433DION, GERARD M.     315 WASHINGTON ST.      EAST POINT, GA    30344
CM00155250A12220020CHOW, SHUI          140 ESSEX ST.           ATLANTA, GA       30339
CM00155723C-2232132PETE'S AUTO SUPPLIES440 JEFFERSON BLVD.     N. ATLANTA, GA    30344
CM00155800A10136714SCARPETTI, JAMES A. 120 JEPSON LANE         FOREST PARK, GA   30050
CM00155800A10241694LAMOUNTAIN, LOUISE  770 BEDFORD ST.         DECATUR, GA       30033
CM01201450A12245400PATALANO, SAMANTHA  50 AETNA ST.            COLLEGE PARK, GA  30337
CM01204300A10248375CADY, RAYMOND F.    70 NORTH COURT          N. ATLANTA, GA    30331
CM01204375A10252100GASPAR, RAOUL       86 COPLEY DR.           MARIETTA, GA      30060
CM01204423A11262025KLEIN, LAURALYNN    105 ALBION ST.          MABLETON, GA      30059
CM01204715C-2275364DORIS BAKERY SHOP   74 SIDNEY AVE.          SMYRNA, GA        30080
CM01523741A10275690HENNESSY, ROBERT J. 46 PALMER ST.           ATLANTA, GA       30305
CM01523742A10278170LUDOVICI, LUIGI     780 COTTAGE AVE.        FOREST PARK, GA   30050
CM01524001A12282985HUMMEL, STELLA      228 POWELL ST.          ATLANTA, GA       30316
CM01524023A10285374PARKS, EMERY R.     131 BARLOW ST.          MABLETON, GA      30059
CM01525200A11345113COFFEY, KENNETH W.  530 BEDFORD ST.         DECATUR, GA       30033
CM01530437A10302010BENNETT, CLARENCE W.5021 KNIGHT ST.         SMYRNA, GA        30080
CM01680142A12305327PETRUSKA, MARIE     379 EAST MAIN RD.       EAST POINT, GA    30312
CM01700150C-2268375LUCIA MUSIC CO.     225 ESSEX ST.           ATLANTA, GA       30339
CM01702325C-2320400MARK MARINE SERVICE 270 COURTNEY ST.        ATLANTA, GA       30306
CM01702465A10331166DIGUILIO, EMILIO M. 52 WALNUT AVE.          MARIETTA, GA      30064
CM01702580A11345943MCCARTHY, EUGENE F. 68 FARNUM ST.           DECATUR, GA       30032
CM01702640C-2363770GERRY'S SEAFOODS    86 WARREN AVE.          COLLEGE PARK, GA  30337
CM01705314A10367150BROWN, GEORGE W.    3964 NORTH MAIN ST.     N. ATLANTA, GA    30318
CM01705520A11384000PRECOURT, JEAN M.   140 JEPSON LANE         FOREST PARK, GA   30050
CM01721325A10391450DEWEY, FRANCES D.   532 BEAVER RD.          FOREST PARK, GA   30050
CM01734250A12394765GARDNER, LEO F.     25 GARDEN AVE.          COLLEGE PARK, GA  30337
```

3X2: Data Set for Chapter 3, Programming Exercise II, Ponagansett Electric Company

```
CM00154324A12100140NARDONE, MARY E.    152 JEFFERSON ST.         ATLANTA, GA        30315
CM00154352A10101235FLYNN, ROGER P.     21 NOTRE DAME ST.         N. ATLANTA, GA     30341
CM00154365C-2103041BEST FURNITURE INC. 550 SAKONNET POINT        EAST POINT, GA     30328
CM00154381A10106176KOLAKOWSKI, CASIMIR 386 CLARKSON ST.          DECATUR, GA        30035
CM00154388A12110025ASSELIN, JANICE M.  245 NO. MARION ST.        ATLANTA, GA        30312
CM00154395C-2115722GLORIA'S BEAUTY SHOP260 WM. SOUZA RD.         HAPEVILLE, GA      30354
CM00154405A11131211KEATING, SUSAN A.   106 FAIRHAVEN AVE.        FOREST PARK, GA    30050
CM00154413A12135400CONNELL, FRED C.    645 CHERRY ST.            EAST POINT, GA     30315
CM00155800A10136714SCARPETTI, JAMES A. 120 JEPSON LANE           FOREST PARK, GA    30050
CM00154417A10138625FRYE, LOUISE N.     43 STEWART ST.            EMORY, GA          30307
CM00154422C-2150950TINY-TOT NURSERY    142 SPRUCE ST.            ATLANTA, GA        30307
CM00154427A11153276BERGERON, FRANK S.  73 DOVER ST.              N. ATLANTA, GA     30331
CM00154438A12155900LOUGHERY, KATRINA   298 SOUTH MAIN ST.        MARIETTA, GA       30060
CM00154444A10157133GOUDREAU, ELIZABETH 24 DAVIS ST.              DECATUR, GA        30030
CM00154452C-2159005COPTER SERVICE      29 PERSHING AVE.          COLLEGE PARK, GA   30337
CM00154469A11160216GATTO, JANICE L.    55 CRESTWOOD AVE.         EAST POINT, GA     30316
CM00154473A10161394JOZEFOWICZ, SANDRA  45 DUKE AVE.              HAPEVILLE, GA      30354
CM00154560C-2173502NATIONWIDE TRAVEL   300 SOUTH MAIN ST.        MARIETTA, GA       30060
CM00154485A12173731MCFADDEN, MICHAEL R.780 ATLANTIC BLVD.        FOREST PARK, GA    30050
CM00154499A12175571LETENDRE, THOMAS F. 205 MASON ST.             ATLANTA, GA        30349
CM00154550A10177505MASSE, EUGENE       131 CENTER AVE.           FOREST PARK, GA    30050
CM00154785C-2182162EVA'S FRUIT STORE   10 SPRING LANE            MARIETTA, GA       30060
CM00154830A10193005SCULLY, CLARA B.    383 NICHOLS ST.           COLLEGE PARK, GA   30337
CM00154942A12201055NICOLETTA, JOHN J.  1012 MADISON AVE.         DECATUR, GA        30030
CM00155010C-2205182RAY TRUCKING CO.    81 STAFFORD RD.           DECATUR, GA        30032
CM00155100A10212433DION, GERARD M.     315 WASHINGTON ST.        EAST POINT, GA     30344
CM00155250A12220020CHOW, SHUI          140 ESSEX ST.             ATLANTA, GA        30339
CM00155723C-2232132PETE'S AUTO SUPPLIES440 JEFFERSON BLVD.       N. ATLANTA, GA     30344
CM01201450A12245400PATALANO, SAMANTHA  50 AETNA ST.              COLLEGE PARK, GA   30337
CM01204300A10248375CADY, RAYMOND F.    70 NORTH COURT            N. ATLANTA, GA     30331
CM01204375A10252100GASPAR, RAOUL       86 COPLEY DR.             MARIETTA, GA       30060
CM01204423A11262025KLEIN, LAURALYNN    105 ALBION ST.            MABLETON, GA       30059
CM01700150C-2268375LUCIA MUSIC CO.     225 ESSEX ST.             ATLANTA, GA        30339
CM01204715C-2275364DORIS BAKERY SHOP   74 SIDNEY AVE.            SMYRNA, GA         30080
CM01523741A10275690HENNESSY, ROBERT J. 46 PALMER ST.             ATLANTA, GA        30305
CM01523742A10278170LUDOVICI, LUIGI     780 COTTAGE AVE.          FOREST PARK, GA    30050
CM01524001A12282985HUMMEL, STELLA      228 POWELL ST.            ATLANTA, GA        30316
CM01524023A10285374PARKS, EMERY R.     131 BARLOW ST.            MABLETON, GA       30059
CM01530437A10302010BENNETT, CLARENCE W.5021 KNIGHT ST.           SMYRNA, GA         30080
CM01680142A12305327PETRUSKA, MARIE     379 EAST MAIN RD.         EAST POINT, GA     30312
CM01702325C-2320400MARK MARINE SERVICE 270 COURTNEY ST.          ATLANTA, GA        30306
CM01702465A10331166DIGUILIO, EMILIO M. 52 WALNUT AVE.            MARIETTA, GA       30064
CM01525200A11345113COFFEY, KENNETH W.  530 BEDFORD ST.           DECATUR, GA        30033
CM01702580A11345943MCCARTHY, EUGENE F. 68 FARNUM ST.             DECATUR, GA        30032
CM00154430A12357118DUVAL, ROBERT J.    25 CENTER AVE.            FOREST PARK, GA    30050
CM01702640C-2363770GERRY'S SEAFOODS    86 WARREN AVE.            COLLEGE PARK, GA   30337
CM01705314A10367150BROWN, GEORGE W.    3964 NORTH MAIN ST.       N. ATLANTA, GA     30318
CM01705520A11384000PRECOURT, JEAN M.   140 JEPSON LANE           FOREST PARK, GA    30050
CM01721325A10391450DEWEY, FRANCES D.   532 BEAVER RD.            FOREST PARK, GA    30050
CM01734250A12394765GARDNER, LEO F.     25 GARDEN AVE.            COLLEGE PARK, GA   30337
```

■ 3X3-I: Data Set for Chapter 3, Programming Exercise III, Ponagansett Electric Company

```
300187450A10100140PETRUSKA, MARY E.   75 WILLIAMS ST.
300175500    212433
300178300A11136714
300185500    159050
2            161394
2            155900
2            175500
100154401A10135510ZUCKER, MARILYN     287 BROADWAY AVE.         DECATUR, GA       30030
100154450A11155920DUNLEVY, JOHN R.    135 PINE ST.              EAST POINT, GA    30312
100155150A10105230MEYERS, DONNALYN    70 ASHLEY BLVD.           EMORY, GA         30307
101524050C-2174200EAST COAST FASTENERS1240 COMMERCIAL WAY       ATLANTA, GA       30316
101201120A12143550YOUNG, ARTHUR J.    358 MONTVALE AVE.         MARIETTA, GA      30060
101524001A12232130BERGERON, ALBERT A. 1530 SOUTH MAIN ST.       MARIETTA, GA      30060
```

■ 3X3-II: Data Set for Chapter 3, Programming Exercise III, Ponagansett Electric Company

```
CM00154324A12100140NARDONE, MARY E.    152 JEFFERSON ST.         ATLANTA, GA         30315
CM00154352A10101235FLYNN, ROGER P.     21 NOTRE DAME ST.         N. ATLANTA, GA      30341
CM00154365C-2103041BEST FURNITURE INC. 550 SAKONNET POINT        EAST POINT, GA      30328
CM00154381A10106176KOLAKOWSKI, CASIMIR 386 CLARKSON ST.          DECATUR, GA         30035
CM00154388A12110025ASSELIN, JANICE M.  245 NO. MARION ST.        ATLANTA, GA         30312
CM00154395C-2115722GLORIA'S BEAUTY SHOP260 WM. SOUZA RD.         HAPEVILLE, GA       30354
CM00154405A11131211KEATING, SUSAN A.   106 FAIRHAVEN AVE.        FOREST PARK, GA     30050
CM00154413A12135400CONNELL, FRED C.    645 CHERRY ST.            EAST POINT, GA      30315
CM00155800A10136714SCARPETTI, JAMES A. 120 JEPSON LANE           FOREST PARK, GA     30050
CM00154417A10138625FRYE, LOUISE N.     43 STEWART ST.            EMORY, GA           30307
CM00154422C-2150950TINY-TOT NURSERY    142 SPRUCE ST.            ATLANTA, GA         30307
CM00154427A11153276BERGERON, FRANK S.  73 DOVER ST.              N. ATLANTA, GA      30331
CM00154438A12155900LOUGHERY, KATRINA   298 SOUTH MAIN ST.        MARIETTA, GA        30060
CM00154444A10157133GOUDREAU, ELIZABETH 24 DAVIS ST.              DECATUR, GA         30030
CM00154452C-2159005COPTER SERVICE      29 PERSHING AVE.          COLLEGE PARK, GA    30337
CM00154469A11160216GATTO, JANICE L.    55 CRESTWOOD AVE.         EAST POINT, GA      30316
CM00154473A10161394JOZEFOWICZ, SANDRA  45 DUKE AVE.              HAPEVILLE, GA       30354
CM00154560C-2173502NATIONWIDE TRAVEL   300 SOUTH MAIN ST.        MARIETTA, GA        30060
CM00154485A12173731MCFADDEN, MICHAEL R.780 ATLANTIC BLVD.        FOREST PARK, GA     30050
CM00154499A12175571LETENDRE, THOMAS F. 205 MASON ST.             ATLANTA, GA         30349
CM00154550A10177505MASSE, EUGENE       131 CENTER AVE.           FOREST PARK, GA     30050
CM00154785C-2182162EVA'S FRUIT STORE   10 SPRING LANE            MARIETTA, GA        30060
CM00154830A10193005SCULLY, CLARA B.    383 NICHOLS ST.           COLLEGE PARK, GA    30337
CM00154942A12201055NICOLETTA, JOHN J.  1012 MADISON AVE.         DECATUR, GA         30030
CM00155010C-2205182RAY TRUCKING CO.    81 STAFFORD RD.           DECATUR, GA         30032
CM00155100A10212433DION, GERARD M.     315 WASHINGTON ST.        EAST POINT, GA      30344
CM00155250A12220020CHOW, SHUI          140 ESSEX ST.             ATLANTA, GA         30339
CM00155723C-2232132PETE'S AUTO SUPPLIES440 JEFFERSON BLVD.       N. ATLANTA, GA      30344
CM01201450A12245400PATALANO, SAMANTHA  50 AETNA ST.              COLLEGE PARK, GA    30337
CM01204300A10248375CADY, RAYMOND F.    70 NORTH COURT            N. ATLANTA, GA      30331
CM01204375A10252100GASPAR, RAOUL       86 COPLEY DR.             MARIETTA, GA        30060
CM01204423A11262025KLEIN, LAURALYNN    105 ALBION ST.            MABLETON, GA        30059
CM01700150C-2268375LUCIA MUSIC CO.     225 ESSEX ST.             ATLANTA, GA         30339
CM01204715C-2275364DORIS BAKERY SHOP   74 SIDNEY AVE.            SMYRNA, GA          30080
CM01523741A10275690HENNESSY, ROBERT J. 46 PALMER ST.             ATLANTA, GA         30305
CM01523742A10278170LUDOVICI, LUIGI     780 COTTAGE AVE.          FOREST PARK, GA     30050
CM01524001A12282985HUMMEL, STELLA      228 POWELL ST.            ATLANTA, GA         30316
CM01524023A10285374PARKS, EMERY R.     131 BARLOW ST.            MABLETON, GA        30059
CM01530437A10302010BENNETT, CLARENCE W.5021 KNIGHT ST.           SMYRNA, GA          30080
CM01680142A12305327PETRUSKA, MARIE     379 EAST MAIN RD.         EAST POINT, GA      30312
CM01702325C-2320400MARK MARINE SERVICE 270 COURTNEY ST.          ATLANTA, GA         30306
CM01702465A10331166DIGUILIO, EMILIO M. 52 WALNUT AVE.            MARIETTA, GA        30064
CM01525200A11345113COFFEY, KENNETH W.  530 BEDFORD ST.           DECATUR, GA         30033
CM01702580A11345943MCCARTHY, EUGENE F. 68 FARNUM ST.             DECATUR, GA         30032
CM00154430A12357118DUVAL, ROBERT J.    25 CENTER AVE.            FOREST PARK, GA     30050
CM01702640C-2363770GERRY'S SEAFOODS    86 WARREN AVE.            COLLEGE PARK, GA    30337
CM01705314A10367150BROWN, GEORGE W.    3964 NORTH MAIN ST.       N. ATLANTA, GA      30318
CM01705520A11384000PRECOURT, JEAN M.   140 JEPSON LANE           FOREST PARK, GA     30050
CM01721325A10391450DEWEY, FRANCES D.   532 BEAVER RD.            FOREST PARK, GA     30050
CM01734250A12394765GARDNER, LEO F.     25 GARDEN AVE.            COLLEGE PARK, GA    30337
```

3X4-I: Data Set for Chapter 3, Programming Exercise IV, Modern Plastics Company

```
12060231423019SIMMONS, CHARLES E. 08753890401
13010053274178NICKERSON, EARLE B. 10002890405
11080002745283KNEELAND, LORRAINE M22501890407
15040157052215FRATES, DENISE      14504890403
12050326571782NYMAN, ROBERT G.    12502890406
2    461602956
2    313905926
2    463239232
2    274010516
320  456235100                    22501
3  60394740218                    10502
350  331952867                    24001
3  40425545014                    15001
3    724844532                    22501
3    217415641                    08502
3    418712334                    0850
```

3x4-II: Data Set for Chapter 3, Programming Exercise IV, Modern Plastics Company

```
EM1030017429976PESARE, KAROLYN S.  18002750205
EM1080125263028CANARIO, MARGARETTA 12502820701
EM3010170347173SHERMAN, MILTON L.  20002700701
EM3050177032815JOUBERT, BERTHA M.  09501700501
EM2040215311637CANTWELL, CLAUDIA   12501820515
EM3050217415641PERRY, CHARLENE     06254800601
EM3050227460634GOSSELIN, ANDREW P. 12003631001
EM5050228728353BELANGER, NORMAND   10502700315
EM2020231769472LOISELLE, CYNTHIA   16501700701
EM3060235596158KOSTEER, RICHARD G. 08003750901
EM3020246302715PAPADOPOULOS, JOE E.18001680601
EM3050261197635SANTOS, MANUELA     10004680601
EM2010288916795SILVIA, ROBERTA S.  18004680805
EM5060294933154WOLFE, LILETH       08752760910
EM3060312251653WINFIELD, LEWIS     06502800701
EM3050313905926ANDREWS, EARLE M.   08002741001
EM3050315631121SOSNICKI, STANLEY   05503820505
EM4050322114268BARBER, MICHELLE K. 08753720101
EM5060325042172AIKEN, MARTINA      07004800505
EM1020325123315GRAHAM, JUDITH L.   12501780501
EM4010331952867PELLETIER, VINCENT  20004680101
EM3070346795384LYNCH, WILLIAM S.   06002760601
EM1080349231175JACKSON, JESSICA    16501740601
EM2040387428531CALIFANO, CONCETTA  16001751201
EM4050392407915SAULNIER, ROBERT J. 07502741201
EM2070394740218ALMEIDA, RICHARD    07504720420
EM5050399168704CELANO, LOUISE      06001801201
EM1030407265788KRAUS, DONALD D.    17504790520
EM5050419426056SORAFINE, JULIO     10502700701
EM4050419712334ABRUZZI, GENE D.    07002780901
EM3050425545014CHAN, SUKOM         12002630901
EM5070426435893JUSTINO, KIRA       06503790604
EM4020433405713POPKIN, ISABELLA M. 14501740220
EM1010456235100PALMER, WALTER R.   20002600306
EM5050461602956GREENE, WILMA       09003740906
EM2040463239232MACDONALD, PHILIP A.18503640601
EM3050466219366CHAPPELLE, BARBARA  08001741201
EM4050544287696ROCK, DONALD R.     07503741001
EM4060585731346HIGGINS, DANIEL J.  07504770520
EM2040587311472PAINE, JAMES H.     15954720101
EM5050673372239LOBO, ALBERT P.     08001781101
EM5020674337414KLINGER, MICHAEL A. 16003700815
EM4070713390477CAMPBELL, ROBIN     04501800601
EM5050722199235POTTER, RICHARD     09004740601
EM1010723510611READY, MARIA ELENA  18001750605
EM1080724844532CHARNIAK, NELSON T. 20003700601
EM2040737565186AFFLECK, SCOTT      14503780901
EM4050739394862PROULX, OSCAR R.    06504800701
EM1010781207315CAPARCO, DOMENIC A. 15503820925
EM5010834615944CAPPUCCI, NAOMI     20001660901
EM1020861745201JACKVONY, WEBSTER P.20002650605
```

4X2: Data Set for Chapter 4, Programming Exercise II, Allied Stock Company

```
CM0003HALEY, ETHEL          99 SUNSET DR.             PORT LAVACA, TX    77979        890215
CM0008PANNONNI, NICHOLAS    3 COLT DRIVE              WHARTON, TX        77488        890207
CM0015HARVEY, SIDNEY        814 REAGAN AVE.           GEORGETOWN, TX     78628        890214
CM0037CORREIA, HERMAN       293 CRESCENT DR.          AUSTIN, TX         78722        890124
CM0046WARD, BRUNO           289 ALMY RD.              AUSTIN, TX         78734        890216
CM0061OLSON, HELENA         2050 EAST KING RD.        WHARTON, TX        77488        890110
CM0105COUSIN, RAYMOND       698 WALNUT AVE.           MIDLAND, TX        79701        890124
CM0210TYRELL, ROBERT T.     292 STOCKTON AVE.         FORT WORTH, TX     76106        890223
CM0432ALVES, HERMANO        350 PILOT DR.             BROWNSVILLE, TX    78521        890125
CM0530RAPOZA, JUDITH        609 DAVOL ST.             WACO, TX           76704        890112
CM0700ROY, ALBERT F.        655 N. MAIN ST.           EL PASO, TX        79901        890224
CM0701O'NEIL, EUGENE        151 RANCHERO DR.          PECOS, TX          79772        890301
CM0702TAYLOR, MAXINE        64 ANAWAN AVE.            LAREDO, TX         78040        890126
CM0703FARNHAM, NORMAN       1255 WILSON RD.           BROWNSVILLE, TX    78521        890112
CM0704FAY, MARGO            815 BEDFORD ST.           CRYSTAL CITY, TX   78839        890217
CM0705BORDEN REPAIR         1 TINMAN RD.              SWEETWATER, TX     79556        890303
CM0706GOVERNO, MARY T.      170 WILLIAM ST.           WACO, TX           76705        890221
CM0707LOU'S PLACE           190 NEWHALL AVE.          LUFKIN, TX         75901        890118
CM0708POCASSET JEWELERS     201 SOUTH MAIN ST.        LAREDO, TX         78040        890120
CM0709LOFTY BALLOONS        45 FREEDOM RD.            FORT WORTH, TX     76104        890209
CM0711PIPEIRA, MARCIA       835 VALENTINE DR.         GEORGETOWN, TX     78626        890206
CM0713PIELA, ELIZABETH      360 BUFFINGTON AVE.       PECOS, TX          79772        890123
CM0715TYSON, URSULA         594 MAPLE AVE             ABILENE, TX        79602        890203
CM0717TRIPLE-A AUTO PARTS 4095 COUNTY RD.             LAREDO, TX         78041        890314
CM0819DUPRE, DIANE          345 DURFEE AVE.           DALLAS, TX         75223        890206
CM1723CARPENTER, HAZEL      189 DENHAM DR.            MIDLAND, TX        79705        890210
CM1765BURNS SERVICE CENTER480 RIDGE RD.               BIG SPRING, TX     79721        890201
CM2150HAGUE, RUSSELL        126 PRESIDENT AVE.        SAN ANTONIO, TX    78219        890303
CM2200WALLACE, EDWARD       64 WILLOW LANE            GEORGETOWN, TX     78628        890207
CM2201BELMORE, ALICE        15 STEVEN AVE.            TEMPLE, TX         76503        890119
CM2203BARRY, JEAN           177 MARKET DR.            KILLEEN, TX        76544        890320
CM2205DOSTER, MARY          287 BROADWAY ST.          SAN ANGELO, TX     76902        890209
CM2207PLUNKETT, GARY A.     750 RODEO BLVD.           ABILENE, TX        79608        890301
CM2520PLUNKETT, LILLIAN     110 CAMPION AVE.          DALLAS, TX         75223        890208
CM2875TURCOTTE, THEODORE    530 S. MAIN ST.           CRYSTAL CITY, TX   78839        890302
CM3200UNDERWOOD, LLOYD      25 ISLAND VIEW RD.        PORT LAVACA, TX    77979        890310
```

4X2: Continued

```
CM3201HAMILTON, RUTH       13 BAKER ST.              AUSTIN, TX         78721               890111
CM3203HANCOCK, LENA        229 RIVERSIDE DR.         SWEETWATER, TX     79556               890209
CM3205LECKY, PAUL M.       111 BORDEN ST.            MIDLAND, TX        79707               890306
CM3207MCNERNEY, MARIE J.   144 MAPLE AVE             SAN ANTONIO, TX    78212               890309
CM3209PERRY, MARY T.       75 HIGH HILL RD.          SAN ANGELO, TX     76904               890126
CM4100PINTO, VICTOR        540 ALDEN ST.             ABILENE, TX        79601               890213
CM4121AMIDON, PATRICIA     35 BANK ST.               MIDLAND, TX        79701               890308
CM4203SAHADY, MARY L.      207 STAFFORD RD.          ODESSA, TX         79764               890317
CM5213HAYES, EDNA          750 MAPLE AVE.            ABILENE, TX        79602               890222
CM5645CABRAL, CAROL        1530 COUNTY RD.           TEMPLE, TX         76504               890116
CM6001PRUITT, LARRY        603 ROCK ST.              ATHENS, TX         75751               890310
CM7752ROY, VICTOR          135 WILCOX ST.            PORT LAVACA, TX    77979               890215
CM8342LATANO, CATHERINE    2120 MAIN RD.             SEGUIN, TX         78156               890125
CM8515OLSON, ROBERT M.     108 FRESNO LANE           LAREDO, TX         78040               890316
CM8611SUTCLIFFE, LOUISE F.1384 PLEASANT ST.          WICHITA FALLS, TX 76304                890207
CM8612BELANGER, AIME       1685 PLEASANT ST.         WICHITA FALLS, TX 76304                890313
CM8614GOULART, GALE M.     740 WILLOW RANCH RD.      DALLAS, TX         75244               890206
CM8617O'NEIL, FRANCIS L.   37 ADAMS RD.              FORT WORTH, TX     76106               890323
CM8618BARTLETT, MICHELLE   96 BAYSIDE DR.            BIG SPRING, TX     79721               890118
CM8619HOOKS, TRUDY         491 WARREN AVE.           ODESSA, TX         79763               890220
CM8633HAYES, TOM           35 COMMONS RD.            BIG SPRING, TX     79721               890320
CM9009PONTES, EDMUND       195 FROST ST.             HOUSTON, TX        77058               890216
CM9551DELICIO, RAYMOND     52 KILBURN ST.            ALVIN, TX          77511               890310
CM9999BENTSON, JAMES R.    254 WEST MAIN RD.         JACKSONVILLE, TX   75766               890227
```

4X3: Data Set for Chapter 4, Programming Exercise III, Allied Stock Company

```
32200                    170 WILLISTON RD.
30707DIANE'S NOOK
32202                    230 MAIN RD.             SAN ANTONIO, TX    78219
33203MARVIN, MRS. LENA   75 TINMAN RD.
26001
22510
20713
20432
28515
18610KIMTO, SANDY W.     251 BEDFORD ST.          CRYSTAL CITY, TX   78839
10900MORRIS, STANFIELD   233 MAPLE AVE.           ABILENE, TX        79602
11765ZAVECKAS, FRANCES   125 RIDGE RD.            BIG SPRING, TX     79721
10432DORAN, MAX          210 FRESNO LANE          LAREDO, TX         78040
```

4X5: Data Set for Chapter 4, Programming Exercise V, Allied Stock Company

```
IM0110PROG-TAPE PUNCH     1120013250
IM0306TAPE-END RETAIN FP  0018000250
IM04732-PLY TAPE ROLL HP  1622519320
IM0710CARR-CONTROL TAPE FP0680008000
IM1131TYPING ELEMENT      0252503290
IM1208TYPEWRITER RIBBON TP0708008250
IM1295HI-YLD CORRECTIBLE R0510006340
IM1298TYPE-SUPPLY KIT     1203014375
IM1404PRINTWHEEL          0307503950
IM1607COPIER TRANSPARENCY 0667508140
IM1637FF TAB DIVIDERS     0038500625
IM1693COPIER STARTER-PAC  0600007130
IM1699COPIER TONER        0542506375
IM23308-IN DP-DISKETTE TP 0400004890
IM2563MAG-TAPE CRIMPER    0600007250
IM7003PC-CRT TURNTABLE    0439505995
IM7011PC-TABLE WH         1990022375
IM70192-PLY JOURNAL-R HP  1050013250
IM70228-IN WP/DW DISKETTE 2750030550
IM7023PC-GENERAL RIBBON TP0176002250
IM70388-IN DP-DISKETTE FF 1625019525
IM7042MAG-TAPE BOX TP     0625007150
IM70435-DISK MAGAZINE KIT 4380051025
IM70458-IN DISK-MAILER    0156001945
IM7048COPIER PAPER 8.5X11 0390005150
IM7049LETTER-W RIBBON TP  0294503625
IM70558-IN DISK-LIB-CASE  0230002995
IM7063DISK MEGAFILE       3180037675
IM7064PALM REST           0300004225
IM7069COPY HOLDER         0790008790
IM7242MOB-PRINTER BASKET  0850010250
IM7302MOBILE COPIER TABLE 1950022550
IM7335HANGING-BINDER TP LB0280003450
IM7343DATA-PAK BOX TP     0714001975
IM7347DATA-PAK MAILER TP  0216002810
IM7380REPORT-BINDER TP BL 0280003650
IM7389REPORT-BINDER TB GR 0299503575
IM7862ADJ WORKTABLE       5700061050
IM7903ADJ TERMINAL BASE   6300071050
IM7905TERM-BASE W/CRT PLAT7100077599
IM7943LO-PRO PRINTER STAND2650032475
IM7952MOBILE STORAGE-CAB  3900043600
IM79612-DR MODULE W/LOCK  2900032450
IM7983OFFICE SWIVEL CHAIR 5950064550
IM7989RECT-X TERM-BASE/CRT2440027950
```

4X6: Data Set for Chapter 4, Programming Exercise VI, Allied Stock Company

```
37989                    2495028750
37335                    0312503890
34073                    1699519850
31404                    0355004325
32563                    0630007625
31637                    0039500000
21693
27347
20109
16038LASER TONER CARTRIDG1190013250
18085PRINTOUT BASKET     0399504850
11298MAC MONITOR CABLE KI0397504425
19045FULL FLOAT VALET    2999534225
16989CPU STAND           0790008575
```

5X1: Data Set for Chapter 5, Programming Exercises I and II, Allied Stock Company

```
9999  0001  76750  0600
6001  0003  10500  0016
9009  0007  01000  0013
0046  0012  03800  0082
9551  0013  01250  0040
2150  0036  00999  0003
0008  0064  01510  0001
7752  0369  03999  3500
2200  0400  00100  1200
2201  0401  02199  0003
2203  0403  87500  0002
2205  0405  10000  0001
2207  0407  00300  0610
8611  0408  03650  0009
8612  0409  10130  0004
8614  0501  01299  0016
8617  0503  31000  0001
8618  0506  03100  0063
0105  0561  05915  0045
8619  0583  00250  0027
0061  0600  00900  0010
0700  0601  02800  0002
0701  0602  10001  0001
0702  0603  50000  0005
0703  0604  05112  0010
0704  0605  08999  0003
0705  0606  02500  1001
0706  0607  01289  0004
0707  0608  00500  0013
0708  0609  01389  0102
0709  0611  40000  0007
0711  0613  07189  0003
0713  0615  00125  0017
0715  0617  12589  0003
0717  0619  00360  0100
4121  0801  12009  5000
0037  1010  09999  0005
5213  1012  95000  0002
8515  1022  00399  0120
8633  1022  00399  0005
0530  1025  05500  3010
0003  1030  00099  0041
0210  1034  06760  0031
4203  1091  25099  0002
3200  1200  80050  0002
3201  1201  30000  0001
3203  1203  45000  0004
3205  1205  01199  0011
3207  1207  01500  0004
3209  1209  00500  0017
```

5X3: Data Set for Chapter 5, Programming Exercise III, Reliable Auto Parts Company

```
010232115142BLACK, GEORGIA           4022504M4
010321643310CONDON, DANIEL           4008751S2
010143227630DINGLE, PATRICIA         3811500S1
010342675521DONNELY, BETH            4009002H2
010622742102GARCIA, ALBERT           4014253M3
010310227540KOZIOR, STANLEY          4016752M4
010111223452LARKIN, JOHN R.          4010500S2
010442782144PIETRASZEK, JAN          4018504M4
010132114679ZINKIE, KRISTA LYNN      2507751S1
020120407526ANTHONY, TONY            4012502M3
020052742813EGLESTON, MARY           4020000M4
020101591271ENDICOTT, MARVIN         4016254M4
020071994322FOGARTY, DOROTHY         4014502M4
020222117532MORONEY, PAUL D.         3508500S1
020444321222NELLY, SHELLY            4010501H2
020522059782PONTARELLI, ARTHUR       3508500S1
020346719113RONDILEAU, PHILIP        4012754M4
020101666214RUDON, MARIA             3009501S2
020600195812WINSPEARE, MARGARET      4011200H3
020411851423ZANIELLO, DAVID          4017503M4
020491112793ZITANO, MARIO            3006501S1
030139416674AYASH, LOUISE            4012500M4
030523335402AZEVEDO, MANUEL          4015253M4
030411562230BEAUDOIN, SUZANNE        4014751S2
030142651998CONDON, ELIZABETH        4017000S2
030614225667JONES, ALFRED            2009503M4
030391667533JUST, HELEN              4011251S2
030882751116LEONARD, WALTER          4014752M4
030552882246LEONARDO, ALBANY         4017252H4
030114332225PRENDERGAST, JACK        4014500S2
030625734622PURCELL, NANCY           3010500S2
030222691532RIGBY, NORMAN            4015253M4
030615766791TANGUAY, ROSEMARY        3010751S2
```

■ 5X4: Data Set for Chapter 5, Programming Exercise IV, Jocelyn Originals Company

```
1ABBRUZZI, KENNETH L.     01057550012960000152705002078080
4AITKEN, THOMAS R.        00898000011250500125600001645050
3ALTERMAN, MAUREEN E.     01432250014850700153805002035050
1BAHR, LENA M.            00995050012760000138790001654250
4BLAZUCK, JOSEPH A.       01254350015395500171900002233000
2BUCCI, ELEANOR F.        01066550012397500156225001888550
2BUXBAUM, JOAN M.         00825000012580500143505002175050
1CARTER, AMELIA L.        01129000013590500097555001995550
2COLETTI, SARAH T.        01067500014100500166850002347000
3COUGHLIN, AILEEN M.      01153000009700000147905001837450
1CYR, ROSARIO             01256350014384000182605002598400
3DURANT, MARIE L.         01098050013788400113255002077050
3GAFFNEY, MARILYN         01231050014450500168285002174025
4HOGAN, RALPH             00000000000000000082450001326850
2KACHADOURIAN, NATALIE A. 01437500016470500198500002437550
1KRUGER, ALLEN            01011050012750500142785001679000
2MARKARIAN, MARIAM        01137250009885000137000001938440
2MCGEE, BERNARD W.        01246450012950500166845002034200
1MOONEY, RONALD           01019050012825500152945001848450
3NUNES, ALICIA            01234525014384500000000000000000
2OVERDEEP, CYNTHIA        00962550014330000162655001997000
4PACCASASSI, DEBBIE       01194250013792500172255002347500
4PRIMEAU, ISABEL          01244550014960000173690002174550
2ROMA, GILDA              01158000013364500169475002077550
4SHERIDAN, RICHARD J.     01065075014280500184500002348550
3STURDAHL, DEBRA          01299000015325500194708002265000
3VELTRI, JOHN A.          01033500012286500174805002174000
```

6X1: Data Set for Chapter 6, Programming Exercise I, Express Auto Parts Warehouse

```
Part #: 0346R
Description: CB ANTENNA
Unit price: $ 33.29


Part #: 0348N
Description: 23 CHANNEL MOBILE CB
Unit price: $208.29


Part #: 0359B
Description: CB CONVERTER
Unit price: $ 20.79


Part #: 0368W
Description: FM ANTENNA
Unit price: $  6.65


Part #: 0382N
Description: STEREO SPEAKERS/PR
Unit price: $ 20.79


Part #: 0462U
Description: FLEXSOCKET WRENCH
Unit price: $  1.91


Part #: 1048T
Description: HITCH BALL COVER
Unit price: $  0.66


Part #: 1033W      (TO BE ENTERED OUT OF SEQUENCE!)
Description: FM RADIO AMPLIFIER
Unit price: $ 10.82


Part #: 1219X
Description: RW DEFOGGER
Unit price: $ 24.98


Part #: 1242W
Description: RV ALARM SYSTEM
Unit price: $ 16.63
```

6X1: Continued

```
Part #: 1263P
Description: TORQUE WRENCH
Unit price: $ 14.98


Part #: 1264Y
Description: 8000 LB. JACK STAND
Unit price: $ 10.82


Part #: 1352V
Description: TUNE-UP TESTER
Unit price: $ 33.29


Part #: 1517A
Description: SPARE TIRE LOCK
Unit price: $  3.74


Part #: 1503W       (TO BE ENTERED OUT OF SEQUENCE!)
Description: ELECTRONIC FILTER
Unit price: $ 10.82


Part #: 1584A
Description: RV ANTENNA
Unit price: $ 41.63


Part #: 1593X
Description: HD. TIE DOWN
Unit price: $ 14.98


Part #: 1685T
Description: BRAKE CABLE ADJUSTER
Unit price: $  0.66


Part #: 1616W       (TO BE ENTERED OUT OF SEQUENCE!)
Description: AIR DIESEL HORN
Unit price: $ 14.15


Part #: 1762N
Description: BUMPER GUARDS
Unit price: $ 14.15
```

6X1: Continued

```
Part #: 1775B
Description: BOLT-ON HITCH
Unit price: $ 56.63


Part #: 1787A
Description: 1000-WATT CONVERTER
Unit price: $289.96


Part #: 1914Y
Description: C-11 TRAILER HITCH
Unit price: $ 14.15


Part #: 16" F           (TO BE ENTERED OUT OF SEQUENCE!)
Description: 16" FULL WHEEL COVER
Unit price: $ 20.79


Part #: 2181X
Description: EXHAUST HEADERS
Unit price: $ 56.63


Part #: 2326R
Description: POWER MUFFLER
Unit price: $ 14.13


Part #: 3734N
Description: CAMSHAFT
Unit price: $ 66.63


Part #: 3731W           (TO BE ENTERED OUT OF SEQUENCE!)
Description: 3-2 BBL MANIFOLD
Unit price: $ 83.29


Part #: 5507R
Description: BONDED BRAKE SHOE
Unit price: $  6.65


Part #: 5524Y
Description: DISC BRAKE PADS
Unit price: $ 12.46
```

6X1: Continued

```
Part #: 5534A
Description: MASTER CYLINDER
Unit price: $ 12.46


Part #: 5557P
Description: SOLENOID SWITCH
Unit price: $  4.58


Part #: 7519Y
Description: SOLID STATE TACH
Unit price: $ 33.29


Part #: 5596W          (TO BE ENTERED OUT OF SEQUENCE!)
Description: HD STAINLESS-ST FAN
Unit price: $ 14.15


Part #: 7568Y
Description: 30-PC TUNE-UP KIT
Unit price: $ 33.29


Part #: 7580X
Description: RAM AIR SYSTEM
Unit price: $ 16.63


Part #: 8419A
Description: HOLLEY CARBURETOR
Unit price: $ 91.63


Part #: 8572V
Description: REAR END LIFT KIT
Unit price: $  6.65


Part #: 8583N
Description: WL-BEARING CAPS/PR
Unit price: $  3.32


Part #: 8776N
Description: RING & PINION GEARS
Unit price: $ 83.29
```

■ 6X4: Data Set for Chapter 6, Programming Exercise IV, Express Auto Parts Warehouse

```
A.  Records to be deleted from the master file

      Part numbers:  1842N (not in master file)
                     1593X
                     1787A

B.  New records to be added to the master file

      1. Part number: 3731W
         Part description: 3-2 BBL MANIFOLD
         Part unit price: $83.29

      2. Part number: 5524Y (duplicate part number)
         Part description: DISC BRAKE PADS
         Part unit price: $12.46

      3. Part number: 8896N
         Part description: ENGINE COOLER KIT
         Part unit price: $33.29

      4. Part number: 8931R
         Part description: SHOCK ABSORBERS/PR
         Part unit price: $20.79

      5. Part number: 8823U
         Part description: DUAL RHEOSTAT DIMMER
         Part unit price: $10.82

      6. Part number: 9998F
         Part description: FIBERGLASS HARDTOP
         Part unit price: $283.32

C.  Price changes to existing master records

      1. Part number: 8836E (no such part number)
         Part unit price: $24.50

      2. Part number: 5534A
         Part unit price: $15.25

      3. Part number: 2181X
         Part unit price: $62.50

      4. Part number: 1242W
         Part unit price: $21.35
```

Appendix E

COBOL Reference Formats

The general COBOL Reference Formats listed in this appendix are contained in the American National Standard ANSI X3.23–1985.

IDENTIFICATION DIVISION Formats

```
IDENTIFICATION DIVISION.

PROGRAM-ID. program-name [ IS { |COMMON| } PROGRAM ].
                                |INITIAL|

[AUTHOR. [comment-entry] . . .]
[INSTALLATION. [comment-entry] . . .]
[DATE-WRITTEN. [comment-entry] . . .]
[DATE-COMPILED. [comment-entry] . . .]
[SECURITY. [comment-entry] . . .]
```

ENVIRONMENT DIVISION Formats

```
[ENVIRONMENT DIVISION.
[CONFIGURATION SECTION.
[SOURCE-COMPUTER. [computer-name [with DEBUGGING MODE].]]
[OBJECT-COMPUTER. [computer-name
                                  { WORDS      }
      [MEMORY SIZE integer        { CHARACTERS } ]
                                  { MODULES    }
      [PROGRAM COLLATING SEQUENCE IS alphabet-name]
      [SEGMENT-LIMIT IS segment-number].]]
[SPECIAL-NAMES. [[implementor-name-1
 { IS mnemonic-name-1 [ON STATUS IS condition-name-1 [OFF STATUS IS condition-name-2]] } ]
 { IS mnemonic-name-2 [OFF STATUS IS condition-name-2 [ON STATUS IS condition-name-1]] } ] . . .
 { ON STATUS IS condition-name-1 [OFF STATUS IS condition-name-2]                       } ]
 { OFF STATUS IS condition-name-2 [ON STATUS IS condition-name-1]                       } ]
                                   { STANDARD-1                                              } ]
                                   { STANDARD-2                                              } ]
                                   { NATIVE                                                  } ]
[ALPHABET alphabet-name-1 IS       { implementor-name-2                                      } ] . . .
                                   {            [ { THROUGH }             ] }                } ]
                                   { { literal-1 [ { THRU    } literal-2  ] } . . .           } ]
                                   {            [                         ] }                } ]
                                   {            [ {ALSO literal-3} . . .   ] }               } ]
                                                            { IS  }
[SYMBOLIC CHARACTERS { { {symbolic-character-1} . . .        {     } {integer-1} . . . } . . . [IN alphabet-name-2] } ] . . .
                                                            { ARE }
                                          { THROUGH }
[CLASS class-name IS { literal-4 [ [      {         } literal-5 ] ] } . . . ] . . .
                                          { THRU    }
[CURRENCY SIGN IS literal-6
```

```
[DECIMAL-POINT IS COMMA].]]]
[INPUT-OUTPUT SECTION.
FILE-CONTROL.
    {file-control-entry} . . .
[I-O-CONTROL.

                                                      ⎧ integer-1 RECORDS                    ⎫
                                                      ⎪            ⎧REEL⎫                     ⎪
  ⎡         ⎡    ⎧file-name-1         ⎫⎤              ⎪ [END OF] ⎨    ⎬ OF file-name-2     ⎪⎤
  ⎢[RERUN   ⎢ON ⎨                    ⎬⎥  EVERY      ⎨            ⎩UNIT⎭                     ⎬⎥ . . .
  ⎣         ⎣    ⎩implementor-name    ⎭⎦              ⎪ integer-2 CLOCK-UNITS                 ⎪⎦
                                                      ⎩ condition-name-1                     ⎭

  ⎡        ⎡RECORD     ⎤
  ⎢[SAME   ⎢SORT       ⎥  AREA FOR file-name-3 {file-name-4} . . .] . . .
  ⎣        ⎣SORT-MERGE ⎦
  [MULTIPLE FILE TAPE CONTAINS {file-name-5 [POSITION integer-3]} . . .].]]]
```

FILE-CONTROL ENTRY Formats

Sequential File

```
                                         ⎧implementor-name-1⎫
SELECT [OPTIONAL] file-name-1 ASSIGN TO ⎨                  ⎬ . . .
                                         ⎩literal-1         ⎭

                      ⎡AREA ⎤⎤
[RESERVE integer-1    ⎣AREAS⎦⎦
[[ORGANIZATION IS] SEQUENTIAL]
                           ⎧data-name-1⎫⎤
[PADDING CHARACTER IS     ⎨           ⎬⎦
                           ⎩literal-2  ⎭
                            ⎧STANDARD-1        ⎫⎤
[RECORD DELIMITER IS       ⎨                  ⎬⎦
                            ⎩implementor-name-2⎭
[ACCESS MODE IS SEQUENTIAL]
[FILE STATUS IS data-name-2].
```

Relative File

```
                                         ⎧implementor-name-1⎫
SELECT [OPTIONAL] file-name-1 ASSIGN TO ⎨                  ⎬ . . .
                                         ⎩literal-1         ⎭

                      ⎡AREA ⎤⎤
[RESERVE integer-1    ⎣AREAS⎦⎦
[ORGANIZATION IS] RELATIVE
                   ⎧ SEQUENTIAL [RELATIVE KEY IS data-name-1]  ⎫⎤
[ACCESS MODE IS   ⎨ ⎧RANDOM ⎫                                 ⎬⎥
                   ⎩ ⎩DYNAMIC⎭ RELATIVE KEY IS data-name-1      ⎭⎦
[FILE STATUS IS data-name-2].
```

Indexed File

```
                                         ⎧implementor-name-1⎫
SELECT [OPTIONAL] file-name-1 ASSIGN TO ⎨                  ⎬ . . .
                                         ⎩literal-1         ⎭

                      ⎡AREA ⎤⎤
[RESERVE integer-1    ⎣AREAS⎦⎦
[ORGANIZATION IS] INDEXED
                   ⎧SEQUENTIAL⎫⎤
[ACCESS MODE IS   ⎨RANDOM    ⎬⎥
                   ⎩DYNAMIC   ⎭⎦
RECORD KEY IS data-name-1
[ALTERNATE RECORD KEY IS data-name-2 [WITH DUPLICATES]] . . .
[FILE STATUS IS data-name-3].
```

Report File

```
SELECT [OPTIONAL] file-name-1 ASSIGN TO {implementor-name-1} . . .
                                        {literal-1         }
[RESERVE integer-1 [AREA ]]
                   [AREAS]
[[ORGANIZATION IS] SEQUENTIAL]
[PADDING CHARACTER IS {data-name-1}]
                      {literal-1  }
[RECORD DELIMITER IS {STANDARD-1        }]
                     {implementor-name-2}
[ACCESS MODE IS SEQUENTIAL]
[FILE STATUS IS data-name-2].
```

Sort or Merge File

```
SELECT file-name-1 ASSIGN TO {implementor-name-1} . . .
                             {literal-1         }
```

DATA DIVISION Formats

```
[DATA DIVISION.
[FILE SECTION.
    [file-description-entry {record-description entry} . . .                  ]     ]
    [sort-merge-file-description-entry {record-description-entry} . . .        ] . . . ]
    [report-file-description-entry                                             ]     ]
[WORKING-STORAGE SECTION.
    [77-level-description-entry] . . . ]
    [record-description-entry  ]
[LINKAGE SECTION.
    [77-level-description-entry] . . . ]
    [record-description-entry  ]
[COMMUNICATION SECTION.
    [communication-description-entry {record-description-entry} . . . ]
[REPORT SECTION.
    [report-description-entry
    {report-group-description-entry} . . . ] . . . ]]
```

FILE DESCRIPTION ENTRY Formats

Sequential File

```
FD file-name-1
  [IS EXTERNAL]
  [IS GLOBAL]
  [BLOCK CONTAINS [integer-1 TO] integer-2 {RECORDS   }]
                                           {CHARACTERS}
  [        {CONTAINS integer-3 CHARACTERS                                         }]
  [RECORD  {IS VARYING IN SIZE [[FROM integer-4] [TO integer-5] CHARACTERS]        }]
  [        {    [DEPENDING ON data-name-1]                                         }]
  [        {CONTAINS integer-6 TO integer-7 CHARACTERS                             }]
```

```
[LABEL {RECORD IS | RECORDS ARE} {STANDARD | OMITTED}]
[VALUE OF {implementor-name-1 IS {data-name-2 | literal-1}} . . .]
[DATA {RECORD IS | RECORDS ARE} {data-name-3} . . .]
[LINAGE IS {data-name-4 | integer-8} LINES [WITH FOOTING AT {data-name-5 | integer-9}]
    [LINES AT TOP {data-name-6 | integer-10}] [LINES AT BOTTOM {data-name-7 | integer-11}]]

[CODE-SET IS alphabet-name-1].
```

Relative File

```
FD file-name-1
 [IS EXTERNAL]
 [IS GLOBAL]
 [BLOCK CONTAINS [integer-1 TO] integer-2 {RECORDS | CHARACTERS}]
 [RECORD { CONTAINS integer-3 CHARACTERS
         | IS VARYING IN SIZE [[FROM integer-4] [TO integer-5] CHARACTERS]
              [DEPENDING ON data-name-1]
         | CONTAINS integer-6 TO integer-7 CHARACTERS }]
 [LABEL {RECORD IS | RECORDS ARE} {STANDARD | OMITTED}]
 [VALUE OF {implementor-name-1 IS {data-name-2 | literal-1}} . . .]
 [DATA {RECORD IS | RECORDS ARE} {data-name-3} . . .].
```

Indexed File

```
FD file-name-1
 [IS EXTERNAL]
 [IS GLOBAL]
 [BLOCK CONTAINS [integer-1 TO] integer-2 {RECORDS | CHARACTERS}]
 [RECORD { CONTAINS integer-3 CHARACTERS
         | IS VARYING IN SIZE [[FROM integer-4] [TO integer-5] CHARACTERS]
              [DEPENDING ON data-name-1]
         | CONTAINS integer-6 TO integer-7 CHARACTERS }]
 [LABEL {RECORD IS | RECORDS ARE} {STANDARD | OMITTED}]
 [VALUE OF {implementor-name-1 IS {data-name-2 | literal-1}} . . .]
 [DATA {RECORD IS | RECORDS ARE} {data-name-3} . . .].
```

Report File

```
FD file-name-1
   [IS EXTERNAL]
   [IS GLOBAL]
   [BLOCK CONTAINS [integer-1 TO] integer-2 {RECORDS   }]
                                            {CHARACTERS}
   [RECORD {CONTAINS integer-3 CHARACTERS               }]
           {CONTAINS integer-4 TO integer-5 CHARACTERS  }
   [LABEL {RECORD IS  } {STANDARD}]
          {RECORDS ARE} {OMITTED }
   [VALUE OF {implementor-name-1 IS {data-name-2}} . . . ]
                                    {literal-1  }
   [CODE-SET IS alphabet-name-1]
   {REPORT IS  } {report-name-1} . . . .
   {REPORTS ARE}
```

Sort-Merge File

```
SD file-name-1
   [        ( CONTAINS integer-1 CHARACTERS                                      )]
   [RECORD  ( IS VARYING IN SIZE [[FROM integer-2] [TO integer-3 CHARACTERS]     )]
   [        (     [DEPENDING ON data-name-1]                                     )]
   [        ( CONTAINS integer-4 TO integer-5 CHARACTERS                         )]
   [DATA {RECORD IS  } {data-name-2} . . . ].
         {RECORDS ARE}
```

DATA DESCRIPTION ENTRY Formats

Format 1

```
level-number [data-name-1]
             [FILLER     ]
             [REDEFINES data-name-2]
             [IS EXTERNAL]
             [IS GLOBAL]
             [{PICTURE} IS character-string]
             [{PIC    }                    ]
             [             {INDEX          }]
             [             {DISPLAY        }]
             [[USAGE IS]   {COMPUTATIONAL  }]
             [             {COMP           }]
             [             {BINARY         }]
             [             {PACKED-DECIMAL }]
             [[SIGN IS] {LEADING } [SEPARATE CHARACTER]]
                        {TRAILING}
             [OCCURS {integer-1 TO integer-2 TIMES DEPENDING ON data-name-4}
                     {integer-2 TIMES                                       }
                    [{ASCENDING } KEY IS {data-name-3} . . . ] . . .
                    [{DESCENDING}                           ]
                    [INDEXED BY {index-name-1} . . .]]
             [{SYNCHRONIZED} [LEFT ]]
             [{SYNC        } [RIGHT]]
             [{JUSTIFIED} RIGHT]
             [{JUST     }      ]
             [BLANK WHEN ZERO]
             [VALUE IS literal-1].
```

Format 2

66 data-name-1 RENAMES data-name-2 [{THROUGH | THRU} data-name-3].

Format 3

88 condition-name-1 {VALUE IS | VALUES ARE} {literal-1 [{THROUGH | THRU} literal-2]} . . . .

COMMUNICATION DESCRIPTION ENTRY Formats

Format 1

```
CD cd-name-1

                    [[SYMBOLIC QUEUE IS data-name-1]
                         [SYMBOLIC SUB-QUEUE-1 IS data-name-2]
                         [SYMBOLIC SUB-QUEUE-2 IS data-name-3]
                         [SYMBOLIC SUB-QUEUE-3 IS data-name-4]
                         [MESSAGE DATE IS data-name-5]
                         [MESSAGE TIME IS data-name-6]
FOR [INITIAL] INPUT      [SYMBOLIC SOURCE IS data-name-7]
                         [TEXT LENGTH IS data-name-8]
                         [END KEY IS data-name-9]
                         [STATUS KEY IS data-name-10]
                         [MESSAGE COUNT IS data-name-11]]
                    [data-name-1, data-name-2, data-name-3, data-name-4, data-name-5, data-name-6,
                         data-name-7, data-name-8, data-name-9, data-name-10, data-name-11]
```

Format 2

```
CD cd-name-1 FOR OUTPUT
     [DESTINATION COUNT IS data-name-1]
     [TEXT LENGTH IS data-name-2]
     [STATUS KEY IS data-name-3]
     [DESTINATION TABLE OCCURS integer-1 TIMES [INDEXED BY {index-name-1} . . . ]]
     [ERROR KEY IS data-name-4]
     [SYMBOLIC DESTINATION IS data-name-5].
```

Format 3

```
CD cd-name-1
                    [[MESSAGE DATE IS data-name-1]
                         [MESSAGE TIME IS data-name-2]
                         [SYMBOLIC TERMINAL IS data-name-3]
FOR [INITIAL] I-O        [TEXT LENGTH IS data-name-4]
                         [END KEY IS data-name-5]
                         [STATUS KEY IS data-name-6]]
                    [data-name-1, data-name-2, data-name-3, data-name-4, data-name-5, data-name-6]
```

REPORT DESCRIPTION ENTRY Format

```
RD report-name-1
  [IS GLOBAL]
  [CODE literal-1]
  [ {CONTROL IS   } { {data-name-1} . . .          } ]
  [ {CONTROLS ARE } { FINAL [data-name-1] . . .    } ]
  [ PAGE [LIMIT IS  ] integer-1 [LINE ] [HEADING integer-2]
  [      [LIMITS ARE]           [LINES]
            [FIRST DETAIL integer-3] [LAST DETAIL integer-4]
            [FOOTING integer-5] ]
```

REPORT GROUP DESCRIPTION ENTRY Formats

Format 1

```
01  [data-name-1]
             { {REPORT HEADING}                                }
             { {RH            }                                }
             { {PAGE HEADING}                                  }
             { {PH          }                                  }
             { {CONTROL HEADING} {data-name-2}                 }
             { {CH             } {FINAL      }                 }
    TYPE IS  { {DETAIL}                                        }
             { {DE    }                                        }
             { {CONTROL FOOTING} {data-name-3}                 }
             { {CF             } {FINAL      }                 }
             { {PAGE FOOTING}                                  }
             { {PF          }                                  }
             { {REPORT FOOTING}                                }
             { {RF            }                                }
    [ LINE NUMBER IS {integer-1 [ON NEXT PAGE]} ]
    [                {PLUS integer-2          } ]
    [                 {integer-3     } ]
    [ NEXT GROUP IS   {PLUS integer-4} ]
    [                 {NEXT PAGE     } ]
    [[USAGE IS] DISPLAY].
```

Format 2

```
level-number [data-name-1]
    [ LINE NUMBER IS {integer-1 [ON NEXT PAGE]} ]
    [                {PLUS integer-2          } ]
    [[USAGE IS] DISPLAY].
```

Format 3

```
level-number [data-name-1]
 {PICTURE}
 {PIC    } IS character-string
 [[USAGE IS] DISPLAY]
 [[SIGN IS] {LEADING } SEPARATE CHARACTER]
 [          {TRAILING}                   ]
 [{JUSTIFIED} RIGHT]
 [{JUST     }      ]
 [BLANK WHEN ZERO]
 [LINE NUMBER IS {integer-1 [ON NEXT PAGE]}]
 [               {PLUS integer-2          }]
 [COLUMN NUMBER IS integer-3]
 { SOURCE IS identifier-1                                       }
 { VALUE IS literal-1                                           }
 { {SUM {identifier-2} . . . [UPON {data-name-2} . . . ]} . . . }
 {      [RESET ON {data-name-3}]                                }
 {      [         {FINAL      }]                                }
 [GROUP INDICATE].
```

■ PROCEDURE DIVISION Formats

Format 1

```
[PROCEDURE DIVISION [USING {data-name-1} . . . ] .
[DECLARATIVES.
    {section-name SECTION [segment-number].
        USE statement.
    [paragraph-name.
        [sentence] . . . ] . . . } . . .
 END DECLARATIVES.]
{section-name SECTION [segment-number].
[paragraph-name.
    [sentence] . . . ] . . . } . . . ]
```

Format 2

```
[PROCEDURE DIVISION [USING {data-name-1} . . . ].
 {paragraph-name.
    [sentence] . . . } . . . ]
```

Formats for COBOL Verbs

```
ACCEPT identifier-1 [FROM mnemonic-name-1]

                              { DATE        }
ACCEPT identifier-2 FROM      { DAY         }
                              { DAY-OF-WEEK }
                              { TIME        }

ACCEPT cd-name-1 MESSAGE COUNT

    {identifier-1}
ADD {literal-1   } . . . TO {identifier-2 [ROUNDED]} . . .
    [ON SIZE ERROR imperative-statement-1]
    [NOT ON SIZE ERROR imperative-statement-2]
    [END-ADD]

    {identifier-1}         {identifier-2}
ADD {literal-1   } . . . TO {literal-2   } GIVING {identifier-3 [ROUNDED]} . . .
    [ON SIZE ERROR imperative-statement-1]
    [NOT ON SIZE ERROR imperative-statement-2]
    [END-ADD]

    {CORRESPONDING}
ADD {CORR         } identifier-1 TO identifier-2 [ROUNDED]
    [ON SIZE ERROR imperative-statement-1]
    [NOT ON SIZE ERROR imperative-statement-2]
    [END-ADD]

ALTER {procedure-name-1 TO [PROCEED TO] procedure-name-2} . . .

     {identifier-1} [       {[BY REFERENCE] {identifier-2} . . .}      ]
CALL {literal-1   } [ USING {BY CONTENT {identifier-2} . . .     } . . . ]
     [ON OVERFLOW imperative-statement-1] [END-CALL]

     {identifier-1} [       {[BY REFERENCE] {identifier-2} . . .}      ]
CALL {literal-1   } [ USING {BY CONTENT {identifier-2} . . .     } . . . ]
     [ON EXCEPTION imperative-statement-1]
     [NOT ON EXCEPTION imperative-statement-2]
     [END-CALL]

       {identifier-1}
CANCEL {literal-1   } . . .

      {              [ {REEL} [FOR REMOVAL]   ] }
CLOSE { file-name-1  [ {UNIT}                 ] } . . .
      {              [      {NO REWIND}       ] }
      {              [ WITH {LOCK     }       ] }

CLOSE {file-name-1 [WITH LOCK]} . . .
COMPUTE {identifier-1 [ROUNDED]} . . . = arithmetic-expression-1
    [ON SIZE ERROR imperative-statement-1]
    [NOT ON SIZE ERROR imperative-statement-2]
    [END-COMPUTE]
CONTINUE
DELETE file-name-1 RECORD
    [INVALID KEY imperative-statement-1]
    [NOT INVALID KEY imperative-statement-2]
    [END-DELETE]

        {INPUT [TERMINAL]}
DISABLE {I-O TERMINAL    } cd-name-1 [ WITH KEY {identifier-1} ]
        {OUTPUT          }           [          {literal-1   } ]

        {identifier-1}
DISPLAY {literal-1   } . . . [UPON mnemonic-name-1] [WITH NO ADVANCING]
```

```
DIVIDE {identifier-1} INTO {identifier-2 [ROUNDED]} . . .
       {literal-1   }
    [ON SIZE ERROR imperative-statement-1]
    [NOT ON SIZE ERROR imperative-statement-2]
    [END-DIVIDE]

DIVIDE {identifier-1} {INTO} {identifier-2} GIVING {identifier-3 [ROUNDED]} . . .
       {literal-1   } {BY  } {literal-2   }
    [ON SIZE ERROR imperative-statement-1]
    [NOT ON SIZE ERROR imperative-statement-2]
    [END-DIVIDE]

DIVIDE {identifier-1} {INTO} {identifier-2} GIVING identifier-3 [ROUNDED]
       {literal-1   } {BY  } {literal-2   }
    REMAINDER identifier-4
    [ON SIZE ERROR imperative-statement-1]
    [NOT ON SIZE ERROR imperative-statement-2]
    [END-DIVIDE]

       {INPUT [TERMINAL]}
ENABLE {I-O TERMINAL    } cd-name-1 [WITH KEY {identifier-1}]
       {OUTPUT          }                     {literal-1   }

ENTER language-name-1 [routine-name-1]

         {identifier-1}        {identifier-2}
         {literal-1   }        {literal-2   }
EVALUATE {expression-1} [ALSO  {expression-2}] . . .
         {TRUE        }        {TRUE        }
         {FALSE       }        {FALSE       }

{ {WHEN
  {   {ANY
  {   {condition-1
  {   {TRUE
  {   {FALSE
  {   {[NOT] {{identifier-3              }} [{THROUGH} {identifier-4              }]}
  {   {      {{literal-3                 }} [{THRU   } {literal-4                 }]}
  {   {      {{arithmetic-expression-1   }} [          {arithmetic-expression-2   }]}
  {
  { [ALSO
  {   {ANY
  {   {condition-2
  {   {TRUE
  {   {FALSE
  {   {[NOT] {{identifier-5              }} [{THROUGH} {identifier-6              }]}
  {   {      {{literal-5                 }} [{THRU   } {literal-6                 }]}
  {   {      {{arithmetic-expression-3   }} [          {arithmetic-expression-4   }]}  ] . . . } . . .
{
  imperative-statement-1} . . .
    [WHEN OTHER imperative-statement-2]
    [END-EVALUATE]

EXIT
EXIT PROGRAM

GENERATE {data-name-1  }
         {report-name-1}

GO TO [procedure-name-1]
```

```
GO TO {procedure-name-1} . . . DEPENDING ON identifier-1

IF condition-1 THEN { {statement-1} . . . } [ { ELSE {statement-2} . . . [END-IF] } ]
                    { NEXT SENTENCE       } [ { ELSE NEXT SENTENCE                 } ]
                                            [ { END-IF                             } ]

INITIALIZE {identifier-1} . . .
    [ REPLACING { { ALPHABETIC             }                 {identifier-2} } . . . ]
    [           { { ALPHANUMERIC           }                 {literal-1   } }       ]
    [           { { NUMERIC                }  DATA BY                       }       ]
    [           { { ALPHANUMERIC-EDITED    }                                }       ]
    [           { { NUMERIC-EDITED         }                                }       ]

INITIATE {report-name-1} . . .

INSPECT identifier-1 TALLYING
    { identifier-2 FOR { CHARACTERS [ {BEFORE} INITIAL {identifier-4} ] . . .                                  } } . . . } . . .
    {                  {            [ {AFTER }         {literal-2   } ]                                        }
    {                  { {ALL    } { {identifier-3} [ {BEFORE} INITIAL {identifier-4} ] . . . } . . .          }
    {                  { {LEADING} { {literal-1   } [ {AFTER }         {literal-2   } ]       }                }

INSPECT identifier-1 REPLACING
    { CHARACTERS BY {identifier-5} [ {BEFORE} INITIAL {identifier-4} ] . . .                                          } . . .
    {               {literal-3   } [ {AFTER }         {literal-2   } ]                                                }
    { {ALL    } { {identifier-3} BY {identifier-5} [ {BEFORE} INITIAL {identifier-4} ] . . . } . . .                  }
    { {LEADING} { {literal-1   }    {literal-3   } [ {AFTER }         {literal-2   } ]       }                        }
    { {FIRST  }                                                                                                       }

INSPECT identifier-1 TALLYING
    { identifier-2 FOR { CHARACTERS [ {BEFORE} INITIAL {identifier-4} ] . . .                                  } } . . . } . . .
    {                  {            [ {AFTER }         {literal-2   } ]                                        }
    {                  { {ALL    } { {identifier-3} [ {BEFORE} INITIAL {identifier-4} ] . . . } . . .          }
    {                  { {LEADING} { {literal-1   } [ {AFTER }         {literal-2   } ]       }                }
  REPLACING
    { CHARACTERS BY {identifier-5} [ {BEFORE} INITIAL {identifier-4} ] . . .                                          } . . .
    {               {literal-3   } [ {AFTER }         {literal-2   } ]                                                }
    { {ALL    } { {identifier-3} BY {identifier-5} [ {BEFORE} INITIAL {identifier-4} ] . . . } . . .                  }
    { {LEADING} { {literal-1   }    {literal-3   } [ {AFTER }         {literal-2   } ]       }                        }
    { {FIRST  }                                                                                                       }

INSPECT identifier-1 CONVERTING {identifier-6} TO {identifier-7}
                                {literal-4   }    {literal-5   }
    [ {BEFORE} INITIAL {identifier-4} ] . . .
    [ {AFTER }         {literal-2   } ]

MERGE file-name-1 { ON {ASCENDING } KEY {data-name-1} . . . } . . .
                  {    {DESCENDING}                         }
    [COLLATING SEQUENCE IS alphabet-name-1]
    USING file-name-2 {file-name-3} . . .
    { OUTPUT PROCEDURE IS procedure-name-1 [ {THROUGH} procedure-name-2 ] }
    {                                      [ {THRU   }                  ] }
    { GIVING {file-name-4} . . .                                          }

MOVE {identifier-1} TO {identifier-2} . . .
     {literal-1   }

MOVE {CORRESPONDING} identifier-1 TO identifier-2
     {CORR         }
```

```
MULTIPLY {identifier-1} BY {identifier-2 [ROUNDED]} . . .
         {literal-1   }

    [ON SIZE ERROR imperative-statement-1]
    [NOT ON SIZE ERROR imperative-statement-2]
    [END-MULTIPLY]

MULTIPLY {identifier-1} BY {identifier-2} GIVING {identifier-3 [ROUNDED]} . . .
         {literal-1   }    {literal-2   }

    [ON SIZE ERROR imperative-statement-1]
    [NOT ON SIZE ERROR imperative-statement-2]
    [END-MULTIPLY]

       { INPUT {file-name-1 [REVERSED      ]} . . .            }
       {                    [WITH NO REWIND]                   }
OPEN   { OUTPUT {file-name-2 [WITH NO REWIND]} . . .           } . . .
       { I-O {file-name-3} . . .                               }
       { EXTEND {file-name-4} . . .                            }

OPEN {OUTPUT {file-name-1 [WITH NO REWIND]} . . .} . . .
     {EXTEND {file-name-2} . . .                 }

PERFORM [procedure-name-1 [{THROUGH} procedure-name-2]]
                          [{THRU   }                 ]
    [imperative-statement-1 END-PERFORM]

PERFORM [procedure-name-1 [{THROUGH} procedure-name-2]]
                          [{THRU   }                 ]
    {identifier-1} TIMES [imperative-statement-1 END-PERFORM]
    {integer-1   }

PERFORM [procedure-name-1 [{THROUGH} procedure-name-2]]
                          [{THRU   }                 ]
    [WITH TEST {BEFORE}] UNTIL condition-1
    [          {AFTER }]
    [imperative-statement-1 END-PERFORM]

PERFORM [procedure-name-1 [{THROUGH} procedure-name-2]]
                          [{THRU   }                 ]
    [WITH TEST {BEFORE}]
    [          {AFTER }]

                                  {identifier-3  }
    VARYING {identifier-2  } FROM {index-name-2  } BY {identifier-4} UNTIL condition-1
            {index-name-1  }      {literal-1     }    {literal-2   }

                                  {identifier-6  }
    [AFTER  {identifier-5  } FROM {index-name-4  } BY {identifier-7} UNTIL condition-2] . . .
    [       {index-name-3  }      {literal-3     }    {literal-4   }                  ]

    [imperative-statement-1 END-PERFORM]

PURGE cd-name-1

READ file-name-1 [NEXT] RECORD [INTO identifier-1]
    [AT END imperative-statement-1]
    [NOT AT END imperative-statement-2]
    [END-READ]

READ file-name-1 RECORD [INTO identifier-1]
    [INVALID KEY imperative-statement-3]
    [NOT INVALID KEY imperative-statement-4]
    [END-READ]
```

```
READ file-name-1 RECORD [INTO identifier-1]
     [KEY IS data-name-1]
     [INVALID KEY imperative-statement-3]
     [NOT INVALID KEY imperative-statement-4]
     [END-READ]

RECEIVE cd-name-1 {MESSAGE} INTO identifier-1
                  {SEGMENT}
     [NO DATA imperative-statement-1]
     [WITH DATA imperative-statement-2]
     [END-RECEIVE]

RELEASE record-name-1 [FROM identifier-1]

RETURN file-name-1 RECORD [INTO identifier-1]
     AT END imperative-statement-1
     [NOT AT END imperative-statement-2]
     [END-RETURN]

REWRITE record-name-1 [FROM identifier-1]

REWRITE record-name-1 [FROM identifier-1]
     [INVALID KEY imperative-statement-1]
     [NOT INVALID KEY imperative-statement-2]
     [END-REWRITE]

SEARCH identifier-1 [VARYING {identifier-2  }]
                             {index-name-1  }
     [AT END imperative-statement-1]
     {WHEN condition-1 {imperative-statement-2}} . . .
                       {NEXT SENTENCE         }
     [END-SEARCH]

SEARCH ALL identifier-1 [AT END imperative-statement-1]
          { data-name-1 {IS EQUAL TO} {identifier-3             } }
     WHEN {             {IS =       } {literal-1                } }
          {                           {arithmetic-expression-1  } }
          { condition-name-1                                      }
   [      { data-name-2 {IS EQUAL TO} {identifier-4             } } ]
   [  AND {             {IS =       } {literal-2                } } ] . . .
   [      {                           {arithmetic-expression-2  } } ]
   [      { condition-name-2                                      } ]
     {imperative-statement-2}
     {NEXT SENTENCE         }
     [END-SEARCH]

SEND cd-name-1 FROM identifier-1

                                       { WITH identifier-2 }
SEND cd-name-1 [FROM identifier-1]     { WITH ESI          }
                                       { WITH EMI          }
                                       { WITH EGI          }
   [                      { {identifier-3} [LINE ] } ]
   [ {BEFORE}             { {integer-1   } [LINES] } ]
   [ {AFTER } ADVANCING   {                        } ]
   [                      { {mnemonic-name-1}      } ]
   [                      { {PAGE           }      } ]
     [REPLACING LINE]

                              {index-name-2}
SET {index-name-1} . . . TO   {identifier-2}
    {identifier-1}            {integer-1   }

SET {index-name-3} . . . {UP BY  } {identifier-2}
                         {DOWN BY} {integer-2   }

SET {{mnemonic-name-1} . . . TO {ON }} . . .
                                {OFF}

SET {condition-name-1} . . . TO TRUE
```

```
SORT file-name-1 {ON {ASCENDING | DESCENDING} KEY {data-name-1} . . .} . . .
    [WITH DUPLICATES IN ORDER]
    [COLLATING SEQUENCE IS alphabet-name-1]
    { INPUT PROCEDURE IS procedure-name-1 [{THROUGH | THRU} procedure-name-2] }
    { USING {file-name-2} . . .                                              }
    { OUTPUT PROCEDURE IS procedure-name-3 [{THROUGH | THRU} procedure-name-4] }
    { GIVING {file-name-3} . . .                                               }

START file-name-1 [ KEY IS { EQUAL TO                    } data-name-1 ]
                           { =                           }
                           { GREATER THAN                }
                           { >                           }
                           { NOT LESS THAN               }
                           { NOT <                       }
                           { GREATER THAN OR EQUAL TO    }
                           { >=                          }
    [INVALID KEY imperative-statement-1]
    [NOT INVALID KEY imperative-statement-2]
    [END-START]

STOP {RUN | literal-1}

STRING {{identifier-1 | literal-1} . . . DELIMITED BY {identifier-2 | literal-2 | SIZE}} . . . INTO identifier-3
    [WITH POINTER identifier-4]
    [ON OVERFLOW imperative-statement-1]
    [NOT ON OVERFLOW imperative-statement-2]
    [END-STRING]

SUBTRACT {identifier-1 | literal-1} . . . FROM {identifier-3 [ROUNDED]} . . .
    [ON SIZE ERROR imperative-statement-1]
    [NOT ON SIZE ERROR imperative-statement-2]
    [END-SUBTRACT]

SUBTRACT {identifier-1 | literal-1} . . . FROM {identifier-2 | literal-2} GIVING {identifier-3 [ROUNDED]} . . .
    [ON SIZE ERROR imperative-statement-1]
    [NOT ON SIZE ERROR imperative-statement-2]
    [END-SUBTRACT]

SUBTRACT {CORRESPONDING | CORR} identifier-1 FROM identifier-2 [ROUNDED]
    [ON SIZE ERROR imperative-statement-1]
    [NOT ON SIZE ERROR imperative-statement-2]
    [END-SUBTRACT]

SUPPRESS PRINTING

TERMINATE {report-name-1} . . .

UNSTRING identifier-1 [DELIMITED BY [ALL] {identifier-2 | literal-1} [OR [ALL] {identifier-3 | literal-2}] . . .]
    INTO {identifier-4 [DELIMITER IN identifier-5] [COUNT IN identifier-6]} . . .
    [WITH POINTER identifier-7]
    [TALLYING IN identifier-8]
    [ON OVERFLOW imperative-statement-1]
    [NOT ON OVERFLOW imperative-statement-2]
    [END-UNSTRING]
```

```
                                                        ⎧ {file-name-1} . . . ⎫
                                                        ⎪ INPUT               ⎪
USE [GLOBAL] AFTER STANDARD {EXCEPTION} PROCEDURE ON    ⎨ OUTPUT              ⎬
                            {ERROR    }                 ⎪ I-O                 ⎪
                                                        ⎩ EXTEND              ⎭

                                                   ⎧ {file-name-3} . . . ⎫
USE AFTER STANDARD {EXCEPTION} PROCEDURE ON        ⎨ OUTPUT              ⎬
                   {ERROR    }                     ⎩ EXTEND              ⎭

USE [GLOBAL] BEFORE REPORTING identifier-1

                         ⎧ cd-name-1                            ⎫
                         ⎪ [ALL REFERENCES OF] identifier-1     ⎪
USE FOR DEBUGGING ON     ⎨ file-name-1                          ⎬ . . .
                         ⎪ procedure-name-1                     ⎪
                         ⎩ ALL PROCEDURES                       ⎭

WRITE record-name-1 [FROM identifier-1]
   ⎡                       ⎧ {identifier-2} [LINE ]  ⎫ ⎤
   ⎢ {BEFORE}  ADVANCING   ⎨ {integer-1   } [LINES]  ⎬ ⎥
   ⎢ {AFTER }              ⎪ {mnemonic-name-1}       ⎪ ⎥
   ⎣                       ⎩ {PAGE           }       ⎭ ⎦
   [AT {END-OF-PAGE} imperative-statement-1]
       {EOP        }
   [NOT AT {END-OF-PAGE} imperative-statement-2]
           {EOP        }
   [END-WRITE]

WRITE record-name-1 [FROM identifier-1]
   [INVALID KEY imperative-statement-1]
   [NOT INVALID KEY imperative-statement-2]
   [END-WRITE]
```

COPY and REPLACE Statement Formats

```
COPY text-name-1 [{OF} library-name-1]
                  {IN}
   ⎡            ⎧ ⎧ ==pseudo-text-1== ⎫      ⎧ ==pseudo-text-2== ⎫ ⎫       ⎤
   ⎢ REPLACING  ⎨ ⎨ identifier-1      ⎬  BY  ⎨ identifier-2      ⎬ ⎬ . . . ⎥
   ⎢            ⎪ ⎪ literal-1         ⎪      ⎪ literal-2         ⎪ ⎪       ⎥
   ⎣            ⎩ ⎩ word-1            ⎭      ⎩ word-2            ⎭ ⎭       ⎦

REPLACE {==pseudo-text-1== BY ==pseudo-text-2==} . . .
REPLACE OFF
```

Condition Formats

Relation Condition

```
                               ⎧ IS [NOT] GREATER THAN         ⎫
                               ⎪ IS [NOT] >                    ⎪
                               ⎪ IS [NOT] LESS THAN            ⎪
⎧ identifier-1            ⎫    ⎪ IS [NOT] <                    ⎪    ⎧ identifier-2            ⎫
⎪ literal-1               ⎪    ⎨ IS [NOT] EQUAL TO             ⎬    ⎪ literal-2               ⎪
⎨ arithmetic-expression-1 ⎬    ⎪ IS [NOT] =                    ⎪    ⎨ arithmetic-expression-2 ⎬
⎩ index-name-1            ⎭    ⎪ IS GREATER THAN OR EQUAL TO   ⎪    ⎩ index-name-2            ⎭
                               ⎪ IS >=                         ⎪
                               ⎪ IS LESS THAN OR EQUAL TO      ⎪
                               ⎩ IS <=                         ⎭
```

Class Condition

$$\text{identifier IS } [\underline{\text{NOT}}] \left\{ \begin{array}{l} \underline{\text{NUMERIC}} \\ \underline{\text{ALPHABETIC}} \\ \underline{\text{ALPHABETIC-LOWER}} \\ \underline{\text{ALPHABETIC-UPPER}} \\ \text{class-name} \end{array} \right\}$$

Sign Condition

$$\text{arithmetic-expression IS } [\underline{\text{NOT}}] \left\{ \begin{array}{l} \underline{\text{POSITIVE}} \\ \underline{\text{NEGATIVE}} \\ \underline{\text{ZERO}} \end{array} \right\}$$

Condition-name Condition

condition-name-1

Negated Condition

$\underline{\text{NOT}}$ condition-1

Switch-status Condition

condition-name-1

Combined Condition

$$\text{condition-1} \left\{ \left\{ \begin{array}{l} \underline{\text{AND}} \\ \underline{\text{OR}} \end{array} \right\} \text{ condition-2} \right\} \ldots$$

Abbreviated Combined Relation Condition

$$\text{relation-condition} \left\{ \left\{ \begin{array}{l} \underline{\text{AND}} \\ \underline{\text{OR}} \end{array} \right\} [\underline{\text{NOT}}] \text{ [relational-operator] object} \right\} \ldots$$

Qualification Formats

Format 1

$$\left\{ \begin{array}{l} \text{data-name-1} \\ \text{condition-name} \end{array} \right\} \left\{ \begin{array}{l} \left\{ \left\{ \begin{array}{l} \underline{\text{IN}} \\ \underline{\text{OF}} \end{array} \right\} \text{ data-name-2} \right\} \ldots \left[\left\{ \begin{array}{l} \underline{\text{IN}} \\ \underline{\text{OF}} \end{array} \right\} \left\{ \begin{array}{l} \text{file-name} \\ \text{cd-name} \end{array} \right\} \right] \\ \left\{ \begin{array}{l} \underline{\text{IN}} \\ \underline{\text{OF}} \end{array} \right\} \left\{ \begin{array}{l} \text{file-name} \\ \text{cd-name} \end{array} \right\} \end{array} \right\}$$

Format 2

$$\text{paragraph-name} \left\{ \begin{array}{l} \underline{\text{IN}} \\ \underline{\text{OF}} \end{array} \right\} \text{ section-name}$$

Format 3

$$\text{text-name} \left\{ \begin{array}{l} \underline{\text{IN}} \\ \underline{\text{OF}} \end{array} \right\} \text{ library-name}$$

Format 4

LINAGE-COUNTER {IN | OF} report-name

Format 5

{PAGE-COUNTER | LINE-COUNTER} {IN | OF} report-name

Format 6

data-name-3 { {IN | OF} data-name-4 [{IN | OF} report-name] | {IN | OF} report-name }

Miscellaneous Formats

Subscripting

{condition-name-1 | data-name-1} ({integer-1 | data-name-2 [{±} integer-2] | index-name-1 [{±} integer-3]} . . .)

Reference Modification

data-name-1 (leftmost-character-position: [length])

Identifier

data-name-1 [{IN | OF} data-name-2] . . . [{IN | OF} {cd-name | file-name | report-name}]

[({subscript} . . .)] [(leftmost-character-position: [length])]

General Format for Nested Source Programs

IDENTIFICATION DIVISION.
PROGRAM-ID. program-name-1 [IS INITIAL PROGRAM].
[ENVIRONMENT DIVISION. environment-division-content]
[DATA DIVISION. data-division-content]
[PROCEDURE DIVISION. procedure-division-content]
[[nested-source-program] . . .
END PROGRAM program-name-1.]

General Format for Nested-Source-Program

IDENTIFICATION DIVISION.

PROGRAM-ID. program-name-2 [IS { | COMMON | INITIAL | } PROGRAM].

[ENVIRONMENT DIVISION. environment-division-content]
[DATA DIVISION. data-division-content]
[PROCEDURE DIVISION. procedure-division-content]
[nested-source-program] . . .
END PROGRAM program-name-2.

General Format for Multiple Source Programs

{IDENTIFICATION DIVISION.
PROGRAM-ID. program-name-3 [IS INITIAL PROGRAM].
[ENVIRONMENT DIVISION. environment-division-content]
[DATA DIVISION. data-division-content]
[PROCEDURE DIVISION. procedure-division-content]
[nested-source-program] . . .
END PROGRAM program-name-3} . . .
IDENTIFICATION DIVISION.
PROGRAM-ID. program-name-4 [IS INITIAL PROGRAM].
[ENVIRONMENT DIVISION. environment-division-content]
[DATA DIVISION. data-division-content]
[PROCEDURE DIVISION. procedure-division-content]
[[nested-source-program] . . .
END PROGRAM program-name-4.]

Appendix F

ANSI COBOL 1985 Reserved Words

ACCEPT
ACCESS
ADD
ADVANCING
AFTER
ALL
ALPHABET
ALPHABETIC
ALPHABETIC-LOWER
ALPHABETIC-UPPER
ALPHANUMERIC
ALPHANUMERIC-EDITED
ALSO
ALTER
ALTERNATE
AND
ANY
ARE
AREA
AREAS
ASCENDING
ASSIGN
AT
AUTHOR

BEFORE
BINARY
BLANK
BLOCK
BOTTOM
BY

CALL
CANCEL
CD
CF
CH
CHARACTER
CHARACTERS
CLASS
CLOCK-UNITS
CLOSE
COBOL
CODE
CODE-SET
COLLATING
COLUMN
COMMA
COMMON
COMMUNICATION
COMP
COMPUTATIONAL
COMPUTE
CONFIGURATION
CONTAINS
CONTENT
CONTINUE
CONTROL
CONTROLS
CONVERTING
COPY
CORR
CORRESPONDING
COUNT
CURRENCY

DATA
DATE
DATE-COMPILED
DATE-WRITTEN
DAY
DAY-OF-WEEK
DE
DEBUG-CONTENTS
DEBUG-ITEM
DEBUG-LINE
DEBUG-NAME
DEBUG-SUB-1
DEBUG-SUB-2
DEBUG-SUB-3
DEBUGGING
DECIMAL-POINT
DECLARATIVES
DELETE
DELIMITED
DELIMITER
DEPENDING
DESCENDING
DESTINATION
DETAIL
DISABLE
DISPLAY
DIVIDE
DIVISION
DOWN
DUPLICATES
DYNAMIC

EGI
ELSE
EMI
ENABLE
END
END-ADD
END-CALL
END-COMPUTE
END-DELETE
END-DIVIDE
END-EVALUATE
END-IF
END-MULTIPLY
END-OF-PAGE
END-PERFORM
END-READ
END-RECEIVE
END-RETURN
END-REWRITE
END-SEARCH
END-START
END-STRING
END-SUBTRACT
END-UNSTRING
END-WRITE
ENTER
ENVIRONMENT
EOP
EQUAL
ERROR
ESI
EVALUATE
EVERY
EXCEPTION
EXIT
EXTEND
EXTERNAL

FALSE
FD
FILE
FILE-CONTROL
FILLER
FINAL
FIRST
FOOTING
FOR
FROM

GENERATE
GIVING
GLOBAL
GO
GREATER
GROUP

HEADING
HIGH-VALUE
HIGH-VALUES

I-O
I-O-CONTROL
IDENTIFICATION
IF
IN
INDEX
INDEXED
INDICATE
INITIAL
INITIALIZE
INITIATE
INPUT
INPUT-OUTPUT
INSPECT
INSTALLATION
INTO
INVALID
IS

JUST
JUSTIFIED

KEY

LABEL
LAST
LEADING
LEFT
LENGTH
LESS
LIMIT
LIMITS
LINAGE
LINAGE-COUNTER
LINE
LINE-COUNTER
LINES

LINKAGE
LOCK
LOW-VALUE
LOW-VALUES

MEMORY
MERGE
MESSAGE
MODE
MODULES
MOVE
MULTIPLE
MULTIPLY

NATIVE
NEGATIVE
NEXT
NO
NOT
NUMBER
NUMERIC
NUMERIC-EDITED

OBJECT-COMPUTER
OCCURS
OF
OFF
OMITTED
ON
OPEN
OPTIONAL
OR
ORDER
ORGANIZATION
OTHER
OUTPUT
OVERFLOW

PACKED-DECIMAL
PADDING
PAGE
PAGE-COUNTER
PERFORM
PF
PH
PIC
PICTURE
PLUS
POINTER
POSITION
POSITIVE
PRINTING
PROCEDURE
PROCEDURES
PROCEED
PROGRAM
PROGRAM-ID
PURGE

QUEUE
QUOTE
QUOTES

RANDOM
RD
READ
RECEIVE
RECORD
RECORDS
REDEFINES
REEL
REFERENCE
REFERENCES
RELATIVE
RELEASE
REMAINDER
REMOVAL
RENAMES
REPLACE
REPLACING
REPORT
REPORTING
REPORTS
RERUN
RESERVE
RESET
RETURN
REVERSED
REWIND
REWRITE
RF
RH
RIGHT
ROUNDED
RUN

SAME
SD
SEARCH
SECTION
SECURITY
SEGMENT
SEGMENT-LIMIT
SELECT
SEND
SENTENCE
SEPARATE
SEQUENCE
SEQUENTIAL
SET
SIGN
SIZE
SORT
SORT-MERGE
SOURCE
SOURCE-COMPUTER
SPACE
SPACES
SPECIAL-NAMES
STANDARD
STANDARD-1
STANDARD-2
START
STATUS
STOP
STRING
SUB-QUEUE-1
SUB-QUEUE-2
SUB-QUEUE-3
SUBTRACT
SUM
SUPPRESS
SYMBOLIC
SYNC
SYNCHRONIZED

TABLE
TALLYING
TAPE
TERMINAL
TERMINATE
TEST
TEXT
THAN
THEN
THROUGH
THRU
TIME
TIMES
TO
TOP
TRAILING
TRUE
TYPE

UNIT
UNSTRING
UNTIL
UP
UPON
USAGE
USE
USING

VALUE
VALUES
VARYING

WHEN
WITH
WORDS
WORKING-STORAGE
WRITE

ZERO
ZEROES
ZEROS

COBOL Symbols:
+
−
*
/
**
>
<
=
>=
<=

Note: Each COBOL compiler has its own set of reserved words. It generally contains most or all of the words in the ANSI set, but may also contain others.

GLOSSARY

Abend
Abnormal ending of program execution usually caused by a data error or a logic error.

Absolute Line Number
A nonnegative integer that specifies a fixed line number on a logical page where a Report Writer report group must be printed.

Access Mode
The manner in which a program accesses records of a file. Records may be accessed sequentially, randomly, or dynamically.

Adding a Record
The process by which new records are inserted into an existing file, in particular, a master file.

Alphabet-name
A user-defined word that names a specific collating sequence or character set. It must be defined in the SPECIAL-NAMES paragraph of the ENVIRONMENT DIVISION.

Alphabetic Character
A character that belongs to the set of uppercase letters (A–Z), lowercase letters (a–z), and a space.

Alphanumeric Character
Any character that belongs to the computer's character set.

Alternate Record Key
A key, other than the prime record key, whose contents identify a particular record of an indexed file.

Ascending Key
A key whose values are used in the ordering of data. Ascending order begins with the lowest key value and ends with the highest key value, as determined by the rules for comparing data.

At End Condition
A condition that may occur during

1. a READ statement execution for a sequentially accessed file. The condition occurs when no next logical record exists for the file.
2. a RETURN statement execution for a sort or merge file. The condition occurs when no next logical record exists in the file.
3. a SEARCH statement execution. The condition occurs when all table elements have been examined without satisfying the condition in any of the statement's WHEN clauses.

Audit Report
A report generally produced by a program designed to do some file maintenance activity on a file. The report provides documentation of the maintenance activity.

Batch Program
A program designed to process data that has previously been collected (batched) into a file, as opposed to processing data supplied interactively by the user during the execution of the program.

Binary Search
A method of searching elements of an ordered table. The procedure removes from further consideration half of the remaining portion of the table every time a test for a matching element fails. The procedure terminates when a matching element is found or when no matching element is found in the table.

Bit
The smallest unit in the computer's storage area. It stands for *bi*nary digi*t*. It has two states, magnetized (ON) and not magnetized (OFF).

Block
A group of logical records stored and/or transferred as a unit. A block is also called a physical record.

Blocking Factor
The number of logical records or characters contained in one block.

Body Group
Generic name for a Report Writer report group defined by TYPE DETAIL, TYPE CONTROL HEADING, or TYPE CONTROL FOOTING.

BPI
*B*its-*p*er-*i*nch. A measure of the density of a magnetic storage medium.

Buffer
A portion of main memory into which a physical record is read or from which it is written.

Byte
The basic unit of a computer's memory, usually consisting of 8 bits. One byte stores one character of the COBOL character set.

Called Program
A program that is the object of a CALL statement. It must be linked with the calling program to form a run unit.

Calling Program
A program that executes a CALL to another program.

Character
The basic, indivisible unit of the COBOL language.

Character Position
The amount of physical storage needed to store one standard data format character whose usage is DISPLAY. In COBOL, this is one byte.

Character String
A sequence of contiguous characters that form a COBOL word, literal, PICTURE clause character string, or comment-entry.

Class Condition
A test to determine if the characters contained in a data item are all alphabetic, or all numeric, or all belong to a defined class-name.

Class-name
A user-defined word in the SPECIAL-NAMES paragraph associated with a specified set of characters.

Clause
A subdivision of a COBOL sentence. It is a set of consecutive COBOL character strings that specifies an attribute of an entry.

COBOL Character Set
The following set of characters used in the COBOL language:

0, 1, 2, . . . 9	digit
A, B, C, . . . Z	letter
a, b, c, . . . z	lowercase letter
+	plus sign
−	minus sign (hyphen)
*	asterisk
/	division sign (slash or stroke)
=	equal sign
$	currency sign
>	greater than symbol
<	less than symbol
:	colon
_	underscore
	space
tab	horizontal tab (equivalent to space)
(	left parenthesis

)	right parenthesis
,	comma (decimal point)
;	semicolon
.	period (decimal point, full stop)
"	double quotation mark
'	apostrophe (single quotation mark)
\	backslash

COBOL Statement Format
A description of the specific arrangement of elements, required and optional, of a COBOL statement.

Collating Sequence
The sequence in which the characters of a specified or default character set are ordered for sorting, merging, and comparing purposes. The two most common collating sequences are ASCII and EBCDIC.

Column
A character position within a print line or a line on a video terminal screen. Columns are numbered from 1 by 1, starting at the leftmost and extending to the rightmost character position.

Common Program
A program contained within a program that may be called by any program directly or indirectly contained in the containing program except the contained program itself and any program it contains directly or indirectly.

Compiler-directing Statement
A statement beginning with a compiler-directing verb that causes the compiler to take a specific action during compilation.

Computer Character Set
The set of characters available on the computer.

Contained Program
A source program nested within another source program.

Containing Program
A source program that contains a contained program.

Control Footing
A report group presented to a report at the end of the control group to which it belongs.

Control Group
A set of body groups presented to a report for a given value of a control data item or of a FINAL clause. Each control group may begin with a control heading report group, contain detail report groups, and end with a control footing report group.

Control Heading
A report group presented at the beginning of the control group to which it belongs.

Control Hierarchy
The sequence in which the subdivisions of a report must be presented to the report. It is specified by the positional ordering of data names and the reserved word FINAL in a report's CONTROL clause.

Counter
A data item used to store numbers or number representations in a manner that allows the number to be increased or decreased by another number, or changed or reset to zero or some other arbitrary positive or negative value.

Crossfooting
The totaling of sum counters that belong to the same control footing report group. It is a horizontal sum of sums, executed only when the control footing report group is presented to the report.

Current Record
In sequential, indexed, or relative file processing, the record currently available in the file's record area.

Cylinders
The vertical alignment of identically numbered tracks of the disks in a disk pack.

■ D

DASD
Direct-Access Storage Device. A device that supports direct access to records of a file. The most common DASD is the disk drive.

Data Clause
A clause in the data description of an item that specifies an attribute of the data item.

Declarative Sentence
A compiler-directing sentence consisting of a single USE statement and terminated by a separator period.

Declaratives
A set of one or more special-purpose sections at the beginning of the PROCEDURE DIVISION, the first of which is preceded by the key word DECLARATIVES and the last of which is followed by the key words END DECLARATIVES. A declarative consists of a section header, followed by a single USE statement, and zero, one, or more paragraphs.

De-edit
The process of removing all editing characters from a numeric-edited data item in order to store its unedited numeric value.

Delimited Scope Statement
A statement that ends with its specific scope terminator. It belongs to a special category of imperative statements.

Delimiter
One or more contiguous characters that mark the end of a string of characters. It separates a string of characters from the next string of characters. The delimiter does not belong to either string.

Density
The number of characters that can be stored per inch of a magnetic tape or disk.

Descending Key
A key whose values determine the ordering of data. Descending order begins with the highest key value and ends with the lowest key value, in accordance with the rules for comparing data items.

Design Implementation Phase
The second phase of the problem-solving procedure. In this phase, the program is coded; it is entered into a file; it is compiled by the compiler, debugged if necessary, and executed with sample data.

Design Phase
The first phase of the problem-solving procedure. In this phase, the layouts of input and output records are prepared, the system flowchart and the structure chart are developed, and the program pseudocode is written and/or the program flowchart is drawn.

Detail File
The file in a master file updating program that contains data on the records involved in the update.

Direct-Access File
A file whose organization allows each record to be accessed directly by specifying its address or its key field value. Direct access is synonymous with random access.

DISPLAY
A COBOL verb that executes an output function. All literals that follow the verb and the values of all data items that follow the verb are output by the program either on the screen of a terminal or into an output file.

Division Algorithm Method
In relative file handling, a particular procedure used in transforming a record's key field value to a relative key number. The relative key number is the record's location in the file.

Dynamic Access
An access mode specified for an indexed or relative file that allows records to be accessed either sequentially or randomly during the same program run.

■ E

END DECLARATIVES
The entry that terminates declaratives in a program.

END PROGRAM
A header used to denote the end of a source program in a multiple-program run unit.

END-ACCEPT
The explicit scope terminator for the ACCEPT statement.

END-CALL
The explicit scope terminator for the CALL statement.

END-DELETE
The explicit scope terminator for the DELETE statement.

END-REWRITE
The explicit scope terminator for the REWRITE statement.

END-SEARCH
The explicit scope terminator for the SEARCH statement.

END-START
The explicit scope terminator for the START statement.

END-UNSTRING
The explicit scope terminator for the UNSTRING statement.

EXIT PROGRAM
The last statement to be executed in a called program.

EXTEND
An open mode for a file whose access mode is sequential that allows records to be written beyond the previous end-of-file marker.

External Data
Data described in a program as external to the program. Such data is not local to a program, and it may be referenced by any program that describes it as external.

■ **File Backup**
A separate copy of a file kept as a safeguard against destruction or corruption of the original file.

File Organization
The permanent structure of a file established at the time the file is first created. The three standard file organizations are sequential, indexed, and relative.

File Position Indicator
Also called a record pointer, it is an entity that points to the next logical record in a sequential, indexed, or relative file.

FILE STATUS
A clause of the file's SELECT statement that names the data item that will store status codes identifying the outcome of input/output operations on the file.

File Status Code
A two-character code generated during input/output operations on a file. If the SELECT statement for the file contains a FILE STATUS clause, the code is stored in the clause's data item and may be referenced by the program.

Fixed-length Record
A record of a file whose description requires that all records contain the same number of character positions.

Folding Technique
A technique that may be used in assigning a relative number to a record of a relative file.

Footing Area
A subdivision of a page body toward the bottom of the logical page.

Format
A specific arrangement of a set of data.

Format a File
In creating a relative file, a procedure that may be used to separate a file's storage area into a number of fixed-length record areas.

Free-form Data Entry
Data entry in which data item values are separated by delimiters instead of being entered in conformity with the data structure of the record receiving the values.

■ **GENERATE**
The Report Writer statement that presents report groups to a report as specified in the REPORT SECTION of the DATA DIVISION.

Global Data
Data defined by the GLOBAL qualifier. Global data may be referenced by the program that defines it and by any program contained within the defining program.

■ **Hard-Coded Table**
A table whose elements are specified in VALUE clauses within the table definition.

Hashing Algorithm
A procedure used to transform a record key value into an address in a file.

Heading Area
A subdivision of a page body toward the top of the logical page.

Horizontal Sum of Sums
See Crossfooting.

■ **I/O Mode**
The mode of a file subsequent to the execution of an OPEN statement and prior to the execution of a CLOSE statement.

IBG
*I*nter*b*lock *g*ap. The space that separates physical records on a magnetic tape.

Index
A computer storage area or register whose contents identify the occurrence of a table element.

Index Data Item
A data item defined by the USAGE IS INDEX clause. It may be used to store the value associated with an index-name.

Index-Name
The name of an index associated with a table. The name is specified by the programmer.

Index Record
A record in the index block (or table) associated with an indexed file. It contains the record key value of a record in the file and a pointer that indicates the location of the record in the file.

Index Table
The table (or block) at the beginning of an indexed file that contains the index records for the file.

INDEXED BY
The phrase used in a table description to name the index (or indexes) associated with the table.

Indexed Data Name
The name of an element in an indexed table. The data name is followed by a pair of parentheses that contain one or more index-names.

Indexed File
A file with indexed organization.

Indexed Organization
The permanent logical structure of a file in which each record contains one or more keys whose values are used to identify it.

Indexed Table
A table whose description contains one or more INDEXED BY phrases.

INITIAL
A program qualifier. When specified, the program is always in its initial state whenever it is called. Local data items whose descriptions contain VALUE clauses are initialized with those values. Other data items are initialized to system-specific default values.

INITIATE
A Report Writer statement that initializes special registers and the sum counters of a report.

Input-Output File
A file opened in I-O mode.

Interactive Dialogue
The exchange of program prompts and user responses that occurs during the execution of an interactive program.

Interactive Program
A program designed to obtain data input from the user during the execution of the program, as opposed to accessing data records previously stored in a file.

Interblock Gap
See IBG.

Internal Data
The data described in a program except for those items qualified as EXTERNAL.

Invalid Key Condition
A condition at run time caused when the value of a key associated with an indexed or relative file is determined to be invalid.

■ **Key**
A data item that identifies the location of a record or a set of one or more data items that serves to identify the ordering of data.

Key of Reference
The key, either prime or alternate, that is currently being used to access records in an indexed file.

Key Word
A reserved word required in a general format.

Kilobyte
One thousand bytes. Usually represented as KB.

Library Name
A user-defined word that names a COBOL library to be used during a compilation.

Library Text
A sequence of text words and other character strings, including separator spaces, in a COBOL library.

Line Number
An integer that denotes the vertical position of a line on a video terminal screen or on a page of a print file.

LINE NUMBER
A Report Writer clause that provides information for the vertical positioning of a report group on a logical page.

LINE-COUNTER
A Report Writer special register whose value indicates the current line on a logical page.

LINKAGE SECTION
The section in the DATA DIVISION of a called program that describes the data items available from the calling program. These data items can be referenced by the called program and the calling program.

Local Name
The name of a data item that is declared in only one program and that may be referenced only by statements in that program.

Logical Page
A conceptual entity which consists of a top margin, a page body, and a bottom margin.

Logical Record
The most inclusive data item processed by a COBOL program. Its level number is 01, and it may be an elementary or a group item. A physical record usually contains one or more logical records.

Main Menu
A screen displayed during the execution of an interactive program that lists the choices (courses of action) available to the user.

Main Program
In a multiple-program run unit, the program that first calls a subprogram. The subprogram may be a contained or a separately compiled program.

Mass Storage
A storage medium in which data records can be organized and maintained either sequentially or randomly.

Mass Storage File
A file on a mass storage device.

Master File
A file containing a management unit's permanent records. Examples are a company's employee file and an inventory file.

Megabyte
One million bytes. Usually represented as MB.

Native Collating Sequence
The default collating sequence used by an operating system. The two most common collating sequences are ASCII and EBCDIC.

Nested OCCURS
An OCCURS clause in the description of a data item that is subordinate to a data item that is also defined by an OCCURS clause or that is subordinate to one that is.

Nested Programs
Programs that are contained within another program.

Next Executable Sentence
The next sentence to which control transfers after execution of the current sentence is complete.

Next Executable Statement
The next statement to which control transfers after execution of the current statement is complete.

NEXT GROUP
A Report Writer clause that provides information for the vertical positioning of the next report group on a logical page following the printing of the last line of the current report group.

NEXT PAGE
An option of the NEXT GROUP clause of the Report Writer.

Next Record
The record that logically follows the current record of a file.

Optional File
A file qualified as OPTIONAL in its SELECT statement. When an OPEN statement is issued for the file, the program checks for its presence or absence.

Optional Word
An optional reserved word included in a format for the purpose of increasing a program's self-documentation.

ORGANIZATION Clause
The clause in a file's SELECT statement that specifies the file's permanent logical structure as SEQUENTIAL, INDEXED, or RELATIVE.

Packing Factor
A number expressed as a percent that represents the ratio of the number of actual records stored in a relative file to the total number of records that file can contain.

PAGE-COUNTER
A Report Writer special register whose value indicates the current page in a report.

Page Footing
A Report Writer report group that is presented at the end of a logical page.

Page Heading
A Report Writer report group that is presented at the beginning of a logical page.

Physical Record
Same as a block.

Prime Record Key
A key that uniquely identifies a record in an indexed file.

Print File
A file whose description contains a LINAGE clause, or whose records are written with the ADVANCING phrase of the WRITE statement, or that is generated by the Report Writer.

Printable Group
A Report Writer report group that contains at least one print line.

Printable Item
A data item defined in the REPORT SECTION as an elementary report entry. Its description must contain a COLUMN clause, a PICTURE clause, and a SOURCE, SUM, or VALUE clause.

Printer Spacing Chart
A preprinted form used to prepare the layout of each type of line to be printed on a report.

Problem-Solving Procedure
A procedure whose systematic application facilitates the programmer's task of designing a program, coding it, debugging it, and running it.

PROCEDURE DIVISION USING
The division header in a subprogram that contains a LINKAGE SECTION, or equivalently, that is called by a CALL USING statement.

Program Flowchart
A graphical representation of the functions to be executed or operations to be performed within a program, as well as the sequence in which they are to be executed or performed.

Program Pseudocode
The set of instructions that must be executed in a program, written in a form that is English-like, which is not restricted by the COBOL language rules of syntax and yet maps out the complete logic of the program.

Prompt/Response Technique
A procedure used in interactive programs that issues prompts or queries to the user for the data that must be entered.

Pseudo-text
A sequence of text words and/or character strings, including the separator space, bounded by pseudo-text delimiters, used in the REPLACING phrase of the COPY statement.

Pseudo-text Delimiter
Two contiguous equal sign (=) characters that delimit pseudo-text.

Random Access
An access mode in which a logical record is read from, or written to, or deleted from an indexed or a relative file on the basis of a program-specified key data item value that identifies the logical record.

Random Update
A master file update in which the access mode is specified as random. The file must have indexed or relative organization.

Randomization Procedure
A generic term applied to transformation techniques used to generate a record's relative number in relative files.

RD
The first entry in a report description within the REPORT SECTION of the DATA DIVISION.

Record Collision
The conflict that occurs when a randomization procedure initially produces the same relative number for two (or more) records in a relative file.

Record Key
A data item in a record of an indexed file whose value is used to identify the record. The key may be the prime record key or an alternate record key.

Relative File
A file with relative organization.

Relative Key
A key whose contents identify a logical record in a relative file.

Relative Line Number
A nonnegative integer that must be added to the current value of the Report Writer register LINE-COUNTER to specify a print line on a logical page for the printing of a report group.

Relative Organization
The permanent logical structure of a file in which each record is uniquely identified by a positive integer. The integer specifies the record's ordinal position within the file.

Repeating Group
A group data item whose description contains an OCCURS clause or that is subordinate to a data item whose description contains an OCCURS clause.

Report Clause
A clause in a report description entry or in a report group description entry.

Report Description Entry
An entry in the REPORT SECTION of the DATA DIVISION that begins with the indicator RD, followed by the report name and one or more report clauses.

Report File
An output file whose file description contains a REPORT clause. The records of this file are produced by the Report Writer.

Report Footing
A report group that is presented to a report only at the end of the report.

Report Group
A 01-level entry, including its subordinate items, in the REPORT SECTION of the DATA DIVISION.

Report Group Description Entry
An entry in the REPORT SECTION of the DATA DIVISION composed of a 01-level number, an optional data name, a TYPE clause, and a set of optional clauses.

Report Heading
A report group that is presented to a report only at the beginning of the report.

Report Line
A division of a report group that produces one line on the report. The characters on the line are positioned by the COLUMN clauses of the entry. Report lines are numbered from 1, by 1, starting at the top of the logical page.

Report Name
A user-defined word that names the report. The name is first used in the REPORT clause and then in the report's RD entry.

REPORT SECTION
The section of the DATA DIVISION that contains one or more report descriptions and their associated report group description entries.

Report Writer Control System
An object-time control system that produces a report according to the specifications in a program's REPORT SECTION.

Report Writer Logical Record
A record that consists of the Report Writer print line and associated control information necessary for the vertical positioning of the report line.

Rolling Forward
The totaling of sum counters of a lower-level control footing report group into sum counters of a higher-level control footing report group. It is a vertical sum of sums and occurs when the lower-level control footing report group is presented to the report.

Run Unit
One or more object programs linked to form a single executable program.

Scope Terminator
An entry that terminates the scope of a statement. The scope may be terminated implicitly by a period or explicitly by a terminator of the form END- . . . , where . . . is the statement verb, as in END-PERFORM.

Screen Layout Form
A preprinted video form generally consisting of 24 lines and 80 columns used by programmers to facilitate the design of menus used in interactive programs.

Screen Management Facility
The combination of hardware and software provided by particular vendors of computers and operating systems designed to facilitate screen handling tasks for interactive programs. (ANSI standards are being developed but have not yet been published.)

Section
A set of zero, one, or more paragraphs or entries, called a section body, that follow a section header. A section consists of the section header and its related section body.

Section Header
A combination of two words followed by a period and a space that indicates the beginning of a section in the ENVIRONMENT, DATA, and PROCEDURE divisions. Every section header must contain the reserved word SECTION.

Section Name
A user-defined word that names a section in the PROCEDURE DIVISION.

Separately Compiled Programs
A program that, together with any contained program, is compiled separately from all other programs.

Separator
A character or two contiguous characters that delimit character strings.

Sequential Access
An access mode in which logical records are obtained from or placed into a file in consecutive sequence. The order in which records were written to the file determines the predecessor-successor logical record sequence.

Sequential File
A file with sequential organization.

Sequential Organization
The permanent logical file structure in which a record is identified by a predecessor-successor relationship established when the record is placed into the file.

Serial Search
A method of searching elements in a table. The search for a match begins with the first table element or another specified table element, and proceeds through successive table elements until a match is found, or until the last table element has been examined without finding a match.

Source Item
An identifier designated by a SOURCE clause of the Report Writer that provides the value of a printable item. The term is also generally applied to operands referenced by the MOVE verb in a MOVE statement.

Storage File
A file that remains on magnetic media for future reference or processing.

Structure Chart
A programmer's design tool that shows the hierarchy of tasks that must be accomplished by a program.

Submenu
A menu displayed on a screen resulting from a user selection from a set of menu choices on a previous screen.

Subprogram
Same as called program.

Subscript
An integer whose value identifies a table element.

Subscripted Data Name
An identifier that consists of a data name followed by one or more subscripts enclosed in parentheses.

Subtotaling
The accumulation of numeric data items during detail processing. In the Report Writer, subtotaling accumulates numeric data items into sum counters during execution of the GENERATE statement. The data items must not themselves be sum counters.

Sum Counter
A signed numeric data item established by a SUM clause in the REPORT SECTION of the DATA DIVISION. The sum counter is used by the Report Writer Control System to contain the result of specified summing operations that take place during the production of a report.

Symbolic Character
A user-defined word that specifies a user-defined figurative constant.

Synonym
A record in a relative file whose relative number initially generated by the application of a randomization procedure matches the relative number of an existing record.

System Flowchart
A flowchart that illustrates the data flow requirements of a particular program.

■ **Terminal Input**
Data entered by an operator at a terminal during the execution of a program.

Terminal Operator
The person who enters data at the terminal in response to prompts issued by a program.

TERMINATE
The Report Writer statement that completes the processing of the specified report.

Text-name
A user-defined word that identifies library text.

Top Margin
An empty area on a logical page that precedes the page body.

Tracks
Concentric circles of a magnetic disk.

■ **Updating a File**
A master file maintenance activity in which new records are added and existing records are either updated or deleted.

Updating a Record
Changing values of selected data items in an existing record.

User Friendly
A characteristic of interactive programs designed to facilitate user interaction with the program.

■ **Vertical Sum of Sums**
See Rolling Forward.

Video Form
See Screen Layout Form.

Index

Record Layout Forms

1 2 3 4 5 6 7 8 9 10 11 12 13 14 15 16 17 18 19 20 21 22 23 24 25 26 27 28 29 30 31 32 33 34 35 36 37 38 39 40 41 42 43 44 45 46 47 48 49 50 51 52 53 54 55 56 57 58 59 60 61 62 63 64 65 66 67 68 69 70 71 72 73 74 75 76 77 78 79 80

Record Name: ______________________

1 2 3 4 5 6 7 8 9 10 11 12 13 14 15 16 17 18 19 20 21 22 23 24 25 26 27 28 29 30 31 32 33 34 35 36 37 38 39 40 41 42 43 44 45 46 47 48 49 50 51 52 53 54 55 56 57 58 59 60 61 62 63 64 65 66 67 68 69 70 71 72 73 74 75 76 77 78 79 80

Record Name: ______________________

1 2 3 4 5 6 7 8 9 10 11 12 13 14 15 16 17 18 19 20 21 22 23 24 25 26 27 28 29 30 31 32 33 34 35 36 37 38 39 40 41 42 43 44 45 46 47 48 49 50 51 52 53 54 55 56 57 58 59 60 61 62 63 64 65 66 67 68 69 70 71 72 73 74 75 76 77 78 79 80

Record Name: ______________________

1 2 3 4 5 6 7 8 9 10 11 12 13 14 15 16 17 18 19 20 21 22 23 24 25 26 27 28 29 30 31 32 33 34 35 36 37 38 39 40 41 42 43 44 45 46 47 48 49 50 51 52 53 54 55 56 57 58 59 60 61 62 63 64 65 66 67 68 69 70 71 72 73 74 75 76 77 78 79 80

Record Name: ______________________

Photocopy Master

Printer Spacing Chart

Line	0	10	20	30	40	50	60	70	80	90	100	110	120	130
	1234567890	1234567890	1234567890	1234567890	1234567890	1234567890	1234567890	1234567890	1234567890	1234567890	1234567890	1234567890	1234567890	1234567890
1														
2														
3														
4														
5														
6														
7														
8														
9														
10														
11														
12														
13														
14														
15														
16														
17														
18														
19														
20														
21														
22														
23														
24														
25														
26														
27														
28														
29														
30														
31														
32														
33														
34														
35														
36														
37														
38														
39														
40														
41														
42														
43														
44														
45														
46														
47														
48														
49														
50														
51														
52														
53														
54														
55														
56														
57														
58														

Photocopy Master

Display Layout Sheet

COLUMN

ROW	1–10	11–20	21–30	31–40	41–50	51–60	61–70	71–80
	1 2 3 4 5 6 7 8 9 0	1 2 3 4 5 6 7 8 9 0	1 2 3 4 5 6 7 8 9 0	1 2 3 4 5 6 7 8 9 0	1 2 3 4 5 6 7 8 9 0	1 2 3 4 5 6 7 8 9 0	1 2 3 4 5 6 7 8 9 0	1 2 3 4 5 6 7 8 9 0
01								
02								
03								
04								
05								
06								
07								
08								
09								
10								
11								
12								
13								
14								
15								
16								
17								
18								
19								
20								
21								
22								
23								
24								
	1–10	11–20	21–30	31–40	41–50	51–60	61–70	71–80
	1 2 3 4 5 6 7 8 9 0	1 2 3 4 5 6 7 8 9 0	1 2 3 4 5 6 7 8 9 0	1 2 3 4 5 6 7 8 9 0	1 2 3 4 5 6 7 8 9 0	1 2 3 4 5 6 7 8 9 0	1 2 3 4 5 6 7 8 9 0	1 2 3 4 5 6 7 8 9 0

Photocopy Master